Bond's Franchise Guide

2002 Edition

14th Annual Edition

Robert E. Bond, Publisher

Stephanie Woo, Editor

Source Book Publications
Serving the Franchising Industry
P.O. Box 12488, Oakland, CA 94604
510.839.5471

ISBN 1-887137-30-0

DISCLAIMER

BOND'S FRANCHISE GUIDE is based on data submitted by the franchisors themselves. Every effort has been made to obtain up-to-date, reliable information. As the information returned has not been independently verified, we assume no responsibility for errors or omissions and reserve the right to include or eliminate listings and otherwise edit and present the data based on our discretion and judgment as to what is useful to the readers of this directory. Inclusion in the publication does not imply endorsement by the editors or the publisher. Errors brought to the attention of the publisher and verified to the satisfaction of the publisher will be corrected in future editions. The publisher specifically disclaims all warranties, including the implied warranties of merchantability and fitness for a specific purpose.

BOND'S FRANCHISE GUIDE was previously published as *The Source Book of Franchise Opportunities. The Source Book of Franchise Opportunities* went through 7 Editions before the name was changed in 1995 to *Bond's Franchise Guide.*

This publication is designed to provide its readers with accurate and authoritative information with regard to the subject matter covered. It is sold with the understanding that neither the author nor the publisher is engaged in rendering legal, accounting or other professional services. If legal advice or other expert assistance is required, the services of a competent professional person should be sought.

From a Declaration of Principles jointly adopted by a Committee of the American Bar Association and a Committee of Publishers.

Cover Design by Joyce Coffland, Artistic Concepts, Oakland, CA.

ISBN 1-887137-30-0

Printed in the United States of America.
10 9 8 7 6 5 4 3 2 1

BOND'S FRANCHISE GUIDE is available at special discounts for bulk purchase. Special editions or book excerpts can also be created to specifications. For details, contact **Source Book Publications**, P.O. Box 12488, Oakland, CA 94604. Phone: (510) 839-5471; FAX: (510) 839-2104.

Preface

At its best, purchasing a franchise is a time-tested, paint-by-the-numbers method of starting a new business. It avoids many of the myriad pitfalls normally encountered by someone starting anew and vastly improves the odds of success. It represents an exceptional blend of operating independence with a proven system that includes a detailed blueprint on starting and managing the business, as well as the all-important on-going support.

But purchasing a franchise is clearly not a foolproof investment that somehow guarantees the investor financial independence.

At its worst, if the evaluation and investment decision is sloppy or haphazard, franchising can be a nightmare. You can lose your original investment plus any assets used to personally secure your debt, not to mention your marriage and your self-confidence.

Your ultimate success as a franchisee will be determined by two factors:

1. The homework you do at the front-end to ensure that you are selecting the optimal franchise for your particular needs, experience and financial resources.

2. Your commitment to work hard and play by the rules once you have signed a binding, long-term franchise agreement. A franchise system is only as good as you make it. In most cases, this involves working 60+ hours per week until you can justify delegating some of the day-to-day responsibilities. It also requires being a team player within the system — not acting as an entrepreneur who does his or her own thing without regard for the system as a whole.

The motivation for writing this annual directory has always been to assist in the evaluation phase of the equation: to provide accurate, in-depth data on the many legitimate companies actively selling franchises. The book is written for the sophisticated businessperson seriously interested in the process of selecting an optimal franchise opportunity: someone willing to commit the time and resources necessary to find the best franchise for his or her particular needs; someone with the wisdom to know that the franchise selection process is exceedingly difficult and filled with potholes; someone keenly aware of the risks — including missed opportunities — of going through the process in a half-hearted way.

We hope we can facilitate the evaluation process by ensuring that the potential franchisee is exposed to the full range of options open to him or her and that he or she goes about the selection process in a logical and systematic manner.

ꝏ

Over 2,150 franchising opportunities are listed on the following pages. An in-depth profile is available on over 1,000 of these. This franchisor profile is the result of the detailed three-page questionnaire noted in Appendix A. The names, addresses, telephone and fax numbers, contact and industry categories are provided on over 1,150 additional active North American franchisors.

No doubt you will be familiar with a large number of the listings. Many are household names. That, incidentally, is one of the primary benefits of franchising. Most people would agree that AAMCO Transmissions has a better ring to it than Bill's Transmission Shop. Apart from the proven systems and procedures, you are buying a recognized name and the reputation that the name enjoys in the marketplace.

ꝏ

After you have decided which of the 45 industry groups hold the most interest, contact **all** of the companies listed and request a marketing brochure. Thoroughly read their literature and pick out the companies that interest you and that represent a natural fit with your talents and financial resources. You should be able to narrow your choices down to a manageable list of six or eight franchises that fit these criteria. Initiate an in-depth analysis of and dialogue with each of these franchisors. Concurrently, develop a thorough knowledge of the business and/or services that you are considering. Seek the advice of professionals, even if you are experienced in various elements of the evaluation process. Don't leave any stone unturned.

ꝏ

Remember, this is not a game! You are quite literally betting the ranch on your ability to pick a well-managed, market-oriented franchise. You want one that will take advantage of your unique talents and experience and not take advantage of you in the process! Don't take short-cuts. Listen to what the franchisor and your advisors tell you. Don't think you are so clever or independent that you can't benefit from the advice of outside professionals. Don't assume that the franchisor's guidelines regarding the amount of investment, experience, temperament, etc., somehow don't apply to you. Don't accept any promises or "understandings" from the franchisor that are not committed in writing to the franchise agreement. Spend the extra money to talk to and/or meet with other franchisees in the system. The additional front-end investment you make, both in time and money, will pay off handsomely if it saves you from making a marginal, or poor, investment decision. This is one of the few times in business when second chances are rare. Make the extra effort to do it right the first time.

ꝏ

Good luck and Godspeed.

Table of Contents

Section Three — Appendix

Section Four — Index

30 Minute Overview

In presenting this data, we have made some unilateral assumptions about our readers. The first is that you purchased the book because of the depth and accuracy of the data provided — not as a how-to manual. Chapter 3, Recommended Reading, lists several resources for anyone requiring additional background information on the franchising industry and on the process of evaluating a company. Clearly, dedication to hard work, adequate financing, commitment, good business sense and access to trusted professional counsel will determine your ultimate success as a franchisee. A strong working knowledge of the industry, however, will help ensure that you have made the best choice of franchise opportunities. I advise you to acquaint yourself with the dynamics of the industry before you initiate the evaluation and negotiation phases of selecting a franchise.

The second assumption is that you have already devoted the time necessary to conduct a detailed personal inventory. This self-assessment should result in a clear understanding of your skills, aptitudes, weaknesses, long-term personal goals, commitment to succeed and financial capabilities. Most of the books in the Recommended Reading Chapter provide worksheets to accomplish this important step.

ꝏ

There are three primary stages to the franchise selection process: 1) the investigation stage, 2) the evaluation stage and 3) and the negotiation stage. This book is intended primarily to assist the reader in the investigation stage by providing a thorough list of the options available. Chapters 1 and 2 include various observations based on my 15 or so years of involvement with the franchising industry. Hopefully, they will provide some insights that you will find of value.

Understand at the outset that the entire process will take many months and involve a great deal of frustration. I suggest that you set up a realistic timeline for signing a franchise agreement and that you stick with that schedule. There will be a lot of pressure on you to prematurely complete the selection and negotiation phases. Resist the temptation. The penalties are too severe for a seat-of-the-pants attitude. A decision of this magnitude clearly deserves your full attention. Do your homework!

Before starting the selection process, you would be well advised to briefly review the areas that follow.

Franchise Industry Structure

The franchising industry is made up of two distinct types of franchises. The first, and by far the larger, encompasses product and trade name franchising. Automotive and truck dealers, soft drink bottlers and gasoline service stations are included in this group. For the most part, these are essentially distributorships.

The second group encompasses business format franchisors. This book only includes information on this latter category.

Layman's Definition of Franchising

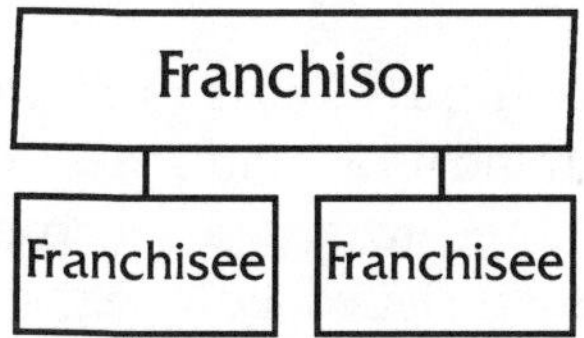

Classic Business Format Model

Business format franchising is a method of market expansion by which one business entity expands the distribution of its products and/or services through independent, third-party operators. Franchising occurs when the operator of a concept or system (the **franchisor**) grants an independent businessperson (the **franchisee**) the right to duplicate its entire business format at a particular location and for a specified period, under terms and conditions set forth in the contract (**franchise agreement**). The franchisee has full access to all of the trademarks, logos, marketing techniques, controls and systems that have made the franchisor successful. In effect, the franchisee acts as a surrogate for a company-owned store in the distribution of the franchisor's goods and/or services. It is important to keep in mind that the franchisor and the franchisee are separate legal entities.

In return for a front-end **franchise fee** — which usually ranges from $15,000–35,000 — the franchisor is obligated to "set up" the franchisee in business. This generally includes assistance in selecting a location, negotiating a lease, obtaining financing, building and equipping a site and providing the necessary training, operating manuals, etc. Once the training is completed and the store is open, the new franchisee should have a carbon copy of other units in the system and enjoy the same benefits they do, whether they are company-owned or not.

Business format franchising is unique because it is a long-term relationship characterized by an on-going, mutually beneficial partnership. On-going services include research and development, marketing strategies, advertising campaigns, group buying, periodic field visits, training updates, and whatever else is required to make the franchisee competitive and profitable. In effect, the franchisor acts as the franchisee's "back office" support organization. To reimburse the franchisor for this support, the franchisee pays the franchisor an on-going **royalty fee**, generally four to eight percent of gross sales or income. In many cases, franchisees also contribute an **advertising fee** to reimburse the franchisor for expenses incurred in maintaining a national or regional advertising campaign.

For the maximum advantage, both the franchisor and the franchisees should share common objectives and goals. Both parties must accept the premise that their fortunes are mutually intertwined and that they are each better off working in a co-operative effort, rather than toward any self-serving goals. Unlike the parent/child relationship that has dominated franchising over the past 30 years, franchising is now becoming a true and productive relationship of partners.

Legal Definition of Franchising

The Federal Trade Commission (FTC) has its own definition of franchising. So do each of the 16 states that have separate franchise registration statutes. The State of California's definition, which is the model for the FTC's definition, follows:

Franchise means a contract or agreement, express or implied, whether oral or written, between two or more persons by which:

> *A franchisee is granted the right to engage in the business of offering, selling or distributing goods or services under a marketing plan or system prescribed in substantial part by a franchisor;*
>
> *The operation of the franchisee's business pursuant to that plan or system as substantially associated with the franchisor's trademark, service mark, trade name, logotype, advertising or other commercial symbol designating the franchisor or its affiliates; and*
>
> *The franchisee is required to pay, directly or indirectly, a franchise fee.*

Multi-Level Franchising

With franchisors continually exploring new ways to expand their distribution, the classic business format model shown above has evolved over the years. Modifications have allowed franchisors to grow more rapidly and at less cost than might have otherwise been possible.

If a franchisor wishes to expand at a faster rate than its financial resources or staff levels allow, it might choose to sell development rights in an area (state, national or international) and let the new entity do the development work. No matter which development method is chosen, the franchisee should still receive the same benefits and support provided under the standard model. The major difference is the entity providing the training and on-going support and receiving the franchise and royalty fees changes.

Three variations of the master franchising model include: 1) master (or regional) franchising, 2) sub-franchising and 3) area development franchising.

In **master (or regional) franchising**, the franchisor sells the development rights in a particular market to a master franchisee who, in turn, sells individual franchises within the territory. In return for a front-end master franchise fee, the master franchisee has sole responsibility for developing that area under a mutually agreed upon schedule. This includes attracting, screening, signing and training all new franchisees within the territory. Once established, on-going support is generally provided by the parent franchisor.

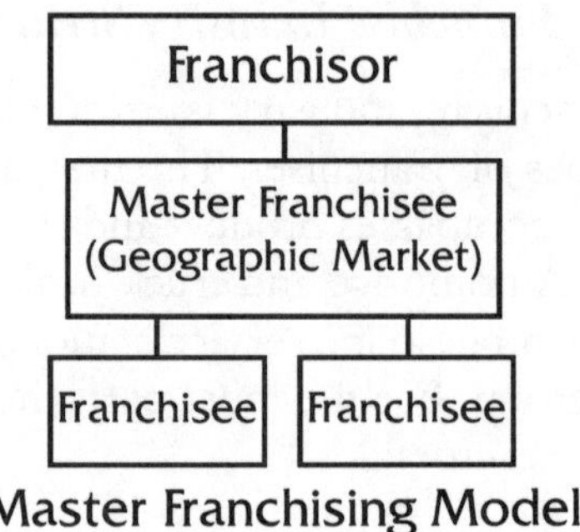

Master Franchising Model

The master franchisee is rewarded by sharing in the franchise fees and the on-going royalties paid to the parent franchisor by the franchisees within the territory.

Sub-franchising is similar to master franchising in that the franchisor grants development rights in a specified territory to a sub-franchisor. After the agreement is signed, however, the parent franchisor has no on-going involvement with the individual franchisees in the territory. Instead, the sub-franchisor becomes the focal point. All fees and royalties are paid directly to the sub-franchisor. It is solely responsible for all recruiting, training and on-going support, and passes on an agreed upon percentage of all incoming fees and royalties to the parent franchisor.

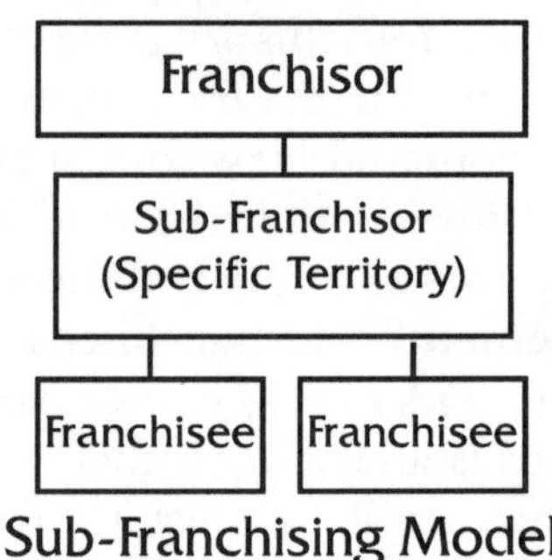

Sub-Franchising Model

In a sub-franchising relationship, the potential franchisee has to be doubly careful in his or her investigation. He or she must first make sure that the sub-franchisor has the necessary financial, managerial and marketing skills to make the program work. Secondarily, the potential franchisee has to feel comfortable that the parent franchisor can be relied upon to come to his or her rescue if the sub-franchisor should fail.

The third variation is an **area development agreement**. Here again, the franchisor grants exclusive development rights for a particular geographic area to an area development investment group. Within its territory, the area developer may either develop individual franchise units for its own account or find independent franchisees to develop units. In the latter case, the area developer has a residual equity position in the profits of its "area franchisees."

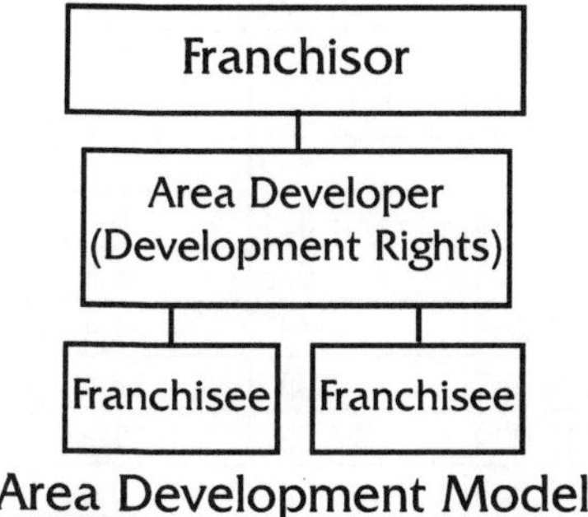

Area Development Model

In return for the rights to an exclusive territory, the area developer pays the franchisor a front-end development fee and commits to develop a certain number of units within a specified time period. (The front-end fee is generally significantly less than the sum of the individual unit fees.) Individual franchisees within the territory pay all contractual franchise, royalty and advertising fees directly to the parent franchisor. The area developer shares in neither the franchise fee nor in on-going royalty or advertising fees. Instead, the area developer shares only in the profitability of the individual franchises that it "owns." In essence, the area developer is buying multiple locations over time at a discount, since the franchise fee and (frequently) the royalty fee are less than the per unit rate.

Franchise Industry Statistics

The International Franchise Association (IFA) estimated that product and trade name franchising accounted for $554 billion in sales in 1992. This represents roughly 28% of all retail sales.

Business format franchising produced total sales of $249 billion in 1992, roughly 13% of all retail sales. In layman's language, this means that for every $1.00 spent at the retail level, more than $0.13 went to franchised establishments. There is no question that franchising has had a profound impact on the way business is conducted in the U.S. Most analysts anticipate that the overall numbers and market share of retail business will continue to grow well into the foreseeable future and at a faster rate than the economy in general.

Exhibits 1–5, noted on the following pages, and the other charts at the beginning of each chapter, are the result of querying our proprietary franchisor database (which has some 30 fields of information on 2,500 franchisors) and the database of some 1,020 detailed questionnaires that were returned as a result of our 2002 industry survey. You should spend some time reviewing the various Exhibits to get a better idea of the relative size, fees and investment levels required in various industry categories. The industry specific statistics in each chapter provide an excellent overview of the various firms in that category. If the size of the franchise fee, total investment or royalty fee fall far outside the averages noted, the franchisor should have a ready explanation as to why.

The Players

Franchisors

Roughly 2,050 U.S. and Canadian franchisors are shown on the following pages.

In past publications, we have always included the names, addresses and contacts of all active franchisors. We felt there was value in touting the coverage of as many franchisors as possible. In retrospect, we did our readers a disservice. We have subsequently changed our listing criteria. We now include supplemental franchisors only under the following circumstances: 1) a company representative was reached directly by phone, 2) they gave us at least some cursory information about the franchise and 3) they confirmed they were still actively franchising. Firms that answered our call with an answering machine, used an uninformed answering service or had children screaming in the background are not listed in the 2002 Edition's Supplemental Listing of Franchisors. Similarly, we

BOND'S FRANCHISE GUIDE
ANNUAL FRANCHISING INDUSTRY OVERVIEW
(As of 1/1/2002)

Exhibit 1

CATEGORY	# of Fran-chisors	Fran-chised Units	Company-Owned Units	Total Operating Units	See Chapter
Automotive Products & Services	159	25,083	2,961	28,044	4
Auto / Truck / Trailer Rental	29	9,600	1,260	10,860	5
Building & Remodeling/Furniture/Appliance Repair	106	8,747	142	8,889	6
Business: Financial Services	42	13,028	7,189	20,217	7
Business: Advertising & Promotion	35	2,081	78	2,159	8
Business: Internet/Telecommunications/Misc.	83	6,464	1,871	8,335	9
Child Development / Education / Products	82	5,389	296	5,685	10
Education / Personal Development / Training	54	3,692	683	4,375	11
Employment & Personnel	76	5,098	3,524	8,622	12
Food: Donuts / Cookies / Bagels	73	13,125	1,516	14,641	13
Food: Coffee	26	1,288	137	1,425	14
Food: Ice Cream / Yogurt	44	16,387	1,058	17,445	15
Food: Quick Service / Take-out	357	115,029	26,587	141,616	16
Food: Restaurant / Family-Style	181	18,805	10,286	29,091	17
Food: Specialty Foods	96	7,194	943	8,137	18
Hairstyling Salons	28	5,568	1,238	6,806	19
Health / Fitness / Beauty	78	15,928	1,950	17,878	20
Laundry & Dry Cleaning	23	2,374	36	2,410	21
Lawn and Garden	23	1,385	416	1,801	22
Lodging	74	28,676	3,581	32,257	23
Maid Service & Home Cleaning	24	3,526	170	3,696	24
Maintenance / Cleaning / Sanitation	129	37,044	604	37,648	25
Medical / Optical / Dental Products & Services	18	1,832	353	2,185	26
Packaging & Mailing	20	9,099	49	9,148	27
Printing & Graphics	26	5,200	40	5,240	28
Publications	27	1,077	61	1,138	29
Real Estate Inspection Services	21	2,237	362	2,599	30
Real Estate Services	57	18,465	471	18,936	31
Recreation & Entertainment	41	2,547	151	2,698	32
Rental Services	10	2,442	533	2,975	33
Retail: Art, Art Supplies & Framing	11	684	31	715	34
Retail: Athletic Wear / Sporting Goods	17	1,753	243	1,996	35
Retail: Clothing / Shoes / Accessories	6	105	113	218	36
Retail: Convenience Stores / Supermarkets / Drugs	28	29,583	6,451	36,034	37
Retail: Home Furnishings	44	2,743	128	2,871	38
Retail: Home Improvement & Hardware	16	10,785	308	11,093	39
Retail: Pet Products & Services	29	1,403	239	1,642	40

CATEGORY	# of Fran-chisors	Fran-chised Units	Company-Owned Units	Total Operating Units	See Chapter
Retail: Photographic Products & Services	19	942	173	1,115	41
Retail: Specialty	112	8,175	2,494	10,669	42
Retail: Video / Audio / Electronics	19	4,160	8,452	12,612	43
Retail: Miscellaneous	13	1,311	150	1,461	44
Security & Safety Systems	16	757	112	869	45
Signs	17	2,007	7	2,014	46
Travel	22	5,199	577	5,776	47
Miscellaneous	111	14,189	1,116	15,305	48
Industry Total	**2,522**	**472,206**	**89,140**	**561,346**	
% of Total		**84.1%**	**15.9%**	**100.0%**	

Exhibit 2

Relative Size - By Number of Total Operating Units:	**#**	**%**	Cum. %
> 5,000 Total Operating Units	19	0.8%	0.8%
1,000 - 4,999 Total Operating Units	72	2.9%	3.6%
500 - 999 Total Operating Units	104	4.1%	7.7%
250 - 499 Total Operating Units	156	6.2%	13.9%
100 - 249 Total Operating Units	344	13.6%	27.6%
50 - 99 Total Operating Units	324	12.8%	40.4%
25 - 49 Total Operating Units	337	13.4%	53.8%
15 - 24 Total Operating Units	250	9.9%	63.7%
Less Than 15 Total Operating Units	916	36.3%	100.0%
Total	**2,522**	**100.0%**	

Exhibit 3

Country of Origin:	**#**	**%**
United States	2,202	87.3%
Canada	320	12.7%
Total	**2,522**	**100.0%**

All of the data in Exhibits 1 - 3 are proprietary and should not be used or quoted without specifically acknowledging Bond's Franchise Guide as the source.

BOND'S FRANCHISE GUIDE
ANNUAL FRANCHISING INDUSTRY OVERVIEW
(As of 1/1/2002)

Exhibit 4

CATEGORY	Average Franchise Fee	Average Total Investment	Average Royalty Fee	# Survey Partici-pants	% of Industry Represent.
Automotive Products & Services	23.0K	199.9K	5.7%	73	45.9%
Auto / Truck / Trailer Rental	31.5K	232.3K	8.6%	17	58.6%
Building & Remodeling/Furniture/Appliance Repair	20.5K	67.7K	5.6%	45	42.5%
Business: Financial Services	21.5K	76.3K	8.9%	11	26.2%
Business: Advertising & Promotion	18.0K	48.7K	5.5%	7	20.0%
Business: Internet/Telecommunications/Misc.	22.7K	74.4K	20.9%	24	28.9%
Child Development / Education / Products	21.3K	144.1K	15.9%	38	46.3%
Education / Personal Development / Training	30.3K	128.4K	8.2%	24	44.4%
Employment & Personnel	25.5K	104.4K	7.2%	29	38.2%
Food: Donuts / Cookies / Bagels	25.4K	231.9K	5.3%	34	46.6%
Food: Coffee	20.7K	218.2K	6.0%	13	50.0%
Food: Ice Cream / Yogurt	22.7K	185.7K	5.4%	23	52.3%
Food: Quick Service / Take-out	21.2K	337.3K	4.9%	144	40.3%
Food: Restaurant / Family-Style	33.4K	875.8K	4.5%	62	34.3%
Food: Specialty Foods	22.3K	230.8K	5.3%	33	34.4%
Hairstyling Salons	17.1K	102.6K	5.6%	11	39.3%
Health / Fitness / Beauty	19.1K	194.3K	6.5%	26	33.3%
Laundry & Dry Cleaning	19.2K	224.3K	6.6%	11	47.8%
Lawn and Garden	34.0K	80.0K	6.9%	11	47.8%
Lodging	31.7K	3,621.0K	4.8%	21	28.4%
Maid Service & Home Cleaning	13.1K	49.3K	5.4%	14	58.3%
Maintenance / Cleaning / Sanitation	19.3K	63.5K	9.9%	66	51.2%
Medical / Optical / Dental A52Products & Services	27.4K	214.7K	5.0%	4	22.2%
Packaging & Mailing	25.3K	93.0K	5.7%	14	70.0%
Printing & Graphics	25.7K	271.3K	5.6%	15	57.7%
Publications	12.0K	21.4K	8.1%	6	22.2%
Real Estate Inspection Services	20.4K	29.3K	7.1%	11	52.4%
Real Estate Services	13.6K	99.1K	5.8%	21	36.8%
Recreation & Entertainment	20.6K	371.9K	8.5%	12	29.3%
Rental Services	16.4K	208.8K	5.3%	8	80.0%
Retail: Art, Art Supplies & Framing	28.2K	127.6K	5.5%	7	63.6%
Retail: Athletic Wear / Sporting Goods	31.4K	256.0K	11.3%	13	76.5%
Retail: Clothing / Shoes / Accessories	21.7K	104.5K	5.7%	3	50.0%
Retail: Convenience Stores / Supermarkets / Drugs	22.7K	353.2K	4.3%	11	39.3%
Retail: Home Furnishings	21.1K	163.5K	4.1%	17	38.6%
Retail: Home Improvement & Hardware	30.2K	303.5K	4.7%	6	37.5%
Retail: Pet Products & Services	17.6K	149.3K	5.4%	10	34.5%

CATEGORY	Average Franchise Fee	Average Total Investment	Average Royalty Fee	# Survey Partici-pants	% of Industry Represent.
Retail: Photographic Products & Services	20.2K	132.2K	6.0%	6	31.6%
Retail: Specialty	25.1K	193.6K	5.3%	46	41.1%
Retail: Video / Audio / Electronics	20.0K	95.3K	4.0%	4	21.1%
Retail: Miscellaneous	24.2K	139.8K	4.3%	5	38.5%
Security & Safety Systems	26.1K	217.1K	6.8%	4	25.0%
Signs	23.7K	114.8K	5.9%	8	47.1%
Travel	20.0K	52.2K	2.3%	6	27.3%
Miscellaneous	37.4K	152.3K	7.8%	23	20.7%
Total Participants				**997**	

Exhibit 5

CATEGORY	Average Franchise Fee	Average Total Investment	Average Royalty Fee	# Survey Partici-pants	% of Industry Represent.
Categories with Lowest Avg. Franchise Fee:					
Publications	$12.0K	21.4K	8.1%	6	22.2%
Maid Service & Home Cleaning	13.1K	49.3K	5.4%	14	58.3%
Real Estate Services	13.6K	99.1K	5.8%	21	36.8%
Categories with Lowest Avg. Total Investment:					
Publications	$12.0K	21.4K	8.1%	6	22.2%
Real Estate Inspection Services	20.4K	29.3K	7.1%	11	52.4%
Business: Advertising & Promotion	18.0K	48.7K	5.5%	7	20.0%
Categories with Lowest Avg. Royalty Fee:					
Travel	$20.0K	52.2K	2.3%	6	27.3%
Retail: Video / Audio / Electronics	20.0K	95.3K	4.0%	4	21.1%
Retail: Home Furnishings	21.1K	163.5K	4.1%	17	38.6%

All of the data in Exhibits 4 - 5 are proprietary and should not be used or quoted without specifically acknowledging Bond's Franchise Guide as the source.

excluded those franchisors who had no operating units or had no active franchised units. Some 300 companies listed in our database fall into one of these categories.

By unilaterally restricting the franchising universe, we are effectively acting as a screen. The objective is to save the prospective franchisee the unnecessary time and aggravation associated with trying to get in touch with a franchisor that isn't substantial enough to answer its phones professionally. After you become a franchisee, occasions will undoubtedly arise in which you will have a major problem that has to be resolved immediately. That is clearly not the time to be connected to an answering machine or an uninformed answering service. You want a substantial organization behind you — not a one- or two-man shop that may have priorities other than supporting its franchisees.

The Regulatory Agencies

The offer and sale of franchises are regulated at both the federal and state levels. Federal requirements cover all 50 states. In addition, certain states have adopted their own requirements.

In 1979, after many years of debate, the Federal Trade Commission (FTC) implemented Rule 436. This Rule requires that franchisors provide prospective franchisees with a disclosure statement (called an offering circular) containing specific information about a company's franchise offering. The Rule has two objectives: to ensure that the potential franchisee has sufficient background information to make an educated investment decision and to provide him or her with adequate time to do so.

Certain "registration states" require additional safeguards to protect potential franchisees. Their requirements are generally more stringent than the FTC's requirements. These states include California, Florida, Hawaii, Illinois, Indiana, Maryland, Michigan, Minnesota, New York, North Dakota, Oregon, Rhode Island, South Dakota, Virginia, Washington and Wisconsin. Separate registration is also required in the province of Alberta, Canada.

For the most part, registration states require a disclosure format know as the Uniform Franchise Offering Circular (UFOC). As a matter of convenience and because the state requirements are more demanding, most franchisors have adopted the UFOC format. This format requires that the franchisor provides a prospective franchisee with the required information at their first face-to-face meeting or at least 10 business days prior to the signing of the franchise agreement, whichever is earlier. Required information includes:

1. The Franchisor and Any Predecessors.
2. Identity and Business Experience of Persons Affiliated with the Franchisor.
3. Litigation.
4. Bankruptcy.
5. Franchisee's Initial Fee/Other Initial Payments.
6. Other Fees.
7. Franchisee's Initial Investment.
8. Obligations of Franchisee to Purchase or Lease from Designated Sources.
9. Obligations of Franchisee to Purchase or Lease in Accordance with Specifications or from Approved Suppliers.
10. Financing Arrangements.
11. Obligations of the Franchisor; Other Supervision, Assistance or Services.
12. Exclusive Area of Territory.
13. Trademarks, Service Marks, Trade Names, Logotypes and Commercial Symbols.
14. Patents and Copyrights.
15. Obligations of the Franchisee to Participate in the Actual Operation of the Franchise Business.
16. Restrictions on Goods and Services Offered by Franchisee.
17. Renewal, Termination, Repurchase, Modification and Assignment of the Franchise Agreement and Related Information.
18. Arrangements with Public Figures.
19. Actual, Average, Projected or Forecasted Franchise Sales, Profits or Earnings.
20. Information Regarding Franchises of the Franchisor.

21. Financial Statements.
22. Contracts.
23. Acknowledgment of Receipt by Respective Franchisee.

If you live in a registration state, make sure that the franchisor you are evaluating is, in fact, registered to sell franchises there. If not, and the franchisor has no near-term plans to register in your state, you should consider other options.

Keep in mind that neither the FTC nor any of the states has reviewed the offering circular to determine whether the information submitted is true or not. They merely require that the franchisor make representations based upon a prescribed format. If the information provided is false, franchisors are subject to civil penalties. That may not help a franchisee, however, who cannot undo a very expensive mistake.

It is up to you to read and thoroughly understand all elements of the offering circular. There is no question that it is tedious reading. Know exactly what you can expect from the franchisor and what your own obligations are. Under what circumstances can the relationship be unilaterally terminated by the franchisor? What is your protected territory? Specifically, what front-end assistance will the franchisor provide? You should have a professional review the UFOC. Shame on you if you don't take full advantage of the documentation that is available to you. The penalties are severe, and you will have no one to blame but yourself.

The Trade Associations

The **International Franchise Association** (IFA) was established as a non-profit trade association to promote franchising as a responsible method of doing business. The IFA currently represents over 650 franchisors in the U.S. and around the world. It is recognized as the leading spokesperson for responsible franchising. For most of its 30+ years, the IFA has represented the interests of franchisors only. In recent years, however, it has initiated an aggressive campaign to recruit franchisees into its membership and represent their interests as well. The IFA's address is 1350 New York Ave., NW, # 900, Washington, DC 20005. (202) 628-8000; FAX (202) 628-0812; www.franchise.org.

The **Canadian Franchise Association** (CFA), which has some 250+ members, is the Canadian equivalent of the IFA. Information on the CFA can be obtained from its offices at 2585 Skymark Ave., # 300, Mississauga, ON L4W 4L5, Canada. (905) 625-2896; FAX (905) 625-9076; www.cfa.ca.

The **American Association of Franchisees & Dealers** (AAFD) represents the rights and interests of franchisees and independent dealers. Formed in 1992 with the mission of "Bringing Fairness to Franchising," the AAFD represents thousands of franchised businesses, representing over 250 different franchise systems. It provides a broad range of services designed to help franchisees build market power, create legislative support, provide legal and financial support and provide a wide range of general member benefits. P.O. Box 81887, San Diego, CA 92138. (800) 733-9858, (619) 209-3775; FAX: (619) 209-3777.

Franchise Survival/Failure Rate

In order to promote the industry's attractiveness, most literature on the subject of franchising includes the same often-quoted, but very misleading, statistics that leave the impression that franchising is a near risk-free investment.

In the 1970s, the Small Business Administration produced a poorly documented report that 38% of all small businesses fail within their first year of operation and 77% fail within their first five years. With franchising, however, comparative failure rates miraculously drop to only three percent after the first year and eight percent after five years. No effort was made to define failure. Instead, "success" was defined as an operating unit still in business under the same name at the same location.

While most people would agree that the failure rates for franchised businesses are substantially lower than the failure rates for independent businesses, that assumption is not substantiated by reliable statistics. Part of the problem is definitional. Part is the fact that the industry has a vested interest in perpetuating the myth rather than debunking it.

FRANDATA, a Washington, DC-based franchise research firm, recently conducted a review of franchise terminations and renewals. It found that 4.4% of all franchisees left their franchise system each year for a variety of reasons. This figure does not include sales to third parties, however. To be fully meaningful, the data should include sales to third parties and the underlying reasons behind a sale.

The critical issue is to properly define failure and success, and then require franchisors to report changes in ownership based on these universally accepted definitions. A logical starting point in defining success should be whether the franchisee can "make an honest living" as a franchisee. A "success" would occur when the franchisee prefers to continue as a franchisee rather than sell the business. A "failure" would occur when the franchisee is forced to sell his or her business at a loss.

A reasonable measure of franchise success would be to ask franchisees "would you do it again?" If a legitimate survey were conducted of all franchisees of all systems, my guess is that the answer to this question would indicate a "success rate" well under 70% after a five-year period. Alternatively, one could ask the question "has the franchise investment met your expectations?" I estimate that fewer than 50% would say "yes" after a five-year period. These are just educated guesses. Like the franchising industry, I have no basis in fact for these estimates.

The failure rate is unquestionably lower for larger, more mature companies in the industry that have proven their systems and carefully chosen their franchisees. It is higher for smaller, newer companies that have unproven products and are less demanding in whom they accept as a franchisee.

As it now stands, the Uniform Franchise Offering Circular (UFOC) only requires the franchisor to provide the potential franchisee with the names of owners who have left the system within the past 12 months. In my opinion, this is a severe shortcoming of the regulatory process. Unless required, franchisors will not willingly provide information about failures to prospective franchisees. There is no question in my mind, however, that franchisors are fully aware of when and why past failures have occurred.

It is patently unfair that a potential investor should not have access to this critical information. To ensure its availability, I propose that the UFOC be amended to require that franchisors provide franchisee turn-over information for the most recent five-year period. Underlying reasons for a change in ownership would be provided by a departing franchisee on a universal, industry-approved questionnaire filled out during an "exit" interview. The questionnaire would then be returned to some central clearing house.

The only way to make up for this lack of information is to aggressively seek out as many previous and current franchisees as possible. Request past UFOCs to get the names of previous owners, and then contact them. Whether successful or not, these owners are an invaluable resource. Try to determine the reason for their failure and/or disenchantment. Most failures are the result of poor management or inadequate finances on the part of the departing franchisee. But people give up franchises for other reasons.

Current franchisees are even better sources of meaningful information. For systems with under 25 units, I strongly encourage you to talk to all franchisees. For those having between 25 and 100 units, I recommend talking to at least half. And for all others, interview a minimum of 50.

What Makes a Winning Franchise

Virtually every writer on the subject of franchising has his or her own idea of what determines a winning franchise. I maintain that there are five primary factors.

1. A product or service with a clear advantage over the competition. The advantage may be

in brand recognition, a unique, proprietary product or 30 years of proven experience.

2. A standardized franchise system that has been time-tested. Look for a company in which most of the bugs in the system have been worked out through the cumulative experience of both company-owned and franchised units. By the time a system has 30 or more operating units, it should be thoroughly tested.

3. Exceptional franchisor support. This includes not only the initial training program, but the on-going support (R&D, refresher training, [800] help-lines, field representatives and on-site training, annual meetings, advertising and promotion, central purchasing, etc.).

4. The financial wherewithal and management experience to carry out any announced growth plans without short-changing its franchisees. Sufficient depth of management is often lacking in high-growth franchises.

5. A strong mutuality of interest between franchisor and franchisees. Unless both parties realize that their relationship is one of long-term partners, it is unlikely that the system will ever achieve its full potential. Whether they have the necessary rapport is easily determined by a few telephone calls.

Financial Projections

The single most important factor in buying a franchise — or any business for that matter — is having a realistic projection of sales, expenses and profits. Specifically, how much can you expect to make after working 65 hours a week for 52 weeks a year? No one is in a better position to supply accurate information (subject to caveats) about a franchise opportunity than the franchisor itself. A potential franchisee often does not have the experience to sit down and project what his or her sales and profits will be over the next five years. This is especially true if he or she has no applied experience in that particular business.

Earnings claim statements (Item 19 of the UFOC) present franchisor-supplied sales, expense and/or profit summaries based on actual operating results for company-owned and/or franchised units. Since no format is prescribed, however, the data may be cursory or detailed. The only constraint is that the franchisor must be able to substantiate the data presented. Further complicating the process is the fact that providing an earnings claim statement is strictly optional. Accordingly, less than 15% of franchisors provide one.

Virtually everyone agrees that the information included in an earnings claim statement can be exceedingly helpful to a potential franchisee. Unfortunately, there are many reasons why franchisors might not willingly choose to make their actual results available to the public. Many franchisors feel that a prospective investor would be turned off if he or she had access to actual operating results. Others may not want to go to the trouble and expense of collecting the data.

Other franchisors are legitimately afraid of being sued for "misrepresentation." There is considerable risk to a franchisor if a published earnings claim statement is interpreted in any way as a "guarantee" of sales or income for new units. Given today's highly litigious society, and the propensity of courts to award large settlements to the "little guy," it's not surprising that so few franchisors provide the information.

As an assist to prospective franchisees, Source Book Publications has recently published a book entitled *"How Much Can I Make?"*. It includes over 143 earnings claim statements covering a diverse group of industries. It is the only publication that contains current earnings claim statements submitted by the franchisors. Given the scarcity of industry projections, this is an invaluable resource for potential franchisees or investors in determining what he or she might make by investing in a franchise or similar business. The book is $29.95, plus $5.00 for shipping. See the inside rear cover of this book for additional detail on the book and the companies that have submitted earnings claim statements. The book can be obtained from Source Book Publications, P.O. Box 12488, Oakland, CA 94604, or by calling (510) 839-5471, or by faxing a request to (510) 839-2104.

New vs. Used

As a potential franchisee, you have the option of becoming a franchisee in a new facility at a new location or purchasing an existing franchise. It is not an easy decision. Your success in making that choice will depend upon your business acumen and your insight into people

Purchasing a new franchise unit will mean that everything is current, clean and under warranty. Purchasing an existing franchise will probably involve a smaller investment and allow greater financial leverage. However, you will have to assess the seller's reason for selling. Is the business not performing to expectations because of poor management, poor location, poor support from the franchisor, an indifferent staff, obsolete equipment and/or facilities, etc.? The decision is further clouded because you may be working through a business broker who may or may not be giving you good information. Regardless of the obstacles, considering a "used" franchise merits your consideration. Apply the same analytical tools you would to a new franchise. Do your homework. Be thorough. Be unrelenting.

The Negotiation Process

Once you have narrowed your options down to your top two or three choices, you must negotiate the best deal you can with the franchisor. In most cases, the franchisor will tell you that the franchise agreement cannot be changed. If you accept this explanation, shame on you. Notwithstanding the legal requirement that all of a franchisor's agreements be **substantially** the same at any point in time, there are usually a number of variables in the equation. If the franchisor truly wants you as a franchisee, it may be willing to make concessions not available to the next applicant. Will the franchisor take a short-term note for all or part of the franchise fee? Can you expand from your initial unit after you have proven yourself? If so, can the franchise fee be eliminated or reduced on a second unit? Can you get a right of first refusal on adjacent territories? Can the term of the agreement be extended from 10–15 years? Can you include a franchise cancellation right if the training and/or initial support don't meet your expectations or the franchisor's promises? The list goes on ad infinitum.

To successfully negotiate, you must have a thorough knowledge of the industry, the franchise agreement you are negotiating (and agreements of competitive franchise opportunities) and access to experienced professional advice. This can be a lawyer, an accountant or a franchise consultant. Above all else, they should have proven experience in negotiating franchise agreements. Franchising is a unique method of doing business. Don't pay someone $100+ per hour to learn the industry. Make them demonstrate that they have been through the process several times before. Negotiating a long-term agreement of this type is extremely tricky and fraught with pitfalls. The risks are extremely high. Don't be so smug as to think that you can handle the negotiations yourself. Don't be so frugal as to think you can't afford outside counsel. In point of fact, you can't afford not to employ an experienced professional.

The Four Rs of Franchising

We are told as children that the three Rs of reading, 'riting and 'rithmetic are critical to our scholastic success. Success in franchising depends on four Rs — realism, research, reserves and resolve.

Realism

At the outset of your investigation, it is important that you be realistic about your strengths and weaknesses, your goals and your capabilities. I strongly recommend that you take the time necessary to do a personal audit — possibly with the help of outside professionals — before investing your life's savings in a franchise.

Franchising is not a money machine. It involves hard work, dedication, set-backs and long hours. Be realistic about the nature of the business you are buying. What traits will ultimately determine your success? Do you have them? If it is a service-oriented business, will you be able to keep smiling when you know the client/customer is a fool? If it is a fast-food business, will you be able to properly manage a minimum-wage staff? How well will you handle the uncertainties that will invariably arise? Can you make day-to-day decisions based on imperfect information? Can you count on your spouse's support after you have gone through all of your working capital reserves, and the future looks cloudy and uncertain?

Be equally realistic about your franchise selection process. Have you thoroughly evaluated all of the alternatives? Have you talked with everyone you can to ensure that you have left no stone unturned? Have you carefully and realistically assessed the advantages and disadvantages of the system offered, the unique demographics of your territory, near-term market trends, the financial projections, etc.? The selection process is tiring. It is easy to convince yourself that the franchise opportunity in your hand is really the best one for you. The penalties for doing so, however, are extreme.

Research

There is no substitute for exhaustive research!

Bond's Franchise Guide contains over 2,000 franchise listings, broken into 45 distinct business categories. This represents a substantial number of options from which to choose. It is up to you to spend the time required to come up with an optimal selection. At a minimum, you will probably be in that business for five years. More likely, you will be in it 10 years or more. Given the long-term commitment, allow yourself the necessary time to ensure you won't regret having made a hasty decision. Research is a tedious, boring process. But doing it carefully and thoroughly can greatly reduce your risk and exposure. The benefits are measurable.

I suggest you first determine which industry groups hold your interest. Don't arbitrarily limit yourself to a particular industry in which you have first-hand experience. Next, request information from all of the companies that are listed in those industries. The incremental cost of mailing (or calling) requests to an additional 15 or 20 companies is insignificant in the larger picture. Based on personal experience, you may feel you already know the best franchise. Step back. Assume there is a competing franchise out there with a comparable product or service, comparable management, etc., that charges a royalty fee 2% of sales less than your intuitive choice. Over a 10-year period, that could add up to a great deal of money. It certainly justifies your requesting initial information.

A thorough analysis of the literature you receive should allow you to reduce the list of prime candidates down to six to eight companies. Aggressively evaluate each firm. Talking with current and former franchisees is the single best source of information you can get. Where possible, site visits are invaluable. My experience is that franchisees tend to be candid in their level of satisfaction with the franchisor. However, since they don't know you, they may be less candid about their sales, expenses and income. Go to the library and get studies that forecast industry growth, market saturation, industry problems, technical breakthroughs, etc. Don't find out a year after becoming a franchisee of a coffee company that earlier reports suggested that the coffee market was oversaturated or that coffee was linked to some form of colon cancer.

Reserves

As a new business, franchising is replete with uncertainty, uneven cash flows and unforeseen problems. It is an imperfect world that might not bear any relation to the pro formas you originally prepared to justify getting into the business. Any one of these unforeseen contingencies could cause a severe drain on your cash reserves. At the same time, you will have fixed and/or contractual payments that must be met on a current basis regardless of sales: rent, employee salaries, insurance, etc. Adequate back-up reserves may be in the form of savings, commitments from relatives, bank loans, etc. Just make certain that the funds are available when, and if, you need them. To be absolutely safe, I suggest you double the level of reserves recommended by the franchisor.

Keep in mind that the most common cause of business failure is inadequate working capital. Plan properly so you don't become a statistic.

Resolve

Let's assume for the time being that you have demonstrated exceptional levels of realism, research and reserves. You have picked an optimal franchise that takes full advantage of your strengths. You are in business and bringing in enough money to achieve a positive cash flow. The future looks bright. Now the fourth R — resolve — comes into play. Remember why you chose franchising in the first place: to take full advantage of a system that has been time-tested in the marketplace. Remember also what makes franchising work so well: the franchisor and franchisees maximize their respective success by working within the system for the common good. Invariably, two obstacles arise.

The first is the physical pain associated with writing that monthly royalty check. Annual sales of $250,000 and a 6% royalty fee result in a monthly royalty check of $1,250 that must be sent to the franchisor. Every month. As a franchisee, you may look for any justification to reduce this sizable monthly outflow. Resist the temptation. Accept the fact that royalty fees are simply another cost of doing business. They are also a legal obligation that you willingly agreed to pay when you signed the franchise agreement. They are the dues you agreed to pay when you joined the club.

Although there may be an incentive, don't look for loopholes in the contract that might allow you to sue the franchisor or get out of the relationship. Don't report lower sales than actual in an effort to reduce royalties. If you have received the support that you were promised, continue to play by the rules. Honor your commitment. Let the franchisor enjoy the rewards it has earned from your success.

The second obstacle is the desire to change the system. You need to honor your commitment to be a "franchisee" and to live within the franchise system. What makes franchising successful as far as your customers are concerned is uniformity and consistency of appearance, product/service quality and corporate image. The most damaging thing an individual franchisee can do is to suddenly and unilaterally introduce changes to a proven system. While these modifications may work in one market, they only serve to diminish the value of the system as a whole. Imagine what would happen to the national perception of your franchise if every franchisee had the latitude to make unilateral changes in his or her operations. Accordingly, any ideas you have on improving the system should be submitted directly to the franchisor for its evaluation. Accept the franchisor's decision on whether or not to pursue an idea.

If you suspect that you may be a closet entrepreneur who needs unrestrained experimenting and tinkering, you are probably not cut out to be a franchisee. Seriously consider this question before you get into a relationship, instead of waiting until you are locked into an untenable situation.

Summary

I hope that I have been clear in suggesting that the selection of an optimal franchise is both time- and energy-consuming. Done properly, the process may take six to nine months and involve the expenditure of several thousand dollars. The difference between a hasty, gut-feel investigation and an exhaustive, well-thought out investigation may mean the difference between finding a poorly-conceived, or even fraudulent, franchise and an exceptional one.

My sense is that there is a strong correlation between the efforts you put into the investigative process and the ultimate degree of success you enjoy as a franchisee. The process is to investigate, evaluate and negotiate. Don't try to bypass any one of these critical elements.

How to Use the Data

Chapter 2

The appendix includes the original questionnaire sent to some 2,500 U.S. and Canadian franchisors. Franchisors who did not respond to the original mailing received a follow-up package roughly one month later. The end result was that roughly 40% of the contacted franchisors returned a completed questionnaire. Those franchisors who did not respond to either mailing, but who still actively franchise (subject to the restrictions noted in Chapter 1), are noted in the Supplemental Listing of Franchisors at the end of each chapter.

The data returned has been condensed into the profiles shown on the following pages. In some cases, an answer has been abbreviated to conserve room and to make the profiles more directly comparable. All of the data is displayed with the objective of providing as much background data as possible. In those cases where no answer was provided to a particular question within the questionnaire, an "NR" is used to signify "No Response."

Please take a few minutes to acquaint yourself with the composition of the sample profile. Supplementary comments have been added where some interpretation of the franchisor's response is required.

Keep in mind that all of the profile data is based on questionnaires returned by the franchisors themselves, with no effort to verify its accuracy independently. There is no doubt that franchisors had some latitude to exaggerate their responses in order to make themselves appear bigger, more mature and/or more franchisee-oriented than they really are. I am confident that some small percentage did just that. The vast majority, however, would see any such deception as dishonest, counter-productive and a general waste of everyone's time.

ꟸ

BLIMPIE SUBS AND SALADS, an extremely well-established fast-food concept, has been selected to illustrate how this book uses the collected data.

BLIMPIE SUBS AND SALADS

1775 The Exchange, # 600
Atlanta, GA 30339
Tel: (800) 447-6256 (770) 984-2707
Fax: (770) 980-9176
E-Mail: chuckt@blimpie.com
Web Site: www.blimpie.com

Mr. Chuck Taylor, National Business Development

National submarine sandwich chain, serving fresh-sliced, high-quality meats and cheeses on fresh-baked bread. Also offering an assortment of fresh-made salads and other quality products.

BACKGROUND: IFA MEMBER

Established: 1964;	1st Franchised: 1977
Franchised Units:	1,954
Company-Owned Units	1
Total Units:	1,955
Dist.:	US-1,881; CAN-13; O'seas-61
North America:	50 States. 4 Provinces
Density:	205 in GA, 203 in FL, 121 in TX
Projected New Units (12 Months):	20
Qualifications:	4,3,2,2,2,5

Registered: CA, FL, HI, IL, IN, MI, MN, NY, ND, OR, RI, SD, WA, WI

FINANCIAL/TERMS:

Cash Investment:	$25-100K
Total Investment:	$60-200K
Minimum Net Worth:	$50K
Fees: Franchise —	$10-18K
Royalty — 6%;	Ad. — 4%
Earnings Claim Statement:	No
Term of Contract (Years):	20/5
Avg. # Of Employees:	4 FT, 8 PT
Passive Ownership:	Discouraged
Encourage Conversions:	Yes
Area Develop. Agreements:	Yes
Sub-Franchising Contracts:	Yes
Expand In Territory:	Yes

Space Needs: 1,200 SF; FS, SF, SC, RM

SUPPORT & TRAINING PROVIDED:

Financial Assistance Provided:	Yes(I)
Site Selection Assistance:	Yes
Lease Negotiation Assistance:	Yes
Co-Operative Advertising:	Yes
Franchisee Assoc./Member:	Yes/Yes
Size Of Corporate Staff:	109
On-Going Support:	B,C,D,E,F,G,H,I

Training: 120 Hours in Local Franchise.

SPECIFIC EXPANSION PLANS:

US:	All United States
Canada:	All Canada
Overseas:	All Except Anti-American Countries

Bond's Top 50 Franchises:

As the industry leader in publishing books on franchising, Source Book Publications is constantly asked *"What are the best franchises?"* Given that there are over 2,500 active North American franchise systems, there clearly is no simple answer. This is especially true given the individual needs, experience and financial wherewithal of a widely-divergent pool of prospective franchisees.

At least to answer the question partially, our staff has broken the franchising industry into three major segments — food-service, service-based and retail franchises. Within each group a rigorous, in-depth analysis was performed on literally hundreds of proven franchise systems to arrive at what we feel are the top 50 franchises in each of these segments. Companies were evaluated on the basis of historical performance, brand identification, market dynamics, franchisee satisfaction, the level of initial training and on-going support, financial stability and other key factors.

The end result was the publication of three separate new publications — *Bond's Top 50 Food-Service Franchises, Bond's Top 50 Service-Based Franchises* and *Bond's Top 50 Retail Franchises.* Each of the 50 companies identified in these books is also identified in this book with an icon that says "Top 50" next to their company logo.

To ensure that we provide the most current information to our readers and are able to stay on top of the dynamics of the industry and its individual participants, the publication of the Top 50 Series will be an annual effort. Companies that are not in a Top 50 publication this year will be considered for inclusion in subsequent years. Inclusion will be based solely on merit. There is absolutely no favoritism shown toward any particular franchise. And, since we do not permit advertising in our publications, there is also no correlation between selection as a Top 50 company and advertising revenues.

Address/Contact:

1. **Company name, address, telephone and fax numbers.**

Comment: All of the data published in the book was current at the time the completed questionnaire was received or upon subsequent verification by phone. Over a 12-month period between annual publications, 10–15% of the addresses and/or telephone numbers become obsolete for various reasons. If you are unable to contact a franchisor at the address/telephone number listed, please give us a call at (510) 839-5471 (or fax [510] 839-2104) and we will provide you with the current address and telephone number.

2. **(800) 447-6256 (770) 984-2707.** In many cases, you may find that you cannot access the (800) number from your area. Do not conclude that the company has gone out of business. Simply call the local number.

Comment: An (800) number serves two important functions. The first is to provide an efficient, no-cost way for potential franchisees to contact the franchisor. Making the prospective franchisee foot the bill artificially limits the number of people who might otherwise make the initial contact. The second function is to demonstrate to existing franchisees that the franchisor is doing everything it can to efficiently respond to problems in the field as they occur. Many companies have a restricted (800) line for their franchisees that the general public cannot access. Since you will undoubtedly be talking with the franchisor's staff on a periodic basis, it is important to determine whether an (800) line is available to franchisees.

Over two-thirds of the companies listed in the book have (800) numbers. Extreme competition among telephone companies today makes the incremental cost of an (800) number relatively minor. My feeling is that it is an expense a franchisor should incur if it wants to stay competitive.

3. **Contact.** You should honor the wishes of the franchisor and address all initial correspondence to the contact listed. It would be counter-productive to try to reach the president directly if the designated contact is the director of franchising.

Comment: The president is the designated contact in approximately half of the profiles noted below. The reason for this varies among franchisors. The president is the best spokesperson for his or her operation, and no doubt it flatters the franchisee to talk directly with the president, or perhaps there is no one else around. Regardless of the justification, it is important to determine if the operation is a one-man show in which the president does everything or if the president merely feels that having an open line to potential franchisees is the best way for him or her to sense the "pulse" of the company and the market. Convinced that the president can only do so many things well, I would want assurances that, by taking all incoming calls, he or she is not neglecting the day-to-day responsibilities of managing the business.

Description of Business:

4. **Description of Business:** The questionnaire provides franchisors with adequate room to differentiate their franchise from the competition. In a minor number of cases, some editing was required.

Comment: In instances where franchisors show no initiative or imagination in describing their operations, you must decide whether this is symptomatic of the company or simply a reflection of the individual who responded to the questionnaire.

Background:

5. **IFA MEMBER.** There are two primary affinity groups associated with the franchising industry — the International Franchise Association (IFA) and the Canadian Franchise Association (CFA). Both the IFA and the CFA are described in Chapter 1.

6. **Established: 1964.** BLIMPIE SUBS AND SALADS was founded in 1964, and, accordingly, has almost 40 years of experience in its primary business. It should be intuitively obvious that a firm that has been in existence for over 20 years has a greater likelihood of being around five years from now than a firm that was founded only last year.

7. **1st Franchised: 1977.** 1977 was the year that BLIMPIE SUBS AND SALADS's first franchised unit(s) were established.

Comment: Over ten years of continuous operation, both as an operator and as a franchisor, is compelling evidence that a firm has staying power. The number of years a franchisor has been in business is one of the key variables to consider in choosing a franchise. This is not to say that a new franchise should not receive your full attention. Every company has to start from scratch. Ultimately, a prospective franchisee has to be convinced that the franchise has 1) been in operation long enough, or 2) its key management personnel have adequate industry experience to have worked out the bugs normally associated with a new business. In most cases, this experience can only be gained through on-the-job training. Don't be the guinea pig that provides the franchisor with the experience it needs to develop a smoothly running operation.

8. **Franchised Units: 1,954.** As of 1/1/2002, BLIMPIE SUBS AND SALADS had 1,954 franchisee-owned and operated units.

9. **Company-Owned Units: 1.** As of 1/1/2002, BLIMPIE SUBS AND SALADS had one company-owned and -operated unit.

Comment: A younger franchise should prove that its concept has worked successfully in several company-owned units before it markets its "system" to a franchisee. Without company-owned prototype stores, the new franchisee may well end up being the "testing kitchen" for the franchise concept itself.

If a franchise concept is truly exceptional, why doesn't the franchisor commit some of its resources to take advantage of the investment opportunity? Clearly a financial decision on the part of the franchisor, the absence of company-owned units should not be a negative in and of itself. This is especially true of proven franchises, which may have previously sold their company-owned operations to franchisees.

Try to determine if there is a noticeable trend in the percentage of company-owned units. If the franchisor is buying back units from franchisees, it may be doing so to preclude litigation. Some firms also "churn" their operating units with some regularity. If the sales pitch is compelling, but the follow-through is not competitive, a franchisor may sell a unit to a new franchisee, wait for him or her to fail, buy it back for $0.60 cents on the dollar and then sell that same unit to the next unsuspecting franchisee. Each time the unit is resold, the franchisor collects a franchise fee, plus the negotiated discount from the previous franchisee.

Alternatively, an increasing or high percentage of company-owned units may well mean the company is convinced of the long-term profitability of such an approach. The key is to determine whether a franchisor is building new units from scratch or buying them from failing and/or unhappy franchisees.

10. **Total Units: 1,955.** As of 1/1/2002, BLIMPIE SUBS AND SALADS had a total of 1,955 franchisee-owned and company-owned units.

Comment: Like a franchisor's longevity, its experience in operating multiple units offers considerable comfort. Those franchisors with over 15–25 operating units have proven that their system works and have probably encountered and overcome most of the problems that plague a new operation. Alternatively, the management of franchises with less than 15 operating units may have gained considerable industry experience before joining the current franchise. It is up to the franchisor to convince you that it is providing you with as risk-free an operation as possible. You don't want to be providing a company with its basic experience in the business.

11. **Distribution: US-1,881; CAN-13; O'seas-61.** As of 1/1/2002, BLIMPIE SUBS AND SALADS had 1,881 operating units in the U.S., 13 in Canada and 61 Overseas.

12. **Distribution: North America: 50 States, 4 Provinces.** As of 1/1/2002, BLIMPIE SUBS AND SALADS had operations in all 50 states in the U.S. and four provinces in Canada.

Comment: It should go without saying that the wider the geographic distribution, the greater the franchisor's level of success. For the most part, such distribution can only come from a large number of operating units. If, however, the franchisor has operations in 15 states but only 18 total operating units, it is unlikely that it can efficiently service these accounts because of geographic constraints. Other things being equal, a prospective franchisee would vastly prefer a franchisor with 15 units in New York to one with 15 units scattered throughout the U.S., Canada and overseas.

13. **Distribution: Density: 205 in GA, 203 in FL, 121 in TX.** The franchisor was asked to list the three states/provinces with the largest number of operating units. (No distinction was made between company-owned and franchisee-owned units.) As of 1/1/2002, BLIMPIE SUBS AND SALADS had 205 units in Georgia, 203 units in Florida and 121 units in Texas.

Comment: For smaller, regional franchises, geographic distribution could be a key variable in deciding whether to buy. If the franchisor has a concentration of units in your immediate geographic area, it is likely that you will be well-served.

For those far removed geographically from the franchisor's current areas of operation, however, there can be problems. It is both time consuming and expensive to support a franchisee 2,000 miles away from company headquarters. To the extent that a franchisor can visit four franchisees in one area on one trip, there is no problem. If, however, your operation is the only one west of the Mississippi, you may not receive the on-site assistance you would like. Don't be a missionary who has to rely on his or her own devices to survive. Don't accept a franchisor's idle promises of support. If on-site assistance is important to your ultimate success, get assurances in writing that the necessary support will be forthcoming. Remember, you are buying into a system, and the availability of day-to-day support is one of the key ingredients of any successful franchise system.

14. **Projected New Units (12 Months): 20.** BLIMPIE SUBS AND SALADS plans to open 20 new units within the following 12 months. Again, there was no distinction between franchised and company-owned units.

Comment: In business, growth has become a highly visible symbol of success. Rapid growth is generally perceived as preferable to slower, more controlled growth. I maintain, however, that the opposite is frequently the case. It is highly unlikely that a new franchise with only five operating units can successfully attract, screen, train and bring multiple new units on-stream in a 12-month period. If it suggests that it can, or even wants to, be properly wary. You must be confident a company has the financial and managerial resources necessary to pull off such a Herculean feat. If management is already thin, concentrating on attracting new units will clearly diminish the time it can and should spend supporting you. It takes many months, if not years, to develop and train a second level of management. You don't want to depend upon new hires teaching you systems and procedures they themselves know little or nothing about.

15. **Qualifications: 4,3,2,2,2,5.** Question 34 of the questionnaire in the Appendix was posed to determine which specific evaluation criteria were important to the franchisor. The franchisor was asked the following: "In qualifying a potential franchisee, please rank the following criteria from Unimportant (1) to Very Important (5)." The responses should be self-explanatory.

Financial Net Worth (Rank from 1–5)

General Business Experience (Rank from 1–5)

Specific Industry Experience (Rank from 1–5)

Formal Education (Rank from 1–5)

Psychological Profile (Rank from 1–5)

Personal Interview(s) (Rank from 1–5)

16. **Registered** refers to the 16 states that require specific formal registration at the state level before the franchisor may offer franchises in that state. State registration and disclosure to the Federal Trade Commission are separate issues that are discussed in Chapter 1.

Capital Requirements/Rights:

17. **Cash Investment: $25-100K.** On average, a BLIMPIE SUBS AND SALADS franchisee will have made a cash investment of $25,000–100,000 by the time he or she finally opens the initial operating unit.

Comment: It is important that you be realistic about the amount of cash you can comfortably invest in a business. Stretching beyond your means can have grave and far-reaching consequences. Assume that you will encounter periodic setbacks and that you will have to draw on your reserves. The demands of starting a new business are harsh enough without adding the uncertainties associated with inadequate working capital. Trust the franchisor's recommendations regarding the suggested minimum cash investment. If anything, there is an incentive for setting the recommended level of investment too low, rather than too high. The franchisor will want to qualify you to the extent that you have adequate financing. No legitimate franchisor wants you to invest if there is a chance that you might fail because of a shortage of funds.

Keep in mind that you will probably not achieve a positive cash flow from the business before six months or more. In your discussions with the franchisor, be absolutely certain that its calculations include an adequate working capital reserve.

18. **Total Investment: $60–200K.** On average, BLIMPIE SUBS AND SALADS franchisees will invest a total of $60,000–200,000, including both cash and debt, by the time the franchise opens its doors.

Comment: The total investment should be the cash investment noted above plus any debt that you will incur in starting the new business. The form of the debt could be a promissory note to the franchisor for all or part of the franchise fee, an equipment lease, building and facilities leases, etc. Make sure that the total includes all of the obligations that you assume, especially any long-term lease obligations.

Be conservative in assessing what your real exposure is. If you are leasing highly specialized equipment or if you are leasing a single-purpose building, it is naive to think that you will recoup your investment if you have to sell or sub-lease those assets in a buyer's market. If there is any specialized equipment that may have been manufactured to the franchisor's specifications, determine if the franchisor has any form of buy-back provision.

19. **Minimum Net Worth: $50K.** In this case, BLIMPIE SUBS AND SALADS feels that a potential franchisee should have a minimum net worth of $50,000. Although net worth can be defined in vastly different ways, the franchisor's response should suggest a minimum level of equity that the prospective franchisee should possess. Net worth is the combination of both liquid and non-liquid assets. Again, don't think that franchisor-determined guidelines somehow don't apply to you.

20. **Fees (Franchise): $10-18K.** BLIMPIE SUBS AND SALADS requires a front-end, one-time-only payment of $10,000-18,000 to grant a franchise for a single location. As noted in Chapter 1, the franchise fee is a payment to reimburse the franchisor for the incurred costs of setting the franchisee up in business — from recruiting through training and manuals. The fee usually ranges from $15,000–30,000. It is a function of competitive franchise fees and the actual out-of-pocket costs incurred by the franchisor.

Depending upon the franchisee's particular circumstances and how well the franchisor thinks he or she might fit into the system, the franchisor may finance all or part of the franchise fee. (See below to see if a franchisor provides any direct or indirect financial assistance.)

The franchise fee is one area in which the franchisor frequently provides either direct or indirect financial support.

Comment: Ideally, the franchisor should do no more than recover its costs on the initial franchise fee. Profits come later in the form of royalty fees, which are a function of the franchisee's sales. Whether the franchise fee is $5,000 or $35,000, the total should be carefully evaluated. What are competitive fees and are they financed? How much training will you actually receive? Are the fees reflective of the franchisor's expenses? If the fees appear to be non-competitive, address your concerns with the franchisor.

Realize that a $5,000 differential in the one-time franchise fee is a secondary consideration in the overall scheme of things. You are in the relationship for the long-term.

By the same token, don't get suckered by an extremely low fee if there is any doubt about the franchisor's ability to fulfill its obligations. Franchisors need to collect reasonable fees to cover their actual costs. If they don't recoup these costs, they cannot recruit and train new franchisees on whom your own future success partially depends.

21. **Fees (Royalty): 6%** means that 6% of gross sales (or other measure, as defined in the franchise agreement) must be periodically paid directly to the franchisor in the form of royalties. This on-going expense is your cost for being part of the larger franchise system and for all of the "back-office" support you receive. In a few cases, the amount of the royalty fee is fixed rather than variable. In others, the fee decreases as the volume of sales (or other measure) increases (i.e., 6% on the first $200,000 of sales, 5% on the next $100,000 and so on). In others, the fee is held at artificially low levels during the start-up phase of the franchisee's business, then increases once the franchisee is better able to afford it.

Comment: Royalty fees represent the mechanism by which the franchisor finally recoups the costs it has incurred in developing its business. It may take many years and many operating units before the franchisor is able to make a true operating profit.

Consider a typical franchisor who might have been in business for three years. With a staff of five, rent, travel, operating expenses, etc., assume it has annual operating costs of $300,000 (including reasonable owner's salaries). Assume also that there are 25 franchised units with average annual sales of $250,000 respectively. Each franchise is required to pay a 6% royalty fee. Total annual royalties in this scenario would total only $375,000. The franchisor is making a $75,000 profit. Then consider the personal risk the franchisor took in developing a new business and the initial years of negative cash flows. Alternatively, evaluate what it would cost you, as a sole proprietor, to provide the myriad services included in the royalty payment.

In assessing alternative investments, the amount of the royalty percentage is a major on-going expense. Assuming average annual sales of $250,000 per year over a 15-year period, the total royalties at 5% would be $187,500. At 6%, the cumulative fees would be $225,000. You have to be fully convinced that the $37,500 difference is justified. While this is clearly a meaningful number, what you are really evaluating is the quality of management and the unique competitive advantages of the goods and/or services offered by the franchisor.

22. **Fees (Advertising): 4%.** Most national or regional franchisors require their franchisees to contribute a certain percentage of their sales (or other measure, as determined in the franchise agreement) into a corporate advertising fund. These individual advertising fees are pooled to develop a corporate advertising/marketing effort that produces great economies of scale. The end result is a national or regional advertising program that promotes the franchisor's products and services. Depending upon the nature of the business, this percentage usually ranges from two to six percent and is in addition to the royalty fee.

Comment: One of the greatest advantages of a franchised system is its ability to promote, on a national or regional basis, its products and services. The promotions may be through television, radio, print medias or direct mail. The objective is name recognition and, over time, the assumption that the product and/or service has been "time-tested." An individual business owner could never justify the expense of mounting a major advertising program at the local level. For a smaller franchise that may not yet have an advertising program or fee, it is important to know when an advertising program will start, how it will be monitored and its expected cost.

23. **Earnings Claim Statement: No** means BLIMPIE SUBS AND SALADS does not provide an Earnings Claim statement to potential franchisees. Unfortunately, only 15–18% of franchisors provide an earnings claim statement in their Uniform Franchise Offering Circular (UFOC). The franchising industry's failure to require earnings claim statements does a serious disservice to the potential franchisee. See Chapter 1 for comments on this important document.

24. **Term of Contract (Years): 20/5.** BLIMPIE SUBS AND SALADS's initial franchise period runs for 20 years. The first renewal period runs for an additional 5 years. Assuming that the franchisee operates within the terms of the franchise agreement, he or she has 40 years within which to develop and, ultimately, sell the business.

Comment: The potential value of any business (or investment) is the discounted sum of the operating income that is generated each year plus its value upon liquidation. Given this truth, the length of the franchise agreement and any renewals are extremely important to the franchisee. It is essential that he or she has adequate time to develop the business to its full potential. At that time, he or she will have maximized the value of the business as an on-going concern. The value of the business to a potential buyer, however, is largely a function of how long the franchise agreement runs. If there are only two years remaining before the agreement expires, or if the terms of extension are vague, the business will be worth only a fraction of the value assigned to it with 15 years to go. For the most part, the longer the agreement and the subsequent extension, the better. (The same logic applies to a lease. If your sales are largely a function of your location and traffic count, then it is important that you have options to extend the lease under known terms. Your lease should never be longer than the remaining term of your franchise agreement however.)

Assuming the length of the agreement is acceptable, be clear under what circumstances renewals might not be granted. Similarly, know the circumstances under which a franchise agreement might be prematurely and unilaterally canceled by the franchisor. I strongly recommend that you have an experienced lawyer review this section of the franchise agreement. It would be devastating if, after spending years developing your business, there were a loophole in the contract that allowed the franchisor to arbitrarily cancel the relationship.

25. **Avg. # of Employees: 4 FT, 8 PT.** The franchisors were asked "Including the owner/operator, how many employees are recommended to properly staff the average franchised unit?" In BLIMPIE SUBS AND SALADS's case, four full-time employees and eight part-time employees are required.

Comment: Most entrepreneurs start a new business based on their intuitive feel that it will be "fun" and that their talents and experience will be put to good use. They will be doing what they enjoy and what they are good at. Times change. Your business prospers. The number of employees increases. You are spending an increasing percentage of your time taking care of personnel problems and less and less on the fun parts of the business. In Chapter 1, the importance of conducting a realistic self-appraisal was stressed. If you found that you have difficulties managing people, or you don't have the patience to manage a large minimum wage staff, cut your losses before you are locked into doing just that.

26. **Passive Ownership: Discouraged.** Depending on the nature of the business, many franchisors are indifferent as to whether you manage the business directly or hire a full-time manager to run it. Others are insistent that, at least for the initial franchise, the franchisee be a full-time owner/operator. BLIMPIE SUBS AND SALADS allows franchisees to hire full-time managers to run their retail outlets, but does not encourage it.

Comment: Unless you have a great deal of experience in the business you have chosen or in managing similar businesses, I feel strongly that you should initially commit your personal time and energies to make the system work. After you have developed a full understanding of the business and have competent, trusted staff members who can assume day-to-day operations, consider delegating these responsibilities. Running the business through a manager can be fraught with peril unless you have mastered all aspects of the business and there are strong economic incentives and sufficient safeguards to ensure the manager will perform as desired.

27. **Conversions Encouraged: Yes.** This section pertains primarily to sole proprietorships or "mom and pop" operations. To the extent that there truly are centralized operating savings associated with the franchise, the most logical people to join a franchise system are those sole practitioners who are working hard but only eking out a living. The implementation of proven systems and marketing clout could significantly reduce operating costs and increase profits.

Comment: The franchisor has the option of 1) actively encouraging such independent operators to become members of the franchise team, 2) seeking out franchisees with limited or no applied experience or 3) going after both groups. Concerned that it will be very difficult to break independent operators of the bad habits they have picked up over the years, many only choose course two. They might say to themselves: "I will continue to do things my way. I won't, or can't, accept corporate direction." Others are simply selective in the conversions they allow. In many cases, the franchise fee is reduced or eliminated for conversions.

28. **Area Development Agreements: Yes.** Area development agreements are more fully described in Chapter 1. Essentially, they allow an investor or investment group to develop an entire area or region. The schedule for development is clearly spelled out in the area development agreement. (Note: "Var." indicates varies and "Neg." indicates negotiable.)

Comment: Area development agreements represent an opportunity for the franchisor to choose a single franchisee or investment group to develop an entire area. The franchisee's qualifications should be strong and include proven business experience and the financial depth to pull it off. An area development agreement represents a great opportunity for an investor to tie up a large geographical area and develop a concept that may not have proven itself on a national basis. Keep in mind that this is a quantum leap from making an investment in a single franchise and is relevant only to those with development experience and deep pockets.

29. **Sub-Franchising Agreements: Yes.** BLIMPIE SUBS AND SALADS does grant sub-franchising agreements. (See Chapter 1 for a more thorough explanation.) Like area development agreements, sub-franchising also allows an investor or investment group to develop an entire area or region. The difference is that the

sub-franchisor becomes a self-contained business, responsible for all relations with franchisees within its area, from initial training to on-going support. Franchisees pay their royalties to the sub-franchisor, who in turn pays a portion to the master franchisor.

Comment: Sub-franchising is used primarily by smaller franchisors who have a relatively easy concept and who are prepared to sell a portion of the future growth of their business to someone for some front-end cash and a percentage of the future royalties they receive from their franchisees.

30. **Expand in Territory: Yes.** Under conditions spelled out in the franchise agreement, BLIMPIE SUBS AND SALADS will allow its franchisees to expand within their exclusive territory.

Comment: Some franchisors define the franchisee's exclusive territory so tightly that there would never be room to open additional outlets within an area. Others provide a larger area in the hopes that the franchisee will do well and have the incentive to open additional units.

There are clearly economic benefits to both parties from having franchisees with multiple units. There is no question that it is in your best interest to have the option to expand once you have proven to both yourself and the franchisor that you can manage the business successfully. Many would concur that the real profits in franchising come from managing multiple units rather than being locked into a single franchise in a single location. Additional fees may or may not be required with these additional units.

31. **Space Needs: 1,200 SF; FS, SF, SC, RM.** The average BLIMPIE SUBS AND SALADS retail outlet will require 1,200 square feet in a Free-Standing (FS) building, Storefront (SF) location, Strip Center (SC) or Regional Mall (RM). Other types of leased space might be Executive Suite (ES), Home Based (HB), Industrial Park (IP), Kiosk (KI), Office Building (OB), Power Center (PC), Regional Mall (RM) or Warehouse (WH).

Comment: Armed with the rough space requirements, you can better project your annual occupancy costs. It should be relatively easy to get comparable rental rates for the type of space required. As annual rent and related expenses can be as high as 15% of your annual sales, be as accurate as possible in your projections.

Franchisor Support and Training Provided:

32. **Financial Assistance Provided: Yes (I)** notes that BLIMPIE SUBS AND SALADS is indirectly (I) involved in providing financial assistance. Indirect assistance might include making introductions to the franchisor's financial contacts, providing financial templates for preparing a business plan or actually assisting in the loan application process. In some cases, the franchisor becomes a co-signer on a financial obligation (equipment lease, space lease, etc.). Other franchisors are (D) directly involved in the process. In this case, the assistance may include a lease or loan made directly by the franchisor. Any loan would generally be secured by some form of collateral. A very common form of assistance is a note for all or part of the initial franchise fee. Yes (B) indicates that the franchisor provides both direct and indirect financial assistance. The level of assistance will generally depend upon the relative strengths of the franchisee.

Comment: The best of all possible worlds is one in which the franchisor has enough confidence in the business and in you to co-sign notes on the building and equipment leases and allow you to pay off the franchise fee over a specified period of time. Depending upon your qualifications, this could happen. Most likely, however, the franchisor will only give you some assistance in raising the necessary capital to start the business. Increasingly, franchisors are testing a franchisee's business acumen by letting him or her assume an increasing level of personal responsibility in securing financing. The objective is to find out early in the process how competent a franchisee really is.

33. **Site Selection Assistance: Yes** means that BLIMPIE SUBS AND SALADS will assist the franchisee in selecting a site location. While the phrase "location, location, location" may be hack-

phrase "location, location, location" may be hackneyed, its importance should not be discounted, especially when a business depends upon retail traffic counts and accessibility. If a business is home- or warehouse-based, assistance in this area is of negligible or minor importance.

Comment: Since you will be locked into a lease for a minimum of three, and probably five, years, optimal site selection is absolutely essential. Even if you were somehow able to sub-lease and extricate yourself from a bad lease or bad location, the franchise agreement may not allow you to move to another location. Accordingly, it is imperative that you get it right the first time.

If a franchisor is truly interested in your success, it should treat your choice of a site with the same care it would use in choosing a company-owned site. Keep in mind that many firms provide excellent demographic data on existing locations at a very reasonable cost.

34. **Lease Negotiation Assistance: Yes.** Once a site is selected, BLIMPIE SUBS AND SALADS will be actively involved in negotiating the terms of the lease.

Comment: Given the complexity of negotiating a lease, an increasing number of franchisors are taking an active role in lease negotiations. There are far too many trade-offs that must be considered — terms, percentage rents, tenant improvements, pass-throughs, kick-out clauses, etc. This responsibility is best left to the professionals. If the franchisor doesn't have the capacity to support you directly, enlist the help of a well-recommended broker. The penalties for signing a bad long-term lease are very severe.

35. **Co-operative Advertising: Yes** refers to the existence of a joint advertising program in which the franchisor and franchisees each contribute to promote the company's products and/or services (usually within the franchisee's specific territory).

Comment: Co-op advertising is a common and mutually-beneficial effort. By agreeing to split part of the advertising costs, whether for television, radio or direct mail, the franchisor is not only supporting the franchisee, but guaranteeing itself royalties from the incremental sales. A franchisor that is not intimately involved with the advertising campaign — particularly when it is an important part of the business — may not be fully committed to your overall success.

36. **Franchisee Assoc./Member: Yes/Yes.** This response notes that the BLIMPIE SUBS AND SALADS system does include an active association made up of BLIMPIE SUBS AND SALADS franchisees. A Yes/Yes response indicates that BLIMPIE SUBS AND SALADS has both an association and is also a member of the franchisee association.

Comment: The empowerment of franchisees has become a major rallying cry within the industry over the past four years. Various states have recently passed laws favoring franchisee rights, and the subject has been widely discussed in congressional staff hearings. Political groups even represent franchisee rights on a national basis. Similarly, the IFA is now actively courting franchisees to become active members. Whether they are equal members remains to be seen.

Franchisees have also significantly increased their clout with respect to the franchisor. If a franchise is to grow and be successful in the long term, it is critical that the franchisor and its franchisees mutually agree that they are partners rather than adversaries.

37. **Size of Corporate Staff: 109.** BLIMPIE SUBS AND SALADS has 109 full-time employees on its staff to support its six operating units.

Comment: There are no magic ratios that tell you whether the franchisor has enough staff to provide the proper level of support. It would appear, however, that BLIMPIE SUBS AND SALADS's staff of 109 is more than adequate to support 1,955 operating units. Less clear is whether a staff of three, including the company president and his wife, can adequately support 15 fledgling franchisees in the field.

Many younger franchises may be managed by a skeleton staff, assisted by outside consultants who are performing various management functions during the start-up phase. From the perspective of the franchisee, it is essential that the franchisor have actual in-house franchising experience, and that the franchisee not be forced to rely on outside consultants to make the system work. Whereas a full-time, salaried employee will probably have the franchisee's objectives in mind, an outside consultant may easily not have the same priorities. Franchising is a unique form of business that requires specific skills and experience — skills and experience that are markedly different from those required to manage a non-franchised business. If you are thinking about establishing a long-term relationship with a firm just starting out in franchising, you should insist that the franchisor prove that it has an experienced, professional team on board and in place to provide the necessary levels of support.

38. **On-Going Support: B,C,D,E,F,G,H,I**

Like initial training, the on-going support services provided by the franchisor are of paramount importance. Having a solid and responsive team behind you can certainly make your life much easier and allow you to concentrate your energies on other areas. As noted below, the franchisors were asked to indicate their support of nine separate on-going services:

Service Provided	Included in Fees	At Add'l. Cost	NA
Central Data Processing	A	a	NA
Central Purchasing	B	b	NA
Field Operations Evaluation	C	c	NA
Field Training	D	d	NA
Initial Store Opening	E	e	NA
Inventory Control	F	f	NA
Franchisee Newsletter	G	g	NA
Regional or National Meetings	H	h	NA
800 Telephone Hotline	I	i	NA

If the franchisor provides the service at no additional cost to the franchisee (as indicated by letters A–I), a capital letter indicates this. If the service is provided only at an additional cost, this is indicated by a lower case letter. If the franchisor responded not applicable, or failed to note an answer for a particular service, the corresponding letter was omitted from the data sheet.

39. **Training: 120 Hours in Local Franchise.**

Comment: Assuming that the underlying business concept is sound and competitive, adequate training and on-going support are among the most important determinants of your success as a franchisee. The initial training should be as lengthy and as "hands-on" as necessary to allow the franchisee to operate alone and with confidence. Obviously, every potential situation cannot be covered in any training program. But the franchisee should come away with a basic understanding of how the business operates and where to go to resolve problems when they originate. Depending on the business, there should be operating manuals, procedure manuals, company policies, training videos, (800) help-lines, etc. It may be helpful at the outset to establish how satisfied recent franchisees are with a company's training. I would also have a clear understanding about how often the company updates its manuals and training programs, the cost of sending additional employees through training, etc.

Remember, you are part of an organization that you are paying (in the form of a franchise fee and on-going royalties) to support you. Training is the first component of this fulfillment. On-going support is the second.

Specific Expansion Plans:

40. **U.S.: All United States.** BLIMPIE SUBS AND SALADS is currently focusing its growth on the entire United States. Alternatively, the franchisor could have listed particular states or regions into which it wishes to expand.

41. **Canada: All Canada.** BLIMPIE SUBS AND SALADS currently seeks additional franchisees in Canada. Specific markets or provinces could have also been indicated.

42. **Overseas: All Except Anti-American Countries.** BLIMPIE SUBS AND SALADS is currently expanding overseas.

Comment: You will note that many smaller companies suggest that they will concurrently expand throughout the U.S., Canada and internationally. In many cases, these are the same companies that foresee more than a 50% growth rate in operating units over the next 12 months. Generally, the chances of this happening are negligible. As a prospective franchisee, you should be wary of any company that thinks it can expand throughout the world without a solid base of experience, staff and financial resources. Even if adequate financing is available, the demands on existing management will be extreme. New management cannot adequately fill the void until they are able to understand the system fully and absorb the corporate culture. If the management's end objective is expansion purely for its own sake, the existing franchisees will suffer.

Supplemental Listings of Franchisors

For those franchisors who chose not to participate in this year's survey, we have added their company names, addresses, telephone numbers (their 800 numbers, if available, as well as their local numbers) and, lastly, their fax numbers. The telephone number(s) and fax numbers are separated by semi-colons.

If you have not already done so, I would strongly encourage you to invest the modest time required to read Chapter 1 — 30 Minute Overview.

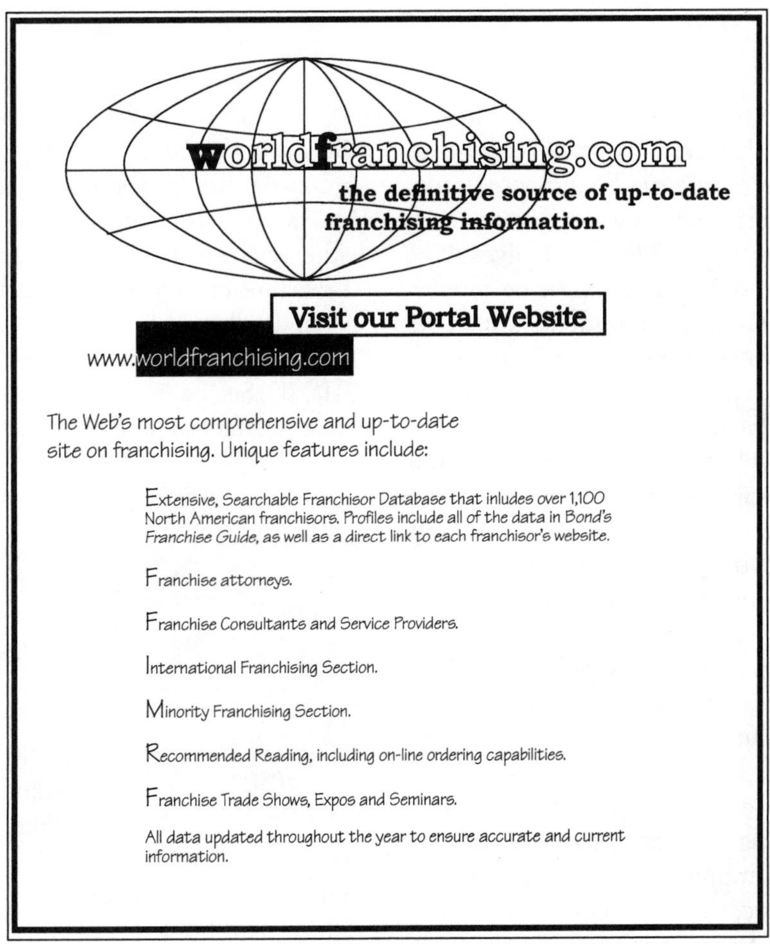

Recommended Reading

Chapter 3

My strong sense is that every potential franchisee should be well-versed in the underlying fundamentals of the franchising industry before he or she commits to the way of life it involves. The better you understand the industry, the better prepared you will be to take maximum advantage of the relationship with your franchisor. There is no doubt that it will also place you in a better position to negotiate the franchise agreement — the conditions of which will dictate every facet of your life as a franchisee for the term of the agreement. The few extra dollars spent on educating yourself could well translate into tens of thousand of dollars to the bottom line in the years ahead.

In addition to general franchising publications, we have included several special interest books that relate to specific, but critical, parts of the start-up and on-going management process — site selection, hiring and managing minimum wage employees, preparing accurate cash flow projections, developing comprehensive business and/or marketing plans, etc. Also included are several audio tapes and software packages that we feel represent good values.

We have also attempted to make the purchasing process easier by allowing readers to purchase the books directly from Source Book Publications, either via our 800-line or our website. All of the books are currently available in inventory and are generally sent the same day an order is received. A 15% discount is available on all orders over $100.00. See page 40 for an order form. Your complete satisfaction is 100% guaranteed on all books.

Background/Evaluation

Franchise Bible: A Comprehensive Guide, 3rd Edit., Keup, Oasis Press. 1996. 314 pp. $24.95.

This recently updated classic is equally useful for prospective franchisees and franchisors alike. The comprehensive guide and workbook explain in detail what the franchise system entails and the precise benefits it offers. The book features the new franchise laws that became effective January, 1995. To assist the prospective franchisee in rating a potential franchisor, Keup provides necessary checklists and forms.

Also noted are the franchisor's contractual obligations to the franchisee and what the franchisee should expect from the franchisor in the way of services and support.

How to Buy and Manage a Franchise, Mancuso and Boroian, Simon & Schuster. 1993. 287 pp. $11.00.

If your objective is to either be your own boss or to expand a business you already own, you should seriously consider franchising. The authors share their expert advice on purchasing, owning and operating a franchise. Keen insights into the mechanics and advantages of franchising. Good starter book.

Tips & Traps When Buying a Franchise, Revised 2nd Edition, Tomzack, Source Book Publications. 1999. 236 pp. $19.95.

Many a green franchisee is shocked to discover that the road to success in franchising is full of hidden costs, inflated revenue promises, reneged marketing support and worse. In this candid, hard-hitting book, Tomzack steers potential franchisees around the pitfalls and guides them in making a smart, lucrative purchase. Topics include: matching a franchise with personal finances and lifestyle, avoiding the five most common pitfalls, choosing a prime location, asking the right questions, etc.

Franchising 101, Dugan, Up-start Publishing Company. 1998. 267 pp. $22.95.

A thoughtful, thorough guide that offers indispensable advice on everything you need to know about evaluating, buying and growing a franchise — from choosing the right franchise to handling taxes and banks to keep records. It will help you evaluate your needs and your personality in order to determine the type of franchise that will make you happy — and prosperous — for the long term. You'll also learn how to scout for a franchise company that is a leader within the strong, vibrant and growing franchise industry. This book offers valuable guidance and support from respected professionals in the franchising industry.

Databases

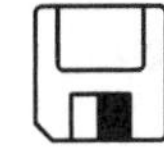

Franchisor Database, Source Book Publications. (800) 841-0873/(510) 839-5471.

Listing of over 2,300 active North American franchisors. 23 fields of information per company: full address, telephone/800/fax numbers, Internet address, contact/title/salutation, president/title/salutation, # of franchised units, # of company-owned units, # total units, IFA/CFA Member, etc. 54 industry categories. Unlimited use. Guaranteed deliverability — $0.50 rebate for any returned mail. $700 for initial database, $75 per quarter for updates. See page 7 for details.

Directories

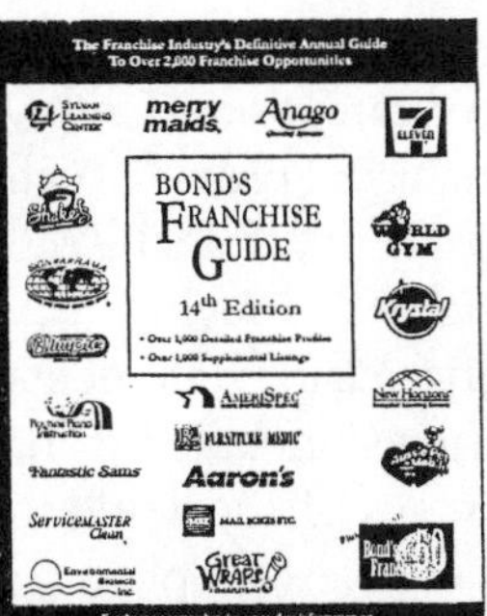

Bond's Franchise Guide — 2002 Edition, Bond, Source Book Publications, 2001. 496 pp. $29.95.
The definitive and most comprehensive franchising directory available. Over 2,150 listings, including over 1,050 detailed franchisor profiles resulting from an exhaustive 40-point questionnaire. 45 distinct business categories. Excellent industry overview.

Minority Franchise Guide — 2002 Edition, Bond/Wallace, Source Book Publications, 2002. 304 pp. $19.95.
The only minority franchising directory! Contains detailed profiles and company logos of over 550

forward-looking franchisors that encourage and actively support the inclusion of minority franchisees. It also includes a listing of resources available to prospective minority franchisees.

Earnings Claims

"How Much Can I Make?", Bond, Source Book Publications. 2000. 476 pp. $29.95.

The single most important task for a prospective investor is to prepare a realistic cash flow statement that accurately reflects the economic potential of that business. *"How Much Can I Make?"* is an invaluable "insider's guide" that details historical sales, expense and/or profit data on actual franchise operations, **as provide by the franchisors themselves**. Whether you plan to buy a franchise or start your own business, these actual performance statistics will ensure that you have a realistic starting point in determining how much you can expect to make in a similar business. 140 current Earnings Claims Statements, in their entirety, are included for 33 major industry categories. Unfortunately, less than 15% of franchisors provide such projections/guidelines to prospective franchisees. *"How Much Can I Make?"* includes roughly half of the total universe of earnings claim statements available. The list of companies included runs from the McDonald's and Subways of the world to newer, smaller franchises with only a few operating units. Any serious investor would be short-sighted not to take full advantage of this extra-ordinary resource.

General

Guide to Negotiating a Business Lease, Kanouse, Professional Press. 1995. 167 pp. $15.95. This book clearly defines words and phrases unique to leases that will enable you to commu-

nicate with your landlord, leasing agent and attorney in an educated manner. It also includes 77 lease provisions that might need to be renegotiated in your best interest and "tenant-oriented" business lease forms. In addition, the book addresses the special issues involved in sub-leasing from a franchisor.

International Franchising

International Herald Tribune International Franchise Guide, Bond/ Thompson, Source Book Publications. 1999. 192 pp. $34.95.

This annual publication, sponsored by the International Herald Tribune, is the definitive guide to international franchising. It lists comprehensive, in-depth profiles of major franchisors who are committed (not just the usual lip service) to promote and support overseas expansion. Details specific geographic areas of desired expansion for each company, country by country — as well as the number of units in each foreign country as of the date of publication. Geared specifically to the needs and requirements of prospective international area developers, master franchisees and investors. Investors must be prepared to assume responsibility for the development of large geographic areas. Also listed are international franchise consultants, attorneys and service providers. Covers 32 distinct business categories.

Ranking of Franchises

Bond's Top 50 Food-Service Franchises, Bond/ Schiller, Source Book Publications, 2000. 288 pp. $19.95

In response to the constantly asked question, *"What are the best franchises?"*, Bond's new book focuses on the top 50 franchises. Over 500 food-service systems were evaluated for inclusion. Companies

were analyzed on the basis of historical performance, brand identification, market dynamics, franchisee satisfaction, the level of training and on-going support, financial stability, etc. Detailed four to five page profiles on each company, as well as key statistics and industry overview. All companies are proven performers and most have a national presence. Excellent starting point for someone focusing on the food-service industry.

Bond's Top 50 Retail Franchises, Bond/Schiller/Tong, Source Book Publications, 2001. 288 pp. $19.95

In response to the constantly asked question, *"What are the best franchises?"*, Bond's new book focuses on the top 50 franchises. Over 350 retail systems were evaluated for inclusion. Companies were analyzed on the basis of historical performance, brand identification, market dynamics, franchisee satisfaction, the level of training and on-going support, financial stability, etc. Detailed four to five page profiles on each company, as well as key statistics and industry overview. All companies are proven performers and most have a national presence. Excellent starting point for someone focusing on the retail industry.

Bond's Top 50 Service-Based Franchises, Bond/Schiller, Source Book Publications, 2000. 300 pp. $19.95

In response to the constantly asked question, *"What are the best franchises?"*, Bond's new book focuses on the top 50 franchises. Over 400 service-based systems were evaluated for inclusion. Companies were analyzed on the basis of historical performance, brand identification, market dynamics, franchisee satisfaction, the level of training and on-going support, financial stability, etc. Detailed four to five page profiles on each company, as well as key statistics and industry overview. All companies are proven performers and most have a national presence. Excellent starting point for someone focusing on the service-based industry.

Site Selection

Location, Location, Location: How to Select the Best Site for Your Business, Salvaneschi, Oasis Press. 1996. 280 pp. $19.95.

Whether you are searching for a new business site or relocating an existing business, you have the power to dramatically increase your profits by choosing the right location. For any business that depends on a customer's ability to find it, location is the most important ingredient for success. Learn how to: spot the essential characteristics of the best location; understand why and how people move from one point to another; analyze and learn from your competitor's business; and learn about the retail trading zone and how to use it to capture the most customers.

Other Franchise Publications

Franchise Times, Restaurant Finance Corp., 2500 Cleveland Ave., North, # D-South, Roseville, MN 55113; (651) 631-4995; FAX (651) 633-8749.

Published 10 times per year, *Franchise Times* magazine focuses on the issues multi-unit franchisees and franchisors need to take their businesses to the next level. Issues such as financing (where is it; who's doing it), real estate (tips for site selection, leases, etc.) and legal issues are tackled. The magazine also highlights successful franchisees and franchisors. In these profiles, the reveal how they have grown their companies to be large franchise businesses and discuss the problems they have conquered along the way. Along with those profiles, *Franchise Times* covers the constantly changing relationship between franchisors and franchisees; how they offer support to each other and conversely the never-ending legal battles that sometimes ensue. The franchise owner survey and the top 200 franchise businesses are eagerly anticipated issues.

The Franchise Bookstore
Order Form

Call (800) 841-0873 or (510) 839-5471; or FAX (510) 839-2104

Item #	Title	Price	Qty.	Total
			Basic postage (1 Book)	$5.00
			Each additional book add $4.00	
			California tax @ 8.25% (if CA resident)	
			Total due in U.S. dollars	
			Deduct 15% if total due is over $100.00	
			Net amount due in U.S. dollars	

Please include credit card number and expiration date for all charge card orders! Checks should be made payable to Source Book Publications. All prices are in U.S. dollars.

Mailing Information: All books shipped by USPS Priority Mail (2nd Day Air). Please print clearly and include your phone number in case we need to contact you. Postage and handling rates are for shipping within the U.S. Please call for international rates.

❑ Check enclosed or

Charge my:

❑ MasterCard ❑ VISA

Card #: ______________________________

Expiration Date: ______________________

Signature: ___________________________

Name: ______________________________

Company: ___________________________

Address: ____________________________

City: _______________________________

Title: _______________________________

Telephone No.: (____)_________________

State/Prov.: ________ Zip: ____________

Special Offer — Save 15%

If your total order above exceeds $100.00, deduct 15% from your bill.

Please send order to:
Source Book Publications
P.O. Box 12488, Oakland, CA 94604
Satisfaction Guaranteed. If not fully satisfied, return for a prompt, 100% refund.

Automotive Products & Services

Chapter 4

Automotive Products & Services Industry Profile

Total # Franchisors in Industry Group	159
Total # Franchised Units in Industry Group	25,083
Total # Company-Owned Units in Industry Group	2,961
Total # Operating Units in Industry Group	28,044
Average # Franchised Units/Franchisor	162.9
Average # Company-Owned Units/Franchisor	19.2
Average # Total Units/Franchisor	182.1
Ratio of Total # Franchised Units/Total # Company-Owned Units	8.5:1
Industry Survey Participants	73
Representing % of Industry	45.9%
Average Franchise Fee*:	$23.0K
Average Total Investment*:	$199.9K
Average On-Going Royalty Fee*:	5.7%

*If a range was provided, the mid-point of the range was used. See detailed profiles for actual ranges.

Five Largest Participants in Survey

Company	# Franchised Units	# Co-Owned Units	# Total Units	Franchise Fee	On-Going Royalty	Total Investment
1. Midas Auto Service Experts	2,614	108	2,722	20K	10%	360-487K
2. Novus	2,510	2	2,512	8.4-20K	5-6%	25-142K
3. Custom Auto Restoration	841	257	1,098	N/A	0%	1-10K
4. Meineke Discount Mufflers	844	25	869	25K	3-7%	154-285K
5. AAMCO Transmissions	715	2	717	2K	7%	200K

All of the data provided are proprietary and should not be quoted without acknowledging *Bond's Franchise Guide.*

AAMCO TRANSMISSIONS

1 Presidential Blvd.
Bala Cynwyd, PA 19004
Tel: (800) 223-8887 (610) 668-2900
Fax: (610) 617-9532
E-Mail: franchise@aamco.com
Web Site: www.aamcotransmissions.com
Mr. Brian O'Donnell, SVP Operations/Sales

AAMCO is the world's largest chain of transmission specialists with 37 years' experience as the undisputed industry leader. An American icon, AAMCO's trademark is recognized by 94% of the driving public.

BACKGROUND:
Established: 1963; 1st Franchised: 1963
Franchised Units: 715
Company-Owned Units 2
Total Units: 717
Dist.: US-685; CAN-29; O'seas-0
North America: 48 States, 4 Provinces
Density: 101 in CA, 61 in FL, 44 NY
Projected New Units (12 Months): 40
Qualifications: 4, 4, 3, 3, 4, 4
Registered: All States

FINANCIAL/TERMS:
Cash Investment: $75K
Total Investment: $200K
Minimum Net Worth: $250K
Fees: Franchise - $30K
Royalty - 7%; Ad. - Varies
Earnings Claim Statement: Yes
Term of Contract (Years): 15/15
Avg. # Of Employees: 4 FT, 1 PT
Passive Ownership: Not Allowed
Encourage Conversions: Yes
Area Develop. Agreements: No
Sub-Franchising Contracts: No
Expand In Territory: Yes
Space Needs: 4,000 SF; FS, SF, Auto Mall

SUPPORT & TRAINING PROVIDED:
Financial Assistance Provided: Yes(I)
Site Selection Assistance: Yes
Lease Negotiation Assistance: Yes
Co-Operative Advertising: No
Franchisee Assoc./Member: Yes/No
Size Of Corporate Staff: 180
On-Going Support: A,B,C,D,E,G,H,I
Training: 5 Weeks Home Office, Philadelphia, PA.

SPECIFIC EXPANSION PLANS:
US: NE, Great Lakes Region
Canada: All Canada
Overseas: No

<< >>

ABRA AUTO BODY & GLASS

6601 Shingle Creek Pkwy., # 200
Brooklyn Center, MN 55430
Tel: (800) 536-2334 (612) 585-6289
Fax: (612) 561-7433
E-Mail: earl@abraauto.com
Web Site: www.abraauto.com
Mr. Timothy R. Adelmann, Executive Vice President

One of the first automobile collision and glass franchises. Operating company and franchised auto body collision and auto glass replacement shops. We offer support with marketing, business management, equipment and material purchases. Investment opportunities for qualifying owners and managers.

BACKGROUND:
Established: 1984; 1st Franchised: 1987
Franchised Units: 36
Company-Owned Units 18
Total Units: 54
Dist.: US-54; CAN-0; O'seas-0
North America: 12 States
Density: 28 in MN, 7 in TN, 6 in WI
Projected New Units (12 Months): 12
Qualifications: 5, 5, 5, 3, 3, 5
Registered: IL,IN,MI,MN,ND,SD,WI

FINANCIAL/TERMS:
Cash Investment: $60-100K
Total Investment: $229.6-422.6K
Minimum Net Worth: $500K
Fees: Franchise - $22.5K
Royalty - 5%; Ad. - 3%
Earnings Claim Statement: Yes
Term of Contract (Years): 10/10
Avg. # Of Employees: NR
Passive Ownership: Allowed
Encourage Conversions: Yes
Area Develop. Agreements: Yes/Varies
Sub-Franchising Contracts: No
Expand In Territory: Yes
Space Needs: 8,000-15,000 SF; FS, SF

SUPPORT & TRAINING PROVIDED:
Financial Assistance Provided: No
Site Selection Assistance: Yes
Lease Negotiation Assistance: Yes
Co-Operative Advertising: N/A
Franchisee Assoc./Member: NR
Size Of Corporate Staff: 53
On-Going Support: a,B,C,D,E,F,g,h,I
Training: 2-4 Weeks ABRA Training Center, Minneapolis, MN; 6 Weeks On-Site.

SPECIFIC EXPANSION PLANS:
US: Central, South, Southeast
Canada: No
Overseas: No

<< >>

ACTIVE GREEN + ROSS TIRE & AUTOMOTIVE CENTRE

580 Evans Ave.
Toronto, ON M8W 2W1 CANADA
Tel: (416) 255-5581
Fax: (416) 255-4793
E-Mail: acttire@idirect.com
Web Site: www.activegreenross.com
Mr. Ralph Chiodo, President

Tire and automotive sales and service. The company currently has locations in Toronto and surrounding area and is one of the largest independent groups of tire and automotive service centres in Canada. Company operations began in 1982. Franchised first outlet in 1983; Training provided for up to 2 months; Dealers elect representatives on Dealer Advisory Committee.

BACKGROUND:
Established: 1982; 1st Franchised: 1983
Franchised Units: 25
Company-Owned Units 5
Total Units: 30
Dist.: US-0; CAN-29; O'seas-0
North America: 1 Province
Density: 29 in ON
Projected New Units (12 Months): NR
Qualifications: 4, 4, 4, 4, 4, 4
Registered: None

FINANCIAL/TERMS:
Cash Investment: $NR
Total Investment: $115-200K
Minimum Net Worth: $250K
Fees: Franchise - $25K
Royalty - 5%; Ad. - 2.5%
Earnings Claim Statement: No
Term of Contract (Years): 5/5
Avg. # Of Employees: 4+ FT
Passive Ownership: Not Allowed
Encourage Conversions: Yes
Area Develop. Agreements: No
Sub-Franchising Contracts: Yes
Expand In Territory: Yes

Space Needs: 3,000-5,000 SF; NR

SUPPORT & TRAINING PROVIDED:

Financial Assistance Provided:	Yes(I)
Site Selection Assistance:	Yes
Lease Negotiation Assistance:	N/A
Co-Operative Advertising:	Yes
Franchisee Assoc./Member:	Yes
Size Of Corporate Staff:	9
On-Going Support:	NR

Training: Head Office and On-Site.

SPECIFIC EXPANSION PLANS:

US:	N/A
Canada:	ON
Overseas:	No

AERO-COLOURS

6971 Washington Ave. S., # 102
Minneapolis, MN 55439-1508
Tel: (800) 696-2376 (612) 942-0490
Fax: (612) 942-0624
E-Mail: spellmire@qwest.net
Web Site: www.aerocolours.com
Mr. James F. Spellmire, President

AERO-COLOURS is an exclusive mobile automotive paint repair process, providing service to dealerships, fleet operations and individual vehicle owners. Our solid support system, complemented by our industry-leading training, allows our franchisees to provide unmatched service. We will show you how to operate, market and grow your own business.

BACKGROUND: IFA MEMBER

Established: 1985; 1st Franchised: 1993

Franchised Units:	171
Company-Owned Units	61
Total Units:	232
Dist.:	US-229; CAN-0; O'seas-3
North America:	28 States
Density:	60 in CA, 15 in TX
Projected New Units (12 Months):	50
Qualifications:	5, 3, 5, 3, 5, 5

Registered: CA,FL,IL,IN,MD,MI,MN,ND,NY,OR,VA,WI

FINANCIAL/TERMS:

Cash Investment:	$5-30K
Total Investment:	$5-60K
Minimum Net Worth:	$100K
Fees: Franchise -	$25K
Royalty - 7%;	Ad. - 0%
Earnings Claim Statement:	No
Term of Contract (Years):	10/10
Avg. # Of Employees:	4-5 FT
Passive Ownership:	Allowed
Encourage Conversions:	No
Area Develop. Agreements:	No
Sub-Franchising Contracts:	Yes
Expand In Territory:	Yes

Space Needs: 2,000 SF; Warehouse

SUPPORT & TRAINING PROVIDED:

Financial Assistance Provided:	Yes(I)
Site Selection Assistance:	Yes
Lease Negotiation Assistance:	Yes
Co-Operative Advertising:	No
Franchisee Assoc./Member:	Yes/Yes
Size Of Corporate Staff:	14
On-Going Support:	A,B,C,D,E,G,H,I

Training: 2 Weeks Tampa, FL; 2 Weeks Territory.

SPECIFIC EXPANSION PLANS:

US:	All United States
Canada:	No
Overseas:	All Countries

AIRBAG SERVICE

9675 SE 36th St., # 100
Mercer Island, WA 98040
Tel: (800) 224-7224 (206) 275-4105
Fax: (206) 275-4122
E-Mail: marketing@airbagservice.com
Web Site: www.airbagservice.com
Ms. Elaine Credelle, Sales/Marketing Mgr.

Automotive service company, specializing in airbag system repair. Our mobile service supplies a needed expertise to the automotive collision repair industry. Specialized software and tools allow us to work on any system right on site for increased efficiency.

BACKGROUND: IFA MEMBER

Established: 1992; 1st Franchised: 1995

Franchised Units:	40
Company-Owned Units	1
Total Units:	40
Dist.:	US-37; CAN-2; O'seas-0
North America:	20 States, 2 Province
Density:	7 in TX, 4 in CA, 3 in WA
Projected New Units (12 Months):	18
Qualifications:	3, 5, 4, 1, 1, 4

Registered: CA,FL,HI,IL,IN,MD,MI,NY,VA

FINANCIAL/TERMS:

Cash Investment:	$50-100K
Total Investment:	$50-125K
Minimum Net Worth:	$75K
Fees: Franchise -	$25-30K
Royalty - 8.5% Net;	Ad. - 2% Net
Earnings Claim Statement:	No
Term of Contract (Years):	10/5+5
Avg. # Of Employees:	2 FT
Passive Ownership:	Discouraged
Encourage Conversions:	N/A
Area Develop. Agreements:	Yes/10
Sub-Franchising Contracts:	No
Expand In Territory:	Yes

Space Needs: 1,000 SF; Commercial Office

SUPPORT & TRAINING PROVIDED:

Financial Assistance Provided:	Yes(I)
Site Selection Assistance:	No
Lease Negotiation Assistance:	No
Co-Operative Advertising:	Yes
Franchisee Assoc./Member:	No
Size Of Corporate Staff:	10
On-Going Support:	C,D,G,H,I

Training: 3 Weeks Seattle, WA.

SPECIFIC EXPANSION PLANS:

US:	All United States
Canada:	No
Overseas:	No

ALL NIGHT AUTO

3872 Rochester Rd.
Troy, MI 48083
Tel: (800) 745-1415 (248) 619-9020
Fax: (248) 557-7931
E-Mail: wfcnet@cris.com
Web Site: www.allnightauto.net
Mr. Dennis Spencer, President

ALL NIGHT AUTO is an exciting new franchise putting a new and innovative spin on the automotive repair business. Franchisees don't need an automotive background or to be mechanically inclined. All you need is some quality business sense. ALL NIGHT AUTO will provide the rest. The system is designed to provide the highest level of support possible with profitability always being the main focus. The high-tech facilities are state-of-the-art, with the latest computerized equipment. Turn-key package.

BACKGROUND:

Established: 1994; 1st Franchised: 1998

Franchised Units:	1
Company-Owned Units	1
Total Units:	2
Dist.:	US-2; CAN-0; O'seas-0
North America:	1 State
Density:	2 in MI
Projected New Units (12 Months):	3
Qualifications:	3, 4, 1, 3, 3, 4

Registered: MI

FINANCIAL/TERMS:

Cash Investment:	$100-150K

Total Investment: $150-245K
Minimum Net Worth: $100K
Fees: Franchise - $25K
Royalty - 6%; Ad. - 1.5%
Earnings Claim Statement: No
Term of Contract (Years): 10/10
Avg. # Of Employees: 4 FT, 2 PT
Passive Ownership: Allowed
Encourage Conversions: Yes
Area Develop. Agreements: Yes/10
Sub-Franchising Contracts: No
Expand In Territory: Yes
Space Needs: 5,000 SF; FS, Auto Mall

SUPPORT & TRAINING PROVIDED:
Financial Assistance Provided: Yes(I)
Site Selection Assistance: Yes
Lease Negotiation Assistance: Yes
Co-Operative Advertising: Yes
Franchisee Assoc./Member: No
Size Of Corporate Staff: 5
On-Going Support: C,D,E,F,I
Training: 18 Days Corporate Store; 7 Days on Location.

SPECIFIC EXPANSION PLANS:
US: Michigan Only
Canada: No
Overseas: No

<< >>

ALTA MERE COMPLETE AUTO IMAGING

4444 W. 147th St.
Midlothian, IL 60445
Tel: (800) 377-9247 (708) 389-5922
Fax: (708) 389-9882
E-Mail: vsmithson@moranindustries.com
Web Site: www.altamere.com
Mr. Nick Micholai, VP Franchise Development

ALTA MERE offers complete auto imaging; window tinting, auto security, cellular phones, beepers and auto accessories. This specialty division of Moran Industries franchises complete auto imaging service centers throughout the US. We offer our franchisees a superior business system, strong brand name, customized marketing and a service that is in strong demand. Our exclusive business system, along with the skills of our franchisees, create customer experiences that result in satisfaction and loyalty.

BACKGROUND: IFA MEMBER
Established: 1993; 1st Franchised: 1993
Franchised Units: 36
Company-Owned Units 1
Total Units: 37
Dist.: US-37; CAN-0; O'seas-0
North America: 9 States
Density: 15 in TX, 7 in OK, 4 in AK
Projected New Units (12 Months): 12
Qualifications: 4, 3, 1, 2, 4, 5
Registered: IL

FINANCIAL/TERMS:
Cash Investment: $35-40K
Total Investment: $93K
Minimum Net Worth: $90K
Fees: Franchise - $27.5K
Royalty - 7%; Ad. - $100/Mo.
Earnings Claim Statement: Yes
Term of Contract (Years): 20/20
Avg. # Of Employees: 3 FT
Passive Ownership: Discouraged
Encourage Conversions: Yes
Area Develop. Agreements: Yes
Sub-Franchising Contracts: No
Expand In Territory: Yes
Space Needs: 2,500 SF; FS, SF, SC, RM

SUPPORT & TRAINING PROVIDED:
Financial Assistance Provided: Yes(I)
Site Selection Assistance: Yes
Lease Negotiation Assistance: Yes
Co-Operative Advertising: Yes
Franchisee Assoc./Member: Yes/Yes
Size Of Corporate Staff: 55
On-Going Support: A,C,D,E,G,H,I
Training: Training is Provided.

SPECIFIC EXPANSION PLANS:
US: All United States
Canada: No
Overseas: No

<< >>

ALTRACOLOR SYSTEMS

P.O. Box 1626
Pearl River, LA 70452
Tel: (800) 678-5220 (504) 454-7233
Fax: (985) 863-9962
E-Mail: altra@altracolor.com
Web Site: www.altracolor.com
Mr. Jeff Richards, President

ALTRACOLOR SYSTEMS is the state-of-the-art mobile, on-site touch-up and spot repair system for automotive paint repair.

BACKGROUND: IFA MEMBER
Established: 1988; 1st Franchised: 1991
Franchised Units: 82
Company-Owned Units 92
Total Units: 174
Dist.: US-174; CAN-0; O'seas-0
North America: 27 States
Density: 14 in NC, 13 in VA, 13 in SC
Projected New Units (12 Months): 23
Qualifications: 3, 3, 1, 1, 2, 4
Registered: CA,FL,IN,MI,MN,NY,OR, VA,WA,WI,DC

FINANCIAL/TERMS:
Cash Investment: $5-11.7K
Total Investment: $16.9-25.2K
Minimum Net Worth: $N/A
Fees: Franchise - $9.95K
Royalty - $95/Wk.; Ad. - 0%
Earnings Claim Statement: Yes
Term of Contract (Years): 15/5
Avg. # Of Employees: 1 FT
Passive Ownership: Not Allowed
Encourage Conversions: Yes
Area Develop. Agreements: Yes/15
Sub-Franchising Contracts: Yes
Expand In Territory: Yes
Space Needs: N/A SF; Mobile Bus

SUPPORT & TRAINING PROVIDED:
Financial Assistance Provided: Yes(D)
Site Selection Assistance: N/A
Lease Negotiation Assistance: N/A
Co-Operative Advertising: N/A
Franchisee Assoc./Member: No
Size Of Corporate Staff: 5
On-Going Support: C,D,G,H,I
Training: 1 Week in Metairie, LA.

SPECIFIC EXPANSION PLANS:
US: All United States
Canada: No
Overseas: No

<< >>

AMERICAN BRAKE SERVICE

1325 Franklin Ave., # 165
Garden City, NY 11530
Tel: (800) TILDENS (516) 746-7911
Fax: (516) 746-1288
E-Mail: info@tildencarcare.com
Web Site: www.tildencarcare.com
Mr. Jason Basking, Dir. Franchise Development

We're not just brakes. The total care concept allows you to offer a full menu of automotive services for maximum customer procurement - rather than a limited niche market. You benefit from a management team whose concept system and training were proven and perfected before we even considered offering franchises.

BACKGROUND:
Established: 1923; 1st Franchised: 1996
Franchised Units: 60
Company-Owned Units 0

Total Units: 60
Dist.: US-60; CAN-0; O'seas-0
North America: 13 States
Density: 24 in FL, 15 in NY, 6 in GA
Projected New Units (12 Months): 10
Qualifications: 3, 4, 3, 3, 3, 4
Registered: CA,FL,IL,IN,MN,NY,VA,wa

FINANCIAL/TERMS:
Cash Investment: $50-60K
Total Investment: $131-171K
Minimum Net Worth: $150K
Fees: Franchise - $25K
Royalty - 6%/$350/Wk.;
Ad. - 3%/$175/Wk.
Earnings Claim Statement: No
Term of Contract (Years): 10/5/5
Avg. # Of Employees: 4 FT, 2 PT
Passive Ownership: Discouraged
Encourage Conversions: Yes
Area Develop. Agreements: Yes/10
Sub-Franchising Contracts: No
Expand In Territory: Yes
Space Needs: 3,500 SF; FS, Auto Mall

SUPPORT & TRAINING PROVIDED:
Financial Assistance Provided: Yes(I)
Site Selection Assistance: Yes
Lease Negotiation Assistance: Yes
Co-Operative Advertising: Yes
Franchisee Assoc./Member: Yes/Yes
Size Of Corporate Staff: 4
On-Going Support: C,d,E,F,G,H,I
Training: 2 Weeks Home Office.

SPECIFIC EXPANSION PLANS:
US: All United States
Canada: All Canada
Overseas: No

<< >>

APPLE AUTO GLASS

360 Applewood Crescent
Concord, ON L4K 4V2 CANADA
Tel: (905) 669-7800
Fax: (905) 669-7821
Web Site: www.tcgi.com/apple
Mr. Calvin Hughes, President

APPLE AUTO GLASS is a Canadian franchise network specializing in automotive glass replacement and stone chip repair, the repair of automotive upholstery, and the sale and installation of vehicle accessories. Franchisees benefit by joining an established network with national name recognition, national and local marketing programs, purchasing strength and the ability to increase sales through new products and services.

BACKGROUND:
Established: 1983; 1st Franchised: 1983
Franchised Units: 126
Company-Owned Units 2
Total Units: 128
Dist.: US-0; CAN-128; O'seas-0
North America: 8 Provinces
Density: 86 in ON, 12 in NS, 11 in NB
Projected New Units (12 Months): 5
Qualifications: 4, 4, 5, 3, 3, 4
Registered: AB

FINANCIAL/TERMS:
Cash Investment: $40-60K
Total Investment: $65-95K
Minimum Net Worth: $75K
Fees: Franchise - $5K
Royalty - 5%; Ad. - 2.5%
Earnings Claim Statement: No
Term of Contract (Years): 10/10
Avg. # Of Employees: 3 FT
Passive Ownership: Discouraged
Encourage Conversions: Yes
Area Develop. Agreements: No
Sub-Franchising Contracts: No
Expand In Territory: Yes
Space Needs: 2,500 SF; SC

SUPPORT & TRAINING PROVIDED:
Financial Assistance Provided: Yes(I)
Site Selection Assistance: Yes
Lease Negotiation Assistance: Yes
Co-Operative Advertising: Yes
Franchisee Assoc./Member: Yes/No
Size Of Corporate Staff: 23
On-Going Support: a,B,d,e,G,h,I
Training: Head Office for Varied Duration.

SPECIFIC EXPANSION PLANS:
US: No
Canada: Western Canada
Overseas: No

<< >>

ATL INTERNATIONAL

8334 Veterans Hwy.
Millersville, MD 21108-2543
Tel: (800) 935-8863 (410) 987-1011
Fax: (410) 987-9080
E-Mail: alltune@erols.com
Web Site: www.alltuneandlube.com
Mr. Louis Kibler, VP Franchise Dev.

ALL TUNE AND LUBE is the leader in 'One Stop' total car care. Our full-service centers provide vehicle maintenance and repair, such as engine performance, brakes, ride control and oil changes. Franchise owners also have the option of adding the ATL MOTOR MATE franchise, which specializes in engine installation, and the ALL TUNE TRANSMISSIONS franchise, which provides transmission service. This co-branding concept provides three times the potential at one location.

BACKGROUND: IFA MEMBER
Established: 1985; 1st Franchised: 1985
Franchised Units: 450
Company-Owned Units 0
Total Units: 450
Dist.: US-448; CAN-2; O'seas-0
North America: 34 States
Density: 50 in CA, 35 in TX, 30 in MD
Projected New Units (12 Months): 450
Qualifications: 3, 4, 1, 2, 1, 4
Registered: All States

FINANCIAL/TERMS:
Cash Investment: $25K
Total Investment: $120-130K
Minimum Net Worth: $75K
Fees: Franchise - $25K
Royalty - 7%; Ad. - 8%
Earnings Claim Statement: No
Term of Contract (Years): 15/3x5
Avg. # Of Employees: 4-6 FT
Passive Ownership: Not Allowed
Encourage Conversions: Yes
Area Develop. Agreements: No
Sub-Franchising Contracts: No
Expand In Territory: Yes
Space Needs: 3,000 SF; FS, SC, Auto Mall

SUPPORT & TRAINING PROVIDED:
Financial Assistance Provided: Yes(B)
Site Selection Assistance: Yes
Lease Negotiation Assistance: Yes
Co-Operative Advertising: Yes
Franchisee Assoc./Member: No
Size Of Corporate Staff: 75
On-Going Support: B,C,D,E,F,G,H,I
Training: 2 Weeks Corporate Office; 1 Week in Center.

SPECIFIC EXPANSION PLANS:
US: All United States
Canada: All Canada
Overseas: All Countries

<< >>

AUTO ACCENT CENTERS

6550 Pearl Rd.
Parma Heights, OH 44130
Tel: (800) 567-3120 (440) 888-8886
Fax: (440) 888-4333
Mr. Walter E. Poston, VP Franchising

AUTO ACCENTS specializes in the sales and installation of the most in-demand automotive after-market products, such as cellular phones, pagers, alarms, stereos, sunroofs, auto and truck accessories (including auto dealership on-site installation).

BACKGROUND:
Established: 1985; 1st Franchised: 1992
Franchised Units: 2
Company-Owned Units 4
Total Units: 6
Dist.: US-12; CAN-0; O'seas-0
North America: 1 State
Density: 10 in OH
Projected New Units (12 Months): 15
Qualifications: 4, 4, 3, 3, 1, 5
Registered: NR

FINANCIAL/TERMS:
Cash Investment: $50K
Total Investment: $70-120K
Minimum Net Worth: $250K
Fees: Franchise - $14.9K
Royalty - 5%; Ad. - 1%
Earnings Claim Statement: No
Term of Contract (Years): 10/10
Avg. # Of Employees: 3 FT, 1 PT
Passive Ownership: Discouraged
Encourage Conversions: Yes
Area Develop. Agreements: Yes/Negot.
Sub-Franchising Contracts: No
Expand In Territory: No
Space Needs: 2,000-2,500 SF; FS, SC

SUPPORT & TRAINING PROVIDED:
Financial Assistance Provided: Yes
Site Selection Assistance: Yes
Lease Negotiation Assistance: Yes
Co-Operative Advertising: Yes
Franchisee Assoc./Member: No
Size Of Corporate Staff: 25
On-Going Support: A,B,C,D,E,F,G,H,I
Training: 2 Weeks Corporate Headquarters; 1 Week On-Site.

SPECIFIC EXPANSION PLANS:
US: All U.S. (OH and Bordering)
Canada: No
Overseas: No

<< >>

BATTERIES PLUS
925 Walnut Ridge Dr., # 100
Hartland, WI 53029-9389
Tel: (800) 274-9155 (262) 369-0690
Fax: (262) 369-0680
E-Mail: franchising@batteriesplus.com
Web Site: www.batteriesplus.com
Mr. Rod Tremelling, Franchise Marketing

BATTERIES PLUS is America's Battery Experts (TM), providing 1,000's of batteries for 1,000's of items, serving both retail and commercial customers. The $19 billion battery market, growing 6.5% annually, is driven by technology and lifestyles. BATTERIES PLUS is a unique opportunity in this growth industry not yet saturated with competitors. Our turn-key program includes a unique store design, graphics, signage and product brands and proven operating methods.

BACKGROUND: IFA MEMBER
Established: 1988; 1st Franchised: 1992
Franchised Units: 231
Company-Owned Units 23
Total Units: 254
Dist.: US-254; CAN-0; O'seas-0
North America: 35 States
Density: 17 in WI, 15 in MN, 14 in MI
Projected New Units (12 Months): 35
Qualifications: 5, 5, 2, 3, 2, 3
Registered: All Except HI

FINANCIAL/TERMS:
Cash Investment: $100K
Total Investment: $173-216K
Minimum Net Worth: $400K
Fees: Franchise - $25K
Royalty - 4%; Ad. - 1%
Earnings Claim Statement: No
Term of Contract (Years): 10/10
Avg. # Of Employees: 3-4 FT
Passive Ownership: Not Allowed
Encourage Conversions: No
Area Develop. Agreements: Yes
Sub-Franchising Contracts: No
Expand In Territory: No
Space Needs: 1,800-2,000 SF; FS, SF, SC

SUPPORT & TRAINING PROVIDED:
Financial Assistance Provided: Yes(I)
Site Selection Assistance: Yes
Lease Negotiation Assistance: Yes
Co-Operative Advertising: No
Franchisee Assoc./Member: No
Size Of Corporate Staff: 65
On-Going Support: C,D,E,F,G,I
Training: 3 Weeks Corporate Training Center; 2 Weeks On-Site Franchisee's Store.

SPECIFIC EXPANSION PLANS:
US: All United States
Canada: No
Overseas: No

<< >>

Top 50

BIG O TIRES
12650 E. Briarwood Ave. # 2D
Englewood, CO 80112
Tel: (800) 321-2446 (303) 728-5500
Fax: (303) 728-5700
Web Site: www.bigotires.com
Ms. Susan Hay, Franchise Qual. Specialist

BIG O TIRES is the fastest-growing retail tire and under-car service center franchisor in North America. We offer over 30 years' experience and proven success, site selection assistance, comprehensive training and on-going field support, protected territory, exclusive product lines, consistent product supply, unique marketing programs, contemporary building designs, effective advertising support, and proven business system.

BACKGROUND: IFA MEMBER
Established: 1962; 1st Franchised: 1967
Franchised Units: 485
Company-Owned Units 0
Total Units: 485
Dist.: US-484; CAN-1; O'seas-0
North America: 20 States, 1 Province
Density: 175 in CA, 56 in AZ, 44 CO
Projected New Units (12 Months): 40
Qualifications: 5, 5, 1, 2, 1, 5
Registered: NR

FINANCIAL/TERMS:
Cash Investment: $100K
Total Investment: $NR
Minimum Net Worth: $300K
Fees: Franchise - $25K
Royalty - 2%; Ad. - 4%
Earnings Claim Statement: No
Term of Contract (Years): 10
Avg. # Of Employees: NR
Passive Ownership: Discouraged
Encourage Conversions: Yes
Area Develop. Agreements: Yes/Varies
Sub-Franchising Contracts: Yes
Expand In Territory: Yes
Space Needs: NR SF; FS

SUPPORT & TRAINING PROVIDED:
Financial Assistance Provided: Yes(I)
Site Selection Assistance: Yes
Lease Negotiation Assistance: Yes
Co-Operative Advertising: Yes
Franchisee Assoc./Member: NR
Size Of Corporate Staff: 100
On-Going Support: A,B,C,d,E,F,G,h,I

Training: 5 Weeks Littleton, CO.

SPECIFIC EXPANSION PLANS:

US: All United States
Canada: BC and AB
Overseas: No

BRAKE MASTERS

6179 E. Broadway Blvd.
Tucson, AZ 85711
Tel: (800) 888-5545 (520) 512-0000
Fax: (520) 512-1000
E-Mail: franchisee@brakemasters.com
Web Site: www.brakemasters.com
Mr. Richard A. Beuzekom, Dir. Franchise Development

Brake repair, brake-related services and lubrication.

BACKGROUND: IFA MEMBER
Established: 1983; 1st Franchised: 1994
Franchised Units: 40
Company-Owned Units 35
Total Units: 75
Dist.: US-100; CAN-0; O'seas-0
North America: 9 States
Density: 26 in CA, 35 in AZ, 11 in TX
Projected New Units (12 Months): NR
Registered: CA,IL,IN,WA

FINANCIAL/TERMS:
Cash Investment: $25-50K
Total Investment: $125-200K
Minimum Net Worth: $NR
Fees: Franchise - $22.95K
Royalty - 5%; Ad. - 4%
Earnings Claim Statement: No
Term of Contract (Years): 20
Avg. # Of Employees: 6 FT, 2 PT
Passive Ownership: Discouraged
Encourage Conversions: Yes
Area Develop. Agreements: Yes/20
Sub-Franchising Contracts: Yes
Expand In Territory: Yes
Space Needs: 4,000 SF; FS

SUPPORT & TRAINING PROVIDED:
Financial Assistance Provided: NR
Site Selection Assistance: Yes
Lease Negotiation Assistance: Yes
Co-Operative Advertising: Yes
Franchisee Assoc./Member: NR
Size Of Corporate Staff: 22
On-Going Support: B,C,D,E,F,I
Training: 2 Weeks Tucson, AZ; 2 Weeks Location Near Franchisee.

SPECIFIC EXPANSION PLANS:
US: West, Southwest, Midwest, SE
Canada: NR
Overseas: NR

<< >>

CARTEX LIMITED

42816 Mound Rd.
Sterling Heights, MI 48314-3256
Tel: (800) 421-7328 (810) 739-4330
Fax: (810) 739-4331
E-Mail: crismar@aol.com
Web Site: www.fabrion.net
Mr. Laurence P. Klukowski, CEO

CARTEX LIMITED, better known as Fabrion, is a mobile service business, specializing in automotive interior repair. The Fabrion repair process electrostatically repairs auto cloth, velour and carpet. Due to our specialization, we have revolutionized auto upholstery repair. Updating on current (OEM) original equipment materials and providing the tools to match all current patterns being used in auto interiors are our strong points.

BACKGROUND:
Established: 1980; 1st Franchised: 1988
Franchised Units: 87
Company-Owned Units 2
Total Units: 89
Dist.: US-73; CAN-0; O'seas-0
North America: 23 States
Density: 13 in CA, 11 in FL, 7 in TX
Projected New Units (12 Months): 10
Qualifications: 3, 3, 3, 3, 3, 3
Registered: CA,FL,HI,IL,MD,MI,MN,NY, OR,VA,WA,DC,AB

FINANCIAL/TERMS:
Cash Investment: $23.5-36.5K
Total Investment: $23.5-36.5K
Minimum Net Worth: $N/A
Fees: Franchise - $23.5-36.5K
Royalty - 7%,min month fee; Ad. - N/A
Earnings Claim Statement: No
Term of Contract (Years): 5/5
Avg. # Of Employees: 3 FT
Passive Ownership: Discouraged
Encourage Conversions: Yes
Area Develop. Agreements: No
Sub-Franchising Contracts: No
Expand In Territory: Yes
Space Needs: N/A SF; N/A

SUPPORT & TRAINING PROVIDED:
Financial Assistance Provided: Yes
Site Selection Assistance: N/A
Lease Negotiation Assistance: N/A
Co-Operative Advertising: N/A
Franchisee Assoc./Member: No
Size Of Corporate Staff: 8
On-Going Support: B,C,D,G,H,I
Training: 3 Weeks On-Site Under Development.

SPECIFIC EXPANSION PLANS:
US: All United States and Europe
Canada: All Canada
Overseas: All Countries

<< >>

CAR-X AUTO SERVICE

8750 Bryn Mawr Ave., # 410
Chicago, IL 60631
Tel: (800) 359-2359 (773) 693-1000
Fax: (773) 693-0309
E-Mail: dmaltzman@carx.com
Web Site: www.carx.com
Mr. David Maltzman, Dir. Franchise Sales

Retail auto repair specialists providing service in brakes, exhaust, road handling, tune-ups, steering systems, air conditioning, tires, and oil changes for all makes of cars and light trucks.

BACKGROUND:
Established: 1971; 1st Franchised: 1973
Franchised Units: 133
Company-Owned Units 53
Total Units: 186
Dist.: US-186; CAN-0; O'seas-0
North America: 10 States
Density: 59 in IL, 27 in MN, 23 in MO
Projected New Units (12 Months): 8
Qualifications: 5, 3, 2, 2, 2, 5
Registered: FL,IL,IN,MI,MN,SD,WI

FINANCIAL/TERMS:
Cash Investment: $75-100K
Total Investment: $250-310K
Minimum Net Worth: $250K
Fees: Franchise - $22.5K
Royalty - 5%; Ad. - 5-7%
Earnings Claim Statement: Yes
Term of Contract (Years): 15/5
Avg. # Of Employees: 4 FT
Passive Ownership: Discouraged
Encourage Conversions: Yes
Area Develop. Agreements: Yes
Sub-Franchising Contracts: No
Expand In Territory: Yes
Space Needs: 5,000 SF; FS

SUPPORT & TRAINING PROVIDED:
Financial Assistance Provided: Yes(I)
Site Selection Assistance: Yes
Lease Negotiation Assistance: Yes
Co-Operative Advertising: No
Franchisee Assoc./Member: Yes/No

Size Of Corporate Staff: 24
On-Going Support: C,D,E,F,G,H,I
Training: 5 Weeks Headquarters; 2 Weeks at Franchisee's Shop.

SPECIFIC EXPANSION PLANS:
US: MW, SW, SE
Canada: No
Overseas: No

<< >>

CERTIGARD (PETRO-CANADA)

2489 North Sheridan Way
Mississauga, ON L5K 1A8 CANADA
Tel: (800) 668-0220 (905) 804-4555
Fax: (905) 804-4595
E-Mail: Bridger@petro-canada.ca
Web Site: www.certigard.com
Mr. Peter Bridger, Category Manager - Certigard

Petro-Canada is a major integrated oil and gasoline company in Canada. CERTIGARD is Petro-Canada's franchise organization of automotive repair/service outlets across Canada. In operation since 1987, the CERTIGARD franchisee network is supported by a team of dedicated, corporate specialists. The top sales performers now measure annual sales/bay in excess of $260,000. Competitive pricing; convenient locations; national warranties on repairs, lifetime on certain products.

BACKGROUND:
Established: 1975; 1st Franchised: 1987
Franchised Units: 156
Company-Owned Units 0
Total Units: 156
Dist.: US-0; CAN-155; O'seas-0
North America: 9 Provinces
Density: 53 in ON, 30 in BC, 24 in AB
Projected New Units (12 Months): 6
Qualifications: 4, 5, 4, 3, 3, 4
Registered: AB

FINANCIAL/TERMS:
Cash Investment: $40-60K
Total Investment: $100-150K
Minimum Net Worth: $30K
Fees: Franchise - $20K
Royalty - 5%; Ad. - 2%
Earnings Claim Statement: No
Term of Contract (Years): 5/5
Avg. # Of Employees: 6 FT
Passive Ownership: Not Allowed
Encourage Conversions: Yes
Area Develop. Agreements: No
Sub-Franchising Contracts: No
Expand In Territory: Yes
Space Needs: 4,000 SF; FS

SUPPORT & TRAINING PROVIDED:
Financial Assistance Provided: No
Site Selection Assistance: Yes
Lease Negotiation Assistance: No
Co-Operative Advertising: Yes
Franchisee Assoc./Member: Yes/Yes
Size Of Corporate Staff: 25
On-Going Support: C,D,E,F,G,H,I
Training: 3 Days System Training -- Local Classroom; 3 Days Automation Training (Class & On-Site).

SPECIFIC EXPANSION PLANS:
US: No
Canada: All Canada
Overseas: No

<< >>

CLUTCH DOCTORS

2701 NW Vaughn St., # 438
Portland, OR 97210
Tel: (888) 258-8248 (503) 525-5808
Fax: (503) 525-5812
E-Mail: bill@clutchdoctor.com
Web Site: www.clutchdoctor.com
Mr. Bill Nootenboom, Chief Executive Officer

CLUTCH DOCTORS is the leading, innovative automotive clutch and brake repair franchise, offering our exclusive QuoteBase clutch pricing software, state-of-the-art POS system, in-house bookkeeping and nationally and internationally award-winning advertising program. We offer complete training for the franchisee and employees, site selection assistance and a proven profitable automotive repair facility.

BACKGROUND:
Established: 1995; 1st Franchised: 2000
Franchised Units: 2
Company-Owned Units 6
Total Units: 8
Dist.: US-8; CAN-0; O'seas-0
North America: 2 States
Density: 6 in OR, 2 in WA
Projected New Units (12 Months): 6
Qualifications: 3, 2, 1, 2, 3, 5
Registered: WA

FINANCIAL/TERMS:
Cash Investment: $10K
Total Investment: $60-130K
Minimum Net Worth: $100K
Fees: Franchise - $10K
Royalty - 8%; Ad. - 7%
Earnings Claim Statement: NR
Term of Contract (Years): 5/5
Avg. # Of Employees: 3 FT
Passive Ownership: Not Allowed
Encourage Conversions: Yes
Area Develop. Agreements: No
Sub-Franchising Contracts: No
Expand In Territory: Yes
Space Needs: 2,000 SF; RM

SUPPORT & TRAINING PROVIDED:
Financial Assistance Provided: No
Site Selection Assistance: Yes
Lease Negotiation Assistance: Yes
Co-Operative Advertising: Yes
Franchisee Assoc./Member: No
Size Of Corporate Staff: 20
On-Going Support: a,C,D,E,F,G,H,I
Training: 3 Weeks in Portland, OR; 2 Weeks On-Site.

SPECIFIC EXPANSION PLANS:
US: Pacific NW
Canada: No
Overseas: No

COLLISION SHOP, THE

15965 Jeanette St.
Southfield, MI 48075
Tel: (248) 557-1415
Fax: (248) 557-7931
E-Mail: wfcnet@cris.com
Web Site: www.wfcnet.com
Dr. Geoffrey Stebbins, Franchise Sales

THE COLLISION SHOP has developed a time-proven system for repairing today's vehicles. THE COLLISION SHOP focuses on body and paint repairs, including unibody repair, metal finishing, two-stage painting system and detailing. THE COLLISION SHOP has body and paint specialists, and retail auto collision service.

BACKGROUND:
Established: 1991; 1st Franchised: 1998
Franchised Units: 21
Company-Owned Units 4
Total Units: 25
Dist.: US-21; CAN-0; O'seas-0
North America: 2 States
Density: 19 in MI, 2 in FL
Projected New Units (12 Months): 8
Qualifications: 3, 3, 2, 3, 1, 5
Registered: FL,MI

FINANCIAL/TERMS:
Cash Investment: $65K
Total Investment: $150K
Minimum Net Worth: $100K

Fees: Franchise - $35K
Royalty - 6%; Ad. - $250
Earnings Claim Statement: Yes
Term of Contract (Years): 10/5
Avg. # Of Employees: 5 FT
Passive Ownership: Discouraged
Encourage Conversions: Yes
Area Develop. Agreements: Yes
Sub-Franchising Contracts: Yes
Expand In Territory: Yes
Space Needs: 6,000-8,000 SF; FS

SUPPORT & TRAINING PROVIDED:

Financial Assistance Provided: Yes(I)
Site Selection Assistance: Yes
Lease Negotiation Assistance: Yes
Co-Operative Advertising: Yes
Franchisee Assoc./Member: NR
Size Of Corporate Staff: NR
On-Going Support: D,E
Training: 10 Days Headquarters; 10 Days On-Site.

SPECIFIC EXPANSION PLANS:

US: All United States
Canada: Regional
Overseas: Regional

<< >>

COLOR SEAL WAX NO MORE

P.O. Box 2302
Brandon, FL 33509
Tel: (888) 801-0333 (813) 643-0320
Fax: (813) 689-7522
E-Mail: colorsealusa1@aol.com
Web Site: www.colorsealusa.com
Mr. Bill Bonneau, Consultant

Detailing with the COLOR SEAL WAX NO MORE SYSTEM. A 2-step process, using orbital polishers to deoxidize cars, trucks, boats, planes, RVs and any other painted surface. We polish in our Teflon PTFE COLOR SEAL Sealant, which provides a mirror gloss finish, guaranteed in writing for 1-5 years. We offer a mobile and a shop set-up in an automotive complex. The COLOR SEAL Cleaning Process is for engines, interior and exterior surfaces, using only 8 ounces of water and taking only 10 minutes.

BACKGROUND:

Established: 1954; 1st Franchised: 1998
Franchised Units: 381
Company-Owned Units 0
Total Units: 381
Dist.: US-373; CAN-1; O'seas-7
North America: NR
Density: NR
Projected New Units (12 Months): 50
Qualifications: 5, 1, 1, 1, 1, 5
Registered: FL

FINANCIAL/TERMS:

Cash Investment: $13K
Total Investment: $15-25K
Minimum Net Worth: $15-25K
Fees: Franchise - $0
Royalty - 0; Ad. - 0%
Earnings Claim Statement: NR
Term of Contract (Years): Varies
Avg. # Of Employees: 1 FT, 4 PT
Passive Ownership: Allowed
Encourage Conversions: Yes
Area Develop. Agreements: Yes/5
Sub-Franchising Contracts: Yes
Expand In Territory: Yes
Space Needs: 1,000-1,500 SF; FS, HB, Automotive Centers

SUPPORT & TRAINING PROVIDED:

Financial Assistance Provided: Yes
Site Selection Assistance: Yes
Lease Negotiation Assistance: Yes
Co-Operative Advertising: NR
Franchisee Assoc./Member: No
Size Of Corporate Staff: 3
On-Going Support: D,I
Training: 2-3 Days On-Site.

SPECIFIC EXPANSION PLANS:

US: All United States
Canada: All Canada
Overseas: All Countries

<< >>

COLORS ON PARADE

642 Century Cir.
Conway, SC 29526
Tel: (800) 7-COLORS (843) 347-8818
Fax: (843) 347-0349
E-Mail: hemingwayi@colorsfranchise.com
Web Site: www.colorsfranchise.com
Ms. Isha Hemingway

We use our patented and proprietary techniques to make minor auto body damage disappear. We perform our quick and economical services on-site for dealers and fleet operators. COLORS ON PARADE franchisees ranked number one in financial satisfaction in the Success Magazine Gold 100 Survey. Extensive training and support provided. Major metropolitan markets available.

BACKGROUND: IFA MEMBER

Established: 1988; 1st Franchised: 1991
Franchised Units: 358
Company-Owned Units 2
Total Units: 360
Dist.: US-360; CAN-0; O'seas-0
North America: 26 States
Density: 35 in CA, 34 in FL, 18 in TX
Projected New Units (12 Months): 50
Qualifications: 3, 3, 2, 3, 5, 5
Registered: All States

FINANCIAL/TERMS:

Cash Investment: $7.5-75K
Total Investment: $50K+
Minimum Net Worth: $50-250K
Fees: Franchise - $5K
Royalty - Varies; Ad. - 0%
Earnings Claim Statement: No
Term of Contract (Years): 10/5
Avg. # Of Employees: 4 FT
Passive Ownership: Discouraged
Encourage Conversions: Yes
Area Develop. Agreements: Yes/10
Sub-Franchising Contracts: No
Expand In Territory: Yes
Space Needs: N/A SF; N/A

SUPPORT & TRAINING PROVIDED:

Financial Assistance Provided: Yes(I)
Site Selection Assistance: N/A
Lease Negotiation Assistance: N/A
Co-Operative Advertising: Yes
Franchisee Assoc./Member: Yes/No
Size Of Corporate Staff: 21
On-Going Support: A,B,C,D,F,G,H,I
Training: 2 Weeks Conway, SC.

SPECIFIC EXPANSION PLANS:

US: All United States
Canada: All Canada
Overseas: Mexico

<< >>

COTTMAN TRANSMISSION SYSTEMS

240 New York Dr.
Fort Washington, PA 19034

Tel: (800) 394-6116 (215) 643-5885
Fax: (215) 643-2519
E-Mail: cottman@cottman.com
Web Site: www.cottman.com
Mr. Barry Auchenbach, Franchise Dir.

Automotive service franchise with centers nationwide. A market leader with opportunities for solid growth. A highly-supportive company that offers intensive training, outstanding advertising and on-site support. A forty-year reputation of treating customers with fairness, integrity and honesty.

BACKGROUND: IFA MEMBER
Established: 1962; 1st Franchised: 1964
Franchised Units: 325
Company-Owned Units 5
Total Units: 330
Dist.: US-325; CAN-4; O'seas-1
North America: 40 States, 2 Province
Density: 45 in PA, 36 in TX, 22 in NJ
Projected New Units (12 Months): 50
Qualifications: 4, 4, 1, 2, 3, 3
Registered: CA,FL,IL,IN,MD,MI,MN,NY, OR,RI,VA,WA,WI,DC,AB

FINANCIAL/TERMS:
Cash Investment: $50K
Total Investment: $150-175K
Minimum Net Worth: $150K
Fees: Franchise - $27.5K
Royalty - 7.5%; Ad. - $675/Wk.
Earnings Claim Statement: Yes
Term of Contract (Years): 15/15
Avg. # Of Employees: 4 FT
Passive Ownership: Not Allowed
Encourage Conversions: Yes
Area Develop. Agreements: Yes/4
Sub-Franchising Contracts: Yes
Expand In Territory: Yes
Space Needs: 3,000 SF; FS,SC,SC, Auto Mall

SUPPORT & TRAINING PROVIDED:
Financial Assistance Provided: Yes(I)
Site Selection Assistance: Yes
Lease Negotiation Assistance: Yes
Co-Operative Advertising: No
Franchisee Assoc./Member: No
Size Of Corporate Staff: 60
On-Going Support: C,D,E,F,G,H,I
Training: 3 Weeks Home Office; 1 Week Franchise Location.

SPECIFIC EXPANSION PLANS:
US: All United States
Canada: All Canada
Overseas: Open

<< >>

CUSTOM AUTO RESTORATION SYSTEMS

479 Interstate Ct.
Sarasota, FL 34240
Tel: (800) 736-1307 (941) 378-1193
Fax: (941) 378-3472
Web Site: www.autorestoration.com/cars/
Mr. Robert Wyatt, President

C.A.R.S. Inc. offers a wide variety of automobile reconditioning systems for people wishing to service dealerships and the retail market as well. These services include paint repair, paintless dent repair, interior repair, odor removal and windshields.

BACKGROUND:
Established: 1984; 1st Franchised: 1986
Franchised Units: 841
Company-Owned Units 257
Total Units: 1,098
Dist.: US-584; CAN-131; O'seas-126
North America: NR
Density: PA, AL, TX
Projected New Units (12 Months): 60
Qualifications: 3, 3, 3, 3, 3, 3
Registered: FL

FINANCIAL/TERMS:
Cash Investment: $1-10K
Total Investment: $1-10K
Minimum Net Worth: $N/A
Fees: Franchise - $N/A
Royalty - 0%; Ad. - 0%
Earnings Claim Statement: No
Term of Contract (Years): N/A
Avg. # Of Employees: 1 FT
Passive Ownership: NR
Encourage Conversions: NR
Area Develop. Agreements: No
Sub-Franchising Contracts: No
Expand In Territory: Yes
Space Needs: NR SF; N/A

SUPPORT & TRAINING PROVIDED:
Financial Assistance Provided: No
Site Selection Assistance: No
Lease Negotiation Assistance: No
Co-Operative Advertising: No
Franchisee Assoc./Member: No
Size Of Corporate Staff: 6
On-Going Support: G,I
Training: 1-2 Weeks Sarasota, FL.

SPECIFIC EXPANSION PLANS:
US: All United States
Canada: All Canada
Overseas: All Countries

<< >>

CV PROS

2556 Advance Rd., # A
Madison, WI 53704
Tel: (888) 287-7671 (608) 222-0728
Fax: (608) 222-0759
E-Mail: badfwd@aol.com
Mr. Ed Grzelinski

CV PROS Service Centers specialize in the rapid repaid/service of constant velocity (CV) axles and boots for today's ever-increasing front and 4-wheel drive vehicle market.

BACKGROUND:
Established: 1993; 1st Franchised: 1997
Franchised Units: 4
Company-Owned Units 6
Total Units: 10
Dist.: US-9; CAN-0; O'seas-0
North America: 3 States
Density: 5 in FL, 3 in WI, 1 in AZ
Projected New Units (12 Months): 10
Qualifications: 3, 3, 4, 3, 3, 5
Registered: FL,IL,WI

FINANCIAL/TERMS:
Cash Investment: $30K
Total Investment: $65-79K
Minimum Net Worth: $60K
Fees: Franchise - $20K
Royalty - 4.5%; Ad. - 1%
Earnings Claim Statement: No
Term of Contract (Years): 5/5/5/5
Avg. # Of Employees: 3 FT
Passive Ownership: Discouraged
Encourage Conversions: Yes
Area Develop. Agreements: No
Sub-Franchising Contracts: No
Expand In Territory: Yes
Space Needs: 2,000 SF; FS

SUPPORT & TRAINING PROVIDED:
Financial Assistance Provided: Yes(I)
Site Selection Assistance: Yes
Lease Negotiation Assistance: Yes
Co-Operative Advertising: Yes
Franchisee Assoc./Member: No
Size Of Corporate Staff: 4
On-Going Support: C,D,E,F,G,I
Training: 2 Weeks Madison, WI.

SPECIFIC EXPANSION PLANS:
US: All United States
Canada: No
Overseas: No

<< >>

DENT DOCTOR

11301 W. Markham St.
Little Rock, AR 72211

Tel: (800) 946-3368 (501) 224-0500
Fax: (501) 224-0507
E-Mail: info@dentdoctor.com
Web Site: www.dentdoctor.com
Mr. Tom Harris, President

DENT DOCTOR gives you a strategy to succeed. Earn extraordinary rewards removing minor dents, door dings and hail damage from vehicles without painting. Customers receive same day service. No automotive experience is required. You can operate from a retail shop along with providing mobile service.

BACKGROUND: IFA MEMBER
Established: 1988; 1st Franchised: 1990
Franchised Units: 34
Company-Owned Units 4
Total Units: 38
Dist.: US-37; CAN-1; O'seas-0
North America: 24 States, 1 Province
Density: 5 in CO, 4 in TN, 3 in TX
Projected New Units (12 Months): 20
Qualifications: 4, 4, 2, 3, 4, 5
Registered: CA,FL,IL,IN,MI,NY,WA,WI
FINANCIAL/TERMS:
Cash Investment: $9.9-49.9K
Total Investment: $22.9-79.9K
Minimum Net Worth: $25K
Fees: Franchise - $9.9-22.8K
Royalty - 6%; Ad. - 0%
Earnings Claim Statement: No
Term of Contract (Years): 10/20
Avg. # Of Employees: 4 FT
Passive Ownership: Allowed
Encourage Conversions: Yes
Area Develop. Agreements: Yes/10
Sub-Franchising Contracts: No
Expand In Territory: Yes
Space Needs: 1,200 SF; FS, SF
SUPPORT & TRAINING PROVIDED:
Financial Assistance Provided: No
Site Selection Assistance: Yes
Lease Negotiation Assistance: Yes
Co-Operative Advertising: Yes
Franchisee Assoc./Member: No
Size Of Corporate Staff: 6
On-Going Support: B,C,E,G,H,I
Training: 4 Weeks Little Rock, AR; 1 Week Franchisee's Home Area (Optional).
SPECIFIC EXPANSION PLANS:
US: All United States
Canada: All Canada
Overseas: All Countries

<< >>

DETAIL GUYS, THE
74478 Hwy. 111, PMB 378
Palm Desert, CA 92260
Tel: (888) 879-8783 (818) 519-9344
Fax: (888) 927-4425
E-Mail: lance@carwashguys.com
Web Site: www.detailguys.com
Mr. Lance Winslow, III, President/CEO

Successful mobile detailing franchise with 4-bay shops and 8-bay super-shops.

BACKGROUND:
Established: 1997; 1st Franchised: 1998
Franchised Units: 39
Company-Owned Units 10
Total Units: 49
Dist.: US-49; CAN-0; O'seas-0
North America: NR
Density: NR
Projected New Units (12 Months): 100+
Qualifications: 1, 1, 1, 1, 1, 5
Registered: CA,FL,WA
FINANCIAL/TERMS:
Cash Investment: $NR
Total Investment: $15-40K
Minimum Net Worth: $N/A
Fees: Franchise - $7.5K
Royalty - $280/Mo.; Ad. - 0%
Earnings Claim Statement: Yes
Term of Contract (Years): 5/20
Avg. # Of Employees: 1 FT, 1 PT
Passive Ownership: Allowed
Encourage Conversions: No
Area Develop. Agreements: No
Sub-Franchising Contracts: No
Expand In Territory: Yes
Space Needs: NR SF; FS, HB
SUPPORT & TRAINING PROVIDED:
Financial Assistance Provided: Yes(I)
Site Selection Assistance: Yes
Lease Negotiation Assistance: Yes
Co-Operative Advertising: Yes
Franchisee Assoc./Member: No
Size Of Corporate Staff: 0
On-Going Support: A,B,C,D,E,F,G,h,I
Training: 1 Week in Reno, NV.
SPECIFIC EXPANSION PLANS:
US: All United States
Canada: All Canada
Overseas: No

<< >>

ECONO LUBE N' TUNE
4911 Birch St.
Newport Beach, CA 92660
Tel: (800) 628-0253 (949) 851-2259
Fax: (714) 852-6688
Mr. David Wisok,

Turn-key automotive service franchise. Lubrications, tune-ups, brake and other general services. Drive-through oil change

BACKGROUND:
Established: 1974; 1st Franchised: 1974
Franchised Units: 173
Company-Owned Units 95
Total Units: 268
Dist.: US-281; CAN-0; O'seas-0
North America: NR
Density: NR
Projected New Units (12 Months): 10
Qualifications: 4, 4, 2, 4, 3, 5
Registered: CA,FL,VA,WA
FINANCIAL/TERMS:
Cash Investment: $50-100K
Total Investment: $200K
Minimum Net Worth: $300-500K
Fees: Franchise - $49.5K
Royalty - 5%/$500; Ad. - 5%/.5% Natl
Earnings Claim Statement: Yes
Term of Contract (Years): 15/5
Avg. # Of Employees: 6-7 FT
Passive Ownership: Discouraged
Encourage Conversions: N/A
Area Develop. Agreements: No
Sub-Franchising Contracts: No
Expand In Territory: Yes
Space Needs: NR SF; NR
SUPPORT & TRAINING PROVIDED:
Financial Assistance Provided: Yes(D)
Site Selection Assistance: N/A
Lease Negotiation Assistance: NR
Co-Operative Advertising: NR
Franchisee Assoc./Member: Yes/No
Size Of Corporate Staff: 100
On-Going Support: B,C,D,E,F,G,H,I
Training: 1 Week Ontario, CA; 1 Week Cypress, CA.
SPECIFIC EXPANSION PLANS:
US: East Coast, VA,NC,SC,GA
Canada: No
Overseas: No

<< >>

ENDRUST AUTO APPEARANCE CENTERS
1155 Greenbriar Dr.
Bethel Park, PA 15102
Tel: (412) 831-1255
Fax: (412) 833-3409
E-Mail: fboei@sqi.net
Mr. William Griser, Vice President

Car preservation services, including wash, wax, detailing, interior shampoo, rust-proofing, sound deadening, exterior paint sealant, fabric protection, etc. There is no franchise fee, and it can be operated as a separate center or an add-on if already in business. Excellent high-profit.

BACKGROUND:

Established: 1969; 1st Franchised: 1970

Franchised Units:	55
Company-Owned Units	0
Total Units:	55
Dist.:	US-55; CAN-0; O'seas-0
North America:	6 States
Density:	20 in PA, 12 in OH, 8 in WV
Projected New Units (12 Months):	10
Qualifications:	4, 3, 2, 2, 2, 5

Registered: All States

FINANCIAL/TERMS:

Cash Investment:	$30K
Total Investment:	$90K
Minimum Net Worth:	$Varies
Fees: Franchise -	$Varies
Royalty - 0%;	Ad. - 0%
Earnings Claim Statement:	No
Term of Contract (Years):	Indefin.
Avg. # Of Employees:	2 FT, 1 PT
Passive Ownership:	Allowed
Encourage Conversions:	N/A
Area Develop. Agreements:	Yes/5
Sub-Franchising Contracts:	Yes
Expand In Territory:	Yes

Space Needs: 2,000 SF; FS, SF, SC, RM, HB

SUPPORT & TRAINING PROVIDED:

Financial Assistance Provided:	Yes(I)
Site Selection Assistance:	Yes
Lease Negotiation Assistance:	Yes
Co-Operative Advertising:	No
Franchisee Assoc./Member:	No
Size Of Corporate Staff:	6
On-Going Support:	C,D,E,F,G,H

Training: 1 Week On-Site; Continual Follow-Up.

SPECIFIC EXPANSION PLANS:

US:	All United States
Canada:	No
Overseas:	No

<< >>

ESTRELLA INSURANCE

7480 NW 186th St.
Miami, Fl 33015
Tel: (888) 511-7722 (305) 828-2444
Fax: (305) 556-7788
E-Mail: estrella@sunnyweb.com
Web Site: www.estrellainsurance.net
Mr. Jose E. Merille, President

ESTRELLA INSURANCE is the leader in the state of Florida in the auto insurance agency field and currently insures close to 100,000 autos in Dade and Broward county alone. Future expansion plans are to West Palm, Tampa, Orlando and other large cities. We offer outstanding support and advertising (TV, radio, outdoor, direct mail, etc.).

BACKGROUND:

Established: 1980; 1st Franchised: 1997

Franchised Units:	5
Company-Owned Units	35
Total Units:	40
Dist.:	US-40; CAN-0; O'seas-0
North America:	1 State
Density:	40 in FL
Projected New Units (12 Months):	8
Qualifications:	5, 3, 1, 4, 3, 5

Registered: FL

FINANCIAL/TERMS:

Cash Investment:	$20-30K
Total Investment:	$79.5-99.5K
Minimum Net Worth:	$75-100K
Fees: Franchise -	$39.5K
Royalty - 2-4%;	Ad. - 1%
Earnings Claim Statement:	Yes
Term of Contract (Years):	7/7
Avg. # Of Employees:	3 FT, 1 PT
Passive Ownership:	Discouraged
Encourage Conversions:	Yes
Area Develop. Agreements:	Yes/10
Sub-Franchising Contracts:	No
Expand In Territory:	No

Space Needs: 800 SF; FS, SF, SC, RM

SUPPORT & TRAINING PROVIDED:

Financial Assistance Provided:	Yes
Site Selection Assistance:	Yes
Lease Negotiation Assistance:	Yes
Co-Operative Advertising:	Yes
Franchisee Assoc./Member:	Yes/Yes
Size Of Corporate Staff:	30
On-Going Support:	A,B,C,D,E,H

Training: 8 Weeks Miami, FL.

SPECIFIC EXPANSION PLANS:

US:	FL
Canada:	No
Overseas:	No

<< >>

EXPRESS OIL CHANGE

190 W. Valley Ave.
Birmingham, AL 35209-3621
Tel: (888) 945-1771 (205) 945-1771
Fax: (205) 940-6026
Web Site: www.expressoil.com
Mr. R. Kent Feazell, VP Development

We are among the top ten fast oil change chains in the world. Per unit, sales out-pace our competitors by over 40%. Attractive, state-of-the-art facilities offer expanded, highly profitable services in addition to our ten minute oil change. We also provide transmission service, air conditioning service, brake repair, tire rotation and balancing and miscellaneous light repairs... Most extensive training and franchise support in the industry.

BACKGROUND: IFA MEMBER

Established: 1979; 1st Franchised: 1986

Franchised Units:	125
Company-Owned Units	12
Total Units:	137
Dist.:	US-137; CAN-0; O'seas-0
North America:	5 States
Density:	62 in AL, 35 in GA, 6 in TN
Projected New Units (12 Months):	20
Qualifications:	5, 5, 1, 3, 3, 5

Registered: NR

FINANCIAL/TERMS:

Cash Investment:	$115-227K
Total Investment:	$706-907K
Minimum Net Worth:	$450K
Fees: Franchise -	$17.5K
Royalty - 5%;	Ad. - 3%
Earnings Claim Statement:	Yes
Term of Contract (Years):	10/10
Avg. # Of Employees:	7 FT
Passive Ownership:	Allowed
Encourage Conversions:	Yes
Area Develop. Agreements:	Yes
Sub-Franchising Contracts:	No
Expand In Territory:	Yes

Space Needs: 22,000 SF; FS

SUPPORT & TRAINING PROVIDED:

Financial Assistance Provided:	Yes(I)
Site Selection Assistance:	Yes
Lease Negotiation Assistance:	Yes
Co-Operative Advertising:	Yes
Franchisee Assoc./Member:	No
Size Of Corporate Staff:	37
On-Going Support:	A,B,C,D,E,F,G,H,I

Training: 8 Weeks Closest Training Center; 1 Yr. On-Site, Post-OpeningTraining;

Continuous Training.

SPECIFIC EXPANSION PLANS:

US: Southeast
Canada: No
Overseas: No

<< >>

GLASS DOCTOR

1020 N. University Parks Dr.
Waco, TX 76710-5098
Tel: (800) 280-9858 (254) 745-2439
Fax: (800) 209-7621
E-Mail: mhawkins@dwyergroup.com
Web Site: www.glassdr.com
Mr. Mike Hawkins, VP Franchising

GLASS DOCTOR is an exclusive, world-wide glass replacement franchise organization. The bulk of our business is replacing auto windshields and tempered glass.

BACKGROUND: IFA MEMBER
Established: 1962; 1st Franchised: 1977
Franchised Units: 73
Company-Owned Units 0
Total Units: 73
Dist.: US-72; CAN-1; O'seas-0
North America: 27 States, 1 Province
Density: NR
Projected New Units (12 Months): 36
Qualifications: 3, 4, 2, 3, 3, 5
Registered: All States

FINANCIAL/TERMS:

Cash Investment: $25-50K
Total Investment: $109.9-252.5K
Minimum Net Worth: $Open
Fees: Franchise - $18.9K
Royalty - 6% or $200/Wk.; Ad. - 2%
Earnings Claim Statement: Yes
Term of Contract (Years): 10/10
Avg. # Of Employees: 4 FT
Passive Ownership: NR
Encourage Conversions: Yes
Area Develop. Agreements: NR
Sub-Franchising Contracts: No
Expand In Territory: Yes
Space Needs: 1,500 SF; NR

SUPPORT & TRAINING PROVIDED:

Financial Assistance Provided: Yes
Site Selection Assistance: No
Lease Negotiation Assistance: No
Co-Operative Advertising: NR
Franchisee Assoc./Member: No
Size Of Corporate Staff: 20
On-Going Support: C,D,E,F,G,H,I
Training: 1 Week in Headquarters in Waco, TX.

SPECIFIC EXPANSION PLANS:

US: All United States
Canada: All Canada
Overseas: No

<< >>

GREASE MONKEY INTERNATIONAL

633 17th St., # 400
Denver, CO 80202
Tel: (800) 364-0352 (303) 308-1660
Fax: (303) 308-5908
E-Mail: danah@greasemonkeyintl.com
Web Site: www.greasemonkeyintl.com
Mr. Michael Brunetti, VP Franchise Sales/Dev.

GREASE MONKEY Centers provide convenient vehicle preventive maintenance services. We provide comprehensive technical training for all franchisees, including instruction performing all GREASE MONKEY approved services thoroughly and safely. You will also learn basic accounting, computer marketing and customer satisfaction techniques to help you operate your business.

BACKGROUND:
Established: 1978; 1st Franchised: 1979
Franchised Units: 186
Company-Owned Units 44
Total Units: 230
Dist.: US-183; CAN-0; O'seas-34
North America: 28 States
Density: 57 in CO, 14 in CA, 13 in WA
Projected New Units (12 Months): 20
Qualifications: 5, 4, 2, 2, 3, 5
Registered: All States Except HI,SD

FINANCIAL/TERMS:

Cash Investment: $120-220K
Total Investment: $300K
Minimum Net Worth: $300K
Fees: Franchise - $28K
Royalty - 5%; Ad. - 6%
Earnings Claim Statement: Yes
Term of Contract (Years): 15/15
Avg. # Of Employees: 3 FT, 3 PT
Passive Ownership: Discouraged
Encourage Conversions: Yes
Area Develop. Agreements: Yes/Negot.
Sub-Franchising Contracts: No
Expand In Territory: Yes
Space Needs: 1,800 SF; FS, SC

SUPPORT & TRAINING PROVIDED:

Financial Assistance Provided: Yes(I)
Site Selection Assistance: Yes
Lease Negotiation Assistance: Yes
Co-Operative Advertising: Yes
Franchisee Assoc./Member: Yes
Size Of Corporate Staff: 45
On-Going Support: A,B,C,D,E,F,G,H,I
Training: 1 Week Corporate Headquarters, Denver, CO; 1 Week Market Center.

SPECIFIC EXPANSION PLANS:

US: All United States
Canada: No
Overseas: Mexico

<< >>

INDY LUBE

6515 E. 82nd St., # 209
Indianapolis, IN 46250
Tel: (800) 326-5823 (317) 845-9444
Fax: (317) 577-3169
E-Mail: rance@1quest.net
Web Site: www.indylube.com
Mr. James C. Yates, President/CEO

INDY LUBE oil change centers specialize in fluid maintenance of both passenger and light industrial vehicles. Each INDY LUBE facility is up-scale with a spacious reception room with television, wallpaper and courtesy phone. The INDY LUBE full-service oil change includes a 20-point safety and fluid check. Each center also has a point-of-sale computer system.

BACKGROUND:
Established: 1986; 1st Franchised: 1989
Franchised Units: 10
Company-Owned Units 18
Total Units: 28
Dist.: US-28; CAN-0; O'seas-0
North America: 2 States
Density: 22 in IN, 6 in MN
Projected New Units (12 Months): 5
Qualifications: 4, 5, 4, 3, 1, 4
Registered: IN

FINANCIAL/TERMS:

Cash Investment: $50-90K
Total Investment: $250-450K
Minimum Net Worth: $100K
Fees: Franchise - $7.5K
Royalty - 5%; Ad. - 5%
Earnings Claim Statement: No
Term of Contract (Years): 20/5-10
Avg. # Of Employees: 4 FT, 2 PT
Passive Ownership: Discouraged

Encourage Conversions: No
Area Develop. Agreements: Yes/20
Sub-Franchising Contracts: No
Expand In Territory: Yes
Space Needs: 2,100 SF; FS

SUPPORT & TRAINING PROVIDED:
Financial Assistance Provided: Yes(I)
Site Selection Assistance: Yes
Lease Negotiation Assistance: Yes
Co-Operative Advertising: Yes
Franchisee Assoc./Member: No
Size Of Corporate Staff: 10
On-Going Support: a,b,C,D,E,F,G,H,I
Training: 2-3 Weeks Headquarters.

SPECIFIC EXPANSION PLANS:
US: Midwest
Canada: No
Overseas: No

<< >>

KING BEAR AUTO SERVICE CENTERS

130 - 29 Merrick Blvd.
Springfield Gardens, NY 11434-4131
Tel: (800) 311-5464 (718) 527-1252
Fax: (718) 527-4985
E-Mail: kingbearauto@aol.com
Web Site: www.kingbearauto.com
Mr. Melvin D. Messinger, Dir. Franchising

KING BEAR AUTO SERVICE CENTER was the first organized automotive franchise in the state of New York. Founded in 1973, it has been a household name known for quality auto service at a reasonable cost. KING BEAR has retained its status as a complete one-stop auto service center.

BACKGROUND: IFA MEMBER
Established: 1973; 1st Franchised: 1973
Franchised Units: 35
Company-Owned Units 0
Total Units: 35
Dist.: US-28; CAN-0; O'seas-0
North America: 1 State
Density: 33 in NY
Projected New Units (12 Months): 12
Qualifications: 2, 3, 1, 1, 1, 5
Registered: NY

FINANCIAL/TERMS:
Cash Investment: $65-90K
Total Investment: $159-294K
Minimum Net Worth: $50K
Fees: Franchise - $29.5K
Royalty - 5% or Fee; Ad. - 7% or Fee
Earnings Claim Statement: No
Term of Contract (Years): 25/25
Avg. # Of Employees: 3 FT
Passive Ownership: Allowed
Encourage Conversions: Yes
Area Develop. Agreements: Yes/25
Sub-Franchising Contracts: No
Expand In Territory: Yes
Space Needs: 2,000-6,000 SF; FS, SC

SUPPORT & TRAINING PROVIDED:
Financial Assistance Provided: Yes(I)
Site Selection Assistance: Yes
Lease Negotiation Assistance: Yes
Co-Operative Advertising: Yes
Franchisee Assoc./Member: No
Size Of Corporate Staff: 6
On-Going Support: B,C,D,E,F,H,I
Training: 2 Weeks at Corporate Office; On-Site as Needed.

SPECIFIC EXPANSION PLANS:
US: All United States
Canada: No
Overseas: No

LEE MYLES TRANSMISSIONS

140 Rte. 17 N., # 200
Paramus, NJ 07652
Tel: (800) 533-6953 (201) 262-0555
Fax: (201) 262-5177
E-Mail: info@leemyles.com
Web Site: www.leemyles.com
Mr. Mark Savel, Marketing/Sales

Service, repair and replace automatic and standard transmissions for the car and light truck market. Turn-key and existing locations are available. On-going operational support, business and technical assistance. Major expansion into new markets. Area developers are welcome.

BACKGROUND: IFA MEMBER
Established: 1947; 1st Franchised: 1964
Franchised Units: 86
Company-Owned Units 0
Total Units: 86
Dist.: US-86; CAN-0; O'seas-0
North America: 10 States
Density: 30 in NY, 15 in NJ, 13 in AZ
Projected New Units (12 Months): 10
Qualifications: 4, 4, 4, 5, 5, 5
Registered: CA,FL,MD,NY,OR,RI,VA,WA,DC

FINANCIAL/TERMS:
Cash Investment: $40-60K
Total Investment: $98-127K
Minimum Net Worth: $60K
Fees: Franchise - $25K
Royalty - 7%; Ad. - 4.5%
Earnings Claim Statement: No
Term of Contract (Years): 25/15/5/5
Avg. # Of Employees: 4 FT
Passive Ownership: Not Allowed
Encourage Conversions: Yes
Area Develop. Agreements: Yes/15
Sub-Franchising Contracts: No
Expand In Territory: Yes
Space Needs: 3,000 SF; FS, SC, HB, Auto Mall

SUPPORT & TRAINING PROVIDED:
Financial Assistance Provided: N/A
Site Selection Assistance: Yes
Lease Negotiation Assistance: Yes
Co-Operative Advertising: Yes
Franchisee Assoc./Member: Yes/Yes
Size Of Corporate Staff: 15
On-Going Support: C,D,E,F,G,I
Training: 1-2 Weeks Corporate Office.

SPECIFIC EXPANSION PLANS:
US: All United States
Canada: All Canada
Overseas: No

LENTZ USA SERVICE CENTERS

1001 Riverview Dr.
Kalamazoo, MI 49048
Tel: (800) 354-2131 (616) 342-2200
Fax: (616) 342-9461
E-Mail: quietcar@lentzusa.com
Web Site: www.lentzusa.com
Mr. Gary R. Thomas, Franchise Liaison

Specialty automotive repairs -- features direct to you product purchases from manufacturers at the best cost, allowing for greater profit opportunities. Great expansion areas available for multiple location ownership.

BACKGROUND: IFA MEMBER
Established: 1972; 1st Franchised: 1989
Franchised Units: 15
Company-Owned Units 11
Total Units: 26
Dist.: US-36; CAN-0; O'seas-0
North America: 5 States
Density: 28 in MI, 6 in IN, 2 in NC
Projected New Units (12 Months): 6
Qualifications: 4, 3, 1, 3, 4, 5
Registered: FL,IL,IN,MD,MI

FINANCIAL/TERMS:
Cash Investment: $35-70K
Total Investment: $90-112K
Minimum Net Worth: $100K
Fees: Franchise - $20K
Royalty - 0-7%; Ad. - 0%

Earnings Claim Statement: No
Term of Contract (Years): 10/10
Avg. # Of Employees: 3-5 FT
Passive Ownership: Not Allowed
Encourage Conversions: Yes
Area Develop. Agreements: Yes/10
Sub-Franchising Contracts: No
Expand In Territory: Yes
Space Needs: 3,600 SF; FS, SC

SUPPORT & TRAINING PROVIDED:
Financial Assistance Provided: Yes(I)
Site Selection Assistance: Yes
Lease Negotiation Assistance: Yes
Co-Operative Advertising: No
Franchisee Assoc./Member: No
Size Of Corporate Staff: 10
On-Going Support: B,C,D,E,F,G,H,I
Training: 2 Weeks Kalamazoo, MI; 1 Week Franchise Site; On-Going Visits.

SPECIFIC EXPANSION PLANS:
US: Midwest
Canada: All Canada
Overseas: Middle East, India, Europe

<< >>

LINE-X SPRAY-ON TRUCK BED-LINERS
2525-A Birch St.
Santa Ana, CA 92707
Tel: (800) 831-3232 (714) 850-1662
Fax: (714) 850-8759
E-Mail: sales@linexcorp.com
Web Site: www.linexcorp.com
Mr. Scott Jewett, General Manager

A LINE-X franchisee operates a retail/industrial location that applies sprayed on coatings. LINE-X has a number of applications from flooring to industrial applications. LINE-X is in a growing, new and unsaturated market with extraordinary opportunities for minority entrepreneurs.

BACKGROUND:
Established: 1993; 1st Franchised: 1998
Franchised Units: 108
Company-Owned Units 0
Total Units: 108
Dist.: US-334; CAN-0; O'seas-27
North America: 50 States
Density: 20 in CA, 15 in WA, 10 in GA
Projected New Units (12 Months): NR
Registered: All States

FINANCIAL/TERMS:
Cash Investment: $25K
Total Investment: $68-147K
Minimum Net Worth: $20K
Fees: Franchise - $20K
Royalty - 0%; Ad. - 1.5%
Earnings Claim Statement: No
Term of Contract (Years): 5/15
Avg. # Of Employees: 2 FT
Passive Ownership: Discouraged
Encourage Conversions: NR
Area Develop. Agreements: Yes
Sub-Franchising Contracts: Yes
Expand In Territory: Yes
Space Needs: 2,500 SF; Industrial/Commercial

SUPPORT & TRAINING PROVIDED:
Financial Assistance Provided: NR
Site Selection Assistance: Yes
Lease Negotiation Assistance: Yes
Co-Operative Advertising: No
Franchisee Assoc./Member: No
Size Of Corporate Staff: 14
On-Going Support: C,D,E,G,H,I
Training: Up to 5 Days at Our Location; up to 7 Days at Franchisee's Location.

SPECIFIC EXPANSION PLANS:
US: All United States
Canada: All Canada
Overseas: All Countries

<< >>

LUBEPRO'S INTERNATIONAL, INC.
1630 Colonial Pkwy.
Inverness, IL 60067
Tel: (800) 654-5823 (847) 776-2500
Fax: (847) 776-2542
Mr. Phil Robinson, Franchise Director

Our building design, our training program and our unique approach to marketing truly set us ahead of our competitors.

BACKGROUND:
Established: 1978; 1st Franchised: 1985
Franchised Units: 22
Company-Owned Units 14
Total Units: 36
Dist.: US-36; CAN-0; O'seas-0
North America: 4 States
Density: 28 in IL, 6 in WI
Projected New Units (12 Months): 4
Qualifications: 4, 3, 1, 2, 2, 4
Registered: IL,IN,MN,WI

FINANCIAL/TERMS:
Cash Investment: $100K
Total Investment: $170-200K
Minimum Net Worth: $300K
Fees: Franchise - $25K
Royalty - 5%; Ad. - 5%
Earnings Claim Statement: No
Term of Contract (Years): 20/10/10
Avg. # Of Employees: 6 FT
Passive Ownership: Allowed
Encourage Conversions: N/A
Area Develop. Agreements: No
Sub-Franchising Contracts: No
Expand In Territory: Yes
Space Needs: 1,800 SF; FS

SUPPORT & TRAINING PROVIDED:
Financial Assistance Provided: No
Site Selection Assistance: Yes
Lease Negotiation Assistance: No
Co-Operative Advertising: Yes
Franchisee Assoc./Member: No
Size Of Corporate Staff: 7
On-Going Support: C,D,E,G,H,I
Training: 10 Days Rockford, IL.

SPECIFIC EXPANSION PLANS:
US: Central, North Central
Canada: No
Overseas: No

<< >>

Top 50

MAACO AUTO PAINTING & BODYWORKS
381 Brooks Rd.
King of Prussia, PA 19406
Tel: (800) 296-2226 (610) 265-6606
Fax: (610) 337-6176
E-Mail: franchise@maaco.com
Web Site: www.maaco.com
Mr. Bill Chaffee, VP Franchise Dev.

MAACO has developed a system relating to the establishment and operation of centers specializing in auto painting and body repair. The system includes market analysis, research and development, sales and merchandising methods, training, record keeping, advertising and business management, all of which are constantly being improved, up-dated and further developed by a fully-staffed and knowledgeable corporate structure to service its owners.

BACKGROUND: IFA MEMBER
Established: 1972; 1st Franchised: 1972

Franchised Units: 575
Company-Owned Units 0
Total Units: 575
Dist.: US-510; CAN-42; O'seas-4
North America: 47 States, 7 Provinces
Density: 42 in CA, 26 in NJ, 21 in PA
Projected New Units (12 Months): 50
Qualifications: 3, 3, 1, 1, 3, 5
Registered: All States

FINANCIAL/TERMS:
Cash Investment: $60K
Total Investment: $249K
Minimum Net Worth: $250K
Fees: Franchise - $30K
Royalty - 8%; Ad. - $850/Wk.
Earnings Claim Statement: No
Term of Contract (Years): 15/5
Avg. # Of Employees: 10 FT
Passive Ownership: Not Allowed
Encourage Conversions: No
Area Develop. Agreements: No
Sub-Franchising Contracts: No
Expand In Territory: Yes
Space Needs: 7,500-10,000 SF; FS

SUPPORT & TRAINING PROVIDED:
Financial Assistance Provided: Yes(I)
Site Selection Assistance: Yes
Lease Negotiation Assistance: Yes
Co-Operative Advertising: Yes
Franchisee Assoc./Member: No
Size Of Corporate Staff: 125
On-Going Support: A,B,C,D,E,F,G,H,I
Training: 4 Weeks King of Prussia, PA; 3 Weeks On-Site.

SPECIFIC EXPANSION PLANS:
US: All United States
Canada: All Canada
Overseas: No

<< >>

MAACO AUTO PAINTING & BODYWORKS (CANADA)
10 Kingsbridge Garden Cir., # 501
Mississauga, ON L5R 3K6 CANADA
Tel: (800) 387-6780 (905) 501-1212
Fax: (905) 501-1218
E-Mail: hdelisle@maaco.com
Web Site: www.maaco.com
Mr. Hermann Delisle, Mgr. Franchise Development

Production car painting and bodyworks center.

BACKGROUND:
Established: 1972; 1st Franchised: 1972
Franchised Units: 560
Company-Owned Units 0
Total Units: 560
Dist.: US-515; CAN-45; O'seas-0
North America: 47 States, 7 Provinces
Density: 18 in ON, 7 in AB, 6 in BC
Projected New Units (12 Months): 6-8
Qualifications: 4, 4, 1, 3, 3, 3
Registered: All States and AB

FINANCIAL/TERMS:
Cash Investment: $80K
Total Investment: $240K
Minimum Net Worth: $NR
Fees: Franchise - $25K
Royalty - 8%; Ad. - $700/Wk.
Earnings Claim Statement: No
Term of Contract (Years): 15/5
Avg. # Of Employees: 8 FT
Passive Ownership: Not Allowed
Encourage Conversions: Yes
Area Develop. Agreements: NR
Sub-Franchising Contracts: Yes
Expand In Territory: Yes
Space Needs: 8,000 SF; FS, SF, SC

SUPPORT & TRAINING PROVIDED:
Financial Assistance Provided: N/A
Site Selection Assistance: Yes
Lease Negotiation Assistance: Yes
Co-Operative Advertising: Yes
Franchisee Assoc./Member: No
Size Of Corporate Staff: 10
On-Going Support: A,B,C,D,E,F,G,H,I
Training: 3 Weeks in King of Prussia, PA; 2 Weeks On-Site.

SPECIFIC EXPANSION PLANS:
US: No
Canada: All Canada
Overseas: No

<< >>

MASTER MECHANIC, THE
1989 Dundas St. E.
Mississauga, ON L4X 1M1 CANADA
Tel: (800) 383-8523 (905) 629-3773
Fax: (905) 629-3864
E-Mail: andrew@mastermechanic.ca
Web Site: www.mastermechanic.ca
Mr. Andrew Wanie, President

General auto repair and emission testing center, with a reputation in high-tech automotive excellence that provides to its customers the convenience of one-stop shopping for all of their automotive maintenance and repair needs.

BACKGROUND:
Established: 1979; 1st Franchised: 1983
Franchised Units: 33
Company-Owned Units 2
Total Units: 35
Dist.: US-0; CAN-35; O'seas-0
North America: 1 Province
Density: 35 in ON
Projected New Units (12 Months): 4
Qualifications: 4, 3, 4, 3, 4, 5
Registered: NR

FINANCIAL/TERMS:
Cash Investment: $60-80K
Total Investment: $125-175K
Minimum Net Worth: $200K
Fees: Franchise - $25K
Royalty - 6%; Ad. - 3% (Varies)
Earnings Claim Statement: Yes
Term of Contract (Years): 20/Open
Avg. # Of Employees: 3-5 FT, 1-2 PT
Passive Ownership: Discouraged
Encourage Conversions: Yes
Area Develop. Agreements: Yes/20
Sub-Franchising Contracts: Yes
Expand In Territory: Yes
Space Needs: 4,000 SF; FS, SF, SC, RM

SUPPORT & TRAINING PROVIDED:
Financial Assistance Provided: Yes(I)
Site Selection Assistance: Yes
Lease Negotiation Assistance: Yes
Co-Operative Advertising: Yes
Franchisee Assoc./Member: Yes/Yes
Size Of Corporate Staff: 6
On-Going Support: a,B,C,D,E,F,G,H,I
Training: 1 Week Classroom; 4 Weeks Training Shop; On-Going -- 2 Weeks/ Yr. On-Site.

SPECIFIC EXPANSION PLANS:
US: No
Canada: ON
Overseas: No

<< >>

Top 50

MEINEKE DISCOUNT MUFFLERS
128 S. Tryon St., # 900
Charlotte, NC 28202
Tel: (800) 275-5200 (704) 377-8855
Fax: (704) 372-4826
E-Mail: franchise.info@meineke.com
Web Site: www.meineke.com
Ms. Lois Calloway, Franchise Development Coord.

MEINEKE DISCOUNT MUFFLERS is the nation's largest discount muffler and brake repair specialist with more than 860 shops across the nation. They have been offering great service at discount prices for more than 25 years. Their franchisees come from all walks of life and represent many nationalities.

BACKGROUND: IFA MEMBER
Established: 1972; 1st Franchised: 1973
Franchised Units: 844
Company-Owned Units 25
Total Units: 869
Dist.: US-830; CAN-30; O'seas-9
North America: 49 States, 5 Provinces
Density: 73 in NY, 73 in PA, 55 in TX
Projected New Units (12 Months): 65
Qualifications: 4, 3, 3, 2, 2, 5
Registered: All States

FINANCIAL/TERMS:
Cash Investment: $50K
Total Investment: $154-285K
Minimum Net Worth: $150K
Fees: Franchise - $25K
Royalty - 3-7%; Ad. - 8%
Earnings Claim Statement: Yes
Term of Contract (Years): 15/15
Avg. # Of Employees: 4 FT
Passive Ownership: Not Allowed
Encourage Conversions: Yes
Area Develop. Agreements: Yes/Varies
Sub-Franchising Contracts: No
Expand In Territory: Yes
Space Needs: 2,880-3,880 SF; FS

SUPPORT & TRAINING PROVIDED:
Financial Assistance Provided: Yes(I)
Site Selection Assistance: Yes
Lease Negotiation Assistance: No
Co-Operative Advertising: Yes
Franchisee Assoc./Member: Yes/Yes
Size Of Corporate Staff: 88
On-Going Support: A,B,C,D,G,h,I
Training: 4 Weeks Charlotte, NC.

SPECIFIC EXPANSION PLANS:
US: All United States
Canada: All Canada
Overseas: Caribbean, Central America--All Countries

<< >>

MERLIN'S MUFFLER & BRAKE

1 N. River Ln., # 206
Geneva, IL 60134-2267
Tel: (800) 652-9900 (630) 208-9900
Fax: (630) 208-8601
E-Mail: wecare@merlins.com
Web Site: www.merlins.com
Mr. Mark M. Hameister, Dir. Franchise Development

MERLIN'S is an upscale 'under-car' service chain with one of the highest average sales per shop statistics in the industry. Its marketing strategies are rooted in long-term customer relationships. Merlin offers a special equity assistance program to 'proven' industry veterans. Industry experience is not always necessary. Candidates must have significant experience managing employees and serving customers. MERLIN'S is expanding in IL, IN, MI, GA, TX, and WI.

BACKGROUND: IFA MEMBER
Established: 1975; 1st Franchised: 1975
Franchised Units: 61
Company-Owned Units 4
Total Units: 65
Dist.: US-65; CAN-0; O'seas-0
North America: 6 States
Density: 50 in IL, 5 in TX, 4 in GA
Projected New Units (12 Months): 6
Qualifications: 3, 5, 4, 3, 4, 5
Registered: IL,IN,MI,WI

FINANCIAL/TERMS:
Cash Investment: $20-50K
Total Investment: $185-210K
Minimum Net Worth: $75K
Fees: Franchise - $26-30K
Royalty - 6.9%; Ad. - 5%
Earnings Claim Statement: Yes
Term of Contract (Years): 20/20
Avg. # Of Employees: 3-4 FT, 1 PT
Passive Ownership: Not Allowed
Encourage Conversions: Yes
Area Develop. Agreements: No
Sub-Franchising Contracts: No
Expand In Territory: Yes
Space Needs: 3,850 SF; FS, SC, RM, Other Center

SUPPORT & TRAINING PROVIDED:
Financial Assistance Provided: Yes(I)
Site Selection Assistance: Yes
Lease Negotiation Assistance: Yes
Co-Operative Advertising: Yes
Franchisee Assoc./Member: No
Size Of Corporate Staff: 20
On-Going Support: B,C,D,E,F,G,H,I
Training: 6 Weeks Corporate Headquarters; in Shop as Needed.

SPECIFIC EXPANSION PLANS:
US: IL, MI, GA, TX, WI, IN
Canada: No
Overseas: No

<< >>

MERMAID CAR WASH

526 Grand Canyon Dr.
Madison, WI 53719
Tel: (608) 833-9273
Fax: (608) 833-9272
Mr. Peter H. Aspinwall, President

Own a MERMAID franchise. MERMAID CAR WASH was designed with the feeling that our customers have a love affair with their vehicle. It is our desire to have customers visit an enjoyable, attractive business run by friendly, helpful, well-groomed, well-trained employees and leave MERMAID with a pleasant experience and a professionally-cleaned vehicle.

BACKGROUND:
Established: 1984; 1st Franchised: 1986
Franchised Units: 4
Company-Owned Units 2
Total Units: 6
Dist.: US-8; CAN-0; O'seas-0
North America: 3 States
Density: 5 in MN, 2 in WI, 1 in IL
Projected New Units (12 Months): 1
Qualifications: 5, 3, 1, 1, 2, 2
Registered: IL,MN,WI

FINANCIAL/TERMS:
Cash Investment: $NR
Total Investment: $1.75-2.0MM
Minimum Net Worth: $NR
Fees: Franchise - $50K
Royalty - 2%; Ad. - 0%
Earnings Claim Statement: No
Term of Contract (Years): 20/20
Avg. # Of Employees: 30 FT
Passive Ownership: Allowed
Encourage Conversions: Yes
Area Develop. Agreements: No
Sub-Franchising Contracts: No
Expand In Territory: Yes
Space Needs: 16,000-68,000 SF; FS

SUPPORT & TRAINING PROVIDED:
Financial Assistance Provided: Yes(I)
Site Selection Assistance: Yes
Lease Negotiation Assistance: Yes
Co-Operative Advertising: No
Franchisee Assoc./Member: No
Size Of Corporate Staff: 3
On-Going Support: b,C,D,E,F,H
Training: 3 Weeks Madison, WI.

SPECIFIC EXPANSION PLANS:
US: All United States
Canada: Not Actively
Overseas: No

<< >>

MIDAS AUTO SERVICE EXPERTS

1300 Arlington Heights Rd.
Itasca, IL 60143
Tel: (800) 365-0007 (630) 438-3000
Fax: (630) 438-3700
E-Mail: bkorus@midas.com
Web Site: www.midasfran.com
Ms. Barbara Korus, Franchise Recruitment Coord.

MIDAS is one of the world's largest providers of automotive service, offering exhaust, brake, steering and suspension services, as well as batteries, climate control and maintenance services at 2,700 franchised, company-owned and licensed MIDAS shops in 19 countries, including nearly 2,000 in the United States and Canada.

BACKGROUND: IFA MEMBER
Established: 1956; 1st Franchised: 1956
Franchised Units: 2,614
Company-Owned Units 108
Total Units: 2,722
Dist.: US-1845; CAN-241; O'seas-636
North America: NR
Density: NR
Projected New Units (12 Months): 40
Qualifications: 4, 4, 2, 2, 3, 5
Registered: All States

FINANCIAL/TERMS:
Cash Investment: $100-150K
Total Investment: $360-487K
Minimum Net Worth: $300K
Fees: Franchise - $20K
Royalty - 10%; Ad. - Incl. Roy.
Earnings Claim Statement: No
Term of Contract (Years): 20/20
Avg. # Of Employees: 6 FT, 4 PT
Passive Ownership: Discouraged
Encourage Conversions: Yes
Area Develop. Agreements: Varies
Sub-Franchising Contracts: No
Expand In Territory: Yes
Space Needs: 4,000-5,000 SF; FS

SUPPORT & TRAINING PROVIDED:
Financial Assistance Provided: Yes(I)
Site Selection Assistance: Yes
Lease Negotiation Assistance: Yes
Co-Operative Advertising: Yes
Franchisee Assoc./Member: Yes/Yes
Size Of Corporate Staff: NR
On-Going Support: B,C,D,e,f,G,H,I
Training: 1-2 Weeks of Self Study; 1-2 Weeks In-Shop Assignment; 3 Weeks in Palatine, IL.

SPECIFIC EXPANSION PLANS:
US: All United States
Canada: All Canada
Overseas: No

<< >>

MIGHTY DISTRIBUTING SYSTEM OF AMERICA

650 Engineering Dr.
Norcross, GA 30092
Tel: (800) 829-3900 (770) 448-3900
Fax: (770) 446-8627
E-Mail: tracy.brown@mightyautoparts.com
Web Site: www.mightyautoparts.com
Ms. Tracy Brown, Franchise Marketing Mgr.

Wholesale distribution of original equipment-quality, MIGHTY-branded auto parts. Franchisees operate in exclusive territories, supplying automotive maintenance and repair facilities with undercar and underhood products, such as filters, belts, tune-up and brake parts.

BACKGROUND: IFA MEMBER
Established: 1963; 1st Franchised: 1970
Franchised Units: 142
Company-Owned Units 5
Total Units: 147
Dist.: US-147; CAN-0; O'seas-0
North America: 45 States
Density: 12 in PA, 10 in FL, 9 in CA
Projected New Units (12 Months): 12
Qualifications: 5, 4, 3, 3, 3, 4
Registered: CA,FL,HI,IL,IN,MD,MI,MN,NY,ND,OR,RI,SD,VA,WA,WI

FINANCIAL/TERMS:
Cash Investment: $42-95K
Total Investment: $84-190K
Minimum Net Worth: $200K
Fees: Franchise - $5K+ $.035/Vcl
Royalty - 5%; Ad. - 0.5%
Earnings Claim Statement: Yes
Term of Contract (Years): 10
Avg. # Of Employees: 4 FT
Passive Ownership: Not Allowed
Encourage Conversions: Yes
Area Develop. Agreements: No
Sub-Franchising Contracts: No
Expand In Territory: N/A
Space Needs: 2,500 SF; Warehouse

SUPPORT & TRAINING PROVIDED:
Financial Assistance Provided: Yes(I)
Site Selection Assistance: No
Lease Negotiation Assistance: No
Co-Operative Advertising: Yes
Franchisee Assoc./Member: Yes/No
Size Of Corporate Staff: 50
On-Going Support: C,D,F,G,h
Training: 1 Week Home Office; 1 Week On-the-Job Training.

SPECIFIC EXPANSION PLANS:
US: All United States
Canada: All Canada
Overseas: No

<< >>

MILEX, TUNE-UP AND BRAKES

4444 W. 147th St.
Midlothian, IL 60445
Tel: (800) 377-9247 (708) 389-5922
Fax: (708) 389-9492
E-Mail: vsmithson@moranindustries.com
Web Site: www.milextuneupbrake.com
Ms. Virginia Smithson, Franchise Coordinator

MILEX TUNE-UPS, BRAKES AND AIR CONDITIONING is a division of Moran Industries that franchises service centers throughout the US. We offer our franchisees a superior business system, strong brand name, customized marketing and a service that is in strong demand. Comprehensive training and continuous support ensure our franchisee's potential. Our exclusive business system, along with the skills of our franchisees, create customer experiences that result in satisfaction and loyalty.

BACKGROUND: IFA MEMBER
Established: 1967; 1st Franchised: 1967
Franchised Units: 9
Company-Owned Units 0
Total Units: 9
Dist.: US-9; CAN-0; O'seas-0
North America: 2 States
Density: 8 in IL, 1 in CT
Projected New Units (12 Months): 5
Qualifications: 4, 3, 2, 2, 4, 5
Registered: IL

FINANCIAL/TERMS:

Cash Investment:	$60K
Total Investment:	$144K
Minimum Net Worth:	$120K
Fees: Franchise -	$27.5K
Royalty - 7%;	Ad. - $100/Mo.
Earnings Claim Statement:	Yes
Term of Contract (Years):	20/20
Avg. # Of Employees:	4-6 FT
Passive Ownership:	Discouraged
Encourage Conversions:	Yes
Area Develop. Agreements:	Yes/Varies
Sub-Franchising Contracts:	No
Expand In Territory:	Yes

Space Needs: 3,500 SF; FS

SUPPORT & TRAINING PROVIDED:

Financial Assistance Provided:	Yes(I)
Site Selection Assistance:	Yes
Lease Negotiation Assistance:	Yes
Co-Operative Advertising:	Yes
Franchisee Assoc./Member:	Yes/Yes
Size Of Corporate Staff:	55
On-Going Support:	C,D,E,G,H,I

Training: 3 Weeks at Various Locations.

SPECIFIC EXPANSION PLANS:

US:	Midwest
Canada:	No
Overseas:	No

MINUTE MUFFLER AND BRAKE

1600 - 3rd Ave. S.
Lethbridge, AB T1J 0L2 CANADA
Tel: (888) 646-6833 (403) 329-1020
Fax: (403) 328-9030
E-Mail: minmuff@agt.net
Web Site: www.minutemuffler.com
Mr. Robb Sloan, VP Sales/Marketing

Retail exhaust, brake, suspension outlets with 0% royalty, 0% advertising fee. Your 65-70% average gross profit goes in your pocket, not ours. Unsurpassed support systems by actual store owner/operators. Service is our business!!

BACKGROUND:

Established: 1969;	1st Franchised: 1977
Franchised Units:	120
Company-Owned Units	1
Total Units:	121
Dist.:	US-0; CAN-119; O'seas-2
North America:	NR
Density:	25 in BC, 24 in AB, 18 in ON
Projected New Units (12 Months):	12
Qualifications:	4, 3, 2, 3, 3, 5

Registered: AB

FINANCIAL/TERMS:

Cash Investment:	$50-100K
Total Investment:	$150-250K
Minimum Net Worth:	$75-100K
Fees: Franchise -	$0-25K
Royalty - 0%;	Ad. - 0%
Earnings Claim Statement:	No
Term of Contract (Years):	On-Going
Avg. # Of Employees:	3-5 FT, 1 PT
Passive Ownership:	Discouraged
Encourage Conversions:	Yes
Area Develop. Agreements:	No
Sub-Franchising Contracts:	Yes
Expand In Territory:	Yes

Space Needs: 3,200-3,500 SF; FS

SUPPORT & TRAINING PROVIDED:

Financial Assistance Provided:	No
Site Selection Assistance:	Yes
Lease Negotiation Assistance:	Yes
Co-Operative Advertising:	N/A
Franchisee Assoc./Member:	No
Size Of Corporate Staff:	13
On-Going Support:	B,C,D,e,F,G,h,I

Training: 1-10 Weeks Head Office; 1-2 Weeks On-Site.

SPECIFIC EXPANSION PLANS:

US:	No
Canada:	All Canada
Overseas:	Carribean, South/Central America, Europe

<< >>

MIRACLE AUTO PAINTING & BODY REPAIR

3157 Corporate Pl.
Hayward, CA 94545
Tel: (877) MIR-ACLE (510) 887-2211
Fax: (510) 887-3092
E-Mail: jim@miracleautopainting.com
Web Site: www.miracleautopainting.com
Mr. Jim Jordan, Vice President

MIRACLE is a production collision repair and refinishing company that specializes in complete paint jobs. MIRACLE caters to individual vehicle owners, insurance carriers, other body shop facilities and new and used automobile dealers.

BACKGROUND: IFA MEMBER

Established: 1953;	1st Franchised: 1964
Franchised Units:	27
Company-Owned Units	3
Total Units:	30
Dist.:	US-30; CAN-0; O'seas-0
North America:	4 States
Density:	23 in CA, 6 in TX, 1 in AZ
Projected New Units (12 Months):	2
Qualifications:	3, 3, 3, 1, 2, 5

Registered: CA,OR,WA

FINANCIAL/TERMS:

Cash Investment:	$75-100K
Total Investment:	$215-275K
Minimum Net Worth:	$400K
Fees: Franchise -	$35K
Royalty - 5%;	Ad. - 5%
Earnings Claim Statement:	No
Term of Contract (Years):	10/10
Avg. # Of Employees:	10 FT, 2 PT
Passive Ownership:	Discouraged
Encourage Conversions:	Yes
Area Develop. Agreements:	Yes/5
Sub-Franchising Contracts:	Yes
Expand In Territory:	Yes

Space Needs: 9,000-11,000 SF; FS, SF

SUPPORT & TRAINING PROVIDED:

Financial Assistance Provided:	Yes(I)
Site Selection Assistance:	Yes
Lease Negotiation Assistance:	Yes
Co-Operative Advertising:	No
Franchisee Assoc./Member:	Yes/Yes
Size Of Corporate Staff:	20
On-Going Support:	B,C,D,E,G,H

Training: 10 Days Headquarters; 10 Days On-Site.

SPECIFIC EXPANSION PLANS:

US:	West, Southwest
Canada:	No
Overseas:	No

<< >>

MISTER TRANSMISSION (INTERNATIONAL) LIMITED

9675 Yonge St.
Richmond Hill, ON L4C 1V7 CANADA
Tel: (800) 373-8432 (905) 884-1511
Fax: (905) 884-4727
E-Mail: info@MisterTransmission.com
Web Site: www.MisterTransmission.com
Mr. Kevin Brillinger, VP Corp. Development

With over 30 years' experience, MISTER

TRANSMISSION is the established name for transmission repair service in Canada. We make sales, training, advertising, a computer program, national fleet accounts, site selection and a warranty program available to all franchisees. MISTER TRANSMISSION is Canadian-owned.

BACKGROUND:
Established: 1963; 1st Franchised: 1969
Franchised Units: 89
Company-Owned Units 0
Total Units: 89
Dist.: US-0; CAN-89; O'seas-0
North America: 7 Provinces
Density: 63 in ON, 14 in BC, 3 in PQ
Projected New Units (12 Months): 3
Qualifications: 3, 3, 3, 2, 3, 4
Registered: NR

FINANCIAL/TERMS:
Cash Investment: $60-80K
Total Investment: $125-150K
Minimum Net Worth: $300K
Fees: Franchise - $25K
Royalty - 7%; Ad. - Varies
Earnings Claim Statement: No
Term of Contract (Years): 10/10
Avg. # Of Employees: 5 FT
Passive Ownership: Discouraged
Encourage Conversions: Yes
Area Develop. Agreements: No
Sub-Franchising Contracts: No
Expand In Territory: NR
Space Needs: 2,800 SF; FS, SC

SUPPORT & TRAINING PROVIDED:
Financial Assistance Provided: No
Site Selection Assistance: Yes
Lease Negotiation Assistance: Yes
Co-Operative Advertising: N/A
Franchisee Assoc./Member: Yes/Yes
Size Of Corporate Staff: 12
On-Going Support: C,D,E,G,H,I
Training: 1 Week Head Office.

SPECIFIC EXPANSION PLANS:
US: No
Canada: All Canada
Overseas: No

MR. TRANSMISSION

4444 W. 147th St.
Midlothian, IL 60445
Tel: (800) 377-9247 (708) 389-5922
Fax: (240) 524-8894
E-Mail: vsmithson@moranindustries.com
Web Site: www.mrtransmission.com
Ms. Virginia Smithson, Qualification Specialist

MR. TRANSMISSION, a division of Moran Industries, franchises transmission service centers throughout the US. We offer our franchisees a superior business system, strong brand name, customized marketing and a service that is in strong demand. In addition, comprehensive training and continuous support help to ensure our franchisees maximize their potential. Our exclusive business system, along with the skills of our franchisees, create customer experiences that result in satisfaction and loyalty.

BACKGROUND: IFA MEMBER
Established: 1956; 1st Franchised: 1990
Franchised Units: 86
Company-Owned Units 1
Total Units: 87
Dist.: US-87; CAN-0; O'seas-0
North America: 14 States
Density: 21 in GA, 12 in IN, 12 in FL
Projected New Units (12 Months): 24
Qualifications: 4, 5, 1, 3, 4, 5
Registered: IL,IN,VA

FINANCIAL/TERMS:
Cash Investment: $50K
Total Investment: $149K
Minimum Net Worth: $100K
Fees: Franchise - $27.5K
Royalty - 7%; Ad. - $100/Mo.
Earnings Claim Statement: Yes
Term of Contract (Years): 20/20
Avg. # Of Employees: 3-5 FT
Passive Ownership: Discouraged
Encourage Conversions: No
Area Develop. Agreements: Yes/Varies
Sub-Franchising Contracts: No
Expand In Territory: Yes
Space Needs: 4,000 SF; FS, SC, Automotive Use

SUPPORT & TRAINING PROVIDED:
Financial Assistance Provided: Yes(I)
Site Selection Assistance: Yes
Lease Negotiation Assistance: Yes
Co-Operative Advertising: No
Franchisee Assoc./Member: Yes
Size Of Corporate Staff: 55
On-Going Support: A,C,D,E,F,G,H,I
Training: Yes.

SPECIFIC EXPANSION PLANS:
US: All United States
Canada: No
Overseas: Limited

<< >>

NOVUS

10425 Hampshire Ave., S.
Minneapolis, MN 55438-2176
Tel: (800) 328-1117 (612) 944-8000
Fax: (612) 946-0481
E-Mail: dougs@novuswsr.com
Web Site: www.novusglass.com
Mr. Doug Dusbury, Mgr. Franchise Sales

NOVUS WINDSHIELD REPAIR®

NOVUS invented windshield repair. Factory-trained NOVUS franchisees have successfully repaired over 18 million windshields in the US, Canada and over 40 other countries. Today, many NOVUS franchisees are also trained and equipped to replace windshields too badly damaged to be repaired. In 1999, NOVUS added automotive paint restoration to their list of services.

BACKGROUND: IFA MEMBER
Established: 1972; 1st Franchised: 1985
Franchised Units: 2,510
Company-Owned Units 2
Total Units: 2,512
Dist.: US-453; CAN-58; O'seas-2000
North America: 50 States,10 Provinces
Density: 31 in WA, 22 in IL, 18 in WI
Projected New Units (12 Months): 20
Qualifications: 5, 3, 1, 3, 3, 5
Registered: All States and AB

FINANCIAL/TERMS:
Cash Investment: $8.4-36K
Total Investment: $25-142K
Minimum Net Worth: $100K
Fees: Franchise - $8.4-20K
Royalty - 5-6%; Ad. - 2-4%
Earnings Claim Statement: No
Term of Contract (Years): 10/10
Avg. # Of Employees: 2-4 FT
Passive Ownership: Discouraged
Encourage Conversions: Yes
Area Develop. Agreements: Yes
Sub-Franchising Contracts: No
Expand In Territory: Yes
Space Needs: 3,000 SF; FS, SF, SC, RM, HB

SUPPORT & TRAINING PROVIDED:
Financial Assistance Provided: Yes(D)
Site Selection Assistance: No
Lease Negotiation Assistance: No
Co-Operative Advertising: No
Franchisee Assoc./Member: Yes
Size Of Corporate Staff: 39
On-Going Support: C,D,G,H,I
Training: 7.5 Days Windshield Repair Minneapolis; 10 Days Replacement in 1 of 4 Locations.

SPECIFIC EXPANSION PLANS:
US: All United States
Canada: All Canada
Overseas: All Countries

<< >>

OIL BUTLER INTERNATIONAL

1599 Rte. 22 W.
Union, NJ 07083
Tel: (908) 687-3283
Fax: (908) 687-7617
Web Site: www.oilbutlerinternational.com
Mr. Pete Rosin,

OIL BUTLER INTERNATIONAL is a mobile oil-change service and windshield repair franchise combining two money-making opportunities in one. Our uniquely designed vehicle provides the corporate image and service your customers will expect from the leader in the field of on-site service. Low-investment, low-overhead, complete training and on-going support.

BACKGROUND:
Established: 1987; 1st Franchised: 1991
Franchised Units: 149
Company-Owned Units 1
Total Units: 150
Dist.: US-89; CAN-4; O'seas-12
North America: 22 States
Density: 21 in TX, 13 in CA, 8 in CO
Projected New Units (12 Months): 100
Qualifications: 3, 3, 2, 2, 5, 5
Registered: CA,IL,IN,MD,MI,NY,VA,WA,WI

FINANCIAL/TERMS:
Cash Investment: $8-15K
Total Investment: $9-18K
Minimum Net Worth: $NR
Fees: Franchise - $4-7K
Royalty - 7%; Ad. - 2%
Earnings Claim Statement: No
Term of Contract (Years): 10/5
Avg. # Of Employees: 1 FT
Passive Ownership: Discouraged
Encourage Conversions: N/A
Area Develop. Agreements: Yes
Sub-Franchising Contracts: No
Expand In Territory: Yes
Space Needs: NR SF; Mobile Unit

SUPPORT & TRAINING PROVIDED:
Financial Assistance Provided: Yes(I)
Site Selection Assistance: Yes
Lease Negotiation Assistance: N/A
Co-Operative Advertising: Yes
Franchisee Assoc./Member: No
Size Of Corporate Staff: 9
On-Going Support: B,C,D,F,G,H
Training: 4 Days to 2 Weeks Union, NJ.

SPECIFIC EXPANSION PLANS:
US: All United States
Canada: All Canada
Overseas: All Countries

<< >>

OIL CAN HENRY'S INTERNATIONAL

1200 NW Naito Pkwy., # 690
Portland, OR 97209
Tel: (800) 765-6244 (503) 243-6311
Fax: (503) 228-5227
Web Site: www.oilcanhenry.com
Ms. Kaye Branche, Dir. Franchising

Automotive lubrication and filter specialist. Our concept blends old-fashioned American service values with high technology. Staff wear striped shirts, bow ties and Gatsby caps. Customers remain in the car and watch service on the monitors. We offer a high-profile building design and impeccably clean facilities and state-of-the-art point-of-sale computers.

BACKGROUND:
Established: 1978; 1st Franchised: 1989
Franchised Units: 47
Company-Owned Units 2
Total Units: 49
Dist.: US-38; CAN-0; O'seas-0
North America: 6 States
Density: 19 in OR, 6 in CA, 4 in FL
Projected New Units (12 Months): 8
Qualifications: 5, 5, 3, 2, 4, 5
Registered: CA,FL,MD,VA,WA

FINANCIAL/TERMS:
Cash Investment: $120-150K
Total Investment: $150-800K
Minimum Net Worth: $300K
Fees: Franchise - $35K
Royalty - 5.5%; Ad. - 1%
Earnings Claim Statement: Yes
Term of Contract (Years): 10/5+
Avg. # Of Employees: 4-6 FT, 5-9 PT
Passive Ownership: Not Allowed
Encourage Conversions: Yes
Area Develop. Agreements: Yes/Negot.
Sub-Franchising Contracts: No
Expand In Territory: Yes
Space Needs: 15,000 SF; FS

SUPPORT & TRAINING PROVIDED:
Financial Assistance Provided: Yes(I)
Site Selection Assistance: Yes
Lease Negotiation Assistance: Yes
Co-Operative Advertising: Yes
Franchisee Assoc./Member: No
Size Of Corporate Staff: 11
On-Going Support: C,d,E,G,h,I
Training: 5 Weeks Portland, OR.

SPECIFIC EXPANSION PLANS:
US: Northwest, Southwest, FL
Canada: No
Overseas: No

<< >>

PETRO STOPPING CENTERS

6080 Surety Dr.
El Paso, TX 79905
Tel: (800) 331-8809 (915) 779-4711
Fax: (915) 774-7373
E-Mail: lglines@petrotruckstops.com
Web Site: www.petrotruckstops.com
Mr. Larry Glines, Exec. Dir. Fran. Business

PETRO STOPPING CENTERS is a nationwide network of premier, full-service, interstate Travel Plazas. PETRO offers the Iron Skillet Restaurant, Petro Lube Truck Service, featuring Mobil Oil products and Volvo and Cummings light warranty service, Mercantile Travel Stores and quality Mobil fuels. PETRO provides the expertise and systems to help develop successful businesses.

BACKGROUND:
Established: 1975; 1st Franchised: 1985
Franchised Units: 22
Company-Owned Units 35
Total Units: 57
Dist.: US-57; CAN-0; O'seas-0
North America: 33 States
Density: 6 in TX, 6 in PA, 4 in OH
Projected New Units (12 Months): 4
Qualifications: 5, 4, 4, 3, 3, 4
Registered: CA,FL,IL,IN,MD,MI,NY,ND,SD,VA,WA,WI

FINANCIAL/TERMS:
Cash Investment: $NR
Total Investment: $NR
Minimum Net Worth: $NR
Fees: Franchise - $NR
Royalty - NR; Ad. - NR
Earnings Claim Statement: No
Term of Contract (Years): 10/5/5
Avg. # Of Employees: 125 FT, 40 PT
Passive Ownership: Discouraged
Encourage Conversions: No
Area Develop. Agreements: No
Sub-Franchising Contracts: No
Expand In Territory: Yes

Space Needs: 20 Acres SF; Other

SUPPORT & TRAINING PROVIDED:

Financial Assistance Provided: No
Site Selection Assistance: No
Lease Negotiation Assistance: No
Co-Operative Advertising: Yes
Franchisee Assoc./Member: Yes/No
Size Of Corporate Staff: NR
On-Going Support: B,C,D,E,G,H,I
Training: 8 Weeks at Various US Locations.

SPECIFIC EXPANSION PLANS:

US: All US Except TX, AZ, NM
Canada: All Canada
Overseas: No

<< >>

Top 50

PRECISION TUNE AUTO CARE CENTER

748 Miller Dr. SE
Leesburg, VA 20175
Tel: (800) 438-8863 (703) 669-2311
Fax: (703) 669-1539
E-Mail: Kevin.Rooney@precisionac.com
Web Site: www.precisionAC.com
Mr. Jim Barger, VP Franchise Development

PRECISION TUNE AUTO CARE is America's largest engine performance car care company, specializing in tune-up, quick oil and lube and brake services. Also offered are complete diagnostics, engine performance, fluid and maintenance services, with 20 years' experience. We provide quality support in site selection, training, marketing, operations, management, business profitability and much more. Comprehensive training program for everyone.

BACKGROUND:

Established: 1975; 1st Franchised: 1978
Franchised Units: 556
Company-Owned Units 1
Total Units: 557
Dist.: US-478; CAN-1; O'seas-90
North America: 36 States
Density: 40 in MI, 38 in FL, 32 in GA
Projected New Units (12 Months): 55
Qualifications: 4, 5, 2, 2, 3, 5
Registered: CA,HI,IL,IN,MD,MN,NY,ND,RI,SD,VA,WA,WI

FINANCIAL/TERMS:

Cash Investment: $75-100K
Total Investment: $142-203K
Minimum Net Worth: $NR
Fees: Franchise - $25K
Royalty - 7.5%; Ad. - 9.0%
Earnings Claim Statement: No
Term of Contract (Years): 10/5
Avg. # Of Employees: 6 FT, 1-2 PT
Passive Ownership: Discouraged
Encourage Conversions: Yes
Area Develop. Agreements: Yes/5
Sub-Franchising Contracts: Yes
Expand In Territory: Yes
Space Needs: 3,000 SF; FS, SF, SC

SUPPORT & TRAINING PROVIDED:

Financial Assistance Provided: Yes
Site Selection Assistance: Yes
Lease Negotiation Assistance: Yes
Co-Operative Advertising: Yes
Franchisee Assoc./Member: Yes
Size Of Corporate Staff: 52
On-Going Support: B,C,D,E,F,G,H,I
Training: 2 Weeks Leesburg, VA.

SPECIFIC EXPANSION PLANS:

US: All United States
Canada: All Canada
Overseas: All Countries

<< >>

RYAN ENGINE EXCHANGE

2465 W. Evans
Denver, CO 80215
Tel: (800) 466-1664 (303) 232-0012
Fax: (303) 205-0172
Web Site: www.ryanengineexchange.com
Mr. Johnny M. Wilson,

RYAN ENGINE EXCHANGE installs and exchanges remanufactured engines. The old engine is exchanged for a new engine and the new engine is installed on the premises. Using the system developed by Ryan, the turn around time is 3 days and a factory warranty of 5 years - 50,000 miles is given.

BACKGROUND:

Established: 1987; 1st Franchised: 1999
Franchised Units: 1
Company-Owned Units 1
Total Units: 2
Dist.: US-1; CAN-0; O'seas-0
North America: 1 State
Density: 1 in CO
Projected New Units (12 Months): 4
Qualifications: 3, 4, 2, 1, 2, 5
Registered: NR

FINANCIAL/TERMS:

Cash Investment: $40K
Total Investment: $78-112.8K
Minimum Net Worth: $50K
Fees: Franchise - $20K
Royalty - 3% or $30/engine;
Ad. - 5% Local
Earnings Claim Statement: No
Term of Contract (Years): 15/5
Avg. # Of Employees: 4 FT, 1 PT
Passive Ownership: Discouraged
Encourage Conversions: Yes
Area Develop. Agreements: No
Sub-Franchising Contracts: No
Expand In Territory: Yes
Space Needs: 2,500 SF; Warehouse

SUPPORT & TRAINING PROVIDED:

Financial Assistance Provided: Yes(I)
Site Selection Assistance: Yes
Lease Negotiation Assistance: Yes
Co-Operative Advertising: No
Franchisee Assoc./Member: No
Size Of Corporate Staff: 3
On-Going Support: B,C,D,E,F,G,H,I
Training: 1 Week in Denver; 3 Days at Factory in Nebraska.

SPECIFIC EXPANSION PLANS:

US: All United States
Canada: No
Overseas: No

<< >>

SAF-T AUTO CENTERS

121-H N. Plains Industrial Rd.
Wallingford, CT 06492
Tel: (800) 382-7238 (203) 294-1094
Fax: (203) 269-2532
E-Mail: rbilodeau@saftauto.com
Web Site: www.saftauto.com
Mr. Richard Biladeau, President

SAF-T AUTO CENTERS is an owner-operated, auto repair shop offering steering, suspension, brakes, muffler, lubrication and minor repair. Our main effort is to put good technicians in a business opportunity, where they can capitalize on their trade.

BACKGROUND:

Established: 1978; 1st Franchised: 1985

Franchised Units: 5
Company-Owned Units 1
Total Units: 6
Dist.: US-9; CAN-0; O'seas-0
North America: 1 State
Density: 6 in CT
Projected New Units (12 Months): 2
Qualifications: 1, 1, 4, 2, 4, 5
Registered: Fed. Registered Trademark

FINANCIAL/TERMS:

Cash Investment: $25K
Total Investment: $32-65K
Minimum Net Worth: $50K
Fees: Franchise - $15K
Royalty - $500/Mo.; Ad. - 1%
Earnings Claim Statement: No
Term of Contract (Years): 10/10
Avg. # Of Employees: 2 FT
Passive Ownership: Discouraged
Encourage Conversions: No
Area Develop. Agreements: Yes
Sub-Franchising Contracts: No
Expand In Territory: Yes
Space Needs: 2,000 SF; FS, SC

SUPPORT & TRAINING PROVIDED:

Financial Assistance Provided: Yes(D)
Site Selection Assistance: Yes
Lease Negotiation Assistance: Yes
Co-Operative Advertising: Yes
Franchisee Assoc./Member: No
Size Of Corporate Staff: 3
On-Going Support: A,B,C,E,F,G,H,I
Training: 1 Month On-Site.

SPECIFIC EXPANSION PLANS:

US: CT
Canada: No
Overseas: No

<< >>

SHINE FACTORY

320 Monument Pl., SE
Calgary, AB T2A 1X3 CANADA
Tel: (403) 243-3030
Fax: (403) 243-3031
Mr. Bruce H. Cousens, President

A solid, proven program to put entrepreneurs into the automotive protection and detail business. Car wash combinations are available.

BACKGROUND:

Established: 1979; 1st Franchised: 1979
Franchised Units: 31
Company-Owned Units 0
Total Units: 31
Dist.: US-0; CAN-31; O'seas-0
North America: 6 Provinces
Density: 12 in NS, 12 in AB, 4 in BC
Projected New Units (12 Months): 3-4
Qualifications: 4, 4, 3, 3, 3, 5
Registered: AB

FINANCIAL/TERMS:

Cash Investment: $100K
Total Investment: $125K
Minimum Net Worth: $60K
Fees: Franchise - $10-50K
Royalty - 8%; Ad. - 5%
Earnings Claim Statement: No
Term of Contract (Years): 5/5
Avg. # Of Employees: 3 FT, 2 PT
Passive Ownership: Discouraged
Encourage Conversions: Yes
Area Develop. Agreements: Yes/5
Sub-Franchising Contracts: Yes
Expand In Territory: Yes
Space Needs: 4,000 SF; FS, SC

SUPPORT & TRAINING PROVIDED:

Financial Assistance Provided: No
Site Selection Assistance: Yes
Lease Negotiation Assistance: Yes
Co-Operative Advertising: Yes
Franchisee Assoc./Member: No
Size Of Corporate Staff: 4
On-Going Support: C,D,E,F,H,I
Training: 2 Weeks Training Center; 2 Weeks On-Site.

SPECIFIC EXPANSION PLANS:

US: No
Canada: All Canada
Overseas: No

<< >>

SPEEDEE OIL CHANGE & TUNE-UP

159 Hwy. 22 East
Madisonville, LA 70447-1035
Tel: (800) 451-7461 (985) 845-1969
Fax: (985) 845-1936
Web Site: www.speedeecorp.com
Ms. Donna L. Ward, Admin. Assistant

SPEEDEE offers preventive auto maintenance services, specializing in a 17-point quick oil change, diagnostic tune-up and brake services. Also offered: fuel system cleanings, a/c services, radiator flushes, emission/smog checks and transmission/differential services. No appointment necessary. Performed while you wait. Successful franchisees are enthusiastic, have a strong commitment to customer service and people management skills. Retail experience preferred.

BACKGROUND:

Established: 1980; 1st Franchised: 1982
Franchised Units: 141
Company-Owned Units 2
Total Units: 143
Dist.: US-121; CAN-0; O'seas-13
North America: 15 States
Density: 50 in CA, 22 in LA, 10 in MA
Projected New Units (12 Months): 14
Qualifications: 5, 5, 3, 3, 3, 4
Registered: CA,VA,FL,HI

FINANCIAL/TERMS:

Cash Investment: $100-150K
Total Investment: $186-765.5K
Minimum Net Worth: $250K
Fees: Franchise - $30K
Royalty - 6%; Ad. - 8%
Earnings Claim Statement: No
Term of Contract (Years): 21/5/5
Avg. # Of Employees: 5 FT, 2 PT
Passive Ownership: Discouraged
Encourage Conversions: Yes
Area Develop. Agreements: No
Sub-Franchising Contracts: No
Expand In Territory: Yes
Space Needs: 2,800 SF; FS

SUPPORT & TRAINING PROVIDED:

Financial Assistance Provided: No
Site Selection Assistance: Yes
Lease Negotiation Assistance: Yes
Co-Operative Advertising: Yes
Franchisee Assoc./Member: No
Size Of Corporate Staff: 16
On-Going Support: C,D,E,G,H
Training: 3-Day Orientation Headquarters; 2-4 Weeks Local Office; 1-2 Weeks Shop.

SPECIFIC EXPANSION PLANS:

US: All United States
Canada: All Canada
Overseas: All Countries

<< >>

SPEEDY TRANSMISSION CENTERS

74 NE 4th Ave., # 1
Delray Beach, FL 33483
Tel: (800) 336-0310 (561) 274-0445
Fax: (561) 274-6456
E-Mail: speedytrans@mindspring.com
Web Site: www.speedytransmission.com
Mr. Bob Petron, Operations Manager

Centers repair, rebuild and recondition automatic and standard transmissions. Other drive train repair services also available. Training, marketing and operational assistance. Warranties are honored throughout the U.S. and Canada.

BACKGROUND: IFA MEMBER
Established: 1974; 1st Franchised: 1974
Franchised Units: 28
Company-Owned Units 0
Total Units: 28
Dist.: US-28; CAN-0; O'seas-0
North America: 6 States
Density: 18 in FL, 7 in GA, 2 in CA
Projected New Units (12 Months): 8
Qualifications: 3, 3, 2, 4, 4, 3
Registered: FL

FINANCIAL/TERMS:
Cash Investment: $40K
Total Investment: $80-100K
Minimum Net Worth: $NR
Fees: Franchise - $19.5K
Royalty - 7%; Ad. - $100/Mo.
Earnings Claim Statement: No
Term of Contract (Years): 20/10
Avg. # Of Employees: 4 FT, 1 PT
Passive Ownership: Discouraged
Encourage Conversions: Yes
Area Develop. Agreements: Yes/10
Sub-Franchising Contracts: Yes
Expand In Territory: Yes
Space Needs: 2,400 SF; FS, SC

SUPPORT & TRAINING PROVIDED:
Financial Assistance Provided: Yes(I)
Site Selection Assistance: Yes
Lease Negotiation Assistance: Yes
Co-Operative Advertising: No
Franchisee Assoc./Member: Yes/Yes
Size Of Corporate Staff: 4
On-Going Support: C,D,E,F,G,H,I
Training: 2 Weeks Home Office; 1 Week On-Site.

SPECIFIC EXPANSION PLANS:
US: Southeast, Northeast
Canada: No
Overseas: Latin America

<< >>

SPOT-NOT CAR WASHES
2011 W. 4th St.
Joplin, MO 64801-3297
Tel: (800) 682-7629 (417) 781-2140
Fax: (417) 781-3906
E-Mail: doug@spot-not.com
Web Site: www.spot-not.com
Mr. Doug Myers, Executive VP

High-pressure spray brushless automatic car wash, complemented by full-featured, self-service wash bays. Each facility offers canopied, lighted vacuum areas. An all cash business with few employees.

BACKGROUND: IFA MEMBER
Established: 1968; 1st Franchised: 1985
Franchised Units: 36
Company-Owned Units 0
Total Units: 36
Dist.: US-36; CAN-0; O'seas-0
North America: 6 States
Density: 10 in AR, 10 in IL, 8 in IN
Projected New Units (12 Months): 3
Registered: IL,IN,MI,WI

FINANCIAL/TERMS:
Cash Investment: $300K
Total Investment: $622K-1.1MM
Minimum Net Worth: $NR
Fees: Franchise - $25K
Royalty - 5%; Ad. - 1%
Earnings Claim Statement: No
Term of Contract (Years): 10/5/5
Avg. # Of Employees: 2 FT, 3 PT
Passive Ownership: Discouraged
Encourage Conversions: Yes
Area Develop. Agreements: Yes/Varies
Sub-Franchising Contracts: No
Expand In Territory: Yes
Space Needs: 40,000 SF; FS

SUPPORT & TRAINING PROVIDED:
Financial Assistance Provided: Yes(I)
Site Selection Assistance: Yes
Lease Negotiation Assistance: Yes
Co-Operative Advertising: Yes
Franchisee Assoc./Member: No
Size Of Corporate Staff: 18
On-Going Support: B,C,D,E,F,G,H,I
Training: 3 Sessions -- 17 Days Total Joplin, MO and OJT Site.

SPECIFIC EXPANSION PLANS:
US: Midwest, South and Southwest
Canada: No
Overseas: No

<< >>

SUPERGLASS WINDSHIELD REPAIR
6101 Chancellor Dr., # 200
Orlando, FL 32809
Tel: (888) 771-2700 (407) 240-1920
Fax: (407) 240-3266
E-Mail: sgwr@aol.com
Web Site: www.sgwr.com
Mr. David A. Casey, President

SUPERGLASS WINDSHIELD REPAIR is the largest repair-only franchisor in the United States, with locations in 43 states. Two weeks of training, including one week in Orlando and one week in the franchisee's exclusive territory, are provided along with all equipment, uniforms, manuals, printing and bookkeeping systems.

BACKGROUND:
Established: 1992; 1st Franchised: 1993
Franchised Units: 204
Company-Owned Units 0
Total Units: 204
Dist.: US-182; CAN-1; O'seas-13
North America: 43 States, 1 Province
Density: 14 in GA, 13 in FL, 11 in CO
Projected New Units (12 Months): 25
Qualifications: 2, 4, 1, 2, 3, 4
Registered: CA,FL,MI,SD

FINANCIAL/TERMS:
Cash Investment: $9.5-11.5K
Total Investment: $9.5-28.5K
Minimum Net Worth: $15K
Fees: Franchise - $5.4K
Royalty - 3%; Ad. - 1%/$20 Min.
Earnings Claim Statement: No
Term of Contract (Years): 10/10
Avg. # Of Employees: 2 FT
Passive Ownership: Discouraged
Encourage Conversions: Yes
Area Develop. Agreements: Yes/10/10
Sub-Franchising Contracts: No
Expand In Territory: Yes
Space Needs: N/A SF; N/A

SUPPORT & TRAINING PROVIDED:
Financial Assistance Provided: Yes(D)
Site Selection Assistance: N/A
Lease Negotiation Assistance: Yes
Co-Operative Advertising: Yes
Franchisee Assoc./Member: No
Size Of Corporate Staff: 6
On-Going Support: a,B,C,D,E,F,G,H,I
Training: 5 Days Orlando, FL; 5 Days Exclusive Franchisee Territory.

SPECIFIC EXPANSION PLANS:
US: All United States
Canada: All Canada
Overseas: Portugal, Mexico, Brazil

<< >>

TILDEN CAR CARE CENTERS

1325 Franklin Ave., # 165
Garden City, NY 11530
Tel: (800) 845-3367 (516) 746-7911
Fax: (516) 746-1288
E-Mail: info@tildencarcare.com
Web Site: www.tildencarcare.com
Mr. Jason Baskind, Dir. Franchise Development

We're not just brakes. The total care concept allows you to offer a full menu of automotive services for maximum customer procurement - rather than a limited niche market. You benefit from a management team whose concept system and training were proven and perfected before we even considered offering franchises.

BACKGROUND: IFA MEMBER
Established: 1923; 1st Franchised: 1996
Franchised Units: 60
Company-Owned Units 0
Total Units: 60
Dist.: US-60; CAN-0; O'seas-0
North America: 13 States
Density: 24 in FL, 15 in NY, 5 in GA
Projected New Units (12 Months): 10
Qualifications: 3, 4, 3, 3, 3, 4
Registered: CA,FL,IL,IN,NY,VA,WA

FINANCIAL/TERMS:
Cash Investment: $50-60K
Total Investment: $131-171.5K
Minimum Net Worth: $150K
Fees: Franchise - $25K
Royalty - 6%/$350/Wk.;
Ad. - 3%/$175/Wk.
Earnings Claim Statement: No
Term of Contract (Years): 10/5/5
Avg. # Of Employees: 4 FT, 2 PT
Passive Ownership: Discouraged
Encourage Conversions: Yes
Area Develop. Agreements: Yes/10
Sub-Franchising Contracts: No
Expand In Territory: Yes
Space Needs: 3,500+ SF; FS, Auto Mall

SUPPORT & TRAINING PROVIDED:
Financial Assistance Provided: Yes(I)
Site Selection Assistance: Yes
Lease Negotiation Assistance: Yes
Co-Operative Advertising: Yes
Franchisee Assoc./Member: Yes/Yes
Size Of Corporate Staff: 6
On-Going Support: A,B,C,D,E,F,G,H,I
Training: 2 Weeks Home Office.

SPECIFIC EXPANSION PLANS:
US: All United States
Canada: All Canada
Overseas: No

<< >>

TIRE WAREHOUSE

492 Main St., P.O. Box 486
Keene, NH 03431-4035
Tel: (800) 756-9876 (603) 352-4478
Fax: (603) 358-6620
E-Mail: franchising@tirewarehouse.net
Web Site: www.tirewarehouse.net
Mr. Eric Stanley, Franchise Dev. Director

TIRE WAREHOUSE, 'Quality Tires For Less,' is a retail tire, wheel and auto parts franchise, offering quality products and services in a 'warehouse-style' setting. Franchisees will utilize the unique TW system to produce volume sales and profits. On-going training and support are provided.

BACKGROUND: IFA MEMBER
Established: 1971; 1st Franchised: 1989
Franchised Units: 25
Company-Owned Units 25
Total Units: 50
Dist.: US-48; CAN-0; O'seas-0
North America: 6 States
Density: 18 in NH, 11 in ME, 11 in MA
Projected New Units (12 Months): 10
Qualifications: 4, 5, 1, 3, 3, 5
Registered: NY,RI

FINANCIAL/TERMS:
Cash Investment: $50-100K
Total Investment: $150-350K
Minimum Net Worth: $150K
Fees: Franchise - $0
Royalty - 3%; Ad. - 2%
Earnings Claim Statement: Yes
Term of Contract (Years): 7/5
Avg. # Of Employees: 5 FT, 2 PT
Passive Ownership: Discouraged
Encourage Conversions: Yes
Area Develop. Agreements: No
Sub-Franchising Contracts: No
Expand In Territory: Yes
Space Needs: 5,000 SF; FS

SUPPORT & TRAINING PROVIDED:
Financial Assistance Provided: Yes(I)
Site Selection Assistance: Yes
Lease Negotiation Assistance: Yes
Co-Operative Advertising: Yes
Franchisee Assoc./Member: No
Size Of Corporate Staff: 32
On-Going Support: A,B,C,D,E,F,G,H,I
Training: 2-4 Weeks in Keene, NH; 1-3 Weeks Field Training.

SPECIFIC EXPANSION PLANS:
US: New England
Canada: No
Overseas: No

<< >>

TIRES PLUS TOTAL CAR CARE

2021 Sunnydale Blvd.
Clearwater, FL 33765
Tel: (800) 754-6519 (651) 255-6279
Fax: (651) 365-1868
E-Mail: franchise@tiresplus.com
Web Site: www.tiresplus.com
Mr. Alan Storry, Franchise Development Dir.

TIRES PLUS is one of the fastest growing retail tire store franchisors in the U.S. We are taking a new and innovative approach to tire retailing. Our franchisees enjoy thorough education programs, in-field support, marketing and advertising assistance, name brand product lines, exclusive territories and a proven operational system.

BACKGROUND: IFA MEMBER
Established: 1976; 1st Franchised: 1981
Franchised Units: 66
Company-Owned Units 495
Total Units: 561
Dist.: US-561; CAN-0; O'seas-0
North America: 24 States
Density: 173 in FL, 55 in MN, 47 GA
Projected New Units (12 Months): 50
Qualifications: 5, 4, 1, 3, 1, 5
Registered: IL,FL,MI,MN,ND,SD,VA,WI

FINANCIAL/TERMS:
Cash Investment: $125-150K
Total Investment: $322-509K
Minimum Net Worth: $300K
Fees: Franchise - $20-30K
Royalty - 4%; Ad. - 1%
Earnings Claim Statement: No
Term of Contract (Years): 20/20
Avg. # Of Employees: 10 FT, 5 PT
Passive Ownership: Discouraged
Encourage Conversions: Yes
Area Develop. Agreements: Yes
Sub-Franchising Contracts: No
Expand In Territory: NR
Space Needs: 6,000 SF; FS

SUPPORT & TRAINING PROVIDED:
Financial Assistance Provided: No
Site Selection Assistance: Yes
Lease Negotiation Assistance: Yes

Co-Operative Advertising: NR
Franchisee Assoc./Member: No
Size Of Corporate Staff: 130
On-Going Support: B,C,D,E,F,I
Training: 1 Week in Classroom; 15 Weeks at Various Store Locations.

SPECIFIC EXPANSION PLANS:
US: All United States
Canada: No
Overseas: No

<< >>

TOP VALUE CAR & TRUCK SERVICE CENTERS

36887 Schoolcraft
Livonia, MI 48150
Tel: (800) 860-8258 (734) 462-3633
Fax: (734) 462-1088
E-Mail: franchiseinfo@top-value.com
Web Site: www.top-value.com
Mr. Richard E. Zimmer, Dir. Franchise Development

We fix cars. People are holding onto and maintaining their vehicles longer than ever. Our menu of repair specialization includes: brakes, exhaust, suspension, shocks, struts, air conditioning, general maintenance and general repair. We focus on customer service and franchisee satisfaction, with on-going training, strong purchasing power and field support that you can count on!

BACKGROUND:
Established: 1977; 1st Franchised: 1980
Franchised Units: 32
Company-Owned Units 8
Total Units: 40
Dist.: US-40; CAN-0; O'seas-0
North America: 3 States
Density: 27 in MI, 3 in OH, 1 in IN
Projected New Units (12 Months): 8
Qualifications: 3, 3, 3, 3, 3, 4
Registered: MI,IN,IL

FINANCIAL/TERMS:
Cash Investment: $30-60K
Total Investment: $125K
Minimum Net Worth: $125K
Fees: Franchise - $17.5K
Royalty - 2-5%; Ad. - 3%
Earnings Claim Statement: Yes
Term of Contract (Years): 10/5
Avg. # Of Employees: 2-3 FT
Passive Ownership: Discouraged
Encourage Conversions: Yes
Area Develop. Agreements: Yes
Sub-Franchising Contracts: Yes
Expand In Territory: Yes
Space Needs: 2,500-3,500 SF; FS

SUPPORT & TRAINING PROVIDED:
Financial Assistance Provided: Yes(I)
Site Selection Assistance: Yes
Lease Negotiation Assistance: Yes
Co-Operative Advertising: Yes
Franchisee Assoc./Member: No
Size Of Corporate Staff: 12
On-Going Support: B,C,D,E,F,G,H,I
Training: 3 Weeks in Livonia, MI; 1 Week On-Site.

SPECIFIC EXPANSION PLANS:
US: MI, OH, IN, IL, N. KY
Canada: No
Overseas: No

<< >>

TUFFY AUTO SERVICE CENTERS

1414 Baronial Plaza Dr.
Toledo, OH 43615
Tel: (800) 228-8339 (419) 865-6900
Fax: (419) 865-7343
E-Mail: Jacobs@tuffy.com
Web Site: www.tuffy.com
Mr. Jim Jacobs, Dir. Franchising

TUFFY AUTO SERVICE CENTERS have been ranked by Success and Entrepreneur Magazines as one of the top franchises in the country. We are an upscale automotive repair franchise specializing in brakes, exhaust, shocks, alignments, air conditioning, batteries, starting and charging, lube-oil-filter, and more. We provide initial and on-going operations, technical and marketing support. Excellent sites being developed in IN, IA, WI, VA, FL, OH, MN, ND, SD, NE and IL

BACKGROUND: IFA MEMBER
Established: 1970; 1st Franchised: 1971
Franchised Units: 238
Company-Owned Units 8
Total Units: 246
Dist.: US-247; CAN-0; O'seas-0
North America: 16 States
Density: 67 in MI, 63 in OH, 32 in FL
Projected New Units (12 Months): 25
Qualifications: 4, 4, 2, 2, 2, 4
Registered: FL,IL,IN,MD,MI,MN,NY,ND,VA,WI

FINANCIAL/TERMS:
Cash Investment: $75K
Total Investment: $127.5-273K
Minimum Net Worth: $250K
Fees: Franchise - $25K
Royalty - 5%; Ad. - 5%
Earnings Claim Statement: No
Term of Contract (Years): 15/10
Avg. # Of Employees: 4 FT, 1 PT
Passive Ownership: Discouraged
Encourage Conversions: Yes
Area Develop. Agreements: Yes/Negot.
Sub-Franchising Contracts: Yes
Expand In Territory: Yes
Space Needs: 3,800 SF; FS

SUPPORT & TRAINING PROVIDED:
Financial Assistance Provided: Yes(I)
Site Selection Assistance: Yes
Lease Negotiation Assistance: Yes
Co-Operative Advertising: Yes
Franchisee Assoc./Member: Yes/Yes
Size Of Corporate Staff: 36
On-Going Support: C,D,E,G,H,I
Training: 3-4 Weeks in Toledo, OH; 3 Weeks On-Site at Franchise.

SPECIFIC EXPANSION PLANS:
US: North Central U.S., FL
Canada: No
Overseas: No

<< >>

TUNEX INTERNATIONAL

556 East 2100 S.
Salt Lake City, UT 84106
Tel: (800) 448-8639 (801) 486-8133
Fax: (801) 484-4740
E-Mail: info@tunex.com
Web Site: www.tunex.com
Mr. Frank C. Hauber, Franchise Sales

We offer diagnostic, engine performance, tune-up services and repairs of engine related systems, i.e. ignition, carburetion, fuel injection, emission controls, computer controls, cooling, air conditioning, emission inspections, used-car evaluations, and lubrication services. For maximum customer satisfaction, we always analyze systems for the problem and maintenance requirements, so the customer can make service and repair decisions.

BACKGROUND: IFA MEMBER
Established: 1974; 1st Franchised: 1975
Franchised Units: 27
Company-Owned Units 2
Total Units: 29
Dist.: US-26; CAN-0; O'seas-1
North America: 6 States
Density: 16 in UT, 4 in CO, 1 in AZ
Projected New Units (12 Months): 5
Qualifications: 4, 3, 2, 3, 2, 5
Registered: NR

FINANCIAL/TERMS:
Cash Investment: $50-60K

Total Investment: $122.5-163.1K
Minimum Net Worth: $200K
Fees: Franchise - $19K
Royalty - 5%; Ad. - $600/Mo.
Earnings Claim Statement: No
Term of Contract (Years): 10/10
Avg. # Of Employees: 4 FT
Passive Ownership: Discouraged
Encourage Conversions: N/A
Area Develop. Agreements: Yes/10
Sub-Franchising Contracts: Yes
Expand In Territory: No
Space Needs: 2,750 SF; FS, SF, SC

SUPPORT & TRAINING PROVIDED:
Financial Assistance Provided: Yes(I)
Site Selection Assistance: Yes
Lease Negotiation Assistance: Yes
Co-Operative Advertising: Yes
Franchisee Assoc./Member: No
Size Of Corporate Staff: 7
On-Going Support: C,D,E,G,H,I
Training: 1 Week Corporate Headquarters; 1 Week On-Site.

SPECIFIC EXPANSION PLANS:
US: Inter-Mountain, Southwest
Canada: Master Franchise
Overseas: Mexico

<< >>

CARS. WE KNOW 'EM. WE LOVE 'EM.

VALVOLINE INSTANT OIL CHANGE

3499 Blazer Pkwy.
Lexington, KY 40509
Tel: (800) 622-6846 (606) 357-7070
Fax: (606) 357-7049
E-Mail: jjtaylor@ashland.com
Web Site: www.viocfranchise.com
Ms. Josie Taylor, Mgr. Franchise Sales

Offers licenses for the establishment and operation of a business which provides a quick oil change, chassis lubrication and routine maintenance checks on automobiles. The licensor and/or its affiliates will offer (to qualified prospects) leasing programs for equipment, signage, POS systems and mortgage based financing for land, building.

BACKGROUND:
Established: 1988; 1st Franchised: 1988
Franchised Units: 310
Company-Owned Units 362
Total Units: 672
Dist.: US-633; CAN-0; O'seas-0
North America: 35 States
Density: 73 in OH, 62 in MI, 53 in MN
Projected New Units (12 Months): 65
Qualifications: 5, 4, 2, 3, 5, 5
Registered: All States

FINANCIAL/TERMS:
Cash Investment: $150K
Total Investment: $96-201.8K
Minimum Net Worth: $200K
Fees: Franchise - $30K
Royalty - 6%; Ad. - 2%
Earnings Claim Statement: Yes
Term of Contract (Years): 15/5/5
Avg. # Of Employees: 4 FT, 2 PT
Passive Ownership: Allowed
Encourage Conversions: Yes
Area Develop. Agreements: No
Sub-Franchising Contracts: No
Expand In Territory: Yes
Space Needs: 15,000 SF; FS

SUPPORT & TRAINING PROVIDED:
Financial Assistance Provided: Yes(I)
Site Selection Assistance: Yes
Lease Negotiation Assistance: Yes
Co-Operative Advertising: Yes
Franchisee Assoc./Member: No
Size Of Corporate Staff: 84
On-Going Support: A,B,C,D,E,F,G,h,I
Training: 3+ Weeks Classroom/OJT/On-Site Training.

SPECIFIC EXPANSION PLANS:
US: All United States
Canada: No
Overseas: No

<< >>

YIPES STRIPES

520 Court St., P.O. Box 775
Dover, DE 19903-0775
Tel: (800) 947-3755 (302) 736-1735
Fax: (302) 736-2693
Ms. Diane M. Scinto, President

YIPES STRIPES offers custom striping, graphics and lettering. Exclusive Insta-dry paint formula, on-site servicing of new and used automobile dealerships, total products/inventory package, comprehensive training program and protected territories.

BACKGROUND:
Established: 1972; 1st Franchised: 1988
Franchised Units: 25
Company-Owned Units 1
Total Units: 26
Dist.: US-26; CAN-0; O'seas-0
North America: 16 States
Density: 7 in OH, 3 in MO, 3 in PA
Projected New Units (12 Months): 12
Qualifications: 3, 4, 2, 2, 2, 4
Registered: NR

FINANCIAL/TERMS:
Cash Investment: $40K
Total Investment: $40-75K
Minimum Net Worth: $N/A
Fees: Franchise - $32K
Royalty - 5%/$500; Ad. - 0%
Earnings Claim Statement: No
Term of Contract (Years): 5/5
Avg. # Of Employees: 1 FT
Passive Ownership: Discouraged
Encourage Conversions: NR
Area Develop. Agreements: Yes/10
Sub-Franchising Contracts: No
Expand In Territory: Yes
Space Needs: NR SF; HB

SUPPORT & TRAINING PROVIDED:
Financial Assistance Provided: Yes(I)
Site Selection Assistance: Yes
Lease Negotiation Assistance: N/A
Co-Operative Advertising: No
Franchisee Assoc./Member: No
Size Of Corporate Staff: 2
On-Going Support: B,c,d,e,G,H,I
Training: 2 Weeks Dover, DE.

SPECIFIC EXPANSION PLANS:
US: All United States
Canada: No
Overseas: No

<< >>

Top 50

ZIEBART INTERNATIONAL

1290 E. Maple Rd., P.O. Box 1290
Troy, MI 48007-1290
Tel: (800) 877-1312 (248) 588-4100
Fax: (248) 588-0718
E-Mail: info@ziebart.com
Web Site: www.ziebart.com
Mr. Gregory D. Longe, VP Franchise Development

Business format consists of automobile detailing, accessories and protection services. Ultra-modern showrooms maximize the exposure for the services offered by the franchisee. The customer base consists of retail, wholesale and fleet - making ZIEBART # 1 in the world.

BACKGROUND: IFA MEMBER
Established: 1954; 1st Franchised: 1962
Franchised Units: 475
Company-Owned Units 22
Total Units: 499
Dist.: US-265; CAN-50; O'seas-253
North America: 39 States, 7 Provinces
Density: NR
Projected New Units (12 Months): 50
Qualifications: 5, 4, 2, 3, 4, 5
Registered: All States

FINANCIAL/TERMS:
Cash Investment: $60K
Total Investment: $100-161K
Minimum Net Worth: $250K
Fees: Franchise - $24K
Royalty - 8%; Ad. - 5%
Earnings Claim Statement: No
Term of Contract (Years): 10/10
Avg. # Of Employees: 2 FT, 3 PT
Passive Ownership: Discouraged
Encourage Conversions: Yes
Area Develop. Agreements: Yes
Sub-Franchising Contracts: No
Expand In Territory: Yes
Space Needs: 500 SF; FS

SUPPORT & TRAINING PROVIDED:
Financial Assistance Provided: Yes(I)
Site Selection Assistance: Yes
Lease Negotiation Assistance: Yes
Co-Operative Advertising: Yes
Franchisee Assoc./Member: Yes/Yes
Size Of Corporate Staff: 100
On-Going Support: a,B,C,D,E,F,G,h,I
Training: 3-6 Weeks Sales, Management and Technical Training at Home Office.

SPECIFIC EXPANSION PLANS:
US: All United States
Canada: All Canada
Overseas: All Countries

≪ ≫

SUPPLEMENTAL LISTING OF FRANCHISORS

21ST CENTURY AUTO ALLIANCE, P.O. Box 3167, Independence, MO 64055-8167 ; (800) 580-8696 (861) 252-1322; (861) 254-9727

AFTERMARKET APPEARANCE INDUSTRIES, P.O. Box 1626, Pearl River LA, LA 70452-1626 ; (800) 678-5220 ; (504) 454-7233

ALTRATOUCH SYSTEMS, 111 Phlox Ave., Metairie, LA 70001 ; (800) 678-5220 (504) 863-9962; (504) 863-9962

AMERICAN TRANSMISSIONS, 340 N. Main, # 207, Plymouth, MI 48170-1237 ; (734) 459-3104; (734) 459-1836

ARMOR FUELING, 1900 Country Rd., # 1, Wrenshall, MN 55797 ; (888) 827-1122 (218) 384-3504; (218) 384-3087

AUTO-LAB DIAGNOSTIC & TUNE-UP CENTERS, 1050 W. Columbia Ave., Battle Creek, MI 49015 ; (877) 349-4968 (616) 966-0500; (616) 966-0520

AUTOMOTIVE TECHNOLOGIES, 1807 Berlin Turnpike, Wethersfield, CT 06109 ; (860) 571-7600; (860) 257-7109

AUTOPRO, 7025 Ontario St. E., Montreal, PQ H1N 2B3 CANADA; (514) 899-0044; (514) 256-5497

AUTOQUAL U.S.A., 4 West Dry Creek Cir. # 245, Littleton, CO 80120 ; (303) 798-7695; (303) 789-7695

AVIS LUBE FAST OIL CHANGE, 900 Old Country Rd., Garden City, NY 11530; (516) 222-3172; (516) 222-4381

BANDAG, 2905 N. Hwy. 61, Muscatine, IA 52761-5886 ; (319) 262-1400; (319) 262-1218

BOOMER MCCLOUD, 14 Industrial Park Pl., # 12V, Middletown, CT 06457 ; (860) 632-4874; (860) 632-4877

BRAKE CENTERS OF AMERICA, 35 Old Battery Rd., Bridgeport, CT 06605 ; (203) 336-1995; (203) 336-1995

BRAKE DEPOT SYSTEMS, 840 B St., # 200, San Diego, CA 92101-4602 ; (619) 696-7200; (619) 687-7370

BUDGET BRAKE & MUFFLER, 4940 Canada Way, # 422, Burnaby, BC V5G 4K6 CANADA; (800) 746-9659 (604) 294-6114; (604) 294-1648

CANADIAN TIRE ASSOCIATE STORE, Sta. K, 2180 Yonge, P.O. Box 770, Toronto, ON M4P 2V8 CANADA; (416) 480-3000; (416) 480-8165

CAP-IT FRANCHISE INTERNATIONAL, 4428 Juneau Street, Burnably, BC V5C 4C8 CANADA; (604) 473-7979; (403) 473-7999

CARSTAR AUTOMOTIVE, 8400 W. 110th St., # 200, Overland Park, KS 66210 ; (800) 999-1949 (913) 451-1294; (913) 451-4436

CARSTAR AUTOMOTIVE (CANADA), 1124 Rymal Rd. E., Hamilton, ON L8W 3N7 CANADA; (905) 388-4720; (905) 388- 1124

CHAMPION AUTO STORES, 2565 Kasota Ave., St. Paul, MN 55108 ; (800) 899-6528 (651) 644-6448; (651) 644-7204

CHEM-GLASS WINDSHIELD REPAIR, 7111-7115 Ohms Ln., Minneapolis, MN 55439 ; (800) 333-8523 (612) 835-1338; (612) 835-1395

COLOR TECH SYSTEMS, 479 Interstate Ct., Sarasota, FL 34240 ; (800) 736-1307 (941) 378-1193; (941) 378-3472

DEALER SPECIALTIES INTERNATIONAL, 4665 Emerill Way, Middletown, OH 45044 ; (800) 647-8425 (513) 539-2200; (513) 539-2202

DENTPRO, 4075 Nelson Ave., # A, Concord, CA 94520 ; (800) 868-3368 (925) 288-8900; (925) 288-8905

DENTS PLUS, 2960 Hartley Rd. W., Jacksonville, FL 32257 ; (904) 268-9916; (904) 268-8666

DING KING, 1280 Bison Ave., # B-9, Newport Beach, CA 92660 ; (800) 304-3464 (949) 979-0966; (949) 442-7611

DOAN & COMPANY AUTO APPRAISING, 5090 Hwy. 212, Covington, GA 30016 ; (800) 647-DOAN (770) 788-8328; (770) 788-0135

END-A-FLAT TIRE SAFETY SEALANT, 1155 Greenbriar Dr., Bethel Park, PA 15102 ; (412) 831-1255; (412) 833-3409

FAS-BREAK FRANCHISE CORPORATION, 4014 E. Broadway Rd., # 408, Phoenix, AZ 85040 ; (800) 777-5169 (602) 437-8282; (602) 437-8848

FIRESTONE TIRE & AUTOMOTIVE CENTRES, 5770 Hurontario St., # 400, Mississauga, ON L5R 3G5 CANADA; (800) 267-1318 (905) 890-1990; (905) 890-1991

GAS TANK RENU-USA, 12727 Greenfield St., Detroit, MI 48227 ; (800) 932-2766 (313) 837-6122; (313) 273-4759

GOODEAL DISCOUNT TRANSMISSIONS, P.O. Box 50, National Park, NJ 08063 ; (800) 626-8695 (609) 665-5225; (609) 273-6913

HAWKINSON TREAD SERVICE, 1325 Winter St., NE, Minneapolis, MN 55413 ; (612) 331-1397; (612) 331-6569

INTERSTATE BATTERIES, P.O. 3284, Des Moines, IA 50316 ; (800) 203-6549 ; (800) 246-1024

J.D. BYRIDER FRANCHISING INC., 5780 W. 71 St., Indianapolis, IN 46278 ; (800) 947-4532 ; (317) 387-2373

JIFFY LUBE INTERNATIONAL, P.O. Box 2967, Houston, TX 77252-2967 ; (800) 327-9532 (713) 546-6940; (713) 546-8762

KENNEDY TRANSMISSION, 2225 Daniels St., Longlake, MN 55356 ; (612) 894-7020; (612) 476-1983

MING AUTO BEAUTY CENTERS, 4608 S. State St., Murray, UT 84107 ; (800) 443-3213 (801) 521-8799; (801) 521-4723

MITEY MUFFLER SHOPS/ MITEYFAST CENTERS, 3530 Jefferson Hwy., Jefferson, LA 70121 ; (504) 832-7925; (504) 832-4931

MOTORCADE INDUSTRIES LTD., 90 Kincart St., Toronto, ON M6M 5G1 CANADA; (604) 532- 8896; (604) 532-8841

MOTORWORKS, 4210 Salem St., Philadelphia, PA 19124 ; (800) 327-9905 (215) 533-4456; (215) 533-7801

MR. FRONT-END, 192 North Queen St., Etobicoke, ON M9C 1A8 CANADA; (416) 622-9998; (416) 622-9999

MR. LUBE, 111 Brunel Rd., # 210, Mississauga, ON L4Z 1X3 CANADA; (800) 667-7809 (905) 890-5503; (905) 890-6977

MR. MOTOR, 4444 W. 147th Street, Midlothian, IL 60445 ; (800) 377-9247 (708) 389-5922; (240) 524-8894

MULTI-TUNE & TIRE, 2457 Covington Pk., Memphis, TN 38128; (901) 386-9600

OIL GARD ANTI-RUST CANADA LTD., 4065 Meadowbrook Dr., # 101, London, ON N6L 1E4 CANADA; (519) 652-9944; (519) 652-9614

OILSTOP-DRIVE-THRY OIL CHANGE, 6111 Redwood Dr., Rohnert Park, CA 94928-2018; (707) 586-1399; (707) 586-2296

ONE STOP UNDERCAR, 2938 S. Daimler St., Santa Ana, CA 92705 ; (714) 505-2600; (714) 505-1817

OWNER'S AUTO MART, 3100 W. 12th St., # 108, Sioux Fall, SD 57104 ; (800) 308-9042 (605) 333-0199; (605) 336-7357

PACIFIC PRIDE, P.O. Box 2099, Salem, OR 97308 ; (800) 367-5066 (503) 588-0455; (503) 371-6708

PAINT SHUTTLE, THE, P.O. Box 478, Monee, IL 60449 ; (219) 534-1419; (219) 534-9475

PICK-UPS PLUS, 5180 Natorp Blvd., # 530, Mason, OH 45040 ; (888) 249-7587 (513) 398-4344; (513) 398-4271

PRECISION AUTO CARE, 748 Miller Dr., SE, Leesburg, VA 20175 ; (800) 438-8863 (703) 669-2311; (703) 669-1539

PRECISION LUBE EXPRESS, P.O. Box 5000, 748 Miller Dr., SE, Leesburg, VA 20177 ; (800) 438-8863 (703) 777-9095; (703) 779-9190

RENT A TIRE, 501 Jones St., Fort Worth, TX 76102 ; (817) 810-9600; (817) 810-9595

RIP N' TEAR VINYL REPAIR SYSTEMS INC., 6832 King George Highway, # 316, Surrey, BC V3W 4Z9 CANADA; (604) 880-5094; (604) 536-1870

SPRAYGLO AUTO REFINISHING & BODY REPAIR, 1959 Parker Ct. SW, # F, Stone Mountain, GA 30087 ; (912) 794-3446; (912) 794-3502

SUPER WASH, 707 W. Lincolnway, Morrison, IL 61270-2004 ; (800) 633-7625 (815) 772-2111; (815) 772-7160

TINT KING AUTO WORLD SUPERMARKETS, 136 Castle Rock Dr., Richmond Hill, ON L4C 5K5 CANADA; (416) 464-TINT;

TOTAL CAR FRANCHISING, 642 Century Cir., Conway, SC 29526-8279 ; (843) 347-8818; (843) 347-0349

TRANSMISSION USA, 4444 W. 147th St., Midlothian, IL 60445 ; (800) 377-9247 (708) 389-5922; (708) 389-9882

TRAVELCENTERS OF AMERICA, 24601 Center Ridge Rd., # 200, Westlake, OH 44145-5634 ; (800) 872-7496 (440) 808-9100; (440) 808-4458

TRUCK OPTIONS, 5865 University Blvd. W., Jacksonville, FL 32216 ; (800) 463-7978 (904) 731-7548; (904) 731-3558

TRUCKIN' AMERICA, 2120 Veasley St. #A, Greensboro, NC 27407-4736 ; (336) 852-5799; (336) 854-5858

VEHICARE, 701 E. Franklin St., # 1501, Richmond, VA 23219 ; (800) 836-2468 (804) 225-0982; (804) 225-0946

WINZER CORPORATION, 10560 Markison Rd., Dallas, TX 75238 ; (800) 527-4126 (214) 341-2122; (800) 867-7714

XPRESS AUTO, 1200 Spears Rd., # 16, Oakville, ON L6L 2X4 CANADA; (905) 815-1121; (905) 815-1196

Auto/Truck/Trailer Rental

Chapter

5

Auto/Truck/Trailer Rental Industry Profile

Total # Franchisors in Industry Group	29
Total # Franchised Units in Industry Group	9,600
Total # Company-Owned Units in Industry Group	1,260
Total # Operating Units in Industry Group	10,860
Average # Franchised Units/Franchisor	331.0
Average # Company-Owned Units/Franchisor	43.4
Average # Total Units/Franchisor	374.4
Ratio of Total # Franchised Units/Total # Company-Owned Units	7.6:1
Industry Survey Participants	17
Representing % of Industry	58.6%
Average Franchise Fee*:	$31.5K
Average Total Investment*:	$232.3K
Average On-Going Royalty Fee*:	8.6%

*If a range was provided, the mid-point of the range was used. See detailed profiles for actual ranges.

Five Largest Participants in Survey

Company	# Franchised Units	# Co-Owned Units	# Total Units	Franchise Fee	On-Going Royalty	Total Investment
1. Budget Car & Truck Rental	2,490	750	3,240	20K	5%	Varies
2. Dollar Rent A Car	2,700	97	2,797	12.5K+	8%	100K-2MM
3. Thrifty Car Rental	1,217	65	1,282	Varies	3%	200-250K+
4. Rent-A-Wreck of America	684	0	684	2.5K+	$30/Car	32.8-209K
5. U-Save Auto Rental of America	454	15	469	20K	$32/Car	56.5-103.5K

All of the data provided are proprietary and should not be quoted without acknowledging *Bond's Franchise Guide.*

AFFORDABLE CAR RENTAL

96 Freneau Ave., # 2
Matawan, NJ 07747
Tel: (800) 631-2290 (732) 290-8300
Fax: (732) 290-8305
Mr. Charles A. Vitale, Vice President

We offer a rental car program which provides training, insurance and management support.

BACKGROUND:

Established: 1981; 1st Franchised: 1981
Franchised Units: 100
Company-Owned Units 0
Total Units: 100
Dist.: US-85; CAN-0; O'seas-0
North America: 15 States
Density: NR
Projected New Units (12 Months): 20
Qualifications: 2, 3, 4, 2, 2, 5
Registered: All States Except CA,WI,LA.

FINANCIAL/TERMS:

Cash Investment: $30K-50K
Total Investment: $Varies
Minimum Net Worth: $Varies
Fees: Franchise - $3.5K Min.
Royalty - $10-15/Car; Ad. - 0%
Earnings Claim Statement: No
Term of Contract (Years): Perpetual
Avg. # Of Employees: 1 FT, 2 PT
Passive Ownership: Not Allowed
Encourage Conversions: N/A
Area Develop. Agreements: No
Sub-Franchising Contracts: No
Expand In Territory: Yes
Space Needs: NR SF; FS

SUPPORT & TRAINING PROVIDED:

Financial Assistance Provided: No
Site Selection Assistance: N/A
Lease Negotiation Assistance: N/A
Co-Operative Advertising: N/A
Franchisee Assoc./Member: Yes/Yes
Size Of Corporate Staff: 9
On-Going Support: C,D,F,G,H,I
Training: 2 Days Corporate in NJ.

SPECIFIC EXPANSION PLANS:

US: All United States
Canada: No
Overseas: No

<< >>

BARGAIN BUGGIES RENT A CAR SYSTEMS

3140 N. Washington Blvd.
Arlington, VA 22201
Tel: (888) 644-9001 (703) 841-0000
Fax: (703) 841-1934
E-Mail: info@bargainbuggies.com
Web Site: www.bargainbuggies.com
Mr. Patrick A. Maloy, Director Franchise Sales

BARGAIN BUGGIES RENT-A-CAR SYSTEMS currently operates 6 company-owned stores and 15 franchises in the Washington metropolitan area. BARGAIN BUGGIES employs 19 permanent staff members with over 200 years combined experience, who manage a fleet ranging in size from 300 to 500 vehicles. BARGAIN BUGGIES plans to continue to expand Internet capabilities and implement new marketing strategies. All of this will take place while focusing on offering exceptional customer service.

BACKGROUND:

Established: 1970; 1st Franchised: 1984
Franchised Units: 12
Company-Owned Units 6
Total Units: 18
Dist.: US-18; CAN-0; O'seas-0
North America: NR
Density: 8 in MD, 4 in VA
Projected New Units (12 Months): 12
Qualifications: 4, 5, 4, 3, 2, 3
Registered: MD, VA, DC

FINANCIAL/TERMS:

Cash Investment: $25-75K
Total Investment: $50-250K
Minimum Net Worth: $150K
Fees: Franchise - $5-25K
Royalty - $25/car/mo.; Ad. - Adv. Fund
Earnings Claim Statement: No
Term of Contract (Years): 5/5
Avg. # Of Employees: 3 FT, 2 PT
Passive Ownership: Not Allowed
Encourage Conversions: Yes
Area Develop. Agreements: No
Sub-Franchising Contracts: No
Expand In Territory: Yes
Space Needs: 1,000 SF; FS, SC, Hotel, Car Dealership

SUPPORT & TRAINING PROVIDED:

Financial Assistance Provided: Yes(I)
Site Selection Assistance: Yes
Lease Negotiation Assistance: Yes
Co-Operative Advertising: Yes
Franchisee Assoc./Member: No
Size Of Corporate Staff: 25
On-Going Support: b,C,D,E,F,G,h,I
Training: 1 Week Corporate Headquarters; 1 Week On-Site.

SPECIFIC EXPANSION PLANS:

US: Mid-Atlantic
Canada: No
Overseas: No

BUDGET CAR & TRUCK RENTAL

4225 Naperville Rd.
Lisle, IL 60532-3662
Tel: (630) 955-7039
Fax: (630) 955-7811
Web Site: www.budget.com
Mr. Vance Watson

Car and truck rental, both in airports and local markets.

BACKGROUND:

Established: 1958; 1st Franchised: 1960
Franchised Units: 2,490
Company-Owned Units 750
Total Units: 3,240
Dist.: US-960; CAN-375; O'seas-1458
North America: 50 States, 9 Provinces
Density: 108 in CA, 107 in FL, 57 AZ
Projected New Units (12 Months): 25
Qualifications: 4, 5, 5, 3, 3, 5
Registered: All States

FINANCIAL/TERMS:

Cash Investment: $55K
Total Investment: $Varies
Minimum Net Worth: $NR
Fees: Franchise - $20K
Royalty - 5%; Ad. - 2.5%
Earnings Claim Statement: No
Term of Contract (Years): 5/5
Avg. # Of Employees: Varies
Passive Ownership: Discouraged
Encourage Conversions: Yes
Area Develop. Agreements: No
Sub-Franchising Contracts: Yes
Expand In Territory: Yes
Space Needs: 15,000 SF; FS

SUPPORT & TRAINING PROVIDED:

Financial Assistance Provided: Yes(D)
Site Selection Assistance: Yes
Lease Negotiation Assistance: Yes
Co-Operative Advertising: Yes
Franchisee Assoc./Member: Yes/Yes
Size Of Corporate Staff: 300
On-Going Support: b,C,D,E,G,H,I
Training: 1 Week Corporate Office; On-Site as Necessary.

SPECIFIC EXPANSION PLANS:

US: All United States

Canada: All Canada
Overseas: All Countries

<< >>

BUDGET RENT A CAR OF CANADA

3080 Yonge St., # 4000
Toronto, ON M4N 3N1 CANADA
Tel: (800) 268-8941 (416) 622-3366
Fax: (416) 622-5555
Mr. Ron Groves, Mgr. Franchising/Bus. Dev.

Car and truck rental, both in airports and local markets.

BACKGROUND:
Established: 1963; 1st Franchised: 1963
Franchised Units: 380
Company-Owned Units 8
Total Units: 388
Dist.: US-0; CAN-388; O'seas-0
North America: NR
Density: NR
Projected New Units (12 Months): 5
Qualifications: 4, 4, 5, 3, 3, 3
Registered: AB

FINANCIAL/TERMS:
Cash Investment: $100K
Total Investment: $100K+
Minimum Net Worth: $1MM
Fees: Franchise - $20K
Royalty - 7.5%; Ad. - 0%
Earnings Claim Statement: No
Term of Contract (Years): 5/5
Avg. # Of Employees: 2 FT, 2 PT
Passive Ownership: Discouraged
Encourage Conversions: No
Area Develop. Agreements: No
Sub-Franchising Contracts: Yes
Expand In Territory: Yes
Space Needs: NR SF; FS, SF, Dealership

SUPPORT & TRAINING PROVIDED:
Financial Assistance Provided: No
Site Selection Assistance: Yes
Lease Negotiation Assistance: Yes
Co-Operative Advertising: No
Franchisee Assoc./Member: Yes/Yes
Size Of Corporate Staff: 40
On-Going Support: A,B,C,D,E,f,G,H,I
Training: 3 Days in Chicago, IL.

SPECIFIC EXPANSION PLANS:
US: No
Canada: AB,SK,MB,ON,PQ
Overseas: No

<< >>

DOLLAR RENT A CAR

5330 E. 31st St.
Tulsa, OK 74135
Tel: (800) 555-9893 (918) 669-0000
Fax: (918) 669-3006
E-Mail: pfritz@dollar.com
Web Site: www.dollar.com
Mr. Peter Fritz, Dir. Franchise Development

DOLLAR RENT A CAR operates and licenses others to operate daily car rental operations. Established over 30 years ago, DOLLAR RENT A CAR now serves the worldwide car rental market.

BACKGROUND:
Established: 1965; 1st Franchised: 1966
Franchised Units: 2,700
Company-Owned Units 97
Total Units: 2,797
Dist.: US-266; CAN-76; O'seas-554
North America: NR
Density: CA, TX, FL
Projected New Units (12 Months): 24
Qualifications: 5, 5, 4, 4, 4, 5
Registered: All States

FINANCIAL/TERMS:
Cash Investment: $100K-2MM
Total Investment: $100K-2MM
Minimum Net Worth: $250K
Fees: Franchise - $12.5K+
Royalty - 8%; Ad. - Included
Earnings Claim Statement: No
Term of Contract (Years): 10/10
Avg. # Of Employees: Varies
Passive Ownership: Not Allowed
Encourage Conversions: Yes
Area Develop. Agreements: No
Sub-Franchising Contracts: No
Expand In Territory: Yes
Space Needs: 2,000+ SF; FS, SF, SC

SUPPORT & TRAINING PROVIDED:
Financial Assistance Provided: Yes(I)
Site Selection Assistance: No
Lease Negotiation Assistance: No
Co-Operative Advertising: Yes
Franchisee Assoc./Member: Yes/No
Size Of Corporate Staff: 400
On-Going Support: a,B,C,D,E,G,H,I
Training: 3 Days Headquarters Orientation; 2 Weeks On-Site Field Training; 1 Week Automation.

SPECIFIC EXPANSION PLANS:
US: Not FL,MA,VT,NH,NV,AR,UT,MT
Canada: 2 Master Fran.
Overseas: Australia, China, Southeast Asia

<< >>

DOLLAR RENT A CAR (CANADA)

1027 Yonge St., 3rd Fl.
Toronto, ON M4W 2K9 CANADA
Tel: (800) 254-7561 (416) 969-1190
Fax: (416) 969-9582
E-Mail: rmohammed@dollarcanada.com
Mr. Ray Mohammed, Franchise Operations

Daily, weekly, monthly car and truck rental.

BACKGROUND:
Established: 1966; 1st Franchised: 1990
Franchised Units: 40
Company-Owned Units 0
Total Units: 40
Dist.: US-0; CAN-42; O'seas-0
North America: 9 Provinces
Density: ON, BC, PQ
Projected New Units (12 Months): 20
Qualifications: 5, 5, 5, 3, 3, 3
Registered: AB

FINANCIAL/TERMS:
Cash Investment: $100-160K
Total Investment: $150-300K
Minimum Net Worth: $250K
Fees: Franchise - $10-50K
Royalty - 7%; Ad. - 2%
Earnings Claim Statement: Yes
Term of Contract (Years): 5/5
Avg. # Of Employees: 3 FT, 1 PT
Passive Ownership: Discouraged
Encourage Conversions: Yes
Area Develop. Agreements: Yes/3
Sub-Franchising Contracts: Yes
Expand In Territory: Yes
Space Needs: 1,200 SF; FS

SUPPORT & TRAINING PROVIDED:
Financial Assistance Provided: Yes(I)
Site Selection Assistance: Yes
Lease Negotiation Assistance: Yes
Co-Operative Advertising: Yes
Franchisee Assoc./Member: No
Size Of Corporate Staff: 10
On-Going Support: B,C,D,E,F,H,I
Training: 5 Days Toronto, ON.

SPECIFIC EXPANSION PLANS:
US: No
Canada: All Canada
Overseas: No

<< >>

EAGLERIDER MOTORCYCLE RENTAL

11860 S. La Cienega Blvd.
Los Angeles, CA 90250-3461
Tel: (800) 501-8687 (310) 536-6777

Fax: (310) 536-6770
E-Mail: rent@eaglerider.com
Web Site: www.eaglerider.com
Mr. Marcelino Orozco, Vice President Franchising

EAGLERIDER is the world's largest motorcycle rental & tour company that specializes in Harley-Davidson motorcycles, ATVs, dirt bike, watercraft and snowmobile rentals. Why buy it when you can rent it?

BACKGROUND:
Established: 1992; 1st Franchised: 1997
Franchised Units: 21
Company-Owned Units 4
Total Units: 25
Dist.: US-21; CAN-4; O'seas-25
North America: 11 States
Density: 6 in CA, 4 in TX, 2 FL
Projected New Units (12 Months): 10
Qualifications: 3, 2, 4, 2, 3, 5
Registered: All States

FINANCIAL/TERMS:
Cash Investment: $69.5-184K
Total Investment: $219.5-684K
Minimum Net Worth: $225K
Fees: Franchise - $30K
Royalty - 10%; Ad. - 0%
Earnings Claim Statement: No
Term of Contract (Years): 10/10
Avg. # Of Employees: 2 FT, 2 PT
Passive Ownership: Discouraged
Encourage Conversions: Yes
Area Develop. Agreements: Yes/10
Sub-Franchising Contracts: No
Expand In Territory: Yes
Space Needs: 3,500 SF; FS, SF, Industrial

SUPPORT & TRAINING PROVIDED:
Financial Assistance Provided: Yes(I)
Site Selection Assistance: Yes
Lease Negotiation Assistance: No
Co-Operative Advertising: No
Franchisee Assoc./Member: No
Size Of Corporate Staff: 31
On-Going Support: A,B,C,d,E,F,G,h,I
Training: 2 Weeks in Los Angeles, CA.

SPECIFIC EXPANSION PLANS:
US: All United States
Canada: All Canada
Overseas: All Tourist Destinations with 6 months or greater rental season

<< >>

PAYLESS CAR RENTAL SYSTEM

2350 34th St. N.
St. Petersburg, FL 33713
Tel: (800) 729-5255 (727) 321-6352
Fax: (727) 323-6856
E-Mail: fran@paylesscarrental.com
Web Site: www.paylesscarrental.com
Mr. Marty Juarez, Dir. Franchise Sales

PAYLESS CAR RENTAL SYSTEM, Inc., has been a recognized name in the car rental industry for almost 30 years. Car rental expertise and an experienced corporate office staff give each franchisee individual assistance and the competitive edge. We offer the tools to become successful in the vehicle rental and sales business. The franchise fee includes an innovative rental industry computer system and image items worth $10K-25K.

BACKGROUND:
Established: 1971; 1st Franchised: 1971
Franchised Units: 120
Company-Owned Units 0
Total Units: 120
Dist.: US-76; CAN-0; O'seas-56
North America: 20 States
Density: 14 in FL, 7 in CA, 5 in AK
Projected New Units (12 Months): 75
Qualifications: 5, 4, 3, 1, 3, 5
Registered: All States

FINANCIAL/TERMS:
Cash Investment: $100K (Varies)
Total Investment: $Varies
Minimum Net Worth: $Varies
Fees: Franchise - $35-500K
Royalty - 5%; Ad. - 3%
Earnings Claim Statement: No
Term of Contract (Years): 5/5
Avg. # Of Employees: Varies
Passive Ownership: Discouraged
Encourage Conversions: Yes
Area Develop. Agreements: Yes/5
Sub-Franchising Contracts: Int
Expand In Territory: Yes
Space Needs: Varies SF; FS

SUPPORT & TRAINING PROVIDED:
Financial Assistance Provided: Yes(I)
Site Selection Assistance: Yes
Lease Negotiation Assistance: No
Co-Operative Advertising: Yes
Franchisee Assoc./Member: Yes/Yes
Size Of Corporate Staff: 55
On-Going Support: A,B,C,D,E,G,h,I
Training: 3-5 Days Corporate Office; 3-5 Days Franchisee's Location.

SPECIFIC EXPANSION PLANS:
US: All United States
Canada: All Canada
Overseas: All Countries

RENT 'N DRIVE

7231 S. 33rd St.
Lincoln, NE 68516
Tel: (888) 917-3959 (402) 421-1606
Fax: (503) 961-1103
E-Mail: info@franchisedevelopers.com
Web Site: www.franchisedevelopers.com
Mr. James E. Hogg

When people need a car for a few days or a few weeks, they don't want to pay high prices. RENT 'N DRIVE provides an affordable alternative to high-priced new car rentals. RENT 'N DRIVE offers dependable vehicles at a fraction of the prices of 'new' car rental services. Offering more flexible rental terms also means a larger customer base! This is an established industry with minimal selling required, reasonable hours and repeat customer traffic.

BACKGROUND:
Established: 1990; 1st Franchised: 1996
Franchised Units: 1
Company-Owned Units 1
Total Units: 2
Dist.: US-2; CAN-0; O'seas-0
North America: 1 State
Density: 2 in NE
Projected New Units (12 Months): 6
Qualifications: 4, 3, 3, 1, 4, 4
Registered: NR

FINANCIAL/TERMS:
Cash Investment: $28.8-46.3K
Total Investment: $95.8-199.3K
Minimum Net Worth: $100K
Fees: Franchise - $20K
Royalty - 6%; Ad. - 1%
Earnings Claim Statement: No
Term of Contract (Years): 10/5/5
Avg. # Of Employees: 1 FT, 2 PT
Passive Ownership: Discouraged
Encourage Conversions: Yes

Area Develop. Agreements: No
Sub-Franchising Contracts: No
Expand In Territory: Yes
Space Needs: 650 + 6,400 SF; FS, SF
SUPPORT & TRAINING PROVIDED:
Financial Assistance Provided: Yes(I)
Site Selection Assistance: Yes
Lease Negotiation Assistance: Yes
Co-Operative Advertising: No
Franchisee Assoc./Member: No
Size Of Corporate Staff: 6
On-Going Support: a,b,C,d,E,f,G,h,I
Training: 1 Week at Lincoln, NE; 1 Week On-Site.
SPECIFIC EXPANSION PLANS:
US: All United States
Canada: No
Overseas: No

<< >>

RENT-A-WRECK

7710 5th St., SE, # 204
Calgary, AB T2H 2L9 CANADA
Tel: (800) 668-8591 (403) 259-6666
Fax: (403) 259-6776
E-Mail: psi@rentawreck.ca
Web Site: www.rentawreck.ca
Ms. Susan Hunt, Vice President Financing

Our success is based upon teaching our franchisees how to achieve their professional goals. Our reputation is based upon providing the lowest car and truck rental rates across Canada.

BACKGROUND:
Established: 1976; 1st Franchised: 1976
Franchised Units: 66
Company-Owned Units 0
Total Units: 66
Dist.: US-0; CAN-66; O'seas-0
North America: 8 Provinces
Density: 16 in BC, 11 in AB, 8 in NF
Projected New Units (12 Months): 21
Qualifications: 5, 5, 3, 3, 5, 5
Registered: AB
FINANCIAL/TERMS:
Cash Investment: $75K+
Total Investment: $Varies
Minimum Net Worth: $75K
Fees: Franchise - $10-30K
Royalty - 6%; Ad. - 4%
Earnings Claim Statement: No
Term of Contract (Years): 5/5
Avg. # Of Employees: 3 FT, 2 PT
Passive Ownership: Discouraged
Encourage Conversions: Yes
Area Develop. Agreements: No
Sub-Franchising Contracts: No
Expand In Territory: Yes
Space Needs: 1,000 SF; SF
SUPPORT & TRAINING PROVIDED:
Financial Assistance Provided: Yes(I)
Site Selection Assistance: Yes
Lease Negotiation Assistance: Yes
Co-Operative Advertising: Yes
Franchisee Assoc./Member: Yes/Yes
Size Of Corporate Staff: 9
On-Going Support: C,D,E,F,G,H,I
Training: 2 Weeks Calgary, AB.
SPECIFIC EXPANSION PLANS:
US: No - US Affiliate
Canada: All Canada
Overseas: No

<< >>

RENT-A-WRECK OF AMERICA

10324 S. Dolfield Rd.
Owings Mills, MD 21117
Tel: (800) 421-7253 (410) 581-5755
Fax: (410) 581-1566
E-Mail: raw@rent-a-wreck.com
Web Site: www.rent-a-wreck.com
Mr. Alan Wagner, Director Sales

America's # 1 neighborhood car rental company, RENT-A-WRECK has attained the highest ratings in the franchising industry. For 5 successive years, Entrepreneur Magazine rated RENT-A-WRECK # 1 in its category for the prestigious Franchise 500 awards. The annual Success Magazine named RENT-A-WRECK 'one of the best-managed franchises in America.' Success surveyed over 2,800 franchise companies in all industries and ranked RENT-A-WRECK 4th.

BACKGROUND: IFA MEMBER
Established: 1973; 1st Franchised: 1978
Franchised Units: 684
Company-Owned Units 0
Total Units: 684
Dist.: US-663; CAN-0; O'seas-21
North America: 49 States
Density: 53 in CA, 33 in NY, 24 in NJ
Projected New Units (12 Months): 75
Qualifications: 3, 5, 2, 3, 3, 3
Registered: All States
FINANCIAL/TERMS:
Cash Investment: $32.8K
Total Investment: $32.8-209K
Minimum Net Worth: $50K
Fees: Franchise - $2.5K+
Royalty - $30/Car; Ad. - $7/Car
Earnings Claim Statement: Yes
Term of Contract (Years): 10/5
Avg. # Of Employees: 1 FT
Passive Ownership: Discouraged
Encourage Conversions: No
Area Develop. Agreements: No
Sub-Franchising Contracts: No
Expand In Territory: Yes
Space Needs: 1,500 SF; FS, SF, SC
SUPPORT & TRAINING PROVIDED:
Financial Assistance Provided: Yes(D)
Site Selection Assistance: No
Lease Negotiation Assistance: Yes
Co-Operative Advertising: Yes
Franchisee Assoc./Member: Yes/Yes
Size Of Corporate Staff: 25
On-Going Support: C,D,e,G,h,I
Training: 1 Week Baltimore, MD.
SPECIFIC EXPANSION PLANS:
US: All United States
Canada: No
Overseas: All Countries

<< >>

SENSIBLE CAR RENTAL

96 Freneau Ave., # 2
Matawan, NJ 07747
Tel: (800) 367-5159 (732) 583-8500
Fax: (732) 290-8305
E-Mail: sensible96@aol.com
Web Site: www.sensiblecarrental.com
Mr. Charles A. Vitale, VP General Manager

We offer a rental car program which provides training, insurance and support. Majority of franchisee are used car dealers and other automotive related businesspersons.

BACKGROUND:
Established: 1986; 1st Franchised: 1986
Franchised Units: 107
Company-Owned Units 0
Total Units: 107
Dist.: US-110; CAN-0; O'seas-0
North America: 22 States
Density: 25 in NY, 24 in NJ, 10 in MA
Projected New Units (12 Months): 25
Qualifications: 2, 3, 4, 2, 2, 5
Registered: All States Except CA,WI,LA
FINANCIAL/TERMS:
Cash Investment: $20-25K
Total Investment: $25-30K

Minimum Net Worth: $Varies
Fees: Franchise - $4-7K
Royalty - $10-15/Car; Ad. - 0%
Earnings Claim Statement: No
Term of Contract (Years): Perpetual
Avg. # Of Employees: 1 FT, 1 PT
Passive Ownership: Not Allowed
Encourage Conversions: N/A
Area Develop. Agreements: No
Sub-Franchising Contracts: No
Expand In Territory: Yes
Space Needs: NR SF; FS

SUPPORT & TRAINING PROVIDED:
Financial Assistance Provided: Yes
Site Selection Assistance: No
Lease Negotiation Assistance: No
Co-Operative Advertising: Yes
Franchisee Assoc./Member: Yes/Yes
Size Of Corporate Staff: 10
On-Going Support: C,d,F,G,H,I
Training: 2 Days in Matawan, NJ.

SPECIFIC EXPANSION PLANS:
US: All United States
Canada: No
Overseas: No

<< >>

THRIFTY CAR RENTAL

5310 E. 31st St.
Tulsa, OK 74135
Tel: (800) 532-3401 (918) 669-2219
Fax: (918) 669-2061
E-Mail: franchisesales@thrifty.com
Web Site: www.thrifty.com
Mr. Gary Valentine, Director

THRIFTY operates in over 65 countries and territories, with over 1,200 locations throughout North and South America, Europe, the Middle East, Caribbean, Asia and the Pacific, and is the fastest-growing car rental company in Canada and Australia. THRIFTY has a significant presence both in the airport and local car rental markets. Approximately 51% of its business is in the airport market, 49% in the local market.

BACKGROUND:
Established: 1950; 1st Franchised: 1970
Franchised Units: 1,217
Company-Owned Units 65
Total Units: 1,282
Dist.: US-500; CAN-140; O'seas-642
North America: 48 States
Density: 54 in CA, 28 in TX, 28 in FL
Projected New Units (12 Months): 50-100
Qualifications: 5, 5, 5, 3, 3, 5
Registered: All States

FINANCIAL/TERMS:
Cash Investment: $150K+
Total Investment: $200-250K+
Minimum Net Worth: $600K+
Fees: Franchise - $Varies
Royalty - 3%; Ad. - 2.5-5%
Earnings Claim Statement: No
Term of Contract (Years): 10/5
Avg. # Of Employees: 4-6 FT Min.
Passive Ownership: Not Allowed
Encourage Conversions: Yes
Area Develop. Agreements: No
Sub-Franchising Contracts: No
Expand In Territory: Yes
Space Needs: Varies SF; FS, SF, SC, RM

SUPPORT & TRAINING PROVIDED:
Financial Assistance Provided: Yes(B)
Site Selection Assistance: No
Lease Negotiation Assistance: Yes
Co-Operative Advertising: Yes
Franchisee Assoc./Member: No
Size Of Corporate Staff: 650
On-Going Support: A,B,C,D,E,F,G,h,I
Training: 8 Days + Mentor Program at Headquarters in Tulsa, OK.

SPECIFIC EXPANSION PLANS:
US: Selected Markets Remaining
Canada: All Canada
Overseas: All Countries

<< >>

THRIFTY CAR RENTAL (CANADA)

6050 Indian Line
Mississauga, ON L4V 1G5 CANADA
Tel: (800) 667-5925 (905) 612-1881
Fax: (905) 612-1893
E-Mail: jforrester@thrifty.com
Web Site: www.thrifty.com
Mr. Jack Forrester, Mgr. Franchise Sales

THRIFTY CAR RENTAL's high name awareness and consistent image of quality and reliable service have resulted in THRIFTY becoming one of North America's fastest-growing car rental companies. THRIFTY has over 1,200 locations in 60 countries worldwide, with approximately 145 locations in Canada. Represented at all major Canadian airport locations, also the largest off-airport car rental in the U. S. and the 5th largest in # of locations throughout North America. Full range of innovative support services.

BACKGROUND:
Established: 1958; 1st Franchised: 1984
Franchised Units: 120
Company-Owned Units 25
Total Units: 145
Dist.: US-560; CAN-145; O'seas-500
North America: NR
Density: NR
Projected New Units (12 Months): 10
Qualifications: 5, 4, 3, 4, 3, 3
Registered: All States

FINANCIAL/TERMS:
Cash Investment: $50-300K
Total Investment: $200-500K
Minimum Net Worth: $250K
Fees: Franchise - $15K+
Royalty - 5%; Ad. - 3%
Earnings Claim Statement: No
Term of Contract (Years): 5/5
Avg. # Of Employees: 3 FT, 2 PT
Passive Ownership: Not Allowed
Encourage Conversions: Yes
Area Develop. Agreements: No
Sub-Franchising Contracts: No
Expand In Territory: Yes
Space Needs: Varies SF; FS, SF, SC, RM, Dealership

SUPPORT & TRAINING PROVIDED:
Financial Assistance Provided: Yes(I)
Site Selection Assistance: Yes
Lease Negotiation Assistance: Yes
Co-Operative Advertising: Yes
Franchisee Assoc./Member: Yes/Yes
Size Of Corporate Staff: 465
On-Going Support: B,C,D,e,F,G,h,I
Training: 1 Week On-Site; 1 Week at Headquarters.

SPECIFIC EXPANSION PLANS:
US: All United States
Canada: All Canada
Overseas: All Countries

<< >>

U-SAVE AUTO RENTAL OF AMERICA

4780 I-55 N., # 300
Jackson, MS 39211
Tel: (800) 438-2300 (601) 713-4333
Fax: (601) 713-4330
E-Mail: info@usave.net
Web Site: www.usave.net
Franchise Sales,

U-SAVE is strategically positioned as the #2 operator in the local neighborhood rental car market, providing superior customer service and affordable rental cars to consumers who need a rental car to temporarily augment their personal use vehicle, or who need a car to replace a vehicle being repaired, and to local businesses that rent vehicles on an an-needed basis.

BACKGROUND: IFA MEMBER
Established: 1979; 1st Franchised: 1979
Franchised Units: 454
Company-Owned Units 15
Total Units: 469
Dist.: US-456; CAN-0; O'seas-6
North America: 47 States
Density:
Projected New Units (12 Months): NR
Qualifications: 5, 4, 3, 2, 1, 4
Registered: All States

FINANCIAL/TERMS:
Cash Investment: $60K Liquid
Total Investment: $56.5-103.5K
Minimum Net Worth: $250K
Fees: Franchise - $20K
Royalty - $32/Vehicle; Ad. - $0.50/Car
Earnings Claim Statement: No
Term of Contract (Years): 10/10
Avg. # Of Employees: 2 FT, 2 PT
Passive Ownership: Discouraged
Encourage Conversions: Yes
Area Develop. Agreements: No
Sub-Franchising Contracts: No
Expand In Territory: Yes
Space Needs: 1,500-2,000 SF; FS, SF, SC, Other Businesses

SUPPORT & TRAINING PROVIDED:
Financial Assistance Provided: Yes(D)
Site Selection Assistance: No
Lease Negotiation Assistance: No
Co-Operative Advertising: Yes
Franchisee Assoc./Member: Yes/Yes
Size Of Corporate Staff: 50
On-Going Support: B,C,D,E,F,G,H,I
Training: 5 Days Jackson, MS.

SPECIFIC EXPANSION PLANS:
US: All United States
Canada: No
Overseas: No

<< >>

WHEELCHAIR GETAWAYS
P.O. Box 605
Versailles, KY 40383-0605
Tel: (800) 536-5518 (859) 873-4973
Fax: (859) 873-8039
E-Mail: sgatewood@aol.com
Web Site: www.wheelchairgetaways.com
Mr. Richard Gatewood, President

WHEELCHAIR GETAWAYS rents wheelchair-accessible vans to wheelchair users by the day, week, month or year. We receive referrals from the major car rental companies and travel agencies. We are the leader in our field and encourage any and all applicants. We will train and continue to support you in every aspect of ownership and management. Affordable, accessible transportation is becoming a necessity as a result of the Americans With Disabilities Act.

BACKGROUND:
Established: 1988; 1st Franchised: 1989
Franchised Units: 42
Company-Owned Units 0
Total Units: 42
Dist.: US-39; CAN-0; O'seas-0
North America: 43 States, Puerto Rico
Density: 5 in FL, 3 in NY, 2 in CA
Projected New Units (12 Months): 5
Qualifications: 3, 5, 3, 3, 4, 4
Registered: CA,FL,IL,IN,MD,MI,NY,VA,WA,DC

FINANCIAL/TERMS:
Cash Investment: $38-100K
Total Investment: $38-100K
Minimum Net Worth: $75K
Fees: Franchise - $17.5K
Royalty - $550/Van/Yr.;
Ad. - $550/Van/Yr
Earnings Claim Statement: No
Term of Contract (Years): 10/10
Avg. # Of Employees: 2 FT
Passive Ownership: Discouraged
Encourage Conversions: No
Area Develop. Agreements: No
Sub-Franchising Contracts: No
Expand In Territory: Yes
Space Needs: 500 SF; FS, SF, RM, HB

SUPPORT & TRAINING PROVIDED:
Financial Assistance Provided: Yes(I)
Site Selection Assistance: Yes
Lease Negotiation Assistance: No
Co-Operative Advertising: N/A
Franchisee Assoc./Member: No
Size Of Corporate Staff: 3
On-Going Support: E,G,h,I
Training: 1 Day Corporate Headquarters or at Franchisee Site.

SPECIFIC EXPANSION PLANS:
US: IL,WI,SC,TX,AL,OR,Northwest
Canada: All Canada
Overseas: All Countries

<< >>

WHEELS 4 RENT USED CAR RENTALS
77 Nassau St.
Toronto, ON M5T 1M6 CANADA
Tel: (877) 707-2500 (416) 585-7782
Fax: (416) 585-4797
E-Mail: wheels@istar.ca
Web Site: www.infoamp.net/nwheels/
Mr. Ernest Weintraub, President

Used car rentals.

BACKGROUND:
Established: 1991; 1st Franchised: 1995
Franchised Units: 5
Company-Owned Units 1
Total Units: 6
Dist.: US-0; CAN-5; O'seas-0
North America: 1 Province
Density: 5 in ON
Projected New Units (12 Months): NR
Qualifications: 3, 3, 4, 1, 2, 2
Registered: NR

FINANCIAL/TERMS:
Cash Investment: $15-20K
Total Investment: $20-25K
Minimum Net Worth: $25K
Fees: Franchise - $5K
Royalty - $25/Car; Ad. - Co-op
Earnings Claim Statement: No
Term of Contract (Years): 5/5
Avg. # Of Employees: 1 FT, 1 PT
Passive Ownership: Discouraged
Encourage Conversions: N/A
Area Develop. Agreements: Available
Sub-Franchising Contracts: No
Expand In Territory: Yes
Space Needs: NR SF; Open Parking/Storage

SUPPORT & TRAINING PROVIDED:
Financial Assistance Provided: No
Site Selection Assistance: Yes
Lease Negotiation Assistance: N/A
Co-Operative Advertising: Yes
Franchisee Assoc./Member: No
Size Of Corporate Staff: 2
On-Going Support: C,D,E,I
Training: As Long as Needed at Corporate Store.

SPECIFIC EXPANSION PLANS:

US:	NR
Canada:	All Canada
Overseas:	NR

≪ ≫

SUPPLEMENTAL LISTING OF FRANCHISORS

AVISCAR INC. AVIS CAR & TRUCK RENTAL, 1 Convair Dr. E., Etobicoke, ON M9W 6Z9 CANADA; (416) 213-4274; (416) 213-8511

BATES MOTOR HOME RENTAL SYSTEMS, 3690 S. Eastern Ave., # 220, Las Vegas, NV 89109 ; (800) 732-2283 (702) 737-9050; (702) 737-9149

DISCOUNT CAR & TRUCK RENTALS, 720 Arrow Rd., North York, ON M9M 2M1 CANADA; (800) 263-2355 (416) 744-0123; (416) 744-0624

NATIONAL CAR RENTAL LICENSING, 208 St. James Ave., Goose Creek, SC 29445 ; (888) 659-3046 (843) 553-6229; (843) 818-6053

PRACTICAL RENT A CAR, 4780 I-55 N., # 300, Jackson, MS 39211 ; (800) 424-7722 (601) 713-4333; (601) 713-4330

PRICE KING RENT-A-CAR, 203 W. Mulberry, Ft. Collins, CO 80521 ; (800) 985-4647 (970) 490-2000; (970) 490-1514

PRICELESS RENT-A-CAR, 10324 S. Dolfield Rd., Owings Mills, MD 21117 ; (800) 662-8322 (410) 581-5755; (410) 581-1566

SELECT LEASING, 2942 N. 16th St., Phoenix, AZ 85016 ; (800) 782-2522 (602) 279-3430; (602) 279-6188

WHEEL FUN RENTALS, 802 E. Yanonali St., Santa Barbara, CA 93103-3242 ; (877) 943-3538 (805) 962-1234; (805) 962-2464

For a full explanation of the data provided in the Franchisor Profiles, please refer to **Chapter 2, "How to Use the Data."**

Building & Remodeling/Furniture & Appliance Repair

Chapter 6

Building & Remodeling/Furniture & Appliance Repair Industry Profile

Total # Franchisors in Industry Group	106
Total # Franchised Units in Industry Group	8,747
Total # Company-Owned Units in Industry Group	142
Total # Operating Units in Industry Group	8,889
Average # Franchised Units/Franchisor	82.5
Average # Company-Owned Units/Franchisor	1.3
Average # Total Units/Franchisor	83.8
Ratio of Total # Franchised Units/Total # Company-Owned Units	61.6:1
Industry Survey Participants	45
Representing % of Industry	42.5%
Average Franchise Fee*:	$20.5K
Average Total Investment*:	$67.7K
Average On-Going Royalty Fee*:	5.6%

*If a range was provided, the mid-point of the range was used. See detailed profiles for actual ranges.

Five Largest Participants in Survey

Company	# Franchised Units	# Co-Owned Units	# Total Units	Franchise Fee	On-Going Royalty	Total Investment
1. Furniture Medic	620	0	620	18.4K	7%/$200 Min.	25-35K
2. Dreammaker Bath & Kitchen	300	0	300	27K	3-6%	35-70K
3. Kitchen Tune-Up	291	0	291	16.5K	4.5-7%	28-35K
4. Color-Glo International	230	1	231	7.5K	2-4%	18-30K
5. Four Seasons Sunrooms	200	3	203	7.5-15K	0%	13.3-82.5K

All of the data provided are proprietary and should not be quoted without acknowledging *Bond's Franchise Guide.*

ABC SEAMLESS

3001 Fiechtner Dr.
Fargo, ND 58103
Tel: (800) 732-6577 (701) 293-5952
Fax: (701) 293-3107
E-Mail: theduck@abcseamless.com
Web Site: www.abcseamless.com
Mr. Veryl Vick, Franchise Director

Franchisor of seamless steel siding, gutters, soffit and fascia. A portable machine embosses and creates seamless siding profiles of any length on the job site.

BACKGROUND:
Established: 1978; 1st Franchised: 1978
Franchised Units: 123
Company-Owned Units 11
Total Units: 134
Dist.: US-132; CAN-0; O'seas-0
North America: 38 States
Density: 22 in MN, 16 in WI, 12 in IL
Projected New Units (12 Months): 10
Qualifications: 5, 4, 5, 4, 4, 4
Registered: CA,FL,HI,IL,IN,MD,MI,MN, NY,ND,OR,RI,SD,VA,WA,WI,DC

FINANCIAL/TERMS:
Cash Investment: $20-40K
Total Investment: $73.8-212K
Minimum Net Worth: $150K
Fees: Franchise - $12K
Royalty - 2-5%; Ad. - 0.05%
Earnings Claim Statement: No
Term of Contract (Years): 10/10
Avg. # Of Employees: 4 FT
Passive Ownership: Discouraged
Encourage Conversions: No
Area Develop. Agreements: Yes/Varies
Sub-Franchising Contracts: No
Expand In Territory: Yes
Space Needs: NR SF; NR

SUPPORT & TRAINING PROVIDED:
Financial Assistance Provided: Yes(I)
Site Selection Assistance: N/A
Lease Negotiation Assistance: Yes
Co-Operative Advertising: N/A
Franchisee Assoc./Member: No
Size Of Corporate Staff: 15
On-Going Support: C,D,E,G,H,I
Training: 2 Weeks at Franchisee's Site; On-Going at Corporate Location.

SPECIFIC EXPANSION PLANS:
US: All United States
Canada: No
Overseas: No

AIRE SERV HEATING & AIR CONDITIONING

1020 N. University Parks Dr.
Waco, TX 76707
Tel: (800) 583-2662 (254) 745-2439
Fax: (800) 209-7621
E-Mail: mhawkins@dwyergroup.com
Web Site: www.aireserv.com
Mr. Mike Hawkins, VP Franchising

Serving the heating, cooling and air balancing needs of all residential and light commercial buildings, including the repair and installation of systems and "whole house" analysis involving infiltrometer testing, duct cleaning, etc.

BACKGROUND: IFA MEMBER
Established: 1992; 1st Franchised: 1994
Franchised Units: 68
Company-Owned Units 0
Total Units: 68
Dist.: US-62; CAN-1; O'seas-5
North America: 31 States, 2 Provinces
Density: 5 in GA, 4 in TX, 3 in NJ
Projected New Units (12 Months): 24
Qualifications: 4, 3, 5, 3, 2, 4
Registered: All States

FINANCIAL/TERMS:
Cash Investment: $15-71K
Total Investment: $52-91K
Minimum Net Worth: $100K
Fees: Franchise - $25K
Royalty - 2.5-4.5%; Ad. - 2%
Earnings Claim Statement: No
Term of Contract (Years): 10/5
Avg. # Of Employees: Varies
Passive Ownership: Discouraged
Encourage Conversions: Yes
Area Develop. Agreements: No
Sub-Franchising Contracts: No
Expand In Territory: No
Space Needs: NR SF; N/A

SUPPORT & TRAINING PROVIDED:
Financial Assistance Provided: Yes(B)
Site Selection Assistance: N/A
Lease Negotiation Assistance: N/A
Co-Operative Advertising: No
Franchisee Assoc./Member: Yes
Size Of Corporate Staff: 7
On-Going Support: C,D,E,G,h,I
Training: 6 Days Corporate Office; 3 Days On-Site.

SPECIFIC EXPANSION PLANS:
US: All United States
Canada: All Canada
Overseas: U.K., Latin America

<< >>

AMERICAN ASPHALT SEALCOATING

8735 Palomino Trail, # 700
Kirtland, OH 44094
Tel: (888) 603-7325 (440) 256-0333
Fax: (440) 256-6325
E-Mail: asphaltusa@aol.com
Web Site: www.american-sealcoating.com
Mr. John Jonz

Get your share at the billion dollar pavement maintenance industry with our franchise. Residential, commercial and industrial sealcoating and pavement services. 94% of all pavement is asphalt that needs our service. (50 million driveways, 7+ million parking lots, 4 million miles of road.) Our expert training staff and low start-up investment of $20K will get you up and running within 60 days. Your trained crew will perform the work while you manage the business from your home-based office.

BACKGROUND:
Established: 1988; 1st Franchised: 1998
Franchised Units: 6
Company-Owned Units 1
Total Units: 7
Dist.: US-7; CAN-0; O'seas-0
North America: 4 States
Density: 4 in OH, 1 in MI, 1 in VA
Projected New Units (12 Months): 10
Qualifications: 4, 3, 1, 1, 1, 3
Registered: NR

FINANCIAL/TERMS:
Cash Investment: $10-30K
Total Investment: $25-40K
Minimum Net Worth: $50K
Fees: Franchise - $9.5-12.5K
Royalty - 7%; Ad. - 1%
Earnings Claim Statement: No
Term of Contract (Years): 15/15
Avg. # Of Employees: 1-2 FT, 1-2 PT
Passive Ownership: Not Allowed
Encourage Conversions: Yes
Area Develop. Agreements: Yes/5
Sub-Franchising Contracts: No
Expand In Territory: Yes
Space Needs: N/A SF; N/A

SUPPORT & TRAINING PROVIDED:
Financial Assistance Provided: Yes(I)

Site Selection Assistance:	Yes
Lease Negotiation Assistance:	Yes
Co-Operative Advertising:	No
Franchisee Assoc./Member:	No
Size Of Corporate Staff:	6
On-Going Support:	B,C,d,H,I

Training: 1-3 Days.

SPECIFIC EXPANSION PLANS:

US:	All United States
Canada:	No
Overseas:	No

<< >>

ARCHADECK

2112 W. Laburnam Ave., # 100
Richmond, VA 23227
Tel: (800) 722-4668 (804) 353-6999
Fax: (804) 358-1878
E-Mail: petew@ussi.net
Web Site: www.archadeck.com
Mr. Pete Wiggins, Vice President

The leading resources for franchise information all list ARCHADECK as one of the top franchise opportunities available today. Without any construction experience, our franchisees are at the forefront of a $122 billion market, enhancing the home environment with custom decks, gazebos, porches and more! If you have sales and/or management experience and the drive to succeed, ARCHADECK will provide the rest with on-going support.

BACKGROUND: IFA MEMBER

Established: 1980;	1st Franchised: 1984
Franchised Units:	62
Company-Owned Units	1
Total Units:	63
Dist.:	US-60; CAN-1; O'seas-2
North America:	27 States, 1 Province
Density:	5 in GA, 4 in NC, 3 in CT
Projected New Units (12 Months):	8
Qualifications:	4, 3, 2, 2, 3, 4

Registered: CA,FL,HI,IL,IN,MD,MI,MN, NY,OR,RI,VA,WA,WI

FINANCIAL/TERMS:

Cash Investment:	$46-96K
Total Investment:	$46-96K
Minimum Net Worth:	$100K
Fees: Franchise -	$26K
Royalty - 6.5%;	Ad. - 1%
Earnings Claim Statement:	No
Term of Contract (Years):	10/10
Avg. # Of Employees:	2 PT
Passive Ownership:	Allowed
Encourage Conversions:	Yes
Area Develop. Agreements:	No
Sub-Franchising Contracts:	No
Expand In Territory:	Yes

Space Needs: N/A SF; N/A

SUPPORT & TRAINING PROVIDED:

Financial Assistance Provided:	Yes(D)
Site Selection Assistance:	N/A
Lease Negotiation Assistance:	N/A
Co-Operative Advertising:	No
Franchisee Assoc./Member:	Yes/Yes
Size Of Corporate Staff:	17
On-Going Support:	C,D,G,H,I

Training: 4 Weeks in Richmond, VA.; 9 Days On Location.

SPECIFIC EXPANSION PLANS:

US:	All United States
Canada:	All Canada
Overseas:	Europe, Australia, New Zealand

ARTHUR RUTENBERG HOMES

13922 58th St., N.
Clearwater, FL 33760
Tel: (800) 274-6637 (727) 536-5900
Fax: (727) 538-9089
E-Mail: rjaghab@arhomes.com
Web Site: www.arhomes.com
Mr. Raja Jaghab, Senior Vice President

Home building franchisor. Master working drawings provided. All necessary forms, manuals, purchasing systems, computer software training and business planning systems provided.

BACKGROUND:

Established: 1980;	1st Franchised: 1980
Franchised Units:	26
Company-Owned Units	1
Total Units:	27
Dist.:	US-27; CAN-0; O'seas-0
North America:	1 State
Density:	27 in FL
Projected New Units (12 Months):	6
Qualifications:	5, 5, 5, 5, 5, 5

Registered: NR

FINANCIAL/TERMS:

Cash Investment:	$350K
Total Investment:	$250-400K
Minimum Net Worth:	$100K
Fees: Franchise -	$20K
Royalty - 4%;	Ad. - 0%
Earnings Claim Statement:	No
Term of Contract (Years):	10
Avg. # Of Employees:	Varies
Passive Ownership:	Allowed
Encourage Conversions:	No
Area Develop. Agreements:	No
Sub-Franchising Contracts:	No
Expand In Territory:	Yes

Space Needs: NR SF; N/A

SUPPORT & TRAINING PROVIDED:

Financial Assistance Provided:	No
Site Selection Assistance:	Yes
Lease Negotiation Assistance:	N/A
Co-Operative Advertising:	N/A
Franchisee Assoc./Member:	No
Size Of Corporate Staff:	75
On-Going Support:	A,B,C,D,H,I

Training: Yes.

SPECIFIC EXPANSION PLANS:

US:	FL
Canada:	No
Overseas:	No

BASEMENTS, BASEMENTS, BASEMENTS

9521 Camelot St.
Pickerington, OH 43147
Tel: (614) 860-1985
Fax: (614) 575-9801
E-Mail: factroydirectohio@yahoo.com
Web Site: www.xteriorexpertsofohio.com
Mr. Michael Pirwitz, President

One of a kind basement remodeling system with few professional competitors. Low cash investment with a high return on your investment. From advertising and sales to installations, we have a competitive system with excellent support. No construction experience necessary to excel in this $128 billion market. We offer a turn-key operation that can be managed from your home or retail front. We are the only franchisor in the basement industry providing a complete system to the home improvement sector.

BACKGROUND:

Established: 1999;	1st Franchised: 2002
Franchised Units:	0

Company-Owned Units 1
Total Units: 1
Dist.: US-1; CAN-0; O'seas-0
North America: 1 State
Density: 1 in OH
Projected New Units (12 Months): 10
Qualifications: 5, 5, 4, 2, 3, 5
Registered: None

FINANCIAL/TERMS:
Cash Investment: $20-30K
Total Investment: $30-45K
Minimum Net Worth: $75K
Fees: Franchise - $12-14.5K
Royalty - 5%; Ad. - N/A
Earnings Claim Statement: Yes
Term of Contract (Years): 10/10
Avg. # Of Employees: 2 FT, 1 PT
Passive Ownership: Not Allowed
Encourage Conversions: Yes
Area Develop. Agreements: No
Sub-Franchising Contracts: Yes
Expand In Territory: Yes
Space Needs: 200 SF; SF, HB

SUPPORT & TRAINING PROVIDED:
Financial Assistance Provided: No
Site Selection Assistance: Yes
Lease Negotiation Assistance: No
Co-Operative Advertising: Yes
Franchisee Assoc./Member: No
Size Of Corporate Staff: 5
On-Going Support: C,D,E,F,G,H,I
Training: 3 Weeks Columbus, OH.

SPECIFIC EXPANSION PLANS:
US: Midwest
Canada: No
Overseas: No

<< >>

BATH FITTER

27 Berard Dr., # 2701
South Burlington, VT 05403-5810
Tel: (800) 892-2847 (802) 860-2919
Fax: (802) 862-7976
E-Mail: bathfitter@together.net
Web Site: www.bathfitter.com
Ms. Linda F. Brakel, VP Franchise Operations

Since 1984, BATH FITTER has been installing custom-molded acrylic bathtub liners, shower bases and one-piece, seamless wall surrounds over existing fixtures in just a few hours in countless residential and commercial properties. We provide full training, specialized tools, marketing and technical manuals and on-going support through regular visits to your location. We award exclusive territories with enormous residential and commercial market potential to qualified franchise owners.

BACKGROUND:
Established: 1984; 1st Franchised: 1992
Franchised Units: 92
Company-Owned Units 3
Total Units: 95
Dist.: US-76; CAN-27; O'seas-0
North America: 24 States, 8 Provinces
Density: 9 in PA, 8 in NY, 8 in ON
Projected New Units (12 Months): 14
Qualifications: 3, 3, 2, 1, 4, 5
Registered: CA,FL,IL,IN,MD,MN,MI,MN,NY,OR,RI,VA,WA,WI,DC,AB

FINANCIAL/TERMS:
Cash Investment: $N/A
Total Investment: $60-100K
Minimum Net Worth: $N/A
Fees: Franchise - $24.5K
Royalty - N/A; Ad. - N/A
Earnings Claim Statement: Yes
Term of Contract (Years): 5/5
Avg. # Of Employees: 3 FT
Passive Ownership: Not Allowed
Encourage Conversions: No
Area Develop. Agreements: Yes/Varies
Sub-Franchising Contracts: No
Expand In Territory: Yes
Space Needs: 2,000-2,500 SF; Industrial Park

SUPPORT & TRAINING PROVIDED:
Financial Assistance Provided: No
Site Selection Assistance: Yes
Lease Negotiation Assistance: N/A
Co-Operative Advertising: N/A
Franchisee Assoc./Member: No
Size Of Corporate Staff: 13
On-Going Support: B,C,D,E,G,h,I
Training: 10 Days Headquarters; 10 Days Franchisee Site.

SPECIFIC EXPANSION PLANS:
US: All United States
Canada: All Canada
Overseas: No

<< >>

BATHCREST

2425 S. Progress Dr.
Salt Lake City, UT 84119
Tel: (800) 826-6790 (801) 972-1110
Fax: (801) 977-0328
E-Mail: info@bathcrest.com
Web Site: www.bathcrest.com
Mr. Lloyd Peterson, VP Franchise Sales

Same-day bathroom remodeling that's highly profitable. You'll get multi-surface restoration processes and products to capitalize on the booming home improvement market. Our comprehensive business system shows you how to update a bathroom in less than a day with no percentage-based royalty to hold you back. You earn it, so you get to keep it.

BACKGROUND:
Established: 1979; 1st Franchised: 1985
Franchised Units: 173
Company-Owned Units 1
Total Units: 174
Dist.: US-166; CAN-6; O'seas-0
North America: 30 States, 3 Provinces
Density: 15 in CA, 15 in PA, 12 in FL
Projected New Units (12 Months): 12
Qualifications: 3, 4, 2, 2, 5, 4
Registered: FL,VA,WI

FINANCIAL/TERMS:
Cash Investment: $12.5-24.5K
Total Investment: $24.5-44.5K
Minimum Net Worth: $200K
Fees: Franchise - $12.5K
Royalty - $250/Mo.; Ad. - N/A
Earnings Claim Statement: No
Term of Contract (Years): 15/15
Avg. # Of Employees: 3-5 FT
Passive Ownership: Allowed
Encourage Conversions: N/A
Area Develop. Agreements: No
Sub-Franchising Contracts: No
Expand In Territory: No
Space Needs: 500-1,200 SF; HB, Industrial Center

SUPPORT & TRAINING PROVIDED:
Financial Assistance Provided: Yes(D)
Site Selection Assistance: N/A
Lease Negotiation Assistance: No
Co-Operative Advertising: No
Franchisee Assoc./Member: No
Size Of Corporate Staff: 11
On-Going Support: B,D,G,H,I
Training: 5 Days Headquarters; 3 Days (30-60 Days after Initial Training) Headquarters.

SPECIFIC EXPANSION PLANS:
US: All United States
Canada: All Except AB
Overseas: No

<< >>

B-DRY SYSTEM

1341 Copley Rd.
Akron, OH 44320
Tel: (800) 321-0985 (330) 867-2576
Fax: (330) 867-7693
Mr. Carl A. Rakich, Vice President

Basement waterproofing system. Low cash investment - high return on investment. Intensive and continuous training. No high-cost site expenditure. No previous experience necessary. Unique patented system. Full customer warranty for the life of the structure.

BACKGROUND: IFA MEMBER
Established: 1958; 1st Franchised: 1978
Franchised Units: 61
Company-Owned Units 6
Total Units: 67
Dist.: US-68; CAN-0; O'seas-0
North America: NR
Density: 10 in OH, 8 in PA, 7 in NY
Projected New Units (12 Months): 3
Qualifications: 2, 3, 2, 2, 3, 5
Registered: NR

FINANCIAL/TERMS:
Cash Investment: $25-50K
Total Investment: $40-74K
Minimum Net Worth: $NR
Fees: Franchise - $15-60K
Royalty - 6%; Ad. - 0%
Earnings Claim Statement: No
Term of Contract (Years): 5/5
Avg. # Of Employees: 6 FT, 1 PT
Passive Ownership: Discouraged
Encourage Conversions: No
Area Develop. Agreements: No
Sub-Franchising Contracts: No
Expand In Territory: Yes
Space Needs: 4,000 SF; FS, HB

SUPPORT & TRAINING PROVIDED:
Financial Assistance Provided: Yes(D)
Site Selection Assistance: No
Lease Negotiation Assistance: No
Co-Operative Advertising: No
Franchisee Assoc./Member: Yes/No
Size Of Corporate Staff: 10
On-Going Support: B,C,D,F,G,h,I
Training: 2 Wks. National Office in Akron, OH; 2 Wks. On-Site; 1-2 Days On-Going Regional Seminars.

SPECIFIC EXPANSION PLANS:
US: Northeast, Northwest
Canada: No
Overseas: No

<< >>

BMR BATH MASTER REGLAZING
4498 Trepanier Rd.
Peachland, BC V0H 1X3 CANADA
Tel: (877) 767-2336 (250) 767-2336
Fax: (250) 767-2718
E-Mail: sales@bathmaster.com
Web Site: www.bathmaster.com
Mr. Trevor Dixon, President

Quality bathtub, tile reglazing, acrylic bathtub liners, tub walls, porcelain restoration and countertop resurfacing with superior materials. Transform dull, worn, unsightly fixtures to a brilliant new finish in just a few hours. This system leaves no mess or odor behind and offers same day use. This franchise includes equipment, training and on-going support. We do it all!

BACKGROUND:
Established: 1989; 1st Franchised: 1992
Franchised Units: 24
Company-Owned Units 0
Total Units: 24
Dist.: US-1; CAN-23; O'seas-0
North America: 5 Provinces
Density: 12 in ON, 6 in BC, 2 in SK
Projected New Units (12 Months): 5
Qualifications: 3, 2, 4, 3, 4, 3
Registered: NR

FINANCIAL/TERMS:
Cash Investment: $17K
Total Investment: $17-41K
Minimum Net Worth: $N/A
Fees: Franchise - $0
Royalty - 5%/$200/Mo.; Ad. - 2%
Earnings Claim Statement: No
Term of Contract (Years): 5/5
Avg. # Of Employees: 1 FT
Passive Ownership: Discouraged
Encourage Conversions: Yes
Area Develop. Agreements: No
Sub-Franchising Contracts: No
Expand In Territory: Yes
Space Needs: 300 SF; HB

SUPPORT & TRAINING PROVIDED:
Financial Assistance Provided: No
Site Selection Assistance: N/A
Lease Negotiation Assistance: No
Co-Operative Advertising: N/A
Franchisee Assoc./Member: Yes/Yes
Size Of Corporate Staff: 2
On-Going Support: B,C,D,F,G,H,I
Training: 15 Days Minimum Peachland, BC.

SPECIFIC EXPANSION PLANS:
US: All United States
Canada: All Canada
Overseas: No

<< >>

CALIFORNIA CLOSETS.
Simplify Your Life.

CALIFORNIA CLOSET COMPANY
1000 Fourth St., # 800
San Rafael, CA 94901-3142
Tel: (800) 241-3222 (415) 256-8500
Fax: (415) 256-8501
Web Site: www.calclosets.com
Ms. Terri Blackburn, Dir. Administration

The CALIFORNIA CLOSET brand is the leader in customized closet, garage and storage space design and installation services. As part of this exciting franchise system, you will receive specialized training, management and marketing support. Newsletters, seminars, conventions and a top notch corporate staff keep you current. A formula for success!

BACKGROUND: IFA MEMBER
Established: 1979; 1st Franchised: 1982
Franchised Units: 153
Company-Owned Units 2
Total Units: 155
Dist.: US-127; CAN-10; O'seas-18
North America: 35 States, 5 Provinces
Density: 14 in CA, 10 in NY, 10 in FL
Projected New Units (12 Months): 4
Registered: CA,IL,IN,MD,MI,MN,NY,RI,VA,WA,WI

FINANCIAL/TERMS:
Cash Investment: $75-225K
Total Investment: $75-225K
Minimum Net Worth: $NR
Fees: Franchise - $39.5K
Royalty - 6%; Ad. - 3%
Earnings Claim Statement: No
Term of Contract (Years): 10/10
Avg. # Of Employees: 3-25 FT
Passive Ownership: Discouraged
Encourage Conversions: N/A
Area Develop. Agreements: No
Sub-Franchising Contracts: No
Expand In Territory: Yes
Space Needs: 2,000-6,000 SF; Light Industrial

SUPPORT & TRAINING PROVIDED:
Financial Assistance Provided: Yes(I)
Site Selection Assistance: Yes
Lease Negotiation Assistance: Yes
Co-Operative Advertising: Yes
Franchisee Assoc./Member: NR
Size Of Corporate Staff: 28

On-Going Support: A,B,C,D,E,F,G,H,I
Training: 1 Week Headquarters; 2 Weeks On-Site.

SPECIFIC EXPANSION PLANS:
US: Various U.S. Locations
Canada: PQ
Overseas: Europe, Asia, Mexico, South America

<< >>

CLOSET & STORAGE CONCEPTS
1000 Laurel Oak Corporate Center, # 208
Voorhees, NJ 08043
Tel: (800) 862-1919 (856) 627-5700
Fax: (856) 627-7447
E-Mail: boblewis@closetandstoragecon cepts.co
Web Site: www.closetandstorageconcept s.com
Mr. Bob Lewis, President

Closet & Storage Concepts designs, manufacturers and installs a wide variety of custom closet, garage, laundry room, home office and storage units. All franchisees receive complete training in all aspects of the operation of the business, both prior to opening and on an on-going basis. Call 1-888-862-1919.

BACKGROUND: IFA MEMBER
Established: 1987; 1st Franchised: 2000
Franchised Units: 7
Company-Owned Units 1
Total Units: 8
Dist.: US-2; CAN-0; O'seas-0
North America: NR
Density: NR
Projected New Units (12 Months): 5
Qualifications: 3, 4, 1, 3, 4, 5
Registered: All States

FINANCIAL/TERMS:
Cash Investment: $20-40K
Total Investment: $95-135K
Minimum Net Worth: $100K
Fees: Franchise - $40K
Royalty - 5%; Ad. - 0%
Earnings Claim Statement: No
Term of Contract (Years): 10/10
Avg. # Of Employees: 8 FT
Passive Ownership: Discouraged
Encourage Conversions: N/A
Area Develop. Agreements: No
Sub-Franchising Contracts: No
Expand In Territory: Yes
Space Needs: 4,000 SF; FS

SUPPORT & TRAINING PROVIDED:
Financial Assistance Provided: No
Site Selection Assistance: Yes
Lease Negotiation Assistance: Yes
Co-Operative Advertising: N/A
Franchisee Assoc./Member: Yes
Size Of Corporate Staff: 4
On-Going Support: C,D,E,G,H,I
Training: 2 Weeks in NJ.

SPECIFIC EXPANSION PLANS:
US: All United States
Canada: All Canada
Overseas: No

<< >>

CLOSET FACTORY, THE
12800 S. Broadway
Los Angeles, CA 90061-1116
Tel: (800) 318-8800 (310) 715-1000
Fax: (310) 576-8065
Web Site: www.closet-factory.com
Ms. Katherine LaBarbara, VP Franchise Development

Join the industry leader, ranked #1 in custom closets by Entrepreneur Magazine worldwide. Franchisees design, sell, manufacture and install custom closet systems, garage organizers, kitchen pantries, entertainment centers and custom office systems. Operate a large, vertically integrated cash business during normal business hours in an exclusive territory. A complete turn-key business through training and on-going support. No technical experience is necessary.

BACKGROUND:
Established: 1983; 1st Franchised: 1985
Franchised Units: 90
Company-Owned Units 27
Total Units: 117
Dist.: US-97; CAN-5; O'seas-10
North America: 39 States, 2 Provinces
Density: 14 in CA, 8 in NY, 7 in FL
Projected New Units (12 Months): 15
Qualifications: 5, 5, 2, 4, 3, 3
Registered: CA,FL,IL,IN,MD,MI,MN,NY, OR,VA,WA,WI,DC,AB

FINANCIAL/TERMS:
Cash Investment: $40-50K
Total Investment: $99.5-185K
Minimum Net Worth: $150-350K
Fees: Franchise - $28.5-39.5K
Royalty - 5.8%; Ad. - 1%
Earnings Claim Statement: No
Term of Contract (Years): 5/5
Avg. # Of Employees: 5-6 FT
Passive Ownership: Allowed
Encourage Conversions: Yes
Area Develop. Agreements: No
Sub-Franchising Contracts: No
Expand In Territory: No
Space Needs: 3,500-4,000 SF; Warehouse or Industrial Park

SUPPORT & TRAINING PROVIDED:
Financial Assistance Provided: Yes(I)
Site Selection Assistance: Yes
Lease Negotiation Assistance: Yes
Co-Operative Advertising: No
Franchisee Assoc./Member: No
Size Of Corporate Staff: NR
On-Going Support: B,C,D,E,G,h
Training: 2 Weeks Corporate Headquarters; 4 Weeks On-Site.

SPECIFIC EXPANSION PLANS:
US: All United States
Canada: All Canada
Overseas: All Countries

<< >>

CLOSETS BY DESIGN
13151 S. Western Ave.
Gardena, CA 90249
Tel: (800) 377-5737 (310) 965-2040
Fax: (310) 527-8955
E-Mail: info@closetsbydesign.com
Web Site: www.closetsbydesign.com
Mr. Gerald Egner, President

CLOSETS BY DESIGN has been creating the custom space industry's most attractive

& functional closets, garage organizers, media & entertainment centers, & home office systems since 1982. We have become the industry benchmark through our unyielding dedication to quality, value, selection, service and customer satisfaction. It all begins with a design that is custom tailored to meet your unique space requirements. Consultants receive the industry's most comprehensive training.

BACKGROUND: IFA MEMBER
Established: 1982; 1st Franchised: 1998
Franchised Units: 32
Company-Owned Units 8
Total Units: 40
Dist.: US-40; CAN-; O'seas-
North America: 8 States
Density: 7 in CA, 4 in OH, 4 in TX
Projected New Units (12 Months): 10
Qualifications: 5, 5, 1, 4, 2, 5
Registered: CA,FL,IL,IN,MD,MI,MN,NY,VA,WI,DC

FINANCIAL/TERMS:
Cash Investment: $30-75K
Total Investment: $88-275K
Minimum Net Worth: $500K
Fees: Franchise - $19.5-34.9K
Royalty - 6%; Ad. - 2%
Earnings Claim Statement: No
Term of Contract (Years): 5/5
Avg. # Of Employees: 6 FT
Passive Ownership: Not Allowed
Encourage Conversions: Yes
Area Develop. Agreements: No
Sub-Franchising Contracts: No
Expand In Territory: Yes
Space Needs: 6-10,000 SF; Business or Industrial Parks

SUPPORT & TRAINING PROVIDED:
Financial Assistance Provided: No
Site Selection Assistance: No
Lease Negotiation Assistance: No
Co-Operative Advertising: Yes
Franchisee Assoc./Member: Yes/No
Size Of Corporate Staff: 3
On-Going Support: c,d,h,I
Training: 2 Weeks Corporate HQ; 1 Week Corporate Location; 2 Weeks On-Site.

SPECIFIC EXPANSION PLANS:
US: NE and NW
Canada: BC and ON
Overseas: No

<< >>

CLOSETTEC

55 Carnegie Row
Norwood, MA 02062
Tel: (800) 365-2021 (781) 769-9997
Fax: (781) 769-9996
E-Mail: closettec@closettec.com
Web Site: www.closettec.com
Mr. David Rogers, President

CLOSETTEC sells, manufactures and installs residential and commercial storage systems, using the finest melamine laminates and exclusive European hardware. We offer comprehensive training, field support, site selection, sales/marketing programs and on-going design assistance to every franchisee. Exclusive CAD and database programs.

BACKGROUND:
Established: 1985; 1st Franchised: 1986
Franchised Units: 35
Company-Owned Units 0
Total Units: 35
Dist.: US-35; CAN-0; O'seas-0
North America: NR
Density: 4 in MA, 2 in NY, 2 in OH
Projected New Units (12 Months): 2
Qualifications: 4, 4, 2, 3, 3, 5
Registered: NR

FINANCIAL/TERMS:
Cash Investment: $NR
Total Investment: $128-240K
Minimum Net Worth: $NR
Fees: Franchise - $30K
Royalty - 4.5%; Ad. - NR
Earnings Claim Statement: No
Term of Contract (Years): 15/15
Avg. # Of Employees: 3-5 FT
Passive Ownership: Discouraged
Encourage Conversions: Yes
Area Develop. Agreements: No
Sub-Franchising Contracts: No
Expand In Territory: Yes
Space Needs: 2,500-3,000 SF; Light Industrial

SUPPORT & TRAINING PROVIDED:
Financial Assistance Provided: No
Site Selection Assistance: Yes
Lease Negotiation Assistance: Yes
Co-Operative Advertising: No
Franchisee Assoc./Member: No
Size Of Corporate Staff: 9
On-Going Support: C,D,E,H,I
Training: 2 Weeks Norwood, MA.

SPECIFIC EXPANSION PLANS:
US: All United States
Canada: No
Overseas: No

<< >>

COLOR-GLO INTERNATIONAL

7111-7115 Ohms Ln.
Minneapolis, MN 55439-2158
Tel: (800) 333-8523 (952) 835-1338
Fax: (952) 835-1395
E-Mail: info@color-glo.com
Web Site: www.color-glo.com
Mr. Scott L. Smith, VP Franchise Sales

The leader in the leather and fabric restoration and repair industry. From automotive to marine to aircraft to all-leather furniture, COLOR-GLO leads the way with innovative products and protected application techniques. We serve all US and foreign car manufacturers.

BACKGROUND: IFA MEMBER
Established: 1975; 1st Franchised: 1984
Franchised Units: 230
Company-Owned Units 1
Total Units: 231
Dist.: US-188; CAN-1; O'seas-21
North America: NR
Density: 15 in FL, 12 in OR, 10 in CA
Projected New Units (12 Months): 50
Qualifications: 4, 4, 3, 4, 3, 3
Registered: All States

FINANCIAL/TERMS:
Cash Investment: $15-20K
Total Investment: $18-30K
Minimum Net Worth: $20K
Fees: Franchise - $7.5K
Royalty - 2-4%; Ad. - 0%
Earnings Claim Statement: Yes
Term of Contract (Years): 10/5
Avg. # Of Employees: 1 FT
Passive Ownership: Allowed
Encourage Conversions: N/A
Area Develop. Agreements: Yes/10
Sub-Franchising Contracts: Yes
Expand In Territory: Yes
Space Needs: N/A SF; N/A

SUPPORT & TRAINING PROVIDED:
Financial Assistance Provided: Yes(I)
Site Selection Assistance: N/A
Lease Negotiation Assistance: N/A
Co-Operative Advertising: Yes
Franchisee Assoc./Member: Yes/Yes
Size Of Corporate Staff: 20
On-Going Support: B,C,D,G,H,I
Training: 2 Weeks On-Location.

SPECIFIC EXPANSION PLANS:
US: All United States
Canada: All Canada
Overseas: All Countries

<< >>

CRACK TEAM, THE

10767 Indian Head Industrial Blvd.
St. Louis, MO 63132-1101
Tel: (866) CRACK-TEAM (314) 426-0900
Fax: (314) 426-0915
E-Mail: info@thecrackteam.com
Web Site: www.thecrackteam.com
Mr. Randy Hove, Director of Franchising

THE CRACK TEAM offers a unique specialty service repairing cracks in foundation walls. Cracked and leaking basements can be repaired permanently, quickly and inexpensively using our proven marketing strategies and exclusively-formulated materials.

BACKGROUND: IFA MEMBER
Established: 1985; 1st Franchised: 2001
Franchised Units: 4
Company-Owned Units 6
Total Units: 10
Dist.: US-10; CAN-0; O'seas-0
North America: 2 States
Density: 8 in Mo, 2 in IL
Projected New Units (12 Months): 50
Qualifications: 5, 3, 1, 2, 2, 3
Registered: IL,IN

FINANCIAL/TERMS:
Cash Investment: $50K
Total Investment: $50-100K
Minimum Net Worth: $75-100K
Fees: Franchise - $25K
Royalty - 6%; Ad. - 0%
Earnings Claim Statement: No
Term of Contract (Years): 20/20
Avg. # Of Employees: 2 FT
Passive Ownership: Discouraged
Encourage Conversions: No
Area Develop. Agreements: Yes/5
Sub-Franchising Contracts: No
Expand In Territory: No
Space Needs: 300 SF; HB

SUPPORT & TRAINING PROVIDED:
Financial Assistance Provided: Yes(I)
Site Selection Assistance: Yes
Lease Negotiation Assistance: N/A
Co-Operative Advertising: No
Franchisee Assoc./Member: No
Size Of Corporate Staff: 6
On-Going Support: A,B,C,D,E,F,G,h,I
Training: NR

SPECIFIC EXPANSION PLANS:
US: Midwest
Canada: No
Overseas: No

<< >>

CREATIVE COLORS INTERNATIONAL

P.O. Box 552
Oak Forest, IL 60452
Tel: (800) 933-2656 (708) 614-7786
Fax: (708) 614-9685
E-Mail: mark@creativecolorsintl.com
Web Site: www.creativecolorsintl.com
Mr. Mark J. Bollman, President

Mobile units providing repair and restoration in all markets that have leather, vinyl, fabric, velour, plastics and fiberglass. These markets include car dealerships (new and used), furniture retailers and manufactures, hotels, airports, car rental agencies and company fleet cars.

BACKGROUND:
Established: 1980; 1st Franchised: 1991
Franchised Units: 52
Company-Owned Units 2
Total Units: 54
Dist.: US-53; CAN-1; O'seas-0
North America: 20 States, 1 Province
Density: IL, FL, OH
Projected New Units (12 Months): 10+
Qualifications: 4, 4, 3, 4, 4, 5
Registered: CA,FL,IL,IN,MI,NY,OR,WI,AB

FINANCIAL/TERMS:
Cash Investment: $19.5K+
Total Investment: $19.5K+
Minimum Net Worth: $50K+
Fees: Franchise - $27.5K
Royalty - 6%/$175/mo.; Ad. - 1%
Earnings Claim Statement: Yes
Term of Contract (Years): 10
Avg. # Of Employees: 5 FT
Passive Ownership: Discouraged
Encourage Conversions: Yes
Area Develop. Agreements: Yes/10
Sub-Franchising Contracts: No
Expand In Territory: Yes
Space Needs: N/A SF; HB

SUPPORT & TRAINING PROVIDED:
Financial Assistance Provided: Yes(D)
Site Selection Assistance: Yes
Lease Negotiation Assistance: N/A
Co-Operative Advertising: Yes
Franchisee Assoc./Member: Yes/Yes
Size Of Corporate Staff: 8
On-Going Support: A,B,C,D,E,F,G,H,I
Training: 3 Weeks Headquarters, Tinley Park, IL; 1 Week in Franchisee's Territory.

SPECIFIC EXPANSION PLANS:
US: All United States
Canada: All Canada
Overseas: All Countries

<< >>

DECKARE SERVICES

1501 Raff Rd., SW
Canton, OH 44710-2356
Tel: (800) 711-3325 (330) 478-3665
Fax: (330) 478-0311
E-Mail: deckcare1@aol.com
Web Site: www.deckcare.com
Mr. Dan Fuline, Jr., VP Communications

Rejuvenating exterior wood surfaces such as decks, fences, docks, gazebos and bridges with a total commitment to being the first nationally-recognized franchise based on image and quality. Franchisees will receive complete business and field training with on-going support services.

BACKGROUND: IFA MEMBER
Established: 1995; 1st Franchised: 1997
Franchised Units: 40
Company-Owned Units 0
Total Units: 40
Dist.: US-25; CAN-0; O'seas-0
North America: 16 States
Density: 4 in OH, 3 in MO, 3 in TN
Projected New Units (12 Months): 40
Qualifications: 5, 4, 3, 3, 2, 5
Registered: CA,IL,IN,MD,MI,MN,NY,VA

FINANCIAL/TERMS:
Cash Investment: $25K
Total Investment: $45K
Minimum Net Worth: $50K
Fees: Franchise - $14.5K
Royalty - 5%; Ad. - N/A
Earnings Claim Statement: No
Term of Contract (Years): 5/5
Avg. # Of Employees: 1 FT, 1 PT

Passive Ownership: Allowed
Encourage Conversions: No
Area Develop. Agreements: No
Sub-Franchising Contracts: No
Expand In Territory: Yes
Space Needs: NR SF; HB

SUPPORT & TRAINING PROVIDED:
Financial Assistance Provided: No
Site Selection Assistance: N/A
Lease Negotiation Assistance: N/A
Co-Operative Advertising: N/A
Franchisee Assoc./Member: No
Size Of Corporate Staff: 5
On-Going Support: C,D,G,H,I
Training: 5 Days at Corporate Office; 4 Days Franchisee's Location.

SPECIFIC EXPANSION PLANS:
US: All United States
Canada: No
Overseas: No

<< >>

DELBE HOME SERVICES

5185 MacArthur Blvd. NW, # 115
Washington, DC 20016
Tel: (800) 753-3523 (202) 237-0187
Fax: (202) 237-0348
E-Mail: hjm@delbefranchise.com
Web Site: www.delbefranchise.com
Mr. Howard J. Margolis, Dir. Bus. Dev.

DHS is a membership-based service company that assists homeowners (members) in solving their home's maintenance, repair and improvement problems and needs. DHS provides its members with licensed and insured contractors, handles scheduling and assigns a personal service representative to manage every member's job. As a full-service company, DHS is able to meet all of the homeowner's needs.

BACKGROUND: IFA MEMBER
Established: 2000; 1st Franchised: 2000
Franchised Units: 1
Company-Owned Units 0
Total Units: 1
Dist.: US-1; CAN-0; O'seas-0
North America: DC
Density: 1 in DC
Projected New Units (12 Months): 13
Qualifications: 5, 4, 3, 3, 2, 5
Registered: FL,MD,VA,DC

FINANCIAL/TERMS:
Cash Investment: $8.4-20.6K
Total Investment: $25.3-61.9K
Minimum Net Worth: $225K
Fees: Franchise - $18.5-40K
Royalty - 3%; Ad. - N/A
Earnings Claim Statement: No
Term of Contract (Years): 10/10
Avg. # Of Employees: 1 FT, 1PT
Passive Ownership: Not Allowed
Encourage Conversions: N/A
Area Develop. Agreements: No
Sub-Franchising Contracts: No
Expand In Territory: No
Space Needs: 100 SF; HB

SUPPORT & TRAINING PROVIDED:
Financial Assistance Provided: Yes(I)
Site Selection Assistance: N/A
Lease Negotiation Assistance: N/A
Co-Operative Advertising: Yes
Franchisee Assoc./Member: Yes/Yes
Size Of Corporate Staff: 3
On-Going Support: C,D,I
Training: 7 Days, Washington, DC.

SPECIFIC EXPANSION PLANS:
US: PA,NJ,DE,MD,VA,NC,SC,GA,FL
Canada: No
Overseas: No

<< >>

DR. VINYL & ASSOCIATES

821 NW Commerce St.
Lee's Summit, MO 64086-9381
Tel: (800) 531-6600 (816) 525-6060
Fax: (816) 525-6333
E-Mail: tbuckley@drvinyl.com
Web Site: www.drvinyl.com
Mr. Tom Buckley, Jr., President

We offer vinyl, leather and velour fabric repair and coloring, auto windshield repair, dashboard and hard plastic repair, vinyl striping, exterior paint touch-up and paintless dent repair to new and used car dealers.

BACKGROUND: IFA MEMBER
Established: 1972; 1st Franchised: 1980
Franchised Units: 190
Company-Owned Units 1
Total Units: 191
Dist.: US-160; CAN-1; O'seas-30
North America: NR
Density: 18 in MO, 10 in IL, 7 in OH
Projected New Units (12 Months): 30
Qualifications: 3, 2, 2, 2, 2, 4
Registered: CA,FL,IL,IN,MD,MI,OR,VA,WI

FINANCIAL/TERMS:
Cash Investment: $26K
Total Investment: $38-61K
Minimum Net Worth: $27K
Fees: Franchise - $23.5K
Royalty - 7%; Ad. - 1%
Earnings Claim Statement: Yes
Term of Contract (Years): 10/10
Avg. # Of Employees: 1 FT
Passive Ownership: Discouraged
Encourage Conversions: N/A
Area Develop. Agreements: Yes/10
Sub-Franchising Contracts: Yes
Expand In Territory: Yes
Space Needs: N/A SF; N/A

SUPPORT & TRAINING PROVIDED:
Financial Assistance Provided: Yes(B)
Site Selection Assistance: N/A
Lease Negotiation Assistance: N/A
Co-Operative Advertising: No
Franchisee Assoc./Member: Yes
Size Of Corporate Staff: 15
On-Going Support: b,C,D,F,G,h,I
Training: 2 Weeks Corporate Office; 2 Weeks Field Training.

SPECIFIC EXPANSION PLANS:
US: All United States
Canada: All Canada
Overseas: All Countries

<< >>

DREAMMAKER BATH & KITCHEN REMODELING

1020 N. University Parks Dr.
Waco, TX 76707
Tel: (800) 583-9099 (254) 745-2477
Fax: (254) 745-2588
E-Mail: dminfo@dwyergroup.com
Ms. Karen Cagle, VP Franchising

DreamMaker has pioneered a full-service remodeling franchise. Support includes training, research and development, marketing, group buying power, ongoing support, better pricing for profits in both residential and commercial remodeling. A unique combination of traditional remodeling and alternatives such as cabinet refacing, refinishing, and tubliners.

BACKGROUND: IFA MEMBER
Established: 1970; 1st Franchised: 1971
Franchised Units: 300
Company-Owned Units 0
Total Units: 300
Dist.: US-120; CAN-5; O'seas-175
North America: 50 States, 3 Provinces
Density: 14 in TX, 7 in IL, 6 in NY
Projected New Units (12 Months): 20
Qualifications: 4, 2, 5, 2, 2, 5
Registered: All States Except VA

FINANCIAL/TERMS:
Cash Investment: $20-35K
Total Investment: $35-70K
Minimum Net Worth: $100K
Fees: Franchise - $27K
Royalty - 3-6%; Ad. - 1-2%
Earnings Claim Statement: No
Term of Contract (Years): 10/10
Avg. # Of Employees: 2 FT
Passive Ownership: Discouraged
Encourage Conversions: Yes
Area Develop. Agreements: No
Sub-Franchising Contracts: No
Expand In Territory: Yes
Space Needs: 700 SF; SF

SUPPORT & TRAINING PROVIDED:
Financial Assistance Provided: Yes(B)
Site Selection Assistance: Yes
Lease Negotiation Assistance: Yes
Co-Operative Advertising: Yes
Franchisee Assoc./Member: Yes/Yes
Size Of Corporate Staff: 10
On-Going Support: B,C,D,e,g,H,I
Training: 3 Weeks Headquarters, Waco, TX.

SPECIFIC EXPANSION PLANS:
US: All United States
Canada: All Except PQ
Overseas: All Countries

<< >>

ESSENTIALS PROTECTIVE COATINGS

5209 Capital Blvd.
Raleigh, NC 27616-2925
Tel: (888) 372-8827 (919) 785-3015
Fax: (919) 785-3319
E-Mail: a.huffman@epc-tubs.com
Web Site: www.epc-tubs.com
Mr. Adam Huffman, Fran. Dev.

Application of proprietary EPC 2000 coating to protect bath fixtures during the construction process. Franchises call on general contractors.

BACKGROUND: IFA MEMBER
Established: 1996; 1st Franchised: 1997
Franchised Units: 6
Company-Owned Units 1
Total Units: 7
Dist.: US-18; CAN-0; O'seas-1
North America: 7 States
Density: 7 in NC, 6 in GA, 2 in VA
Projected New Units (12 Months): 10
Qualifications: 5, 4, 4, 3, 3, 4
Registered: FL,VA,AB

FINANCIAL/TERMS:
Cash Investment: $30-75K
Total Investment: $46.1-91.7K
Minimum Net Worth: $150K
Fees: Franchise - $25K
Royalty - 8%; Ad. - 3%
Earnings Claim Statement: No
Term of Contract (Years): 5/5
Avg. # Of Employees: 2 FT
Passive Ownership: Not Allowed
Encourage Conversions: No
Area Develop. Agreements: Yes
Sub-Franchising Contracts: No
Expand In Territory: No
Space Needs: N/A SF; N/A

SUPPORT & TRAINING PROVIDED:
Financial Assistance Provided: Yes(I)
Site Selection Assistance: N/A
Lease Negotiation Assistance: Yes
Co-Operative Advertising: Yes
Franchisee Assoc./Member: Yes/No
Size Of Corporate Staff: 6
On-Going Support: B,C,D,E,F,G,I
Training: 1 Week at Corporate Office; 1 Week on Location.

SPECIFIC EXPANSION PLANS:
US: SE, SW, W
Canada: AB
Overseas: Europe, Asia

<< >>

Top 50

FOUR SEASONS SUNROOMS

5005 Veterans Memorial Hwy.
Holbrook, NY 11741
Tel: (800) 521-0179 (516) 563-4000
Fax: (516) 563-4010
E-Mail: tonyr@four-seasons-sunrooms.com
Web Site: www.four-seasons-sunrooms.com
Mr. Tony Russo, VP Business Dev.

FOUR SEASONS SUNROOMS is the largest manufacturer of sunrooms, conservatories and solariums in the Unites States. The FOUR SEASONS franchise opportunity is targeted to the $121 billion remodeling industry. We offer comprehensive training and exclusive products.

BACKGROUND: IFA MEMBER
Established: 1974; 1st Franchised: 1985
Franchised Units: 200
Company-Owned Units 3
Total Units: 203
Dist.: US-188; CAN-12; O'seas-47
North America: 48 States, 5 Provinces
Density: 17 in CA, 21 in NY, 16 in PA
Projected New Units (12 Months): 24
Qualifications: 2, 5, 4, 3, 3, 4
Registered: All States

FINANCIAL/TERMS:
Cash Investment: $10-25K
Total Investment: $13.3-82.5K
Minimum Net Worth: $100K
Fees: Franchise - $7.5-15K
Royalty - 0%; Ad. - 0%
Earnings Claim Statement: No
Term of Contract (Years): 10/10
Avg. # Of Employees: 2 FT, 1 PT
Passive Ownership: Not Allowed
Encourage Conversions: Yes
Area Develop. Agreements: No
Sub-Franchising Contracts: No
Expand In Territory: Yes
Space Needs: 750 SF; FS, SF

SUPPORT & TRAINING PROVIDED:
Financial Assistance Provided: No
Site Selection Assistance: Yes
Lease Negotiation Assistance: Yes
Co-Operative Advertising: Yes
Franchisee Assoc./Member: Yes
Size Of Corporate Staff: 250
On-Going Support: C,D,E,F,G,H,I
Training: 5 Days Holbrook, NY; 5 Days Hayward, CA; 5 Days Regionally.

SPECIFIC EXPANSION PLANS:
US: All United States
Canada: All Canada
Overseas:
U.K., Spain, France, Germany, Italy

<< >>

FURNITURE MEDIC

860 Ridge Lake Blvd.
Memphis, TN 38120
Tel: (800) 255-9687 (901) 820-8600
Fax: (901) 820-8660

E-Mail: furnmedic@attglobal.net
Web Site: www.furnituremedicfranchise.com
Mr. David Messenger, VP Market Expansion

FURNITURE MEDIC is a division of ServiceMaster Consumer Services. It has grown into an international franchise operation providing complete on-site precision repair as well as furniture stripping and refinishing. Targeting the residential, commercial and insurance markets, their patented Restoration-Refinishing process yields efficiency plus cost saving to customers. A solid training program and strong business support has effectively positioned FURNITURE MEDIC as the premier furniture repair company.

BACKGROUND: IFA MEMBER
Established: 1992; 1st Franchised: 1992
Franchised Units: 600
Company-Owned Units 0
Total Units: 600
Dist.: US-450; CAN-65; O'seas-85
North America: 47 States,10 Provinces
Density: 36 in CA, 35 in FL, 28 in VA
Projected New Units (12 Months): 60
Qualifications: 4, 4, 2, 3, 3, 5
Registered: All States

FINANCIAL/TERMS:
Cash Investment: $15-25K
Total Investment: $32.7-78.9K
Minimum Net Worth: $75-100K
Fees: Franchise - $20.5K
Royalty - 7%/$250 Min.;
Ad. - 1%/$50 Min.
Earnings Claim Statement: No
Term of Contract (Years): 5/5
Avg. # Of Employees: 1 FT, 1 PT
Passive Ownership: Not Allowed
Encourage Conversions: N/A
Area Develop. Agreements: No
Sub-Franchising Contracts: No
Expand In Territory: Yes
Space Needs: NR SF; N/A

SUPPORT & TRAINING PROVIDED:
Financial Assistance Provided: Yes(D)
Site Selection Assistance: N/A
Lease Negotiation Assistance: No
Co-Operative Advertising: No
Franchisee Assoc./Member: Yes/Yes
Size Of Corporate Staff: 21
On-Going Support: A,B,G,h,I
Training: 2 Weeks Memphis, TN.

SPECIFIC EXPANSION PLANS:
US: All United States
Canada: All Canada
Overseas: All Countries

<< >>

FURNITURE MEDIC OF CANADA
6540 Tomken Rd.
Mississauga, ON L5T 2E9 CANADA
Tel: (800) 263-5928 (905) 670-0000
Fax: (905) 670-0077
E-Mail: mgreenwood@svm.com
Web Site: www.furnituremedic.com
Mr. Murray Greenwood, Market Expansion Mgr.

The first franchise network of mobile furniture touch-up and restoration. Exclusive patented, environmentally conscious restoration techniques allow FURNITURE MEDIC to restore wood and furniture damage on-site for a fraction of replacement costs.

BACKGROUND:
Established: 1992; 1st Franchised: 1993
Franchised Units: 55
Company-Owned Units 0
Total Units: 55
Dist.: US-0; CAN-28; O'seas-0
North America: 8 Provinces
Density: 15 in ON, 5 in AB, 3 in PQ
Projected New Units (12 Months): 20
Qualifications: 2, 3, 1, 3, 3, 4
Registered: AB

FINANCIAL/TERMS:
Cash Investment: $20K (Can)
Total Investment: $28-40K
Minimum Net Worth: $50K
Fees: Franchise - $19.9K
Royalty - 7%; Ad. - 1%
Earnings Claim Statement: No
Term of Contract (Years): 5/5
Avg. # Of Employees: 1 FT
Passive Ownership: Not Allowed
Encourage Conversions: Yes
Area Develop. Agreements: No
Sub-Franchising Contracts: No
Expand In Territory: Yes
Space Needs: NR SF; HB

SUPPORT & TRAINING PROVIDED:
Financial Assistance Provided: Yes(D)
Site Selection Assistance: N/A
Lease Negotiation Assistance: N/A
Co-Operative Advertising: N/A
Franchisee Assoc./Member: Yes
Size Of Corporate Staff: 18
On-Going Support: B,C,D,G,h,I
Training: 2 Weeks Memphis, TN; 1 Week at Home Study Program.

SPECIFIC EXPANSION PLANS:
US: All United States
Canada: All Canada
Overseas: All Countries

<< >>

GUARDSMAN WOODPRO
4999 36th St. SE
Grand Rapids, MI 49512
Tel: (800) 496-6377 (616) 285-7877
Fax: (616) 285-7882
E-Mail: woodpro@valspar.com
Web Site: www.guardsman.com
Franchise Development

Partner and profit with a world leader. As a business unit of Lilly Industries, the largest manufacturer of furniture finishes in N. America, GUARDSMAN WOODPRO is the premier choice of residential and commercial customers alike for furniture repair and refinishing services. Lilly has been involved in the furniture industry for 130 years, supplying finishes, furniture care products and now furniture repair services. If you want to be in the furniture business, you want to be with us.

BACKGROUND:
Established: 1865; 1st Franchised: 1994
Franchised Units: 128
Company-Owned Units 0
Total Units: 128
Dist.: US-110; CAN-14; O'seas-0
North America: 36 States, 2 Provinces
Density: 9 in MI, 6 in OH, 6 in TX
Projected New Units (12 Months): 36
Qualifications: 4, 4, 4, 3, 5, 5
Registered: All States

FINANCIAL/TERMS:
Cash Investment: $10-25K
Total Investment: $7-25K
Minimum Net Worth: $50K
Fees: Franchise - $7K
Royalty - Fixed; Ad. - Fixed
Earnings Claim Statement: No
Term of Contract (Years): 5/5
Avg. # Of Employees: 1-3 FT, 1-2 PT
Passive Ownership: Discouraged
Encourage Conversions: Yes
Area Develop. Agreements: Yes/2-5 Yrs.
Sub-Franchising Contracts: Yes
Expand In Territory: Yes
Space Needs: NR SF; HB

SUPPORT & TRAINING PROVIDED:
Financial Assistance Provided: Yes(D)
Site Selection Assistance: N/A
Lease Negotiation Assistance: N/A
Co-Operative Advertising: Yes
Franchisee Assoc./Member: Yes/Yes

Size Of Corporate Staff: 80
On-Going Support: A,C,D,G,H,I
Training: 2 Weeks Grand Rapids, MI.
SPECIFIC EXPANSION PLANS:
US: All United States
Canada: All Canada
Overseas: All Countries

<< >>

Handyman CONNECTION®

HANDYMAN CONNECTION
227 Northland Blvd.
Cincinnati, OH 45246
Tel: (800) 466-5530 (513) 771-3003
Fax: (513) 771-6439
E-Mail: mbogert@handymanconnection.com
Web Site: www.handymanconnection.com
Mr. Matt Borgert, Dir. Franchise Sales

HANDYMAN CONNECTION specializes in the small to medium size home repair and remodeling industry. We offer a turnkey package that includes marketing, advertising and a complete training program. 90%of our franchise partners had NO handyman experience.

BACKGROUND: IFA MEMBER
Established: 1990; 1st Franchised: 1993
Franchised Units: 140
Company-Owned Units 4
Total Units: 144
Dist.: US-48; CAN-15; O'seas-0
North America: 35+ States
Density: 24 in CA, 7 in OH, 4 in TN
Projected New Units (12 Months): 20
Qualifications: 4, 3, 1, 2, 2, 4
Registered: NR
FINANCIAL/TERMS:
Cash Investment: $65-150K
Total Investment: $50-250K
Minimum Net Worth: $150K+
Fees: Franchise - $Varies
Royalty - 5%; Ad. - 2%
Earnings Claim Statement: No
Term of Contract (Years): 10/10
Avg. # Of Employees: 2 FT
Passive Ownership: Allowed
Encourage Conversions: N/A
Area Develop. Agreements: Yes/10
Sub-Franchising Contracts: No
Expand In Territory: Yes
Space Needs: 500-600 SF; FS, Industrial Warehouse
SUPPORT & TRAINING PROVIDED:
Financial Assistance Provided: Yes
Site Selection Assistance: No
Lease Negotiation Assistance: Yes
Co-Operative Advertising: No
Franchisee Assoc./Member: Yes/Yes
Size Of Corporate Staff: 10
On-Going Support: B,C,D,E,G,h,I
Training: 2 Weeks Flagship (Cincinnati, OH); 1 Week Franchisee Location.
SPECIFIC EXPANSION PLANS:
US: All United States
Canada: All Canada
Overseas: All Countries

<< >>

JET-BLACK SEALCOATING & REPAIR
25 West Cliff Rd., # 103
Burnsville, MN 55337
Tel: (888) 538-2525 (952) 890-8343
Fax: (952) 890-7022
E-Mail: hoiland@earthlink.net
Web Site: www.jet-black.com
Mr. Rick Clark, Franchise Development

We provide blacktop driveway sealcoating, hot-rubber crack and joint filling, heat-treat oil spots, grass edging and patching. We beautify and protect driveways.

BACKGROUND: IFA MEMBER
Established: 1988; 1st Franchised: 1993
Franchised Units: 106
Company-Owned Units 0
Total Units: 106
Dist.: US-106; CAN-0; O'seas-0
North America: 24 States
Density: NR
Projected New Units (12 Months): 80
Qualifications: 3, 3, 3, 3, 5, 5
Registered: All States
FINANCIAL/TERMS:
Cash Investment: $20K
Total Investment: $49K
Minimum Net Worth: $50K
Fees: Franchise - $15K
Royalty - 8%; Ad. - N/A
Earnings Claim Statement: Yes
Term of Contract (Years): 15/15
Avg. # Of Employees: 1 FT
Passive Ownership: Not Allowed
Encourage Conversions: No
Area Develop. Agreements: No
Sub-Franchising Contracts: No
Expand In Territory: Yes
Space Needs: NR SF; HB
SUPPORT & TRAINING PROVIDED:
Financial Assistance Provided: Yes(I)
Site Selection Assistance: Yes
Lease Negotiation Assistance: N/A
Co-Operative Advertising: Yes
Franchisee Assoc./Member: Yes
Size Of Corporate Staff: 3
On-Going Support: A,B,C,D,E,F,G,H
Training: 1 Week Burnsville, MN.
SPECIFIC EXPANSION PLANS:
US: All United States
Canada: All Canada
Overseas: No

<< >>

KITCHEN SOLVERS
401 Jay St.
La Crosse, WI 54601
Tel: (800) 845-6779 (608) 791-5516
Fax: (608) 784-2917
E-Mail: dave@kitchensolvers.com
Web Site: www.kitchensolvers.com
Mr. David Woggon, SVP Franchise Operations

Specialize or diversify... It's your option. '10 in 1' business concept offered by the most experienced kitchen remodeling franchise system in the United States. Home-based business with no inventory required. Complete start-up and on-going marketing program, experienced technical support.

BACKGROUND:
Established: 1982; 1st Franchised: 1984
Franchised Units: 114
Company-Owned Units 3
Total Units: 117
Dist.: US-114; CAN-3; O'seas-0
North America: 31 States, 4 Provinces
Density: 12 in WI, 11 in IA, 12 in IL
Projected New Units (12 Months): 15
Qualifications: 2, 2, 2, 2, , 5
Registered: CA,FL,IL,IN,MD,MI,MN,ND,OR,SD,VA,WA,WI,AB
FINANCIAL/TERMS:
Cash Investment: $25K
Total Investment: $27.8-40K
Minimum Net Worth: $NR
Fees: Franchise - $14K
Royalty - 6; Ad. - 1%
Earnings Claim Statement: No
Term of Contract (Years): 10/10
Avg. # Of Employees: 1 FT
Passive Ownership: Not Allowed
Encourage Conversions: Yes

Area Develop. Agreements: No
Sub-Franchising Contracts: No
Expand In Territory: Yes
Space Needs: N/A SF; HB

SUPPORT & TRAINING PROVIDED:
Financial Assistance Provided: Yes(D)
Site Selection Assistance: N/A
Lease Negotiation Assistance: N/A
Co-Operative Advertising: N/A
Franchisee Assoc./Member: Yes/Yes
Size Of Corporate Staff: 8
On-Going Support: a,B,C,D,G,h,I
Training: 2 Weeks LaCrosse, WI Corporate Headquarters; 3 Days Houston, TX.

SPECIFIC EXPANSION PLANS:
US: All United States
Canada: All Canada
Overseas: No

<< >>

KITCHEN TUNE-UP

813 Circle Dr.
Aberdeen, SD 57401-2670
Tel: (800) 333-6385 (605) 225-4049
Fax: (605) 225-1371
E-Mail: craig@kitchentuneup.com
Web Site: www.kitchentuneup.com
Mr. Craig Green, Franchise Acquisitions Dir.

America's #1 home improvement franchise. We offer 'Kitchen Solutions For Any Budget.' Cabinet and wood restoration, cabinet refacing and custom cabinetry, along with shelf lining, replacement hardware and cabinet organization systems. Excellent initial and on-going training and support. High residential and commercial potential. Home-based and retail locations available.

BACKGROUND: IFA MEMBER
Established: 1975; 1st Franchised: 1988
Franchised Units: 291
Company-Owned Units 0
Total Units: 291
Dist.: US-290; CAN-1; O'seas-0
North America: 35 States, 1 Province
Density: 13 in CA, 10 in IL, 7 in CO
Projected New Units (12 Months): 20
Qualifications: 3, 4, 2, 2, 4, 4
Registered: All States Except HI,RI

FINANCIAL/TERMS:
Cash Investment: $18-25K
Total Investment: $28-35K
Minimum Net Worth: $N/A
Fees: Franchise - $16.5K
Royalty - 4.5-7%; Ad. - 0%
Earnings Claim Statement: Yes
Term of Contract (Years): 10/10
Avg. # Of Employees: 1-2 FT, As Needed PT
Passive Ownership: Discouraged
Encourage Conversions: Yes
Area Develop. Agreements: Yes/10
Sub-Franchising Contracts: No
Expand In Territory: Yes
Space Needs: 500-2,500 SF; FS, SF, SC, HB

SUPPORT & TRAINING PROVIDED:
Financial Assistance Provided: Yes(D)
Site Selection Assistance: Yes
Lease Negotiation Assistance: Yes
Co-Operative Advertising: No
Franchisee Assoc./Member: Yes
Size Of Corporate Staff: 8
On-Going Support: A,B,C,D,E,G,H,I
Training: 2 Weeks Pre-Training Home Study; 6-10 Days Corporate Office; 12 Wks. Home Study; On-Going.

SPECIFIC EXPANSION PLANS:
US: All United States
Canada: All Canada
Overseas: No

<< >>

MARBLELIFE

805 W. North Carrier Pkwy., # 220
Grand Prairie, TX 75050-1044
Tel: (800) 627-4569 (972) 623-0500
Fax: (972) 623-0220
E-Mail: rcross@marblelife.com
Web Site: www.marblelife.com
Mr. Rick Cross, VP Operations

Specializes in the restoration, preservation and maintenance services for natural stones and other surfaces.

BACKGROUND: IFA MEMBER
Established: 1987; 1st Franchised: 1993
Franchised Units: 49
Company-Owned Units 0
Total Units: 49
Dist.: US-39; CAN-1; O'seas-9
North America: 38 States, 1 Province
Density: 3 in TX, 3 in CA, 3 in FL
Projected New Units (12 Months): 10
Qualifications: 4, 4, 2, 2, 2, 4
Registered: CA,FL,IL,NY,VA,WI

FINANCIAL/TERMS:
Cash Investment: $50K+
Total Investment: $15-100K
Minimum Net Worth: $Varies/Terr.
Fees: Franchise - $5K/100K pop.
Royalty - 6%; Ad. - 2%
Earnings Claim Statement: No
Term of Contract (Years): 10/10
Avg. # Of Employees: 3+ FT
Passive Ownership: Discouraged
Encourage Conversions: Yes
Area Develop. Agreements: Yes
Sub-Franchising Contracts: No
Expand In Territory: No
Space Needs: N/A SF; N/A

SUPPORT & TRAINING PROVIDED:
Financial Assistance Provided: Yes(I)
Site Selection Assistance: N/A
Lease Negotiation Assistance: No
Co-Operative Advertising: No
Franchisee Assoc./Member: Yes/Yes
Size Of Corporate Staff: 12
On-Going Support: C,D,E,G,H,I
Training: 2 Weeks at Grand Prairie, TX.

SPECIFIC EXPANSION PLANS:
US: All United States
Canada: All Canada
Overseas: All Europe and Middle East

<< >>

MIRACLE METHOD BATH & KITCHEN RESTORATION

4239 N. Nevada, # 115
Colorado Springs, CO 80907
Tel: (800) 444-8827 (719) 594-9196
Fax: (719) 594-9282
E-Mail: sales@miraclemethod.com
Web Site: www.miraclemethod.com
Mr. Paul Leonard, Vice President

Make money in the growing remodeling industry by running your own bath and kitchen refinishing business. Save customers money by refinishing instead of replacing. Bathtubs, tile, showers, counter tops and more. Excellent income potential!

BACKGROUND: IFA MEMBER
Established: 1979; 1st Franchised: 1980
Franchised Units: 100
Company-Owned Units 0
Total Units: 100
Dist.: US-75; CAN-0; O'seas-25

North America: 30 States
Density: 20 in CA, 5 in TX, 3 in CT
Projected New Units (12 Months): 12+
Qualifications: 3, 5, 4, 3, 3, 5
Registered: CA,FL,WA

FINANCIAL/TERMS:
Cash Investment: $13-15K
Total Investment: $20-30K
Minimum Net Worth: $20K
Fees: Franchise - $15K
Royalty - 5%; Ad. - 3%
Earnings Claim Statement: Yes
Term of Contract (Years): 5
Avg. # Of Employees: 1-5 FT & PT
Passive Ownership: Discouraged
Encourage Conversions: Yes
Area Develop. Agreements: No
Sub-Franchising Contracts: Yes
Expand In Territory: No
Space Needs: N/A SF; HB

SUPPORT & TRAINING PROVIDED:
Financial Assistance Provided: Yes(D)
Site Selection Assistance: No
Lease Negotiation Assistance: No
Co-Operative Advertising: Yes
Franchisee Assoc./Member: Yes
Size Of Corporate Staff: 4
On-Going Support: C,D,G,H,I
Training: 1 Week at Headquarters Location.

SPECIFIC EXPANSION PLANS:
US: All United States
Canada: All Canada
Overseas: All Countries

<< >>

Mr Appliance
EXPERT APPLIANCE REPAIR

MR. APPLIANCE CORPORATION
P.O. Box 3146
Waco, TX 76707
Tel: (800) 290-1422 (254) 745-2439
Fax: (800) 209-7621
E-Mail: mhawkins@dwyergroup.com
Web Site: www.mrappliance.com
Mr. Mike Hawkins, VP Franchising

Full-service appliance repair service for all brands; residential and commercial business.

BACKGROUND: IFA MEMBER
Established: 1996; 1st Franchised: 1997
Franchised Units: 39
Company-Owned Units 0
Total Units: 39
Dist.: US-39; CAN-0; O'seas-0
North America: 15 States
Density: 9 in TX, 4 in FL, 2 in CA
Projected New Units (12 Months): 48
Qualifications: 4, 4, 4, 2, 3, 4
Registered: All States

FINANCIAL/TERMS:
Cash Investment: $NR
Total Investment: $NR
Minimum Net Worth: $Varies
Fees: Franchise - $13.5K
Royalty - 3-6%; Ad. - 2%
Earnings Claim Statement: No
Term of Contract (Years): 10/10
Avg. # Of Employees: Depends on Sales
Passive Ownership: Discouraged
Encourage Conversions: Yes
Area Develop. Agreements: No
Sub-Franchising Contracts: Yes
Expand In Territory: Yes
Space Needs: NR SF; N/A

SUPPORT & TRAINING PROVIDED:
Financial Assistance Provided: Yes(I)
Site Selection Assistance: N/A
Lease Negotiation Assistance: N/A
Co-Operative Advertising: N/A
Franchisee Assoc./Member: No
Size Of Corporate Staff: 4
On-Going Support: A,C,D,E,F,G,H,I
Training: 1 Week Waco, TX.

SPECIFIC EXPANSION PLANS:
US: All United States
Canada: Master Franchise
Overseas: Master Franchise Only

<< >>

Top 50

MR. ELECTRIC CORP.
P.O. Box 3146
Waco, TX 76707
Tel: (800) 805-0575 (254) 745-2439
Fax: (800) 209-7621
E-Mail: mhawkins@dwyergroup.com
Web Site: www.mrelectric.com
Mr. Mike Hawkins, VP Franchising

Serving the electrical repair needs of residential and light commercial establishments, in addition to offering other electrical products to the 'same user,' including such items as surcharge protectors, communication and data cabling, ceiling fans, decorative light fixtures, security and landscape lighting, etc.

BACKGROUND: IFA MEMBER
Established: 1994; 1st Franchised: 1994
Franchised Units: 117
Company-Owned Units 0
Total Units: 117
Dist.: US-109; CAN-4; O'seas-4
North America: 37 States, 2 Province
Density: 11 in CA, 5 in IL, 4 in TX
Projected New Units (12 Months): 18
Qualifications: 3, 2, 5, 3, 2, 4
Registered: All States

FINANCIAL/TERMS:
Cash Investment: $30.2-68K
Total Investment: $64-157K
Minimum Net Worth: $75K
Fees: Franchise - $19.5K
Royalty - 3-6%; Ad. - 2%
Earnings Claim Statement: No
Term of Contract (Years): 10/5
Avg. # Of Employees: 3 FT, 1 PT
Passive Ownership: Discouraged
Encourage Conversions: Yes
Area Develop. Agreements: No
Sub-Franchising Contracts: Yes
Expand In Territory: Yes
Space Needs: 500-1,000 SF; FS, HB

SUPPORT & TRAINING PROVIDED:
Financial Assistance Provided: Yes(B)
Site Selection Assistance: N/A
Lease Negotiation Assistance: N/A
Co-Operative Advertising: No
Franchisee Assoc./Member: No
Size Of Corporate Staff: 8
On-Going Support: C,D,E,G,h,I
Training: 5 Business Days at Corporate Offices; 3 Business Days On-Site in Business.

SPECIFIC EXPANSION PLANS:
US: All United States
Canada: Not This Year
Overseas: Most Latin American and Asian Countries

MR. HANDYMAN
3948 Ranchero Dr.
Ann Arbor, MI 48108-2775
Tel: (800) 289-4600 (734) 822-6800
Fax: (734) 822-6888
E-Mail: info@mrhandyman.com
Web Site: www.mrhandyman.com
Mr. Steve Olsen, Franchise Director

Seeking a business with tremendous consumer demand? Stop right here. MR. HANDYMAN is the solution to today's fix-it problems for millions of time-starved families. An affordable investment gives you a franchise catering to 100 million homeowners and commercial customers needing property maintenance and repair. Technicians do the work. You manage the business.

BACKGROUND: IFA MEMBER
Established: 2000; 1st Franchised: 2000
Franchised Units: 10
Company-Owned Units 0
Total Units: 10
Dist.: US-10; CAN-0; O'seas-0
North America: 10 States
Density: NR
Projected New Units (12 Months): 25
Qualifications: 3, 3, 1, 3, 4, 5
Registered: CA,FL,IL,IN,MD,MI,MN,NY, OR,RI,VA,WA,WI,DC

FINANCIAL/TERMS:
Cash Investment: $10-20K
Total Investment: $47-76K
Minimum Net Worth: $150K
Fees: Franchise - $6.9K
Royalty - 7%; Ad. - 0%
Earnings Claim Statement: No
Term of Contract (Years): 10/10
Avg. # Of Employees: 6 FT
Passive Ownership: Discouraged
Encourage Conversions: Yes
Area Develop. Agreements: No
Sub-Franchising Contracts: No
Expand In Territory: Yes
Space Needs: 200 SF; HB

SUPPORT & TRAINING PROVIDED:
Financial Assistance Provided: Yes(I)
Site Selection Assistance: N/A
Lease Negotiation Assistance: N/A
Co-Operative Advertising: N/A
Franchisee Assoc./Member: No
Size Of Corporate Staff: 15
On-Going Support: C,D,E,G,h,I
Training: 4 Days Home Office; 1 Day Field; 6 Months Right Start Program; 2 Days Franchise Location.

SPECIFIC EXPANSION PLANS:
US: All United States
Canada: All Canada
Overseas: All Countries

<< >>

PERMACRETE SYSTEMS
21 Williams Ave.
Dartmouth, NS B3B 1X3 CANADA
Tel: (800) 565-5325 (902) 468-1700
Fax: (902) 468-7474
E-Mail: permacrete@aol.com
Ms. Colleen Cole, Franchise Sales

Provision of services in the restoration of concrete surfaces and structures, using products and following a repair system prescribed and developed by the franchisor. These crack repair and concrete specialists are encouraged to expand and diversify their business in any area where concrete products are used or repairs are required.

BACKGROUND:
Established: 1980; 1st Franchised: 1990
Franchised Units: 19
Company-Owned Units 2
Total Units: 21
Dist.: US-4; CAN-16; O'seas-1
North America: 3 States, 6 Provinces
Density: 7 in NS, 4 in NB, 2 in AB
Projected New Units (12 Months): 6
Qualifications: 3, 3, 3, 2, 5, 5
Registered: AB

FINANCIAL/TERMS:
Cash Investment: $18.5-25K
Total Investment: $18.5-35K
Minimum Net Worth: $N/A
Fees: Franchise - $18.5K
Royalty - 5%; Ad. - 0%
Earnings Claim Statement: Yes
Term of Contract (Years): 5/5
Avg. # Of Employees: 1 FT, 1 PT
Passive Ownership: Discouraged
Encourage Conversions: N/A
Area Develop. Agreements: No
Sub-Franchising Contracts: No
Expand In Territory: Yes
Space Needs: NR SF; HB, Garage Storage

SUPPORT & TRAINING PROVIDED:
Financial Assistance Provided: Yes(I)
Site Selection Assistance: N/A
Lease Negotiation Assistance: No
Co-Operative Advertising: Yes
Franchisee Assoc./Member: No
Size Of Corporate Staff: 7
On-Going Support: A,C,D,G,H,I
Training: 2 Weeks Minimum at Head Office in Dartmouth, NS.

SPECIFIC EXPANSION PLANS:
US: All United States
Canada: Exclude PI,NS,NB
Overseas: Great Britain

<< >>

PERMA-GLAZE
1638 S. Research Loop Rd., # 160
Tucson, AZ 85710
Tel: (800) 332-7397 (520) 722-9718
Fax: (520) 296-4393
E-Mail: permaglaze@permaglaze.com
Web Site: www.permaglaze.com
Mr. Dale R. Young, President/CEO

PERMA GLAZE specializes in multi-surface restoration of bathtubs, sinks, countertops, appliances, porcelain, metal, acrylics, cultured marble and more. PERMA GLAZE licensed representatives provide valued services to hotels/motels, private residences, apartments, schools, hospitals, contractors, property managers and many others.

BACKGROUND: IFA MEMBER
Established: 1978; 1st Franchised: 1981
Franchised Units: 177
Company-Owned Units 1
Total Units: 178
Dist.: US-124; CAN-3; O'seas-51
North America: 36 States, 1 Province
Density: 15 in CA, 7 in AZ, 6 in PA
Projected New Units (12 Months): 20
Qualifications: 4, 2, 1, 3, 4, 3
Registered: CA,IL,IN,MD,MI,MN,NY,ND ,OR,SD,VA,WA,WI

FINANCIAL/TERMS:
Cash Investment: $2.5-3K
Total Investment: $22-25K+
Minimum Net Worth: $21.5K
Fees: Franchise - $21.5K+
Royalty - 6/5/4%/$200 Min.; Ad. - NR
Earnings Claim Statement: Yes
Term of Contract (Years): 10/10
Avg. # Of Employees: 1 FT
Passive Ownership: Not Allowed
Encourage Conversions: N/A
Area Develop. Agreements: Yes/10
Sub-Franchising Contracts: No
Expand In Territory: No
Space Needs: N/A SF; HB

SUPPORT & TRAINING PROVIDED:
Financial Assistance Provided: No
Site Selection Assistance: Yes
Lease Negotiation Assistance: N/A
Co-Operative Advertising: N/A
Franchisee Assoc./Member: No

Size Of Corporate Staff: 6
On-Going Support: C,D,G,H,I
Training: 5 Days Tucson, AZ.

SPECIFIC EXPANSION PLANS:

US: All United States
Canada: All Canada
Overseas: All Countries

<< >>

RE-BATH CORPORATION

1055 S. Country Club Dr.
Mesa, AZ 85210-4613
Tel: (800) 426-4573 (480) 844-1575
Fax: (480) 833-7199
E-Mail: jhausner@re-bath.com
Web Site: www.re-bath.com
Mr. John Hausner, VP Sales & Marketing

Acrylic tubs, shower bases, and wall systems that retrofit old ones. We have innovated the one day bath remodeling program.

BACKGROUND:

Established: 1979; 1st Franchised: 1991
Franchised Units: 112
Company-Owned Units 1
Total Units: 113
Dist.: US-111; CAN-1; O'seas-1
North America: 39 States, 1 Province
Density: 11 in NY, 10 in PA, 7 in OH
Projected New Units (12 Months): 25
Qualifications: 4, 4, 3, 3, 4, 5
Registered: All Except ND,SD

FINANCIAL/TERMS:

Cash Investment: $6.5-40K
Total Investment: $33-150K
Minimum Net Worth: $100K
Fees: Franchise - $3.5-40K
Royalty - $25/Unit; Ad. - 0%
Earnings Claim Statement: No
Term of Contract (Years): 7/7
Avg. # Of Employees: 3 FT
Passive Ownership: Discouraged
Encourage Conversions: NR
Area Develop. Agreements: No
Sub-Franchising Contracts: No
Expand In Territory: Yes
Space Needs: 200 SF; SF, Showroom

SUPPORT & TRAINING PROVIDED:

Financial Assistance Provided: No
Site Selection Assistance: Yes
Lease Negotiation Assistance: Yes
Co-Operative Advertising: Yes
Franchisee Assoc./Member: Yes/Yes
Size Of Corporate Staff: 14
On-Going Support: C,D,E,F,G,h,I
Training: 9 Days Pheonix, AZ.

SPECIFIC EXPANSION PLANS:

US: All United States
Canada: All Canada
Overseas: No

<< >>

SCREEN MACHINE, THE

1522A Second Ave.
Walnut Creek, CA 94596
Tel: (877) 505-1985 (925) 256-9981
Fax: (925) 256-9983
E-Mail: screens@screen-machine.com
Web Site: www.screen-machine.com
Ms. Suzy Schantz, Vice President

A mobile repair and replacement service for window and door screens. Unique mobile workshop complete with all tools, materials and supplies including a portable generator and chop saw, allows franchisees to quickly take care of customers screen repairs at the customer's home. Very limited competition. High profit margins, low material costs.

BACKGROUND:

Established: 1986; 1st Franchised: 1988
Franchised Units: 22
Company-Owned Units 1
Total Units: 23
Dist.: US-23; CAN-0; O'seas-0
North America: 1 State
Density: 23 in CA
Projected New Units (12 Months): 5
Qualifications: 3, 2, 1, 1, 4, 4
Registered: CA, FL, VA

FINANCIAL/TERMS:

Cash Investment: $20-30K
Total Investment: $44-73K
Minimum Net Worth: $50K
Fees: Franchise - $25K
Royalty - 5%; Ad. - 0%
Earnings Claim Statement: No
Term of Contract (Years): 10/10
Avg. # Of Employees: 1 FT, 3 PT
Passive Ownership: Discouraged
Encourage Conversions: Yes
Area Develop. Agreements: Yes/10
Sub-Franchising Contracts: Yes
Expand In Territory: Yes
Space Needs: 800 SF; HB, Warehouse

SUPPORT & TRAINING PROVIDED:

Financial Assistance Provided: Yes(I)
Site Selection Assistance: N/A
Lease Negotiation Assistance: No
Co-Operative Advertising: No
Franchisee Assoc./Member: No
Size Of Corporate Staff: 3
On-Going Support: c,d,G,h,I
Training: 7 Days Walnut Creek, CA.

SPECIFIC EXPANSION PLANS:

US: SE, SW
Canada: No
Overseas: No

SCREENMOBILE, THE

72-050A Corporate Way
Thousand Palms, CA 92276
Tel: (909) 593-5775
Fax: (909) 593-3119
E-Mail: smcorp@screenmobile.com
Web Site: www.screenmobile.com
Mr. Monty M. Walker, President

SCREENMOBILE provides quality window and door screens. SCREENMOBILE is a mobile outdoor service business offering custom design and installations of high-quality screening products right at the job site on the very first visit.

BACKGROUND:

Established: 1982; 1st Franchised: 1984
Franchised Units: 52
Company-Owned Units 1
Total Units: 53
Dist.: US-56; CAN-0; O'seas-0
North America: 15 States
Density: CA, AZ, CO
Projected New Units (12 Months): 5
Qualifications: 3, 1, 1, 1, 3, 5
Registered: CA,IN

FINANCIAL/TERMS:

Cash Investment: $25K
Total Investment: $56.3K
Minimum Net Worth: $50K
Fees: Franchise - $12.3K
Royalty - 5%; Ad. - 0%
Earnings Claim Statement: No
Term of Contract (Years): 5/5
Avg. # Of Employees: 1 FT
Passive Ownership: Not Allowed
Encourage Conversions: No

Area Develop. Agreements: No
Sub-Franchising Contracts: No
Expand In Territory: Yes
Space Needs: 400 SF; HB

SUPPORT & TRAINING PROVIDED:
Financial Assistance Provided: Yes(I)
Site Selection Assistance: Yes
Lease Negotiation Assistance: No
Co-Operative Advertising: No
Franchisee Assoc./Member: No
Size Of Corporate Staff: 6
On-Going Support: C,D,E,F,G,H
Training: 1 Week Palm Springs, CA.

SPECIFIC EXPANSION PLANS:
US: All United States
Canada: No
Overseas: No

SURFACE DOCTOR

4239 N. Nevada Ave., # 115
Colorado Springs, CO 80907-4380
Tel: (800) 735-5055 (719) 594-4112
Fax: (719) 594-9282
E-Mail: sales@surfacedoctor.com
Web Site: www.surfacedoctor.com
Mr. Charles Pistor, President

SURFACE DOCTOR provides an alternative to conventional remodeling, saving our customers up to 70% over the cost of conventional renovation. Services include: cabinet refacing, resurfacing of cabinets, counter tops, appliances and bathroom fixtures. We provide services to both residential and a variety of commercial markets. SURFACE DOCTOR can give almost any fixture a new look, for a fraction of the cost of replacement.

BACKGROUND: IFA MEMBER
Established: 1993; 1st Franchised: 1994
Franchised Units: 70
Company-Owned Units 0
Total Units: 70
Dist.: US-84; CAN-6; O'seas-3
North America: 42 States, 5 Provinces
Density: 7 in NC, 6 in GA, 5 in FL
Projected New Units (12 Months): 50
Qualifications: 3, 3, 3, 3, 3, 3
Registered: All States

FINANCIAL/TERMS:
Cash Investment: $20-30K
Total Investment: $20-30K
Minimum Net Worth: $N/A
Fees: Franchise - $19.5K
Royalty - 6%; Ad. - 2%
Earnings Claim Statement: No
Term of Contract (Years): 10/10
Avg. # Of Employees: 5 FT
Passive Ownership: Not Allowed
Encourage Conversions: N/A
Area Develop. Agreements: No
Sub-Franchising Contracts: No
Expand In Territory: Yes
Space Needs: 1,000 +/- SF; Small Office Warehouse

SUPPORT & TRAINING PROVIDED:
Financial Assistance Provided: No
Site Selection Assistance: No
Lease Negotiation Assistance: No
Co-Operative Advertising: No
Franchisee Assoc./Member: No
Size Of Corporate Staff: 55
On-Going Support: G,H,I
Training: 2 Weeks Charlotte, NC.

SPECIFIC EXPANSION PLANS:
US: All United States
Canada: All Canada
Overseas: All Countries

SURFACE SPECIALISTS SYSTEMS

5168 Country Club Dr.
High Ridge, MO 63049
Tel: (888) 376-4468 (314) 376-4468
Fax: (314) 376-8889
Web Site: www.surfacespecialists.com
Mr. John G. Lucas, President

SURFACE SPECIALISTS franchisees specialize in repairing and refinishing kitchen and bathroom surfaces. These surfaces include acrylic spas, fiberglass tubs and showers, porcelain tubs, cultured marble, Formica countertops, and PVC/ABS (plastic). Become a factory authorized warranty service provider for more than 34 manufacturers nationwide. We are the only franchisor in the industry providing full service to the new construction market. Excellent opportunity of high profit potential at low investment.

BACKGROUND:
Established: 1981; 1st Franchised: 1982
Franchised Units: 31
Company-Owned Units 0
Total Units: 31
Dist.: US-26; CAN-0; O'seas-0
North America: 16 States
Density: 5 in MI, 4 in WI, 2 in FL
Projected New Units (12 Months): 4
Qualifications: 4, 3, 2, 3, 3, 5
Registered: FL,IL,MI,DC

FINANCIAL/TERMS:
Cash Investment: $10-15K
Total Investment: $13.9-42K
Minimum Net Worth: $90K
Fees: Franchise - $9.5-30K
Royalty - 5%; Ad. - N/A
Earnings Claim Statement: No
Term of Contract (Years): 10/10
Avg. # Of Employees: 2 FT, 2 PT
Passive Ownership: Discouraged
Encourage Conversions: Yes
Area Develop. Agreements: Yes
Sub-Franchising Contracts: No
Expand In Territory: Yes
Space Needs: 300 SF; HB

SUPPORT & TRAINING PROVIDED:
Financial Assistance Provided: Yes(D)
Site Selection Assistance: N/A
Lease Negotiation Assistance: N/A
Co-Operative Advertising: No
Franchisee Assoc./Member: No
Size Of Corporate Staff: 4
On-Going Support: B,c,D,G,h,I
Training: 3 Weeks High Ridge, MO.

SPECIFIC EXPANSION PLANS:
US: All United States
Canada: No
Overseas: No

<< >>

UBUILDIT

12006 98th Ave., # 200
Kirkland, WA 98034
Tel: (800) 992-4357 (425) 821-6200
Fax: (425) 821-6876
E-Mail: franchiseinfo@ubuildit.com
Web Site: www.ubuildit.com
Mr. Kurt Kempfer, SVP Franchise Development

For over 10 years, the UBuildIt system has been assisting homeowners to act as their own general contractor for both remodeling and new home construction. By teaming a homeowner with a construction professional, the project is efficiently completed while avoiding the common pitfalls and saving thousands. Providing subcontractors, bank financing, site visits, etc., UBuildIt is a perfect complementary service for the building professional or entrepreneur looking for a huge untapped niche.

BACKGROUND:
Established: 1988; 1st Franchised: 1998
Franchised Units: 44
Company-Owned Units 0
Total Units: 44
Dist.: US-44; CAN-0; O'seas-0
North America: 18 States
Density: 12 in WA
Projected New Units (12 Months): 30
Qualifications: 4, 5, 4, 3, 4, 5
Registered: CA,IN,MD,MN,VA,WA

FINANCIAL/TERMS:
Cash Investment: $40.1-106.6K
Total Investment: $40.1-106.6K
Minimum Net Worth: $100K
Fees: Franchise - $25K
Royalty - 5-7%/$300;Ad. - 2%/$50/Mo.
Earnings Claim Statement: No
Term of Contract (Years): 10/10
Avg. # Of Employees: 1 FT, 1 PT
Passive Ownership: Not Allowed
Encourage Conversions: Yes
Area Develop. Agreements: No
Sub-Franchising Contracts: No
Expand In Territory: No
Space Needs: 400 SF; Class B Office

SUPPORT & TRAINING PROVIDED:
Financial Assistance Provided: No
Site Selection Assistance: No
Lease Negotiation Assistance: No
Co-Operative Advertising: Yes
Franchisee Assoc./Member: No
Size Of Corporate Staff: 7
On-Going Support: C,D,E,H,I
Training: 2 Weeks Seattle, WA.

SPECIFIC EXPANSION PLANS:
US: All United States
Canada: All Canada
Overseas: No

<< >>

WISE CRACKS RESTORATIONS

2 Lakeside Pl., # 9
Halifax, NS B3T 1L7 CANADA
Tel: (800) 587-7325 (902) 876-8480
Fax: (902) 876-8863
Web Site: www.wisecraksrestoration.com
Ms. Andrea Mackey, President

Foundation and concrete repair specialists.

BACKGROUND:
Established: 1991; 1st Franchised: 1994
Franchised Units: 10
Company-Owned Units 2
Total Units: 12
Dist.: US-0; CAN-10; O'seas-0
North America: NR
Density: NR
Projected New Units (12 Months): 3
Registered: NR

FINANCIAL/TERMS:
Cash Investment: $15-30K
Total Investment: $15-30K
Minimum Net Worth: $15K
Fees: Franchise - $15K/Dwelling
Royalty - 4.5%; Ad. - Co-op
Earnings Claim Statement: Yes
Term of Contract (Years): 5/5
Avg. # Of Employees: 1 FT, 1 PT
Passive Ownership: Discouraged
Encourage Conversions: N/A
Area Develop. Agreements: No
Sub-Franchising Contracts: No
Expand In Territory: No
Space Needs: N/A SF; HB

SUPPORT & TRAINING PROVIDED:
Financial Assistance Provided: No
Site Selection Assistance: N/A
Lease Negotiation Assistance: N/A
Co-Operative Advertising: Yes
Franchisee Assoc./Member: No
Size Of Corporate Staff: 5
On-Going Support: a,B,C,D,E,F,G,H,I
Training: 1 Week at Head Office.

SPECIFIC EXPANSION PLANS:
US: NR
Canada: All Canada
Overseas: No

<< >>

XTERIOR EXPERTS

9521 Camelot St.
Pickerington, OH 43147
Tel: (614) 860-1985
Fax: (614) 575-9801
E-Mail: factorydirectohio@yahoo.com
Web Site: www.xteriorexpertsofohio.com
Mr. Michael Pirwitz, President

We provide a unique opportunity in the exterior home improvement industry. Low cash investment with great returns. From advertising and sales to installation, we have a turn-key system to manage your franchise. We offer vinyl/wood fences and various sunrooms. No construction experience necessary to excel in this $12 billion market. We are the only franchisor to offer vinyl/wood decks, fences and sunrooms in a complete package. Excellent profit potential.

BACKGROUND:
Established: 1999; 1st Franchised: 2002
Franchised Units: 0
Company-Owned Units 1
Total Units: 1
Dist.: US-1; CAN-0; O'seas-0
North America: 1 State
Density: 1 in OH
Projected New Units (12 Months): 10
Qualifications: 5, 5, 4, 2, 3, 5
Registered: None

FINANCIAL/TERMS:
Cash Investment: $20-30K
Total Investment: $30-45K
Minimum Net Worth: $75K
Fees: Franchise - $12-14.5K
Royalty - 5; Ad. - N/A
Earnings Claim Statement: Yes
Term of Contract (Years): 10/10
Avg. # Of Employees: 2 FT, 1 PT
Passive Ownership: Not Allowed
Encourage Conversions: Yes
Area Develop. Agreements: No
Sub-Franchising Contracts: Yes
Expand In Territory: Yes
Space Needs: 200 SF; SF, HB

SUPPORT & TRAINING PROVIDED:
Financial Assistance Provided: No
Site Selection Assistance: Yes
Lease Negotiation Assistance: No
Co-Operative Advertising: Yes
Franchisee Assoc./Member: No
Size Of Corporate Staff: 5
On-Going Support: C,D,E,F,G,H,I
Training: 3 Weeks Columbus, OH.

SPECIFIC EXPANSION PLANS:
US: Midwest
Canada: No
Overseas: No

<< >>

SUPPLEMENTAL LISTING OF FRANCHISORS

A-1 CONCRETE LEVELING, 1 Cascade Plz., # 2100, Akron, OH 44308 ; (800) 675-3835 (330) 848-1804; (330) 253-1261

AMERICAN CONCRETE RAISING, 916 Westwood Ave., Addison, IL 60101 ; (630) 543-5775; (630) 543-5930

AMERICAN RESTORATION SERVICES, 2061 Monongahela Ave., Pittsburgh, PA 15218 ; (800) 245-1617 (412) 351-7100; (412) 351-2544

AMERLINK, P.O. Box 669, Battleboro, NC 27809 ; (800) 872-4254 (252) 977-2545; (252) 442-6900

BASEMENT REFINISHING SYSTEMS, 1 Owens Corning Pkwy., Toledo, OH 43659 ; (419) 248-6091; (419) 321-1091

BATH GENIE, 20 River St., Marlboro, MA 01752 ; (800) 255-8827 (508) 481-8338; (508) 624-6444

C. G. I., 7111-7115 Ohms Ln., Minneapolis, MN 55439 ; (800) 328-6347 (612) 835-1338; (612) 835-1395

CASTART, 1041 E. Miles St., Tucson, AZ 85719 ; (800) 871-8838 (520) 623-8858; (520) 670-0062

CERTA PROPAINTERS, 150 Green Tree Rd., # 1003, Oaks, PA 19456-0836 ; (800) 452-3782 (610) 650-9999; (610) 650-9997

CERTA PROPAINTERS OF CANADA, 5397 Eglinton Ave. W., # 109, Toronto, ON M9C 5K6 CANADA; (888) 295-3555 (416) 620-4600; (800) 446-6840

COLLEGE PRO PAINTERS, 341 Broadway, Cambridge, MA 02139 ; (888) 427-7672 (617) 576-6822; (617) 576-6827

DOORS UNLIMITED, 301 W. Hunting Park Ave., # B, Philadelphia, PA 19140-2697 ; (800) 338-5330 (215) 455-2100; (215) 843-4066

DRY-B-LO-DESIGNER DECK DRAIN SYSTEM, 475 Tribble Gap Rd., # B, Cumming, GA 30040 ; (800) 437-9256 (770) 781-4754; (770) 886-7408

ELDORADO STONE, P.O. Box 489, Carnation, WA 98014 ; (800) 925-1491 (425) 333-6722; (425) 333-4755

ELEVATORS ETC., 6802 Ringgold Rd., Chattanooga, TN 37412 ; (800) 451-8336 (423) 267-5438; (423) 265-7477

EPMARK, 6277 Riverside Dr., Dublin, OH 43017-5067 ; (800) 783-3838 (614) 761-1010; (614) 761-1155

EVERDRY WATERPROOFING, 365 Highland Rd. E., Macedonia, OH 44056 (800) 383-7379 (330) 467-1055; (330) 468-3231

HONKA HOMES USA, 35715 US Hwy. 40, # D-303, Evergreen, CO 80439 ; (877) 874-6652 (303) 679-0568; (303) 679-0641

IDRS, 152 SE Fifth Ave., Hillsboro, OR 97123 ; (800) 779-1357 (503) 693-1619; (503) 693-1993

INSULATED DRY ROOF SYSTEMS, 152 SE 5th Ave., Hillsboro, OR 97123 (800) 779-1357 (503) 693-1619; (503) 693-1993

JET-BLACK SEALCOATING & REPAIR, 25 West Cliff Rd., # 103, Burnsville, MN 55337 ; (888) 538-2525 (952) 890-8343; (952) 890-7022

K.T.U. WORLDWIDE, 813 Circle Dr., Aberdeen, SD 57401-2670 ; (800) 333-6385 (605) 225-4049; (605) 225-1305

KITCHEN WIZARDS, 1020 N. University Parks Dr., p.o. Box 3146, Waco, TX 76707 ; (800) 893-6777 (254) 745-2488; (254) 745-5073

KOTT KOATINGS, 27161 Burbank St., Foothill Ranch, CA 92610 ; (800) 452-6161 (949) 770-5055; (949) 770-5101

LINC CORPORATION, THE, 4 Northshore Center, 106 Isabella, Pittsburgh, PA 15212 ; (412) 359-2197; (412) 321-3809

LUXURY BATH SYSTEMS, 1958 Brandon Ct., Glendale Heights, IL 60139-2086 (800) 354-2284 (630) 295-9084; (630) 295-9418

OUTDOOR LIGHTING PERSPECTIVES, 6930 Ancient Oak Ln., Charlotte, NC 28277; (704) 849-8808; (704) 841-1822

OWENS CORNING REMODELING SYSTEMS, 1 Owens Corning Pkwy., Toledo, OH 43569 ; (800) GET-PINK (419) 248-8000; (419) 248-6091

PERMA CERAM ENTERPRISES, 65 Smithtown Blvd., Smithtown, NY 11788 (800) 645-5039 (516) 724-1205; (516) 724-9626

PERMA-JACK COMPANY, 9066 Watson Rd., St. Louis, MO 63126-2234 ; (800) 843-1888 (314) 843-1957; (314) 843-7898

POLLMER TECHNOLOGIES, P.O. Box 14, Wilmington, NC 28402 ; (888) 296-2558 ; (910) 251-8359

REFACE IT KITCHEN SYSTEMS, P.O. Box 874, Ferndale, WA 98248 ; (360) 384-3546; (360) 384-0246

SOLID / FLUE CHIMNEY SYSTEMS, 4937 Starr St., SE, Grand Rapids, MI 49546 ; (800) 444-FLUE (616) 940-8809; (616) 940-0921

SUPERIOR WALLS OF AMERICA, 937 E. Earl Rd., New Holland, PA 17557; (800) 452-9255 (717) 351-9255; (717) 351-9263

TIFFANY MARBLE MOLDS INTERNATIONAL, 1999 S. Bascom Ave., # 470, Campbell, CA 95008 ; (800) 654-9093 (408) 559-4888; (408) 559-7771

WOOD RE NEW, 1540 F E Stoneridge, Springfield, MO 65803 ; (888) 244-3303 (417) 833-3303; (417) 833-5479

Business: Financial Services

Chapter

7

Business: Financial Services Industry Profile

Total # Franchisors in Industry Group	42
Total # Franchised Units in Industry Group	13,028
Total # Company-Owned Units in Industry Group	7,189
Total # Operating Units in Industry Group	20,217
Average # Franchised Units/Franchisor	310.2
Average # Company-Owned Units/Franchisor	171.2
Average # Total Units/Franchisor	481.4
Ratio of Total # Franchised Units/Total # Company-Owned Units	1.8:1
Industry Survey Participants	11
Representing % of Industry	26.2%
Average Franchise Fee*:	$21.5K
Average Total Investment*:	$76.3K
Average On-Going Royalty Fee*:	8.9%

*If a range was provided, the mid-point of the range was used. See detailed profiles for actual ranges.

Five Largest Participants in Survey

Company	# Franchised Units	# Co-Owned Units	# Total Units	Franchise Fee	On-Going Royalty	Total Investment
1. Jackson Hewitt Tax Service	3,390	414	3,804	25K	15%	47.4-75.2K
2. Liberty Tax Service	604	22	626	20K	Varies	53.05-64.1K
3. Padgett Business Services	423	1	424	34.5K	9-4.5%	40-60K
4. Ledgerplus	143	8	151	16K	6%	16.4-29.4K
5. United Check Cashing	96	3	99	24.6K	.002%	186.5K

CASH PLUS

3002 Dow Ave., # 120
Tustin, CA 92780
Tel: (888) 707-2274 (714) 731-2274
Fax: (714) 731-2099
E-Mail: cpcorp@cashplusinc.com
Web Site: www.cashplusinc.com
Mr. Mike Carter, VP Franchise Operations

We are meeting America's changing financial needs with tasteful, attractive, retail stores that have proven to be appealing to customers across the socio-economic spectrum. Our unique style shows genuine care for our customers - this is good for business. A powerful marketing program is designed to be cost-effective and offers support from major retailers. Shorter hours, fewer employees, computer management systems and training - it's all here for you.

BACKGROUND:	IFA MEMBER
Established: 1985;	1st Franchised: 1988
Franchised Units:	70
Company-Owned Units	3
Total Units:	73
Dist.:	US-62; CAN-1; O'seas-0
North America:	8 States, 1 Province
Density:	46 in CA, 3 in NV, 3 in FL
Projected New Units (12 Months):	30
Qualifications:	4, 5, 1, 3, 4, 5
Registered: CA,MD,WA	

FINANCIAL/TERMS:	
Cash Investment:	$50-100K
Total Investment:	$124-204K
Minimum Net Worth:	$200K
Fees: Franchise -	$22.5K
Royalty - 6%;	Ad. - 3%
Earnings Claim Statement:	Yes
Term of Contract (Years):	10/10
Avg. # Of Employees:	2 FT, 2 PT
Passive Ownership:	Allowed
Encourage Conversions:	Yes
Area Develop. Agreements:	Yes/5
Sub-Franchising Contracts:	No
Expand In Territory:	Yes
Space Needs: 1,200 SF; FS, SF, SC	

SUPPORT & TRAINING PROVIDED:	
Financial Assistance Provided:	Yes(I)
Site Selection Assistance:	Yes
Lease Negotiation Assistance:	Yes
Co-Operative Advertising:	Yes
Franchisee Assoc./Member:	Yes/Yes
Size Of Corporate Staff:	9
On-Going Support:	a,b,C,D,E,F,G,h,I
Training: 1 Week Tustin, CA; 3 Days at Franchisee Store.	

SPECIFIC EXPANSION PLANS:	
US:	West, SW, NW, Midwest, SE
Canada:	No
Overseas:	No

<< >>

CHECKCARE SYSTEMS

P.O. Box 9636
Columbus, GA 31908
Tel: (706) 596-1306
Fax: (706) 596-0337
Web Site: www.checkcare.com
Mr. William Brandon, SVP Finance

CHECKCARE SYSTEMS is the fastest-growing check guarantee and verification company in the U.S. Proprietary software and hardware configuration included in total investment. Our national account base makes this opportunity a 'must investigate.'

BACKGROUND:	
Established: 1982;	1st Franchised: 1984
Franchised Units:	71
Company-Owned Units	0
Total Units:	71
Dist.:	US-71; CAN-0; O'seas-0
North America:	22 States
Density:	7 in GA, 6 in FL, 5 in TX
Projected New Units (12 Months):	3
Qualifications:	4, 3, 2, 3, 3, 3
Registered: CA,FL,IL,IN,MD,MI,MN,VA, DC	

FINANCIAL/TERMS:	
Cash Investment:	$65-85K
Total Investment:	$110-169K
Minimum Net Worth:	$100K
Fees: Franchise -	$12.5-45K
Royalty - 5%;	Ad. - 0.5%
Earnings Claim Statement:	Yes
Term of Contract (Years):	7/7
Avg. # Of Employees:	13 FT, 2 PT
Passive Ownership:	Discouraged
Encourage Conversions:	Yes
Area Develop. Agreements:	Yes/1
Sub-Franchising Contracts:	No
Expand In Territory:	No
Space Needs: 2,000 SF; Office Park	

SUPPORT & TRAINING PROVIDED:	
Financial Assistance Provided:	Yes
Site Selection Assistance:	Yes
Lease Negotiation Assistance:	No
Co-Operative Advertising:	Yes
Franchisee Assoc./Member:	Yes/Yes
Size Of Corporate Staff:	20
On-Going Support:	b,c,d,e,f,G,h
Training: 2 Weeks Columbus, GA.	

SPECIFIC EXPANSION PLANS:	
US:	West Coast, Northeast
Canada:	All Canada
Overseas:	No

ECONOTAX

P.O. Box 13829
Jackson, MS 39236
Tel: (800) 748-9106 (601) 956-0500
Fax: (601) 956-0583
E-Mail: opportunity@econotox.com
Web Site: www.econotax.com
Mr. James T. Marsh, President

ECONOTAX provides full support for the establishment and operation of tax offices that provide the public individual and small business tax services, including audit representation, tax preparation, electronic tax filing, and refund loan services. This includes software for tax preparation and electronic filing and training and research services.

BACKGROUND:	
Established: 1965;	1st Franchised: 1968
Franchised Units:	68
Company-Owned Units	0
Total Units:	68
Dist.:	US-52; CAN-0; O'seas-0
North America:	7 States
Density:	40 in MS, 6 in AL, 3 in FL
Projected New Units (12 Months):	5
Qualifications:	2, 3, 1, 1, 5, 5
Registered: FL	

FINANCIAL/TERMS:	
Cash Investment:	$5-15K
Total Investment:	$10-25K
Minimum Net Worth:	$25K
Fees: Franchise -	$10K
Royalty - 15%;	Ad. - 4%
Earnings Claim Statement:	Yes
Term of Contract (Years):	5/1
Avg. # Of Employees:	2 FT, 2 PT
Passive Ownership:	Discouraged
Encourage Conversions:	N/A
Area Develop. Agreements:	No
Sub-Franchising Contracts:	No
Expand In Territory:	Yes
Space Needs: 600 SF; SC	

SUPPORT & TRAINING PROVIDED:	
Financial Assistance Provided:	Yes(D)
Site Selection Assistance:	No
Lease Negotiation Assistance:	Yes
Co-Operative Advertising:	Yes
Franchisee Assoc./Member:	No
Size Of Corporate Staff:	5

On-Going Support: A,b,C,d,G,H,I
Training: 5 Days, Jackson, MS.

SPECIFIC EXPANSION PLANS:

US: All United States
Canada: No
Overseas: No

ELECTRONIC TAX FILERS

P.O. Box 2077
Cary, NC 27512-2077
Tel: (800) 945-9277 (919) 469-0651
Fax: (919) 460-5935
E-Mail: RachelWishon@aol.com
Web Site: www.ElectronicTaxFilers.com
Ms. Rachel Wishon, President

We do no tax preparation! Instead, we provide a local, reasonably-priced, walk-in retail location where the 51% of the taxpayers who prepare their own returns can obtain electronic filing without being pressured into tax preparation they do not need. We transmit the data from self-prepared returns to the IRS and states in order that the taxpayer may receive his refunds in days, not months, via direct deposit into his bank, mail or refund loan.

BACKGROUND:

Established: 1990; 1st Franchised: 1990
Franchised Units: 42
Company-Owned Units 2
Total Units: 44
Dist.: US-44; CAN-0; O'seas-0
North America: 15 States
Density: NC
Projected New Units (12 Months): 6
Qualifications: 3, 4, 1, 3, , 4
Registered: All States

FINANCIAL/TERMS:

Cash Investment: $22.5K
Total Investment: $22.5K
Minimum Net Worth: $25K
Fees: Franchise - $9K
Royalty - 8%; Ad. - 4%
Earnings Claim Statement: No
Term of Contract (Years): 3/17
Avg. # Of Employees: 2 FT, 4 PT
Passive Ownership: Discouraged
Encourage Conversions: No
Area Develop. Agreements: No
Sub-Franchising Contracts: No
Expand In Territory: Yes
Space Needs: 1,000 SF; FS, SF, SC, RM

SUPPORT & TRAINING PROVIDED:

Financial Assistance Provided: Yes(D)
Site Selection Assistance: Yes
Lease Negotiation Assistance: Yes
Co-Operative Advertising: Yes
Franchisee Assoc./Member: No
Size Of Corporate Staff: Varies
On-Going Support: A,C,D,h,I
Training: 1 Week in Cary, NC; 2-3 Days On-Site.

SPECIFIC EXPANSION PLANS:

US: Eastern United States
Canada: No
Overseas: No

JACKSON HEWITT TAX SERVICE

339 Jefferson Rd.
Parsippany, NJ 07054
Tel: (800) 475-2904 (973) 496-1040
Fax: (973) 496-2760
E-Mail: william.scavone@jtax.com
Web Site: www.jacksonhewitt.com
Mr. William Scavone, SVP Franchise Sales/Dev.

JACKSON HEWITT TAX SERVICE is the fastest-growing national tax preparation service and the second largest company in this category. With more than 3,800 locations in 47 states and DC, the company provides full service, individual Federal and state income tax preparation and bank products. A leader and pioneer in electronic filing, the company has always provided the service to its tax preparation customers at no cost.

BACKGROUND: IFA MEMBER

Established: 1960; 1st Franchised: 1986
Franchised Units: 3,390
Company-Owned Units 414
Total Units: 3,804
Dist.: US-3804; CAN-0; O'seas-0
North America: 47 States, DC
Density: 411 in TX, 336 in FL, 281 IL
Projected New Units (12 Months): 350
Qualifications: 5, 5, 3, 4, 4, 5
Registered: All States

FINANCIAL/TERMS:

Cash Investment: $25-50K
Total Investment: $47.4-75.2K
Minimum Net Worth: $100K
Fees: Franchise - $25K
Royalty - 15%; Ad. - 6%
Earnings Claim Statement: No
Term of Contract (Years): 10/10
Avg. # Of Employees: 1 FT, 6 PT
Passive Ownership: Allowed
Encourage Conversions: Yes
Area Develop. Agreements: No
Sub-Franchising Contracts: No
Expand In Territory: Yes
Space Needs: 400-1,000 SF; SF, SC, RM

SUPPORT & TRAINING PROVIDED:

Financial Assistance Provided: Yes(I)
Site Selection Assistance: Yes
Lease Negotiation Assistance: No
Co-Operative Advertising: Yes
Franchisee Assoc./Member: Yes/Yes
Size Of Corporate Staff: 235
On-Going Support: A,B,C,D,G,H,I
Training: 5 Days in Parsippany, NJ.

SPECIFIC EXPANSION PLANS:

US: All United States
Canada: No
Overseas: No

LEDGERPLUS

401 St. Francis St.
Tallahassee, FL 32301
Tel: (888) 643-1348 (850) 681-1941
Fax: (850) 561-1374
E-Mail: rbaker@ledgerplus.com
Web Site: www.ledgerplus.com
Mr. Ron Baker, Vice President

Accounting and tax franchise, offering services to America's small business clients. Reports they can understand and use, professional services at affordable prices.

BACKGROUND:

Established: 1989; 1st Franchised: 1990
Franchised Units: 143
Company-Owned Units 8
Total Units: 151
Dist.: US-148; CAN-2; O'seas-1
North America: NR
Density: Fl, NC, CA
Projected New Units (12 Months): 66

Qualifications: 3, 5, 5, 3, 2, 4
Registered: All States Except ND,SD

FINANCIAL/TERMS:

Cash Investment: $16.4-29.4K
Total Investment: $16.4-29.4K
Minimum Net Worth: $NR
Fees: Franchise - $16K
Royalty - 6%; Ad. - 2%
Earnings Claim Statement: No
Term of Contract (Years): 10/10
Avg. # Of Employees: 1 FT
Passive Ownership: Allowed
Encourage Conversions: Yes
Area Develop. Agreements: Yes
Sub-Franchising Contracts: No
Expand In Territory: Yes
Space Needs: 400 SF; OB

SUPPORT & TRAINING PROVIDED:

Financial Assistance Provided: No
Site Selection Assistance: N/A
Lease Negotiation Assistance: No
Co-Operative Advertising: Yes
Franchisee Assoc./Member: No
Size Of Corporate Staff: 7
On-Going Support: b,C,D,G,H
Training: 5 Days Chicago, IL.

SPECIFIC EXPANSION PLANS:

US: All United States
Canada: All Canada
Overseas: No

<< >>

LIBERTY TAX SERVICE

4575 Bonney Rd., # 1040
Virginia Beach, VA 23462
Tel: (800) 790-3863 (757) 493-8855
Fax: (757) 493-0694
E-Mail: sales@libtax.com
Web Site: www.libertytax.com
Mr. Charles Lovelace, VP Fran. Dev.

LIBERTY TAX SERVICE is ranked #50 on Entrepreneur Magazine's list of top 500 franchises. The ratings are based on financial strength, stability, growth rate, size of the system, start-up costs and financing options. IN the September 2001 issue of Black Enterprise Magazine, LIBERTY TAX SERVICE is rated as one of the 15 top affordable franchise opportunities. We offer low start-up costs and a proven operating system including marketing, training, software, research, development, tax and technical support.

BACKGROUND: IFA MEMBER

Established: 1996; 1st Franchised: 1996
Franchised Units: 604
Company-Owned Units 22
Total Units: 626
Dist.: US-412; CAN-214; O'seas-0
North America: 40 States
Density: 54 in VA, 21 in IL, 17 in TX
Projected New Units (12 Months): NR
Registered: NR

FINANCIAL/TERMS:

Cash Investment: $33.05-44.1K
Total Investment: $53.05-64.1K
Minimum Net Worth: $N/A
Fees: Franchise - $20K
Royalty - Varies; Ad. - 6-7K/Yr rec
Earnings Claim Statement: No
Term of Contract (Years): 5/5
Avg. # Of Employees: 6 FT, 2 PT
Passive Ownership: Discouraged
Encourage Conversions: NR
Area Develop. Agreements: Yes
Sub-Franchising Contracts: No
Expand In Territory: Yes
Space Needs: 400+ SF; FS, SF, SC, RM

SUPPORT & TRAINING PROVIDED:

Financial Assistance Provided: NR
Site Selection Assistance: Yes
Lease Negotiation Assistance: Yes
Co-Operative Advertising: Yes
Franchisee Assoc./Member: No
Size Of Corporate Staff: 66
On-Going Support: A,B,C,D,G,H,I
Training: 5 Days, VB Higher Education Center.

SPECIFIC EXPANSION PLANS:

US: All United States
Canada: NR
Overseas: NR

<< >>

PADGETT BUSINESS SERVICES

160 Hawthorne Park
Athens, GA 30606-2147
Tel: (800) 323-7292 (706) 548-1040
Fax: (706) 543-8537
E-Mail: bgrimes@smallbizpros.com
Web Site: www.smallbizpros.com
Mr. Greg Williams, VP Franchise Development

America's top-rated and fastest-growing tax and accounting franchise - serving the fastest-growing segment of the economy - America's small business owners. Initial training. Specialized software. On-going support.

BACKGROUND: IFA MEMBER

Established: 1966; 1st Franchised: 1975
Franchised Units: 423
Company-Owned Units 1
Total Units: 424
Dist.: US-304; CAN-120; O'seas-0
North America: 45 States, 8 Provinces
Density: 67 in ON, 38 in QC, 26 in GA
Projected New Units (12 Months): 25
Qualifications: 3, 3, 4, 4, 2, 4
Registered: All States

FINANCIAL/TERMS:

Cash Investment: $15-35K
Total Investment: $40-60K
Minimum Net Worth: $60K
Fees: Franchise - $34.5K
Royalty - 9-4.5%; Ad. - 0%
Earnings Claim Statement: No
Term of Contract (Years): 20/20
Avg. # Of Employees: 1 FT, 2 PT
Passive Ownership: Discouraged
Encourage Conversions: Yes
Area Develop. Agreements: No
Sub-Franchising Contracts: No
Expand In Territory: Yes
Space Needs: 200-400 SF; HB, OB, ES

SUPPORT & TRAINING PROVIDED:

Financial Assistance Provided: Yes(I)
Site Selection Assistance: N/A
Lease Negotiation Assistance: N/A
Co-Operative Advertising: N/A
Franchisee Assoc./Member: Yes/No
Size Of Corporate Staff: 20
On-Going Support: C,D,G,H,I
Training: 2.5 Weeks Athens, GA; 3 (2.5 Day) Site Visits.

SPECIFIC EXPANSION PLANS:

US: All United States
Canada: All Canada
Overseas: No

<< >>

PEOPLES INCOME TAX

4915 Radford Ave., # 100A
Richmond, VA 23230
Tel: (800) 984-1040 (804) 204-1040
Fax: (804) 213-4248
E-Mail: peoplesinc@aol.com
Web Site: www.peoplestax.com
Mr. Charles E. McCabe, President/CEO

Professional income tax preparation service specializing in middle-income and upwardly-mobile individual and small business taxpayers. Proven marketing and operating methods. Income tax school. Business training and support provided. Minimal start-up cost.

BACKGROUND:

Established: 1987; 1st Franchised: 1998
Franchised Units: 0
Company-Owned Units 16
Total Units: 16
Dist.: US-0; CAN-0; O'seas-0
North America: 1 State
Density: 13 in VA
Projected New Units (12 Months): NR
Registered: NR

FINANCIAL/TERMS:

Cash Investment: $40-60K
Total Investment: $51-86K
Minimum Net Worth: $100K
Fees: Franchise - $16K
Royalty - 9%; Ad. - 6%
Earnings Claim Statement: No
Term of Contract (Years): 5
Avg. # Of Employees:
1 Ft, 9 PT (seasonal)
Passive Ownership: Not Allowed
Encourage Conversions: NR
Area Develop. Agreements: No
Sub-Franchising Contracts: No
Expand In Territory: Yes
Space Needs: 600-1,000 SF; SF, SC, RM

SUPPORT & TRAINING PROVIDED:

Financial Assistance Provided: NR
Site Selection Assistance: Yes
Lease Negotiation Assistance: Yes
Co-Operative Advertising: No
Franchisee Assoc./Member: No
Size Of Corporate Staff: 10
On-Going Support: C,d,E,G,H,I
Training: 25 Hours Richmond, VA.

SPECIFIC EXPANSION PLANS:

US: VA Only
Canada: NR
Overseas: NR

<< >>

TRADEBANK INTERNATIONAL

4220 Pleasantdale Rd.
Atlanta, GA 30340
Tel: (678) 568-5680
Fax: (678) 533-7113
E-Mail: jdavis@tradebank.com
Web Site: www.tradebank.com
Mr. John Davis, President

TRADEBANK is a national retail/ commercial trade exchange, arranging barter transactions for manufacturers, wholesalers, distributors, retailers, professional services or anyone with a product or services to sell. For this service, we collect a 10% brokerage fee.

BACKGROUND:

Established: 1987; 1st Franchised: 1995
Franchised Units: 26
Company-Owned Units 0
Total Units: 26
Dist.: US-20; CAN-6; O'seas-0
North America: 8 States, 2 Provinces
Density: 7 in GA, 4 in AL, 3 in TN
Projected New Units (12 Months): 10
Qualifications: 3, 4, 2, 3, 3, 5
Registered: FL,MI,OR

FINANCIAL/TERMS:

Cash Investment: $20K
Total Investment: $50K
Minimum Net Worth: $50K
Fees: Franchise - $30K
Royalty - 0%; Ad. - N/A
Earnings Claim Statement: No
Term of Contract (Years): 5/2-5
Avg. # Of Employees: 1 FT
Passive Ownership: Discouraged
Encourage Conversions: No
Area Develop. Agreements: No
Sub-Franchising Contracts: No
Expand In Territory: Yes
Space Needs: 600-1,000 SF; FS, SF, SC, OB

SUPPORT & TRAINING PROVIDED:

Financial Assistance Provided: Yes(D)
Site Selection Assistance: Yes
Lease Negotiation Assistance: Yes
Co-Operative Advertising: No
Franchisee Assoc./Member: No
Size Of Corporate Staff: 15
On-Going Support: A,C,D,E,h,I
Training: 1 Week Atlanta, GA; 1 Week Franchised Territory.

SPECIFIC EXPANSION PLANS:

US: All United States
Canada: BC, PQ
Overseas: Europe, Asia

<< >>

UNITED CHECK CASHING

400 Market St., # 1030
Philadelphia, PA 19106
Tel: (800) 626-0787 (215) 238-0300
Fax: (215) 238-9056
E-Mail: sschonberg@united.com
Web Site: www.unitedcheckcashing.com
Mr. Seth N. Schonberg, VP Franchise Development

It may be surprising to most people that 20 to 30% of Americans have no formal banking relationship. Most of these hard working people need a service that will give them immediate access to the cash they need. Even those Americans with established banking patterns are discovering the convenience of the alternative financial services industry. Our customers need more convenient hours than most banks provide. Our industry is happy to provide for these customers.

BACKGROUND:

Established: 1977; 1st Franchised: 1992
Franchised Units: 96
Company-Owned Units 3
Total Units: 99
Dist.: US-100; CAN-0; O'seas-0
North America: 13 States
Density: 41 in PA, 37 in NJ, 5 in DE
Projected New Units (12 Months): 20
Qualifications: 5, 3, 2, 2, 4, 5
Registered: All States

FINANCIAL/TERMS:

Cash Investment: $50-75K
Total Investment: $186.5K
Minimum Net Worth: $200K
Fees: Franchise - $24.5K
Royalty - 0.002% of Volume;
Ad. - 3% income
Earnings Claim Statement: Yes
Term of Contract (Years): 15/15
Avg. # Of Employees: 1 FT, 2 PT
Passive Ownership: Discouraged
Encourage Conversions: Yes
Area Develop. Agreements: Yes/Negot.
Sub-Franchising Contracts: No
Expand In Territory: Yes
Space Needs: 1000-1200 SF; SC

SUPPORT & TRAINING PROVIDED:

Financial Assistance Provided: Yes(I)
Site Selection Assistance: Yes
Lease Negotiation Assistance: Yes
Co-Operative Advertising: Yes
Franchisee Assoc./Member: Yes/No
Size Of Corporate Staff: 16
On-Going Support: A,C,D,E,G,H,I
Training: 1 Week Corporate Headquarters; 1 Week on Premises.

SPECIFIC EXPANSION PLANS:

US: All United States
Canada: No
Overseas: No

SUPPLEMENTAL LISTING OF FRANCHISORS

ABS SYSTEMS, 374 Morning Glory Dr., # 5, Lake Mary, FL 32746 ; (800) ABS-7504 (407) 324-1693; (407) 324-0589

ACCOUNTAX SERVICES, 499 Ray Lawson Blvd., # 32, Brampton, ON L6Y 4E6 CANADA; (905) 453-3220; (905) 453-9562

ADVANTAGE PAYROLL SERVICES, 126 Merrow Rd., P.O. Box 1330, Auburn, ME 04211-1330 ; (800) 876-0178 (207) 784-0178; (207) 786-0490

AMERICAN CREDIT SYSTEMS, 41743 Enterprise Circle N., # 204, Temecula, CA 92598 ; (800) 305-9561 (909) 694-9394; (909) 694-4300

ATM BANKING SRVICES, 4115 Tiverton Rd., Randallstown, MD 21133-2019 (800) 992-1615 (410) 655-3201; (410) 655-0262

BROOKE CORP., 205 F. St., Phillipsburg, KS 67661-1918 ; (800) 642-1872 (785) 543-3199; (785) 543-3098

DONE RIGHT ACCOUNTING, 410 Registration Dr., Kelowna, BC V48 4T5 CANADA; (888) 573-1136 ; (204) 957-0265

FAST BUCKS CHECK CASHING SERVICE, 3615 N. 44th St., # 1, Lincoln, NE 68504 ; (402) 464-3949; (402) 464-3181

FEDERAL INCOME TAX SERVICES, 250 Auburn Ave., # 304, Atlanta, GA 30303 ; (800) 691-0636 (404) 659-5644; (404) 659-5646

FED-USA INSURANCE, 4161 NW Fifth St., Plantation, FL 33317-2158 ; (888) 440-6875 (954) 581-9993; (954) 316-9201

FIDUCIAL CENTURY SMALL BUSINESS SERVICES, 2441 Honolulu Ave., Montrose, CA 91020-1864 ; (800) 283-1040 ; (818)249-5344

FRENCH COMPANY, THE, 31005 Bainbridge Rd., Cleveland, OH 44139 ; (800) 321-8875 ; (404) 349-4344

H & R BLOCK CANADA, 340 Midpark Way, SE, # 200, Calgary, AB T2X 1P1 CANADA; (403) 254-8689; (403) 254-9949

H & R BLOCK TAX SERVICES, 4400 Main St., Kansas City, MO 64111-1812 (800) 869-9220 (816) 932-8439; (816) 932-8489

HOMEOWNERS MARKETING SERVICES, 1625 NW 136th Ave., # 200, Ft. Lauderdale, FL 33233 ; (954) 845-9100

LEDGERPLUS, 401 St. Francis St., Tallahassee, FL 32301 ; (888) 643-1348 (850) 681-1941; (850) 561-1374

LIBERTY TAX SERVICE (CANADA), 1245 Pembina Hwy., Winnipeg, MB R3T 2B6 CANADA; (800) 665-5144 ; (204) 284-8954

NATIONAL LOAN CONSULTANTS, 70 Paris Snow Dr., # 14, Caribou, ME 04736 ; (888) 887-6559 ; (760) 675-8184

NEO FINANCIAL SERVICES, 2629 Production Ave., # 6, Hayward, CA 94545 (510) 259-0234; (510) 784-9959

NEXT DAY TAX CASH, 2854 S. Broadway, Englewood, CO 80110 ; (303) 761-8080

PADGETT BUSINESS SERVICES (CANADA), 6700 Cote-de Liesse, # 105, Montreal, QC H4T 1E3 CANADA; (888) PADGETT ; (800) 428-5297

PAID INC., 1600 Lake Air Dr., Waco, TX 76710 ; (877) 674-7543 (254) 772-8131; (254) 772-4642

TAX CENTERS OF AMERICA, 1611 E. Main St., Russellville, AR 72801-5328 (800) 364-2012 (501) 968-4796; (501) 968-8012

TAXPRO ELECTRONIC FILING, P.O. Box 13829, Jackson, MS 39236 ; (800) 748-9106 (601) 956-0500; (601) 956-0583

TRIPLE CHECK INCOME TAX SERVICE, 2441 Honolulu Ave., Montrose, CA 91020 ; (800) 283-1040 (818) 236-2944; (818) 249-5344

U & R TAX SERVICES, 1345 Pembina Hwy., # 201, Winnipeg, MB R3T 2B6 CANADA; (800) 665-5144 (204) 949-3636; (204) 284-8954

UNITED FINANCIAL SERVICES, 400 Market St., # 1030, Philadelphia, PA 19106-2513 ; (800) 626-0787 (215) 238-0300; (215) 238-9056

X-BANKERS CHECK CASHING, 1155 Main St., Bridgeport, CT 06604 ; (800) 873-9226 (203) 374-1377; (203) 773-0418

Business: Advertising & Promotion

Chapter 8

Business: Advertising & Promotion Industry Profile

Total # Franchisors in Industry Group	35
Total # Franchised Units in Industry Group	2,081
Total # Company-Owned Units in Industry Group	78
Total # Operating Units in Industry Group	2,159
Average # Franchised Units/Franchisor	59.5
Average # Company-Owned Units/Franchisor	2.2
Average # Total Units/Franchisor	61.7
Ratio of Total # Franchised Units/Total # Company-Owned Units	26.7:1
Industry Survey Participants	7
Representing % of Industry	20.0%
Average Franchise Fee*:	$18.0K
Average Total Investment*:	$48.7K
Average On-Going Royalty Fee*:	5.5%

*If a range was provided, the mid-point of the range was used. See detailed profiles for actual ranges.

Five Largest Participants in Survey

Company	# Franchised Units	# Co-Owned Units	# Total Units	Franchise Fee	On-Going Royalty	Total Investment
1. Adventures in Advertising	405	0	405	5-27.5K	4-7%	11.9-47.7K
2. Val-Pak Direct Marketing	248	5	253	7K	0%	32-85K
3. Money Mailer	244	8	252	25-35K	Varies	37-71.5K
4. Super Coups	210	0	210	32K	$148/Mailing	41K
5. Trimark	34	0	34	Included	0%	31-122K

All of the data provided are proprietary and should not be quoted without acknowledging *Bond's Franchise Guide.*

ADVENTURES IN ADVERTISING

400 Crown Colony Dr.
Quincy, MA 02169
Tel: (800) 432-6332 (617) 472-9900
Fax: (617) 472-9976
E-Mail: discoveraia@advinadv.com
Web Site: www.discoveraia.com
Mr. Dan Carlson, Chairman/CEO

Adventures in Advertising Franchise, Inc. (AIAFI) is an international network of over 450 individually-owned and operated, professional promotional product distributorships. Ranked in Entrepreneur Magazine as the #1 franchise in its category, AIAFI offers unlimited capital to grow your business, a complete training and education program, and support from top industry professionals.

BACKGROUND:

Established: 1980; 1st Franchised: 1993
Franchised Units: 405
Company-Owned Units 0
Total Units: 405
Dist.: US-350; CAN-55; O'seas-0
North America: 44 States
Density: 26 in CA, 18 in FL, 16 in TX
Projected New Units (12 Months): 60
Qualifications: 3, 3, 3, 2, 5, 5
Registered: All States and AB

FINANCIAL/TERMS:

Cash Investment: $5-35K
Total Investment: $11.9-47.7K
Minimum Net Worth: $10K
Fees: Franchise - $5-27.5K
Royalty - 4-7%; Ad. - .25-1%
Earnings Claim Statement: No
Term of Contract (Years): 5/5
Avg. # Of Employees: 1-2 FT
Passive Ownership: Discouraged
Encourage Conversions: Yes
Area Develop. Agreements: No
Sub-Franchising Contracts: No
Expand In Territory: Yes
Space Needs: N/A SF; HB

SUPPORT & TRAINING PROVIDED:

Financial Assistance Provided: Yes(D)
Site Selection Assistance: No
Lease Negotiation Assistance: No
Co-Operative Advertising: Yes
Franchisee Assoc./Member: Yes/Yes
Size Of Corporate Staff: 60
On-Going Support: A,B,C,D,G,H,I
Training: NR

SPECIFIC EXPANSION PLANS:

US: All United States and Canada
Canada: All Canada
Overseas: No

<< >>

COUPON TABLOID INTERNATIONAL, THE

5775 SW Jean Rd., # 101
Lake Oswego, OR 97035
Tel: (800) 888-8575 (503) 697-1968
Fax: (503) 697-1978
E-Mail: jon@coupontabloid.com
Web Site: www.coupontabloid.com
Mr. Jonathan D. Crane, President

COUPON TABLOID INTERNATIONAL is a publisher of a direct mail coupon newspaper that has a price point attractive to smaller retailers. Clean look, affordable advertising at 80% plus renewal rate. Bankers hours, no inventory, plenty of freedom and unlimited earning potential. Ideal home-based business. Franchise fee is a low $4,500.

BACKGROUND:

Established: 1986; 1st Franchised: 1994
Franchised Units: 23
Company-Owned Units 1
Total Units: 24
Dist.: US-24; CAN-0; O'seas-0
North America: 23 States
Density: 11 in AZ, 11 in OR, 2 in ID
Projected New Units (12 Months): 5-10
Qualifications: 2, 3, 3, 2, 3, 4
Registered: CA,WA

FINANCIAL/TERMS:

Cash Investment: $10K
Total Investment: $7-12K
Minimum Net Worth: $10K
Fees: Franchise - $4.5K
Royalty - Graphic fee; Ad. - 0%
Earnings Claim Statement: Yes
Term of Contract (Years): 5/5
Avg. # Of Employees: 1 FT
Passive Ownership: Discouraged
Encourage Conversions: N/A
Area Develop. Agreements: No
Sub-Franchising Contracts: No
Expand In Territory: Yes
Space Needs: N/A SF; HB

SUPPORT & TRAINING PROVIDED:

Financial Assistance Provided: Yes(D)
Site Selection Assistance: Yes
Lease Negotiation Assistance: N/A
Co-Operative Advertising: N/A
Franchisee Assoc./Member: No
Size Of Corporate Staff: 5
On-Going Support: E,G,H,I
Training: 4 Days at Your Franchise Location.

SPECIFIC EXPANSION PLANS:

US: Northwest, Southwest
Canada: No
Overseas: No

<< >>

EFFECTIVE MAILERS

28510 Hayes Rd.
Roseville, MI 48066-2314
Tel: (810) 777-3223
Fax: (810) 777-4141
E-Mail: jgupta@couponvalue.com
Web Site: www.couponvalue.com
Mr. Jai Gupta, President

Co-op direct mail coupons design, print, insert and mail. Training and on-going support in all aspects of business. Our clients get one of the best coupon redemptions when they advertise with us. Four color coupons. Cutting edge technology. Price competitive in envelope type direct mail.

BACKGROUND:

Established: 1982; 1st Franchised: 1993
Franchised Units: 5
Company-Owned Units 1
Total Units: 6
Dist.: US-0; CAN-0; O'seas-0
North America: 3 States
Density: 2 in MA, 2 in NJ, 1 in MI
Projected New Units (12 Months): NR
Registered: NR

FINANCIAL/TERMS:

Cash Investment: $25K+
Total Investment: $25-50K
Minimum Net Worth: $25K
Fees: Franchise - $18K
Royalty - 0%; Ad. - 0%
Earnings Claim Statement: No
Term of Contract (Years): 10/10
Avg. # Of Employees: 1 FT
Passive Ownership: Not Allowed
Encourage Conversions: NR
Area Develop. Agreements: No
Sub-Franchising Contracts: No
Expand In Territory: No
Space Needs: NR SF; HB

SUPPORT & TRAINING PROVIDED:

Financial Assistance Provided: NR
Site Selection Assistance: N/A
Lease Negotiation Assistance: N/A
Co-Operative Advertising: N/A
Franchisee Assoc./Member: No
Size Of Corporate Staff: 60
On-Going Support: NR
Training: 1 Week at Headquarters.

SPECIFIC EXPANSION PLANS:
US: All United States
Canada: NR
Overseas: NR

<< >>

MONEY MAILER

14271 Corporate Dr.
Garden Grove, CA 92843-4937
Tel: (888) 446-4648 (714) 265-8498
Fax: (714) 265-8311
E-Mail: franchiseleads@moneymailer.net
Web Site: www.moneymailer.net
Ms. Maria McCoy, Franchise Licensing

MONEY MAILER is one of America's leading direct mail advertising companies with over 300 franchises in the U.S. and Canada. Over its 20 year history, MONEY MAILER has been at the forefront of introducing innovative direct mail advertising products and programs to the marketplace - helping businesses get and keep more customers and helping consumers save money everyday.

BACKGROUND: IFA MEMBER
Established: 1978; 1st Franchised: 1980
Franchised Units: 244
Company-Owned Units 8
Total Units: 252
Dist.: US-312; CAN-6; O'seas-1
North America: NR
Density: 31 in CA, 23 in NJ, 20 in NC
Projected New Units (12 Months): 40
Qualifications: 4, 3, 4, 3, 4, 5
Registered: CA,FL,IL,IN,NY,VA,WA,WI

FINANCIAL/TERMS:
Cash Investment: $37-71.5K
Total Investment: $37-71.5K
Minimum Net Worth: $Varies
Fees: Franchise - $25-35K
Royalty - Varies; Ad. - N/A
Earnings Claim Statement: No
Term of Contract (Years): 10/10
Avg. # Of Employees: 1 FT, 1 PT
Passive Ownership: Not Allowed
Encourage Conversions: N/A
Area Develop. Agreements: No
Sub-Franchising Contracts: Yes
Expand In Territory: Yes
Space Needs: NR SF; HB

SUPPORT & TRAINING PROVIDED:
Financial Assistance Provided: No
Site Selection Assistance: N/A
Lease Negotiation Assistance: N/A
Co-Operative Advertising: No
Franchisee Assoc./Member: Yes/Yes
Size Of Corporate Staff: 300
On-Going Support: C,D,H,I
Training: 1 Week Regional Office; 2 Weeks Corporate Headquarters; 1 Week Regional Office.

SPECIFIC EXPANSION PLANS:
US: All United States
Canada: No
Overseas: No

<< >>

SUPER COUPS

180 Bodwell St.
Avon, MA 02322-1177
Tel: (800) 508-8960 (508) 580-4340
Fax: (508) 580-3347
E-Mail: opportunities@supercoups.com
Web Site: www.supercoups.com
Mr. Mark Franklin, VP Franchise Licensing

SUPER COUPS is one of the top co-op direct mail companies in America. We specialize in developing an integrated marketing solution for local and regional businesses, featuring co-op coupon mailings, co-op TV and internet advertising. We are known for our personalized training, outstanding field support and state-of-the-art production facilities.

BACKGROUND: IFA MEMBER
Established: 1984; 1st Franchised: 1983
Franchised Units: 210
Company-Owned Units 0
Total Units: 210
Dist.: US-438; CAN-0; O'seas-0
North America: 29 States
Density: 47 in MA, 38 in NY, 38 in NJ
Projected New Units (12 Months): 50
Qualifications: 5, 5, 4, 3, 1, 5
Registered: CA,DC,FL,IL,IN,MD,MI,MN, NY,ND,OR,SD,VA,WA,WI

FINANCIAL/TERMS:
Cash Investment: $5-10K
Total Investment: $41K
Minimum Net Worth: $50K
Fees: Franchise - $32K
Royalty - $148/Mailing; Ad. - $500/Yr.
Earnings Claim Statement: Yes
Term of Contract (Years): 10/10
Avg. # Of Employees: 1 FT
Passive Ownership: Not Allowed
Encourage Conversions: Yes
Area Develop. Agreements: No
Sub-Franchising Contracts: Yes
Expand In Territory: Yes
Space Needs: N/A SF; HB

SUPPORT & TRAINING PROVIDED:
Financial Assistance Provided: Yes(I)
Site Selection Assistance: No
Lease Negotiation Assistance: No
Co-Operative Advertising: Yes
Franchisee Assoc./Member: Yes/Yes
Size Of Corporate Staff: 180
On-Going Support: C,D,F,G,H,I
Training: 1 Week Headquarters, Avon, MA; 1 Week in Field.

SPECIFIC EXPANSION PLANS:
US: All United States
Canada: All Canada
Overseas: No

<< >>

TRIMARK

621 Delaware St., # 200
Newcastle, DE 19720
Tel: (888) 321-MARK (302) 322-2143
Fax: (302) 322-9910
E-Mail: trimark@universal.dca.net
Web Site: www.trimarkinc.om
Mr. John E. Kinch, President

Multiple-unit TRIMARK master franchises offer excellent opportunities for former corporate executives and entrepreneurs with the desire to build a big and profitable business in the growing, dynamic direct-mail advertising industry. No store-front real estate or inventory. Low start-up costs, low overhead and full corporate support. An outstanding franchise business. Single unit franchises also available.

BACKGROUND:
Established: 1969; 1st Franchised: 1978
Franchised Units: 34
Company-Owned Units 0
Total Units: 34
Dist.: US-34; CAN-0; O'seas-0
North America: 18 States
Density: 4 in PA, 3 in NY, 3 in FL
Projected New Units (12 Months): 12
Qualifications: 4, 5, 3, 3, 3, 5
Registered: FL,HI,MI,NY

FINANCIAL/TERMS:
Cash Investment: $25-100K
Total Investment: $31-122K
Minimum Net Worth: $50-150K
Fees: Franchise - $Included
Royalty - 0%; Ad. - N/A
Earnings Claim Statement: No
Term of Contract (Years): 10/10
Avg. # Of Employees: 1 FT, 1 PT
Passive Ownership: Allowed

Encourage Conversions:	No
Area Develop. Agreements:	Yes/2
Sub-Franchising Contracts:	Yes
Expand In Territory:	Yes

Space Needs: NR SF; HB

SUPPORT & TRAINING PROVIDED:

Financial Assistance Provided:	No
Site Selection Assistance:	N/A
Lease Negotiation Assistance:	N/A
Co-Operative Advertising:	N/A
Franchisee Assoc./Member:	No
Size Of Corporate Staff:	15
On-Going Support:	b,c,D,G,h

Training: 40-80 Hours Corporate Headquarters; 80 Hours On-Site.

SPECIFIC EXPANSION PLANS:

US:	All United States
Canada:	All Except AB
Overseas:	U.K.

<< >>

VALPAK DIRECT MARKETING

8605 Largo Lakes Dr.
Largo, FL 33773
Tel: (800) 237-6266 (727) 393-1270
Fax: (727) 392-0049
franchiseinformation@coxtarget.com
Web Site: www.valpak.net
Ms. Shari Kay, Director Franchise Sales

North America's oldest and largest local co-operative direct mail advertising franchisor, with distribution of over 490 million coupon envelopes annually to over 53 million unduplicated homes and businesses. Subsidiary of Cox Enterprises, Inc. VALPAK OF CANADA is the Canadian franchisor.

BACKGROUND: IFA MEMBER

Established: 1968; 1st Franchised: 1989

Franchised Units:	248
Company-Owned Units	5
Total Units:	253
Dist.:	US-209; CAN-36; O'seas-1
North America:	48 States,10 Provinces
Density:	19 in ON, 15 in CA, 14 in NY
Projected New Units (12 Months):	10
Qualifications:	4, 3, 3, 2, 1, 4

Registered: All States

FINANCIAL/TERMS:

Cash Investment:	$25K+
Total Investment:	$32-85K
Minimum Net Worth:	$Varies
Fees: Franchise -	$7K
Royalty - 0%;	Ad. - 0%
Earnings Claim Statement:	No
Term of Contract (Years):	10/5
Avg. # Of Employees:	Varies
Passive Ownership:	Discouraged
Encourage Conversions:	Yes
Area Develop. Agreements:	No
Sub-Franchising Contracts:	No
Expand In Territory:	No

Space Needs: N/A SF; HB

SUPPORT & TRAINING PROVIDED:

Financial Assistance Provided:	Yes(I)
Site Selection Assistance:	N/A
Lease Negotiation Assistance:	N/A
Co-Operative Advertising:	Yes
Franchisee Assoc./Member:	Yes/Yes
Size Of Corporate Staff:	1,100
On-Going Support:	C,D,G,h,I

Training: 5 Days Home Study with Trainer; 1 Week Corporate Headquarters; On-Going, On- and Off-Site.

SPECIFIC EXPANSION PLANS:

US:	All US, Limited Areas Remain
Canada:	All Canada
Overseas:	No

<< >>

SUPPLEMENTAL LISTING OF FRANCHISORS

ADVERTISING ON THE MOVE, 1900 NW 32nd St., Pompano Beach, FL 33064 (800) 566-2450 (954) 969-8558; (954) 969-8171

CONSUMER NETWORK OF AMERICA, 2650 E. Beltline, Grand Rapids, MI 49546-5942 ; (800) 288-1135 (616) 942-8165; (616) 942-0347

COUPON-CASH SAVER, 1020 Milwaukee Ave., # 240, Deerfield, IL 60015-3513 (847) 537-6420; (847) 537-6499

CREATIVWORKS, 4818 Washington Blvd., St. Louis, MO 63108-1829 ; (888) 304-4332 (314) 367-8500; (314) 367-5510

FOCUS ON SALES, 5689 S. Ouray St., Aurora, CO 80015 ; (888) 373-6287 (303) 617-9526; (303) 617-9431

GIFTS REMEMBERED, 5678 C.T.H., # R, Denmark, WI 54208-9107 ; (888) 685-9484 (920) 863-8326; (920) 863-5241

GREETINGS, P.O. Box 25623, Lexington, KY 40524 ; (606) 272-5624

MERCHANT ADVERTISING SYSTEMS, 4115 Tiverton Rd., Randallstown, MD 21133-2019 ; (410) 655-3201; (410) 655-0262

MOBIL' AMBITION USA, 1900 NW 32nd St., Pompano Beach, FL 33064-1304 (800) 566-2450 (954) 493-8440; (954) 493-8604

NEWMETHOD DIRECT, 14 Inverness Dr. E., Bldg. C-108, Englewood, CO 80112-5625 ; (800) 824-3983 (303) 799-6090; (303) 799-6087

POINTS FOR PROFIT, P.O. Box 2424, La Mesa, CA 91943 ; (619) 588-0664; (619) 588-0664

PROFIT-ON-HOLD, 3401 Ridgelake Dr., # 108, Metairie, LA 70002 ; (800) 569-4653 (504) 832-8000; (504) 828-2141

SCORECARD PLUS, 1101 Portage St., NW, North Canton, OH 44720-2353 ; (800) 767-9273 (330) 493-9900; (330) 493-9274

UNITED COUPON CORPORATION, 8380 Alban Rd., Springfield, VA 22150 (800) 368-3501 (703) 644-0200; (703) 569-1465

VALPAK OF CANADA, 40 Wynford Dr., # 301, Don Mills, ON M3C 1J5 CANADA; (800) 237-6266 (727) 392-0049; (416) 510-5002

WELCOME HOST OF AMERICA, 13953 Perkins Rd., Baton Rouge, LA 70810-3438 ; (800) 962-5431 (504) 769-3000; (504) 751-9039

WHEELS AMERICA ADVERTISING, 545 Charles St., Luzerne, PA 18709 ; (800) 823-0044 (570) 283-5000; (570) 283-3245

YELLOW JACKET DIRECT MAIL ADVERTISING, 23101 Moulton Pkwy., # 110, Laguna Hills, CA 92653 ; (800) 893-5569 (949) 951-9500; (949) 859-0899

Business: Internet/Telecommunications/Miscellaneous

Chapter 9

Business: Internet/Telecommunications/ Miscellaneous Industry Profile

Total # Franchisors in Industry Group	83
Total # Franchised Units in Industry Group	6,464
Total # Company-Owned Units in Industry Group	1,871
Total # Operating Units in Industry Group	8,335
Average # Franchised Units/Franchisor	77.9
Average # Company-Owned Units/Franchisor	22.5
Average # Total Units/Franchisor	100.4
Ratio of Total # Franchised Units/Total # Company-Owned Units	3.5:1
Industry Survey Participants	24
Representing % of Industry	28.9%
Average Franchise Fee*:	$22.7K
Average Total Investment*:	$74.4K
Average On-Going Royalty Fee*:	20.9%

*If a range was provided, the mid-point of the range was used. See detailed profiles for actual ranges.

Five Largest Participants in Survey

Company	# Franchised Units	# Co-Owned Units	# Total Units	Franchise Fee	On-Going Royalty	Total Investment
1. Ace Cash Express	159	919	1,078	15-30K	5%, $850 Min.	77.5-186.1K
2. Fiducial	693	20	713	7.5-25K	1.5-6%	39-116K
3. Quik Internet	210	0	210	35K	10%	65-75K
4. Sunbelt Business Brokers	178	1	179	5-10K	$3-6K/Year	5-50K
5. VR Business Brokers	112	0	112	12K	6%	40-75K

ACE CASH EXPRESS

1231 Greenway Dr., # 800
Irving, TX 75038-2531
Tel: (800) 713-3338 (972) 550-5110
Fax: (972) 582-1406
E-Mail: hjohnson@acecashexpress.com
Web Site: www.acecashexpress.com
Mr. Herman Johnson, President Franchise Group

Cash in with the leader in retail financial services! ACE is a 30-year-old publicly-traded company operating and franchising over 900+ locations across 29 states. ACE offers customers a number of financial services, including check cashing, bill payments, money orders, wire transfers, short-term loans or cash advances, pre-paid telecommunication products and other related services.

BACKGROUND: IFA MEMBER
Established: 1968; 1st Franchised: 1996
Franchised Units: 159
Company-Owned Units 919
Total Units: 1,078
Dist.: US-911; CAN-0; O'seas-0
North America: 29 States
Density: 237 in TX, 53 in AZ, 44 MD
Projected New Units (12 Months): 120+
Qualifications: 5, 4, 2, 2, 4, 5
Registered: All States and AB

FINANCIAL/TERMS:
Cash Investment: $50K
Total Investment: $77.5-186.1K
Minimum Net Worth: $150K
Fees: Franchise - $15-30K
Royalty - 5%/$850 Min.; Ad. - 3%
Earnings Claim Statement: Yes
Term of Contract (Years): 10/5
Avg. # Of Employees: 2 FT
Passive Ownership: Discouraged
Encourage Conversions: Yes
Area Develop. Agreements: Yes
Sub-Franchising Contracts: No
Expand In Territory: Varies
Space Needs: 250-1,500 SF; FS, SC, Kiosk

SUPPORT & TRAINING PROVIDED:
Financial Assistance Provided: Yes(I)
Site Selection Assistance: Yes
Lease Negotiation Assistance: N/A
Co-Operative Advertising: Yes
Franchisee Assoc./Member: Yes/Yes
Size Of Corporate Staff: 151
On-Going Support: A,C,G,I
Training: 10 Days Corporate Office (Excludes Travel and Lodging Expenses).

SPECIFIC EXPANSION PLANS:
US: All United States
Canada: No
Overseas: No

<< >>

ALTERNATIVE BOARD, THE (TAB)

225 E. 16th Ave.,# 580
Denver, CO 80203-1608
Tel: (800) 727-0126 (303) 839-1200
Fax: (303) 839-9012
E-Mail: tamyra@TABoards.com
Web Site: www.TABoards.com
Ms. Tamyra A. Wallace, Dir. Facilitator Dev.

TAB Facilitators develop and facilitate small peer advisory groups of presidents, CEOs, and business owners who meet once a month. Each business owner discusses challenges or opportunities he or she is having in his or her business. Solutions and strategies are provided by the facilitator and other group members. Senior level executive and/or business consulting experience required.

BACKGROUND: IFA MEMBER
Established: 1990; 1st Franchised: 1996
Franchised Units: 38
Company-Owned Units 41
Total Units: 79
Dist.: US-47; CAN-3; O'seas-0
North America: 22 States, 3 Provinces
Density: NR
Projected New Units (12 Months): 24
Qualifications: 3, 5, 5, 5, 5, 5
Registered: All Except VA

FINANCIAL/TERMS:
Cash Investment: $8-34.9K
Total Investment: $32.4-51.7K
Minimum Net Worth: $N/A
Fees: Franchise - $34.9K
Royalty - 10%; Ad. - 1%
Earnings Claim Statement: No
Term of Contract (Years): 10/10
Avg. # Of Employees: 1 FT
Passive Ownership: Not Allowed
Encourage Conversions: N/A
Area Develop. Agreements: No
Sub-Franchising Contracts: No
Expand In Territory: Yes
Space Needs: N/A SF; HB or Executive Office Suite

SUPPORT & TRAINING PROVIDED:
Financial Assistance Provided: No
Site Selection Assistance: N/A
Lease Negotiation Assistance: N/A
Co-Operative Advertising: Yes
Franchisee Assoc./Member: Yes
Size Of Corporate Staff: 12
On-Going Support: A,C,D,d,E,G,H,h,I
Training: 4 Days Denver, CO; 3 Weeks Franchisee's Territory Field Support Training.

SPECIFIC EXPANSION PLANS:
US: All United States
Canada: All Canada
Overseas: All Countries

<< >>

AMERICAN INSTITUTE OF SMALL BUSINESS

7515 Wayzata Blvd., # 129
Minneapolis, MN 55426
Tel: (800) 328-2906 (953) 545-7001
Fax: (953) 545-7020
E-Mail: aisbofmn@aol.com
Web Site: www.aisbofmn.com
Mr. Max Fallek, President

THE AMERICAN INSTITUTE OF SMALL BUSINESS provides educational materials, including books, on small business and entrepreneurship. It also provides a seminar for training people on how to set up and operate their own small business. THE INSTITUTE also supplies business software sold by franchisees.

BACKGROUND:
Established: 1985; 1st Franchised: 1988
Franchised Units: 8
Company-Owned Units 1
Total Units: 9
Dist.: US-4; CAN-0; O'seas-2
North America: 7 States
Density: 1 in MN, 1 in CO, 1 in IL
Projected New Units (12 Months): NR
Qualifications: 3, 4, 3, 2, 1, 1
Registered: MN

FINANCIAL/TERMS:
Cash Investment: $5K
Total Investment: $10K
Minimum Net Worth: $NR
Fees: Franchise - $5K
Royalty - 0%; Ad. - 0%
Earnings Claim Statement: NR
Term of Contract (Years): 2/Varies
Avg. # Of Employees: 1 PT
Passive Ownership: Allowed
Encourage Conversions: N/A
Area Develop. Agreements: No

Sub-Franchising Contracts: No
Expand In Territory: Yes
Space Needs: 600 SF; NR

SUPPORT & TRAINING PROVIDED:
Financial Assistance Provided: Yes
Site Selection Assistance: Yes
Lease Negotiation Assistance: N/A
Co-Operative Advertising: N/A
Franchisee Assoc./Member: NR
Size Of Corporate Staff: 5
On-Going Support: B,D,E,h,I
Training: 1 Day Headquarters.

SPECIFIC EXPANSION PLANS:
US: All United States
Canada: All Canada
Overseas: All Countries

<< >>

CONFIDENTIAL BUSINESS CONNECTION

4155 E. Jewell Ave., # 1010
Denver, CO 80222
Tel: (888) 446-1414 (303) 759-2334
Fax: (303) 584-0793
E-Mail: rwbert@ix.netcom.com
Mr. Chris W. Sales, President

Reorganized in 1997, CBC offers a unique alternative to the traditional business brokerage market by providing a non-exclusive clearinghouse for business/franchise buyers and sellers. Services range from 'List & Match' to full valuation and total structuring. CBC relies on confidential profiles, matching capabilities and heavy advertising/telemarketing on a national level to ensure the right connection is made.

BACKGROUND:
Established: 1997; 1st Franchised: 1997
Franchised Units: 1
Company-Owned Units 0
Total Units: 1
Dist.: US-1; CAN-0; O'seas-0
North America: 1 State
Density: 1 in CO
Projected New Units (12 Months): 8
Qualifications: 4, 3, 3, 4, 2, 5
Registered: NR

FINANCIAL/TERMS:
Cash Investment: $50-100K
Total Investment: $50-100K
Minimum Net Worth: $70K
Fees: Franchise - $15.5-31K
Royalty - 6%; Ad. - 2%
Earnings Claim Statement: No
Term of Contract (Years): 10/10
Avg. # Of Employees: 3 FT, 1 PT
Passive Ownership: Discouraged
Encourage Conversions: No
Area Develop. Agreements: No
Sub-Franchising Contracts: No
Expand In Territory: Yes
Space Needs: 700 SF; Class A Office

SUPPORT & TRAINING PROVIDED:
Financial Assistance Provided: No
Site Selection Assistance: Yes
Lease Negotiation Assistance: Yes
Co-Operative Advertising: Yes
Franchisee Assoc./Member: No
Size Of Corporate Staff: 2
On-Going Support: c,d,E,G,h,I
Training: 1 Week Denver, CO; 3 Days On-Site.

SPECIFIC EXPANSION PLANS:
US: All United States
Canada: All Canada
Overseas: No

<< >>

CORPORATE MINUTES MADE FRANCHISING

5631 E. Le Mauche Ave.
Scottsdale, AZ 85265
Tel: (480) 510-9000
Fax: (480) 473-2323
E-Mail: duncan@franchise1.net
Web Site: www.franchise1.net
Mr. Duncan McGillivray, EVP Managing Director

Our franchises sell corporate minutes to their clients. Truly home-based opportunity with low investment and very high potential return. No inventory, employees, leases or franchisor performance reporting necessary. Personal computer, printer, telephone and fax required. Territory protected. Founder offers 24 years of experience. Software provided.

BACKGROUND:
Established: 1995; 1st Franchised: 1995
Franchised Units: 17
Company-Owned Units 0
Total Units: 17
Dist.: US-17; CAN-0; O'seas-0
North America: 6 States
Density: 6 in WS, 2 in CA, 2 in AZ
Projected New Units (12 Months): NR
Registered: NR

FINANCIAL/TERMS:
Cash Investment: $NR
Total Investment: $12.5-17.5
Minimum Net Worth: $N/A
Fees: Franchise - $12.5K
Royalty - $250/month; Ad. - 0%
Earnings Claim Statement: No
Term of Contract (Years): 10/10
Avg. # Of Employees: 1 FT
Passive Ownership: Discouraged
Encourage Conversions: NR
Area Develop. Agreements: NR
Sub-Franchising Contracts: No
Expand In Territory: Yes
Space Needs: NR SF; NR

SUPPORT & TRAINING PROVIDED:
Financial Assistance Provided: NR
Site Selection Assistance: N/A
Lease Negotiation Assistance: N/A
Co-Operative Advertising: No
Franchisee Assoc./Member: No
Size Of Corporate Staff: NR
On-Going Support: NR
Training: Optional Half-Day, Scottsdale, AZ.

SPECIFIC EXPANSION PLANS:
US: All United States
Canada: NR
Overseas: NR

<< >>

ENTREPRENEUR'S SOURCE, THE

900 Main St. S., Bldg. # 2
Southbury, CT 06488
Tel: (800) 289-0086 (203) 264-2006
Fax: (203) 264-3516
E-Mail: info@TheESource.com
Web Site: www.franchisematch.com
Mr. Chris Otter, Franchise Director

We provide consulting, education and guidance to people exploring self-employment as an additional career option. Using a unique profiling system, ENTREPRENEUR'S SOURCE consultants help people discover the best options for them.

BACKGROUND: IFA MEMBER
Established: 1984; 1st Franchised: 1998
Franchised Units: 50
Company-Owned Units 0
Total Units: 50
Dist.: US-43; CAN-1; O'seas-0
North America: 27 States
Density: 5 in GA, 5 in FL, 3 in SC,
Projected New Units (12 Months): 40
Qualifications: 4, 4, 1, 1, 2, 5
Registered: CA,FL,MD,MI,MN,NY,VA, WA,WI

FINANCIAL/TERMS:
Cash Investment: $50K

Total Investment: $45-50K
Minimum Net Worth: $100K
Fees: Franchise - $35K
Royalty - 0%; Ad. - $350/Mo.
Earnings Claim Statement: No
Term of Contract (Years): 10/10
Avg. # Of Employees: 1 FT
Passive Ownership: Not Allowed
Encourage Conversions: Yes
Area Develop. Agreements: No
Sub-Franchising Contracts: Yes
Expand In Territory: Yes
Space Needs: NR SF; N/A

SUPPORT & TRAINING PROVIDED:
Financial Assistance Provided: Yes(I)
Site Selection Assistance: N/A
Lease Negotiation Assistance: N/A
Co-Operative Advertising: Yes
Franchisee Assoc./Member: No
Size Of Corporate Staff: 6
On-Going Support: D,H,I
Training: 8 Days in CT.

SPECIFIC EXPANSION PLANS:
US: All United States
Canada: All Canada
Overseas: Most Countries

<< >>

FIDUCIAL℠

FIDUCIAL

10480 Little Patuxent Pkwy., 3rd Fl.
Columbia, MD 21044
Tel: (800) 323-9000 (410) 910-5885
Fax: (410) 910-5903
E-Mail: franchise@fiducial.com
Web Site: www.fiducial.com
Mr. Howard Margolis, Manager Field Operations/Dev.

A FIDUCIAL franchise is a sophisticated professional service firm providing small businesses and individuals with back office support and accounting and financial management, tax, financial, business counseling and payroll services. Franchise offices operate out of commercial spaces that will impress customers that their needs will be taken care of by qualified individuals, who will be there for them year after year. Package includes initial and on-going training, proprietary software and full support

BACKGROUND:
Established: 1999; 1st Franchised: 1999
Franchised Units: 693
Company-Owned Units 20
Total Units: 713
Dist.: US-713; CAN-0; O'seas-0
North America: 48 States
Density: 60 in CA, 37 in TX, 34 FL
Projected New Units (12 Months): 100
Qualifications: 4, 4, 2, 3, 3, 4
Registered: All States

FINANCIAL/TERMS:
Cash Investment: $25-75K
Total Investment: $39-116K
Minimum Net Worth: $150K
Fees: Franchise - $7.5-25K
Royalty - 1.5-6%; Ad. - 2%
Earnings Claim Statement: No
Term of Contract (Years): 10/5
Avg. # Of Employees: 1 FT, 1 PT
Passive Ownership: Not Allowed
Encourage Conversions: Yes
Area Develop. Agreements: No
Sub-Franchising Contracts: No
Expand In Territory: No
Space Needs: 600 SF; OB

SUPPORT & TRAINING PROVIDED:
Financial Assistance Provided: Yes(I)
Site Selection Assistance: Yes
Lease Negotiation Assistance: No
Co-Operative Advertising: No
Franchisee Assoc./Member: Yes/Yes
Size Of Corporate Staff: 80+
On-Going Support: A,B,C,D,E,F,G,H,I
Training: 10 Days in Columbia, MD; 2 Weeks Self-Administered.

SPECIFIC EXPANSION PLANS:
US: All United States
Canada: No
Overseas: No

<< >>

FORTUNE PRACTICE MANAGEMENT

9191 Towne Centre Dr., # 600
San Diego, CA 92122
Tel: (800) 628-1052 (858) 535-6287
Fax: (858) 535-6387
E-Mail: Bradfpm@aol.com
Web Site: www.fortunepractice.com
Mr. Brad Hunsaker, General Manager

FORTUNE PRACTICE MANAGEMENT is a comprehensive health care coaching / management company. We offer franchisees a set program to help health care professional run successful practices.

BACKGROUND:
Established: 1990; 1st Franchised: 1991
Franchised Units: 41
Company-Owned Units 0
Total Units: 41
Dist.: US-37; CAN-1; O'seas-0
North America: 23 States
Density: 7 in CA, 3 in FL, 3 in WA
Projected New Units (12 Months): 4
Qualifications: 2, 5, 2, 3, 4, 5
Registered: CA,FL,IL,IN,MD,MI,NY

FINANCIAL/TERMS:
Cash Investment: $20-60K
Total Investment: $43.9-114.7K
Minimum Net Worth: $100K
Fees: Franchise - $42K
Royalty - 10%; Ad. - 5%
Earnings Claim Statement: No
Term of Contract (Years): 5/5
Avg. # Of Employees: 1 FT
Passive Ownership: Discouraged
Encourage Conversions: N/A
Area Develop. Agreements: No
Sub-Franchising Contracts: No
Expand In Territory: Yes
Space Needs: N/A SF; HB

SUPPORT & TRAINING PROVIDED:
Financial Assistance Provided: Yes(I)
Site Selection Assistance: N/A
Lease Negotiation Assistance: N/A
Co-Operative Advertising: Yes
Franchisee Assoc./Member: Yes/No
Size Of Corporate Staff: 3
On-Going Support: B,C,D,G,H,I
Training: 1 Week in Memphis, TN.

SPECIFIC EXPANSION PLANS:
US: Midwest, Northeast
Canada: AB, ON
Overseas: No

<< >>

FRANKLIN TRAFFIC SERVICE

P.O. Box 100
Ransomville, NY 14131
Tel: (716) 731-3131
Fax: (716) 731-2705
Mr. James C. Knox, President

We provide a full range of traffic management services to clients including, but not limited to, freight bill audit and payment, carrier selection and negotiation, loss and damage servicing, international audit/payment and compliance services, etc.

BACKGROUND:
Established: 1969; 1st Franchised: 1985
Franchised Units: 2

Company-Owned Units 0
Total Units: 2
Dist.: US-3; CAN-0; O'seas-0
North America: 2 States
Density: 2 in NY, 1 in MN
Projected New Units (12 Months): 3
Qualifications: 3, 5, 5, 3, , 5
Registered: NY

FINANCIAL/TERMS:
Cash Investment: $25K
Total Investment: $25K
Minimum Net Worth: $N/A
Fees: Franchise - $25K
Royalty - Varies; Ad. - N/A
Earnings Claim Statement: No
Term of Contract (Years): 5/5
Avg. # Of Employees: 1 FT
Passive Ownership: Allowed
Encourage Conversions: N/A
Area Develop. Agreements: No
Sub-Franchising Contracts: No
Expand In Territory: Yes
Space Needs: NR SF; N/A

SUPPORT & TRAINING PROVIDED:
Financial Assistance Provided: Yes(D)
Site Selection Assistance: N/A
Lease Negotiation Assistance: N/A
Co-Operative Advertising: N/A
Franchisee Assoc./Member: No
Size Of Corporate Staff: 70
On-Going Support: A,B,C,d,G
Training: 3 Weeks Ransomville, NY.

SPECIFIC EXPANSION PLANS:
US: Southeast, Midwest
Canada: No
Overseas: No

<< >>

FULL CIRCLE IMAGE

6256 34th Ave., NW
Rochester, MN 55901
Tel: (800) 584-7244 (507) 280-0136
Fax: (507) 280-4425
E-Mail: fullinfo@fullcircleimage.com
Web Site: www.fullcircleimage.com
Mr. Charles Benson, President

FULL CIRCLE IMAGE is a direct sales franchise specializing in remanufactured laser toner, ink jet and printer ribbon cartridges. Tap into the $15 billion industry of imaging products used in every business every day. Help reduce waste through recycling while presenting your customers with guaranteed product with guaranteed savings.

BACKGROUND:
Established: 1991; 1st Franchised: 1997
Franchised Units: 31
Company-Owned Units 0
Total Units: 31
Dist.: US-23; CAN-0; O'seas-3
North America: NR
Density: 11 in MN, 2 in WI
Projected New Units (12 Months): 20
Qualifications: 2, 2, 1, 1, 1, 3
Registered: CA,FL,IL,IN,MD,MI,MN,NY, ND,OR,SD,WI

FINANCIAL/TERMS:
Cash Investment: $3K
Total Investment: $20-25K
Minimum Net Worth: $20K
Fees: Franchise - $20K
Royalty - 5%; Ad. - 3%
Earnings Claim Statement: No
Term of Contract (Years): 10/10
Avg. # Of Employees: 1 FT
Passive Ownership: Not Allowed
Encourage Conversions: N/A
Area Develop. Agreements: No
Sub-Franchising Contracts: No
Expand In Territory: Yes
Space Needs: NR SF; N/A

SUPPORT & TRAINING PROVIDED:
Financial Assistance Provided: Yes(I)
Site Selection Assistance: N/A
Lease Negotiation Assistance: N/A
Co-Operative Advertising: Yes
Franchisee Assoc./Member: No
Size Of Corporate Staff: 30
On-Going Support: a,B,C,D,F,G,h,I
Training: 1 Week at Home Office; 1 Week at Your Center Location.

SPECIFIC EXPANSION PLANS:
US: All United States
Canada: All Canada
Overseas: Panama, Costa Rica, Mexico, Guatemala, El Slavador, Venezuela, Columbia

<< >>

IMPRESSIONS ON HOLD

4880 S. Lewis Ave., # 200
Tulsa, OK 74105-5100
Tel: (800) 580-4653 (918) 744-0988
Fax: (918) 744-0989
E-Mail: jmiller@impressionsonhold.com
Web Site: www.impressionsonhold.com
Mr. John Miller, Dir. Franchise Development

We are an advertising company tied to the tele-communications industry. We enable businesses to use the "on-hold" time of their phone system as a marketing tool. Our franchisees market and sell the "on-hold" service to businesses on a local level, and corporate offices then custom-produce the work that is sold on behalf of the franchise owner.

BACKGROUND: IFA MEMBER
Established: 1991; 1st Franchised: 1994
Franchised Units: 74
Company-Owned Units 10
Total Units: 84
Dist.: US-75; CAN-0; O'seas-0
North America: NR
Density: NR
Projected New Units (12 Months): 18
Qualifications: 3, 4, 3, 3, 3, 5
Registered: CA,FL,HI,MD,MI,NY,VA,WA

FINANCIAL/TERMS:
Cash Investment: $47K
Total Investment: $50K
Minimum Net Worth: $150K
Fees: Franchise - $47K
Royalty - 4%; Ad. - 1%
Earnings Claim Statement: No
Term of Contract (Years): 10/10
Avg. # Of Employees: NR
Passive Ownership: Discouraged
Encourage Conversions: N/A
Area Develop. Agreements: No
Sub-Franchising Contracts: No
Expand In Territory: Yes
Space Needs: NR SF; HB

SUPPORT & TRAINING PROVIDED:
Financial Assistance Provided: Yes(I)
Site Selection Assistance: N/A
Lease Negotiation Assistance: N/A
Co-Operative Advertising: N/A
Franchisee Assoc./Member: Yes
Size Of Corporate Staff: 50
On-Going Support: A,B,C,D,G,h,I
Training: 5 Days at Corporate Office; 2 Days On-Site.

SPECIFIC EXPANSION PLANS:
US: All United States
Canada: All Canada
Overseas: No

<< >>

INTELLIGENT OFFICE, THE

4450 Arapahoe Ave.
Boulder, CO 80303-9123
Tel: (800) 800-1956 (303) 447-9000
Fax: (303) 415-2500

E-Mail: dballen@mfvexpo.com
Web Site: www.intelligentoffice.com
Mr. Dennis A. Ballen, Exclusive Agent

This highly-evolved alternative to the traditional office provides a prestigious address, anywhere communications and a live receptionist for businesses, corporate executives and professionals, releasing them from the limitations and expense of a residential office. THE INTELLIGENT OFFICE offers private offices, conference rooms and professional office services on an as-needed basis and at only a fraction of the cost of a traditional office.

BACKGROUND: IFA MEMBER
Established: 1999; 1st Franchised: 1999
Franchised Units: 23
Company-Owned Units 3
Total Units: 26
Dist.: US-2; CAN-0; O'seas-0
North America: 3 States
Density: 9 in FL, 2 in CO
Projected New Units (12 Months): 18
Qualifications: 1, 5, 1, 3, 1, 1
Registered: NR

FINANCIAL/TERMS:
Cash Investment: $120K+
Total Investment: $350-500
Minimum Net Worth: $N/A
Fees: Franchise - $38K
Royalty - 5%; Ad. - $250/Mo.
Earnings Claim Statement: No
Term of Contract (Years): 20/20
Avg. # Of Employees: 5 FT
Passive Ownership: Allowed
Encourage Conversions: No
Area Develop. Agreements: Yes
Sub-Franchising Contracts: Yes
Expand In Territory: Yes
Space Needs: 4,500-6,500 SF; OB

SUPPORT & TRAINING PROVIDED:
Financial Assistance Provided: Yes(I)
Site Selection Assistance: Yes
Lease Negotiation Assistance: Yes
Co-Operative Advertising: Yes
Franchisee Assoc./Member: Yes/IFA
Size Of Corporate Staff: 6
On-Going Support: C,D,E,H,G
Training: 1 Week Boulder, CO; 1 Week On-Site.

SPECIFIC EXPANSION PLANS:
US: All United States
Canada: All Canada
Overseas: All Countries

<< >>

INTERFACE FINANCIAL GROUP, THE

4521 PGA Blvd., # 211
Palm Beach Gardens, FL 33418
Tel: (800) 387-0860 (905) 475-5701
Fax: (905) 475-8688
E-Mail: ifg@interfacefinancial.com
Web Site: www.interfacefinancial.com
Mr. David T. Banfield, President

Franchise buys quality accounts receivables from client companies at a discount to provide short-term working capital to expanding businesses.

BACKGROUND:
Established: 1971; 1st Franchised: 1991
Franchised Units: 76
Company-Owned Units 0
Total Units: 76
Dist.: US-29; CAN-47; O'seas-0
North America: 11 States, 6 Provinces
Density: 7 in ON, 9 in CA
Projected New Units (12 Months): 12
Qualifications: 3, 3, 4, 2, 2, 3
Registered: CA,FL,IL,MD,MI,MN,NY,VA ,WA & FTC Disclosure States

FINANCIAL/TERMS:
Cash Investment: $50K
Total Investment: $50-100K
Minimum Net Worth: $150K
Fees: Franchise - $25K
Royalty - 8%; Ad. - 1%
Earnings Claim Statement: No
Term of Contract (Years): 10/10
Avg. # Of Employees: 1 PT
Passive Ownership: Discouraged
Encourage Conversions: N/A
Area Develop. Agreements: Yes
Sub-Franchising Contracts: NR
Expand In Territory: Yes
Space Needs: N/A SF; HB

SUPPORT & TRAINING PROVIDED:
Financial Assistance Provided: Yes
Site Selection Assistance: N/A
Lease Negotiation Assistance: N/A
Co-Operative Advertising: No
Franchisee Assoc./Member: No
Size Of Corporate Staff: NR
On-Going Support: D,E,I
Training: 2 Days + Minimum 3 Days On-Site.

SPECIFIC EXPANSION PLANS:
US: All United States
Canada: All Canada
Overseas: All Countries

INTERNATIONAL MERGERS & ACQUISITIONS

4300 N. Miller Rd., # 230
Scottsdale, AZ 85251
Tel: (480) 990-3899
Fax: (480) 990-7480
E-Mail: imahq@aol.com
Web Site: www.ima-world.com
Mr. Neil D. Lewis, President/CEO

An international affiliation of members engaged in the profession of serving merger and acquisitions-minded companies, offering consulting services, financing services, M & A services and other services of a distinctive nature. A one-stop service for corporate needs.

BACKGROUND:
Established: 1969; 1st Franchised: 1979
Franchised Units: 65
Company-Owned Units 0
Total Units: 65
Dist.: US-60; CAN-0; O'seas-8
North America: 24 States
Density: 7 in AZ, 4 in CA, 3 in NY
Projected New Units (12 Months): 6-12
Qualifications: 3, 5, 5, 4, 1, 5
Registered: All States

FINANCIAL/TERMS:
Cash Investment: $10-50K
Total Investment: $10-50K
Minimum Net Worth: $N/A
Fees: Franchise - $10K
Royalty - $375/Qtr.; Ad. - N/A
Earnings Claim Statement: No
Term of Contract (Years): 10/10
Avg. # Of Employees: 2 FT
Passive Ownership: Not Allowed
Encourage Conversions: N/A
Area Develop. Agreements: No
Sub-Franchising Contracts: Yes
Expand In Territory: No
Space Needs: N/A SF; N/A

SUPPORT & TRAINING PROVIDED:
Financial Assistance Provided: No
Site Selection Assistance: N/A
Lease Negotiation Assistance: N/A
Co-Operative Advertising: N/A
Franchisee Assoc./Member: No
Size Of Corporate Staff: 3
On-Going Support: A,G,H

Training: 3 Days World Headquarters; 2 Days Creative Work Sessions; As Needed World Headquarters.

SPECIFIC EXPANSION PLANS:

US: All United States
Canada: All Canada
Overseas: All Countries

<< >>

JAY ROBERTS & ASSOCIATES

608 Mack St.
Joliet, IL 60435
Tel: (815) 726-9359
Fax: (815) 722-4750
E-Mail: jayroberts_sbs@msn.com
Mr. John S. Meers, President

JAY ROBERTS & ASSOCIATES is a management/financial consultant firm started in 1965. It specializes in start-up, general and turn-around consulting to small and medium-sized businesses. An emphasis is put on loan brokerage, particularly government loans.

BACKGROUND:

Established: 1965; 1st Franchised: 1981
Franchised Units: 30
Company-Owned Units 2
Total Units: 32
Dist.: US-32; CAN-0; O'seas-0
North America: 16 States
Density: 2 in IL, 2 in NY, 2 in CA
Projected New Units (12 Months): 12
Qualifications: 3, 4, 2, 3, 4, 3
Registered: NR

FINANCIAL/TERMS:

Cash Investment: $25-50K
Total Investment: $Varies
Minimum Net Worth: $NR
Fees: Franchise - $2K
Royalty - Varies; Ad. - N/A
Earnings Claim Statement: No
Term of Contract (Years): Open/Open
Avg. # Of Employees: 2 FT
Passive Ownership: Not Allowed
Encourage Conversions: N/A
Area Develop. Agreements: Yes
Sub-Franchising Contracts: No
Expand In Territory: Yes
Space Needs: Varies SF; HB

SUPPORT & TRAINING PROVIDED:

Financial Assistance Provided: Yes(D)
Site Selection Assistance: No
Lease Negotiation Assistance: No
Co-Operative Advertising: No
Franchisee Assoc./Member: No
Size Of Corporate Staff: 5
On-Going Support: A,C,D,G,h
Training: 1 Week Joliet, IL.

SPECIFIC EXPANSION PLANS:

US: All United States
Canada: No
Overseas: No

<< >>

MANUFACTURING MANAGEMENT ASSOCIATES

2625 W. Butterfield Rd., # 212E
Oak Brook, IL 60523
Tel: (800) 574-0308 (630) 574-0300
Fax: (630) 574-0309
E-Mail: franchising@consult-mma.com
Web Site: www.consult-mma.com
Mr. Roger Dykstra, President

Manufacturing consulting: for the small- and medium-size company. Teaching you the market development and sales techniques that made the 'big guys' big. We use your experience and knowledge with our proven methodologies to deliver a quality service.

BACKGROUND:

Established: 1982; 1st Franchised: 1992
Franchised Units: 10
Company-Owned Units 0
Total Units: 10
Dist.: US-8; CAN-2; O'seas-0
North America: 6 States
Density: 2 in IN, 2 in IL
Projected New Units (12 Months): 4
Qualifications: 4, 5, 4, 4, 3, 5
Registered: IL,MI,KS

FINANCIAL/TERMS:

Cash Investment: $10-15K
Total Investment: $15-25K
Minimum Net Worth: $25-50K
Fees: Franchise - $6-8K
Royalty - 5%; Ad. - 1%/$500
Earnings Claim Statement: No
Term of Contract (Years): 10/10
Avg. # Of Employees: 1 FT
Passive Ownership: Not Allowed
Encourage Conversions: Yes
Area Develop. Agreements: No
Sub-Franchising Contracts: No
Expand In Territory: Yes
Space Needs: NR SF; N/A

SUPPORT & TRAINING PROVIDED:

Financial Assistance Provided: N/A
Site Selection Assistance: Yes
Lease Negotiation Assistance: Yes
Co-Operative Advertising: Yes
Franchisee Assoc./Member: No
Size Of Corporate Staff: 20
On-Going Support: a,E,G,H,I
Training: 8-10 Days Chicago, IL.

SPECIFIC EXPANSION PLANS:

US: All United States
Canada: All Canada
Overseas: No

<< >>

MISTER MONEY - USA

238 Walnut St.
Ft. Collins, CO 80524
Tel: (800) 827-7296 (970) 493-0574
Fax: (970) 490-2099
E-Mail: tim@mistermoney.com
Web Site: www.mistermoney.com
Mr. Don Ettinger, Franchise Sales Dir.

MISTER MONEY - USA franchises offer pawn loans, payday loans, check cashing, money orders, and other financial services. Franchisees operate full-service retail stores or loan only outlets. MISTER MONEY - USA stores are modern, customer friendly and located in solid blue collar areas.

BACKGROUND:

Established: 1976; 1st Franchised: 1996
Franchised Units: 35
Company-Owned Units 14
Total Units: 49
Dist.: US-48; CAN-0; O'seas-2
North America: 11 States
Density: 13 in IA, 9 in CO, 4 in WI
Projected New Units (12 Months): 12
Qualifications: 5, 4, 3, 3, 5, 5
Registered: FL,IL,IN,MN,ND,WI

FINANCIAL/TERMS:

Cash Investment: $65-150K
Total Investment: $65-200K
Minimum Net Worth: $65K
Fees: Franchise - $21.5-24.5K
Royalty - 3-5%; Ad. - 3%
Earnings Claim Statement: Yes
Term of Contract (Years): 5/5
Avg. # Of Employees: 3 FT, 1 PT
Passive Ownership: Discouraged

Encourage Conversions: Yes
Area Develop. Agreements: No
Sub-Franchising Contracts: Yes
Expand In Territory: Yes
Space Needs: 4,000-10,000 SF; FS, SF, SC

SUPPORT & TRAINING PROVIDED:
Financial Assistance Provided: Yes(D)
Site Selection Assistance: Yes
Lease Negotiation Assistance: Yes
Co-Operative Advertising: Yes
Franchisee Assoc./Member: Yes/Yes
Size Of Corporate Staff: 25
On-Going Support: a,B,C,D,E,F,G,I
Training: 10-14 Days Fort Collins, CO.

SPECIFIC EXPANSION PLANS:
US: All United States
Canada: No
Overseas: Mexico

<< >>

MONEY CONCEPTS (CANADA)

180 Attwell Dr., # 501
Etobicoke, ON M9W 6A9 CANADA
Tel: (800) 661-7296 (416) 674-0450
Fax: (416) 674-4785
Mr. Rob Sylvester, President

MONEY CONCEPTS offers financial planning control. We are the fastest-growing independent franchise in financial services in Canada, specializing in complete financial planning and searching the market for financial products to implement our plan.

BACKGROUND:
Established: 1984; 1st Franchised: 1985
Franchised Units: 94
Company-Owned Units 0
Total Units: 94
Dist.: US-0; CAN-94; O'seas-0
North America: 8 Provinces
Density: 53 in ON, 21 in BC, 5 in NB
Projected New Units (12 Months): 25
Qualifications: 3, 4, 1, 2, 4, 5
Registered: AB

FINANCIAL/TERMS:
Cash Investment: $50K
Total Investment: $80K
Minimum Net Worth: $200K+
Fees: Franchise - $49.5K
Royalty - Varies; Ad. - 2%/$5K Max.
Earnings Claim Statement: No
Term of Contract (Years): 5/1
Avg. # Of Employees: 4 FT
Passive Ownership: Discouraged
Encourage Conversions: N/A
Area Develop. Agreements: Yes/5
Sub-Franchising Contracts: No
Expand In Territory: Yes
Space Needs: 750-1,000 SF; N/A

SUPPORT & TRAINING PROVIDED:
Financial Assistance Provided: No
Site Selection Assistance: Yes
Lease Negotiation Assistance: No
Co-Operative Advertising: Yes
Franchisee Assoc./Member: Yes/Yes
Size Of Corporate Staff: 25
On-Going Support: A,b,C,D,G,H,I
Training: 2 Weeks Head Office.

SPECIFIC EXPANSION PLANS:
US: No
Canada: All Canada
Overseas: No

NETSPACE

2801 NE 208 Ter., 2nd Fl.
Miami, FL 33180
Tel: (800) 638-7722 (305) 931-4000
Fax: (305) 931-7772
E-Mail: info@netfrancorp.com
Web Site: www.netfrancorp.com
Mr. Dellray Lefevere, VP Franchise Development

Netspace offers full-service Internet consulting for small and mid-sized businesses, including website development, hosting, promotion and e-business solutions. Netspace marketing directors help franchisees build their business through phone and email support, virtual meetings and visits to the franchisee's location. Franchisees need not be techies, although some working knowledge of the computers and the Internet and strong people skills are preferable.

BACKGROUND: IFA MEMBER
Established: 1996; 1st Franchised: 2000
Franchised Units: 25
Company-Owned Units 0
Total Units: 25
Dist.: US-25; CAN-0; O'seas-0
North America: 17 States
Density: 2 in FL, 2 in NJ, 2 in NY
Projected New Units (12 Months): NR
Registered: NR

FINANCIAL/TERMS:
Cash Investment: $35-40K
Total Investment: $35-40K
Minimum Net Worth: $250K
Fees: Franchise - $30K
Royalty - 10%; Ad. - 1%
Earnings Claim Statement: No
Term of Contract (Years): 10/5
Avg. # Of Employees: 1 FT
Passive Ownership: Not Allowed
Encourage Conversions: NR
Area Develop. Agreements: Yes
Sub-Franchising Contracts: 10
Expand In Territory: Yes
Space Needs: NR SF; Other

SUPPORT & TRAINING PROVIDED:
Financial Assistance Provided: NR
Site Selection Assistance: Yes
Lease Negotiation Assistance: Yes
Co-Operative Advertising: No
Franchisee Assoc./Member: Yes
Size Of Corporate Staff: 20
On-Going Support: A,B,C,D,E,G,H,I
Training: 1 Week, Home Office; 1 Week, Franchisee's Location.

SPECIFIC EXPANSION PLANS:
US: All United States
Canada: NR
Overseas: NR

PROVENTURE BUSINESS GROUP

P.O. Box 338
Needham Heights, MA 02494
Tel: (781) 444-8278
Fax: (781) 444-0565
E-Mail: proventure@aol.com
Mr. William J. Tedoldi, President

PROVENTURE is an all-inclusive, New England-based business brokerage, consulting and management company. The group lists and sells going businesses including franchises (up to $100 million in value), and other business opportunities on a fee basis. We also offer a moderately-priced consulting service for new franchise start-ups.

BACKGROUND:
Established: 1979; 1st Franchised: 1981
Franchised Units: 9
Company-Owned Units 4
Total Units: 13
Dist.: US-9; CAN-0; O'seas-0
North America: 2 States
Density: 8 in MA, 1 in NH
Projected New Units (12 Months): 2
Qualifications: 3, 5, 3, 3, 4, 4
Registered: NR

FINANCIAL/TERMS:
Cash Investment: $35K
Total Investment: $35-50K
Minimum Net Worth: $N/A
Fees: Franchise - $10K

Royalty - 6%; Ad. - 0%
Earnings Claim Statement: No
Term of Contract (Years): 10/10
Avg. # Of Employees: 2 FT, 2 PT
Passive Ownership: Discouraged
Encourage Conversions: Yes
Area Develop. Agreements: No
Sub-Franchising Contracts: No
Expand In Territory: Yes
Space Needs: 500 SF; OB

SUPPORT & TRAINING PROVIDED:
Financial Assistance Provided: No
Site Selection Assistance: Yes
Lease Negotiation Assistance: Yes
Co-Operative Advertising: No
Franchisee Assoc./Member: No
Size Of Corporate Staff: 2
On-Going Support: C,D,E,G,h
Training: 1 Week Headquarters.

SPECIFIC EXPANSION PLANS:
US: New England
Canada: PQ, ON
Overseas: Mexico, Europe, Asia

QUIK INTERNET

170 E. 17th St., # 101
Costa Mesa, CA 92627-3701
Tel: (888) 784-5266 (949) 548-2171
Fax: (949) 548-0569
E-Mail: murray@quik.com
Web Site: www.quik/007.com
Mr. Murray Mead, CEO

QUIK INTERNET is the world's first and largest Internet services franchise, with over 200 franchises worldwide. Provide highly-demanded Internet services in your local community, including Internet access, Web design, on-line marketing and more. Prime territories, low fees - apply today!

BACKGROUND: IFA MEMBER
Established: 1996; 1st Franchised: 1996
Franchised Units: 210
Company-Owned Units 0
Total Units: 210
Dist.: US-200; CAN-0; O'seas-0
North America: NR
Density: CA, TX, FL
Projected New Units (12 Months): 250
Qualifications: 5, 5, 1, 4, 4, 4
Registered: All States and AB

FINANCIAL/TERMS:
Cash Investment: $65-75K
Total Investment: $65-75K
Minimum Net Worth: $N/A
Fees: Franchise - $35K
Royalty - 10%; Ad. - 3%
Earnings Claim Statement: No
Term of Contract (Years): 10/10
Avg. # Of Employees: 1 FT
Passive Ownership: NR
Encourage Conversions: N/A
Area Develop. Agreements: NR
Sub-Franchising Contracts: No
Expand In Territory: N/A
Space Needs: N/A SF; N/A

SUPPORT & TRAINING PROVIDED:
Financial Assistance Provided: No
Site Selection Assistance: N/A
Lease Negotiation Assistance: N/A
Co-Operative Advertising: No
Franchisee Assoc./Member: No
Size Of Corporate Staff: 30
On-Going Support: A,P,C,D,F
Training: 1 Week Costa Mesa, CA.

SPECIFIC EXPANSION PLANS:
US: All United States
Canada: All Canada
Overseas: All Countries

<< >>

SUNBELT BUSINESS BROKERS

2 Amherst St.
Charleston, SC 29413-0549
Tel: (800) 771-7866 (843) 853-4781
Fax: (843) 853-4135
E-Mail: sunset@sunbeltnetwork.com
Web Site: www.sunbeltnetwork.com
Mr. Edward T. Pendarvis, President

We offer business brokerage/merger and acquisition franchises. SUNBELT is the largest and fastest-growing business brokerage firm in the world. Our success comes from our name recognition, quality training programs and hands-on assistance. We are the leaders in computerized office management, networking and Internet technology. We take no percentage fees. All of our services are covered in our low semi-annual fee.

BACKGROUND: IFA MEMBER
Established: 1978; 1st Franchised: 1993
Franchised Units: 178
Company-Owned Units 1
Total Units: 179
Dist.: US-199; CAN-0; O'seas-6
North America: 38 States
Density: 16 in FL, 10 in NC, 10 in VA
Projected New Units (12 Months): 50
Registered: CA,FL,HI,IL,IN,MD,MI,MN, NY,OR,RI,SD,VA,WA,WI

FINANCIAL/TERMS:
Cash Investment: $5-15K
Total Investment: $5-50K
Minimum Net Worth: $N/A
Fees: Franchise - $5-10K
Royalty - $3-6K/Yr.; Ad. - 0%
Earnings Claim Statement: No
Term of Contract (Years): On-Going
Avg. # Of Employees:
Independent Contrac.
Passive Ownership: Not Allowed
Encourage Conversions: Yes
Area Develop. Agreements: No
Sub-Franchising Contracts: No
Expand In Territory: Yes
Space Needs: 1,000 SF; FS

SUPPORT & TRAINING PROVIDED:
Financial Assistance Provided: Yes(D)
Site Selection Assistance: N/A
Lease Negotiation Assistance: N/A
Co-Operative Advertising: N/A
Franchisee Assoc./Member: Yes/Yes
Size Of Corporate Staff: 9
On-Going Support: C,D,G,H,I
Training: 4 Days Various Regional Centers.

SPECIFIC EXPANSION PLANS:
US: All United States
Canada: All Canada
Overseas: All Countries

VR BUSINESS BROKERS

2601 E. Oakland Park Blvd., # 205
Ft. Lauderdale, FL 33306
Tel: (800) 377-8722 (954) 565-1555
Fax: (954) 565-6855
E-Mail: pking@vrbusinessbrokers.com
Web Site: www.vrbusinessbrokers.com
Mr. Richard Brinkley, Principal

Oldest established chain of franchised business brokers in the nation. We also publish 'Today's Business Owner Magazine' for exclusive use of franchisees at no additional cost.

BACKGROUND:
Established: 1978; 1st Franchised: 1979
Franchised Units: 112
Company-Owned Units 0
Total Units: 112
Dist.: US-85; CAN-0; O'seas-0
North America: 37 States
Density: 12 in FL, 10 in CA, 5 in NC
Projected New Units (12 Months): NR
Qualifications: 3, 3, 3, 3, 2, 5
Registered: CA,FL,IL,MD,MI, OR,WA

FINANCIAL/TERMS:
Cash Investment: $40-75K
Total Investment: $40-75K
Minimum Net Worth: $150K
Fees: Franchise - $12K
Royalty - 6%; Ad. - $150/Mo.
Earnings Claim Statement: No
Term of Contract (Years): 10/10
Avg. # Of Employees: 2 FT, 1 PT
Passive Ownership: Not Allowed
Encourage Conversions: Yes
Area Develop. Agreements: No
Sub-Franchising Contracts: No
Expand In Territory: No
Space Needs: Varies SF; OB
SUPPORT & TRAINING PROVIDED:
Financial Assistance Provided: No
Site Selection Assistance: Yes
Lease Negotiation Assistance: Yes
Co-Operative Advertising: Yes
Franchisee Assoc./Member: Yes/Yes
Size Of Corporate Staff: 10
On-Going Support: A,B,C,d,G,H,I
Training: 2.5 Weeks Greensboro, NC; 2.5 Weeks Ft. Lauderdale, FL.
SPECIFIC EXPANSION PLANS:
US: All United States
Canada: Soon
Overseas: Soon

WORLD TRADE NETWORK

580 Lincoln Park Blvd., # 300
Dayton, OH 45429
Tel: (800) 227-3772 (937) 298-3383
Fax: (937) 298-2550
E-Mail: wtnet@infinet.com
Web Site: www.wnetwork.com
Mr. Michael J. Wenzler, President/CEO

WORLD TRADE NETWORK has created a structure and system for the import/export business and combined it with the franchise/licensing industry to create an international trading company with self-motivated entrepreneurs and existing import/export companies. The WTN structure was created over a 9-year period. In 4 years, it has trained over 40 offices in over 30 countries. The international trading business is booming!

BACKGROUND:
Established: 1993; 1st Franchised: 1993
Franchised Units: 40
Company-Owned Units 1
Total Units: 41
Dist.: US-5; CAN-1; O'seas-35
North America: NR
Density: 2 in CA, 1 in WI, 1 in OH
Projected New Units (12 Months): 5
Qualifications: 4, 4, 3, 2, 3, 2
Registered: FL
FINANCIAL/TERMS:
Cash Investment: $85K
Total Investment: $135K
Minimum Net Worth: $Varies
Fees: Franchise - $12K
Royalty - 7%; Ad. - 3%
Earnings Claim Statement: No
Term of Contract (Years): 10/15
Avg. # Of Employees: 1 FT, 1 PT
Passive Ownership: Discouraged
Encourage Conversions: Yes
Area Develop. Agreements: No
Sub-Franchising Contracts: No
Expand In Territory: No
Space Needs: 400 SF; OB
SUPPORT & TRAINING PROVIDED:
Financial Assistance Provided: Yes(D)
Site Selection Assistance: No
Lease Negotiation Assistance: No
Co-Operative Advertising: No
Franchisee Assoc./Member: No
Size Of Corporate Staff: 3
On-Going Support: d,G,h
Training: 5 Days in Dayton, OH.
SPECIFIC EXPANSION PLANS:
US: All United States
Canada: All Canada
Overseas: All Countries

WSI INTERNET

5915 Airport Rd., # 300
Mississauga, ON L4V 1T1 CANADA
Tel: (888) 678-7588 (905) 678-7588
Fax: (905) 678-7242
E-Mail: ralvarado@wsicorporate.com
Web Site: www.wsicorporate.com
Mr. Roberto Alvarado, Senior Marketing Executive

WSI INTERNET is proud to have been rated in the Top 100 Franchises by Entrepreneur Magazine. You can be part of this successful franchise and profit from the Internet! In 7 years, WSI has established 700 independent franchise owners in 87 countries worldwide. Home-based or office-based. Complete training and support. No technical experience required. The WSI Formula is simple - Successful Franchise Owners + Successful Clients = Successful Franchise Opportunity. Call for free info package & CD.

BACKGROUND:
Established: 1995; 1st Franchised: 1996
Franchised Units: 700
Company-Owned Units 0
Total Units: 700
Dist.: US-151; CAN-54; O'seas-345
North America: 9 States
Density: 4 in TX, FL Mast. Fran, WA
Projected New Units (12 Months): 400
Qualifications: 2, 2, 1, 1, 4, 5
Registered: FL,AB
FINANCIAL/TERMS:
Cash Investment: $39K+
Total Investment: $39K+
Minimum Net Worth: $NR
Fees: Franchise - $39.7K
Royalty - 10%; Ad. - NR
Earnings Claim Statement: No
Term of Contract (Years): 5/5
Avg. # Of Employees: 1-2 FT
Passive Ownership: Allowed
Encourage Conversions: N/A
Area Develop. Agreements: Yes/5
Sub-Franchising Contracts: No
Expand In Territory: Yes
Space Needs: N/A SF; HB
SUPPORT & TRAINING PROVIDED:
Financial Assistance Provided: No
Site Selection Assistance: N/A
Lease Negotiation Assistance: N/A
Co-Operative Advertising: Yes
Franchisee Assoc./Member: Yes/Yes
Size Of Corporate Staff: 42
On-Going Support: b,c,G,H,I
Training: 1 Week Mississauga, ON.
SPECIFIC EXPANSION PLANS:
US: All United States
Canada: All Canada
Overseas: All Countries

SUPPLEMENTAL LISTING OF FRANCHISORS

ACCUTRAK INVENTORY SPECIALISTS, P.O. Box 20549, Charleston, SC 29413 ; (866) 7ACCUTRAK (843) 853-0901; (843) 853-4135

ACTION INTERNATIONAL, 55670 Wynn Rd., # C, Las Vegas, NV 89118

(888) 483-2828 (702) 795-3188; (702) 795-3183

AD COM EXPRESS, 7424 W. 78th St., P.O. Box 390048, Edina, MN 55439 ; (800) 829-7991 (612) 829-7990; (612) 829-7995

AMERICAN LENDERS SERVICE CO., P.O. Box 7238, Odessa, TX 79760 ; (915) 332-0361; (915) 335-3412

ASSET VERIFICATION, 510 S. Batavia Ave., Batavia, IL 60510 ; (800) 335-0513 (630) 406-8874; (630) 406-9783

BARTERCARD USA, 1845 W. Orangewood, # 320, Orange, CA 92868 ; (866) 462-2783 (714) 876-2444; (714) 876-2440

BRAD SUGARS ACTION INTERNATIONAL, 5670 Wynn Rd., # C, Las Vegas, NV 89118-2356 ; (888) 483-2828 (702) 795-3188; (702) 795-3183

CASH AMERICA PAWN, 1600 W. Seventh St., Fort Worth, TX 76102 ; (800) 223-8738 (817) 335-1100; (817) 377-0400

CLICKTOWN INTERNATIONAL, 2444 Morris Ave., # 305, Union, NJ 07083-5711 ; (908) 964-5566; (908) 964-7772

COMM PLUS, 317 NE Killingsworth St., # A, Portland, OR 97211 ; (800) 735-1422 (503) 735-1422; (503) 735-0482

COMMWORLD INTERNATIONAL, 7388 S. Revere Pkwy., # 1000, Englewood, CO 80112 ; (800) 525-3200 (303) 721-8200; (303) 721-8299

CONNECT.AD, 1000 W. McNab Rd., # 236, Pompano Beach, FL 33069 ; (954) 942-5070; (954) 942-0701

ENROLLMENT CENTER, THE, 320 Nautilus St., La Jolla, CA 92037 ; (800) 336-9222 (619) 459-7020; (619) 459-7086

FAX-9, 1235 Lake Plaza Dr., Colorado Springs, CO 80906 ; (719) 579-0955; (719) 579-0952

FIDUCIAL TRIPLE CHECK, 2441 Honolulu Ave., Montrose, CA 91020-1864 (800) 283-1040 (818) 236-2944; (818) 249-5344

FRANCHISE COMPANY, THE, 5397 Eglinton Ave. W., # 108, Toronto, ON M9C 5K6 CANADA; (416) 620-4700; (416) 620-9955

FRANCHISE CONSORTIUM INTERNATIONAL, 245 S. 84th St., # 200, Lincoln, NE 68510 ; (800) 301-9504 (402) 484-7100; (402) 484-7811

FRANCHISE SERVICES, INC., 26722 Plaza Dr., Mission Viejo, CA 92691 ; (949) 348-5400; (949) 348-5062

FREEFONE, 1001 W. Loop South, # 603, Houston, TX 77027 ; (888) 373-3971 (713) 355-1886; (713) 355-1855

GEEKS ON CALL, 814 Kempsville Rd., # 106, Norfolk, VA 23502 ; (888) 667-4577 (757) 466-3448; (757) 466-3457

GETLOCALCANADA.COM, 30444 Great Northern Ave., # 100, Abbotsford, BC V2T 6H4 CANADA; (866) 438-5622 (604) 854-5508; (604) 854-5578

GLOBENETIX, 10375 Richmond Ave., # 800, Houston, TX 77042 ; (888) 570-5278 (713) 570-7450; (713) 570-7550

INNER CIRCLE INTERNATIONAL LTD., 3320 Louisiana Ave. South, # 305, Minneapolis, MN 55426-4129 ; (612) 933-6629; (612) 935-5269

INTERFORM GRAPHICS, 1264 West 50 So., Centerville, UT 84014-4507 ; (800) 488-7961 (801) 292-7971; (801) 292-7990

LOCALWEB4U, 3310 S. Main St., Tower Bldg. E1, Anderson, IN 46013-4264 ; (877) 463-5401 (765) 683-9436; (765) 653-7552

NETSAVINGS, 2630 Sand Lake Rd., Longwood, FL 32779 ; (407) 287-0840; (877) 649-5125

NUTRITION CLUB, 10540 72nd St., Largo, FL 33777-1500 ; (877) 474-2582 (412) 490-2929; (412) 490-2955

PACIFIC MEDICAL, 16516 Bernardo Center Dr., # 300, San Diego, CA 92128 ; (800) 815-6334 (858) 676-9840

PAYTRAK PAYROLL SERVICES, 541 High St., Westwood, MA 02090 ; (877) 729-8725 (781) 251-9410; (781) 251-9520

PRIME BUSINESS COMMUNICATIONS, 3900 Skyhawk Dr., Chantilly, VA 20151 ; (888) 767-4PBC

REGIONAL INTERNET GALAXY NETWORK, 27475 Ynez Rd., # 642, Temecula, CA 92591 ; (909) 696-3954; (909) 694-0639

REGUS BUSINESS CENTRES, 1925 Vaughn Rd., # 105, Kennesaw, GA 30144-4566 ; (866) REGUS4U (678) 290-0555; (678) 290-0660

SABERCOR, P.O. Box 17, Sussex, WI 53089 ; (888) 773-9234 (262) 246-4521; (262) 246-4528

SERVICE CENTER, 5202 E. Mt. View Rd., Scottsdale, AZ 85253 ; (800) 729-7424 (480) 998-1616; (480) 998-4091

STRATEGIC LIVING INTERNATIONAL, 10409 Stevenson Village, Stevenson, MD 21153 ; (800) 727-4754 (410) 653-1993; (301) 358-7858

VETSMART PET HOSPITAL & HEALTHCENTER, 11815 NE Glen Widing Dr., Portland, OR 97220 ; (800) 838-6929 (503) 345-5200; (503) 256-7636

VIRTUAL CEO, 27128A Paseo Espada, # 1521, San Juan Capistrano, CA 92675 (877) 367-8236 (949) 248-2404; (949) 248-2413

WIRELESS TOYZ, 1486 Washtenaw Ave., Ypsilanti, MI 48197 ; (866) 237-2624 (734) 482-8000; (801) 858-8285

WIRELESS ZONE, 34 Industrial Park Pl., Middletown, CT 06457 ; (860) 632-9494; (860) 632-9343

Child Development/Education/Products

Chapter 10

Child Development/Education/Products Industry Profile

Total # Franchisors in Industry Group	82
Total # Franchised Units in Industry Group	5,389
Total # Company-Owned Units in Industry Group	296
Total # Operating Units in Industry Group	5,685
Average # Franchised Units/Franchisor	65.7
Average # Company-Owned Units/Franchisor	3.6
Average # Total Units/Franchisor	69.3
Ratio of Total # Franchised Units/Total # Company-Owned Units	18.2:1
Industry Survey Participants	38
Representing % of Industry	46.3%
Average Franchise Fee*:	$21.3K
Average Total Investment*:	$144.1K
Average On-Going Royalty Fee*:	15.9%

*If a range was provided, the mid-point of the range was used. See detailed profiles for actual ranges.

Five Largest Participants in Survey

Company	# Franchised Units	# Co-Owned Units	# Total Units	Franchise Fee	On-Going Royalty	Total Investment
1. Kumon North America	1,389	0	1,389	1K	$30-33.8K	5.9-30.6K
2. Futurekids (Canada)	596	0	596	50K	$360+10%	100-142.9K
3. Gymboree Play and Music	408	27	435	35K	6%	80-150K
4. Technokids	250	1	251	15K+	7%	25-50K
5. Fourth R, The	244	0	244	16K	$400/Month, 5% Sales	69-85K

All of the data provided are proprietary and should not be quoted without acknowledging *Bond's Franchise Guide.*

BABY NEWS CHILDRENS STORES
6909 Las Postas Rd.
Livermore, CA 94550
Tel: (866) 437-2229 (925) 245-1370
Fax: (925) 245-1376
E-Mail: info@babynewsstores.com
Web Site: www.babynewsonline.com
Mr. Roger O'Callaghan, President

BABY NEWS is the oldest established association of individually-owned baby stores.

BACKGROUND:
Established: 1950; 1st Franchised: 1961
Franchised Units: 44
Company-Owned Units 1
Total Units: 45
Dist.: US-35; CAN-0; O'seas-10
North America: 35 States
Density: 20 in CA
Projected New Units (12 Months): 2
Qualifications: 5, 3, 3, 3, 3, 5
Registered: CA

FINANCIAL/TERMS:
Cash Investment: $100K
Total Investment: $150-250K
Minimum Net Worth: $NR
Fees: Franchise - $15K
Royalty - 1%; Ad. - 0%
Earnings Claim Statement: Yes
Term of Contract (Years): 5/5
Avg. # Of Employees: 3 FT, 4 PT
Passive Ownership: Not Allowed
Encourage Conversions: Yes
Area Develop. Agreements: No
Sub-Franchising Contracts: No
Expand In Territory: Yes
Space Needs: 5,000 SF; FS, SC, RM

SUPPORT & TRAINING PROVIDED:
Financial Assistance Provided: No
Site Selection Assistance: Yes
Lease Negotiation Assistance: Yes
Co-Operative Advertising: No
Franchisee Assoc./Member: No
Size Of Corporate Staff: 14
On-Going Support: A,B,C,d,E,F,G,H
Training: 1-2 Weeks at Various Locations.

SPECIFIC EXPANSION PLANS:
US: All United States
Canada: All Canada
Overseas: All Countries

<< >>

Top 50

BABY USA
857 N. Larch Ave.
Elmhurst, IL 60126
Tel: (800) 323-4108 (630) 832-9880
Fax: (630) 832-0139
E-Mail: franchise@usababy.com
Web Site: www.usababy.com
Mr. James L. Courtney, Sr. Mgr. Franchise Dev.

USA BABY is North America's leading specialty retailer of infant and juvenile furniture and accessories. Franchisees receive market evaluation, site selection, store design, financing, opening, advertising, merchandising and on-going operational support. Exclusive territories and substantial single, multi-unit and area development opportunities exist for candidates with a passion for serving customers, developing employee teams and participating in a proven retail environment.

BACKGROUND: IFA MEMBER
Established: 1975; 1st Franchised: 1986
Franchised Units: 61
Company-Owned Units 0
Total Units: 61
Dist.: US-44; CAN-15; O'seas-2
North America: 22 States
Density: 8 in IL, 7 in NY, 6 in OH
Projected New Units (12 Months): 15
Qualifications: 4, 4, 1, 3, 2, 5
Registered: CA,FL,HI,IL,IN,MD,MI,MN, NY,VA,WA,WI

FINANCIAL/TERMS:
Cash Investment: $120-150K
Total Investment: $450-600K
Minimum Net Worth: $180K
Fees: Franchise - $42.5K
Royalty - 3%; Ad. - 5%
Earnings Claim Statement: Yes
Term of Contract (Years): 10/10
Avg. # Of Employees: 5 FT, 4 PT
Passive Ownership: Not Allowed
Encourage Conversions: Yes
Area Develop. Agreements: Yes/Varies
Sub-Franchising Contracts: No
Expand In Territory: Yes
Space Needs: 12,000 SF; SC

SUPPORT & TRAINING PROVIDED:
Financial Assistance Provided: Yes(I)
Site Selection Assistance: Yes
Lease Negotiation Assistance: Yes
Co-Operative Advertising: N/A
Franchisee Assoc./Member: Yes/Yes
Size Of Corporate Staff: 12
On-Going Support: C,D,E,G,H,I
Training: 14 Days Corporate Office/Store; 4 Days Pre-Opening; 4 Days Opening; 4-5 Days Post-Opening.

SPECIFIC EXPANSION PLANS:
US: All United States
Canada: All Canada
Overseas: No

<< >>

Top 50

CHILDREN'S ORCHARD
2100 S. Main St., # B
Ann Arbor, MI 48103
Tel: (800) 999-5437 (734) 994-9199
Fax: (734) 994-9323
E-Mail: childrensorchard@ameritech.net
Web Site: www.childorch.com
Ms. Josephine Gonzalez, Franchise Development Dir.

Upscale children's retail/resale stores, featuring clothing, toys, furniture, equipment, books and parenting products. We buy top-brand items from area families by appointment, and re-sell in lovely stores, along with top-quality new children's items from over 100 suppliers. These are large volume stores selling thousands of items per week.

BACKGROUND: IFA MEMBER
Established: 1980; 1st Franchised: 1985
Franchised Units: 99
Company-Owned Units 1
Total Units: 100
Dist.: US-100; CAN-0; O'seas-0
North America: 25 States
Density: 22 in CA, 15 in MA, 8 in MI
Projected New Units (12 Months): 9
Qualifications: 5, 3, 2, 4, 2, 5
Registered: CA,FL,IL,IN,MD,MI,MN,NY ,VA, WA, WI

FINANCIAL/TERMS:
Cash Investment: $30-35K
Total Investment: $69-145K

Minimum Net Worth: $200K
Fees: Franchise - $19.5K
Royalty - 5%; Ad. - 1.5%
Earnings Claim Statement: No
Term of Contract (Years): 10/5
Avg. # Of Employees: 1 FT, 3 PT
Passive Ownership: Discouraged
Encourage Conversions: Yes
Area Develop. Agreements: Yes/Open
Sub-Franchising Contracts: No
Expand In Territory: No
Space Needs: 2,000 SF; SF, SC

SUPPORT & TRAINING PROVIDED:
Financial Assistance Provided: Yes(I)
Site Selection Assistance: Yes
Lease Negotiation Assistance: Yes
Co-Operative Advertising: Yes
Franchisee Assoc./Member: Yes/Yes
Size Of Corporate Staff: 7
On-Going Support: B,C,D,E,F,G,H,I
Training: 2 Weeks in Ann Arbor, MI; 2 Weeks in Lake Forest, CA.

SPECIFIC EXPANSION PLANS:
US: All United States
Canada: No
Overseas: No

<< >>

COMPUTERTOTS

Top 50

COMPUTERTOTS/ COMPUTER EXPLORERS

10132 Colvin Run Rd.
Great Falls, VA 22066
Tel: (800) 531-5053 (703) 759-2556
Fax: (703) 759-1938
E-Mail: sgould@computertots.com
Web Site: www.computertots.com
Ms. Sandy Gould, Franchise Development Dir.

A network of computer education services for children 3 - 12. The program was established in 1984 and offers programs through outreach programs at private and public educational sites.

BACKGROUND: IFA MEMBER
Established: 1984; 1st Franchised: 1988
Franchised Units: 190
Company-Owned Units 2
Total Units: 192
Dist.: US-110; CAN-0; O'seas-82
North America: 38 States
Density: 12 in CA, 8 in TX, 7 in OH
Projected New Units (12 Months): 6
Qualifications: 3, 4, 4, 3, 3, 5
Registered: All States

FINANCIAL/TERMS:
Cash Investment: $45K
Total Investment: $45K
Minimum Net Worth: $100K
Fees: Franchise - $10-29.9K
Royalty - 8%/$350; Ad. - 1%
Earnings Claim Statement: Yes
Term of Contract (Years): 10/10
Avg. # Of Employees: 1 FT, 5 PT
Passive Ownership: Discouraged
Encourage Conversions: N/A
Area Develop. Agreements: No
Sub-Franchising Contracts: No
Expand In Territory: No
Space Needs: N/A SF; HB

SUPPORT & TRAINING PROVIDED:
Financial Assistance Provided: No
Site Selection Assistance: N/A
Lease Negotiation Assistance: N/A
Co-Operative Advertising: N/A
Franchisee Assoc./Member: Yes/Yes
Size Of Corporate Staff: 10
On-Going Support: b,c,d,g,h,I
Training: 7 Days Great Falls, VA.

SPECIFIC EXPANSION PLANS:
US: All United States
Canada: No
Overseas: No

<< >>

DANCERCISE KIDS

P.O. Box 219
Anoka, MN 55303-0219
Tel: (800) 613-8231 (952) 920-9880
Fax: (952) 925-1141
E-Mail: franchiseinfo@dancercise.com
Web Site: www.dancercise.com
Ms. Jennifer Gordon, Franchise Operations Director

DANCERCISE KIDS is a comprehensive dance program designed for young children at child care facilities. Our unique educational curriculum and lesson plans are provided along with marketing materials, computer software, ongoing training and corporate support. DANCERCISE KIDS offers an exciting opportunity to impact children's lives and enjoy a rewarding career. Call us today!

BACKGROUND: IFA MEMBER
Established: 1988; 1st Franchised: 1999
Franchised Units: 3
Company-Owned Units 9
Total Units: 12
Dist.: US-12; CAN-0; O'seas-0
North America: 7 States
Density: 3 in MN, 3 in IL, 2 in VA
Projected New Units (12 Months): 5
Qualifications: 3, 4, 3, 3, 5, 5
Registered: CA,FL,MD,MI,MN,WI

FINANCIAL/TERMS:
Cash Investment: $3-9.5K
Total Investment: $16.8-23.3K
Minimum Net Worth: $25K
Fees: Franchise - $9.5K
Royalty - 10%; Ad. - 0%
Earnings Claim Statement: Yes
Term of Contract (Years): 10/15
Avg. # Of Employees: 1 FT
Passive Ownership: Discouraged
Encourage Conversions: Yes
Area Develop. Agreements: No
Sub-Franchising Contracts: No
Expand In Territory: Yes
Space Needs: N/A SF; HB

SUPPORT & TRAINING PROVIDED:
Financial Assistance Provided: Yes(I)
Site Selection Assistance: Yes
Lease Negotiation Assistance: N/A
Co-Operative Advertising: N/A
Franchisee Assoc./Member: No
Size Of Corporate Staff: 5
On-Going Support: B,C,D,E,G,H,I
Training: 1 Week at Corporate Office in Minneapolis.

SPECIFIC EXPANSION PLANS:
US: All United States
Canada: All Canada
Overseas: No

<< >>

FASTRACKIDS INTERNATIONAL LTD.

6900 E. Belleview Ave.
Greenwood Village, CO 80111-1619
Tel: (888) 576-6888 (303) 224-0200
Fax: (303) 224-0222
E-Mail: info@fastrackids.com
Web Site: www.fastrackids.com
Mr. Kevin Krause, Dir. Franchise Development

FASTRACKIDS® is an exciting advancement in the education of young children, powered by innovative technology, a strong curriculum, and the leadership of franchise owners throughout the world. Based on the premise that, given proper instruction and reinforcement, most children can perform at the level we now call gifted, FasTracKids fosters the early development of creativity, leadership and communication skills.

BACKGROUND: IFA MEMBER
Established: 1998; 1st Franchised: 1998
Franchised Units: 130
Company-Owned Units 0
Total Units: 130
Dist.: US-16; CAN-7; O'seas-107
North America: 7 States
Density: NR
Projected New Units (12 Months): 30
Qualifications: 4, 4, 4, 4, 5, 5
Registered: All States

FINANCIAL/TERMS:
Cash Investment: $10.4-36.2K
Total Investment: $10.4-36.2K
Minimum Net Worth: $NR
Fees: Franchise - $5-15K
Royalty - 1.5%; Ad. - 5%
Earnings Claim Statement: Yes
Term of Contract (Years): 5/5
Avg. # Of Employees: 1-5 FT
Passive Ownership: Discouraged
Encourage Conversions: N/A
Area Develop. Agreements: Yes/5
Sub-Franchising Contracts: No
Expand In Territory: Yes
Space Needs: 700 SF; N/A

SUPPORT & TRAINING PROVIDED:
Financial Assistance Provided: Yes(B)
Site Selection Assistance: Yes
Lease Negotiation Assistance: No
Co-Operative Advertising: Yes
Franchisee Assoc./Member: No
Size Of Corporate Staff: 12
On-Going Support: C,G,h,I
Training: 3-4 Days in Denver, CO.

SPECIFIC EXPANSION PLANS:
US: All United States
Canada: All Canada
Overseas: All Countries

<< >>

FIT BY FIVE PRESCHOOL

29520 Center Ridge Rd.
Westlake, OH 44145
Tel: (440) 835-8558
Fax: (440) 835-8838
Ms. Michelle DeMarsh, Owner

Active approach to preschool education. Serving children 20 months to 5 years. Fun business to own especially for physically active people.

BACKGROUND:
Established: 1969; 1st Franchised: 1976
Franchised Units: 3
Company-Owned Units 1
Total Units: 4
Dist.: US-5; CAN-0; O'seas-0
North America: 3 States
Density: NR
Projected New Units (12 Months): 1
Qualifications: 4, 2, 2, 2, 5, 5
Registered: NR

FINANCIAL/TERMS:
Cash Investment: $60K
Total Investment: $50-75K
Minimum Net Worth: $NR
Fees: Franchise - $25K
Royalty - $3.6K/Yr; Ad. - NR
Earnings Claim Statement: No
Term of Contract (Years): 10/1
Avg. # Of Employees: 3 FT, 3 PT
Passive Ownership: Discouraged
Encourage Conversions: NR
Area Develop. Agreements: NR
Sub-Franchising Contracts: Yes
Expand In Territory: Yes
Space Needs: 3,000 SF; FS

SUPPORT & TRAINING PROVIDED:
Financial Assistance Provided: No
Site Selection Assistance: Yes
Lease Negotiation Assistance: No
Co-Operative Advertising: No
Franchisee Assoc./Member: No
Size Of Corporate Staff: 3
On-Going Support: b,D,E,G,h
Training: 2 Weeks at the Home-Office in Cleveland; 1 Week On-Site.

SPECIFIC EXPANSION PLANS:
US: OH
Canada: No
Overseas: No

<< >>

THE FOURTH R®
Computer Training Solutions

FOURTH R, THE

1715 Market St., # 103
Kirkland, WA 98033-4968
Tel: (800) 821-8653 (425) 828-0336
Fax: (425) 828-0192
E-Mail: fourthR@fourthR.com
Web Site: www.FourthR.com
Mr. Robert L. McCauley, President

Computers have changed virtually all aspects of our lives. As we move into the information age, many experts agree that computer literacy has become THE FOURTH R in education today. As an international leader in computer training, THE FOURTH R is one of the fastest-growing companies in the computer training sector and has been highlighted in prominent national publications as one of the top franchisors both in the U. S. and abroad.

BACKGROUND: IFA MEMBER
Established: 1991; 1st Franchised: 1992
Franchised Units: 244
Company-Owned Units 0
Total Units: 244
Dist.: US-45; CAN-8; O'seas-191
North America: 21 States, 2 Provinces
Density: 6 in CA, 6 in PA, 5 in WA,
Projected New Units (12 Months): 54
Qualifications: 2, 4, 3, 4, 2, 3
Registered: CA,HI,IL,IN,MD,MI,MN,NY, OR,VA,WA,WI,DC,AB

FINANCIAL/TERMS:
Cash Investment: $N/A
Total Investment: $69-85K
Minimum Net Worth: $None
Fees: Franchise - $16K
Royalty - 400/month,5%sale; Ad. - 0%
Earnings Claim Statement: No
Term of Contract (Years): 5/5
Avg. # Of Employees: Varies
Passive Ownership: Allowed
Encourage Conversions: Yes
Area Develop. Agreements: Yes/5
Sub-Franchising Contracts: No
Expand In Territory: Yes
Space Needs: 800-3,000 SF; SF, SC, HB, Commercial

SUPPORT & TRAINING PROVIDED:
Financial Assistance Provided: Yes(I)
Site Selection Assistance: Yes
Lease Negotiation Assistance: Yes
Co-Operative Advertising: Yes
Franchisee Assoc./Member: Yes/Yes
Size Of Corporate Staff: 7
On-Going Support: B,C,G,H,I
Training: 5 Days Seattle, WA.

SPECIFIC EXPANSION PLANS:
US: All United States
Canada: All Canada
Overseas: All Countries

<< >>

FUTUREKIDS (CANADA)
18 Crimson Millway
Willowdale, ON M2L 1T6 CANADA
Tel: (416) 445-6488
Fax: (416) 445-5750
Mr. Elliot Sachar, President

Computer-training centers. We train children and adults how to use the computer as a tool. Teach out of learning centers through regular classes, camps and special interest groups. We also go out on-location to work with schools, daycares, etc., and provide teacher training for public and private schools.

BACKGROUND:
Established: 1983; 1st Franchised: 1989
Franchised Units: 596
Company-Owned Units 0
Total Units: 596
Dist.: US-243; CAN-31; O'seas-322
North America: 38 States, 7 Provinces
Density: 58 in CA, 26 in NY, 14 in ON
Projected New Units (12 Months): 20
Qualifications: 5, 5, 4, 3, 3, 5
Registered: AB

FINANCIAL/TERMS:
Cash Investment: $48K
Total Investment: $100-142.9K
Minimum Net Worth: $100K
Fees: Franchise - $50K
Royalty - 10% + $360; Ad. - 2%/$250
Earnings Claim Statement: No
Term of Contract (Years): 10/10
Avg. # Of Employees: Varies
Passive Ownership: Discouraged
Encourage Conversions: No
Area Develop. Agreements: Yes/1.5
Sub-Franchising Contracts: Yes
Expand In Territory: Yes
Space Needs: 1,000 SF; SF, SC

SUPPORT & TRAINING PROVIDED:
Financial Assistance Provided: No
Site Selection Assistance: Yes
Lease Negotiation Assistance: Yes
Co-Operative Advertising: Yes
Franchisee Assoc./Member: NR
Size Of Corporate Staff: 1
On-Going Support: B,C,D,e,G,H,I
Training: 2 Weeks Los Angeles, CA.

SPECIFIC EXPANSION PLANS:
US: No
Canada: All Canada
Overseas: All Countries

GYMBOREE
PLAY PROGRAMS

GYMBOREE PLAY & MUSIC
700 Airport Blvd., # 200
Burlingame, CA 94010-1912
Tel: (800) 520-7529 (650) 373-7628
Fax: (650) 696-7452
E-Mail: play_franchise@gymboree.com
Web Site: www.playandmusic.com
Mr. Burt Yarkin, Dir. Franchise Development

GYMBOREE, the world's largest development play and music program, offers weekly classes to parents and their children, ages newborn through 4 years, on custom-designed equipment. The program is based on sensory integration theory, positive parenting, child development principles and the importance of play. GYMBOREE has recently rolled out a new Music Program designed to support your child's development through an array of enriching experiences and Fun!

BACKGROUND: IFA MEMBER
Established: 1976; 1st Franchised: 1978
Franchised Units: 408
Company-Owned Units 27
Total Units: 435
Dist.: US-280; CAN-22; O'seas-100
North America: 40 States, 3 Provinces
Density: 52 in CA, 30 in NY, 28 in NJ
Projected New Units (12 Months): 25
Qualifications: 4, 4, 3, 3, 2, 4
Registered: CA,FL,HI,IL,IN,MD,MI,MN, NY,OR,RI,SD,VA,WA,WI,DC,AB

FINANCIAL/TERMS:
Cash Investment: $35-60K
Total Investment: $80-150K
Minimum Net Worth: $150K
Fees: Franchise - $35K
Royalty - 6%; Ad. - 2.25%
Earnings Claim Statement: No
Term of Contract (Years): 10/10
Avg. # Of Employees: 1 FT, 3 PT
Passive Ownership: Not Allowed
Encourage Conversions: No
Area Develop. Agreements: No
Sub-Franchising Contracts: No
Expand In Territory: Yes
Space Needs: 1,800 SF; SF, SC, RM

SUPPORT & TRAINING PROVIDED:
Financial Assistance Provided: No
Site Selection Assistance: Yes
Lease Negotiation Assistance: Yes
Co-Operative Advertising: Yes
Franchisee Assoc./Member: Yes
Size Of Corporate Staff: 19
On-Going Support: B,D,G,h,I
Training: 6 Days Headquarters.

SPECIFIC EXPANSION PLANS:
US: All United States
Canada: All Canada
Overseas: Asia, Europe

GYMN' AROUND KIDS
1036 Blythwood Rd.
Blythwood, SC 29016
Tel: (803) 359-0433
Fax: (803) 892-5631
Ms. Kelly S. Coyle, President

A unique mobile business serving children. Circus/gymnastics equipment used for fitness classes. Summer camps and kids parties. A great way to work at home with flexible hours, year round or seasonal, and incredible income available.

BACKGROUND:
Established: 1987; 1st Franchised: 1994
Franchised Units: 2
Company-Owned Units 2
Total Units: 4
Dist.: US-4; CAN-0; O'seas-0
North America: 2 States
Density: 3 in SC, 1 in NC
Projected New Units (12 Months): 6
Qualifications: 2, 4, 3, 3, 3, 5
Registered: NR

FINANCIAL/TERMS:
Cash Investment: $9.5K
Total Investment: $5-9.5K
Minimum Net Worth: $100K
Fees: Franchise - $8.5K
Royalty - 8%; Ad. - 0%
Earnings Claim Statement: No
Term of Contract (Years): 3/1
Avg. # Of Employees: 1 FT, 1-2 PT
Passive Ownership: Not Allowed
Encourage Conversions: NR
Area Develop. Agreements: NR
Sub-Franchising Contracts: No
Expand In Territory: Yes
Space Needs: NR SF; Mobile

SUPPORT & TRAINING PROVIDED:
Financial Assistance Provided: No
Site Selection Assistance: Yes
Lease Negotiation Assistance: No
Co-Operative Advertising: Yes

Franchisee Assoc./Member: Yes/Yes
Size Of Corporate Staff: 1
On-Going Support: b,d,f,G,h,I
Training: 3-5 Days in SC.

SPECIFIC EXPANSION PLANS:
US: All United States
Canada: No
Overseas: No

<< >>

GYMSTERS

6135 E. Danbury Rd.
Scottsdale, AZ 85254-6447
Tel: (480) 315-0351
Fax: (480) 315-0311
E-Mail: gymsters.inc@home.com
Ms. Lonnie Coppock, President

The GYMSTERS® system brings physical education to children from two to twelve by providing the equipment, the staff and the program. Experts in education and health agree that learning through physical movement is the primary way that children develop. The children's fitness industry offers a vast and huge market place whose potential has become even greater, due to budget cuts, and GYMSTERS® is the answer.

BACKGROUND:
Established: 1980; 1st Franchised: 1988
Franchised Units: 8
Company-Owned Units 1
Total Units: 9
Dist.: US-9; CAN-0; O'seas-0
North America: 4 States
Density: 6 in CA, 1 in OH, 1 in AZ
Projected New Units (12 Months): 6
Qualifications: 4, 3, 5, 5, 5, 5
Registered: All States

FINANCIAL/TERMS:
Cash Investment: $19.8-24.5K
Total Investment: $19.8-24.5K
Minimum Net Worth: $NR
Fees: Franchise - $12K
Royalty - 7%; Ad. - 3%
Earnings Claim Statement: Yes
Term of Contract (Years): 5/5
Avg. # Of Employees: 1 PT
Passive Ownership: Discouraged
Encourage Conversions: N/A
Area Develop. Agreements: No
Sub-Franchising Contracts: No
Expand In Territory: NR
Space Needs: NR SF; N/A

SUPPORT & TRAINING PROVIDED:
Financial Assistance Provided: No
Site Selection Assistance: Yes
Lease Negotiation Assistance: N/A
Co-Operative Advertising: N/A
Franchisee Assoc./Member: No
Size Of Corporate Staff: 1
On-Going Support: b,C,D,f,G,h,I
Training: Initially 5 Days in Scottsdale, AZ.

SPECIFIC EXPANSION PLANS:
US: All United States
Canada: No
Overseas: No

<< >>

HIGH TOUCH-HIGH TECH

12352 Wiles Rd.
Coral Springs, FL 33076
Tel: (800) 444-4968 (954) 755-2900
Fax: (954) 755-1242
E-Mail: info@hightouch-hightech.com
Web Site: www.hightouch-hightech.com
Mr. Daniel Shaw, President/CEO

Provides hands-on science experiences that go right into the classroom. We provide in-school field trips. We also provide fun, science-oriented birthday parties.

BACKGROUND:
Established: 1992; 1st Franchised: 1994
Franchised Units: 79
Company-Owned Units 2
Total Units: 81
Dist.: US-21; CAN-0; O'seas-1
North America: 12 States
Density: 5 in FL, 2 in NJ, 2 in IL
Projected New Units (12 Months): 8-10
Qualifications: 5, 5, 3, 5, 3, 3
Registered: CA,FL,IL,NY,VA,WI

FINANCIAL/TERMS:
Cash Investment: $5-8K
Total Investment: $28-42K
Minimum Net Worth: $NR
Fees: Franchise - $20-35K
Royalty - 7%; Ad. - 0%
Earnings Claim Statement: Yes
Term of Contract (Years): 10/10
Avg. # Of Employees: 2-3 PT
Passive Ownership: NR
Encourage Conversions: N/A
Area Develop. Agreements: No
Sub-Franchising Contracts: Yes
Expand In Territory: Yes
Space Needs: NR SF; HB

SUPPORT & TRAINING PROVIDED:
Financial Assistance Provided: Yes(D)
Site Selection Assistance: Yes
Lease Negotiation Assistance: N/A
Co-Operative Advertising: N/A
Franchisee Assoc./Member: No
Size Of Corporate Staff: 6
On-Going Support: D,G,H,I
Training: 5 Full Days National Programming Offices.

SPECIFIC EXPANSION PLANS:
US: All United States, Global
Canada: All Canada
Overseas: Europe, Asia, Pacific Region

<< >>

IMAGINE THAT DISCOVERY MUSEUMS

P.O. Box 493
New Vernon, NJ 07976
Tel: (800) 820-1145 (973) 267-2907
Fax: (973) 445-1917
Ms. Deborah Bodnar, Founder

Children's hands-on interactive museum with over 50 exhibit areas. Field trips, parties, general admission, café, retail area, drop-off service and enrichment programs are how we earn our revenue.

BACKGROUND:
Established: 1994; 1st Franchised: 1996
Franchised Units: 2
Company-Owned Units 1
Total Units: 3
Dist.: US-3; CAN-0; O'seas-0
North America: 3 States
Density: NR
Projected New Units (12 Months): 1
Qualifications: 5, 5, 3, 3, 4, 5
Registered: FL,NY

FINANCIAL/TERMS:
Cash Investment: $325K
Total Investment: $450-550K
Minimum Net Worth: $325K
Fees: Franchise - $25K
Royalty - 6%; Ad. - 0%
Earnings Claim Statement: No
Term of Contract (Years): 10/10
Avg. # Of Employees: 3 FT, 15 PT
Passive Ownership: Discouraged
Encourage Conversions: Yes
Area Develop. Agreements: Yes
Sub-Franchising Contracts: No
Expand In Territory: No
Space Needs: 15,000 SF; FS, SC

SUPPORT & TRAINING PROVIDED:
Financial Assistance Provided: No
Site Selection Assistance: Yes
Lease Negotiation Assistance: Yes
Co-Operative Advertising: Yes
Franchisee Assoc./Member: NR

Size Of Corporate Staff: 2
On-Going Support: B,C,D,E,I
Training: 2 Weeks E. Hanover, NJ; 2 Weeks On-Site.

SPECIFIC EXPANSION PLANS:
US: All United States
Canada: No
Overseas: No

<< >>

J. W. TUMBLES, A CHILDREN'S GYM

12750 Carmel Country Rd., # 102
San Diego, CA 92130
Tel: (800) 886-2532 (619) 756-8718
Fax: (619) 756-7719
Web Site: www.jwtumbles.com
Mr. Jeff Woods, President

A gym just for children, ages 4 months to 9 years, with a 2,000 sq. ft. space of colorful equipment. We have instructional class formats designed to teach young children basic physical education fundamentals, all in a non-competitive environment where building self-esteem and having fun are #1! Birthday parties, summer and winter camps, and mobile programs available.

BACKGROUND:
Established: 1985; 1st Franchised: 1993
Franchised Units: 5
Company-Owned Units 3
Total Units: 8
Dist.: US-5; CAN-0; O'seas-1
North America: NR
Density: NR
Projected New Units (12 Months): 4
Qualifications: 5, 3, 2, 3, 5, 5
Registered: CA,OR

FINANCIAL/TERMS:
Cash Investment: $85-110K
Total Investment: $85-110K
Minimum Net Worth: $200K
Fees: Franchise - $25K
Royalty - $2.4K/Yr.; Ad. - 0%
Earnings Claim Statement: No
Term of Contract (Years): 5/5
Avg. # Of Employees: 1 FT, 2 PT
Passive Ownership: Discouraged
Encourage Conversions: N/A
Area Develop. Agreements: No
Sub-Franchising Contracts: No
Expand In Territory: Yes
Space Needs: 2,000 SF; SC

SUPPORT & TRAINING PROVIDED:
Financial Assistance Provided: No
Site Selection Assistance: Yes
Lease Negotiation Assistance: Yes
Co-Operative Advertising: Yes
Franchisee Assoc./Member: No
Size Of Corporate Staff: 8
On-Going Support: E,G,H,I
Training: 2-4 Weeks San Diego, CA.

SPECIFIC EXPANSION PLANS:
US: All United States
Canada: All Canada
Overseas: All Countries

<< >>

JACADI

72 Parkway E.
Mount Vernon, NY 10552
Tel: (914) 667-2183
Fax: (914) 665-0416
E-Mail: jacadi@juno.com
Web Site: www.jacadiusa.com
Mr. Bruce Pettibone, President/COO

JACADI is a childrenswear retail company whose collections include clothing, shoes, accessories, furniture and nursery items in newborn through size 12 for both boys and girls. The merchandise is a European-style which adapts the latest trends to classic design and allows the customer to mix and match the various styles and color groups. JACADI also strives to give excellent customer service and the highest price/quality ratio.

BACKGROUND: IFA MEMBER
Established: 1988; 1st Franchised: 1992
Franchised Units: 23
Company-Owned Units 3
Total Units: 26
Dist.: US-26; CAN-3; O'seas-350
North America: 10 States, 1 Province
Density: 8 in CA, 4 in NY, 3 in FL
Projected New Units (12 Months): 8
Qualifications: 5, 3, 1, 2, 4, 5
Registered: CA,FL,IL,NY

FINANCIAL/TERMS:
Cash Investment: $120-250K
Total Investment: $183-313K
Minimum Net Worth: $750K Liquid
Fees: Franchise - $20K
Royalty - 4%; Ad. - 1%
Earnings Claim Statement: No
Term of Contract (Years): 7/7
Avg. # Of Employees: 2-3 FT, 2-3 PT
Passive Ownership: Not Allowed
Encourage Conversions: N/A
Area Develop. Agreements: Yes/7
Sub-Franchising Contracts: No
Expand In Territory: Yes
Space Needs: 1,100 SF; FS, SF, RM

SUPPORT & TRAINING PROVIDED:
Financial Assistance Provided: No
Site Selection Assistance: Yes
Lease Negotiation Assistance: Yes
Co-Operative Advertising: No
Franchisee Assoc./Member: No
Size Of Corporate Staff: 4
On-Going Support: B,C,d,E,f,G,h
Training: 3-5 Days in Subsidiary Shop; 3 Days Franchisee's Shop Before Opening; On-Going Corporate.

SPECIFIC EXPANSION PLANS:
US: All United States
Canada: All Canada
Overseas: All Countries

<< >>

KID TO KID

452 E. 500 S.
Salt Lake City, UT 84111
Tel: (888) KID-2-KID (801) 359-0071
Fax: (801) 359-3207
E-Mail: k2kcorp@aol.com
Web Site: www.kidtokid.com
Mr. Michael Petroff, Director of Development

KID TO KID is an up-scale children's resale store based on the premise that 'kids grow faster than paychecks.' Parents buy and sell better-quality used children's clothing, toys, equipment and accessories. If you enjoy working with people and want to increase your financial security as you grow your own business, call KID TO KID today!

BACKGROUND:
Established: 1992; 1st Franchised: 1994
Franchised Units: 35
Company-Owned Units 0
Total Units: 35
Dist.: US-35; CAN-0; O'seas-0
North America: 13 States
Density: 12 in UT, 5 in TX, 3 in PA
Projected New Units (12 Months): 10

Qualifications: 4, 3, 1, 2, 4, 5
Registered: All States

FINANCIAL/TERMS:

Cash Investment: $25-35K
Total Investment: $88-116K
Minimum Net Worth: $150K
Fees: Franchise - $20K
Royalty - 4.75%; Ad. - 0.5%
Earnings Claim Statement: Yes
Term of Contract (Years): 10/5
Avg. # Of Employees: 3 FT, 2 PT
Passive Ownership: Discouraged
Encourage Conversions: Yes
Area Develop. Agreements: Yes/Varies
Sub-Franchising Contracts: No
Expand In Territory: No
Space Needs: 2,000 SF; FS, SF, SC

SUPPORT & TRAINING PROVIDED:

Financial Assistance Provided: No
Site Selection Assistance: Yes
Lease Negotiation Assistance: Yes
Co-Operative Advertising: Yes
Franchisee Assoc./Member: No
Size Of Corporate Staff: 4
On-Going Support: B,C,d,E,f,G,H
Training: 10 Days Salt Lake City, UT.

SPECIFIC EXPANSION PLANS:

US: All United States
Canada: All Canada
Overseas: No

<< >>

KIDDIE ACADEMY INTERNATIONAL

108 Wheel Rd., # 200
Bel Air, MD 21015
Tel: (800) 554-3343 (410) 515-0788
Fax: (410) 569-2729
E-Mail: sales@kiddieacademy.com
Web Site: www.kiddieacademy.com
Ms. Jennifer Garrett, Franchise Admissions Dir.

We offer comprehensive training and support without additional cost. KIDDIE ACADEMY'S step-by-step program assists with staff recruitment, training, accounting support, site selection, marketing, advertising and curriculum. A true turn-key opportunity that provides on-going support so you can focus on running a successful business.

BACKGROUND: IFA MEMBER
Established: 1981; 1st Franchised: 1992
Franchised Units: 78
Company-Owned Units 12
Total Units: 90
Dist.: US-51; CAN-0; O'seas-0
North America: 10 States
Density: 15 in MD, 5 in NJ, 4 in IL
Projected New Units (12 Months): 100
Qualifications: 4, 4, 2, 3, 2, 4
Registered: CA,FL,IL,IN,MD,MI,MN,NY,OR,RI,VA,WI,DC

FINANCIAL/TERMS:

Cash Investment: $60K
Total Investment: $180-260K
Minimum Net Worth: $250K
Fees: Franchise - $40K
Royalty - 7%; Ad. - 0%
Earnings Claim Statement: No
Term of Contract (Years): 10/5
Avg. # Of Employees: 10-20 FT, 2 PT
Passive Ownership: Discouraged
Encourage Conversions: No
Area Develop. Agreements: Yes/10
Sub-Franchising Contracts: No
Expand In Territory: Yes
Space Needs: 6,500-12,000 SF; FS, SF, SC

SUPPORT & TRAINING PROVIDED:

Financial Assistance Provided: Yes(I)
Site Selection Assistance: Yes
Lease Negotiation Assistance: Yes
Co-Operative Advertising: Yes
Franchisee Assoc./Member: No
Size Of Corporate Staff: 30
On-Going Support: a,B,C,D,E,G,I
Training: 2 Weeks Owner Train., Corp. HQ; 1 Wk. Director Train., Corp. HQ; 3-5 Day Staff Training.

SPECIFIC EXPANSION PLANS:

US: All United States
Canada: No
Overseas: No

<< >>

KIDDIE KOBBLER

68 Robertson Rd., # 106
Nepean, ON K2H 8P5 CANADA
Tel: (800) 561-9762 (613) 820-0505
Fax: (613) 820-8250
E-Mail: kiddiekobblerltd@sprint.ca
Web Site: www.kiddiekobbler.com
Mr. Fred Norman, President

Children's shoe stores, located in major shopping malls and strip centers. The extensive marketing program is designed to develop new and repeat business through intensive customer service, selection and value.

BACKGROUND:
Established: 1951; 1st Franchised: 1968
Franchised Units: 29
Company-Owned Units 0
Total Units: 29
Dist.: US-0; CAN-31; O'seas-0
North America: 6 Provinces
Density: 25 in ON, 2 in NS, 2 in PQ
Projected New Units (12 Months): 2
Qualifications: 5, 3, 3, 3, 5, 5
Registered: NR

FINANCIAL/TERMS:

Cash Investment: $50K
Total Investment: $100K
Minimum Net Worth: $150K
Fees: Franchise - $25K
Royalty - 4%; Ad. - 1%
Earnings Claim Statement: No
Term of Contract (Years): 10/5/5
Avg. # Of Employees: 2 FT, 2 PT
Passive Ownership: Not Allowed
Encourage Conversions: Yes
Area Develop. Agreements: Yes
Sub-Franchising Contracts: Yes
Expand In Territory: Yes
Space Needs: 1,000-1,200 SF; SC, RM, SF

SUPPORT & TRAINING PROVIDED:

Financial Assistance Provided: N/A
Site Selection Assistance: Yes
Lease Negotiation Assistance: Yes
Co-Operative Advertising: Yes
Franchisee Assoc./Member: Yes
Size Of Corporate Staff: 6
On-Going Support: b,C,D,E,f,G,H,I
Training: 4 Weeks On-Site; 6 Weeks Supervised Home Study.

SPECIFIC EXPANSION PLANS:

US: Area & Master Franchise Terr
Canada: All Canada
Overseas: No

KINDERDANCE INTERNATIONAL

268 N. Babcock St.
Melbourne, FL 32935-6766
Tel: (800) 554-2334 (321) 242-0590
Fax: (321) 254-3388
E-Mail: kindercorp@kinderdance.com
Web Site: www.kinderdance.net
Mr. Jerry M. Perch, VP Sales/Marketing

KINDERDANCE franchisees are trained to teach 4 developmentally-unique dance and motor development programs: KINDERDANCE, KINDERGYM, KINDERTOTS and KINDERCOMBO, which are designed for boys and girls ages 2-8. They learn the basics of ballet, tap, gymnastics and creative dance, as well as learning numbers, colors, shapes and words. No studio or dance experience required. Franchisee teaches at child care center sites. Area development agreements available.

BACKGROUND: IFA MEMBER
Established: 1979; 1st Franchised: 1985
Franchised Units: 75
Company-Owned Units 2
Total Units: 77
Dist.: US-70; CAN-3; O'seas-3
North America: 29 States, 3 Provinces
Density: 7 in CA, 7 in FL, 7 in TX
Projected New Units (12 Months): 12
Qualifications: 2, 2, 1, 2, 2, 5
Registered: CA,FL,HI,IL,MD,MI,MN,NY, OR,VA,WA,DC,AB

FINANCIAL/TERMS:
Cash Investment: $6.4-25.6K
Total Investment: $9-25.6K
Minimum Net Worth: $N/A
Fees: Franchise - $6.5-20K
Royalty - 6-15%; Ad. - 3%
Earnings Claim Statement: No
Term of Contract (Years): 10/10
Avg. # Of Employees: 1 PT
Passive Ownership: Discouraged
Encourage Conversions: Yes
Area Develop. Agreements: Yes/10
Sub-Franchising Contracts: No
Expand In Territory: Yes
Space Needs: NR SF; NR

SUPPORT & TRAINING PROVIDED:
Financial Assistance Provided: Yes(D)
Site Selection Assistance: N/A
Lease Negotiation Assistance: N/A
Co-Operative Advertising: Yes
Franchisee Assoc./Member: Yes/Yes
Size Of Corporate Staff: 7
On-Going Support: A,B,C,D,E,F,G,H,I
Training: 6 Days in Melbourne, FL and On-Site.

SPECIFIC EXPANSION PLANS:
US: All United States
Canada: All Canada
Overseas: All Countries

KUMON®
MATH & READING CENTERS
Learning How To Learn™

KUMON NORTH AMERICA

300 Frank W. Burr Blvd., 2nd Fl.
Teaneck, NJ 07666
Tel: (800) 222-6284 (201) 928-0444
Fax: (201) 928-0044
E-Mail: mmele@kumon.com
Web Site: www.kumon.com
Mr. Mark Mele, Asst. VP Fran. Recruitment

Kumon is the world's largest provider of supplemental math and reading programs. Our neighborhood learning centers serve students of all ages and abilities, from preschool through high school.

BACKGROUND: IFA MEMBER
Established: 1958; 1st Franchised: 1980
Franchised Units: 1,389
Company-Owned Units 0
Total Units: 1,389
Dist.: US-1052; CAN-337; O'seas-0
North America: 50 States, 9 Provinces
Density: 232 in CA, 93 in NY, 92 NJ
Projected New Units (12 Months): NR
Qualifications: 4, 3, 3, 4, 4, 4
Registered: All States

FINANCIAL/TERMS:
Cash Investment: $NR
Total Investment: $5.9-30.6K
Minimum Net Worth: $NR
Fees: Franchise - $1K
Royalty - $30-33.75; Ad. - N/A
Earnings Claim Statement: No
Term of Contract (Years): 2/5
Avg. # Of Employees: 1 FT, 1-3 PT
Passive Ownership: Not Allowed
Encourage Conversions: N/A
Area Develop. Agreements: No
Sub-Franchising Contracts: No
Expand In Territory: Yes
Space Needs: Varies SF; FS, SF, SC, RM

SUPPORT & TRAINING PROVIDED:
Financial Assistance Provided: N/A
Site Selection Assistance: Yes
Lease Negotiation Assistance: Yes
Co-Operative Advertising: N/A
Franchisee Assoc./Member: Yes
Size Of Corporate Staff: NR
On-Going Support: B,C,D,E,G,H,I
Training: 9-12 Weeks Local Branch Office; 9-12 Weeks Local Kumon Center.

SPECIFIC EXPANSION PLANS:
US: All United States
Canada: All Canada
Overseas: All Countries

LEARNING EXPRESS

29 Buena Vista St.
Ayer, MA 01432-5026
Tel: (888) 725-8697 (978) 889-1000
Fax: (978) 889-1010
E-Mail: steve@learningexpress.com
Web Site: www.learningexpress.com
Mr. Jamie Levy, President

Largest franchisor of specialty toy stores in the United states, currently operating in 20 states. Average sales significantly outperforms independent operators. Comprehensive training and turn-key services by franchisor.

BACKGROUND: IFA MEMBER
Established: 1987; 1st Franchised: 1990
Franchised Units: 142
Company-Owned Units 0
Total Units: 142
Dist.: US-63; CAN-0; O'seas-0
North America: 20 States
Density: 14 in MA, 6 in TX, 6 in NJ
Projected New Units (12 Months): 38
Qualifications: 4, 3, 2, 3, 2, 4
Registered: All Except HI

FINANCIAL/TERMS:
Cash Investment: $75-125K
Total Investment: $203-354K
Minimum Net Worth: $300K
Fees: Franchise - $30K
Royalty - 5%; Ad. - 2%
Earnings Claim Statement: No
Term of Contract (Years): 10/5
Avg. # Of Employees: 2 FT, 8-10 PT
Passive Ownership: Discouraged
Encourage Conversions: N/A
Area Develop. Agreements: Yes/10
Sub-Franchising Contracts: No
Expand In Territory: NR
Space Needs: 3,000 SF; FS, SF, SC, RM

SUPPORT & TRAINING PROVIDED:
Financial Assistance Provided: Yes(I)
Site Selection Assistance: Yes
Lease Negotiation Assistance: Yes
Co-Operative Advertising: No
Franchisee Assoc./Member: No
Size Of Corporate Staff: 12
On-Going Support: C,D,E,F,G,H,I
Training: 1 Week Brookline, MA; 1 Week

Sunnyvale, CA; 1 Week Dallas, TX.

SPECIFIC EXPANSION PLANS:

US: All United States
Canada: No
Overseas: No

<< >>

LITTLE GYM, THE

8970 E. Raintree Dr., # 200
Scottsdale, AZ 85260
Tel: (888) 228-2878 (480) 948-2878
Fax: (480) 948-2765
E-Mail: sales@thelittlegym.com
Web Site: www.thelittlegym.com
Mr. Ron Cordova, Dir. Franchise Development

THE LITTLE GYM child development centers are for children 4 months to 12 years, and offer a unique, integrated approach to child development. THE LITTLE GYM'S highly-motivational and individualized programs are curriculum-based and provide physical, social and intellectual development. Classes develop basic motor skills, build self-esteem and encourage risk-taking through gymnastics, karate and sports skills development.

BACKGROUND:

Established: 1992; 1st Franchised: 1992
Franchised Units: 110
Company-Owned Units 6
Total Units: 116
Dist.: US-95; CAN-0; O'seas-5
North America: 27 States
Density: 11 in TX, 9 in NY, 6 in NC
Projected New Units (12 Months): 24
Qualifications: 5, 5, 2, 3, 5, 5
Registered: CA,FL,IL,IN,MD,MI,MN,NY,OR,WA

FINANCIAL/TERMS:

Cash Investment: $51.2K
Total Investment: $125-160K
Minimum Net Worth: $160K
Fees: Franchise - $37.5K
Royalty - 8%; Ad. - 1%
Earnings Claim Statement: No
Term of Contract (Years): 10/10
Avg. # Of Employees: 2 FT, 2-3 PT
Passive Ownership: Discouraged
Encourage Conversions: Yes
Area Develop. Agreements: Yes/10
Sub-Franchising Contracts: No
Expand In Territory: No
Space Needs: 3,500 SF; SC, Destination

SUPPORT & TRAINING PROVIDED:

Financial Assistance Provided: Yes(I)
Site Selection Assistance: Yes
Lease Negotiation Assistance: Yes
Co-Operative Advertising: No
Franchisee Assoc./Member: No
Size Of Corporate Staff: 18
On-Going Support: C,D,G,H,I
Training: 1 Week Raynham, MA; 1 Week Bellevue, WA.

SPECIFIC EXPANSION PLANS:

US: All United States
Canada: All Canada
Overseas: All Countries

<< >>

LITTLE SCIENTISTS

200 Main St., 3rd Fl.
Ansonia, CT 06401
Tel: (800) FACT-FUN (203) 732-3522
Fax: (203) 736-2165
E-Mail: Dr_Heidi@little-scientists.com
Web Site: www.little-scientists.com
Ms. Ronda Margolis, VP Franchise Development

LITTLE SCIENTISTS is a leader in hands-on science education for children ages 3 to 9. Nearly 200 hands-on lessons make up a innovative science curriculum. The curriculum has been developed by renowned scientists and educators. The market is growing at a remarkable rate. Owning a LITTLE SCIENTIST franchise is a highly profitable endeavor yielding great community benefits.

BACKGROUND:

Established: 1993; 1st Franchised: 1996
Franchised Units: 27
Company-Owned Units 2
Total Units: 29
Dist.: US-17; CAN-0; O'seas-1
North America: 7 States
Density: 5 in CT, 2 in NJ
Projected New Units (12 Months): 14
Qualifications: 3, 5, 4, 4, 5, 5
Registered: CA,FL,IL,NY,VA,WI

FINANCIAL/TERMS:

Cash Investment: $25K
Total Investment: $35K
Minimum Net Worth: $50K
Fees: Franchise - $20K
Royalty - 6%/$250/Mo.; Ad. - 1%
Earnings Claim Statement: No
Term of Contract (Years): 10/10
Avg. # Of Employees: 2 FT, 6-10 PT
Passive Ownership: Discouraged
Encourage Conversions: Yes
Area Develop. Agreements: Yes/10
Sub-Franchising Contracts: Yes
Expand In Territory: Yes
Space Needs: 500 SF; HB

SUPPORT & TRAINING PROVIDED:

Financial Assistance Provided: Yes(I)
Site Selection Assistance: N/A
Lease Negotiation Assistance: N/A
Co-Operative Advertising: N/A
Franchisee Assoc./Member: Yes/Yes
Size Of Corporate Staff: 15
On-Going Support: A,B,C,D,G,H,I
Training: 1 Week at HQ; 1-3 Day Seminars/Training 2 Times/Year at HQ; 2-4 Times/Year On Site.

SPECIFIC EXPANSION PLANS:

US: All United States
Canada: All Canada
Overseas: All Countries Except Korea

<< >>

MAD SCIENCE GROUP, THE

3400 Jean Talon W. # 101
Montreal, PQ H3R 2E8 CANADA
Tel: (800) 586-5231 (514) 344-4181
Fax: (514) 444-6695
E-Mail: joel@madscience.org
Web Site: www.madscience.org
Mr. Joel Lazarovitz, Marketing/Sales

Your staff provides hands-on, interactive science shows for children ages 4-12. Turn kids onto science! Home based, profitable, rewarding.

BACKGROUND: IFA MEMBER

Established: 1985; 1st Franchised: 1995
Franchised Units: 120
Company-Owned Units 0
Total Units: 120
Dist.: US-50; CAN-10; O'seas-6
North America: 15 States, 7 Provinces
Density: 9 in CA, 5 in NJ, 4 in BC
Projected New Units (12 Months): 50
Qualifications: 2, 5, 3, 3, 5, 5
Registered: All States

FINANCIAL/TERMS:

Cash Investment: $10K
Total Investment: $55K
Minimum Net Worth: $23.5K
Fees: Franchise - $23.5K
Royalty - 8%; Ad. - 0%
Earnings Claim Statement: Yes
Term of Contract (Years): 10/5
Avg. # Of Employees: 1 FT, 3-5 PT
Passive Ownership: Not Allowed
Encourage Conversions: N/A
Area Develop. Agreements: No
Sub-Franchising Contracts: No

Expand In Territory: Yes
Space Needs: NR SF; HB

SUPPORT & TRAINING PROVIDED:
Financial Assistance Provided: Yes(I)
Site Selection Assistance: N/A
Lease Negotiation Assistance: N/A
Co-Operative Advertising: N/A
Franchisee Assoc./Member: Yes/Yes
Size Of Corporate Staff: 30
On-Going Support: A,b,C,D,E,F,G,h,i
Training: 2 Weeks Montreal, PQ.

SPECIFIC EXPANSION PLANS:
US: All United States
Canada: All Canada
Overseas: All Countries

<< >>

MY GYM CHILDREN'S FITNESS CENTER

15300 Ventura Blvd., # 307A
Sherman Oaks, CA 91403
Tel: (800) 469-4967 (818) 907-6966
Fax: (818) 907-0735
E-Mail: info@my-gym.com
Web Site: www.my-gym.com
Mr. Gene Barr, Dir. Franchise Development

MY GYM CHILDREN'S FITNESS CENTER's structured, age-appropriate weekly classes incorporates music, dance, relays, games, special rides, gymnastics, sports and other original activities. MY GYM kids have so much fun as they gain strength, balance, gross motor skills, agility, flexibility and social skills. Our programs' biggest benefit is the building of confidence and self esteem. We help design our state-of-the-art facility and assist in every aspect of getting you started.

BACKGROUND:
Established: 1983; 1st Franchised: 1994
Franchised Units: 88
Company-Owned Units 11
Total Units: 99
Dist.: US-98; CAN-0; O'seas-1
North America: 29 States
Density: 24 in CA, 18 in FL, 8 in IL
Projected New Units (12 Months): 40
Qualifications: 2, 3, 3, 3, 4, 5
Registered: All States Exc. ND and SD

FINANCIAL/TERMS:
Cash Investment: $30-60K
Total Investment: $130-180K
Minimum Net Worth: $N/A
Fees: Franchise - $39K
Royalty - 6%; Ad. - 1%
Earnings Claim Statement: No
Term of Contract (Years): 12/12
Avg. # Of Employees: 3 FT, 4 PT
Passive Ownership: Discouraged
Encourage Conversions: N/A
Area Develop. Agreements: Yes/12
Sub-Franchising Contracts: No
Expand In Territory: Yes
Space Needs: 2,400 SF; SF, SC

SUPPORT & TRAINING PROVIDED:
Financial Assistance Provided: Yes(I)
Site Selection Assistance: Yes
Lease Negotiation Assistance: Yes
Co-Operative Advertising: Yes
Franchisee Assoc./Member: No
Size Of Corporate Staff: 15
On-Going Support: B,C,D,E,F,I
Training: 19 Days Corporate Headquarters in Los Angeles, CA; Regional Pre-and Post-Training.

SPECIFIC EXPANSION PLANS:
US: All United States
Canada: All Canada
Overseas: All Countries

<< >>

Once upon a child®

Top 50

ONCE UPON A CHILD

4200 Dahlberg Dr.
Minneapolis, MN 55422-4837
Tel: (800) 445-1006 (763) 520-8500
Fax: (763) 520-8501
E-Mail: lmjensen@winmarkcorporation.com
Web Site: www.ouac.com
Ms. Lynn Jensen, Franchise Development

ONCE UPON A CHILD is an ultra high-value retail store that buys and sells new and used brand-name children's apparel, furniture, equipment and toys.

BACKGROUND: IFA MEMBER
Established: 1985; 1st Franchised: 1993
Franchised Units: 232
Company-Owned Units 1
Total Units: 233
Dist.: US-204; CAN-0; O'seas-0
North America: NR
Density: 15 in OH
Projected New Units (12 Months): 140
Registered: All States

FINANCIAL/TERMS:
Cash Investment: $30-50K
Total Investment: $85-145K
Minimum Net Worth: $NR
Fees: Franchise - $20K
Royalty - 5%; Ad. - $500/Yr.
Earnings Claim Statement: Yes
Term of Contract (Years): 10/10
Avg. # Of Employees: 3 FT, 2 PT
Passive Ownership: Discouraged
Encourage Conversions: Yes
Area Develop. Agreements: No
Sub-Franchising Contracts: No
Expand In Territory: Yes
Space Needs: 2,000-3,000 SF; FS, SC

SUPPORT & TRAINING PROVIDED:
Financial Assistance Provided: Yes(I)
Site Selection Assistance: Yes
Lease Negotiation Assistance: Yes
Co-Operative Advertising: Yes
Franchisee Assoc./Member: NR
Size Of Corporate Staff: 200
On-Going Support: B,C,D,E,F,G,H,I
Training: 12 Days Minneapolis, MN.

SPECIFIC EXPANSION PLANS:
US: All United States
Canada: All Canada
Overseas: No

PEE WEE WORKOUT

34976 Aspenwood Ln.
Willoughby, OH 44094
Tel: (800) 356-6261 (440) 946-7888
Fax: (440) 946-7888
E-Mail: PeeWeeWork@aol.com
Web Site: www.peeweeworkout.com
Ms. Margaret J. Carr, President

Mission Statement: to reach and educate children about the benefits of healthy living. Program teaches healthy living to preschoolers and grade school children. Classes consist of movement to original music that covers components of fitness and concludes with educational lessons. Trained instructors have weekly visits to day schools and recreation departments.

BACKGROUND:
Established: 1986; 1st Franchised: 1987
Franchised Units: 25
Company-Owned Units 1

Total Units: 26
Dist.: US-37; CAN-1; O'seas-1
North America: 18 States
Density: NR
Projected New Units (12 Months): 5
Qualifications: 2, 4, 5, 3, 5, 5
Registered: NR

FINANCIAL/TERMS:
Cash Investment: $NR
Total Investment: $2-2.3K
Minimum Net Worth: $N/A
Fees: Franchise - $1.5K
Royalty - 10%; Ad. - 0%
Earnings Claim Statement: Yes
Term of Contract (Years): 5/5
Avg. # Of Employees: 1 PT
Passive Ownership: Discouraged
Encourage Conversions: N/A
Area Develop. Agreements: No
Sub-Franchising Contracts: Yes
Expand In Territory: Yes
Space Needs: NR SF; HB

SUPPORT & TRAINING PROVIDED:
Financial Assistance Provided: No
Site Selection Assistance: No
Lease Negotiation Assistance: N/A
Co-Operative Advertising: No
Franchisee Assoc./Member: No
Size Of Corporate Staff: NR
On-Going Support: B,G,I
Training: Video Based.

SPECIFIC EXPANSION PLANS:
US: All United States
Canada: All Canada
Overseas: All Countries

<< >>

PLAYTIME PIANO INSTRUCTION
4800 Dromoland Ct., # G
Owings Mills, MD 21117
Tel: (877) 823-6664 x.6227 (410) 654-9131
Fax: (410) 654-9042
E-Mail: playtimepiano@comcast.net
Web Site: www.playtimepiano.com
Ms. Harlene McGowan, Co-Owner/Creative Director

PLAYTIME PIANO INSTRUCTION provides in-home piano instruction (plus other instruments). Individually-tailored programs consider each student's learning style/musical preferences. Lessons are fun and keep students motivated. We teach theory hands-on through our composition program. Practice Incentive Program provides prizes. Home-based business with low overhead/low start-up cost. We provide everything a franchisee needs to become successful in this largely untapped market.

BACKGROUND:
Established: 1997; 1st Franchised: 2002
Franchised Units: 0
Company-Owned Units 1
Total Units: 1
Dist.: US-1; CAN-0; O'seas-0
North America: 1 State
Density: 1 in MD
Projected New Units (12 Months): 10-15
Qualifications: 4, 3, 1, 3, 5, 5
Registered: None

FINANCIAL/TERMS:
Cash Investment: $17.5-25K
Total Investment: $30.9-50.1K
Minimum Net Worth: $35K
Fees: Franchise - $17.5K
Royalty - 8%; Ad. - 1%
Earnings Claim Statement: No
Term of Contract (Years): 10/10
Avg. # Of Employees: 1 FT, 1 PT
Passive Ownership: Not Allowed
Encourage Conversions: N/A
Area Develop. Agreements: No
Sub-Franchising Contracts: No
Expand In Territory: Yes
Space Needs: N/A SF; Home Based

SUPPORT & TRAINING PROVIDED:
Financial Assistance Provided: N/A
Site Selection Assistance: N/A
Lease Negotiation Assistance: N/A
Co-Operative Advertising: Yes
Franchisee Assoc./Member: No
Size Of Corporate Staff: 3
On-Going Support: C,d,G,hHI
Training: 1 Week and 2 Full Weekends.

SPECIFIC EXPANSION PLANS:
US: MD and Non-Reg. States First
Canada: No
Overseas: No

<< >>

PRE-FIT
10926 S. Western Ave.
Chicago, IL 60643
Tel: (773) 233-7771
Fax: (773) 233-7121
E-Mail: prefit@ameritech.net
Web Site: www.pre-fit.com
Ms. Latrice Lee, Franchise Director

PRE-FIT, INC offers America's premier sports, exercise and health systems for children. These systems include: PRE-FIT, a mobile preschool fitness program; FITNESS IS ELEMENTARY, our mobile elementary physical education program; and CHEC, the Children's Health and Executive Club. All of these programs are offered through our success-oriented franchise system that provides marketing, administrative and instructional training, an exclusive territory, and continuous support.

BACKGROUND:
Established: 1987; 1st Franchised: 1992
Franchised Units: 50
Company-Owned Units 2
Total Units: 52
Dist.: US-40; CAN-1; O'seas-0
North America: 13 States
Density: 19 in IL, 6 in PA, 2 in MI
Projected New Units (12 Months): 10
Qualifications: 4, 4, 4, 3, 3, 5
Registered: CA,FL,IL,MD,MI,MN,VA,WA

FINANCIAL/TERMS:
Cash Investment: $10-41K
Total Investment: $10-118.2K
Minimum Net Worth: $25K
Fees: Franchise - $8.5-24.5K
Royalty - 8-10%; Ad. - 2%
Earnings Claim Statement: No
Term of Contract (Years): 10/10
Avg. # Of Employees: 1-2 FT, 2-5 PT
Passive Ownership: Discouraged
Encourage Conversions: N/A
Area Develop. Agreements: No
Sub-Franchising Contracts: No
Expand In Territory: Yes
Space Needs: 2,000-4,000 SF; SC, RM, HB

SUPPORT & TRAINING PROVIDED:
Financial Assistance Provided: Yes(I)
Site Selection Assistance: Yes
Lease Negotiation Assistance: Yes
Co-Operative Advertising: No
Franchisee Assoc./Member: No
Size Of Corporate Staff: 6
On-Going Support: D,E,G,h,I
Training: Chicago, IL.

SPECIFIC EXPANSION PLANS:
US: All United States
Canada: All Canada
Overseas: All Countries

<< >>

PREMIER LEARNING FRANCHISE INTERNATIONAL

3591 Habersham at Northlake,
Tucker, GA 30084-4009
Tel: (888) 592-8020 (770) 939-5441
Fax: (770) 939-8858
E-Mail: rescoffery@mindspring.com
Web Site: www.premierlearningcenters.com
Mr. Ron Escoffery, President/CEO

The outstanding value, along with PLCS franchise success, is centered around: high quality care, affordable facilities, reasonable lease and conversion options, dedication to your total success with PLC franchisee, you'll have all the tools you need to effectively manage and grow your business, while experienced caregivers provide superior child care services for you. Success-support-training-flexibility.

BACKGROUND: IFA MEMBER
Established: 1987; 1st Franchised: 1999
Franchised Units: 0
Company-Owned Units 2
Total Units: 2
Dist.: US-2; CAN-0; O'seas-0
North America: 1 State
Density: 2 in GA
Projected New Units (12 Months): NR
Registered: NR

FINANCIAL/TERMS:
Cash Investment: $50-150K
Total Investment: $250K-1.2MM
Minimum Net Worth: $N/A
Fees: Franchise - $30K
Royalty - 4%; Ad. - 1%
Earnings Claim Statement: No
Term of Contract (Years): 7/7
Avg. # Of Employees: 12 FT, 3 PT
Passive Ownership: Discouraged
Encourage Conversions: NR
Area Develop. Agreements: No
Sub-Franchising Contracts: No
Expand In Territory: Yes
Space Needs: 6000 SF; FS, SC, Renovated Building

SUPPORT & TRAINING PROVIDED:
Financial Assistance Provided: NR
Site Selection Assistance: Yes
Lease Negotiation Assistance: Yes
Co-Operative Advertising: No
Franchisee Assoc./Member: Yes/Yes
Size Of Corporate Staff: 2
On-Going Support: C,D,E,H
Training: 1 Week Head Office; 2 Weeks Operating Unit

SPECIFIC EXPANSION PLANS:
US: SE United States
Canada: NR
Overseas: NR

PRIMROSE SCHOOLS

199 S. Erwin St.
Cartersville, GA 30120
Tel: (800) 745-0677 (770) 606-9600
Fax: (770) 606-0020
E-Mail: psfcfranchise@mindspring.com
Web Site: www.primroseschoolsfranchise.com
Ms. Kim Calvert, Franchise Sales Mgr.

Educational child-care franchise, offering a traditional pre-school curriculum and programs while also providing quality childcare services. Site selection assistance, extensive training, operations manuals, building plans, marketing plans and on-going support.

BACKGROUND: IFA MEMBER
Established: 1982; 1st Franchised: 1989
Franchised Units: 124
Company-Owned Units 1
Total Units: 125
Dist.: US-118; CAN-0; O'seas-0
North America: 14 States
Density: 37 in GA, 37 in TX, 10 in NC
Projected New Units (12 Months): 22
Qualifications: 5, 5, 1, 4, 5, 5
Registered: FL,MN,WA

FINANCIAL/TERMS:
Cash Investment: $150-200K
Total Investment: $1.3-2MM
Minimum Net Worth: $250K
Fees: Franchise - $50K
Royalty - 7%; Ad. - 1%
Earnings Claim Statement: Yes
Term of Contract (Years): 11/10/10
Avg. # Of Employees: 25 FT, 5 PT
Passive Ownership: Not Allowed
Encourage Conversions: N/A
Area Develop. Agreements: No
Sub-Franchising Contracts: No
Expand In Territory: No
Space Needs: 8,500 SF; FS

SUPPORT & TRAINING PROVIDED:
Financial Assistance Provided: Yes(I)
Site Selection Assistance: Yes
Lease Negotiation Assistance: Yes
Co-Operative Advertising: Yes
Franchisee Assoc./Member: Yes/Yes
Size Of Corporate Staff: 23
On-Going Support: A,C,D,E,f,G,h,I
Training: 1 Week Home Office; 1 Week at Existing School; 1 Week at Franchisee's New School.

SPECIFIC EXPANSION PLANS:
US: SW, SE, TX, OH, CO
Canada: No
Overseas: No

SAFE-T-CHILD

203 Barsana Ave.
Austin, TX 78737
Tel: (512) 288-2882
Fax: (512) 288-2898
E-Mail: dennis@yellodyno.com
Web Site: www.safe-t-child.com
Mr. Dennis Wagner, Vice President

Experience the joy of empowering children to stay safe in today's exciting but dangerous world. You'll offer an important array of I. D. and entertainment-driven educational safety products that has families and experts raving. Personal security is booming. Home-based, proven, part-time/full-time, training and support. From $12,500.

BACKGROUND:
Established: 1986; 1st Franchised: 1992
Franchised Units: 71
Company-Owned Units 1
Total Units: 72
Dist.: US-67; CAN-4; O'seas-1
North America: NR
Density: 8 in CA, 6 in TX, 4 in NY
Projected New Units (12 Months): 36
Qualifications: 2, 3, 2, 2, 3, 5
Registered: CA,FL,HI,MI,MN,NY,OR

FINANCIAL/TERMS:
Cash Investment: $5-10K
Total Investment: $15-30K
Minimum Net Worth: $N/A
Fees: Franchise - $12.5K
Royalty - 6%; Ad. - 0%
Earnings Claim Statement: No
Term of Contract (Years): 10/20
Avg. # Of Employees: 2 FT, 2 PT
Passive Ownership: Allowed
Encourage Conversions: N/A
Area Develop. Agreements: Yes
Sub-Franchising Contracts: No
Expand In Territory: No
Space Needs: NR SF; N/A

SUPPORT & TRAINING PROVIDED:
Financial Assistance Provided: No
Site Selection Assistance: N/A
Lease Negotiation Assistance: N/A

Co-Operative Advertising: N/A
Franchisee Assoc./Member: Pending
Size Of Corporate Staff: 9
On-Going Support: C,d,g,h
Training: NR

SPECIFIC EXPANSION PLANS:
US: All United States
Canada: All Canada
Overseas: New Zealand, England, Europe, Latin America, Australia

<< >>

STORK NEWS OF AMERICA

1305 Hope Mills Rd., # A
Fayetteville, NC 28304
Tel: (800) 633-6395 (910) 426-1357
Fax: (910) 426-2473
E-Mail: no2stork@netquick.net
Web Site: www.storknews.com
Mr. John M. Young, VP Franchise Development

The number one and the original newborn yard display business. New mothers, fathers, grandmothers and grandfathers, or any family relations want to tell the world about their new arrival. Rated in many publications as the best buy in home-operated businesses. Almost all operators are Mom's and some Mr. Mom's that don't want to have to ship their kids to day care and then go to work. With a STORK NEWS franchise, kids can go along to work, too.

BACKGROUND:
Established: 1983; 1st Franchised: 1986
Franchised Units: 137
Company-Owned Units 1
Total Units: 138
Dist.: US-124; CAN-2; O'seas-3
North America: 23 States, 1 Province
Density: 14 in VA, 12 in FL, 11 in CA
Projected New Units (12 Months): 12
Qualifications: 1, 4, 1, 1, 3, 5
Registered: CA,FL,HI,IL,MD,MI,MN,NY,VA,WA

FINANCIAL/TERMS:
Cash Investment: $8-20K
Total Investment: $7-12K
Minimum Net Worth: $N/A
Fees: Franchise - $7-10K
Royalty - $0.50-1K; Ad. - N/A
Earnings Claim Statement: No
Term of Contract (Years): Perpetual
Avg. # Of Employees: 1 FT
Passive Ownership: Allowed
Encourage Conversions: N/A
Area Develop. Agreements: No
Sub-Franchising Contracts: No
Expand In Territory: Yes
Space Needs: N/A SF; HB

SUPPORT & TRAINING PROVIDED:
Financial Assistance Provided: Yes(D)
Site Selection Assistance: No
Lease Negotiation Assistance: No
Co-Operative Advertising: No
Franchisee Assoc./Member: No
Size Of Corporate Staff: 0
On-Going Support: D,F,G,I
Training: Manual.

SPECIFIC EXPANSION PLANS:
US: All United States
Canada: All Canada
Overseas: No

<< >>

STRETCH-N-GROW INTERNATIONAL

3912 Tumbil Ln., P.O. Box 261397
Plano, TX 75023
Tel: (800) 348-0166 (972) 519-1635
Fax: (972) 612-5819
Web Site: www.stretch-n-grow.com
Mr. Robert E. Manly, Chief Executive Officer

STRETCH-N-GROW is a comprehensive mobile fitness program for children ages 2 1/2 to 8. It is taught primarily in child care facilities. We provide a corporate marketing system and a curriculum package which covers health-related issues and exercise that is age-appropriate, but adaptable to the age ranges above. The investment and time demands are minimal, the rewards, both financial and personal, immense.

BACKGROUND:
Established: 1992; 1st Franchised: 1994
Franchised Units: 82
Company-Owned Units 0
Total Units: 82
Dist.: US-67; CAN-1; O'seas-0
North America: 24 States, 1 Province
Density: 10 in TX, 5 in NY, 5 in PA
Projected New Units (12 Months): 12
Qualifications: 3, 3, 4, 4, , 5
Registered: CA,FL,NY

FINANCIAL/TERMS:
Cash Investment: $7.6-12.6K
Total Investment: $8.3-13.3K
Minimum Net Worth: $N/A
Fees: Franchise - $7.6-12.6K
Royalty - $100/Mo.; Ad. - $100/Yr.
Earnings Claim Statement: No
Term of Contract (Years): N/A
Avg. # Of Employees: 1 FT, 1-2 PT
Passive Ownership: Discouraged
Encourage Conversions: N/A
Area Develop. Agreements: No
Sub-Franchising Contracts: No
Expand In Territory: No
Space Needs: N/A SF; HB

SUPPORT & TRAINING PROVIDED:
Financial Assistance Provided: No
Site Selection Assistance: N/A
Lease Negotiation Assistance: N/A
Co-Operative Advertising: Yes
Franchisee Assoc./Member: No
Size Of Corporate Staff: 2
On-Going Support: b,D,G,h,I
Training: 3 Days in Dallas, TX.

SPECIFIC EXPANSION PLANS:
US: All United States
Canada: No
Overseas: Australia

<< >>

TECHNOKIDS

2232 Sheridan Garden Dr.
Oakville, ON L6J 7T1 CANADA
Tel: (800) 221-7921 (905) 829-4171
Fax: (905) 829-4172
E-Mail: info@technokids.com
Web Site: www.technokids.com
Mr. Scott Gerard, President

TECHNOKIDS teaches computing and technology skills to children aged 4 to 17 using proprietary thematic-based curriculum. Our program is licensed and sold to schools and delivered through stand-alone computer learning centers.

BACKGROUND:
Established: 1993; 1st Franchised: 1994
Franchised Units: 250
Company-Owned Units 1
Total Units: 251
Dist.: US-2; CAN-3; O'seas-10
North America: 3 States, 2 Provinces
Density: 1 in NM, 1 in VA, 1 in CA
Projected New Units (12 Months): 6
Qualifications: 3, 3, 3, 3, 3, 3
Registered: NR

FINANCIAL/TERMS:
Cash Investment: $25K
Total Investment: $25-50K
Minimum Net Worth: $100K
Fees: Franchise - $15K+
Royalty - 7%; Ad. - 0%
Earnings Claim Statement: No

Term of Contract (Years): 10/10
Avg. # Of Employees: 1 FT, 1 PT
Passive Ownership: Discouraged
Encourage Conversions: Yes
Area Develop. Agreements: Yes/15
Sub-Franchising Contracts: Yes
Expand In Territory: Yes
Space Needs: NR SF; HB

SUPPORT & TRAINING PROVIDED:
Financial Assistance Provided: Yes(D)
Site Selection Assistance: N/A
Lease Negotiation Assistance: N/A
Co-Operative Advertising: Yes
Franchisee Assoc./Member: No
Size Of Corporate Staff: 6
On-Going Support: D,G,H,I
Training: 5-10 Days at Head Office.

SPECIFIC EXPANSION PLANS:
US: All United States
Canada: All Canada
Overseas: All Countries

<< >>

WEE WATCH

3948 Ranchero Dr.
Ann Arbor, MI 48108-2775
Tel: (888) 822-6888 (734) 822-6800
Fax: (734) 822-6888
E-Mail: info@weewatch.com
Web Site: www.weewatch.com
Mr. Marc A. Kiekenapp, Vice President

WEE WATCH - a private home day care franchise company, offering 13 years of experience. Total investment under $30,000. Our sysetm trains you to manage day care providers, expand your customer base and provide safe, educational child care environments. WEE WATCH - an exceptional day care system for today's families.

BACKGROUND: IFA MEMBER
Established: 1987; 1st Franchised: 1987
Franchised Units: 54
Company-Owned Units 0
Total Units: 54
Dist.: US-0; CAN-54; O'seas-0
North America: NR
Density: NR
Projected New Units (12 Months): 25
Qualifications: 3, 3, 1, 3, 4, 5
Registered: CA,FL,IL,IN,MD,MI,MN,NY,OR,RI,VA,WA,WI,DC

FINANCIAL/TERMS:
Cash Investment: $10-20K
Total Investment: $27-47K
Minimum Net Worth: $100K
Fees: Franchise - $6.9K
Royalty - 8%; Ad. - N/A
Earnings Claim Statement: No
Term of Contract (Years): 10/10
Avg. # Of Employees: 3 FT
Passive Ownership: Discouraged
Encourage Conversions: Yes
Area Develop. Agreements: No
Sub-Franchising Contracts: No
Expand In Territory: Yes
Space Needs: 200 SF; HB

SUPPORT & TRAINING PROVIDED:
Financial Assistance Provided: Yes(I)
Site Selection Assistance: Yes
Lease Negotiation Assistance: N/A
Co-Operative Advertising: N/A
Franchisee Assoc./Member: No
Size Of Corporate Staff: 15
On-Going Support: C,D,E,G,h,I
Training: 5 Days Home Office; 1 Week Right Start Program; 2 Days Franchise Location.

SPECIFIC EXPANSION PLANS:
US: All United States
Canada: All Canada
Overseas: All Countries

WEE WATCH PRIVATE HOME DAY CARE

105 Main St.
Unionville, ON L3R 2G1 CANADA
Tel: (905) 479-4274
Fax: (905) 479-9047
E-Mail: weewatch@weewatch.com
Web Site: www.weewatch.com
Mr. Terry Fullerton, President

WEE WATCH is a private home day care agency, catering to children ages 6 weeks and older. Full-time and part-time. The franchisee trains and supervises providers who provide day care in their homes.

BACKGROUND:
Established: 1984; 1st Franchised: 1987
Franchised Units: 50
Company-Owned Units 0
Total Units: 50
Dist.: US-0; CAN-50; O'seas-0
North America: 3 Provinces
Density: 38 in ON, 11 in BC, 1 IN nb
Projected New Units (12 Months): 6
Registered: NR

FINANCIAL/TERMS:
Cash Investment: $24K
Total Investment: $24K
Minimum Net Worth: $NR
Fees: Franchise - $12.5K
Royalty - 6-8%; Ad. - 2%
Earnings Claim Statement: Yes
Term of Contract (Years): 5/20
Avg. # Of Employees: 2 FT, 1 PT
Passive Ownership: Not Allowed
Encourage Conversions: Yes
Area Develop. Agreements: No
Sub-Franchising Contracts: No
Expand In Territory: No
Space Needs: N/A SF; N/A

SUPPORT & TRAINING PROVIDED:
Financial Assistance Provided: No
Site Selection Assistance: N/A
Lease Negotiation Assistance: N/A
Co-Operative Advertising: Yes
Franchisee Assoc./Member: No
Size Of Corporate Staff: 9
On-Going Support: B,C,D,G,H,I
Training: 4 Days Home Office; 3 Days On-Site.

SPECIFIC EXPANSION PLANS:
US: All United States
Canada: All Canada
Overseas: No

SUPPLEMENTAL LISTING OF FRANCHISORS

A CHOICE NANNY, 5110 Ridgefield Rd., # 403 B, Bethesda, MD 20816 ; (800) 73-NANNY (301) 652-2229; (301) 596-9939

BELLINI JUVENILE DESIGNER FURNITURE, 301 N. Main St., New City, NY 10956 ; (800) 332-2229 (914) 638-4111; (914) 638-3878

CHILD CARE CHOICES, P.O. Box 691, Bensalem, PA 19020 ; (877) 748-4968 (215) 969-0276; (215) 969-7662

CREATIVE WORLD SCHOOL, 13315 Orange Grove Dr., Tampa, FL 33618; (800) 362-5940 (813) 968-9154; (813) 264-7266

DISCOVERY POINT, 1140 Old Peachtree Rd., # A, Duluth, GA 30097 ; (770) 622-2112; (770) 622-2388

DRAMA KIDS INTERNATIONAL, 3225-B Corporate Ct., Ellicott City, MD 21042 ; (877) 543-7456 (410) 480-2015; (410) 480-2026

FUTUREKIDS, 1000 N. Studebaker Rd., # 1, Long Beach, CA 90815 ; (800) 876-5444 (562) 296-1111; (562) 296-1110

GENIUS KID ACADEMY, 398 Steeles Ave. W., # 214, Thornhill, ON L4J 6X3 CANADA; (905) 886-1920; (905) 886-4919

GODDARD SCHOOL, THE, 381 Brooks Rd., King of Prussia, PA 19406 (800) 272-4901 (610) 265-7128; (610) 265-7194

HAND ME DOWNS, 3201 Tooley's Rd., Courtice, ON L1E 2K7 CANADA; (905) 720-3328

HIGH TOUCH-HIGH TECH, 12352 Wiles Rd., Coral Springs, FL 33076 ; (800) 444-4968 (954) 755-2900; (954) 755-1242

KIDDIE PROOFERS, 3011 Dufferin St., Toronto, ON M6B 3T4 CANADA; (800) 601-5437 (416) 785-5437; (416) 785-4780

KIDS "R" KIDS QUALITY LEARNING CENTERS, 1625 Executive Drive S., Duluth, GA 30096 ; (800) 279-0033 (770) 279-8500; (770) 279-9699

KIDS COACH, 7 - 3331 Viking Way, Richmond, BC V6V 1X7 CANADA; (604) 270-2360; (604) 220-6442

KIDSPORTS INTERNATIONAL, 240 Penn Ave., Sinking Spring, PA 19608 ; (610) 372-6830; (610) 372-8045

KUMON MATH & READING CENTRES, 344 Consumer Rd., North York, ON M2J 1P8 CANADA; (416) 490-1722; (416) 490-1694

OTHER MOTHERS, 18425 N. Division Rd., Colbert, WA 93005 ; (888) 467-5133 (509) 467-5133; (509) 467-5147

PUCKMASTERS HOCKEY TRAINING CENTERS, 1260 Hornby St., # 102, Vancouver, BC V6Z 1W2 CANADA; (800) 663-2331 (604) 683-7825; (604) 683-7841

RAINBOW STATION, 3307 Church Rd., # 205, Richmond, VA 23233 ; (888) 747-1552 (804) 747-5900; (804) 747-8016

SAFE & SOUND, 530 S. Henderson Rd., # D, King of Prussia, PA 19406 ; (800) 384-SAFE (610) 265-5155; (610) 265-5149

SPRINGSTONE FRANCHISE LEARNING CENTERS, 1615 Randolph Ct., # B, Albuquerque, NM 87106 ; (866) 915-3276 (505) 242-1888; (505) 242-1115

THEATER FUN, 3400 Jean Talon W., # 101, Montreal, PQ H3R 2E8 CANADA; (800) 586-5231 (514) 344-4181; (514) 344-6695

TUTORING CLUB, 6964 Almaden Expy., San Jose, CA 95120-3201 ; (888) 674-6425 (408) 997-7590; (408) 997-7024

WEE WATCH PRIVATE HOME DAY CARE, 105 Main St., Unionville, ON L3R 2G1 CANADA; (905) 479-4274; (905) 479-9047

WHOLE CHILD LEARNING CO., THE, 921 Belvin St., San Marcos, TX 78666 ; (888) 317-3535 (512) 396-2740; (512) 392-7820

WONDERS OF WISDOM CHILDREN'S CENTERS, 13420 Minnieville Rd., Woodbridge, VA 22192-4104 ; (800) 424-0550 (703) 670-9344; (703) 670-2851

For a full explanation of the data provided in the Franchisor Profiles, please refer to **Chapter 2, "How to Use the Data."**

Education/Personal Development/Training

Education/Personal Development/Training Industry Profile

Total # Franchisors in Industry Group	54
Total # Franchised Units in Industry Group	3,692
Total # Company-Owned Units in Industry Group	683
Total # Operating Units in Industry Group	4,375
Average # Franchised Units/Franchisor	68.4
Average # Company-Owned Units/Franchisor	12.6
Average # Total Units/Franchisor	81.0
Ratio of Total # Franchised Units/Total # Company-Owned Units	5.4:1
Industry Survey Participants	24
Representing % of Industry	44.4 %
Average Franchise Fee*:	$30.3K
Average Total Investment*:	$128.4K
Average On-Going Royalty Fee*:	8.2%

*If a range was provided, the mid-point of the range was used. See detailed profiles for actual ranges.

Five Largest Participants in Survey

Company	# Franchised Units	# Co-Owned Units	# Total Units	Franchise Fee	On-Going Royalty	Total Investment
1. Sylvan Learning Centers	765	82	847	38-46K	8-9%	121-219K
2. Berlitz International	65	336	401	30-50K	10%	150-300K
3. New Horizons Computer Learning Centers	269	29	298	25-75K	6%	400-500K
4. Huntington Learning Centers	171	50	221	34K	8%/1.2K Min.	139-192K
5. Executrain	166	35	201	30K	6-9%	200-250K

ACADEMY FOR MATHEMATICS & SCIENCE

30 Glen Cameron Rd., # 200
Thornhill, ON L3T 1N7 CANADA
Tel: (800) 809-5555 (905) 709-3233
Fax: (905) 709-3045
E-Mail: info@acadfor.com
Web Site: www.acadfor.com
Mr. Balti Sauer, President/CEO

Licensees provide math, science, English and computer tutoring to school age children from kindergarten to the end of high school. Individualized, self-paced learning is provided in learning centers located in major malls, using a unique audio-visual learning program.

BACKGROUND:
Established: 1992; 1st Franchised: 1993
Franchised Units: 29
Company-Owned Units 7
Total Units: 36
Dist.: US-0; CAN-36; O'seas-0
North America: 3 Provinces
Density: 25 in ON, 6 in BC, 5 in AB
Projected New Units (12 Months): 6
Qualifications: 2, 3, 1, 4, 1, 5
Registered: AB

FINANCIAL/TERMS:
Cash Investment: $50-70K
Total Investment: $50-70K
Minimum Net Worth: $N/A
Fees: Franchise - $35K
Royalty - 10-12%; Ad. - 2%
Earnings Claim Statement: No
Term of Contract (Years): 5/5
Avg. # Of Employees: 2 FT, 6 PT
Passive Ownership: Not Allowed
Encourage Conversions: N/A
Area Develop. Agreements: Yes/10
Sub-Franchising Contracts: Yes
Expand In Territory: Yes
Space Needs: 1,000 SF; SC, RM

SUPPORT & TRAINING PROVIDED:
Financial Assistance Provided: Yes(I)
Site Selection Assistance: Yes
Lease Negotiation Assistance: Yes
Co-Operative Advertising: No
Franchisee Assoc./Member: Yes/No
Size Of Corporate Staff: 13
On-Going Support: C,D,E,G,H,I
Training: 1 Week Corporate Office; 1 Week Training Center.

SPECIFIC EXPANSION PLANS:
US: Not Yet
Canada: All Canada
Overseas: Yes

<< >>

ACADEMY OF LEARNING

Five Bank St., # 202
Attleboro, MA 02703
Tel: (508) 222-0000
Fax: (508) 222-0005
Web Site: www.academyol.com
Mr. Jeffrey A. Goldwasser, U.S. Director of Operations

Computer training centers, utilizing unique 'Integrated Learning System.' This self-paced, flex-time system uses audio instruction, workbooks and PCs with full individual supervision.

BACKGROUND:
Established: 1987; 1st Franchised: 1987
Franchised Units: 154
Company-Owned Units 3
Total Units: 157
Dist.: US-7; CAN-140; O'seas-10
North America: 3 States, 9 Provinces
Density: 50 in ON, 16 in BC, 9 in AB
Projected New Units (12 Months): 50
Qualifications: 4, 4, 3, 4, 2, 5
Registered: NY,RI,AB

FINANCIAL/TERMS:
Cash Investment: $100K
Total Investment: $200-300K
Minimum Net Worth: $200K
Fees: Franchise - $30K
Royalty - 0%; Ad. - $400/Mo.
Earnings Claim Statement: No
Term of Contract (Years): 10/10
Avg. # Of Employees: 5 FT, 2 PT
Passive Ownership: Not Allowed
Encourage Conversions: Yes
Area Develop. Agreements: Yes
Sub-Franchising Contracts: No
Expand In Territory: Yes
Space Needs: 3,000 SF; Other

SUPPORT & TRAINING PROVIDED:
Financial Assistance Provided: No
Site Selection Assistance: Yes
Lease Negotiation Assistance: Yes
Co-Operative Advertising: Yes
Franchisee Assoc./Member: Yes/Yes
Size Of Corporate Staff: 30
On-Going Support: C,D,E,G,h,I
Training: 2 Weeks Training Center; 2 Days Head Office; 1 Week On-Site.

SPECIFIC EXPANSION PLANS:
US: Northeast
Canada: All Canada
Overseas: All Countries

<< >>

AMRON SCHOOL OF THE FINE ARTS

1315 Medlin Rd.
Monroe, NC 28112
Tel: (704) 283-4290
Fax: (704) 283-7290
E-Mail: normawilliams@verizon.net
Ms. Norma W. Williams, President/CEO

(Educational) Teach modeling, acting, cosmetics and photography for portfolios. Agency to get clients jobs in acting and modeling.

BACKGROUND:
Established: 1979; 1st Franchised: 1986
Franchised Units: 0
Company-Owned Units 1
Total Units: 1
Dist.: US-0; CAN-0; O'seas-0
North America: 1 State
Density: 1 in NC
Projected New Units (12 Months): NR
Registered: NR

FINANCIAL/TERMS:
Cash Investment: $15K
Total Investment: $20K
Minimum Net Worth: $20K
Fees: Franchise - $20K
Royalty - Sliding Scale; Ad. - 1%
Earnings Claim Statement: Yes
Term of Contract (Years): 5/5
Avg. # Of Employees: 2 PT
Passive Ownership: Allowed
Encourage Conversions: NR
Area Develop. Agreements: No
Sub-Franchising Contracts: No
Expand In Territory: Yes
Space Needs: NR SF; FS, SF, SC, RM, HB

SUPPORT & TRAINING PROVIDED:
Financial Assistance Provided: NR
Site Selection Assistance: N/A
Lease Negotiation Assistance: N/A
Co-Operative Advertising: N/A
Franchisee Assoc./Member: No
Size Of Corporate Staff: 2
On-Going Support: A,B,D,d,E,F,G,H,h
Training: 1 Week at Home Office in Monroe, NC.

SPECIFIC EXPANSION PLANS:
US: All United States

Canada: NR
Overseas: NR

<< >>

BARBIZON SCHOOLS OF MODELING

2240 Woolbright Rd., # 300
Boynton Beach, FL 33426
Tel: (888) 999-9404 (561) 369-8600
Fax: (561) 369-1299
E-Mail: franchise@barbizonmodeling.com
Web Site: www.barbizonmodeling.com
Mr. Tom Blangiardo, President

Proprietary, private schools of modeling and related creative arts.

BACKGROUND: IFA MEMBER
Established: 1939; 1st Franchised: 1968
Franchised Units: 60
Company-Owned Units 0
Total Units: 60
Dist.: US-56; CAN-1; O'seas-3
North America: 27 States
Density: 7 in CA, 5 in NY, 5 in NJ
Projected New Units (12 Months): 7
Qualifications: 4, 3, 1, 4, 2, 5
Registered: CA,HI,IL,MD,MN,NY,VA,WA

FINANCIAL/TERMS:
Cash Investment: $30-50K
Total Investment: $47-67.5K
Minimum Net Worth: $NR
Fees: Franchise - $35K
Royalty - 7.5%; Ad. - 2.5%
Earnings Claim Statement: No
Term of Contract (Years): 10/10
Avg. # Of Employees: NR
Passive Ownership: Discouraged
Encourage Conversions: Yes
Area Develop. Agreements: No
Sub-Franchising Contracts: No
Expand In Territory: Yes
Space Needs: NR SF; NR

SUPPORT & TRAINING PROVIDED:
Financial Assistance Provided: Yes(D)
Site Selection Assistance: Yes
Lease Negotiation Assistance: Yes
Co-Operative Advertising: N/A
Franchisee Assoc./Member: Yes/Yes
Size Of Corporate Staff: NR
On-Going Support: C,D,E,G,H
Training: Varies Home Office; Varies On-Site.

SPECIFIC EXPANSION PLANS:
US: All United States
Canada: All Canada
Overseas: All Countries

<< >>

BERLITZ INTERNATIONAL

400 Alexander Park Dr.
Princeton, NJ 08540-6306
Tel: (800) 626-6419 (609) 514-3046
Fax: (609) 514-9675
E-Mail: frank.garton@berlitz.com
Web Site: www.berlitz.com
Mr. Frank Garton, VP Worldwide Franchising

Language instruction, publishing and translation services

BACKGROUND: IFA MEMBER
Established: 1900; 1st Franchised: 1996
Franchised Units: 65
Company-Owned Units 336
Total Units: 401
Dist.: US-61; CAN-11; O'seas-328
North America: NR
Density: 18 in NY, 18 in CA, 18 in FL
Projected New Units (12 Months): 50
Qualifications: 4, 5, 2, 3, 4, 5
Registered: CA,FL,IL,MD,MI,NY,OR,VA,WA

FINANCIAL/TERMS:
Cash Investment: $150-300K
Total Investment: $150-300K
Minimum Net Worth: $300K
Fees: Franchise - $30-50K
Royalty - 10%; Ad. - 2%
Earnings Claim Statement: No
Term of Contract (Years): 10/10
Avg. # Of Employees: 1 FT, 1 PT
Passive Ownership: Discouraged
Encourage Conversions: Yes
Area Develop. Agreements: Yes/10
Sub-Franchising Contracts: No
Expand In Territory: No
Space Needs: 1,500-3,000 SF; N/A

SUPPORT & TRAINING PROVIDED:
Financial Assistance Provided: No
Site Selection Assistance: Yes
Lease Negotiation Assistance: Yes
Co-Operative Advertising: No
Franchisee Assoc./Member: No
Size Of Corporate Staff: 7000
On-Going Support: B,C,D,E,F,G,H
Training: 2 Weeks Home Office; 2 Weeks Division Training; 2 Weeks On-Site.

SPECIFIC EXPANSION PLANS:
US: Southeast, West
Canada: NB
Overseas: Africa, Central Asia, Asia

<< >>

BOSTON BARTENDERS SCHOOL ASSOCIATES

P.O. Box 176
Wilbraham, MA 01095
Tel: (800) 357-3210 (413) 596-4600
Fax: (413) 596-4630
Mr. William Green, Chief Operating Officer

BBS offers a 35-hour course in Mixology and alcohol awareness to men and women ages 18 and up. College students, people in-between or changing jobs or those moving to a new area will be interested in a job bartending. It's easy, fun, quick and affordable. The program takes one or two weeks of evenings to complete. The program costs $400-600, paid up front.

BACKGROUND:
Established: 1968; 1st Franchised: 1995
Franchised Units: 10
Company-Owned Units 3
Total Units: 13
Dist.: US-9; CAN-0; O'seas-0
North America: NR
Density: 4 in MA, 2 in CT, 2 in RI
Projected New Units (12 Months): 3
Qualifications: 1, 1, 1, 1, 1, 4
Registered: RI

FINANCIAL/TERMS:
Cash Investment: $30K
Total Investment: $30K
Minimum Net Worth: $50K
Fees: Franchise - $6.9K
Royalty - 10%; Ad. - NR
Earnings Claim Statement: No
Term of Contract (Years): 10/10
Avg. # Of Employees: 2 FT, 1 PT
Passive Ownership: Discouraged
Encourage Conversions: N/A
Area Develop. Agreements: No
Sub-Franchising Contracts: No
Expand In Territory: Yes
Space Needs: 1,000 SF; N/A

SUPPORT & TRAINING PROVIDED:
Financial Assistance Provided: No
Site Selection Assistance: Yes
Lease Negotiation Assistance: Yes
Co-Operative Advertising: N/A
Franchisee Assoc./Member: No
Size Of Corporate Staff: 2
On-Going Support: A,E,F,H,I
Training: 2 Weeks in Springfield, MA.

SPECIFIC EXPANSION PLANS:
US: All United States
Canada: All Canada
Overseas: No

<< >>

CAREER BLAZERS LEARNING CENTERS

290 Madison Ave.
New York, NY 10017-6308
Tel: (212) 725-7900
Fax: (212) 725-8767
E-Mail: hkane@cblazers.com
Web Site: www.cblazers.com
Mr. Paul Viboch, Vice President

State-of-the-art computer and information technology training centers, which are state licensed business schools, serving corporations, governmentally funded/entitled groups and the public. The need for technology training increases exponentially every day and theses skills are essential to the individual, at the workplace and at home.

BACKGROUND:
Established: 1948; 1st Franchised: 1993
Franchised Units: 46
Company-Owned Units 11
Total Units: 57
Dist.: US-54; CAN-3; O'seas-0
North America: 20 States, 1 Province
Density: 9 in PA, 4 in MA, 4 in OH
Projected New Units (12 Months): 10
Qualifications: 4, 4, 3, 3, 3, 4
Registered: CA,FL,IL,MI

FINANCIAL/TERMS:
Cash Investment: $150K
Total Investment: $350K
Minimum Net Worth: $300K
Fees: Franchise - $25K
Royalty - 8-10%; Ad. - 2%
Earnings Claim Statement: No
Term of Contract (Years): 10/10
Avg. # Of Employees: 4 FT, 2 PT
Passive Ownership: Allowed
Encourage Conversions: Yes
Area Develop. Agreements: No
Sub-Franchising Contracts: No
Expand In Territory: Yes
Space Needs: 3,000 SF; SF, SC, OB

SUPPORT & TRAINING PROVIDED:
Financial Assistance Provided: No
Site Selection Assistance: Yes
Lease Negotiation Assistance: Yes
Co-Operative Advertising: Yes
Franchisee Assoc./Member: No
Size Of Corporate Staff: 25
On-Going Support: b,C,D,E,G,H,I
Training: At Least 1 Week in Either New York City, NY or Atlanta, GA.

SPECIFIC EXPANSION PLANS:
US: All United States
Canada: No
Overseas: No

<< >>

COMPUTER U LEARNING CENTERS

75850 Osage Trl.
Indian Wells, CA 92210
Tel: (888) 708-7877 (760) 340-2453
Fax: (760) 340-0306
E-Mail: info@computeru.com
Web Site: www.computeru.com
Mr. Russ Beckner, Vice President

COMPUTER U LEARNING CENTERS provides computer training to mature adults through classroom instruction and private tutoring. We teach in the context of mid-life and retirement, with tested programs developed especially for adults ago 50 and over. We make it simple to learn computers. We keep it simple for our franchise partners with comprehensive training and continuing on-line support. Come GROW with us!

BACKGROUND: IFA MEMBER
Established: 1992; 1st Franchised: 1997
Franchised Units: 9
Company-Owned Units 6
Total Units: 15
Dist.: US-15; CAN-0; O'seas-0
North America: 4 States
Density: CA, NV, FL
Projected New Units (12 Months): 10
Qualifications: 3, 3, 1, 4, 5, 5
Registered: CA,FL,MI,OR,WI,DC

FINANCIAL/TERMS:
Cash Investment: $30-40K
Total Investment: $30-40K
Minimum Net Worth: $N/A
Fees: Franchise - $20K
Royalty - 6%; Ad. - 1%
Earnings Claim Statement: Yes
Term of Contract (Years): 10/5
Avg. # Of Employees: 1 FT, 2 PT
Passive Ownership: Allowed
Encourage Conversions: N/A
Area Develop. Agreements: Yes
Sub-Franchising Contracts: No
Expand In Territory: Yes
Space Needs: 400 SF; N/A

SUPPORT & TRAINING PROVIDED:
Financial Assistance Provided: No
Site Selection Assistance: Yes
Lease Negotiation Assistance: Yes
Co-Operative Advertising: No
Franchisee Assoc./Member: No
Size Of Corporate Staff: 4
On-Going Support: NR
Training: 2 Days On-Site; 6 Days Headquarters, Palm Springs, CA.

SPECIFIC EXPANSION PLANS:
US: Where Registered
Canada: No
Overseas: No

<< >>

CRESTCOM INTERNATIONAL, LTD.

6900 E. Belleview Ave.
Greenwood Village, CO 80111
Tel: (888) 273-7826 (303) 267-8200
Fax: (303) 267-8207
E-Mail: franchiseinfo@crestcom.com
Web Site: www.crestcom.com
Mr. Kelly Krause, Dir. International Marketing

Recognized by Entrepreneur and Success magazines as the #1 management/sales training franchise, CRESTCOM INTERNATIONAL offers business executives and professionals the opportunity to put their experience to work for themselves as the CEO of their own training company. CRESTCOM training combines live-facilitated instruction by franchisees and videos featuring internationally known business experts.

BACKGROUND: IFA MEMBER
Established: 1987; 1st Franchised: 1992
Franchised Units: 125
Company-Owned Units 0
Total Units: 125
Dist.: US-42; CAN-6; O'seas-77
North America: 20 States, 4 Provinces
Density: NR
Projected New Units (12 Months): 25
Qualifications: 4, 5, 2, 4, 5, 5
Registered: All States

FINANCIAL/TERMS:
Cash Investment: $35-52.5K
Total Investment: $44.4-73.2K
Minimum Net Worth: $NR

Fees: Franchise - $35-52.5K
Royalty - 1.5%; Ad. - N/A
Earnings Claim Statement: Yes
Term of Contract (Years): 7/7/7
Avg. # Of Employees: 2-5 FT
Passive Ownership: Discouraged
Encourage Conversions: N/A
Area Develop. Agreements: No
Sub-Franchising Contracts: No
Expand In Territory: Yes
Space Needs: NR SF; SF, HB

SUPPORT & TRAINING PROVIDED:
Financial Assistance Provided: Yes
Site Selection Assistance: N/A
Lease Negotiation Assistance: N/A
Co-Operative Advertising: Yes
Franchisee Assoc./Member: No
Size Of Corporate Staff: 15
On-Going Support: D,G,H
Training: 7-10 Days Denver, CO, Phoenix, AZ or Sacramento, CA.

SPECIFIC EXPANSION PLANS:
US: All United States
Canada: All Canada
Overseas: All Countries

ELS LANGUAGE CENTERS

400 Alexander Park
Princeton, NJ 08540-6306
Tel: (800) 468-8978 (609) 750-3508
Fax: (609) 750-3596
E-Mail: info@els.com
Web Site: www.els.com
Mr. Charles J. Gilbert, VP Franchising

Leader in teaching English to the world. Franchises English-language schools overseas, students learn business English, conversational English, TOEFL and other programs. Franchisees also offer study-abroad programs and university placement assistance.

BACKGROUND: IFA MEMBER
Established: 1956; 1st Franchised: 1978
Franchised Units: 51
Company-Owned Units 34
Total Units: 85
Dist.: US-33; CAN-1; O'seas-50
North America: 21 States, 1 Province
Density: 5 in CA, 2 in NY, 2 in FL
Projected New Units (12 Months): Unsure
Qualifications: 4, 4, 4, 3, 4, 5
Registered: None

FINANCIAL/TERMS:
Cash Investment: $100-300K
Total Investment: $100-300K
Minimum Net Worth: $250K
Fees: Franchise - $30K
Royalty - 5%; Ad. - 0%
Earnings Claim Statement: No
Term of Contract (Years): 10/10
Avg. # Of Employees: 6-20 FT
Passive Ownership: Discouraged
Encourage Conversions: Yes
Area Develop. Agreements: Yes/10-20
Sub-Franchising Contracts: No
Expand In Territory: Yes
Space Needs: Feasible SF; N/A

SUPPORT & TRAINING PROVIDED:
Financial Assistance Provided: No
Site Selection Assistance: Yes
Lease Negotiation Assistance: No
Co-Operative Advertising: Yes
Franchisee Assoc./Member: No
Size Of Corporate Staff: 65
On-Going Support: C,D,G,H
Training: 2 Weeks Princeton, NJ.

SPECIFIC EXPANSION PLANS:
US: No
Canada: No
Overseas: Case by Case Basis

EXECUTRAIN

4800 Northpoint Pkwy.
Alpharetta, GA 30022-3766
Tel: (800) 437-2034 (770) 667-7700
Fax: (770) 664-2006
Web Site: www.executrain.com
Ms. Michelle Beekman, International Support

EXECUTRAIN is the world's leading computer-training franchise. EXECUTRAIN offers over 800+ courses in the most popular business-applications software in order to increase the productivity of business people from all levels. This is achieved through instructor-led, hands-on training in a classroom setting.

BACKGROUND:
Established: 1984; 1st Franchised: 1986
Franchised Units: 166
Company-Owned Units 35
Total Units: 201
Dist.: US-173; CAN-4; O'seas-41
North America: NR
Density: NR
Projected New Units (12 Months): 18
Qualifications: 5, 5, 3, 3, 1, 5
Registered: All States

FINANCIAL/TERMS:
Cash Investment: $200K
Total Investment: $200-250K
Minimum Net Worth: $250K
Fees: Franchise - $30K
Royalty - 6-9%; Ad. - 1.5%
Earnings Claim Statement: No
Term of Contract (Years): 7/7
Avg. # Of Employees: 15-20 FT/PT
Passive Ownership: Discouraged
Encourage Conversions: No
Area Develop. Agreements: No
Sub-Franchising Contracts: No
Expand In Territory: Yes
Space Needs: 3,500 SF; FS

SUPPORT & TRAINING PROVIDED:
Financial Assistance Provided: Yes(D)
Site Selection Assistance: Yes
Lease Negotiation Assistance: Yes
Co-Operative Advertising: No
Franchisee Assoc./Member: NR
Size Of Corporate Staff: 110
On-Going Support: NR
Training: 5 Days GM Training; 5 Days Instructor Training; 5 Days Sale Training -- all Atlanta, GA.

SPECIFIC EXPANSION PLANS:
US: No
Canada: All Canada
Overseas: All Countries

GWYNNE LEARNING ACADEMY

P.O. Box 41701
Mesa, AZ 85274-1701
Tel: (480) 644-1434
Fax: (480) 644-1434
Ms. Penny Gwynne, Treasurer

Video-based interactive training, based on the latest scientific training technology for individuals, blue chip groups in the business, government and education sectors.

BACKGROUND:
Established: 1991; 1st Franchised: 1991
Franchised Units: 14
Company-Owned Units 1
Total Units: 15
Dist.: US-2; CAN-0; O'seas-12
North America: 1 State
Density: 2 in AZ
Projected New Units (12 Months): 6
Registered: NR

FINANCIAL/TERMS:
Cash Investment: $45K
Total Investment: $45-65K
Minimum Net Worth: $NR

Fees: Franchise - $25K
Royalty - 7%; Ad. - 2%
Earnings Claim Statement: No
Term of Contract (Years): 10/10
Avg. # Of Employees: 2 FT
Passive Ownership: Allowed
Encourage Conversions: N/A
Area Develop. Agreements: No
Sub-Franchising Contracts: No
Expand In Territory: Yes
Space Needs: 600 SF; FS, SF, SC, RM

SUPPORT & TRAINING PROVIDED:
Financial Assistance Provided: Yes(I)
Site Selection Assistance: Yes
Lease Negotiation Assistance: Yes
Co-Operative Advertising: Yes
Franchisee Assoc./Member: No
Size Of Corporate Staff: 2
On-Going Support: b,D,e,I
Training: 7 Days Phoenix, AZ.

SPECIFIC EXPANSION PLANS:
US: All United States
Canada: All Canada
Overseas: Australia, Malaysia

<< >>

HONORS LEARNING CENTER, THE

5959 Shallowford Rd., # 515
Chattanooga, TN 37421
Tel: (423) 892-1803
Fax: (423) 892-1803
E-Mail: honorsman@aol.com
Web Site: www.honorslearningcenter.com
Mr. Gary Miller, President

THE HONORS LEARNING CENTER franchisees offers students in grades K-12 supplemental, individualized, academic programs in reading, math, study skills, SAT/ACT prep, etc. Comprehensive academic testing (pre-admission) used to develop the instruction prescription of materials and curricula to deal with the student's special needs. Remedial programs to catch up and enrichment programs for advanced students are also offered.

BACKGROUND:
Established: 1987; 1st Franchised: 1992
Franchised Units: 1
Company-Owned Units 1
Total Units: 2
Dist.: US-2; CAN-0; O'seas-0
North America: 2 States
Density: 1 in TN, 1 in FL
Projected New Units (12 Months): 6
Qualifications: 4, 4, 4, 5, 4, 4
Registered: FL

FINANCIAL/TERMS:
Cash Investment: $65-132K
Total Investment: $65-132K
Minimum Net Worth: $100K
Fees: Franchise - $15K
Royalty - 8%; Ad. - 0%
Earnings Claim Statement: No
Term of Contract (Years): 10/10
Avg. # Of Employees: 2 FT, 8 PT
Passive Ownership: Not Allowed
Encourage Conversions: Yes
Area Develop. Agreements: No
Sub-Franchising Contracts: No
Expand In Territory: Yes
Space Needs: 1,100-1,300 SF; SC, Professional Building

SUPPORT & TRAINING PROVIDED:
Financial Assistance Provided: No
Site Selection Assistance: Yes
Lease Negotiation Assistance: No
Co-Operative Advertising: No
Franchisee Assoc./Member: No
Size Of Corporate Staff: 2
On-Going Support: C,d,E,G,h
Training: 2-3 Weeks at Corporate Office.

SPECIFIC EXPANSION PLANS:
US: All United States
Canada: No
Overseas: No

<< >>

HUNTINGTON LEARNING CENTER

496 Kinderkamack Rd.
Oradell, NJ 07649
Tel: (800) 653-8400 (201) 261-8400
Fax: (201) 261-3233
E-Mail: hlcorp@aol.com
Web Site: www.huntingtonlearning.com
Mr. Richard C. Pittius, VP Franchise

Offers services to 5-19 year-olds, and occasionally to adults, in reading, spelling, phonics, language development study skills and mathematics, as well as programs to prepare for standardized entrance exams. Instruction is offered in a tutorial setting and is predominately remedial in nature, although some enrichment is offered.

BACKGROUND:
Established: 1977; 1st Franchised: 1985
Franchised Units: 171
Company-Owned Units 50
Total Units: 221
Dist.: US-226; CAN-0; O'seas-0
North America: 29 States
Density: 26 in NY, 19 in NJ, 18 in FL
Projected New Units (12 Months): 25
Qualifications: 5, 3, 1, 3, 1, 5
Registered: CA,FL,IL,IN,MD,MI,NY,RI, VA,WA,WI

FINANCIAL/TERMS:
Cash Investment: $100K
Total Investment: $139.3-191.6K
Minimum Net Worth: $300K
Fees: Franchise - $34K
Royalty - 8%/$1.2K Min.;
Ad. - 2%/$300 Min
Earnings Claim Statement: Yes
Term of Contract (Years): 10/10
Avg. # Of Employees: 2-4 FT
Passive Ownership: Not Allowed
Encourage Conversions: No
Area Develop. Agreements: Yes
Sub-Franchising Contracts: No
Expand In Territory: No
Space Needs: 2,800 SF; SF, SC, RM

SUPPORT & TRAINING PROVIDED:
Financial Assistance Provided: Yes(D)
Site Selection Assistance: Yes
Lease Negotiation Assistance: Yes
Co-Operative Advertising: Yes
Franchisee Assoc./Member: Yes/Yes
Size Of Corporate Staff: 70
On-Going Support: B,C,D,E,F,G,h,I
Training: 2 1/2 Weeks at Oradell, NJ.

SPECIFIC EXPANSION PLANS:
US: NW, SW, MW, South
Canada: All Canada
Overseas: No

<< >>

John Casablancas
MODELING & CAREER CENTER

JOHN CASABLANCAS MODELING/CAREER CENTERS

111 E. 22nd St., 4th Fl.
New York, NY 10010
Tel: (212) 420-0655
Fax: (212) 473-2725
E-Mail: mmi11122@aol.com
Web Site: www.jc-centers.com
Ms. Charyn Parker Urban, Dir. Franchise Development

Our franchised schools and in-house modeling agencies provide cutting-edge professional modeling, personal image development and film and TV acting programs and workshops. Created by John Casablancas, former Chairman of Elite Model Management.

BACKGROUND: IFA MEMBER
Established: 1979; 1st Franchised: 1979
Franchised Units: 44
Company-Owned Units 0
Total Units: 44
Dist.: US-36; CAN-1; O'seas-8
North America: 25 States, 1 Province
Density: 5 in FL, 2 in OH, 3 in PA
Projected New Units (12 Months): 2
Qualifications: 5, 5, 5, 4, 5, 5
Registered: CA,FL,HI,IL,IN,MD,MN.NB, NY,RI,VA,WA,WI

FINANCIAL/TERMS:
Cash Investment: $50-100K
Total Investment: $100-200K
Minimum Net Worth: $NR
Fees: Franchise - $40K
Royalty - 7%; Ad. - 3%
Earnings Claim Statement: No
Term of Contract (Years): 10/10
Avg. # Of Employees: 4 FT, 6-8 PT
Passive Ownership: Not Allowed
Encourage Conversions: Yes
Area Develop. Agreements: No
Sub-Franchising Contracts: No
Expand In Territory: Yes
Space Needs: 1,800-2,500 SF; SC, RM

SUPPORT & TRAINING PROVIDED:
Financial Assistance Provided: No
Site Selection Assistance: Yes
Lease Negotiation Assistance: N/A
Co-Operative Advertising: Yes
Franchisee Assoc./Member: Yes
Size Of Corporate Staff: 8
On-Going Support: b,C,D,E,g,h
Training: 2-3 Days NY.

SPECIFIC EXPANSION PLANS:
US: Northwest, Southwest
Canada: All Canada
Overseas: Far East, Europe, Latin America

<< >>

LEADERSHIP MANAGEMENT, INC.

4567 Lake Shore Dr.
Waco, TX 76710
Tel: (800) 365-7437 (254) 776-2060
Fax: (254) 757-4600
Web Site: www.lmi-inc.com
Mr. Tony Stigliano, Dir. Development Opportunities

Own a professional training dealership that helps companies achieve success. Producing measurable results for clients since 1966; interface with business executives; programs and a process to develop leaders, managers and executives; proven success system; long-term client relationships; national network. Call (800) 365-7437 or send resume.

BACKGROUND:
Established: 1965; 1st Franchised: 1965
Franchised Units: 177
Company-Owned Units 0
Total Units: 177
Dist.: US-365; CAN-0; O'seas-0
North America: NR
Density: NR
Projected New Units (12 Months): 60
Registered: All States

FINANCIAL/TERMS:
Cash Investment: $NR
Total Investment: $N/A
Minimum Net Worth: $NR
Fees: Franchise - $NR
Royalty - 0%; Ad. - 0%
Earnings Claim Statement: No
Term of Contract (Years): 1
Avg. # Of Employees: Varies
Passive Ownership: Discouraged
Encourage Conversions: N/A
Area Develop. Agreements: No
Sub-Franchising Contracts: No
Expand In Territory: No
Space Needs: NR SF; NR

SUPPORT & TRAINING PROVIDED:
Financial Assistance Provided: Yes(D)
Site Selection Assistance: N/A
Lease Negotiation Assistance: N/A
Co-Operative Advertising: N/A
Franchisee Assoc./Member: NR
Size Of Corporate Staff: 25
On-Going Support: D,C,H,I
Training: 1-3 Weeks.

SPECIFIC EXPANSION PLANS:
US: All United States
Canada: All Canada
Overseas: No

<< >>

Top 50

NEW HORIZONS COMPUTER LEARNING CENTER

1900 S. State College Blvd., # 200
Anaheim, CA 92806
Tel: (714) 940-8230
Fax: (714) 938-6008
E-Mail: ralph.loberger@newhorizons.com
Web Site: www.newhorizons.com
Mr. Ralph Loberger, VP N. Amer. Franchise Dev.

NEW HORIZONS COMPUTER LEARNING CENTERS, Inc. is the world's largest independent IT training company, meeting the needs of more than 2.4 million students each year. NEW HORIZONS offers a variety of flexible training choices: instructor-led classes, Web-based training, computer-based training via CD-ROM, computer labs, certification exam preparation tools and 24-hour, 7-day-a-week help-desk support.

BACKGROUND: IFA MEMBER
Established: 1982; 1st Franchised: 1992
Franchised Units: 269
Company-Owned Units 29
Total Units: 298
Dist.: US-145; CAN-4; O'seas-120
North America: 44 States, 9 Provinces
Density: 20 in CA, 13 in FL, 10 in NY
Projected New Units (12 Months): 28
Qualifications: 5, 5, 2, 3, 3, 5
Registered: All States

FINANCIAL/TERMS:
Cash Investment: $100-150K
Total Investment: $400-500K
Minimum Net Worth: $500K
Fees: Franchise - $25-75K
Royalty - 6%; Ad. - 1%
Earnings Claim Statement: No
Term of Contract (Years): 10/5
Avg. # Of Employees: 15 FT
Passive Ownership: Discouraged
Encourage Conversions: Yes
Area Develop. Agreements: Yes/10
Sub-Franchising Contracts: Yes
Expand In Territory: Yes
Space Needs: 4,000-5,000 SF; FS, OB, IP, Business Park

SUPPORT & TRAINING PROVIDED:
Financial Assistance Provided: Yes(D)
Site Selection Assistance: Yes
Lease Negotiation Assistance: Yes
Co-Operative Advertising: Yes
Franchisee Assoc./Member: Yes/Yes
Size Of Corporate Staff: 200+
On-Going Support: B,C,D,E,G,H
Training: 2 Weeks Headquarters; 1 Week Franchise Location; 2 Days Regional.

SPECIFIC EXPANSION PLANS:
US: All United States
Canada: All Canada
Overseas: All Countries

<< >>

OXFORD LEARNING CENTRES

312 Commissioners Rd. W.
London, ON N6J 1Y3 CANADA
Tel: (888) 559-2212 (519) 473-1207
Fax: (519) 473-6086
E-Mail: lenkaw@oxfordlearning.com
Web Site: www.oxfordlearning.com
Ms. Lenka Whitehead, Dir. Fran. Dev.

Join the leaders in supplemental education. Our proprietary curriculum developed over the past 10 years, ensures that your students will make impressive academic gains while developing higher self-esteem. Successful, confident students and happy parents mean referrals and a growing business. We will assist you every step of the way, providing the proven training, marketing, and business expertise you will need. Excellent territories available.

BACKGROUND:
Established: 1984; 1st Franchised: 1990
Franchised Units: 49
Company-Owned Units 8
Total Units: 57
Dist.: US-5; CAN-51; O'seas-0
North America: 2 States, 5 Provinces
Density: 38 in ON, 4 in MI
Projected New Units (12 Months): 18
Qualifications: 4, 4, 1, 3, 4, 5
Registered: MI,AB

FINANCIAL/TERMS:
Cash Investment: $35K
Total Investment: $85K
Minimum Net Worth: $300-500K
Fees: Franchise - $30K
Royalty - 9%; Ad. - 2%
Earnings Claim Statement: No
Term of Contract (Years): 10/10
Avg. # Of Employees: Varies
Passive Ownership: Allowed
Encourage Conversions: No
Area Develop. Agreements: No
Sub-Franchising Contracts: No
Expand In Territory: Yes
Space Needs: 2,000 SF; FS, SC

SUPPORT & TRAINING PROVIDED:
Financial Assistance Provided: Yes(I)
Site Selection Assistance: Yes
Lease Negotiation Assistance: Yes
Co-Operative Advertising: Yes
Franchisee Assoc./Member: Yes/Yes
Size Of Corporate Staff: 12
On-Going Support: B,C,D,E,F,G,H,I
Training: 2 Weeks London, ON; 1 Week + On-Site.

SPECIFIC EXPANSION PLANS:
US: NR
Canada: All Canada
Overseas: India, Hong Kong, Japan, Germany, Korea

<< >>

PROFESSIONAL DYNAMETRIC PROGRAMS/PDP

750 E. Hwy. 24, Bldg. I
Woodland Park, CO 80863
Tel: (719) 687-6074
Fax: (719) 687-8587
Web Site: www.pdpnet.com
Mr. Brent W. Hubby, President

PDP is a business-to-business license that offers independence with lucrative opportunity in the executive management market. Sell, train, consult and service large and small businesses in highly-successful and proven programs for hiring, motivating, stress managing and evaluating. There is automatic, repeat business, low overhead, no inventory and no leases.

BACKGROUND:
Established: 1978; 1st Franchised: 1980
Franchised Units: 24
Company-Owned Units 0
Total Units: 24
Dist.: US-17; CAN-4; O'seas-3
North America: 28 States, 3 Provinces
Density: 4 in TX, 3 in CO, 2 in CA.
Projected New Units (12 Months): 5
Qualifications: 4, 4, 4, 4, 5, 4
Registered: CA

FINANCIAL/TERMS:
Cash Investment: $5-19.5K
Total Investment: $31.5-49.5K
Minimum Net Worth: $250K
Fees: Franchise - $29.5K
Royalty - 0%; Ad. - 0%
Earnings Claim Statement: No
Term of Contract (Years): 7
Avg. # Of Employees: 1 FT
Passive Ownership: Discouraged
Encourage Conversions: N/A
Area Develop. Agreements: No
Sub-Franchising Contracts: Yes
Expand In Territory: Yes
Space Needs: N/A SF; HB, ES, OB

SUPPORT & TRAINING PROVIDED:
Financial Assistance Provided: No
Site Selection Assistance: N/A
Lease Negotiation Assistance: N/A
Co-Operative Advertising: N/A
Franchisee Assoc./Member: No
Size Of Corporate Staff: 7
On-Going Support: c,d,F,G,h,i,
Training: 1 Week Corporate; 2 Days Field; 3 Days Corporate.

SPECIFIC EXPANSION PLANS:
US: All United States
Canada: All Canada
Overseas: All Countries

RENAISSANCE EXECUTIVE FORUMS

7855 Ivanhoe Ave., # 300
La Jolla, CA 92037-4500
Tel: (858) 551-6600
Fax: (858) 551-8777
E-Mail: moreinfo@executiveforums.com
Web Site: www.executiveforums.com
Ms. Cyndi Sudberry, Coordinator, Franchise Dev.

RENAISSANCE EXECUTIVE FORUMS bring together top executives from similarly-sized, non-competing companies into an advisory board process in which thousands of chief executives throughout the world participate. These CEOs, presidents and owners meet once a month in small groups of approximately 8 -12 individuals. The meetings provide an environment designed to address the opportunities and challenges they face as individuals and leaders of their respective organizations.

BACKGROUND: IFA MEMBER
Established: 1994; 1st Franchised: 1994
Franchised Units: 29
Company-Owned Units 0
Total Units: 29
Dist.: US-27; CAN-1; O'seas-1
North America: 13 States
Density: 10 in CA, 3 in AZ
Projected New Units (12 Months): 5
Qualifications: 4, 5, 4, 4, 4, 5
Registered: All States

FINANCIAL/TERMS:
Cash Investment: $60-100K
Total Investment: $60-100K
Minimum Net Worth: $500K
Fees: Franchise - $49.5K
Royalty - 20%; Ad. - 0%

Earnings Claim Statement: No
Term of Contract (Years): 10/10
Avg. # Of Employees: 1 FT
Passive Ownership: Not Allowed
Encourage Conversions: N/A
Area Develop. Agreements: Yes/5
Sub-Franchising Contracts: No
Expand In Territory: Yes
Space Needs: NR SF; Executive Suite

SUPPORT & TRAINING PROVIDED:

Financial Assistance Provided: No
Site Selection Assistance: No
Lease Negotiation Assistance: No
Co-Operative Advertising: No
Franchisee Assoc./Member: Yes/Yes
Size Of Corporate Staff: 13
On-Going Support: A,b,c,d,G,H,h
Training: 5 Days La Jolla, CA.

SPECIFIC EXPANSION PLANS:

US: All United States
Canada: All Canada
Overseas: All Countries

SANDLER SALES INSTITUTE

10411 Stevenson Rd.
Stevenson, MD 21153
Tel: (800) 669-3537 (410) 653-1993
Fax: (410) 358-7858
E-Mail: rtaylor@sandler.com
Web Site: www.sandler.com
Mr. Ron Taylor, Dir. Franchising

SANDLER SALES INSTITUTE offers a distinctive style of training to companies and individuals in the fields of sales, management consulting and leadership development through on-going seminars and workshops. SANDLER SALES INSTITUTE provides intensive training, a unique lead generation program, on-going day-to-day support and protected territories to help you succeed in business.

BACKGROUND: IFA MEMBER

Established: 1967; 1st Franchised: 1983
Franchised Units: 162
Company-Owned Units <u>0</u>
Total Units: 162
Dist.: US-151; CAN-11; O'seas-0
North America: NR
Density: 15 in PA, 14 in OH, 12 in TX
Projected New Units (12 Months): 20
Qualifications: 3, 5, 5, 3, 1, 5
Registered: All States Except HI,AB

FINANCIAL/TERMS:

Cash Investment: $45K
Total Investment: $51.5-68.5K
Minimum Net Worth: $N/A
Fees: Franchise - $39.5K
Royalty - $908/Mo.; Ad. - N/A
Earnings Claim Statement: No
Term of Contract (Years): 5/5/5/5
Avg. # Of Employees: 1 FT, 1 PT
Passive Ownership: Discouraged
Encourage Conversions: N/A
Area Develop. Agreements: No
Sub-Franchising Contracts: No
Expand In Territory: Yes
Space Needs: N/A SF; N/A

SUPPORT & TRAINING PROVIDED:

Financial Assistance Provided: No
Site Selection Assistance: Yes
Lease Negotiation Assistance: N/A
Co-Operative Advertising: No
Franchisee Assoc./Member: Yes/Yes
Size Of Corporate Staff: 26
On-Going Support: g,H,I
Training: 5 Days Home Office/Other; 1 Day Home Office/Other.

SPECIFIC EXPANSION PLANS:

US: All United States
Canada: All Canada
Overseas: All Countries

SCOOTER'S PLACE

221 Bonita Ave., # 240
Piedmont, CA 94611
Tel: (510) 839-5471
Fax: (510) 547-3245
Mr. Jeffe Y. Hoserr, President

Unique opportunity in the highly profitable, growth business of removing unwanted facial and body hair. Specializing in Scooter's Bikini Cuts, guaranteed to last 3 months. Custom merkin fitting. Free initial consultation. Average customer spends $225 per year for services. Great customer loyalty. Complete turn-key operation. Initial investment under $25,000.

BACKGROUND:

Established: 1982; 1st Franchised: 1986
Franchised Units: 28
Company-Owned Units <u>10</u>
Total Units: 38
Dist.: US-12; CAN-4; O'seas-5
North America: 5 States, 1 Province
Density: 7 in CA, 2 in KY, 1 in TN
Projected New Units (12 Months): 3
Registered: NR

FINANCIAL/TERMS:

Cash Investment: $25-45K
Total Investment: $35-75K
Minimum Net Worth: $NR
Fees: Franchise - $12K
Royalty - 4%; Ad. - 1%
Earnings Claim Statement: Yes
Term of Contract (Years): 10/10
Avg. # Of Employees: 2 FT, 3 PT
Passive Ownership: Discouraged
Encourage Conversions: Yes
Area Develop. Agreements: Yes/10
Sub-Franchising Contracts: No
Expand In Territory: No
Space Needs: 1,500-1,800 SF; FS, SF, SC, RM

SUPPORT & TRAINING PROVIDED:

Financial Assistance Provided: Yes(D)
Site Selection Assistance: Yes
Lease Negotiation Assistance: Yes
Co-Operative Advertising: Yes
Franchisee Assoc./Member: NR
Size Of Corporate Staff: 5
On-Going Support: A,C,D,G,H,I
Training: 4 Weeks Headquarters; 2 Weeks On-Site.

SPECIFIC EXPANSION PLANS:

US: All United States
Canada: BC, ON
Overseas: No

SYLVAN LEARNING CENTERS

1001 Fleet St.
Baltimore, MD 21202
Tel: (800) 284-8214 (410) 843-8000
Fax: (410) 843-6265
E-Mail: greg.helwig@educate.com
Web Site: www.sylvanfranchise.com
Mr. Greg Helwig, VP Franchise Sales/Dev.

SYLVAN is the leading provider of educational services to families, schools and industry. SYLVAN services kindergarten through adult-levels from more than 800 SYLVAN LEARNING CENTERS worldwide.

BACKGROUND: IFA MEMBER

Established: 1979; 1st Franchised: 1980
Franchised Units: 765
Company-Owned Units <u>82</u>
Total Units: 847
Dist.: US-762; CAN-72; O'seas-3

North America: 50 States
Density: CA, TX, NY
Projected New Units (12 Months): 70
Qualifications: 4, 4, 2, 3, 2, 5
Registered: All States

FINANCIAL/TERMS:

Cash Investment: $101.1-171.3K
Total Investment: $121.1-219.3K
Minimum Net Worth: $N/A
Fees: Franchise - $38-46K
Royalty - 8-9%; Ad. - 1.5%
Earnings Claim Statement: Yes
Term of Contract (Years): 10/10
Avg. # Of Employees: 2 FT, 5 PT
Passive Ownership: Not Allowed
Encourage Conversions: No
Area Develop. Agreements: Yes/Varies
Sub-Franchising Contracts: No
Expand In Territory: Yes
Space Needs: 1,600-2,500 SF; FS, SF, SC

SUPPORT & TRAINING PROVIDED:

Financial Assistance Provided: Yes(B)
Site Selection Assistance: Yes
Lease Negotiation Assistance: No
Co-Operative Advertising: Yes
Franchisee Assoc./Member: Yes
Size Of Corporate Staff: 500
On-Going Support: B,C,D,E,G,H,I
Training: 6 Days Baltimore, MD; 5 Days in Various Other Locations.

SPECIFIC EXPANSION PLANS:

US: All United States
Canada: All Canada
Overseas: Asia, Europe, South America

<< >>

TURBO MANAGEMENT SYSTEMS

36280 NE Wilsonville Rd.
Newberg, OR 97132
Tel: (800) 574-4373 (503) 625-1867
Fax: (503) 625-2699
E-Mail: turbo@turbomgmt.com
Web Site: www.turbomgmt.com
Ms. Chris Tipp, Office Manager

TMS is a leadership development and training company. You help your clients tap the resource that allows them to dramatically improve their sales, profits and market share. You deliver behavior changing programs that impact habit change culture. Leverage your experience as a manager, trainer and sales person.

BACKGROUND:

Established: 1985; 1st Franchised: 1997
Franchised Units: 2
Company-Owned Units 1
Total Units: 3
Dist.: US-3; CAN-0; O'seas-0
North America: 2 States
Density: NR
Projected New Units (12 Months): 10
Qualifications: 2, 5, 3, 4, 5, 5
Registered: NR

FINANCIAL/TERMS:

Cash Investment: $25-50K
Total Investment: $25-50K
Minimum Net Worth: $250K
Fees: Franchise - $24K
Royalty - 10%; Ad. - N/A
Earnings Claim Statement: NR
Term of Contract (Years): 10/10
Avg. # Of Employees: 2 FT
Passive Ownership: Not Allowed
Encourage Conversions: N/A
Area Develop. Agreements: Yes/10
Sub-Franchising Contracts: No
Expand In Territory: Yes
Space Needs: N/A SF; N/A

SUPPORT & TRAINING PROVIDED:

Financial Assistance Provided: Yes(I)
Site Selection Assistance: N/A
Lease Negotiation Assistance: N/A
Co-Operative Advertising: N/A
Franchisee Assoc./Member: No
Size Of Corporate Staff: 6
On-Going Support: d,h,I
Training: 30 Days Portland, OR.

SPECIFIC EXPANSION PLANS:

US: All United States
Canada: All Canada
Overseas: All Countries

<< >>

SUPPLEMENTAL LISTING OF FRANCHISORS

A THOUSAND POINTS OF KNOWLEDGE, 3016 S. Grand Blvd., Spokane, WA 99203 ; (800) 647-7114 (509) 838-0882; (509) 838-0314

ALAMO LEARNING SYSTEMS, 3160 Crow Canyon Rd., # 280, San Ramon, CA 94583 ; (800) 829-8081 (925) 277-1818; (925) 277-1919

ARTHUR MURRAY INTERNATIONAL, 1077 Ponce De Leon Blvd., Coral Gables, FL 33134 ; (305) 445-9645; (305) 445-0451

CLUB Z! IN-HOME TUTORING SERVICES, 12000 N. Dale Mabry Hwy., # 262, Tampa, FL 33618 ; (800) 434-2582 (813) 264-0197; (813) 908-9001

CPR SERVICES, 22 Stoneybrook Dr., Ashland, MA 01721 ; (800) 547-5107 (508) 881-5107; (508) 881-4718

DALE CARNEGIE & ASSOCIATES, 290 Motor Pkwy., Hauppaguge, NY 11788-5105; (631) 435-2800; (631) 435-2830

DREAMCATCHER LEARNING CENTERS, 427 Main St., Windsor, CO 80550 (888) 937-3121 (970) 686-9282; (970) 686-7045

JEI - JAENEUNG EDUCATIONAL INSTITUTE, 4221 Wilshire Blvd., # 224, Los Angeles, CA 90010 ; (800) 954-0777 (323) 936-3300; (323) 936-0300

PERSONAL BEST KARATE, 250 E. Main St., Norton, MA 02766-2436 ; (508) 285-5425; (508) 285-7064

PERSONAL PRODUCTIVITY PLUS, 1600 Merivale Rd., # 213, Nepean, ON K2G 5J8 CANADA; (877) 611-7587 (613) 225-0083; (613) 225-9469

POSITIVE CHANGES HYPNOSIS CENTERS, P.O. Box 20549, Charleston, SC 29413 ; (877) POSITIVE (843) 853-4781; (843) 853-4135

PRIORITY MANAGEMENT SYSTEMS, 13200 Delf Pl., # 180, Richmond, BC V6V 2A2 CANADA; (800) 665-5448 (604) 214-7772; (800) 665-2556

SANDLER SALES INSTITUTE OF CANADA, 745 Clark Dr., Vancouver, BC V5L 3J3 CANADA; (800) 670-1400 (604) 254-4363; (604) 251-8060

SEARS DRIVER TRAINING, 247 N. Service Rd. W., # 301, Oakville, ON L6M 3E6 CANADA; (416) 363-7483; (905) 842-4251

SUCCESS MOTIVATION INSTITUTE, 5000 Lakewood Dr., Waco, TX 76702 (800) 678-6103 (254) 776-1230; (254) 741-0001

WALL STREET INSTITUTE, 1000 E. Lancaster St., Baltimore, MD 21202-4373 (410) 843-8000; (410) 843-8717

Employment & Personnel

Chapter **12**

Employment & Personnel Industry Profile

Total # Franchisors in Industry Group	76
Total # Franchised Units in Industry Group	5,098
Total # Company-Owned Units in Industry Group	3,524
Total # Operating Units in Industry Group	8,622
Average # Franchised Units/Franchisor	67.1
Average # Company-Owned Units/Franchisor	46.4
Average # Total Units/Franchisor	113.5
Ratio of Total # Franchised Units/Total # Company-Owned Units	1.4:1
Industry Survey Participants	29
Representing % of Industry	38.2%
Average Franchise Fee*:	$25.5K
Average Total Investment*:	$104.4K
Average On-Going Royalty Fee*:	7.2%

*If a range was provided, the mid-point of the range was used. See detailed profiles for actual ranges.

Five Largest Participants in Survey

Company	# Franchised Units	# Co-Owned Units	# Total Units	Franchise Fee	On-Going Royalty	Total Investment
1. Management Recruiters/Sales Con.	1,000	32	1,032	72.5K	7%	110-145K
2. Express Personnel Services	407	1	408	17.5-20.5K	8-9%	120-160K
3. Home Instead Senior Care	340	1	341	19.5K	5%	26.8-34.8K
4. Interim Healthcare	219	94	313	10K	7%	150-200K
5. Remedy Intelligent Staffing	154	101	255	18K	Varies	95-150K

ACCOUNTANTS INC.

111 Anza Blvd., # 400
Burlingame, CA 94010-1932
Tel: (800) 491-9411 (650) 579-1111
Fax: (650) 579-1927
E-Mail: contactai@accountantsinc.com
Web Site: www.accountantsinc.com
Ms. Pam Egbert, Franchise Operations Mgr.

Temporary and full time placement of accounting and finance professionals.

BACKGROUND: IFA MEMBER
Established: 1986; 1st Franchised: 1994
Franchised Units: 16
Company-Owned Units 21
Total Units: 37
Dist.: US-40; CAN-0; O'seas-0
North America: 13 States
Density: 19 in CA, 3 in WA
Projected New Units (12 Months): 5
Qualifications: 4, 5, 1, 1, 1, 5
Registered: CA,FL,IL,IN,MD,MI,MN,NY, OR,VA,WA,WI

FINANCIAL/TERMS:
Cash Investment: $174.5-224K
Total Investment: $NR
Minimum Net Worth: $145-200K
Fees: Franchise - $30K
Royalty - 7.5-10%/4K;
Ad. - 2.5 W/Co-Op
Earnings Claim Statement: Yes
Term of Contract (Years): 10/10
Avg. # Of Employees: 4 FT
Passive Ownership: Not Allowed
Encourage Conversions: NR
Area Develop. Agreements: NR
Sub-Franchising Contracts: No
Expand In Territory: Yes
Space Needs: NR SF; Class A Office

SUPPORT & TRAINING PROVIDED:
Financial Assistance Provided: No
Site Selection Assistance: Yes
Lease Negotiation Assistance: Yes
Co-Operative Advertising: Yes
Franchisee Assoc./Member: No
Size Of Corporate Staff: 35
On-Going Support: E,h,I
Training: Burlingame, CA; Franchisee's Location.

SPECIFIC EXPANSION PLANS:
US: All United States
Canada: No
Overseas: No

<< >>

AHEAD HUMAN RESOURCES

2209 Heather Ln.
Louisville, KY 40218
Tel: (877) 485-5858 (502) 485-1000
Fax: (502) 485-0810
E-Mail: franchise@aheadhr.com
Web Site: www.aheadr.com
Mr. Rick Mabrey, Dir. Franchise

AHEAD HR brings a totally unique concept to the human resource franchise industry. SEE OUR WEBSITE! We're offering an industry-leading, top-flight temporary staffing franchise AND a PEO/HR outsourcing franchise, which is one-of-a-kind in the nation. If you want to be on the cutting edge of THE growth industry, SEE OUR WEBSITE!

BACKGROUND: IFA MEMBER
Established: 1995; 1st Franchised: 2001
Franchised Units: 2
Company-Owned Units 7
Total Units: 9
Dist.: US-11; CAN-0; O'seas-0
North America: 5 States
Density: 3 in KY, 4 in IN, 2 in CT
Projected New Units (12 Months): NR
Registered: NR

FINANCIAL/TERMS:
Cash Investment: $25-50K
Total Investment: $75-170K
Minimum Net Worth: $Varies
Fees: Franchise - $15.5-30K
Royalty - Varies; Ad. - Varies
Earnings Claim Statement: No
Term of Contract (Years): 5/5
Avg. # Of Employees: 1 FT, 1 PT
Passive Ownership: Discouraged
Encourage Conversions: NR
Area Develop. Agreements: No
Sub-Franchising Contracts: No
Expand In Territory: Yes
Space Needs: 100-1500 SF; SF, SC, HB, Office

SUPPORT & TRAINING PROVIDED:
Financial Assistance Provided: NR
Site Selection Assistance: No
Lease Negotiation Assistance: No
Co-Operative Advertising: No
Franchisee Assoc./Member: No
Size Of Corporate Staff: 50
On-Going Support: A,C,d,h,I
Training: 2 to 4 Weeks Louisville, KY.

SPECIFIC EXPANSION PLANS:
US: All United States
Canada: NR
Overseas: NR

<< >>

ATC HEALTH CARE SERVICES

1983 Marcus Ave., # E122
New Hyde Park, NY 11042-1016
Tel: (888) 262-7823 (516) 327-3379
Fax: (516) 358-3678
Web Site: www.atchealthcare.com
Mr. Peter Berry, VP Franchising

ATC HEALTH CARE SERVICES provide temporary staffing and T. L. C.

BACKGROUND: IFA MEMBER
Established: 1984; 1st Franchised: 1995
Franchised Units: 37
Company-Owned Units 0
Total Units: 37
Dist.: US-40; CAN-0; O'seas-0
North America: NR
Density: 5 in Ga, 5 in TN, 3 in PA
Projected New Units (12 Months): 15
Qualifications: 4, 4, 4, 5, 2, 5
Registered: All States

FINANCIAL/TERMS:
Cash Investment: $30-50K
Total Investment: $110K
Minimum Net Worth: $150K
Fees: Franchise - $19.5K
Royalty - Varies; Ad. - 0%
Earnings Claim Statement: No
Term of Contract (Years): 10/5/5
Avg. # Of Employees: 3 FT, 2 PT
Passive Ownership: Allowed
Encourage Conversions: Yes
Area Develop. Agreements: Yes/20
Sub-Franchising Contracts: No
Expand In Territory: Yes
Space Needs: 1,000 SF; FS, SF, SC

SUPPORT & TRAINING PROVIDED:
Financial Assistance Provided: Yes(D)
Site Selection Assistance: Yes
Lease Negotiation Assistance: No
Co-Operative Advertising: No
Franchisee Assoc./Member: No
Size Of Corporate Staff: 35
On-Going Support: A,B,C,D,E,G,H
Training: 1 Week Corporate Headquarters.

SPECIFIC EXPANSION PLANS:
US: All United States
Canada: All Canada
Overseas: No

<< >>

ATWORK PERSONNEL SERVICES

7855 E. Evans, # C
Scottsdale, AZ 85260-2949

Tel: (800) 383-0804 (480) 922-9959
Fax: (480) 922-7283
opportunity@atworkpersonnel.com
Web Site: www.atworkpersonnel.com
Ms. Melody Philipp, Dir. Franchise Sales

ATWORK PERSONNEL SERVICES announces its new 3-for-1 Franchise Program. For the cost of one franchise, ATWORK offers temporary help, staff leasing and permanent placement programs for its franchisees. Here are some benefits of becoming a member of ATWORK's network: franchise fee - $11,500; training fee - $2,500; sliding volume discount sale for royalty and service fees. Call our franchise sales department today to receive our information package.

BACKGROUND: IFA MEMBER
Established: 1990; 1st Franchised: 1992
Franchised Units: 62
Company-Owned Units 1
Total Units: 63
Dist.: US-40; CAN-0; O'seas-0
North America: 12 States
Density: 15 in TN, 3 in NC, 2 in ME
Projected New Units (12 Months): 24
Qualifications: 3, 2, 3, 2, 3, 3
Registered: All States

FINANCIAL/TERMS:
Cash Investment: $15K
Total Investment: $35-75K
Minimum Net Worth: $75K
Fees: Franchise - $1K
Royalty - 8%; Ad. - 0%
Earnings Claim Statement: No
Term of Contract (Years): 10/5
Avg. # Of Employees: 3 FT, 1 PT
Passive Ownership: Discouraged
Encourage Conversions: Yes
Area Develop. Agreements: No
Sub-Franchising Contracts: No
Expand In Territory: Yes
Space Needs: 800 SF; FS, SF, SC, RM

SUPPORT & TRAINING PROVIDED:
Financial Assistance Provided: Yes
Site Selection Assistance: Yes
Lease Negotiation Assistance: No
Co-Operative Advertising: No
Franchisee Assoc./Member: No
Size Of Corporate Staff: 15
On-Going Support: A,C,D,H,I
Training: 4-5 Days in Corporate Office.

SPECIFIC EXPANSION PLANS:
US: All United States
Canada: No
Overseas: No

<< >>

CAREERS USA

6501 Congress Ave., # 200
Boca Raton, Fl 33487-2829
Tel: (888) 227-3377 (561) 995-7000
Fax: (561) 995-7001
E-Mail: lgordon@careersusa.com
Web Site: www.careersusa.com
Mr. Leo X. Gordon, Dir. Franchise Operations

CAREERS USA provides temporary, temp to hire, and permanent personnel to businesses and corporations in your market area. CAREERS USA's proprietary computer software program computes the franchisee's temporary payroll, taxes and insurance. You, the franchisee, can download and analyze your sales, margins, rates, cash flow, etc. CAREERS USA finances 100% of your temporary payroll and 100% of your accounts receivable, helping you eliminate cash flow problems. Territories available nationally.

BACKGROUND: IFA MEMBER
Established: 1981; 1st Franchised: 1987
Franchised Units: 4
Company-Owned Units 17
Total Units: 21
Dist.: US-23; CAN-0; O'seas-0
North America: 8 States
Density: 5 in PA, 5 in FL, 3 in IL
Projected New Units (12 Months): 12
Qualifications: 3, 4, 2, 3, 3, 4
Registered: All States

FINANCIAL/TERMS:
Cash Investment: $40-50K
Total Investment: $84-130K
Minimum Net Worth: $150K
Fees: Franchise - $14.5K
Royalty - 7%/Varies; Ad. - N/A
Earnings Claim Statement: No
Term of Contract (Years): 10/5
Avg. # Of Employees: 3 FT
Passive Ownership: Discouraged
Encourage Conversions: Yes
Area Develop. Agreements: N/A
Sub-Franchising Contracts: No
Expand In Territory: Yes
Space Needs: 1,000-1,500 SF; OB

SUPPORT & TRAINING PROVIDED:
Financial Assistance Provided: No
Site Selection Assistance: Yes
Lease Negotiation Assistance: Yes
Co-Operative Advertising: Yes
Franchisee Assoc./Member: No
Size Of Corporate Staff: 38
On-Going Support: A,b,C,D,E,G,H,I
Training: 2 Weeks Boca Raton, FL Headquarters; 1 Week Your Center Location.

SPECIFIC EXPANSION PLANS:
US: All United States
Canada: All Canada
Overseas: All Countries

CHECKMATE SYSTEMS

661 St. Andrews Blvd.
Charleston, SC 29407
Tel: (800) 964-6298 (843) 763-9393
Fax: (843) 571-1851
E-Mail: checkmate@checkmatepeo.com
Web Site: www.checkmatepeo.com
Mr. Ed Arrington, VP Marketing

Employee leasing companies, also known as professional employers, are growing at over 33% per year. This new and largely untapped market has little competition and CHECKMATE is the only franchise in this new field which allows you to operate independently.

BACKGROUND:
Established: 1992; 1st Franchised: 1993
Franchised Units: 19
Company-Owned Units 0
Total Units: 19
Dist.: US-19; CAN-0; O'seas-0
North America: 11 States
Density: 4 in LA, 2 in SC, 2 in AZ
Projected New Units (12 Months): 8
Qualifications: 3, 5, 1, 3, 4, 4
Registered: NR

FINANCIAL/TERMS:
Cash Investment: $35-85K
Total Investment: $30-75K
Minimum Net Worth: $100K
Fees: Franchise - $27.5K
Royalty - 7.5%; Ad. - 0%
Earnings Claim Statement: No
Term of Contract (Years): 10/5
Avg. # Of Employees: 3 FT, 1-2 PT
Passive Ownership: Not Allowed
Encourage Conversions: Yes
Area Develop. Agreements: No
Sub-Franchising Contracts: No
Expand In Territory: Yes
Space Needs: N/A SF; HB, Rented Office

SUPPORT & TRAINING PROVIDED:
Financial Assistance Provided: No
Site Selection Assistance: N/A
Lease Negotiation Assistance: N/A

Co-Operative Advertising: N/A
Franchisee Assoc./Member: No
Size Of Corporate Staff: 7
On-Going Support: G,h,I
Training: 1 Week New Orleans, LA.

SPECIFIC EXPANSION PLANS:

US: All United States
Canada: No
Overseas: No

<< >>

DUNHILL STAFFING SYSTEMS

150 Motor Pkwy.
Hauppauge, NY 11788
Tel: (800) 386-7823 (631) 952-3000
Fax: (631) 952-3500
E-Mail: rrs@Dunhillstaff.com
Web Site: www.dunhillstaff.com
Mr. Robert Stidham, VP Business Dev.

DUNHILL offers Professional Search and Temporary Staffing franchises. Our franchisees provide permanent executives, mid-level management, professionals, technical staffing and temporaries. Professional Search franchisees benefit from the industry's best interview-to-placement ratio and leading edge computerized placement matching system. All DUNHILL executives have 'front line' industry experience. Our temporary offices are supported with back-office accounting, including payroll and accounts receivable.

BACKGROUND: IFA MEMBER

Established: 1952; 1st Franchised: 1961
Franchised Units: 150
Company-Owned Units 25
Total Units: 175
Dist.: US-151; CAN-4; O'seas-0
North America: 50 States
Density: 21 in TX, 19 in IN, 12 in CT
Projected New Units (12 Months): 12
Qualifications: 4, 3, 1, 3, 3, 5
Registered: All States

FINANCIAL/TERMS:

Cash Investment: $15-38K
Total Investment: $70-140K
Minimum Net Worth: $250K
Fees: Franchise - $15-38K
Royalty - 7% Perm./Varies;
Ad. - 1% Perm.
Earnings Claim Statement: No
Term of Contract (Years): 10/10/5
Avg. # Of Employees: 2-3 FT
Passive Ownership: Discouraged
Encourage Conversions: Yes
Area Develop. Agreements: No
Sub-Franchising Contracts: No
Expand In Territory: Yes
Space Needs: 700-1,500 SF; FS, SF, SC, RM, Suites

SUPPORT & TRAINING PROVIDED:

Financial Assistance Provided: Yes(D)
Site Selection Assistance: Yes
Lease Negotiation Assistance: Yes
Co-Operative Advertising: Yes
Franchisee Assoc./Member: Yes
Size Of Corporate Staff: 45
On-Going Support: A,B,C,D,E,G,H,I
Training: 1-2 Weeks Corporate; 1-2 Weeks Field.

SPECIFIC EXPANSION PLANS:

US: All United States
Canada: All Canada
Overseas: No

<< >>

Top 50

EXPRESS PERSONNEL SERVICES

8516 Northwest Expy., # 200
Oklahoma City, OK 73162
Tel: (877) 652-6400 (405) 840-5000
Fax: (405) 717-5665
E-Mail: franchising@expresspersonnel.com
Web Site: www.expressfranchising.com
Mr. Jeffrey C. Bevis, VP Franchising

Three divisions - permanent placement, temporary placement and executive search - offering full and complete coverage of the employment field.

BACKGROUND: IFA MEMBER

Established: 1983; 1st Franchised: 1985
Franchised Units: 407
Company-Owned Units 1
Total Units: 408
Dist.: US-393; CAN-11; O'seas-4
North America: 45 States
Density: 48 in TX, 32 in OK, 24 in WA
Projected New Units (12 Months): 50
Qualifications: 4, 4, 3, 4, 4, 4
Registered: All States

FINANCIAL/TERMS:

Cash Investment: $120-160K
Total Investment: $120-160K
Minimum Net Worth: $100K
Fees: Franchise - $17.5-20.5K
Royalty - 8-9%; Ad. - 0.6%
Earnings Claim Statement: No
Term of Contract (Years): 5/5
Avg. # Of Employees: 2 FT, 1 PT
Passive Ownership: Not Allowed
Encourage Conversions: Yes
Area Develop. Agreements: Yes
Sub-Franchising Contracts: No
Expand In Territory: Yes
Space Needs: 1,200 SF; SC, RM, SF

SUPPORT & TRAINING PROVIDED:

Financial Assistance Provided: Yes(D)
Site Selection Assistance: Yes
Lease Negotiation Assistance: Yes
Co-Operative Advertising: Yes
Franchisee Assoc./Member: No
Size Of Corporate Staff: 169
On-Going Support: A,C,D,E,G,H,I
Training: 2 Weeks Oklahoma City, OK; Plus 1 Week On-Site.

SPECIFIC EXPANSION PLANS:

US: All United States
Canada: ON Only
Overseas: No

<< >>

F-O-R-T-U-N-E PERSONNEL CONSULTANTS

1140 Avenue of the Americas, 5th Fl.
New York, NY 10036-2711
Tel: (800) 886-7839 (212) 302-1141
Fax: (212) 302-2422
E-Mail: nsarnataro@pfcnyc.com
Web Site: www.fpcweb.com
Ms. Nicole Sarnataro, Dir. Franchise Development

As one of the largest and most successful executive recruiting firms in the world, F-O-R-T-U-N-E PERSONNEL CONSULTANTS has set a distinguished standard of leadership and integrity in the executive placement industry. Franchisees enjoy all of today's technologies, along with good old-fashioned service. Intensive training and unparalleled support by industry experienced professionals securely places qualified candidates in their own professional business. Extensive on-going training.

BACKGROUND: IFA MEMBER

Established: 1959; 1st Franchised: 1973
Franchised Units: 98
Company-Owned Units 1
Total Units: 99
Dist.: US-100; CAN-0; O'seas-0
North America: 28 States
Density: 7 in FL, 7 in MA, 7 in NJ
Projected New Units (12 Months): 12-15
Qualifications: 4, 3, 3, 4, 2, 4

Registered: All Except AB

FINANCIAL/TERMS:

Cash Investment:	$31.4-63.9K
Total Investment:	$71.4-103.9K
Minimum Net Worth:	$250K
Fees: Franchise -	$40K
Royalty - 7%;	Ad. - 1%
Earnings Claim Statement:	Yes
Term of Contract (Years):	20/10
Avg. # Of Employees:	3-5 FT, 1-2 PT
Passive Ownership:	Discouraged
Encourage Conversions:	N/A
Area Develop. Agreements:	No
Sub-Franchising Contracts:	No
Expand In Territory:	Yes

Space Needs: 1,000 SF; Commercial Office

SUPPORT & TRAINING PROVIDED:

Financial Assistance Provided:	Yes(D)
Site Selection Assistance:	Yes
Lease Negotiation Assistance:	Yes
Co-Operative Advertising:	Yes
Franchisee Assoc./Member:	Yes
Size Of Corporate Staff:	15
On-Going Support:	A,B,C,D,E,F,G,H,I

Training: 2 Weeks Home Office, New York, NY: 5 Days Franchise Location.

SPECIFIC EXPANSION PLANS:

US:	All United States
Canada:	All Canada
Overseas:	No

<< >>

HOME HELPERS

4338 Glendale-Milford Rd.
Cincinnati, OH 45242
Tel: (800) 216-4196 (513) 563-8339
Fax: (513) 563-2691
E-Mail: inquiry@homehelpers.com
Web Site: www.homehelpers.com
Franchise Sales Department

HOME HELPERS is the #1 franchise offering the demand for non-medical, in-home companion care. Our clients are among the 33 million elderly, millions of new moms and those recuperating from illness. We now offer financing up to 100% of the franchise fee. As a franchisee, you are eligible to become a Direct Link (offering clients 24-hour emergency and medical monitoring in their home) Dealer without any up-front fees. It's based on monthly residual income, has huge margins and requires no added employees.

BACKGROUND:

Established: 1997; 1st Franchised: 1997

Franchised Units:	135
Company-Owned Units	0
Total Units:	135
Dist.:	US-135; CAN-0; O'seas-0
North America:	28 States
Density:	NR
Projected New Units (12 Months):	75
Qualifications:	, , 1, , 3, 5

Registered: All States

FINANCIAL/TERMS:

Cash Investment:	$7.5-11.5K
Total Investment:	$19-39K
Minimum Net Worth:	$N/A
Fees: Franchise -	$13.9-23.9K
Royalty - 4-6% Varies;	Ad. - 0%
Earnings Claim Statement:	No
Term of Contract (Years):	10/10/10
Avg. # Of Employees:	N/A
Passive Ownership:	Discouraged
Encourage Conversions:	N/A
Area Develop. Agreements:	No
Sub-Franchising Contracts:	No
Expand In Territory:	N/A

Space Needs: N/A SF; HB

SUPPORT & TRAINING PROVIDED:

Financial Assistance Provided:	100%
Site Selection Assistance:	N/A
Lease Negotiation Assistance:	N/A
Co-Operative Advertising:	N/A
Franchisee Assoc./Member:	No
Size Of Corporate Staff:	9
On-Going Support:	B,C,D,G,H,I

Training: 5 Days Cincinnati, OH.

SPECIFIC EXPANSION PLANS:

US:	All United States
Canada:	All Canada
Overseas:	All Countries

<< >>

HOME INSTEAD SENIOR CARE

604 N. 109th Ct.
Omaha, NE 68154
Tel: (888) 484-5759 (402) 498-4466
Fax: (402) 498-5757
E-Mail: mmaguire@homeinstead.com
Web Site: www.homeinstead.com
Mr. Mike Maguire, Franchise Development

HOME INSTEAD SENIOR CARE is America's largest, most successful, non-medical companionship and home care franchise. Entrepreneur and other leading business publications have ranked us one of the top opportunities in all of franchising. The elderly market we serve is the fastest-growing segment of the population. Services such as companionship, light housework, errands and meal preparation assist the elderly in remaining in their homes rather than being institutionalized.

BACKGROUND: IFA MEMBER

Established: 1994; 1st Franchised: 1995

Franchised Units:	340
Company-Owned Units	1
Total Units:	341
Dist.:	US-331; CAN-6; O'seas-3
North America:	43 States, 2 Provinces
Density:	41in CA, 21 FL, 19 in TX
Projected New Units (12 Months):	70
Qualifications:	4, 3, 1, 3, 1, 5

Registered: All States and AB

FINANCIAL/TERMS:

Cash Investment:	$7.3-14.3K
Total Investment:	$26.8-34.8K
Minimum Net Worth:	$Varies
Fees: Franchise -	$19.5K
Royalty - 5%;	Ad. - 0%
Earnings Claim Statement:	Yes
Term of Contract (Years):	10/10
Avg. # Of Employees:	2 FT, 45 PT
Passive Ownership:	Discouraged
Encourage Conversions:	Yes
Area Develop. Agreements:	No
Sub-Franchising Contracts:	No
Expand In Territory:	Yes

Space Needs: 300-500 SF; Industrial/ Office

SUPPORT & TRAINING PROVIDED:

Financial Assistance Provided:	No
Site Selection Assistance:	Yes
Lease Negotiation Assistance:	No
Co-Operative Advertising:	No
Franchisee Assoc./Member:	No
Size Of Corporate Staff:	38
On-Going Support:	B,C,D,E,F,G,H,I

Training: 2 Weeks Corporate Headquarters; 2 Days Field Visit Franchise Office.

SPECIFIC EXPANSION PLANS:

US:	All United States

Canada: All Canada
Overseas: All Countries

<< >>

HOMEWATCH CAREGIVERS

2865 S. Colorado Blvd.
Denver, CO 80222
Tel: (800) 777-9770 (303) 758-7290
Fax: (303) 758-1724
E-Mail: pasauer@homewatch-intl.com
Web Site: www.homewatch-intl.com
Mr. David MacDonald, VP Franchising

The mission of Homewatch Caregivers is to be the best provider of non-medical personal care services to seniors and others who are recovering, rehabilitating and convalescing within the communities we serve. The elderly make up 25% of the population. This unique franchise opportunity is not only financially rewarding, but offers the chance to make a difference in rendering a variety of basic need and personal care assistance to the elderly.

BACKGROUND:
Established: 1973; 1st Franchised: 1986
Franchised Units: 19
Company-Owned Units 0
Total Units: 19
Dist.: US-14; CAN-0; O'seas-0
North America: 6 States
Density: 3 in CO, 2 in MN
Projected New Units (12 Months): 15
Qualifications: 5, 3, 2, 3, 4, 4
Registered: CA,IL,IN,MD,MI,WA

FINANCIAL/TERMS:
Cash Investment: $15-49K
Total Investment: $35-49K
Minimum Net Worth: $150K
Fees: Franchise - $17.5K
Royalty - 5%/on Gross; Ad. - 0%
Earnings Claim Statement: Yes
Term of Contract (Years): 10/10
Avg. # Of Employees: 4 FT
Passive Ownership: Allowed
Encourage Conversions: Yes
Area Develop. Agreements: Yes/10
Sub-Franchising Contracts: No
Expand In Territory: No
Space Needs: N/A SF; N/A

SUPPORT & TRAINING PROVIDED:
Financial Assistance Provided: Yes(D)
Site Selection Assistance: N/A
Lease Negotiation Assistance: N/A
Co-Operative Advertising: No
Franchisee Assoc./Member: No
Size Of Corporate Staff: 6
On-Going Support: C,D,G,H,I
Training: 5 Days Denver, CO; Grand Opening at Franchisee Location.

SPECIFIC EXPANSION PLANS:
US: All United States
Canada: All Canada
Overseas: All Countries

<< >>

HUNT PERSONNEL/ TEMPORARILY YOURS

P.O. Box 1564
Niagara On The Lake, ON L05 1J0
CANADA
Tel: (416) 920-4141
Fax: (905) 468-8174
E-Mail: info@hunt.ca
Web Site: www.hunt.ca
Mr. Ted Turner, President

Established in 1967, we have an unequalled reputation for quality service. Prefer local industry experience or conversion. Specialization encouraged.

BACKGROUND:
Established: 1967; 1st Franchised: 1974
Franchised Units: 12
Company-Owned Units 0
Total Units: 12
Dist.: US-0; CAN-12; O'seas-0
North America: 4 Provinces
Density: 7 in ON, 3 in PQ, 1 in BC
Projected New Units (12 Months): 3
Qualifications: 5, 5, 5, 3, 4, 4
Registered: NR

FINANCIAL/TERMS:
Cash Investment: $100K
Total Investment: $150K
Minimum Net Worth: $200K
Fees: Franchise - $Varies
Royalty - Varies; Ad. - ~0.25%
Earnings Claim Statement: No
Term of Contract (Years): 5/5
Avg. # Of Employees: 3+ FT
Passive Ownership: Not Allowed
Encourage Conversions: Yes
Area Develop. Agreements: No
Sub-Franchising Contracts: Yes
Expand In Territory: Yes
Space Needs: 1,200 SF; OB

SUPPORT & TRAINING PROVIDED:
Financial Assistance Provided: No
Site Selection Assistance: Yes
Lease Negotiation Assistance: Yes
Co-Operative Advertising: No
Franchisee Assoc./Member: No
Size Of Corporate Staff: 4
On-Going Support: a,B,C,D,G,H
Training: 2-3 Weeks Local.

SPECIFIC EXPANSION PLANS:
US: No
Canada: ON,PQ,AB,MB,SKMR
Overseas: No

<< >>

INTERIM HEALTHCARE

2050 Spectrum Blvd.
Ft. Lauderdale, FL 33309
Tel: (800) 840-6568 (954) 938-7600
Fax:
E-Mail: gigigarcia@interim.com
Web Site: www.interim.com
Mr. Phil Baird

INTERIM HEALTHCARE is one of the nation's largest proprietary home health care and staffing services. Since 1966, INTERIM has provided a wide variety of health care personnel to people in need at home as well as in traditional facilities, such as hospitals, physicians groups, convalescent centers and HMO's. From highly-skilled nursing to home companions, INTERIM HEALTHCARE offers its services 24 hours a day, 7 days a week.

BACKGROUND:
Established: 1946; 1st Franchised: 1966
Franchised Units: 219
Company-Owned Units 94
Total Units: 313
Dist.: US-378; CAN-13; O'seas-3
North America: 46 States, 4 Provinces
Density: 36 in FL, 32 in NC, 29 in CA
Projected New Units (12 Months): 5
Qualifications: 5, 5, 2, 3, 3, 5
Registered: All States

FINANCIAL/TERMS:
Cash Investment: $50-75K
Total Investment: $150-200K
Minimum Net Worth: $NR
Fees: Franchise - $10K
Royalty - 7%; Ad. - 0.0025%
Earnings Claim Statement: No
Term of Contract (Years): 5/5
Avg. # Of Employees: 3 FT
Passive Ownership: Discouraged
Encourage Conversions: Yes
Area Develop. Agreements: No
Sub-Franchising Contracts: No
Expand In Territory: Yes
Space Needs: 1,000-1,200 SF; SC, OB

SUPPORT & TRAINING PROVIDED:
Financial Assistance Provided: Yes(I)
Site Selection Assistance: Yes

Lease Negotiation Assistance: Yes
Co-Operative Advertising: Yes
Franchisee Assoc./Member: Yes
Size Of Corporate Staff: 500
On-Going Support: A,C,D,E,G,H,I
Training: 2 Weeks Headquarters; 1 Week On-Site.

SPECIFIC EXPANSION PLANS:
US: ID, IN, MI, ND Only
Canada: No
Overseas: Latin America, Mexico, Europe

<< >>

LABOR FINDERS INTERNATIONAL

3910 RCA Blvd., # 1001
Palm Beach Gardens, FL 33410
Tel: (800) 864-7749 (561) 627-6507
Fax: (561) 627-6556
E-Mail: lfi@laborfinders.com
Web Site: www.laborfinders.com
Mr. Robert R. Gallagher, VP Marketing

LABOR FINDERS is a specialized labor staffing service that supplies highly productive skilled, semi-skilled and unskilled workers to companies in construction, industrial and commercial business segments.

BACKGROUND: IFA MEMBER
Established: 1975; 1st Franchised: 1975
Franchised Units: 157
Company-Owned Units 8
Total Units: 165
Dist.: US-165; CAN-0; O'seas-0
North America: 24 States
Density: 42 in FL, 12 in GA, 11 in AL
Projected New Units (12 Months): 20
Qualifications: 4, 4, 3, 3, 4, 4
Registered: CA,FL,IL,IN,MD,MN,VA,WA,WI

FINANCIAL/TERMS:
Cash Investment: $45-75K
Total Investment: $66.8-110.5K
Minimum Net Worth: $500K
Fees: Franchise - $10K
Royalty - % Billable Wages; Ad. - 0%
Earnings Claim Statement: No
Term of Contract (Years): 10/5/5
Avg. # Of Employees: 2 FT, 1 PT
Passive Ownership: Discouraged
Encourage Conversions: Yes
Area Develop. Agreements: No
Sub-Franchising Contracts: No
Expand In Territory: Yes
Space Needs: 800-1,000 SF; FS, SF, SC

SUPPORT & TRAINING PROVIDED:
Financial Assistance Provided: Yes(D)
Site Selection Assistance: Yes
Lease Negotiation Assistance: No
Co-Operative Advertising: Yes
Franchisee Assoc./Member: Yes/Yes
Size Of Corporate Staff: 15
On-Going Support: C,D,E,G,h,I
Training: 2 Weeks Operating Unit; 2 Weeks On-Site; 1 Week Classroom.

SPECIFIC EXPANSION PLANS:
US: All United States
Canada: No
Overseas: No

<< >>

LABOR FORCE

2550 South Parker Rd., #201
Aurora, CO 80014
Tel: (800) 299-4312 (713) 802-1284
Fax: (713) 802-1288
Web Site: www.laborforce.com
Mr. A. F. Nagel, President

We have small to large light industrial offices and finance 90% of weekly sales for 49 days to give instant cash flow. Enjoy instant recognition with national companies.

BACKGROUND:
Established: 1970; 1st Franchised: 1992
Franchised Units: 23
Company-Owned Units 16
Total Units: 39
Dist.: US-39; CAN-0; O'seas-0
North America: 15 States
Density: 17 in TX, 5 in GA, 3 in AZ
Projected New Units (12 Months): 10
Qualifications: 5, 5, 3, 3, 4, 4
Registered: NR

FINANCIAL/TERMS:
Cash Investment: $25-50K
Total Investment: $111-127K
Minimum Net Worth: $50K
Fees: Franchise - $15-25K
Royalty - 6%; Ad. - 0%
Earnings Claim Statement: No
Term of Contract (Years): 10/10
Avg. # Of Employees: 3 FT
Passive Ownership: Discouraged
Encourage Conversions: Yes
Area Develop. Agreements: No
Sub-Franchising Contracts: No
Expand In Territory: Yes
Space Needs: 800-1,200 SF; SC

SUPPORT & TRAINING PROVIDED:
Financial Assistance Provided: No
Site Selection Assistance: Yes
Lease Negotiation Assistance: Yes
Co-Operative Advertising: Yes
Franchisee Assoc./Member: No
Size Of Corporate Staff: 20
On-Going Support: B,C,D,E,G,H,I
Training: 2 Weeks at National Training Center; 1 Week On-Site.

SPECIFIC EXPANSION PLANS:
US: All Non-Registration States
Canada: All Canada
Overseas: Mexico

<< >>

LAWCORPS LEGAL STAFFING

1819 L St., NW, 9th Fl.
Washington, DC 20036-3807
Tel: (800) 437-8809 (202) 785-5996
Fax: (202) 785-1118
E-Mail: info@lawcorps.com
Web Site: www.lawcorps.com
Ms. Elaine Altamar, Dir. Training/Development

Temporary legal staffing: attorneys, law clerks, paralegals and support staff. LAWCORPS Franchise Corporation is the first and only exclusively legal temporary service to franchise. Join the fastest-growing segment of the fastest-growing industry.

BACKGROUND: IFA MEMBER
Established: 1988; 1st Franchised: 1995
Franchised Units: 3
Company-Owned Units 4
Total Units: 7
Dist.: US-7; CAN-0; O'seas-0
North America: NR
Density: DC, NY, IL
Projected New Units (12 Months): 4-6
Qualifications: 5, 5, 5, 5, 5, 5
Registered: HI,IL,MI,MN,NY

FINANCIAL/TERMS:
Cash Investment: $88-110K
Total Investment: $88-110K
Minimum Net Worth: $N/A
Fees: Franchise - $25K
Royalty - 8%; Ad. - N/A
Earnings Claim Statement: No
Term of Contract (Years): 7/7
Avg. # Of Employees: 2 FT, 1 PT
Passive Ownership: Discouraged
Encourage Conversions: Yes
Area Develop. Agreements: No

Sub-Franchising Contracts: No
Expand In Territory: No
Space Needs: 200-500 SF; Executive Suite

SUPPORT & TRAINING PROVIDED:
Financial Assistance Provided: N/A
Site Selection Assistance: Yes
Lease Negotiation Assistance: No
Co-Operative Advertising: Yes
Franchisee Assoc./Member: No
Size Of Corporate Staff: 5
On-Going Support: a,b,C,D,E,g,H,I
Training: 2 Weeks Headquarters; 1 Week On-Site.

SPECIFIC EXPANSION PLANS:
US: All United States
Canada: All Canada
Overseas: No

<< >>

LINK STAFFING SERVICES

1800 Bering Dr., # 800
Houston, TX 77057-3129
Tel: (800) 848-5465 (713) 784-4400
Fax: (713) 784-4454
E-Mail: franchise@linkstaffing.com
Web Site: www.linkstaffing.com
Mr. Don Lawrence, VP Franchise Development

LINK STAFFING SERVICES provides a wide variety of flexible staffing/productivity solutions. We allow our clients to build their own business while providing them the staff they need; they tell us one thing that sets us apart from other staffing services is our comprehensive screening process, which consistently delivers higher quality workers. Many fieldstaff have accepted full-time positions with our clients. Join a team with top-notch employees and the experience to support you all the way to success!

BACKGROUND: IFA MEMBER
Established: 1980; 1st Franchised: 1993
Franchised Units: 28
Company-Owned Units <u>14</u>
Total Units: 42
Dist.: US-42; CAN-0; O'seas-0
North America: 13 States
Density: 19 in TX, 7 in FL, 6 in CA
Projected New Units (12 Months): 6
Qualifications: 3, 4, 2, 4, 4, 5
Registered: All Except HI,AB

FINANCIAL/TERMS:
Cash Investment: $25-35K
Total Investment: $95-166K
Minimum Net Worth: $N/A
Fees: Franchise - $17K
Royalty - Varies; Ad. - 0.05%
Earnings Claim Statement: No
Term of Contract (Years): 10/5/5/5
Avg. # Of Employees: 2 FT
Passive Ownership: Discouraged
Encourage Conversions: Yes
Area Develop. Agreements: No
Sub-Franchising Contracts: No
Expand In Territory: Yes
Space Needs: 1,200-1,800 SF; SF, SC, Industrial Office Park

SUPPORT & TRAINING PROVIDED:
Financial Assistance Provided: Yes(I)
Site Selection Assistance: Yes
Lease Negotiation Assistance: Yes
Co-Operative Advertising: Yes
Franchisee Assoc./Member: Yes/Yes
Size Of Corporate Staff: 44
On-Going Support: A,B,C,D,E,G,H,I
Training: 3-5 Days Existing Franchise; 5 Days (Sales), 5 Days (Operations) Support Center, TX.

SPECIFIC EXPANSION PLANS:
US: All United States
Canada: No
Overseas: No

LLOYD STAFFING

445 Broadhollow Rd., # 119
Melville, NY 11747-3601
Tel: (888) 292-6678 (631) 777-7600
Fax: (631) 777-7620
E-Mail: jbondi@lloydstaffing.com
Web Site: www.lloydstaffing.com
Ms. Jeanine L. Bondi, VP Natl. Fran. Ops.

Since 1971, we have successfully served thousands of employers, job seekers and temporary employees. Our blended service concept truly embodies the entire spectrum of staffing, including temporary personnel, consultant referrals, contingency placement and executive search. And because we recognize that the field of human resources has significantly changed its structure and focus over the years, we've added several complimentary and compatible staffing components to enhance the support we provide.

BACKGROUND: IFA MEMBER
Established: 1971; 1st Franchised: 1986
Franchised Units: 8
Company-Owned Units <u>7</u>
Total Units: 15
Dist.: US-11; CAN-0; O'seas-0
North America: NR
Density: 5 in NY, 2 in NJ, 2 in CT
Projected New Units (12 Months): 3
Qualifications: 4, 5, 4, 3, 3, 5
Registered: FL,MD

FINANCIAL/TERMS:
Cash Investment: $75-100K
Total Investment: $85-150K
Minimum Net Worth: $100-150K
Fees: Franchise - $15-22K
Royalty - 60/40-7%; Ad. - N/A
Earnings Claim Statement: No
Term of Contract (Years): 10/10
Avg. # Of Employees: 4 FT
Passive Ownership: Not Allowed
Encourage Conversions: No
Area Develop. Agreements: No
Sub-Franchising Contracts: No
Expand In Territory: Yes
Space Needs: 1,500 SF; FS, SF, SC

SUPPORT & TRAINING PROVIDED:
Financial Assistance Provided: Yes(I)
Site Selection Assistance: Yes
Lease Negotiation Assistance: Yes
Co-Operative Advertising: No
Franchisee Assoc./Member: No
Size Of Corporate Staff: 123
On-Going Support: A,C,D,E,g,h,I
Training: 2 Weeks in Melville, NY; 1 Week at Your Location.

SPECIFIC EXPANSION PLANS:
US: Southeast, Northeast
Canada: No
Overseas: No

<< >>

MANAGEMENT RECRUITERS/ SALES CONSULTANTS

200 Public Sq., 31st Fl.
Cleveland, OH 44114-2301
Tel: (800) 875-4000 (216) 416-8245
Fax: (216) 696-6612
E-Mail: jennifer.wood@brilliantpeople.com
Web Site: www.brilliantpeople.com
Ms. Jennifer Wood, Franchise Marketing Coord.

Complete range of recruitment and human resource services, including: permanent executive, mid-management, professional, marketing, sales management and sales placement; temporary professional and sales staffing; video-conferencing; permanent and temporary office support personnel; with coverage on all continents. Franchises available outside of North America through our wholly-owned subsidiary, the Humana Group International.

BACKGROUND: IFA MEMBER
Established: 1957; 1st Franchised: 1965
Franchised Units: 1,000
Company-Owned Units 32
Total Units: 1,032
Dist.: US-829; CAN-0; O'seas-1
North America: 48 States
Density: 64 in FL, 62 in CA,60 in NC
Projected New Units (12 Months): 50
Qualifications: 3, 4, 1, 4, 3, 3
Registered: All States

FINANCIAL/TERMS:
Cash Investment: $110-145K
Total Investment: $110-145K
Minimum Net Worth: $N/A
Fees: Franchise - $72.5K
Royalty - 7%; Ad. - 0.5%
Earnings Claim Statement: Yes
Term of Contract (Years): 5-20/10
Avg. # Of Employees: 3-4 FT
Passive Ownership: Discouraged
Encourage Conversions: Yes
Area Develop. Agreements: No
Sub-Franchising Contracts: No
Expand In Territory: Yes
Space Needs: 600-1,000 SF; FS

SUPPORT & TRAINING PROVIDED:
Financial Assistance Provided: Yes(I)
Site Selection Assistance: Yes
Lease Negotiation Assistance: Yes
Co-Operative Advertising: N/A
Franchisee Assoc./Member: Yes
Size Of Corporate Staff: 91
On-Going Support: C,D,E,G,H,I
Training: 3 Weeks Headquarters, Cleveland, OH; 10 Days Franchisee's Location.

SPECIFIC EXPANSION PLANS:
US: All United States
Canada: No
Overseas: No

<< >>

NURSEFINDERS

1701 E. Lamar Blvd., # 200
Arlington, TX 76006
Tel: (800) 445-0459 (817) 460-1181
Fax: (817) 462-9139
Web Site: www.nursefinders.com
Mr. Ed McGuinness, VP Franchising

Largest provider in United States of temporary medical staffing to hospitals and other health care facilities. Ranked Number 1 in category by Entrepreneur Magazine. We also provide the full spectrum of home health care.

BACKGROUND:
Established: 1974; 1st Franchised: 1978
Franchised Units: 54
Company-Owned Units 68
Total Units: 122
Dist.: US-113; CAN-0; O'seas-0
North America: 31 States
Density: 14 in FL, 8 in IL, 7 in CA
Projected New Units (12 Months): 10
Registered: All States

FINANCIAL/TERMS:
Cash Investment: $50-100K
Total Investment: $110-200K
Minimum Net Worth: $250K
Fees: Franchise - $19.6K
Royalty - 7%; Ad. - 0%
Earnings Claim Statement: No
Term of Contract (Years): 10/5/5
Avg. # Of Employees: 5 FT, 100 PT
Passive Ownership: Discouraged
Encourage Conversions: Yes
Area Develop. Agreements: Yes/5/5
Sub-Franchising Contracts: No
Expand In Territory: Yes
Space Needs: 1,500-2,000 SF; Profess. Office. Bldg.

SUPPORT & TRAINING PROVIDED:
Financial Assistance Provided: Yes(D)
Site Selection Assistance: Yes
Lease Negotiation Assistance: Yes
Co-Operative Advertising: N/A
Franchisee Assoc./Member: No
Size Of Corporate Staff: 62
On-Going Support: A,B,C,D,E,G,h,I
Training: 2 Weeks Arlington, TX; 1 Week Company Office; 2 Weeks On-Site.

SPECIFIC EXPANSION PLANS:
US: All United States
Canada: No
Overseas: No

<< >>

PMA FRANCHISE SYSTEMS

1950 Spectrum Cir., # B-310
Marietta, GA 30067
Tel: (800) 466-7822 (770) 916-1668
Fax: (770) 916-1429
E-Mail: jobs@pmasearch.com
Web Site: www.pmasearch.com
Mr. Bill Lins, Director Operations

A national executive search firm specializing in store and mid-level management through vice president level positions in the retail, hospitality and service industries.

BACKGROUND: IFA MEMBER
Established: 1984; 1st Franchised: 1998
Franchised Units: 6
Company-Owned Units 1
Total Units: 7
Dist.: US-7; CAN-0; O'seas-0
North America: 6 States
Density: 2 in TN, 1 in OR, 1 in OK
Projected New Units (12 Months): NR
Registered: NR

FINANCIAL/TERMS:
Cash Investment: $25K
Total Investment: $25-35K
Minimum Net Worth: $N/A
Fees: Franchise - $20K
Royalty - 10%; Ad. - 0%
Earnings Claim Statement: NR
Term of Contract (Years): 5/5
Avg. # Of Employees: NR
Passive Ownership: Not Allowed
Encourage Conversions: NR
Area Develop. Agreements: Yes/Varies
Sub-Franchising Contracts: NR
Expand In Territory: Yes
Space Needs: 150+ SF; NR

SUPPORT & TRAINING PROVIDED:
Financial Assistance Provided: NR
Site Selection Assistance: No
Lease Negotiation Assistance: Yes
Co-Operative Advertising: Yes
Franchisee Assoc./Member: Yes/Yes
Size Of Corporate Staff: 12
On-Going Support: A,C,E,G,h,I
Training: 4 Weeks Atlanta, GA.

SPECIFIC EXPANSION PLANS:
US: All United States
Canada: NR
Overseas: NR

<< >>

REMEDY INTELLIGENT STAFFING

101 Enterprise
Aliso Viejo, CA 92656
Tel: (800) 736-3392 (949) 425-7600
Fax: (800) 291-2060
E-Mail: gerryr@remedystaff.com
Web Site: www.remedyfranchise.com
Mr. Gerry Rhydderch, VP Fran. Dev.

A national full-service staffing company, providing contingent workers in the disciplines of law, accounting, professional office auditing, clerical and light industrial. Fully-automated office, with exclusive, validated behavioral testing. Entire back-office support and exclusive territories.

BACKGROUND: IFA MEMBER
Established: 1965; 1st Franchised: 1988
Franchised Units: 154
Company-Owned Units 101
Total Units: 255
Dist.: US-277; CAN-0; O'seas-0
North America: 40 States
Density: 88 in CA, 24 in FL, 18 in TX
Projected New Units (12 Months): 30
Qualifications: 4, 4, 4, 3, 4, 5
Registered: CA,FL,HI,IL,IN,MD,MI,MN, NY,OR,RI,VA,WA,WI,DC,AB

FINANCIAL/TERMS:
Cash Investment: $30-60K
Total Investment: $95-150K
Minimum Net Worth: $250K
Fees: Franchise - $18K
Royalty - Varies; Ad. - 0%
Earnings Claim Statement: No
Term of Contract (Years): 10/5
Avg. # Of Employees: 5 FT, 1 PT
Passive Ownership: Discouraged
Encourage Conversions: Yes
Area Develop. Agreements: Yes/10
Sub-Franchising Contracts: No
Expand In Territory: Yes
Space Needs: 1,400 SF; OB

SUPPORT & TRAINING PROVIDED:
Financial Assistance Provided: Yes(I)
Site Selection Assistance: Yes
Lease Negotiation Assistance: Yes
Co-Operative Advertising: Yes
Franchisee Assoc./Member: Yes/Yes
Size Of Corporate Staff: 160
On-Going Support: A,C,D,E,G,H,I
Training: 2 Weeks Home Office; 1 Week On-Site.

SPECIFIC EXPANSION PLANS:
US: All Except CA,WA,OR,NM,CO
Canada: All Canada
Overseas: No

<< >>

SALES CONSULTANTS

200 Public Sq., 31st Fl.
Cleveland, OH 44114-2301
Tel: (800) 875-4000 (216) 696-1122
Fax: (216) 696-6612
E-Mail: raa@@mricorp.mrinet.com
Web Site: www.mrinet.com
Mr. Robert A. Angel, VP Franchise Marketing

Complete range of recruitment and human resource services for sales, sales management and marketing professionals, including permanent placement, interim staffing; video-conferencing; with coverage on all continents through strategic alliances with leading search firms.

BACKGROUND: IFA MEMBER
Established: 1957; 1st Franchised: 1966
Franchised Units: 170
Company-Owned Units 17
Total Units: 187
Dist.: US-226; CAN-0; O'seas-0
North America: 39 States
Density: 20 in CA, 15 in FL, 14 in MI
Projected New Units (12 Months): 20
Qualifications: 3, 4, 1, 4, 3, 3
Registered: All States

FINANCIAL/TERMS:
Cash Investment: $113-154K
Total Investment: $113-154K
Minimum Net Worth: $N/A
Fees: Franchise - $75-80K
Royalty - 7%; Ad. - 1%
Earnings Claim Statement: Yes
Term of Contract (Years): 10-20/5
Avg. # Of Employees: 3-4 FT or PT
Passive Ownership: Discouraged
Encourage Conversions: Yes
Area Develop. Agreements: No
Sub-Franchising Contracts: No
Expand In Territory: Yes
Space Needs: 600-1,000 SF; FS

SUPPORT & TRAINING PROVIDED:
Financial Assistance Provided: Yes(I)
Site Selection Assistance: Yes
Lease Negotiation Assistance: Yes
Co-Operative Advertising: N/A
Franchisee Assoc./Member: Yes
Size Of Corporate Staff: 128
On-Going Support: C,D,E,G,H,I
Training: 3 Weeks Headquarters, Cleveland, OH; 2 Weeks Franchisee's Location.

SPECIFIC EXPANSION PLANS:
US: All United States
Canada: No
Overseas: No

<< >>

SANFORD ROSE ASSOCIATES

3737 Embassy Dr., # 200
Akron, OH 44333-8369
Tel: (800) 731-7724 (330) 670-9797
Fax: (330) 670-9798
E-Mail: masweeterman@franchiseSRA.com
Web Site: www.franchiseSRA.com
Mr. Mark A. Sweeterman, Dir. Franchise Development

Executive search is distinct within the SRA organization. We provide a highly-reliable service to fill critical openings with our corporate clients. Only the most qualified candidates are presented. Our adaptability allows us to work at virtually all professional levels, developing repeat business.

BACKGROUND: IFA MEMBER
Established: 1959; 1st Franchised: 1970
Franchised Units: 60
Company-Owned Units 0
Total Units: 60
Dist.: US-51; CAN-0; O'seas-2
North America: 23 States
Density: 7 in OH, 7 in IL, 5 in CA
Projected New Units (12 Months): 15
Qualifications: 3, 5, 3, 5, 5, 5
Registered: CA,IL,MD,NY,VA,WA

FINANCIAL/TERMS:
Cash Investment: $70-95K
Total Investment: $70-95K
Minimum Net Worth: $80K
Fees: Franchise - $40K
Royalty - 3-7%; Ad. - 0%
Earnings Claim Statement: Yes
Term of Contract (Years): 7/1
Avg. # Of Employees: 10 FT, 1 PT
Passive Ownership: NR
Encourage Conversions: Yes
Area Develop. Agreements: No
Sub-Franchising Contracts: No
Expand In Territory: No
Space Needs: 600-1,000 SF; OB

SUPPORT & TRAINING PROVIDED:
Financial Assistance Provided: Yes(D)
Site Selection Assistance: Yes
Lease Negotiation Assistance: Yes
Co-Operative Advertising: No
Franchisee Assoc./Member: Yes/Yes
Size Of Corporate Staff: 6
On-Going Support: C,G,H,I
Training: 10 Days National Headquarters; 5 Days On-Site.

SPECIFIC EXPANSION PLANS:
US: All United States
Canada: All Canada
Overseas: All Developed Countries

STAFF BUILDERS HOME HEALTH CARE

1983 Marcus Ave., # C115
Lake Success, NY 11042-1016

Tel: (800) 444-4633 (516) 358-1000
Fax: (516) 358-3678
Web Site: www.staffbuildersintl.com
Mr. Rob Laufer, VP Franchising

STAFF BUILDERS provides home health care services to patients in their home ranging from hi-tech nursing to para-professional services.

BACKGROUND: IFA MEMBER
Established: 1967; 1st Franchised: 1967
Franchised Units: 200
Company-Owned Units 20
Total Units: 220
Dist.: US-248; CAN-0; O'seas-2
North America: 38 States
Density: 20 in PA, 19 in NY, 18 in OH
Projected New Units (12 Months): 30
Qualifications: 4, 4, 5, 5, 1, 5
Registered: All States

FINANCIAL/TERMS:
Cash Investment: $50K
Total Investment: $110-150K
Minimum Net Worth: $200-250K
Fees: Franchise - $29.5K
Royalty - Varies; Ad. - N/A
Earnings Claim Statement: No
Term of Contract (Years): 10/5
Avg. # Of Employees: 4 FT, 2 PT
Passive Ownership: Allowed
Encourage Conversions: Yes
Area Develop. Agreements: No
Sub-Franchising Contracts: No
Expand In Territory: Yes
Space Needs: 1,000 SF; FS, SF, SC

SUPPORT & TRAINING PROVIDED:
Financial Assistance Provided: Yes(D)
Site Selection Assistance: Yes
Lease Negotiation Assistance: No
Co-Operative Advertising: No
Franchisee Assoc./Member: Yes/Yes
Size Of Corporate Staff: 350
On-Going Support: A,B,C,D,E,G,H
Training: 5 Days at Corporate Office in NY; 5 Days Regional Location.

SPECIFIC EXPANSION PLANS:
US: All United States
Canada: All Canada
Overseas: Asia, Europe, Latin America

<< >>

TALENT TREE
9703 Richmond Ave., # 216
Houston, TX 77042-4620
Tel: (800) 999-1515 (713) 789-1818
Fax: (713) 785-1986
E-Mail: franchise@talenttree.com
Web Site: www.talenttree.com
Ms. Shelly Oldner, Franchise Business Dev.

TALENT TREE offers full-service staffing franchise opportunities with the placement of clerical, administrative, technical support and light industrial staff. Franchisees are offered intensive on-going training and hands-on support by industry experts. Our franchisees have the advantage of our proven system and innovative, proprietary programs.

BACKGROUND: IFA MEMBER
Established: 1976; 1st Franchised: 1990
Franchised Units: 24
Company-Owned Units 156
Total Units: 180
Dist.: US-234; CAN-0; O'seas-0
North America: 30 States
Density: 32 in CA, 14 in TX, 14 in GA
Projected New Units (12 Months): 3-5
Qualifications: 4, 4, 5, 1, 2, 4
Registered: All States

FINANCIAL/TERMS:
Cash Investment: $100-150K
Total Investment: $120-170K
Minimum Net Worth: $150-250K
Fees: Franchise - $20K
Royalty - Varies; Ad. - 0%
Earnings Claim Statement: No
Term of Contract (Years): 10/5
Avg. # Of Employees: 2 FT
Passive Ownership: Allowed
Encourage Conversions: Yes
Area Develop. Agreements: Yes
Sub-Franchising Contracts: No
Expand In Territory: Yes
Space Needs: 1,000 SF; FS, SF, SC

SUPPORT & TRAINING PROVIDED:
Financial Assistance Provided: Yes(I)
Site Selection Assistance: Yes
Lease Negotiation Assistance: Yes
Co-Operative Advertising: Yes
Franchisee Assoc./Member: No
Size Of Corporate Staff: 180
On-Going Support: A,B,C,D,E,H,I
Training: 3-4 Weeks at Corporate Office & On-Going; 1st 120 Days and as Needed at Franchise.

SPECIFIC EXPANSION PLANS:
US: All United States
Canada: No
Overseas: No

<< >>

TRC STAFFING SERVICES
100 Ashford Center N., # 500
Atlanta, GA 30338
Tel: (800) 488-8008 (770) 392-1411
Fax: (770) 698-7885
E-Mail: sasanders@trcstaff.com
Web Site: www.trcstaff.com
Mr. Steve Sanders, VP Franchise Operations

TRC offers a unique freedom franchise that provides special financing for experienced, temporary industry professionals. Start-up capital, computer equipment, payroll, workers' compensation, taxes and field and classroom support are all provided for an approved candidate.

BACKGROUND:
Established: 1980; 1st Franchised: 1984
Franchised Units: 48
Company-Owned Units 27
Total Units: 75
Dist.: US-69; CAN-0; O'seas-0
North America: 17 States
Density: 21 in GA, 10 in TX, 7 in CA
Projected New Units (12 Months): 12
Qualifications: 2, 2, 5, 2, 3, 5
Registered: CA,FL,HI,IL,IN,MD,MN,NY, OR,RI,VA,WA,WI,DC

FINANCIAL/TERMS:
Cash Investment: $25K
Total Investment: $25K
Minimum Net Worth: $150K
Fees: Franchise - $0
Royalty - 9.5%; Ad. - 0%
Earnings Claim Statement: No
Term of Contract (Years): 5/5
Avg. # Of Employees: 2 FT
Passive Ownership: Not Allowed
Encourage Conversions: Yes
Area Develop. Agreements: No
Sub-Franchising Contracts: No
Expand In Territory: Yes
Space Needs: 800 SF; Class A Office

SUPPORT & TRAINING PROVIDED:
Financial Assistance Provided: Yes(D)
Site Selection Assistance: Yes
Lease Negotiation Assistance: Yes
Co-Operative Advertising: No
Franchisee Assoc./Member: No
Size Of Corporate Staff: 117
On-Going Support: A,b,C,D,E,G,h,I
Training: 1 Week Atlanta, GA; 1 Week On-Site.

SPECIFIC EXPANSION PLANS:
US: All United States
Canada: No
Overseas: No

<< >>

WESTERN MEDICAL SERVICES

220 N. Wiget Ln.
Walnut Creek, CA 94598
Tel: (800) 872-8367 (925) 256-1561
Fax: (925) 952-2591
E-Mail: franchise@westaff.com
Web Site: www.westaff.com
Ms. Bobbi George, VP Business Dev.

Full-service home health agency (staffing, home care). WESTERN offers exclusive territories, comprehensive training, Medicare certification, JCAHO accreditation, Medicare and non-Medicare billing, integrated payroll, billing, accounting and cost reporting services, complete caregiver payroll and accounts receivable financing, managed care contracts, professional risk management, credit and legal expertise, advertising/promotional support and more.

BACKGROUND:

Established: 1967; 1st Franchised: 1975
Franchised Units: 24
Company-Owned Units 30
Total Units: 54
Dist.: US-54; CAN-0; O'seas-0
North America: 20 States
Density: 10 in IN, 8 in CA, 5 in OH
Projected New Units (12 Months): 20
Qualifications: 5, 2, 5, 4, 2, 5
Registered: CA,FL,IL,IN,MD,MI,MN,NY, OR,SD,VA,WA,WI

FINANCIAL/TERMS:

Cash Investment: $100-200K
Total Investment: $200-250K
Minimum Net Worth: $100K
Fees: Franchise - $30-40K
Royalty - 8%; Ad. - Included
Earnings Claim Statement: No
Term of Contract (Years): Indefin.
Avg. # Of Employees: 3 FT
Passive Ownership: Not Allowed
Encourage Conversions: Yes
Area Develop. Agreements: No
Sub-Franchising Contracts: No
Expand In Territory: Yes
Space Needs: 500-750 SF; FS, SF, SC

SUPPORT & TRAINING PROVIDED:

Financial Assistance Provided: No
Site Selection Assistance: Yes
Lease Negotiation Assistance: No
Co-Operative Advertising: Yes
Franchisee Assoc./Member: Yes/Yes
Size Of Corporate Staff: 250
On-Going Support: A,B,C,D,E,G,H,I
Training: 5 Days Corporate Headquarters; 5 Days On-Site.

SPECIFIC EXPANSION PLANS:

US: All United States
Canada: No
Overseas: No

<< >>

SUPPLEMENTAL LISTING OF FRANCHISORS

AAA EMPLOYMENT, 4914-A Creekside Dr., Clearwater, FL 33760 ; (800) 237-2853 (727) 573-0202; (727) 572-8709

ACCOUNTANTS ON CALL, Park 80 West, Plaza II, 9th Fl., Saddle Brook, NJ 07663 ; (201) 843-0006; (201) 712-1033

ACCUSTAFF, 177 Crossways Park Dr., Woodbury, NY 11797 ; (888) 536-1200 (516) 682-1432; (516) 677-6023

AMERICAN RECRUITERS, 800 W. Cypress Creek Rd., # 300, Ft. Lauderdale, FL 33309-2075 ; (800) 493-9201 (954) 493-9200; (954) 493-9582

ATS PERSONNEL, 9700 Philips Hwy., # 101, Jacksonville, FL 32256 ; (800) 346-5574 (904) 645-9505; (904) 645-0390

BELCAN TECHSERVICES, 10200 Anderson Way, Cincinnati, OH 45242 (800) 423-5226 (513) 891-0972; (513) 985-7421

CARDINAL SERVICES, 1721 Indianwood Cir., # A, Maumee, OH 43537-4008 (419) 893-5400; (419) 893-8640

CAREER BLAZERS, 590 Fifth Ave., New York, NY 10036-4702 ; (212) 719-3232; (212) 921-1827

COMFORCARE SENIOR SERVICES, 42505 Woodward Ave., # 250, Bloomfield Hills, MI 48304-5146 ; (800) 886-4044 (248) 745-9700; (248) 745-9763

CONSULTIS, 1615 S. Federal Hwy., # 300, Boca Raton, FL 33432-7434 ; (800) 275-2667 (561) 362-9104; (561) 367-9802

DRAKE INTERNATIONAL, P.O. Box 800, Toronto, ON M4Y 2N8 CANADA; (800) GO DRAKE (416) 967-7700; (416) 216-1109

GRISWOLD SPECIAL CARE, 717 Bethlehem Pk., # 300, Erdenheim, PA 19038; (888) 777-7630 (215) 402-0200; (215) 402-0202

HEALTH FORCE, 185 Crossways Park Dr., Woodbury, NY 11797-2047 ; (800) 967-1001 (516) 490-1200; (516) 496-3283

HOMEWATCH CAREGIVERS, 2865 S. Colorado Blvd., Denver, CO 80222 ; (800) 777-9770 (303) 758-7290; (303) 758-1724

INTERIM PERSONNEL SERVICES, 2050 Spectrum Blvd., Ft. Lauderdale, FL 33309 ; (888) 840-6568 (954) 938-7600; (954) 938-7770

OUTSOURCE INTERNATIONAL, 1690 S. Congress Ave., #210, Delray Beach, FL 33445 ; (800) 275-5000 (561) 454-3509; (561) 454-3642

PHARMACISTS: prn, 44 Wycliffe Rd., East Walpole, MA 02032 ; (800) 832-5560 (508) 660-1469; (508) 668-5663

PRIDESTAFF, 6780 N. West Ave., # 103, Fresno, CA 93711-1393 ; (800) 774-3316 (559) 432-7780; (559) 432-4371

PROFESSIONAL EMPLOYEE MANAGEMENT (PEM), 1819 Main St., 8th Fl., Sarasota, FL 34236 ; (800) 329-7823 (941) 957-1444; (941) 364-5799

RECRUITERS PROFESSIONAL NETWORK, 8 Grenada Circle, Nashua, NH 03062-1429 ; (888) 598-6633 (603) 598-6633; (603) 598-6622

RESUME HUT, THE, 743 View St., Victoria, BC V8W 1J9 CANADA; (800) 441-6488 (250) 383-3983; (250) 383-1580

ROTH YOUNG PERSONNEL SERVICE, 535 5th Ave., 33rd Fl., New York, NY 10017 ; (800) 343-8518 (212) 557-4900; (212) 972-5367

RUSSOLI TEMPS, 7510 Brouse Ave., Philadelphia, PA 19152-3906 ; (800) 779-0401 (215) 953-1620;

SARAH ADULT DAY SERVICES, 800 Market Ave., N., # 1230, Canton, OH 44702-1083 ; (800) 472-5544 (330) 454-3200; (330) 454-6807

SENIORS FOR SENIORS/SENIORS FOR BUSINESS, 55 Eglinton Ave. E., # 311, Toronto, ON M4P 1G8 CANADA; (416) 481-4579; (416) 481-6752

SNELLING PERSONNEL SERVICES, 12801 N. Central Expy., # 700, Dallas, TX 75243 ; (800) 766-5556 (972) 239-7575; (972) 383-3871

SPHERION CORP., 2050 Spectrum Blvd., Ft. Lauderdale, FL 33309-3008 (800) 388-7783 (954) 489-6564; (954) 938-7770

TANDEM, 1690 S. Congress Ave., # 210, Delray Beach, FL 33445 ; (800) 275-5000 (954) 454-3509; (954) 454-3642

TECHSTAFF, 11270 W. Park Pl., # 460, Milwaukee, WI 53224 ; (800) 515-4440 (414) 359-4444; (414) 359-4949

TEMPFORCE, 177 Crossways Park Dr., Woodbury, NY 11797 ; (888) 536-1200 (516) 682-1432; (516) 677-6023

TIME SERVICES, 6422 Lima Rd., Fort Wayne, IN 46818 ; (800) 837-8463 (219) 489-2020; (219) 489-1466

TODAYS STAFFING, 18111 Preston Rd., # 700, Dallas, TX 75252-4383 ; (800) 822-7868 (972) 380-9380; (972) 713-4198

USA EMPLOYMENT, 5533 Central Ave., St. Petersburg, FL 33710 ; (800) 801-5627 (727) 343-3044; (727) 343-2953

WESTAFF, 301 Lennon Ln., Walnut Creek, CA 94598 ; (800) USA-TEMP (925) 930-5000; (925) 952-2555

Food: Donuts/Cookies/Bagels

Chapter 13

Food: Donuts/Cookies/Bagels Industry Profile

Total # Franchisors in Industry Group	73
Total # Franchised Units in Industry Group	13,125
Total # Company-Owned Units in Industry Group	1,516
Total # Operating Units in Industry Group	14,641
Average # Franchised Units/Franchisor	179.8
Average # Company-Owned Units/Franchisor	20.8
Average # Total Units/Franchisor	200.6
Ratio of Total # Franchised Units/Total # Company-Owned Units	8.7:1
Industry Survey Participants	34
Representing % of Industry	46.6%
Average Franchise Fee*:	$25.4K
Average Total Investment*:	$231.9K
Average On-Going Royalty Fee*:	5.3%

*If a range was provided, the mid-point of the range was used. See detailed profiles for actual ranges.

Five Largest Participants in Survey

Company	# Franchised Units	# Co-Owned Units	# Total Units	Franchise Fee	On-Going Royalty	Total Investment
1. Dunkin' Donuts	5,000	0	5,000	50K	5.9%	356K-1MM
2. Tim Hortons	1,553	145	1,698	35-50K	3-4.5%	300-360K
3. Mrs. Fields Cookies	457	150	607	30K	6%	180-247K
4. Cinnabon	309	172	481	35K	5%	178-255K
5. Great American Cookies	280	100	380	30K	7%	121-631K

All of the data provided are proprietary and should not be quoted without acknowledging *Bond's Franchise Guide.*

BETWEEN ROUNDS BAGEL DELI & BAKERY

19A John Fitch Blvd.
South Windsor, CT 06074
Tel: (860) 291-0323
Fax: (860) 289-2732
E-Mail: betweenrounds@snet.net
Mr. Jerry Puiia, President

Providing customers with more choices than just bagels, cream cheese and gourmet coffee, BETWEEN ROUNDS sells a wide variety of bakery and deli items, as well as offers extensive catering. BETWEEN ROUNDS BAGEL DELI & BAKERY is your competitive edge in the explosive bagel franchise field because, soon, selling bagels won't be enough!

BACKGROUND: IFA MEMBER
Established: 1990; 1st Franchised: 1993
Franchised Units: 4
Company-Owned Units 3
Total Units: 7
Dist.: US-7; CAN-0; O'seas-0
North America: 3 States
Density: 4 in CT, 2 in MA, 1 in WV
Projected New Units (12 Months): 5
Qualifications: 4, 3, 3, 1, 3, 3
Registered: N/A

FINANCIAL/TERMS:
Cash Investment: $50-80K
Total Investment: $160-210K
Minimum Net Worth: $100K
Fees: Franchise - $18K
Royalty - 4%; Ad. - 2%
Earnings Claim Statement: Yes
Term of Contract (Years): 10/15
Avg. # Of Employees: 3 FT, 5 PT
Passive Ownership: Discouraged
Encourage Conversions: Yes
Area Develop. Agreements: Yes
Sub-Franchising Contracts: No
Expand In Territory: Yes
Space Needs: 1,600 SF; SC

SUPPORT & TRAINING PROVIDED:
Financial Assistance Provided: Yes(I)
Site Selection Assistance: Yes
Lease Negotiation Assistance: Yes
Co-Operative Advertising: Yes
Franchisee Assoc./Member: No
Size Of Corporate Staff: 3
On-Going Support: a,C,D,E,F,G
Training: 2 Weeks Company Stores in CT; 1-2 Weeks Own Unit.

SPECIFIC EXPANSION PLANS:
US: Mid-Atlantic, Northeast
Canada: No
Overseas: No

<< >>

Top 50

BIG APPLE BAGELS

8501 W. Higgins Rd., # 320
Chicago, IL 60631
Tel: (800) 251-6101 (773) 380-6100
Fax: (773) 380-6183
E-Mail: tcervini@babcorp.com
Web Site: www.babcorp.com
Mr. Anthony Cervini, Dir. Fran. Dev.

Bakery-café featuring three brands, fresh-from-scratch Big Apple Bagels and My Favorite Muffin, and freshly roasted Brewster's specialty coffee. Our product offering covers many day parts with a delicious assortment of made-to-order gourmet sandwiches, salads, soups, espresso beverages, and fruit smoothies. Franchisees can develop beyond their stores with corporate catering and gift basket opportunities, as well as wholesaling opportunities within their market area.

BACKGROUND: IFA MEMBER
Established: 1992; 1st Franchised: 1993
Franchised Units: 172
Company-Owned Units 6
Total Units: 178
Dist.: US-171; CAN-0; O'seas-7
North America: 26 States
Density: 31 in Michigan, 27, 23 in WI
Projected New Units (12 Months): 25
Qualifications: 3, 4, 3, 3, 3, 5
Registered: All States

FINANCIAL/TERMS:
Cash Investment: $40-70K
Total Investment: $250-325K
Minimum Net Worth: $250K
Fees: Franchise - $25K
Royalty - 5%; Ad. - 1%
Earnings Claim Statement: No
Term of Contract (Years): 10/10
Avg. # Of Employees: 3 FT, 11 PT
Passive Ownership: Allowed
Encourage Conversions: Yes
Area Develop. Agreements: Yes/Varies
Sub-Franchising Contracts: No
Expand In Territory: Yes
Space Needs: 1,400-2,000 SF; SC

SUPPORT & TRAINING PROVIDED:
Financial Assistance Provided: No
Site Selection Assistance: Yes
Lease Negotiation Assistance: Yes
Co-Operative Advertising: No
Franchisee Assoc./Member: No
Size Of Corporate Staff: 34
On-Going Support: C,D,E,F,G,H,I
Training: 2 Weeks Milwaukee, WI.

SPECIFIC EXPANSION PLANS:
US: All United States
Canada: All Canada
Overseas: All Countries

<< >>

BLUE CHIP COOKIES

157 Barnwood Dr.
Edgewood, KY 41017
Tel: (800) 888-9866 (859) 331-7600
Fax: (859) 331-7604
E-Mail: bluechip@fuse.net
Web Site: www.bluechipcookies.com
Mr. Mark D. Hannahan, President/CEO

BLUE CHIP COOKIES brings pleasure to our customers by making the world's best gourmet cookies and brownies, fresh from scratch, everyday, at every one of our retail locations. We have won numerous awards, and our wonderful cookies and brownies continue to bring joy to young and old alike!

BACKGROUND:
Established: 1983; 1st Franchised: 1986
Franchised Units: 12
Company-Owned Units 18
Total Units: 30
Dist.: US-35; CAN-0; O'seas-0
North America: 11 States
Density: 10 in OH, 10 in CA, 2 in KY
Projected New Units (12 Months): 4
Qualifications: 5, 4, 4, 3, 1, 5
Registered: N/A

FINANCIAL/TERMS:
Cash Investment: $50-100K
Total Investment: $120-200K
Minimum Net Worth: $200K
Fees: Franchise - $19.5K
Royalty - 6%; Ad. - 0%
Earnings Claim Statement: No
Term of Contract (Years): 10/10
Avg. # Of Employees: 2-3 FT, 4-8 PT
Passive Ownership: Allowed
Encourage Conversions: Yes
Area Develop. Agreements: No
Sub-Franchising Contracts: No
Expand In Territory: Yes
Space Needs: 600+ SF; SC, RM, Airport, Tourist Site

SUPPORT & TRAINING PROVIDED:
Financial Assistance Provided: No
Site Selection Assistance: Yes
Lease Negotiation Assistance: Yes
Co-Operative Advertising: No
Franchisee Assoc./Member: No
Size Of Corporate Staff: 6
On-Going Support: C,D,E,G,H,I
Training: 1-2 Weeks Cincinnati, OH.

SPECIFIC EXPANSION PLANS:
US: All United States
Canada: Would Consider
Overseas: Would Consider

<< >>

BREADSMITH

409 E. Silver Spring Dr.
Whitefish Bay, WI 53217
Tel: (414) 962-1965
Fax: (414) 962-5888
E-Mail: jock@breadsmith.com
Web Site: www.breadsmith.com
Mr. Jock Mutschler, Franchising

Award-winning, European, hearth-bread bakery, featuring fresh-from-scratch crusty breads, gourmet jams and coffee. Open kitchen concept reveals a six-ton, stone hearth oven imported from Europe used to bake the hand-crafted loaves each morning. BREADSMITH has been ranked by Bon Appetit, Best in 11 cities across the country.

BACKGROUND:
Established: 1993; 1st Franchised: 1994
Franchised Units: 40
Company-Owned Units 1
Total Units: 41
Dist.: US-41; CAN-0; O'seas-0
North America: 12 States
Density: 10 in IL, 9 in MI
Projected New Units (12 Months): 10
Qualifications: 5, 4, 2, 3, 5, 5
Registered: CA,FL,IL,IN,MI,MN,NY,OR, SD,VA,WA,WI

FINANCIAL/TERMS:
Cash Investment: $200-260K
Total Investment: $217.5-416K
Minimum Net Worth: $750K
Fees: Franchise - $30K
Royalty - 7%; Ad. - 0%
Earnings Claim Statement: Yes
Term of Contract (Years): 15/15
Avg. # Of Employees: 2 FT, 12 PT
Passive Ownership: Not Allowed
Encourage Conversions: N/A
Area Develop. Agreements: No
Sub-Franchising Contracts: No
Expand In Territory: Yes
Space Needs: 2,000 SF; FS, SF, SC

SUPPORT & TRAINING PROVIDED:
Financial Assistance Provided: Yes(I)
Site Selection Assistance: Yes
Lease Negotiation Assistance: Yes
Co-Operative Advertising: No
Franchisee Assoc./Member: Yes
Size Of Corporate Staff: 9
On-Going Support: C,D,E,F,G,I
Training: 3 Weeks Corporate Store; 2 Weeks Franchisee Store.

SPECIFIC EXPANSION PLANS:
US: All United States
Canada: All Canada
Overseas: No

BRUEGGER'S BAGELS

159 Bank St., 3rd Floor, P.O. Box 374
Burlington, VT 05401
Tel: (802) 660-4020
Fax: (802) 652-9293
E-Mail: franchising@brueggers.com
Web Site: www.brueggers.com
Ms. Joan Giard, Franchise Coordinator

Our mission is to be the dominant, first choice, neighborhood bagel bakery in all markets where we operate.

BACKGROUND: IFA MEMBER
Established: 1983; 1st Franchised: 1983
Franchised Units: 269
Company-Owned Units 0
Total Units: 269
Dist.: US-285; CAN-0; O'seas-0
North America: 16 States
Density: 35 in MN, 33 in OH, 32 in MA
Projected New Units (12 Months): 25
Qualifications: 4, 3, 5, 1, 4, 5
Registered: CA,FL,IN,MD,MI,MN,NY,RI ,VA,WA,WI

FINANCIAL/TERMS:
Cash Investment: $NR
Total Investment: $250-706K
Minimum Net Worth: $400K
Fees: Franchise - $20K
Royalty - 2-5%; Ad. - 2-4%
Earnings Claim Statement: Yes
Term of Contract (Years): 10/5
Avg. # Of Employees: NR
Passive Ownership: Discouraged
Encourage Conversions: Yes
Area Develop. Agreements: No
Sub-Franchising Contracts: No
Expand In Territory: Yes
Space Needs: 1,500-2,200 SF; SF, SC, RM

SUPPORT & TRAINING PROVIDED:
Financial Assistance Provided: No
Site Selection Assistance: Yes
Lease Negotiation Assistance: No
Co-Operative Advertising: Yes
Franchisee Assoc./Member: NR
Size Of Corporate Staff: 25
On-Going Support: a,b,C,D,E,f,G,H
Training: NR

SPECIFIC EXPANSION PLANS:
US: All United States
Canada: No
Overseas: No

<< >>

BUNS MASTER BAKERY SYSTEMS

2 E. Beaver Creek Rd., Bldg. #1
Richmond Hill, ON L4B 2N3 CANADA
Tel: (905) 764-7066
Fax: (905) 764-7634
Mr. Peter A. Mertens, General Manager

Retail and commercial bakery, with a wide variety of self-serve products made and baked fresh on-site.

BACKGROUND:
Established: 1970; 1st Franchised: 1977
Franchised Units: 106
Company-Owned Units 0
Total Units: 106
Dist.: US-1; CAN-105; O'seas-0
North America: 1 State, 9 Provinces
Density: 50 in ON, 30 in BC, 9 in SK
Projected New Units (12 Months): 10
Qualifications: 4, 4, 1, 2, , 5
Registered: AB

FINANCIAL/TERMS:
Cash Investment: $95K
Total Investment: $275K
Minimum Net Worth: $NR
Fees: Franchise - $25K
Royalty - 5%; Ad. - 1%
Earnings Claim Statement: No
Term of Contract (Years): 20
Avg. # Of Employees: 6 FT, 12 PT
Passive Ownership: Not Allowed
Encourage Conversions: Yes
Area Develop. Agreements: No
Sub-Franchising Contracts: No
Expand In Territory: Yes

Space Needs: NR SF; SC

SUPPORT & TRAINING PROVIDED:

Financial Assistance Provided: Yes(I)
Site Selection Assistance: Yes
Lease Negotiation Assistance: Yes
Co-Operative Advertising: Yes
Franchisee Assoc./Member: No
Size Of Corporate Staff: 44
On-Going Support: A,B,C,D,E,F,G,h,I
Training: 7 Days Head Office; 14 Days On-Site.

SPECIFIC EXPANSION PLANS:

US: All United States
Canada: All Canada
Overseas: No

CINDY'S CINNAMON ROLLS

P.O. Box 1480
Fallbrook, CA 92028
Tel: (800) 468-7655 (760) 723-1121
Fax: (760) 723-4143
E-Mail: cindyscin@aol.com
Mr. Thomas Harris, President

Fresh-baked cinnamon rolls and muffins. All shops in major shopping malls. Great family business. All products made in the shop and baked fresh all day.

BACKGROUND:

Established: 1985; 1st Franchised: 1986
Franchised Units: 30
Company-Owned Units 0
Total Units: 30
Dist.: US-29; CAN-0; O'seas-3
North America: 14 States
Density: 8 in NY, 3 in CA, 2 in NJ
Projected New Units (12 Months): 5
Qualifications: 3, 3, 3, 3, 3, 3
Registered: NY,CA

FINANCIAL/TERMS:

Cash Investment: $130K
Total Investment: $130K
Minimum Net Worth: $100K
Fees: Franchise - $25K
Royalty - 5%; Ad. - 0%
Earnings Claim Statement: No
Term of Contract (Years): 10/10
Avg. # Of Employees: 8 FT
Passive Ownership: Allowed
Encourage Conversions: Yes
Area Develop. Agreements: No
Sub-Franchising Contracts: No
Expand In Territory: Yes
Space Needs: 800 SF; RM

SUPPORT & TRAINING PROVIDED:

Financial Assistance Provided: No
Site Selection Assistance: Yes
Lease Negotiation Assistance: Yes
Co-Operative Advertising: No
Franchisee Assoc./Member: No
Size Of Corporate Staff: 3
On-Going Support: B,C,D,E,F,G,H,I
Training: 1 Week New York, NY; 4 Days in Store.

SPECIFIC EXPANSION PLANS:

US: All United States
Canada: All Canada
Overseas: All Countries

CINNABON

6 Concourse Pkwy., # 1700
Atlanta, GA 30328-6117
Tel: (800) 639-3826 (770) 353-3271
Fax: (770) 353-3093
E-Mail: whaas@afce.com
Web Site: www.cinnabon.com
Ms. Wanda Haas, Specialist

Since 1985, CINNABON has created a winning formula for leadership and growth in the industry. As the category leader in the U.S., CINNABON currently enjoys an 80% brand awareness. Millions throughout the world who have had the CINNABON experience will confirm that CINNABON has the perfect recipe for baking delicious, classic sweet rewards. Multi-unit development, limited exclusivity and world-class franchisor support services are key tenets to our goal of becoming the world's franchisor of choice.

BACKGROUND: IFA MEMBER

Established: 1985; 1st Franchised: 1986
Franchised Units: 309
Company-Owned Units 172
Total Units: 481
Dist.: US-385; CAN-17; O'seas-40
North America: NR
Density: NR
Projected New Units (12 Months): 135
Qualifications: 5, 5, 4, 3, 4, 5
Registered: All States

FINANCIAL/TERMS:

Cash Investment: $NR
Total Investment: $178-253K
Minimum Net Worth: $600K
Fees: Franchise - $35K
Royalty - 5%; Ad. - 1.5-3%
Earnings Claim Statement: Yes
Term of Contract (Years): 10/5/5
Avg. # Of Employees: NR
Passive Ownership: Not Allowed
Encourage Conversions: N/A
Area Develop. Agreements: Yes
Sub-Franchising Contracts: No
Expand In Territory: Yes
Space Needs: 850 SF; RM

SUPPORT & TRAINING PROVIDED:

Financial Assistance Provided: Yes(I)
Site Selection Assistance: Yes
Lease Negotiation Assistance: Yes
Co-Operative Advertising: No
Franchisee Assoc./Member: Yes/Yes
Size Of Corporate Staff: 50
On-Going Support: A,B,C,D,E,f,G,H,I
Training: 3 Weeks Atlanta, GA.

SPECIFIC EXPANSION PLANS:

US: LA, OK, MA, TN, FL, OH
Canada: All Canada
Overseas:
Taiwan, South America, Far East

CINNZEO

6910 Farrell Rd. E., SE
Calgary, AB T2H 0T1 CANADA
Tel: (877) 246-6036 (403) 255-4556
Fax: (403) 259-5124
E-Mail: chucka@cinnzeo.com
Web Site: www.cinnzeo.com
Mr. Chuck Arcand, Dir. Franchise Sales

CINNZEO is home of the Best Tasting Cinnamon Rolls on Earth. An open concept bakery featuring upfront preparation in public view with the aroma of sweet cinnamon. This franchise is commanding worldwide appeal. A modern-looking CINNZEO features modern artwork, design and architecture. Franchise support is our strength. CINNZEO is currently looking for master franchisee opportunities worldwide!

BACKGROUND:

Established: 1986; 1st Franchised: 1997
Franchised Units: 20
Company-Owned Units 7
Total Units: 27
Dist.: US-0; CAN-21; O'seas-3
North America: 3 Provinces
Density: 12 in AB, 7 in BC
Projected New Units (12 Months): 50
Qualifications: 4, 3, 1, 3, 3, 5
Registered: CA,AB

FINANCIAL/TERMS:

Cash Investment: $17K
Total Investment: $11.6-16.7K
Minimum Net Worth: $NR
Fees: Franchise - $17K

Royalty - 5%; Ad. - 2%
Earnings Claim Statement: No
Term of Contract (Years): 10/5
Avg. # Of Employees: 5 FT, 14 PT
Passive Ownership: Discouraged
Encourage Conversions: Yes
Area Develop. Agreements: Yes/10
Sub-Franchising Contracts: No
Expand In Territory: Yes
Space Needs: 350+ SF; FS, SF, SC, RM

SUPPORT & TRAINING PROVIDED:
Financial Assistance Provided: No
Site Selection Assistance: Yes
Lease Negotiation Assistance: Yes
Co-Operative Advertising: Yes
Franchisee Assoc./Member: Yes/Yes
Size Of Corporate Staff: 12
On-Going Support: A,B,C,D,E,F,G,h,I
Training: 21 Days at the Calgary Corporate Training Facility; 7 Days at Your Bakery during Opening.

SPECIFIC EXPANSION PLANS:
US: All United States
Canada: ON
Overseas: Australia, New Zealand, Europe, Middle East, Japan, Korea, Africa

<< >>

COFFEE TIME DONUTS

477 Ellesmere Rd.
Scarborough, ON M1R 4E5 CANADA
Tel: (416) 288-8515
Fax: (416) 288-8895
Ms. Helen Keletzis, Director of Marketing

A quick-service restaurant-type donut chain, with great-tasting coffee, muffins, donuts, salads and sandwiches. Fresh, quality products are what set us apart from the competition.

BACKGROUND:
Established: 1982; 1st Franchised: 1987
Franchised Units: 300
Company-Owned Units 11
Total Units: 311
Dist.: US-0; CAN-324; O'seas-0
North America: 3 Provinces
Density: 319 in ON, 3 in MB, 1 in AB
Projected New Units (12 Months): 65
Qualifications: 3, 3, 2, 2, 3, 5
Registered: NR

FINANCIAL/TERMS:
Cash Investment: $NR
Total Investment: $160-250K
Minimum Net Worth: $150K
Fees: Franchise - $NR
Royalty - 4.5%; Ad. - 2%
Earnings Claim Statement: No
Term of Contract (Years): NR
Avg. # Of Employees: 6 FT, 4 PT
Passive Ownership: Not Allowed
Encourage Conversions: Yes
Area Develop. Agreements: NR
Sub-Franchising Contracts: No
Expand In Territory: Yes
Space Needs: NR SF; FS, SF, RM

SUPPORT & TRAINING PROVIDED:
Financial Assistance Provided: NR
Site Selection Assistance: NR
Lease Negotiation Assistance: N/A
Co-Operative Advertising: NR
Franchisee Assoc./Member: No
Size Of Corporate Staff: 50
On-Going Support: b,C,D,E,F,G,H
Training: 3-6 Weeks Scarborough, ON.

SPECIFIC EXPANSION PLANS:
US: All United States
Canada: All Canada
Overseas: All Countries

<< >>

COOKIE BOUQUET / COOKIES BY DESIGN

1865 Summit Ave., # 605
Plano, TX 75074-8147
Tel: (800) 945-2665 (972) 398-9536
Fax: (972) 398-9542
E-Mail: frandevopment@mgwmail.com
Web Site: www.cookiebydesign.com or www.cookiesbydesign.com
Mr. David Patterson, VP Fran. Dev.

Unique retail opportunity! Gift bakery, specializing in hand-decorated cookie arrangements and gourmet cookies, decorated for special events, holidays, centerpieces, etc. Clientele include both individual and corporate customers. A wonderfully delicious alternative to flowers or balloons.

BACKGROUND: IFA MEMBER
Established: 1983; 1st Franchised: 1987
Franchised Units: 218
Company-Owned Units 1
Total Units: 219
Dist.: US-228; CAN-0; O'seas-0
North America: 43 States
Density: 32 in TX, 21 in FL, 20 in CA
Projected New Units (12 Months): 30
Qualifications: 3, 5, 4, 4, 4, 5
Registered: CA,FL,HI,IL,IN,MD,MI,NY, OR,RI,SD,VA,WA,WI

FINANCIAL/TERMS:
Cash Investment: $80-145K
Total Investment: $80-145K
Minimum Net Worth: $NR
Fees: Franchise - $22.5K
Royalty - 6%; Ad. - 1%
Earnings Claim Statement: No
Term of Contract (Years): 5/5
Avg. # Of Employees: 3 FT, 2 PT
Passive Ownership: Discouraged
Encourage Conversions: No
Area Develop. Agreements: Yes
Sub-Franchising Contracts: No
Expand In Territory: Yes
Space Needs: 1,200-1,500 SF; SC

SUPPORT & TRAINING PROVIDED:
Financial Assistance Provided: No
Site Selection Assistance: Yes
Lease Negotiation Assistance: Yes
Co-Operative Advertising: Yes
Franchisee Assoc./Member: No
Size Of Corporate Staff: 19
On-Going Support: C,D,E,G,h,I
Training: 2 Weeks Dallas, TX.

SPECIFIC EXPANSION PLANS:
US: All United States
Canada: No
Overseas: No

<< >>

COOKIES IN BLOOM

5437 N. MacArthur Blvd.
Irving, TX 75038
Tel: (800) 222-3104 (972) 518-1749
Fax: (972) 580-1831
E-Mail: re-pinac@verizon.net
Web Site: www.cookiesinbloom.com
Mr. Robert E. Pinac, Vice President

Operation of retail cookie gift baking shops that produce and sell decorated cookies, gourmet cookies and whimsical cookie arrangements packaged as floral bouquets and related products for retail sale to the public.

BACKGROUND:
Established: 1988; 1st Franchised: 1992
Franchised Units: 18
Company-Owned Units 0
Total Units: 18

Dist.: US-14; CAN-0; O'seas-0
North America: 14 States
Density: 6 in TX, 2 in LA
Projected New Units (12 Months): 5
Qualifications: 4, 5, 1, 2, 3, 4
Registered: CA,FL,IL,MD,MI,NY,OR,VA,WA,WI

FINANCIAL/TERMS:
Cash Investment: $53-107K
Total Investment: $53-107K
Minimum Net Worth: $100K
Fees: Franchise - $17.5K
Royalty - 5%; Ad. - 2%
Earnings Claim Statement: No
Term of Contract (Years): 5/5
Avg. # Of Employees: 3 FT, 2 PT
Passive Ownership: Discouraged
Encourage Conversions: N/A
Area Develop. Agreements: Yes/5
Sub-Franchising Contracts: No
Expand In Territory: Yes
Space Needs: 1,200-1,500 SF; SC

SUPPORT & TRAINING PROVIDED:
Financial Assistance Provided: No
Site Selection Assistance: Yes
Lease Negotiation Assistance: Yes
Co-Operative Advertising: Yes
Franchisee Assoc./Member: No
Size Of Corporate Staff: 2
On-Going Support: b,C,D,E,G,H,I
Training: 2 Weeks in Irving, TX.

SPECIFIC EXPANSION PLANS:
US: All United States
Canada: No
Overseas: No

<< >>

DUNKIN' DONUTS
14 Pacella Park Dr., P.O. Box 317
Randolph, MA 02368
Tel: (800) 777-9983 (781) 961-4020
Fax: (781) 961-4207
Web Site: www.dunkin-baskin-togos.com
Mr. Anthony Padulo, VP Business Dev.

DUNKIN' DONUTS is the world's largest coffee and doughnut chain. We offer a full array of quick-service menu items, including muffins, bagels and donuts. In some markets DUNKIN' DONUTS, together with TOGO's and/or BASKIN-ROBBINS, offers multiple brand combinations of the three brands. TOGO's, BASKIN-ROBBINS, and DUNKIN' DONUTS are all subsidiaries of Allied Domecq PLC.

BACKGROUND: IFA MEMBER
Established: 1950; 1st Franchised: 1955
Franchised Units: 5,000
Company-Owned Units 0
Total Units: 5,000
Dist.: US-3390; CAN-500; O'seas-1110
North America: 39 States
Density: 490 in MA, 359 in NY, 237 IL
Projected New Units (12 Months): 350
Qualifications: 5, 4, 2, 2, 5, 4
Registered: CA,FL,IL,IN,MD,MI,MN,NY,OR,RI,VA,WA,WI,DC

FINANCIAL/TERMS:
Cash Investment: $200K
Total Investment: $255.7-1139.7K
Minimum Net Worth: $400K/unit
Fees: Franchise - $50K
Royalty - 5.9%; Ad. - 5%
Earnings Claim Statement: Yes
Term of Contract (Years): 20
Avg. # Of Employees: NR
Passive Ownership: Allowed
Encourage Conversions: Yes
Area Develop. Agreements: Yes/3-5
Sub-Franchising Contracts: No
Expand In Territory: Yes
Space Needs: NR SF; FS, SF, SC, RM

SUPPORT & TRAINING PROVIDED:
Financial Assistance Provided: Yes(I)
Site Selection Assistance: N/A
Lease Negotiation Assistance: Yes
Co-Operative Advertising: Yes
Franchisee Assoc./Member: Yes/No
Size Of Corporate Staff: NR
On-Going Support: B,C,E,G,H,I
Training: 51 Days in Randolph, MA; 3.5 Days in another Location.

SPECIFIC EXPANSION PLANS:
US: All Regions
Canada: PQ, ON
Overseas: All Countries

<< >>

GREAT AMERICAN BAGEL, THE
519 N. Cass Ave., # 1W
Westmont, IL 60559
Tel: (888) BAGEL-ME (630) 963-3393
Fax: (630) 963-7799
Ms. Linda Rog, Dir. Franchising

Bagel bakery and restaurant, specializing in freshly-made bagels - made daily from scratch on the store premises. Stores feature monthly specials along with 28 varieties of bagels daily. In addition, each store also prepares it's own fresh cream cheeses!

BACKGROUND:
Established: 1987; 1st Franchised: 1994
Franchised Units: 201
Company-Owned Units 14
Total Units: 215
Dist.: US-40; CAN-0; O'seas-0
North America: 10 States
Density: 25 in IL, 3 in WA, 2 in IN
Projected New Units (12 Months): 20
Qualifications: 5, 3, 2, 3, 4, 5
Registered: FL,IL,IN,MI,MN,ND,WA,WI

FINANCIAL/TERMS:
Cash Investment: $60-80K
Total Investment: $230-280K
Minimum Net Worth: $250K
Fees: Franchise - $20K
Royalty - 4%; Ad. - 2%
Earnings Claim Statement: No
Term of Contract (Years): 20/5
Avg. # Of Employees: 3 FT, 9 PT
Passive Ownership: Not Allowed
Encourage Conversions: N/A
Area Develop. Agreements: No
Sub-Franchising Contracts: No
Expand In Territory: Yes
Space Needs: 2,000 SF; FS, SF, SC, RM

SUPPORT & TRAINING PROVIDED:
Financial Assistance Provided: No
Site Selection Assistance: Yes
Lease Negotiation Assistance: Yes
Co-Operative Advertising: N/A
Franchisee Assoc./Member: Yes
Size Of Corporate Staff: NR
On-Going Support: B,C,D,E,g,h
Training: 4 Weeks Western Springs, IL.

SPECIFIC EXPANSION PLANS:
US: All United States
Canada: No
Overseas: No

<< >>

GREAT AMERICAN COOKIES
2855 E. Cottonwood Pkwy., # 400
Salt Lake City, UT 84121
Tel: (800) 348-6311 (801) 736-5600
Fax: (801) 736-5936
E-Mail: squireji@greatamcookie.com
Web Site: www.greatamericancookies.com
Mr. Scott Moffitt, SVP Franchise Development

'Share the Fun of Cookies.' Established cookie concept with a great old family recipe, attractive retail price point, unique cookie cake program, available in combination store formats for traditional and non-traditional venues.

BACKGROUND: IFA MEMBER
Established: 1977; 1st Franchised: 1977
Franchised Units: 280
Company-Owned Units 100
Total Units: 380
Dist.: US-380; CAN-0; O'seas-0
North America: 39 States
Density: 47 in TX, 24 in GA, 24 in FL
Projected New Units (12 Months): 23
Qualifications: 5, 3, 1, 1, 3, 5
Registered: All States

FINANCIAL/TERMS:
Cash Investment: $122-493K
Total Investment: $121-631K
Minimum Net Worth: $75-150K
Fees: Franchise - $30K
Royalty - 7%; Ad. - N/A
Earnings Claim Statement: No
Term of Contract (Years): NR
Avg. # Of Employees: Varies
Passive Ownership: Allowed
Encourage Conversions: Yes
Area Develop. Agreements: No
Sub-Franchising Contracts: No
Expand In Territory: Yes
Space Needs: 625 SF; RM

SUPPORT & TRAINING PROVIDED:
Financial Assistance Provided: No
Site Selection Assistance: Yes
Lease Negotiation Assistance: Yes
Co-Operative Advertising: N/A
Franchisee Assoc./Member: Yes
Size Of Corporate Staff: 65
On-Going Support: B,C,D,E,G,H,I
Training: 6 Days Atlanta, GA.

SPECIFIC EXPANSION PLANS:
US: All United States
Canada: No
Overseas: No

<< >>

GREAT CANADIAN BAGEL, THE
270 Central Pkwy. W., # 301
Mississauga, ON L5C 4P4 CANADA
Tel: (905) 803-7796
Fax: (905) 566-1402
E-Mail: greatcanadianbagel.com
Web Site: www.greatcanadianbagel.com
Mr. Glen Tucker, Dir. Franchising

Canada's largest chain devoted to bagels has elevated the bagel to a new culinary experience. The chain offers a healthy way to enjoy a sandwich, snack or meal, while providing an alternative to higher fat, fast-food establishments. The bagel has become the ideal convenience food of the 90's - low in fat, high in taste, nutritious and now, convenient, thanks to the expansion of THE GREAT CANADIAN BAGEL.

BACKGROUND:
Established: 1993; 1st Franchised: 1994
Franchised Units: 151
Company-Owned Units 7
Total Units: 158
Dist.: US-0; CAN-152; O'seas-4
North America: 9 Provinces
Density: 90 in ON, 24 in BC, 13 Marit
Projected New Units (12 Months): 20
Qualifications: 5, 4, 3, 3, 2, 5
Registered: AB

FINANCIAL/TERMS:
Cash Investment: $100K
Total Investment: $260-300K
Minimum Net Worth: $10K
Fees: Franchise - $30K
Royalty - 6%; Ad. - 1.5%
Earnings Claim Statement: Yes
Term of Contract (Years): 10/5
Avg. # Of Employees: 7 FT, 5 PT
Passive Ownership: Discouraged
Encourage Conversions: No
Area Develop. Agreements: No
Sub-Franchising Contracts: Yes
Expand In Territory: Yes
Space Needs: 2,000 SF; N/A

SUPPORT & TRAINING PROVIDED:
Financial Assistance Provided: Yes
Site Selection Assistance: Yes
Lease Negotiation Assistance: N/A
Co-Operative Advertising: Yes
Franchisee Assoc./Member: Yes/Yes
Size Of Corporate Staff: NR
On-Going Support: A,B,C,D,E,F,G,h
Training: 4-6 Weeks Toronto, ON.

SPECIFIC EXPANSION PLANS:
US: See The Great American Bagel
Canada: All Canada
Overseas: All Countries

<< >>

GREAT HARVEST BREAD CO.
28 S. Montana St.
Dillon, MT 59725-2434
Tel: (800) 442-0424 (406) 683-6842
Fax: (406) 683-5537
E-Mail: inquiry@greatharvest.com
Web Site: www.greatharvest.com
Ms. Lisa WagnerMr. Andy Bills, Executive Vice President

GREAT HARVEST BREAD CO. stores are neighborhood, retail bread bakeries, specializing in the best tasting, made-from-scratch, whole wheat breads you ever had. These unique stores also serve scratch-made cookies, scones, muffins and specialty breads.

BACKGROUND: IFA MEMBER
Established: 1976; 1st Franchised: 1978
Franchised Units: 167
Company-Owned Units 1
Total Units: 168
Dist.: US-168; CAN-0; O'seas-0
North America: 35 States
Density: 16 in MI, 11 in UT, 10 in IL
Projected New Units (12 Months): 24
Qualifications: 4, 4, 3, 4, 5, 3
Registered: All States

FINANCIAL/TERMS:
Cash Investment: $50-70K
Total Investment: $108-249K
Minimum Net Worth: $200K
Fees: Franchise - $29K
Royalty - 5-7%; Ad. - 0%
Earnings Claim Statement: Yes
Term of Contract (Years): 10/10
Avg. # Of Employees: 3 FT, 6 PT
Passive Ownership: Discouraged
Encourage Conversions: N/A
Area Develop. Agreements: Yes/2
Sub-Franchising Contracts: No
Expand In Territory: Yes
Space Needs: 1,500-2,200 SF; FS, SC

SUPPORT & TRAINING PROVIDED:
Financial Assistance Provided: Yes(I)
Site Selection Assistance: Yes
Lease Negotiation Assistance: Yes
Co-Operative Advertising: No
Franchisee Assoc./Member: Yes/No
Size Of Corporate Staff: 29
On-Going Support: B,C,D,E,G,H,I
Training: 1 Wk Dillon, MT; 1 Wk ea. 2 Host Trainings; 3-5 Days Store Opening; 5-10 Days 3 Trainers.

SPECIFIC EXPANSION PLANS:
US: All United States
Canada: Alberta
Overseas: No

<< >>

HOUSE OF BREAD

858 Higuera St.
San Luis Obispo, CA 93401
Tel: (800) 545-5146 (805) 542-0257
Fax: (805) 542-0255
E-Mail: houseofbread@mail.com
Web Site: www.houseofbread.com
Ms. Sheila McCann, Chief Executive Officer

Healthy, premium bread bakery, with over 20 varieties of delicious breads - from traditional honey whole wheat to irresistible sourdough pesto artichoke or the decadent triple chocolate bread. HOUSE OF BREAD's unique recipes use no dairy, refined sugar or fat, yet taste incredible.

BACKGROUND:
Established: 1996; 1st Franchised: 1998
Franchised Units: 4
Company-Owned Units 3
Total Units: 7
Dist.: US-9; CAN-0; O'seas-0
North America: 2 States
Density: 7 in CA
Projected New Units (12 Months): 6
Qualifications: 3, 3, 1, 3, 3, 5
Registered: CA

FINANCIAL/TERMS:
Cash Investment: $24-65K
Total Investment: $75-204K
Minimum Net Worth: $50K
Fees: Franchise - $24K
Royalty - 6%; Ad. - 2%
Earnings Claim Statement: No
Term of Contract (Years): 10/10
Avg. # Of Employees: 2 FT, 8 PT
Passive Ownership: Discouraged
Encourage Conversions: NR
Area Develop. Agreements: Yes
Sub-Franchising Contracts: NR
Expand In Territory: Yes
Space Needs: 1,500 SF; SC, RM

SUPPORT & TRAINING PROVIDED:
Financial Assistance Provided: Yes(B)
Site Selection Assistance: Yes
Lease Negotiation Assistance: Yes
Co-Operative Advertising: Yes
Franchisee Assoc./Member: No
Size Of Corporate Staff: 2
On-Going Support: C,D,E,F,G,H,I
Training: Minimum 9 Days San Luis Obispo, CA; Minimum 7 Days Franchisee Location.

SPECIFIC EXPANSION PLANS:
US: All United States
Canada: All Canada
Overseas: All Countries

<< >>

LAMAR'S DONUTS

245 S. 84th St., # 210
Lincoln, NE 68510-2600
Tel: (800) 533-7489 (402) 484-5900
Fax: (402) 484-7911
E-Mail: franinfo@lamars.com
Web Site: www.lamars.com
Mr. Joseph J. Field, President/CEO

LAMAR'S DONUTS is a rapidly growing chain of retail donut shops, founded in Kansas City, specializing in 53 varieties of handmade donuts and specialties since 1933, served in an atmosphere rich in hospitality and authenticity. A K.C. institution and Chamber of Commerce tourist attraction, LAMAR's has received acclaim nationwide, creating what critics call "the perfect donut."

BACKGROUND: IFA MEMBER
Established: 1933; 1st Franchised: 1993
Franchised Units: 22
Company-Owned Units 5
Total Units: 27
Dist.: US-27; CAN-0; O'seas-0
North America: 8 States
Density: 11 in MO, 6 in KS, 2 in VA
Projected New Units (12 Months): 10-20
Qualifications: 4, 5, 3, 2, 5, 5
Registered: FL,VA

FINANCIAL/TERMS:
Cash Investment: $Varies
Total Investment: $200-240K
Minimum Net Worth: $Varies
Fees: Franchise - $26.5K
Royalty - 5%; Ad. - 2%
Earnings Claim Statement: No
Term of Contract (Years): 10/10
Avg. # Of Employees: 4-6 FT, 5-10 PT
Passive Ownership: Allowed
Encourage Conversions: Yes
Area Develop. Agreements: Yes/Negot.
Sub-Franchising Contracts: Yes
Expand In Territory: Yes
Space Needs: 2,000 SF; SF, SC

SUPPORT & TRAINING PROVIDED:
Financial Assistance Provided: Yes(I)
Site Selection Assistance: Yes
Lease Negotiation Assistance: Yes
Co-Operative Advertising: Yes
Franchisee Assoc./Member: No
Size Of Corporate Staff: 10
On-Going Support: a,b,C,D,E,F,G,H,I
Training: 2-4 Weeks Training Store in Kansas City; 3-5 On-Site in Franchise Store.

SPECIFIC EXPANSION PLANS:
US: All U.S., Midwest, Southeast
Canada: No
Overseas: No

<< >>

MANHATTAN BAGEL COMPANY

246 Industrial Way W.
Eatontown, NJ 07724-2206
Tel: (800) 872-2243 (732) 544-0155
Fax: (732) 544-1315
E-Mail: mphillips@bgls.com
Web Site: www.manhattanbagel.com
Mr. Mike Phillips, Vice President Franchising

MANHATTAN BAGEL CO. offers upscale, efficient, bagel eateries, offering authentic New York bagels in 21 varieties, as well as gourmet spreads and deli items, plus full breakfast fare. Stores are configured 100% turn-key, including site selection and negotiation. We have comprehensive training with a detailed operations manual and continuing assistance in marketing, merchandising and food preparation. No baking experience is required.

BACKGROUND: IFA MEMBER
Established: 1987; 1st Franchised: 1988
Franchised Units: 300
Company-Owned Units 11
Total Units: 311
Dist.: US-311; CAN-0; O'seas-0
North America: 21 States
Density: 33 in NJ, 18 in PA, 17 in CA
Projected New Units (12 Months): 35
Qualifications: 3, 3, 1, 1, 3, 5
Registered: All States

FINANCIAL/TERMS:
Cash Investment: $80-100K
Total Investment: $150-337K
Minimum Net Worth: $150K
Fees: Franchise - $20K
Royalty - 5%; Ad. - 2.5-4%
Earnings Claim Statement: No
Term of Contract (Years): 10/10
Avg. # Of Employees: 3 FT, 9 PT
Passive Ownership: Discouraged

Encourage Conversions: Yes
Area Develop. Agreements: Yes
Sub-Franchising Contracts: Yes
Expand In Territory: Yes
Space Needs: 1,200-1,600 SF; FS, SC

SUPPORT & TRAINING PROVIDED:
Financial Assistance Provided: No
Site Selection Assistance: Yes
Lease Negotiation Assistance: Yes
Co-Operative Advertising: Yes
Franchisee Assoc./Member: Yes
Size Of Corporate Staff: 313
On-Going Support: B,C,D,E,F,G,h
Training: 2 Weeks in Corporate Office; 1 Week in Store.

SPECIFIC EXPANSION PLANS:
US: All United States
Canada: No
Overseas: Middle East, Iceland

<< >>

MMMARVELLOUS MMMUFFINS (CANADA)

3300 Bloor St. W., # 2900
Etobicoke, ON M8X 2X3 CANADA
Tel: (416) 236-0055
Fax: (416) 236-0054
E-Mail: lboyd@richmont.com
Web Site: www.mmmuffins.com
Ms. Gale Galea, President

Fresh, high-quality specialty baked goods including over 100 varieties of muffins as well as scones, cinnamon swirls, cookies and streusel cakes. In addition, we offer a selection of gourmet coffee, teas, and fruit juices.

BACKGROUND: IFA MEMBER
Established: 1979; 1st Franchised: 1980
Franchised Units: 105
Company-Owned Units 5
Total Units: 110
Dist.: US-0; CAN-116; O'seas-6
North America: 8 Provinces
Density: 43 in ON, 26 in PQ, 13 in BC
Projected New Units (12 Months): 10
Qualifications: 5, 4, 3, 3, 4, 5
Registered: AB

FINANCIAL/TERMS:
Cash Investment: $40-60K+
Total Investment: $160K
Minimum Net Worth: $200K
Fees: Franchise - $25K
Royalty - 7%; Ad. - 1%
Earnings Claim Statement: No
Term of Contract (Years): 10/10
Avg. # Of Employees: 2-3 FT, 4-7 PT
Passive Ownership: Not Allowed
Encourage Conversions: Yes
Area Develop. Agreements: Yes (I'ntl.)
Sub-Franchising Contracts: Yes
Expand In Territory: Yes
Space Needs: 300 SF; SF, SC, RM

SUPPORT & TRAINING PROVIDED:
Financial Assistance Provided: Yes(I)
Site Selection Assistance: Yes
Lease Negotiation Assistance: Yes
Co-Operative Advertising: Yes
Franchisee Assoc./Member: No
Size Of Corporate Staff: 35
On-Going Support: A,B,C,D,E,F,G,h
Training: 4 Weeks Toronto, ON.

SPECIFIC EXPANSION PLANS:
US: N/A
Canada: All Canada
Overseas: Asia, Eastern Europe, Middle East, South America

<< >>

Top 50

MRS. FIELDS COOKIES

2855 E. Cottonwood Pkwy., # 400
Salt Lake City, UT 84121-7037
Tel: (800) 348-6311 (801) 736-5730
Fax: (801) 736-5936
E-Mail: frandev@mrsfields.com
Web Site: www.mrsfields.com
Mr. Scott Moffitt, SVP Franchise Development

Premier retail cookie business with 'uncompromising quality,' 94% brand recognition, easy to operate, flexible designs and combination store options that operate in traditional and non-traditional venues.

BACKGROUND: IFA MEMBER
Established: 1977; 1st Franchised: 1990
Franchised Units: 457
Company-Owned Units 150
Total Units: 607
Dist.: US-528; CAN-5; O'seas-74
North America: 35 States, 1 Province
Density: 86 in CA, 27 in IL, 19 in NY
Projected New Units (12 Months): 14
Qualifications: 4, 4, 2, 2, 2, 5
Registered: All States

FINANCIAL/TERMS:
Cash Investment: $10-73.5K
Total Investment: $180-247K
Minimum Net Worth: $75-150K
Fees: Franchise - $30K
Royalty - 6%; Ad. - 1%
Earnings Claim Statement: No
Term of Contract (Years): 7/7
Avg. # Of Employees: 3 FT, 4 PT
Passive Ownership: Not Allowed
Encourage Conversions: Yes
Area Develop. Agreements: Yes
Sub-Franchising Contracts: No
Expand In Territory: Yes
Space Needs: 650-800 SF; RM, SC, SF, Stadium

SUPPORT & TRAINING PROVIDED:
Financial Assistance Provided: Yes(I)
Site Selection Assistance: Yes
Lease Negotiation Assistance: Yes
Co-Operative Advertising: No
Franchisee Assoc./Member: Yes/Yes
Size Of Corporate Staff: 60
On-Going Support: A,B,C,D,E,F,G,H,I
Training: 10 Days Park City, UT; 5-10 Days Field Training.

SPECIFIC EXPANSION PLANS:
US: All United States
Canada: All Canada
Overseas: All Countries

<< >>

MRS. POWELL'S BAKERY EATERY

3380 S. Service Rd.
Burlington, ON L7N 3J5 CANADA
Tel: (905) 681-8448
Fax: (905) 637-7745
E-Mail: franchisedept@aftonfood.com
Web Site: www.aftonfood.com
Mr. Andrew Diveky, Dir. Franchising

Production and baking of fresh cinnamon rolls, custom sandwiches, European-style sandwiches, soup, desserts and assorted beverages.

BACKGROUND:
Established: 1984; 1st Franchised: 1986
Franchised Units: 26
Company-Owned Units 1
Total Units: 27
Dist.: US-23; CAN-0; O'seas-2
North America: 14 States
Density: 6 in ID, 3 in WA, 3 in CA
Projected New Units (12 Months): 8
Qualifications: 3, 4, 2, 3, 3, 4
Registered: IN,WA,AB

FINANCIAL/TERMS:

Cash Investment:	$50K
Total Investment:	$125-160K
Minimum Net Worth:	$100K
Fees: Franchise -	$25K
Royalty - 5%;	Ad. - 3%
Earnings Claim Statement:	No
Term of Contract (Years):	10/10
Avg. # Of Employees:	2 FT, 4 PT
Passive Ownership:	Discouraged
Encourage Conversions:	Yes
Area Develop. Agreements:	Yes/20
Sub-Franchising Contracts:	Yes
Expand In Territory:	Yes

Space Needs: 500-2,000 SF; SF, SC, RM

SUPPORT & TRAINING PROVIDED:

Financial Assistance Provided:	No
Site Selection Assistance:	Yes
Lease Negotiation Assistance:	Yes
Co-Operative Advertising:	No
Franchisee Assoc./Member:	No
Size Of Corporate Staff:	10
On-Going Support:	C,D,E,F,G,h

Training: 1 Week Head Office; 1 Week Franchised Store; 1 Week Own Store.

SPECIFIC EXPANSION PLANS:

US:	All United States
Canada:	All Canada
Overseas:	Europe, Far East

<< >>

MUFFIN BREAK

3300 Bloor St., W., # 2900
Etobicoke, ON M8X 2X3 CANADA
Tel: (416) 236-0055
Fax: (416) 236-0054
Web Site: www.muffinbreak.com
Mr. Tim Grech, Franchise Administration

Muffins and pastries baked on premises complement our gourmet coffees, teas and refreshing fruit juices. Eat-in or take-out.

BACKGROUND:

Established: 1980; 1st Franchised: 1981

Franchised Units:	30
Company-Owned Units	0
Total Units:	30
Dist.:	US-0; CAN-30; O'seas-0
North America:	4 Provinces
Density:	25 in BC, 2 in AB, 2 in ON
Projected New Units (12 Months):	0
Qualifications:	5, 3, 2, 3, 4, 5

Registered: AB

FINANCIAL/TERMS:

Cash Investment:	$60-80K
Total Investment:	$160-200K
Minimum Net Worth:	$80K
Fees: Franchise -	$25K
Royalty - 6%;	Ad. - 2%
Earnings Claim Statement:	Yes
Term of Contract (Years):	10/10
Avg. # Of Employees:	4 FT, 5-7 PT
Passive Ownership:	Not Allowed
Encourage Conversions:	No
Area Develop. Agreements:	No
Sub-Franchising Contracts:	Yes
Expand In Territory:	No

Space Needs: 1,500 SF; FS, SF, SC, RM

SUPPORT & TRAINING PROVIDED:

Financial Assistance Provided:	Yes(I)
Site Selection Assistance:	Yes
Lease Negotiation Assistance:	Yes
Co-Operative Advertising:	Yes
Franchisee Assoc./Member:	Yes/Yes
Size Of Corporate Staff:	30
On-Going Support:	A,B,C,D,E,G

Training: 10-14 Days Vancouver, BC.

SPECIFIC EXPANSION PLANS:

US:	No
Canada:	All Canada
Overseas:	No

<< >>

MY FAVORITE MUFFIN

8501 W. Higgins Rd., # 320
Chicago, IL 60631
Tel: (800) 251-6101 (773) 380-6100
Fax: (773) 380-6183
E-Mail: hmarks@babholdings.com
Web Site: www.babholdings.com
Ms. Ruth Stern, Mgr. Administration

As a MY FAVORITE MUFFIN franchisee, you get to create and sell over 300 varieties of our special muffins in both regular and fat-free varieties. Where applicable, you can add BIG APPLE BAGELS and BREWSTER'S COFFEE to complement your wonderful muffins.

BACKGROUND:

Established: 1987; 1st Franchised: 1988

Franchised Units:	63
Company-Owned Units	8
Total Units:	71
Dist.:	US-71; CAN-0; O'seas-0
North America:	19 States
Density:	18 in NJ, 10 in PA, 8 in FL
Projected New Units (12 Months):	15
Qualifications:	3, 3, 5, 2, 2, 5

Registered: All States

FINANCIAL/TERMS:

Cash Investment:	$NR
Total Investment:	$234-382.3K
Minimum Net Worth:	$50K Min.
Fees: Franchise -	$25K
Royalty - 5%;	Ad. - 2%
Earnings Claim Statement:	No
Term of Contract (Years):	10/10
Avg. # Of Employees:	3 FT, 15 PT
Passive Ownership:	Discouraged
Encourage Conversions:	N/A
Area Develop. Agreements:	Yes
Sub-Franchising Contracts:	No
Expand In Territory:	Yes

Space Needs: 1,800-2,200 SF; FS, SC, RM

SUPPORT & TRAINING PROVIDED:

Financial Assistance Provided:	Yes(I)
Site Selection Assistance:	Yes
Lease Negotiation Assistance:	Yes
Co-Operative Advertising:	No
Franchisee Assoc./Member:	NR
Size Of Corporate Staff:	34
On-Going Support:	B,C,D,E,F,G,H,I

Training: 2 Weeks Milwaukee, WI; 5 Days Store Location Prior to Opening.

SPECIFIC EXPANSION PLANS:

US:	All United States
Canada:	All Canada
Overseas:	All Countries

<< >>

Top 50

PANERA BREAD COMPANY

6710 Clayton Rd.
Richmond Heights, MO 63117
Tel: (800) 301-5566 (314) 633-7100
Fax: (314) 633-7200
E-Mail: jane.friedrick@panerabread.com
Web Site: www.panerabread.com
Mr. P. J. Evans, VP Franchise Development

Founded in Saint Louis in 1987, SAINT LOUIS BREAD has expanded into new markets over the past few years, with strong consumer acceptance for its unique concept. Each SAINT LOUIS BREAD bakery-cafe features a comfortable neighborhood setting where residents can relax and enjoy a wide range of fresh-baked sourdough breads, along with other fresh-baked goods, bagels and hearty made-to-order sandwiches, salads and soups.

BACKGROUND:

Established: 1987; 1st Franchised: 1993

Franchised Units:	212

Company-Owned Units 100
Total Units: 312
Dist.: US-104; CAN-0; O'seas-0
North America: 14 States
Density: 36 in MO, 25 in IL, 8 in GA
Projected New Units (12 Months): 108
Qualifications: 5, 5, 5, 3, 3, 4
Registered: All States

FINANCIAL/TERMS:

Cash Investment: $135-165K
Total Investment: $550-650K
Minimum Net Worth: $3MM
Fees: Franchise - $35K
Royalty - 5%; Ad. - Up to 5%
Earnings Claim Statement: Yes
Term of Contract (Years): 20/Agrmt.
Avg. # Of Employees: 17 FT, 17 PT
Passive Ownership: Not Allowed
Encourage Conversions: No
Area Develop. Agreements: Yes/3-13
Sub-Franchising Contracts: No
Expand In Territory: No
Space Needs: 3,500 SF; FS, SF, SC, RM

SUPPORT & TRAINING PROVIDED:

Financial Assistance Provided: No
Site Selection Assistance: Yes
Lease Negotiation Assistance: No
Co-Operative Advertising: Yes
Franchisee Assoc./Member: No
Size Of Corporate Staff: 54
On-Going Support: B,C,D,E,F,H,I
Training: 10 Weeks St. Louis, MO.

SPECIFIC EXPANSION PLANS:

US: All United States
Canada: No
Overseas: No

<< >>

PARADISE BAKERY & CAFE

5150 Fair Oaks Blvd., # 101-185
Carmichael, CA 95608-5758
Tel: (800) 951-9582 (916) 335-5166
Fax: (916) 568-1240
Mr. Karl Thompson, VP Franchise Development

Over 20 years of bakery and cafe experience, offering our signature fresh-baked goods, made from scratch and baked right on the premises all day long. Made-to-order sandwiches, soups, salads and gourmet coffee and a large selection of beverages.

BACKGROUND:

Established: 1976; 1st Franchised: 1987
Franchised Units: 36
Company-Owned Units 16
Total Units: 52
Dist.: US-52; CAN-0; O'seas-0
North America: 8 States
Density: 20 in CA, 8 in TX, 7 in AZ
Projected New Units (12 Months): 30
Registered: CA,HI

FINANCIAL/TERMS:

Cash Investment: $75-150K
Total Investment: $222-439K
Minimum Net Worth: $150K
Fees: Franchise - $35K
Royalty - 6%; Ad. - 2%
Earnings Claim Statement: No
Term of Contract (Years): 10/5
Avg. # Of Employees: 5 FT, 11 PT
Passive Ownership: Allowed
Encourage Conversions: No
Area Develop. Agreements: Yes/10
Sub-Franchising Contracts: No
Expand In Territory: Yes
Space Needs: 1,000-2,000 SF; NR

SUPPORT & TRAINING PROVIDED:

Financial Assistance Provided: Yes(I)
Site Selection Assistance: Yes
Lease Negotiation Assistance: Yes
Co-Operative Advertising: Yes
Franchisee Assoc./Member: No
Size Of Corporate Staff: 17
On-Going Support: B,C,D,E,F,G,I
Training: 5 Weeks.

SPECIFIC EXPANSION PLANS:

US: All United States
Canada: All Canada
Overseas: No

<< >>

ROBIN'S DONUTS

2001 - 715 Hewitson St.
Thunder Bay, ON P7B 6B5 CANADA
Tel: (807) 623-4453
Fax: (807) 623-4682
E-Mail: robins@robinsdonuts.com
Web Site: www.robinsdonuts.com
Mr. Ian Sharp, Vice President

Since 1975, ROBIN'S DONUTS has grown to be the largest chain in Western Canada and the second largest in Canada, due to its proven system of providing consistent, high-quality donuts, coffee, deli-products, soups, sandwiches and salads in a contemporary, family-oriented environment.

BACKGROUND:

Established: 1975; 1st Franchised: 1977
Franchised Units: 216
Company-Owned Units 25
Total Units: 241
Dist.: US-0; CAN-242; O'seas-0
North America: 9 Provinces
Density: 65 in ON, 49 in MB, 37 in AB
Projected New Units (12 Months): 10
Qualifications: 5, 5, 1, 3, 3, 5
Registered: MN,WA,AB

FINANCIAL/TERMS:

Cash Investment: $120K
Total Investment: $240-260K
Minimum Net Worth: $150K
Fees: Franchise - $25K
Royalty - 4%; Ad. - 3%
Earnings Claim Statement: Yes
Term of Contract (Years): 10/10
Avg. # Of Employees: 12 FT, 6 PT
Passive Ownership: Not Allowed
Encourage Conversions: Yes
Area Develop. Agreements: No
Sub-Franchising Contracts: No
Expand In Territory: Yes
Space Needs: 2,250 SF; FS, SC

SUPPORT & TRAINING PROVIDED:

Financial Assistance Provided: Yes(I)
Site Selection Assistance: Yes
Lease Negotiation Assistance: Yes
Co-Operative Advertising: Yes
Franchisee Assoc./Member: No
Size Of Corporate Staff: 65
On-Going Support: B,C,D,E,F,G,H
Training: 4 Weeks Thunder Bay, ON; 2 Weeks Store Opening.

SPECIFIC EXPANSION PLANS:

US: No
Canada: All Canada
Overseas: No

<< >>

SAINT CINNAMON BAKE SHOPPE

7181 Woodbine Ave., # 222
Markham, ON L3R 1A3 CANADA
Tel: (905) 470-1517
Fax: (905) 470-8112
E-Mail: info@saintcinnamon.com
Web Site: www.saintcinnamon.com
Mr. Mark Halpern, Executive VP

Largest cinnamon-roll franchise in Canada. The rolls are made and baked daily at each location. The franchisee is given two weeks of intensive training in all aspects of the business.

BACKGROUND:
Established: 1986; 1st Franchised: 1986
Franchised Units: 104
Company-Owned Units 3
Total Units: 107
Dist.: US-3; CAN-70; O'seas-34
North America: 3 States, 3 Provinces
Density: 42 in ON, 25 in PQ, 3 in NB
Projected New Units (12 Months): 15
Qualifications: 4, 4, 4, 4, 4, 5
Registered: NR

FINANCIAL/TERMS:
Cash Investment: $40-75K
Total Investment: $144-265K
Minimum Net Worth: $NR
Fees: Franchise - $25K
Royalty - 6%; Ad. - 3%
Earnings Claim Statement: No
Term of Contract (Years): 10/5
Avg. # Of Employees: 2 FT, 5 PT
Passive Ownership: Not Allowed
Encourage Conversions: N/A
Area Develop. Agreements: Yes/10
Sub-Franchising Contracts: Yes
Expand In Territory: Yes
Space Needs: 300-600 SF; RM

SUPPORT & TRAINING PROVIDED:
Financial Assistance Provided: N/A
Site Selection Assistance: Yes
Lease Negotiation Assistance: Yes
Co-Operative Advertising: No
Franchisee Assoc./Member: No
Size Of Corporate Staff: 7
On-Going Support: A,B,C,D,e,F,G,h
Training: 2 Weeks in ON.

SPECIFIC EXPANSION PLANS:
US: All United States
Canada: All Canada
Overseas:
Middle East, Europe, South America

SOUTHERN MAID DONUTS

3615 Cavalier Dr.
Garland, TX 75042-7599
Tel: (800) 936-6887 (972) 272-6425
Fax: (972) 276-3549
E-Mail: dunker@gte.net
Web Site: www.southernmaiddonuts.com
Ms. Doris Franklin, Vice President

Since 1937, we have offered personal service to assist each franchisee in producing the finest-quality donuts at low initial cost and continuing fees. Our motto is 'The Taste You Remember - Since 1937. SOUTHERN MAID DONUTS.'

BACKGROUND:
Established: 1937; 1st Franchised: 1941
Franchised Units: 86
Company-Owned Units 0
Total Units: 86
Dist.: US-85; CAN-0; O'seas-0
North America: 12 States
Density: 65 in TX, 10 in LA, 3 in WA
Projected New Units (12 Months): 12
Qualifications: 3, 3, 1, 1, 3, 5
Registered: CA,OR,VA

FINANCIAL/TERMS:
Cash Investment: $50K+
Total Investment: $50-125K
Minimum Net Worth: $50K+
Fees: Franchise - $5K
Royalty - 0%; Ad. - 0%
Earnings Claim Statement: No
Term of Contract (Years): 10/10
Avg. # Of Employees: 4 FT,2 PT
Passive Ownership: Allowed
Encourage Conversions: Yes
Area Develop. Agreements: Yes/5
Sub-Franchising Contracts: No
Expand In Territory: Yes
Space Needs: 1,000-1,500 SF; SF, SC

SUPPORT & TRAINING PROVIDED:
Financial Assistance Provided: Yes(I)
Site Selection Assistance: Yes
Lease Negotiation Assistance: Yes
Co-Operative Advertising: No
Franchisee Assoc./Member: No
Size Of Corporate Staff: 6
On-Going Support: B,C,D,e,I
Training: 7 Days at Franchisee's Location (Not Included in Initial Fee.)

SPECIFIC EXPANSION PLANS:
US: All United States
Canada: All Canada
Overseas: All Countries

STONE HEARTH BREADS U. S. A.

12301 Coller Hwy.
Tipton, MI 49287
Tel: (517) 431-2593
Fax: (517) 431-3408
E-Mail: StoneHearthBreads@msn.com
Mr. Vincent D. Cassone, President

Production and ales of traditional and ethnic breads using proprietary ovens and equipment, complete for mulation, production and sales instruction.

BACKGROUND:
Established: 1995; 1st Franchised: 1997
Franchised Units: 0
Company-Owned Units 1
Total Units: 1
Dist.: US-1; CAN-0; O'seas-0
North America: 1 State
Density: 1 in MI
Projected New Units (12 Months): NR
Registered: NR

FINANCIAL/TERMS:
Cash Investment: $25K
Total Investment: $200K
Minimum Net Worth: $NR
Fees: Franchise - $20K (incl.)
Royalty - 4%; Ad. - 2%
Earnings Claim Statement: Yes
Term of Contract (Years): 10
Avg. # Of Employees: 4 FT, 3 PT
Passive Ownership: Discouraged
Encourage Conversions: NR
Area Develop. Agreements: Yes
Sub-Franchising Contracts: Yes
Expand In Territory: No
Space Needs: 1,500 SF; SF, SC, RM

SUPPORT & TRAINING PROVIDED:
Financial Assistance Provided: NR
Site Selection Assistance: No
Lease Negotiation Assistance: Yes
Co-Operative Advertising: Yes
Franchisee Assoc./Member: Yes
Size Of Corporate Staff: 2
On-Going Support: D,E,G,H
Training: 30 Days Brooklyn, MI; 30 Days at Franchise Outlet; 2 Years Monthly.

SPECIFIC EXPANSION PLANS:
US: All United States
Canada: NR
Overseas: NR

TIM HORTONS

874 Sinclair Rd.
Oakville, ON L6K 2Y1 CANADA
Tel: (888) 376-4835 (905) 845-6511
Fax: (905) 845-0265
Web Site: www.timhortons.com
Ms. Lilian Longdo, Mgr. Franchising

TIM HORTONS is Canada's largest franchised retail coffee, donuts and specialty baked goods chain, with over 1,300 stores in Canada and the U. S. The franchisee purchases a turn-key operation, the right to use TIM HORTONS trademarks and tradenames, as well as a comprehensive 8-week training program and on-going operational and marketing support.

BACKGROUND: IFA MEMBER
Established: 1964; 1st Franchised: 1965

Franchised Units: 1,553
Company-Owned Units 145
Total Units: 1,698
Dist.: US-108; CAN-1772; O'seas-0
North America: 4 States, 12 Provinces
Density: ON, PQ, NS
Projected New Units (12 Months): 200
Qualifications: 5, 4, 3, 3, 3, 5
Registered: IN,MI,MN,NY,RI,WI,AB

FINANCIAL/TERMS:
Cash Investment: $100-110K
Total Investment: $300-360K
Minimum Net Worth: $NR
Fees: Franchise - $35-50K
Royalty - 3-4.5%; Ad. - 4%
Earnings Claim Statement: No
Term of Contract (Years): 20/10/10
Avg. # Of Employees: 22-25 FT or PT
Passive Ownership: Not Allowed
Encourage Conversions: Yes
Area Develop. Agreements: No
Sub-Franchising Contracts: No
Expand In Territory: Yes
Space Needs: 2,650-3,000 SF; FS, SF, SC, RM

SUPPORT & TRAINING PROVIDED:
Financial Assistance Provided: No
Site Selection Assistance: Yes
Lease Negotiation Assistance: Yes
Co-Operative Advertising: Yes
Franchisee Assoc./Member: No
Size Of Corporate Staff: 580
On-Going Support: B,C,D,E,G,H
Training: 8 Weeks Oakville, ON.

SPECIFIC EXPANSION PLANS:
US: NY,MI,OH, North Central U.S.
Canada: All Canada
Overseas: No

TREATS

418 Preston St.
Ottawa, ON K1S 4N2 CANADA
Tel: (800) 461-4003 (613) 563-4073
Fax: (613) 563-1982
Web Site: www.treats.com
Ms. Shirley Adams, Franchise Relations

Micro-bakery concept, featuring gourmet and specialty coffees and fresh-baked, on-site baked goods, including muffins, cookies and bagels. Three concept variations are available: TREATS BAKERY (~400 SF) serves the base menu offering; TREATS CAFE (~1,200 SF) also serves sandwiches (baguettes), soups and salads; TREATS COFFEE EMPORIUM (~1,200 SF) also offers coffee beans, coffee-related merchandise and sandwiches.

BACKGROUND:
Established: 1977; 1st Franchised: 1979
Franchised Units: 142
Company-Owned Units 3
Total Units: 145
Dist.: US-5; CAN-140; O'seas-0
North America: 3 States, 9 Provinces
Density: 75 in ON, 25 in PQ, 10 in AB
Projected New Units (12 Months): 12
Qualifications: 3, 3, 3, 2, 3, 5
Registered: CA,FL,IL,IN,MD,MI,MN,NY, OR,RI,VA,WA,WI,DC,AB

FINANCIAL/TERMS:
Cash Investment: $40-50K
Total Investment: $100-150K
Minimum Net Worth: $200K
Fees: Franchise - $25K
Royalty - 7%; Ad. - 1%
Earnings Claim Statement: No
Term of Contract (Years): Lease
Avg. # Of Employees: 3 FT, 2 PT
Passive Ownership: Discouraged
Encourage Conversions: Yes
Area Develop. Agreements: Yes/15
Sub-Franchising Contracts: Yes
Expand In Territory: Yes
Space Needs: 500-1,500 SF; SF, SC, RM

SUPPORT & TRAINING PROVIDED:
Financial Assistance Provided: No
Site Selection Assistance: Yes
Lease Negotiation Assistance: Yes
Co-Operative Advertising: Yes
Franchisee Assoc./Member: No
Size Of Corporate Staff: 15
On-Going Support: B,C,D,E,G,H,I
Training: 2 Weeks Training Center; 1 Week On-Site.

SPECIFIC EXPANSION PLANS:
US: East Coast
Canada: All Canada
Overseas: Chile, Brazil, Middle East

SUPPLEMENTAL LISTING OF FRANCHISORS

AU BON PAIN, 19 Fid Kennedy Ave., Boston, MA 02210 ; (617) 423-2100; (617) 423-7879

BAGEL PATCH, 71-58 Austin St., Forest Hills, NY 11375 ; (718) 261-8882;

BAGELSMITH RESTAURANTS & FOOD STORES, 37 Van Syckel Rd., Hampton, NJ 08827 ; (908) 730-8600; (908) 730-8165

BAGELZ, 95 Oak St., Glastonbury, CT 06033 ; (800) 270-7900 (860) 657-4400;

BENNY'S BAGELS, 2636 Walnut Hill Ln., # 110, Dallas, TX 75229 ; (214) 351-2600; (214) 351-2604

BEST BAGELS IN TOWN, 480-19 Patchogue-Holbrook Rd., Holbrook, NY 11741 ; (631) 472-4104; (631) 472-4105

BEST BAGELS IN TOWN, 480-19 Patchogue Holbrook Rd., Holbrook, NY 11741 ; (516) 472-4104; (516) 472-4105

BIG CITY BAGELS, 620 Johnson Ave, # 1B, Bohemia, NY 11716 ; (800) 88-BAGEL (714) 515-9300; (714) 515-7743

BUN KING BAKERIES, 1173 N. Service Rd., E., Oakville, ON L6H 1A7 CANADA; (905) 842-8770; (905) 842-8772

CHESAPEAKE BAGEL BAKERY, 6 Concourse Pkwy., # 1700, Atlanta, GA 30328 ; (800) 848-8248 (770) 321-6827; (770) 350-3652

CINNAMON STREET BAKERY & COFFEE CO., 2930 W. Maple Ave., P.O. Box 780, Sioux Falls, SD 57101 ; (800) 648-6227 (605) 336-6961; (605) 336-0141

CINNAMONSTER, 7346 S. Alton Way, # 10-A, Englewood, CO 80112 ; (303) 770-5075; (303) 770-5083

COMPANY'S COMING BAKERY CAFE, 1121 Centre St. N., # 440, Calgary, AB T2E 7K6 CANADA; (800) 361-1151 (403) 230-1151; (403) 230-2182

COOKIE FACTORY BAKERY, 1010 W. St. Martins Dr., St. Joseph, MO 64506 (800) 968-2902 (816) 364-1088; (816) 364-3739

COUNTRY STYLE DONUTS, 2 E. Beaver Creek Rd., Bldg. 1, Richmond Hill, ON L3T 3R7 CANADA; (905) 764-7066; (905) 764-8426

CREATIVE CAKERY, 636 Redondo Blvd., Long Beach, CA 90814 ; (800) 224-4261 (562) 438-2301; (562) 433-2423

DONUT DELITE CAFE, 3380 S. Service Rd., Burlington, ON L7N 3J5 CANADA; (905) 681-8448; (905) 637-7745

EINSTEIN/NOAH BAGEL, 1687 Cole Blvd., Golden, CO 80401-3316 ; (303) 568-8026; (303) 568-8199

GREAT HARVEST BREAD CO., 28 S. Montana St., Dillon, MT 59725-2434 (800) 442-0424 (406) 683-6842; (406) 683-5537

HONEY DEW DONUTS, 35 Braintree Hill Office Park, # 203, Braintree, MA 02184 ; (781) 849-3000; (781) 849-3111

INCREDIBLE CHOCOLATE CHIP COOKIE CO., 640 Lower Poplar St., Macon, GA 31201 ; (912) 742-8455; (618) 281-6888

JOLLY PIRATE DONUTS, 3923 E. Broad St., Columbus, OH 43213 ; (614) 235-4501; (614) 235-4533

KRISPY KREME DOUGHNUTS, P.O. Box 83, Winston-Salem, NC 27102 ; (800) 242-8880 (336) 725-2981; (336) 733-3791

LOX OF BAGELS, 3028 Palos Verdes Dr. W., Palos Verdes, CA 90274 ; (800) 879-6927

MICHEL'S BAGUETTE (CANADA), 3300 Bloor St. W., # 2910, Etobicoke, ON M8X 2X3 CANADA; (877) 7-BAKERY (416) 236-0055; (416) 236-0054

T. J. CINNAMON'S, 1000 Corporate Dr., Ft. Lauderdale, FL 33334 ; (800) 487-272945 (954) 351-5100; (954) 351-5222

WHOLE DONUT, THE, 894 New Britain Ave., Hartford, CT 06106 ; (860) 953-3569; (860) 953-1692

Food: Coffee

Chapter 14

Food: Coffee Industry Profile

Total # Franchisors in Industry Group	26
Total # Franchised Units in Industry Group	1,288
Total # Company-Owned Units in Industry Group	137
Total # Operating Units in Industry Group	1,425
Average # Franchised Units/Franchisor	49.5
Average # Company-Owned Units/Franchisor	5.3
Average # Total Units/Franchisor	54.8
Ratio of Total # Franchised Units/Total # Company-Owned Units	9.4:1
Industry Survey Participants	13
Representing % of Industry	50.0%
Average Franchise Fee*:	$20.7K
Average Total Investment*:	$218.2K
Average On-Going Royalty Fee*:	6.0%

*If a range was provided, the mid-point of the range was used. See detailed profiles for actual ranges.

Five Largest Participants in Survey

Company	# Franchised Units	# Co-Owned Units	# Total Units	Franchise Fee	On-Going Royalty	Total Investment
1. Second Cup, The	391	8	399	25K	9%	335K
2. Gloria Jean's Gourmet Coffees	250	25	275	15-25K	6%	132.8-307.6K
3. Coffee Beanery, The	158	13	171	5-25K	6%	200-400K
4. Quikava	65	3	68	3-20K	5%	95-425K
5. Grabbajabba	59	0	59	25K	8%	150-225K

All of the data provided are proprietary and should not be quoted without acknowledging *Bond's Franchise Guide.*

ARABICA COFFEEHOUSE
5755 Granger Rd., # 200
Independence, OH 44131-1410
Tel: (800) 837-9599 (216) 351-1000
Fax: (216) 398-0707
E-Mail: tsozio@mrhero.com
Web Site: www.mrhero.com
Ms. Terri Sozio, Franchise Sales Admin.

Built to reflect the personality of the community, an ARABICA COFFEEHOUSE is more than a place to enjoy 50 flavors of coffee, specialty drinks, unique teas, health-conscious sandwiches, decadent pastries and desserts. Superior food and beverages in well-appointed, comfortable surroundings is a perfect venue for any purpose.

BACKGROUND:
Established: 1994; 1st Franchised: 1994
Franchised Units: 46
Company-Owned Units 1
Total Units: 47
Dist.: US-47; CAN-0; O'seas-0
North America: 1 State
Density: 47 in OH
Projected New Units (12 Months): 25
Qualifications: 5, 3, 3, 2, 3, 5
Registered: NR

FINANCIAL/TERMS:
Cash Investment: $75K
Total Investment: $126-363K
Minimum Net Worth: $300K
Fees: Franchise - $22.5K
Royalty - 5.5%; Ad. - 2.5%
Earnings Claim Statement: No
Term of Contract (Years): 10/10
Avg. # Of Employees: 4 FT, 6 PT
Passive Ownership: Discouraged
Encourage Conversions: Yes
Area Develop. Agreements: Yes/3-5
Sub-Franchising Contracts: Yes
Expand In Territory: Yes
Space Needs: 2,500 SF; FS, SF, SC, RM, Co-Brand

SUPPORT & TRAINING PROVIDED:
Financial Assistance Provided: Yes(I)
Site Selection Assistance: Yes
Lease Negotiation Assistance: Yes
Co-Operative Advertising: Yes
Franchisee Assoc./Member: No
Size Of Corporate Staff: 40
On-Going Support: B,C,D,E,F,G,H,I
Training: 3 Weeks Cleveland, OH.

SPECIFIC EXPANSION PLANS:
US: MI, OH, PA, KY, IN
Canada: No
Overseas: No

<< >>

BLENZ COFFEE
535 Thurlow St., # 300
Vancouver, BC V6E 3L2 CANADA
Tel: (604) 682-2995
Fax: (604) 684-2542
Ms. Sarah Moen,

Retailer of specialty coffees and teas in a warm, service-oriented environment. Capitalizing on the consumer trend towards better service and quality coffee-based beverages.

BACKGROUND:
Established: 1990; 1st Franchised: 1991
Franchised Units: 25
Company-Owned Units 2
Total Units: 27
Dist.: US-0; CAN-15; O'seas-1
North America: 1 Province
Density: 15 in BC
Projected New Units (12 Months): 6
Qualifications: 3, 2, 2, 1, 5, 5
Registered: NR

FINANCIAL/TERMS:
Cash Investment: $40-75K
Total Investment: $135-190K
Minimum Net Worth: $NR
Fees: Franchise - $25K
Royalty - 8%; Ad. - 2%
Earnings Claim Statement: Yes
Term of Contract (Years): 10
Avg. # Of Employees: 4 FT, 10 PT
Passive Ownership: Not Allowed
Encourage Conversions: No
Area Develop. Agreements: Yes/20
Sub-Franchising Contracts: Yes
Expand In Territory: Yes
Space Needs: 750-2,000 SF; FS, SF, SC, RM

SUPPORT & TRAINING PROVIDED:
Financial Assistance Provided: Yes(I)
Site Selection Assistance: Yes
Lease Negotiation Assistance: Yes
Co-Operative Advertising: Yes
Franchisee Assoc./Member: Yes/No
Size Of Corporate Staff: 4
On-Going Support: A,B,C,D,E,H
Training: 2 Weeks Exisitng Operation; 2 Weeks New Location.

SPECIFIC EXPANSION PLANS:
US: All United States
Canada: All Canada
Overseas: All Countries

<< >>

BREWSTER'S COFFEE
8501 W. Higgins Rd., # 320
Chicago, IL 60631-2801
Tel: (800) 251-6101 (773) 380-6100
Fax: (773) 380-6183
Web Site: www.babcorp.com
Mr. Tony Cervini, Dir. Domestic Franchise Dev.

Our BREWSTER'S COFFEE franchisees expertly prepare coffee and espresso beverages from the freshest coffee, roasted to the peak of flavor for each varietal and unique blend we offer. They also offer the same fresh coffee on a bulk basis for customers to enjoy at home. BREWSTER'S franchisees learn to consult with their customers and suggest the appropriate coffee to match any food or occasion.

BACKGROUND: IFA MEMBER
Established: 1996; 1st Franchised: 1996
Franchised Units: 7
Company-Owned Units 2
Total Units: 9
Dist.: US-9; CAN-0; O'seas-0
North America: 3 States
Density: 7 in IL, 1 in OH
Projected New Units (12 Months): 5
Qualifications: 3, 3, 5, 2, 2, 5
Registered: All States

FINANCIAL/TERMS:
Cash Investment: $50K Min.
Total Investment: $125.1-282.4K
Minimum Net Worth: $Not Required
Fees: Franchise - $25K
Royalty - 5%; Ad. - 2%
Earnings Claim Statement: No
Term of Contract (Years): 10/10
Avg. # Of Employees: 5 FT, 10PT
Passive Ownership: Discouraged
Encourage Conversions: Yes
Area Develop. Agreements: Yes/Varies
Sub-Franchising Contracts: No
Expand In Territory: Yes
Space Needs: 1,200-1,400 SF; FS, SF, SC

SUPPORT & TRAINING PROVIDED:
Financial Assistance Provided: Yes(I)
Site Selection Assistance: Yes
Lease Negotiation Assistance: Yes
Co-Operative Advertising: Yes
Franchisee Assoc./Member: No
Size Of Corporate Staff: 34
On-Going Support: B,C,D,E,F,G,H,I

Training: 2 Weeks Milwaukee, WI; 5 Days Store Location Prior to Opening.
SPECIFIC EXPANSION PLANS:
US: All United States
Canada: All Canada
Overseas: All Countries

<< >>

Top 50

COFFEE BEANERY, THE

3429 Pierson Pl.
Flushing, MI 48433
Tel: (800) 728-2326 (810) 733-1020
Fax: (810) 244-8151
E-Mail: franchiseinfo@beanerysupport.com
Web Site: www.coffeebeanery.com
Ms. JoAnne Shaw, CEO/President

THE COFFEE BEANERY, LTD. offers a variety of investment levels with storefront cafes being the main growth vehicle in the future. The cornerstone and foundation of the business is the exceptional quality of its own hand-roasted coffee. Our customers enjoy the best coffee and assorted products available from a network of over 180 opened franchised and corporate locations. Our operations department and training are superb.

BACKGROUND: IFA MEMBER
Established: 1976; 1st Franchised: 1985
Franchised Units: 158
Company-Owned Units 13
Total Units: 171
Dist.: US-167; CAN-0; O'seas-0
North America: 30 States
Density: 32 in MI, 12 in FL, 16 in NY
Projected New Units (12 Months): 25
Qualifications: 5, 5, 1, 1, 1, 5
Registered: CA,FL,IL,IN,MD,MI,MN,NY,VA
FINANCIAL/TERMS:
Cash Investment: $50-80K
Total Investment: $200-400K
Minimum Net Worth: $250K
Fees: Franchise - $5-25K
Royalty - 6%; Ad. - 2%
Earnings Claim Statement: Yes
Term of Contract (Years): 5,10,15+
Avg. # Of Employees: 2-3 FT, 10-15 PT
Passive Ownership: Allowed
Encourage Conversions: Yes
Area Develop. Agreements:Yes/5,10,15+
Sub-Franchising Contracts: No
Expand In Territory: Yes
Space Needs: 2,000 SF; FS, SF, SC, RM
SUPPORT & TRAINING PROVIDED:
Financial Assistance Provided: Yes(I)
Site Selection Assistance: Yes
Lease Negotiation Assistance: Yes
Co-Operative Advertising: Yes
Franchisee Assoc./Member: Yes/Yes
Size Of Corporate Staff: 40
On-Going Support: B,C,D,E,F,G,H,I
Training: 21 Days Café; 14 Days Mallat Michigan Corporate Center
SPECIFIC EXPANSION PLANS:
US: All United States
Canada: No
Overseas: Yes, Guam (2)

<< >>

Top 50

GLORIA JEAN'S GOURMET COFFEES

2144 Michelson Dr.
Irvine, CA 92612
Tel: (800) 333-0050 (949) 260-6701
Fax: (949) 260-1610
Web Site: www.greatbeans.com
Mr. Mike Zorehkey, VP Franchising/Real Estate

American's largest retail gourmet coffee franchisor offers the highest-quality gourmet coffees, teas and accessories. Our unique store design and exclusive coffee bean counter are the focal points of our nationally-honored company. Each store has up to 64 varieties of coffees.

BACKGROUND:
Established: 1979; 1st Franchised: 1986
Franchised Units: 250
Company-Owned Units 25
Total Units: 275
Dist.: US-248; CAN-0; O'seas-27
North America: 38 States
Density: 38 in CA, 28 in IL, 9 in WI
Projected New Units (12 Months): 20
Qualifications: 4, 4, 3, 3, 4, 5
Registered: All States
FINANCIAL/TERMS:
Cash Investment: $75K
Total Investment: $132.8-307.6K
Minimum Net Worth: $150K
Fees: Franchise - $15-25K
Royalty - 6%; Ad. - 2%
Earnings Claim Statement: No
Term of Contract (Years): Lease
Avg. # Of Employees: 2 FT, 8 PT
Passive Ownership: Discouraged
Encourage Conversions: N/A
Area Develop. Agreements: Yes
Sub-Franchising Contracts: No
Expand In Territory: Yes
Space Needs: 600-1,200 SF; RM
SUPPORT & TRAINING PROVIDED:
Financial Assistance Provided: Yes(I)
Site Selection Assistance: Yes
Lease Negotiation Assistance: Yes
Co-Operative Advertising: Yes
Franchisee Assoc./Member: Yes/Yes
Size Of Corporate Staff: 150
On-Going Support: B,C,D,E,G,H,I
Training: 3 Weeks Corporate Office, Castroville, CA.
SPECIFIC EXPANSION PLANS:
US: All United States
Canada: No
Overseas: All Countries

<< >>

GRABBAJABBA

1121 Centre St. N., # 440
Calgary, AB T2E 7K6 CANADA
Tel: (800) 361-1151 (403) 230-1151
Fax: (403) 230-2182
Mr. Sheldon Jones, Franchise Development Mgr.

Up-scale European coffee house, specializing in over 50 varieties of Arabica whole bean and liquid coffees, cappuccino and other specialty coffees. European sandwiches, soups, salads, freshly-baked goods, decadent desserts and pastries.

BACKGROUND:
Established: 1987; 1st Franchised: 1990
Franchised Units: 59
Company-Owned Units 0
Total Units: 59
Dist.: US-0; CAN-59; O'seas-0
North America: 5 Provinces
Density: 30 in AB, 7 in BC, 13 in ON
Projected New Units (12 Months): 17
Registered: AB

FINANCIAL/TERMS:

Cash Investment: $60-85K
Total Investment: $150-225K
Minimum Net Worth: $175K
Fees: Franchise - $25K
Royalty - 8%; Ad. - 0%
Earnings Claim Statement: Yes
Term of Contract (Years): 10/10
Avg. # Of Employees: 2 FT, 4 PT
Passive Ownership: Discouraged
Encourage Conversions: Yes
Area Develop. Agreements: No
Sub-Franchising Contracts: No
Expand In Territory: Yes
Space Needs: 1,100 SF; SF, SC, RM

SUPPORT & TRAINING PROVIDED:

Financial Assistance Provided: Yes(I)
Site Selection Assistance: Yes
Lease Negotiation Assistance: Yes
Co-Operative Advertising: Yes
Franchisee Assoc./Member: Yes
Size Of Corporate Staff: 12
On-Going Support: C,D,E,f,G,h
Training: 14 Days Comprehensive Hands-On Training.

SPECIFIC EXPANSION PLANS:

US: No
Canada: All Canada
Overseas: No

JAVA DAVE'S COFFEE

6239 E. 15th St.
Tulsa, OK 74112
Tel: (800) 725-7315 (918) 836-5570
Fax: (918) 835-4348
E-Mail: davebeans@aol.com
Web Site: www.javadavescoffee.com
Mr. Mike Blair, Franchise Marketing Mgr.

The JAVA DAVE'S COFFEE House System is a thrifty franchise that allows the franchisee an opportunity to participate in the higher level retail purveyance of products which includes the world's finest Arabica bean coffees, teas, cocoas and cappuccino mixes, as well as 200 other related products. The espresso and specialty drinks bar compliments the retail.

BACKGROUND: IFA MEMBER

Established: 1981; 1st Franchised: 1993
Franchised Units: 12
Company-Owned Units 2
Total Units: 14
Dist.: US-14; CAN-0; O'seas-0
North America: 2 States
Density: 13 in OK, 1 in TX
Projected New Units (12 Months): 5-7
Qualifications: 5, 5, 3, 4, 3, 5
Registered: IL

FINANCIAL/TERMS:

Cash Investment: $150K
Total Investment: $150-195K
Minimum Net Worth: $200K
Fees: Franchise - $17.5K
Royalty - 3%; Ad. - 2%
Earnings Claim Statement: No
Term of Contract (Years): 10/10
Avg. # Of Employees: 2 FT, 4-5 PT
Passive Ownership: Not Allowed
Encourage Conversions: Yes
Area Develop. Agreements: Yes/10
Sub-Franchising Contracts: No
Expand In Territory: Yes
Space Needs: 1,500-1,800 SF; FS, SF, SC, RM

SUPPORT & TRAINING PROVIDED:

Financial Assistance Provided: Yes(D)
Site Selection Assistance: Yes
Lease Negotiation Assistance: Yes
Co-Operative Advertising: Yes
Franchisee Assoc./Member: Yes/Yes
Size Of Corporate Staff: 60
On-Going Support: C,d,E,G,h,I
Training: 1 Week in Tulsa, OK; 2 Days On -Site.

SPECIFIC EXPANSION PLANS:

US: MW, SE,SW
Canada: No
Overseas: No

JAVA'S BREWIN

150 Main St., # 3
Reading, MA 01867
Tel: (800) 413-2376 (781) 944-1757
Fax: (781) 944-3808
Mr. Chris Gregoris, President

Exceptional gourmet coffee house and bakery concept.

BACKGROUND: IFA MEMBER

Established: 1997; 1st Franchised: 1998
Franchised Units: 3
Company-Owned Units 1
Total Units: 4
Dist.: US-0; CAN-0; O'seas-0
North America: 1 State
Density: 3 in MA
Projected New Units (12 Months): NR
Registered: NR

FINANCIAL/TERMS:

Cash Investment: $50-100K
Total Investment: $120-150K
Minimum Net Worth: $75K
Fees: Franchise - $17.5K
Royalty - 5%; Ad. - 2%
Earnings Claim Statement: No
Term of Contract (Years): 10/5/5
Avg. # Of Employees: 4 FT, 2 PT
Passive Ownership: Discouraged
Encourage Conversions: NR
Area Develop. Agreements: No
Sub-Franchising Contracts: No
Expand In Territory: Yes
Space Needs: 750-1,500 SF; FS, SF, SC

SUPPORT & TRAINING PROVIDED:

Financial Assistance Provided: NR
Site Selection Assistance: Yes
Lease Negotiation Assistance: Yes
Co-Operative Advertising: Yes
Franchisee Assoc./Member: No
Size Of Corporate Staff: 1
On-Going Support: B,C,D,E,F,H,I
Training: 2 Weeks in Company Store.

SPECIFIC EXPANSION PLANS:

US: Northeast
Canada: NR
Overseas: NR

MCBEANS

1560 Church Ave., # 6
Victoria, BC V8P 2H1 CANADA
Tel: (250) 721-2411
Fax: (250) 721-3213
Mr. Arne Andersson, President

Gourmet coffee stores in B. C. and Alberta, Canada that offer simply the finest in gourmet coffee by the cup, as well as lattes, cappuccino, espresso, a wide selection of beans (40 varieties), gourmet tea and the very best name-brand coffee-related merchandise. We offer our franchisees a well-researched and developed concept, lease negotiation, design and construction, and prime locations. We also provide continued and on-going support.

BACKGROUND:

Established: 1983; 1st Franchised: 1985
Franchised Units: 16
Company-Owned Units 1

Total Units: 17
Dist.: US-0; CAN-17; O'seas-0
North America: 2 Provinces
Density: 8 in BC, 9 in AB
Projected New Units (12 Months): 3
Qualifications: 5, 4, 4, 3, 5, 5
Registered: NR

FINANCIAL/TERMS:
Cash Investment: $60K
Total Investment: $126-174K
Minimum Net Worth: $NR
Fees: Franchise - $25K
Royalty - 7%; Ad. - 0%
Earnings Claim Statement: No
Term of Contract (Years): Lease
Avg. # Of Employees: 1-3 FT, 3-5 PT
Passive Ownership: Allowed
Encourage Conversions: Yes
Area Develop. Agreements: No
Sub-Franchising Contracts: No
Expand In Territory: Yes
Space Needs: 600 SF; SC, RM

SUPPORT & TRAINING PROVIDED:
Financial Assistance Provided: Yes(I)
Site Selection Assistance: Yes
Lease Negotiation Assistance: Yes
Co-Operative Advertising: N/A
Franchisee Assoc./Member: Yes/Yes
Size Of Corporate Staff: 5
On-Going Support: C,D,E,F
Training: 2 Weeks Corporate Training Center.

SPECIFIC EXPANSION PLANS:
US: BC and AB
Canada: BC, AB
Overseas: No

<< >>

NEW WORLD COFFEE

246 Industrial Way W.
Eatontown, NJ 07724
Tel: (800) 308-2457 (732) 544-0155
Fax: (732) 544-1315
Web Site: www.nwcbl.com
Franchise Development

Full service bagel bakery - Manhattan Bagel. Upscale coffee bar/espresso - New World Coffee.

BACKGROUND: IFA MEMBER
Established: 1987; 1st Franchised: 1990
Franchised Units: 43
Company-Owned Units 0
Total Units: 43
Dist.: US-380; CAN-0; O'seas-5
North America: NR
Density: NR
Projected New Units (12 Months): 40
Qualifications: 5, 3, 1, 1, 4, 5
Registered: All States

FINANCIAL/TERMS:
Cash Investment: $50-75K
Total Investment: $150-350K
Minimum Net Worth: $225K+
Fees: Franchise - $20K
Royalty - 5%; Ad. - 2.5-4%
Earnings Claim Statement: No
Term of Contract (Years): 10/10
Avg. # Of Employees: 3 FT, 5 PT
Passive Ownership: Allowed
Encourage Conversions: Yes
Area Develop. Agreements: Yes
Sub-Franchising Contracts: No
Expand In Territory: Yes
Space Needs: NR SF; FS, SF, SC, RM

SUPPORT & TRAINING PROVIDED:
Financial Assistance Provided: Yes(I)
Site Selection Assistance: Yes
Lease Negotiation Assistance: Yes
Co-Operative Advertising: Yes
Franchisee Assoc./Member: Yes
Size Of Corporate Staff: 200+
On-Going Support: C,D,E,G,H
Training: NR

SPECIFIC EXPANSION PLANS:
US: All United States
Canada: All Canada
Overseas: All Countries

<< >>

P. J.'S COFFEE & TEA

110 Poydras St., # 1150
New Orleans, LA 70163
Tel: (800) 749-5547 (504) 486-2827
Fax: (504) 486-2345
E-Mail: pjs@pjscoffee.com
Web Site: www.pjscoffee.com
Mr. Bryan K. O'Rourke, Chief Executive Officer

P. J.'S COFFEE & TEA has long been regarded as a leader in the specialty coffee industry in the southeast. Our neighborhood-based cafes are set apart from others because we roast and distribute only the highest-quality coffee and serve it in warm, comfortable settings. Our customer base is extremely varied. We provide an unusually high level of service to our franchisees because quality is of the utmost importance to us.

BACKGROUND:
Established: 1978; 1st Franchised: 1987
Franchised Units: 18
Company-Owned Units 4
Total Units: 22
Dist.: US-22; CAN-0; O'seas-0
North America: 4 States
Density: 17 in LA, 2 in MS, 2 in FL
Projected New Units (12 Months): 7
Qualifications: 5, 5, 3, 3, 2, 3
Registered: FL

FINANCIAL/TERMS:
Cash Investment: $30-40K
Total Investment: $100-190K
Minimum Net Worth: $120K
Fees: Franchise - $20K
Royalty - 5%; Ad. - 1%
Earnings Claim Statement: No
Term of Contract (Years): 10/10
Avg. # Of Employees: 1 FT, 6 PT
Passive Ownership: Allowed
Encourage Conversions: Yes
Area Develop. Agreements: Yes/Varies
Sub-Franchising Contracts: No
Expand In Territory: Yes
Space Needs: 1,200 SF; SF, SC

SUPPORT & TRAINING PROVIDED:
Financial Assistance Provided: No
Site Selection Assistance: Yes
Lease Negotiation Assistance: Yes
Co-Operative Advertising: Yes
Franchisee Assoc./Member: No
Size Of Corporate Staff: 74
On-Going Support: B,C,D,E,G,h,I
Training: 2 Days Corporate Office; 10 Days Corporate Store; 3 Days On-Location Sites.

SPECIFIC EXPANSION PLANS:
US: Southeast
Canada: No
Overseas: No

<< >>

QUIKAVA

100 Foxborough Blvd., # 200
Foxborough, MA 02035
Tel: (800) 381-6303 (508) 698-2223
Fax: (508) 698-2224
E-Mail: jazzyjavas@aol.com
Web Site: www.quikava.com
Mr. Gerry Pelissier, VP Franchise Sales

QUIKAVA, a wholly-owned subsidiary of CHOCK FULL O'NUTS, has created a unique coffee concept geared to today's lifestyle. We're franchising a "drive-thru coffee café!" We offer three formats to fit your needs and budget: * free standing building (700 SF) * strip mall café style * gas/convenience location.

BACKGROUND:
Established: 1990; 1st Franchised: 1993
Franchised Units: 65
Company-Owned Units 3
Total Units: 68
Dist.: US-46; CAN-0; O'seas-0
North America: 11 States
Density: 14 in MA, 10 in NY, 4 in NH
Projected New Units (12 Months): 20
Qualifications: 4, 2, 1, 2, 4, 5
Registered: MD,NY,RI,VA,DC

FINANCIAL/TERMS:
Cash Investment: $35-150K
Total Investment: $95-425K
Minimum Net Worth: $400K
Fees: Franchise - $3-20K
Royalty - 5%; Ad. - 4%
Earnings Claim Statement: No
Term of Contract (Years): 3-10/3-10
Avg. # Of Employees: 2 FT, 16 PT
Passive Ownership: Not Allowed
Encourage Conversions: Yes
Area Develop. Agreements: Yes/5
Sub-Franchising Contracts: No
Expand In Territory: No
Space Needs: 20,000 SF; FS, SC, Convenience Location

SUPPORT & TRAINING PROVIDED:
Financial Assistance Provided: No
Site Selection Assistance: Yes
Lease Negotiation Assistance: Yes
Co-Operative Advertising: No
Franchisee Assoc./Member: Yes/Yes
Size Of Corporate Staff: 11
On-Going Support: B,C,D,E,F,H,I
Training: 1 Week Hingham, MA; 1 Week Warwick, RI.

SPECIFIC EXPANSION PLANS:
US: Northeast, Mid-Atlantic
Canada: No
Overseas: No

<< >>

SECOND CUP, THE

175 Bloor St. E., S. Tower, # 801
Toronto, ON M4W 3R8 CANADA
Tel: (800) 569-6318 (416) 975-5541
Fax: (416) 975-5207
Web Site: www.secondcup.com
Ms. Kavita Hildenbrand, Dir. Franchising

As the largest retailer of specialty coffee in Canada with over 370 locations coast to coast, we are committed in attracting quality franchisees. Together, with outstanding location and store operations, we are dedicated to serving the best coffee in the world in an inviting atmosphere with uncompromising standards of customer service, quality and freshness.

BACKGROUND:
Established: 1975; 1st Franchised: 1975
Franchised Units: 391
Company-Owned Units 8
Total Units: 399
Dist.: US-0; CAN-399; O'seas-0
North America: 10 Provinces
Density: 170 in ON, 55 in AB, 30 PQ
Projected New Units (12 Months): 40
Qualifications: 4, 5, 4, 4, 4, 5
Registered: AB

FINANCIAL/TERMS:
Cash Investment: $90-140K
Total Investment: $~335K
Minimum Net Worth: $N/A
Fees: Franchise - $25K
Royalty - 9%; Ad. - 3%
Earnings Claim Statement: No
Term of Contract (Years): Lease
Avg. # Of Employees: 5 FT, 10 PT
Passive Ownership: Not Allowed
Encourage Conversions: Yes
Area Develop. Agreements: No
Sub-Franchising Contracts: No
Expand In Territory: Yes
Space Needs: 1,000-1,500 SF; FS, SF, SC, RM, Power Center

SUPPORT & TRAINING PROVIDED:
Financial Assistance Provided: No
Site Selection Assistance: Yes
Lease Negotiation Assistance: Yes
Co-Operative Advertising: Yes
Franchisee Assoc./Member: Yes/Yes
Size Of Corporate Staff: 60
On-Going Support: A,B,C,D,E,F,G,h,I
Training: 3 Weeks Toronto, ON.

SPECIFIC EXPANSION PLANS:
US: No
Canada: All Canada
Overseas: No

<< >>

SUPPLEMENTAL LISTING OF FRANCHISORS

ARIZONA BLENDS, 4699 Keele St., # 1, Downsview, ON M3J 2N8 CANADA; (416) 661-9916; (416) 661-9706

BEANER'S GOURMET COFFEE, 206 E. Grand River, Lansing, MI 48906 ; (877) 423-2637 (517) 482-8145; (517) 482-8625

COFFEE WAY, 123 Rexdale Blvd., Rexdale, ON M9W 1P3 CANADA; (416) 741-4144; (416) 741-5878

MR. MUGS, P.O. Box 20019 Global Courier, Brantford, ON N3P 2A4 CANADA; (519) 752-9890; (519) 752-0978

P. A. M.'S COFFEE & TEA CO., 2900 John St., # 202, Markham, ON L3R 5G3 CANADA; (905) 305-9595; (905) 305-9597

PJ'S COFFEE & TEA, 1100 Poydras St., # 1150, New Orleans, LA 70163 ; (800) 527-1055 (504) 582-2264; (504) 582-2265

SEATTLE'S BEST COFFEE, 1321 2nd Ave., # 200, Seattle, WA 98101-2005 ; (888) 232-4405 (206) 624-8858; (206) 442-2468

Food: Ice Cream/Yogurt

Chapter 15

Food: Ice Cream/Yogurt Industry Profile

Total # Franchisors in Industry Group	44
Total # Franchised Units in Industry Group	16,387
Total # Company-Owned Units in Industry Group	1,058
Total # Operating Units in Industry Group	17,445
Average # Franchised Units/Franchisor	372.4
Average # Company-Owned Units/Franchisor	24.0
Average # Total Units/Franchisor	396.4
Ratio of Total # Franchised Units/Total # Company-Owned Units	15.5:1
Industry Survey Participants	23
Representing % of Industry	52.3%
Average Franchise Fee*:	$22.7K
Average Total Investment*:	$185.7K
Average On-Going Royalty Fee*:	5.4%

*If a range was provided, the mid-point of the range was used. See detailed profiles for actual ranges.

Five Largest Participants in Survey

Company	# Franchised Units	# Co-Owned Units	# Total Units	Franchise Fee	On-Going Royalty	Total Investment
1. Yogen Fruz	5,196	33	5,239	25K	6%	130-250K
2. Baskin-Robbins	4,500	0	4,500	40K	5-5.9%	146-528K
3. TCBY Treats	2,104	1	2,105	20K	4%	192-337K
4. I Can't Believe It's Yogurt	400	940	1,340	15K	0%	110-203K
5. Dippin' Dots Ice Cream	569	2	571	12.5K	4%	46-190K

All of the data provided are proprietary and should not be quoted without acknowledging *Bond's Franchise Guide.*

ALL AMERICAN DELI & ICE CREAM SHOPS

812 SW Washington St., # 1110
Portland, OR 97205-3222
Tel: (800) 311-3930 (503) 224-6199
Fax: (503) 224-5042
E-Mail: franchise@allamericanicecream.com
Web Site: www.allamericanicecream.com
Mr. R. Scott Earl, Franchise Development

Owner/operator-oriented franchisor with deli & ice cream and ice cream & frozen yogurt shops located in shopping malls and strip centers. Expanded menu for increased sales and profits. Low food costs, extensive training programs and a fun business to operate.

BACKGROUND: IFA MEMBER
Established: 1986; 1st Franchised: 1988
Franchised Units: 32
Company-Owned Units 1
Total Units: 33
Dist.: US-33; CAN-0; O'seas-0
North America: 4 States
Density: 17 in OR, 3 in WA, 3 in CA
Projected New Units (12 Months): 10
Qualifications: 4, 4, 2, 3, 3, 5
Registered: CA,HI,OR,WA

FINANCIAL/TERMS:
Cash Investment: $30-40K
Total Investment: $81-182K
Minimum Net Worth: $200K
Fees: Franchise - $4-20K
Royalty - 5%; Ad. - 1%
Earnings Claim Statement: No
Term of Contract (Years): 10/10
Avg. # Of Employees: 1 FT, 8 PT
Passive Ownership: Discouraged
Encourage Conversions: Yes
Area Develop. Agreements: Yes
Sub-Franchising Contracts: No
Expand In Territory: Yes
Space Needs: 1,400 SF; SC, RM

SUPPORT & TRAINING PROVIDED:
Financial Assistance Provided: Yes(I)
Site Selection Assistance: Yes
Lease Negotiation Assistance: Yes
Co-Operative Advertising: N/A
Franchisee Assoc./Member: No
Size Of Corporate Staff: 4
On-Going Support: B,C,D,E,F,G,I
Training: 7 Days in Portland, OR; 8 Days On-Site.

SPECIFIC EXPANSION PLANS:
US: West, Inter-Mountain, SW
Canada: No
Overseas: No

<< >>

Top 50

BASKIN-ROBBINS

14 Pacella Park Dr., P.O. Box 317
Randolph, MA 02368
Tel: (800) 777-9983 (781) 961-4020
Fax: (781) 961-4207
Web Site: www.dunkin-baskin-togos-com
Mr. Anthony Padulo, VP Business Dev.

BASKIN-ROBBINS develops, operates and franchises retail stores that sell ice cream, frozen yogurt and other approved services. In some markets, BASKIN-ROBBINS, together with TOGO'S and/or DUNKIN' DONUTS, offers multiple brand combinations of the three brands. TOGO'S, BASKIN-ROBBINS and DUNKIN' DONUTS are all subsidiaries of Allied Domecq PLC.

BACKGROUND: IFA MEMBER
Established: 1946; 1st Franchised: 1948
Franchised Units: 4,500
Company-Owned Units 0
Total Units: 4,500
Dist.: US-2286; CAN-620; O'seas-1594
North America: 41 States
Density: 554 in CA, 195 in IL, 181 NY
Projected New Units (12 Months): 27
Registered: All States

FINANCIAL/TERMS:
Cash Investment: $145.8-527.8K
Total Investment: $145.7-527.8K
Minimum Net Worth: $400K/unit
Fees: Franchise - $40K
Royalty - 5-5.9%; Ad. - 5%
Earnings Claim Statement: Yes
Term of Contract (Years): 20
Avg. # Of Employees: N/A
Passive Ownership: Allowed
Encourage Conversions: NR
Area Develop. Agreements: Yes/3-5
Sub-Franchising Contracts: No
Expand In Territory: Yes
Space Needs: NR SF; FS, SF, SC, RM

SUPPORT & TRAINING PROVIDED:
Financial Assistance Provided: Yes(I)
Site Selection Assistance: N/A
Lease Negotiation Assistance: Yes
Co-Operative Advertising: Yes
Franchisee Assoc./Member: Yes/No
Size Of Corporate Staff: N/A
On-Going Support: B,C,D,G,H,I
Training: 51 Days in Randolph, MA; 3.5 Days at another Location.

SPECIFIC EXPANSION PLANS:
US: All Regions
Canada: All Canada
Overseas: All Countries

<< >>

Top 50

BEN & JERRY'S

30 Community Dr.
South Burlington, VT 05403
Tel: (802) 846-1543
Fax: (802) 846-1538
E-Mail: will@benjerry.com
Web Site: www.benjerry.com
Mr. Will Patten, Director Retail Operations

BEN & JERRY'S was started in 1978 in a renovated gas station in Burlington, VT, by childhood friends Ben Cohen and Jerry Greenfield. They soon became popular for their funky, chunky flavors, made from fresh Vermont milk and cream. The scoop shops feature a fun environment with a varied menu including cakes, gifts, baked goods and coffee drinks created from ice cream, frozen yogurt and sorbet flavors. Community involvement is an important element in being a successful BEN & JERRY'S franchisee.

BACKGROUND: IFA MEMBER
Established: 1978; 1st Franchised: 1981
Franchised Units: 234
Company-Owned Units 6
Total Units: 240
Dist.: US-211; CAN-4; O'seas-16
North America: 28 States, 1 Province
Density: 39 in CA, 21 in NY, 12 in MA
Projected New Units (12 Months): 60
Qualifications: 5, 5, 4, 4, 4, 5
Registered: CA,FL,IL,IN,MD,MI,MN,NY,OR,RI,VA,WA

FINANCIAL/TERMS:
Cash Investment: $86K+
Total Investment: $199-481K
Minimum Net Worth: $150K
Fees: Franchise - $30K
Royalty - 0%; Ad. - 4%
Earnings Claim Statement: No
Term of Contract (Years): 10/10
Avg. # Of Employees: 2 FT, 10 PT
Passive Ownership: Not Allowed
Encourage Conversions: Yes
Area Develop. Agreements: No
Sub-Franchising Contracts: No
Expand In Territory: No
Space Needs: Avg. 1,000 SF; FS, SF, SC, RM, KI

SUPPORT & TRAINING PROVIDED:
Financial Assistance Provided: No
Site Selection Assistance: Yes
Lease Negotiation Assistance: No
Co-Operative Advertising: Yes
Franchisee Assoc./Member: No
Size Of Corporate Staff: 30
On-Going Support: C,D,E,F,G,H,I
Training: 10 Days in VT.

SPECIFIC EXPANSION PLANS:
US: Various Markets
Canada: Not Currently
Overseas: Call International Division

BRUSTER'S OLD-FASHIONED ICE CREAM & YOGURT

730 Mulberry St.
Bridgewater, PA 15009
Tel: (724) 774-4250
Fax: (724) 774-0666
Web Site: www.brustersicecream.com
Mr. David Guido, President

BRUSTER'S ICE CREAM features fresh, delicious homemade ice cream which is made fresh daily on-site at each of our stores. Quality products and exceptional customer service are our main goals. Our products feature only the best ingredients - whole nuts, cherries and the best caramels and fudges. Homemade waffle cones are a great complement to our homemade ice cream.

BACKGROUND:
Established: 1989; 1st Franchised: 1993
Franchised Units: 85
Company-Owned Units 4
Total Units: 89
Dist.: US-45; CAN-0; O'seas-0
North America: 8 States
Density: 21 in PA, 15 in GA, 2 in OH
Projected New Units (12 Months): 30
Qualifications: 3, 2, 1, 1, 4, 4
Registered: IN,NY,VA

FINANCIAL/TERMS:
Cash Investment: $150K
Total Investment: $150-761K
Minimum Net Worth: $None
Fees: Franchise - $30K
Royalty - 5%; Ad. - Up to 3%
Earnings Claim Statement: No
Term of Contract (Years): 10/10/10
Avg. # Of Employees: 2-3 FT, 25 PT
Passive Ownership: Discouraged
Encourage Conversions: No
Area Develop. Agreements: Yes/Varies
Sub-Franchising Contracts: No
Expand In Territory: Yes
Space Needs: 988 SF; FS

SUPPORT & TRAINING PROVIDED:
Financial Assistance Provided: No
Site Selection Assistance: Yes
Lease Negotiation Assistance: Yes
Co-Operative Advertising: Yes
Franchisee Assoc./Member: No
Size Of Corporate Staff: 10
On-Going Support: B,C,D,E,G,H
Training: 4 Weeks Western PA or Atlanta, GA.

SPECIFIC EXPANSION PLANS:
US: Eastern United States
Canada: No
Overseas: No

<< >>

CARVEL ICE CREAM BAKERY

20 Batterson Park Rd.
Farmington, CT 06032
Tel: (800) 322-4848 (860) 677-6811
Fax: (860) 677-8211
E-Mail: cdobosh@carvelcorp.com
Web Site: www.carvelcorp.com
Ms. Carla Dobosh, Fran. Recruiting Mgr.

CARVEL ICE CREAM BAKERIES manufacture and sell ice cream and no-fat desserts through retail stores. CARVEL ICE CREAM cakes are designed to compete not only in the frozen dessert markets, but in the $13 billion dollar retail bakery market. Franchise operators can open additional branch units in malls, tourist areas and stadiums for no additional licensing fee. Franchisee can also purchase a license to sell products to supermarket through CARVEL Branded-Products Program.

BACKGROUND:
Established: 1934; 1st Franchised: 1947
Franchised Units: 450
Company-Owned Units 5
Total Units: 455
Dist.: US-392; CAN-3; O'seas-29
North America: 12 States, 1 Province
Density: 220 in NY, 63 in NJ, 37 FL
Projected New Units (12 Months): 20
Qualifications: 5, 5, 3, 3, 3, 5
Registered: CA,MD,NY,RI,VA

FINANCIAL/TERMS:
Cash Investment: $100-125K
Total Investment: $185-240K
Minimum Net Worth: $100K
Fees: Franchise - $10K
Royalty - $1.63/Gal.; Ad. - $1.42/Gal.
Earnings Claim Statement: No
Term of Contract (Years): 10/5/5
Avg. # Of Employees: 2 FT, 6 PT
Passive Ownership: Not Allowed
Encourage Conversions: Yes
Area Develop. Agreements: Yes
Sub-Franchising Contracts: No
Expand In Territory: Yes
Space Needs: 1,200-1,500 SF; FS, SF, RM

SUPPORT & TRAINING PROVIDED:
Financial Assistance Provided: Yes(I)
Site Selection Assistance: Yes
Lease Negotiation Assistance: Yes
Co-Operative Advertising: Yes
Franchisee Assoc./Member: Yes/Yes
Size Of Corporate Staff: 50
On-Going Support: A,B,C,D,E,G,H,I
Training: 11 Days Farmington, CT.

SPECIFIC EXPANSION PLANS:
US: East Coast
Canada: All Canada
Overseas: China, Mexico, Caribbean

COLD STONE CREAMERY

16101 N. 82nd St., # A-4
Scottsdale, AZ 85260
Tel: (888) 218-3349 (480) 348-1704
Fax: (480) 348-1718
E-Mail: franchisenecreamery.com.com
Web Site: www.coldstonecreamery.com
Mr. Ray Flores

The COLD STONE CREAMERY team is made up of seasoned professionals who deliver a proven system for providing the world's best ice cream experience to more people more often. Making our franchisee's successful is our number one priority. Our super-premium ice cream, yogurt, sorbet and waffle cones are made fresh daily right in our stores. Fresh-baked brownies and brand-name mix-ins like Snickers and M&Ms are blended on our frozen granite stones to make every dessert pure delight.

BACKGROUND: IFA MEMBER
Established: 1988; 1st Franchised: 1995
Franchised Units: 400
Company-Owned Units <u>3</u>
Total Units: 403
Dist.: US-320; CAN-0; O'seas-0
North America: 25 States
Density: 135 in CA, 30 in AZ, 6 in NV
Projected New Units (12 Months): 150
Qualifications: 2, 3, 1, 1, 3, 5
Registered: All States

FINANCIAL/TERMS:
Cash Investment: $50K
Total Investment: $199-298K
Minimum Net Worth: $NR
Fees: Franchise - $25K
Royalty - 6%; Ad. - 3%
Earnings Claim Statement: No
Term of Contract (Years): 10/5/5/5
Avg. # Of Employees: 3 FT, 9 PT
Passive Ownership: Discouraged
Encourage Conversions: NR
Area Develop. Agreements: Yes
Sub-Franchising Contracts: No
Expand In Territory: Yes
Space Needs: 1,200 SF; SC

SUPPORT & TRAINING PROVIDED:
Financial Assistance Provided: No
Site Selection Assistance: Yes
Lease Negotiation Assistance: Yes
Co-Operative Advertising: Yes
Franchisee Assoc./Member: No
Size Of Corporate Staff: 36
On-Going Support: C,D,E,G,H
Training: 6 Days Scottsdale, AZ; 2 Days Franchisee Location.

SPECIFIC EXPANSION PLANS:
US: All United States
Canada: All Canada
Overseas: All Countries

DIPPIN' DOTS ICE CREAM OF THE FUTURE

5110 Charter Oak Dr.
Paducah, KY 42001-5209
Tel: (270) 575-6990
Fax: (270) 575-6997
E-Mail: franchiseinfo@dippindots.com
Web Site: www.dippindots.com
Ms. Vanessa Riley, Franchise Dev. Specialist

DIPPIN' DOTS are those tiny beads of ice cream that are super-cold, creamy, and delicious. Here's your invitation to look at our exciting alternative to traditional ice cream, yogurt, and flavored ice products.

BACKGROUND: IFA MEMBER
Established: 1988; 1st Franchised: 1999
Franchised Units: 569
Company-Owned Units <u>2</u>
Total Units: 571
Dist.: US-571; CAN-0; O'seas-0
North America: 42 States
Density: 49 in TX, 37 in CA, 29 in FL
Projected New Units (12 Months): Unknown
Qualifications: 5, 4, 2, 3, 3, 5
Registered: All States

FINANCIAL/TERMS:
Cash Investment: $75K
Total Investment: $45.6-189.8K
Minimum Net Worth: $250K
Fees: Franchise - $12.5K
Royalty - 4%; Ad. - .05%
Earnings Claim Statement: No
Term of Contract (Years): 5/5/5
Avg. # Of Employees: 1 FT
Passive Ownership: Discouraged
Encourage Conversions: No
Area Develop. Agreements: No
Sub-Franchising Contracts: No
Expand In Territory: Yes
Space Needs: 100 SF; RM

SUPPORT & TRAINING PROVIDED:
Financial Assistance Provided: No
Site Selection Assistance: Yes
Lease Negotiation Assistance: Yes
Co-Operative Advertising: No
Franchisee Assoc./Member: No
Size Of Corporate Staff: 130
On-Going Support: B,C,D,E,G,H
Training: 2 Days in Paducah, KY; 2 Days On-Site.

SPECIFIC EXPANSION PLANS:
US: All United States
Canada: No
Overseas: No

<< >>

EMACK & BOLIO'S ICE CREAM & YOGURT

P.O. Box 703
Brookline Village, MA 02447
Tel: (617) 739-7995
Fax: (617) 232-1102
E-Mail: enbic@aol.com
Mr. Robert Rook, President

Best Ice Cream in NYC - 2000; Best Buy in NYC - 1999 Zagat Survey; Best Ice Cream Cape Cod; Best Ice Cream New Jersey; Best Ice Cream L.A. 1998; Best Smoothie in Boston 1999. We train in our Macy's NYC Store and give additional training in your store at opening. Manuals and videos provided, ad slicks. No fees or royalties. 25 years' experience.

BACKGROUND:
Established: 1975; 1st Franchised: 1977
Franchised Units: 40
Company-Owned Units <u>4</u>
Total Units: 44
Dist.: US-37; CAN-0; O'seas-0
North America: 10 States
Density: 13 in MA, 5 in NJ, 4 in NY
Projected New Units (12 Months): 6
Qualifications: 3, 3, 1, 2, 4, 4
Registered: All States

FINANCIAL/TERMS:
Cash Investment: $60-90K
Total Investment: $60-90K
Minimum Net Worth: $N/A
Fees: Franchise - $0
Royalty - 0%; Ad. - 0%
Earnings Claim Statement: No
Term of Contract (Years): 20/10
Avg. # Of Employees: 2 FT, 4-10 PT
Passive Ownership: Discouraged
Encourage Conversions: Yes
Area Develop. Agreements: Yes/20
Sub-Franchising Contracts: Yes
Expand In Territory: Yes
Space Needs: 200-1,500 SF; SF

SUPPORT & TRAINING PROVIDED:
Financial Assistance Provided: No
Site Selection Assistance: No
Lease Negotiation Assistance: Yes
Co-Operative Advertising: No
Franchisee Assoc./Member: No
Size Of Corporate Staff: 3
On-Going Support: B,C,D,E,F,G
Training: 1 Week Macy's NYC.

SPECIFIC EXPANSION PLANS:
US: All United States
Canada: No
Overseas: No

<< >>

GOOD FOR YOU! YOGURT

24-4567 Lougheed Hwy.
Burnaby, BC V5C 3Z6 CANADA
Tel: (604) 570-0570
Fax: (604) 299-2797
Mr. Karim Rahemtulla, General Manager

Fresh fruit and frozen yogurt business, combined with serving healthy breakfast and lunches.

BACKGROUND:
Established: 1983; 1st Franchised: 1983

Franchised Units:	15
Company-Owned Units	0
Total Units:	15
Dist.:	US-0; CAN-16; O'seas-0
North America:	2 Provinces
Density:	9 in AB, 7 in BC
Projected New Units (12 Months):	5
Qualifications:	4, 4, 3, 3, 3, 5

Registered: AB

FINANCIAL/TERMS:

Cash Investment:	$30K
Total Investment:	$70-110K
Minimum Net Worth:	$50K
Fees: Franchise -	$25K
Royalty - 6%;	Ad. - 2%
Earnings Claim Statement:	No
Term of Contract (Years):	5/5
Avg. # Of Employees:	1 FT, 1 PT
Passive Ownership:	Discouraged
Encourage Conversions:	Yes
Area Develop. Agreements:	Yes/5
Sub-Franchising Contracts:	No
Expand In Territory:	Yes

Space Needs: 500 SF; RM

SUPPORT & TRAINING PROVIDED:

Financial Assistance Provided:	Yes(I)
Site Selection Assistance:	Yes
Lease Negotiation Assistance:	Yes
Co-Operative Advertising:	Yes
Franchisee Assoc./Member:	No
Size Of Corporate Staff:	3
On-Going Support:	C,D,E,G,h,I

Training: 5 Days in AB.

SPECIFIC EXPANSION PLANS:

US:	No
Canada:	All Canada
Overseas:	Japan, Chile, South Africa

<< >>

HAPPY & HEALTHY PRODUCTS

1600 S. Dixie Hwy., # 200
Boca Raton, FL 33432
Tel: (800) 764-6114 (561) 367-0739
Fax: (561) 368-5267
E-Mail: franchiseinfo@fruitfull.com
Web Site: www.fruitfull.com
Ms. Susan Scotts, VP Sales & Marketing

A wholesale distributorship for the sale of FRUITFULL frozen fruit bars and other delicious novelties through dedicated freezers placed in retail locations or in retailer's own freezers. Super Grand, Grand and Standard wholesale franchisees will receive the services of a marketing consultant who will provide on-site training in identifying and negotiating agreements to place freezers. Training includes stocking, collection and route service procedures ..

BACKGROUND: IFA MEMBER
Established: 1991; 1st Franchised: 1993

Franchised Units:	85
Company-Owned Units	0
Total Units:	85
Dist.:	US-85; CAN-0; O'seas-0
North America:	39 States
Density:	11 in CA, 7 in NJ, 5 in IL
Projected New Units (12 Months):	12
Qualifications:	5, 5, 3, 3, 3, 5

Registered: All States Except ND, WA

FINANCIAL/TERMS:

Cash Investment:	$23-55K
Total Investment:	$23-55K
Minimum Net Worth:	$23-55K
Fees: Franchise -	$17-24K
Royalty - 0%;	Ad. - 0%
Earnings Claim Statement:	No
Term of Contract (Years):	10/5
Avg. # Of Employees:	1 FT or 1 PT
Passive Ownership:	Discouraged
Encourage Conversions:	No
Area Develop. Agreements:	No
Sub-Franchising Contracts:	No
Expand In Territory:	Yes

Space Needs: N/A SF; N/A

SUPPORT & TRAINING PROVIDED:

Financial Assistance Provided:	No
Site Selection Assistance:	N/A
Lease Negotiation Assistance:	N/A
Co-Operative Advertising:	N/A
Franchisee Assoc./Member:	No
Size Of Corporate Staff:	10
On-Going Support:	b,C,D,G,H

Training: 1 or 2 Weeks in Franchise MSA.

SPECIFIC EXPANSION PLANS:

US:	All Except WA,LA,ND,ME
Canada:	No
Overseas:	No

<< >>

I CAN'T BELIEVE IT'S YOGURT

4175 Veterans Hwy.
Ronkonkoma, NY 11779
Tel: (800) 423-2763 (631) 737-9700
Fax:
Web Site: www.yogenfruz.com
Mr. Joe Arancio, VP Franchise Development

We are the leading premier yogurt franchisor domestically and internationally. I CAN'T BELIEVE IT'S YOGURT is noted for developing smooth, creamy, sweet-tasting frozen yogurt in more than 100 self-serve flavor combinations in original, non-fat, and sugar- free varieties.

BACKGROUND:
Established: 1977; 1st Franchised: 1983

Franchised Units:	400
Company-Owned Units	940
Total Units:	1,340
Dist.:	US-1025; CAN-0; O'seas-317
North America:	33 States
Density:	33 in TX, 16 in NC, 15 in FL
Projected New Units (12 Months):	NR
Qualifications:	4, 2, 3, 2, 2, 4

Registered: CA,IL,IN,MN,OR,RI,WA,WI, DC

FINANCIAL/TERMS:

Cash Investment:	$50K
Total Investment:	$110-203K
Minimum Net Worth:	$200K
Fees: Franchise -	$15K
Royalty - 0%;	Ad. - 2.3%
Earnings Claim Statement:	NR
Term of Contract (Years):	10/10
Avg. # Of Employees:	2 FT, 6 PT
Passive Ownership:	Discouraged
Encourage Conversions:	Yes
Area Develop. Agreements:	Yes
Sub-Franchising Contracts:	Yes
Expand In Territory:	Yes

Space Needs: 1,200 SF; SC, RM

SUPPORT & TRAINING PROVIDED:

Financial Assistance Provided:	No
Site Selection Assistance:	Yes
Lease Negotiation Assistance:	Yes

Co-Operative Advertising: N/A
Franchisee Assoc./Member: Yes
Size Of Corporate Staff: 60
On-Going Support: E,G
Training: 10 Days Corporate Headquarters; 1 Week Store.

SPECIFIC EXPANSION PLANS:

US: All United States
Canada: No
Overseas: All Countries

<< >>

ICE CREAM CHURN

4175 Veterans Hwy.
Ronkonkoma, NY 11779
Tel: (800) 423-2763 (631) 737-9700
Fax: (516) 737-9792
Web Site: www.yogenfruz.com
Mr. Lee Anderson, President

ICE CREAM CHURN's concept is to add an old-fashioned ice cream parlor within another existing location, such as delis, bakeries, video stores, convenience stores, truckstops. ICE CREAM CHURN sets up location, trains employees, installs exterior signs and supports location with on-going promotions and training. 32 flavors of ice cream and yogurt are available. Master franchise available. New mall kiosk also available!

BACKGROUND:

Established: 1973; 1st Franchised: 1979
Franchised Units: 470
Company-Owned Units 0
Total Units: 470
Dist.: US-516; CAN-0; O'seas-10
North America: 32 States
Density: 117 in FL, 83 in AR, 42 AL
Projected New Units (12 Months): 100
Registered: FL,IL,IN,MD,RI,VA,DC

FINANCIAL/TERMS:

Cash Investment: $5-35K
Total Investment: $5-35K
Minimum Net Worth: $NR
Fees: Franchise - $5K
Royalty - $1.40/Tub; Ad. - $0.25/Tub
Earnings Claim Statement: No
Term of Contract (Years): 10/5
Avg. # Of Employees: 1 PT
Passive Ownership: Allowed
Encourage Conversions: Yes
Area Develop. Agreements: No
Sub-Franchising Contracts: Yes
Expand In Territory: Yes
Space Needs: 135 SF; Existing Business

SUPPORT & TRAINING PROVIDED:

Financial Assistance Provided: Yes
Site Selection Assistance: Yes
Lease Negotiation Assistance: Yes
Co-Operative Advertising: Yes
Franchisee Assoc./Member: No
Size Of Corporate Staff: 7
On-Going Support: D,E,F,G,I
Training: As Needed.

SPECIFIC EXPANSION PLANS:

US: Seeking Master Franchisees
Canada: All Canada
Overseas: All Countries

<< >>

JULIE ANN'S FROZEN CUSTARD

4314 F Crystal Lake Rd.
McHenry, IL 60050
Tel: (815) 459-9193
Fax: (815) 459-9195
Web Site: www.julieanns.com
Mr. Peter Wisniewski, President

JULIE ANN'S FROZEN CUSTARD is famous for its freshly-made frozen custard. It's like ultra ice cream. We make our product into sundaes, shakes, cones and 40 flavors of carry-out flavors. Fast food is available for year-round business. Our recipe is believed to be the finest in the world. Voted 'Best of Chicago' by New City magazine.

BACKGROUND:

Established: 1985; 1st Franchised: 1997
Franchised Units: 4
Company-Owned Units 1
Total Units: 5
Dist.: US-5; CAN-0; O'seas-0
North America: 1 State
Density: 5 in IL
Projected New Units (12 Months): 5
Qualifications: 5, 2, 1, 3, 4, 5
Registered: IL

FINANCIAL/TERMS:

Cash Investment: $150-200K
Total Investment: $150-280K
Minimum Net Worth: $500K
Fees: Franchise - $25-35K
Royalty - 4-4.5%; Ad. - 0-2%
Earnings Claim Statement: Yes
Term of Contract (Years): 10/5/5
Avg. # Of Employees: 3 FT, 22 PT
Passive Ownership: Discouraged
Encourage Conversions: No
Area Develop. Agreements: Yes
Sub-Franchising Contracts: No
Expand In Territory: Yes
Space Needs: 22,000 SF; FS, SC, RM

SUPPORT & TRAINING PROVIDED:

Financial Assistance Provided: No
Site Selection Assistance: Yes
Lease Negotiation Assistance: Yes
Co-Operative Advertising: Yes
Franchisee Assoc./Member: No
Size Of Corporate Staff: 1
On-Going Support: B,C,D,E,F
Training: 1-2 Weeks Chicago, IL; 1-2 Weeks Franchisee Location.

SPECIFIC EXPANSION PLANS:

US: IL Only
Canada: No
Overseas: No

<< >>

KOHR BROS. FROZEN CUSTARD

2115 Berkmar Dr.
Charlottesville, VA 22901
Tel: (888) 527-9783 (434) 975-1500
Fax: (434) 975-1505
E-Mail: dennispoletti@kohrbros.com
Web Site: www.kohrbros.com
Mr. Dennis G. Poletti, Executive Director Franchising

KOHR BROS. is the original frozen custard since 1919. Our stores, which are bright and easily maintained, offer a simple and unique frozen dessert concept.

BACKGROUND: IFA MEMBER

Established: 1919; 1st Franchised: 1994
Franchised Units: 37
Company-Owned Units 11
Total Units: 48
Dist.: US-39; CAN-0; O'seas-0
North America: 11 States
Density: 10 in NJ, 6 in VA, 5 in FL
Projected New Units (12 Months): 24
Qualifications: 5, 5, 2, 4, 4, 5
Registered: FL,MD,MI,NY,VA

FINANCIAL/TERMS:

Cash Investment: $75K
Total Investment: $145.9-277.5K
Minimum Net Worth: $300K
Fees: Franchise - $27.5K
Royalty - 5%; Ad. - 1%
Earnings Claim Statement: No
Term of Contract (Years): 5/3/5
Avg. # Of Employees: 6 FT, 4 PT
Passive Ownership: Allowed
Encourage Conversions: Yes
Area Develop. Agreements: Yes
Sub-Franchising Contracts: No
Expand In Territory: Yes
Space Needs: 500 SF; FS, SC, RM, Kiosk

SUPPORT & TRAINING PROVIDED:

Financial Assistance Provided: Yes(I)
Site Selection Assistance: Yes
Lease Negotiation Assistance: Yes

Co-Operative Advertising: Yes
Franchisee Assoc./Member: No
Size Of Corporate Staff: 11
On-Going Support: A,B,C,D,E,F,G,H,I
Training: 6 Days in Corporate Offices; 3 Days at Franchisee Unit.

SPECIFIC EXPANSION PLANS:

US: All United States
Canada: No
Overseas: No

<< >>

MAGGIEMOO'S INTERNATIONAL

10290 Old Columbia Rd., # 305
Columbia, MD 21046
Tel: (800) 949-8114 (410) 309-6001
Fax: (410) 309-6006
E-Mail: info@maggiemoos.com
Web Site: www.maggiemoos.com
Ms. Suzy Amette, Mgr. Franchise Development

Unique and exciting retail shop, featuring homemade, super-premium ice cream, non-fat ice cream, custom-made cones, sorbet, smoothies, homemade fudge, plus a line of specialty merchandise. We make our ice cream fresh in the store and serve it in fresh- baked waffle cones. Featuring over 40 mix-ins and folded in on a frozen granite slab to create 1,000s of great combos. Association with a marketable spokes character - MAGGIE MOO - in a fun, contemporary store design.

BACKGROUND: IFA MEMBER
Established: 1996; 1st Franchised: 1996
Franchised Units: 100
Company-Owned Units 1
Total Units: 101
Dist.: US-51; CAN-0; O'seas-0
North America: 19 States
Density: 6 in KS, 6 in MO, 4 in TX
Projected New Units (12 Months): 30
Qualifications: 4, 5, 3, 2, 3, 5
Registered: CA,FL,IL,MD,MI,OR,RI,VA, WA,WI,DC

FINANCIAL/TERMS:

Cash Investment: $50-70K
Total Investment: $150-285K
Minimum Net Worth: $250K
Fees: Franchise - $23K
Royalty - 6%; Ad. - 2%
Earnings Claim Statement: No
Term of Contract (Years): 10/5/5
Avg. # Of Employees: 3 FT, 8 PT
Passive Ownership: Discouraged
Encourage Conversions: Yes
Area Develop. Agreements: Yes/3
Sub-Franchising Contracts: No
Expand In Territory: Yes
Space Needs: 900-1,400 SF; SC

SUPPORT & TRAINING PROVIDED:

Financial Assistance Provided: No
Site Selection Assistance: Yes
Lease Negotiation Assistance: Yes
Co-Operative Advertising: Yes
Franchisee Assoc./Member: Yes/Yes
Size Of Corporate Staff: 14
On-Going Support: B,C,D,E,F,G,h,I
Training: 11 Days Alexandria, VA; 6 Days Grand Opening On-Site.

SPECIFIC EXPANSION PLANS:

US: All United States
Canada: No
Overseas: No

<< >>

MARBLE SLAB CREAMERY

3100 S. Gessner Dr., # 305
Houston, TX 77063
Tel: (713) 780-3601
Fax: (713) 780-0264
E-Mail: cdull@marbleslab.com
Web Site: www.marbleslab.com
Mr. Chris Dull, VP Fran. Dev.

Retail ice cream stores, featuring super-premium homemade ice cream, cones baked fresh daily, frozen yogurt, frozen pies and cakes, homemade cookies and brownies and specialty coffees. Ice cream is custom-designed for customer on frozen marble slab and made daily in the store.

BACKGROUND: IFA MEMBER
Established: 1983; 1st Franchised: 1984
Franchised Units: 218
Company-Owned Units 1
Total Units: 219
Dist.: US-219; CAN-0; O'seas-0
North America: 24 States
Density: 106 in TX, 20 in FL,12 in GA
Projected New Units (12 Months): 15
Qualifications: 5, 3, 1, 3, 3, 5
Registered: All States

FINANCIAL/TERMS:

Cash Investment: $40-60K
Total Investment: $178-238K
Minimum Net Worth: $250K
Fees: Franchise - $23K
Royalty - 6%; Ad. - 2%
Earnings Claim Statement: Yes
Term of Contract (Years): 10/10
Avg. # Of Employees: 2 FT, 8 PT
Passive Ownership: Discouraged
Encourage Conversions: Yes
Area Develop. Agreements: Yes/Varies
Sub-Franchising Contracts: No
Expand In Territory: No
Space Needs: 500-1,800 SF; SC, RM

SUPPORT & TRAINING PROVIDED:

Financial Assistance Provided: No
Site Selection Assistance: Yes
Lease Negotiation Assistance: Yes
Co-Operative Advertising: Yes
Franchisee Assoc./Member: Yes/No
Size Of Corporate Staff: 25
On-Going Support: B,C,D,E,H
Training: 10 Days Franchisor Location; 6 Days Franchisee Site.

SPECIFIC EXPANSION PLANS:

US: SW, S, SE, W, Midwest, East
Canada: All Canada
Overseas: All Countries

<< >>

MORRONE'S ITALIAN ICES & HOMEMADE ICE CREAM

200 N. 63rd St.
Philadelphia, PA 19151
Tel: (888) MORRONES (610) 446-5668
Fax: (610) 446-2388
E-Mail: morronesices@cs.com
Web Site: www.morrones.com
Mr. Steve D. Aleardi, Director of Sales

Retail outlets selling Italian Ices and a special blend of homemade ice cream made right on the premises. Also offering walk-in, year- round operations.

BACKGROUND:
Established: 1910; 1st Franchised: 2002

Franchised Units: 2
Company-Owned Units 1
Total Units: 3
Dist.: US-3; CAN-0; O'seas-0
North America: 2 States
Density: 2 in PA
Projected New Units (12 Months): 10-15
Qualifications: 5, 2, 2, 3, 5, 5
Registered: NR

FINANCIAL/TERMS:

Cash Investment: $20K
Total Investment: $115-150K
Minimum Net Worth: $100K
Fees: Franchise - $20K
Royalty - 0%; Ad. - 0%
Earnings Claim Statement: No
Term of Contract (Years): 10
Avg. # Of Employees: 2 FT, 6 PT
Passive Ownership: Discouraged
Encourage Conversions: Yes
Area Develop. Agreements: Yes
Sub-Franchising Contracts: Yes
Expand In Territory: Yes
Space Needs: 500-1,000 SF; FS, SF, SC, RM

SUPPORT & TRAINING PROVIDED:

Financial Assistance Provided: Yes(I)
Site Selection Assistance: Yes
Lease Negotiation Assistance: Yes
Co-Operative Advertising: No
Franchisee Assoc./Member: No
Size Of Corporate Staff: 8
On-Going Support: A,C,D,E,F,G,I
Training: 40-100 Hours at Location.

SPECIFIC EXPANSION PLANS:

US: All United States
Canada: No
Overseas: No

<< >>

PETRUCCI'S ICE CREAM CO.

2362 State Rd.
Bensalem, PA 19020
Tel: (888) 738-7822 (215) 245-6688
Fax: (215) 245-1563
E-Mail: mpmogul@aol.com
Web Site: www.petruccis.com
Mr. Mice Petrucci, President

Retailing '50' wild whirling flavors of soft ice cream, homemade fresh fruit Italian ices, frozen yogurt and premium hand-dipped ice cream. All shops feature custom decorated ice cream cakes and proprietary take home frozen novelties.

BACKGROUND:

Established: 1983; 1st Franchised: 1996
Franchised Units: 41
Company-Owned Units 5
Total Units: 46
Dist.: US-0; CAN-0; O'seas-0
North America: 5 States
Density: 18 in PA, 8 in NJ, 2 in MD
Projected New Units (12 Months): 25
Registered: MD

FINANCIAL/TERMS:

Cash Investment: $20K
Total Investment: $139.9-229.9K
Minimum Net Worth: $150K
Fees: Franchise - $20K
Royalty - 5%; Ad. - 2%
Earnings Claim Statement: No
Term of Contract (Years): 10/5
Avg. # Of Employees: 5 FT, 3 PT
Passive Ownership: Discouraged
Encourage Conversions: Yes
Area Develop. Agreements: Yes/10
Sub-Franchising Contracts: No
Expand In Territory: Yes
Space Needs: 1,250 SF; FS, RM

SUPPORT & TRAINING PROVIDED:

Financial Assistance Provided: Yes
Site Selection Assistance: Yes
Lease Negotiation Assistance: Yes
Co-Operative Advertising: Yes
Franchisee Assoc./Member: Yes/Yes
Size Of Corporate Staff: 7
On-Going Support: C,D,E,F,G,H
Training: 3 Days Langhorne, PA; 3 Days Local Shop Training; 3-4 Days at Your Location When Open.

SPECIFIC EXPANSION PLANS:

US: NE, SE
Canada: NR
Overseas: NR

<< >>

Rita's
Ices • Cones • Shakes and other Cool Stuff

Top 50

RITA'S ITALIAN ICE

1525 Ford Rd.
Bensalem, PA 19020
Tel: (800) 677-7482 (215) 633-9899
Fax: (215) 633-9922
Web Site: www.ritasice.com
Mr. Steve Beagelman, VP Franchising

Retail outlets selling Italian ices.

BACKGROUND: IFA MEMBER

Established: 1984; 1st Franchised: 1989
Franchised Units: 222
Company-Owned Units 3
Total Units: 225
Dist.: US-225; CAN-0; O'seas-0
North America: 9 States
Density: 104 in PA, 44 in NJ,10 in MD
Projected New Units (12 Months): 36
Qualifications: 5, 3, 2, 3, 5, 5
Registered: CA,MD,NY,VA

FINANCIAL/TERMS:

Cash Investment: $50-70K
Total Investment: $135-242K
Minimum Net Worth: $250K
Fees: Franchise - $25K
Royalty - 6.5%; Ad. - 2.5%
Earnings Claim Statement: Yes
Term of Contract (Years): 10/10
Avg. # Of Employees: 1 FT, 9 PT
Passive Ownership: Discouraged
Encourage Conversions: Yes
Area Develop. Agreements: Yes
Sub-Franchising Contracts: No
Expand In Territory: Yes
Space Needs: 600-1,500 SF; FS

SUPPORT & TRAINING PROVIDED:

Financial Assistance Provided: Yes(I)
Site Selection Assistance: Yes
Lease Negotiation Assistance: Yes
Co-Operative Advertising: Yes
Franchisee Assoc./Member: Yes/Yes
Size Of Corporate Staff: 33
On-Going Support: B,C,D,E,G,h
Training: 6 Days Corporate Office; 2-4 Days On-Site.

SPECIFIC EXPANSION PLANS:

US: FL,MD,OH,VA,PA,NE,SC,WV
Canada: No
Overseas: No

SCOOPERS ICE CREAM

22 Woodrow Ave.
Youngstown, OH 44512-3306
Tel: (330) 758-3857
Fax: (330) 758-4405
Mr. Norman J. Hughes, Jr., President

SCOOPERS ICE CREAM is a made-fresh-daily concept at each location. Using only the finest ingredients in a homemade, low over-run, high-butterfat, gourmet ice cream. As many as 100 flavors and yogurts and sherbets are made fresh at your location.

BACKGROUND:
Established: 1981; 1st Franchised: 1991
Franchised Units: 8
Company-Owned Units 2
Total Units: 10
Dist.: US-10; CAN-0; O'seas-0
North America: 3 States
Density: 7 in PA, 2 in OH, 1 in FL
Projected New Units (12 Months): 8
Qualifications: 2, 1, 1, 2, 3, 3
Registered: NR

FINANCIAL/TERMS:
Cash Investment: $50K
Total Investment: $50-80K
Minimum Net Worth: $75K
Fees: Franchise - $15K
Royalty - 5%; Ad. - 0%
Earnings Claim Statement: No
Term of Contract (Years): 10/10
Avg. # Of Employees: 2 FT, 20 PT
Passive Ownership: Allowed
Encourage Conversions: Yes
Area Develop. Agreements: Yes/5
Sub-Franchising Contracts: Yes
Expand In Territory: Yes
Space Needs: 700-1,200 SF; FS, SF, SC, RM

SUPPORT & TRAINING PROVIDED:
Financial Assistance Provided: No
Site Selection Assistance: Yes
Lease Negotiation Assistance: Yes
Co-Operative Advertising: Yes
Franchisee Assoc./Member: No
Size Of Corporate Staff: 5
On-Going Support: E
Training: 2-4 Days at Main Store Location; 1 Day at Store Opening.

SPECIFIC EXPANSION PLANS:
US: All United States
Canada: All Canada
Overseas: NR

SHAKE'S FROZEN CUSTARD
244 W. Dickson St.
Fayetteville, AR 72701
Tel: (866) 742-5648 (501) 587-9115
Fax: (501) 587-0780
E-Mail: info@shakesfrozencustard.com
Web Site: www.shakesfrozencustard.com
Mr. Jim Buckner, Executive Vice President

SHAKE'S FROZEN CUSTARD is where friends gather, couples fall in love, and people of all ages come to enjoy the vibrant nostalgic atmosphere of the 40's and 50's. Featuring an extensive menu consisting of our one-of-a-kind, delicious frozen custard and a wide variety of innovative concepts, SHAKE'S is a rapidly growing franchise system. With intensive training and continuous support, we will always ensure your business is operating to its maximum potential.

BACKGROUND:
Established: 1991; 1st Franchised: 1999
Franchised Units: 25
Company-Owned Units 3
Total Units: 28
Dist.: US-28; CAN-0; O'seas-0
North America: 8 States
Density: 12 in AR, 5 in MO, 3 OK
Projected New Units (12 Months): 25
Qualifications: 4, 4, 2, 1, 3, 5
Registered: FL,IL,IN,VA,WI

FINANCIAL/TERMS:
Cash Investment: $50-250K
Total Investment: $166-800K
Minimum Net Worth: $250K
Fees: Franchise - $30K
Royalty - 5; Ad. - 3%
Earnings Claim Statement: Yes
Term of Contract (Years): 15/5
Avg. # Of Employees: 2 FT, 12 PT
Passive Ownership: Discouraged
Encourage Conversions: No
Area Develop. Agreements: Yes/15
Sub-Franchising Contracts: No
Expand In Territory: Yes
Space Needs: 1,200 SF; FS

SUPPORT & TRAINING PROVIDED:
Financial Assistance Provided: Yes(I)
Site Selection Assistance: Yes
Lease Negotiation Assistance: Yes
Co-Operative Advertising: Yes
Franchisee Assoc./Member: Yes
Size Of Corporate Staff: 10
On-Going Support: A,B,C,D,E,F,G,h
Training: 1 Week in Fayetteville, AR and 1 Week in Joplin, MO.

SPECIFIC EXPANSION PLANS:
US: Southeast Southwest Midwest
Canada: No
Overseas: No

SWEET LICKS
1525 Ashbury Ln.
Pittsburgh, PA 15237
Tel: (412) 366-6531
Fax: (412) 366-6531
E-Mail: sweetlicks77@hotmail.com
Mr. Tony Battaglia, President

SWEET LICKS features REAL soft ice cream, non-fat yogurt and over 40 flavors of premium, hand-packed ice cream. Our extensive variety of reasonably-priced products is second to none. Outstanding customer service is a result of our 'hands on' training. Delicious, elegant ice cream cakes and pies are made daily in our stores for all occasions. Spacious outdoor decks provide a relaxed atmosphere while our loyal customers enjoy our refreshing ice cream treats.

BACKGROUND:
Established: 1980; 1st Franchised: 1999
Franchised Units: 1
Company-Owned Units 2
Total Units: 3
Dist.: US-3; CAN-0; O'seas-0
North America: 1 State
Density: 3 in PA
Projected New Units (12 Months): 10
Qualifications: 4, 3, 3, 3, 3, 5
Registered: NR

FINANCIAL/TERMS:
Cash Investment: $40-115K
Total Investment: $115K
Minimum Net Worth: $None
Fees: Franchise - $20K
Royalty - 6%; Ad. - 0%
Earnings Claim Statement: No
Term of Contract (Years): 10/5
Avg. # Of Employees: 2-3 FT, 12-18 PT
Passive Ownership: Discouraged
Encourage Conversions: No
Area Develop. Agreements: Yes/Varies
Sub-Franchising Contracts: No
Expand In Territory: Yes
Space Needs: 1,200-1,500 SF; FS

SUPPORT & TRAINING PROVIDED:
Financial Assistance Provided: Yes(I)
Site Selection Assistance: Yes
Lease Negotiation Assistance: Yes

Co-Operative Advertising: No
Franchisee Assoc./Member: No
Size Of Corporate Staff: 3
On-Going Support: B,C,D,E,F,G
Training: 2 Weeks SWEET LICKS Stores in Western PA.

SPECIFIC EXPANSION PLANS:
US: Eastern United States
Canada: No
Overseas: No

<< >>

TCBY TREATS

2855 E. Cottonwood Pkwy., # 400
Salt Lake City, UT 84121-7050
Tel: (800) 348-6311 (801) 736-5600
Fax: (801) 736-5936
E-Mail: frandev@mrsfields.com
Web Site: www.tcby.com
Mr. Scott Moffitt, SVP Development

TCBY TREATS shops offer yogurt, sorbet and ice cream products, as well as a complete line of pies and cakes. TCBY Systems, Inc. offers franchises for traditional locations, and for 'combined concept' locations, wherein TCBY TREATS shops are operated within another business.

BACKGROUND: IFA MEMBER
Established: 1981; 1st Franchised: 1982
Franchised Units: 2,104
Company-Owned Units 1
Total Units: 2,105
Dist.: US-1827; CAN-42; O'seas-236
North America: 50 States, 2 Provinces
Density: NR
Projected New Units (12 Months): NR
Qualifications: 5, 3, 2, 2, 2, 4
Registered: All States and AB

FINANCIAL/TERMS:
Cash Investment: $N/A
Total Investment: $192-337K
Minimum Net Worth: $75-150K
Fees: Franchise - $20K
Royalty - 4%; Ad. - 3%
Earnings Claim Statement: No
Term of Contract (Years): 10/10
Avg. # Of Employees: 2 FT, 8 PT
Passive Ownership: Discouraged
Encourage Conversions: Yes
Area Develop. Agreements: No
Sub-Franchising Contracts: No
Expand In Territory: Yes
Space Needs: 100-2,000 SF; FS, SF, SC, RM, C-Store, QSR

SUPPORT & TRAINING PROVIDED:
Financial Assistance Provided: No
Site Selection Assistance: Yes
Lease Negotiation Assistance: No
Co-Operative Advertising: Yes
Franchisee Assoc./Member: Yes/Yes
Size Of Corporate Staff: 400+
On-Going Support: C,D,E,G,H,I
Training: 6.5 Days Little Rock, AR.

SPECIFIC EXPANSION PLANS:
US: All United States
Canada: All Canada
Overseas: All Countries

<< >>

YOGEN FRUZ

8300 Woodbine Ave., 5th Fl.
Markham, ON L3R 94Y CANADA
Tel: (905) 479-8762
Fax: (905) 479-5235
E-Mail: yogenfruz@yogenfruz.com
Web Site: www.yogenfruz.com
Mr. Aaron Serruya, President

YOGEN FRUZ is a frozen yogurt franchise chain. Frozen yogurt and fresh fruit are blended in front of the customer's eyes! We also sell shakes, pies, juices, ice cream, smoothies and fruity ice.

BACKGROUND:
Established: 1986; 1st Franchised: 1987
Franchised Units: 5,196
Company-Owned Units 33
Total Units: 5,239
Dist.: US-1687; CAN-795; O'seas-2747
North America: 50 States,10 Provinces
Density: 375 in ON, 200 in TX
Projected New Units (12 Months): 500
Qualifications: 5, 4, 1, 1, 3, 5
Registered: All States and AB

FINANCIAL/TERMS:
Cash Investment: $50% Total Inv
Total Investment: $130-250K
Minimum Net Worth: $200K
Fees: Franchise - $25K
Royalty - 6%; Ad. - 3%
Earnings Claim Statement: No
Term of Contract (Years): 5-10/5-10
Avg. # Of Employees: 2 FT, 4 PT
Passive Ownership: Not Allowed
Encourage Conversions: Yes
Area Develop. Agreements: Yes/10
Sub-Franchising Contracts: Yes
Expand In Territory: No
Space Needs: 150-1,500 SF; SF, SC, RM

SUPPORT & TRAINING PROVIDED:
Financial Assistance Provided: Yes(I)
Site Selection Assistance: Yes
Lease Negotiation Assistance: Yes
Co-Operative Advertising: Yes
Franchisee Assoc./Member: Yes/No
Size Of Corporate Staff: 60
On-Going Support: C,D,E,F,G,H
Training: 2 Weeks in Dallas, TX; 1.5 Weeks in Toronto, ON.

SPECIFIC EXPANSION PLANS:
US: All United States
Canada: All Canada
Overseas: All Countries

<< >>

SUPPLEMENTAL LISTING OF FRANCHISORS

ABBOTT'S FROZEN CUSTARD, 4791 Lake Ave., Rochester, NY 14612 ; (716) 865-7400; (716) 865-6034

BRESLER'S ICE CREAM, 4175 Vererans Hwy., Ronkonkoma, NY 11779 ; (800) 423-2763

HAAGEN-DAZS, 200 S. Sixth St., MS29 R1, Minneapolis, MN 55402-1464 ; (800) 793-6872 (6120 330-4490; (612) 330-7074

ICE CREAM CLUB, THE, 1580 High Ridge Rd., Boynton Beach, FL 33426 ; (561) 731-3331; (561) 731-0311

JOE'S ITALIAN ICES, 2362 State Rd., Rear Bldg., Bensalem, PA 19020 ; (800) 563-7423 (215) 338-0100; (215) 338-7262

PERKITS YOGURT SHOPS, P.O. Box 2862, Cleveland, TN 37320 ; (423) 559-9505; (423) 559-9914

PICKLES AND ICE CREAM, 203 Main St., Thomson, GA 30824-2616 ; (706) 595-9779; (706) 595-9560

RITTER'S FROZEN CUSTARD, 5222 Southeast St., Bldg. B, # 1, Indianapolis, IN 46227 ; (317) 786-3000; (317) 786-9361

Food: Quick Service/Take-Out

Chapter **16**

FOOD: QUICK SERVICE/TAKE-OUT INDUSTRY PROFILE

Total # Franchisors in Industry Group	357
Total # Franchised Units in Industry Group	115,029
Total # Company-Owned Units in Industry Group	26,587
Total # Operating Units in Industry Group	141,616
Average # Franchised Units/Franchisor	322.2
Average # Company-Owned Units/Franchisor	74.5
Average # Total Units/Franchisor	396.7
Ratio of Total # Franchised Units/Total # Company-Owned Units	4.3:1
Industry Survey Participants	144
Representing % of Industry	40.3%
Average Franchise Fee*:	$21.2K
Average Total Investment*:	$337.3K
Average On-Going Royalty Fee*:	4.9%

*If a range was provided, the mid-point of the range was used. See detailed profiles for actual ranges.

FIVE LARGEST PARTICIPANTS IN SURVEY

Company	# Franchised Units	# Co-Owned Units	# Total Units	Franchise Fee	On-Going Royalty	Total Investment
1. McDonald's	21,702	7,354	29,056	45K	12.5%	489.8K-1.5MM
2. Subway Restaurants	16,232	1	16,233	10K	8%	66.8-188.5K
3. KFC	6,663	2,975	9,638	25K	4%	700K-1.2MM
4. Taco Bell	4,600	3,044	7,644	45K	5.5%	236-503K
5. Dairy Queen	6,032	63	6,095	20-35K	4-6%	200-950K

All of the data provided are proprietary and should not be quoted without acknowledging *Bond's Franchise Guide.*

Top 50

A & W RESTAURANTS

101 Yorkshire Blvd., P.O. Box 11988
Lexington, KY 40509
Tel: (800) 545-8360 (859) 543-6000
Fax: (859) 543-6190
E-Mail: fsales@ygrest.com
Web Site: www.ygrest.com
VP Franchising

A & W has been a successful, all-American icon for more than 80 years. Since repositioning A & W as the home of 'All American Food' with a menu of burgers, hot dogs, coney dogs, french fries, onion rings, and our signature A & W Root Beer and Root Beer floats, we have entered the ranks of the most rapidly-growing quick-service restaurants in the world. Opportunities to develop are now even greater with our new co-branded restaurants that combine A & W and our sister brand, LONG JOHN SILVER'S.

BACKGROUND: IFA MEMBER
Established: 1919; 1st Franchised: 1925
Franchised Units: 966
Company-Owned Units 131
Total Units: 1,097
Dist.: US-907; CAN-; O'seas-190
North America: 48 States
Density: NR
Projected New Units (12 Months): 300
Qualifications: 5, 5, 3, 4, 5, 5
Registered: All States Except DC,HI

FINANCIAL/TERMS:
Cash Investment: $75-150K
Total Investment: $75K-1.5MM
Minimum Net Worth: $100K
Fees: Franchise - $15-20K
Royalty - 5-5.5%; Ad. - 4%
Earnings Claim Statement: No
Term of Contract (Years): 10-20/1/5
Avg. # Of Employees: 50-60 FT & PT
Passive Ownership: Allowed
Encourage Conversions: Yes
Area Develop. Agreements: NR
Sub-Franchising Contracts: NR
Expand In Territory: Yes
Space Needs: 1,200+ SF; FS, SF, SC, RM, Non-Tradit.

SUPPORT & TRAINING PROVIDED:
Financial Assistance Provided: No
Site Selection Assistance: Yes
Lease Negotiation Assistance: Yes
Co-Operative Advertising: Yes
Franchisee Assoc./Member: Yes/Yes
Size Of Corporate Staff: 300
On-Going Support: B,C,D,E,F,G,H,I
Training: 2 Weeks Training with Pre-Opening and Opening Assistance.

SPECIFIC EXPANSION PLANS:
US: All United States
Canada: No
Overseas: All Countries

<< >>

AMECI PIZZA & PASTA

6603 Independence Ave., # B
Canoga Park, CA 91303
Tel: (818) 712-0110
Fax: (818) 712-0792
Web Site: www.imal.com
Mr. Nick Andrisano, President

Italian fast foods, such as pizza, pasta, salads and subs.

BACKGROUND:
Established: 1979; 1st Franchised: 1987
Franchised Units: 41
Company-Owned Units 2
Total Units: 43
Dist.: US-43; CAN-0; O'seas-0
North America: 1 State
Density: 43 in CA
Projected New Units (12 Months): 5
Qualifications: 5, 2, 1, 2, 2, 5
Registered: CA

FINANCIAL/TERMS:
Cash Investment: $185K
Total Investment: $135-235K
Minimum Net Worth: $250K
Fees: Franchise - $25K
Royalty - 4%; Ad. - 2%
Earnings Claim Statement: No
Term of Contract (Years): 10/10
Avg. # Of Employees: 4 FT, 5 PT
Passive Ownership: Discouraged
Encourage Conversions: Yes
Area Develop. Agreements: Yes/10/10
Sub-Franchising Contracts: No
Expand In Territory: Yes
Space Needs: 1,200 SF; SC

SUPPORT & TRAINING PROVIDED:
Financial Assistance Provided: No
Site Selection Assistance: Yes
Lease Negotiation Assistance: Yes
Co-Operative Advertising: Yes
Franchisee Assoc./Member: No
Size Of Corporate Staff: 7
On-Going Support: A,B,C,D,E,F,G,H,I
Training: 4 Weeks of School at Home Office; 2 Weeks at Unit Location.

SPECIFIC EXPANSION PLANS:
US: NR
Canada: No
Overseas: All Latin Countries

<< >>

ANDERSON'S RESTAURANTS

6075 Main St.
Williamsville, NY 14221
Tel: (716) 633-2302
Fax: (716) 633-2671
E-Mail: info@andersonscustard.com
Web Site: www.andersonscustard.com
Mr. Kirk P. Wildermuth, President

A Western New York tradition, serving award-winning roast beef, BBQ, chicken and ham sandwiches. Also, we are famous for our one-of-a-kind frozen custard, plus homemade ice cream. We also specialize in ice cream cakes and pies. We are the Northeast's premium lunch, dinner and dessert fast casual concept.

BACKGROUND: IFA MEMBER
Established: 1946; 1st Franchised: 1996
Franchised Units: 8
Company-Owned Units 3
Total Units: 11
Dist.: US-10; CAN-0; O'seas-0
North America: 1 State
Density: 9 in NY
Projected New Units (12 Months): NR
Registered: NR

FINANCIAL/TERMS:
Cash Investment: $400-500K
Total Investment: $900K-1.1MM
Minimum Net Worth: $500K
Fees: Franchise - $30K
Royalty - 4%; Ad. - 2%
Earnings Claim Statement: No
Term of Contract (Years): 20
Avg. # Of Employees: 10 FT, 25 PT
Passive Ownership: Not Allowed
Encourage Conversions: NR
Area Develop. Agreements: Yes/20
Sub-Franchising Contracts: No
Expand In Territory: Yes
Space Needs: 3,800 SF; FS, End Cap

SUPPORT & TRAINING PROVIDED:
Financial Assistance Provided: NR
Site Selection Assistance: Yes
Lease Negotiation Assistance: Yes
Co-Operative Advertising: Yes
Franchisee Assoc./Member: No
Size Of Corporate Staff: 7
On-Going Support: B,C,D,E,G
Training: 12-16 Weeks Buffalo, NY.
SPECIFIC EXPANSION PLANS:
US: OH, NY, PA
Canada: NR
Overseas: NR

<< >>

ARBY'S

1000 Corporate Dr.
Ft. Lauderdale, FL 33334-3655
Tel: (800) 487-2729 (954) 351-5100
Fax: (954) 351-5783
E-Mail: roshins@arby.com
Web Site: www.arby.com
Ms. Roni Oshins, VP Business Dev.

The leader in the roast beef segment, ARBY'S offers cut above menu options including a complete line of roast beef and chicken sandwiches, chicken fingers, a light sandwich menu, salads and three fry varieties. Development opportunities available. An experienced brand with over 3,200 locations.

BACKGROUND: IFA MEMBER
Established: 1964; 1st Franchised: 1965
Franchised Units: 3,256
Company-Owned Units 0
Total Units: 3,256
Dist.: US-3043; CAN-122; O'seas-36
North America: 48 States, 8 Provinces
Density: 248 in OH, 167 in CA, 166 MI
Projected New Units (12 Months): 150
Qualifications: 5, 5, 4, 3, 3, 5
Registered: All States
FINANCIAL/TERMS:
Cash Investment: $0-2,253,200
Total Investment: $212.9K-2.25MM
Minimum Net Worth: $1.0MM
Fees: Franchise - $37.5K
Royalty - 4%; Ad. - Min 3.7%
Earnings Claim Statement: Yes
Term of Contract (Years): 20/Varies
Avg. # Of Employees: 15 FT, 25 PT
Passive Ownership: Allowed
Encourage Conversions: Yes
Area Develop. Agreements: Yes/Varies
Sub-Franchising Contracts: No
Expand In Territory: Yes
Space Needs: 2,000-3,000 SF; FS

SUPPORT & TRAINING PROVIDED:
Financial Assistance Provided: No
Site Selection Assistance: Yes
Lease Negotiation Assistance: No
Co-Operative Advertising: Yes
Franchisee Assoc./Member: Yes/Yes
Size Of Corporate Staff: 150
On-Going Support: B,C,D,E,G,I
Training: 5 Weeks MTP-Certified Training Locations.
SPECIFIC EXPANSION PLANS:
US: NE, W, S
Canada: All Canada
Overseas: Canada, Mexico, Australia, U.K., Middle East

<< >>

ARTHUR TREACHER'S FISH & CHIPS

S. Dakota Dr., # 302
Lake Success, NY 11042
Tel: (516) 358-0600
Fax: (516) 358-0600
E-Mail: pudgiestreachers@aol.com
Mr. John Ryley, Dir. Franchising

Fast-food fish and chips, chicken and seafood.

BACKGROUND: IFA MEMBER
Established: 1969; 1st Franchised: 1970
Franchised Units: 65
Company-Owned Units 11
Total Units: 76
Dist.: US-59; CAN-9; O'seas-0
North America: 15 States
Density: 51 in OH, 27 in PA, 25 in FL
Projected New Units (12 Months): 60
Qualifications: 4, 4, 3, 3, 3, 4
Registered: FL,MI,NY
FINANCIAL/TERMS:
Cash Investment: $75-100K
Total Investment: $175-225K
Minimum Net Worth: $250K
Fees: Franchise - $30K
Royalty - 5%; Ad. - 3%
Earnings Claim Statement: No
Term of Contract (Years): 10/10
Avg. # Of Employees: 3 FT, 12 PT
Passive Ownership: Discouraged
Encourage Conversions: Yes
Area Develop. Agreements: Yes/Varies
Sub-Franchising Contracts: Yes
Expand In Territory: Yes
Space Needs: 500-2,000 SF; FS, SF, SC, RM
SUPPORT & TRAINING PROVIDED:
Financial Assistance Provided: No
Site Selection Assistance: Yes
Lease Negotiation Assistance: Yes
Co-Operative Advertising: Yes
Franchisee Assoc./Member: No
Size Of Corporate Staff: 50
On-Going Support: B,C,D,E,F,G,H,I
Training: 10 Days Long Island, NY.
SPECIFIC EXPANSION PLANS:
US: Northeast, Southeast
Canada: No
Overseas: No

<< >>

BACK YARD BURGERS

1657 N. Shelby Oaks Dr., #105
Memphis, TN 38134
Tel: (800) 292-6939 (901) 367-0888
Fax: (901) 367-0999
E-Mail: mpearce@backyardburgers.com
Web Site: www.backyardburgers.com
Mr. Mike Pearce, Dir. Franchise Development

BACK YARD BURGERS operates and franchises quick casual restaurants, serving 1/3 lb. gourmet hamburgers, boneless, skinless chicken fillet sandwiches, fresh lemonade, hand-dipped shakes and malts and other menu items. Our theme emphasizes charbroiled, fresh, great-tasting food as the customers would cook in their own back yard.

BACKGROUND:
Established: 1987; 1st Franchised: 1988
Franchised Units: 68
Company-Owned Units 37
Total Units: 105
Dist.: US-105; CAN-0; O'seas-0
North America: 17 States
Density: 32 in TN, 12 in AR, 10 in NC
Projected New Units (12 Months): 15
Qualifications: 4, 4, 3, 2, 1, 3
Registered: FL,IL,IN,MI,VA
FINANCIAL/TERMS:
Cash Investment: $200-300K
Total Investment: $400K-1.2MM
Minimum Net Worth: $300K
Fees: Franchise - $25K
Royalty - 4%; Ad. - 1%
Earnings Claim Statement: No
Term of Contract (Years): 10/5
Avg. # Of Employees: 8 FT, 22 PT
Passive Ownership: Discouraged
Encourage Conversions: Yes
Area Develop. Agreements: Yes/12
Sub-Franchising Contracts: No
Expand In Territory: Yes

Space Needs: 2,500 SF; FS

SUPPORT & TRAINING PROVIDED:

Financial Assistance Provided: Yes(I)
Site Selection Assistance: Yes
Lease Negotiation Assistance: Yes
Co-Operative Advertising: Yes
Franchisee Assoc./Member: Yes/Yes
Size Of Corporate Staff: 30
On-Going Support: B,C,D,E,F,G,H
Training: 8 Weeks Corporate Headquarters.

SPECIFIC EXPANSION PLANS:

US: SE, MW, Mid-Atlantic, SW
Canada: No
Overseas: No

<< >>

BIG TOWN HERO

912 SW Third Ave.
Portland, OR 97204
Tel: (503) 228-4376
Fax: (503) 228-8778
Web Site: www.bth.com
Mr. Rick Olson, Director of Franchising

Sub sandwich franchise. We bake our bread from scratch everyday. We have the "Ultimate Sandwich" and the "Ultimate Franchise."

BACKGROUND:

Established: 1982; 1st Franchised: 1987
Franchised Units: 36
Company-Owned Units 0
Total Units: 36
Dist.: US-36; CAN-0; O'seas-0
North America: 3 States
Density: 34 in OR, 1 in CA, 1 in WA
Projected New Units (12 Months): 12
Qualifications: 5, 4, 3, 1, 1, 5
Registered: CA, HI, OR, WA

FINANCIAL/TERMS:

Cash Investment: $25-70K
Total Investment: $25-125K
Minimum Net Worth: $100K
Fees: Franchise - $14.5K
Royalty - 6%; Ad. - $300/mo.
Earnings Claim Statement: No
Term of Contract (Years): 5/5
Avg. # Of Employees: 1 FT, 4 PT
Passive Ownership: Not Allowed
Encourage Conversions: No
Area Develop. Agreements: Yes/10
Sub-Franchising Contracts: No
Expand In Territory: Yes
Space Needs: 1,500 SF; FS, SF, SC, RM

SUPPORT & TRAINING PROVIDED:

Financial Assistance Provided: No
Site Selection Assistance: Yes
Lease Negotiation Assistance: Yes
Co-Operative Advertising: No
Franchisee Assoc./Member: No
Size Of Corporate Staff: 6
On-Going Support: C,D,E,F,G,h
Training: 3 Weeks in Portland, OR.

SPECIFIC EXPANSION PLANS:

US: NW, SW
Canada: No
Overseas: No

<< >>

BLIMPIE SUBS AND SALADS

1775 The Exchange, # 600
Atlanta, GA 30339
Tel: (800) 447-6256 (770) 984-2707
Fax: (770) 980-9176
E-Mail: chuckt@blimpie.com
Web Site: www.blimpie.com
Mr. Chuck Taylor, National Business Dev.

National submarine sandwich chain, serving fresh-sliced, high-quality meats and cheeses on fresh-baked bread. Also offering an assortment of fresh-made salads and other quality products. Awarding more than 1 new franchise daily and opening a new restaurant every day. Single and multi-unit opportunities.

BACKGROUND: IFA MEMBER

Established: 1964; 1st Franchised: 1977
Franchised Units: 1,955
Company-Owned Units 1
Total Units: 1,956
Dist.: US-1,882; CAN-13; O'seas-61
North America: 50 States, 4 Provinces
Density: 205 in GA, 203 in FL, 121 TX
Projected New Units (12 Months): NR
Qualifications: 4, 3, 2, 2, 2, 5
Registered: CA,FL,HI,IL,IN,MI,MN,NY, ND,OR,RI,SD,WA,WI

FINANCIAL/TERMS:

Cash Investment: $50K
Total Investment: $60-200K
Minimum Net Worth: $100K
Fees: Franchise - $10-18K
Royalty - 6%; Ad. - 4%
Earnings Claim Statement: No
Term of Contract (Years): 20/5
Avg. # Of Employees: 4 FT, 8 PT
Passive Ownership: Discouraged
Encourage Conversions: Yes
Area Develop. Agreements: Yes
Sub-Franchising Contracts: Yes
Expand In Territory: Yes
Space Needs: 1,500 SF; FS, SF, SC, RM

SUPPORT & TRAINING PROVIDED:

Financial Assistance Provided: Yes(I)
Site Selection Assistance: Yes
Lease Negotiation Assistance: Yes
Co-Operative Advertising: Yes
Franchisee Assoc./Member: Yes/Yes
Size Of Corporate Staff: 109
On-Going Support: B,C,D,E,F,G,H,I
Training: 120 Hours in Atlanta, GA; 40 Hours in Local Franchise.

SPECIFIC EXPANSION PLANS:

US: All United States
Canada: All Canada
Overseas: All Except Anti-American Countries

<< >>

BOARDWALK FRIES

8980 Route 108, # J
Columbia, MD 21045
Tel: (410) 715-0500
Fax: (410) 715-0711
E-Mail: brandedbwf@aol.com
Web Site: www.boardwalkfries.com
Mr. David DiFerdinando, President

We specialize in serving gourmet fries, fresh-cut and cooked in peanut oil with assorted toppings, prepared on location. We also have hot dogs, hamburgers, assorted sub sandwiches, drinks, fresh-squeezed lemonade. Our locations range from fries-only to full-menu restaurants.

BACKGROUND:

Established: 1981; 1st Franchised: 1981
Franchised Units: 25
Company-Owned Units 1
Total Units: 26

Dist.: US-25; CAN-1; O'seas-26
North America: 26 States
Density: 8 in MD, 6 in PA, 3 in IL
Projected New Units (12 Months): 18-24
Qualifications: 4, 3, 3, 3, 5, 5
Registered: MD

FINANCIAL/TERMS:

Cash Investment: $30-90K
Total Investment: $30-150K
Minimum Net Worth: $100K
Fees: Franchise - $15-25K
Royalty - 5-7%; Ad. - 0-2%
Earnings Claim Statement: No
Term of Contract (Years): 10/10
Avg. # Of Employees: Varies
Passive Ownership: Not Allowed
Encourage Conversions: Yes
Area Develop. Agreements: Yes/10
Sub-Franchising Contracts: No
Expand In Territory: Yes
Space Needs: 400-1,200 SF; RM

SUPPORT & TRAINING PROVIDED:

Financial Assistance Provided: Yes(I)
Site Selection Assistance: Yes
Lease Negotiation Assistance: Yes
Co-Operative Advertising: Yes
Franchisee Assoc./Member: No
Size Of Corporate Staff: 9
On-Going Support: C,D,E,F
Training: 6 Days in MD.

SPECIFIC EXPANSION PLANS:

US: East Coast
Canada: No
Overseas: Korea

<< >>

BOJANGLES' FAMOUS CHICKEN 'N BISCUITS

9432 Southern Pine Blvd.
Charlotte, NC 28273
Tel: (800) 366-9921 (704) 527-2675
Fax: (704) 523-6676
E-Mail: msandefer@bojangles.com
Web Site: www.bojangles.com
Mr. Mike Sandefer, Dir. Fran. Dev.

BOJANGLES OPERATES DURING ALL 3 DAY-PARTS. Breakfast items are available all day long. Our menu in unique, and flavorful, with chicken prepared either spicy or traditional Southern-style. Restaurants operate in traditional locations and non-traditional locations in convenience stores.

BACKGROUND: IFA MEMBER
Established: 1977; 1st Franchised: 1979
Franchised Units: 140
Company-Owned Units 149
Total Units: 289
Dist.: US-286; CAN-0; O'seas-3
North America: 10 States
Density: 130 in NC, 55 in SC,18 in GA
Projected New Units (12 Months): 30
Qualifications: 5, 4, 4, 3, 3, 5
Registered: FL,IL,MD,VA

FINANCIAL/TERMS:

Cash Investment: $225-350K
Total Investment: $740K
Minimum Net Worth: $750K
Fees: Franchise - $12-20K
Royalty - 4%; Ad. - 1%
Earnings Claim Statement: No
Term of Contract (Years): 20/10
Avg. # Of Employees: 12 FT, 20 PT
Passive Ownership: Discouraged
Encourage Conversions: Yes
Area Develop. Agreements: Yes/10
Sub-Franchising Contracts: No
Expand In Territory: Yes
Space Needs: 2,000+ SF; FS

SUPPORT & TRAINING PROVIDED:

Financial Assistance Provided: No
Site Selection Assistance: Yes
Lease Negotiation Assistance: No
Co-Operative Advertising: Yes
Franchisee Assoc./Member: Yes/Yes
Size Of Corporate Staff: 80
On-Going Support: B,C,D,E,F,G,H,I
Training: 5 Weeks Training in Training Units.

SPECIFIC EXPANSION PLANS:

US: Southeast, Midwest
Canada: No
Overseas:
Central America, Caribbean Areas

<< >>

BOX LUNCH, THE

50 Briar Ln.
Wellfleet, MA 02667
Tel: (508) 349-3509
Fax: (508) 349-3661
E-Mail: boxlunch@capecod.net
Web Site: www.boxlunch.com
Mr. Owen MacNutt, President

We are Darwin's theory applied to the sandwich. We have served only rolled pita sandwiches (Rollwiches) for 23 years. No cooking, no fried food, yet we are fast enough to feed 200+ people per hour, each Rollwich custom-made from over 40 selections. Voted best on Cape Cod last 6 years.

BACKGROUND:
Established: 1977; 1st Franchised: 1986
Franchised Units: 10
Company-Owned Units 1
Total Units: 11
Dist.: US-11; CAN-0; O'seas-0
North America: 2 States
Density: 10 in MA, 1 in CT
Projected New Units (12 Months): 3
Qualifications: 4, 3, 1, 2, 2, 5
Registered: N/A

FINANCIAL/TERMS:

Cash Investment: $60-100K
Total Investment: $125-200K
Minimum Net Worth: $500K
Fees: Franchise - $15K
Royalty - 4.5%; Ad. - 3%
Earnings Claim Statement: No
Term of Contract (Years): 5/5
Avg. # Of Employees: 4 FT, 2 PT
Passive Ownership: Not Allowed
Encourage Conversions: N/A
Area Develop. Agreements: Yes/10
Sub-Franchising Contracts: No
Expand In Territory: No
Space Needs: 1,200 SF; FS, SF, SC, RM

SUPPORT & TRAINING PROVIDED:

Financial Assistance Provided: No
Site Selection Assistance: Yes
Lease Negotiation Assistance: Yes
Co-Operative Advertising: Yes
Franchisee Assoc./Member: No
Size Of Corporate Staff: 2
On-Going Support: A,B,C,d,E,F,G,H,i
Training: 2-4 Weeks Wellfleet, MA.

SPECIFIC EXPANSION PLANS:

US: Northeast, New England
Canada: All Canada
Overseas: No

<< >>

BREADEAUX PIZZA

P.O. Box 6158
St. Joseph, MO 64506

Tel: (800) 835-6534 (816) 364-1088
Fax: (816) 364-3739
E-Mail: scott@breadeauxpizza.com
Web Site: www.breadeauxpizza.com
Mr. Scott J. Henze, VP Sales/Marketing

BREADEAUX PIZZA is a growing regional chain, stressing quality and service. Our acclaimed pizza is made with a double raised crust that is chewy and sweet like fine french bread and our meat toppings have no fillers or additives. We also offer pastas, subs, baked potatoes, hot wings and salads to give customers plenty of variety. Our customers say 'Best Pizza in Town.'

BACKGROUND:
Established: 1985; 1st Franchised: 1985
Franchised Units: 95
Company-Owned Units 3
Total Units: 98
Dist.: US-95; CAN-3; O'seas-0
North America: 8 States, 1 Province
Density: 45 in IA, 28 MO, 6 KS
Projected New Units (12 Months): 10
Qualifications: 3, 5, 2, 2, 3, 5
Registered: IL,MI,SD,WI

FINANCIAL/TERMS:
Cash Investment: $30-80K
Total Investment: $58-313K
Minimum Net Worth: $50K
Fees: Franchise - $15K
Royalty - 5%; Ad. - 3%
Earnings Claim Statement: Yes
Term of Contract (Years): 15/15
Avg. # Of Employees: 2 FT, 12 PT
Passive Ownership: Discouraged
Encourage Conversions: Yes
Area Develop. Agreements: Yes/10
Sub-Franchising Contracts: Yes
Expand In Territory: Yes
Space Needs: 1,200-2,500 SF; FS, SF, SC, RM

SUPPORT & TRAINING PROVIDED:
Financial Assistance Provided: Yes(I)
Site Selection Assistance: Yes
Lease Negotiation Assistance: Yes
Co-Operative Advertising: No
Franchisee Assoc./Member: Yes/Yes
Size Of Corporate Staff: 14
On-Going Support: A,B,C,D,E,F,G,H,I
Training: 2 Weeks Corporate Headquarters; 1 Week Franchisee Location; On-Going as Needed.

SPECIFIC EXPANSION PLANS:
US: Midwest
Canada: All Canada
Overseas: No

<< >>

BROWN'S CHICKEN & PASTA

1200 Jorie Blvd.
Oak Brook, IL 60523
Tel: (630) 571-5300
Fax: (630) 571-5378
Mr. Frank Portillo, Jr., President

High-quality, quick-service franchisor of BROWN'S CHICKEN & PASTA RESTAURANTS. Featuring various fresh-made side dishes. Stores can have take-out, dine-in and drive-up service. Our products, service and franchisee support exceed both customer and franchisee expectations. Expanded into corporate and home catering. Oven-baked chicken and full-service grill and pan pasta catering.

BACKGROUND:
Established: 1965; 1st Franchised: 1965
Franchised Units: 70
Company-Owned Units 24
Total Units: 94
Dist.: US-74; CAN-0; O'seas-0
North America: 3 States
Density: 80 in IL, 5 in FL
Projected New Units (12 Months): 3-5
Qualifications: 3, 3, 2, 3, 5, 5
Registered: FL,IL,IN

FINANCIAL/TERMS:
Cash Investment: $25K
Total Investment: $150-160K
Minimum Net Worth: $200K
Fees: Franchise - $25K
Royalty - 5%; Ad. - 4%
Earnings Claim Statement: Yes
Term of Contract (Years): 15/5
Avg. # Of Employees: 3 FT, 12 PT
Passive Ownership: Not Allowed
Encourage Conversions: Yes
Area Develop. Agreements: Yes/15
Sub-Franchising Contracts: No
Expand In Territory: No
Space Needs: 1,500 SF; FS, SC

SUPPORT & TRAINING PROVIDED:
Financial Assistance Provided: No
Site Selection Assistance: Yes
Lease Negotiation Assistance: Yes
Co-Operative Advertising: Yes
Franchisee Assoc./Member: Yes/Yes
Size Of Corporate Staff: 12
On-Going Support: B,C,D,E,F,G,H,I
Training: 6 Weeks Oakbrook, IL Corporate Office.

SPECIFIC EXPANSION PLANS:
US: FL, IL, IN
Canada: No
Overseas: Russia, Asia

<< >>

BUCK'S PIZZA

P.O. Box 405
DuBois, PA 15801
Tel: (800) 310-8848 (814) 371-3076
Fax: (814) 371-4214
E-Mail: lance@buckspizza.com
Web Site: www.buckspizza.com
Mr. Lance Benton, President

We at BUCK'S PIZZA pride ourselves on the best-quality pizza we can prepare. To do that, we buy only select ingredients and prepare them in our own special way. BUCK'S PIZZA is a delicious blend of natural ingredients delicately, flavored with special spices. We have expanded to 22 states in a few short years. Towns of any size offer the opportunity for BUCK'S low start-up costs and low overhead concept. When you are ready, BUCK'S is ready to train and then support you in your business!

BACKGROUND:
Established: 1994; 1st Franchised: 1994
Franchised Units: 83
Company-Owned Units 0
Total Units: 83
Dist.: US-80; CAN-0; O'seas-0
North America: 22 States
Density: 21 in TX, 10 in GA, 10 in SC
Projected New Units (12 Months): 24
Qualifications: 3, 4, 5, 3, 3, 5
Registered: FL,IL,MD,MN,NY,VA,WA,WI

FINANCIAL/TERMS:
Cash Investment: $15-30K
Total Investment: $100-120K
Minimum Net Worth: $30-40K
Fees: Franchise - $10K
Royalty - 3%; Ad. - 2%
Earnings Claim Statement: No
Term of Contract (Years): 10/10
Avg. # Of Employees: 4 FT, 11 PT
Passive Ownership: Discouraged
Encourage Conversions: Yes
Area Develop. Agreements: Yes/Varies
Sub-Franchising Contracts: No
Expand In Territory: Yes
Space Needs: 1,000 SF; FS, SF, SC

SUPPORT & TRAINING PROVIDED:
Financial Assistance Provided: Yes(I)
Site Selection Assistance: Yes

Lease Negotiation Assistance: Yes
Co-Operative Advertising: Yes
Franchisee Assoc./Member: No
Size Of Corporate Staff: 10
On-Going Support: B,C,d,E,F,h,I
Training: 1-2 Day(s) Seminar in Headquarters; 10-14 Days On-Site.

SPECIFIC EXPANSION PLANS:
US: All United States
Canada: No
Overseas: No

<< >>

BUMPERS DRIVE-IN

1554 West Peace St.
Canton, MS 39046
Tel: (888) 840-6601 (601) 855-0146
Fax: (601) 855-0516
E-Mail: amberrigdon@bumpersdrivein.com
Ms. Monica Harrigill, VP Operations

Fast food drive-in providing quality hamburgers, chicken, catfish, hot dogs, ice creams, shakes, french fries, potato pearls (tots), soft drinks, tea, coffee and desserts, namely apple pies, banana splits, short cakes with various toppings with the friendliest service possible.

BACKGROUND:
Established: 1985; 1st Franchised: 1985
Franchised Units: 5
Company-Owned Units 25
Total Units: 30
Dist.: US-30; CAN-0; O'seas-0
North America: 3 States
Density: 28 in MS, 1 in TN, 1 in TX
Projected New Units (12 Months): 1
Registered: NR

FINANCIAL/TERMS:
Cash Investment: $75-125K
Total Investment: $400-550K
Minimum Net Worth: $300K
Fees: Franchise - $10K
Royalty - 4%; Ad. - 6%
Earnings Claim Statement: No
Term of Contract (Years): 20/10
Avg. # Of Employees: 8 FT, 12 PT
Passive Ownership: Not Allowed
Encourage Conversions: NR
Area Develop. Agreements: Yes/10
Sub-Franchising Contracts: No
Expand In Territory: Yes
Space Needs: 24,000 SF; FS

SUPPORT & TRAINING PROVIDED:
Financial Assistance Provided: NR
Site Selection Assistance: Yes
Lease Negotiation Assistance: Yes
Co-Operative Advertising: Yes
Franchisee Assoc./Member: No
Size Of Corporate Staff: 70+
On-Going Support: a,B,C,D,E,F,G,h,I
Training: Nine Weeks (Two Hours Each) in Classroom; Five Weeks In-store Training.

SPECIFIC EXPANSION PLANS:
US: All United States
Canada: NR
Overseas: NR

<< >>

BURGER KING (CANADA)

401 The West Mall, 7th Fl.
Etobicoke, ON M9C 5J4 CANADA
Tel: (416) 626-7423
Fax: (416) 626-6691
E-Mail: gheos@whopper.com
Web Site: www.burgerking.com
Mr. George Heos, Fran. Dev. Mgr.

Second largest hamburger chain in the world. BURGER KING is currently recruiting franchisees qualified to develop multiple units in markets throughout Canada.

BACKGROUND: IFA MEMBER
Established: 1954; 1st Franchised: 1969
Franchised Units: 190
Company-Owned Units 110
Total Units: 300
Dist.: US-0; CAN-256; O'seas-0
North America: 10 Provinces
Density: 143 in ON, 59 in PQ, 30 BC
Projected New Units (12 Months): 35
Qualifications: 5, 4, 2, 3, 2, 5
Registered: AB

FINANCIAL/TERMS:
Cash Investment: $150-250K
Total Investment: $300K-1.1MM
Minimum Net Worth: $800K
Fees: Franchise - $55K
Royalty - 4%; Ad. - 4%
Earnings Claim Statement: Yes
Term of Contract (Years): 20/20
Avg. # Of Employees: 15 FT, 35 PT
Passive Ownership: Allowed
Encourage Conversions: Yes
Area Develop. Agreements: Yes/1-5
Sub-Franchising Contracts: No
Expand In Territory: Yes
Space Needs: 3,000-3,800 SF; FS, SF, SC, RM

SUPPORT & TRAINING PROVIDED:
Financial Assistance Provided: N/A
Site Selection Assistance: Yes
Lease Negotiation Assistance: Yes
Co-Operative Advertising: Yes
Franchisee Assoc./Member: Yes
Size Of Corporate Staff: 70
On-Going Support: B,C,D,E,F,H
Training: 15 Weeks Combined Classroom and Restaurant Training in Various Locations.

SPECIFIC EXPANSION PLANS:
US: No
Canada: All Canada
Overseas: No

<< >>

CAP'N TACO

16099 Brook Park Rd.
Brookpark, OH 44142
Tel: (216) 621-3777
Fax: (216) 676-9830
Mr. Raymond Brown, President

Aviation Theme/Top Gun Decor. CAP'N TACO as a 'Topgun' Pilot. TV's, foreground music, murals, set the theme. Hot sauce is called Nitro, + Jet fuel.

BACKGROUND:
Established: 1976; 1st Franchised: 1986
Franchised Units: 2
Company-Owned Units 3
Total Units: 5
Dist.: US-4; CAN-0; O'seas-0
North America: 1 State
Density: 4 in OH
Projected New Units (12 Months): 3
Qualifications: 5, 5, 4, 2, 5, 5
Registered: NR

FINANCIAL/TERMS:
Cash Investment: $20-150K
Total Investment: $80-175K
Minimum Net Worth: $100K
Fees: Franchise - $15K
Royalty - 5%; Ad. - 2%
Earnings Claim Statement: No
Term of Contract (Years): 10/5/5
Avg. # Of Employees: 2 FT, 4 PT
Passive Ownership: Discouraged
Encourage Conversions: Yes
Area Develop. Agreements: No
Sub-Franchising Contracts: No
Expand In Territory: Yes
Space Needs: 1,000 SF; SC

SUPPORT & TRAINING PROVIDED:
Financial Assistance Provided: No
Site Selection Assistance: Yes
Lease Negotiation Assistance: Yes
Co-Operative Advertising: Yes

Franchisee Assoc./Member: No
Size Of Corporate Staff: 2
On-Going Support: B,C,D,E,F,G,h
Training: 2 Weeks Brook Park, OH.

SPECIFIC EXPANSION PLANS:
US: All United States
Canada: All Canada
Overseas: All Countries

<< >>

CAPTAIN D'S SEAFOOD

1717 Elm Hill Pk., # A-1
Nashville, TN 37210
Tel: (800) 550-4877 (615) 391-5202
Fax: (615) 231-2790
E-Mail: darin_harris@captainds.com
Web Site: www.captainds.com
Mr. Darin S. Harris, VP Franchise Development

Quick-service, sit-down/take-out seafood restaurant, serving broiled, baked and fried fish, shrimp and crab entrees, as well as chicken, specialty salads and a wide range of vegetables and desserts.

BACKGROUND: IFA MEMBER
Established: 1969; 1st Franchised: 1969
Franchised Units: 230
Company-Owned Units 334
Total Units: 564
Dist.: US-564; CAN-0; O'seas-0
North America: 23 States
Density: 95 in GA, 77 in TN, 40 in KY
Projected New Units (12 Months): 3
Registered: All States

FINANCIAL/TERMS:
Cash Investment: $150K
Total Investment: $572K-1.6MM
Minimum Net Worth: $400K
Fees: Franchise - $20K
Royalty - 3%; Ad. - 5.25%
Earnings Claim Statement: Yes
Term of Contract (Years): 20/20
Avg. # Of Employees: 5 FT, 15 PT
Passive Ownership: Discouraged
Encourage Conversions: Yes
Area Develop. Agreements: Yes/Varies
Sub-Franchising Contracts: No
Expand In Territory: Yes
Space Needs: 1,800-2,700 SF; FS,SC,C-Store,Food Court

SUPPORT & TRAINING PROVIDED:
Financial Assistance Provided: No
Site Selection Assistance: Yes
Lease Negotiation Assistance: No
Co-Operative Advertising: Yes
Franchisee Assoc./Member: Yes
Size Of Corporate Staff: 85
On-Going Support: C,D,e,G,h,I
Training: Approximately 6 Weeks Nashville, TN; Depends on Franchisee's Experience.

SPECIFIC EXPANSION PLANS:
US: South, Southeast
Canada: No
Overseas: No

<< >>

CAPTAIN TONY'S PIZZA & PASTA EMPORIUM

2607 S. Woodland Blvd., # 300
Deland, FL 32720
Tel: (800) 332-8669 (904) 736-9855
Fax: (904) 736-7237
E-Mail: captain-tonys@wati.com
Web Site: www.captain-tonys.wati.com
Mr. Michael J. Martella, President

We have pizza, pasta, etc. for take-out, delivery and dining-in.

BACKGROUND:
Established: 1985; 1st Franchised: 1985
Franchised Units: 10
Company-Owned Units 0
Total Units: 10
Dist.: US-10; CAN-0; O'seas-2
North America: NR
Density: 2 in CA, 3 in OH
Projected New Units (12 Months): NR
Qualifications: 3, 3, 2, 3, 3, 5
Registered: FL,NY

FINANCIAL/TERMS:
Cash Investment: $25-75K
Total Investment: $65-250K
Minimum Net Worth: $250K
Fees: Franchise - $10-20K
Royalty - 4.5% $500/Wk cap; Ad. - 0%
Earnings Claim Statement: No
Term of Contract (Years): 20
Avg. # Of Employees: NR
Passive Ownership: Discouraged
Encourage Conversions: Yes
Area Develop. Agreements: NR
Sub-Franchising Contracts: NR
Expand In Territory: NR
Space Needs: 1,200 SF; NR

SUPPORT & TRAINING PROVIDED:
Financial Assistance Provided: Yes(I)
Site Selection Assistance: Yes
Lease Negotiation Assistance: Yes
Co-Operative Advertising: No
Franchisee Assoc./Member: No
Size Of Corporate Staff: NR
On-Going Support: D,E,I
Training: 3 Weeks Orlando, FL.

SPECIFIC EXPANSION PLANS:
US: All United States
Canada: No
Overseas: All Countries

<< >>

CENTRAL PARK OF AMERICA

537 Market St., #301
Chattanooga, TN 37402
Tel: (423) 267-6575
Fax: (423) 267-4361
Web Site: www.centralparkamerica.com
Mr. Mike Clifford

Central Park is the originator of the Double Drive Thru concept. Central Park specializes in serving the highest quality burgers, chicken sandwiches, fries, and soft drinks in a smooth and efficient operation. Because of our building size, our overhead is reduced and we are able to be located on small, inexpensive pieces of real estate. Call today to realize the joy of business ownership.

BACKGROUND:
Established: 1982; 1st Franchised: 1988
Franchised Units: 47
Company-Owned Units 17
Total Units: 64
Dist.: US-55; CAN-0; O'seas-0
North America: 9 States
Density: 17 in TN, 11 in GA, 6 in NC
Projected New Units (12 Months): NR
Registered: NR

FINANCIAL/TERMS:
Cash Investment: $150K
Total Investment: $300-400K
Minimum Net Worth: $300K
Fees: Franchise - $20K
Royalty - 5%; Ad. - 2%
Earnings Claim Statement: Yes
Term of Contract (Years): 15/15
Avg. # Of Employees: NR
Passive Ownership: Discouraged
Encourage Conversions: NR
Area Develop. Agreements: No
Sub-Franchising Contracts: No

Expand In Territory: Yes
Space Needs: 500 SF; NR

SUPPORT & TRAINING PROVIDED:
Financial Assistance Provided: NR
Site Selection Assistance: Yes
Lease Negotiation Assistance: Yes
Co-Operative Advertising: NR
Franchisee Assoc./Member: Yes
Size Of Corporate Staff: NR
On-Going Support: B,C,D,E,F,G,H,I
Training: 2 Weeks on Site, 2 Weeks Classroom, Chattanooga, TN.

SPECIFIC EXPANSION PLANS:
US: All United States
Canada: NR
Overseas: NR

<< >>

CHECKERS DRIVE-IN RESTAURANTS

4300 W. Cypress St., # 600
Tampa, FL 33607
Tel: (800) 275-3628 (813) 283-7000
Fax: (813) 283-7001
E-Mail: fransales@checkers.com
Web Site: www.checkers.com
Mr. Dick Sveum, VP Fran. Sales/Dev.

Quick-service, fast-food restaurant (double drive-thru).

BACKGROUND: IFA MEMBER
Established: 1986; 1st Franchised: 1989
Franchised Units: 300
Company-Owned Units 128
Total Units: 428
Dist.: US-481; CAN-0; O'seas-0
North America: 24 States
Density: 191 in FL, 85 in GA, 32 AL
Projected New Units (12 Months): 35
Qualifications: 5, 4, 5, 4, 4, 4
Registered: FL,IL,IN,MD,MI,MN,NY,VA,WA,WI,DC

FINANCIAL/TERMS:
Cash Investment: $100-250K
Total Investment: $382.1-522.7K
Minimum Net Worth: $500K
Fees: Franchise - $30K
Royalty - 4%; Ad. - 0.25%+4.75%
Earnings Claim Statement: No
Term of Contract (Years): 20/Agrmt.
Avg. # Of Employees: 10 FT, 20 PT
Passive Ownership: Not Allowed
Encourage Conversions: Yes
Area Develop. Agreements: Yes
Sub-Franchising Contracts: Yes
Expand In Territory: Yes
Space Needs: 15,000 SF; FS

SUPPORT & TRAINING PROVIDED:
Financial Assistance Provided: No
Site Selection Assistance: Yes
Lease Negotiation Assistance: N/A
Co-Operative Advertising: Yes
Franchisee Assoc./Member: Yes
Size Of Corporate Staff: ~100
On-Going Support: A,B,C,D,E,F,G,H,I
Training: 4-6 Weeks Atlanta, GA; 4-6 Weeks Clearwater, FL.

SPECIFIC EXPANSION PLANS:
US: Eastern United States
Canada: No
Overseas: No

<< >>

CHEEBURGER CHEEBURGER

15951 McGregor Blvd., # 2A
Fort Myers, FL 33908
Tel: (800) 487-6211 (941) 437-1611
Fax: (941) 437-1512
E-Mail: cheeburger@minospring.com
Mr. Bruce Zicari, President/CEO

Full-service, gourmet, specialty-sandwich restaurant, serving high-quality, freshly-prepared products and featuring burgers in various sizes, fresh-cut fries and big, thick milk shakes.

BACKGROUND:
Established: 1986; 1st Franchised: 1990
Franchised Units: 14
Company-Owned Units 4
Total Units: 18
Dist.: US-18; CAN-0; O'seas-0
North America: 5 States
Density: 11 in FL, 2 in AR
Projected New Units (12 Months): 6
Qualifications: 5, 5, 3, 3, 4, 5
Registered: MI,NY

FINANCIAL/TERMS:
Cash Investment: $150-200K
Total Investment: $180-280K
Minimum Net Worth: $350K Liquid
Fees: Franchise - $17.5K
Royalty - 4.5%; Ad. - 1%
Earnings Claim Statement: No
Term of Contract (Years): 10/5
Avg. # Of Employees: 5 FT, 10 PT
Passive Ownership: NR
Encourage Conversions: Yes
Area Develop. Agreements: Yes
Sub-Franchising Contracts: No
Expand In Territory: Yes
Space Needs: 2,000 SF; FS, SF, SC

SUPPORT & TRAINING PROVIDED:
Financial Assistance Provided: No
Site Selection Assistance: Yes
Lease Negotiation Assistance: Yes
Co-Operative Advertising: Yes
Franchisee Assoc./Member: Yes
Size Of Corporate Staff: 5
On-Going Support: C,D,E,F,H,I,G
Training: 17 Days.

SPECIFIC EXPANSION PLANS:
US: East of Mississippi
Canada: All Canada
Overseas: No

<< >>

CHICAGO'S PIZZA

1111 N. Broadway
Greenfield, IN 46140
Tel: (317) 462-9878
Fax: (317) 467-1877
E-Mail: colips@freewooeb.com
Mr. Robert L. McDonald, Chief Executive Officer

Franchise designed for owner/operator. Flexibility allowed to ensure success. Can be adapted to large and small operations. Inside dining/carry-out/delivery.

BACKGROUND:
Established: 1979; 1st Franchised: 1981
Franchised Units: 12
Company-Owned Units 0
Total Units: 12
Dist.: US-12; CAN-0; O'seas-0
North America: 4 States
Density: 10 in IN, 2 in OH
Projected New Units (12 Months): 2
Qualifications: 4, 4, 4, 3, 4, 5
Registered: IN

FINANCIAL/TERMS:
Cash Investment: $25-50K
Total Investment: $100-300K
Minimum Net Worth: $50K
Fees: Franchise - $18K
Royalty - 4%; Ad. - 2%
Earnings Claim Statement: No
Term of Contract (Years): 10/10
Avg. # Of Employees: 3 FT, 12 PT
Passive Ownership: Not Allowed
Encourage Conversions: Yes

Area Develop. Agreements: Yes/Open
Sub-Franchising Contracts: No
Expand In Territory: Yes
Space Needs: 1,800-3,000 SF; FS, SC

SUPPORT & TRAINING PROVIDED:
Financial Assistance Provided: No
Site Selection Assistance: Yes
Lease Negotiation Assistance: Yes
Co-Operative Advertising: Yes
Franchisee Assoc./Member: No
Size Of Corporate Staff: 3
On-Going Support: C,D,E,F,H
Training: 2 Weeks at Existing Store.

SPECIFIC EXPANSION PLANS:
US: IN, OH, MI, KY, IL
Canada: No
Overseas: No

<< >>

CHICKEN DELIGHT

395 Berry St.
Winnipeg, MB R3J 1N6 CANADA
Tel: (204) 885-7570
Fax: (204) 831-6176
E-Mail: info@chickendelight.com
Web Site: www.chickendelight.com
Mr. Larry Millar, Marketing Manager

CHICKEN DELIGHT has been in business for 50 years, featuring our famous pressure-fried chicken, BBQ ribs and fresh dough pizzas. We cater to the fast-food market with dine-in, take-out, delivery and drive-thru. Our focus on 3 staple products for take-out and delivery broadens your market potential.

BACKGROUND:
Established: 1952; 1st Franchised: 1952
Franchised Units: 35
Company-Owned Units 15
Total Units: 50
Dist.: US-10; CAN-38; O'seas-2
North America: 2 States, 4 Provinces
Density: 34 in MB, 3 in SK, 1 in ON
Projected New Units (12 Months): 3
Qualifications: 4, 5, 3, 4, 3, 5
Registered: CA, AB

FINANCIAL/TERMS:
Cash Investment: $70-100K
Total Investment: $275-600K
Minimum Net Worth: $70K
Fees: Franchise - $25K
Royalty - 5%; Ad. - 3%
Earnings Claim Statement: No
Term of Contract (Years): 10/10
Avg. # Of Employees: 6 FT, 6 PT
Passive Ownership: Discouraged
Encourage Conversions: Yes
Area Develop. Agreements: Yes/10
Sub-Franchising Contracts: No
Expand In Territory: Yes
Space Needs: 1,800 SF; SC

SUPPORT & TRAINING PROVIDED:
Financial Assistance Provided: No
Site Selection Assistance: Yes
Lease Negotiation Assistance: Yes
Co-Operative Advertising: Yes
Franchisee Assoc./Member: No
Size Of Corporate Staff: 20
On-Going Support: C,D,e,F,G,h
Training: Minimum 1 Month Winnipeg, MB.

SPECIFIC EXPANSION PLANS:
US: All United States
Canada: All Canada
Overseas: Any Master License

<< >>

Top 50

CHURCHS CHICKEN

980 Hammond Dr. NE, # 1100, Bldg. # 2
Atlanta, GA 30328
Tel: (800) 639-3495 (770) 350-3800
Fax: (770) 512-3972
E-Mail: jrobinson@afce.com
Web Site: www.churchs.com
Mr. Hannibal Myers, Worldwide Development Officer

CHURCHS is the 2nd largest chicken restaurant chain in the country. CHURCHS offers Southern fried chicken with signature side items such as fried okra, corn-on-the-cob, jalapenos and honey butter biscuits. CHURCHS has a proven business system niche customer base, low square footage requirements (as little as 750 square feet) and world class franchise support.

BACKGROUND: IFA MEMBER
Established: 1952; 1st Franchised: 1972
Franchised Units: 761
Company-Owned Units 468
Total Units: 1,219
Dist.: US-1032; CAN-80; O'seas-107
North America: 28 States
Density: 416 in TX, 103 in GA, 74 CA
Projected New Units (12 Months): 125
Qualifications: 5, 4, 3, 3, 3, 5
Registered: All States

FINANCIAL/TERMS:
Cash Investment: $200K
Total Investment: $194-750K
Minimum Net Worth: $400K
Fees: Franchise - $5-15K
Royalty - 5%; Ad. - 4%
Earnings Claim Statement: No
Term of Contract (Years): 20/10
Avg. # Of Employees: 15 FT, 6 PT
Passive Ownership: Discouraged
Encourage Conversions: Yes
Area Develop. Agreements: Yes/Varies
Sub-Franchising Contracts: No
Expand In Territory: Yes
Space Needs: 750-22,000 SF; FS, C-Store

SUPPORT & TRAINING PROVIDED:
Financial Assistance Provided: No
Site Selection Assistance: Yes
Lease Negotiation Assistance: Yes
Co-Operative Advertising: Yes
Franchisee Assoc./Member: Yes/Yes
Size Of Corporate Staff: 70
On-Going Support: C,D,E,F,G,h,I
Training: 6 Weeks Regional.

SPECIFIC EXPANSION PLANS:
US: All United States
Canada: All Canada
Overseas:
Europe, Asia, Middle East, Australia

<< >>

CICI'S PIZZA

1080 W. Bethel Rd.
Coppell, TX 75019-4427
Tel: (972) 745-4200
Fax: (972) 745-4204
E-Mail: jsheahan@cicispizza.com
Web Site: www.cicispizza.com
Mr. Jim Sheahan, Dir. Franchise Sales

Highest Rated Pizza Chain in America 2 years in a row. CiCi's Pizza provides its guests with delicious pizza, pasta, salad bar and dessert on an all-you-can-eat buffet for only $3.99 for adults and $2.99 for kids. Our low price, combined with quality food, great service and sparkling clean restaurants is making CiCi's among the fastest growing franchises in America!

BACKGROUND: IFA MEMBER
Established: 1985; 1st Franchised: 1987
Franchised Units: 344
Company-Owned Units 31
Total Units: 375
Dist.: US-375; CAN-0; O'seas-0
North America: 18 States
Density: NR
Projected New Units (12 Months): 50
Qualifications: 5, 4, 1, 1, 3, 5
Registered: FL,IN,MI,VA

FINANCIAL/TERMS:
Cash Investment: $116.5-147.8K
Total Investment: $388-492.5K
Minimum Net Worth: $NR
Fees: Franchise - $30K
Royalty - 4%; Ad. - 3%/$2.3K
Earnings Claim Statement: Yes
Term of Contract (Years): 10
Avg. # Of Employees: 8 FT, 15 PT
Passive Ownership: Not Allowed
Encourage Conversions: No
Area Develop. Agreements: Yes
Sub-Franchising Contracts: No
Expand In Territory: Yes
Space Needs: 4,200 SF; FS, SC

SUPPORT & TRAINING PROVIDED:
Financial Assistance Provided: Yes(I)
Site Selection Assistance: Yes
Lease Negotiation Assistance: Yes
Co-Operative Advertising: Yes
Franchisee Assoc./Member: No
Size Of Corporate Staff: 48
On-Going Support: B,C,D,E,F,G,H
Training: 7-11 Weeks in Dallas, TX.

SPECIFIC EXPANSION PLANS:
US: South, Southeast, N. Central
Canada: No
Overseas: No

CLUCK-U CHICKEN

261 Raymond Rd.
Princeton, NJ 08540
Tel: (732) 438-1900
Fax: (732) 438-0055
Web Site: www.clucku.com
Mr. Bob Alex, VP Franchise Development

Our objective is to exceed the expectations of our customers and develop a system full of great people. We sell chicken, BBQ and related products.

BACKGROUND:
Established: 1985; 1st Franchised: 1991
Franchised Units: 34
Company-Owned Units 1
Total Units: 35
Dist.: US-35; CAN-0; O'seas-0
North America: 6 States
Density: NJ, MO, PA
Projected New Units (12 Months): 12
Qualifications: 3, 4, 4, 3, 5, 5
Registered: CA,MD

FINANCIAL/TERMS:
Cash Investment: $50K
Total Investment: $125-225K
Minimum Net Worth: $200K
Fees: Franchise - $2.5K
Royalty - 5%; Ad. - 2%
Earnings Claim Statement: No
Term of Contract (Years): 20/10
Avg. # Of Employees: 8 FT
Passive Ownership: Not Allowed
Encourage Conversions: Yes
Area Develop. Agreements: No
Sub-Franchising Contracts: Yes
Expand In Territory: Yes
Space Needs: 1,500 SF; FS, SF, SC

SUPPORT & TRAINING PROVIDED:
Financial Assistance Provided: Yes(I)
Site Selection Assistance: Yes
Lease Negotiation Assistance: Yes
Co-Operative Advertising: Yes
Franchisee Assoc./Member: No
Size Of Corporate Staff: 5
On-Going Support: B,C,D,E,F,G,H,I
Training: 6 Weeks at DE, CA, or NJ.

SPECIFIC EXPANSION PLANS:
US: All United States
Canada: No
Overseas: No

<< >>

COUSINS SUBS

N83 W13400 Leon Rd.
Menomenee Falls, WI 53051
Tel: (800) 238-9736 (262) 253-7700
Fax: (800) 820-1762
E-Mail: rhanson@cousinssubs.com
Web Site: www.cousinssubs.com
Mr. Rich Hanson, Franchise Sales Manager

COUSINS SUBS celebrates over 30 years as an exceptionally high-volume, fast service concept in up-scale, in-line, free-standing and non-traditional locations. #1 sub sandwich chain for five years running (Income Opportunities Magazine). Midwest and Southwest development available for single and multiple unit operators.

BACKGROUND: IFA MEMBER
Established: 1972; 1st Franchised: 1985
Franchised Units: 130
Company-Owned Units 40
Total Units: 170
Dist.: US-170; CAN-0; O'seas-0
North America: 10 States
Density: 100 in WI, 26 in AZ, 18 MN
Projected New Units (12 Months): 24
Qualifications: 5, 4, 5, 3, 3, 5
Registered: CA,IL,IN,MI,MN,ND,SD,WI

FINANCIAL/TERMS:
Cash Investment: $50-100K
Total Investment: $159-287K
Minimum Net Worth: $300K
Fees: Franchise - $15K
Royalty - 4-6%; Ad. - 2%
Earnings Claim Statement: Yes
Term of Contract (Years): 10/10
Avg. # Of Employees: 2 FT, 12 PT
Passive Ownership: Not Allowed
Encourage Conversions: Yes
Area Develop. Agreements: No
Sub-Franchising Contracts: No
Expand In Territory: Yes
Space Needs: 1,600 SF; FS, SF, SC, C-Store

SUPPORT & TRAINING PROVIDED:
Financial Assistance Provided: Yes(D)
Site Selection Assistance: Yes
Lease Negotiation Assistance: Yes
Co-Operative Advertising: Yes
Franchisee Assoc./Member: Yes/Yes
Size Of Corporate Staff: 50
On-Going Support: C,D,E,G,h,I
Training: Up to 5 Days HQ;4 Wks. Training Store;10 Days Franchisee Store; 3 Field Visits/Mo. Yr 1.

SPECIFIC EXPANSION PLANS:
US: Southwest,CA,TX,IL,IN,MN,WI
Canada: No
Overseas: No

<< >>

CROISSANT + PLUS

2020 St. Patrick
Montreal, PQ H3K 1A9 CANADA
Tel: (800) 267-4896 (514) 931-5550
Fax: (514) 931-3749

E-Mail: madi@toa.ca
Mr. Tony Vanvari, President

A fast-food chain, offering healthy menu items such as soups, salads, sandwiches, bake-off products and gourmet coffees.

BACKGROUND:
Established: 1980; 1st Franchised: 1981
Franchised Units: 19
Company-Owned Units 6
Total Units: 25
Dist.: US-0; CAN-40; O'seas-0
North America: 3 Provinces
Density: 37 in PQ, 2 in ON, 1 in BC
Projected New Units (12 Months): 10
Qualifications: 4, 5, 2, 2, 4, 5
Registered: NR

FINANCIAL/TERMS:
Cash Investment: $50-75K
Total Investment: $100-200K
Minimum Net Worth: $80-150K
Fees: Franchise - $10-30K
Royalty - 5%; Ad. - 3%
Earnings Claim Statement: No
Term of Contract (Years): 10/5
Avg. # Of Employees: 2 FT, 3-5 PT
Passive Ownership: Discouraged
Encourage Conversions: N/A
Area Develop. Agreements: Yes/10/10
Sub-Franchising Contracts: Yes
Expand In Territory: Yes
Space Needs: 300-1,000 SF; FS, SF,SC, RM, Office Bldg.

SUPPORT & TRAINING PROVIDED:
Financial Assistance Provided: Yes(I)
Site Selection Assistance: Yes
Lease Negotiation Assistance: Yes
Co-Operative Advertising: Yes
Franchisee Assoc./Member: Yes/Yes
Size Of Corporate Staff: 10
On-Going Support: B,C,D,E,F,H,I
Training: 2-6 Weeks Montreal, PQ; 2-6 Weeks Quebec City, PQ.

SPECIFIC EXPANSION PLANS:
US: All United States
Canada: All Canada
Overseas: No

<< >>

CULVERS FROZEN CUSTARD
540 Water St.
Prairie du Sac, WI 53578-1129
Tel: (608) 643-7980
Fax: (608) 643-7982
E-Mail: ksto@culvers.com
Web Site: www.culvers.com
Mr. Phil Keiser, Chief Operating Officer

Culver's Frozen Custard specializes in ButterBurgers and Frozen Custard. All food items are prepared to order and delivered to the customer's table in about five minutes. Our system is based on franchisees as owner/operators with the operator working full time in their restaurant to ensure guest satisfaction and involvement in the local community.

BACKGROUND: IFA MEMBER
Established: 1984; 1st Franchised: 1988
Franchised Units: 138
Company-Owned Units 5
Total Units: 143
Dist.: US-143; CAN-0; O'seas-0
North America: 11 States
Density: 86 in WI, 21 in IL, 15 in MN
Projected New Units (12 Months): 30
Qualifications: 4, 3, 3, 3, 1, 5
Registered: Midwest States

FINANCIAL/TERMS:
Cash Investment: $150-500K
Total Investment: $400K-2.8MM
Minimum Net Worth: $Varies
Fees: Franchise - $50K
Royalty - 4%; Ad. - 2%
Earnings Claim Statement: Yes
Term of Contract (Years): 15/10
Avg. # Of Employees: 18 FT, 52 PT
Passive Ownership: Not Allowed
Encourage Conversions: Yes
Area Develop. Agreements: No
Sub-Franchising Contracts: No
Expand In Territory: No
Space Needs: 55000 SF; FS

SUPPORT & TRAINING PROVIDED:
Financial Assistance Provided: No
Site Selection Assistance: No
Lease Negotiation Assistance: Yes
Co-Operative Advertising: No
Franchisee Assoc./Member: No
Size Of Corporate Staff: 45
On-Going Support: B,C,D,E,F,G,H
Training: 16 Weeks in South Central, WI.

SPECIFIC EXPANSION PLANS:
US: Midwest, TX
Canada: No
Overseas: No

<< >>

DAIRY BELLE FREEZE
P.O. Box 360830
Milpitas, CA 95036-0830
Tel: (408) 433-9337
Fax: (408) 433-9395
E-Mail: stone557@aol.com
Web Site: www.dairybelle.com
Ms. Patricia (Pat) Souza, President

Locally-owned and operated since 1957, DAIRY BELLE restaurants have provided quality food that is cooked to order to ensure the satisfaction of each customer. Our menu has expanded from soft-serve cones, hamburgers, fries and soft drinks to now include specialty sandwiches, Mexican food and a variety of soft-serve desserts.

BACKGROUND:
Established: 1957; 1st Franchised: 1981
Franchised Units: 13
Company-Owned Units 0
Total Units: 13
Dist.: US-13; CAN-0; O'seas-0
North America: 1 State
Density: 13 in CA
Projected New Units (12 Months): 2
Qualifications: 5, 3, 4, 2, 2, 5
Registered: CA

FINANCIAL/TERMS:
Cash Investment: $50-100K
Total Investment: $50-200K
Minimum Net Worth: $100K
Fees: Franchise - $12.5K
Royalty - 4.5%/$600; Ad. - 2%
Earnings Claim Statement: Yes
Term of Contract (Years): 10/10
Avg. # Of Employees: 4 FT, 3-10 PT
Passive Ownership: Not Allowed
Encourage Conversions: Yes
Area Develop. Agreements: No
Sub-Franchising Contracts: No
Expand In Territory: Yes
Space Needs: 1,500 SF; FS

SUPPORT & TRAINING PROVIDED:
Financial Assistance Provided: Yes(I)
Site Selection Assistance: Yes
Lease Negotiation Assistance: Yes
Co-Operative Advertising: Yes
Franchisee Assoc./Member: No
Size Of Corporate Staff: 6
On-Going Support: B,C,D,E,H
Training: 2-3 Weeks at Existing Franchisee's Restaurant; 2-3 Weeks at New Franchisee's Restaurant.

SPECIFIC EXPANSION PLANS:
US: Northern CA
Canada: No
Overseas: No

<< >>

DAIRY QUEEN
7505 Metro Blvd.
Minneapolis, MN 55439-3020
Tel: (800) 285-8515 (952) 830-0200

Fax: (952) 830-0450
E-Mail: development@idq.com
Web Site: www.dairyqueen.com
Development Department

A subsidiary of Berkshire Hathaway, Inc., DAIRY QUEEN offers several franchise concepts and development programs from single unit to multi-unit agreements. Our concepts are designed for various location types--from free-standing restaurants to regional shopping malls. With over sixty years and 6000 units we offer great experience and brand recognition.

BACKGROUND: IFA MEMBER
Established: 1940; 1st Franchised: 1940
Franchised Units: 6,032
Company-Owned Units 63
Total Units: 6,095
Dist.: US-5166; CAN-635; O'seas-294
North America: 49 States,12 Provinces
Density: 629 in TX, 287 in IL, 282 OH
Projected New Units (12 Months): 100
Qualifications: 5, 4, 5, 3, , 4
Registered: All States

FINANCIAL/TERMS:
Cash Investment: $200-300K
Total Investment: $200-950K
Minimum Net Worth: $200-500K
Fees: Franchise - $20-35K
Royalty - 4-6%; Ad. - 3-6%
Earnings Claim Statement: No
Term of Contract (Years): 20/10
Avg. # Of Employees: Varies
Passive Ownership: Allowed
Encourage Conversions: Yes
Area Develop. Agreements: Yes/Varies
Sub-Franchising Contracts: Yes
Expand In Territory: No
Space Needs: 40,000 SF; FS, RM

SUPPORT & TRAINING PROVIDED:
Financial Assistance Provided: No
Site Selection Assistance: Yes
Lease Negotiation Assistance: Yes
Co-Operative Advertising: Yes
Franchisee Assoc./Member: Yes/No
Size Of Corporate Staff: 470
On-Going Support: C,D,E,G,H,I
Training: 4 Weeks in Existing Restaurants; 1-2 Weeks at Headquarters; 1-2 Weeks On-Site.

SPECIFIC EXPANSION PLANS:
US: All United States
Canada: BC, AB, ON
Overseas: Mexico

<< >>

DAIRY QUEEN CANADA

5245 Harvester Rd., P.O. Box 430
Burlington, ON L7R 3Y3 CANADA
Tel: (905) 639-1492
Fax: (905) 681-3623
Mr. Larry Carver, Franchise Development

Fast-food restaurant, featuring soft-serve products.

BACKGROUND: IFA MEMBER
Established: 1940; 1st Franchised: 1950
Franchised Units: 480
Company-Owned Units 0
Total Units: 480
Dist.: US-0; CAN-505; O'seas-0
North America: 10 Provinces
Density: 165 in ON, 95 in AB, 88 BC
Projected New Units (12 Months): 35
Qualifications: 5, 3, 3, 3, 3, 5
Registered: AB

FINANCIAL/TERMS:
Cash Investment: $150-350K
Total Investment: $400K-1.2MM
Minimum Net Worth: $NR
Fees: Franchise - $30K
Royalty - 4%; Ad. - 3-6%
Earnings Claim Statement: No
Term of Contract (Years): N/A
Avg. # Of Employees: 20 FT, 40 PT
Passive Ownership: Discouraged
Encourage Conversions: Yes
Area Develop. Agreements: No
Sub-Franchising Contracts: No
Expand In Territory: Yes
Space Needs: 2,000-3,000 SF; FS

SUPPORT & TRAINING PROVIDED:
Financial Assistance Provided: Yes(I)
Site Selection Assistance: Yes
Lease Negotiation Assistance: Yes
Co-Operative Advertising: Yes
Franchisee Assoc./Member: Yes/Yes
Size Of Corporate Staff: 70
On-Going Support: A,B,C,D,E,F,G,H,I
Training: 3 Weeks Minneapolis, MN.

SPECIFIC EXPANSION PLANS:
US: All United States
Canada: All Canada
Overseas: All Countries

<< >>

DEL TACO

23041 Avenida de La Carlota
Laguna Hills, CA 92653
Tel: (949) 462-9322
Fax: (949) 462-7444
E-Mail: dlangston@deltaco.net
Web Site: www.deltaco.net
Mr. Ron Petty, President

Mexican-American fast-food restaurant.

BACKGROUND: IFA MEMBER
Established: 1964; 1st Franchised: 1967
Franchised Units: 133
Company-Owned Units 249
Total Units: 382
Dist.: US-382; CAN-0; O'seas-0
North America: 10 States
Density: 307 in CA, 25 in NV, 23 AZ
Projected New Units (12 Months): 50
Qualifications: 4, 5, 5, 4, 4, 4
Registered: CA,IL,NY

FINANCIAL/TERMS:
Cash Investment: $250K
Total Investment: $466-679K
Minimum Net Worth: $750K
Fees: Franchise - $25K
Royalty - 5%; Ad. - 4%
Earnings Claim Statement: No
Term of Contract (Years): 20/15
Avg. # Of Employees: 2 FT, 24 PT
Passive Ownership: Not Allowed
Encourage Conversions: No
Area Develop. Agreements: Yes/Varies
Sub-Franchising Contracts: No
Expand In Territory: Yes
Space Needs: 2,100 SF; FS

SUPPORT & TRAINING PROVIDED:
Financial Assistance Provided: No
Site Selection Assistance: No
Lease Negotiation Assistance: Yes
Co-Operative Advertising: Yes
Franchisee Assoc./Member: No
Size Of Corporate Staff: 120
On-Going Support: C,D,E,G,H
Training: 2 Days Laguna Hills, CA; 6 Weeks Restaurant, CA.

SPECIFIC EXPANSION PLANS:
US: W, SW, Central United States
Canada: No
Overseas: No

<< >>

DIAMOND DAVE'S TACO COMPANY

201 S. Clinton St., # 281
Iowa City, IA 52240
Tel: (319) 337-7690
Fax: (319) 337-4707
Web Site: www.diamonddaves.com
Mr. Stanley J. White, President

DIAMOND DAVE'S TACO COMPANY is a regional restaurant chain, featuring great family-priced Mexican/American cuisine. Opportunities include full-service restaurant/bar concept. Locations available in enclosed regional malls, strip centers and free-standing units.

BACKGROUND:

Established: 1980;	1st Franchised: 1981
Franchised Units:	36
Company-Owned Units	4
Total Units:	40
Dist.:	US-36; CAN-0; O'seas-0
North America:	5 States
Density:	14 in IA, 9 in IL, 5 in WI
Projected New Units (12 Months):	2
Registered: IL,MN,SD,WI	

FINANCIAL/TERMS:

Cash Investment:	$50-75K
Total Investment:	$150-250K
Minimum Net Worth:	$NR
Fees: Franchise -	$15K
Royalty - 4%;	Ad. - 1%
Earnings Claim Statement:	No
Term of Contract (Years):	10/10
Avg. # Of Employees:	5 FT, 15 PT
Passive Ownership:	Discouraged
Encourage Conversions:	Yes
Area Develop. Agreements:	Yes
Sub-Franchising Contracts:	No
Expand In Territory:	Yes
Space Needs: 2,000-3,000 SF; SC, RM	

SUPPORT & TRAINING PROVIDED:

Financial Assistance Provided:	N/A
Site Selection Assistance:	Yes
Lease Negotiation Assistance:	Yes
Co-Operative Advertising:	Yes
Franchisee Assoc./Member:	NR
Size Of Corporate Staff:	4
On-Going Support:	C,D,E,F,G,H
Training: 2-4 Weeks Local Restaurant.	

SPECIFIC EXPANSION PLANS:

US:	Midwest Only
Canada:	No
Overseas:	No

<< >>

DONATOS PIZZA

1 Easton Oval, # 200
Columbus, OH 43219-6061
Tel: (800) 366-2867 (614) 416-7700
Fax: (614) 416-7701
Web Site: www.donatospizza.com
Mr. Brian Oaks, Exec. Dir. Of Franchise Dev.

DONATOS PIZZA is a retail outlet specializing in the sale of pizzas, subs and salads, featuring delivery, carryout and dine-in service. DONATOS is committed to serving the best pizza and promoting goodwill through product, principle and people. DONATOS PIZZA strives to be the best pizza on the block where the stores are located.

BACKGROUND: IFA MEMBER

Established: 1963;	1st Franchised: 1991
Franchised Units:	46
Company-Owned Units	83
Total Units:	129
Dist.:	US-114; CAN-0; O'seas-0
North America:	4 States
Density:	94 in OH, 13 in IN, 4 in KY
Projected New Units (12 Months):	25
Qualifications:	5, 4, 5, 3, 2, 4
Registered: FL,IL,IN,MD,MI,MN,VA,DC	

FINANCIAL/TERMS:

Cash Investment:	$25% of Total
Total Investment:	$250-600K
Minimum Net Worth:	$350K
Fees: Franchise -	$30K
Royalty - 4%;	Ad. - 4%
Earnings Claim Statement:	Yes
Term of Contract (Years):	20/5
Avg. # Of Employees:	15 FT, 20 PT
Passive Ownership:	Discouraged
Encourage Conversions:	Yes
Area Develop. Agreements:	Yes/Varies
Sub-Franchising Contracts:	No
Expand In Territory:	Yes
Space Needs: 2,000 SF; FS, SF, SC	

SUPPORT & TRAINING PROVIDED:

Financial Assistance Provided:	No
Site Selection Assistance:	Yes
Lease Negotiation Assistance:	Yes
Co-Operative Advertising:	Yes
Franchisee Assoc./Member:	No
Size Of Corporate Staff:	90
On-Going Support:	B,C,D,E,G,H,I
Training: 6-8 Weeks Colombus, OH.	

SPECIFIC EXPANSION PLANS:

US:	Midwest, Southeast
Canada:	No
Overseas:	No

<< >>

EAST OF CHICAGO PIZZA COMPANY

318 W. Walton
Willard, OH 44890
Tel: (419) 935-3033
Fax: (419) 935-3278
E-Mail: development@eastofchicago.com
Web Site: www.eastofchicago.com
Ms. Nina L. Blanton, Dev. Coord.

EAST OF CHICAGO PIZZA COMPANY is a young, determined franchising company that utilizes dine-in and delivery/carry-out units to achieve market dominance. Established in 1990, EOC has grown to over 100 units, with plans to expand. Combining proven marketing and operational systems, with ideal franchisee strategic partnerships, EOC meets demands of customers with unique products, which, when combined with superior customer service, creates an atmosphere of tremendous customer loyalty/repeat business.

BACKGROUND:

Established: 1990;	1st Franchised: 1991
Franchised Units:	134
Company-Owned Units	9
Total Units:	143
Dist.:	US-128; CAN-0; O'seas-0
North America:	5 States
Density:	115 in OH, 9 in IN, 4 in PA
Projected New Units (12 Months):	30
Qualifications:	4, 3, 3, 3, 4, 4
Registered: FL,IN,VA	

FINANCIAL/TERMS:

Cash Investment:	$50K
Total Investment:	$150-300K
Minimum Net Worth:	$N/A
Fees: Franchise -	$20K
Royalty - 5%;	Ad. - 2%
Earnings Claim Statement:	Yes
Term of Contract (Years):	10/10
Avg. # Of Employees:	10 FT, 10 PT
Passive Ownership:	Allowed
Encourage Conversions:	Yes
Area Develop. Agreements:	No
Sub-Franchising Contracts:	No
Expand In Territory:	No
Space Needs: 1,200-3,000 SF; FS, SC	

SUPPORT & TRAINING PROVIDED:

Financial Assistance Provided:	No
Site Selection Assistance:	Yes
Lease Negotiation Assistance:	No
Co-Operative Advertising:	Yes
Franchisee Assoc./Member:	Yes/Yes
Size Of Corporate Staff:	40

On-Going Support: A,B,C,D,E,F,G,H
Training: 4 Weeks in Willard, OH.

SPECIFIC EXPANSION PLANS:

US: OH, IN, PA, FL, VA Only.
Canada: No
Overseas: No

<< >>

Top 50

EL POLLO LOCO

3333 Michelson Dr., # 550
Irvine, CA 92612
Tel: (800) 997-6556 (949) 399-2055
Fax: (949) 399-2025
E-Mail: franchise@elpolloloco.com
Web Site: www.elpolloloco.com
Mr. Stephen Dunn, Dir. Franchise Development

The nation's leading flame-broiled chicken, quick-service restaurant, specializing in great tasting Mexican food that offers customers a wholesome alternative to traditional fast-food.

BACKGROUND: IFA MEMBER

Established: 1975; 1st Franchised: 1983
Franchised Units: 156
Company-Owned Units 127
Total Units: 283
Dist.: US-270; CAN-0; O'seas-4
North America: 4 States
Density: 250 in CA, 9 in AZ, 7 in NV
Projected New Units (12 Months): 20
Qualifications: 5, 5, 5, 3, 3, 5
Registered: CA

FINANCIAL/TERMS:

Cash Investment: $300K minimum
Total Investment: $502K-1MM
Minimum Net Worth: $1MM
Fees: Franchise - $40K
Royalty - 4%; Ad. - 4-5%
Earnings Claim Statement: Yes
Term of Contract (Years): 20
Avg. # Of Employees: 8 FT, 17 PT
Passive Ownership: Discouraged
Encourage Conversions: Yes
Area Develop. Agreements: Yes/Varies
Sub-Franchising Contracts: No
Expand In Territory: Yes
Space Needs: 2,600 SF; FS, SF, SC

SUPPORT & TRAINING PROVIDED:

Financial Assistance Provided: No
Site Selection Assistance: Yes
Lease Negotiation Assistance: No
Co-Operative Advertising: Yes
Franchisee Assoc./Member: Yes/Yes
Size Of Corporate Staff: 75
On-Going Support: B,C,D,E,F,H,I
Training: 6 Weeks in Southern CA.

SPECIFIC EXPANSION PLANS:

US: CA, AZ, NV, TX
Canada: No
Overseas: No

<< >>

Erbert & Gerbert's
SUBS CLUBS

ERBERT & GERBERT'S SUBS & CLUBS

205 E. Grand Ave
Eau Claire, WI 54701
Tel: (800) 283-5241 (715) 833-1375
Fax: (715) 833-8523
Web Site: www.erbertandgerberts.com
Mr. Kevin Schippers, President

ERBERT AND GERBERT'S SUBS & CLUBS offer the gourmet sandwich product in the fast-food niche. Growing rapidly, the market is wide open for this top-quality, service-oriented company. Immaculate shops and outstanding service complement the gourmet product.

BACKGROUND:

Established: 1987; 1st Franchised: 1992
Franchised Units: 15
Company-Owned Units 1
Total Units: 16
Dist.: US-16; CAN-0; O'seas-0
North America: 3 States
Density: 9 in WI, 6 in MN, 1 in ND
Projected New Units (12 Months): 12
Qualifications: 4, 5, 1, 3, 4, 5
Registered: FL,IL,MN,ND,SD,WI

FINANCIAL/TERMS:

Cash Investment: $30-35K
Total Investment: $158-289K
Minimum Net Worth: $250K
Fees: Franchise - $25K
Royalty - 6.5%; Ad. - 5%
Earnings Claim Statement: Yes
Term of Contract (Years): 15/5
Avg. # Of Employees: 2-3 FT, 10 PT
Passive Ownership: Discouraged
Encourage Conversions: Yes
Area Develop. Agreements: Yes/Varies
Sub-Franchising Contracts: No
Expand In Territory: NR
Space Needs: 1,000-2,000 SF; SF, SC

SUPPORT & TRAINING PROVIDED:

Financial Assistance Provided: Yes(I)
Site Selection Assistance: Yes
Lease Negotiation Assistance: Yes
Co-Operative Advertising: Yes
Franchisee Assoc./Member: Yes
Size Of Corporate Staff: 5
On-Going Support: C,D,d,E,G,H,I
Training: 2 Weeks Home Office; 1 Week On-Site during Opening.

SPECIFIC EXPANSION PLANS:

US: All U.S., Primarily Midwest
Canada: No
Overseas: No

<< >>

FAMILY PIZZA

318 105th St. E., Bay 10
Saskatoon, SK S7N 1Z3 CANADA
Tel: (306) 955-0215
Fax: (306) 955-0215
Mr. Hal Schmidt, President

2-for-1 gourmet pizza and pasta. Take-out and delivery - 39 minute guarantee or your order is free.

BACKGROUND:

Established: 1983; 1st Franchised: 1987
Franchised Units: 17
Company-Owned Units 7
Total Units: 24
Dist.: US-0; CAN-24; O'seas-0
North America: 3 Provinces
Density: 13 in SK, 5 in AB, 5 in BC
Projected New Units (12 Months): 10
Qualifications: 3, 3, 2, 3, 3, 4
Registered: AB

FINANCIAL/TERMS:

Cash Investment: $40K
Total Investment: $75-120K
Minimum Net Worth: $50K
Fees: Franchise - $15K
Royalty - 4%; Ad. - 5%
Earnings Claim Statement: Yes
Term of Contract (Years): 5/5

Avg. # Of Employees: 5 FT, 10 PT
Passive Ownership: Discouraged
Encourage Conversions: No
Area Develop. Agreements: Yes/5
Sub-Franchising Contracts: No
Expand In Territory: Yes
Space Needs: 900-1,500 SF; FS, SC

SUPPORT & TRAINING PROVIDED:
Financial Assistance Provided: Yes(I)
Site Selection Assistance: Yes
Lease Negotiation Assistance: Yes
Co-Operative Advertising: Yes
Franchisee Assoc./Member: No
Size Of Corporate Staff: 3
On-Going Support: A,B,C,D,E,F,G,H
Training: 2-4 Weeks in Store.

SPECIFIC EXPANSION PLANS:
US: No
Canada: All Canada
Overseas: No

<< >>

FARMER BOYS HAMBURGERS

3452 University Ave.
Riverside, CA 92501
Tel: (888) 930-3276 (909) 275-9900
Fax: (909) 275-9930
E-Mail: bfoss@farmerboys.com
Web Site: www.farmerboys.com
Mr. Bill Foss, Franchise Sales Mgr.

FARMER BOYS RESTAURANTS fill a unique food service niche by offering greater choice to both fast food and traditional sit-down restaurant customers. Concept offers over 100 fresh breakfast, lunch or dinner items, prepared and cooked to order in 5 - 7 minutes - with a choice of sit-down, take-out or drive-thru service.

BACKGROUND:
Established: 1981; 1st Franchised: 1997
Franchised Units: 11
Company-Owned Units 10
Total Units: 21
Dist.: US-21; CAN-0; O'seas-0
North America: 1 State
Density: 20 in CA
Projected New Units (12 Months): 10
Qualifications: 4, 4, 2, 3, 1, 5
Registered: CA

FINANCIAL/TERMS:
Cash Investment: $200K
Total Investment: $393-582K
Minimum Net Worth: $500K
Fees: Franchise - $30K
Royalty - 5%; Ad. - 2%
Earnings Claim Statement: Yes
Term of Contract (Years): 20/10/10
Avg. # Of Employees:7-10 FT, 10-15 PT
Passive Ownership: Discouraged
Encourage Conversions: No
Area Develop. Agreements: Yes/Varies
Sub-Franchising Contracts: No
Expand In Territory: Yes
Space Needs: 2,500-3,000 SF; FS

SUPPORT & TRAINING PROVIDED:
Financial Assistance Provided: NR
Site Selection Assistance: Yes
Lease Negotiation Assistance: Yes
Co-Operative Advertising: Yes
Franchisee Assoc./Member: No
Size Of Corporate Staff: 15
On-Going Support: B,C,D,E,F,I
Training: 3 Months at Company-Operated Unit.

SPECIFIC EXPANSION PLANS:
US: CA Only
Canada: No
Overseas: No

<< >>

FAST EDDIE'S

129 Wellington St., # 102
Brantford, ON N3T 5Z9 CANADA
Tel: (519) 758-0111
Fax: (519) 758-1393
E-Mail: fasteddies@sympatico.ca
Mr. Mike Gorski, President

FAST EDDIE'S is a hamburger-based, fast-food, double-drive-thru restaurant with no inside seating. We have 100% pure-beef, quality hamburgers with shakes and fries to go. Try our crazy fries!

BACKGROUND:
Established: 1989; 1st Franchised: 1989
Franchised Units: 0
Company-Owned Units 9
Total Units: 9
Dist.: US-0; CAN-6; O'seas-0
North America: 1 Province
Density: 6 in ON
Projected New Units (12 Months): 1
Qualifications: 5, 5, 4, 3, 3, 5
Registered: None

FINANCIAL/TERMS:
Cash Investment: $50-100K
Total Investment: $200-400K
Minimum Net Worth: $300K
Fees: Franchise - $15K
Royalty - 4-6%; Ad. - 2%
Earnings Claim Statement: Yes
Term of Contract (Years): N/A
Avg. # Of Employees: 3 FT, 15 PT
Passive Ownership: Not Allowed
Encourage Conversions: No
Area Develop. Agreements: No
Sub-Franchising Contracts: No
Expand In Territory: Yes
Space Needs: 900 SF; FS

SUPPORT & TRAINING PROVIDED:
Financial Assistance Provided: No
Site Selection Assistance: Yes
Lease Negotiation Assistance: Yes
Co-Operative Advertising: Yes
Franchisee Assoc./Member: Yes/Yes
Size Of Corporate Staff: 18
On-Going Support: C,D,E,F
Training: 2 Weeks Brantford, ON.

SPECIFIC EXPANSION PLANS:
US: No
Canada: ON
Overseas: No

<< >>

FATBURGER

1218 Third St. Promenade
Santa Monica, CA 90401-1308
Tel: (310) 319-1850
Fax: (310) 319-1863
Web Site: www.fatburger.com
Ms. Angelina Morse, Dir. Franchise Relations

The classic hamburger stand, serving cooked-to-order burgers at an open grill since 1952. Also serving grilled chicken-breast sandwiches, freshly-made onion rings and real milkshakes in a fun environment with a unique R & B jukebox.

BACKGROUND: IFA MEMBER
Established: 1952; 1st Franchised: 1980
Franchised Units: 28
Company-Owned Units 13
Total Units: 41
Dist.: US-36; CAN-0; O'seas-0
North America: 3 States
Density: 28 in CA, 7 in NV
Projected New Units (12 Months): 8
Qualifications: 4, 5, 3, 2, 5, 5
Registered: CA,IL,MD,NY,WA

FINANCIAL/TERMS:
Cash Investment: $150-250K
Total Investment: $370-730K

Minimum Net Worth: $NR
Fees: Franchise - $30K
Royalty - 5%; Ad. - 2%
Earnings Claim Statement: Yes
Term of Contract (Years): 15/10/10
Avg. # Of Employees: 16-40 PT
Passive Ownership: Allowed
Encourage Conversions: Yes
Area Develop. Agreements: Yes/5
Sub-Franchising Contracts: No
Expand In Territory: No
Space Needs: 1,800-2,000 SF; FS, SF, SC

SUPPORT & TRAINING PROVIDED:
Financial Assistance Provided: No
Site Selection Assistance: Yes
Lease Negotiation Assistance: No
Co-Operative Advertising: No
Franchisee Assoc./Member: No
Size Of Corporate Staff: 10
On-Going Support: C,D,E,H
Training: 10 Weeks Orange County, CA; 7-10 Days On-Site.

SPECIFIC EXPANSION PLANS:
US: All United States
Canada: All Canada
Overseas: No

FIGARO'S PIZZA

1500 Liberty St., S. E., # 160
Salem, OR 97302
Tel: (888) 344-2767 (503) 371-9318
Fax: (503) 363-5364
E-Mail: franchisedev@figaros.com
Web Site: www.figaros.com
Mr. Steve Nilsby, Dir. Franchise Development

A Figaro's Pizza franchise is a complete business system. It's easy to run, has low initial investment, low labor costs, simple equipment package and low-cost locations. Figaro's is unique because it offers the consumer the choice of fresh, made-to-order "Take-and-Bake" pizza made with the freshest, highest quality ingredients or one that is "Baked-to-Order" in the store and ready-to-eat. And most importantly, pizza delivers and excellent profit margin.

BACKGROUND: IFA MEMBER
Established: 1981; 1st Franchised: 1986
Franchised Units: 97
Company-Owned Units 0
Total Units: 97
Dist.: US-94; CAN-0; O'seas-0
North America: 7 States
Density: 64 in OR, 17 in WA, 6 in ID
Projected New Units (12 Months): 25
Qualifications: 5, 4, 2, 3, 4, 5
Registered: CA,FL,IN,MN,ND,OR,SD,TX,UT,WA

FINANCIAL/TERMS:
Cash Investment: $50-65K
Total Investment: $97.5-191.5K
Minimum Net Worth: $150-225K
Fees: Franchise - $18.5K
Royalty - 5%; Ad. - 3%
Earnings Claim Statement: No
Term of Contract (Years): 5/5/5/5
Avg. # Of Employees: 1 FT, 12 PT
Passive Ownership: Discouraged
Encourage Conversions: Yes
Area Develop. Agreements: Yes
Sub-Franchising Contracts: Yes
Expand In Territory: Yes
Space Needs: 1200 SF; FS, SF, SC

SUPPORT & TRAINING PROVIDED:
Financial Assistance Provided: Yes
Site Selection Assistance: Yes
Lease Negotiation Assistance: Yes
Co-Operative Advertising: Yes
Franchisee Assoc./Member: Yes
Size Of Corporate Staff: 27
On-Going Support: B,C,D,E,G,H,I
Training: 21 Days, Salem, OR.

SPECIFIC EXPANSION PLANS:
US: All United States
Canada: No
Overseas: No

FOUR STAR PIZZA

P.O. Box W
Claysville, PA 15323
Tel: (800) 628-3398
Fax: (724) 484-9235
E-Mail: fourstarza@aol.com
Web Site: www.fourstarpizza.net
Mr. David Roderick, President

Four Star Pizza is looking for aggressive, hard-driving entrepreneur as a four star franchisee you will feature a popular premium quality product, a great location, and an unbeatable, low start-up cost. Add a dash of entrepreneurial spirit and you're on your way to an exciting and profitable future.

BACKGROUND:
Established: 1981; 1st Franchised: 1985
Franchised Units: 40
Company-Owned Units 3
Total Units: 43
Dist.: US-19; CAN-0; O'seas-0
North America: 5 States
Density: 10 in PA, 4 in MO, 2 in OH
Projected New Units (12 Months): 6
Qualifications: 3, 4, 2, 3, 1, 5
Registered: MD,NY,VA

FINANCIAL/TERMS:
Cash Investment: $NR
Total Investment: $47.5-142K
Minimum Net Worth: $NR
Fees: Franchise - $7K
Royalty - 5%; Ad. - 1%
Earnings Claim Statement: No
Term of Contract (Years): 10/10
Avg. # Of Employees: 3 FT, 4-10 PT
Passive Ownership: Discouraged
Encourage Conversions: Yes
Area Develop. Agreements: Yes
Sub-Franchising Contracts: No
Expand In Territory: Yes
Space Needs: 800-1200 SF; FS, SC

SUPPORT & TRAINING PROVIDED:
Financial Assistance Provided: Yes(I)
Site Selection Assistance: No
Lease Negotiation Assistance: Yes
Co-Operative Advertising: Yes
Franchisee Assoc./Member: No
Size Of Corporate Staff: 3
On-Going Support: B,C,D,E,H,I
Training: 1-2 Weeks Varied Location.

SPECIFIC EXPANSION PLANS:
US: PA, VA, OH, WV, MD
Canada: No
Overseas: No

FOX'S PIZZA DEN

3243 Old Frankstown Rd.
Pittsburgh, PA 15239
Tel: (800) 899-3697 (724) 733-7888
Fax: (724) 325-5479
E-Mail: foxs@alltel.net
Web Site: www.foxspizza.com
Mr. James R. Fox, President

FOX'S PIZZA DEN believes in one philosophy - you earned it, you keep it! FOX'S royalties are $200 a month - no percentages of sales. FOX'S PIZZA DENS offers the finest pizza, specialty sandwiches, salads and sides and our house special - the 'wedgie.'

BACKGROUND:
Established: 1971; 1st Franchised: 1974
Franchised Units: 207
Company-Owned Units 0
Total Units: 207

Dist.: US-205; CAN-0; O'seas-0
North America: 19 States
Density: 105 in PA, 42 in WV, 12 OH
Projected New Units (12 Months): 30
Qualifications: 2, 4, 4, 2, 2, 5
Registered: FL,MD,MI,NY,VA

FINANCIAL/TERMS:

Cash Investment:	$50-80K
Total Investment:	$50-80K
Minimum Net Worth:	$N/A
Fees: Franchise -	$8K
Royalty - $200/Mo.;	Ad. - 0%
Earnings Claim Statement:	No
Term of Contract (Years):	5/5
Avg. # Of Employees:	2-3 FT, 8-10 PT
Passive Ownership:	Discouraged
Encourage Conversions:	Yes
Area Develop. Agreements:	Yes
Sub-Franchising Contracts:	Yes
Expand In Territory:	Yes

Space Needs: 1,000-2,000 SF; FS, SF, SC

SUPPORT & TRAINING PROVIDED:

Financial Assistance Provided:	Yes(I)
Site Selection Assistance:	Yes
Lease Negotiation Assistance:	No
Co-Operative Advertising:	Yes
Franchisee Assoc./Member:	NR
Size Of Corporate Staff:	8
On-Going Support:	B,C,D,E,F,G,H,I

Training: 7 Days On-Site.

SPECIFIC EXPANSION PLANS:

US:	All United States
Canada:	No
Overseas:	No

<< >>

Top 50

FRULLATI CAFÉ & BAKERY

7730 E. Greenway Rd., # 230
Scottsdale, AZ 85260
Tel: (800) 289-8291 (972) 401-9730
Fax: (972) 401-9731
E-Mail: comments@frullati.com
Web Site: www.frulatti.com
Ms. Nicole Rayborn, Franchise Director

FRULLATI CAFÉ & BAKERY, the fresh franchise alternative in fast food. Featuring something fresh for every taste, FRULLATI's lite fare menu includes: fruit smoothies, frozen yogurt, deli sandwiches, healthy snacks, fresh baked bread, cookies and gourmet coffee. If the taste of success by owning one or a chain of FRULLATI CAFÉs sounds appetizing, here's the opportunity for you. We have FRULLATI CAFÉ & BAKERY franchise opportunities coming to your neighborhood.

BACKGROUND:

Established: 1985; 1st Franchised: 1994

Franchised Units:	57
Company-Owned Units	37
Total Units:	94

Dist.: US-100; CAN-0; O'seas-0
North America: 14 States
Density: 29 in TX, 12 in IL, 7 in FL
Projected New Units (12 Months): 28
Qualifications: 5, 4, , 3, , 5
Registered: CA,FL,IL,IN,MD,MI,MN,ND, OR,VA,WA,WI

FINANCIAL/TERMS:

Cash Investment:	$50K
Total Investment:	$150-275K
Minimum Net Worth:	$150K
Fees: Franchise -	$20K
Royalty - 6%;	Ad. - 1%
Earnings Claim Statement:	Yes
Term of Contract (Years):	10/10
Avg. # Of Employees:	3 FT, 5 PT
Passive Ownership:	Discouraged
Encourage Conversions:	Yes
Area Develop. Agreements:	Yes/Varies
Sub-Franchising Contracts:	No
Expand In Territory:	Yes

Space Needs: 600 SF; RM

SUPPORT & TRAINING PROVIDED:

Financial Assistance Provided:	Yes(I)
Site Selection Assistance:	Yes
Lease Negotiation Assistance:	Yes
Co-Operative Advertising:	Yes
Franchisee Assoc./Member:	Yes/Yes
Size Of Corporate Staff:	350
On-Going Support:	C,D,E,G,H,I

Training: 3 Weeks Dallas, TX.

SPECIFIC EXPANSION PLANS:

US:	All United States
Canada:	No
Overseas:	No

<< >>

GODFATHER'S PIZZA

9140 W. Dodge Rd., # 300
Omaha, NE 68114
Tel: (800) 456-8347 (402) 391-1452
Fax: (402) 255-2685
E-Mail: brucec@godfathers.com
Web Site: www.godfathers.com
Mr. Bruce N. Cannon, VP Franchising

GODFATHER'S PIZZA is consistently recognized by consumers and independent research as having a superior quality product. Couple this with consistent operations, innovative new products, attention to service and full support services and GODFATHER'S PIZZA is positioned to retain its reputation for high quality and service.

BACKGROUND:

Established: 1973; 1st Franchised: 1974

Franchised Units:	480
Company-Owned Units	111
Total Units:	591

Dist.: US-590; CAN-1; O'seas-0
North America: 38 States
Density: 67 in WA, 60 in IA, 39 in MN
Projected New Units (12 Months): 27
Qualifications: 5, 5, 5, 3, ,
Registered: CA,FL,IL,IN,MD,MI,MN, OR,SD,WA

FINANCIAL/TERMS:

Cash Investment:	$55-120K
Total Investment:	$82.5-358K
Minimum Net Worth:	$200K
Fees: Franchise -	$20K
Royalty - 5%;	Ad. - 0%
Earnings Claim Statement:	No
Term of Contract (Years):	15/10
Avg. # Of Employees:	6 FT, 20 PT
Passive Ownership:	Discouraged
Encourage Conversions:	Yes
Area Develop. Agreements:	Yes/5
Sub-Franchising Contracts:	No
Expand In Territory:	Yes

Space Needs: 3,500 SF; FS, SC

SUPPORT & TRAINING PROVIDED:

Financial Assistance Provided:	No
Site Selection Assistance:	Yes
Lease Negotiation Assistance:	No
Co-Operative Advertising:	Yes
Franchisee Assoc./Member:	Yes
Size Of Corporate Staff:	92
On-Going Support:	D,G,I

Training: 35 Days Omaha, NE.

SPECIFIC EXPANSION PLANS:

US:	All United States
Canada:	No
Overseas:	No

<< >>

GOLDEN CHICK

11488 Luna Rd., # 100B
Dallas, TX 75234

Tel: (972) 831-0911
Fax: (972) 831-0401
Mr. Kelly Creighton, Vice President

GOLDEN CHICK is a fast-food chicken restaurant, offering indoor dining, drive-thru, carry-out and delivery service. GC's menu consists of fresh, golden fried chicken, golden tenders, country-style biscuits, gravy, french fries, cole slaw, mashed potatoes, corn on the cob, sandwiches and fountain soft drinks.

BACKGROUND:
Established: 1967; 1st Franchised: 1972
Franchised Units: 62
Company-Owned Units 10
Total Units: 72
Dist.: US-68; CAN-0; O'seas-4
North America: 3 States
Density: 66 in TX, 2 in OK, 4 in MX
Projected New Units (12 Months): 6
Qualifications: 4, 4, 5, 2, 2, 5
Registered: NR

FINANCIAL/TERMS:
Cash Investment: $NR
Total Investment: $400-750K
Minimum Net Worth: $N/A
Fees: Franchise - $15K
Royalty - 4%; Ad. - 1%
Earnings Claim Statement: Yes
Term of Contract (Years): 20/N/A
Avg. # Of Employees: NR
Passive Ownership: Not Allowed
Encourage Conversions: Yes
Area Develop. Agreements: No
Sub-Franchising Contracts: No
Expand In Territory: No
Space Needs: 1,800 SF; FS

SUPPORT & TRAINING PROVIDED:
Financial Assistance Provided: Yes
Site Selection Assistance: Yes
Lease Negotiation Assistance: No
Co-Operative Advertising: Yes
Franchisee Assoc./Member: No
Size Of Corporate Staff: 12
On-Going Support: a,B,C,D,d,E,F,G,H
Training: 6 Weeks Dallas, TX.

SPECIFIC EXPANSION PLANS:
US: South, Southwest
Canada: No
Overseas: No

<< >>

GORIN'S HOMEMADE CAFE & GRILL

57 Executive Park S., # 440
Atlanta, GA 30329
Tel: (888) 489-7277 (404) 248-9900
Fax: (404) 248-0180
E-Mail: franchise@gorins.com
Web Site: www.gorins.com
Mr. Mark Kaplan, Chief Executive Officer

GORIN'S offers a unique, high quality sandwich concept, featuring its proprietary Melt Sandwiches such as the Almond Chicken Melt, Turkey Bacon Melt and the Honey Ham Melt. Additionally, GORIN'S serves a full line of deli sandwiches, cheesesteaks, soups and a proprietary line of ice cream. Combines the comfort and quality of casual dining with the price and convenience of quick serve.

BACKGROUND: IFA MEMBER
Established: 1981; 1st Franchised: 1983
Franchised Units: 31
Company-Owned Units 1
Total Units: 31
Dist.: US-30; CAN-0; O'seas-1
North America: 4 States
Density: 32 in GA, 4 in AL, 1 in NC
Projected New Units (12 Months): 8-10
Qualifications: 5, 4, 3, 3, 3, 4
Registered: FL

FINANCIAL/TERMS:
Cash Investment: $85-95K
Total Investment: $190-250K
Minimum Net Worth: $300K
Fees: Franchise - $17.5K
Royalty - 5%; Ad. - 0.5-2.5%
Earnings Claim Statement: No
Term of Contract (Years): 10/10
Avg. # Of Employees: 7 FT, 6 PT
Passive Ownership: Discouraged
Encourage Conversions: Yes
Area Develop. Agreements: Yes/Varies
Sub-Franchising Contracts: No
Expand In Territory: Yes
Space Needs: 1,800-2,400 SF; FS, SF, SC, RM, OB

SUPPORT & TRAINING PROVIDED:
Financial Assistance Provided: Yes(I)
Site Selection Assistance: Yes
Lease Negotiation Assistance: Yes
Co-Operative Advertising: Yes
Franchisee Assoc./Member: Yes/Yes
Size Of Corporate Staff: 11
On-Going Support: C,D,E,F,G
Training: 3 Weeks Atlanta, GA.

SPECIFIC EXPANSION PLANS:
US: Southeast
Canada: No
Overseas: Asia, Europe, Open Countries

<< >>

GREAT OUTDOOR SUB SHOPS

900 E. Parker Rd.
Plano, TX 75074
Tel: (972) 423-2693
Fax: (972) 424-7798
E-Mail: GOSUBS1973@aol.com
Ms. Gail Voelcker, President

G. O. FRANCHISE, INC. is a quick-service restaurant which offers freshly-prepared submarine sandwiches, salads and ice cream under the trade name GREAT OUTDOOR SUB SHOP. Over the last 26 years, we have excelled and perfected the system and are now offering G. O. FRANCHISE opportunities to qualified individuals who are interested in the franchise restaurant industry.

BACKGROUND:
Established: 1973; 1st Franchised: 1996
Franchised Units: 3
Company-Owned Units 6
Total Units: 9
Dist.: US-9; CAN-0; O'seas-0
North America: 1 State
Density: 9 in TX
Projected New Units (12 Months): 3
Qualifications: 3, 4, 4, 3, 4, 5
Registered: NR

FINANCIAL/TERMS:
Cash Investment: $75-265K
Total Investment: $75-265K
Minimum Net Worth: $150K
Fees: Franchise - $25K
Royalty - 4%; Ad. - 3%
Earnings Claim Statement: Yes
Term of Contract (Years): 10/10
Avg. # Of Employees: 6 FT, 5 PT
Passive Ownership: Not Allowed
Encourage Conversions: Yes
Area Develop. Agreements: Yes/10
Sub-Franchising Contracts: No
Expand In Territory: Yes
Space Needs: 1,800-2,200 SF; FS, SC

SUPPORT & TRAINING PROVIDED:
Financial Assistance Provided: No
Site Selection Assistance: Yes

Lease Negotiation Assistance:	Yes
Co-Operative Advertising:	No
Franchisee Assoc./Member:	No
Size Of Corporate Staff:	8
On-Going Support:	b,C,d,E,f

Training: 8 Weeks Dallas, TX.

SPECIFIC EXPANSION PLANS:

US:	TX, SW
Canada:	No
Overseas:	No

<< >>

GREAT WRAPS!

4 Executive Park E., # 315
Atlanta, GA 30329
Tel: (888) 489-7277 (404) 248-9900
Fax: (404) 248-0180
E-Mail: franchise@greatwraps.com
Web Site: www.greatwraps.com
Mr. Mark Kaplan, Chairman

GREAT WRAPS, the original and #1 wrapped sandwich franchise, is leading this explosive, new food category into malls, shopping centers, airports and business districts. GREAT WRAPS features a powerful line-up of hot wrapped sandwiches, burritos, cheesesteaks and frozen smoothies. With over 15 years of proven success, GREAT WRAPS offers you an established business system, excellent training and tremendous growth potential.

BACKGROUND: IFA MEMBER

Established: 1978; 1st Franchised: 1986

Franchised Units:	45
Company-Owned Units	0
Total Units:	45
Dist.:	US-45; CAN-0; O'seas-0
North America:	8 States
Density:	19 in GA, 6 in FL, 4 in TX
Projected New Units (12 Months):	8-10
Qualifications:	5, 3, 3, 3, 4, 4

Registered: FL,MI,NY,VA

FINANCIAL/TERMS:

Cash Investment:	$70-80K
Total Investment:	$175-250K
Minimum Net Worth:	$250K
Fees: Franchise -	$17.5K
Royalty - 5%;	Ad. - 0.5%
Earnings Claim Statement:	No
Term of Contract (Years):	10/10
Avg. # Of Employees:	5 FT, 6 PT
Passive Ownership:	Discouraged
Encourage Conversions:	Yes
Area Develop. Agreements:	Yes/Varies
Sub-Franchising Contracts:	No
Expand In Territory:	Yes

Space Needs: 600-1,500 SF; RM, SC, Airport, Univer.

SUPPORT & TRAINING PROVIDED:

Financial Assistance Provided:	Yes(I)
Site Selection Assistance:	Yes
Lease Negotiation Assistance:	Yes
Co-Operative Advertising:	Yes
Franchisee Assoc./Member:	Yes
Size Of Corporate Staff:	11
On-Going Support:	B,C,D,E,G,H

Training: 3 Weeks Atlanta, GA.

SPECIFIC EXPANSION PLANS:

US:	NE, SE, SW, MW
Canada:	No
Overseas:	No

<< >>

GRECO PIZZA DONAIR

105 Walker St., P.O. Box 1040
Truro, NS B2N 5G9 CANADA
Tel: (902) 893-4141
Fax: (902) 895-7635
E-Mail: grinners@greco.ca
Web Site: www.greco.ca
Mr. Guy Gallant, Director Development

Atlantic Canada's largest home delivery pizza chain, specializing in pizza, donair products, oven sub sandwiches and pita-wrapped sandwiches.

BACKGROUND:

Established: 1977; 1st Franchised: 1981

Franchised Units:	101
Company-Owned Units	2
Total Units:	103
Dist.:	US-0; CAN-54; O'seas-0
North America:	4 Provinces
Density:	21 in NB, 23 in NS, 5 in NF
Projected New Units (12 Months):	5

Registered: NR

FINANCIAL/TERMS:

Cash Investment:	$40K
Total Investment:	$150-180K
Minimum Net Worth:	$40K
Fees: Franchise -	$15K
Royalty - 5%;	Ad. - 3%
Earnings Claim Statement:	No
Term of Contract (Years):	10/5/5
Avg. # Of Employees:	5 FT, 10 PT
Passive Ownership:	Discouraged
Encourage Conversions:	Yes
Area Develop. Agreements:	Yes/Varies
Sub-Franchising Contracts:	Yes
Expand In Territory:	Yes

Space Needs: 1,200 SF; FS, SF, SC, RM

SUPPORT & TRAINING PROVIDED:

Financial Assistance Provided:	No
Site Selection Assistance:	Yes
Lease Negotiation Assistance:	Yes
Co-Operative Advertising:	Yes
Franchisee Assoc./Member:	NR
Size Of Corporate Staff:	19
On-Going Support:	a,b,C,D,E,F,G,h,I

Training: 4 Weeks Correspondence; 2 Days Headquarters; 3 Weeks On-Site.

SPECIFIC EXPANSION PLANS:

US:	No
Canada:	PQ, Atlantic Can
Overseas:	No

<< >>

HAMBURGER MARY'S

P.O. Box 456
Corona Del Mar, CA 92625
Tel: (888) 834-6279 (949) 729-8000
Fax: (949) 675-9979
E-Mail: hamburgermary@home.com
Web Site: www.franchisemarys.com
Mr. Stan Sax, President

Hamburger Mary's Bar & Grille is the only and the largest restaurant franchise catering to the Gay and Lesbian community (as well as the general public). With over 30 years of successful operations, we have totally re-organized under HMI to become a major franchise. In 2001 alone 7 new stores have been sold across the U.S. Our Owner's Manual, Bar Guide/Recipe book, Ad program and In-store training program are just a few of the plus features offered.

BACKGROUND:

Established: 1972; 1st Franchised: 1997

Franchised Units:	9
Company-Owned Units	0
Total Units:	9
Dist.:	US-9; CAN-0; O'seas-0
North America:	6 States, DC
Density:	4 in CA, 1 in AZ, 1 in OH

Projected New Units (12 Months): NR
Registered: NR

FINANCIAL/TERMS:

Cash Investment: $45K (Fee)
Total Investment: $195-500K
Minimum Net Worth: $150K
Fees: Franchise - $45K
Royalty - 4%; Ad. - 2%
Earnings Claim Statement: No
Term of Contract (Years): 15/5
Avg. # Of Employees:35-40 FT, 5-10 PT
Passive Ownership: Not Allowed
Encourage Conversions: NR
Area Develop. Agreements: Yes/Lifetime
Sub-Franchising Contracts: Yes
Expand In Territory: Yes
Space Needs: 4000+ SF; FS

SUPPORT & TRAINING PROVIDED:

Financial Assistance Provided: NR
Site Selection Assistance: Yes
Lease Negotiation Assistance: Yes
Co-Operative Advertising: No
Franchisee Assoc./Member: No
Size Of Corporate Staff: 2
On-Going Support: B,C,D,E,f,H,I
Training: 2 Weeks, Long Beach, CA or Washington DC.

SPECIFIC EXPANSION PLANS:

US: All United States
Canada: NR
Overseas: Australia, Europe

HAMBURGER STAND

4440 Von Karman Ave., # 222
Newport Bech, CA 92660
Tel: (800) 764-9353 (949) 752-5800
Fax: (949) 851-2618
E-Mail: fcoyle@galardigroup.com
Web Site: www.hamburgerstand.com
Mr. Frank R. Coyle, Franchise Sales Dir.

HAMBURGER STAND has successfully positioned itself in the highly competitive quick-serve hamburger business by providing the highest-quality products at lower than market prices. As a Division of Galardi Group, HAMBURGER STAND is part of a network of over 300 restaurants.

BACKGROUND:

Established: 1982; 1st Franchised: 1982
Franchised Units: 23
Company-Owned Units 0
Total Units: 23
Dist.: US-23; CAN-0; O'seas-0
North America: NR
Density: NR

Projected New Units (12 Months): 1
Qualifications: 4, 3, 3, 2, 1, 4
Registered: CA

FINANCIAL/TERMS:

Cash Investment: $150-200K
Total Investment: $250-800K
Minimum Net Worth: $150K
Fees: Franchise - $20K
Royalty - 5%; Ad. - 5%
Earnings Claim Statement: No
Term of Contract (Years): 20
Avg. # Of Employees: 2 FT, 25-35 PT
Passive Ownership: Discouraged
Encourage Conversions: Yes
Area Develop. Agreements: Yes/5
Sub-Franchising Contracts: No
Expand In Territory: Yes
Space Needs: 20,000 SF; FS

SUPPORT & TRAINING PROVIDED:

Financial Assistance Provided: Yes(I)
Site Selection Assistance: Yes
Lease Negotiation Assistance: No
Co-Operative Advertising: Yes
Franchisee Assoc./Member: Yes/Yes
Size Of Corporate Staff: 48
On-Going Support: A,B,C,d,E,F,H,I
Training: 5 Weeks Denver, CO; 1 Week Newport Beach, CA.

SPECIFIC EXPANSION PLANS:

US: Denver, Tucson Only.
Canada: No
Overseas: No

<< >>

HAPPY JOE'S PIZZA & ICE CREAM PARLOR

2705 Happy Joe Dr.
Bettendorf, IA 52722
Tel: (563) 332-8811
Fax: (563) 332-5822
Web Site: www.happyjoes.com
Mr. Tim Anderson, Dir. Franchising

Pizza and ice cream in a fun atmosphere. Birthday party packages available. Very involved with special programs for youth in the community. Diversified pizza, pasta, sandwiches, salad bar and ice cream menu, candy, soft drinks and beer. Several parlors offer Family Fun Centers with redemption games and adventure-style golf.

BACKGROUND:

Established: 1972; 1st Franchised: 1973
Franchised Units: 56
Company-Owned Units 7
Total Units: 63
Dist.: US-64; CAN-0; O'seas-0
North America: 6 States, 1 Province
Density: 34 in IA, 12 in IL, 7 in WI
Projected New Units (12 Months): 3
Qualifications: 5, 4, 3, 3, 3, 4
Registered: IL,ND,WI

FINANCIAL/TERMS:

Cash Investment: $50K
Total Investment: $50K-1.5MM
Minimum Net Worth: $200K
Fees: Franchise - $20K
Royalty - 4.5%; Ad. - 1%
Earnings Claim Statement: No
Term of Contract (Years): 15/10
Avg. # Of Employees: 4 FT, 30 PT
Passive Ownership: Discouraged
Encourage Conversions: Yes
Area Develop. Agreements: Yes/15
Sub-Franchising Contracts: No
Expand In Territory: Yes
Space Needs: 3,500 SF; FS, SF, SC

SUPPORT & TRAINING PROVIDED:

Financial Assistance Provided: Yes(I)
Site Selection Assistance: Yes
Lease Negotiation Assistance: Yes
Co-Operative Advertising: Yes
Franchisee Assoc./Member: Yes/Yes
Size Of Corporate Staff: 30
On-Going Support: B,C,D,E,G,h
Training: 6-12 Weeks in IA.

SPECIFIC EXPANSION PLANS:

US: Midwest
Canada: No
Overseas: No

<< >>

HARDEE'S FOOD SYSTEMS

1200 N. Harbor Blvd., P.O. Box 4349
Anaheim, CA 92801-8349
Tel: (800) 997-8435 (714) 520-4452
Fax: (714) 520-4409
Web Site: www.hardeesrestaurants.com
Mr. Don McLean

Fast food.

BACKGROUND: IFA MEMBER

Established: 1960; 1st Franchised: 1961
Franchised Units: 2,787
Company-Owned Units 1,126
Total Units: 3,913
Dist.: US-2778; CAN-0; O'seas-106
North America: 38 States
Density: 315 in NC, 207 in VA,186 SC
Projected New Units (12 Months): 50-70
Qualifications: 5, 5, 5, 1, 1, 5
Registered: All States

FINANCIAL/TERMS:

Cash Investment: $300K

Total Investment: $1.19-1.25MM
Minimum Net Worth: $1MM
Fees: Franchise - $35K
Royalty - 4%; Ad. - 5%
Earnings Claim Statement: No
Term of Contract (Years): 20/5
Avg. # Of Employees: 40 PT Total
Passive Ownership: Allowed
Encourage Conversions: N/A
Area Develop. Agreements: Yes/Varies
Sub-Franchising Contracts: No
Expand In Territory: Yes
Space Needs: 2,000 SF; FS, SC, RM, Univer.

SUPPORT & TRAINING PROVIDED:
Financial Assistance Provided: No
Site Selection Assistance: Yes
Lease Negotiation Assistance: No
Co-Operative Advertising: Yes
Franchisee Assoc./Member: Yes/No
Size Of Corporate Staff: 300
On-Going Support: A,B,C,D,E,f,h,I
Training: 3 Days Local Restaurant Orientation; 360 Hours Formal Training.

SPECIFIC EXPANSION PLANS:
US: Southeast, Midwest
Canada: No
Overseas: Bahrain, Costa Rica, Hong Kong, Korea, Kuwait, Lebanon, Oman, Qatar, Saudi Arabia, United Arab Em.

HARTZ CHICKEN

14451 Cornerstone Village Dr., # 250
Houston, TX 77014
Tel: (281) 583-0020
Fax: (281) 580-3752
E-Mail: hartz@hartz-chicken.com
Web Site: www.hartz-chicken.com
Mr. John Bergeron, Controller

All-you-can-eat chicken buffet restaurant, featuring crispy and rotisserie chicken, Southern-style fish, fresh steamed vegetables, cold salads, casseroles, homestyle desserts and fresh homemade yeast rolls. Drive-thru and take-out service available at units. Delivery available in 1/3 of the domestic units. International program expanding - units open in Malaysia, Indonesia and China.

BACKGROUND:
Established: 1972; 1st Franchised: 1975
Franchised Units: 50
Company-Owned Units 1
Total Units: 51
Dist.: US-42; CAN-0; O'seas-9
North America: 2 States
Density: 41 in TX, 1 in MS
Projected New Units (12 Months): 20
Qualifications: 4, 5, 3, 1, 3, 5
Registered: NR

FINANCIAL/TERMS:
Cash Investment: $250K
Total Investment: $300K-1MM
Minimum Net Worth: $250K
Fees: Franchise - $20K
Royalty - 4%; Ad. - 2-3%
Earnings Claim Statement: Yes
Term of Contract (Years): 20/5
Avg. # Of Employees: 7 FT, 6 PT
Passive Ownership: Discouraged
Encourage Conversions: Yes
Area Develop. Agreements: Yes
Sub-Franchising Contracts: Yes
Expand In Territory: Yes
Space Needs: 3,000 SF; FS

SUPPORT & TRAINING PROVIDED:
Financial Assistance Provided: No
Site Selection Assistance: Yes
Lease Negotiation Assistance: Yes
Co-Operative Advertising: Yes
Franchisee Assoc./Member: Yes
Size Of Corporate Staff: 10
On-Going Support: B,C,D,E,G,I
Training: 6 Weeks in Houston, TX.

SPECIFIC EXPANSION PLANS:
US: South
Canada: No
Overseas: Far East, Asia

<< >>

HO-LEE-CHOW

658 Danforth Ave., # 201
Toronto, ON M4J 5B9 CANADA
Tel: (800)HO-LEE-CHOW (416) 778-6660
Fax: (416) 778-6818
E-Mail: holeechow@holeechow.com
Web Site: www.holeechow.com
Mr. Jake Cappiello, President

Great Chinese food delivered fast and fresh. Each entree in our restaurants is cooked-to-order with no added MSG or preservatives. Each order is delivered in under 45 minutes. All locations are brightly lit and have our open kitchen concept so customers can view their food being cooked in the most pristine kitchens.

BACKGROUND:
Established: 1989; 1st Franchised: 1989
Franchised Units: 18
Company-Owned Units 4
Total Units: 22
Dist.: US-0; CAN-22; O'seas-0
North America: 1 Province
Density: 22 in ON
Projected New Units (12 Months): 15
Qualifications: 3, 3, 1, 2, 3, 5
Registered: NR

FINANCIAL/TERMS:
Cash Investment: $50-75K
Total Investment: $150-175K
Minimum Net Worth: $100K
Fees: Franchise - $Included
Royalty - 6%; Ad. - 3%
Earnings Claim Statement: Yes
Term of Contract (Years): 5/15
Avg. # Of Employees: 3 FT, 1 PT
Passive Ownership: Discouraged
Encourage Conversions: Yes
Area Develop. Agreements: Yes/10
Sub-Franchising Contracts: Yes
Expand In Territory: Yes
Space Needs: 900 SF; FS, SF, SC

SUPPORT & TRAINING PROVIDED:
Financial Assistance Provided: Yes(I)
Site Selection Assistance: Yes
Lease Negotiation Assistance: Yes
Co-Operative Advertising: Yes
Franchisee Assoc./Member: Yes/Yes
Size Of Corporate Staff: 50+
On-Going Support: A,B,C,D,E,F,G,H,I
Training: 1 Week Head Office in Toronto, ON; 4 Weeks On-Site.

SPECIFIC EXPANSION PLANS:
US: All United States
Canada: ON
Overseas: No

<< >>

HOT 'N NOW HAMBURGERS

4205 Charlar, # 3
Holt, MI 48842
Tel: (888) 350-3146 (517) 694-4240
Fax: (517) 694-6370
E-Mail: tomv@voyager.net
Mr. Tom VanAlstine, VP/CFO

Hot 'N Now operates and franchises drive thru only quick service restaurants, with the goal of serving great food fast. By keeping our operations as simple as possible we are able to keep our focus on what on what is really important, customer service.

BACKGROUND:
Established: 1984; 1st Franchised: 1987
Franchised Units: 30
Company-Owned Units 32
Total Units: 62
Dist.: US-62; CAN-0; O'seas-0
North America: 3 States
Density: 55 in MI, 3 in IN, 4 in WI
Projected New Units (12 Months): NR
Registered: NR

FINANCIAL/TERMS:
Cash Investment: $50K+
Total Investment: $400K-1MM
Minimum Net Worth: $100K
Fees: Franchise - $22K
Royalty - 4%; Ad. - .5%
Earnings Claim Statement: No
Term of Contract (Years): 20/20
Avg. # Of Employees: 4 FT, 15 PT
Passive Ownership: Discouraged
Encourage Conversions: NR
Area Develop. Agreements: Yes/Varies
Sub-Franchising Contracts: No
Expand In Territory: Yes
Space Needs: 1000 SF; FS

SUPPORT & TRAINING PROVIDED:
Financial Assistance Provided: NR
Site Selection Assistance: N/A
Lease Negotiation Assistance: Yes
Co-Operative Advertising: Yes
Franchisee Assoc./Member: No
Size Of Corporate Staff: 10
On-Going Support: B,C,D,E,G,H,I
Training: Eight Hours at a To Be Determined Location.

SPECIFIC EXPANSION PLANS:
US: MidWest
Canada: NR
Overseas: NR

<< >>

HUNGRY HOWIE'S PIZZA & SUBS
30300 Stephenson Hwy., # 200
Madison Heights, MI 48071-1600
Tel: (800) 624-8122 (248) 414-3300
Fax: (248) 414-3301
E-Mail: franchiseinfo@hungryhowies.com
Web Site: www.hungryhowies.com
Mr. Bob Cuffaro, Dir. Franchise Development

HUNGRY HOWIE'S, the innovator of the award-winning Flavored-Crust Pizza, is the nation's 9th largest carry-out / delivery pizza company. Menu offerings include 8 varieties of Flavored-Crust pizzas, delicious oven-baked subs and fresh and crispy salads.

BACKGROUND: IFA MEMBER
Established: 1973; 1st Franchised: 1982
Franchised Units: 445
Company-Owned Units 0
Total Units: 445
Dist.: US-434; CAN-1; O'seas-0
North America: 19 States, 1 Province
Density: 180 in FL, 180 in MI, 15 CA
Projected New Units (12 Months): 20
Qualifications: 4, 3, 2, 3, 4, 5
Registered: CA,FL,IL,IN,MD,MI,MN,NY, OR,RI,VA,WA,WI,DC

FINANCIAL/TERMS:
Cash Investment: $50K
Total Investment: $85-125K
Minimum Net Worth: $150K
Fees: Franchise - $15K
Royalty - 5%; Ad. - 3%
Earnings Claim Statement: No
Term of Contract (Years): 20/20
Avg. # Of Employees: 4 FT, 8 PT
Passive Ownership: Discouraged
Encourage Conversions: Yes
Area Develop. Agreements: Yes/20
Sub-Franchising Contracts: Yes
Expand In Territory: Yes
Space Needs: 1,200 SF; SC

SUPPORT & TRAINING PROVIDED:
Financial Assistance Provided: Yes(I)
Site Selection Assistance: Yes
Lease Negotiation Assistance: Yes
Co-Operative Advertising: Yes
Franchisee Assoc./Member: No
Size Of Corporate Staff: 20
On-Going Support: B,C,D,E,F,G,h
Training: 5 Weeks Madison Heights, MI.

SPECIFIC EXPANSION PLANS:
US: All United States
Canada: No
Overseas: No

<< >>

INTERSTATE DAIRY QUEEN
8555 16th St., # 850
Silver Spring, MD 20910
Tel: (800) 423-6171 (301) 587-4411
Fax: (301) 585-8997
E-Mail: wtellegen@interstatedq.com
Web Site: www.interstatedq.com
Mr. Walt Tellegen, President

Fast food treat franchisor on interstate highways. `

BACKGROUND:
Established: 1977; 1st Franchised: 1978
Franchised Units: 170
Company-Owned Units 0
Total Units: 170
Dist.: US-170; CAN-0; O'seas-0
North America: 29 States
Density: 23 in GA,9 in FL, 9 in NC
Projected New Units (12 Months): 13
Qualifications: 4, 5, 2, 2, 2, 5
Registered: CA,FL,IL,IN,MD,MI,NY,RI

FINANCIAL/TERMS:
Cash Investment: $100-300K
Total Investment: $Varies
Minimum Net Worth: $Varies
Fees: Franchise - $25K
Royalty - 4-7%; Ad. - 3-5%
Earnings Claim Statement: No
Term of Contract (Years): Permanent
Avg. # Of Employees: Varies
Passive Ownership: Allowed
Encourage Conversions: Yes
Area Develop. Agreements: No
Sub-Franchising Contracts: No
Expand In Territory: Yes
Space Needs: 1,000-3,000 SF; FS, SC, Travel Plaza

SUPPORT & TRAINING PROVIDED:
Financial Assistance Provided: No
Site Selection Assistance: Yes
Lease Negotiation Assistance: Yes
Co-Operative Advertising: No
Franchisee Assoc./Member: Yes/No
Size Of Corporate Staff: 13
On-Going Support: a,B,C,D,e,F,G,H,I
Training: 2-4 Weeks in Minneapolis, MN.

SPECIFIC EXPANSION PLANS:
US: Eastern United States
Canada: No
Overseas: No

<< >>

JERRY'S SUBS & PIZZA
15942 Shady Grove Rd.
Gaithersburg, MD 20877
Tel: (800) 990-9176 (301) 921-8777
Fax: (301) 948-3508
E-Mail: robbinb@jerrys-subs.com
Web Site: www.jerrys-subs.com

Ms. Robbin Brinkhoff

High-volume, high-traffic locations are selected, featuring our 'overstuffed' subs and NY-style pizza. Decor is bright and up-scale and provides a warm, friendly environment.

BACKGROUND:
Established: 1954; 1st Franchised: 1980
Franchised Units: 135
Company-Owned Units 3
Total Units: 138
Dist.: US-100; CAN-0; O'seas-0
North America: 7 States
Density: MD, VA, DC
Projected New Units (12 Months): 12
Qualifications: 4, 2, 1, 1, 4, 2
Registered: CA,FL,MD,NY,VA,WI,DC

FINANCIAL/TERMS:
Cash Investment: $50-75K
Total Investment: $150-225K
Minimum Net Worth: $NR
Fees: Franchise - $10-25K
Royalty - 5%; Ad. - 4%
Earnings Claim Statement: No
Term of Contract (Years): 20/Open
Avg. # Of Employees: NR
Passive Ownership: Discouraged
Encourage Conversions: Yes
Area Develop. Agreements: Yes/20
Sub-Franchising Contracts: No
Expand In Territory: Yes
Space Needs: 2,000 SF; FS, SC, RM

SUPPORT & TRAINING PROVIDED:
Financial Assistance Provided: Yes
Site Selection Assistance: Yes
Lease Negotiation Assistance: Yes
Co-Operative Advertising: Yes
Franchisee Assoc./Member: No
Size Of Corporate Staff: 20
On-Going Support: B,C,D,E,F,G,H,I
Training: 10 Weeks Aspen Hill, MD.

SPECIFIC EXPANSION PLANS:
US: All U.S. - Esp. East Coast
Canada: No
Overseas: No

<< >>

JERSEY MIKE'S SUBMARINES & SALADS

1973 Hwy. 34, # E 21
Wall, NJ 07719
Tel: (800) 321-7676 (732) 282-2323
Fax: (732) 282-2233
E-Mail: sales@jerseymikes.com
Web Site: www.jerseymikes.com
Mr. Victor F. Merlo, VP Sales

JERSEY MIKE'S is a submarine sandwich franchise company which prides itself on producing the freshest submarine sandwich in the industry. They bake bread daily in the store. Roast beefs are cooked on premises and meats and cheeses are sliced in front of the customer. Awards include 'Best Sub' in Nashville, Charlotte, RTP, Wilmington, Greenville and Ocean/Monmouth, NJ.

BACKGROUND:
Established: 1956; 1st Franchised: 1986
Franchised Units: 201
Company-Owned Units 4
Total Units: 205
Dist.: US-131; CAN-0; O'seas-0
North America: 13 States
Density: 83 in NC, 25 in OH, 15 in TN
Projected New Units (12 Months): NR
Registered: NR

FINANCIAL/TERMS:
Cash Investment: $NR
Total Investment: $150-200K
Minimum Net Worth: $NR
Fees: Franchise - $18.5K
Royalty - 5.5%; Ad. - 3.5%
Earnings Claim Statement: NR
Term of Contract (Years): 10/10
Avg. # Of Employees: 7 FT, 8 PT
Passive Ownership: Discouraged
Encourage Conversions: NR
Area Develop. Agreements: Yes/10
Sub-Franchising Contracts: No
Expand In Territory: NR
Space Needs: 1,500 SF; FS, SC

SUPPORT & TRAINING PROVIDED:
Financial Assistance Provided: NR
Site Selection Assistance: Yes
Lease Negotiation Assistance: Yes
Co-Operative Advertising: Yes
Franchisee Assoc./Member: No
Size Of Corporate Staff: 30
On-Going Support: B,C,D,E,G,H,I
Training: 3-4 Weeks Nashville, TN.

SPECIFIC EXPANSION PLANS:
US: All United States
Canada: NR
Overseas: NR

<< >>

Top 50

JIMMY JOHN'S GOURMET SANDWICH SHOPS

600 Tollgate Rd., # B
Elgin, IL 60123
Tel: (800) 546-6904 (847) 888-7206
Fax: (847) 888-7070
E-Mail: mandc@tbcnet.com
Web Site: www.jimmyjohns.com
Mr. Bobby Morena, Sales Representative

World's greatest gourmet sandwich shop. All the sandwiches are made on fresh-baked french bread or 7-grain honey wheat bread. We only use the highest-quality meats available with garden fresh veggies that are brought in and sliced each morning.

BACKGROUND: IFA MEMBER
Established: 1983; 1st Franchised: 1993
Franchised Units: 90
Company-Owned Units 10
Total Units: 101
Dist.: US-91; CAN-0; O'seas-7
North America: 16 States
Density: 39 in IL, 12 in WI, 10 in MI
Projected New Units (12 Months): 25
Qualifications: 5, 4, 2, 4, 4, 5
Registered: FL,IL,IN,MI,MN,RI,VA,WI,DC

FINANCIAL/TERMS:
Cash Investment: $25-50K
Total Investment: $116-303K
Minimum Net Worth: $100K
Fees: Franchise - $15-25K
Royalty - 6%; Ad. - 4.5%
Earnings Claim Statement: Yes
Term of Contract (Years): 10/5/5
Avg. # Of Employees: 2 FT, 20 PT
Passive Ownership: Discouraged
Encourage Conversions: N/A
Area Develop. Agreements: Yes/Varies
Sub-Franchising Contracts: No
Expand In Territory: Yes
Space Needs: 800-1,200 SF; FS, SC, SF

SUPPORT & TRAINING PROVIDED:
Financial Assistance Provided: No
Site Selection Assistance: Yes
Lease Negotiation Assistance: No
Co-Operative Advertising: Yes
Franchisee Assoc./Member: Yes
Size Of Corporate Staff: 12
On-Going Support: C,D,E,F,G,H,I
Training: 3 Weeks in Champaign, IL.

SPECIFIC EXPANSION PLANS:
US: All United States
Canada: All Canada
Overseas: All Countries

<< >>

JOHNNY ROCKETS, THE ORIGINAL HAMBURGER

26970 Laguna Hills Dr., # 100
Aliso Viejo, CA 92656-2621
Tel: (949) 643-6119
Fax: (949) 643-6200
E-Mail: crabe@johnnyrockets.com
Web Site: www.johnnyrockets.com
Ms. Cyndi Rabe, Mgr. Franchise Relations

Johnny Rockets is more than a restaurant. It's like taking a bite out of the good ol' days. A 1950's "magical" experience at the neighborhood malt shop. It's two straws in a shake, red vinyl bar stools, chrome, and jukeboxes at a nickel a play. It's juicy hamburgers on a seared bun, crisp golden fries and waiters that always dance on the half-hour, twirl straws and serve ketchup with a smile! Johnny Rockets is a place that feels like a stroll down memory lane back to those simpler times.

BACKGROUND: IFA MEMBER
Established: 1986; 1st Franchised: 1989
Franchised Units: 82
Company-Owned Units 60
Total Units: 142
Dist.: US-82; CAN-0; O'seas-60
North America: 26 States, 9 Countries
Density: 38 in CA, 13 in FL, 9 in GA
Projected New Units (12 Months): NR
Registered: NR

FINANCIAL/TERMS:
Cash Investment: $800K-1MM
Total Investment: $595-695K
Minimum Net Worth: $1MM+
Fees: Franchise - $45K
Royalty - 5% or gross sale;
Ad. - 2% of Gross
Earnings Claim Statement: No
Term of Contract (Years): 10/2 or 5
Avg. # Of Employees:
1 Server/12 Guests
Passive Ownership: Allowed
Encourage Conversions: NR
Area Develop. Agreements: Yes/10
Sub-Franchising Contracts: No
Expand In Territory: Yes
Space Needs: 800-2000 SF; FS, SF, SC, RM

SUPPORT & TRAINING PROVIDED:
Financial Assistance Provided: NR
Site Selection Assistance: Yes
Lease Negotiation Assistance: Yes
Co-Operative Advertising: No
Franchisee Assoc./Member: No
Size Of Corporate Staff: 40
On-Going Support: B,C,D,E,G,H,I
Training: 6 Weeks, 1 of 6 Locations.

SPECIFIC EXPANSION PLANS:
US: All United States
Canada: NR
Overseas: All Countries

<< >>

KFC

1441 Gardiner Ln.
Louisville, KY 40213
Tel: (800) 544-5774 (502) 872-2021
Fax: (502) 874-5306
E-Mail: terrian.barnes@tricon-yum.com
Web Site: www.kfc.com
Ms. Kellie Vogt, Franchise Recruiter

World's largest quick-service restaurant with a chicken-dominant menu. KFC offers full-service restaurants and non-traditional express units for captive markets.

BACKGROUND: IFA MEMBER
Established: 1954; 1st Franchised: 1959
Franchised Units: 6,663
Company-Owned Units 2,975
Total Units: 9,638
Dist.: US-3122; CAN-3555; O'seas-3192
North America: 50 States,10 Provinces
Density: CA, TX, IL
Projected New Units (12 Months): 100
Qualifications: 5, 4, 5, 3, 3, 5
Registered: All States

FINANCIAL/TERMS:
Cash Investment: $500K
Total Investment: $700K-1.2MM
Minimum Net Worth: $1MM
Fees: Franchise - $25K
Royalty - 4%; Ad. - 4.5%
Earnings Claim Statement: No
Term of Contract (Years): 20/10
Avg. # Of Employees: 2 FT, 22 PT
Passive Ownership: Not Allowed
Encourage Conversions: No
Area Develop. Agreements: No
Sub-Franchising Contracts: No
Expand In Territory: Yes
Space Needs: 2,000-3,000 SF; FS

SUPPORT & TRAINING PROVIDED:
Financial Assistance Provided: No
Site Selection Assistance: Yes
Lease Negotiation Assistance: No
Co-Operative Advertising: Yes
Franchisee Assoc./Member: Yes/Yes
Size Of Corporate Staff: 820
On-Going Support: C,d,E,G,h,I
Training: 14 Weeks at Varied Sites.

SPECIFIC EXPANSION PLANS:
US: All United States
Canada: All Canada
Overseas: All Countries

KOYA JAPAN

720 Broadway, # 207
Winnipeg, MB R3G 0X1 CANADA
Tel: (888) 569-2872 (204) 783-4433
Fax: (204) 783-1749
E-Mail: jo-ann@koyajapan.com
Web Site: www.koyajapan.com
Mr. Steve M. Sabbagh, President

Delicious Japanese food served fast from the freshest of ingredients and complimented by or unique sauce. What makes us successful is our cooking techniques, each meal is made to order in full view of the customer. KOYA JAPAN -- where freshness sizzles before your eyes.

BACKGROUND:
Established: 1985; 1st Franchised: 1986
Franchised Units: 24
Company-Owned Units 0
Total Units: 24
Dist.: US-2; CAN-22; O'seas-0
North America: 6 Provinces
Density: 7 in BC, 6 in MB, 5 in ON
Projected New Units (12 Months): 12
Qualifications: 4, 4, 3, 2, 3, 5
Registered: FL

FINANCIAL/TERMS:
Cash Investment: $50% of Total
Total Investment: $165-250K
Minimum Net Worth: $100K
Fees: Franchise - $25K
Royalty - 6-7%; Ad. - 2%
Earnings Claim Statement: No
Term of Contract (Years): Up to 10
Avg. # Of Employees: 3 FT, 1 PT
Passive Ownership: Allowed
Encourage Conversions: Yes
Area Develop. Agreements: Yes/20
Sub-Franchising Contracts: No
Expand In Territory: Yes

Space Needs: 300-400 SF; RM

SUPPORT & TRAINING PROVIDED:

Financial Assistance Provided: No
Site Selection Assistance: Yes
Lease Negotiation Assistance: Yes
Co-Operative Advertising: Yes
Franchisee Assoc./Member: No
Size Of Corporate Staff: 3
On-Going Support: C,d,E,I
Training: Up to 1 Month in Operating Location; up to 1 Month On-Site; 2-3 Days at Head Office.

SPECIFIC EXPANSION PLANS:

US: All United States
Canada: All Canada
Overseas: Bahrain, United Arab Emirates, Kuwait, Quatar, Saudi Arabia

<< >>

KRYSTAL COMPANY, THE

1 Union Square, 10th Fl.
Chattanooga, TN 37402
Tel: (800) 458-5912 (423) 757-1581
Fax: (423) 757-5644
E-Mail: jschmidt@krystalco.com
Web Site: www.krystal.com
Mr. Jamie Schmidt, Dir. Fran. Dev.

The KRYSTAL COMPANY, a 'cultural icon' in the Southeast, is a unique brand with 70 years of success As a niche franchisor, we provide quality service and thoughtful leadership to our franchise partners. We have made major changes in re-engineering and reducing the size of the initial investment. We offer a protected development territory, requiring a minimum 3-restaurant development agreement, minimum liquidity of $600K and a net worth of $1.2 million. KRYSTAL, fresh, hot, small and square.

BACKGROUND:

Established: 1932; 1st Franchised: 1990
Franchised Units: 172
Company-Owned Units <u>246</u>
Total Units: 418
Dist.: US-418; CAN-0; O'seas-0
North America: 13 States
Density: 104 in GA, 105 in TN, 53 AL
Projected New Units (12 Months): 52
Qualifications: 5, 4, 5, 2, 2, 5
Registered: FL,VA

FINANCIAL/TERMS:

Cash Investment: $5,000/Rest.
Total Investment: $900K-1MM
Minimum Net Worth: $1.2MM
Fees: Franchise - $32.5K
Royalty - 4.5%; Ad. - 4%
Earnings Claim Statement: No
Term of Contract (Years): 20/20
Avg. # Of Employees: 14 FT, 15 PT
Passive Ownership: Allowed
Encourage Conversions: Yes
Area Develop. Agreements: Yes/10
Sub-Franchising Contracts: No
Expand In Territory: Yes
Space Needs: 33,000 SF; FS,SC,C-Store

SUPPORT & TRAINING PROVIDED:

Financial Assistance Provided: No
Site Selection Assistance: Yes
Lease Negotiation Assistance: No
Co-Operative Advertising: Yes
Franchisee Assoc./Member: Yes/No
Size Of Corporate Staff: 100
On-Going Support: A,B,C,D,E,F,G,H,I
Training: 4 Weeks Company Store; 1 Week Corporate Computer Center.

SPECIFIC EXPANSION PLANS:

US: Southeast, TX, OK, VA, NC,SC
Canada: No
Overseas: No

<< >>

LA SALSA FRESH MEXICAN GRILL

3938 State St., # 200
Santa Barbara, CA 93105
Tel: (800) 527-2572 (805) 563-3644
Fax: (805) 898-2365
Web Site: www.lasalsa.com
Mr. Frank Holdraker, VP Franchising

Quick-service fresh Mexican grill restaurant.

BACKGROUND:

Established: 1979; 1st Franchised: 1988
Franchised Units: 47
Company-Owned Units <u>50</u>
Total Units: 97
Dist.: US-96; CAN-0; O'seas-0
North America: NR
Density: 62 in CA, 7 in AZ, 6 in UT
Projected New Units (12 Months): 36
Qualifications: 4, 4, 4, 2, 2, 5
Registered: CA,FL,IL,IN,MD,MI,MN,NY, VA,WA,WI

FINANCIAL/TERMS:

Cash Investment: $NR
Total Investment: $222-371K
Minimum Net Worth: $Varies
Fees: Franchise - $29.5K
Royalty - 5%; Ad. - 1%
Earnings Claim Statement: Yes
Term of Contract (Years): 10/10
Avg. # Of Employees: 12 FT, 4 PT
Passive Ownership: Not Allowed
Encourage Conversions: Yes
Area Develop. Agreements: Yes/Varies
Sub-Franchising Contracts: No
Expand In Territory: No
Space Needs: 1,800-2,000 SF; SF, SC, RM

SUPPORT & TRAINING PROVIDED:

Financial Assistance Provided: No
Site Selection Assistance: No
Lease Negotiation Assistance: No
Co-Operative Advertising: Yes
Franchisee Assoc./Member: No
Size Of Corporate Staff: NR
On-Going Support: B,C,D,E,G,H,I
Training: 5-8 Weeks Los Angeles, CA.

SPECIFIC EXPANSION PLANS:

US: All United States
Canada: All Canada
Overseas: No

<< >>

LARRY'S GIANT SUBS

8616 Baymeadows Rd.
Jacksonville, FL 32256
Tel: (800) 358-6870 (904) 739-9069
Fax: (904) 739-1218
E-Mail: bigone@larryssubs.com
Web Site: www.larryssubs.com
Mr. Mitchell Raikes, Vice President

Upscale submarine sandwich franchise, featuring top-quality foods, such as USDA choice roast beef, oven-roasted turkey, whitemeat chicken salad, store décor, custom table tops, laser logo steel chairs and huge ape display.

BACKGROUND:

Established: 1982; 1st Franchised: 1986
Franchised Units: 80

Company-Owned Units 2
Total Units: 82
Dist.: US-82; CAN-0; O'seas-0
North America: 5 States
Density: 53 in FL, 28 in GA, 2 in TX
Projected New Units (12 Months): 15
Qualifications: 3, 3, 3, 3, 3, 5
Registered: FL

FINANCIAL/TERMS:
Cash Investment: $25-40K
Total Investment: $110-170K
Minimum Net Worth: $150K
Fees: Franchise - $17K
Royalty - 6%; Ad. - 2%
Earnings Claim Statement: No
Term of Contract (Years): 10/10
Avg. # Of Employees: 6 FT, 10 PT
Passive Ownership: Discouraged
Encourage Conversions: No
Area Develop. Agreements: Yes/2
Sub-Franchising Contracts: Yes
Expand In Territory: Yes
Space Needs: 1,400 SF; FS, SC

SUPPORT & TRAINING PROVIDED:
Financial Assistance Provided: No
Site Selection Assistance: Yes
Lease Negotiation Assistance: Yes
Co-Operative Advertising: Yes
Franchisee Assoc./Member: No
Size Of Corporate Staff: 10
On-Going Support: A,B,C,D,E,F,G,H,I
Training: 30 Days at Corporate Office; 1 - 2 Weeks Franchise Store.

SPECIFIC EXPANSION PLANS:
US: Southeast
Canada: No
Overseas: No

<< >>

LE CROISSANT SHOP
227 W. 40th St.
New York, NY 10018
Tel: (212) 719-5940
Fax: (212) 944-0269
E-Mail: franchise_info@lecroissantshop.com
Web Site: www.lecroissantshop.com
Mr. Arnaud Thieffry, Vice President

French bakery cafe - specialty croissants, bread, soups, french sandwiches and gourmet salads. Breakfast-Lunch-Dinner.

BACKGROUND:
Established: 1981; 1st Franchised: 1984
Franchised Units: 11
Company-Owned Units 4
Total Units: 15
Dist.: US-15; CAN-0; O'seas-13
North America: 3 States
Density: 12 in NY, 1 in PA, 1 in FL
Projected New Units (12 Months): 2-3
Qualifications: 4, 4, 3, 3, 3, 5
Registered: FL,IL,MD,NY,VA

FINANCIAL/TERMS:
Cash Investment: $1/3 Invest.
Total Investment: $140-576K
Minimum Net Worth: $NR
Fees: Franchise - $22.5K
Royalty - 5%; Ad. - NR
Earnings Claim Statement: No
Term of Contract (Years): 10/5/5
Avg. # Of Employees: 10 FT
Passive Ownership: Allowed
Encourage Conversions: No
Area Develop. Agreements: Yes/10
Sub-Franchising Contracts: No
Expand In Territory: Yes
Space Needs: 500-2,000 SF; FS, SF, SC, RM

SUPPORT & TRAINING PROVIDED:
Financial Assistance Provided: No
Site Selection Assistance: Yes
Lease Negotiation Assistance: Yes
Co-Operative Advertising: N/A
Franchisee Assoc./Member: No
Size Of Corporate Staff: 6
On-Going Support: C,D,E
Training: 2 Weeks Headquarters in NY.

SPECIFIC EXPANSION PLANS:
US: East Coast
Canada: No
Overseas: South America, India, Asia

<< >>

LEDO PIZZA SYSTEM
2568A Riva Rd., # 202
Annapolis, MD 21401
Tel: (410) 721-6887
Fax: (410) 266-6888
E-Mail: ledo@aol.com
Web Site: www.ledopizza.com
Mr. Will Robinson, Asst. Dir. Of System Marketing

Ledo Pizza is a full service dining experience with a menu that features fresh salads, pastas, sandwiches, and our critically acclaimed Ledo Pizza.

BACKGROUND: IFA MEMBER
Established: 1955; 1st Franchised: 1989
Franchised Units: 51
Company-Owned Units 0
Total Units: 51
Dist.: US-51; CAN-0; O'seas-0
North America: 5 States
Density: 41 in MD, 7 in VA, 2 in PA
Projected New Units (12 Months): NR
Registered: NR

FINANCIAL/TERMS:
Cash Investment: $50-150K
Total Investment: $119-419K
Minimum Net Worth: $Varies
Fees: Franchise - $20K
Royalty - 5%; Ad. - 2%
Earnings Claim Statement: No
Term of Contract (Years): 5/15
Avg. # Of Employees: 15 FT, 30 PT
Passive Ownership: Discouraged
Encourage Conversions: NR
Area Develop. Agreements: No
Sub-Franchising Contracts: No
Expand In Territory: Yes
Space Needs: 1800+ SF; FS, SC, Hotels

SUPPORT & TRAINING PROVIDED:
Financial Assistance Provided: NR
Site Selection Assistance: Yes
Lease Negotiation Assistance: Yes
Co-Operative Advertising: Yes
Franchisee Assoc./Member: Yes/No
Size Of Corporate Staff: 12
On-Going Support: B,C,D,E,F,G,H
Training: Varies.

SPECIFIC EXPANSION PLANS:
US: NE, SE
Canada: NR
Overseas: NR

<< >>

LITTLE KING
11811 I St.
Omaha, NE 68137
Tel: (800) 788-9478 (402) 330-8019
Fax: (402) 330-3221
E-Mail: rw68137@aol.com
Web Site: www.littlekinginc.com
Mr. Bob B. Wertheim, President

Deli and sub restaurant, featuring fresh, fast-food concept - sandwiches. Products are prepared in full view of customers, breads are all baked fresh on premises. All meats are sliced fresh to order. Top-of-the-line food quality, utilizing major nationally-known brands. Concept is adaptable to various locations and configurations.

BACKGROUND:
Established: 1968; 1st Franchised: 1978
Franchised Units: 30
Company-Owned Units 0
Total Units: 30
Dist.: US-30; CAN-0; O'seas-0
North America: 5 States
Density: 29 in NE, 3 in IA, 2 in SD
Projected New Units (12 Months): 5-7
Qualifications: 5, 4, 4, 4, 1, 5
Registered: NR

FINANCIAL/TERMS:
Cash Investment: $Varies
Total Investment: $75-95K
Minimum Net Worth: $100K
Fees: Franchise - $12K
Royalty - 6%; Ad. - 2.5%
Earnings Claim Statement: No
Term of Contract (Years): 10/10
Avg. # Of Employees: 1-3 FT, 6-9 PT
Passive Ownership: Discouraged
Encourage Conversions: Yes
Area Develop. Agreements: Yes
Sub-Franchising Contracts: No
Expand In Territory: Yes
Space Needs: 1,200-1,800 SF; FS, SF, SC

SUPPORT & TRAINING PROVIDED:
Financial Assistance Provided: Yes(I)
Site Selection Assistance: Yes
Lease Negotiation Assistance: Yes
Co-Operative Advertising: Yes
Franchisee Assoc./Member: No
Size Of Corporate Staff: 2
On-Going Support: B,C,E,F,G,H,I
Training: 15 Days Omaha, NE Headquarters; 8 Days On-Site; Follow Up Training as Needed.

SPECIFIC EXPANSION PLANS:
US: All United States
Canada: No
Overseas: No

LONG JOHN SILVER'S
P.O. Box 11988
Lexington, KY 40579-1988
Tel: (800) 545-8360 (859) 543-6000
Fax: (859) 543-6190
E-Mail: fsales@ljsilvers.com
Web Site: www.ljsilvers.com
Ms. Jaynie Royal

LONG JOHN SILVER'S is the largest, quick-service seafood restaurant chain in the world. We continue to aggressively grow with new units and sales. Opportunities are available in new and existing markets and with our sister brand, A & W in our new co-brand facilities.

BACKGROUND: IFA MEMBER
Established: 1969; 1st Franchised: 1970
Franchised Units: 491
Company-Owned Units 742
Total Units: 1,233
Dist.: US-1233; CAN-0; O'seas-18
North America: 35 States
Density: 185 in TX, 114 in OH, 101 IN
Projected New Units (12 Months): NR
Qualifications: 5, 5, 3, 4, 5, 5
Registered: ALL

FINANCIAL/TERMS:
Cash Investment: $150-250K
Total Investment: $150K-1MM
Minimum Net Worth: $250K
Fees: Franchise - $15-20K
Royalty - 5%; Ad. - 5%
Earnings Claim Statement: NR
Term of Contract (Years): 10-20-5
Avg. # Of Employees: NR
Passive Ownership: Allowed
Encourage Conversions: NR
Area Develop. Agreements: NR
Sub-Franchising Contracts: No
Expand In Territory: Yes
Space Needs: NR SF; FS, C-Store, Food Court

SUPPORT & TRAINING PROVIDED:
Financial Assistance Provided: No
Site Selection Assistance: Yes
Lease Negotiation Assistance: NR
Co-Operative Advertising: Yes
Franchisee Assoc./Member: Yes
Size Of Corporate Staff: 300
On-Going Support: C,D,E,G,h,I
Training: 24 Days of Training.

SPECIFIC EXPANSION PLANS:
US: All United States
Canada: All Canada
Overseas: Asia, Europe, Caribbean, Latin America, Middle East

<< >>

MAGIC WOK
2060 Laskey Rd.
Toledo, OH 43613
Tel: (800) 447-8998 (419) 471-0696
Fax: (419) 471-0405
E-Mail: tpipatjz@pop3.utoledo.edu
Mr. Tommy Pipatjarasgit, Vice President

Quick-service, made-to-order, hot oriental concept. Stand alone, mall, drive-thru, delivery, school lunch and other non-traditional operations. Low barrier to entry, high return on investment. Domestic and international.

BACKGROUND:
Established: 1983; 1st Franchised: 1991
Franchised Units: 12
Company-Owned Units 10
Total Units: 22
Dist.: US-11; CAN-0; O'seas-2
North America: 5 States
Density: 7 in OH, 3 in MI
Projected New Units (12 Months): 2
Qualifications: 3, 2, 2, 2, 2, 4
Registered: FL,IL,IN,MD,MI,VA

FINANCIAL/TERMS:
Cash Investment: $50K
Total Investment: $95-150K
Minimum Net Worth: $100K
Fees: Franchise - $12.5K
Royalty - 5%; Ad. - 3%
Earnings Claim Statement: No
Term of Contract (Years): 10/10
Avg. # Of Employees: 2 FT, 8 PT
Passive Ownership: Discouraged
Encourage Conversions: Yes
Area Develop. Agreements: Yes
Sub-Franchising Contracts: Yes
Expand In Territory: Yes
Space Needs: 1,600 SF; FS

SUPPORT & TRAINING PROVIDED:
Financial Assistance Provided: No
Site Selection Assistance: Yes
Lease Negotiation Assistance: Yes
Co-Operative Advertising: Yes
Franchisee Assoc./Member: No
Size Of Corporate Staff: 7
On-Going Support: C,D,E,F,H,I
Training: 3-4 Weeks Toledo, OH.

SPECIFIC EXPANSION PLANS:
US: Midwest
Canada: No
Overseas: Saudi Arabia, Mexico

MAMMA ILARDO'S

3600 Clipper Mill Rd., # 260
Baltimore, MD 21211
Tel: (410) 662-1930
Fax: (410) 662-1936
E-Mail: john@mammailardos.com
Web Site: www.mammailardos.com
Mr. John A. Filipiak, VP Ops./Dev.

MAMMA ILARDO'S prepares fresh, delicious pizza. Choose from a variety of whole pies and pizza by the slice, featuring New York-style and our signature pan pizza. We offer great side items to complement our pizza, including calzones, pasta, salads and subs. Pizzeria and Express formats available--no franchising fees, no royalty fees, no marketing fees.

BACKGROUND:

Established: 1976; 1st Franchised: 1984
Franchised Units: 48
Company-Owned Units 2
Total Units: 50
Dist.: US-50; CAN-0; O'seas-0
North America: 16 States, Wash. DC
Density: 16 in MD, 6 in NV, 4 in NY
Projected New Units (12 Months): 40
Qualifications: 3, 4, 4, 4, 4, 5
Registered: N/A

FINANCIAL/TERMS:

Cash Investment: $40-100K
Total Investment: $175-320K
Minimum Net Worth: $150K
Fees: Franchise - $0
Royalty - 0%; Ad. - 0%
Earnings Claim Statement: No
Term of Contract (Years): 10/10
Avg. # Of Employees: 8 FT, 10 PT
Passive Ownership: Discouraged
Encourage Conversions: Yes
Area Develop. Agreements: Yes/10
Sub-Franchising Contracts: Yes
Expand In Territory: Yes
Space Needs: 350-1,200 SF; SF, RM, Cart

SUPPORT & TRAINING PROVIDED:

Financial Assistance Provided: Yes(I)
Site Selection Assistance: Yes
Lease Negotiation Assistance: Yes
Co-Operative Advertising: N/A
Franchisee Assoc./Member: No
Size Of Corporate Staff: 7
On-Going Support: B,C,D,E,F,G,H
Training: 3 Days to 3 Weeks at Corporate Office and Stores in Baltimore, MD.

SPECIFIC EXPANSION PLANS:

US: All United States
Canada: All Canada
Overseas: All Countries

<< >>

Top 50

MANCHU WOK (USA)

816 S. Military Trail, # 6
Deerfield Beach, FL 33442
Tel: (800) 423-4009 (954) 481-9555
Fax: (954) 481-9670
E-Mail: alec_hudson@manchuwok.com
Web Site: www.manchuwok.com/index2.html
Mr. Alec Hudson, Franchise Sales Mgr.

MANCHU WOK is one of the largest Chinese quick service franchises in North America. MANCHU WOK operates in over 225 food court locations in large regional malls. MANCHU WOK franchisees are enjoying profitable growth; many owning multiple locations.

BACKGROUND: IFA MEMBER

Established: 1980; 1st Franchised: 1980
Franchised Units: 142
Company-Owned Units 47
Total Units: 189
Dist.: US-111; CAN-76; O'seas-2
North America: 28 States, 10 Provinces
Density: 45 in ON, 14 in FL, 13 in IL
Projected New Units (12 Months): 50
Qualifications: 4, 4, 4, 3, 4, 4
Registered: All States and AB

FINANCIAL/TERMS:

Cash Investment: $100-150K
Total Investment: $265.5-316.75K
Minimum Net Worth: $100-150K
Fees: Franchise - $20K
Royalty - 7%; Ad. - 1%
Earnings Claim Statement: Yes
Term of Contract (Years): 5/5
Avg. # Of Employees: 2-3 FT, 6-10 PT
Passive Ownership: Discouraged
Encourage Conversions: Yes
Area Develop. Agreements: No
Sub-Franchising Contracts: No
Expand In Territory: Yes
Space Needs: 600 SF; RM

SUPPORT & TRAINING PROVIDED:

Financial Assistance Provided: Yes(I)
Site Selection Assistance: Yes
Lease Negotiation Assistance: Yes
Co-Operative Advertising: N/A
Franchisee Assoc./Member: No
Size Of Corporate Staff: 500
On-Going Support: B,C,D,E,F,G,H,I
Training: 3-4 Weeks Corporate Site.

SPECIFIC EXPANSION PLANS:

US: Northeast, Southeast
Canada: All Canada
Overseas: All Countries

<< >>

MANNY AND OLGA'S PIZZA

13707 N. Gate Dr.
Silver Spring, MD 20906
Tel: (301) 588-2500
Fax: (301) 608-8203
E-Mail: mannyandolgas@webtvnt.com
Mr. Bobby Athanasakis, President

MANNY AND OLGA'S PIZZA offers a full menu of pizza, subs, salads, pasta, wings, gyros and desserts - everything made fresh daily. Delivery or carry-out.

BACKGROUND:

Established: 1983; 1st Franchised: 1998
Franchised Units: 2
Company-Owned Units 3
Total Units: 5
Dist.: US-5; CAN-0; O'seas-0
North America: 3 States
Density: NR
Projected New Units (12 Months): 4
Qualifications: 5, 2, 1, 3, 3, 3
Registered: MD,DC,VA

FINANCIAL/TERMS:

Cash Investment: $50K
Total Investment: $90-160K
Minimum Net Worth: $100K
Fees: Franchise - $15K
Royalty - 5%; Ad. - 4%
Earnings Claim Statement: No
Term of Contract (Years): 10/10
Avg. # Of Employees: 3 FT, 3 PT
Passive Ownership: Not Allowed
Encourage Conversions: Yes
Area Develop. Agreements: Yes/10
Sub-Franchising Contracts: Yes
Expand In Territory: Yes
Space Needs: 700 SF; FS, SF, SC, RM

SUPPORT & TRAINING PROVIDED:

Financial Assistance Provided: No
Site Selection Assistance: Yes
Lease Negotiation Assistance: Yes
Co-Operative Advertising: Yes
Franchisee Assoc./Member: No
Size Of Corporate Staff: 8
On-Going Support: E
Training: 3 Weeks Silver Spring, MD.

SPECIFIC EXPANSION PLANS:
US: Northeast
Canada: No
Overseas: No

<< >>

MARCO'S PIZZA

5252 Monroe St.
Toledo, OH 43623
Tel: (800) 262-7267 (419) 885-7000
Fax: (419) 885-5215
E-Mail: franchise@marcos.com
Web Site: www.marcos.com
Mr. Jim Strachan, Franchise Director

MARCO'S PIZZA offers pizza, hot sub sandwiches, Cheezybread, salad and soft drinks. There are 3 crust style - hand spun, pan or crispy thin, and 3 types of crust flavors - garlic butter, parmesan, and roma seasoning. MARCO'S PIZZA offers carry-out and fast, hot delivery.

BACKGROUND:
Established: 1978; 1st Franchised: 1979
Franchised Units: 84
Company-Owned Units 41
Total Units: 125
Dist.: US-125; CAN-0; O'seas-0
North America: 3 States
Density: 97 in OH, 21 in MI, 7 in IN
Projected New Units (12 Months): 8
Qualifications: 5, 5, 5, 4, 3, 5
Registered: IN,MI

FINANCIAL/TERMS:
Cash Investment: $60-75K
Total Investment: $118.5-204.5K
Minimum Net Worth: $100K
Fees: Franchise - $15K
Royalty - 3-5%; Ad. - 1%
Earnings Claim Statement: No
Term of Contract (Years): 10/10
Avg. # Of Employees: 6 FT, 10 PT
Passive Ownership: Not Allowed
Encourage Conversions: N/A
Area Develop. Agreements: Yes/10
Sub-Franchising Contracts: No
Expand In Territory: Yes
Space Needs: 1,200-1,400 SF; SF, SC

SUPPORT & TRAINING PROVIDED:
Financial Assistance Provided: Yes(I)
Site Selection Assistance: Yes
Lease Negotiation Assistance: Yes
Co-Operative Advertising: Yes
Franchisee Assoc./Member: No
Size Of Corporate Staff: 40
On-Going Support: B,C,D,E,F,H,I
Training: 2 Weeks Toledo, OH; 6 Weeks in Store.

SPECIFIC EXPANSION PLANS:
US: Midwest
Canada: No
Overseas: No

<< >>

MAUI TACOS

1775 The Exchange, # 600
Atlanta, GA 30339
Tel: (888) 628-4822 (770) 226-8226
Fax: (770) 541-2300
E-Mail: chuckl@mauitacos.com
Web Site: www.mauitacos.com
Mr. Chuck Leaness, Chief Executive Officer

Fast-casual "Maui-Mex" restaurant featuring Mexican Foods created by internationally recognized chef Mark Ellmao, using pineapple and lime juice marinade with island spices. Char-grilled chicken, steak, and lean beef burritos topped with unique salsas is our mainstay. This food experience is like a vacation in Maui.

BACKGROUND: IFA MEMBER
Established: 1993; 1st Franchised: 1998
Franchised Units: 10
Company-Owned Units 1
Total Units: 11
Dist.: US-14; CAN-0; O'seas-0
North America: 2 States
Density: 8 in HI, 3 in GA
Projected New Units (12 Months): 20
Qualifications: 4, 4, 3, 3, 4, 4
Registered: CA,FL,HI,IN,MD,MI,MN,NY, ND,OR,RI,VA,WA,WI,DC

FINANCIAL/TERMS:
Cash Investment: $60-125K
Total Investment: $180-375K
Minimum Net Worth: $300K
Fees: Franchise - $20K
Royalty - 6%; Ad. - 4%
Earnings Claim Statement: Yes
Term of Contract (Years): 20/20
Avg. # Of Employees: 4 FT, 10 PT
Passive Ownership: Discouraged
Encourage Conversions: Yes
Area Develop. Agreements: Yes/50
Sub-Franchising Contracts: Yes
Expand In Territory: Yes
Space Needs: 2,000 SF; FS, SF,SC, RM, HB, Open Air

SUPPORT & TRAINING PROVIDED:
Financial Assistance Provided: Yes(I)
Site Selection Assistance: Yes
Lease Negotiation Assistance: Yes
Co-Operative Advertising: Yes
Franchisee Assoc./Member: Yes/Yes
Size Of Corporate Staff: 6
On-Going Support: A,B,C,D,E,F,G,h,I
Training: 160 Hours in Atlanta, GA.

SPECIFIC EXPANSION PLANS:
US: All United States
Canada: All Canada
Overseas: All Countries

<< >>

MAZZIO'S PIZZA

4441 S. 72nd E. Ave.
Tulsa, OK 74145-4610
Tel: (800) 827-1910 (918) 663-8880
Fax: (918) 641-1236
E-Mail: mlong@mazzios.com
Web Site: www.mazzios.com
Mr. Steve Davis, Dir. Franchise Operations

MAZZIO'S PIZZA is an up-scale Italian restaurant, featuring 3 types of pizza, along with excellent pasta, calzone rings, sandwiches and salad. There is an emphasis on an attractive decor and surroundings as well as a distinctive exterior. Delivery is available from an existing dine-in unit.

BACKGROUND: IFA MEMBER
Established: 1961; 1st Franchised: 1979
Franchised Units: 145
Company-Owned Units 105
Total Units: 250
Dist.: US-235; CAN-0; O'seas-0
North America: 13 States
Density: 116 in OK, 36 in AR, 29 MO
Projected New Units (12 Months): 5
Qualifications: 5, 5, 5, 4, 5, 5
Registered: CA,FL,IL,IN,MI,VA

FINANCIAL/TERMS:
Cash Investment: $200K
Total Investment: $309-976K
Minimum Net Worth: $400K
Fees: Franchise - $25K
Royalty - 3%; Ad. - 1%
Earnings Claim Statement: Yes
Term of Contract (Years): 20/5
Avg. # Of Employees: 2 FT, 25-35 PT

Passive Ownership: Discouraged
Encourage Conversions: Yes
Area Develop. Agreements: Yes/5
Sub-Franchising Contracts: No
Expand In Territory: Yes
Space Needs: 3,000 SF; FS, SF, SC

SUPPORT & TRAINING PROVIDED:
Financial Assistance Provided: No
Site Selection Assistance: Yes
Lease Negotiation Assistance: No
Co-Operative Advertising: Yes
Franchisee Assoc./Member: No
Size Of Corporate Staff: 75
On-Going Support: B,C,D,E,F,G,H,I
Training: 9 Weeks at Corporate Headquarters; 3.5 Weeks On-Site.

SPECIFIC EXPANSION PLANS:
US: South, SW, SE, Midwest
Canada: No
Overseas: No

<< >>

MCDONALD'S

2911 Jorie Blvd.
Oak Brook, IL 60523
Tel: (888) 800-7257 (630) 623-6196
Fax: (630) 623-5645
E-Mail: franchisedept@mcdonalds.com
Web Site: www.mcdonalds.com
Ms. Ann Cotter, Sr. Financial Manager

Quick-service restaurant.

BACKGROUND: IFA MEMBER
Established: 1955; 1st Franchised: 1956
Franchised Units: 21,702
Company-Owned Units 7,354
Total Units: 29,056
Dist.:US-13137; CAN-1223; O'seas-14696
North America: 50 States
Density: 1,226 in CA, 904 TX, 775 FL
Projected New Units (12 Months): NR
Qualifications: 3, 5, 3, 3, 4, 4
Registered: All States

FINANCIAL/TERMS:
Cash Investment: $NR
Total Investment: $489.8K-1.5MM
Minimum Net Worth: $NR
Fees: Franchise - $45K
Royalty - 12.5%; Ad. - 4%
Earnings Claim Statement: No
Term of Contract (Years): 20/20
Avg. # Of Employees: NR
Passive Ownership: Not Allowed
Encourage Conversions: N/A
Area Develop. Agreements: No
Sub-Franchising Contracts: No
Expand In Territory: No
Space Needs: 2,000 SF; FS

SUPPORT & TRAINING PROVIDED:
Financial Assistance Provided: No
Site Selection Assistance: N/A
Lease Negotiation Assistance: N/A
Co-Operative Advertising: Yes
Franchisee Assoc./Member: Yes/Yes
Size Of Corporate Staff: NR
On-Going Support: B,C,D,E,G,H,I
Training: NR

SPECIFIC EXPANSION PLANS:
US: All United States
Canada: All Canada
Overseas: All Countries

<< >>

MICHEL'S BAGUETTE

16251 Dallas Pkwy.
Addison, TX 75001
Tel: (972) 687-4091
Fax: (972) 687-4062
E-Mail: lpolyak@richmont.com
Web Site: www.mmmuffins.com
Ms. Irene La Cota, Chief Executive Officer

European bakery/café, featuring authentic European breads, rolls, and pastries. In addition, we offer gourmet soups, salads, sandwiches, and hot entrees. We also serve a variety of beverages including espresso, gourmet coffee, teas and fruit juices. In addition to our full store, we have a "grab 'n' go" version as well.

BACKGROUND: IFA MEMBER
Established: 1980; 1st Franchised: 1984
Franchised Units: 13
Company-Owned Units 5
Total Units: 18
Dist.: US-0; CAN-15; O'seas-0
North America: 3 Provinces
Density: 13 in ON, 3 in AB, 1 in BC
Projected New Units (12 Months): 10
Qualifications: 5, 4, 3, 3, 4, 5
Registered: AB

FINANCIAL/TERMS:
Cash Investment: $300K+
Total Investment: $750-800K
Minimum Net Worth: $500K
Fees: Franchise - $40K
Royalty - 6%; Ad. - 0.5%
Earnings Claim Statement: No
Term of Contract (Years): 10/10
Avg. # Of Employees: 10 FT, 8-12 PT
Passive Ownership: Not Allowed
Encourage Conversions: Yes
Area Develop. Agreements: Yes (Int'l.)
Sub-Franchising Contracts: Yes
Expand In Territory: Yes
Space Needs: 4,000 SF; SF, SC, RM

SUPPORT & TRAINING PROVIDED:
Financial Assistance Provided: No
Site Selection Assistance: Yes
Lease Negotiation Assistance: Yes
Co-Operative Advertising: Yes
Franchisee Assoc./Member: No
Size Of Corporate Staff: 35
On-Going Support: A,B,C,D,E,F,G,h
Training: 3 Months Toronto, ON or Dallas, TX.

SPECIFIC EXPANSION PLANS:
US: N/A
Canada: All Canada
Overseas:
Middle East, Europe, South America

<< >>

MOE'S ITALIAN SANDWICHES

15 Constitution Dr., # 140
Bedford, NH 03110
Tel: (800) 588-6637 (603) 472-8008
Fax: (603) 472-8025
E-Mail: info@moesitaliansandwiches.com
Web Site: www.moesitaliansandwiches.com
Mr. Stanley R. DeLoid, President

High-quality sandwiches and soups, featuring our flagship sandwich 'The Original Moe.' We have a simple concept that has over 40 years of heritage in New England. Low overhead, turnkey system. Very flexible.

BACKGROUND:
Established: 1959; 1st Franchised: 1993
Franchised Units: 13
Company-Owned Units 0
Total Units: 13
Dist.: US-13; CAN-0; O'seas-0
North America: 2 States

Density: 10 in NH, 3 in ME
Projected New Units (12 Months): 2-5
Qualifications: 4, 4, 3, 3, 4, 5
Registered: None

FINANCIAL/TERMS:

Cash Investment: $30-40K
Total Investment: $60-100K
Minimum Net Worth: $250K
Fees: Franchise - $10K
Royalty - 5%; Ad. - 2%
Earnings Claim Statement: No
Term of Contract (Years): 10/5
Avg. # Of Employees: 2 FT, 4 PT
Passive Ownership: Discouraged
Encourage Conversions: Yes
Area Develop. Agreements: No
Sub-Franchising Contracts: No
Expand In Territory: Yes
Space Needs: 1,000-1,400 SF; SF, SC, RM

SUPPORT & TRAINING PROVIDED:

Financial Assistance Provided: Yes(I)
Site Selection Assistance: Yes
Lease Negotiation Assistance: Yes
Co-Operative Advertising: Yes
Franchisee Assoc./Member: No
Size Of Corporate Staff: 2
On-Going Support: C,D,E,F,G,H,I
Training: 2 Weeks in Store - Various Locations; 3 Days in Class.

SPECIFIC EXPANSION PLANS:

US: NE. Expansion Outside 2002
Canada: No
Overseas: No

<< >>

MR. GOODCENTS SUBS & PASTAS

8997 Commerce Dr.
DeSoto, KS 66018
Tel: (800) 648-2368 (913) 583-8400
Fax: (913) 888-8477
E-Mail: frandev@mrgoodcents.com
Web Site: www.mrgoodcents.com
Ms. Margot Bubien, Franchise Development

Quick-service lunch and dinner restaurant, serving freshly-sliced submarine sandwiches served on bread baked daily on premises, hot pasta dishes, delicious soups and fresh salads, quick-service restaurant for dine-in, carry-out, delivery or catering. Continued business consultant support and in-house 30-day training period.

BACKGROUND: IFA MEMBER
Established: 1989; 1st Franchised: 1990
Franchised Units: 117
Company-Owned Units 7
Total Units: 124
Dist.: US-145; CAN-0; O'seas-0
North America: 13 States
Density: 43 in KS, 54 in MO, 8 in AZ
Projected New Units (12 Months): NR
Qualifications: 3, 3, 2, 2, 1, 5
Registered: All States

FINANCIAL/TERMS:

Cash Investment: $35-50K
Total Investment: $67.8-187.3K
Minimum Net Worth: $NR
Fees: Franchise - $12.5K
Royalty - 5%; Ad. - 2.5%
Earnings Claim Statement: Yes
Term of Contract (Years): 10/10
Avg. # Of Employees: 1-3 FT, 10-20 PT
Passive Ownership: N/A
Encourage Conversions: Yes
Area Develop. Agreements: Yes
Sub-Franchising Contracts: No
Expand In Territory: Yes
Space Needs: 1,700-2,000 SF; FS, SC

SUPPORT & TRAINING PROVIDED:

Financial Assistance Provided: Yes(I)
Site Selection Assistance: Yes
Lease Negotiation Assistance: Yes
Co-Operative Advertising: Yes
Franchisee Assoc./Member: No
Size Of Corporate Staff: 40
On-Going Support: A,B,C,D,E,F,G,H,I
Training: 30 Days DeSoto, KS.

SPECIFIC EXPANSION PLANS:

US: All United States
Canada: No
Overseas: No

<< >>

MR. HERO

5755 Granger Rd., # 200
Independence, OH 44131-1410
Tel: (800) 837-9599 (216) 398-1101
Fax: (216) 398-0707
E-Mail: tsozio@mrhero.com
Web Site: www.mrhero.com
Ms. Terri Sozio, Franchise Sales Admin.

MR. HERO is an exciting alternative to the typical quick-service restaurant. Our difference centers around the food. We have grill-based hot food offerings of Romanburgers, ribeye steak sandwiches, hot buttered cheesesteaks with wafer fries, cold subs and an assortment of sides and desserts. Café Morocco breakfast program included.

BACKGROUND: IFA MEMBER
Established: 1969; 1st Franchised: 1969
Franchised Units: 107
Company-Owned Units 13
Total Units: 120
Dist.: US-120; CAN-0; O'seas-0
North America: 7 States
Density: 112 in OH, 3 in NC, 2 in VA
Projected New Units (12 Months): 20
Qualifications: 5, 3, 3, 2, 5, 4
Registered: IL,IN,MD,MI,NY,VA,DC

FINANCIAL/TERMS:

Cash Investment: $40-75K
Total Investment: $75-300K
Minimum Net Worth: $250K
Fees: Franchise - $16.5K
Royalty - 5.5%; Ad. - 5%
Earnings Claim Statement: No
Term of Contract (Years): 20/20
Avg. # Of Employees: 4 FT, 8 PT
Passive Ownership: Discouraged
Encourage Conversions: Yes
Area Develop. Agreements: Yes/3-5
Sub-Franchising Contracts: Yes
Expand In Territory: Yes
Space Needs: 1,500 SF; FS, SF, SC, RM, Co-Brand

SUPPORT & TRAINING PROVIDED:

Financial Assistance Provided: Yes(I)
Site Selection Assistance: Yes
Lease Negotiation Assistance: Yes
Co-Operative Advertising: Yes
Franchisee Assoc./Member: No
Size Of Corporate Staff: 40
On-Going Support: A,B,C,D,E,F,G,H,I
Training: 4 Weeks Cleveland, OH.

SPECIFIC EXPANSION PLANS:

US: NE, E, SE, S, MW
Canada: No
Overseas: No

<< >>

MR. JIM'S PIZZA

4276 Kellway Cir.
Addison, TX 75001
Tel: (800) 583-5960 (972) 267-5467
Fax: (972) 267-5463
Web Site: www.mrjimspizza.net

Mr. Randall Wooley, Executive Director

Specializing in delivery and take-out operations. Low start-up cost of under $90,000, including franchise fee. Dallas, Ft. Worth's largest locally-owned pizza franchise.

BACKGROUND:
Established: 1974; 1st Franchised: 1976
Franchised Units: 64
Company-Owned Units 0
Total Units: 64
Dist.: US-64; CAN-0; O'seas-0
North America: NR
Density: 58 in TX, 2 in LA, 2 in VA
Projected New Units (12 Months): 6
Qualifications: 4, 4, 5, 2, 3, 4
Registered: OR,VA

FINANCIAL/TERMS:
Cash Investment: $50K
Total Investment: $56-108K
Minimum Net Worth: $100K
Fees: Franchise - $10K
Royalty - 5%; Ad. - 0%
Earnings Claim Statement: No
Term of Contract (Years): 15/15
Avg. # Of Employees: 5 FT, 15 PT
Passive Ownership: Discouraged
Encourage Conversions: Yes
Area Develop. Agreements: Yes
Sub-Franchising Contracts: No
Expand In Territory: Yes
Space Needs: 1,100 SF; SC

SUPPORT & TRAINING PROVIDED:
Financial Assistance Provided: No
Site Selection Assistance: Yes
Lease Negotiation Assistance: Yes
Co-Operative Advertising: Yes
Franchisee Assoc./Member: No
Size Of Corporate Staff: 6
On-Going Support: B,C,D,E,G,H
Training: 2 Months.

SPECIFIC EXPANSION PLANS:
US: All Except FL, MI
Canada: No
Overseas: No

<< >>

MRS. VANELLI'S FRESH ITALIAN FOODS

700 Kerr St.
Oakville, ON L6K 3W5 CANADA
Tel: (800) 555-5726 (905) 337-7777
Fax: (905) 337-0331
E-Mail: info@donatogroup.com
Web Site: www.mrsvanellis.com
Mr. Nik Jurkovic,

Serving pizza, pasta, salad and sandwiches located in mall food courts, airports, universities, hospitals, theme parks and other similar high traffic settings.

BACKGROUND: IFA MEMBER
Established: 1981; 1st Franchised: 1983
Franchised Units: 100
Company-Owned Units 2
Total Units: 102
Dist.: US-0; CAN-87; O'seas-7
North America: NR
Density: 49 in ON, 14 in BC, 5 in AB
Projected New Units (12 Months): 8
Qualifications: 5, 2, 2, 2, 3, 4
Registered: IL,AB

FINANCIAL/TERMS:
Cash Investment: $50-100K
Total Investment: $175-250K
Minimum Net Worth: $200K
Fees: Franchise - $25K
Royalty - 6%; Ad. - 1.5%
Earnings Claim Statement: No
Term of Contract (Years): 8-10/5-10
Avg. # Of Employees: 3 FT, 6 PT
Passive Ownership: Discouraged
Encourage Conversions: Yes
Area Develop. Agreements: Yes/15
Sub-Franchising Contracts: Yes
Expand In Territory: Yes
Space Needs: 400 SF; RM

SUPPORT & TRAINING PROVIDED:
Financial Assistance Provided: Yes(I)
Site Selection Assistance: Yes
Lease Negotiation Assistance: Yes
Co-Operative Advertising: N/A
Franchisee Assoc./Member: No/No
Size Of Corporate Staff: 40
On-Going Support: B,C,D,E,G,H,I
Training: 3-4 Days at Company HQ; 3-4 Days at the Store; 1 Week during your Grand Opening.

SPECIFIC EXPANSION PLANS:
US: All United States
Canada: All Canada
Overseas: All Countries

<< >>

MY FAMILY FOOD COURT

3331 Viking Way, # 7
Richmond, BC V6V 1X7 CANADA
Tel: (604) 270-2360
Fax: (604) 270-6560
Web Site: www.edelweissdeli.com
Mr. Duncan Williams, President

We build food courts for one owner. We have six different franchisees. Customer can have one to four franchises in his location.

BACKGROUND:
Established: 1973; 1st Franchised: 1989
Franchised Units: 20
Company-Owned Units 0
Total Units: 20
Dist.: US-0; CAN-20; O'seas-0
North America: 1 Province
Density: 20 in BC
Projected New Units (12 Months): 6
Qualifications: 5, 3, 2, 4, 2, 5
Registered: CA,OR,WA

FINANCIAL/TERMS:
Cash Investment: $50K
Total Investment: $50-500K
Minimum Net Worth: $50K
Fees: Franchise - $20K
Royalty - 6%/$600/Mo.; Ad. - 2%
Earnings Claim Statement: Yes
Term of Contract (Years): 20/20
Avg. # Of Employees: 3 FT, 3 PT
Passive Ownership: Discouraged
Encourage Conversions: Yes
Area Develop. Agreements: Yes/20
Sub-Franchising Contracts: Yes
Expand In Territory: Yes
Space Needs: 1,000 SF; FS, SF, SC, RM, HB

SUPPORT & TRAINING PROVIDED:
Financial Assistance Provided: Yes(I)
Site Selection Assistance: Yes
Lease Negotiation Assistance: Yes
Co-Operative Advertising: Yes
Franchisee Assoc./Member: Yes/Yes
Size Of Corporate Staff: 5
On-Going Support: C,D,E,F,G
Training: 3 Weeks Richmond, BC; 2 Weeks Customer Location.

SPECIFIC EXPANSION PLANS:
US: Northwest
Canada: BC
Overseas: U.K.

<< >>

MY FRIEND'S PLACE

106 Hammond Dr.
Atlanta, GA 30328
Tel: (404) 843-2803
Fax: (404) 843-0371
Mr. John Thomas, Dir. Franchise Sales

A quality franchise opportunity for your financial independence and future. Our restaurants cater to the quality-oriented customer interested in a quick, yet light and healthy lunch, specializing in sandwiches, salads, soups and home-made desserts. MY FRIEND'S PLACE is a 'Fresh Food Express!'

BACKGROUND:
Established: 1980; 1st Franchised: 1990
Franchised Units: 16
Company-Owned Units 2
Total Units: 18
Dist.: US-13; CAN-0; O'seas-0
North America: 1 State
Density: 13 in GA
Projected New Units (12 Months): 4
Qualifications: 3, 4, 3, 3, 2, 5
Registered: NR

FINANCIAL/TERMS:
Cash Investment: $95-175K
Total Investment: $95-175K
Minimum Net Worth: $200K
Fees: Franchise - $17.5K
Royalty - Flat; Ad. - Flat
Earnings Claim Statement: No
Term of Contract (Years): 15/10
Avg. # Of Employees: 2 FT, 2 PT
Passive Ownership: Not Allowed
Encourage Conversions: Yes
Area Develop. Agreements: No
Sub-Franchising Contracts: Yes
Expand In Territory: Yes
Space Needs: 1,400 SF; SC, FS

SUPPORT & TRAINING PROVIDED:
Financial Assistance Provided: Yes(I)
Site Selection Assistance: Yes
Lease Negotiation Assistance: Yes
Co-Operative Advertising: Yes
Franchisee Assoc./Member: No
Size Of Corporate Staff: 4
On-Going Support: C,d,E,f
Training: 12 Business Days Headquarters; 12 Business Days Franchisee Site.

SPECIFIC EXPANSION PLANS:
US: SE Only, GA,FL,AL,IN,SC,TX
Canada: No
Overseas: No

<< >>

NATHAN'S FAMOUS

1400 Old Country Rd., # 400
Westbury, NY 11590
Tel: (800) NATHANS (516) 338-8500
Fax: (516) 338-7220
E-Mail: nfidevel@webspan.net
Mr. Carl Paley, Senior Vice President

Fast-food restaurant, featuring premium-quality, all beef hot dogs, fresh-cut fries, plus a large variety of menu items - 9 prototypes, ranging from carts, counter modules, food courts and full-service restaurants. Franchise license and area development opportunities available worldwide.

BACKGROUND:
Established: 1916; 1st Franchised: 1979
Franchised Units: 200
Company-Owned Units 28
Total Units: 228
Dist.: US-214; CAN-0; O'seas-0
North America: 37 States
Density: 27 in NY, 19 in NJ, 17 in FL
Projected New Units (12 Months): 35
Qualifications: 5, 3, 4, 2, 3, 5
Registered: CA,FL,HI,IL,IN,MD,MI,MN, NY,VA,WA,WI,DC

FINANCIAL/TERMS:
Cash Investment: $50-250K
Total Investment: $50-550K
Minimum Net Worth: $400K
Fees: Franchise - $15-30K
Royalty - 4.5%; Ad. - 2.5%
Earnings Claim Statement: No
Term of Contract (Years): 20/15
Avg. # Of Employees: 6-7 FT, 10-15 PT
Passive Ownership: Discouraged
Encourage Conversions: Yes
Area Develop. Agreements: Yes/Varies
Sub-Franchising Contracts: Yes
Expand In Territory: Yes
Space Needs: 500-2,500 SF; SF, RM

SUPPORT & TRAINING PROVIDED:
Financial Assistance Provided: Yes(I)
Site Selection Assistance: Yes
Lease Negotiation Assistance: Yes
Co-Operative Advertising: Yes
Franchisee Assoc./Member: No
Size Of Corporate Staff: 42
On-Going Support: B,C,D,E,F,G,H,I
Training: 2-4 Weeks in Long Island, NY and in Store.

SPECIFIC EXPANSION PLANS:
US: All United States
Canada: PQ, ON
Overseas: Europe, Asia

<< >>

NATURE'S TABLE

800 N. Magnolia Ave.
Orlando, FL 32803
Tel: (800) 222-6090
Fax: (407) 843-6057
Mr. Michael W. Karr, Franchise Agent

NATURE'S TABLE is an expanding Florida-based chain with 20 years of experience. Our menu features healthy food such as vegetarian chili, homemade soups, harvest salads, frozen yogurt, smoothies and a variety of sandwiches.

BACKGROUND:
Established: 1977; 1st Franchised: 1985
Franchised Units: 42
Company-Owned Units 6
Total Units: 48
Dist.: US-48; CAN-0; O'seas-0
North America: 1 State
Density: 34 in FL
Projected New Units (12 Months): 12
Qualifications: 5, 3, 3, 4, 5, 4
Registered: FL,MD,MI,MN,VA,WI,DC

FINANCIAL/TERMS:
Cash Investment: $100-175K
Total Investment: $100-175K
Minimum Net Worth: $100K
Fees: Franchise - $25K
Royalty - 5%; Ad. - 1%
Earnings Claim Statement: No
Term of Contract (Years): 10/5
Avg. # Of Employees: 2 FT, 2-4 PT
Passive Ownership: Allowed
Encourage Conversions: N/A
Area Develop. Agreements: Yes/10
Sub-Franchising Contracts: No
Expand In Territory: No
Space Needs: 500-750 SF; RM

SUPPORT & TRAINING PROVIDED:
Financial Assistance Provided: No
Site Selection Assistance: Yes
Lease Negotiation Assistance: Yes
Co-Operative Advertising: No
Franchisee Assoc./Member: Yes
Size Of Corporate Staff: 7
On-Going Support: C,D,E,F,G,h,I
Training: 2 Weeks Orlando, FL; On-Site.

SPECIFIC EXPANSION PLANS:
US: Southeast United States
Canada: No
Overseas: No

<< >>

NEW YORK BURRITO GOURMET WRAPS

955 E. Javelina Ave., # 114
Mesa, AZ 85204
Tel: (800) 711-4036 (480) 503-3363
Fax: (480) 503-1850
E-Mail: info@nybfoods.com
Web Site: www.newyorkburrito.com
Mr. Robert Palmer, President

Casual/up-scale, quick-serve restaurants serving multi-cultural gourmet wraps (burritos). Some restaurants feature breakfast, fruit smoothies, and/or beer and wine. Menu items prepared daily with the highest-quality and variety meats and veggies. Giant tortillas offered in a variety of flavors: tomato basil, whole wheat, spinach, jalapeno and white flour. Low start-up cost and ease of operation. Join the hottest new food trend of the 90s with the leader of the pack.

BACKGROUND: IFA MEMBER
Established: 1995; 1st Franchised: 1996
Franchised Units: 75
Company-Owned Units 1
Total Units: 76
Dist.: US-79; CAN-0; O'seas-0
North America: 27 States
Density: 8 in CA, 8 in CO, 5 in UT
Projected New Units (12 Months): 15
Qualifications: 4, 4, 2, 3, 3, 4
Registered: CA,FL,IN,MI,MN,NY,OR, SD,WI

FINANCIAL/TERMS:
Cash Investment: $25-35K
Total Investment: $75-135K
Minimum Net Worth: $Varies
Fees: Franchise - $15K
Royalty - 7%; Ad. - 4%
Earnings Claim Statement: No
Term of Contract (Years): Perpetual
Avg. # Of Employees: Varies
Passive Ownership: Discouraged
Encourage Conversions: N/A
Area Develop. Agreements: Yes
Sub-Franchising Contracts: No
Expand In Territory: Yes
Space Needs: 1,500-2,500 SF; FS, SC, RM

SUPPORT & TRAINING PROVIDED:
Financial Assistance Provided: Yes
Site Selection Assistance: Yes
Lease Negotiation Assistance: Yes
Co-Operative Advertising: Yes
Franchisee Assoc./Member: No
Size Of Corporate Staff: 9+
On-Going Support: A,B,C,D,E,F,G,H,I
Training: 5 Days at Headquarters/Training Center; 5 Days at Franchise Store.

SPECIFIC EXPANSION PLANS:
US: All United States
Canada: All Except AB
Overseas: No

<< >>

OBEE'S SOUP-SALAD-SUBS

949 Tamiami Trail
Port Charlotte, FL 33953-3152
Tel: (866) 623-3462 (941) 625-0773
Fax: (941) 625-1501
E-Mail: franchisedirector@obees.com
Web Site: www.obees.com
Mr. James Patrick, President

World's greatest fresh food restaurant. Our subs are made from the highest quality meats, cheeses, and condiments available. The vegetables that go into our subs are sliced daily. We use real Italian break baked fresh daily. In addition to the mouth-watering subs, O'Bee's also offers a variety of soups, salads, desserts and soft drinks.

BACKGROUND: IFA MEMBER
Established: 1995; 1st Franchised: 2000
Franchised Units: 21
Company-Owned Units 1
Total Units: 22
Dist.: US-23; CAN-0; O'seas-0
North America: 3 States
Density: 1 in AR, 3 in MI, 19 in FL
Projected New Units (12 Months): NR
Registered: NR

FINANCIAL/TERMS:
Cash Investment: $10-20K
Total Investment: $60-65K
Minimum Net Worth: $NR
Fees: Franchise - $15K
Royalty - 5-6%; Ad. - 1%
Earnings Claim Statement: No
Term of Contract (Years): 10/10
Avg. # Of Employees: 2 FT, 6 PT
Passive Ownership: Discouraged
Encourage Conversions: NR
Area Develop. Agreements: Yes/50
Sub-Franchising Contracts: No
Expand In Territory: Yes
Space Needs: 1000-1400 SF; SF, SC

SUPPORT & TRAINING PROVIDED:
Financial Assistance Provided: NR
Site Selection Assistance: Yes
Lease Negotiation Assistance: Yes
Co-Operative Advertising: Yes
Franchisee Assoc./Member: No
Size Of Corporate Staff: 3
On-Going Support: B,C,D,E,F,G,H,I
Training: 2 Weeks in Port Charlotte, FL;. 1 Week at Franchise Location.

SPECIFIC EXPANSION PLANS:
US: All United States
Canada: NR
Overseas: NR

<< >>

ORION FOOD SYSTEMS

2930 W. Maple Ave., P.O. Box 780
Sioux Falls, SD 57101
Tel: (800) 648-6227 (605) 336-6961
Fax: (605) 336-0141
Web Site: www.orionfoodsys.com
Mr. Tom Coyle, National Development Mgr.

Franchise offers 9 separate brands covering all popular fast food categories: HOT STUFF PIZZA, EDDIE PEPPERS GREAT AMERICAN, CINNAMON STREET BAKERY + COFFEE COMPANY, MEAN GENE'S BURGERS, MACGREGOR'S MARKET SUBS, SMASH HITS SUBS, JOEY PAGODA'S ORIENTAL EXPRESS, CHIX THE CHICKEN STATION.

BACKGROUND:
Established: 1984; 1st Franchised: 1986
Franchised Units: 1,058
Company-Owned Units 7
Total Units: 1,065
Dist.: US-1493; CAN-7; O'seas-1
North America: 50 States, 2 Provinces
Density: 89 in MN, 38 in SD, 34 in WI
Projected New Units (12 Months): 240
Qualifications: 4, 4, 4, 3, 3, 5
Registered: All States and AB

FINANCIAL/TERMS:
Cash Investment: $20K
Total Investment: $35-300K
Minimum Net Worth: $30K
Fees: Franchise - $0
Royalty - 0%; Ad. - 0%
Earnings Claim Statement: No
Term of Contract (Years): 5/5
Avg. # Of Employees: 4 FT, 10 PT
Passive Ownership: Allowed
Encourage Conversions: Yes
Area Develop. Agreements: No
Sub-Franchising Contracts: No
Expand In Territory: Yes
Space Needs: 700 SF; RM

SUPPORT & TRAINING PROVIDED:
Financial Assistance Provided: Yes(I)
Site Selection Assistance: Yes
Lease Negotiation Assistance: Yes
Co-Operative Advertising: No
Franchisee Assoc./Member: Yes/Yes
Size Of Corporate Staff: 700
On-Going Support: B,C,D,E,F,G,I
Training: 2 Weeks at New Franchisee's Site.

SPECIFIC EXPANSION PLANS:
US: All United States
Canada: All Canada
Overseas: No

<< >>

PANCHERO'S MEXICAN GRILL

P.O. Box 1786
Iowa City, IA 52244
Tel: (888) MEX-BEST (319) 351-4551
Fax: (319) 358-6435
E-Mail: fsource@pancheros.com
Web Site: www.pancheros.com
Mr. James Manura, GM of Development

PANCHERO'S MEXICAN GRILLS offer a delicious and affordable alternative to traditional fast-food places. Fast, fresh and at prices that make it easy to come back time and again are the keys to PANCHERO'S success. Qualified franchisees will share in our operating systems, site selection assistance and training.

BACKGROUND:

Established: 1991; 1st Franchised: 1995
Franchised Units: 3
Company-Owned Units 3
Total Units: 6
Dist.: US-6; CAN-0; O'seas-0
North America: 4 States
Density: 2 in IA, 2 in MI
Projected New Units (12 Months): 10
Qualifications: 5, 3, 3, 3, 3, 5
Registered: FL,IL,IN,MI,MN,WI

FINANCIAL/TERMS:

Cash Investment: $100K
Total Investment: $100-350K
Minimum Net Worth: $250K
Fees: Franchise - $15-25K
Royalty - 5%; Ad. - 3%
Earnings Claim Statement: Yes
Term of Contract (Years): 5/5
Avg. # Of Employees: 2 FT, 12 PT
Passive Ownership: Discouraged
Encourage Conversions: Yes
Area Develop. Agreements: Yes
Sub-Franchising Contracts: Yes
Expand In Territory: No
Space Needs: 2,000 SF; FS, SF, SC

SUPPORT & TRAINING PROVIDED:

Financial Assistance Provided: NR
Site Selection Assistance: Yes
Lease Negotiation Assistance: Yes
Co-Operative Advertising: No
Franchisee Assoc./Member: No
Size Of Corporate Staff: 5
On-Going Support: B,C,D,E,F,H
Training: 3 Weeks at Company Store.

SPECIFIC EXPANSION PLANS:

US: Midwest
Canada: No
Overseas: No

<< >>

PASTEL'S CAFE

1121 Centre St. N., # 440
Calgary, AB T2E 7K6 CANADA
Tel: (800) 361-1151 (403) 230-1151
Fax: (403) 230-2182
Mr. Sheldon Jones, Franchise Development Mgr.

PASTEL'S CAFE features a full menu of the finest-quality gourmet sandwiches, a mouth-watering array of specialty salads and hearty homemade soups, all prepared with FRESH, healthy ingredients and presented with style.

BACKGROUND:

Established: 1980; 1st Franchised: 1982
Franchised Units: 20
Company-Owned Units 0
Total Units: 20
Dist.: US-0; CAN-20; O'seas-0
North America: 2 Provinces
Density: 15 in BC
Projected New Units (12 Months): 3
Registered: AB

FINANCIAL/TERMS:

Cash Investment: $75-95K
Total Investment: $160-250K
Minimum Net Worth: $175K
Fees: Franchise - $25K
Royalty - 5%; Ad. - 0%
Earnings Claim Statement: Yes
Term of Contract (Years): 10/10
Avg. # Of Employees: 2 FT, 5 PT
Passive Ownership: Discouraged
Encourage Conversions: Yes
Area Develop. Agreements: No
Sub-Franchising Contracts: No
Expand In Territory: Yes
Space Needs: 1,100 SF; SF, SC, RM

SUPPORT & TRAINING PROVIDED:

Financial Assistance Provided: Yes(I)
Site Selection Assistance: Yes
Lease Negotiation Assistance: Yes
Co-Operative Advertising: Yes
Franchisee Assoc./Member: Yes
Size Of Corporate Staff: 12
On-Going Support: C,D,E,f,G,h
Training: 21 Days Comprehensive Hands-On Training.

SPECIFIC EXPANSION PLANS:

US: No
Canada: All Canada
Overseas: No

<< >>

PAUL REVERE'S PIZZA INTERNATIONAL

1574 42nd St. NE
Cedar Rapids, IA 52402-3062
Tel: (800) 995-9437 (319) 395-9113
Fax: (319) 395-9115
E-Mail: patrickroof@mcleodusa.net
Web Site: www.paulreverespizza.com
Mr. Larry A. Schuster, President

PAUL REVERE'S PIZZA is a low investment, high quality franchise. Our concept is designed to utilize low square footage buildings or spaces. Low overhead equals larger bottomlines. High quality menu items, competitive pricing and excellent service make PAUL REVERE'S PIZZA a great buy for a customer or prospective franchisee.

BACKGROUND:

Established: 1975; 1st Franchised: 1982
Franchised Units: 45
Company-Owned Units 0
Total Units: 45
Dist.: US-0; CAN-0; O'seas-0
North America: 4 States
Density: 29 in IA; 15 in WI; 2 in MO
Projected New Units (12 Months): NR
Registered: NR

FINANCIAL/TERMS:

Cash Investment: $25-75K
Total Investment: $110-210K
Minimum Net Worth: $70K
Fees: Franchise - $15K
Royalty - 4%; Ad. - 0%
Earnings Claim Statement: Yes
Term of Contract (Years): 10/10
Avg. # Of Employees: 6 FT, 8 PT
Passive Ownership: Discouraged
Encourage Conversions: NR
Area Develop. Agreements: Yes/10
Sub-Franchising Contracts: Yes
Expand In Territory: Yes
Space Needs: 1,100 SF; SF, SC

SUPPORT & TRAINING PROVIDED:

Financial Assistance Provided: NR
Site Selection Assistance: Yes
Lease Negotiation Assistance: Yes
Co-Operative Advertising: N/A
Franchisee Assoc./Member: No
Size Of Corporate Staff: 3
On-Going Support: B,C,D,d,E,F,G,H,I
Training: 10-14 Days in Cedar Rapids, IA.

SPECIFIC EXPANSION PLANS:

US: IA,WI,IL,MN,MO,AR,NE,KS
Canada: NR
Overseas: NR

<< >>

PENN STATION/ EAST COAST SUBS

8276 Beechmont Ave.
Cincinnati, OH 45255-3153
Tel: (513) 474-5957
Fax: (513) 474-7116
Web Site: www.penn-station.com
Mr. Mark Partusch, Dir. Sales/Dev.

Retail sale of authentic 'East Coast-style' submarines, including the original Philadelphia cheesesteak, all prepared fresh before the customer. Fresh-cut fries, flash fried in peanut oil, and fresh-squeezed lemonade.

BACKGROUND:
Established: 1985; 1st Franchised: 1987
Franchised Units: 79
Company-Owned Units 4
Total Units: 83
Dist.: US-70; CAN-0; O'seas-0
North America: 4 States
Density: 41 in OH, 14 in IN, 13 in KY
Projected New Units (12 Months): 25
Qualifications: 3, 5, 3, 4, 4, 5
Registered: IN

FINANCIAL/TERMS:
Cash Investment: $40-82.5K
Total Investment: $182.8-328.7K
Minimum Net Worth: $Varies
Fees: Franchise - $17.5K
Royalty - 4-7.5%; Ad. - 1%
Earnings Claim Statement: Yes
Term of Contract (Years): 5/5/5/5
Avg. # Of Employees: 11 FT, 10 PT
Passive Ownership: Allowed
Encourage Conversions: No
Area Develop. Agreements: Yes
Sub-Franchising Contracts: No
Expand In Territory: Yes
Space Needs: 1,600-1,800 SF; FS, SC

SUPPORT & TRAINING PROVIDED:
Financial Assistance Provided: No
Site Selection Assistance: Yes
Lease Negotiation Assistance: Yes
Co-Operative Advertising: Yes
Franchisee Assoc./Member: Yes/Yes
Size Of Corporate Staff: 13
On-Going Support: C,D,E,F,G,H
Training: 2 Weeks Penn Station in Cincinnati, OH; 2-3 Days On-Site Training Prior to Grand Opening.

SPECIFIC EXPANSION PLANS:
US: Midwest, Southeast, South
Canada: No
Overseas: No

<< >>

PHILLY CONNECTION

120 Interstate N. Pkwy., E., # 112
Atlanta, GA 30339-2103
Tel: (800) 886-8826 (770) 952-6152
Fax: (770) 952-3168
E-Mail: phillycon@mindspring.com
Web Site: www.phillyconnection.com
Mr. John D. Pollock, SVP Franchise Development

Quick service restaurant and ice cream parlor. "The Cheesesteak Champion" serves fresh, high quality products prepared to order in front of customers. On premises, take out, drive though, delivery. May operate in strip shopping centers, convenience stores, free-standing buildings and "end cap" space. Franchisor helps in site location, lease negotiation, equipment purchasing, grand opening, initial and ongoing training, toll free helpline.

BACKGROUND: IFA MEMBER
Established: 1984; 1st Franchised: 1987
Franchised Units: 90
Company-Owned Units 2
Total Units: 92
Dist.: US-85; CAN-0; O'seas-0
North America: 5 States
Density: 49 in GA, 13 in NC, 11 in FL
Projected New Units (12 Months): 30
Qualifications: 4, 5, 3, 3, 3, 5
Registered: FL

FINANCIAL/TERMS:
Cash Investment: $30-80K
Total Investment: $130-231K
Minimum Net Worth: $110K
Fees: Franchise - $20K
Royalty - 5%; Ad. - 5%
Earnings Claim Statement: No
Term of Contract (Years): 10/5
Avg. # Of Employees: 2 FT, 10 PT
Passive Ownership: Discouraged
Encourage Conversions: N/A
Area Develop. Agreements: Yes/3
Sub-Franchising Contracts: No
Expand In Territory: Yes
Space Needs: 1,000-1,600 SF; FS, SF, SC, C-Stores

SUPPORT & TRAINING PROVIDED:
Financial Assistance Provided: Yes(I)
Site Selection Assistance: Yes
Lease Negotiation Assistance: Yes
Co-Operative Advertising: Yes
Franchisee Assoc./Member: No
Size Of Corporate Staff: 14
On-Going Support: a,B,C,D,E,F,G,H,I
Training: 2-6 Weeks Existing Restaurant; 1 Week Corporate Headquarters.

SPECIFIC EXPANSION PLANS:
US: Southeast
Canada: All Canada
Overseas: Europe

<< >>

PICKERMAN'S SOUP & SANDWICHES

5714 Nordic Dr., # 400
Cedar Falls, IA 50613-6958
Tel: (800) 273-2172 (319) 266-7141
Fax: (319) 277-1201
E-Mail: bwendling@pickermans.com
Web Site: www.pickermans.com
Ms. Michele Jensen

Pickerman's is a low investment, high-return restaurant that sells distinctive soups, sandwiches and salads. Our service fee is on 4% without hidden fees. We help keep your investment low by providing you with an efficient food system requiring minimal space and capital. The total investment range is generally between $165,000-$185,000.

BACKGROUND:
Established: 1998; 1st Franchised: 1998
Franchised Units: 39
Company-Owned Units 0
Total Units: 39
Dist.: US-39; CAN-0; O'seas-0
North America: 8 States
Density: 12 in IA, 12 in IL, 5 in MN
Projected New Units (12 Months): 100
Qualifications: 2, 2, 1, 2, 3, 3
Registered: IL,MN

FINANCIAL/TERMS:
Cash Investment: $42-46K
Total Investment: $165-185K
Minimum Net Worth: $N/A
Fees: Franchise - $10K
Royalty - 4%; Ad. - 0%
Earnings Claim Statement: No
Term of Contract (Years): 10/10
Avg. # Of Employees: 2 FT, 10 PT
Passive Ownership: Discouraged
Encourage Conversions: Yes
Area Develop. Agreements: No
Sub-Franchising Contracts: No
Expand In Territory: Yes
Space Needs: 1300-2000 SF; SC, RM

SUPPORT & TRAINING PROVIDED:
Financial Assistance Provided: Yes(I)
Site Selection Assistance: Yes
Lease Negotiation Assistance: Yes

Co-Operative Advertising: No
Franchisee Assoc./Member: No
Size Of Corporate Staff: 24
On-Going Support: C,D,E,G
Training: 1 Week Corporate Office; 1 Week Another Store; 1 Week Franchisee's Store.
SPECIFIC EXPANSION PLANS:
US: Midwest
Canada: No
Overseas: No

PIZZA FACTORY

P.O. Box 989, 49430 Road 426
Oakhurst, CA 93644
Tel: (800) 654-4840 (559) 683-3377
Fax: (559) 683-6879
E-Mail: pfinc@sierratel.com
Web Site: www.pizzafactoryinc.com
Ms. Nikki Van Velson, Operations Director

'We Toss 'em, They're Awesome.' PIZZA FACTORY has a proven track record with 107 restaurants in 12 states, The franchisee has a strong support system which includes site location, lease negotiating, on-site training and on-going support from headquarters. Call for brochure. Serving homemade pizza, pasta, sandwiches, beer and wine.

BACKGROUND:
Established: 1979; 1st Franchised: 1985
Franchised Units: 116
Company-Owned Units 0
Total Units: 116
Dist.: US-197; CAN-0; O'seas-8
North America: 12 States
Density: 61 in CA, 17 in WA, 10 in ID
Projected New Units (12 Months): 10
Qualifications: 5, 4, 4, 2, 2, 3
Registered: AZ,CA,CO,FL,ID,MN,OR,SD,WA
FINANCIAL/TERMS:
Cash Investment: $65-80K
Total Investment: $70-262K
Minimum Net Worth: $150K
Fees: Franchise - $20K
Royalty - 5%; Ad. - 2%
Earnings Claim Statement: No
Term of Contract (Years): 20
Avg. # Of Employees: 3 FT, 12-15 PT
Passive Ownership: Allowed
Encourage Conversions: Yes
Area Develop. Agreements: Yes/Varies
Sub-Franchising Contracts: No
Expand In Territory: Yes
Space Needs: 200-1,500 Var SF; SC
SUPPORT & TRAINING PROVIDED:
Financial Assistance Provided: No
Site Selection Assistance: Yes
Lease Negotiation Assistance: Yes
Co-Operative Advertising: Yes
Franchisee Assoc./Member: NR
Size Of Corporate Staff: 7
On-Going Support: C,D,E,G,H,I
Training: 325 Hours Training Stores, Training Fee: $2,500.
SPECIFIC EXPANSION PLANS:
US: All United States
Canada: All Canada
Overseas: All Countries; China

PIZZA MAN

6930 1/2 Tujunga Ave.
North Hollywood, CA 91605
Tel: (818) 766-4395
Fax: (818) 766-1496
Mr. Robert Ohanian, President/CEO

Pizza, chicken, ribs, Italian dishes. Delivery and fast food.

BACKGROUND:
Established: 1964; 1st Franchised: 1973
Franchised Units: 48
Company-Owned Units 0
Total Units: 48
Dist.: US-50; CAN-0; O'seas-0
North America: 1 State
Density: 50 in CA
Projected New Units (12 Months): 3
Qualifications: 3, 5, 5, 4, 5, 5
Registered: All States
FINANCIAL/TERMS:
Cash Investment: $70K
Total Investment: $100K
Minimum Net Worth: $150K
Fees: Franchise - $25K
Royalty - 4%/$140/Wk.;
Ad. - 4%/$140/Wk.
Earnings Claim Statement: No
Term of Contract (Years): 1+/1+
Avg. # Of Employees: 3 FT, 2 PT
Passive Ownership: Discouraged
Encourage Conversions: Yes
Area Develop. Agreements: Yes/2
Sub-Franchising Contracts: No
Expand In Territory: Yes
Space Needs: 1,000 SF; SF, SC
SUPPORT & TRAINING PROVIDED:
Financial Assistance Provided: Yes(I)
Site Selection Assistance: Yes
Lease Negotiation Assistance: Yes
Co-Operative Advertising: Yes
Franchisee Assoc./Member: No
Size Of Corporate Staff: 8
On-Going Support: b,C,D,e,f,H
Training: 3 Weeks Los Angeles, CA.
SPECIFIC EXPANSION PLANS:
US: All United States
Canada: All Canada
Overseas: All Countries

PIZZA OUTLET

2101 Greentree Rd., # A-202
Pittsburgh, PA 15220-1400
Tel: (888) 279-9100 (412) 279-9100
Fax: (412) 279-9781
E-Mail: tcarvell@pizzaoutlet.com
Web Site: www.pizzaoutlet.com
Ms. Tiffini Carvell, Dir. Franchising

PIZZA OUTLET provides delivery and carry-out service of pizza, subs, wings, breadsticks and drinks. Streamlined operations and a compact menu provide for low start-up costs and ease of operation. On-going support at every level is provided, including a marketing effort with a national focus.

BACKGROUND: IFA MEMBER
Established: 1988; 1st Franchised: 1994
Franchised Units: 69
Company-Owned Units 37
Total Units: 106
Dist.: US-106; CAN-0; O'seas-0
North America: 5 States
Density: 83 in PA, 11 in VA, 6 in WV
Projected New Units (12 Months): 15
Qualifications: 5, 4, 4, 2, 2, 4
Registered: NR
FINANCIAL/TERMS:
Cash Investment: $25-50K
Total Investment: $95-185K
Minimum Net Worth: $75K
Fees: Franchise - $15K
Royalty - 4%; Ad. - 1%
Earnings Claim Statement: Yes
Term of Contract (Years): 10/5
Avg. # Of Employees: 8 FT, 12 PT
Passive Ownership: Not Allowed
Encourage Conversions: Yes
Area Develop. Agreements: Yes/Varies
Sub-Franchising Contracts: No
Expand In Territory: Yes
Space Needs: 1,200 SF; FS, SF, SC
SUPPORT & TRAINING PROVIDED:
Financial Assistance Provided: No

Site Selection Assistance: Yes
Lease Negotiation Assistance: No
Co-Operative Advertising: Yes
Franchisee Assoc./Member: No
Size Of Corporate Staff: 38
On-Going Support: B,C,D,E,F,G,H,I
Training: 4 Weeks Corporate Office; 1 Week On-Site during Opening.

SPECIFIC EXPANSION PLANS:
US: OH, PA, WV, VA
Canada: No
Overseas: No

<< >>

PIZZA RANCH, THE
1121 Main St., Box 823
Hull, IA 51239
Tel: (800) 321-3401 (712) 439-1150
Fax: (712) 439-1125
E-Mail: pizzar@mtcnet.net
Web Site: www.pizza-ranch.com
Mr. Lawrence Vander Esch, Co-Founder

THE PIZZA RANCH is a family restaurant, specializing in pizza, pasta and chicken.

BACKGROUND:
Established: 1981; 1st Franchised: 1984
Franchised Units: 86
Company-Owned Units 6
Total Units: 91
Dist.: US-85; CAN-0; O'seas-0
North America: 6 States
Density: 40 in IA, 20 in MN, 16 in SD
Projected New Units (12 Months): 12
Qualifications: 3, 3, 3, 3, 2, 5
Registered: IL,MI,MN,ND,SD, WI

FINANCIAL/TERMS:
Cash Investment: $20-50K
Total Investment: $200-500K
Minimum Net Worth: $25K
Fees: Franchise - $10K
Royalty - 4%; Ad. - $1.7-2.2K
Earnings Claim Statement: No
Term of Contract (Years): 10/10/10
Avg. # Of Employees: 2 FT, 20 PT
Passive Ownership: Allowed
Encourage Conversions: Yes
Area Develop. Agreements: Yes
Sub-Franchising Contracts: Yes
Expand In Territory: Yes
Space Needs: 4,000 SF; Any

SUPPORT & TRAINING PROVIDED:
Financial Assistance Provided: Yes(I)
Site Selection Assistance: Yes
Lease Negotiation Assistance: Yes
Co-Operative Advertising: Yes
Franchisee Assoc./Member: No
Size Of Corporate Staff: 15
On-Going Support: C,D,E,F,G,H,I
Training: 2 Weeks Sioux Center, IA.; 1 Week On-Site.

SPECIFIC EXPANSION PLANS:
US: Midwest
Canada: No
Overseas: No

<< >>

PIZZA ROYALE
650 Graham Bell, # 217
Sainte-Foy, PQ G1N 4H5 CANADA
Tel: (418) 682-5744
Fax: (418) 682-2684
E-Mail: administration@pizzaroyale.com
Web Site: www.pizzaroyale.com
Mr. Rejean Samson, President

PIZZA ROYALE is a chain of Italian restaurants, specializing in pizza cooked in an open wood oven fire in the serving area. It also offers a salad bar and a pasta bar. Take-out orders and delivery are also available. Healthy food and warm atmosphere are the main features of a concept that has proven successful over the years.

BACKGROUND:
Established: 1980; 1st Franchised: 1985
Franchised Units: 7
Company-Owned Units 3
Total Units: 10
Dist.: US-0; CAN-10; O'seas-0
North America: 1 Province
Density: 10 in PQ
Projected New Units (12 Months): 1
Registered: NR

FINANCIAL/TERMS:
Cash Investment: $100-125K
Total Investment: $250-300K
Minimum Net Worth: $NR
Fees: Franchise - $30K
Royalty - 3%; Ad. - 2%
Earnings Claim Statement: NR
Term of Contract (Years): 10/10
Avg. # Of Employees: 20 FT, 5 PT
Passive Ownership: Discouraged
Encourage Conversions: Yes
Area Develop. Agreements: Yes
Sub-Franchising Contracts: No
Expand In Territory: Yes
Space Needs: 3,500 SF; FS, SC, RM

SUPPORT & TRAINING PROVIDED:
Financial Assistance Provided: Yes(I)
Site Selection Assistance: Yes
Lease Negotiation Assistance: Yes
Co-Operative Advertising: Yes
Franchisee Assoc./Member: NR
Size Of Corporate Staff: 6
On-Going Support: B,C,d,E,F,H
Training: 2 Weeks Headquarters; 2 Weeks On-Site.

SPECIFIC EXPANSION PLANS:
US: NE, Master Franchises Avail.
Canada: PQ, ON, Master
Overseas: No

<< >>

Top 50

POPEYES CHICKEN & BISCUITS
5555 Glenridge Connector NE, # 300
Atlanta, GA 30342-4759
Tel: (800) 639-3780 (404) 459-4450
Fax: (404) 459-4533
E-Mail: dphibbs@afce.com
Web Site: www.popeyesfranchising.com
Ms. Diane Phibbs, Development Director

POPEYES CHICKEN & BISCUITS, the world's second-largest chicken chain, is owned by AFC Enterprises, Inc., one of the world's largest restaurant parent companies and the winner of the 1997 MUFSO Operator of the Year and Golden Chain awards. POPEYES is famous for its New Orleans-style chicken, buttermilk biscuits and signature side items. The brand name has a presence in 41 states and 20 countries worldwide. 1999 system sales were $1 billion+.

BACKGROUND: IFA MEMBER
Established: 1972; 1st Franchised: 1976
Franchised Units: 1,419
Company-Owned Units 120
Total Units: 1,539
Dist.: US-945; CAN-12; O'seas-257
North America: 41 States, 2 Provinces
Density: NR
Projected New Units (12 Months): 120
Qualifications: 5, 4, 5, 3, , 3
Registered: All States

FINANCIAL/TERMS:
Cash Investment: $600K
Total Investment: $500K-1.2MM
Minimum Net Worth: $1.2MM
Fees: Franchise - $20K
Royalty - 5%; Ad. - 3%
Earnings Claim Statement: No

Term of Contract (Years): 20/10
Avg. # Of Employees: 15-25 FT
Passive Ownership: Discouraged
Encourage Conversions: Yes
Area Develop. Agreements: Varies
Sub-Franchising Contracts: No
Expand In Territory: Yes
Space Needs: 2,200 SF; FS, SC, RM, Airport, Univer.

SUPPORT & TRAINING PROVIDED:
Financial Assistance Provided: Yes(I)
Site Selection Assistance: Yes
Lease Negotiation Assistance: Yes
Co-Operative Advertising: Yes
Franchisee Assoc./Member: Yes/Yes
Size Of Corporate Staff: NR
On-Going Support: B,C,D,E,F,G,H,I
Training: 4 Weeks Atlanta, GA.

SPECIFIC EXPANSION PLANS:
US: All United States
Canada: All Canada
Overseas: All Countries

<< >>

PORT OF SUBS

5365 Mae Anne Ave., # A-29
Reno, NV 89523
Tel: (800) 245-0245 (775) 747-0555
Fax: (775) 747-1510
E-Mail: ltanaka@portofsubs.com
Web Site: www.portofsubs.com
Ms. Laura Tanaka, Dir. Franchise Development

Port of Subs is an established fast-casual submarine sandwich chain with over 30 years of proven operating systems. Port of Subs specializes in fresh, quality, deli-style products and sandwiches. We serve breakfast, lunch and dinner, and offer catering and special event planning. We offer an assortment of made-to-order submarine type sandwiches, hot sandwiches, salads, pastries, party platters, beverages and other quick service food items for the on-premises consumption or take-out.

BACKGROUND: IFA MEMBER
Established: 1975; 1st Franchised: 1985
Franchised Units: 115
Company-Owned Units 15
Total Units: 130
Dist.: US-130; CAN-0; O'seas-0
North America: 5 States
Density: 66 in NV, 43 in CA, 10 in AZ
Projected New Units (12 Months): 15
Registered: CA,HI,WA

FINANCIAL/TERMS:
Cash Investment: $50-60K
Total Investment: $141.1-219.5K
Minimum Net Worth: $200K
Fees: Franchise - $16K
Royalty - 5.5%; Ad. - 1%
Earnings Claim Statement: No
Term of Contract (Years): 10/10
Avg. # Of Employees: 2-3 FT, 6-7 PT
Passive Ownership: Discouraged
Encourage Conversions: Yes
Area Develop. Agreements: Yes/Varies
Sub-Franchising Contracts: No
Expand In Territory: Yes
Space Needs: 1,200-1,500 SF; SF, SC, Power Center

SUPPORT & TRAINING PROVIDED:
Financial Assistance Provided: Yes(I)
Site Selection Assistance: Yes
Lease Negotiation Assistance: Yes
Co-Operative Advertising: Yes
Franchisee Assoc./Member: Yes
Size Of Corporate Staff: 27
On-Going Support: A,B,C,D,E,F,G,H,I
Training: 3 Weeks Reno, NV.

SPECIFIC EXPANSION PLANS:
US: W, NW, SW
Canada: No
Overseas: No

<< >>

POTTS DOGGIE SHOP

16305 San Carlos Blvd.
Fort Myers, FL 33908
Tel: (941) 466-7747
Fax: (941) 466-1769
Mr. Michael A. Potts, President

Fast food, specializing in hot dogs, Philly steak sandwiches, wings, burgers, etc., open for breakfast, lunch and dinner.

BACKGROUND:
Established: 1971; 1st Franchised: 1985
Franchised Units: 2
Company-Owned Units 4
Total Units: 6
Dist.: US-7; CAN-0; O'seas-0
North America: 3 States
Density: 3 in FL, 3 in PA, 1 in NJ
Projected New Units (12 Months): 3
Qualifications: 5, 4, 4, 4, 4, 4
Registered: FL

FINANCIAL/TERMS:
Cash Investment: $60K
Total Investment: $60K
Minimum Net Worth: $100K
Fees: Franchise - $15K
Royalty - 4%; Ad. - 2%
Earnings Claim Statement: No
Term of Contract (Years): 5/5
Avg. # Of Employees: 4 FT, 5 PT
Passive Ownership: Allowed
Encourage Conversions: N/A
Area Develop. Agreements: Yes/5
Sub-Franchising Contracts: No
Expand In Territory: Yes
Space Needs: 1,400 SF; FS, SF, SC, RM

SUPPORT & TRAINING PROVIDED:
Financial Assistance Provided: No
Site Selection Assistance: Yes
Lease Negotiation Assistance: Yes
Co-Operative Advertising: Yes
Franchisee Assoc./Member: No
Size Of Corporate Staff: 1
On-Going Support: None
Training: 2-3 Weeks Ft. Myers, FL.

SPECIFIC EXPANSION PLANS:
US: Eastern Seaboard
Canada: No
Overseas: No

<< >>

PUDGIE'S FAMOUS CHICKEN

Five Dakota Dr., # 302
Lake Success, NY 11042
Tel: (800) 783-4437 (516) 358-0600
Fax: (516) 358-5076
E-Mail: pudgiestreachers@aol.com
Web Site: www.pudgies.com
Mr. John Ryley, Dir. Franchise Development

Our secret is premium skinless chicken and proprietary breading. 25% less fat and cholesterol . Strong commitment to our franchise owners. Low start-up costs and low rent mean greater profits. Owners receive comprehensive training and extensive operational and marketing support.

BACKGROUND: IFA MEMBER
Established: 1981; 1st Franchised: 1981
Franchised Units: 25
Company-Owned Units 10
Total Units: 35
Dist.: US-24; CAN-0; O'seas-1
North America: 7 States
Density: 14 in NY, 2 in NJ, 2 in CT
Projected New Units (12 Months): 12
Qualifications: 4, 4, 2, 3, 4, 4
Registered: FL,NY,VA,DC

FINANCIAL/TERMS:
Cash Investment: $75-100K

Total Investment: $175-225K
Minimum Net Worth: $250K
Fees: Franchise - $30K
Royalty - 5%; Ad. - 3%
Earnings Claim Statement: No
Term of Contract (Years): 10/10
Avg. # Of Employees: 4 FT, 6 PT
Passive Ownership: Discouraged
Encourage Conversions: Yes
Area Develop. Agreements: Yes
Sub-Franchising Contracts: No
Expand In Territory: Yes
Space Needs: 1,000 SF; SF SC

SUPPORT & TRAINING PROVIDED:
Financial Assistance Provided: Yes(I)
Site Selection Assistance: Yes
Lease Negotiation Assistance: Yes
Co-Operative Advertising: Yes
Franchisee Assoc./Member: Yes/Yes
Size Of Corporate Staff: 200
On-Going Support: A,B,C,D,e,F,G,H,I
Training: 1 Week to 10 Days Long Island, NY.

SPECIFIC EXPANSION PLANS:
US: Northeast, Southeast
Canada: No
Overseas: No

RANCH *1

130 W. 42nd St., 21st Fl.
New York, NY 10036
Tel: (800) 372-6241 (212) 354-8210
Fax: (212) 730-4444
Web Site: www.ranch1.com
Mr. Gary Occhiogrosso, VP Franchising

Up-scale - QSR features - fresh, never-frozen, grilled chicken sandwiches, salads, pasta and wraps.

BACKGROUND:
Established: 1993; 1st Franchised: 1993
Franchised Units: 18
Company-Owned Units 17
Total Units: 35
Dist.: US-35; CAN-0; O'seas-0
North America: 3 States
Density: 32 in NY, 2 in MD, 1 in CA
Projected New Units (12 Months): 25
Qualifications: 4, 4, 5, 1, 3, 4
Registered: All States and AB

FINANCIAL/TERMS:
Cash Investment: $150-200K
Total Investment: $200-350K
Minimum Net Worth: $200K
Fees: Franchise - $40K
Royalty - 5%; Ad. - 3%
Earnings Claim Statement: No
Term of Contract (Years): 15/5
Avg. # Of Employees: 3 FT, 20 PT
Passive Ownership: Discouraged
Encourage Conversions: Yes
Area Develop. Agreements: Yes/3
Sub-Franchising Contracts: No
Expand In Territory: No
Space Needs: 1,500-2,000 SF; FS, SF, SC, RM

SUPPORT & TRAINING PROVIDED:
Financial Assistance Provided: Yes(I)
Site Selection Assistance: Yes
Lease Negotiation Assistance: No
Co-Operative Advertising: Yes
Franchisee Assoc./Member: Yes/Yes
Size Of Corporate Staff: 34
On-Going Support: C,D,E,F,G,H,I
Training: 6 Weeks at New York Ranch *1; 2 Weeks on Site.

SPECIFIC EXPANSION PLANS:
US: All United States
Canada: All Canada
Overseas: Europe, Asia

RENZIOS

4690 S. Yosemite St.
Greenwood Village, CO 80111-1227
Tel: (800) 892-3441 (303) 267-0300
Fax: (303) 267-0088
Web Site: www.renzios.com
Mr. Thomas D. Rentzios, President

You don't have to be Greek to own this unique, fast-service Greek restaurant franchise, operating in a variety of locations such as regional mall food courts, strip centers and gas stations, with future plans in airports and free-standing. RENZIOS fills the gap between fast-food and full-service restaurants. Designed to be easily operated with minimum staff and minimum restaurant experience. Featuring the best all beef or chicken gyros pitas.

BACKGROUND:
Established: 1986; 1st Franchised: 1993
Franchised Units: 9
Company-Owned Units 9
Total Units: 18
Dist.: US-25; CAN-0; O'seas-0
North America: 8 States
Density: 10 in CO, 2 in NV, 4 in TX
Projected New Units (12 Months): 30
Qualifications: 5, 5, 1, 3, 5, 5
Registered: None

FINANCIAL/TERMS:
Cash Investment: $60K
Total Investment: $130-199K
Minimum Net Worth: $100K
Fees: Franchise - $15K
Royalty - 5%; Ad. - 2%
Earnings Claim Statement: No
Term of Contract (Years): 10/5/5
Avg. # Of Employees: 3 FT, 5 PT
Passive Ownership: Discouraged
Encourage Conversions: Yes
Area Develop. Agreements: Yes/10
Sub-Franchising Contracts: No
Expand In Territory: Yes
Space Needs: 500-800 SF; SC, RM

SUPPORT & TRAINING PROVIDED:
Financial Assistance Provided: Yes(I)
Site Selection Assistance: Yes
Lease Negotiation Assistance: Yes
Co-Operative Advertising: Yes
Franchisee Assoc./Member: No
Size Of Corporate Staff: 8
On-Going Support: B,C,D,E,F,G,H,I
Training: 21 Days Corporate Training Center; 5 Days On-Location.

SPECIFIC EXPANSION PLANS:
US: All United States
Canada: All Canada
Overseas: No

RESTAURANT SYSTEMS INTERNATIONAL

1000 South Ave.
Staten Island, NY 10314-3403
Tel: (800) 205-6050 (718) 494-8888
Fax: (718) 494-8776
E-Mail: Treats@restsys.com
Web Site: www.restsys.com
Mr. Larry Feierstein, VP Franchise Development

GREENLEAF'S GRILLE is a perfect combination of healthy menu items presented in a contemporary setting. Featuring grilled chicken and tuna sandwiches and wholesome, made-to-order salads. TREAT STREET was created with the idea of fun foods for the kid in all of us. It consists of mouth-watering, appetizing treats such as frozen yogurt, fruit drinks, smoothies, fresh-made pretzels and more!

BACKGROUND:
Established: 1976; 1st Franchised: 1981
Franchised Units: 239
Company-Owned Units 3
Total Units: 242
Dist.: US-240; CAN-0; O'seas-2

North America: NR
Density: NR
Projected New Units (12 Months): 28
Qualifications: 5, 5, 5, 3, 3, 5
Registered: NY

FINANCIAL/TERMS:

Cash Investment: $50-75K
Total Investment: $120-360K
Minimum Net Worth: $NR
Fees: Franchise - $15-25K
Royalty - 5%; Ad. - 1%
Earnings Claim Statement: No
Term of Contract (Years): 10/10
Avg. # Of Employees: 4 FT, 8 PT
Passive Ownership: NR
Encourage Conversions: NR
Area Develop. Agreements: Yes
Sub-Franchising Contracts: NR
Expand In Territory: Yes
Space Needs: 350-1,200 SF; FS, SC, RM

SUPPORT & TRAINING PROVIDED:

Financial Assistance Provided: Yes(I)
Site Selection Assistance: Yes
Lease Negotiation Assistance: Yes
Co-Operative Advertising: NR
Franchisee Assoc./Member: Yes/Yes
Size Of Corporate Staff: 30
On-Going Support: B,C,D,E,G,H,I
Training: 10 Days per Concept at Staten Island, NY.

SPECIFIC EXPANSION PLANS:

US: All United States
Canada: No
Overseas: All Countries

<< >>

SKYLINE CHILI
4180 Thunderbird Ln.
Fairfield, OH 45014
Tel: (800) 443-4371 (513) 874-1188
Fax: (513) 874-3591
E-Mail: pmlewis@skylinechili.com
Web Site: www.skylinechili.com
Mr. Phil Lewis, VP RE and Franchise

Fast-casual restaurant concept that delivers great Cincinnati style chili in the speed of fast food. Sit down unit with table service that is ideal for owner/operators. Concept has a fanatical following by consumers and is one of the simplest restaurant concepts to run.

BACKGROUND: IFA MEMBER
Established: 1949; 1st Franchised: 1965
Franchised Units: 83
Company-Owned Units 41
Total Units: 124
Dist.: US-124; CAN-0; O'seas-0
North America: 5 States
Density: 94 in OH, 19 in KY, 6 in IN
Projected New Units (12 Months): 12
Qualifications: 5, 4, 4, 3, 4, 5
Registered: FL,IN,MI

FINANCIAL/TERMS:

Cash Investment: $60-200K
Total Investment: $300K-1MM
Minimum Net Worth: $650K
Fees: Franchise - $20K
Royalty - 4%; Ad. - 4%
Earnings Claim Statement: Yes
Term of Contract (Years): 20/20
Avg. # Of Employees: 15 FT, 20 PT
Passive Ownership: Discouraged
Encourage Conversions: Yes
Area Develop. Agreements: Yes/5-10
Sub-Franchising Contracts: No
Expand In Territory: Yes
Space Needs: 2,800 SF; FS, SF, SC, End Cap

SUPPORT & TRAINING PROVIDED:

Financial Assistance Provided: No
Site Selection Assistance: Yes
Lease Negotiation Assistance: Yes
Co-Operative Advertising: Yes
Franchisee Assoc./Member: Yes/No
Size Of Corporate Staff: 40
On-Going Support: a,B,C,D,E,G,I
Training: 6-8 Weeks in Cincinnati, OH.

SPECIFIC EXPANSION PLANS:

US: OH, KY, IN, MI, FL, PA, WV
Canada: No
Overseas: No

<< >>

SMOOTHIE KING
2400 Veterans Blvd., # 110
Kenner, LA 70062
Tel: (800) 577-4200 (504) 467-4006
Fax: (504) 469-1274
E-Mail: mikep@smoothieking.com
Web Site: www.smoothieking.com
Mr. Richard Leveille, Jr., EVP Franchise Development

SMOOTHIE KING is the original nutritional smoothie bar and health marketplace since 1973. Our brand is recognized by Entrepreneur Magazine as being # 1 in our category for 11 consecutive years and has steadily grown to 264 stores. Brand loyalty and recognition, corporate support and innovation are some reasons why SMOOTHIE KING is in the front of the industry.

BACKGROUND: IFA MEMBER
Established: 1973; 1st Franchised: 1989
Franchised Units: 230
Company-Owned Units 1
Total Units: 231
Dist.: US-165; CAN-0; O'seas-0
North America: 10 States
Density: 37 in LA, 28 in TX, 14 in FL
Projected New Units (12 Months): 75
Qualifications: 3, 3, 3, 3, 4, 4
Registered: All States

FINANCIAL/TERMS:

Cash Investment: $40K
Total Investment: $120-220K
Minimum Net Worth: $100K
Fees: Franchise - $20K
Royalty - 5%; Ad. - 1%
Earnings Claim Statement: No
Term of Contract (Years): 10/10
Avg. # Of Employees: 2 FT, 6 PT
Passive Ownership: Discouraged
Encourage Conversions: Yes
Area Develop. Agreements: Yes
Sub-Franchising Contracts: No
Expand In Territory: Yes
Space Needs: 800-1,000 SF; SC

SUPPORT & TRAINING PROVIDED:

Financial Assistance Provided: N/A
Site Selection Assistance: Yes
Lease Negotiation Assistance: Yes
Co-Operative Advertising: No
Franchisee Assoc./Member: No
Size Of Corporate Staff: 16
On-Going Support: C,D,E,F,G,h,I
Training: 7 Days New Orleans, LA.

SPECIFIC EXPANSION PLANS:

US: All United States
Canada: No
Overseas: No

<< >>

Top 50

SONIC DRIVE-IN
101 Park Ave., # 1400
Oklahoma City, OK 73102
Tel: (800) 569-6656 (405) 280-7654

Fax: (405) 290-7478
E-Mail: ttibbits@sonicdrivein.com
Web Site: www.sonicdrivein.com
Mr. David Vernon, VP Franchise Sales

SONIC DRIVE-INS offer made-to-order hamburgers and other sandwiches, and feature signature items, such as extra-long cheese coneys, hand-breaded onion rings, tater tots, fountain favorites, including cherry limeades, slushes and a full ice-cream dessert menu.

BACKGROUND: IFA MEMBER
Established: 1953; 1st Franchised: 1959
Franchised Units: 2,018
Company-Owned Units 405
Total Units: 2,423
Dist.: US-2423; CAN-0; O'seas-0
North America: 30 States
Density: 681 in TX, 221 in OK, 179 TN
Projected New Units (12 Months): 190
Qualifications: 5, 5, 5, 2, 2, 4
Registered: CA,FL,IN,OR,VA,WA,DC

FINANCIAL/TERMS:
Cash Investment: $300K
Total Investment: $500K-1.0MM
Minimum Net Worth: $1MM
Fees: Franchise - $30K
Royalty - 1-5%; Ad. - 4%
Earnings Claim Statement: No
Term of Contract (Years): 20/10
Avg. # Of Employees: 35 FT
Passive Ownership: Not Allowed
Encourage Conversions: No
Area Develop. Agreements: Yes/Varies
Sub-Franchising Contracts: No
Expand In Territory: Yes
Space Needs: 1,450 SF; FS

SUPPORT & TRAINING PROVIDED:
Financial Assistance Provided: Yes(I)
Site Selection Assistance: Yes
Lease Negotiation Assistance: Yes
Co-Operative Advertising: Yes
Franchisee Assoc./Member: Yes/Yes
Size Of Corporate Staff: 210
On-Going Support: B,C,D,E,F,G,H,I
Training: 1 Week Oklahoma City, OK; 11 Weeks at Local Market.

SPECIFIC EXPANSION PLANS:
US: SW, SE, West, Midwest
Canada: No
Overseas: Mexico

<< >>

STEAK ESCAPE
222 Neilston St.
Columbus, OH 43215
Tel: (866) 247-8325 (614) 224-0300
Fax: (614) 224-6460
E-Mail: lallen@steakescape.com
Web Site: www.steakescape.com
Mr. Shane Pratt, VP Fran. Dev.

STEAK ESCAPE prides itself on serving delicious grilled sandwiches, freshly-cut fries and freshly-squeezed lemonade. All of these items are created from fresh ingredients and are prepared in full view of customers using our own unique method of exhibition-style cooking. STEAK ESCAPE's signature item is The Genuine Philadelphia Cheesesteak Sandwich. Today we have opportunities available in free-standing locations, strip center locations and in mall locations!

BACKGROUND:
Established: 1982; 1st Franchised: 1983
Franchised Units: 165
Company-Owned Units 0
Total Units: 165
Dist.: US-166; CAN-0; O'seas-1
North America: 35 States
Density: 18 un CA, 16 in CO, 14 in OH
Projected New Units (12 Months): 40-45
Qualifications: 4, 4, 3, 1, 3, 4
Registered: All States

FINANCIAL/TERMS:
Cash Investment: $70-250K
Total Investment: $180-1.25MM
Minimum Net Worth: $100K
Fees: Franchise - $25K
Royalty - 6-5%; Ad. - 0.5%
Earnings Claim Statement: No
Term of Contract (Years): 20/Varies
Avg. # Of Employees: 4 FT, 12 PT
Passive Ownership: Allowed
Encourage Conversions: Yes
Area Develop. Agreements: Yes
Sub-Franchising Contracts: Yes
Expand In Territory: Yes
Space Needs: 300-2,400 SF; FS, SF, SC, RM

SUPPORT & TRAINING PROVIDED:
Financial Assistance Provided: Yes(I)
Site Selection Assistance: Yes
Lease Negotiation Assistance: Yes
Co-Operative Advertising: Yes
Franchisee Assoc./Member: Yes/Yes
Size Of Corporate Staff: 28
On-Going Support: A,B,C,D,e,F,G,H,I
Training: 3 Weeks in Colombus, OH.

SPECIFIC EXPANSION PLANS:
US: All United States
Canada: All Canada
Overseas: Western Hemisphere

<< >>

STUFT PIZZA
1040 Calle Cordillera, # 103
San Clemente, CA 92673
Tel: (949) 361-2522
Fax: (949) 361-2501
E-Mail: jbertstuft@aol.com
Web Site: www.stuftpizza.com
Mr. Jack S. Bertram, President

Take-outs to full service with pasta and micro-brewery.

BACKGROUND:
Established: 1976; 1st Franchised: 1985
Franchised Units: 26
Company-Owned Units 1
Total Units: 27
Dist.: US-27; CAN-0; O'seas-0
North America: 2 States
Density: 26 in CA, 1 in OR
Projected New Units (12 Months): 5
Qualifications: 4, 3, 2, 3, 3, 4
Registered: CA,OR

FINANCIAL/TERMS:
Cash Investment: $75-150K
Total Investment: $150-750K
Minimum Net Worth: $250K
Fees: Franchise - $25K
Royalty - 3%; Ad. - 0%
Earnings Claim Statement: No
Term of Contract (Years): 10/10
Avg. # Of Employees: 3 FT, 8+ PT
Passive Ownership: Discouraged
Encourage Conversions: Yes
Area Develop. Agreements: Yes
Sub-Franchising Contracts: Yes
Expand In Territory: Yes
Space Needs: 1,800+ SF; FS, SF, SC, RM

SUPPORT & TRAINING PROVIDED:
Financial Assistance Provided: N/A
Site Selection Assistance: Yes
Lease Negotiation Assistance: Yes
Co-Operative Advertising: No
Franchisee Assoc./Member: No
Size Of Corporate Staff: 4
On-Going Support: C,D,E,G,H
Training: 2 Weeks San Clemente, CA.

SPECIFIC EXPANSION PLANS:
US: West
Canada: No
Overseas: No

<< >>

SUB STATION II
425 N. Main St.
Sumter, SC 29150

Tel: (800) 779-2970 (803) 773-4711
Fax: (803) 775-2220
Web Site: www.substationii.com
Ms. Susan H. Vaden, Vice President

SUB STATION II is a chain of submarine sandwich franchises. We currently have 90 stores located in 9 states. Our sandwich shops offer a variety of over 25 submarine sandwiches, along with specialty sandwiches and salads. We have developed an efficient method of preparing each sandwich to the customer's specifications. The emphasis is on high-quality food and cleanliness. We provide our franchisee's with training and on-going support, layout, etc.

BACKGROUND:
Established: 1975; 1st Franchised: 1976
Franchised Units: 82
Company-Owned Units 2
Total Units: 84
Dist.: US-90; CAN-0; O'seas-0
North America: 9 States
Density: 40 in SC, 20 in NC, 15 in CA
Projected New Units (12 Months): 15
Qualifications: 5, 4, 2, 3, 2, 4
Registered: CA,FL,VA

FINANCIAL/TERMS:
Cash Investment: $40-70K
Total Investment: $75-150K
Minimum Net Worth: $200K
Fees: Franchise - $10.5K
Royalty - 4%; Ad. - 2%
Earnings Claim Statement: No
Term of Contract (Years): 10/10
Avg. # Of Employees: 4 FT, 8 PT
Passive Ownership: Allowed
Encourage Conversions: Yes
Area Develop. Agreements: No
Sub-Franchising Contracts: Yes
Expand In Territory: Yes
Space Needs: 1,500 SF; FS, SF, SC, RM

SUPPORT & TRAINING PROVIDED:
Financial Assistance Provided: Yes(I)
Site Selection Assistance: Yes
Lease Negotiation Assistance: Yes
Co-Operative Advertising: Yes
Franchisee Assoc./Member: No
Size Of Corporate Staff: 8
On-Going Support: B,C,D,E,G,h
Training: 7-10 Days Corporate Store; 7-10 Days Franchisee Location.

SPECIFIC EXPANSION PLANS:
US: Southeast, Southern Calif.
Canada: No
Overseas: No

<< >>

SUBMARINA
10225 Barnes Canyon Rd., # A-202
San Diego, CA 92121
Tel: (877) 714-SUBS (858) 784-0760
Fax: (858) 784-0765
Web Site: www.submarina.com
Mr. Jeffrey Warfield, President

SUBMARINA is the quality alternative to the national sub shop franchises. We combine the unique attributes of a back-East deli and the speed and convenience of a quick-serve restaurant. Our menu is filled with an ample variety of hot and cold subs and deli sandwiches containing the uncommon, such as prosciutto and capacolla, and the popular, turkey and avocado. Sliced to order and served in made-from-scratch bakery breads and rolls, with the customer's choice of 11 different toppings.

BACKGROUND:
Established: 1977; 1st Franchised: 1988
Franchised Units: 36
Company-Owned Units 3
Total Units: 39
Dist.: US-39; CAN-0; O'seas-0
North America: 2 States
Density: 38 in CA, 1 in NV
Projected New Units (12 Months): 12
Qualifications: 3, 4, 1, 3, 3, 5
Registered: CA

FINANCIAL/TERMS:
Cash Investment: $25-50K
Total Investment: $140-200K
Minimum Net Worth: $200K
Fees: Franchise - $20K
Royalty - 6%; Ad. - 2%
Earnings Claim Statement: Yes
Term of Contract (Years): 10/10
Avg. # Of Employees: 1 FT, 6 PT
Passive Ownership: Not Allowed
Encourage Conversions: Yes
Area Develop. Agreements: Yes/10
Sub-Franchising Contracts: No
Expand In Territory: Yes
Space Needs: 1,200 SF; FS, SF, SC, RM

SUPPORT & TRAINING PROVIDED:
Financial Assistance Provided: Yes(I)
Site Selection Assistance: Yes
Lease Negotiation Assistance: Yes
Co-Operative Advertising: Yes
Franchisee Assoc./Member: No
Size Of Corporate Staff: 10
On-Going Support: A,B,C,D,E,F,G,H
Training: 2 Weeks Corporate Office/Training Store; 2 Weeks Their Store.

SPECIFIC EXPANSION PLANS:
US: Southern CA, AZ, NV
Canada: No
Overseas: No

<< >>

SUBWAY RESTAURANTS
325 Bic Dr.
Milford, CT 06460-3072
Tel: (800) 888-4848 (203) 877-4281
Fax: (203) 783-7325
E-Mail: franchise@subway.com
Web Site: www.subway.com
Franchise Sales

For more than 37 years, SUBWAY RESTAURANTS has been offering entrepreneurs a chance to build and succeed in their own business through a proven, well-structured sandwich franchise. In 2002, Entrepreneur Magazine again chose SUBWAY as the overall number one franchise in all categories, making that 10 our of the past 14 years. With more than 16,000 independently-owned locations in 74 countries, SUBWAY continues to inspire partnerships worldwide.

BACKGROUND: IFA MEMBER
Established: 1965; 1st Franchised: 1974
Franchised Units: 16,356
Company-Owned Units 1
Total Units: 16,357
Dist.:US-13,467; CAN-1,568; O'seas-1198
North America: All States & Provinces
Density: CA, TX, FL
Projected New Units (12 Months): 1,000+
Qualifications: 5, 4, 3, 4, 3, 3
Registered: All States

FINANCIAL/TERMS:
Cash Investment: $NR
Total Investment: $65-183.7K
Minimum Net Worth: $NR
Fees: Franchise - $10K
Royalty - 8%; Ad. - 3.5%
Earnings Claim Statement: No
Term of Contract (Years): 20/20
Avg. # Of Employees: 2-3 FT, 6-10 PT
Passive Ownership: Not Allowed
Encourage Conversions: N/A
Area Develop. Agreements: Yes/20
Sub-Franchising Contracts: No

Expand In Territory: Yes
Space Needs: 300-2,000 SF; FS, SF, SC, RM, C-Store

SUPPORT & TRAINING PROVIDED:
Financial Assistance Provided: Yes(D)
Site Selection Assistance: Yes
Lease Negotiation Assistance: Yes
Co-Operative Advertising: No
Franchisee Assoc./Member: Yes/Yes
Size Of Corporate Staff: 600
On-Going Support: A,B,C,D,E,F,G,H,I
Training: 2 Weeks in Milford, CT; (Foreign Training in Costa Rica, Australia or China).

SPECIFIC EXPANSION PLANS:
US: All United States
Canada: All Canada
Overseas: All Countries

<< >>

TACO BELL

17901 Von Karman Ave.
Irvine, CA 926146253
Tel: (949) 863-3807
Fax: (949) 863-4793
E-Mail: frecruit@tacobell.com
Web Site: www.tacobell.com
Ms. Sherene Lewis, Mgr. Franchise Recruiting

TACO BELL has been the world's largest Mexican quick-service franchise for the past 38 years.

BACKGROUND: IFA MEMBER
Established: 1962; 1st Franchised: 1964
Franchised Units: 4,600
Company-Owned Units 3,044
Total Units: 7,644
Dist.: US-1597; CAN-600; O'seas-5447
North America: 50 States
Density: 232 in CA, 151 in OH, 150 FL
Projected New Units (12 Months): NR
Registered: All States

FINANCIAL/TERMS:
Cash Investment: $NR
Total Investment: $236-503K
Minimum Net Worth: $NR
Fees: Franchise - $45K
Royalty - 5.5%; Ad. - 4.5%
Earnings Claim Statement: No
Term of Contract (Years): 20
Avg. # Of Employees: NR
Passive Ownership: Allowed
Encourage Conversions: NR
Area Develop. Agreements: Yes
Sub-Franchising Contracts: No
Expand In Territory: Yes
Space Needs: NR SF; FS, SF, RM, Other

SUPPORT & TRAINING PROVIDED:
Financial Assistance Provided: Yes
Site Selection Assistance: Yes
Lease Negotiation Assistance: Yes
Co-Operative Advertising: Yes
Franchisee Assoc./Member: NR
Size Of Corporate Staff: NR
On-Going Support: NR
Training: 18 Weeks at Approved Training Restaurant.

SPECIFIC EXPANSION PLANS:
US: All United States
Canada: All Canada
Overseas: All Countries

<< >>

TACO JOHN'S INTERNATIONAL

808 W. 20th St.
Cheyenne, WY 82001
Tel: (800) 854-0819 (307) 635-0101
Fax: (307) 772-0369
E-Mail: gvanhorn@tacojohns.com
Web Site: www.tacojohns.com
Mr. Gene Van Horne, Chief Operating Officer

Mexican fast-food restaurant franchisor.

BACKGROUND: IFA MEMBER
Established: 1969; 1st Franchised: 1969
Franchised Units: 415
Company-Owned Units 11
Total Units: 426
Dist.: US-426; CAN-0; O'seas-0
North America: 29 States
Density: 66 in MN, 62 in IA, 38 in SD
Projected New Units (12 Months): 30
Qualifications: 4, 5, 3, 3, 1, 5
Registered: All States Except DC

FINANCIAL/TERMS:
Cash Investment: $50-200K
Total Investment: $440-673K
Minimum Net Worth: $100-250K
Fees: Franchise - $15-22.5K
Royalty - 4%; Ad. - 3.5%
Earnings Claim Statement: No
Term of Contract (Years): 20/10
Avg. # Of Employees: 15-25
Passive Ownership: Discouraged
Encourage Conversions: Yes
Area Develop. Agreements: Yes/Varies
Sub-Franchising Contracts: No
Expand In Territory: Yes
Space Needs: 1,200-1,600 SF; FS, SC, RM

SUPPORT & TRAINING PROVIDED:
Financial Assistance Provided: No
Site Selection Assistance: No
Lease Negotiation Assistance: Yes
Co-Operative Advertising: Yes
Franchisee Assoc./Member: Yes/No
Size Of Corporate Staff: 60
On-Going Support: B,C,D,E,G,H,I
Training: 4 Weeks Cheyenne, Wyoming.

SPECIFIC EXPANSION PLANS:
US: Upper Midwest, Central US
Canada: No
Overseas: No

TACO MAKER, THE

4605 Harrison Blvd., 3rd Fl.
Ogden, UT 84403
Tel: (800) 207-5804 (801) 476-9780
Fax: (801) 476-9788
E-Mail: ttm@tacomaker.com
Web Site: www.tacomaker.com
Mr. Corey King, Dir. Franchise Licensing

International Mexican fast-food franchise, specializing in fast, friendly service and a complete menu with made-from-scratch and fresh ingredients. Centralized purchasing, corporate marketing and promotional support and progressive store design provide for the most comprehensive and fun investment opportunity. Available in free-standing, mall or strip center locations and also convenience stores, truck stops and co-branding opportunities.

BACKGROUND:
Established: 1978; 1st Franchised: 1978
Franchised Units: 129
Company-Owned Units 3
Total Units: 132
Dist.: US-84; CAN-0; O'seas-73
North America: 32 States
Density: 13 in UT, 10 in WA, 5 in NY
Projected New Units (12 Months): 50
Qualifications: 4, 4, 5, 2, 4, 4

Registered: All States

FINANCIAL/TERMS:

Cash Investment: $20-140K
Total Investment: $75-650K
Minimum Net Worth: $NR
Fees: Franchise - $5-22.5K
Royalty - 5-7%; Ad. - 3%
Earnings Claim Statement: No
Term of Contract (Years): 15/15
Avg. # Of Employees: 2-6 FT, 5-20 PT
Passive Ownership: Discouraged
Encourage Conversions: Yes
Area Develop. Agreements: Yes/15
Sub-Franchising Contracts: Yes
Expand In Territory: Yes
Space Needs: 200-3,000 SF; FS

SUPPORT & TRAINING PROVIDED:

Financial Assistance Provided: Yes(I)
Site Selection Assistance: Yes
Lease Negotiation Assistance: Yes
Co-Operative Advertising: Yes
Franchisee Assoc./Member: No
Size Of Corporate Staff: 30
On-Going Support: B,C,D,E,F,I
Training: 12-15 Days UT.

SPECIFIC EXPANSION PLANS:

US: All United States
Canada: All Canada
Overseas: All Countries

<< >>

TACO MAYO

10405 Greenbriar Pl.
Oklahoma City, OK 73159
Tel: (405) 691-8226
Fax: (405) 691-2572
E-Mail: franchising@tacomayo.com
Web Site: www.tacomayo.com
Ms. Debbie Jackson, Qualification Specialist

Southwest-based, privately-held chain of quick-service restaurants, serving Tex-Mex favorites, including tacos, nachos, salads, burritos, etc. Over 100 restaurants in 8 states, with active advertising co-ops, centralized purchasing, distribution, training and field service representatives. Free-standing limits (conversion and remodeled) feature drive-thru and dining room seating.

BACKGROUND:

Established: 1978; 1st Franchised: 1980
Franchised Units: 69
Company-Owned Units 34
Total Units: 103
Dist.: US-103; CAN-0; O'seas-0
North America: 8 States
Density: 86 in OK, 9 in TX, 3 in KS
Projected New Units (12 Months): 18
Qualifications: 5, 4, 2, 3, 5, 5
Registered: NR

FINANCIAL/TERMS:

Cash Investment: $80K
Total Investment: $99-499K
Minimum Net Worth: $200K
Fees: Franchise - $15K
Royalty - 4%; Ad. - 3%
Earnings Claim Statement: No
Term of Contract (Years): 10/10
Avg. # Of Employees: 5 FT, 16 PT
Passive Ownership: Not Allowed
Encourage Conversions: Yes
Area Develop. Agreements: Yes/10
Sub-Franchising Contracts: No
Expand In Territory: Yes
Space Needs: 900-2,200 SF; FS

SUPPORT & TRAINING PROVIDED:

Financial Assistance Provided: Yes(I)
Site Selection Assistance: Yes
Lease Negotiation Assistance: Yes
Co-Operative Advertising: Yes
Franchisee Assoc./Member: Yes/Yes
Size Of Corporate Staff: 23
On-Going Support: a,B,C,D,E,G,H
Training: 3 Weeks at Store in Tulsa or Oklahoma City, OK; 2 Weeks at Franchise Store.

SPECIFIC EXPANSION PLANS:

US: OK, KS, AR, MO, LA, N.TX
Canada: No
Overseas: No

<< >>

TACO PALACE

814 E. Hwy. 60, P.O. Box 87
Monett, MO 65708
Tel: (417) 235-6595
Fax: (810) 958-5991
E-Mail: larry@tacopalace.com
Web Site: www.tacopalace.com
Mr. Larry Faria, President

Our concept is targeted at people that normally could not afford the cost and expense that other franchises require. Our low overhead concept translates to more profit to the franchisee. We offer more flexibility. Fresh Tex-Mex food at "down to earth" prices!

BACKGROUND:

Established: 1985; 1st Franchised: 1999
Franchised Units: 5
Company-Owned Units 2
Total Units: 7
Dist.: US-0; CAN-0; O'seas-0
North America: 3 States
Density: 10 in MO, 2 in KS
Projected New Units (12 Months): NR
Registered: NR

FINANCIAL/TERMS:

Cash Investment: $65K
Total Investment: $75K
Minimum Net Worth: $50-65K
Fees: Franchise - $0
Royalty - 0; Ad. - 0%
Earnings Claim Statement: Yes
Term of Contract (Years): N/A
Avg. # Of Employees: 8 FT, 2 PT
Passive Ownership: Allowed
Encourage Conversions: NR
Area Develop. Agreements: Yes
Sub-Franchising Contracts: Yes
Expand In Territory: Yes
Space Needs: 1,000+ SF; FS, SF, SC, RM

SUPPORT & TRAINING PROVIDED:

Financial Assistance Provided: NR
Site Selection Assistance: No
Lease Negotiation Assistance: Yes
Co-Operative Advertising: No
Franchisee Assoc./Member: No/No
Size Of Corporate Staff: 4
On-Going Support: C,D,E,F
Training: Unlimited Days in Monett, MO; 21 Days with Trainers at Franchisee's Location.

SPECIFIC EXPANSION PLANS:

US: All United States
Canada: NR
Overseas: NR

<< >>

TacoTime®

Top 50

TACO TIME INTERNATIONAL

3880 W. 11th Ave.
Eugene, OR 97402
Tel: (800) 547-8907 (541) 687-8222
Fax: (541) 343-5208
E-Mail: bobn@tacotime.com
Web Site: www.tacotime.com
Ms. Lisa Ross, Dir. Fran. Dev.

TACO TIME continues to provide and improve our system for quick-service Mexican restaurants that have stood the test of time for 40 years. TACO TIME quality, focus on customer service, franchisee support and existing new products make us the innovative leader of high-quality Mexican food.

BACKGROUND:
Established: 1959; 1st Franchised: 1960
Franchised Units: 311
Company-Owned Units 4
Total Units: 315
Dist.: US-194; CAN-112; O'seas-9
North America: 14 States, 7 Provinces
Density: 74 in OR, 42 in UT, 34 in BC
Projected New Units (12 Months): 20
Qualifications: 5, 4, 3, 4, 5, 5
Registered: All States Except MD,RI,AB

FINANCIAL/TERMS:
Cash Investment: $100K
Total Investment: $150-200K
Minimum Net Worth: $300K
Fees: Franchise - $25K
Royalty - 5%; Ad. - 4%
Earnings Claim Statement: No
Term of Contract (Years): 15/10
Avg. # Of Employees: 2-3 FT, 15-20 PT
Passive Ownership: Not Allowed
Encourage Conversions: Yes
Area Develop. Agreements: Yes
Sub-Franchising Contracts: Yes
Expand In Territory: Yes
Space Needs: 1,500-2,160 SF; FS, RM

SUPPORT & TRAINING PROVIDED:
Financial Assistance Provided: No
Site Selection Assistance: Yes
Lease Negotiation Assistance: Yes
Co-Operative Advertising: Yes
Franchisee Assoc./Member: Yes/Yes
Size Of Corporate Staff: 25
On-Going Support: B,C,D,E,F,G,h,I
Training: Up to 6 Weeks at Corporate Office.

SPECIFIC EXPANSION PLANS:
US: All United States
Canada: Western Province
Overseas:
Master Licensing Agreement -- Asia

TACO VILLA

3710 Chesswood Dr., # 220
North York, ON M3J 2W4 CANADA
Tel: (800) 608-8226 (416) 636-9348
Fax: (416) 636-9162
Ms. Wendy J. MacKinnon, Fran. Director

TACO VILLA is a quick-service Mexican-food concept. With over 16 years' experience, we offer franchisees a dynamic design concept, full turn-key operation, proven menu and procedures, full training and marketing. We provide today's consumer with a high-quality, high-value food experience. TACO VILLA continues to expand.

BACKGROUND:
Established: 1983; 1st Franchised: 1985
Franchised Units: 20
Company-Owned Units 1
Total Units: 21
Dist.: US-0; CAN-21; O'seas-0
North America: 1 Province
Density: 21 in ON
Projected New Units (12 Months): 10-15
Qualifications: 5, 3, 2, 3, 4, 4
Registered: NR

FINANCIAL/TERMS:
Cash Investment: $40-50K
Total Investment: $140-150K
Minimum Net Worth: $150K
Fees: Franchise - $20K
Royalty - 6%; Ad. - 2%
Earnings Claim Statement: No
Term of Contract (Years): 10/10
Avg. # Of Employees: 3 FT, 5 PT
Passive Ownership: Not Allowed
Encourage Conversions: Yes
Area Develop. Agreements: No
Sub-Franchising Contracts: Yes
Expand In Territory: Yes
Space Needs: 350-400 SF; RM

SUPPORT & TRAINING PROVIDED:
Financial Assistance Provided: Yes(I)
Site Selection Assistance: Yes
Lease Negotiation Assistance: Yes
Co-Operative Advertising: Yes
Franchisee Assoc./Member: NR
Size Of Corporate Staff: 7
On-Going Support: A,B,C,D,E,G,I
Training: 1 Week Head Office; 3 Weeks In Store.

SPECIFIC EXPANSION PLANS:
US: Eastern Seaboard, New Eng.
Canada: All Canada
Overseas: No

TACONE WRAPS

4801 Wilshire, # 280
Los Angeles, CA 90010
Tel: (877) 482-2663 (310) 574-8177
Fax: (310) 574-8179
E-Mail: craig@tacone.com
Web Site: www.tacone.com
Mr. Craig Albert, President

Franchisor of quick-service restaurants serving fresh soups, sandwiches, salads, smoothies and catering.

BACKGROUND:
Established: 1995; 1st Franchised: 1998
Franchised Units: 8
Company-Owned Units 9
Total Units: 17
Dist.: US-0; CAN-0; O'seas-0
North America: 6 States
Density: 9 in CA, 2 in MA, 1 in NJ
Projected New Units (12 Months): NR
Registered: NR

FINANCIAL/TERMS:
Cash Investment: $50K
Total Investment: $125-300K
Minimum Net Worth: $100K
Fees: Franchise - $25K
Royalty - 6%/3K/Mo.; Ad. - 2%
Earnings Claim Statement: Yes
Term of Contract (Years): 10
Avg. # Of Employees: 1 FT, 5-7 PT
Passive Ownership: Discouraged
Encourage Conversions: NR
Area Develop. Agreements: Yes/10
Sub-Franchising Contracts: Yes
Expand In Territory: No
Space Needs: 400-1,500 SF; SF, SC, RM

SUPPORT & TRAINING PROVIDED:
Financial Assistance Provided: NR
Site Selection Assistance: Yes
Lease Negotiation Assistance: Yes
Co-Operative Advertising: Yes
Franchisee Assoc./Member: No
Size Of Corporate Staff: 10
On-Going Support: A,B,C,D,E,F,G,H,I
Training: 6 Weeks Los Angeles, CA.

SPECIFIC EXPANSION PLANS:
US: All United States
Canada: NR
Overseas: NR

TASTEE-FREEZ

48380 Van Dyke Ave.
Utica, MI 48317
Tel: (810) 739-5520
Fax: (810) 739-8351
E-Mail: tfiint@aol.com
Web Site: www.tastee-freez.com
Mr. Bob Lerash, Dir. Operations/Dev.

Restaurant franchise with the flexibility to offer a full menu from chicken, burgers and fries plus hand-dipped and soft serve ice cream treats to offering a very streamlined soft serve treats-only menu for a co-brand or limited space location.

BACKGROUND: IFA MEMBER
Established: 1950; 1st Franchised: 1950
Franchised Units: 250
Company-Owned Units 0
Total Units: 250
Dist.: US-253; CAN-0; O'seas-7
North America: NR
Density: NR
Projected New Units (12 Months): 40-50
Qualifications: 3, 3, 3, 3, 3, 3
Registered: CA,FL,IN,MD,MI,MN,ND, VA,WI

FINANCIAL/TERMS:
Cash Investment: $20-250K
Total Investment: $30K-1MM
Minimum Net Worth: $N/A
Fees: Franchise - $5-15K
Royalty - 4-5%; Ad. - 1%
Earnings Claim Statement: No
Term of Contract (Years): 10/10
Avg. # Of Employees: Varies
Passive Ownership: Discouraged
Encourage Conversions: Yes
Area Develop. Agreements: N/A
Sub-Franchising Contracts: N/A
Expand In Territory: Possible
Space Needs: NR SF; FS, SF, SC, Co-Brand

SUPPORT & TRAINING PROVIDED:
Financial Assistance Provided: No
Site Selection Assistance: No
Lease Negotiation Assistance: No
Co-Operative Advertising: No
Franchisee Assoc./Member: No
Size Of Corporate Staff: 7
On-Going Support: B,C,D,E,F,G,H
Training: Varies.

SPECIFIC EXPANSION PLANS:
US: All United States
Canada: No
Overseas: No

<< >>

THUNDERCLOUD SUBS

1102 W. 6th St.
Austin, TX 78703
Tel: (800) 256-7895 (512) 479-8805
Fax: (512) 479-8806
E-Mail: thunder@onr.com
Web Site: www.ThunderCloud.com
Mr. David E. Cohen, Dir. Franchising

Fresh, fast and healthy sub sandwiches, salads, soup, etc. in a casual atmosphere without the fast-food look. A distinctive trademark, system and product, each store having a unique decor that ties in to the local community. Definitely not a cookie cutter franchise. We train our people to capture the essence of the THUNDERCLOUD experience. The customer service and atmosphere play a large part in overall customer satisfaction. We offer a great value.

BACKGROUND:
Established: 1975; 1st Franchised: 1989
Franchised Units: 30
Company-Owned Units 8
Total Units: 38
Dist.: US-38; CAN-0; O'seas-0
North America: 2 States
Density: 37 in TX
Projected New Units (12 Months): 8-12
Qualifications: 4, 4, 3, 3, 4, 5
Registered: NR

FINANCIAL/TERMS:
Cash Investment: $25-50K
Total Investment: $60-100K
Minimum Net Worth: $100K
Fees: Franchise - $10K
Royalty - 4%; Ad. - Varies
Earnings Claim Statement: No
Term of Contract (Years): 10+8/4/4
Avg. # Of Employees: 2 FT, 6-12 PT
Passive Ownership: Discouraged
Encourage Conversions: Yes
Area Develop. Agreements: Yes/Varies
Sub-Franchising Contracts: No
Expand In Territory: Yes
Space Needs: 1,000-1,500 SF; FS, SF, SC

SUPPORT & TRAINING PROVIDED:
Financial Assistance Provided: No
Site Selection Assistance: Yes
Lease Negotiation Assistance: Yes
Co-Operative Advertising: N/A
Franchisee Assoc./Member: No
Size Of Corporate Staff: 5
On-Going Support: C,D,E,F,G,h,I
Training: 1-2 Weeks at Corporate Headquarters in Austin, TX; 5-10 Days at Franchisee's Store.

SPECIFIC EXPANSION PLANS:
US: Primarily Southwest
Canada: No
Overseas: No

<< >>

TIPPY'S TACO HOUSE

5025 Falcon Hollow
McKinney, TX 75070
Tel: (972) 547-0888
Fax: (972) 547-0888
Mr. W. L. (Jack) Locklier, Owner

Excellent Tex-Mex food. Eat-in/take-out/drive-thru/delivery. Chuckwagon chili enchiladas, tacos, burritos, wraps of all kinds, armadillo eggs, chimichongos, nachos, fried jalapenos, tortilla soup, quesadillas and guacamole.

BACKGROUND:
Established: 1958; 1st Franchised: 1968
Franchised Units: 15
Company-Owned Units 0
Total Units: 15
Dist.: US-15; CAN-0; O'seas-0
North America: 5 States
Density: VA, NC
Projected New Units (12 Months): NR
Qualifications: 1, 3, 2, 2, 5, 5
Registered: NR

FINANCIAL/TERMS:
Cash Investment: $20% of Total
Total Investment: $150K+
Minimum Net Worth: $150K
Fees: Franchise - $20K
Royalty - 3%; Ad. - 0.03%
Earnings Claim Statement: No
Term of Contract (Years): 20/20
Avg. # Of Employees: 5 FT, 3 PT
Passive Ownership: Discouraged
Encourage Conversions: Yes
Area Develop. Agreements: Yes/Varies
Sub-Franchising Contracts: Yes
Expand In Territory: Yes
Space Needs: 1,500-2,000 SF; FS, SF, SC

SUPPORT & TRAINING PROVIDED:
Financial Assistance Provided: No
Site Selection Assistance: Yes
Lease Negotiation Assistance: Yes
Co-Operative Advertising: No
Franchisee Assoc./Member: No
Size Of Corporate Staff: 2
On-Going Support: B,D,E,F,G,H
Training: 1 Week at Closest Approved Unit.

SPECIFIC EXPANSION PLANS:
US: Southwest, Southeast, North
Canada: No
Overseas: No

<< >>

TOGO'S EATERY

14 Pacella Park Dr.
Randolph, MA 02368
Tel: (888) 777-9983 (781) 961-4020
Fax: (781) 961-4207

Web Site: www.dunkin-baskin-togos.com
Mr. Anthony Padulo, VP Business Dev.

As part of Allied Domecq's team of international franchise leaders, TOGO'S joins BASKIN-ROBBINS and DUNKIN' DONUTS in franchising for the future - multi-branding. Allied Domecq's strategic plan includes territorial development.

BACKGROUND: IFA MEMBER
Established: 1971; 1st Franchised: 1977
Franchised Units: 399
Company-Owned Units 0
Total Units: 399
Dist.: US-0; CAN-1; O'seas-0
North America: 1 Province
Density: 1 in BC
Projected New Units (12 Months): 12
Qualifications: 5, 5, 4, 4, 4, 5
Registered: NR

FINANCIAL/TERMS:
Cash Investment: $125-150K
Total Investment: $225-250K
Minimum Net Worth: $500K
Fees: Franchise - $25K
Royalty - 5%; Ad. - 5%
Earnings Claim Statement: No
Term of Contract (Years): 10/10
Avg. # Of Employees: 4 FT, 8 PT
Passive Ownership: Discouraged
Encourage Conversions: No
Area Develop. Agreements: Yes/3
Sub-Franchising Contracts: No
Expand In Territory: No
Space Needs: 1,400-4,400 SF; FS, SF, SC, RM

SUPPORT & TRAINING PROVIDED:
Financial Assistance Provided: No
Site Selection Assistance: Yes
Lease Negotiation Assistance: Yes
Co-Operative Advertising: No
Franchisee Assoc./Member: Yes/Yes
Size Of Corporate Staff: 30
On-Going Support: B,C,d,E,G,H,I
Training: 4 Weeks CA.

SPECIFIC EXPANSION PLANS:
US: No
Canada: BC, ON, PQ
Overseas: No

<< >>

TUBBY'S SUB SHOPS

43191 Dalcoma Dr., # 6
Clinton Township, MI 48038-6308
Tel: (800) 752-0644 (810) 416-1900
Fax: (810) 416-1639
E-Mail: dan@tubby.com
Web Site: www.tubby.com
Mr. Dan Kauble, Franchising

We serve a variety of cold and grilled-to-perfection submarine sandwiches, using only the finest ingredients. We also offer a wide selection of side items, including soups, salads and desserts. TUBBY'S offers many different concepts - each of which easily adapts to any location. Area development territories are available.

BACKGROUND: IFA MEMBER
Established: 1968; 1st Franchised: 1978
Franchised Units: 94
Company-Owned Units 3
Total Units: 97
Dist.: US-97; CAN-0; O'seas-0
North America: 4 States
Density: 80 in MI, 4 in OH, 3 in NJ
Projected New Units (12 Months): 36
Qualifications: 5, 5, 2, 2, 3, 5
Registered: All States

FINANCIAL/TERMS:
Cash Investment: $25-50K
Total Investment: $110-300K
Minimum Net Worth: $150K
Fees: Franchise - $8-15K
Royalty - 4-6%; Ad. - 1%
Earnings Claim Statement: No
Term of Contract (Years): 10/10
Avg. # Of Employees: 2 FT, 3 PT
Passive Ownership: Discouraged
Encourage Conversions: Yes
Area Develop. Agreements: Yes
Sub-Franchising Contracts: Yes
Expand In Territory: Yes
Space Needs: 600-1,200 SF; FS, SF, SC, RM, C-Store

SUPPORT & TRAINING PROVIDED:
Financial Assistance Provided: Yes(I)
Site Selection Assistance: Yes
Lease Negotiation Assistance: Yes
Co-Operative Advertising: Yes
Franchisee Assoc./Member: No
Size Of Corporate Staff: 13
On-Going Support: C,D,E,G,H,I
Training: 3 Weeks Headquarters and Training Store.

SPECIFIC EXPANSION PLANS:
US: All United States
Canada: All Canada
Overseas: All Countries

<< >>

VAN HOUTTE

8300 19th Ave.
Montreal, PQ H1Z 4J8 CANADA
Tel: (800) 361-5628 (514) 593-7711
Fax: (514) 593-8755
Web Site: www.hanhoutte
Mr. Stephane Breault, President

Van Houtte cafes serve the exclusive Café-bistro Collection coffee blends and a wide variety of espresso-based drinks, featured the choicest beans roasted according to our traditional European roasting method. Enjoy any time of the day with a cup of the distinctive, high-quality coffee that has given. Feeling hungry? Our cafes also serve an array of pastries, salad, sandwiches and breakfast products, all prepared with the freshest ingredients.

BACKGROUND:
Established: 1919; 1st Franchised: 1983
Franchised Units: 51
Company-Owned Units 4
Total Units: 55
Dist.: US-0; CAN-55; O'seas-0
North America: 2 Provinces
Density: 54 in PQ, 1 in ON
Projected New Units (12 Months): 10
Qualifications: 4, 3, 4, 3, 4, 4
Registered: NR

FINANCIAL/TERMS:
Cash Investment: $80K
Total Investment: $150-200K
Minimum Net Worth: $80K
Fees: Franchise - $25K
Royalty - 5%; Ad. - 2%
Earnings Claim Statement: No
Term of Contract (Years): 10/5
Avg. # Of Employees: 4 FT, 8 PT
Passive Ownership: Not Allowed
Encourage Conversions: No
Area Develop. Agreements: No
Sub-Franchising Contracts: No
Expand In Territory: No
Space Needs: 1,500 SF; FS, SF, SC, RM

SUPPORT & TRAINING PROVIDED:
Financial Assistance Provided: Yes(I)
Site Selection Assistance: Yes
Lease Negotiation Assistance: Yes
Co-Operative Advertising: Yes
Franchisee Assoc./Member: No
Size Of Corporate Staff: 12
On-Going Support: C,D,E,F,H
Training: 3 Weeks Training School; 1 Week Actual Store.
SPECIFIC EXPANSION PLANS:
US: No
Canada: All Canada
Overseas: No

VILLA PIZZA/COZZOLI'S

17 Elm St.
Morristown, NJ 07960
Tel: (973) 285-4800
Fax: (973) 285-5252
E-Mail: atorine@villapizza.com
Web Site: www.villapizza.com
Mr. Adam Torine, Dir. Business Dev.

Quick-service pizza and Italian restaurant chain, primarily located in regional malls and outlet centers either in food courts or in-line locations. We use only the freshest cheeses, seasonings, vegetables, homemade sauces and other ingredients. Our large, tantalizing food display offers customers a wide variety of homemade dishes.

BACKGROUND:
Established: 1964; 1st Franchised: 1995
Franchised Units: 84
Company-Owned Units 109
Total Units: 193
Dist.: US-116; CAN-0; O'seas-4
North America: 38 States
Density: 11 in TX, 10 in PA, 7 in VA
Projected New Units (12 Months): 25
Qualifications: 4, 4, 5, 3, 3, 4
Registered: CA,FL,IL,KY,MI,NE,NY,ND, RI,SD,TX,UT,VA,WA,WI
FINANCIAL/TERMS:
Cash Investment: $100-250K
Total Investment: $190-400K
Minimum Net Worth: $150K
Fees: Franchise - $25K
Royalty - 5%; Ad. - 0%
Earnings Claim Statement: No
Term of Contract (Years): 10
Avg. # Of Employees: 2 FT, 4-7 PT
Passive Ownership: Not Allowed
Encourage Conversions: Yes
Area Develop. Agreements: No
Sub-Franchising Contracts: No
Expand In Territory: Yes
Space Needs: 650-2,500 SF; RM, Non-Traditional
SUPPORT & TRAINING PROVIDED:
Financial Assistance Provided: Yes(I)
Site Selection Assistance: Yes
Lease Negotiation Assistance: Yes
Co-Operative Advertising: N/A
Franchisee Assoc./Member: No
Size Of Corporate Staff: 25
On-Going Support: B,C,D,E,F,G,I
Training: 2 Weeks.
SPECIFIC EXPANSION PLANS:
US: All United States
Canada: All Canada
Overseas: England, Italy and Spain

WARD'S RESTAURANTS

7 Professional Pkwy.
Hattiesburg, MS 39402
Tel: (800) 748-9273 (601) 268-9273
Fax: (601) 268-9283
E-Mail: wfsinc@netdoor.com
Web Site: www.wardsrestaurants.com
Mr. Kenneth R. Hrdlica, President

Fast-food restaurant, both traditional and non-traditional, featuring chili-burgers, chili-dogs and frosted mugs of homemade root beer. Menu is complemented by full breakfast line and a variety of sandwiches, side orders and beverages. Seating of up to 60 and drive-thru facilities are part of the building package.

BACKGROUND:
Established: 1985; 1st Franchised: 1985
Franchised Units: 18
Company-Owned Units 1
Total Units: 19
Dist.: US-19; CAN-0; O'seas-0
North America: 2 States
Density: 14 in MS, 5 in AL
Projected New Units (12 Months): 2
Qualifications: 5, 4, 3, 3, 3, 4
Registered: NR
FINANCIAL/TERMS:
Cash Investment: $100K
Total Investment: $250-400K
Minimum Net Worth: $100K
Fees: Franchise - $20K
Royalty - 4-5%; Ad. - NR
Earnings Claim Statement: No
Term of Contract (Years): Varies
Avg. # Of Employees: 8 FT, 7 PT
Passive Ownership: Discouraged
Encourage Conversions: Yes
Area Develop. Agreements: Yes/Varies
Sub-Franchising Contracts: No
Expand In Territory: Yes
Space Needs: 2,000 SF; FS
SUPPORT & TRAINING PROVIDED:
Financial Assistance Provided: No
Site Selection Assistance: Yes
Lease Negotiation Assistance: No
Co-Operative Advertising: No
Franchisee Assoc./Member: No
Size Of Corporate Staff: 4
On-Going Support: a,C,D,E,f,G,h,I
Training: 4 Weeks Home Office.
SPECIFIC EXPANSION PLANS:
US: All United States, Southeast
Canada: No
Overseas: No

WENDY'S RESTAURANTS OF CANADA

240 Wyecroft Rd.
Oakville, ON L6K 2G7 CANADA
Tel: (905) 849-7685
Fax: (905) 849-5545
E-Mail: jane_dann@wendys.com
Web Site: www.wendys.com
Ms. Jane Dann, Franchise Sales/Dev.

Our mission is to deliver superior quality products and services for our customers and communities through leadership, innovation and partnerships.

BACKGROUND:
Established: 1969; 1st Franchised: 1975
Franchised Units: 212
Company-Owned Units 120
Total Units: 332
Dist.: US-0; CAN-332; O'seas-0
North America: 10 Provinces
Density: 173 in ON, 56 in AB, 45 BC
Projected New Units (12 Months): 30
Qualifications: 5, 4, 3, 4, 3, 5
Registered: AB
FINANCIAL/TERMS:
Cash Investment: $400K
Total Investment: $590K-1.4MM
Minimum Net Worth: $800K

Fees: Franchise - $40K
Royalty - 4%/$350; Ad. - 4%
Earnings Claim Statement: No
Term of Contract (Years): 20/10
Avg. # Of Employees: 10 FT, 40 PT
Passive Ownership: Not Allowed
Encourage Conversions: Yes
Area Develop. Agreements: Yes/Varies
Sub-Franchising Contracts: No
Expand In Territory: Yes
Space Needs: + -44,000 SF; FS, RM, Other

SUPPORT & TRAINING PROVIDED:
Financial Assistance Provided: Yes(I)
Site Selection Assistance: Yes
Lease Negotiation Assistance: Yes
Co-Operative Advertising: Yes
Franchisee Assoc./Member: Yes/Yes
Size Of Corporate Staff: 121
On-Going Support: B,C,D,E,G,H,I
Training: Regional in a Certified Training Restaurant with Classes. 20 Weeks.

SPECIFIC EXPANSION PLANS:
US: No
Canada: ON, bc AND pq
Overseas: No

<< >>

Top 50

WIENERSCHNITZEL
4440 Von Karman Ave., # 222
Newport Beach, CA 92660
Tel: (800) 764-9353 (949) 851-2609
Fax: (949) 851-2618
E-Mail: fcoyle@galardigroup.com
Web Site: www.wienerschnitzel.com
Mr. Frank R. Coyle, Franchise Sales Dir.

WIENERSCHNITZEL is the world's largest quick service hot dog restaurant chain with over 300 locations selling 90 million hot dogs annually. We are interested in developing new locations throughout California, the Southwest and Pacific Northwest.

BACKGROUND:
Established: 1961; 1st Franchised: 1965
Franchised Units: 321
Company-Owned Units 0
Total Units: 321
Dist.: US-316; CAN-0; O'seas-0
North America: 11 States
Density: 220 in CA, 30 in TX, 7 in NM
Projected New Units (12 Months): 35
Qualifications: 4, 3, 3, 2, 1, 4
Registered: CA,IL,OR,WA

FINANCIAL/TERMS:
Cash Investment: $100-200K
Total Investment: $250K-1.2MM
Minimum Net Worth: $150K
Fees: Franchise - $20K
Royalty - 5%; Ad. - 3-5%
Earnings Claim Statement: No
Term of Contract (Years): 20/1-20
Avg. # Of Employees: 1-3 FT, 25-30 PT
Passive Ownership: Discouraged
Encourage Conversions: Yes
Area Develop. Agreements: Yes/1
Sub-Franchising Contracts: No
Expand In Territory: Yes
Space Needs: 20,000 SF; FS, RM

SUPPORT & TRAINING PROVIDED:
Financial Assistance Provided: Yes(I)
Site Selection Assistance: Yes
Lease Negotiation Assistance: No
Co-Operative Advertising: Yes
Franchisee Assoc./Member: Yes/Yes
Size Of Corporate Staff: 48
On-Going Support: A,B,C,d,E,F,G,H,I
Training: 30 Days Plano, TX; 30 Days Gilroy, CA; 7 Days Corporate Office.

SPECIFIC EXPANSION PLANS:
US: NW, SW, SE, NE
Canada: No
Overseas: No

<< >>

WILLY DOG
120 Clarence St., # 1141
Kingston, ON K7L 4Y5 CANADA
Tel: (800) 915-4683 (613) 389-6118
Fax: (613) 389-6138
E-Mail: willrhodgskiss@aol.com
Web Site: www.willydogs.com
Mr. Will R. Hodgskiss, President

Fully self-contained hot dog and fast-food cart that looks like a giant hot dog. Can be used indoors in malls, etc. or outdoors. We serve a great menu of our all beef "Willy Dog" hot dogs and our smokin' Willy Sausages and drinks. This proven money maker will work anywhere for you.

BACKGROUND:
Established: 1989; 1st Franchised: 1993
Franchised Units: 146
Company-Owned Units 15
Total Units: 190
Dist.: US-114; CAN-76; O'seas-0
North America: 15 States
Density: CA, PA, IL
Projected New Units (12 Months): NR
Registered: NR

FINANCIAL/TERMS:
Cash Investment: $6.5K
Total Investment: $3-6.5K
Minimum Net Worth: $N/A
Fees: Franchise - $NR
Royalty - $500/Yr.; Ad. - N/A
Earnings Claim Statement: Yes
Term of Contract (Years): 10/10
Avg. # Of Employees: 1 FT, 1 PT
Passive Ownership: Discouraged
Encourage Conversions: NR
Area Develop. Agreements: Yes/5
Sub-Franchising Contracts: Yes
Expand In Territory: Yes
Space Needs: 35 SF; RM

SUPPORT & TRAINING PROVIDED:
Financial Assistance Provided: NR
Site Selection Assistance: Yes
Lease Negotiation Assistance: Yes
Co-Operative Advertising: Yes
Franchisee Assoc./Member: No
Size Of Corporate Staff: 15
On-Going Support: B,C,D,E,F,G,H,I
Training: TBA.

SPECIFIC EXPANSION PLANS:
US: All United States
Canada: NR
Overseas: NR

<< >>

WING ZONE
1720 Peachtree St., NW, # 940
Atlanta, GA 30309
Tel: (877) 333-9464 (404) 875-5045
Fax: (404) 875-6631
E-Mail: scott@wingzone.com
Web Site: www.wingzone.com
Mr. Scott C. Bigelow, National Sales Mgr.

WING ZONE is a Buffalo-style chicken

wing restaurant that offers 25 homemade flavors of jumbo wings, salads, grilled sandwiches, appetizers and desserts. We offer take-out and delievery, and have anchored our stores around large college populations.

BACKGROUND: IFA MEMBER
Established: 1993; 1st Franchised: 1999
Franchised Units: 20
Company-Owned Units 6
Total Units: 26
Dist.: US-20; CAN-0; O'seas-0
North America: 12 States
Density: 4 in FL, 2 in GA, 2 in SC
Projected New Units (12 Months): 24
Qualifications: 4, 3, 2, 2, 3, 5
Registered: CA,HI,IL,IN,MN,ND,RI, SD,WI

FINANCIAL/TERMS:
Cash Investment: $50-75K
Total Investment: $130-190K
Minimum Net Worth: $300K
Fees: Franchise - $25K
Royalty - 5%; Ad. - 0.5%
Earnings Claim Statement: No
Term of Contract (Years): 10/10
Avg. # Of Employees: 6 FT, 15 PT
Passive Ownership: Discouraged
Encourage Conversions: Yes
Area Develop. Agreements: No
Sub-Franchising Contracts: No
Expand In Territory: Yes
Space Needs: 1,200-1,500 SF; SF; SC

SUPPORT & TRAINING PROVIDED:
Financial Assistance Provided: No
Site Selection Assistance: Yes
Lease Negotiation Assistance: Yes
Co-Operative Advertising: Yes
Franchisee Assoc./Member: No
Size Of Corporate Staff: 6
On-Going Support: a,b,C,D,E,F,I
Training: 1 Week Home Office in Atlanta, GA; 1-2 Weeks Franchisee's Location.

SPECIFIC EXPANSION PLANS:
US: All United States
Canada: All Canada
Overseas: All Countries

<< >>

WINGSTOP RESTAURANTS

1234 Northwest Hwy.
Garland, TX 75041
Tel: (972) 686-6500
Fax: (972) 686-6502
E-Mail: bruce@wingstop.com
Web Site: www.wingstop.com
Mr. Bruce Evans, Franchise Development Coord.

The Arlington Morning News wrote: ' With the somewhat rough-and-ready air of an early century barnstormers' aircraft hanger, WINGSTOP treads the line between neighborhood hang and a casual, laid-back dinner-snack spot. The place's signature chicken wings, however, are righteously assertive, distinctive and anything but bland . . ' WINGSTOP is fun! WINGSTOP is focused! WINGSTOP is growing fast!

BACKGROUND: IFA MEMBER
Established: 1994; 1st Franchised: 1997
Franchised Units: 61
Company-Owned Units 2
Total Units: 63
Dist.: US-35; CAN-0; O'seas-0
North America: 11 States
Density: 43 in TX, 3 in OK, 3 in LA
Projected New Units (12 Months): 50
Qualifications: 3, 3, 2, 2, 1, 4
Registered: All States except ND, SD

FINANCIAL/TERMS:
Cash Investment: $60-70K
Total Investment: $229K
Minimum Net Worth: $100K
Fees: Franchise - $20K
Royalty - 5%; Ad. - 2%
Earnings Claim Statement: Yes
Term of Contract (Years): 10/10
Avg. # Of Employees: 2 FT, 4 PT
Passive Ownership: Allowed
Encourage Conversions: N/A
Area Develop. Agreements: No
Sub-Franchising Contracts: No
Expand In Territory: No
Space Needs: 1,200-1,500 SF; SC

SUPPORT & TRAINING PROVIDED:
Financial Assistance Provided: Yes(I)
Site Selection Assistance: Yes
Lease Negotiation Assistance: Yes
Co-Operative Advertising: Yes
Franchisee Assoc./Member: Yes/Yes
Size Of Corporate Staff: 13
On-Going Support: A,B,C,D,E,H
Training: 2 Weeks Corporate Store; 1 Week Franchise Store.

SPECIFIC EXPANSION PLANS:
US: All United States
Canada: All Canada
Overseas: All Countries

<< >>

YAYA'S FLAME BROILED CHICKEN

521 S. Dort Hwy.
Flint, MI 48503
Tel: (800) 754-1242 (810) 235-6550
Fax: (810) 235-5210
E-Mail: yayas@yayas.com
Web Site: www.yayas.com
Mr. Gus C. Chinonis, Vice President

Flamed-broiled chicken, health oriented with great flavor. No freezers or fryers in restaurant. Dine-in or take-out. Locations in strips centers or free-standing buildings.

BACKGROUND: IFA MEMBER
Established: 1985; 1st Franchised: 1988
Franchised Units: 14
Company-Owned Units 5
Total Units: 19
Dist.: US-20; CAN-0; O'seas-0
North America: 2 States
Density: 14 in MI, 6 in FL
Projected New Units (12 Months): 5
Qualifications: 4, 4, 3, 3, 4, 4
Registered: FL,MI,MN

FINANCIAL/TERMS:
Cash Investment: $233-336K
Total Investment: $233-336K
Minimum Net Worth: $500K
Fees: Franchise - $15K
Royalty - 4%; Ad. - 4%
Earnings Claim Statement: No
Term of Contract (Years): 10/10
Avg. # Of Employees: 7 FT, 7 PT
Passive Ownership: Not Allowed
Encourage Conversions: N/A
Area Develop. Agreements: Yes/10
Sub-Franchising Contracts: No
Expand In Territory: Yes
Space Needs: 2,800 SF; FS, SF, SC

SUPPORT & TRAINING PROVIDED:
Financial Assistance Provided: No
Site Selection Assistance: N/A
Lease Negotiation Assistance: N/A
Co-Operative Advertising: Yes
Franchisee Assoc./Member: No
Size Of Corporate Staff: 6
On-Going Support: C,D,E,F,H,I
Training: 3 Weeks Flint, MI.

SPECIFIC EXPANSION PLANS:
US: All United States
Canada: All Canada
Overseas: No

<< >>

ZERO'S SUBS
2859 VA Beach Blvd., # 105
Virginia Beach, VA 23452
Tel: (800) 588-0782 (757) 486-8338
Fax: (757) 486-9755
E-Mail: zeros@zeros.com
Web Site: www.zeros.com
Ms. Susan Eller

Quick service restaurant specializing in hot, oven-baked submarines, philly cheese steaks, and pizzas. We cater to families and offer kids meals. Catering and party subs complement any special event. Our uniqueness brings customers back again and again.

BACKGROUND:
Established: 1967; 1st Franchised: 1990
Franchised Units: 61
Company-Owned Units 5
Total Units: 66
Dist.: US-66; CAN-0; O'seas-0
North America: 6 States
Density: 45 in VA, 8 in NC, 5 in SC
Projected New Units (12 Months): 12
Qualifications: 3, 4, 5, 3, 3, 5
Registered: FL, MD, VA
FINANCIAL/TERMS:
Cash Investment: $50-75K
Total Investment: $120-200K
Minimum Net Worth: $150K
Fees: Franchise - $15K
Royalty - 6%; Ad. - 2%
Earnings Claim Statement: No
Term of Contract (Years): 15/15
Avg. # Of Employees: 4 FT, 3 PT
Passive Ownership: Discouraged
Encourage Conversions: Yes
Area Develop. Agreements: Yes/25
Sub-Franchising Contracts: Yes
Expand In Territory: Yes
Space Needs: 1,500 SF; FS, SF, SC
SUPPORT & TRAINING PROVIDED:
Financial Assistance Provided: Yes(I)
Site Selection Assistance: Yes
Lease Negotiation Assistance: Yes
Co-Operative Advertising: Yes
Franchisee Assoc./Member: No
Size Of Corporate Staff: 10
On-Going Support: C,d,E,F,H,I
Training: 2-3 Weeks in Virginia Beach, VA.
SPECIFIC EXPANSION PLANS:
US: East Coast and SW
Canada: No
Overseas: No

<< >>

SUPPLEMENTAL LISTING OF FRANCHISORS

241 PIZZA, 3380 S. Service Rd., # 200, Burlington, ON L7N 3J5 CANADA; (877) 241-0241 (905) 681-8448; (905) 637-7745

3 FOR 1 PIZZA & WINGS, 10 Bay St, # 802, Toronto, ON L7N 3J5 CANADA; (416) 360-0888; (416) 360-5543

5 & DINER, 1140 E. Greenway, # 1, Mesa, AZ 85203 ; (480) 962-7104; (480) 962-0159

A & W FOOD SERVICES OF CANADA, 171 W. Esplanade, # 300, North Vancouver, BC V7M 3K9 CANADA; (604) 988-2141; (604) 988-0553

AFC ENTERPRISES, 6 Concourse Parkway, # 1700, Atlanta, GA 30328-6117 ; (770) 391-9500; (770) 350-3695

ANTONE'S FAMOUS PO' BOYS & DELI, 13100 Northwest Fwy., # 160, Houston, TX 77040 ; (800) 934-6734 (713) 934-2100; (713) 934-2200

ARBY'S (CANADA), 6299 Airport Rd., # 200, Mississauga, ON L4V 1N3 CANADA; (800) 263-7040 (905) 672-2729; (905) 672-2755

ARCTIC CIRCLE, P.O. Box 339, Midvale, UT 84047 ; (801) 561-3620; (801) 561-9646

AURELIO'S IS PIZZA, 18162 Harwood Ave., Homewood, IL 60430 ; (708) 798-8050; (708) 798-6692

BACK YARD BURGERS, 1657 N. Shelby Oaks Dr., #105, Memphis, TN 38134; (800) 292-6939 (901) 367-0888; (901) 367-0999

BALDINOS GIANT JERSEY SUBS, 3823 Roswell Rd., # 204, Marietta, GA 30062 ; (770) 971-9441; (770) 977-1083

BASILS FLAME BROILED CHICKEN & RIBS, 5601 Manatee Ave., Bradenton, FL 34209 ; (800) 809-6300 (941) 795-0848; (941) 795-1776

BENNETT'S PIT BAR-B-QUE, 6551 S. Revere Pkwy., # 285, Englewood, CO 80111 ; (303) 792-3088; (303) 792-5801

BLACKJACK PIZZA, 9137 E. Mineral Circle, # 100, Englewood, CO 80112 ; (303) 790-7057; (303) 790-7162

BOSTON THE GOURMET PIZZA, 1505 LBJ Fwy., # 250, Dallas, TX 75234 ; (866) 277-8721 (972) 484-9022; (972) 484-7630

BOZ HOT DOGS, 770 E. 142nd St., Dolton, IL 60419 ; (708) 841-3747; (708) 841-4770

BRIGHAM'S, 30 Mill St., Millbrook Park, Arlington, MA 02476 ; (800) BRIGHAM (781) 648-9000; (781) 646-0507

BROADWAY STATION RESTAURANTS, 1818 Wooddale Dr., Woodbury, MN 55125 ; (651) 731-0800; (651) 731-9609

BRUCHI'S CHEESESTEAKS AND SUBS, 11801 NE 65th St., Vancouver, WA 98607 ; (360) 882-8823; (360) 882-5988

BUDDY'S BAR-B-Q, 5806 Kingston Pk., Knoxville, TN 37919 ; (800) 368-9208 (423) 588-0051; (423) 588-7211

BULLETS CORPORATION OF AMERICA, 9201 Forest Hill Ave., # 109, Richmond, VA 23235 ; (800) 472-0933 (804) 330-0837; (804) 330-5405

BURGER KING CORPORATION, 17777 Old Cutler Rd., Miami, FL 33157 ; (305) 378-7011; (305) 378-7262

BUSCEMI'S INTERNATIONAL, 30362 Gratiot Ave., Roseville, MI 48066 ; (810) 296-5560; (810) 296-3366

CAFE SUPREME, 1233 Rue de la Montagne, # 201, Montreal, PQ H3G 1Z2 CANADA; (514) 875-9803; (514) 875-9899

CAMILLE'S SIDEWALK CAFÉ, 5128 S. 95th East Ave., # B, Tulsa, OK 74145

(800) 299-6829 (918) 664-9727; (918) 664-9721

CARBONE'S PIZZA, 680 E. 7th St., Saint Paul, MN 55106 ; (651) 771-5553; (651) 771-3320

CARL'S JR. RESTAURANTS, 3916 State St., Garden Suites, Santa Barbara, CA 93105 (800) 422-4141 (805) 898-7119; (805) 898-7110

CATERINA'S, P.O. Box 5587, San Clemente, CA 92674-5587 ; (800) 765-3089

CHARO CHICKEN, 2134 Main St., # 240, Huntington Beach, CA 92648 ; (714) 960-2348; (714) 374-1889

CHICKEN OUT ROTISSERIE, 15952 Shady Grove Rd., Gaithersburg, MD 20877-1315 ; (301) 921-0600; (301) 548-0024

CHICK-FIL-A, 5200 Buffington Rd., Atlanta, GA 30349-2998 ; (800) 232-2677 (404) 765-8000; (404) 765-8942

CHICO'S TACOS, P.O. Box 891269, Temecula, CA 92589-1269 ; (800) 772-4426 (909) 676-3204; (909) 676-6104

CHOCK CAFÉ, 100 Foxborough Blvd., # 200, Foxborough, MA 02035-2882 ; (800) 381-6303 (508) 698-2223; (508) 698-2224

CHOICE PICKS FOOD COURT, 10750 Columbia Pk., Silver Spring, MD 20901-4447 ; (800) 503-2212 (301) 592-6296; (301) 598-6205

COPELANDS OF NEW ORLEANS, 1405 Airline Hwy., Metairie, LA 70001 (800) 401-0401 (504) 830-1000; (504) 830-1038

CORKY'S RIB AND BBQ, 223 Madison St., # 107, Madison, TN 37115 ; (800) 342-1705 (615) 860-7188; (615) 865-8864

COUNTY LINE, THE, 3345 Bee Cave Rd., #150, Austin, TX 78746 ; (512) 327-1959; (512) 327-2622

CROISSANT + PLUS, 2020 St. Patrick, Montreal, PQ H3K 1A9 CANADA; (800) 267-4896 (514) 931-5550; (514) 931-3749

D'ANGELO SANDWICH SHOPS, 600 Providence Hwy., Dedham, MA 02626 (800) 242-1437 (781) 461-1200; (781) 461-1896

DEL'S LEMONADE, 1260 Oaklawn Ave., Cranston, RI 02920 ; (401) 463-6190; (401) 463-7931

DINO'S PIZZA, P.O. Box 97244, Raleigh, NC 27624-7244 ; (919) 676-1080;

DOLLY'S PIZZA, 1097 Union Lake Rd., # B, White Lake, MI 48386-4516 ; (248) 360-6440; (248) 360-7020

DOMINIC'S OF NEW YORK, 4949 Cox Rd., Suite B, Glen Allen, VA 23060 ; (888) DOM-OFNY (804) 273-0600; (804) 273-0152

DOMINO'S PIZZA INTERNATIONAL, 30 Frank Lloyd Wright Dr., P.O. Box 997, Ann Arbor, MI 48106-0997 (734) 668-6055; (734) 668-0342

DOUBLEDAVE'S PIZZAWORKS SYSTEMS, P.O. Box 802216, Dallas, TX 75380 (800) 460-9000 (512) 343-0330; (972) 716-9913

EMPRESS CHILI, 10592 Taconic Ter., Cincinnati, OH 45215 ; (513) 771-1441; (513) 771-1442

FAMOUS SAM'S, 1930 S. Alma School Rd., #C-105, Mesa, AZ 85210 ; (888) 866-8808 (480) 756-9800; (480) 756-9884

FAT BOY'S BAR-B-Q, 1940 10th Ave., # B, Vero Beach, FL 32960-6458 ; (561) 794-1080; (561) 794-9590

FAZOLI'S SYSTEMS, 2470 Palumbo Dr., Lexington, KY 40509 ; (859) 268-1668; (859) 268-2263

FRANK & STEIN DOGS & DRAFTS, 1630 Braeburn Dr., # A, Salem, MA 24153 (540) 389-8435; (540)-389-1780

FRISCH'S RESTAURANTS, 2800 Gilbert Ave., Cincinnati, OH 45206 ; (513) 559-5304

GERALD M. LISS CO., 203 N. Main St., Bowling Green, OH 43402 ; (419) 352-5166; (419) 354-1402

GOLDEN SKILLET, USA, P.O. Box 905, Ahoskie, NC 27910 ; (252) 332-5248; (252) 332-7557

GRANDY'S, 997 Grandy's Ln., Lewisville, TX 75077-2507 ; (877) 457-8145 (972) 317-8026; (972) 317-8174

GUMBY'S PIZZA INTERNATIONAL, 5217 SW 91st Dr., Gainesville, FL 32608 (800) 354-8629 (352) 375-8084; (352) 377-2592

HEALTH FIRST RESTAURANTS, 3321 Greenhill Ln., # 310, Louisville, KY 40207 (510) 839-5471; (510) 547-3245

HOGI YOGI, 4833 N. Edgewood Dr., Provo, UT 84604 ; (801) 222-9004

HOT DOG ON A STICK, 5601 Palmer Way, Carlsbad, CA 92008-7242 ; (800) 321-8400 (760) 930-0456; (760) 431-3703

ITALIAN FRANCHISE COMPANY, THE, 3701 Canal St., # D, New Orleans, LA 70119; (504) 488-4441; (504) 488-4474

ITALO'S PIZZA SHOP, 3560 Middlebranch Rd., NE, Canton, OH 44705 ; (330) 455-7443

IZZY'S PIZZA RESTAURANT, 110 3rd Ave., SE, Albany, OR 97321 ; (541) 926-8693; (541) 928-8127

JACK IN THE BOX, 9330 Balboa Ave., San Diego, CA 92123-1516 ; (858) 571-2121; (858) 694-1556

JAKE'S OVER THE TOP, 4605 Harrison Blvd., Ogden, UT 84403 ; (800) 207-5804 (801) 476-9780; (801) 476-9788

JAKE'S PIZZA, 1911-C Rohlwing Rd., Rolling Meadows, IL 60008-4502 ; (800) 4-A-JAKES (847) 368-1990; (847) 368-1995

JETS PIZZA, 37177 Mound Rd., Sterling Heights, MI 48310-4116 ; (800) 446-5870 (810) 268-5870; (810) 268-6762

JIMBOY'S TACOS, 1485 Response Rd., # 110, Sacramento, CA 95815 ; (800) JIM-BOYS (916) 564-8226; (916) 564-0802

JIMMY'S PIZZA, 2015 First St. S., #119, Willmar, MN 56201 ; (320) 235-7844;

(320) 235-7837

JODY MARONI'S SAUSAGE KINGDOM, 5441 W. 104th St., Los Angeles, CA 90045-6011 ; (800) 628-8364 (310) 348-1500; (310) 348-1510

KFC CANADA, 10 Carlson Ct., # 400, Rexdale, ON M9W 6L2 CANADA; (800) 268-5435 (416) 674-0367; (416) 674-2697

KOJAX, 8150 Marco Polo, Riviere des Prairies, PQ H1E 5Y7 CANADA; (514) 494-2526; (514) 494-8988

LAMPPOST PIZZA, 3002 Dow Ave., #320, Tustin, CA 92780 ; (714) 731-6171; (714) 731-0951

LAROSA'S PIZZERIAS, 2334 Boudinot Ave., Cincinnati, OH 45238 ; (513) 347-5660; (513) 922-2776

LENNY AND VINNY'S NEW YORK PIZZERIA/BAKERY, 3102 W. Waters Ave., # 201, Tampa, FL 33614 ; (888) YO-VINNY (813) 882-4336; (813) 885-1486

LINDY - GERTIE'S, 8437 Park Ave., Burr Ridge, IL 60521 ; (630) 323-8003; (630) 323-5449

LITTLE CAESARS PIZZA, 2211 Woodward Ave., Detroit, MI 48201-3400 ; (800) 553-5776 (313) 983-6469; (313) 983-6197

MAMMA ILARDO'S, 3600 Clipper Mill Rd., # 260, Baltimore, MD 21211 ; (410) 662-1930; (410) 662-1936

MARY BROWN'S FRIED CHICKEN, 250 Shields Ct., # 7, Markham, ON L3R 9W7 CANADA; (905) 513-0044; (905) 513-0050

MASH HOAGIES/MASH SUBS & SALADS, 3164 Lake Washington Rd., Melbourne, FL 32934 ; (321) 242-2066; (321) 752-6026

MCDONALD'S RESTAURANTS OF CANADA, McDonald's Place, Toronto, ON M3C 3L4 CANADA; (416) 443-1000; (416) 446-3429

MELLOW MUSHROOM PIZZA, 695 North Ave. NE, Atlanta, GA 30308 ; (404) 524-6133; (404) 223-5419

ME-N-ED'S PIZZERIAS, 5701 N. West Ave., Fresno, CA 93711 ; (888) 636-3373 (559) 432-0399; (559) 432-0398

MIAMI SUBS GRILL, 6300 NW 31st Ave., Ft. Lauderdale, FL 33309 ; (954) 973-0000; (954) 973-7616

MR. CHICKEN, P.O. Box 23051, Cleveland, OH 44123 ; (440) 585-4800; (440) 585-4815

MR. GATTI'S, 444 Sidney Baker S., P.O. Box 1522, Kerrville, TX 78028 ; (830) 792-5700; (830) 257-2003

MR. GREEK MEDITERRANEAN RESTAURANTS, 18 Wynford Dr., # 504, Toronto, ON M3C 3J2 CANADA; (416) 444-3266; (416) 444-3489

MR. PITA, 48238 Lake Valley Dr., Shelby Township, MI 48317 ; (866) 738-7482 (810) 323-3624; (810) 323-3625

MR. SUBB, 601 Columbia St., Cohoes, NY 12047-3801 ; (800) 267-7822 (518) 783-0276; (518) 783-0294

NACH-O-FAST INTERNATIONAL, 447 N. 300 West, # 200, P.O. Box 47, Kaysville, UT 84037 ; (801) 546-9909; (801) 546-9909

NESTLE TOLL HOUSE CAFÉ BY CHIP, 1900 Preston Rd., # 267-314, Plano, TX 75093-5175 ; (214) 495-9533; (214) 853-5347

NOBLE ROMAN'S PIZZA EXPRESS, 1 Virginia Ave., # 800, Indianapolis, IN 46204 ; (317) 634-3377; (317) 636-3207

O'BRIEN'S IRISH SANDWICH BARS, 223 E. Wacker Dr., # 3610, Chicago, IL 60606 ; (312) 893-3625; (312) 893-3625

ONE WORLD ENTERPRISE, P.O. Box 6955, Bloomington, IN 47402 ; (812) 339-2256; (812) 333-3200

ORANGE JULIUS, P.O. Box 35286, Minneapolis, MN 55435 ; (800) JULIUS-9 (612) 830-0200; (612) 830-0450

ORANGE JULIUS CANADA, P.O. Box 430, Burlington, ON L7R 3Y3 CANADA; (800) 268-9169 (416) 639-1492; (416) 681-3623

ORIGINAL HAMBURGER STAND, P.O. Box 7460, Newport Beach, CA 92658 (949) 752-5800; (949) 851-2615

PAPA GINO'S, 600 Providence Hwy., Dedham, MA 02026 ; (800) 242-1437 (781) 461-1200; (781) 461-1896

PAPA JOHN'S PIZZA, P.O. Box 99900, Louisville, KY 40269-0900 ; (502) 261-4143; (502) 261-4299

PASTA CENTRAL, 1775 The Exchange, # 600, Atlanta, GA 30339 ; (800) 447-6256 (770) 980-9176

PASTA LOVERS TRATTORIAS, 201 W. First St., Sanford, FL 32771 ; (407) 321-1101; (407) 321-3077

PETER PIPER PIZZA, 6263 N. Scottsdale Rd., # 100, Scottsdale, AZ 85250 (888) 912-1333 (602) 609-6400; (602) 609-6522

PETRO'S CHILI & CHIPS, 5614 Kingston Pk., 2nd Fl., Knoxville, TN 37919 ; (800) PETROFY (423) 588-1076; (865) 588-0916

PICCADILLY CIRCUS PIZZA, 1009 Okoboji Ave., Box # 188, Milford, IA 51351 ; (800) 338-4340 (712) 338-2771; (712) 338-2263

PIZZA INN, 5050 Quorum Dr., # 500, Dallas, TX 75254 ; (800) 284-3466 (972) 701-9955; (972) 702-0009

PIZZA OUTLET, 2101 Greentree Rd., # A-202, Pittsburgh, PA 15220-1400 ; (888) 279-9100 (412) 279-9100; (412) 279-9781

PIZZA PIPELINE, THE, 418 W. Sharp, Spokane, WA 99201 ; (509) 326-1977; (509) 326-3017

PIZZA PIT, 1401 Emil St., Madison, WI 53713-2311 ; (608) 221-6777; (608) 221-6771

PIZZA PIZZA INTERNATIONAL, 580 Jarvis St., Toronto, ON M4Y 2H9 CANADA; (800) 263-5556 (416) 967-1010; (416) 967-0891

PIZZA PRO, 2107 North 2nd St., Cabot, AR 72023 ; (800) 777-7554 (501) 605-1175; (501) 605-1204

PIZZERIA REGINO, 999 Broadway, # 400, Saugus, MA 01906 ; (781) 231-7575;

POLLO TROPICAL, 7300 N. Kendall Dr., # 800, Miami, FL 33156 ; (305) 670-7696; (305) 670-6403

PUDGIES PIZZA & SUB SHOPS, 524 530 N. Main St., Elmira, NY 14901 ; (607) 734-3366

RALLY'S HAMBURGERS, 4300 W. Cypress St., # 600, Tampa, FL 33607 ; (813) 283-7000; (813) 283-7001

RESTAURANT SYSTEMS INTERNATIONAL, 1000 South Ave., Staten Island, NY 10314-3403 ; (800) 205-6050 (718) 494-8888; (718) 494-8776

ROLI BOLI, 109 Main St., Sayreville, NJ 08872 ; (732) 257-8100; (732) 257-3255

ROLY POLY, 697 Beach Ave., Atlantic Beach, FL 32233 ; (904) 246-8565; (904) 246-8544

RONZIO PIZZA, 6 Blackstone Valley Pl., Bldg. 202, Lincoln, RI 02865 ; (401) 334-9750; (401) 334-0030

ROTELLI PIZZA & PASTA, 501 E. Atlantic Ave., Delray Beach, FL 33483; (888) 238-4326 (561) 272-4807; (561) 272-8495

RUBIO'S BAJA GRILL, 1902 Wright Pl., # 300, Carlsbad, CA 92008-6583 ; (800) 354-4199 (760) 929-8226; (760) 929-8203

RUBY'S, 110 Newport Center Dr., # 110, Newport Beach, CA 92660 ; (800) HAY-RUBY (714) 644-7829; (714) 644-4625

SALUBRE-PIZZA, SUBSATION'S SANDWICHES, 2337 Perimeter Park Dr., #200, Chamblee, GA 30341 ; (800) 310-9640 (770) 457-7611; (770) 457-2404

SANDWICH BOARD, THE, 10 Plastics Ave., Etobicoke, ON M8Z 4B7 CANADA; (416) 255-0898; (416) 255-8086

SCHOOP'S HAMBURGERS, 215 Ridge Rd., Munster, IN 46321 ; (219) 836-6233

SELECT SANDWICH, 1090 Don Mills Rd., # 401, North York, ON M3C 3R6 CANADA; (416) 391-1244; (416) 391-5244

SIMPLE SIMON'S PIZZA, 6650 S. Lewis, Tulsa, OK 74136 ; (800) 261-6375 (918) 496-1272; (918) 493-6516

SNAPPY TOMATO PIZZA, 7230 Turfway Rd., Florence, KY 41042 ; (888) 463-7627 (606) 525-4680; (606) 525-4686

SNEAKY PETE'S HOT DOGS, 100 Centerview Dr., # 191, Birmingham, AL 35126 ; (205) 824-0855; (205) 824-0852

SONIC DRIVE-IN, 101 Park Ave., # 1400, Oklahoma City, OK 73102 ; (800) 569-6656 (405) 280-7654; (405) 290-7478

STEAK 'N SHAKE, 36 S. Pennsylvania St., # 500, Indianapolis, IN 46204 ; (317) 633-4100; (317) 656-4500

SUBS PLUS, 173 Queenston St., St. Catharines, ON L2R 3A2 CANADA; (888) 549-7777 (905) 641-3696; (905) 641-3696

SUBZONE, 509 Madison St., Huntsville, AL 35801 ; (256) 551-1058; (256) 551-0159

TACO BELL (CANADA), 10 Carlson Ct., # 400, Rexdale, ON M9W 6L2 CANADA; (416) 674-0367; (416) 674-2697

TACO CASA, P.O. Box 4542, Topeka, KS 66604 ; (785) 267-2548; (785) 267-2652

TACO GRANDE, P.O. Box 780066, Wichita, KS 67278 ; (316) 744-0200; (316) 744-0299

TOPPER'S PIZZA, 311 Elm St. W., # 3, Sudbury, ON P3C 1V6 CANADA; (705) 674-0703; (705) 674-5302

VALENTINO'S OF AMERICA, P.O. Box 6206, Lincoln, NE 68506 ; (877) BUY-VALS (402) 434-9000; (402) 434-9860

VITA BURRITO, 4627 N. 1st Ave., # 2, Tucson, AZ 85718-5608 ; (520) 882-8713; (520) 620-6466

W. G. GRINDERS, 200 W. Bridge St., # 200, Dublin, OH 43017 ; (614) 766-2313; (614) 766-4030

WENDY'S INTERNATIONAL, 4288 W. Dublin-Granville Rd., P.O. Box 256, Dublin, OH 43017 ; (800) 443-7266 (614) 764-3100; (614) 764-6894

WETZEL'S PRETZELS, 65 N. Raymond Ave., # 310, Pasadena, CA 91103 ; (626) 432-6900; (626) 432-6904

WG GRINDERS, 220 W. Bridge St., # 200, Dublin, OH 43017 ; (614) 766-2313; (614) 766-4030

WHATABURGER, 4600 Parkdale Dr., Corpus Christi, TX 78411 ; (877) 551-0660 (361) 878-0683; (361) 878-0427

WHITE CASTLE INTERNATIONAL, 555 W. Goodale St., Columbus, OH 43215 (614) 559-2510; (614) 461-4033

WINDMILL GOURMET FAST FOODS, 200 Ocean Ave., Long Branch, NJ 07740 ; (800) 874-8282 (732) 870-8282; (732) 870-9613

WINGERS - AN AMERICAN DINER, 404 E. 4500 South, # A12, Salt Lake City, UT 84107 ; (801) 261-3700; (801) 261-1615

WINGS TO GO, 170 Jennifer Rd., # 250, Annapolis, MD 21401 ; (800) 552-WING (410) 224-5631; (410) 224-5635

WOK TO U EXPRESS, 3331 Viking Way, # 7, Richmond, BC V6V 1X7 CANADA; (604) 270-2360; (604) 270-6560

WOODY'S BAR-B-Q, 6960 Bonniwell Rd., Jacksonville, FL 32216 ; (904) 296-6940; (904) 296-6943

WOODY'S HOT DOGS HAWAII, 23254 Valley High Rd., Morrison, CO 80465 ; (877) GO-WOODY (303) 697-3962; (303) 697-3965

WRAP & ROLL CAFE, 1405 Airline Hwy., Metairie, LA 70001 ; (800) 401-0401 (504) 830-1000; (504) 832-8918

YEUNG'S LOTUS EXPRESS, 4014 Aurora St., Coral Gables, FL 33146-1416 ; (305) 4776-1611; (305) 476-9622

YOSHI'S, 2302 E. Indian School Rd., Phoenix, AZ 85016 ; (602) 955-1825

ZEPPE'S PIZZERIA, 10 Alpha Park, Highland Heights, OH 44143 ; (440) 442-9898; (440) 442-4655

Food: Restaurants/Family-Style

Chapter 17

Food: Restaurants/Family-Style Industry Profile

Total # Franchisors in Industry Group	181
Total # Franchised Units in Industry Group	18,805
Total # Company-Owned Units in Industry Group	10,286
Total # Operating Units in Industry Group	29,091
Average # Franchised Units/Franchisor	103.9
Average # Company-Owned Units/Franchisor	56.8
Average # Total Units/Franchisor	160.7
Ratio of Total # Franchised Units/Total # Company-Owned Units	1.8:1
Industry Survey Participants	62
Representing % of Industry	34.3%
Average Franchise Fee*:	$33.4K
Average Total Investment*:	$875.8K
Average On-Going Royalty Fee*:	4.5%

*If a range was provided, the mid-point of the range was used. See detailed profiles for actual ranges.

Five Largest Participants in Survey

Company	# Franchised Units	# Co-Owned Units	# Total Units	Franchise Fee	On-Going Royalty	Total Investment
1. Denny's	708	884	1,592	35K	4%	858K-1.5MM
2. Applebee's International	852	257	1,109	35K/Unit	4%	1.7-3.2MM
3. Sbarro	293	632	925	45K	7%	250-850K
4. Big Boy Restaurant and Bakery	596	104	700	40K	3%	600K-1.8MM
5. Friendly's Restaurant	157	404	561	35K	4%	875K-1.5MM

APPLEBEE'S INTERNATIONAL

4551 W. 107th St., # 100
Overland Park, KS 66207
Tel: (913) 967-4000
Fax: (913) 967-4135
Web Site: www.applebees.com
Mr. Loyd L. Hill, Chief Executive Officer

Everyone's favorite neighbor is definitely APPLEBEE'S neighborhood grill and bar. This distinguished casual-dining restaurant has a comfortable individuality which reflects the neighborhood in which it is located, making the APPLEBEE'S concept appealing wherever it is built.

BACKGROUND: IFA MEMBER
Established: 1980; 1st Franchised: 1988
Franchised Units: 852
Company-Owned Units 257
Total Units: 1,109
Dist.: US-889; CAN-5; O'seas-8
North America: 47 States, 3 Provinces
Density: 62 in FL, 54 in CA, 48 in OH
Projected New Units (12 Months): 125
Qualifications: 5, 5, 5, , , 5
Registered: All Except AB

FINANCIAL/TERMS:
Cash Investment: $1MM-50% Liq.
Total Investment: $1.74-3.17MM
Minimum Net Worth: $NR
Fees: Franchise - $35K/Unit
Royalty - 4%; Ad. - 3%
Earnings Claim Statement: No
Term of Contract (Years): 20/5
Avg. # Of Employees: 75-100 FT
Passive Ownership: Not Allowed
Encourage Conversions: No
Area Develop. Agreements: Yes
Sub-Franchising Contracts: No
Expand In Territory: Yes
Space Needs: 5,000-5,400 SF; FS, SC, RM

SUPPORT & TRAINING PROVIDED:
Financial Assistance Provided: No
Site Selection Assistance: Yes
Lease Negotiation Assistance: Yes
Co-Operative Advertising: Yes
Franchisee Assoc./Member: Yes
Size Of Corporate Staff: 300
On-Going Support: A,B,C,D,E,G,H,I
Training: 8-12 Weeks Certified Training Unit; 3-Day Seminars at Headquarters.

SPECIFIC EXPANSION PLANS:
US: NY, LA, HI, AK
Canada: All Canada
Overseas: All Countries

<< >>

BEEF O'BRADY'S FAMILY SPORTS PUBS

5510 W. LaSalle St., # 200
Tampa, FL 33607
Tel: (800) 728-8878 (813) 226-2333
Fax: (813) 226-0030
E-Mail: nick@beefobradys.com
Web Site: www.beefobradys.com
Mr. Nick Vojnovic, SVP Corporate Development

Beef O'Brady's Family Sports Pubs are family-friendly, sports-themed, casual pubs that feature signature Buffalo-style crispy chicken wings, burgers, sandwiches and salads. They only serve beer and wine (no hard liquor), have no dart boards or pool tables. They feature many televisions with diverse sports viewing, video games for the kids and a relaxed atmosphere. Our concept is built on the "owner/operator" model, however, our owners do not have to have previous restaurant experience.

BACKGROUND: IFA MEMBER
Established: 1985; 1st Franchised: 1998
Franchised Units: 66
Company-Owned Units 1
Total Units: 67
Dist.: US-67; CAN-0; O'seas-0
North America: 4 States
Density: 61 in FL, 3 in GA, 2 in AL
Projected New Units (12 Months): 16
Qualifications: 3, 4, 2, 2, 4, 4
Registered: FL

FINANCIAL/TERMS:
Cash Investment: $100K
Total Investment: $250-300K
Minimum Net Worth: $150K
Fees: Franchise - $25K
Royalty - 3.5%; Ad. - 1.5%
Earnings Claim Statement: No
Term of Contract (Years): 10/5
Avg. # Of Employees: 15 FT, 10 PT
Passive Ownership: Not Allowed
Encourage Conversions: Yes
Area Develop. Agreements: Yes/10
Sub-Franchising Contracts: Yes
Expand In Territory: Yes
Space Needs: 3,000 SF; SC

SUPPORT & TRAINING PROVIDED:
Financial Assistance Provided: Yes(I)
Site Selection Assistance: Yes
Lease Negotiation Assistance: Yes
Co-Operative Advertising: N/A
Franchisee Assoc./Member: No
Size Of Corporate Staff: 7
On-Going Support: B,C,D,E,G,H,I
Training: 6 Weeks Tampa, FL.

SPECIFIC EXPANSION PLANS:
US: SE United States
Canada: No
Overseas: No

<< >>

BENIHANA OF TOKYO

8685 NW 53rd Ter.
Miami, FL 33166
Tel: (800) 327-3369 (305) 593-0770
Fax: (305) 592-6371
E-Mail: benihana@bellsouth.net
Mr. Tom Vrabel, Dir. Franchising

BENIHANA is not only an internationally famous Japanese steak and seafood restaurant, it is also a genuine 'dining experience.' Both first-time and frequent visitors to BENIHANA are immediately drawn to the unique table top hibachi-style of cuisine, where mouth-watering dishes are prepared before their very eyes.

BACKGROUND:
Established: 1964; 1st Franchised: 1970
Franchised Units: 23
Company-Owned Units 57
Total Units: 80
Dist.: US-57; CAN-1; O'seas-8
North America: 20 States, 1 Province
Density: 15 in CA, 6 in FL, 3 in IL
Projected New Units (12 Months): 3
Qualifications: 5, 4, 3, 2, 2, 4
Registered: CA,HI,NY

FINANCIAL/TERMS:
Cash Investment: $550-650K
Total Investment: $1.3-1.8MM
Minimum Net Worth: $1K
Fees: Franchise - $50K
Royalty - 6%; Ad. - 0.5%
Earnings Claim Statement: No
Term of Contract (Years): 15/Varies
Avg. # Of Employees: 35 FT, 7 PT
Passive Ownership: Discouraged
Encourage Conversions: Yes
Area Develop. Agreements: Yes/15
Sub-Franchising Contracts: No
Expand In Territory: No
Space Needs: 6,000+ SF; FS

SUPPORT & TRAINING PROVIDED:
Financial Assistance Provided: No
Site Selection Assistance: Yes
Lease Negotiation Assistance: N/A
Co-Operative Advertising: Yes
Franchisee Assoc./Member: No
Size Of Corporate Staff: 51
On-Going Support: a,C,d,E,F,H,I
Training: 12-15 Weeks in Miami, FL.

SPECIFIC EXPANSION PLANS:
US: PA,MD,MI,NC,OH,AZ,TX,NY
Canada: All Canada
Overseas: Europe, Pacific Rim

<< >>

BENNIGAN'S GRILL & TAVERN

6500 International Pkwy., # 1000
Plano, TX 75093
Tel: (800) 543-9670 (972) 588-5770
Fax: (972) 588-5806
E-Mail: franchise@metrogroup.com
Web Site: www.bennigans.com
Ms. Lynette McKee, VP Franchise Development

BENNIGAN'S is a leading casual restaurant chain known for the warm hospitality of an Irish pub and the great taste of fun American foods. Established in 1976, BENNIGAN'S has expanded beyond its original tavern image to become more food-focused. Today, each restaurant serves a wide assortment of moderately-priced, quality food, as well as a wide selection of beverages.

BACKGROUND: IFA MEMBER
Established: 1976; 1st Franchised: 1995
Franchised Units: 125
Company-Owned Units 174
Total Units: 299
Dist.: US-280; CAN-0; O'seas-19
North America: 32 States
Density: 59 in TX, 44 in FL, 23 in IL
Projected New Units (12 Months): 12
Qualifications: 5, 5, 4, 4, 4, 5
Registered: All States

FINANCIAL/TERMS:
Cash Investment: $750K
Total Investment: $1.2-2.2MM
Minimum Net Worth: $3MM
Fees: Franchise - $65K
Royalty - 4%; Ad. - 4%
Earnings Claim Statement: No
Term of Contract (Years): 15/NR
Avg. # Of Employees: 5 FT, 65 PT
Passive Ownership: Not Allowed
Encourage Conversions: No
Area Develop. Agreements: No
Sub-Franchising Contracts: No
Expand In Territory: Yes
Space Needs: 6,689 SF; FS, SC

SUPPORT & TRAINING PROVIDED:
Financial Assistance Provided: No
Site Selection Assistance: No
Lease Negotiation Assistance: No
Co-Operative Advertising: Yes
Franchisee Assoc./Member: Yes/NA
Size Of Corporate Staff: 23
On-Going Support: A,B,C,D,E,F,G,H,I
Training: Managers - 1 Week Home Office and 11 Weeks On-Site; Employees - 2-4 Weeks On-Site.

SPECIFIC EXPANSION PLANS:
US: NW, SW, SE, HI
Canada: All Canada
Overseas: Brazil, China, Hong Kong, Japan, Venezuela

<< >>

BIG BOY RESTAURANT & BAKERY

4199 Marcy Dr.
Warren, MI 48091
Tel: (800) 837-3003 (810) 755-8114
Fax: (810) 757-4737
Web Site: www.bigboy.com
Mr. Ronald E. Johnston, Executive Vice President

Full-service family restaurant with over 60 years of success. BIG BOY'S comprehensive menu features a daily breakfast and fruit buffet, soup, salad and fruit bar, in-store bakery and award-winning desserts, in addition to traditional favorites. Industry leader in managed profitability.

BACKGROUND:
Established: 1936; 1st Franchised: 1952
Franchised Units: 596
Company-Owned Units 104
Total Units: 700
Dist.: US-373; CAN-0; O'seas-100
North America: 17 States
Density: 142 in MI, 102 in OH, 25 KY
Projected New Units (12 Months): 7
Qualifications: 5, 5, 4, 3, 4, 5
Registered: All States

FINANCIAL/TERMS:
Cash Investment: $250K
Total Investment: $600K-1.8MM
Minimum Net Worth: $700K
Fees: Franchise - $40K
Royalty - 3%; Ad. - 3%
Earnings Claim Statement: Yes
Term of Contract (Years): 20
Avg. # Of Employees: 10 FT, 25 PT
Passive Ownership: Discouraged
Encourage Conversions: Yes
Area Develop. Agreements: Yes/20
Sub-Franchising Contracts: No
Expand In Territory: Yes
Space Needs: 5,200 SF; FS

SUPPORT & TRAINING PROVIDED:
Financial Assistance Provided: Yes(I)
Site Selection Assistance: Yes
Lease Negotiation Assistance: Yes
Co-Operative Advertising: Yes
Franchisee Assoc./Member: Yes/Yes
Size Of Corporate Staff: 165
On-Going Support: A,B,C,D,E,F,G,H,I
Training: 6-8 Weeks In-Unit; 1-2 Weeks at Corporate Headquarters.

SPECIFIC EXPANSION PLANS:
US: All United States
Canada: All Canada
Overseas: All Countries

<< >>

BOBBY RUBINO'S PLACE FOR RIBS

1990 E. Sunrise Blvd.
Ft. Lauderdale, FL 33304
Tel: (800) 997-7427 (954) 763-9871
Fax: (954) 467-1192
E-Mail: rubinosusa@att.net
Ms. Kay Ferrara, Dir. Franchise Operations

Full-service, including full liquor service. Specializing in BBQ. BOBBY RUBINO'S PLACE FOR RIBS also has a large menu including steak, seafood, salads, etc. served in a casual atmosphere. A kiddie menu is available.

BACKGROUND:
Established: 1978; 1st Franchised: 1982
Franchised Units: 10
Company-Owned Units 0
Total Units: 10
Dist.: US-9; CAN-0; O'seas-1
North America: 5 States
Density: 4 in FL, 1 in CA, 1 in NY
Projected New Units (12 Months): 3
Qualifications: 5, 5, 3, 3, 3, 3
Registered: FL,MI,NY,WI

FINANCIAL/TERMS:
Cash Investment: $200K
Total Investment: $450-650K
Minimum Net Worth: $750K
Fees: Franchise - $50K
Royalty - 4%; Ad. - 3%
Earnings Claim Statement: No
Term of Contract (Years): 15/10
Avg. # Of Employees: 20 FT, 20 PT

Passive Ownership: Discouraged
Encourage Conversions: Yes
Area Develop. Agreements: Yes/Negot.
Sub-Franchising Contracts: No
Expand In Territory: Yes
Space Needs: 6,000 SF; FS, SF, SC, RM

SUPPORT & TRAINING PROVIDED:
Financial Assistance Provided: No
Site Selection Assistance: Yes
Lease Negotiation Assistance: Yes
Co-Operative Advertising: Yes
Franchisee Assoc./Member: No
Size Of Corporate Staff: 1
On-Going Support: a,C,d,E,F,h,I
Training: 6-8 Weeks Ft. Lauderdale, FL.

SPECIFIC EXPANSION PLANS:
US: All United States
Canada: All Canada
Overseas: All Countries

<< >>

BOSTON PIZZA INTERNATIONAL

5500 Parkwood Way, # 200
Richmond, BC V6V 2M4 CANADA
Tel: (800) 887-7757 (604) 270-1108
Fax: (604) 270-4168
E-Mail: franchising@bostonpizza.com
Web Site: www.bostonpizza.com
Mr. Rick Villalpando, Dir. Franchising

BOSTON PIZZA is Canada's most successful casual dining pizza and pasta franchise operation, with over 100 locations and system-wide sales in excess of $200 million. Boston Pizza appeals to four sectors: families at early evening; business people at lunch; after movies; and take-out and delivery.

BACKGROUND:
Established: 1963; 1st Franchised: 1968
Franchised Units: 130
Company-Owned Units 2
Total Units: 132
Dist.: US-3; CAN-129; O'seas-0
North America: 3 States, 5 Provinces
Density: 59 in AB, 44 in BC, 10 in SK
Projected New Units (12 Months): 12
Qualifications: 5, 5, 3, 3, 3, 4
Registered: ND,WA,AB

FINANCIAL/TERMS:
Cash Investment: $300-400K
Total Investment: $900K-1MM
Minimum Net Worth: $1MM
Fees: Franchise - $45-55K
Royalty - 7%; Ad. - 3%
Earnings Claim Statement: Yes
Term of Contract (Years): 10/10
Avg. # Of Employees: 30 FT, 40 PT
Passive Ownership: Not Allowed
Encourage Conversions: No
Area Develop. Agreements: Yes/10
Sub-Franchising Contracts: No
Expand In Territory: Yes
Space Needs: 5,000-6,600 SF; FS

SUPPORT & TRAINING PROVIDED:
Financial Assistance Provided: Yes(I)
Site Selection Assistance: Yes
Lease Negotiation Assistance: Yes
Co-Operative Advertising: Yes
Franchisee Assoc./Member: Yes/Yes
Size Of Corporate Staff: 79
On-Going Support: B,C,D,E,F,G,H
Training: 8 Weeks Richmond, BC, Corporate Training Centre.

SPECIFIC EXPANSION PLANS:
US: Northwest, Southwest, South
Canada: All Canada
Overseas: All Countries

<< >>

BUFFALO WILD WINGS GRILL & BAR

600 S. Highway 169, # 1919
Minneapolis, MN 55426-1919
Tel: (800) 499-9586 (952) 593-9943
Fax: (952) 593-9787
E-Mail: bill@bw3.com
Web Site: www.buffalowildwings.com
Mr. Bill McClintock, VP Franchise Development

Sports theme, family-friendly restaurant, world-famous buffalo wings with 12 proprietary sauces, great burgers & sandwiches, full bar, 25+ TV's, National Trivia Network.

BACKGROUND: IFA MEMBER
Established: 1982; 1st Franchised: 1991
Franchised Units: 107
Company-Owned Units 53
Total Units: 160
Dist.: US-133; CAN-0; O'seas-0
North America: 26 States
Density: 65 in OH, 15 in IN, 7 in KY
Projected New Units (12 Months): 35
Qualifications: 5, 4, 4, 3, 3, 5
Registered: All States

FINANCIAL/TERMS:
Cash Investment: $200K
Total Investment: $586-974K
Minimum Net Worth: $600K/Store
Fees: Franchise - $25-30K
Royalty - 5%; Ad. - 3%
Earnings Claim Statement: Yes
Term of Contract (Years): 10/10
Avg. # Of Employees: 3 FT, 50 PT
Passive Ownership: Not Allowed
Encourage Conversions: Yes
Area Develop. Agreements: Yes/10
Sub-Franchising Contracts: No
Expand In Territory: Yes
Space Needs: 5,000-6,000 SF; FS, SC

SUPPORT & TRAINING PROVIDED:
Financial Assistance Provided: Yes
Site Selection Assistance: Yes
Lease Negotiation Assistance: Yes
Co-Operative Advertising: Yes
Franchisee Assoc./Member: Yes/Yes
Size Of Corporate Staff: 65
On-Going Support: A,B,C,D,E,F,G,H,I
Training: 3 Weeks in Store.

SPECIFIC EXPANSION PLANS:
US: All United States
Canada: No
Overseas: No

BUFFALO WINGS & RINGS

900 Adams Crossing, # B
Cincinnati, OH 45202
Tel: (800) 501-2865 (513) 723-1886
Fax: (513) 723-0465
E-Mail: bwar@fuse.net
Web Site: www.wingsandrings.com
Ms. Linda D. Biciocchi, Executive Vice President

Casual dining featuring our signature wings, hamburgers, salads, specialty fries, homemade soups, chili and more. Our eclectic decor packages and award-winning menu attract customers of all ages. Key factors for our system are operational efficiency and economics.

BACKGROUND:
Established: 1988; 1st Franchised: 1989
Franchised Units: 25
Company-Owned Units 5
Total Units: 30
Dist.: US-25; CAN-0; O'seas-0
North America: NR
Density: 19 in OH, 5 in KY, 1 in IL
Projected New Units (12 Months): 10
Qualifications: 4, 4, 3, 3, 4, 5

Registered: CA,FL,IL,MD,NY,VA,WA,WI

FINANCIAL/TERMS:

Cash Investment: $95-200K
Total Investment: $200-300K
Minimum Net Worth: $400K
Fees: Franchise - $25K
Royalty - 4%; Ad. - 3%
Earnings Claim Statement: No
Term of Contract (Years): 10/10
Avg. # Of Employees:6-10 FT, 10-15 PT
Passive Ownership: Discouraged
Encourage Conversions: Yes
Area Develop. Agreements: Yes/5-10
Sub-Franchising Contracts: No
Expand In Territory: Yes
Space Needs: 2,500-4,500 SF; FS, SF, SC

SUPPORT & TRAINING PROVIDED:

Financial Assistance Provided: No
Site Selection Assistance: Yes
Lease Negotiation Assistance: Yes
Co-Operative Advertising: Yes
Franchisee Assoc./Member: No
Size Of Corporate Staff: 12
On-Going Support: C,d,E,F,H,I
Training: 278 Hours Cincinnati, OH.

SPECIFIC EXPANSION PLANS:

US: All United States
Canada: All Canada
Overseas: Asia, Europe, South America

BUFFALO'S CAFE

707 Whitlock Ave. SW, Bldg. H-13
Marietta, GA 30064
Tel: (800) 459-4647 (770) 420-1800
Fax: (770) 420-1811
E-Mail: kculkin@buffaloscafe.com
Web Site: www.buffaloscafe.com
Mr. William Taylor, VP Franchise Business

BUFFALO'S CAFE offers casual family dining in an 'Old West' cafe atmosphere. Menu is based on a fresh-food concept, featuring Buffalo-style chicken-wings, rotisserie chicken and other charbroiled specialties. Complete training is offered both initially and on-going.

BACKGROUND: IFA MEMBER

Established: 1985; 1st Franchised: 1991
Franchised Units: 42
Company-Owned Units 9
Total Units: 51
Dist.: US-49; CAN-0; O'seas-2
North America: 6 States, Puerto Rico
Density: 35 in GA, 5 in SC, 2 in AL
Projected New Units (12 Months): 20
Qualifications: 4, 4, 2, 2, 4, 4
Registered: FL

FINANCIAL/TERMS:

Cash Investment: $200K
Total Investment: $450K-1.5MM
Minimum Net Worth: $500K
Fees: Franchise - $35K
Royalty - 5%; Ad. - 2%
Earnings Claim Statement: No
Term of Contract (Years): 10/10/10
Avg. # Of Employees: 20 FT, 30 PT
Passive Ownership: Allowed
Encourage Conversions: No
Area Develop. Agreements: Yes/Varies
Sub-Franchising Contracts: No
Expand In Territory: Yes
Space Needs: 4,000-5,000 SF; FS, SC

SUPPORT & TRAINING PROVIDED:

Financial Assistance Provided: Yes(I)
Site Selection Assistance: Yes
Lease Negotiation Assistance: Yes
Co-Operative Advertising: Yes
Franchisee Assoc./Member: Yes
Size Of Corporate Staff: 20
On-Going Support: B,C,D,E,F,G,H,I
Training: 30 Days Corporate Store; 2 Weeks Franchisee's Store -- Pre & Post Opening.

SPECIFIC EXPANSION PLANS:

US: All United States
Canada: All Canada
Overseas: All Countries

CAFÉ SANTA FE

4004 N. College, # I
Fayetteville, AR 72703
Tel: (800) 909-4898 (501) 444-9001
Fax: (501) 444-0434
E-Mail: info@cafesantafe.com
Web Site: www.cafesantafe.com
Mr. Tom D. Flores, President

A unique blend of old-style Mexican food and new wave Southwest fare. CAFÉ SANTA FE is a contemporary Southwest-style concept that appeals to the young and old. It sets itself apart by not yielding to the 'Village' look. Bright, airy and festive! 'Come away with CAFÉ SANTA FE and taste the Southwest.'

BACKGROUND:

Established: 1982; 1st Franchised: 1996
Franchised Units: 11
Company-Owned Units 4
Total Units: 15
Dist.: US-15; CAN-0; O'seas-0
North America: 2 States
Density: 13 in AR, 2 in MO
Projected New Units (12 Months): 7
Qualifications: 3, 5, 3, 3, 5, 5
Registered: NR

FINANCIAL/TERMS:

Cash Investment: $200-250K
Total Investment: $1.1MM
Minimum Net Worth: $300K
Fees: Franchise - $35K
Royalty - 4.5%; Ad. - 1%
Earnings Claim Statement: No
Term of Contract (Years): 10/10
Avg. # Of Employees: 10 FT, 25 PT
Passive Ownership: Not Allowed
Encourage Conversions: Yes
Area Develop. Agreements: Yes/10
Sub-Franchising Contracts: No
Expand In Territory: Yes
Space Needs: 4,500 SF; FS, SC

SUPPORT & TRAINING PROVIDED:

Financial Assistance Provided: No
Site Selection Assistance: Yes
Lease Negotiation Assistance: Yes
Co-Operative Advertising: Yes
Franchisee Assoc./Member: No
Size Of Corporate Staff: 8
On-Going Support: A,B,C,D,E,F,G
Training: 4-6 Weeks in Springdale, AR -- Corporate Training; 2 Weeks, On-Site.

SPECIFIC EXPANSION PLANS:

US: AR, MO, KS, OK
Canada: No
Overseas: No

<< >>

CARLSON RESTAURANTS WORLDWIDE

P.O. Box 59159, Carlson Pkwy.
Minneapolis, MN 55459-8200
Tel: (800) FRIDAYS (612) 212-2181
Fax: (612) 212-2302
Web Site: www.tgifridays.com
Mr. Darwin Klockers, VP Contract Administration

Casual-theme, full-service restaurants.

BACKGROUND:

Established: 1965; 1st Franchised: 1970
Franchised Units: 360
Company-Owned Units 180
Total Units: 540
Dist.: US-414; CAN-1; O'seas-93
North America: 45 States
Density: 49 in FL, 42 in TX, 35 in CA
Projected New Units (12 Months): 100+
Qualifications: 5, 4, 5, 3, 5, 5

Registered: All States

FINANCIAL/TERMS:

Cash Investment: $1MM
Total Investment: $1.7-4MM
Minimum Net Worth: $3MM
Fees: Franchise - $75K
Royalty - 4%; Ad. - 2-4%
Earnings Claim Statement: Yes
Term of Contract (Years): 20/Varies
Avg. # Of Employees: 100-125
Passive Ownership: Discouraged
Encourage Conversions: Yes
Area Develop. Agreements: Yes/5
Sub-Franchising Contracts: No
Expand In Territory: Yes
Space Needs: 6,800 SF; FS

SUPPORT & TRAINING PROVIDED:

Financial Assistance Provided: No
Site Selection Assistance: Yes
Lease Negotiation Assistance: No
Co-Operative Advertising: No
Franchisee Assoc./Member: Yes/Yes
Size Of Corporate Staff: 300+
On-Going Support: b,c,d,e,h,I
Training: 2 Weeks in Dallas, TX.

SPECIFIC EXPANSION PLANS:

US: All United States
Canada: All Canada
Overseas: All Countries

<< >>

CASEY'S BAR/GRILL

10 Kingsbridge Garden Cir., # 600
Mississauga, ON L5R 3K6 CANADA
Tel: (905) 568-0000
Fax: (905) 568-0080
Web Site: www.primerestaurants.com
Mr. H. Ross R. Bain, VP Admin./Legal Counsel

Casual dining, grilled food, burgers, wraps.

BACKGROUND:

Established: 1979; 1st Franchised: 1979
Franchised Units: 20
Company-Owned Units 11
Total Units: 31
Dist.: US-0; CAN-31; O'seas-0
North America: 2 Provinces
Density: 26 in ON, 5 in PQ
Projected New Units (12 Months): 6
Qualifications: 5, 3, 3, 2, 5, 5
Registered: None

FINANCIAL/TERMS:

Cash Investment: $250-350K
Total Investment: $750-1035K
Minimum Net Worth: $500K
Fees: Franchise - $40K
Royalty - 5%; Ad. - 2%/2% Local
Earnings Claim Statement: No
Term of Contract (Years): 10/5/5
Avg. # Of Employees: 35 FT, 25 PT
Passive Ownership: Discouraged
Encourage Conversions: Yes
Area Develop. Agreements: Yes
Sub-Franchising Contracts: No
Expand In Territory: No
Space Needs: 5,168 SF; FS, SC, RM

SUPPORT & TRAINING PROVIDED:

Financial Assistance Provided: No
Site Selection Assistance: Yes
Lease Negotiation Assistance: Yes
Co-Operative Advertising: Yes
Franchisee Assoc./Member: Yes/Yes
Size Of Corporate Staff: 100
On-Going Support: B,C,D,E,h
Training: 6 Weeks in Store; 1 Week at Head Office.

SPECIFIC EXPANSION PLANS:

US: No
Canada: All Canada
Overseas: No

<< >>

Top 50

CHARLEY'S STEAKERY

6610 Busch Blvd., # 100
Columbus, OH 43229
Tel: (800) 437-8325 (614) 847-8100
Fax: (614) 847-8110
E-Mail: franchising@charleyssteakery.com
Web Site: www.charleyssteakery.com
Mr. Rich Page, Dir. National Development

CHARLEY'S STEAKERY is a progressive quick-service restaurant with over 100 locations across the United States and Canada. The heart of CHARLEY'S menu consists of freshly-grilled Steak and Chicken Subs, fresh-cut fries and freshly squeezed lemonade. CHARLEY'S open kitchen environment and freshly-prepared products are unique in the fast-food industry.

BACKGROUND: IFA MEMBER

Established: 1986; 1st Franchised: 1991
Franchised Units: 106
Company-Owned Units 12
Total Units: 118
Dist.: US-96; CAN-8; O'seas-2
North America: 27 States, 1 Province
Density: 15 in OH, 8 in FL,8 in ON
Projected New Units (12 Months): 60
Qualifications: 4, 5, 2, 2, 2, 5
Registered: CA,FL,HI,IL,IN,MD,MI,NY,VA,WI

FINANCIAL/TERMS:

Cash Investment: $NR
Total Investment: $124.5-294.5K
Minimum Net Worth: $200K
Fees: Franchise - $19.5K
Royalty - 5% or $200/Mo.; Ad. - 0.25%
Earnings Claim Statement: Yes
Term of Contract (Years): 10/10
Avg. # Of Employees: NR
Passive Ownership: Discouraged
Encourage Conversions: Yes
Area Develop. Agreements: Yes/10
Sub-Franchising Contracts: Yes
Expand In Territory: Yes
Space Needs: NR SF; SC, RM

SUPPORT & TRAINING PROVIDED:

Financial Assistance Provided: Yes(I)
Site Selection Assistance: Yes
Lease Negotiation Assistance: Yes
Co-Operative Advertising: Yes
Franchisee Assoc./Member: Yes/Yes
Size Of Corporate Staff: 18
On-Going Support: B,C,D,e(required),G,h,I
Training: 3 Weeks at Columbus, OH.

SPECIFIC EXPANSION PLANS:

US: All United States
Canada: ON
Overseas: No

<< >>

COLTER'S BAR-B-Q

5910 N. Central Expy., # 1355
Dallas, TX 75206
Tel: (888) 265-8377 (214) 987-5910
Fax: (214) 987-5938
E-Mail: anne@colter's
Web Site: www.coltersbbq.com
Ms. Marie Bernat, Vice President

Casual, family, cafeteria-style barbeque restaurant, serving Texas barbeque in a western setting.

BACKGROUND:
Established: 1982; 1st Franchised: 1994
Franchised Units: 9
Company-Owned Units 6
Total Units: 15
Dist.: US-13; CAN-0; O'seas-0
North America: 1 State
Density: 13 in TX
Projected New Units (12 Months): 2-4
Qualifications: 5, 4, 4, 3, 4, 3
Registered: NR

FINANCIAL/TERMS:
Cash Investment: $156-250K
Total Investment: $730K-1.03MM
Minimum Net Worth: $1-1.5MM
Fees: Franchise - $30K
Royalty - 4%; Ad. - 0.5%
Earnings Claim Statement: No
Term of Contract (Years): 20/10-20
Avg. # Of Employees: 3 FT, 25 PT
Passive Ownership: Discouraged
Encourage Conversions: No
Area Develop. Agreements: Yes/Open
Sub-Franchising Contracts: No
Expand In Territory: Yes
Space Needs: 4,600 SF; FS

SUPPORT & TRAINING PROVIDED:
Financial Assistance Provided: Yes(I)
Site Selection Assistance: Yes
Lease Negotiation Assistance: N/A
Co-Operative Advertising: Yes
Franchisee Assoc./Member: No
Size Of Corporate Staff: 10
On-Going Support: B,C,D,E,F,H,I
Training: 8 Weeks at Dallas, TX.

SPECIFIC EXPANSION PLANS:
US: Southwest, Northeast
Canada: No
Overseas: No

<< >>

COYOTE CANYON
2908 N. Plum St.
Hutchinson, KS 67502
Tel: (620) 669-9372
Fax: (620) 669-0531
E-Mail: dans@stockagecompanies.com
Web Site: www.stockadecompanies.com
Mr. Dan Spitz, Dir. Franchise Sales

MONTANA CANYON is an 'all you can eat' steak buffet, featuring a self-service salad bar, a hot food buffet, a dessert bar and a display bakery at one affordable price, which also includes your drink.

BACKGROUND:
Established: 1984; 1st Franchised: 1984
Franchised Units: 6
Company-Owned Units 1
Total Units: 7
Dist.: US-7; CAN-0; O'seas-0
North America: 5 States
Density: 2 in TX, 2 in KS
Projected New Units (12 Months): 2
Qualifications: 5, 4, 4, 3, 2, 4
Registered: IL,IN,VA

FINANCIAL/TERMS:
Cash Investment: $250-350K
Total Investment: $1.2-2.2MM
Minimum Net Worth: $1MM
Fees: Franchise - $20K
Royalty - 3%; Ad. - 1%
Earnings Claim Statement: No
Term of Contract (Years): 15/5
Avg. # Of Employees: 20 FT, 50 PT
Passive Ownership: Discouraged
Encourage Conversions: Yes
Area Develop. Agreements: Not Now
Sub-Franchising Contracts: No
Expand In Territory: Yes
Space Needs: 10,000 SF; FS

SUPPORT & TRAINING PROVIDED:
Financial Assistance Provided: No
Site Selection Assistance: Yes
Lease Negotiation Assistance: No
Co-Operative Advertising: No
Franchisee Assoc./Member: NR
Size Of Corporate Staff: 16
On-Going Support: B,C,D,E,G,h,i
Training: 6-8 Weeks Training.

SPECIFIC EXPANSION PLANS:
US: All United States
Canada: No
Overseas: No

<< >>

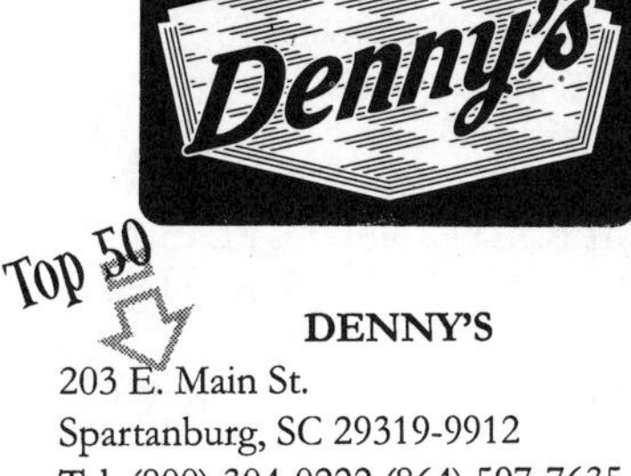

Top 50

DENNY'S
203 E. Main St.
Spartanburg, SC 29319-9912
Tel: (800) 304-0222 (864) 597-7635
Fax: (864) 597-7708
B_Cauthan@Advantica-Dine.Com
Web Site: www.dennys.com/franchise
Ms. Beth Cauthan, Administrator

From its beginning in 1953, DENNY'S has grown into one of America's largest full-service restaurant chains, serving nearly 1 million customers a day at its nearly 1,800 restaurants worldwide. Today, DENNY'S is going back to its roots with the DENNY'S Diner 2000 reimaging program for existing restaurants. DENNY'S is well known for its around-the-clock breakfast entrees and is the only full-service restaurant chain where most restaurants are open 24 hours a day, 7 days a week.

BACKGROUND: IFA MEMBER
Established: 1953; 1st Franchised: 1963
Franchised Units: 708
Company-Owned Units 884
Total Units: 1,592
Dist.: US-1745; CAN-48; O'seas-23
North America: 49 States, 4 Provinces
Density: 207 in CA, 135 in FL, 100 TX
Projected New Units (12 Months): NR
Qualifications: 5, 5, 5, 2, 2, 5
Registered: All States

FINANCIAL/TERMS:
Cash Investment: $250K
Total Investment: $858K-1.5MM
Minimum Net Worth: $750K
Fees: Franchise - $35K
Royalty - 4%; Ad. - 5%
Earnings Claim Statement: Yes
Term of Contract (Years): 20/N/A
Avg. # Of Employees: 80 FT
Passive Ownership: Discouraged
Encourage Conversions: Yes
Area Develop. Agreements: Yes
Sub-Franchising Contracts: No
Expand In Territory: Yes
Space Needs: 30,000-38,364 SF; FS, SC, Other

SUPPORT & TRAINING PROVIDED:
Financial Assistance Provided: Yes(I)
Site Selection Assistance: Yes
Lease Negotiation Assistance: No
Co-Operative Advertising: Yes
Franchisee Assoc./Member: Yes/No
Size Of Corporate Staff: 18
On-Going Support: C,D,E,G,H,I
Training: Up to 10 Weeks at Various Geographical Areas.

SPECIFIC EXPANSION PLANS:
US: All United States
Canada: All Canada
Overseas: No

<< >>

DESERT MOON CAFÉ
612 Corporate Wy., # 1M
Valley Cottage, NY 10989-2021
Tel: (877) JOIN-DMC (845) 267-3300
Fax: (845) 267-2548
E-Mail: desertmooncafe@msn.com
Web Site: www.desertmooncafe.com
Mr. Mike Liedberg, Chief Executive Officer

Fast casual Southwestern / Fresh Mexican Grille in a fun, bold environment.

BACKGROUND: IFA MEMBER
Established: 1998; 1st Franchised: 1999
Franchised Units: 8
Company-Owned Units 5
Total Units: 13
Dist.: US-13; CAN-0; O'seas-0
North America: 7 States
Density: 4 in NY, 2 in CT, 2 in VA
Projected New Units (12 Months): 15
Qualifications: 5, 3, 4, 1, 3, 5
Registered: FL,MD,MI,NY,RI,VA,DC

FINANCIAL/TERMS:
Cash Investment: $100K
Total Investment: $190-350K
Minimum Net Worth: $250K
Fees: Franchise - $25K
Royalty - 5%; Ad. - 3%
Earnings Claim Statement: No
Term of Contract (Years): 10/5
Avg. # Of Employees: 3 FT, 6 PT
Passive Ownership: Discouraged
Encourage Conversions: Yes
Area Develop. Agreements: Yes/3
Sub-Franchising Contracts: No
Expand In Territory: Yes
Space Needs: 1,800 SF; SC

SUPPORT & TRAINING PROVIDED:
Financial Assistance Provided: Yes(I)
Site Selection Assistance: Yes
Lease Negotiation Assistance: Yes
Co-Operative Advertising: Yes
Franchisee Assoc./Member: Yes/Yes
Size Of Corporate Staff: 7
On-Going Support: C,D,E,F,G,I
Training: 3 Weeks Corporate Training; 2 Weeks On-Site.

SPECIFIC EXPANSION PLANS:
US: All United States
Canada: No
Overseas: No

<< >>

DICKEY'S BARBECUE PIT RESTAURANTS
4515 Cole Ave., # 1000
Dallas, TX 75205
Tel: (800) 460-9000 (972) 248-9899
Fax: (972) 248-8667
E-Mail: info@dickeys.com
Web Site: www.dickeys.com
Ms. Cecile E. Fountain, Franchise Development

Original Texas-style, slow-smoked barbecue. 8 meats and 15 hot and cold veggie dishes made fresh every day. Average 4,000 SF, seating 120-140. In-line, conversions and new buildings. Custom exteriors.

BACKGROUND: IFA MEMBER
Established: 1941; 1st Franchised: 1994
Franchised Units: 30
Company-Owned Units 5
Total Units: 35
Dist.: US-21; CAN-0; O'seas-0
North America: 3 States
Density: 18 in TX, 2 in CO, 1 in CA
Projected New Units (12 Months): 40
Qualifications: 5, 4, 1, 4, 1, 5
Registered: CA,FL,RI

FINANCIAL/TERMS:
Cash Investment: $150-250K
Total Investment: $450K-1.3MM
Minimum Net Worth: $500K
Fees: Franchise - $25K
Royalty - 4%; Ad. - 2%
Earnings Claim Statement: Yes
Term of Contract (Years): 10/20
Avg. # Of Employees: 10 FT, 8 PT
Passive Ownership: Discouraged
Encourage Conversions: Yes
Area Develop. Agreements: Yes/5
Sub-Franchising Contracts: No
Expand In Territory: No
Space Needs: 4,000 SF; FS, SC, RM, Conversions

SUPPORT & TRAINING PROVIDED:
Financial Assistance Provided: Yes(I)
Site Selection Assistance: Yes
Lease Negotiation Assistance: Yes
Co-Operative Advertising: Yes
Franchisee Assoc./Member: No
Size Of Corporate Staff: 10
On-Going Support: B,C,D,E,F,h,I
Training: 30 Days Dallas, TX.

SPECIFIC EXPANSION PLANS:
US: West, Tidewater
Canada: No
Overseas: Pacific Rim

<< >>

An American Italian Eatery

EAST SIDE MARIO'S
10 Kingsbridge Garden Cir., # 600
Mississauga, ON L5R 3K6 CANADA
Tel: (800) 361-3111 (905) 568-0000
Fax: (905) 568-0080
Web Site: www.primerestaurants.com
Mr. H. Ross R. Bain, VP Admin./Legal Counsel

American-Italian.

BACKGROUND:
Established: 1979; 1st Franchised: 1989
Franchised Units: 85
Company-Owned Units 7
Total Units: 92
Dist.: US-6; CAN-86; O'seas-0
North America: 5 States, 6 Provinces
Density: 61 in ON, 12 in PQ, 7 in AB
Projected New Units (12 Months): 12
Qualifications: 5, 3, 3, 2, 5, 5
Registered: NR

FINANCIAL/TERMS:
Cash Investment: $300-400K
Total Investment: $850-1135K
Minimum Net Worth: $750K
Fees: Franchise - $50K
Royalty - 5%; Ad. - 3%/1% Local
Earnings Claim Statement: No
Term of Contract (Years): 10/5/5
Avg. # Of Employees: 50 FT, 25 PT
Passive Ownership: Discouraged
Encourage Conversions: Yes
Area Develop. Agreements: Yes
Sub-Franchising Contracts: No
Expand In Territory: No
Space Needs: 5,314 SF; FS, SC, RM

SUPPORT & TRAINING PROVIDED:
Financial Assistance Provided: No
Site Selection Assistance: Yes
Lease Negotiation Assistance: Yes
Co-Operative Advertising: Yes
Franchisee Assoc./Member: Yes/Yes
Size Of Corporate Staff: 100
On-Going Support: B,C,D,E,h
Training: 6 Weeks in Store; 1 Week at Head Office.

SPECIFIC EXPANSION PLANS:
US: No

Canada: All Canada
Overseas: No

<< >>

EDO JAPAN

4838 32nd St. SE
Calgary, AB T2B 2S6 CANADA
Tel: (403) 215-8800
Fax: (403) 215-8801
E-Mail: edo@edojapan.com
Web Site: www.edojapan.com
Ms. Colleen Pickard, Mgr. Legal/Admin.

EDO JAPAN originated the concept of preparing Japanese Teppan Meals inexpensively through fast-food outlets more than 20 years ago. Since that time, EDO has maintained its popularity in the food courts due to EDO's menu placing emphasis on freshness, nutrition, service and very reasonable prices.

BACKGROUND:
Established: 1977; 1st Franchised: 1986
Franchised Units: 93
Company-Owned Units 6
Total Units: 99
Dist.: US-46; CAN-55; O'seas-3
North America: 13 States, 5 Provinces
Density: 28 in AB, 16 in ON, 14 in CA
Projected New Units (12 Months): 6
Qualifications: 5, 4, 4, 3, 4, 5
Registered: CA,FL,HI,MD,OR,WA,AB

FINANCIAL/TERMS:
Cash Investment: $NR
Total Investment: $160-350K
Minimum Net Worth: $NR
Fees: Franchise - $20K
Royalty - 6%; Ad. - 0-2%
Earnings Claim Statement: No
Term of Contract (Years): Lease
Avg. # Of Employees: 2 FT, 4 PT
Passive Ownership: Discouraged
Encourage Conversions: N/A
Area Develop. Agreements: Yes/Varies
Sub-Franchising Contracts: Yes
Expand In Territory: Yes
Space Needs: 350-650 SF; RM

SUPPORT & TRAINING PROVIDED:
Financial Assistance Provided: No
Site Selection Assistance: Yes
Lease Negotiation Assistance: Yes
Co-Operative Advertising: Yes
Franchisee Assoc./Member: No
Size Of Corporate Staff: 10
On-Going Support: B,C,D,E,F,G,H
Training: 2 Weeks Calgary, AB; 10 Days Opening Assistance On-Site.

SPECIFIC EXPANSION PLANS:
US: All United States
Canada: No
Overseas: No

<< >>

Elmer's
BREAKFAST • LUNCH • DINNER

ELMER'S BREAKFAST/LUNCH/ DINNER

11802 SE Stark St.
Portland, OR 97216
Tel: (800) 325-5188 (503) 252-1485
Fax: (503) 252-6706
Web Site: www.elmers-restaurants.com
Mr. Jerry Scott, VP Operations

Full-service, family-oriented restaurant serving three meals a day. All menu items served all day. Banquet facilities.

BACKGROUND:
Established: 1960; 1st Franchised: 1966
Franchised Units: 19
Company-Owned Units 13
Total Units: 32
Dist.: US-32; CAN-0; O'seas-0
North America: 6 States
Density: 17 in OR, 5 in WA, 5 in ID
Projected New Units (12 Months): 3
Qualifications: 5, 5, 3, 3, 4, 5
Registered: CA,OR,WA

FINANCIAL/TERMS:
Cash Investment: $200K
Total Investment: $N/A
Minimum Net Worth: $Varies
Fees: Franchise - $35K
Royalty - 4%; Ad. - 1%
Earnings Claim Statement: No
Term of Contract (Years): 25/Varies
Avg. # Of Employees: 15 FT, 35 PT
Passive Ownership: Not Allowed
Encourage Conversions: Yes
Area Develop. Agreements: Yes/5
Sub-Franchising Contracts: No
Expand In Territory: Yes
Space Needs: 5,500 SF; FS

SUPPORT & TRAINING PROVIDED:
Financial Assistance Provided: Yes(I)
Site Selection Assistance: Yes
Lease Negotiation Assistance: Yes
Co-Operative Advertising: Yes
Franchisee Assoc./Member: No
Size Of Corporate Staff: 20
On-Going Support: B,C,D,E,G,h
Training: 8-12 Weeks Portland, OR.

SPECIFIC EXPANSION PLANS:
US: Northwest
Canada: No
Overseas: No

<< >>

FRIENDLY'S RESTAURANT

1855 Boston Rd.
Wilbraham, MA 01095
Tel: (888) 342-7776 (413) 543-2400
Fax: (413) 543-1015
E-Mail: laurel.adams@friendlys.com
Web Site: www.friendlys.com
Mr. Bill Pierquet, VP Development

FRIENDLY'S is a full-service restaurant chain with ice cream a key point of difference. FRIENDLY'S has enjoyed five years of comparable store sales increases and five years of guest check average increases. The franchise will receive full support for success, including training, marketing, site selection, store openings and on-going operational assistance.

BACKGROUND: IFA MEMBER
Established: 1935; 1st Franchised: 1997
Franchised Units: 157
Company-Owned Units 404
Total Units: 561
Dist.: US-561; CAN-0; O'seas-0
North America: 17 States
Density: 164 in NY, 153 in MA, 67 CT
Projected New Units (12 Months): 41
Registered: FL,IL,IN,MD,MI,NY,RI,VA ,WI

FINANCIAL/TERMS:
Cash Investment: $300-400K
Total Investment: $875K-1.5MM
Minimum Net Worth: $1MM (400Liq)
Fees: Franchise - $35K
Royalty - 4%; Ad. - 3%
Earnings Claim Statement: Yes
Term of Contract (Years): 20/10-20
Avg. # Of Employees: 40 FT, 35 PT
Passive Ownership: Allowed
Encourage Conversions: Yes
Area Develop. Agreements: Yes
Sub-Franchising Contracts: No
Expand In Territory: Yes

Space Needs: 4,100-5,000 SF; FS

SUPPORT & TRAINING PROVIDED:

Financial Assistance Provided: No
Site Selection Assistance: Yes
Lease Negotiation Assistance: Yes
Co-Operative Advertising: Yes
Franchisee Assoc./Member: No
Size Of Corporate Staff: 400
On-Going Support: A,b,C,d,E,F,G,h
Training: 12 Weeks at the Corporate Training Center and in Individual Training Units.

SPECIFIC EXPANSION PLANS:

US: SE, NE, Mid-Atlantic
Canada: No
Overseas: All Countries

<< >>

Top 50

FUDDRUCKERS

35 Old Avon Village, # 347
Avon, CT 06001
Tel: (860) 651-4421
Fax: (860) 651-5218
E-Mail: craig.ahrens@fuddruckers.com
Web Site: www.fuddruckers.com
Mr. Craig Ahrens, SVP Franchise Development

It's an exciting time at FUDDRUCKERS. Our relentless commitment to freshness makes us "Home of the World's Greatest Hamburgers". Our in-house butcher shops and bakeries provide our guests with the freshest products available. FUDDRUCKERS' menu includes not only our famous 1/3 and 1/2 pound hamburgers but now features a 1-lb. burger. We have also added Big Bowl salads, new Steakhouse Platters and fantastic desserts like our Brownie Blast Sundae. We also have a new 50's and 60's rock and roll image.

BACKGROUND: IFA MEMBER

Established: 1980; 1st Franchised: 1982
Franchised Units: 100
Company-Owned Units 108
Total Units: 208
Dist.: US-199; CAN-1; O'seas-12
North America: 30 States, 1 Province
Density: 37 in TX, 12 in VA, 11 in IL
Projected New Units (12 Months): 12
Qualifications: 5, 5, 4, 3, 2, 5
Registered: CA,FL,HI,IL,IN,MD,MI,MN,NY,ND,OR,RI,SD,VA,WA,DC,AB

FINANCIAL/TERMS:

Cash Investment: $300K
Total Investment: $650K-1.28MM
Minimum Net Worth: $1MM
Fees: Franchise - $50K
Royalty - 5%; Ad. - 0-3%
Earnings Claim Statement: No
Term of Contract (Years): 20/20
Avg. # Of Employees: 15 FT, 30 PT
Passive Ownership: Discouraged
Encourage Conversions: Yes
Area Develop. Agreements: Yes/Varies
Sub-Franchising Contracts: No
Expand In Territory: Yes
Space Needs: 6,800 SF; FS

SUPPORT & TRAINING PROVIDED:

Financial Assistance Provided: No
Site Selection Assistance: Yes
Lease Negotiation Assistance: No
Co-Operative Advertising: NR
Franchisee Assoc./Member: No
Size Of Corporate Staff: 70
On-Going Support: C,D,E
Training: 8 Weeks at Regional Training Locations.

SPECIFIC EXPANSION PLANS:

US: All United States
Canada: All Canada
Overseas: All Countries

<< >>

Top 50

GOLDEN CORRAL FAMILY STEAKHOUSE

P.O. Box 29502
Raleigh, NC 27626-0502
Tel: (800) 284-5673 (919) 881-5128
Fax: (919) 881-5252
Web Site: www.goldencorral.net
Mrs. Tammy Sullivan, Fran. Dev.

Golden Corral family restaurants feature 'steaks, buffet and bakery.' The 'Golden Choice Buffet' offers 140 hot and cold items. A special feature is 'The Brass Bell Bakery' which prepares made-from-scratch rolls, cookies, muffins, brownies and pizza. Steak, chicken and fish entrees are also available. Value-driven concept with a $6.72 per person check average in 2000. Open lunch and dinner - 7 days; Breakfast Buffet - weekends or holidays.

BACKGROUND: IFA MEMBER

Established: 1973; 1st Franchised: 1986
Franchised Units: 345
Company-Owned Units 124
Total Units: 469
Dist.: US-469; CAN-0; O'seas-0
North America: 40 States
Density: TX, OK, NC
Projected New Units (12 Months): 25
Registered: All States Exc. HI

FINANCIAL/TERMS:

Cash Investment: $300K
Total Investment: $1.5-3.7MM
Minimum Net Worth: $1.5MM
Fees: Franchise - $40K
Royalty - 4%; Ad. - 2%
Earnings Claim Statement: Yes
Term of Contract (Years): 15/5
Avg. # Of Employees: 80 FT, 40 PT
Passive Ownership: Not Allowed
Encourage Conversions: No
Area Develop. Agreements: Yes/Varies
Sub-Franchising Contracts: No
Expand In Territory: Yes
Space Needs: 7,700-11,500 SF; FS

SUPPORT & TRAINING PROVIDED:

Financial Assistance Provided: No
Site Selection Assistance: Yes
Lease Negotiation Assistance: No
Co-Operative Advertising: Yes
Franchisee Assoc./Member: NR
Size Of Corporate Staff: 190
On-Going Support: C,D,E,G
Training: 12 Weeks Headquarters and Field.

SPECIFIC EXPANSION PLANS:

US: All United States
Canada: All Canada
Overseas: Mexico, Puerto Rico

<< >>

GOLDEN GRIDDLE FAMILY RESTAURANTS

505 Consumers Rd., # 1000
North York, ON M2J 4V8 CANADA
Tel: (416) 493-3800
Fax: (416) 493-3889
E-Mail: gogrill@interlog.com
Web Site: www.goldengriddlecorp.com
Mr. W. W. Hood, President

Full-service, licensed family restaurant, serving all day. We are located primarily in hotels and are totally franchised.

BACKGROUND:
Established: 1964; 1st Franchised: 1976
Franchised Units: 33
Company-Owned Units 0
Total Units: 33
Dist.: US-1; CAN-41; O'seas-0
North America: 1 State, 3 Provinces
Density: 39 in ON, 3 in BC, 1 in MI
Projected New Units (12 Months): 14
Qualifications: 5, 4, 3, 3, 2, 5
Registered: NR
FINANCIAL/TERMS:
Cash Investment: $50-100K
Total Investment: $100-500K
Minimum Net Worth: $100K
Fees: Franchise - $17.5-25K
Royalty - 5%; Ad. - 3%
Earnings Claim Statement: No
Term of Contract (Years): 10/10
Avg. # Of Employees: 3-6 FT, 10-30 PT
Passive Ownership: Discouraged
Encourage Conversions: Yes
Area Develop. Agreements: Yes/5
Sub-Franchising Contracts: No
Expand In Territory: Yes
Space Needs: 3,000 SF; FS, SF, SC, RM
SUPPORT & TRAINING PROVIDED:
Financial Assistance Provided: No
Site Selection Assistance: Yes
Lease Negotiation Assistance: Yes
Co-Operative Advertising: Yes
Franchisee Assoc./Member: No
Size Of Corporate Staff: 20
On-Going Support: B,C,D,d,E,G,H,h
Training: 3-5 Days at Head Offoce; 14-28 Days at Training Store.
SPECIFIC EXPANSION PLANS:
US: Northeast, Southeast
Canada: All Canada
Overseas: No

<< >>

GREAT STEAK & POTATO COMPANY
188 N. Brookwood Ave., # 100
Hamilton, OH 45013
Tel: (513) 896-9695
Fax: (513) 896-3750
E-Mail: franchiseinfo@thegreatsteak.com
Web Site: www.thegreatsteak.com
Mr. Roger J. Burrin, VP Franchise Development

America's premier fresh grilled cheesesteak franchisor, serving hand-cut french fries (cooked in peanut oil), baked potatoes with various toppings, grilled topped salads, homemade soups and fresh-squeezed lemonade.

BACKGROUND:
Established: 1982; 1st Franchised: 1984
Franchised Units: 221
Company-Owned Units 9
Total Units: 230
Dist.: US-214; CAN-12; O'seas-4
North America: 31 States, 1 Provinces
Density: 32 in OH, 27 in CA, 25 in IL
Projected New Units (12 Months): 24
Qualifications: 4, 4, 3, 2, 3, 4
Registered: All States
FINANCIAL/TERMS:
Cash Investment: $75-100K
Total Investment: $200-800K
Minimum Net Worth: $200K
Fees: Franchise - $20K
Royalty - 5%; Ad. - 2%
Earnings Claim Statement: No
Term of Contract (Years): 10/10
Avg. # Of Employees: 2 FT, 15 PT
Passive Ownership: Allowed
Encourage Conversions: Yes
Area Develop. Agreements: Yes/10
Sub-Franchising Contracts: Yes
Expand In Territory: Yes
Space Needs: 600-2,000 SF; FS,SF,SC,RM, Airports,Univ.
SUPPORT & TRAINING PROVIDED:
Financial Assistance Provided: Yes(I)
Site Selection Assistance: Yes
Lease Negotiation Assistance: Yes
Co-Operative Advertising: Yes
Franchisee Assoc./Member: No
Size Of Corporate Staff: 28
On-Going Support: a,B,C,D,E,F,G,H
Training: 2 Weeks Hamilton, OH.
SPECIFIC EXPANSION PLANS:
US: All United States
Canada: All Canada
Overseas: No

<< >>

HARVEY'S RESTAURANTS
6303 Airport Rd.
Mississauga, ON L4V 1R8 CANADA
Tel: (905) 405-6771
Fax: (905) 405-6667
E-Mail: ifong@cara.com
Web Site: www.cara.com
Mr. Claus Etzler, Franchise Manager

Foodservice. Quick-service restaurants.

BACKGROUND:
Established: 1900; 1st Franchised: 1982
Franchised Units: 330
Company-Owned Units 39
Total Units: 369
Dist.: US-0; CAN-350; O'seas-0
North America: NR
Density: ON, PQ, AB
Projected New Units (12 Months): 42
Qualifications: 5, 4, 3, 3, 1, 5
Registered: AB
FINANCIAL/TERMS:
Cash Investment: $155-200K
Total Investment: $510-600K
Minimum Net Worth: $300K
Fees: Franchise - $50-75K
Royalty - 5%; Ad. - 4%
Earnings Claim Statement: Yes
Term of Contract (Years): 20/5x4
Avg. # Of Employees: 3 FT, 40 PT
Passive Ownership: Not Allowed
Encourage Conversions: Yes
Area Develop. Agreements: No
Sub-Franchising Contracts: No
Expand In Territory: Yes
Space Needs: 2,600 SF; FS
SUPPORT & TRAINING PROVIDED:
Financial Assistance Provided: N/A
Site Selection Assistance: Yes
Lease Negotiation Assistance: Yes
Co-Operative Advertising: Yes
Franchisee Assoc./Member: Yes/Yes
Size Of Corporate Staff: 200
On-Going Support: C,D,E,G,h,I
Training: 6-8 Weeks Toronto, ON.
SPECIFIC EXPANSION PLANS:
US: No
Canada: All Canada
Overseas: No

<< >>

HOULIHAN'S RESTAURANT GROUP
2 Brush Creek Blvd., P.O. Box 16000
Kansas City, MO 64112
Tel: (816) 756-2200
Fax: (816) 561-2842
E-Mail: bgrams@houlihans.com
Web Site: www.houlihans.com
Ms. Bridget Grams, Dir. Franchise Sales

HOULIHAN'S is the ONE casual dining

restaurant and bar with a varied menu catering to adults.

BACKGROUND:
Established: 1972; 1st Franchised: 1987
Franchised Units: 47
Company-Owned Units 62
Total Units: 109
Dist.: US-110; CAN-0; O'seas-0
North America: 24 States
Density: NJ, PA
Projected New Units (12 Months): 10
Qualifications: 4, 4, 5, 3, 3, 4
Registered: All States

FINANCIAL/TERMS:
Cash Investment: $1MM
Total Investment: $NR
Minimum Net Worth: $4MM
Fees: Franchise - $40K
Royalty - 4%; Ad. - 1.5%
Earnings Claim Statement: Yes
Term of Contract (Years): 20/10
Avg. # Of Employees: 40 FT, 80 PT
Passive Ownership: Allowed
Encourage Conversions: Yes
Area Develop. Agreements: Yes/Varies
Sub-Franchising Contracts: No
Expand In Territory: NR
Space Needs: 5,000 SF; FS, SF, SC, RM

SUPPORT & TRAINING PROVIDED:
Financial Assistance Provided: No
Site Selection Assistance: Yes
Lease Negotiation Assistance: Yes
Co-Operative Advertising: Yes
Franchisee Assoc./Member: No
Size Of Corporate Staff: 120
On-Going Support: B,C,D,E,F,H,I
Training: 90-120 Days in Various Locations in U.S.

SPECIFIC EXPANSION PLANS:
US: All United States
Canada: No
Overseas: No

HUDDLE HOUSE RESTAURANTS
2969 E. Ponce de Leon Ave.
Decatur, GA 30030
Tel: (800) 686-5700 (404) 377-5700
Fax: (404) 377-0497
E-Mail: franchise@huddlehouse.com
Web Site: www.huddlehouse.com
Mr. Cory Durden, Dir. Franchise Development

HUDDLE HOUSE RESTAURANTS are open 24 hours a day, serving delicious meals, cooked to order - a place where hungry folks gather to enjoy good food, good friends and good hospitality. HUDDLE HOUSE RESTAURANTS offer any meal, any time from our broad menu of breakfast, lunch and dinner entrees, featuring, 'Big House' platters, which are our signature 'Big Meals for Big Appetites.'

BACKGROUND: IFA MEMBER
Established: 1964; 1st Franchised: 1966
Franchised Units: 322
Company-Owned Units 31
Total Units: 354
Dist.: US-360; CAN-0; O'seas-0
North America: 13 States
Density: 166 in GA, 60 in SC, 34 AL
Projected New Units (12 Months): 40
Qualifications: 5, 5, 4, 3, 3, 4
Registered: FL,IL,IN,VA

FINANCIAL/TERMS:
Cash Investment: $120-500K
Total Investment: $120-500K
Minimum Net Worth: $200K
Fees: Franchise - $20K
Royalty - 4%; Ad. - 1%
Earnings Claim Statement: No
Term of Contract (Years): 15/5x3
Avg. # Of Employees: 18 FT, 6 PT
Passive Ownership: Discouraged
Encourage Conversions: Yes
Area Develop. Agreements: Yes/Varies
Sub-Franchising Contracts: Yes
Expand In Territory: Yes
Space Needs: 2,000 SF; FS,SF,SC, Co-Brand, C-Stores

SUPPORT & TRAINING PROVIDED:
Financial Assistance Provided: No
Site Selection Assistance: Yes
Lease Negotiation Assistance: Yes
Co-Operative Advertising: Yes
Franchisee Assoc./Member: Yes/No
Size Of Corporate Staff: 120
On-Going Support: b,C,D,E,f,h,I
Training: 5-6 Weeks Metro Atlanta, GA; 1-2 Weeks On-Site Pre-Opening; 1 Week Training Store.

SPECIFIC EXPANSION PLANS:
US: Southeast, Midwest
Canada: No
Overseas: No

<< >>

HUDSON'S GRILL OF AMERICA
16970 Dallas Pkwy., # 402
Dallas, TX 75248-1928
Tel: (972) 931-9237
Fax: (972) 931-1326
E-Mail: sacco@hudsonsgrill.com
Web Site: www.hudsonsgrill.com
Mr. Tom Sacco

A casual-style, full-service, high-energy, late 50's and early 60's rock 'n' roll theme restaurant and bar. Burgers, chicken sandwiches, salads, desserts and specialty items, such as fajitas. TV monitors throughout restaurant and bar show sporting events while the bubbling Wurlitzer juke box beats out Elvis Presley and Beatles' tunes, bridging the past with the present.

BACKGROUND:
Established: 1985; 1st Franchised: 1986
Franchised Units: 17
Company-Owned Units 2
Total Units: 19
Dist.: US-17; CAN-0; O'seas-0
North America: 4 States
Density: 10 in CA, 4 in TX, 2 in MI
Projected New Units (12 Months): 4
Qualifications: 5, 3, 1, 3, 3, 5
Registered: All Except RI

FINANCIAL/TERMS:
Cash Investment: $125K
Total Investment: $100K-1MM
Minimum Net Worth: $250K
Fees: Franchise - $25K
Royalty - 4%; Ad. - 1%
Earnings Claim Statement: Yes
Term of Contract (Years): 20/20
Avg. # Of Employees: 12 FT, 38 PT
Passive Ownership: Allowed
Encourage Conversions: No
Area Develop. Agreements: Yes/5
Sub-Franchising Contracts: Yes
Expand In Territory: Yes
Space Needs: 4,500 SF; FS

SUPPORT & TRAINING PROVIDED:
Financial Assistance Provided: Yes(I)
Site Selection Assistance: Yes
Lease Negotiation Assistance: Yes
Co-Operative Advertising: Yes
Franchisee Assoc./Member: No
Size Of Corporate Staff: 7
On-Going Support: B,C,D,E,F,H
Training: 5-6 Weeks CA; 5-6 Weeks TX.

SPECIFIC EXPANSION PLANS:
US: All United States
Canada: BC,AB,ON,PQ,NS
Overseas: Latin America, South America, Pacific Rim, Europe

<< >>

HUMPTY'S FAMILY RESTAURANT
2505 Macleod Trail S.
Calgary, AB T2G 5J4 CANADA
Tel: (800) 661-7589 (403) 269-4675
Fax: (403) 266-1973
E-Mail: humpty@cadvision.com
Web Site: www.humptys.com
Mr. Don Koenig, President

A full-service, family-oriented restaurant, offering a varied menu that includes an extensive breakfast menu. Available 24 hours a day at most locations. Many restaurants are highway-located and include gas and convenience-store service.

BACKGROUND:
Established: 1977; 1st Franchised: 1982
Franchised Units: 55
Company-Owned Units 5
Total Units: 60
Dist.: US-0; CAN-52; O'seas-0
North America: 4 Provinces
Density: 30 in AB, 9 in SK, 9 in BC
Projected New Units (12 Months): 17
Qualifications: 5, 4, 2, 3, 4, 5
Registered: AB

FINANCIAL/TERMS:
Cash Investment: $130-200K
Total Investment: $400-500K
Minimum Net Worth: $400K
Fees: Franchise - $25K
Royalty - 5%; Ad. - 2%
Earnings Claim Statement: No
Term of Contract (Years): 10/2-5
Avg. # Of Employees: 26 FT, 8 PT
Passive Ownership: Not Allowed
Encourage Conversions: Yes
Area Develop. Agreements: Yes/20
Sub-Franchising Contracts: No
Expand In Territory: Yes
Space Needs: 4,000 SF; FS, SC

SUPPORT & TRAINING PROVIDED:
Financial Assistance Provided: Yes(I)
Site Selection Assistance: Yes
Lease Negotiation Assistance: Yes
Co-Operative Advertising: Yes
Franchisee Assoc./Member: Yes/Yes
Size Of Corporate Staff: 12
On-Going Support: B,C,D,E,F,G,H,I
Training: 3 Weeks Calgary, AB; 4 Weeks On-Location.

SPECIFIC EXPANSION PLANS:
US: Northwest
Canada: All Canada
Overseas: No

<< >>

JOEY'S ONLY SEAFOOD RESTAURANT
514 42nd Ave. SE
Calgary, AB T2G 1Y6 CANADA
Tel: (800) 661-2123 (403) 243-4584
Fax: (403) 243-8989
E-Mail: admin.joeys@home.com
Web Site: www.joeys-only.com
Mr. David Mossey, Senior Partner

JOEY'S ONLY is a sit down, family-style seafood restaurant, specializing in fish and chips, licensed for beer and wine. Casual atmosphere, affordable prices, high-quality, high-volume restaurants with a wide selection of popular seafood dishes.

BACKGROUND:
Established: 1985; 1st Franchised: 1992
Franchised Units: 82
Company-Owned Units 1
Total Units: 83
Dist.: US-6; CAN-55; O'seas-0
North America: 4 States, 5 Provinces
Density: 20 in AB, 2 in MT, 2 in ND
Projected New Units (12 Months): 10
Qualifications: 4, 4, 3, 3, 5, 5
Registered: CA,FL,ND,AB

FINANCIAL/TERMS:
Cash Investment: $40-80K
Total Investment: $149-202.5K
Minimum Net Worth: $200K
Fees: Franchise - $25K
Royalty - 4.5%; Ad. - 1%
Earnings Claim Statement: No
Term of Contract (Years): 10/5
Avg. # Of Employees: 5 FT, 15 PT
Passive Ownership: Discouraged
Encourage Conversions: Yes
Area Develop. Agreements: Yes/20
Sub-Franchising Contracts: Yes
Expand In Territory: Yes
Space Needs: 2,000-2,400 SF; FS, SF, SC

SUPPORT & TRAINING PROVIDED:
Financial Assistance Provided: No
Site Selection Assistance: Yes
Lease Negotiation Assistance: Yes
Co-Operative Advertising: No
Franchisee Assoc./Member: Yes/Yes
Size Of Corporate Staff: 11
On-Going Support: C,D,E,F,G,H,I
Training: 5 Weeks in Franchise Office and in Corporate Store.

SPECIFIC EXPANSION PLANS:
US: All United States
Canada: All Canada
Overseas: No

<< >>

K-BOB'S STEAKHOUSES
3700 Rio Grande NW, # 6
Albuquerque, NM 87107
Tel: (800) 225-8403 (505) 341-2504
Fax: (505) 341-2490
E-Mail: srkbobs@aol.com
Web Site: www.kbobs.com
Ms. Susan Rosulek, Dir. Administration

K-BOB'S caters to small, rural communities with populations of approximately 10,000 - 50,000 people. It concentrates on expanding with committed owner/operators in rural markets with good highway count and with the potential sales achievement of $900,000+ annually.

BACKGROUND:
Established: 1966; 1st Franchised: 1992
Franchised Units: 21
Company-Owned Units 5
Total Units: 26
Dist.: US-26; CAN-0; O'seas-0
North America: 4 States
Density: 14 in TX, 10 in NM, 3 in CO
Projected New Units (12 Months): 7
Registered: NR

FINANCIAL/TERMS:
Cash Investment: $62.5K
Total Investment: $170-973K
Minimum Net Worth: $NR
Fees: Franchise - $25K
Royalty - 3%; Ad. - 1%
Earnings Claim Statement: No
Term of Contract (Years): 20/10
Avg. # Of Employees: 4 FT, 30 PT
Passive Ownership: Not Allowed
Encourage Conversions: Yes
Area Develop. Agreements: No
Sub-Franchising Contracts: No
Expand In Territory: Yes
Space Needs: 6,300 SF; FS

SUPPORT & TRAINING PROVIDED:
Financial Assistance Provided: No
Site Selection Assistance: Yes
Lease Negotiation Assistance: No
Co-Operative Advertising: Yes
Franchisee Assoc./Member: NR

Size Of Corporate Staff: 5
On-Going Support: a,b,C,D,E,f,G,H,I
Training: 8 Weeks.

SPECIFIC EXPANSION PLANS:
US: Southwest, Midwest
Canada: No
Overseas: Mexico

<< >>

KELSEY'S RESTAURANTS

450 S. Service Rd. W.
Oakville, ON L6K 2H4 CANADA
Tel: (800) 982-1682 (905) 842-5510
Fax: (905) 842-9048
E-Mail: lsantolini@hq.kelseys.ca
Web Site: www.kelseys.ca
Mr. Larry Santolini, Dir. Franchising

Approaching its 20th anniversary, KELSEY'S has been bringing outstanding food, unrivaled service and its celebrated 'good times' to communities throughout Canada since 1998. KELSEY'S new menu features more than 100 exciting items. KELSEY'S warm, friendly decor and fast service make it an appealing place for lunch crowds, the after work gang, as well as families at dinner and late evening adult patrons who come for the good times in a neighborhood atmosphere.

BACKGROUND:
Established: 1978; 1st Franchised: 1983
Franchised Units: 28
Company-Owned Units 77
Total Units: 105
Dist.: US-0; CAN-54; O'seas-0
North America: 5 Provinces
Density: 42 in ON, 8 in AB, 1 in SK
Projected New Units (12 Months): 10
Qualifications: 5, 4, 4, 2, 2, 5
Registered: AB

FINANCIAL/TERMS:
Cash Investment: $250-300K
Total Investment: $600-750K
Minimum Net Worth: $600K
Fees: Franchise - $40K
Royalty - 5%; Ad. - 0.5%
Earnings Claim Statement: No
Term of Contract (Years): 10/5/5
Avg. # Of Employees: 70-90 FT & PT
Passive Ownership: Not Allowed
Encourage Conversions: No
Area Develop. Agreements: NR
Sub-Franchising Contracts: No
Expand In Territory: Yes
Space Needs: 5,000 SF; FS

SUPPORT & TRAINING PROVIDED:
Financial Assistance Provided: Yes(I)
Site Selection Assistance: Yes
Lease Negotiation Assistance: Yes
Co-Operative Advertising: Yes
Franchisee Assoc./Member: Yes/Yes
Size Of Corporate Staff: 30
On-Going Support: a,B,C,D,E,F,G,I
Training: 12 Weeks in Restaurant; 1 Week Office.

SPECIFIC EXPANSION PLANS:
US: N/A
Canada: ON, AB, BC
Overseas: Philippines, Western Europe, Australia

<< >>

MADE IN JAPAN...A TERIYAKI EXPERIENCE

700 Kerr St.
Oakville, ON L6K 3W5 CANADA
Tel: (800) 555-5726 (905) 337-7777
Fax: (905) 337-0331
E-Mail: info@donatogroup.com
Web Site: www.madein-japan.com
Franchise Development

Japanese quick service restaurant located in major mall food courts, airports, universities, hospitals, theme parks, strip plazas and other similar high traffic settings.

BACKGROUND: IFA MEMBER
Established: 1986; 1st Franchised: 1987
Franchised Units: 70
Company-Owned Units 2
Total Units: 72
Dist.: US-0; CAN-50; O'seas-5
North America: 4 Provinces
Density: 36 in ON, 7 in PQ, 4 in BC
Projected New Units (12 Months): 6
Qualifications: 5, 2, 2, 2, 3, 4
Registered: IL,AB

FINANCIAL/TERMS:
Cash Investment: $50-100K
Total Investment: $175-250K
Minimum Net Worth: $200K
Fees: Franchise - $25K
Royalty - 6%; Ad. - 1.5%
Earnings Claim Statement: No
Term of Contract (Years): 8-10/5-10
Avg. # Of Employees: 3 FT, 6 PT
Passive Ownership: Discouraged
Encourage Conversions: Yes
Area Develop. Agreements: Yes/15
Sub-Franchising Contracts: Yes
Expand In Territory: Yes
Space Needs: 400-1,800 SF; SC, RM

SUPPORT & TRAINING PROVIDED:
Financial Assistance Provided: Yes(I)
Site Selection Assistance: Yes
Lease Negotiation Assistance: Yes
Co-Operative Advertising: N/A
Franchisee Assoc./Member: No/No
Size Of Corporate Staff: 40
On-Going Support: B,C,D,E,G,H,I
Training: 3-4 Days at Company HQ; 3-4 Days at the Store; 1 Week during your Grand Opening.

SPECIFIC EXPANSION PLANS:
US: All United States
Canada: All Canada
Overseas: All Countries

<< >>

MAX & ERMA'S RESTAURANTS

4849 Evanswood Dr.
Columbus, OH 43229
Tel: (614) 431-5800
Fax: (614) 854-7957
E-Mail: Rob@max-ermas.com
Web Site: www.max-ermas.com
Mr. Rob Lindeman, VP Franchising

MAX & ERMA'S RESTAURANTS is famous for gourmet burgers, overstuffed sandwiches, homemade pasta dishes, chargrilled chicken specialties, super salads and taste-tempting munchies. Antiques artifacts and local paraphernalia make MAX & ERMA'S a fun, unique place to take friends and family. We work hard every day to help our guests enjoy their total dining experience so they can't wait to come back. And, we believe that experience starts with our food. We use only the freshest, highest-quality ingredients.

BACKGROUND: IFA MEMBER
Established: 1972; 1st Franchised: 1997
Franchised Units: 7
Company-Owned Units 60
Total Units: 67
Dist.: US-67; CAN-0; O'seas-0
North America: 9 States
Density: 22 in OH, 8 in MI, 7 in IL
Projected New Units (12 Months): 10
Qualifications: 3, 4, 4, 2, 3, 5
Registered: VA,WI

FINANCIAL/TERMS:
Cash Investment: $400-500K
Total Investment: $800K-2.7MM
Minimum Net Worth: $3MM
Fees: Franchise - $40K
Royalty - 4%; Ad. - 2%
Earnings Claim Statement: No
Term of Contract (Years): 20/10
Avg. # Of Employees: 40 FT, 50 PT

Passive Ownership: Allowed
Encourage Conversions: Yes
Area Develop. Agreements: Yes
Sub-Franchising Contracts: No
Expand In Territory: Yes
Space Needs: 5,000-6,900 SF; FS, RM

SUPPORT & TRAINING PROVIDED:
Financial Assistance Provided: No
Site Selection Assistance: Yes
Lease Negotiation Assistance: Yes
Co-Operative Advertising: N/A
Franchisee Assoc./Member: No
Size Of Corporate Staff: 55
On-Going Support: B,C,D,E,F,G,H
Training: 14 Weeks Manager Training; 2-6 Weeks Staff Training; 2-3 Weeks Opening Training.

SPECIFIC EXPANSION PLANS:
US: All United States
Canada: No
Overseas: No

<< >>

MELTING POT RESTAURANTS, THE

8810 Twin Lakes Blvd.
Tampa, FL 33614
Tel: (800) 783-0867 (813) 881-0055
Fax: (813) 889-9361
E-Mail: franchisesales@meltingpot.com
Web Site: www.meltingpot.com
Mr. Dan Addison, Franchise Sales

The largest fondue-based restaurant system in the world. Franchise provides numerous areas of expertise and assistance to new and established owners. Large percentage of existing owners become multi-unit operators. A unique dining format that is often referred to as a "fun and gotta be experienced" event.

BACKGROUND:
Established: 1975; 1st Franchised: 1984
Franchised Units: 50
Company-Owned Units 4
Total Units: 54
Dist.: US-54; CAN-0; O'seas-0
North America: 18 States
Density: 16 in FL, 6 in NC, 4 in VA
Projected New Units (12 Months): 15
Registered: CA,FL,IL,IN,MD,MI,MN,NY, OR,VA,WA,WI,DC

FINANCIAL/TERMS:
Cash Investment: $90-150K
Total Investment: $375-750K
Minimum Net Worth: $N/A
Fees: Franchise - $28K
Royalty - 4.5%; Ad. - NR
Earnings Claim Statement: No
Term of Contract (Years): 10
Avg. # Of Employees:10-20 FT, 5-20 PT
Passive Ownership: Discouraged
Encourage Conversions: NR
Area Develop. Agreements: Yes
Sub-Franchising Contracts: No
Expand In Territory: No
Space Needs: 4500-6500 SF; FS, SC

SUPPORT & TRAINING PROVIDED:
Financial Assistance Provided: Yes(I)
Site Selection Assistance: Yes
Lease Negotiation Assistance: Yes
Co-Operative Advertising: No
Franchisee Assoc./Member: No
Size Of Corporate Staff: 21
On-Going Support: A,B,C,D,E,F,G,H,I
Training: Minimum 6 Weeks, Home Office, Tampa, FL; Minimum 2 Weeks, On Location.

SPECIFIC EXPANSION PLANS:
US: All United States
Canada: No
Overseas: No

<< >>

MIKES RESTAURANTS

8250 Decarie Blvd., # 310
Montreal, PQ H4P 2P5 CANADA
Tel: (514) 341-5544
Fax: (514) 341-5635
Web Site: www.mikes.ca
Mr. Carmen Starnino, VP Operations

MIKES RESTAURANTS is the dominant purveyor, in its market area, of Italian-style specialties, featuring pizzas, sandwiches and pastas. Each unit features a very attractive and welcoming decor. MIKES RESTAURANTS also provide a full dessert and alcohol menu.

BACKGROUND:
Established: 1967; 1st Franchised: 1972
Franchised Units: 103
Company-Owned Units 24
Total Units: 127
Dist.: US-0; CAN-127; O'seas-0
North America: 3 Provinces
Density: 125 in PQ, 1 in ON, 1 in NB
Projected New Units (12 Months): 5-7
Qualifications: 4, 5, 3, 3, 5, 5
Registered: NR

FINANCIAL/TERMS:
Cash Investment: $75-175K
Total Investment: $275-550K
Minimum Net Worth: $NR
Fees: Franchise - $45K
Royalty - 8%; Ad. - 0%
Earnings Claim Statement: No
Term of Contract (Years): 20/20
Avg. # Of Employees: 25 FT, 10 PT
Passive Ownership: Not Allowed
Encourage Conversions: Yes
Area Develop. Agreements: Yes/20
Sub-Franchising Contracts: No
Expand In Territory: Yes
Space Needs: 3,500 SF; FS, SC

SUPPORT & TRAINING PROVIDED:
Financial Assistance Provided: Yes(I)
Site Selection Assistance: Yes
Lease Negotiation Assistance: Yes
Co-Operative Advertising: Yes
Franchisee Assoc./Member: Yes
Size Of Corporate Staff: 36
On-Going Support: B,C,D,E,F,H
Training: 6-8 Weeks Montreal, PQ.

SPECIFIC EXPANSION PLANS:
US: Northeast
Canada: ON,NB,NS,NF
Overseas: No

<< >>

MONTANA MIKE'S STEAK HOUSE

2908 North Plum St.
Hutchinson, KS 67502
Tel: (620) 669-9372
Fax: (620) 669-0531
E-Mail: dans@stockadecompanies.com
Web Site: www.stockadecompanies.com
Mr. Dan Spitz, Dir. Franchise Sales

MONTANA MIKE'S STEAK HOUSE is a sit-down, full-service restaurant serving alcohol and a bar area. We are known for very large portions at affordable prices. Open for lunch and dinner Thursday through Sunday.

BACKGROUND:
Established: 1984; 1st Franchised: 1984

Franchised Units: 10
Company-Owned Units 3
Total Units: 13
Dist.: US-13; CAN-0; O'seas-0
North America: 6 States
Density: 5 in KS, 3 in TX
Projected New Units (12 Months): 4
Qualifications: 5, 4, 4, 3, 2, 4
Registered: IL,IN,VA

FINANCIAL/TERMS:

Cash Investment: $250-350K
Total Investment: $1.2-2.2MM
Minimum Net Worth: $1MM
Fees: Franchise - $15K
Royalty - 3%; Ad. - 1%
Earnings Claim Statement: Yes
Term of Contract (Years): 15/5
Avg. # Of Employees: 20 FT, 50 PT
Passive Ownership: Discouraged
Encourage Conversions: Yes
Area Develop. Agreements: Not Now
Sub-Franchising Contracts: No
Expand In Territory: Yes
Space Needs: 10,000 SF; FS

SUPPORT & TRAINING PROVIDED:

Financial Assistance Provided: No
Site Selection Assistance: Yes
Lease Negotiation Assistance: No
Co-Operative Advertising: No
Franchisee Assoc./Member: NR
Size Of Corporate Staff: 16
On-Going Support: B,C,D,E,G,h,i
Training: 6-8 Weeks Training.

SPECIFIC EXPANSION PLANS:

US: All United States
Canada: No
Overseas: No

MOUNTAIN MIKE'S PIZZA

4212 N. Freeway Blvd., # 6
Sacramento, CA 95834
Tel: (916) 929-3946
Fax: (916) 929-6018
Mr. Randy Vogel, President

Casual dining in a family-oriented restaurant, featuring counter service, delivery and take-out, lunch buffet, self-service beverages and video game room. Our pizzas are made-to-order, using only the freshest-quality ingredients available.

BACKGROUND:

Established: 1978; 1st Franchised: 1978
Franchised Units: 79
Company-Owned Units 0
Total Units: 79
Dist.: US-79; CAN-0; O'seas-0
North America: 6 States
Density: 63 in CA, 1 in NV, 1 in OR
Projected New Units (12 Months): 40
Qualifications: 4, 4, 2, 2, 3, 5
Registered: CA,FL,IL,IN,MD,MI,MN, OR,VA,WI

FINANCIAL/TERMS:

Cash Investment: $75-100K
Total Investment: $150-250K
Minimum Net Worth: $150K
Fees: Franchise - $20K
Royalty - 5%/$1K; Ad. - 3%
Earnings Claim Statement: Yes
Term of Contract (Years): 15/15
Avg. # Of Employees: 2 FT, 15 PT
Passive Ownership: Not Allowed
Encourage Conversions: Yes
Area Develop. Agreements: Yes/15
Sub-Franchising Contracts: No
Expand In Territory: Yes
Space Needs: 2,500 SF; SF, SC

SUPPORT & TRAINING PROVIDED:

Financial Assistance Provided: Yes(I)
Site Selection Assistance: Yes
Lease Negotiation Assistance: Yes
Co-Operative Advertising: Yes
Franchisee Assoc./Member: No
Size Of Corporate Staff: 10
On-Going Support: A,B,C,D,E,F,H,I
Training: 3 Weeks Boulder, CO/Northern CA; 2 Weeks On-Site at Opening.

SPECIFIC EXPANSION PLANS:

US: All United States
Canada: No
Overseas: No

MR. MIKE'S WEST COAST GRILL

611 Columbia St.
New Westminster, BC V3M 1A7
CANADA
Tel: (604) 515-1190
Fax: (604) 515-1197
E-Mail: bouthwaite@mrmikes.ca
Web Site: www.mrmikes.ca
Mr. Bill Outhwaite, Executive Vice President

Founded in 1960, MR. MIKE'S WEST COAST GRILL is a full-service casual dining restaurant experience. Our primary focus is beef. We provide "affordable indulgence" of premium spirits and quality grilled entrees in a refreshing restaurant environment that is relaxed and inviting. A full support franchise system. Proven results, a fresh approach -- all uniquely West Coast.

BACKGROUND:

Established: 1960; 1st Franchised: 1961
Franchised Units: 6
Company-Owned Units 4
Total Units: 10
Dist.: US-0; CAN-10; O'seas-0
North America: 1 Province
Density: 10 in BC
Projected New Units (12 Months): 3
Qualifications: 5, 5, 3, 2, 2, 5
Registered: NR

FINANCIAL/TERMS:

Cash Investment: $300-700K
Total Investment: $650K-1.0MM
Minimum Net Worth: $500K
Fees: Franchise - $37.5K
Royalty - 5; Ad. - 2%
Earnings Claim Statement: No
Term of Contract (Years): 10/5
Avg. # Of Employees: 10 FT, 30 PT
Passive Ownership: Discouraged
Encourage Conversions: Yes
Area Develop. Agreements: No
Sub-Franchising Contracts: No
Expand In Territory: No
Space Needs: 3,500-5,000 SF; FS, SC

SUPPORT & TRAINING PROVIDED:

Financial Assistance Provided: Yes
Site Selection Assistance: Yes
Lease Negotiation Assistance: Yes
Co-Operative Advertising: Yes
Franchisee Assoc./Member: No
Size Of Corporate Staff: 10
On-Going Support: A,B,C,D,E,F,G,H,I
Training: 8-12 Weeks in Corporate Store; 2 Weeks On-Site.

SPECIFIC EXPANSION PLANS:

US: None
Canada: BC
Overseas: No

NANCY'S PIZZERIA

8200 W. 185th St., # J
Tinley Park, IL 60477
Tel: (800) 626-2977 (708) 444-4411
Fax: (708) 444-4422
E-Mail: eholly@chicagofranchise.com
Web Site: www.chicagofranchise.com
Mr. George Nordstrom, VP Franchise Development

NANCY'S PIZZERIA is expanding nationally; we have 66 franchisees with stores located in Illinois, Iowa and Michigan. More coming soon in Florida and Indiana. We offer the following advantages: original inventor of stuffed pizza, protected territories, comprehensive classroom and in-store training, pre and past-opening support provided by our "operations" support staff, teamed with the product voted "The Best Pizza in Chicago" by Chicago Magazine and lauded by other publications.

BACKGROUND:
Established: 1974; 1st Franchised: 1993
Franchised Units: 66
Company-Owned Units 0
Total Units: 66
Dist.: US-66; CAN-0; O'seas-0
North America: 3 States
Density: 36 in IL, 1 in IA, 1 in MI
Projected New Units (12 Months): 12
Qualifications: 5, 4, 3, 3, 5, 5
Registered: CA,FL,IL,IN,MD,MI,VA,WI

FINANCIAL/TERMS:
Cash Investment: $50-120K
Total Investment: $190-250K
Minimum Net Worth: $250K
Fees: Franchise - $20K
Royalty - 5%; Ad. - 2%
Earnings Claim Statement: No
Term of Contract (Years): 10/10
Avg. # Of Employees: 3 FT, 15 PT
Passive Ownership: Discouraged
Encourage Conversions: Yes
Area Develop. Agreements: Yes/1-5
Sub-Franchising Contracts: No
Expand In Territory: Yes
Space Needs: 800-1,400 SF; SF

SUPPORT & TRAINING PROVIDED:
Financial Assistance Provided: No
Site Selection Assistance: Yes
Lease Negotiation Assistance: Yes
Co-Operative Advertising: Yes
Franchisee Assoc./Member: No
Size Of Corporate Staff: 12
On-Going Support: b,C,D,E,F,G,H
Training: 230 Hours of Hands-On Training; 40 Hours Office Training.

SPECIFIC EXPANSION PLANS:
US: All United States
Canada: No
Overseas: No

<< >>

PEPE'S MEXICAN RESTAURANT
1325 W. 15th St.
Chicago, IL 60608
Tel: (312) 733-2500
Fax: (312) 733-2564
Mr. Edwin A. Ptak, Corporate Counsel

A full-service Mexican restaurant, serving a complete line of Mexican food, with liquor, beer and wine. Complete training and help in remodeling, site selection, equipment purchasing and running the restaurant provided.

BACKGROUND:
Established: 1967; 1st Franchised: 1968
Franchised Units: 55
Company-Owned Units 0
Total Units: 55
Dist.: US-55; CAN-0; O'seas-0
North America: 3 States
Density: 44 in IL, 11 in IN
Projected New Units (12 Months): 4
Qualifications: 3, 3, 2, 2, 1, 4
Registered: IL,IN,VA

FINANCIAL/TERMS:
Cash Investment: $30-100K
Total Investment: $75-300K
Minimum Net Worth: $NR
Fees: Franchise - $15K
Royalty - 4%; Ad. - 3%
Earnings Claim Statement: Yes
Term of Contract (Years): 20
Avg. # Of Employees: 8 FT, 5 PT
Passive Ownership: Discouraged
Encourage Conversions: Yes
Area Develop. Agreements: Yes/Varies
Sub-Franchising Contracts: No
Expand In Territory: No
Space Needs: 3,000 SF; FS, SF, SC

SUPPORT & TRAINING PROVIDED:
Financial Assistance Provided: No
Site Selection Assistance: Yes
Lease Negotiation Assistance: Yes
Co-Operative Advertising: Yes
Franchisee Assoc./Member: NR
Size Of Corporate Staff: 15
On-Going Support: B,C,D,E,F,G,H
Training: 4 Weeks Headquarters.

SPECIFIC EXPANSION PLANS:
US: Midwest
Canada: No
Overseas: No

<< >>

PERKINS RESTAURANT & BAKERY
6075 Poplar Ave., # 800
Memphis, TN 38119-4717
Tel: (800) 877-7375 (901) 766-6400
Fax: (901) 766-6482
E-Mail: franchise@perkinsrestaurants.com
Web Site: www.perkinsrestaurants.com
Mr. Robert J. Winters, VP Franchise Development

Full-service family-style restaurant, offering breakfast, lunch and dinner, along with proprietary bakery items at moderate prices.

BACKGROUND: IFA MEMBER
Established: 1958; 1st Franchised: 1958
Franchised Units: 354
Company-Owned Units 140
Total Units: 494
Dist.: US-469; CAN-15; O'seas-0
North America: 35 States
Density: 75 in MN, 54 in PA, 51 in OH
Projected New Units (12 Months): 35
Qualifications: 5, 3, 5, 3, 3, 4
Registered: All States Except RI

FINANCIAL/TERMS:
Cash Investment: $100-600K
Total Investment: $1.0-2.0MM
Minimum Net Worth: $750K
Fees: Franchise - $40K
Royalty - 4%; Ad. - 3%
Earnings Claim Statement: Yes
Term of Contract (Years): 10-20/20
Avg. # Of Employees: 20 FT, 40 PT
Passive Ownership: Discouraged
Encourage Conversions: Yes
Area Develop. Agreements: Yes/3-8
Sub-Franchising Contracts: No
Expand In Territory: Yes
Space Needs: 5,000 SF; FS, SC

SUPPORT & TRAINING PROVIDED:
Financial Assistance Provided: No
Site Selection Assistance: Yes
Lease Negotiation Assistance: Yes
Co-Operative Advertising: Yes
Franchisee Assoc./Member: No
Size Of Corporate Staff: 224
On-Going Support: a,B,C,D,E,F,G,H,I
Training: 8-12 Weeks Management Training at Various Locations.

SPECIFIC EXPANSION PLANS:
US: All United States
Canada: All Canada
Overseas: No

<< >>

PIZZA DELIGHT

331 Elmwood Dr., 2nd Fl., P.O. Box 23070
Moncton, NB E1A 6S8 CANADA
Tel: (506) 853-0990
Fax: (506) 853-4131
E-Mail: opportunity@pizzadelight.ca
Web Site: www.pizzadelight.com
Mr. Bernard Imbeault, Chief Executive Officer

Our will and purpose is to get and keep customers. It can be realized through our mission: to be the best pizza place in town! We are a multi-brand organization operating as: PIZZA DELIGHT and LE COQ ROTI (rotisserie chicken).

BACKGROUND:
Established: 1968; 1st Franchised: 1970
Franchised Units: 150
Company-Owned Units 4
Total Units: 154
Dist.: US-0; CAN-145; O'seas-2
North America: 6 Provinces
Density: NB, NF, NS
Projected New Units (12 Months): 15
Qualifications: 5, 3, 2, 2, 4, 5
Registered: None

FINANCIAL/TERMS:
Cash Investment: $50-150K
Total Investment: $150-350K
Minimum Net Worth: $250K
Fees: Franchise - $10-30K
Royalty - 4-6%; Ad. - 4.5%
Earnings Claim Statement: No
Term of Contract (Years): 10/5
Avg. # Of Employees: 5-10 FT, 5-10 PT
Passive Ownership: Discouraged
Encourage Conversions: Yes
Area Develop. Agreements: Yes/20
Sub-Franchising Contracts: Yes
Expand In Territory: Yes
Space Needs: 1,000-4,000 SF; Varies

SUPPORT & TRAINING PROVIDED:
Financial Assistance Provided: Yes(I)
Site Selection Assistance: Yes
Lease Negotiation Assistance: Yes
Co-Operative Advertising: Yes
Franchisee Assoc./Member: No
Size Of Corporate Staff: 25
On-Going Support: a,B,C,D,E,F,G,H,i
Training: 12 Days Head Office; 10 Days On-the-Job Training; 3 Days a Year of Continuous Training.

SPECIFIC EXPANSION PLANS:
US: No
Canada: Central, East
Overseas: No

<< >>

Top 50

PIZZERIA UNO CHICAGO BAR & GRILL

100 Charles Park Rd.
Boston, MA 02132-4985
Tel: (617) 218-5325
Fax: (617) 218-5376
E-Mail: randy.clifton@unos.com
Web Site: www.unos.com
Mr. Randy M. Clifton, VP Worldwide Franchising

A full-service casual theme restaurant with a brand name signature product - UNO's Original Chicago Deep Dish Pizza. A full varied menu with broad appeal featuring steak, shrimp and pasta. A flair for fun including a bar and comfortable décor in a facility that attracts guests of all ages.

BACKGROUND: IFA MEMBER
Established: 1943; 1st Franchised: 1979
Franchised Units: 74
Company-Owned Units 114
Total Units: 188
Dist.: US-181; CAN-0; O'seas-7
North America: 32 States
Density: 27 in MA
Projected New Units (12 Months): 17
Qualifications: 5, 4, 5, 2, 2, 5
Registered: All States

FINANCIAL/TERMS:
Cash Investment: $500K
Total Investment: $900K-1.7MM
Minimum Net Worth: $2MM
Fees: Franchise - $35K
Royalty - 5%; Ad. - 1%
Earnings Claim Statement: Yes
Term of Contract (Years): 15/10
Avg. # Of Employees: 30 FT, 35 PT
Passive Ownership: Allowed
Encourage Conversions: No
Area Develop. Agreements: Yes
Sub-Franchising Contracts: No
Expand In Territory: Yes
Space Needs: 5,500 SF; FS, SC

SUPPORT & TRAINING PROVIDED:
Financial Assistance Provided: Yes(I)
Site Selection Assistance: Yes
Lease Negotiation Assistance: Yes
Co-Operative Advertising: Yes
Franchisee Assoc./Member: Yes/Yes
Size Of Corporate Staff: 135
On-Going Support: a,B,C,D,E,F,G,H,I
Training: 12 Weeks in a Training Restaurant; 2 Weeks On-Site Staff Training.

SPECIFIC EXPANSION PLANS:
US: All United States
Canada: All Canada
Overseas: Asia, South and Central America, Europe

<< >>

PONDEROSA STEAKHOUSE

Top 50

PONDEROSA/ BONANZA STEAKHOUSES

6500 International Pkwy., # 1000
Plano, TX 75093
Tel: (800) 543-9670 (972) 588-5770
Fax: (972) 588-5806
E-Mail: franchise@metrogroup.com
Web Site: www.ponderosasteakhouses.com
Ms. Lynette McKee, VP Franchise Development

PONDEROSA and BONANZA FAMILY STEAKHOUSES serve great-tasting, family-priced steaks and entrees, accompanied by a large variety of all-you-can-eat salad items, soups, appetizers, hot vegetables, breads, sundae and dessert bar and other tasty food. All steaks and entrees come with the salad bar, buffet and dessert bar at no extra cost.

BACKGROUND: IFA MEMBER
Established: 1965; 1st Franchised: 1966
Franchised Units: 419
Company-Owned Units 108
Total Units: 527
Dist.: US-449; CAN-14; O'seas-64
North America: 29 States
Density: 84 in OH, 49 in IN, 40 in NY
Projected New Units (12 Months): 5
Qualifications: 5, 5, 4, 4, 4, 5
Registered: All States and AB

FINANCIAL/TERMS:
Cash Investment: $750K
Total Investment: $1.2-2.1MM
Minimum Net Worth: $3MM
Fees: Franchise - $40K
Royalty - 4%; Ad. - 4%
Earnings Claim Statement: No
Term of Contract (Years): 20
Avg. # Of Employees: 10 FT, 50 PT
Passive Ownership: Not Allowed
Encourage Conversions: No

Area Develop. Agreements: No
Sub-Franchising Contracts: No
Expand In Territory: Yes
Space Needs: 8,639 SF; FS, SC

SUPPORT & TRAINING PROVIDED:
Financial Assistance Provided: No
Site Selection Assistance: No
Lease Negotiation Assistance: No
Co-Operative Advertising: Yes
Franchisee Assoc./Member: Yes/NA
Size Of Corporate Staff: 400
On-Going Support: A,B,C,D,E,F,G,H,I
Training: 9 Weeks Headquarters in Plano, TX and Restaurant in Field.

SPECIFIC EXPANSION PLANS:
US: All United States
Canada: ON,QB,NB,BC,AB
Overseas: Brazil, Canada, China, Hong Kong, Japan, Venezuela

<< >>

R. J. BOAR'S BARBEQUE

3127 Brady St., # 3
Davenport, IA 52803
Tel: (319) 322-2627
Fax: (319) 322-1947
Web Site: www.rjboars.com
Mr. Schuyler (Skip) Moore, Dir. Franchise Sales

R. J. BOAR'S is awarding franchise opportunities in the Midwest to qualified individuals. We specialize in hickory-smoked ribs, chicken and beef. As a niche player in the casual theme restaurant category, we realized very early on that a broad and varied menu of popular items was a crucial factor in determining our formula. That's why R. J. BOAR'S has such a diverse menu, including signature appetizers, specialty salads, fresh fish, tender steaks and award-winning hickory-smoked BBQ.

BACKGROUND:
Established: 1993; 1st Franchised: 1998
Franchised Units: 2
Company-Owned Units 3
Total Units: 5
Dist.: US-5; CAN-0; O'seas-0
North America: 2 States
Density: 3 in IA, 2 in IL
Projected New Units (12 Months): 6-8
Qualifications: 4, 4, 5, 2, 2, 4
Registered: IL,IN,MN,SD,WI

FINANCIAL/TERMS:
Cash Investment: $175-300K
Total Investment: $378-909K
Minimum Net Worth: $1.5MM
Fees: Franchise - $35K
Royalty - 4%; Ad. - 3%
Earnings Claim Statement: No
Term of Contract (Years): 10/5/5
Avg. # Of Employees: 10 FT, 60 PT
Passive Ownership: Not Allowed
Encourage Conversions: Yes
Area Develop. Agreements: Yes/Varies
Sub-Franchising Contracts: No
Expand In Territory: Yes
Space Needs: 5,500 SF; FS

SUPPORT & TRAINING PROVIDED:
Financial Assistance Provided: No
Site Selection Assistance: Yes
Lease Negotiation Assistance: No
Co-Operative Advertising: Yes
Franchisee Assoc./Member: No
Size Of Corporate Staff: 4
On-Going Support: B,C,D,E,f, h
Training: 8-10 Weeks Bettendorf, IA.

SPECIFIC EXPANSION PLANS:
US: Midwest
Canada: No
Overseas: No

<< >>

RED HOT & BLUE

1701 Clarendon Blvd., # 105
Arlington, VA 22209
Tel: (800) 723-0745 (703) 276-8833
Fax: (703) 528-4789
E-Mail: dknutsen@rhbri.com
Web Site: www.redhotandblue.com
Mr. Dave Knutsen, Dir. Franchise Operations

RED HOT & BLUE restaurants serve Memphis-style ribs, pork, beef, chicken plus salads, burgers and a full menu in a casual dining environment, featuring blues memorabilia and recorded blues music. Service is Southern hospitality.

BACKGROUND:
Established: 1988; 1st Franchised: 1991
Franchised Units: 32
Company-Owned Units 6
Total Units: 38
Dist.: US-35; CAN-0; O'seas-0
North America: 10 States
Density: 6 in NC, 5 in TX, 5 in VA
Projected New Units (12 Months): 6
Qualifications: 5, 5, 5, 4, 3, 5
Registered: All States Except RI,SD

FINANCIAL/TERMS:
Cash Investment: $347.7-868K
Total Investment: $397.75K
Minimum Net Worth: $1MM
Fees: Franchise - $35K
Royalty - 5%; Ad. - $375/Mo.
Earnings Claim Statement: No
Term of Contract (Years): 20/10
Avg. # Of Employees: 30 FT, 20 PT
Passive Ownership: Not Allowed
Encourage Conversions: Yes
Area Develop. Agreements: Yes/Varies
Sub-Franchising Contracts: No
Expand In Territory: No
Space Needs: 2,400-5,000 SF; FS, SC

SUPPORT & TRAINING PROVIDED:
Financial Assistance Provided: No
Site Selection Assistance: Yes
Lease Negotiation Assistance: No
Co-Operative Advertising: Yes
Franchisee Assoc./Member: Yes/Yes
Size Of Corporate Staff: 18
On-Going Support: C,D,E,f,G,h
Training: 3 Weeks at Home Office; 2 Weeks On-Site.

SPECIFIC EXPANSION PLANS:
US: All United States
Canada: All Canada
Overseas: No

<< >>

ROUND TABLE PIZZA RESTAURANT

2175 N. California Blvd., # 400
Walnut Creek, CA 94596
Tel: (800) 866-5866 (925) 274-1700
Fax: (925) 974-3978
E-Mail: gfleury@roundtablepizza.com
Web Site: www.roundtablepizza.com
Mr. Greg Fleury, Franchise Sales Mgr.

ROUND TABLE FRANCHISE CORP. offers franchisees the opportunity to establish and operate a ROUND TABLE PIZZA RESTAURANT, which provides the public with pizza and related products in a wholesome, family restaurant setting. ROUND TABLE PIZZA is the nation's fourth largest pizza franchise chain, providing restaurant, take-out and delivery service.

BACKGROUND:
Established: 1959; 1st Franchised: 1962
Franchised Units: 517
Company-Owned Units 19

Total Units: 536
Dist.: US-536; CAN-0; O'seas-17
North America: 11 States
Density: NR
Projected New Units (12 Months): 10
Registered: CA,HI,OR,WA

FINANCIAL/TERMS:
Cash Investment: $135K
Total Investment: $420-496K
Minimum Net Worth: $450K
Fees: Franchise - $25K
Royalty - 4%; Ad. - 4%
Earnings Claim Statement: No
Term of Contract (Years): 10/10
Avg. # Of Employees: 5-7 FT, 10-15 PT
Passive Ownership: Discouraged
Encourage Conversions: Yes
Area Develop. Agreements: Yes/Varies
Sub-Franchising Contracts: Yes
Expand In Territory: Yes
Space Needs: 2,800 SF; SC, RM

SUPPORT & TRAINING PROVIDED:
Financial Assistance Provided: No
Site Selection Assistance: Yes
Lease Negotiation Assistance: Yes
Co-Operative Advertising: Yes
Franchisee Assoc./Member: NR
Size Of Corporate Staff: 70
On-Going Support: C,D,E,G,H,I
Training: 2 Weeks Headquarters; 2 Weeks Field.

SPECIFIC EXPANSION PLANS:
US: Northwest, Southwest
Canada: No
Overseas: All Countries

<< >>

SANDWICH TREE RESTAURANTS
535 Thurlow St., # 300
Vancouver, BC V6E 3L2 CANADA
Tel: (800) 663-8733 (604) 684-3314
Fax: (604) 684-2542
Web Site: www.sandwichtree.ca
Mr. Tony Cardarelli, Director Operations

Famous for our custom sandwiches, creative salads, hearty soups, catering and much more, SANDWICH TREE is a limited-hours operation located in shopping centres, commercial towers and industrial centres. Our quality food, served in our attractive surroundings, makes SANDWICH TREE a number one investment opportunity.

BACKGROUND:
Established: 1978; 1st Franchised: 1979
Franchised Units: 31
Company-Owned Units 0
Total Units: 31
Dist.: US-0; CAN-43; O'seas-0
North America: 6 Provinces
Density: 19 in BC, 7 in NS, 5 in ON
Projected New Units (12 Months): 4
Registered: NR

FINANCIAL/TERMS:
Cash Investment: $35-55K
Total Investment: $90-120K
Minimum Net Worth: $NR
Fees: Franchise - $10-17.5K
Royalty - 5%; Ad. - 3%
Earnings Claim Statement: Yes
Term of Contract (Years): 5/5
Avg. # Of Employees: 4 FT, 7 PT
Passive Ownership: Discouraged
Encourage Conversions: Yes
Area Develop. Agreements: Yes/10
Sub-Franchising Contracts: Yes
Expand In Territory: Yes
Space Needs: 300+ SF; SF, RM, Industrial Park

SUPPORT & TRAINING PROVIDED:
Financial Assistance Provided: Yes(I)
Site Selection Assistance: Yes
Lease Negotiation Assistance: Yes
Co-Operative Advertising: Yes
Franchisee Assoc./Member: NR
Size Of Corporate Staff: 6
On-Going Support: a,B,C,D,E,F,G,H,I
Training: 2 Weeks Headquarters.

SPECIFIC EXPANSION PLANS:
US: No
Canada: All Canada
Overseas: All Countries

<< >>

Top 50

SBARRO
401 Broadhollow Rd.
Melville, NY 11747
Tel: (800) 955-7227 (631) 715-4100
Fax: (631) 715-4183
E-Mail: communications@sbarro.com
Web Site: www.sbarro.com
Mr. Gennaro A. Sbarro, President Franchise/Licensing

Sbarro, the Italian Eatery, is an international QSR serving pizza, pasta and entrees in more than 30 countries. Entrepreneur Magazine has recognized Sbarro three years in a row as the #1 Franchiser for the QSR Italian Segment. Sbarro is currently looking for new Franchisees who share our passion for excellence.

BACKGROUND: IFA MEMBER
Established: 1959; 1st Franchised: 1979
Franchised Units: 293
Company-Owned Units 632
Total Units: 925
Dist.: US-823; CAN-4; O'seas-99
North America: 48 States
Density: 85 in CA, 69 in NY, 43 in FL
Projected New Units (12 Months): NR
Qualifications: 5, 4, 5, 3, 3, 3
Registered: CA,HI,,IL,MD,MI,MN,NY, ND,VA,WI

FINANCIAL/TERMS:
Cash Investment: $150K
Total Investment: $250-850K
Minimum Net Worth: $300K
Fees: Franchise - $45K
Royalty - 7%; Ad. - 2%
Earnings Claim Statement: No
Term of Contract (Years): 10/10
Avg. # Of Employees:8-10 FT, 10-15 PT
Passive Ownership: Not Allowed
Encourage Conversions: N/A
Area Develop. Agreements: Yes/10
Sub-Franchising Contracts: No
Expand In Territory: Yes
Space Needs: 750 minimum SF; RM

SUPPORT & TRAINING PROVIDED:
Financial Assistance Provided: No
Site Selection Assistance: No
Lease Negotiation Assistance: No
Co-Operative Advertising: No
Franchisee Assoc./Member: No
Size Of Corporate Staff: 250
On-Going Support: B,C,D,E,H
Training: 3 Weeks Roosevelt Field Mall, NY.

SPECIFIC EXPANSION PLANS:
US: All United States
Canada: All Canada
Overseas: All Countries

<< >>

SIRLOIN STOCKADE
2908 N. Plum St.
Hutchinson, KS 67502
Tel: (620) 669-9372
Fax: (620) 669-0531
E-Mail: dans@stockadecompanies.com
Web Site: www.stockadecompanies.com
Mr. Dan Spitz, Dir. Franchise Sales

SIRLOIN STOCKADE features a selection of top-quality steaks, chicken and fish, a self-service salad bar, hot food buffet and display bakery at affordable prices. Free-standing buildings of approximately 10,000 square feet, seating 300+ and 70,000 square feet of land required.

BACKGROUND:
Established: 1984; 1st Franchised: 1984
Franchised Units: 51
Company-Owned Units 1
Total Units: 52
Dist.: US-39; CAN-0; O'seas-13
North America: 10 States
Density: 12 in TX, 8 in KS, 6 in OK
Projected New Units (12 Months): 4
Qualifications: 5, 4, 4, 3, 2, 4
Registered: IL,IN,VA

FINANCIAL/TERMS:
Cash Investment: $250-350K
Total Investment: $1.2-2.2MM
Minimum Net Worth: $1MM
Fees: Franchise - $15K
Royalty - 3%; Ad. - 1%
Earnings Claim Statement: No
Term of Contract (Years): 15/5
Avg. # Of Employees: 20 FT, 50 PT
Passive Ownership: Discouraged
Encourage Conversions: Yes
Area Develop. Agreements: Yes/Varies
Sub-Franchising Contracts: No
Expand In Territory: Yes
Space Needs: 10,000 SF; FS

SUPPORT & TRAINING PROVIDED:
Financial Assistance Provided: No
Site Selection Assistance: Yes
Lease Negotiation Assistance: No
Co-Operative Advertising: No
Franchisee Assoc./Member: NR
Size Of Corporate Staff: 16
On-Going Support: B,C,D,E,G,h,i
Training: 6-8 Weeks Training.

SPECIFIC EXPANSION PLANS:
US: All United States
Canada: No
Overseas: Mexico

<< >>

SMITTY'S RESTAURANTS

501 18th Ave. SW, # 600
Calgary, AB T2S 0C7 CANADA
Tel: (403) 229-3838
Fax: (403) 229-3899
E-Mail: ptomlinson@smittys.ca
Web Site: www.smittys.ca
Mr. Paul Tomlinson, VP Franchise Development

Specializing in ALL-DAY breakfast, featuring lunch and dinner menus with a special senior's menu. A truly family restaurant.

BACKGROUND:
Established: 1960; 1st Franchised: 1960
Franchised Units: 107
Company-Owned Units 12
Total Units: 119
Dist.: US-0; CAN-119; O'seas-0
North America: 8 Provinces
Density: 38 in AB, 18 in BC, 18 in SK
Projected New Units (12 Months): 10
Qualifications: 3, 4, 3, 3, 4, 4
Registered: AB

FINANCIAL/TERMS:
Cash Investment: $150K
Total Investment: $300-500K
Minimum Net Worth: $NR
Fees: Franchise - $35K
Royalty - 5%; Ad. - 0%
Earnings Claim Statement: Yes
Term of Contract (Years): 20/10
Avg. # Of Employees: 15 FT, 15 PT
Passive Ownership: Discouraged
Encourage Conversions: Yes
Area Develop. Agreements: Yes/20+
Sub-Franchising Contracts: No
Expand In Territory: Yes
Space Needs: 4,300-5,000 SF; FS, SF, RM, Hotel

SUPPORT & TRAINING PROVIDED:
Financial Assistance Provided: Yes(I)
Site Selection Assistance: Yes
Lease Negotiation Assistance: Yes
Co-Operative Advertising: Yes
Franchisee Assoc./Member: No
Size Of Corporate Staff: 20
On-Going Support: C,D,E,F,G,h
Training: 3-4 Weeks Calgary, AB; 2-3 Weeks Restaurant Location.

SPECIFIC EXPANSION PLANS:
US: HI
Canada: All Canada
Overseas: No

SONNY'S REAL PIT BAR-B-Q

2605 Maitland Center Pkwy., # C
Maitland, FL 32751
Tel: (407) 660-8888
Fax: (407) 660-9050
Ms. Barbara C. Crain, Dir. Franchise Services

SONNY'S is the largest Bar-B-Q chain and concentrates in the Southeast U. S. SONNY'S is a full-service restaurant, specializing in Bar-B-Q beef, pork, chicken and ribs, as well as fast and friendly service.

BACKGROUND:
Established: 1968; 1st Franchised: 1976
Franchised Units: 102
Company-Owned Units 11
Total Units: 113
Dist.: US-113; CAN-0; O'seas-0
North America: 6 States
Density: 66 in FL, 18 in GA, 4 in NC
Projected New Units (12 Months): 10
Qualifications: 3, 4, 5, 2, 3, 4
Registered: FL,VA

FINANCIAL/TERMS:
Cash Investment: $NR
Total Investment: $600K-1.1MM
Minimum Net Worth: $1MM
Fees: Franchise - $25K
Royalty - 3.5%; Ad. - 1%
Earnings Claim Statement: No
Term of Contract (Years): 20/10
Avg. # Of Employees: 25 FT, 15 PT
Passive Ownership: Discouraged
Encourage Conversions: No
Area Develop. Agreements: Yes/Varies
Sub-Franchising Contracts: No
Expand In Territory: Yes
Space Needs: 5,500 SF; FS

SUPPORT & TRAINING PROVIDED:
Financial Assistance Provided: No
Site Selection Assistance: Yes
Lease Negotiation Assistance: No
Co-Operative Advertising: Yes
Franchisee Assoc./Member: Yes/Yes
Size Of Corporate Staff: 17
On-Going Support: a,b,c,d,e,G,h,I
Training: 400-500 Hours or 10-13 Weeks at Orlando, FL.

SPECIFIC EXPANSION PLANS:
US: Southeast
Canada: No
Overseas: No

<< >>

STEAK AND ALE

6500 International Pkwy., # 1000
Plano, TX 75093
Tel: (800) 543-9670 (972) 588-5657
Fax: (972) 588-5806
E-Mail: franchise@metrogroup.com
Web Site: www.metromediarestaruants.com
Mr. Art Kilmer, VP Franchising

STEAK AND ALE is an up-scale restaurant that features a variety of distinctive tastes, such as prime rib, steaks and a fresh salad bar served in a casually elegant atmosphere.

BACKGROUND: IFA MEMBER
Established: 1966; 1st Franchised: 1998
Franchised Units: 1
Company-Owned Units 107
Total Units: 108
Dist.: US-113; CAN-0; O'seas-0
North America: 24 States
Density: 27 in FL, 25 in TX, 7 in NJ
Projected New Units (12 Months): NR
Qualifications: 5, 5, 4, 3, 4, 5
Registered: All States

FINANCIAL/TERMS:
Cash Investment: $500K
Total Investment: $1.0-2.0MM
Minimum Net Worth: $1MM
Fees: Franchise - $50K
Royalty - 4%; Ad. - 4%
Earnings Claim Statement: No
Term of Contract (Years): 20/Varies
Avg. # Of Employees: NR
Passive Ownership: Discouraged
Encourage Conversions: Yes
Area Develop. Agreements: Yes/20
Sub-Franchising Contracts: No
Expand In Territory: Yes
Space Needs: 6,300 SF; FS

SUPPORT & TRAINING PROVIDED:
Financial Assistance Provided: No
Site Selection Assistance: Yes
Lease Negotiation Assistance: No
Co-Operative Advertising: Yes
Franchisee Assoc./Member: Yes/No
Size Of Corporate Staff: 375
On-Going Support: A,B,C,D,E,G,h
Training: Headquarters at Plano, TX; in Unit.

SPECIFIC EXPANSION PLANS:
US: All United States
Canada: All Canada
Overseas: All Countries

<< >>

STRAW HAT PIZZA®

STRAW HAT PIZZA

18 Crow Canyon Ct., # 150
San Ramon, CA 94583
Tel: (925) 837-3400
Fax: (925) 820-1080
E-Mail: info@strawhatpizza.com
Web Site: www.strawhatpizza.com
Mr. Joshua V. Richman, President/CEO

STRAW HAT PIZZA is a cooperative owned by a membership made up of individual store owners. Royalty fees are very low and more than offset by purchasing, insurance and marketing advantages. Stores operate under a detailed system, yet are allowed a great deal of flexibility. Store owners participate in the operation of the parent company.

BACKGROUND: IFA MEMBER
Established: 1959; 1st Franchised: 1969
Franchised Units: 43
Company-Owned Units 0
Total Units: 43
Dist.: US-47; CAN-0; O'seas-0
North America: 2 States
Density: 41 in CA, 2 in NV
Projected New Units (12 Months): 4
Qualifications: 4, 4, 3, 3, 4, 4
Registered: CA,HI,WA

FINANCIAL/TERMS:
Cash Investment: $100-200K
Total Investment: $150-600K
Minimum Net Worth: $250K
Fees: Franchise - $10K
Royalty - 2%; Ad. - 0.75%
Earnings Claim Statement: No
Term of Contract (Years): 10/5
Avg. # Of Employees: 3-5 FT, 8-15 PT
Passive Ownership: Discouraged
Encourage Conversions: Yes
Area Develop. Agreements: No
Sub-Franchising Contracts: No
Expand In Territory: Yes
Space Needs: 4,000 SF; FS,SC

SUPPORT & TRAINING PROVIDED:
Financial Assistance Provided: Yes(I)
Site Selection Assistance: No
Lease Negotiation Assistance: No
Co-Operative Advertising: Yes
Franchisee Assoc./Member: No
Size Of Corporate Staff: 5
On-Going Support: B,C,D,F,G,h
Training: 4 Weeks Long Beach, CA.

SPECIFIC EXPANSION PLANS:
US: West
Canada: No
Overseas: No

<< >>

SWISS CHALET/SWISS CHALET PLUS RESTAURANTS

6303 Airport Rd.
Mississauga, ON L4V 1R8 CANADA
Tel: (905) 405-6500
Fax: (905) 405-6777
Ms. Irene Fong, Dir. Franchise Admin.

Foodservice family restaurants.

BACKGROUND:
Established: 1900; 1st Franchised: 1984
Franchised Units: 173
Company-Owned Units 38
Total Units: 211
Dist.: US-7; CAN-146; O'seas-0
North America: NR
Density: ON, PQ, AB
Projected New Units (12 Months): 20
Qualifications: 5, 4, 3, 3, 1, 5
Registered: AB

FINANCIAL/TERMS:
Cash Investment: $300-360K
Total Investment: $1-1.2MM
Minimum Net Worth: $600K
Fees: Franchise - $75-90K
Royalty - 5%; Ad. - 4%
Earnings Claim Statement: Yes
Term of Contract (Years): 20/5x4
Avg. # Of Employees: 6 FT, 80 PT
Passive Ownership: Not Allowed
Encourage Conversions: Yes
Area Develop. Agreements: No
Sub-Franchising Contracts: No
Expand In Territory: Yes
Space Needs: 6,000 SF; FS

SUPPORT & TRAINING PROVIDED:
Financial Assistance Provided: No
Site Selection Assistance: Yes
Lease Negotiation Assistance: Yes
Co-Operative Advertising: Yes
Franchisee Assoc./Member: Yes/Yes
Size Of Corporate Staff: 200
On-Going Support: C,D,E,G,h,I
Training: 10-12 Weeks Toronto, ON.

SPECIFIC EXPANSION PLANS:
US: No
Canada: All Canada
Overseas: No

<< >>

TAXI'S RESTAURANTS INTERNATIONAL

1840 San Miguel Dr., # 206
Walnut Creek, CA 94596
Tel: (877) 448-8294 (925) 939-5021
Fax: (925) 937-7227
E-Mail: franchise@taxis1.com
Web Site: www.taxishamburgers.com
Mr. Jeffery Neustadt, President/CEO

TAXI'S RESTAURANTS is a chain of fast/casual restaurants, offering a varied menu of gourmet hamburgers, over-sized sandwiches, salads, soups, shakes and a Top-Your-Own Baked Potato Bar. The restaurants feature a lively atmosphere, complete with jukebox music set in the theme of a taxi garage. TAXI'S is open for lunch and dinner and Company unit sales average over $1 million annually.

BACKGROUND: IFA MEMBER
Established: 1991; 1st Franchised: 1995
Franchised Units: 0
Company-Owned Units 5
Total Units: 5
Dist.: US-5; CAN-0; O'seas-0
North America: 1 State
Density: 5 in CA
Projected New Units (12 Months): 7
Qualifications: 4, 5, 5, 3, 1, 4
Registered: CA,WA

FINANCIAL/TERMS:
Cash Investment: $N/A
Total Investment: $395-450K
Minimum Net Worth: $N/A
Fees: Franchise - $25K
Royalty - 4%; Ad. - 3.75%
Earnings Claim Statement: No
Term of Contract (Years): 20/N/A
Avg. # Of Employees: 10 FT, 15 PT
Passive Ownership: Not Allowed
Encourage Conversions: Yes
Area Develop. Agreements: Yes
Sub-Franchising Contracts: No
Expand In Territory: Yes
Space Needs: 2,500 SF; FS, SF, SC, RM

SUPPORT & TRAINING PROVIDED:
Financial Assistance Provided: No
Site Selection Assistance: Yes
Lease Negotiation Assistance: No
Co-Operative Advertising: No
Franchisee Assoc./Member: No
Size Of Corporate Staff: 4
On-Going Support: C,D,E,G,H,I
Training: 4 Weeks Walnut Creek, CA.

SPECIFIC EXPANSION PLANS:
US: NR
Canada: No
Overseas: No

<< >>

VILLAGE INN RESTAURANTS

400 W. 48th Ave., P. O. Box 16601
Denver, CO 80216
Tel: (800) 891-9978 (303) 296-2121
Fax: (303) 672-2212
E-Mail: mcrogle@vicorpinc.com
Web Site: www.vicorpinc.com
Ms. Maxine Crogle, Qualifications Specialist

Full-service, family-style restaurants, offering a variety of menu items and bimonthly features, emphasizing our breakfast heritage in all dayparts.

BACKGROUND: IFA MEMBER
Established: 1958; 1st Franchised: 1961
Franchised Units: 114
Company-Owned Units 109
Total Units: 223
Dist.: US-223; CAN-0; O'seas-0
North America: 22 States
Density: 48 in CO, 25 in FL, 19 AZ
Projected New Units (12 Months): 12
Qualifications: 5, 4, 5, 3, 1, 5
Registered: CA,FL,IL,MD,MN,MS,ND,SD,UT,VA,WA

FINANCIAL/TERMS:
Cash Investment: $Varies
Total Investment: $577K-2.7MM
Minimum Net Worth: $750K
Fees: Franchise - $40K
Royalty - 4%; Ad. - 2%
Earnings Claim Statement: Yes
Term of Contract (Years): 15/20
Avg. # Of Employees: 20 FT, 40 PT
Passive Ownership: Discouraged
Encourage Conversions: Yes
Area Develop. Agreements: Yes/Varies
Sub-Franchising Contracts: No
Expand In Territory: Yes
Space Needs: 4,400 SF; FS, SC, RM

SUPPORT & TRAINING PROVIDED:
Financial Assistance Provided: No
Site Selection Assistance: Yes
Lease Negotiation Assistance: No
Co-Operative Advertising: Yes
Franchisee Assoc./Member: No
Size Of Corporate Staff: 200
On-Going Support: C,d,E,F,G,h,I
Training: Approximately 10-12 Weeks Denver, CO.

SPECIFIC EXPANSION PLANS:
US: Mid-Atlantic,NE,SE,SW
Canada: No
Overseas: No

WESTERN SIZZLIN'

317 Kimball Ave., NE
Roanoke, VA 24016
Tel: (800) 247-8325 (540) 345-3195
Fax: (540) 345-0831
E-Mail: vgardner@western-sizzlin.com
Web Site: www.western-sizzlin.com
Mr. Kert Gennings, Senior Vice President

WESTERN SIZZLIN' restaurants operate a full line of steak-chicken-seafood entrees, as well as a full expanded food bar, featuring proteins, vegetables and bakery items, along with an expanded salad bar. Our focus is on making a quality statement with excellent price/value. Also offering franchises for Great American Steak & Buffet and Austin's Steakhouse and Saloon.

BACKGROUND: IFA MEMBER
Established: 1962; 1st Franchised: 1976
Franchised Units: 236
Company-Owned Units 17
Total Units: 253
Dist.: US-253; CAN-0; O'seas-0
North America: NR
Density: 31 in AR, 24 in VA, 21 in GA
Projected New Units (12 Months): NR
Qualifications: 5, 4, 2, 3, 2, 5
Registered: CA,FL,IL,IN,MD,VA

FINANCIAL/TERMS:
Cash Investment: $NR
Total Investment: $811K-2.3MM
Minimum Net Worth: $NR
Fees: Franchise - $30K
Royalty - 2% Gross; Ad. - 1% Gross
Earnings Claim Statement: No
Term of Contract (Years): 20/10
Avg. # Of Employees: 25 FT, 50 PT
Passive Ownership: NR
Encourage Conversions: Yes
Area Develop. Agreements: Yes/Negot.
Sub-Franchising Contracts: NR

Expand In Territory: Yes
Space Needs: 7,500-8,500 SF; FS

SUPPORT & TRAINING PROVIDED:

Financial Assistance Provided: No
Site Selection Assistance: Yes
Lease Negotiation Assistance: No
Co-Operative Advertising: No
Franchisee Assoc./Member: Yes
Size Of Corporate Staff: 40
On-Going Support: C,D,E,F,G,h,I
Training: 6 Weeks Training Center in Manassas, VA, Knoxville, TN, Little Rock, AR.

SPECIFIC EXPANSION PLANS:

US: All United States
Canada: No
Overseas: No

<< >>

WORLDLY WRAPS

221 Sequoia Rd., # 222
Louisville, KY 40207
Tel: (510) 839-5462
Fax: (510) 839-2104
Mr. McKee Y. Elder, President

Truly the world's best wraps! 17 different varieties. Also, smoothies and health drinks. Low start-up cost. Exceptional training and on-going support. This is a new market that has not yet been tapped. Take advantage of our concept and our growth program. Option to expand within territory.

BACKGROUND:

Established: 1994; 1st Franchised: 1995
Franchised Units: 24
Company-Owned Units <u>6</u>
Total Units: 30
Dist.: US-21; CAN-0; O'seas-0
North America: 6 States
Density: 10 in KY, 4 in TN, 2 in IN
Projected New Units (12 Months): 4
Registered: CA,FL,IL,MN,WA

FINANCIAL/TERMS:

Cash Investment: $90-120K
Total Investment: $200-280K
Minimum Net Worth: $100K
Fees: Franchise - $19.5K
Royalty - 6%; Ad. - 1%
Earnings Claim Statement: No
Term of Contract (Years): 10/10
Avg. # Of Employees: 2 FT, 8 PT
Passive Ownership: Not Allowed
Encourage Conversions: Yes
Area Develop. Agreements: Yes/10
Sub-Franchising Contracts: No

Expand In Territory: No
Space Needs: 3,000-4,000 SF; FS

SUPPORT & TRAINING PROVIDED:

Financial Assistance Provided: Yes(I)
Site Selection Assistance: Yes
Lease Negotiation Assistance: Yes
Co-Operative Advertising: Yes
Franchisee Assoc./Member: NR
Size Of Corporate Staff: 21
On-Going Support: A,B,C,D,E,F,G,H,I
Training: 8 Weeks Headquarters; 3 Weeks Pre-0pening; On-Going.

SPECIFIC EXPANSION PLANS:

US: South, Southeast
Canada: No
Overseas: No

<< >>

SUPPLEMENTAL LISTING OF FRANCHISORS

ABC COUNTRY RESTAURANTS, 15373 Fraser Hwy., #202, Surrey, BC V3R 3P3 CANADA; (604) 583-2919; (604) 583-8488

ALBERT'S FAMILY RESTAURANT, 10544 - 144 St., Edmonton, AB T5H 3J7 CANADA; (403) 429-1259; (403) 426-7391

ARROW NEIGHBORHOOD PUB GROUP, THE, 173 Woolwich St., # 201, Guelph, ON N1H 3V4 CANADA; (519) 836-3948; (519) 836-6749

AUNT SARAH'S PANCAKE HOUSE, P.O. Box 9504, Richmond, VA 23228 ; (804) 264-9189; (804) 266-1255

BANNERS RESTAURANTS, 1965 W. Fourth Ave., # 203, Vancouver, BC V6J 1M8 CANADA; (604) 737-7748; (604) 737-7993

BLUEBERRY HILL, 401 Newport Center Dr., # A103, Newport Beach, CA 92660 ; (949) 644-2705; (949) 760-9525

BOCAZA MEXICAN GRILL, 1420 Kenton St., Aurora, CO 80010-3448 ; (303) 366-4423; (303) 366-4429

BOSTON MARKET INTERNATIONAL, 14123 Denver W. Pkwy., P.O. Box 4086, Golden, CO 80401-3116 ; (303) 278-9500; (303) 216-5460

BRIDGEMAN'S RESTAURANTS, 6201 Brooklyn Blvd., Brooklyn Center, MN 55429 ; (800) 297-5050 (612) 931-3099; (612) 931-3199

BUD'S BROILER, 2337 Tulane Ave., New Orleans, LA 70119 ; (504) 821-3598; (504) 821-3810

BULLWINKLE'S RESTAURANT & THE FAMILY FUN CENTERS, 18300 Von Karman, # 900, Irvine, CA 92612 ; (949) 261-0404; (949) 261-1414

CHEDDAR'S CASUAL CAFÉ, 616 Six Flags Dr., # 116, Arlington, TX 76011 ; (817) 640-4344; (817) 633-4452

COCO'S/CARROWS, 3355 Michelson Dr., # 350, Irvine, CA 92612 ; (949) 251-5700; (949) 251-5231

CONSOLIDATED RESTAURANT OPERATIONS, 12200 Stemmons Frwy., # 100, Dallas, TX 75234-5888 ; (972) 888-8133; (972) 888-4260

COUNTRY KITCHEN INTERNATIONAL, P.O. Box 44434, 6410 Enterprise Ln., Madison, WI 53744-4434 ; (608) 274-5030; (608) 274-9999

CUCOS MEXICAN CAFÉ, 110 Veterans Blvd., # 222, Metairie, LA 70005 ; (800) 888-2826 (504) 835-0306; (504) 835-0336

DAMON'S INTERNATIONAL, 4645 Executive Dr., Columbus, OH 43220 ; (614) 442-7900; (614) 273-3121

DARDEN RESTAURANTS, 5900 Lake Ellenor Dr., Orlando, FL 32809 ; (407) 245-4000; (407) 245-4518

DESERT MOON CAFÉ, 612 Corporate Wy., # 1M, Valley Cottage, NY 10989-2021; (877) JOIN-DMC (845) 267-3300; (845) 267-2548

DON CHERRY'S GRAPEVINE RESTAURANTS, 500 Ray Lawson Blvd., Brampton, ON l6y 5b3 CANADA; (905) 451-5197; (905) 451-1980

DURANGO STEAK HOUSE, 2325 Ulmerton Rd., # 20, Clearwater, FL 33762; (800) 525-8643 (727) 540-0009; (727) 572-8342

EAT AT JOE'S, P.O. Box 500, Yonkers, NY 10704 ; (800) 899-5637 (914) 337-6584; (914) 725-8663

EL TORITO RESTAURANTS, 4001 Via Oro Ave., # 200, Long Beach, CA 90810; (800) 735-3501 (310) 513-7500; (310) 522-9810

ELEPHANT & CASTLES PUB, 13300 Old Branco Rd., # 323, San Antonio, TX 78216 ; (201) 764-1911; (201) 764-1922

EMBERS AMERICA, 1664 University Ave., St. Paul, MN 55104 ; (888) 805-3448 (651) 645-6473; (651) 645-6866

FAMOUS DAVE'S OF AMERICA, 7657 Anagram Dr., Eden Prairie, MN 55344-7310 ; (800) 210-4040 (952) 294-1300; (952) 294-1301

FISH COVE FRANCHISING, 1802 Teall Ave., Syracuse, NY 13206 ; (315) 463-6990; (315) 463-1038

GENGHIS GRILL - THE MONGOLIAN FEAST, 225 Main St., Dallas, TX 75226-1411 ; (888) 436-4447 (214) 742-5426; (214) 749-4329

GEPPETTO'S PIZZA & RIBS, 3314 Warren Rd., Cleveland, OH 44111 ; (216) 251-1354; (216) 251-8960

GIGGLEBEES, 519 S. Minnesota Ave., Sioux Falls, SD 57104 ; (605) 331-4242; (605) 334-4514

GIORGIO RESTAURANTS, 222 St-Laurent Blvd., Montreal, PQ H2Y 2Y3 CANADA; (514) 845-4221; (514) 844-0071

GOLDIES PATIO GRILL, 8332 E. 73rd St. S., Tulsa, OK 74133 ; (918) 254-8100

GOOD TIMES DRIVE THRU, 601 Corporate Cir., Golden, CO 80401 ; (303) 384-1400; (303) 273-0177

GREAT AMERICAN STEAK & BUFFET, 317 Kimball Ave., NE, Roanoke, VA 24016-2005 ; (800) 247-8325 (540) 345-3195; (540) 345-6298

HOOTERS OF AMERICA, 1815 The Exchange, Atlanta, GA 30339-2027 ; (770) 951-2040; (770) 933-9464

INTERNATIONAL HOUSE OF PANCAKES/IHOP, 450 N. Brand Blvd., 3rd Fl., Glendale, CA 91203-2306 ; (818) 240-6055; (818) 240-0270

IRON SKILLET RESTAURANTS, THE, 6080 Surety Dr., El Paso, TX 79905 ; (800) 331-8809 (915) 779-4711; (915) 774-7391

IT'S JUST LUNCH, 835 Fifth Ave., # 300, San Diego, CA 92101-6134 ; (619) 234-7200; (619) 234-8500

JACK ASTOR'S BAR & GRILL, 4405 Knoll View Dr., Plano, TX 75024 ; (972) 801-9376; (972) 801-9415

JB'S FAMILY RESTAURANT, 2207 S. 48th St., # A, Tempe, AZ 85282 ; (800) 995-7555 (602) 426-2660; (602) 426-0480

JOHNNY'S NEW YORK STYLE PIZZA, 834 Virginia Ave., Hapeville, GA 30354 ; (404) 766-3727; (404) 766-3727

KEG RESTAURANTS, 10760 Shellbridge Way, # 150, Richmond, BC V6X 3H1 CANADA; (604) 276-0242; (604) 276-2681

KELLY'S CAJUN GRILL, 4104 Aurora St., Coral Gables, FL 33146-1416 ; (800) 901-0369 (305) 476-1611; (305) 476-9622

KOO KOO ROO ENTERPRISES, INC., P.O. Box 19561, Irvine, CA 92623-9561 ; (949) 757-8015; (714) 757-3047

LE PEEP, 4 W. Dry Creek Circle, # 201, Littleton, CO 80120 ; (303) 730-6300; (303) 730-7105

LOOP, THE, 1 San Jose Pl., # 3, Jacksonville, FL 32257 ; (800) 329-5667 (904) 268-2609; (904) 268-5809

MANCINO'S ITLAIAN EATERY, 1324 W. Milham St., Portage, MI 49024 ; (888) 432-8379 (616) 226-4400; (616) 226-4466

MANDARIN RESTAURANT, 239 Queen St. E., # 18, Brampton, ON L6W 2B6 CANADA; (905) 451-4100; (905) 456-3411

MARIE CALLENDER PIE SHOPS, 1100 Town & Country Rd., # 1300, Orange, CA 92868 ; (714) 542-3355; (714) 542-4702

METROMEDIA FAMILY STEAKHOUSES, 6500 International Pkwy., # 1000, Plano, TX 75093-8222 ; (800) 543-9760 (972) 404-5000; (972) 588-5806

OLD CHICAGO FRANCHISING, 248 Centennial Pwky. # 100, Louisville, CO 80027 ; (303) 664-4200; (303) 664-4007

OLD SAN FRANCISCO STEAKHOUSE, 9809 McCullough, San Antonio, TX 78216 ; (210) 341-3189; (210) 341-3585

OUTBACK STEAKHOUSE INTERNATIONAL, 3355 Lenox Rd., # 600, Atlanta, GA 30326 ; (404) 231-4329; (404) 231-2167

PANTRY FAMILY RESTAURANTS, THE, 1812 152nd St., # 203, South Surrey, BC V4A 4N5 CANADA; (604) 536-4111; (604) 536-4103

PAT O'BRIEN'S INTERNATIONAL, 718 St. Peter St., New Orleans, LA 70116 ; (504) 582-6910; (504) 582 6909

PIZZA HUT, 14841 Dallas Pkwy., Dallas, TX 75240 ; (972) 338-7007; (972) 338-7681

PRIME RESTAURANT GROUP, 10 Kingsbridge Garden Cir., # 600, Mississauga, ON L5R 3K6 CANADA; (800) 361-3111 (905) 568-0000; (905) 568-0080

R. J. GATOR'S FLORIDA FOOD N' FUN, 609 Hepburn Ave., # 103, Jupiter, FL 33458-5014 ; (800) 438-4286 (561) 575-0326; (561) 575-9220

RAGAZZI'S ITALIAN GRILLE, P.O. Box 29511, Raleigh, NC 27626 ; ;

RED ROBIN INTERNATIONAL, 5575 DTC Pkwy., # 110, Englewood, CO 80111 (303) 846-6000; (303) 846-6013

RED'S BACKWOODS BBQ, 2255 Glades Rd., # 110E, Boca Raton, FL 33431 ; (888) 311-7337 (561) 998-2250; (561) 998-2249

RESTAURANT DEVELOPERS CORP., 5755 Granger Rd., #200, Independence, OH 44131 ; (800) 837-9599 (216) 398-1101; (216) 398-0707

RESTAURANTS GIORGIO (AMERIQUE), 222 St-Laurent Blvd., Montreal, PQ H2Y 2Y3 CANADA; (514) 845-4221; (514) 844-0071

RICKY'S RESTAURANTS, 7565 132nd St., # 201, Surrey, BC V3W 1K5 CANADA; (888) 597-7272 (604) 597-7272; (604) 597-8874

ROYAL FORK RESTAURANT, 6874 Fairview Ave., Boise, ID 83704 ; (208) 322-5600; (208) 322-0149

ROYAL WAFFLE KING, P.O. Box 1025, Alpharetta, GA 30009 ; (770) 442-3800; (770) 475-0763

RUBY TUESDAY, 150 W. Church Ave., Maryville, TN 37801 ; (800) 325-0755 (423) 379-5700; (423) 379-6817

RUNZA FAMILY STEAK HOUSE, 5931 S. 58th St., # D, Lincoln, NE 68516 ; (402) 423-2394; (402) 423-5726

RUSS' RESTAURANTS, 390 E. 8th St., Holland, MI 49423 ; (800) 521-1778 (616) 396-6571; (616) 396-6755

SALVATORE SCALLOPINI RESTAURANTS, 1650 E. 12th Mile Rd., Madison Heights, MI 48071 ; (248) 542-9150; (248) 542-9168

SAMUEL MANCINO'S ITALIAN EATERY, 1324 W. Milham St., Portage, MI 49024 ; (888) 432-8379 (616) 226-4400; (616) 226-4466

SAMURAI SAM'S TERIYAKI GRILL, 7720 E. Evans, Scottsdale, AZ 85260 ; (800) 473-2798 (480) 483-8602; (480) 483-4621

SANDELLA'S CAFÉ, 9 Brookside Pl., West Redding, CT 06896 ; (888) 544-9984 (203) 544-9984; (203) 544-7749

SHAKEY'S, 12092 Valley View St., Garden Grove, CA 92845-1737 ; (888) 444-6686 (714) 890-4801; (714) 934-3760

SHONEY'S RESTAURANTS, 1727 Elm Hill Pk., # B-3, Nashville, TN 37210 ; (877) 377-2233 (615) 231-2605; (615) 231-2009

SHOOTERS INTERNATIONAL, 3033 NE 32nd Ave., Ft. Lauderdale, FL 33308 (954) 566-3044; (954) 566-2953

SIZZLER INTERNATIONAL, 6101 W. Centinela Ave., # 200, Culver City, CA 90230-6337 ; (310) 568-0135; (310) 568-8255

SODA FOUNTAIN, THE, 2 Amherst St., Charleston, SC 29403 ; (843) 853-8536; (843) 853-4135

SPAGHETTI WAREHOUSE ITALIAN GRILL, 12200 Stemmons Frwy., # 100, Dallas, TX 75234-5888 ; (972) 888-8153; (972) 888-4260

SPECTRUM RESTAURANT GROUP, 977 Grandy's Ln., Lewisville, TX 75077-2507 ; (972) 317-8104; (972) 317-8174

ST. HUBERT BAR-B-Q, 1515 Chomedey Blvd., # 250, Laval, PQ H7V 3Y7 CANADA; (450) 688-6500; (450) 688-3900

STRINGS ITALIAN CAFE, 11344 Coloma Rd., # 545, Gold River, CA 95670 (916) 635-3990; (916) 631-9775

SUNSHINE CAFE, 7112 Zionsville Rd., Indianapolis, IN 46268-4153 ; (800) 808-4774 (317) 299-3391; (317) 299-3390

TACO CABANA, 8918 Tesoro Dr., # 200, San Antonio, TX 78217 ; (800) 842-0556 (210) 804-0990; (210) 804-2135

TGI FRIDAY'S, 7540 LBJ Frwy., # 100, Dallas, TX 75251 ; (800) 374-3297 (972) 450-5400; (972) 450-3642

TONY ROMA'S - A PLACE FOR RIBS, 9304 Forest Ln., # 200, Dallas, TX 75243-8953 ; (800) 286-7662 (214) 343-7800; (214) 343-2680

TUMBLEWEED INTERNATIONAL, 9016 Taylorsville Rd., # 159, Louisville, KY 40299-1750

WAFFLE HOUSE, P.O. Box 6450, Norcross, GA 30091-6450 ; (877) 992-3353 (770) 729-5700; (770) 729-5870

WALL STREET DELI, 1 Independence Plz., # 100, Birmingham, AL 35209-2628 (888) 351-2514 (205) 868-2566; (205) 868-0875

WHITE SPOT RESTAURANTS, 1126 SE Marine Dr., Vancouver, BC V5X 2V7 CANADA; (604) 321-6631; (604) 325-1499

ZAXBY'S, 1160 S. Millege Ave., Athens, GA 30605-1350 ; (706) 353-8107; (706) 548-6002

ZYNG NOODLERY, 3575 Boul. St. Laurent Blvd., # 188, Montreal, PQ H2X 2T7 CANADA; (888) 9-NOODLE (514) 288-8800; (514) 288-8821

Food: Specialty Foods

Chapter

18

Food: Specialty Foods Industry Profile

Total # Franchisors in Industry Group	96
Total # Franchised Units in Industry Group	7,194
Total # Company-Owned Units in Industry Group	943
Total # Operating Units in Industry Group	8,137
Average # Franchised Units/Franchisor	74.9
Average # Company-Owned Units/Franchisor	9.8
Average # Total Units/Franchisor	84.7
Ratio of Total # Franchised Units/Total # Company-Owned Units	7.6:1
Industry Survey Participants	33
Representing % of Industry	34.4%
Average Franchise Fee*:	$22.3K
Average Total Investment*:	$230.8K
Average On-Going Royalty Fee*:	5.3%

*If a range was provided, the mid-point of the range was used. See detailed profiles for actual ranges.

Five Largest Participants in Survey

Company	# Franchised Units	# Co-Owned Units	# Total Units	Franchise Fee	On-Going Royalty	Total Investment
1. Quizno's Classic Subs	944	28	972	20K	7%	170-225K
2. Auntie Anne's	677	30	707	30K	6%	252K
3. Scholtzsky's Deli	672	30	702	30K	6%	1.3-2.3MM
4. Papa Murphy's	636	12	648	25K	5%	149-200K
5. Candy Bouquet International	514	1	515	3.5-25K	0%	7-43K

AMERICANDY
1401 Lexington Rd.
Louisville, KY 40206-1928
Tel: (502) 583-1776
Fax: (502) 583-6627
E-Mail: omar@americandy.com
Web Site: www.americandy.com
Mr. Omar L. Tatum, President/Founder

A tour of America through candy. 50 state chocolates available by state, region or all 50 state chocolates in our signature collection. Retail store, kiosks, packing center.

BACKGROUND:
Established: 1990; 1st Franchised: 1992
Franchised Units: 0
Company-Owned Units 1
Total Units: 1
Dist.: US-0; CAN-0; O'seas-0
North America: 1 State
Density: 1 in KY
Projected New Units (12 Months): 10
Qualifications: 5, 5, 5, 3, 1, 5
Registered: NR

FINANCIAL/TERMS:
Cash Investment: $75-185K
Total Investment: $200K
Minimum Net Worth: $500K
Fees: Franchise - $N/A
Royalty - N/A; Ad. - N/A
Earnings Claim Statement: No
Term of Contract (Years): 5/5
Avg. # Of Employees: 2 FT, 2 PT
Passive Ownership: Not Allowed
Encourage Conversions: N/A
Area Develop. Agreements: Yes/10
Sub-Franchising Contracts: No
Expand In Territory: Yes
Space Needs: 1,200 SF; SF, SC, RM, Portable Unit

SUPPORT & TRAINING PROVIDED:
Financial Assistance Provided: Yes(I)
Site Selection Assistance: Yes
Lease Negotiation Assistance: Yes
Co-Operative Advertising: No
Franchisee Assoc./Member: No
Size Of Corporate Staff: 4
On-Going Support: C,D,E,F,h
Training: 2 Weeks in Louisville, KY; Two Weeks at Franchise Site.

SPECIFIC EXPANSION PLANS:
US: All United States
Canada: All Canada
Overseas: Japan, India, All Countries

<< >>

ATLANTA BREAD COMPANY
1200 A Wilson Way, # 100
Smyrna, GA 30082-7207
Tel: (800) 398-3728 (770) 432-0933
Fax: (770) 444-9082
E-Mail: franchise-div@atlantabread.com
Web Site: www.atlantabread.com
Mr. John Bryon, VP Franchise Development

Let's make some bread together! The concept behind the ATLANTA BREAD COMPANY BAKERY CAFE is simple: an upscale neighborhood café serving soups, salads, sandwiches, breads and pastries. ATLANTA BREAD COMPANY is riding the crest of the hottest food concept around - and we've experienced over 450% growth in just 12 months. ABC provides a full spectrum of support, from training to real estate assistance. Franchise offer made by offering circular only.

BACKGROUND: IFA MEMBER
Established: 1993; 1st Franchised: 1995
Franchised Units: 104
Company-Owned Units 1
Total Units: 105
Dist.: US-105; CAN-0; O'seas-0
North America: 23 States
Density: GA, NC, SC
Projected New Units (12 Months): 60
Qualifications: 5, 3, 3, 3, 4, 4
Registered: All States Except ND, SD, IA

FINANCIAL/TERMS:
Cash Investment: $120-150K
Total Investment: $533.7-718.8K
Minimum Net Worth: $500-650K
Fees: Franchise - $40K
Royalty - 5%; Ad. - 2%
Earnings Claim Statement: No
Term of Contract (Years): 10/10
Avg. # Of Employees: 34 FT
Passive Ownership: Discouraged
Encourage Conversions: N/A
Area Develop. Agreements: Yes
Sub-Franchising Contracts: No
Expand In Territory: Yes
Space Needs: 4000-4500 SF SF; FS, SF, PC

SUPPORT & TRAINING PROVIDED:
Financial Assistance Provided: Yes(I)
Site Selection Assistance: Yes
Lease Negotiation Assistance: Yes
Co-Operative Advertising: N/A
Franchisee Assoc./Member: No
Size Of Corporate Staff: 34
On-Going Support: B,C,D,E,F,H,I
Training: 7 Weeks Atlanta, GA.

SPECIFIC EXPANSION PLANS:
US: All United States
Canada: No
Overseas: No

<< >>

AUNTIE ANNE'S
160-A, Rt. 41, P.O. Box 529
Gap, PA 17527
Tel: (717) 442-4766
Fax: (717) 442-4139
Web Site: www.auntieannes.com
Ms. Terri Wisdo, VP Franchise Sales

As the founder and leader of what Entrepreneur Magazine calls the pretzel retailing revolution, AUNTIE ANNE'S supports over 600 locations. Customers love to watch our pretzels being rolled, twisted and baked. They choose our pretzels not only for the variety and taste, but also for our commitment to providing a nutritious snack alternative to mall treats. Our innovative mall-based concept has made AUNTIE ANNE'S one of the most sought-after franchises in the industry today.

BACKGROUND: IFA MEMBER
Established: 1988; 1st Franchised: 1989
Franchised Units: 677
Company-Owned Units 30
Total Units: 707
Dist.: US-520; CAN-0; O'seas-30
North America: 42 States
Density: 81 in PA, 41 in CA, 40 in FL
Projected New Units (12 Months): 70
Qualifications: 5, 3, 3, 2, , 5
Registered: All States

FINANCIAL/TERMS:
Cash Investment: $156-252K
Total Investment: $252K
Minimum Net Worth: $300K
Fees: Franchise - $30K
Royalty - 6%; Ad. - 1%
Earnings Claim Statement: No
Term of Contract (Years): 1-5/5
Avg. # Of Employees: 3 FT, 12 PT
Passive Ownership: Discouraged

Encourage Conversions: N/A
Area Develop. Agreements: No
Sub-Franchising Contracts: No
Expand In Territory: Yes
Space Needs: 400-800 SF; RM

SUPPORT & TRAINING PROVIDED:

Financial Assistance Provided: No
Site Selection Assistance: Yes
Lease Negotiation Assistance: Yes
Co-Operative Advertising: No
Franchisee Assoc./Member: Yes/No
Size Of Corporate Staff: 135
On-Going Support: A,B,C,D,E,G,h
Training: 7-14 Days Corporate Headquarters, Gap, PA.

SPECIFIC EXPANSION PLANS:

US: Parts of MW, SE, West. Regns
Canada: All Canada
Overseas: All Countries Except Singapore, Thailand, Indonesia, Malaysia and Philipines

<< >>

BAHAMA BUCK'S ORIGINAL SHAVED ICE CO.

465 E. Chilton Dr., # 5
Chandler, AZ 85225
Tel: (480) 539-6952
Fax: (480) 539-6953
E-Mail: azlee1@aol.com
Web Site: www.bahamabucks.com
Mr. Blake Buchanan, President

BAHAMA BUCK'S offers a unique, low-cost opportunity for anyone interested in a fun, family-oriented business. We concentrate on offering quality products and great customer service. Set in a tropical atmosphere, BAHAMA BUCK'S offers 61 flavors of soft, creamy shaved ice, plus over 14 non-alcoholic tropical drinks. Store layouts and sizes vary and are extremely flexible, but typically range from 1200-1500 square feet.

BACKGROUND:

Established: 1990; 1st Franchised: 1992
Franchised Units: 6
Company-Owned Units 3
Total Units: 9
Dist.: US-10; CAN-0; O'seas-0
North America: 2 States
Density: 5 in AZ, 5 in TX
Projected New Units (12 Months): 6
Qualifications: 4, 3, 1, 3, 4, 4
Registered: NR

FINANCIAL/TERMS:

Cash Investment: $35K
Total Investment: $60-140K
Minimum Net Worth: $120K
Fees: Franchise - $15K
Royalty - 6%; Ad. - 1%
Earnings Claim Statement: No
Term of Contract (Years): 10/10
Avg. # Of Employees: 1 FT, 12 PT
Passive Ownership: Allowed
Encourage Conversions: Yes
Area Develop. Agreements: Yes/10
Sub-Franchising Contracts: No
Expand In Territory: Yes
Space Needs: 1,000-1,500 SF; FS, SC

SUPPORT & TRAINING PROVIDED:

Financial Assistance Provided: Yes(I)
Site Selection Assistance: Yes
Lease Negotiation Assistance: Yes
Co-Operative Advertising: Yes
Franchisee Assoc./Member: No
Size Of Corporate Staff: 5
On-Going Support: B,C,d,E,G,H,I
Training: 60-80 Hours Tempe, AZ; 2 Days On-Site.

SPECIFIC EXPANSION PLANS:

US: Southwest, South
Canada: No
Overseas: No

<< >>

Top 50

CANDY BOUQUET INTERNATIONAL

423 E. 3rd St.
Little Rock, AR 72201
Tel: (877) 226-3901 (501) 375-9990
Fax: (501) 375-9998
E-Mail: yumyum@candybouquet.com
Web Site: www.candybouquet.com
Ms. Gina McNabb, Franchise Development

CANDY BOUQUET franchises are as unique as the people who own them. All franchises offer floral-like arrangements that are crafted from candies and the finest of chocolates. Each bouquet includes a burst of accessories, bright cellophane accents and a unique container. CANDY BOUQUETS are fun to give, fun to receive and fun to eat. They are perfect as corporate gifts and can be shipped anywhere.

BACKGROUND: IFA MEMBER

Established: 1989; 1st Franchised: 1993
Franchised Units: 514
Company-Owned Units 1
Total Units: 515
Dist.: US-466; CAN-42; O'seas-7
North America: 48 States, 7 Provinces
Density: 46 in TX, 39 in AR, 24 in CA
Projected New Units (12 Months): 213
Qualifications: 5, 5, 5, 5, 5, 5
Registered: All States and AB

FINANCIAL/TERMS:

Cash Investment: $7.5-43K
Total Investment: $7-43K
Minimum Net Worth: $N/A
Fees: Franchise - $3.5-25K
Royalty - 0%; Ad. - 0%
Earnings Claim Statement: No
Term of Contract (Years): 5/5
Avg. # Of Employees: 1 FT, 2 PT
Passive Ownership: Not Allowed
Encourage Conversions: N/A
Area Develop. Agreements: Yes/10
Sub-Franchising Contracts: Yes
Expand In Territory: Yes
Space Needs: Appox. 1,000 SF; HB, SF

SUPPORT & TRAINING PROVIDED:

Financial Assistance Provided: No
Site Selection Assistance: Yes
Lease Negotiation Assistance: No
Co-Operative Advertising: Yes
Franchisee Assoc./Member: No
Size Of Corporate Staff: 27
On-Going Support: b,c,d,D,e,G,h,I
Training: 5 Days Little Rock, AR.

SPECIFIC EXPANSION PLANS:

US: All United States
Canada: All Canada
Overseas: All Countries

<< >>

CANDY EXPRESS

10480 Little Patuxent Pkwy., # 400
Columbia, MD 21044

Tel: (800) 511-4438 (410) 964-5500
Fax: (410) 964-6404
E-Mail: jrosenberg@candyexpress.com
Web Site: www.candyexpress.com
Mr. Joel Rosenberg, President

The number-one ranked retail candy store franchise, offering over 1,000 varieties of candy and confections in a self-serve format. This international franchise company provides franchisees with a total turn-key opportunity that is profitable and easy to operate.

BACKGROUND:
Established: 1989; 1st Franchised: 1989
Franchised Units: 37
Company-Owned Units 5
Total Units: 42
Dist.: US-40; CAN-0; O'seas-8
North America: 17 States
Density: 6 in MD, 5 in GA, 4 in VA
Projected New Units (12 Months): 15
Qualifications: 5, 2, 1, 1, 2, 3
Registered: All States

FINANCIAL/TERMS:
Cash Investment: $25-75K
Total Investment: $125-175K
Minimum Net Worth: $200K
Fees: Franchise - $25K
Royalty - 6%; Ad. - 1%
Earnings Claim Statement: No
Term of Contract (Years): 10/10
Avg. # Of Employees: 1 FT, 3 PT
Passive Ownership: Allowed
Encourage Conversions: Yes
Area Develop. Agreements: Yes/20
Sub-Franchising Contracts: Yes
Expand In Territory: Yes
Space Needs: 1,000 SF; SF, RM, Airport

SUPPORT & TRAINING PROVIDED:
Financial Assistance Provided: Yes(I)
Site Selection Assistance: Yes
Lease Negotiation Assistance: Yes
Co-Operative Advertising: Yes
Franchisee Assoc./Member: Yes/No
Size Of Corporate Staff: 10
On-Going Support: A,B,C,D,E,F,G,H
Training: 2 Weeks MD.

SPECIFIC EXPANSION PLANS:
US: All United States
Canada: All Canada
Overseas: All Countries

<< >>

DIFFERENT TWIST PRETZEL CO., THE

6052 Rte. 8, P.O. Box 334
Bakerstown, PA 15007
Tel: (724) 443-8010
Fax: (724) 443-7287
Mr. August P. Maggio, President

Serving hand-rolled, fresh-baked soft pretzels in 10 different flavors. (Licensor)

BACKGROUND:
Established: 1992; 1st Franchised: 1992
Franchised Units: 15
Company-Owned Units 0
Total Units: 15
Dist.: US-18; CAN-1; O'seas-2
North America: 8 States
Density: 2 in WV, 1 in FL, 1 in MA
Projected New Units (12 Months): 20
Qualifications: 4, 4, 1, 2, 1, 4
Registered: FL

FINANCIAL/TERMS:
Cash Investment: $40-80K
Total Investment: $40-80K
Minimum Net Worth: $50K
Fees: Franchise - $5K
Royalty - 5%; Ad. - NR
Earnings Claim Statement: Yes
Term of Contract (Years): 10/10
Avg. # Of Employees: 3 FT, 3 PT
Passive Ownership: Allowed
Encourage Conversions: Yes
Area Develop. Agreements: Yes
Sub-Franchising Contracts: Yes
Expand In Territory: Yes
Space Needs: 150-400 SF; SF, RM, Other

SUPPORT & TRAINING PROVIDED:
Financial Assistance Provided: Yes(D)
Site Selection Assistance: Yes
Lease Negotiation Assistance: Yes
Co-Operative Advertising: Yes
Franchisee Assoc./Member: No
Size Of Corporate Staff: 12
On-Going Support: b,D,e
Training: 1 Week On-Site.

SPECIFIC EXPANSION PLANS:
US: All United States
Canada: All Canada
Overseas: All Countries

<< >>

FUDGE CO.

103 Belvedere Ave.
Charlevoix, MI 49720
Tel: (231) 547-4612
Fax: (231) 547-4612
Mr. Robert L. Hoffman, President

Handmade fudge cooked in copper kettles, using only natural ingredients and no preservatives, cooled and creamed on marble slabs in view of the public.

BACKGROUND:
Established: 1978; 1st Franchised: 1981
Franchised Units: 13
Company-Owned Units 1
Total Units: 14
Dist.: US-7; CAN-0; O'seas-2
North America: 3 States
Density: 2 in AZ, 2 in AL, 2 in VA
Projected New Units (12 Months): 2-4
Qualifications: 4, 4, 1, 3, 4, 4
Registered: FL,HI,MI,OR

FINANCIAL/TERMS:
Cash Investment: $NR
Total Investment: $28-35K
Minimum Net Worth: $100K
Fees: Franchise - $12.5-15K
Royalty - 3%; Ad. - 0%
Earnings Claim Statement: Yes
Term of Contract (Years): 10/10
Avg. # Of Employees: 2 FT, 2 PT
Passive Ownership: Discouraged
Encourage Conversions: N/A
Area Develop. Agreements: Yes
Sub-Franchising Contracts: NR
Expand In Territory: Yes
Space Needs: 300-600 SF; FS, RM, Resort Areas

SUPPORT & TRAINING PROVIDED:
Financial Assistance Provided: No
Site Selection Assistance: Yes
Lease Negotiation Assistance: No
Co-Operative Advertising: Yes
Franchisee Assoc./Member: No
Size Of Corporate Staff: NR
On-Going Support: b,c,D,E
Training: 10-14 Days in AZ.

SPECIFIC EXPANSION PLANS:
US: All United States
Canada: All Canada
Overseas: All Countries

<< >>

GREAT EARTH VITAMINS

140 Lauman Ln.11478 Mission Vista Dr.
Rancho Cucamonga, CA 91730
Tel: (800) 284-8243 (909) 987-8892
Fax: (909) 941-3472
Web Site: www.greatearth.com
Mr. Stephen R. Stern, Chief Executive Officer

Franchise company that understands consumers' needs and lifestyles, enabling franchisees to personalize a program of vitamins and nutritional supplements for consumers based upon the training we conduct for new franchise owners in our own school. This sets us apart from all other vitamin and nutrient supplement franchise systems.

BACKGROUND:
Established: 1971; 1st Franchised: 1974
Franchised Units: 137
Company-Owned Units 0
Total Units: 137
Dist.: US-142; CAN-8; O'seas-1
North America: 15 States
Density: 77 in CA, 11 in TX
Projected New Units (12 Months): 25
Qualifications: 2, 1, 3, 3, 2, 2
Registered: All States

FINANCIAL/TERMS:
Cash Investment: $NR
Total Investment: $75-135K
Minimum Net Worth: $100K
Fees: Franchise - $30K
Royalty - 6%; Ad. - $150/Mo.
Earnings Claim Statement: No
Term of Contract (Years): 10/5
Avg. # Of Employees: 2 FT, 2 PT
Passive Ownership: Discouraged
Encourage Conversions: Yes
Area Develop. Agreements: Yes/Varies
Sub-Franchising Contracts: Yes
Expand In Territory: Yes
Space Needs: 650-1,400 SF; SC, RM

SUPPORT & TRAINING PROVIDED:
Financial Assistance Provided: Yes(D)
Site Selection Assistance: Yes
Lease Negotiation Assistance: Yes
Co-Operative Advertising: Yes
Franchisee Assoc./Member: Yes
Size Of Corporate Staff: 12
On-Going Support: B,C,D,E,G,h,I
Training: 3 Weeks Cerritos, CA.

SPECIFIC EXPANSION PLANS:
US: All United States
Canada: All Canada
Overseas: NR

<< >>

HARD TIMES CAFÉ

112 South West St., # 310
Alexandria, VA 22314
Tel: (800) 422-2435 (703) 683-8545
Fax: (703) 684-6466
E-Mail: danr@hardtimes.com
Web Site: www.hardtimes.com
Mr. Dan A. Rowe, Chief Executive Officer

Authentic western-style chili parlor. Featuring chili, burgers and beer.

BACKGROUND:
Established: 1980; 1st Franchised: 1992
Franchised Units: 10
Company-Owned Units 4
Total Units: 14
Dist.: US-0; CAN-0; O'seas-0
North America: 3 States
Density: 6 in VA, 6 in MD, 2 in NC
Projected New Units (12 Months): NR
Registered: NR

FINANCIAL/TERMS:
Cash Investment: $100-200K
Total Investment: $400-500K
Minimum Net Worth: $250K
Fees: Franchise - $30K
Royalty - 4%; Ad. - 1%
Earnings Claim Statement: No
Term of Contract (Years): 10/10
Avg. # Of Employees: 6 FT, 20 PT
Passive Ownership: Not Allowed
Encourage Conversions: NR
Area Develop. Agreements: Yes/20
Sub-Franchising Contracts: Yes
Expand In Territory: Yes
Space Needs: NR SF; FS, SC

SUPPORT & TRAINING PROVIDED:
Financial Assistance Provided: NR
Site Selection Assistance: Yes
Lease Negotiation Assistance: Yes
Co-Operative Advertising: Yes
Franchisee Assoc./Member: No
Size Of Corporate Staff: 10
On-Going Support: a,C,D,E,F,G,H,I
Training: 4 Weeks in Washington, DC Area.

SPECIFIC EXPANSION PLANS:
US: East Coast, Mid-Atlantic
Canada: NR
Overseas: NR

<< >>

HEAVENLY HAM

1100 Old Ellis Rd., # 100
Roswell, GA 30076-3819
Tel: (800) 899-2228 (770) 752-1999
Fax: (770) 752-4653
E-Mail: rflynn@heavenlyham.com
Web Site: www.heavenlyham.com
Mr. Roger Flynn, Dir. Franchising

The innovative opportunity in high quality specialty foods. Ownership benefits include: minimal labor, low start-up costs, extensive training, marketing support, site selection assistance and more. HEAVEN.Y HAM focuses primarily on two businesses: specialty meats and lunch. We offer signature spiral-sliced, honey and spice glazed ham and delicious tender-smoked turkeys. Other specialty meats include pork chops, hickory smoked ribs, bacon and steaks.

BACKGROUND: IFA MEMBER
Established: 1984; 1st Franchised: 1984
Franchised Units: 212
Company-Owned Units 2
Total Units: 214
Dist.: US-202; CAN-0; O'seas-0
North America: 32 States
Density: 17 in FL, 13 in NC, 13 in IN
Projected New Units (12 Months): 30
Qualifications: 5, 2, 1, 2, 3, 5
Registered: CA,FL,IL,IN,MD,MI,MN,NY, OR,RI,VA,WA,WI,DC

FINANCIAL/TERMS:
Cash Investment: $NR
Total Investment: $184.9-289K
Minimum Net Worth: $250K
Fees: Franchise - $30K
Royalty - 5%; Ad. - 1%
Earnings Claim Statement: Yes
Term of Contract (Years): 10/10
Avg. # Of Employees: 2 FT, 2 PT
Passive Ownership: Not Allowed
Encourage Conversions: No
Area Develop. Agreements: No
Sub-Franchising Contracts: No
Expand In Territory: Yes
Space Needs: 2,500 SF; FS, SC

SUPPORT & TRAINING PROVIDED:
Financial Assistance Provided: Yes(I)
Site Selection Assistance: Yes
Lease Negotiation Assistance: Yes
Co-Operative Advertising: Yes
Franchisee Assoc./Member: No
Size Of Corporate Staff: 30
On-Going Support: C,D,E,F,G,H,I
Training: 10 Days Atlanta, GA.

SPECIFIC EXPANSION PLANS:
US: All United States
Canada: No
Overseas: No

<< >>

JOE CORBI'S ® PIZZA KIT FUND-RAISING PROGRAM

1430 Desoto Rd.
Baltimore, MD 21230
Tel: (800) 587-7677 (410) 525-8331
Fax: (412) 745-1272

Web Site: www.joecorbi.com
Mr. Joseph Violi

Specializing in the sale of fund-raising pizza kits, breads and other food items, as well as related goods and ancillary services, which are marketed to charitable, municipal, civic and other organizations.

BACKGROUND:
Established: 1984; 1st Franchised: 1999
Franchised Units: 5
Company-Owned Units 5
Total Units: 10
Dist.: US-8; CAN-0; O'seas-0
North America: 7 States
Density: 2 in PA, 1 in MD, 1 in VA
Projected New Units (12 Months): 6
Qualifications: 5, 3, 3, 3, 5, 5
Registered: MD,NY

FINANCIAL/TERMS:
Cash Investment: $40-85K
Total Investment: $50.4-105.5K
Minimum Net Worth: $50.4K
Fees: Franchise - $25-50K
Royalty - 0%; Ad. - 0%
Earnings Claim Statement: No
Term of Contract (Years): 10/10
Avg. # Of Employees: 2 FT
Passive Ownership: Discouraged
Encourage Conversions: Yes
Area Develop. Agreements: No
Sub-Franchising Contracts: No
Expand In Territory: Yes
Space Needs: N/A SF; HB

SUPPORT & TRAINING PROVIDED:
Financial Assistance Provided: No
Site Selection Assistance: Yes
Lease Negotiation Assistance: No
Co-Operative Advertising: No
Franchisee Assoc./Member: No
Size Of Corporate Staff: 7
On-Going Support: C,d,F,G,H
Training: 3 Days at Operating Unit.

SPECIFIC EXPANSION PLANS:
US: Eastern United States
Canada: No
Overseas: No

<< >>

M&M MEAT SHOPS

640 Trillium Dr., P.O. Box 2488
Kitchener, ON N2H 6M3 CANADA
Tel: (519) 895-1075
Fax: (519) 895-0762
E-Mail: johannaj@mmms.ca
Web Site: www.mmmeatshops.com
Ms. Johanna Jamnik, Executive Assistant

Canada's largest specialty frozen food chain, providing high-quality meats and specialty frozen food items to the public at reasonable prices. Recipient of 1992 and 1995 Canadian Franchise Association Award of Excellence, 1994 Hall of Fame Award and 1999 Corporate Citizenship Award. Our product caters to a variety of lifestyles - homemakers, seniors, professionals and trades people.

BACKGROUND:
Established: 1980; 1st Franchised: 1981
Franchised Units: 312
Company-Owned Units 3
Total Units: 315
Dist.: US-0; CAN-315; O'seas-0
North America: 10 Provinces
Density: 175 in ON, 38 in PQ,33 in AB
Projected New Units (12 Months): 34
Registered: AB

FINANCIAL/TERMS:
Cash Investment: $150K
Total Investment: $300K
Minimum Net Worth: $300K
Fees: Franchise - $30K
Royalty - 3%; Ad. - 1.5%
Earnings Claim Statement: Yes
Term of Contract (Years): 10/10
Avg. # Of Employees: 2 FT, 1 PT
Passive Ownership: Not Allowed
Encourage Conversions: Yes
Area Develop. Agreements: No
Sub-Franchising Contracts: No
Expand In Territory: Yes
Space Needs: 1,400 SF; SC

SUPPORT & TRAINING PROVIDED:
Financial Assistance Provided: Yes(I)
Site Selection Assistance: Yes
Lease Negotiation Assistance: Yes
Co-Operative Advertising: Yes
Franchisee Assoc./Member: Yes/Yes
Size Of Corporate Staff: 80
On-Going Support: B,C,D,E,F,G,H,I
Training: 2 Weeks Kitchener, ON.

SPECIFIC EXPANSION PLANS:
US: No
Canada: All Canada
Overseas: No

<< >>

MAUI WOWI SMOOTHIES

5601 S. Broadway, # 200
Littleton, CO 80021
Tel: (888) 862-8555 (303) 781-7800
Fax: (303) 781-2438
E-Mail: michael@concentric.net
Web Site: www.mauiwowi.com
Mr. Michael Haith, President

MAIU WOWI is a home-based business using our unique kiosks and carts in mall and high traffic venues. Work when and where you would like using a system which has been proven for 18 years. Perfect for retirees, teachers and people who want to keep their current jobs to start. Healthy and high-end product for schools, events, malls, etc.

BACKGROUND: IFA MEMBER
Established: 1983; 1st Franchised: 1997
Franchised Units: 56
Company-Owned Units 1
Total Units: 57
Dist.: US-56; CAN-0; O'seas-1
North America: 14 States
Density: 10 in CO, 6 in WA, 3 in UT
Projected New Units (12 Months): 30
Qualifications: 2, 2, 1, 1, 1, 5
Registered: NR

FINANCIAL/TERMS:
Cash Investment: $17-37K
Total Investment: $21-54K
Minimum Net Worth: $100K
Fees: Franchise - $20K
Royalty - 0%; Ad. - 5%
Earnings Claim Statement: No
Term of Contract (Years): 5/5
Avg. # Of Employees: 2 PT
Passive Ownership: Allowed
Encourage Conversions: Yes
Area Develop. Agreements: Yes/20
Sub-Franchising Contracts: Yes
Expand In Territory: Yes
Space Needs: 100 SF; HB

SUPPORT & TRAINING PROVIDED:
Financial Assistance Provided: Yes(I)
Site Selection Assistance: Yes
Lease Negotiation Assistance: Yes
Co-Operative Advertising: Yes
Franchisee Assoc./Member: No
Size Of Corporate Staff: 5
On-Going Support: B,C,D,E,F,G,H,I
Training: 1.5 Days at Your Location.

SPECIFIC EXPANSION PLANS:
US: All United States
Canada: All Canada
Overseas: Europe

<< >>

MCALISTER'S DELI

731 S. Pear Orchard Rd., # 51
Ridgeland, MS 39157-4800
Tel: (888) 855-3354 (601) 952-1100
Fax: (601) 952-1138
E-Mail: pwalls@mcalistersdeli.com
Web Site: www.mcallistersdeli.com
Mr. Patrick K. Walls, VP Franchise Sales

Fast, casual restaurant, featuring a complete menu of gourmet deli foods, including hot and cold deli sandwiches, super-stuffed baked potatoes, salads, soups, desserts, iced tea and other food and beverage products.

BACKGROUND: IFA MEMBER
Established: 1989; 1st Franchised: 1994
Franchised Units: 71
Company-Owned Units 14
Total Units: 85
Dist.: US-85; CAN-0; O'seas-0
North America: 13 States
Density: 19 in MS, 10 in TN, 12 in AL
Projected New Units (12 Months): 25
Qualifications: 5, 5, 4, 3, 1, 3
Registered: All States

FINANCIAL/TERMS:
Cash Investment: $80-250K
Total Investment: $329K-1.4MM
Minimum Net Worth: $500K
Fees: Franchise - $30K
Royalty - 5%; Ad. - 2%
Earnings Claim Statement: Yes
Term of Contract (Years): 10/5/5/5
Avg. # Of Employees: 5 FT, 35 PT
Passive Ownership: Allowed
Encourage Conversions: Yes
Area Develop. Agreements: Yes/Varies
Sub-Franchising Contracts: No
Expand In Territory: No
Space Needs: 3,600 SF; FS, SC

SUPPORT & TRAINING PROVIDED:
Financial Assistance Provided: Yes(I)
Site Selection Assistance: Yes
Lease Negotiation Assistance: Yes
Co-Operative Advertising: Yes
Franchisee Assoc./Member: Yes
Size Of Corporate Staff: 32
On-Going Support: a,B,C,D,E,F,G,H,I
Training: 10 Weeks Jackson, MS; 10 Days Franchisee Location.

SPECIFIC EXPANSION PLANS:
US: All United States
Canada: All Canada
Overseas: No

<< >>

MOM'S BAKE AT HOME PIZZA

4457 Main St.
Philadelphia, PA 19128
Tel: (800) 311-MOMS (215) 482-1044
Fax: (215) 482-0402
E-Mail: bakehome@aol.com
Mr. Martin Bair, President

MOM'S PIZZA franchise 'Bake at Home' pizza stores. The franchisee purchases his or her supplies from the main office. The franchisee then retails a fresh, hand-made gourmet pizza, which is baked at the customer's convenience, in the convenience of his or her home.

BACKGROUND:
Established: 1961; 1st Franchised: 1981
Franchised Units: 13
Company-Owned Units 0
Total Units: 13
Dist.: US-18; CAN-0; O'seas-0
North America: 2 States
Density: 12 in PA, 6 in NJ
Projected New Units (12 Months): 2
Registered: NR

FINANCIAL/TERMS:
Cash Investment: $50K
Total Investment: $50K
Minimum Net Worth: $NR
Fees: Franchise - $15K
Royalty - 0%; Ad. - 0%
Earnings Claim Statement: No
Term of Contract (Years): On-Going
Avg. # Of Employees: 1 FT, 2 PT
Passive Ownership: Not Allowed
Encourage Conversions: No
Area Develop. Agreements: No
Sub-Franchising Contracts: No
Expand In Territory: No
Space Needs: 800 SF; SC

SUPPORT & TRAINING PROVIDED:
Financial Assistance Provided: No
Site Selection Assistance: Yes
Lease Negotiation Assistance: Yes
Co-Operative Advertising: No
Franchisee Assoc./Member: No
Size Of Corporate Staff: 12
On-Going Support: B,C,D,E
Training: 7 Days Existing Franchise.

SPECIFIC EXPANSION PLANS:
US: PA, NJ
Canada: No
Overseas: No

<< >>

NEW YORK FRIES

1220 Yonge St., # 400
Toronto, ON M4T 1W1 CANADA
Tel: (416) 963-5005
Fax: (416) 963-4920
E-Mail: mail@newyorkfries.com
Web Site: www.newyorkfries.com
Mr. Bob Okamoto, Bus. Developer Manager

Exceptional product and simplicity of operations make NEW YORK FRIES an outstanding opportunity. Specializing in fresh-cut fries and hot dogs, our concept is simply. Our standards are high. We start with fresh potatoes, hand-cut on site everyday. We cook them in 100% vegetable oil in our special process. Winner, Canada's Best managed Companies award, requalified winner 2001. Winner of numerous advertising awards. Runner-up, Franchisor of the Year award, Canadian Franchise Association 1994.

BACKGROUND:
Established: 1984; 1st Franchised: 1984
Franchised Units: 160
Company-Owned Units 15
Total Units: 175
Dist.: US-0; CAN-171; O'seas-4
North America: 9 Provinces
Density: 94 in ON, 27 in BC, 24 in AB
Projected New Units (12 Months): 10-12
Qualifications: 4, 5, 4, 3, 1, 5
Registered: AB

FINANCIAL/TERMS:
Cash Investment: $50-75K
Total Investment: $125-175K
Minimum Net Worth: $Depends
Fees: Franchise - $30K
Royalty - 6%; Ad. - 2%
Earnings Claim Statement: No
Term of Contract (Years): 10/5/5
Avg. # Of Employees: 2-3 FT, 5-6 PT
Passive Ownership: Allowed
Encourage Conversions: N/A
Area Develop. Agreements: O'seas
Sub-Franchising Contracts: No
Expand In Territory: Yes
Space Needs: 350 SF; RM

SUPPORT & TRAINING PROVIDED:
Financial Assistance Provided: No
Site Selection Assistance: Yes

Lease Negotiation Assistance: Yes
Co-Operative Advertising: Yes
Franchisee Assoc./Member: Yes/yes
Size Of Corporate Staff: 16
On-Going Support: B,C,D,E,G,h
Training: 7-10 Days Toronto, ON; 5-10 Week On-Site.

SPECIFIC EXPANSION PLANS:
US: No
Canada: All Canada
Overseas: England, Pacific Rim

<< >>

PAPA MURPHY'S

8000 NE Parkway Dr., # 350
Vancouver, WA 98662
Tel: (800) 257-7272 (360) 260-7272
Fax: (360) 260-0500
E-Mail: franchise@papamurphys.com
Web Site: www.papamurphys.com
Ms. Tiffany Carvell, Franchise Sales Mgr.

PAPA MURPHY'S produces a great pizza made from top-quality ingredients. Letting customers bake it themselves is smart business. Put the 2 together and you get the largest, fastest-growing Take 'N' Bake franchise in the world. PAPA MURPHY'S now has 565 stores with another 175 stores expected to open in 2000.

BACKGROUND: IFA MEMBER
Established: 1981; 1st Franchised: 1982
Franchised Units: 636
Company-Owned Units 12
Total Units: 648
Dist.: US-640; CAN-0; O'seas-0
North America: 22 States
Density: 163 in CA,117 in WA,85 in OR
Projected New Units (12 Months): 175
Qualifications: 4, 3, 2, 3, 3, 5
Registered: CA,IL,IN,MI,MN,ND,OR,SD,WA,WI

FINANCIAL/TERMS:
Cash Investment: $80K
Total Investment: $148.8-199.5K
Minimum Net Worth: $250K
Fees: Franchise - $25K
Royalty - 5%; Ad. - 1%
Earnings Claim Statement: No
Term of Contract (Years): 10/5
Avg. # Of Employees: 2 FT, 8-10 PT
Passive Ownership: Not Allowed
Encourage Conversions: Yes
Area Develop. Agreements: No
Sub-Franchising Contracts: No
Expand In Territory: Yes
Space Needs: 1,200-1,400 SF; FS, SF, SC

SUPPORT & TRAINING PROVIDED:
Financial Assistance Provided: Yes(I)
Site Selection Assistance: Yes
Lease Negotiation Assistance: Yes
Co-Operative Advertising: Yes
Franchisee Assoc./Member: Yes/No
Size Of Corporate Staff: 106
On-Going Support: B,C,D,E,G,H,I
Training: 3 Days/30 Hours in the Closest Training Store; 6 Weeks in Store; 6 Days Corporate Office.

SPECIFIC EXPANSION PLANS:
US: Midwest
Canada: No
Overseas: No

<< >>

PIZZA NOVA

2247 Midland Ave.
Scarborough, ON M1P 4R1 CANADA
Tel: (416) 439-0051
Fax: (416) 299-3558
Mr. Frank Macri, Franchise Director

PIZZA NOVA specializes in traditional Italian pizza, pastas and chicken wings. All menu items are prepared fresh daily and are available for take-out or delivery. We pride ourselves on quality and service.

BACKGROUND:
Established: 1963; 1st Franchised: 1969
Franchised Units: 85
Company-Owned Units 2
Total Units: 87
Dist.: US-1; CAN-80; O'seas-6
North America: 1 State, 1 Province
Density: 80 in ON
Projected New Units (12 Months): 10
Qualifications: 4, 4, 4, 2, 4, 5
Registered: NR

FINANCIAL/TERMS:
Cash Investment: $40K
Total Investment: $125-135K
Minimum Net Worth: $NR
Fees: Franchise - $N/A
Royalty - 6%; Ad. - 4%
Earnings Claim Statement: Yes
Term of Contract (Years): 5/5
Avg. # Of Employees: 4 FT, 6 PT
Passive Ownership: Not Allowed
Encourage Conversions: Yes
Area Develop. Agreements: No
Sub-Franchising Contracts: No
Expand In Territory: Yes
Space Needs: 800-1,100 SF; SF, SC, RM

SUPPORT & TRAINING PROVIDED:
Financial Assistance Provided: No
Site Selection Assistance: Yes
Lease Negotiation Assistance: Yes
Co-Operative Advertising: Yes
Franchisee Assoc./Member: Yes
Size Of Corporate Staff: 18
On-Going Support: A,B,C,D,E,F,G,H
Training: 3 Weeks.

SPECIFIC EXPANSION PLANS:
US: NR
Canada: ON
Overseas: All Countries

<< >>

POWER SMOOTHIE

8930 W. State Rd. 84, # 170
Davie, FL 33324
Tel: (888) 818-POWER (954) 370-3913
Fax: (954) 370-3902
Mr. Michael Genovese, President

POWER SMOOTHIE offers 'delicious nutrition' with a fast, up-beat atmosphere. We serve healthy smoothies, juices, sandwiches, nutritional supplements and low-fat snacks in a clean, non-cooking environment.

BACKGROUND:
Established: 1991; 1st Franchised: 1994
Franchised Units: 20
Company-Owned Units 0
Total Units: 20
Dist.: US-14; CAN-0; O'seas-0
North America: 3 States
Density: 11 in FL, 2 in NV, 1 in TX
Projected New Units (12 Months): 20
Qualifications: 2, 2, 2, 2, 2, 5
Registered: FL

FINANCIAL/TERMS:
Cash Investment: $80-120K
Total Investment: $80-120K
Minimum Net Worth: $50K
Fees: Franchise - $20K
Royalty - 5%; Ad. - 1.5-3%
Earnings Claim Statement: No
Term of Contract (Years): 10/10
Avg. # Of Employees: 2 FT, 5 PT
Passive Ownership: Allowed
Encourage Conversions: Yes
Area Develop. Agreements: Yes/Negot.
Sub-Franchising Contracts: No
Expand In Territory: Yes
Space Needs: 800-1,500 SF; SC, RM

SUPPORT & TRAINING PROVIDED:
Financial Assistance Provided: Yes(I)

Site Selection Assistance: Yes
Lease Negotiation Assistance: Yes
Co-Operative Advertising: Yes
Franchisee Assoc./Member: No
Size Of Corporate Staff: 5
On-Going Support: C,D,E,F,I
Training: 2 Weeks Plantation, FL.

SPECIFIC EXPANSION PLANS:
US: All United States
Canada: No
Overseas: All Countries

<< >>

PRETZEL MAKER

2855 E. Cottonwood Pkwy., # 400
Salt Lake City, UT 84121-7050
Tel: (800) 348-6311 (801) 736-5600
Fax: (801) 736-5936
Web Site: www.pretzelmaker.com
Mr. Scott Moffitt, SVP Franchise Development

The 'World's Best Soft Pretzels,' hand-rolled and served hot with high consumer acceptance, precision portion control and available in combination store configurations. May be operated in both traditional and non-traditional venues.

BACKGROUND: IFA MEMBER
Established: 1991; 1st Franchised: 1992
Franchised Units: 180
Company-Owned Units 10
Total Units: 190
Dist.: US-148; CAN-33; O'seas-9
North America: 39 States, 9 Provinces
Density: 21 in CA, 13 in UT, 11 in CO
Projected New Units (12 Months): 80
Qualifications: 4, 4, 3, 2, 2, 5
Registered: All States

FINANCIAL/TERMS:
Cash Investment: $10-30K
Total Investment: $100-213K
Minimum Net Worth: $75K
Fees: Franchise - $25K
Royalty - 5%; Ad. - 1.5%
Earnings Claim Statement: No
Term of Contract (Years): 10/10
Avg. # Of Employees: 5 FT, 7 PT
Passive Ownership: Discouraged
Encourage Conversions: Yes
Area Develop. Agreements: Yes/3
Sub-Franchising Contracts: No
Expand In Territory: Yes
Space Needs: 500-700 SF; FS, SC, RM

SUPPORT & TRAINING PROVIDED:
Financial Assistance Provided: Yes(I)
Site Selection Assistance: Yes
Lease Negotiation Assistance: Yes
Co-Operative Advertising: Yes
Franchisee Assoc./Member: No
Size Of Corporate Staff: 37
On-Going Support: B,C,D,E,F,G,H
Training: 5 Days Denver, CO.

SPECIFIC EXPANSION PLANS:
US: All United States
Canada: All Canada
Overseas: Asia, Australia

<< >>

PRETZEL TIME

2855 E. Cottonwood Pkwy., # 400
Salt Lake City, UT 84121-7050
Tel: (800) 348-6311 (801) 736-5600
Fax: (801) 736-5936
Web Site: www.pretzeltime.com
Mr. Scott Moffitt, SVP Franchise Development

'Freshness With A Twist.' Retail pretzel stores, offering a healthy snack alternative that is freshly mixed, rolled and baked. Unique combination store options are available for traditional and non-traditional venues.

BACKGROUND: IFA MEMBER
Established: 1991; 1st Franchised: 1992
Franchised Units: 157
Company-Owned Units 91
Total Units: 248
Dist.: US-175; CAN-73; O'seas-0
North America: 41 States, 2 Provinces
Density: 29 in CA, 20 in NY, 19 in TX
Projected New Units (12 Months): NR
Registered: All States

FINANCIAL/TERMS:
Cash Investment: $175-250K
Total Investment: $120-238K
Minimum Net Worth: $75-150K
Fees: Franchise - $25K
Royalty - 7%; Ad. - 1%
Earnings Claim Statement: No
Term of Contract (Years): 7/7
Avg. # Of Employees: 3 FT, 9 PT
Passive Ownership: Allowed
Encourage Conversions: Yes
Area Develop. Agreements: Yes
Sub-Franchising Contracts: No
Expand In Territory: Yes
Space Needs: 400-1,000 SF; RM

SUPPORT & TRAINING PROVIDED:
Financial Assistance Provided: No
Site Selection Assistance: Yes
Lease Negotiation Assistance: Yes
Co-Operative Advertising: No
Franchisee Assoc./Member: No
Size Of Corporate Staff: 26
On-Going Support: B,C,D,E,F,G,H,I
Training: 6 Days Salt Lake City, UT.

SPECIFIC EXPANSION PLANS:
US: All United States
Canada: All Canada
Overseas: Europe, Japan, Mexico, Australia, Israel

<< >>

PRETZEL TWISTER, THE

2706 S. Horseshoe Dr., # 112
Naples, FL 34102
Tel: (888) 638-8806 (941) 643-2075
Fax: (941) 353-6479
E-Mail: keith@pretzeltwister.com
Web Site: www.pretzeltwister.com
Mr. Keith Johnson, President

THE PRETZEL TWISTER is a gourmet, hand-rolled soft pretzel franchise. Other products sold are fresh, hand-squeezed lemonade, frozen fruit smoothies and soft drinks. The pretzels are served fresh and hot and are available in a wide variety of flavors.

BACKGROUND:
Established: 1992; 1st Franchised: 1993
Franchised Units: 45
Company-Owned Units 0
Total Units: 45
Dist.: US-41; CAN-4; O'seas-0
North America: 14 States, 3 Provinces
Density: 13 in FL, 10 in NC, 3 in SC
Projected New Units (12 Months): NR
Registered: NR

FINANCIAL/TERMS:
Cash Investment: $NR
Total Investment: $105.2-162.5K
Minimum Net Worth: $NR
Fees: Franchise - $22.5K
Royalty - 5%; Ad. - 0.25-1%
Earnings Claim Statement: No
Term of Contract (Years): NR
Avg. # Of Employees: NR
Passive Ownership: Allowed
Encourage Conversions: NR
Area Develop. Agreements: No
Sub-Franchising Contracts: No
Expand In Territory: Yes
Space Needs: 300-900 SF; RN, Kiosk or In-Line

SUPPORT & TRAINING PROVIDED:
Financial Assistance Provided: NR
Site Selection Assistance: No
Lease Negotiation Assistance: Yes

Co-Operative Advertising: No
Franchisee Assoc./Member: NR
Size Of Corporate Staff: NR
On-Going Support: C,D,E,G,h,I
Training: NR

SPECIFIC EXPANSION PLANS:

US: All United States
Canada: NR
Overseas: NR

<< >>

PRETZELS PLUS

639 Frederick St.
Hanover, PA 17331
Tel: (800) 559-7927 (717) 633-7927
Fax: (717) 633-5078
E-Mail: pretzelsplus@pretzelspus.com
Web Site: www.pretzelsplus.com
Mr. Alan Harbaugh, Dir. Franchising

PRETZELS PLUS stores sell soft, hand-rolled pretzels, soups and hearty sandwiches made on our famous pretzel dough rolls. Our mall-based stores provide ample seating for about twenty people in the cafe-styled environment. With our sandwich menu along with our pretzels, we're definitely a twist above the competition.

BACKGROUND:

Established: 1990; 1st Franchised: 1991
Franchised Units: 28
Company-Owned Units 0
Total Units: 28
Dist.: US-30; CAN-0; O'seas-0
North America: 9 States
Density: 13 in PA, 5 in VA, 3 in NC
Projected New Units (12 Months): 24
Qualifications: 5, 2, 1, 1, 2, 2
Registered: MD,VA

FINANCIAL/TERMS:

Cash Investment: $70-90K
Total Investment: $70-90K
Minimum Net Worth: $N/A
Fees: Franchise - $12K
Royalty - 4%; Ad. - 0%
Earnings Claim Statement: No
Term of Contract (Years): 10/10
Avg. # Of Employees: 5 FT, 4 PT
Passive Ownership: Allowed
Encourage Conversions: Yes
Area Develop. Agreements: No
Sub-Franchising Contracts: No
Expand In Territory: Yes
Space Needs: 1,000 SF; RM

SUPPORT & TRAINING PROVIDED:

Financial Assistance Provided: No
Site Selection Assistance: Yes
Lease Negotiation Assistance: No
Co-Operative Advertising: No
Franchisee Assoc./Member: No
Size Of Corporate Staff: 3
On-Going Support: B,D,E,I
Training: 3 Days Before Opening.

SPECIFIC EXPANSION PLANS:

US: Eastern United States
Canada: All Canada
Overseas: No

<< >>

QUIZNO'S CLASSIC SUBS

1415 Larimer St.
Denver, CO 80202
Tel: (800) 335-4782 (720) 359-3300
Fax: (720) 359-3393
E-Mail: pmeyer@quiznos.com
Web Site: www.quiznos.com
Ms. Patricia Meyer, Dir. Franchise Sales

QUIZNO'S CLASSIC SUBS is an upscale, Italian-theme sub sandwich restaurant that features 'the best sandwich you will ever eat.' QUIZNO'S subs are oven-baked and made with our special recipe bread, QUIZNO'S special dressing and the highest-quality meats and cheeses. With over 900 units open across the U. S., Canada and Puerto Rico, our success will continue as we double the number of units open in the coming year. Franchisees are supported at both the corporate level and by one of our 80 area owners.

BACKGROUND: IFA MEMBER

Established: 1981; 1st Franchised: 1984
Franchised Units: 944
Company-Owned Units 28
Total Units: 972
Dist.: US-860; CAN-106; O'seas-6
North America: NR
Density: CO, IL, TX
Projected New Units (12 Months): 400
Qualifications: 5, 4, 2, 2, 2, 5
Registered: All States

FINANCIAL/TERMS:

Cash Investment: $60K
Total Investment: $170-225K
Minimum Net Worth: $125K
Fees: Franchise - $20K
Royalty - 7%; Ad. - 1-3%
Earnings Claim Statement: No
Term of Contract (Years): 15
Avg. # Of Employees: 2 FT, 6 PT
Passive Ownership: Discouraged
Encourage Conversions: Yes
Area Develop. Agreements: Yes/10
Sub-Franchising Contracts: No
Expand In Territory: Yes
Space Needs: 1,400 SF; SC, RM

SUPPORT & TRAINING PROVIDED:

Financial Assistance Provided: Yes(I)
Site Selection Assistance: Yes
Lease Negotiation Assistance: Yes
Co-Operative Advertising: Yes
Franchisee Assoc./Member: No
Size Of Corporate Staff: 103
On-Going Support: C,D,E,F,G,H,I
Training: 11 Days Regional Market; 11 Days Corporate Office Denver, CO.

SPECIFIC EXPANSION PLANS:

US: All United States
Canada: All Canada
Overseas: All Countries

<< >>

ROCKY MOUNTAIN CHOCOLATE FACTORY

265 Turner Dr.
Durango, CO 81303
Tel: (800) 438-7623 (970) 259-0554
Fax: (970) 259-5895
E-Mail: carlson@rmcf.net
Web Site: www.rmcf.net
Mr. Craig Carlson

Retail sale of packaged and bulk chocolates, brittles, truffles, sauces, cocoas, coffees, assorted hard candies and related chocolate and non-chocolate items. In-store preparation of fudges, caramel apples and dipped fruits via interactive cooking demonstrations. Complete line of gift and holiday items. Supplemental retail sale of soft drinks, ice cream, cookies and brewed coffee.

BACKGROUND:

Established: 1981; 1st Franchised: 1982
Franchised Units: 220
Company-Owned Units 4
Total Units: 224
Dist.: US-202; CAN-17; O'seas-1
North America: 41 States, 3 Provinces
Density: 36 in CA, 22 in CO, 12 BC
Projected New Units (12 Months): 12-15
Registered: CA,FL,HI,IL,IN,MD,MI,MN, NY,OR,SD,VA,WA,WI

FINANCIAL/TERMS:

Cash Investment: $50K
Total Investment: $113-213K
Minimum Net Worth: $250K
Fees: Franchise - $19.5K
Royalty - 5%; Ad. - 1%
Earnings Claim Statement: No

Term of Contract (Years): 5/5
Avg. # Of Employees: 2 FT, 4 PT
Passive Ownership: Discouraged
Encourage Conversions: N/A
Area Develop. Agreements: No
Sub-Franchising Contracts: No
Expand In Territory: Yes
Space Needs: 800-1,200 SF; Factory Outlet

SUPPORT & TRAINING PROVIDED:

Financial Assistance Provided: Yes(I)
Site Selection Assistance: Yes
Lease Negotiation Assistance: Yes
Co-Operative Advertising: No
Franchisee Assoc./Member: Yes
Size Of Corporate Staff: 12
On-Going Support: B,C,D,E,F,G,H,I
Training: 7 Days Durango, CO; 5 Days Store Site.

SPECIFIC EXPANSION PLANS:

US: All United States
Canada: No
Overseas: All Countries

<< >>

Top 50

SCHLOTZSKY'S DELI

203 Colorado St.
Austin, TX 78701
Tel: (800) 846-2867 (512) 236-3600
Fax: (512) 236-3650
E-Mail: franchise@schlotzskys.com
Web Site: www.schlotzskys.com
Ms. Joyce Cates, SVP Fran. Operations

SCHLOTZSKY'S DELI is a franchised restaurant, serving a menu of sandwiches, pizza and salads on SCHLOTZSKY'S baked-fresh-daily sourdough bread. Restaurants are designed to provide fresh, clean environments with an in-store bakery.

BACKGROUND:

Established: 1971; 1st Franchised: 1977
Franchised Units: 641
Company-Owned Units 33
Total Units: 674
Dist.: US-653; CAN-1; O'seas-20
North America: 38 States + DC
Density: 197 in TX, 30 in GA, 30 in NC
Projected New Units (12 Months): NR
Qualifications:
Registered: All States

FINANCIAL/TERMS:

Cash Investment: $173-754K
Total Investment: $481K-2.6MM
Minimum Net Worth: NR
Fees: Franchise - $30K
Royalty - 6%; Ad. - 4%
Earnings Claim Statement: Yes
Term of Contract (Years): 20/10
Avg. # Of Employees: 5 FT, 20 PT
Passive Ownership: Not Allowed
Encourage Conversions: No
Area Develop. Agreements: No
Sub-Franchising Contracts: No
Expand In Territory: Yes
Space Needs: 3,200 SF; FS, SC

SUPPORT & TRAINING PROVIDED:

Financial Assistance Provided: Yes
Site Selection Assistance: Yes
Lease Negotiation Assistance: Yes
Co-Operative Advertising: Yes
Franchisee Assoc./Member: Yes/No
Size Of Corporate Staff: 145
On-Going Support: A,C,D,E,F,G,H,I
Training: 4 Weeks in Austin, TX.

SPECIFIC EXPANSION PLANS:

US: All United States
Canada: All Canada
Overseas: Europe, Latin America, Pacific Rim

<< >>

STEAK-OUT CHAR-BROILED DELIVERY

6801 Governors Lake Pkwy., # 100
Norcross, GA 30071
Tel: (877) 878-3257 (678) 533-6000
Fax: (678) 291-0222
E-Mail: jmccord@steakout.com
Web Site: www.steakout.com
Mr. Joseph M. McCord, Vice President

STEAK-OUT franchising specializes in home and office deliveries of charbroiled steaks, chicken and burgers - other menu items include salads and desserts. The only full meal delivery service expanding nationwide. Customers absolutely love our combination of quality food and delivery service. America's finest delivery.

BACKGROUND: IFA MEMBER

Established: 1986; 1st Franchised: 1987
Franchised Units: 78
Company-Owned Units 2
Total Units: 80
Dist.: US-93; CAN-0; O'seas-0
North America: 17 States
Density: 18 in AL, 12 in TN, 8 in GA
Projected New Units (12 Months): 12
Qualifications: 4, 5, 3, 3, 3, 5
Registered: CA,FL,IL,IN,MD,MI,MN,NY, OR,SD,VA,WI

FINANCIAL/TERMS:

Cash Investment: $50-75K
Total Investment: $232.3-330.2K
Minimum Net Worth: $300K
Fees: Franchise - $24.5K
Royalty - 5%; Ad. - 2%
Earnings Claim Statement: Yes
Term of Contract (Years): 10/10
Avg. # Of Employees: 2 FT, 25-30 PT
Passive Ownership: Discouraged
Encourage Conversions: Yes
Area Develop. Agreements: Yes/Varies
Sub-Franchising Contracts: No
Expand In Territory: Yes
Space Needs: 1,600 SF; FS, SF, SC

SUPPORT & TRAINING PROVIDED:

Financial Assistance Provided: Yes(I)
Site Selection Assistance: Yes
Lease Negotiation Assistance: Yes
Co-Operative Advertising: N/A
Franchisee Assoc./Member: No
Size Of Corporate Staff: 25
On-Going Support: B,C,D,E,G,H,I
Training: 4-5 Weeks Training Center at Atlanta, GA.

SPECIFIC EXPANSION PLANS:

US: SE, MW, NE
Canada: No
Overseas: No

<< >>

STUCKEY'S EXPRESS

4601 Willard Ave.
Chevy Chase, MD 20815
Tel: (800) 423-6171 (301) 913-9800
Fax: (301) 913-5424
Mr. Mike Bolin, Dir. Business Development

An innovative way to add the STUCKEY'S name and product line to an existing or new location with minimal investment and no build-ons necessary!!

BACKGROUND:

Established: 1930; 1st Franchised: 1960
Franchised Units: 155
Company-Owned Units 2
Total Units: 157

Dist.: US-132; CAN-0; O'seas-0
North America: 21 States
Density: 10 in MS, 8 in SC, 6 in TN
Projected New Units (12 Months): 12
Qualifications: 5, 4, 4, 2, 1, 4
Registered: CA,IL,IN,MD,MI,VA,DC

FINANCIAL/TERMS:
Cash Investment: $10-25K
Total Investment: $28-135K
Minimum Net Worth: $NR
Fees: Franchise - $2.5K
Royalty - $250/Mo.; Ad. - 0.5%
Earnings Claim Statement: No
Term of Contract (Years): 20/10
Avg. # Of Employees: Varies
Passive Ownership: Allowed
Encourage Conversions: Yes
Area Develop. Agreements: No
Sub-Franchising Contracts: No
Expand In Territory: Yes
Space Needs: Varies SF; Fuel Center

SUPPORT & TRAINING PROVIDED:
Financial Assistance Provided: No
Site Selection Assistance: Yes
Lease Negotiation Assistance: Yes
Co-Operative Advertising: No
Franchisee Assoc./Member: Yes/Yes
Size Of Corporate Staff: 12
On-Going Support: B,C,D,E,G,H,I
Training: 1 Week in Store.

SPECIFIC EXPANSION PLANS:
US: All United States
Canada: No
Overseas: No

<< >>

SWEETS FROM HEAVEN

1830 Forbes Ave.
Pittsburgh, PA 15219-5836
Tel: (412) 434-6711
Fax: (412) 434-6718
E-Mail: sfheaven@aol.com
Web Site: www.sweetsfromheaven.com
Mr. Mark R. Lando, President

Self-serve candy stores with unique selection of international candies. Part of an international chain of over 300 stores.

BACKGROUND: IFA MEMBER
Established: 1992; 1st Franchised: 1993
Franchised Units: 38
Company-Owned Units 15
Total Units: 303
Dist.: US-59; CAN-0; O'seas-124
North America: 16 States
Density: 6 in TX, 5 in FL, 6 in PA
Projected New Units (12 Months): 24
Qualifications: 5, 3, 1, 3, 3, 4
Registered: CA,IL,NY,VA

FINANCIAL/TERMS:
Cash Investment: $50K
Total Investment: $125-232K
Minimum Net Worth: $125K
Fees: Franchise - $30K
Royalty - 6%; Ad. - 0%
Earnings Claim Statement: No
Term of Contract (Years): 10/5
Avg. # Of Employees: 4 FT, 3 PT
Passive Ownership: Allowed
Encourage Conversions: Yes
Area Develop. Agreements: Yes/10
Sub-Franchising Contracts: Yes
Expand In Territory: Yes
Space Needs: 800-1,000 SF; SF, RM, Tourist Areas

SUPPORT & TRAINING PROVIDED:
Financial Assistance Provided: No
Site Selection Assistance: Yes
Lease Negotiation Assistance: Yes
Co-Operative Advertising: No
Franchisee Assoc./Member: No
Size Of Corporate Staff: 13
On-Going Support: B,C,D,E,F,G
Training: 1 Week Corporate Office; 1 Week Company Store; 1 Week Franchisee's Store.

SPECIFIC EXPANSION PLANS:
US: All United States
Canada: All Canada
Overseas: All Countries

<< >>

TROPICAL SMOOTHIE CAFÉ

1190 Eglin Pkwy.
Shalimar, FL 32579
Tel: (888) 292-2522 (850) 609-6022
Fax: (850) 609-6023
E-Mail: tsi@tropicalsmoothie.com
Web Site: www.tropicalsmoothie.com
Mr. Eric Jenrich, President/CEO

At Tropical Smoothie, we believe in serving only the highest quality products to create the ultimate refreshing nutritional beverage. We offer over 40 flavors of smoothies with exact recipes to create the perfect smoothie for everyone. In addition to smoothies we offer high quality gourmet wraps, sandwiches and specialty coffee.

BACKGROUND:
Established: 1997; 1st Franchised: 1997
Franchised Units: 54
Company-Owned Units 0
Total Units: 54
Dist.: US-46; CAN-0; O'seas-0
North America: 9 States
Density: 36 in FL
Projected New Units (12 Months): 30
Qualifications: 4, 3, 3, 3, 4, 5
Registered: FL,VA,DC

FINANCIAL/TERMS:
Cash Investment: $30-50K
Total Investment: $75-150K
Minimum Net Worth: $50-100K
Fees: Franchise - $10K
Royalty - 6%; Ad. - 1-2%
Earnings Claim Statement: No
Term of Contract (Years): 20/20
Avg. # Of Employees: 2 FT, 6-8 PT
Passive Ownership: Discouraged
Encourage Conversions: Yes
Area Develop. Agreements: Yes/25
Sub-Franchising Contracts: Yes
Expand In Territory: Yes
Space Needs: 1200 SF; SC

SUPPORT & TRAINING PROVIDED:
Financial Assistance Provided: Yes(I)
Site Selection Assistance: Yes
Lease Negotiation Assistance: Yes
Co-Operative Advertising: Yes
Franchisee Assoc./Member: No
Size Of Corporate Staff: 4
On-Going Support: A,B,C,D,E,F,G,H,I
Training: 3 Days, Corporate Office; 5 Days, Local Store; 7 Days, Franchisee's New Store.

SPECIFIC EXPANSION PLANS:
US: All United States
Canada: All Canada
Overseas: All Countries

<< >>

TROPIK SUN FRUIT & NUT

37 Sherwood Ter., # 101
Lake Bluff, IL 60044
Tel: (847) 234-3407
Fax: (847) 234-3856
E-Mail: TropikHdqr@aol.com
Ms. Barbara J. Wellard, President

TROPIK SUN FRUIT & NUT is a national franchised chain of over 80 retail stores located in regional malls, featuring candies, nuts, chocolates, fresh popcorn, snacks, drinks, plush toys, balloons and gifts.

BACKGROUND:
Established: 1980; 1st Franchised: 1980
Franchised Units: 80
Company-Owned Units 2

Total Units: 82
Dist.: US-82; CAN-0; O'seas-0
North America: 27 States
Density: 12 in TX, 5 in CT, 5 IN CA
Projected New Units (12 Months): 20
Qualifications: 4, 2, 1, 2, 2, 4
Registered: All States

FINANCIAL/TERMS:

Cash Investment: $30-50K
Total Investment: $100-190K
Minimum Net Worth: $125K
Fees: Franchise - $20K
Royalty - 6%; Ad. - 0%
Earnings Claim Statement: No
Term of Contract (Years): 5-10/5-10
Avg. # Of Employees: 0 FT, 3-6 PT
Passive Ownership: Allowed
Encourage Conversions: Yes
Area Develop. Agreements: No
Sub-Franchising Contracts: No
Expand In Territory: No
Space Needs: 160-1,000 SF; RM

SUPPORT & TRAINING PROVIDED:

Financial Assistance Provided: No
Site Selection Assistance: Yes
Lease Negotiation Assistance: Yes
Co-Operative Advertising: N/A
Franchisee Assoc./Member: Yes/No
Size Of Corporate Staff: 9
On-Going Support: C,D,E,G,H
Training: 5 Days Franchisee's Store.

SPECIFIC EXPANSION PLANS:

US: All United States
Canada: No
Overseas: No

<< >>

We're Rolling PRETZEL COMPANY

WE'RE ROLLING PRETZEL COMPANY

P.O. Box 6106, 2500 W. State St.,
Alliance, OH 44601
Tel: (888) 549-7655 (330) 823-0575
Fax: (330) 821-8908
E-Mail: kkrabill@wererolling.com
Web Site: www.wererolling.com
Mr. Kevin Krabill, President

WE'RE ROLLING PRETZEL COMPANY offers fresh, hand-made pretzel products and exceptional customer service. By serving an expanded menu, creating a strong system to open and operate stores, and recruitng, training, and supporting dedicated franchisees, WE'RE ROLLING PRETZEL COMPANY can effectively meet the needs of a variety of customers.

BACKGROUND:

Established: 1996; 1st Franchised: 1998
Franchised Units: 8
Company-Owned Units 3
Total Units: 11
Dist.: US-11; CAN-0; O'seas-0
North America: 2 States
Density: 10 in OH, 1 in PA
Projected New Units (12 Months): 15
Qualifications: 4, 3, 3, 2, 5, 5
Registered: FL,IN,MI

FINANCIAL/TERMS:

Cash Investment: $40-70K
Total Investment: $63.9-195K
Minimum Net Worth: $150K
Fees: Franchise - $15K
Royalty - 5%; Ad. - 1%
Earnings Claim Statement: No
Term of Contract (Years): 5/5
Avg. # Of Employees: 3 FT, 3 PT
Passive Ownership: Discouraged
Encourage Conversions: Yes
Area Develop. Agreements: No
Sub-Franchising Contracts: No
Expand In Territory: Yes
Space Needs: 400-1,000 SF; RM, SF, Wal-Mart Supercenter

SUPPORT & TRAINING PROVIDED:

Financial Assistance Provided: No
Site Selection Assistance: Yes
Lease Negotiation Assistance: Yes
Co-Operative Advertising: Yes
Franchisee Assoc./Member: No
Size Of Corporate Staff: 6
On-Going Support: b,C,D,E,F,G,H,I
Training: 3 Days Corporate Office; 4 Days Corporate Store; 1 Week On-Site.

SPECIFIC EXPANSION PLANS:

US: Midwest
Canada: No
Overseas: No

<< >>

WINE NOT INTERNATIONAL

15 Heritage Rd., # 1
Markham, ON M5N 1G5 CANADA
Tel: (888) 946-3668 (905) 294-6121
Fax: (905) 294-7772
E-Mail: winenot@global.com
Web Site: www.winenot.com
Mr. Kerry Baskey, VP Sales/Marketing

Turn-key commercial custom wineries, wine pubs and u-vint operations in which we provide equipment and supplies for the on-premises winemaker and provide wine pub services and equipment for restaurants and hotels.

BACKGROUND:

Established: 1993; 1st Franchised: 1993
Franchised Units: 38
Company-Owned Units 0
Total Units: 38
Dist.: US-1; CAN-36; O'seas-0
North America: 1 Province, 1 State
Density: 36 ON, 1 OH, 1 Trinidad
Projected New Units (12 Months): 10
Qualifications: 4, 3, 2, 2, 3, 5
Registered: CA,FL,HI,IL,IN,MD,MI,MN, ND,OR,RI,SD,WA,WI

FINANCIAL/TERMS:

Cash Investment: $40-150K
Total Investment: $110-375K
Minimum Net Worth: $100-500K
Fees: Franchise - $25-35K
Royalty - 5%; Ad. - 2% (for ON)
Earnings Claim Statement: Yes
Term of Contract (Years): 5/5/5
Avg. # Of Employees: 2 FT, 2 PT
Passive Ownership: Discouraged
Encourage Conversions: Yes
Area Develop. Agreements: Yes
Sub-Franchising Contracts: Yes
Expand In Territory: Yes
Space Needs: 1,200-3,000 SF; FS, SC

SUPPORT & TRAINING PROVIDED:

Financial Assistance Provided: Yes(I)
Site Selection Assistance: Yes
Lease Negotiation Assistance: Yes
Co-Operative Advertising: Yes
Franchisee Assoc./Member: Yes/Yes
Size Of Corporate Staff: 10
On-Going Support: A,B,C,D,E,F,G,H,I
Training: 2 Weeks Home Study; 6 Days Head Office; 1-3 Days On-Site..

SPECIFIC EXPANSION PLANS:

US: All United States
Canada: All Canada
Overseas:
U.K., Thailand, Japan, Caribbean

<< >>

SUPPLEMENTAL LISTING OF FRANCHISORS

BAIN'S DELI, 1415 Larimer St., Denver, CO 80202-1743 ; (800) 205-6050 (303) 291-0999; (303) 291-0909

BAKER STREET ARTISAN BREADS & CAFE, P.O. Box 2401, Bala Cynwyd, PA 19004-6401

BEAVERTAILS PASTRY, 38 Antares Dr., # 150, Ottawa, ON K2E 7V2 CANADA; (800) 704-0351 (613) 789-4940; (613) 789-5158

BETSY ANN CHOCOLATES, 322 Perry Hwy., Pittsburgh, PA 15229 ; (888) 4-TRUFFL (412) 931-4288; (412) 931-9777

BOURBON STREET CANDY COMPANY, 266 Elmwood Ave., # 287, Buffalo, NY 14222 ; (800) 949-5115 (905) 894-4819; (905) 894-3072

CANDY BLOSSOMS, 7511 Lemont Rd., Darien, IL 60561 ; (800) 572-5931 (603) 985-9406; (603) 985-6469

CANOPY, THE, 3275 Bethany Ln., # 1, Ellicott City, MD 21042 ; (410) 750-1252; (410) 750-1254

CASSANO'S PIZZA & SUBS, 1700 E. Stroop Rd., Dayton, OH 45429 ; (937) 294-8400; (937) 294-8107

EDELWEISS DELI EXPRESS, 3331 Viking Way, # 7, Richmond, BC V6V 1X7 CANADA; (604) 270-2360; (604) 270-6560

ERIK'S DELICAFE, 365 Coral St., Santa Cruz, CA 95060 ; (831) 458-1818; (831) 458-9797

FIRE GLAZED HAM STORE AND CAFE, 1112 - 7th Ave., Monroe, WI 53566 ; (800) 356-8119 (608) 328-8555; (608) 324-4516

GIULIANO'S DELI EXPRESS, 1117 E. Walnut St., Carson, CA 90746 ; (310) 537-7700; (310) 537-7981

HICKORY FARMS OF OHIO, 1505 Holland Rd., Maumee, OH 43537 ; (800) 433-6008 (419) 893-7611; (419) 893-0164

HONEY BAKED HAM & CAFÉ, 5445 Triangle Pkwy., # 400, Norcross, GA 30092-2584 ; (800) 662-3235 (678) 966-3309; (678) 966-3135

HOT SAM'S PRETZEL BAKERY, 2855 E. Cottonwood Pkwy., # 400, Salt Lake City, UT 84121 ; (800) 677-3435 (801) 736-5600; (801) 736-5970

INCREDIBLY EDIBLE DELITES, 1 Summitt Ave., Broomall, PA 19008-2519 ; (610) 353-8702; (610) 359-9188

JASON'S DELI, 2400 Broadway, Beaumont, TX 77702 ; (800) 444-4825 (409) 832-5055; (409) 832-9994

JUICE CABANA, 222 N. Sepulveda Blvd., # 2000, El Segundo, CA 90245-4341 ; (877) 584-2399 (310) 364-5220; (310) 406-1611

JUICE HEAVEN, 345 N. Pass Ave., Burbank, CA 91505-3859 ; (818) 953-9611; (818) 953-9612

JUICE WORKS, 1200 TCBY Tower, 425 W. Capitol Ave., Little Rock, AR 72201 (800) 449-5842 (501) 688-8267; (501) 688-8549

KARMELKORN, P.O. Box 39286, Minneapolis, MN 55439-0286 ; (800) 285-8515 (612) 830-0200; (612) 830-0498

KERNELS POPCORN, 40 Eglinton Ave. E., # 250, Toronto, ON M4P 3A2 CANADA; (800) CORN-COB (416) 487-4194; (416) 487-3920

KILWIN'S CHOCOLATES, 355 N. Division Rd., Petoskey, MI 49770 ; (888) 454-5946 (231) 347-3800; (231) 347-6951

LI'L DINO DELI & GRILLE, 5601 Roanne Way, # 100, Greensboro, NC 27409 ; (336) 297-4440; (336) 297-4449

LOGAN FARMS HONEY GLAZED HAMS, 10560 Westheimer Rd., # 1040, Houston, TX 77042 ; (800) 833-4267 (713) 781-4335; (713) 977-0532

MAYAN JAMMA JUICE, 4605 Harrison Blvd., Ogden, UT 84403 ; (800) 207-5804 (801) 476-9780; (801) 476-9788

MOUNTAIN MAN NUT & FRUIT CO., 10338 S. Progress Way, Parker, CO 80134 ; (303) 841-4041; (303) 841-4100

PAPA ROMANO'S, 24581 Crestview Court, Farmington Hills, MI 48335 ; (800) 427-2727 (248) 888-7272; (248) 888-0011

PAPA'S PIZZA TO GO, 4465 Commerce Dr., # 101, Buford, GA 30518-9913 ; (770) 614-6676; (770) 614-9095

PARFUMERIES DANS UN JARDIN, 1351 Ampere, # 3, Boucherville, PQ J4B 5Z5 CANADA; (450) 449-2121; (450) 641-1322

PIZZA DELIGHT INTERNATIONAL, 331 Elmwood Dr. Box 23970, Moncton, NB E1A 6S8 CANADA; (905) 477-1600; (905) 477-2207

PLANET SMOOTHIE, 2100 River Edge Pkwy., # 1080, Atlanta, GA 30328 ; (404) 239-0009; (404) 239-0034

POTATO SACK, THE, 201 Monroeville Mall, Monroeville, PA 15146 ; (800) 828-3770 (412) 373-0850; (412) 373-4497

PRETZEL TWISTER, THE, 2706 S. Horseshoe Dr., # 112, Naples, FL 34102 ; (888) 638-8806 (941) 643-2075; (941) 353-6479

SCHAKOLAD CHOCOLATE FACTORY, 480 N. Orlando Ave., # 131, Winter Park, FL 32789-2912 ; (407) 677-4114; (407) 677-4118

SEATTLE SUTTON'S HEALTHY EATING, 1500 Boyce Memorial Dr., Ottawa, IL 61350 ; (888) 442-3438 (815) 433-4444; (815) 795-3493

SMOOTHIE ISLAND, 1775 The Exchange, # 600, Atlanta, GA 30339 ; (888) 628-4822 ; (770) 980-9176

SOUTH BEND CHOCOLATE COMPANY, 3300 W. Sample, South Bend, IN 46619 ; (219) 233-2577; (219) 233-3150

SURF CITY SQUEEZE, 7730 E. Greenway Rd. # 203, Scottsdale, AZ 85260 ; (602) 443-0200; (602) 443-1972

SWEET CITY, 389 Edwin Dr., Virginia Beach, VA 23462-4522 ; (800) 793-3824 (757) 456-0800; (757) 456-9980

TOARMINA'S PIZZA, 673 Barbara St., Westland, MI 48185 ; (734) 729-9067; (734) 727-1882

Hairstyling Salons

Chapter **19**

Hairstyling Salons Industry Profile

Total # Franchisors in Industry Group	28
Total # Franchised Units in Industry Group	5,568
Total # Company-Owned Units in Industry Group	1,238
Total # Operating Units in Industry Group	6,806
Average # Franchised Units/Franchisor	198.9
Average # Company-Owned Units/Franchisor	44.2
Average # Total Units/Franchisor	243.1
Ratio of Total # Franchised Units/Total # Company-Owned Units	4.5:1
Industry Survey Participants	11
Representing % of Industry	39.3%
Average Franchise Fee*:	$17.1K
Average Total Investment*:	$102.6K
Average On-Going Royalty Fee*:	5.6%

*If a range was provided, the mid-point of the range was used. See detailed profiles for actual ranges.

Five Largest Participants in Survey

Company	# Franchised Units	# Co-Owned Units	# Total Units	Franchise Fee	On-Going Royalty	Total Investment
1. Supercuts	902	645	1,547	12.5-22.5K	4-6% Year 1	90-164K
2. Great Clips	1,504	7	1,511	17.5K	6%	87.2-161.5K
3. Fantastic Sams	1,344	6	1,350	20-30K	$235/Week Year 1	75-165K
4. Cost Cutters Family Hair Care	714	113	827	12.5-19.5K	6/4% Year 1	67.7-124K
5. First Choice Haircutters	194	151	345	10-25K	5-7%	92.5-121K

All of the data provided are proprietary and should not be quoted without acknowledging *Bond's Franchise Guide.*

CITY LOOKS SALONS INTERNATIONAL

7201 Metro Blvd.
Edina, MN 55439-2130
Tel: (888) 888-7778 (952) 947-7328
Fax: (952) 947-7301
E-Mail: jennifer.kiewel@regiscorp.com
Web Site: www.regiscorp.com
Ms. Jennifer Kiewel, Development Coord.

CITY LOOKS SALONS INTERNATIONAL provides private, individual consultation and styling in tasteful, comfortable surroundings, filling a need for clients who place a strong emphasis on full-service, personalized hair care. CITY LOOKS franchises generate deep customer loyalty and up-scale sales.

BACKGROUND: IFA MEMBER
Established: 1963; 1st Franchised: 1967
Franchised Units: 49
Company-Owned Units 1
Total Units: 50
Dist.: US-35; CAN-0; O'seas-15
North America: 8 States
Density: 25 in MN, 8 in IA
Projected New Units (12 Months): 10
Qualifications: 5, 5, 3, 3, 1, 5
Registered: All States

FINANCIAL/TERMS:
Cash Investment: $Varies
Total Investment: $60-126K
Minimum Net Worth: $250K
Fees: Franchise - $19.5K
Royalty - 4%; Ad. - 4%
Earnings Claim Statement: No
Term of Contract (Years): 15/15
Avg. # Of Employees: 10 FT
Passive Ownership: Allowed
Encourage Conversions: Yes
Area Develop. Agreements: Yes/Varies
Sub-Franchising Contracts: No
Expand In Territory: Yes
Space Needs: 1,000 SF; SF, SC, RM

SUPPORT & TRAINING PROVIDED:
Financial Assistance Provided: Yes(I)
Site Selection Assistance: Yes
Lease Negotiation Assistance: Yes
Co-Operative Advertising: Yes
Franchisee Assoc./Member: Yes/Yes
Size Of Corporate Staff: 66
On-Going Support: C,d,e,G,h,I
Training: 1 Week Headquarters; 10 Days On-Site.

SPECIFIC EXPANSION PLANS:
US: All United States
Canada: All Canada
Overseas: All Countries

<< >>

COST CUTTERS FAMILY HAIR CARE

7201 Metro Blvd.
Edina, MN 55439-2130
Tel: (888) 888-7008 (952) 947-7777
Fax: (952) 947-7300
E-Mail: jennifer.kiewel@regiscorp.com
Web Site: www.costcutters.com
Ms. Jennifer Kiewel, Development Coord.

COST CUTTERS FAMILY HAIR CARE is a value-priced, family hair salon chain with over 850 locations in 45 states. COST CUTTERS offers its customers high-quality hair care services and products in an attractive atmosphere and at affordable prices.

BACKGROUND: IFA MEMBER
Established: 1968; 1st Franchised: 1982
Franchised Units: 714
Company-Owned Units 113
Total Units: 827
Dist.: US-822; CAN-0; O'seas-0
North America: 45 States
Density: 115 in WI, 82 in MN, 81 CO
Projected New Units (12 Months): 100
Qualifications: 5, 5, 1, 4, 2, 5
Registered: All States

FINANCIAL/TERMS:
Cash Investment: $75K
Total Investment: $67.7K-123.8K
Minimum Net Worth: $250K
Fees: Franchise - $12.5-19.5K
Royalty - 6%/4% Yr. 1; Ad. - 5%
Earnings Claim Statement: Yes
Term of Contract (Years): 15/15
Avg. # Of Employees: 6 FT, 3 PT
Passive Ownership: Discouraged
Encourage Conversions: Yes
Area Develop. Agreements: Yes/Varies
Sub-Franchising Contracts: No
Expand In Territory: Yes
Space Needs: 1,000 SF; SC

SUPPORT & TRAINING PROVIDED:
Financial Assistance Provided: Yes(I)
Site Selection Assistance: Yes
Lease Negotiation Assistance: Yes
Co-Operative Advertising: Yes
Franchisee Assoc./Member: No
Size Of Corporate Staff: 55
On-Going Support: C,D,E,G,h,I
Training: 1 Week at National HQ; 1 Week On-Site; Several On-Site Visits Prior to Opening.

SPECIFIC EXPANSION PLANS:
US: All United States
Canada: All Canada
Overseas: All Countries

<< >>

Fantastic Sams

Top 50

FANTASTIC SAMS

1400 N. Kellogg, # E
Anaheim, CA 92807
Tel: (800) 441-6588 (714) 701-3471
Fax: (714) 537-3869
E-Mail: franchise@fantasticsams.com
Web Site: www.fantasticsams.com
Mr. Terry Cooper, SVP Franchise Licensing

FANTASTIC SAMS is the world's largest full-service hair care franchise, with over 1,350 salons worldwide. Our full service salons offer quality hair care services for the entire family, including cuts, perms and color. When you join the FANTASTIC SAMS family of franchisees, you'll receive both local and national support through on-going management training, educational programs and national conferences, as well as advertising and other benefits. No hair care experience required.

BACKGROUND: IFA MEMBER
Established: 1974; 1st Franchised: 1976
Franchised Units: 1,344
Company-Owned Units 6
Total Units: 1,350
Dist.: US-1251; CAN-15; O'seas-84
North America: 43 States, 4 Provinces
Density: 219 in CA, 131 in FL, 96 MI
Projected New Units (12 Months): 120
Qualifications: 2, 4, 1, 3, 1, 4
Registered: All States

FINANCIAL/TERMS:
Cash Investment: $20-30K
Total Investment: $75-165K
Minimum Net Worth: $Varies
Fees: Franchise - $20-30K
Royalty - $225/Wk.- Vaires; Ad. - $104/Wk.
Earnings Claim Statement: No
Term of Contract (Years): 10/10
Avg. # Of Employees: 8 FT
Passive Ownership: Allowed
Encourage Conversions: Yes
Area Develop. Agreements: Yes/10
Sub-Franchising Contracts: Yes
Expand In Territory: Yes
Space Needs: 1,200 SF; SC

SUPPORT & TRAINING PROVIDED:
Financial Assistance Provided: Yes(I)

Site Selection Assistance: Yes
Lease Negotiation Assistance: Yes
Co-Operative Advertising: Yes
Franchisee Assoc./Member: No
Size Of Corporate Staff: 40
On-Going Support: C,d,E,G,h
Training: 6 Days in Anaheim, CA; On-Going within Region.

SPECIFIC EXPANSION PLANS:
US: All United States
Canada: All Canada
Overseas: Pacific Rim, UK, Australia

<< >>

FIRST CHOICE HAIRCUTTERS

6465 Millcreek Dr., # 210
Mississauga, ON L5N 5R6 CANADA
Tel: (800) 617-3961 (905) 821-8555
Fax: (905) 567-7000
E-Mail: franchise@firstchoice.com
Web Site: www.firstchoice.com
Mr. John Wissent, VP Development

We're a cutting-edge chain of price-value family hair care salons with over 300 locations across Canada and the US. Since 1980, we've built a strong, growing base of loyal customers - over 6 million last year alone. And you don't even have to have any hair experience or become a stylist. We'll provide all the training, tools and on-going support you'll need to manage your thriving salon business. At FIRST CHOICE HAIRCUTTERS, our philosophy is simple: your success is our success.

BACKGROUND: IFA MEMBER
Established: 1980; 1st Franchised: 1982
Franchised Units: 194
Company-Owned Units 151
Total Units: 345
Dist.: US-63; CAN-243; O'seas-0
North America: 2 States, 8 Provinces
Density: 164 in ON, 43 in FL, 24 AB
Projected New Units (12 Months): 40
Registered: N/A

FINANCIAL/TERMS:
Cash Investment: $46-61K
Total Investment: $92.5-121.2K
Minimum Net Worth: $NR
Fees: Franchise - $10-25K
Royalty - 5-7%; Ad. - 3% Fund
Earnings Claim Statement: No
Term of Contract (Years): 10/5
Avg. # Of Employees: 5-7 FT, 2-4 PT
Passive Ownership: Not Allowed
Encourage Conversions: Yes
Area Develop. Agreements: Yes/10
Sub-Franchising Contracts: No
Expand In Territory: Yes
Space Needs: 800-1,000 SF; SC

SUPPORT & TRAINING PROVIDED:
Financial Assistance Provided: Yes(I)
Site Selection Assistance: Yes
Lease Negotiation Assistance: Yes
Co-Operative Advertising: Yes
Franchisee Assoc./Member: No
Size Of Corporate Staff: 20
On-Going Support: B,C,D,E,G,H,I
Training: 1 Week Classroom; 10 Days On-Site. Annual Staff Refresher.

SPECIFIC EXPANSION PLANS:
US: OH, MI, Southeast
Canada: All Canada
Overseas: No

<< >>

Top 50

GREAT CLIPS

3800 W. 80th St., # 400
Minneapolis, MN 55431-4419
Tel: (800) 947-1143 (952) 893-9088
Fax: (952) 999-5959
E-Mail: franchise@greatclips.com
Web Site: www.greatclipsfranchise.com
Mr. Alan Majerko, Franchise Development Mgr.

High-volume haircutting salon, specializing in haircuts for the entire family. Unique, attractive decor, with quality, comprehensive advertising programs. Strong, local support to franchisees, excellent training programs. We offer real value to our customers. Tremendous growth opportunities.

BACKGROUND: IFA MEMBER
Established: 1982; 1st Franchised: 1983
Franchised Units: 1,504
Company-Owned Units 7
Total Units: 1,511
Dist.: US-1366; CAN-48; O'seas-0
North America: 32 States, 2 Provinces
Density: 115 in MN, 107 in CA, 95 OH
Projected New Units (12 Months): 180
Qualifications: 5, 4, 1, 3, 3, 5
Registered: CA,FL,IL,IN,MD,MI,MN,NY,ND,OR,SD,VA,WA,WI,DC,AB

FINANCIAL/TERMS:
Cash Investment: $70-100K
Total Investment: $87.2-161.5K
Minimum Net Worth: $150K
Fees: Franchise - $17.5K
Royalty - 6%; Ad. - 5%
Earnings Claim Statement: Yes
Term of Contract (Years): 10/5/5
Avg. # Of Employees: 3 FT, 5 PT
Passive Ownership: Discouraged
Encourage Conversions: No
Area Develop. Agreements: Yes
Sub-Franchising Contracts: No
Expand In Territory: Yes
Space Needs: 1,000-1,200 SF; SF, SC

SUPPORT & TRAINING PROVIDED:
Financial Assistance Provided: Yes(I)
Site Selection Assistance: Yes
Lease Negotiation Assistance: Yes
Co-Operative Advertising: Yes
Franchisee Assoc./Member: Yes/Yes
Size Of Corporate Staff: 180
On-Going Support: A,B,C,D,E,f,G,H,I
Training: 5 Days Minneapolis, MN; 2.5 Weeks Local Market.

SPECIFIC EXPANSION PLANS:
US: All United States
Canada: Western Canada
Overseas: No

KIDS SUPER SALON

7408 W. Commercial Blvd.
Lauderhill, FL 33319
Tel: (800) 405-9466 (954) 355-2589
Fax: (954) 746-5119
E-Mail: franchise@kidssupersalon.com
Web Site: www.kidssupersalon.com
Mr. Carlos M. Fluxa, President

Childrens' specialty hair salon franchise. KIDS SUPER SALON is well positioned to become a leader of the children's segment of the $40 billion industry. The franchisor provides an extensive operations and management training program, designed to train individuals with no hair care experience. Services include: real estate site selection, lease negotiation, salon design and construction, on-site Grand Opening Celebration team, initial and on-going training, advertising, continuing support and more.

BACKGROUND:
Established: 1994; 1st Franchised: 1998
Franchised Units: 1
Company-Owned Units 1
Total Units: 2
Dist.: US-2; CAN-0; O'seas-0
North America: 1 State

Density: 2 in FL
Projected New Units (12 Months): 10
Qualifications: 4, 5, 1, 4, 4, 5
Registered: FL

FINANCIAL/TERMS:

Cash Investment: $15K
Total Investment: $75-88K
Minimum Net Worth: $125K
Fees: Franchise - $15K
Royalty - $600/Mo.; Ad. - $150/Mo.
Earnings Claim Statement: No
Term of Contract (Years): 10/10
Avg. # Of Employees: 4 FT, 3 PT
Passive Ownership: Allowed
Encourage Conversions: N/A
Area Develop. Agreements: No
Sub-Franchising Contracts: No
Expand In Territory: Yes
Space Needs: 800-1,500 SF; SC, RM

SUPPORT & TRAINING PROVIDED:

Financial Assistance Provided: No
Site Selection Assistance: Yes
Lease Negotiation Assistance: Yes
Co-Operative Advertising: Yes
Franchisee Assoc./Member: No
Size Of Corporate Staff: NR
On-Going Support: C,D,E,F,H,I
Training: 1 Week Corporate Office; 2 Weeks Franchise Outlet (On-Site).

SPECIFIC EXPANSION PLANS:

US: All United States
Canada: All Canada
Overseas: Puerto Rico

≺≺ ≻≻

LEMON TREE - A UNISEX HAIR-CUTTING EST.

3301 Hempstead Tpk.
Levittown, NY 11756
Tel: (800) 345-9156 (516) 735-2828
Fax: (516) 735-1851
E-Mail: lemontree@lemontree.com
Web Site: www.lemontree.com
Mr. Glen Yaris, VP Sales

LEMON TREE serves the haircare needs of all people, offering the entire family affordable prices and quality service. Lemon Tree uses only name brand quality products. Lemon Tree is open from early morning to late evening, 7 days per week. We provide a strong, hands-on training program to each franchisee.

BACKGROUND:

Established: 1975; 1st Franchised: 1975
Franchised Units: 66
Company-Owned Units 0
Total Units: 66
Dist.: US-66; CAN-0; O'seas-0
North America: 5 States
Density: 60 in NY, 2 in PA, 1 in CT
Projected New Units (12 Months): 8-10
Qualifications: 4, 4, 1, 2, 1, 5
Registered: FL,MD,NY

FINANCIAL/TERMS:

Cash Investment: $25-30K
Total Investment: $40-75K
Minimum Net Worth: $40K
Fees: Franchise - $15K
Royalty - 6%; Ad. - $400/Mo.
Earnings Claim Statement: No
Term of Contract (Years): 15/15
Avg. # Of Employees: 4-6 FT, 3 PT
Passive Ownership: Discouraged
Encourage Conversions: Yes
Area Develop. Agreements: Yes/Varies
Sub-Franchising Contracts: No
Expand In Territory: Yes
Space Needs: 800-1,200 SF; FS, SF, SC, RM

SUPPORT & TRAINING PROVIDED:

Financial Assistance Provided: Yes(D)
Site Selection Assistance: Yes
Lease Negotiation Assistance: Yes
Co-Operative Advertising: Yes
Franchisee Assoc./Member: No
Size Of Corporate Staff: 6
On-Going Support: C,D,E,F,H,I
Training: 1 Week at Headquarters; 1 Week plus whatever needed at Store Location.

SPECIFIC EXPANSION PLANS:

US: East Coast
Canada: No
Overseas: No

≺≺ ≻≻

PRO-CUTS

500 Grapevine Hwy., # 400
Hurst, TX 76054-2796
Tel: (888) 776-2887 (817) 788-8000
Fax: (817) 788-0000
E-Mail: gopro@pro-cuts.com
Web Site: www.pro-cuts.com
Mr. James Franks, Dir. Franchise Development

PRO-CUTS provides professional haircuts for the whole family at affordable prices. PRO-CUTS exhibits a friendly, yet professional atmosphere. Our franchisees are provided with support and training in ALL phases of operation, as well as ongoing training and support for employees.

BACKGROUND: IFA MEMBER

Established: 1982; 1st Franchised: 1983
Franchised Units: 189
Company-Owned Units 13
Total Units: 202
Dist.: US-210; CAN-0; O'seas-0
North America: 12 States
Density: 160 in TX, 18 in OK, 9 OH
Projected New Units (12 Months): 25
Qualifications: 4, 5, 1, 3, 3, 4
Registered: CA

FINANCIAL/TERMS:

Cash Investment: $15-60K
Total Investment: $100-130K
Minimum Net Worth: $150K
Fees: Franchise - $10-25K
Royalty - 6%; Ad. - 5%
Earnings Claim Statement: No
Term of Contract (Years): 10/10
Avg. # Of Employees: 6 FT, 2 PT
Passive Ownership: Discouraged
Encourage Conversions: No
Area Develop. Agreements: Yes
Sub-Franchising Contracts: Yes
Expand In Territory: Yes
Space Needs: 1,000-1,200 SF; FS, SC

SUPPORT & TRAINING PROVIDED:

Financial Assistance Provided: Yes(I)
Site Selection Assistance: Yes
Lease Negotiation Assistance: Yes
Co-Operative Advertising: Yes
Franchisee Assoc./Member: Yes/Yes
Size Of Corporate Staff: 28
On-Going Support: b,C,D,E,G,h,I
Training: 3 Days Franchise Support Office; 1 Week Field Training.

SPECIFIC EXPANSION PLANS:

US: All United States
Canada: No
Overseas: No

≺≺ ≻≻

SNIP N' CLIP HAIRCUT SHOPS

11427 Strong Line Rd.
Lenexa, KS 66215
Tel: (800) 622-6804 (913) 345-0077
Fax: (913) 345-1554
E-Mail: info@snipnclip.net
Web Site: www.snipnclip.com
Ms. Donna Massey, VP Franchise Director

Family haircut shops. Fast service, low price, no appointments. Strip mall shopping centers. Least expensive cpt. turn key

BACKGROUND:

Established: 1976; 1st Franchised: 1986

Franchised Units: 46
Company-Owned Units 49
Total Units: 95
Dist.: US-100; CAN-0; O'seas-0
North America: 12 States
Density: 38 in KS, 28 in MO, 9 in AR
Projected New Units (12 Months): 7
Qualifications: 4, 3, 1, 3, , 4
Registered: All States

FINANCIAL/TERMS:

Cash Investment: $60K
Total Investment: $70-82K
Minimum Net Worth: $100K
Fees: Franchise - $10K
Royalty - 5%; Ad. - 0%
Earnings Claim Statement: No
Term of Contract (Years): 10
Avg. # Of Employees: 4 FT, 2 PT
Passive Ownership: Allowed
Encourage Conversions: N/A
Area Develop. Agreements: No
Sub-Franchising Contracts: No
Expand In Territory: Yes
Space Needs: 1,000 SF; SF, SC

SUPPORT & TRAINING PROVIDED:

Financial Assistance Provided: Yes(I)
Site Selection Assistance: Yes
Lease Negotiation Assistance: Yes
Co-Operative Advertising: N/A
Franchisee Assoc./Member: Yes
Size Of Corporate Staff: 10
On-Going Support: C,D,E,G,H,I
Training: 5 Days On-Site.

SPECIFIC EXPANSION PLANS:

US: Midwest, West, Southwest
Canada: No
Overseas: No

<< >>

SPORT CLIPS

PMB 266, P.O. Box 3000
Georgetown, TX 78627-3000
Tel: (800) 872-4247 (512) 869-1201
Fax: (512) 869-0366
E-Mail: beth@sportclips.com
Web Site: www.sportclips.com
Ms. Beth Boecker, Market Development Coord.

Sports-themed haircutting salons, appealing primarily to men and boys. Unique design, proprietary haircutting system and complete support at the unit level. Retail sale of Paul Mitchell hair care products, sports apparel and memorabilia.

BACKGROUND:

Established: 1995; 1st Franchised: 1995
Franchised Units: 55
Company-Owned Units 7
Total Units: 62
Dist.: US-62; CAN-0; O'seas-0
North America: 4 States
Density: 46 in TX, 5 in NY, 2 in OK
Projected New Units (12 Months): 40
Qualifications: 5, 3, 1, 1, 3, 5
Registered: FL,TX

FINANCIAL/TERMS:

Cash Investment: $30-50K
Total Investment: $100-150K
Minimum Net Worth: $250K
Fees: Franchise - $17.5K
Royalty - 6%; Ad. - $250/Wk.
Earnings Claim Statement: Yes
Term of Contract (Years): 5/5
Avg. # Of Employees: 8 FT, 4 PT
Passive Ownership: Allowed
Encourage Conversions: No
Area Develop. Agreements: Yes
Sub-Franchising Contracts: No
Expand In Territory: Yes
Space Needs: 1,200 SF; SC

SUPPORT & TRAINING PROVIDED:

Financial Assistance Provided: Yes
Site Selection Assistance: Yes
Lease Negotiation Assistance: Yes
Co-Operative Advertising: Yes
Franchisee Assoc./Member: Yes/Yes
Size Of Corporate Staff: 15
On-Going Support: B,C,D,E,F,G,H,I
Training: 3 Days in Georgetown, TX for Franchisee + 2 Weeks Locally; 2 Weeks Locally for Manager.

SPECIFIC EXPANSION PLANS:

US: SW, MW, SE
Canada: No
Overseas: No

<< >>

SUPERCUTS

7201 Metro Blvd.
Edina, MN 55439-2103
Tel: (888) 888-7008 (952) 947-7328
Fax: (952) 947-7300
E-Mail: jennifer.Kiewel@regiscorp.com
Web Site: www.supercuts.com
Ms. Jennifer Kiewel, Development Coord.

Top quality, affordable haircare salons.

BACKGROUND: IFA MEMBER

Established: 1975; 1st Franchised: 1977
Franchised Units: 902
Company-Owned Units 645
Total Units: 1,547
Dist.: US-1329; CAN-9; O'seas-0
North America: 50 States
Density: NR
Projected New Units (12 Months): 100
Qualifications: 5, 5, 1, 3, 4, 5
Registered: All States and AB

FINANCIAL/TERMS:

Cash Investment: $75K
Total Investment: $90-164.1K
Minimum Net Worth: $250K
Fees: Franchise - $12.5-22.5K
Royalty - 4-6% Yr. 1; Ad. - 5%
Earnings Claim Statement: No
Term of Contract (Years): Evergreen
Avg. # Of Employees: 6 FT, 4 PT
Passive Ownership: Discouraged
Encourage Conversions: Yes
Area Develop. Agreements: Yes
Sub-Franchising Contracts: No
Expand In Territory: Yes
Space Needs: 1,200 SF; SC

SUPPORT & TRAINING PROVIDED:

Financial Assistance Provided: Yes(D)
Site Selection Assistance: Yes
Lease Negotiation Assistance: Yes
Co-Operative Advertising: Yes
Franchisee Assoc./Member: Yes/Yes
Size Of Corporate Staff: 50
On-Going Support: B,C,D,E,G,H
Training: 4 Days Minneapolis, MN.

SPECIFIC EXPANSION PLANS:

US: All United States
Canada: Toronto,Vancouver
Overseas: No

<< >>

SUPPLEMENTAL LISTING OF FRANCHISORS

CARTOON CUTS, 5501 Backlick Rd., # 115, Springfield, VA 22151 ; (800) 701-2887 (703) 354-3801; (703) 354-4431

COCOZZO, 384 Broadway, Saratoga Springs, NY 12866-3123 ; (518) 581-1958; (518) 581-2941

HAIR PERFORMERS, THE, 7201 Metro Blvd., Edina, MN 55439-2130 ; (888) 888-7778 (952) 947-7777; (952) 947-7300

WE CARE HAIR, 7201 Metro Blvd., Minneapolis, MN 55439-2130 ; (888) 888-7778 (952) 947-7000; (952) 331-2821

Health/Fitness/Beauty

Chapter

20

Health/Fitness/Beauty Industry Profile

Total # Franchisors in Industry Group	78
Total # Franchised Units in Industry Group	15,928
Total # Company-Owned Units in Industry Group	1,950
Total # Operating Units in Industry Group	17,878
Average # Franchised Units/Franchisor	204.2
Average # Company-Owned Units/Franchisor	25.0
Average # Total Units/Franchisor	229.2
Ratio of Total # Franchised Units/Total # Company-Owned Units	8.2:1
Industry Survey Participants	26
Representing % of Industry	33.3%
Average Franchise Fee*:	$19.1K
Average Total Investment*:	$194.3K
Average On-Going Royalty Fee*:	6.5%

*If a range was provided, the mid-point of the range was used. See detailed profiles for actual ranges.

Five Largest Participants in Survey

Company	# Franchised Units	# Co-Owned Units	# Total Units	Franchise Fee	On-Going Royalty	Total Investment
1. Jazzercise	5,302	2	5,304	.7K	20%	1.5-20K
1. Merle Norman Cosmetics	1,895	11	1,906	0K	0%	33-153K
2. Pearle Vision	402	396	798	30K	7%	135K-2.5MM
3. Jenny Craig Weight Loss Centres	137	658	795	50K	7%	160-315K
4. LA Weight Loss Centers	151	250	401	20K	7%	60-95K

All of the data provided are proprietary and should not be quoted without acknowledging *Bond's Franchise Guide.*

ALOETTE COSMETICS

4900 Highlands Pkwy.
Smyrna, GA 30082
Tel: (800) 256-3883 (678) 444-2563
Fax: (678) 444-2564
Web Site: www.aloette.com
Mr. W. James Squire, III, President

ALOETTE is a direct marketer of Aloe Vera-based skin care products. Franchises provide career opportunities to beauty consultants who sell the products through home shows.

BACKGROUND: IFA MEMBER
Established: 1978; 1st Franchised: 1978
Franchised Units: 65
Company-Owned Units 0
Total Units: 65
Dist.: US-50; CAN-32; O'seas-0
North America: 36 States,10 Provinces
Density: 18 in ON, 4 in BC, 3 in PQ
Projected New Units (12 Months): 10
Qualifications: 1, 2, 5, 2, 1, 2
Registered: NR

FINANCIAL/TERMS:
Cash Investment: $10-20K
Total Investment: $55-86.3K
Minimum Net Worth: $10K
Fees: Franchise - $20K
Royalty - 5%; Ad. - N/A
Earnings Claim Statement: No
Term of Contract (Years): 5/10
Avg. # Of Employees: 3 FT
Passive Ownership: Discouraged
Encourage Conversions: N/A
Area Develop. Agreements: No
Sub-Franchising Contracts: No
Expand In Territory: Yes
Space Needs: 1,000 SF; HB, Light Industrial, Retail

SUPPORT & TRAINING PROVIDED:
Financial Assistance Provided: Yes(D)
Site Selection Assistance: No
Lease Negotiation Assistance: No
Co-Operative Advertising: No
Franchisee Assoc./Member: No
Size Of Corporate Staff: 25
On-Going Support: C,D,E,h
Training: 2 Days Operations Training at Franchise; 2 Days Sales Training at Franchise.

SPECIFIC EXPANSION PLANS:
US: All United States
Canada: ON
Overseas: No

<< >>

BEAUTY BRANDS SALON-SPA-SUPERSTORE

4600 Madison, # 400
Kansas City, MO 64112-3012
Tel: (888) 725-6608 (816) 531-2266
Fax: (816) 531-7122
E-Mail: franchising@beautybrands.com
Web Site: www.beautybrands.com
Mr. Steve Eckman, VP Corp. Dev./Fran.

BEAUTY BRANDS SALON/SPA/SUPERSTORE is the cutting-edge concept that offers consumers a "total beauty" experience. We have brought together a full-service salon and spa and have showcased it in a dynamic 6,000-7,000 square-foot retail environment offering nearly 50,000 units of product representing the top salon brands for hair, skin and nails.

BACKGROUND: IFA MEMBER
Established: 1995; 1st Franchised: 1998
Franchised Units: 0
Company-Owned Units 19
Total Units: 19
Dist.: US-19; CAN-0; O'seas-0
North America: 5 States
Density: 4 in KS, 6 in TX, 3 in CO
Projected New Units (12 Months): 8
Qualifications: 5, 5, 5, 4, 4, 4
Registered: All States Except IL

FINANCIAL/TERMS:
Cash Investment: $100-200K
Total Investment: $594.5-936K
Minimum Net Worth: $3MM
Fees: Franchise - $25K
Royalty - 1-5%; Ad. - 1-2%
Earnings Claim Statement: Yes
Term of Contract (Years): 10/10
Avg. # Of Employees: 10, 20 PT
Passive Ownership: Not Allowed
Encourage Conversions: Yes
Area Develop. Agreements: Yes/Varies
Sub-Franchising Contracts: No
Expand In Territory: Yes
Space Needs: 5,000-7,000 SF; FS, SC

SUPPORT & TRAINING PROVIDED:
Financial Assistance Provided: No
Site Selection Assistance: Yes
Lease Negotiation Assistance: Yes
Co-Operative Advertising: Yes
Franchisee Assoc./Member: Yes
Size Of Corporate Staff: 50
On-Going Support: A,B,C,D,E,F,h,I
Training: 4-6 Weeks Kansas City, MO.

SPECIFIC EXPANSION PLANS:
US: All United States
Canada: No
Overseas: No

<< >>

BENEFICIAL HEALTH & BEAUTY

1780 West 500 South
Salt Lake City, UT 84104
Tel: (800) 367-0990 (801) 973-7778
Fax: (801) 973-8836
Ms. Linda T. Nelson, President

BENEFICIAL HEALTH & BEAUTY CENTERS are urban mini-health spas, offering a total wellness and fitness program in each local community. We offer programs that aid in body cleansing, weight-loss, nutrition, body contouring, skin care, massage, personal exercise trainers and many complementary programs.

BACKGROUND:
Established: 1981; 1st Franchised: 1990
Franchised Units: 21
Company-Owned Units 0
Total Units: 21
Dist.: US-10; CAN-0; O'seas-18
North America: 3 States
Density: 6 in CA, 2 in HI, 2 in WI
Projected New Units (12 Months): 10
Qualifications: 5, 5, 3, 3, 4, 4
Registered: CA,HI,IL,MI,MN,NY,ND, OR,WA,WI

FINANCIAL/TERMS:
Cash Investment: $30-80K
Total Investment: $100K
Minimum Net Worth: $NR
Fees: Franchise - $15K
Royalty - 3%; Ad. - 4%
Earnings Claim Statement: No
Term of Contract (Years): 10/5
Avg. # Of Employees: 2 FT, 2 PT
Passive Ownership: Discouraged
Encourage Conversions: Yes
Area Develop. Agreements: Yes/10
Sub-Franchising Contracts: No
Expand In Territory: Yes
Space Needs: 1,200-2,500 SF; FS, SC, SF, HB

SUPPORT & TRAINING PROVIDED:
Financial Assistance Provided: Yes(I)

Site Selection Assistance: Yes
Lease Negotiation Assistance: Yes
Co-Operative Advertising: Yes
Franchisee Assoc./Member: NR
Size Of Corporate Staff: 7
On-Going Support: B,C,D,E,f,G,H,I
Training: 2 Days Local Area; 4 Days Practical Salt Lake City, UT; Weekly On-Site.

SPECIFIC EXPANSION PLANS:
US: All United States
Canada: All Canada
Overseas: All Countries

<< >>

BEVERLY HILLS WEIGHT LOSS & WELLNESS

1106 Union Ave.
Laconia, NH 03246-2127
Tel: (866) 232-5000 (603) 524-4903
Fax: (603) 524-4591
E-Mail: franchisesales@beverlyhillsintl.net
Web Site: www.beverlyhillsintl.net
Mr. Roberto Calderon, Chief Executive Officer

Medically supervised weight loss clinics.

BACKGROUND: IFA MEMBER
Established: 1986; 1st Franchised: 1989
Franchised Units: 28
Company-Owned Units 1
Total Units: 29
Dist.: US-23; CAN-6; O'seas-0
North America: 6 States
Density: 16 in NC, 3 in VA, 2 in RI
Projected New Units (12 Months): 12
Qualifications: 4, 5, 3, 3, 4, 4
Registered: CA,FL,IN,MN,NY,RI,VA

FINANCIAL/TERMS:
Cash Investment: $10-18K
Total Investment: $45-90K
Minimum Net Worth: $N/A
Fees: Franchise - $25K
Royalty - 8%; Ad. - 4%
Earnings Claim Statement: No
Term of Contract (Years): 5/3/5
Avg. # Of Employees: 2 FT, 2 PT
Passive Ownership: Not Allowed
Encourage Conversions: Yes
Area Develop. Agreements: Yes
Sub-Franchising Contracts: Yes
Expand In Territory: Yes
Space Needs: 1300 SF; FS, SF, SC, RM

SUPPORT & TRAINING PROVIDED:
Financial Assistance Provided: Yes(D)
Site Selection Assistance: Yes
Lease Negotiation Assistance: Yes
Co-Operative Advertising: Yes
Franchisee Assoc./Member: No
Size Of Corporate Staff: 15
On-Going Support: B,C,D,E,G,H,I
Training: 4 Weeks Corporate Clinic, 4 Locations; 10 Days on Site.

SPECIFIC EXPANSION PLANS:
US: All United States
Canada: ON
Overseas: All Countries

<< >>

CELSIUS TANNERY

12142A State Line Rd.
Leawood, KS 66209-1254
Tel: (888) 737-6527 (913) 451-7000
Fax: (913) 451-7001
E-Mail: jimb@celsiustan.com
Web Site: www.celsiustannerysalons.com
Mr. Jim Burandt, VP Sales

We are the fastest growing indoor tanning franchise chain in the U.S. With the exclusive STS tanning process, we are the first tanning salon franchise inside a big box retailer. We offer motivating and educational instruction in management, sales, and marketing your salon, and help you with professional guidance as well as on-going administrative and business support. Site location, lease negotiation, construction, financial assistance and a toll-free number for support!

BACKGROUND:
Established: 1995; 1st Franchised: 2000
Franchised Units: 15
Company-Owned Units 3
Total Units: 18
Dist.: US-18; CAN-0; O'seas-0
North America: 3 States
Density: 10 in KS, 7 in MO, 1 in NE
Projected New Units (12 Months): 8-10
Qualifications: 3, 2, 1, 1, 2, 4
Registered: FL,IL,NY,WI

FINANCIAL/TERMS:
Cash Investment: $35-100K
Total Investment: $240-600K
Minimum Net Worth: $150K
Fees: Franchise - $20-35K
Royalty - 1%/250 Min.;
Ad. - $1,200/Mo.
Earnings Claim Statement: No
Term of Contract (Years): 5/5
Avg. # Of Employees: 3 FT, 5 PT
Passive Ownership: Allowed
Encourage Conversions: Yes
Area Develop. Agreements: Yes/5
Sub-Franchising Contracts: No
Expand In Territory: Yes
Space Needs: 2,000 SF; FS, SF, SC

SUPPORT & TRAINING PROVIDED:
Financial Assistance Provided: Yes(I)
Site Selection Assistance: Yes
Lease Negotiation Assistance: Yes
Co-Operative Advertising: Yes
Franchisee Assoc./Member: No
Size Of Corporate Staff: 10
On-Going Support: A,B,C,D,E,F,I
Training: 1 Week at Corporate Headquarters; 3 Week On-Site.

SPECIFIC EXPANSION PLANS:
US: All United States
Canada: No
Overseas: No

<< >>

CHAMPION HOME HEALTH CARE

3247 Northwest 60th St.
Boca Raton, FL 33496
Tel: (561) 999-9276
Fax: (561) 999-9608
E-Mail: rickstewart@championhome.com
Web Site: www.championhome.com
Mr. Richard Stewart, President

Champion Home Health Care is a licensed private pay agency that is able to provide all levels of in-home service from Companions to skilled Nursing as well as institutional staffing. We license only in Florida where we are fully conversant with the market and State Licensure requirements. Within Florida the elderly population is expanding at 20% per year. Exclusive territories are available. Our integrated personnel, client and scheduling software and back office bookkeeping service simplify operations.

BACKGROUND:
Established: 1993; 1st Franchised: 1999
Franchised Units: 3
Company-Owned Units 0
Total Units: 3
Dist.: US-3; CAN-0; O'seas-0
North America: 1 State

Density: 3 in FL
Projected New Units (12 Months): 2
Qualifications: 4, 4, 1, 3, 3, 4
Registered: FL

FINANCIAL/TERMS:

Cash Investment: $30-50K
Total Investment: $50-75K
Minimum Net Worth: $100K
Fees: Franchise - $18K
Royalty - 8%; Ad. - 0%
Earnings Claim Statement: No
Term of Contract (Years): 5/5
Avg. # Of Employees: 2 FT
Passive Ownership: Discouraged
Encourage Conversions: No
Area Develop. Agreements: No
Sub-Franchising Contracts: No
Expand In Territory: Yes
Space Needs: 400-800 SF; FS

SUPPORT & TRAINING PROVIDED:

Financial Assistance Provided: No
Site Selection Assistance: Yes
Lease Negotiation Assistance: No
Co-Operative Advertising: Yes
Franchisee Assoc./Member: No/No
Size Of Corporate Staff: 4
On-Going Support: A,C,d,E
Training: 1-6 Weeks in Boca Raton, FL.

SPECIFIC EXPANSION PLANS:

US: FL
Canada: No
Overseas: No

DIET CENTER

395 Springside Dr.
Akron, OH 44333-2496
Tel: (800) 656-5861 (330) 655-5861
Fax: (330) 666-2197
E-Mail: info@dietcenterworldwide.com
Web Site: www.dietcenterworldwide.com
Mr. Kenneth M. Massey, Dir. Franchise Development

DIET CENTER offers innovative weight management programs.

BACKGROUND:

Established: 1972; 1st Franchised: 1972
Franchised Units: 325
Company-Owned Units 0
Total Units: 325
Dist.: US-238; CAN-11; O'seas-1
North America: 44 States, 4 Provinces
Density: 28 in NY, 19 in NC, 18 in CA
Projected New Units (12 Months): 8-10
Qualifications: 3, 3, 3, 2, 3, 5
Registered: All States

FINANCIAL/TERMS:

Cash Investment: $16.4-34.9K
Total Investment: $16.4-34.9K
Minimum Net Worth: $50-75K
Fees: Franchise - $15K
Royalty - 8%/$100/Wk.;
Ad. - 8%/$500/Mo.
Earnings Claim Statement: No
Term of Contract (Years): 5/5
Avg. # Of Employees: 2 FT, 1 PT
Passive Ownership: Discouraged
Encourage Conversions: Yes
Area Develop. Agreements: No
Sub-Franchising Contracts: No
Expand In Territory: Yes
Space Needs: 700-1,200 SF; FS, SF, SC

SUPPORT & TRAINING PROVIDED:

Financial Assistance Provided: No
Site Selection Assistance: Yes
Lease Negotiation Assistance: Yes
Co-Operative Advertising: No
Franchisee Assoc./Member: No
Size Of Corporate Staff: 40
On-Going Support: C,D,E,G,H,I
Training: 3 Weeks in Akron, OH.

SPECIFIC EXPANSION PLANS:

US: All United States
Canada: All Canada
Overseas: No

DIET LIGHT WEIGHT LOSS SYSTEM

300 Market St., # 101
Lebanon, OR 97355
Tel: (800) 248-7712 (541) 259-3573
Fax: (541) 259-3506
E-Mail: dietlight@juno.com
Web Site: www.busdir.com/dietlight
Ms. Kathy Bengtson, President

A complete weight loss system that incorporates individual counseling with delicious, gourmet meals. The Delight Entrees are vacuum-sealed, contain no preservatives, and require no refrigeration. One day a week clients can eat out or plan their own meals. Some of the centers have incorporated a fitness area with workout equipment for women.

BACKGROUND:

Established: 1983; 1st Franchised: 1989
Franchised Units: 5
Company-Owned Units 10
Total Units: 15
Dist.: US-18; CAN-0; O'seas-0
North America: 4 States
Density: 11 in OR, 4 in CA, 2 in TN
Projected New Units (12 Months): 6
Qualifications: 3, 3, 3, 2, 3, 3
Registered: All States

FINANCIAL/TERMS:

Cash Investment: $10K
Total Investment: $10-20K
Minimum Net Worth: $25K
Fees: Franchise - $5K
Royalty - 0%; Ad. - 0%
Earnings Claim Statement: Yes
Term of Contract (Years): NR
Avg. # Of Employees: 1 FT, 2 PT
Passive Ownership: Discouraged
Encourage Conversions: Yes
Area Develop. Agreements: No
Sub-Franchising Contracts: No
Expand In Territory: Yes
Space Needs: 500-1,000 SF; SC

SUPPORT & TRAINING PROVIDED:

Financial Assistance Provided: No
Site Selection Assistance: Yes
Lease Negotiation Assistance: Yes
Co-Operative Advertising: No
Franchisee Assoc./Member: No
Size Of Corporate Staff: 3
On-Going Support: a,b,c,d,e,F,h,I
Training: 3 Days Lebanon, OR.

SPECIFIC EXPANSION PLANS:

US: All United States
Canada: All Canada
Overseas: No

EXECUTIVE TANS

165 South Union Blvd., # 780
Lakewood, CO 80228-2215
Tel: (877) 393-2826 (303) 988-9999
Fax: (303) 988-5390
E-Mail: sales@executivetans.com
Web Site: www.executivetans.com
Mr. Wayne Smeal, President

Indoor tanning salons along with related products and services.

BACKGROUND: IFA MEMBER

Established: 1991; 1st Franchised: 1995
Franchised Units: 27
Company-Owned Units 1
Total Units: 28
Dist.: US-26; CAN-0; O'seas-0
North America: 1 State
Density: 26 in CO
Projected New Units (12 Months): 10
Qualifications: 3, 3, 3, 4, 3, 3
Registered: IL,FL,WI

FINANCIAL/TERMS:
Cash Investment: $40-60K
Total Investment: $130-150K
Minimum Net Worth: $175K
Fees: Franchise - $15K
Royalty - $795-1,895/Mo;
Ad. - $315/Mo
Earnings Claim Statement: No
Term of Contract (Years): 3/3
Avg. # Of Employees: 2 FT, 3 PT
Passive Ownership: Discouraged
Encourage Conversions: Yes
Area Develop. Agreements: Yes/5
Sub-Franchising Contracts: Yes
Expand In Territory: Yes
Space Needs: 1,500-6,000 SF; SC

SUPPORT & TRAINING PROVIDED:
Financial Assistance Provided: Yes(I)
Site Selection Assistance: Yes
Lease Negotiation Assistance: Yes
Co-Operative Advertising: Yes
Franchisee Assoc./Member: No
Size Of Corporate Staff: 4
On-Going Support: B,C,d,E,G,h,I
Training: 1 Week at Corporate Offices; 1 Week on Location.

SPECIFIC EXPANSION PLANS:
US: All United States
Canada: No
Overseas: No

FACES

3425 Laird Rd., # 5
Mississauga, ON L5L 5R8 CANADA
Tel: (905) 569-8989
Fax: (905) 569-8998
E-Mail: stevensont@faces-cosmetics.com
Web Site: www.faces-cosmetics.com
Ms. Tamara Stevenson, Dir. Franchising

FACES is a retail cosmetics business featuring in-mall, stand-alone boutiques selling FACES' own extensive, affordable and distinct brand of prestige color cosmetics and bath, body and skin care. Twenty-five years of operating history and extensive market research enables FACES to successfully service a critical gap between mass-market merchandisers and expensive department store brands.

BACKGROUND:
Established: 1974; 1st Franchised: 1980
Franchised Units: 75
Company-Owned Units 22
Total Units: 97
Dist.: US-0; CAN-67; O'seas-30
North America: 9 Provinces
Density: 38 in PQ, 19 in ON
Projected New Units (12 Months): NR
Qualifications: 3, 4, 3, 3, 3, 5
Registered: FL,MI,MN,NY,ND,OR,RI,SD, VA,WA,WI,DC

FINANCIAL/TERMS:
Cash Investment: $25-30K
Total Investment: $85-90K
Minimum Net Worth: $Varies
Fees: Franchise - $16.3K
Royalty - 5%; Ad. - 2%
Earnings Claim Statement: No
Term of Contract (Years): 10/10
Avg. # Of Employees: 1 FT, 3-4 PT
Passive Ownership: Allowed
Encourage Conversions: Yes
Area Develop. Agreements: Yes/10
Sub-Franchising Contracts: Yes
Expand In Territory: Yes
Space Needs: 230 SF; SF, SC, RM

SUPPORT & TRAINING PROVIDED:
Financial Assistance Provided: Yes(I)
Site Selection Assistance: Yes
Lease Negotiation Assistance: Yes
Co-Operative Advertising: No
Franchisee Assoc./Member: No
Size Of Corporate Staff: 70
On-Going Support: A,B,D,E,G,h
Training: 4 Weeks Toronto, ON.

SPECIFIC EXPANSION PLANS:
US: All United States
Canada: All Canada
Overseas: All Countries in a Master Franchisee capacity

<< >>

FIT AMERICA

401 Fairway Dr., # 200
Deerfield Beach, FL 33441-1871
Tel: (800) 221-1186 (954) 570-3211
Fax: (954) 570-8608
E-Mail: jackfarland@fitamerica.com
Web Site: www.fitamerica.com
Mr. Jack Farland, Dir. Franchise Development

Retail store operation offering the finest all-natural herbal products, comprehensive education and training, and unparalleled, free customer service, as well as motivation to help people lose weight in integration with health clubs and fitness centers.

BACKGROUND: IFA MEMBER
Established: 1992; 1st Franchised: 1996
Franchised Units: 70
Company-Owned Units 0
Total Units: 70
Dist.: US-31; CAN-0; O'seas-0
North America: 12 States
Density: 13 in NJ, 7 in NY, 2 in FL
Projected New Units (12 Months): 20
Qualifications: 4, 4, 1, 2, 3, 3
Registered: CA,FL,IL,MI,NY,VA

FINANCIAL/TERMS:
Cash Investment: $25-45K
Total Investment: $25-45K
Minimum Net Worth: $N/A
Fees: Franchise - $8.5K
Royalty - $400/Mo.; Ad. - $165/Mo.
Earnings Claim Statement: No
Term of Contract (Years): 2/2
Avg. # Of Employees: 3 FT
Passive Ownership: Discouraged
Encourage Conversions: Yes
Area Develop. Agreements: No
Sub-Franchising Contracts: No
Expand In Territory: Yes
Space Needs: 800-1,200 SF; SC

SUPPORT & TRAINING PROVIDED:
Financial Assistance Provided: Yes
Site Selection Assistance: Yes
Lease Negotiation Assistance: Yes
Co-Operative Advertising: Yes
Franchisee Assoc./Member: Yes/Yes
Size Of Corporate Staff: 22
On-Going Support: A,B,C,D,E,F,G,h,I
Training: 3 Days Corporate Headquarters; 1 Week at Already Existing Site; 2 Weeks Franchisee's Store

SPECIFIC EXPANSION PLANS:
US: All United States
Canada: No
Overseas: No

<< >>

FORM-YOU-3 INTERNATIONAL

395 Springside Dr.
Akron, OH 44333-2496
Tel: (800) 525-6315 (330) 668-1461
Fax: (330) 666-2197
Web Site: www.formyou3.com
Mr. Kenneth M. Massey, Dir. Fran. Dev.

Assisting individuals in weight loss and maintenance by utilizing a proprietary multi-level diet plan, individual and group behavior life modification programs, diet-related products and maintenance programs.

BACKGROUND:

Established: 1982;	1st Franchised: 1983
Franchised Units:	53
Company-Owned Units	3
Total Units:	56
Dist.:	US-34; CAN-0; O'seas-0
North America:	12 States
Density:	12 in OH, 7 in MI, 5 in NC
Projected New Units (12 Months):	10
Qualifications:	5, 4, 3, 3, , 5
Registered: None	

FINANCIAL/TERMS:

Cash Investment:	$23.1-33.7K
Total Investment:	$33-43K
Minimum Net Worth:	$100K
Fees: Franchise -	$15K
Royalty - 6%/$150/Wk.;	Ad. - 6%
Earnings Claim Statement:	No
Term of Contract (Years):	5/5/5/5
Avg. # Of Employees:	2-5 FT
Passive Ownership:	Not Allowed
Encourage Conversions:	Yes
Area Develop. Agreements:	No
Sub-Franchising Contracts:	No
Expand In Territory:	Yes
Space Needs: 700-1,200 SF; SC	

SUPPORT & TRAINING PROVIDED:

Financial Assistance Provided:	N/A
Site Selection Assistance:	Yes
Lease Negotiation Assistance:	Yes
Co-Operative Advertising:	Yes
Franchisee Assoc./Member:	No
Size Of Corporate Staff:	45
On-Going Support:	A,B,c,d,E,G,H,I
Training: 3 Weeks in Akron, OH; 1-3 Days On-Site.	

SPECIFIC EXPANSION PLANS:

US:	All United States
Canada:	No
Overseas:	No

JAZZERCISE

2460 Impala Dr.
Carlsbad, CA 92008
Tel: (800) FIT IS IT (760) 476-1750
Fax: (760) 602-7180
E-Mail: jazzinc@jazzercise.com
Web Site: www.jazzercise.com
Mr. Kenny Harvey, Public Relations Dir.

JAZZERCISE is the world's leading international dance fitness franchisor, with a multi-media division and mail-order catalog business at 1-800-FIT-IS-IT, specializing in active wear and accessories.

BACKGROUND:

Established: 1969;	1st Franchised: 1983
Franchised Units:	5,302
Company-Owned Units	2
Total Units:	5,304
Dist.:	US-4210; CAN-101; O'seas-860
North America:	50 States, 5 Provinces
Density:	626 in CA, 296 in OH, 343 TX
Projected New Units (12 Months):	600
Qualifications:	1, 2, 4, 2, 5, 5
Registered: All States	

FINANCIAL/TERMS:

Cash Investment:	$1.5-3K
Total Investment:	$1.5-20K
Minimum Net Worth:	$N/A
Fees: Franchise -	$0.7K
Royalty - 20%;	Ad. - N/A
Earnings Claim Statement:	No
Term of Contract (Years):	5/5
Avg. # Of Employees:	NR
Passive Ownership:	Allowed
Encourage Conversions:	N/A
Area Develop. Agreements:	No
Sub-Franchising Contracts:	No
Expand In Territory:	Yes
Space Needs: 3,000 SF; Community Building	

SUPPORT & TRAINING PROVIDED:

Financial Assistance Provided:	No
Site Selection Assistance:	No
Lease Negotiation Assistance:	No
Co-Operative Advertising:	Yes
Franchisee Assoc./Member:	No
Size Of Corporate Staff:	125
On-Going Support:	C,D,G,H,I
Training: 3 Days Various Locations.	

SPECIFIC EXPANSION PLANS:

US:	All United States
Canada:	All Canada
Overseas:	All Countries

JENNY CRAIG WEIGHT LOSS CENTRES

11355 N. Torrey Pines Rd.
La Jolla, CA 92038-7010
Tel: (800) 583-6151 (619) 812-7000
Fax: (619) 812-2711
Web Site: www.jennycraig.com
Ms. Tara L. McNeil, Franchise Service Mgr.

JENNY CRAIG INTERNATIONAL is one of the largest weight-management service companies in the world. We believe the key to success in our weight management program lies in a strong emphasis on personalized service, quality products and a highly-trained and motivated staff. We are seeking unique, highly-qualified individuals to meet our expansion plans.

BACKGROUND: IFA MEMBER

Established: 1983;	1st Franchised: 1987
Franchised Units:	137
Company-Owned Units	658
Total Units:	795
Dist.:	US-623; CAN-30; O'seas-117
North America:	46 States, 3 Provinces
Density:	NR
Projected New Units (12 Months):	10
Qualifications:	5, 5, 4, 4, 5, 5
Registered: All States	

FINANCIAL/TERMS:

Cash Investment:	$150K
Total Investment:	$160-315K
Minimum Net Worth:	$250K
Fees: Franchise -	$50K
Royalty - 7%;	Ad. - 0%
Earnings Claim Statement:	No
Term of Contract (Years):	10/10
Avg. # Of Employees:	4 FT
Passive Ownership:	Discouraged
Encourage Conversions:	N/A
Area Develop. Agreements:	Yes/10
Sub-Franchising Contracts:	No
Expand In Territory:	Yes
Space Needs: 1,200-1,500 SF; SC	

SUPPORT & TRAINING PROVIDED:

Financial Assistance Provided:	No
Site Selection Assistance:	Yes
Lease Negotiation Assistance:	Yes
Co-Operative Advertising:	N/A
Franchisee Assoc./Member:	No
Size Of Corporate Staff:	250
On-Going Support:	A,B,C,D,E,F,H,I
Training: 2-3 Days Corporate Office; 2 Weeks Regional Training Sites.	

SPECIFIC EXPANSION PLANS:

US:	All United States
Canada:	All Canada
Overseas:	No

L A WEIGHT LOSS CENTERS

747 Dresher Rd., # 100
Horsham, PA 19044-2247
Tel: (888) 258-7099 (215) 346-8762
Fax: (215) 346-4377
E-Mail: franchise@laweightloss.com
Web Site: www.laweightloss.com
Mr. Tim Britt, Dir. Fran. Dev.

L A WEIGHT LOSS CENTERS combine personalized meal plans, using everyday foods, with professional one-on-one counseling and a line of proprietary products to create one of the hottest new business opportunities in America. This center-based weight loss program features the industry's leading marketing, training and operations systems.

BACKGROUND: IFA MEMBER
Established: 1989; 1st Franchised: 1998
Franchised Units: 151
Company-Owned Units 250
Total Units: 401
Dist.: US-401; CAN-0; O'seas-0
North America: 12 States
Density: 58 in NY, 51 in PA, 38 in FL
Projected New Units (12 Months): 100
Qualifications: 3, 5, 1, 3, 3, 4
Registered: All States Except VA

FINANCIAL/TERMS:
Cash Investment: $60-95K
Total Investment: $60-95K
Minimum Net Worth: $100K
Fees: Franchise - $20K
Royalty - 7%; Ad. - NR
Earnings Claim Statement: Yes
Term of Contract (Years): 10/10
Avg. # Of Employees: 5 FT
Passive Ownership: Allowed
Encourage Conversions: N/A
Area Develop. Agreements: Yes/10
Sub-Franchising Contracts: Yes
Expand In Territory: Yes
Space Needs: 1,200 SF; SC

SUPPORT & TRAINING PROVIDED:
Financial Assistance Provided: Yes(I)
Site Selection Assistance: Yes
Lease Negotiation Assistance: Yes
Co-Operative Advertising: N/A
Franchisee Assoc./Member: No
Size Of Corporate Staff: 1,250
On-Going Support: A,B,C,D,E,G,H,I
Training: 1 Week Corporate Headquarters; 2 Wks. Center; 2 Wks. Classroom.

SPECIFIC EXPANSION PLANS:
US: NW, SW, Midwest, New England
Canada: Yes
Overseas: No

<< >>

LADY OF AMERICA

500 E. Broward Blvd., # 1650
Ft. Lauderdale, FL 33394-3000
Tel: (800) 833-5239 (954) 527-5373
Fax: (815) 425-7118
E-Mail: wlandman@ladyofamerica.com
Web Site: www.ladyofamerica.com
Mr. Bill Landman, VP Franchising

Ladies-only health club, specializing in aerobics, weight training, personal training and the sales of related products and services.

BACKGROUND: IFA MEMBER
Established: 1984; 1st Franchised: 1985
Franchised Units: 280
Company-Owned Units 0
Total Units: 280
Dist.: US-145; CAN-0; O'seas-0
North America: 25 States, 4 Countries
Density: 46 in FL, 25 in TX, 15 in PA
Projected New Units (12 Months): 25
Qualifications: 5, 4, 1, 3, 4, 4
Registered: CA,FL,NY

FINANCIAL/TERMS:
Cash Investment: $20-30K
Total Investment: $40-75K
Minimum Net Worth: $50K
Fees: Franchise - $12.5K
Royalty - 10%; Ad. - 0%
Earnings Claim Statement: No
Term of Contract (Years): 10/5
Avg. # Of Employees: 2 FT, 6 PT
Passive Ownership: Allowed
Encourage Conversions: Yes
Area Develop. Agreements: Yes/10
Sub-Franchising Contracts: Yes
Expand In Territory: Yes
Space Needs: 4,500 SF; SC

SUPPORT & TRAINING PROVIDED:
Financial Assistance Provided: Yes
Site Selection Assistance: Yes
Lease Negotiation Assistance: Yes
Co-Operative Advertising: Yes
Franchisee Assoc./Member: Yes/No
Size Of Corporate Staff: 25
On-Going Support: A,B,C,D,E,F,G,H,I
Training: 2-3 Weeks On-Site; 1-2 Weeks at Corporate Headquarters.

SPECIFIC EXPANSION PLANS:
US: All United States
Canada: All Canada
Overseas: All Countries

<< >>

MADAME ET MONSIEUR

8157 Santa Monica Blvd.
West Hollywood, CA 90046
Tel: (310) 275-8901
Fax: (310) 275-8906
Mr. Robey Taute, President

World leaders in bodyshaping, cellulite and weight loss using non-physical computerized machine programs.

BACKGROUND:
Established: 1983; 1st Franchised: 1983
Franchised Units: 81
Company-Owned Units 2
Total Units: 83
Dist.: US-9; CAN-0; O'seas-74
North America: 1 State
Density: NR
Projected New Units (12 Months): 50
Qualifications: 2, 5, 3, 3, 2, 5
Registered: CA,NY

FINANCIAL/TERMS:
Cash Investment: $60K
Total Investment: $160K
Minimum Net Worth: $100K
Fees: Franchise - $NR
Royalty - $300/Mo.; Ad. - Negotiable
Earnings Claim Statement: Yes
Term of Contract (Years): 5-10/5-10
Avg. # Of Employees: 3 FT
Passive Ownership: Discouraged
Encourage Conversions: No
Area Develop. Agreements: No
Sub-Franchising Contracts: NR
Expand In Territory: Yes
Space Needs: 1,000+ SF; SF, RM

SUPPORT & TRAINING PROVIDED:
Financial Assistance Provided: Yes(I)
Site Selection Assistance: Yes
Lease Negotiation Assistance: Yes
Co-Operative Advertising: Yes
Franchisee Assoc./Member: No
Size Of Corporate Staff: 40
On-Going Support: B,D,E,H,i
Training: 40-60 Hours/2-3 Weeks Beverly Hills, CA.

SPECIFIC EXPANSION PLANS:
US: All United States
Canada: All Canada
Overseas: Europe

<< >>

Top 50

MERLE NORMAN COSMETICS

9130 Bellanca Ave.
Los Angeles, CA 90045
Tel: (800) 421-6648 (310) 641-3000

Fax: (310) 337-2370
E-Mail: mpham@merlenorman.com
Web Site: www.merlenorman.com
Ms. Carol LaPorta, VP Studio Development

MERLE NORMAN
COSMETICS

MERLE NORMAN COSMETICS is a specialty retail store, selling scientifically-developed, state-of-the-art cosmetic products, using the 'free make over' and 'try before you buy' complete customer satisfaction methods of selling.

BACKGROUND: IFA MEMBER
Established: 1931; 1st Franchised: 1989
Franchised Units: 1,895
Company-Owned Units 11
Total Units: 1,906
Dist.: US-1807; CAN-90; O'seas-9
North America: 50 States, 1 Province
Density: 259 in TX, 100 in GA, 97 AL
Projected New Units (12 Months): 88
Qualifications: 3, 4, 3, 3, 4, 4
Registered: All States

FINANCIAL/TERMS:
Cash Investment: $15-65K
Total Investment: $33-153K
Minimum Net Worth: $NR
Fees: Franchise - $0
Royalty - 0%; Ad. - 0%
Earnings Claim Statement: Yes
Term of Contract (Years): Unlimited
Avg. # Of Employees: 2 FT, 2-5 PT
Passive Ownership: Discouraged
Encourage Conversions: No
Area Develop. Agreements: No
Sub-Franchising Contracts: No
Expand In Territory: Yes
Space Needs: 450-800 SF; SC, RM

SUPPORT & TRAINING PROVIDED:
Financial Assistance Provided: Yes(I)
Site Selection Assistance: Yes
Lease Negotiation Assistance: Yes
Co-Operative Advertising: Yes
Franchisee Assoc./Member: No
Size Of Corporate Staff: 630
On-Going Support: a,B,C,D,E,F,G,H,I
Training: 2 Weeks Los Angeles, CA.

SPECIFIC EXPANSION PLANS:
US: All United States
Canada: All Canada
Overseas: No

<< >>

MIRAGE TANNING CENTERS

3122 Logan Valley Rd.
Traverse City, MI 49684
Tel: (248) 559-1415
Fax: (248) 557-7931
E-Mail: wfcnet@cris.com
Web Site: www.wfcnet.com
Mr. Jim Rose, President

MIRAGE TANNING offers their customers the most innovative technology in indoor tanning. Indoor tanning is quickly becoming a very high-tech mega-industry. MIRAGE TANNING provides a market feasibility study, professional consultation, customized design, construction and much more.

BACKGROUND:
Established: 1989; 1st Franchised: 1993
Franchised Units: 14
Company-Owned Units 5
Total Units: 19
Dist.: US-16; CAN-0; O'seas-0
North America: 1 State
Density: 16 in MI
Projected New Units (12 Months): 8
Qualifications: 3, 3, 2, 3, 3, 4
Registered: NR

FINANCIAL/TERMS:
Cash Investment: $50K
Total Investment: $200-500K
Minimum Net Worth: $200K
Fees: Franchise - $15K
Royalty - 8%; Ad. - NR
Earnings Claim Statement: NR
Term of Contract (Years): NR
Avg. # Of Employees: NR
Passive Ownership: Allowed
Encourage Conversions: Yes
Area Develop. Agreements: NR
Sub-Franchising Contracts: Yes
Expand In Territory: Yes
Space Needs: NR SF; FS, SF, SC

SUPPORT & TRAINING PROVIDED:
Financial Assistance Provided: Yes(I)
Site Selection Assistance: Yes
Lease Negotiation Assistance: Yes
Co-Operative Advertising: Yes
Franchisee Assoc./Member: NR
Size Of Corporate Staff: NR
On-Going Support: D,E
Training: NR

SPECIFIC EXPANSION PLANS:
US: All United States
Canada: All Canada
Overseas: All Countries

<< >>

PEARLE VISION

1925 Enterprise Pkwy.
Twinsburg, OH 44087
Tel: (800) 282-3931 (330) 486-4000
Fax: (330) 486-3425
E-Mail: t.murray@mciworldcom.net
Web Site: www.pearlevision.com
Mr. Todd Murray, VP Franchising

PEARLE VISION, the largest optical franchisor, offers the ability for qualified individuals to benefit from PEARLE's strong name recognition and operating systems developed over the past 36 years. We have been franchising for 16 years.

BACKGROUND: IFA MEMBER
Established: 1961; 1st Franchised: 1980
Franchised Units: 402
Company-Owned Units 396
Total Units: 798
Dist.: US-637; CAN-18; O'seas-36
North America: 43 States, 2 Provinces
Density: 65 in PA, 53 in IL, 49 in TX
Projected New Units (12 Months): 45
Qualifications: 5, 4, 5, 3, 2, 4
Registered: CA,FL,HI,IL,IN,MD,MI,MN,NY,ND,OR,RI,SD,VA,WI,DC

FINANCIAL/TERMS:
Cash Investment: $110K Max.
Total Investment: $135K-2.5MM
Minimum Net Worth: $Varies
Fees: Franchise - $30K
Royalty - 7%; Ad. - 9%
Earnings Claim Statement: No
Term of Contract (Years): 10/10
Avg. # Of Employees: Varies
Passive Ownership: Not Allowed
Encourage Conversions: Yes
Area Develop. Agreements: No
Sub-Franchising Contracts: No
Expand In Territory: Yes
Space Needs: 2,000-2,500 SF; FS, SC, RM

SUPPORT & TRAINING PROVIDED:
Financial Assistance Provided: Yes(B)
Site Selection Assistance: NR
Lease Negotiation Assistance: No
Co-Operative Advertising: No
Franchisee Assoc./Member: Yes
Size Of Corporate Staff: 250
On-Going Support: a,B,C,D,d,E,F,G,H,I
Training: Varies Dramatically with Skill Assessment of Franchisee.

SPECIFIC EXPANSION PLANS:
US: All U.S. Except CA, WA
Canada: No
Overseas: No

<< >>

Top 50

PHYSICIANS WEIGHTLOSS CENTERS OF AMERICA

395 Springside Dr.
Akron, OH 44333-2496
Tel: (800) 205-7887 (330) 666-7952
Fax: (330) 666-2197
E-Mail: info@pwlc.com
Web Site: www.pwlc.com
Mr. Ken M. Massey

Supervised weight reduction business, offering the customer a comprehensive program, utilizing individual treatment, personal care, counseling and weight management.

BACKGROUND:
Established: 1979; 1st Franchised: 1980
Franchised Units: 58
Company-Owned Units 2
Total Units: 60
Dist.: US-56; CAN-0; O'seas-0
North America: 12 States
Density: 20 in OH, 10 in SC, 4 in NC
Projected New Units (12 Months): 10
Qualifications: 5, 4, 3, 3, , 5
Registered: All States Except CA,HI,NY

FINANCIAL/TERMS:
Cash Investment: $21-52.1K
Total Investment: $38-70K
Minimum Net Worth: $100K
Fees: Franchise - $20K
Royalty - 5.5%/$115/Wk.;
Ad. - 7%/$600/Wk.
Earnings Claim Statement: No
Term of Contract (Years): 5/5/5
Avg. # Of Employees: 2 FT, 2 PT
Passive Ownership: Not Allowed
Encourage Conversions: Yes
Area Develop. Agreements: No
Sub-Franchising Contracts: No
Expand In Territory: Yes
Space Needs: 1,200 SF; SC

SUPPORT & TRAINING PROVIDED:
Financial Assistance Provided: No
Site Selection Assistance: Yes
Lease Negotiation Assistance: Yes
Co-Operative Advertising: Yes
Franchisee Assoc./Member: No
Size Of Corporate Staff: 45
On-Going Support: A,B,c,d,E,G,H,I
Training: 3 Weeks Akron, OH; 1-3 Days On-Site.

SPECIFIC EXPANSION PLANS:
US: All United States
Canada: No
Overseas: No

<< >>

RIGHT AT HOME

2939 S. 120th St.
Omaha, NE 68144
Tel: (877) 697-7537 (402) 697-7537
Fax: (402) 697-7536
E-Mail: info@rightathome.net
Web Site: www.rightathome.net
Mr. Ron Schiller, Director of Sales

RIGHT AT HOME offers one of the most exciting opportunities in franchising today. RIGHT AT HOME offers in-home senior care and supplemental staffing for the healthcare industry. You double your opportunity with the same franchise system.

BACKGROUND:
Established: 1995; 1st Franchised: 2000
Franchised Units: 16
Company-Owned Units 1
Total Units: 17
Dist.: US-17; CAN-0; O'seas-0
North America: 9 States
Density: NR
Projected New Units (12 Months): 20
Qualifications: 3, 4, 1, 1, 1, 5
Registered: All States Except RI, HI, AB

FINANCIAL/TERMS:
Cash Investment: $25-45K
Total Investment: $NR
Minimum Net Worth: $N/A
Fees: Franchise - $16.5K
Royalty - 5%; Ad. - 2%
Earnings Claim Statement: Yes
Term of Contract (Years): 10/5/5
Avg. # Of Employees: NR
Passive Ownership: Discouraged
Encourage Conversions: No
Area Develop. Agreements: Yes/10
Sub-Franchising Contracts: No
Expand In Territory: Yes
Space Needs: 700 SF; FS

SUPPORT & TRAINING PROVIDED:
Financial Assistance Provided: No
Site Selection Assistance: Yes
Lease Negotiation Assistance: No
Co-Operative Advertising: No
Franchisee Assoc./Member: No
Size Of Corporate Staff: 6
On-Going Support: C,D,G,H,I
Training: 2 Weeks Omaha, NE.

SPECIFIC EXPANSION PLANS:
US: All United States
Canada: No
Overseas: No

<< >>

SANGSTER'S
health centres

SANGSTER'S HEALTH CENTRES

2218 Hanselman Ave.
Saskatoon, SK S7L 6A4 CANADA
Tel: (306) 653-4481
Fax: (306) 653-4688
E-Mail: franchise@sangsters.com
Web Site: www.sangsters.com
Ms. Wendy Sangster, VP Franchising

Health and well being are part of today's lifestyle with an enormous demand for vitamins, minerals, sports nutrition, body care and aromatherapy. SANGSTER'S HEALTH CENTRES has over 30 years of market experience and aggressive growth both in Canada and internationally. SANGSTER'S has received many awards including the CFA's 2001 Marketing Award. SANGSTER'S complete franchise system includes: Exclusive Private Label Supplements, extensive training, ongoing support, and national advertising.

BACKGROUND:
Established: 1971; 1st Franchised: 1978
Franchised Units: 44
Company-Owned Units 4
Total Units: 48
Dist.: US-0; CAN-48; O'seas-0
North America: 7 Provinces
Density: 14 in SK, 11 in ON, 8 in AB
Projected New Units (12 Months): 8
Qualifications: 3, 3, 4, 2, 3, 4
Registered: AB

FINANCIAL/TERMS:
Cash Investment: $30-50K
Total Investment: $50-165K
Minimum Net Worth: $50K
Fees: Franchise - $25K

Royalty - 5%; Ad. - 2%
Earnings Claim Statement: No
Term of Contract (Years): 5/2-5
Avg. # Of Employees: 2 FT, 1 PT
Passive Ownership: Discouraged
Encourage Conversions: Yes
Area Develop. Agreements: No
Sub-Franchising Contracts: No
Expand In Territory: Yes
Space Needs: 600-1,000 SF; SC, RM

SUPPORT & TRAINING PROVIDED:
Financial Assistance Provided: Yes(D)
Site Selection Assistance: Yes
Lease Negotiation Assistance: Yes
Co-Operative Advertising: Yes
Franchisee Assoc./Member: Yes
Size Of Corporate Staff: 13
On-Going Support: B,C,D,E,F,G,H
Training: 2 Weeks in Saskatoon, SK; Minimum of 1 Week at Franchisee Location.

SPECIFIC EXPANSION PLANS:
US: All United States
Canada: All Canada
Overseas: Europe, Asia

<< >>

TOP OF THE LINE FRAGRANCES

515 Bath Ave.
Long Branch, NJ 07740
Tel: (800) 929-3083 (732) 229-0014
Fax: (732) 222-1762
E-Mail: info@tolfranchise.com
Web Site: www.tolfranchise.com
Mr. Steven Ciaverelli, Vice President

T.O.L. specializes in the retail sale of designer fragrances at the lowest discounted prices.

BACKGROUND:
Established: 1987; 1st Franchised: 1987
Franchised Units: 3
Company-Owned Units 1
Total Units: 4
Dist.: US-4; CAN-0; O'seas-0
North America: 3 States
Density: 2 in FL, 1 in TN, 1 in PA
Projected New Units (12 Months): 3
Qualifications: 5, 3, 3, 1, 1, 4
Registered: NR

FINANCIAL/TERMS:
Cash Investment: $150-200K
Total Investment: $150-200K
Minimum Net Worth: $150K
Fees: Franchise - $20K
Royalty - 5%; Ad. - N/A
Earnings Claim Statement: No

Term of Contract (Years): 10/5
Avg. # Of Employees: 3 FT, 3 PT
Passive Ownership: Discouraged
Encourage Conversions: Yes
Area Develop. Agreements: Yes/10
Sub-Franchising Contracts: No
Expand In Territory: Yes
Space Needs: 700-1,200 SF; SC, RM, Outlet Ctr.

SUPPORT & TRAINING PROVIDED:
Financial Assistance Provided: Yes(I)
Site Selection Assistance: Yes
Lease Negotiation Assistance: Yes
Co-Operative Advertising: N/A
Franchisee Assoc./Member: No
Size Of Corporate Staff: 5
On-Going Support: B,C,d,E,F,I
Training: 7-10 Days at Franchise Location.

SPECIFIC EXPANSION PLANS:
US: East
Canada: No
Overseas: No

TROPI-TAN FRANCHISING

5152 Commerce Rd.
Flint, MI 48507
Tel: (800) 642-4826 (810) 230-6789
Fax: (810) 230-1115
Ms. Carol Mills, Franchise Director

In business for 19 years, TROPI-TAN indoor sun-tanning salons are international design and decor award winners. One of the most progressive salon chains, TROPI-TAN salons also feature a full line of tanning lotions, clothing, and related accessories.

BACKGROUND:
Established: 1979; 1st Franchised: 1985
Franchised Units: 5
Company-Owned Units 6
Total Units: 11
Dist.: US-11; CAN-0; O'seas-0
North America: 1 State
Density: 11 in MI
Projected New Units (12 Months): 25
Qualifications: 3, 3, 1, 3, 3, 5
Registered: MI

FINANCIAL/TERMS:
Cash Investment: $50-100K
Total Investment: $175-250K
Minimum Net Worth: $150K
Fees: Franchise - $20K
Royalty - 5%; Ad. - 3%
Earnings Claim Statement: No

Term of Contract (Years): 10/5
Avg. # Of Employees: 1 FT, 3 PT
Passive Ownership: Discouraged
Encourage Conversions: Yes
Area Develop. Agreements: Yes/5
Sub-Franchising Contracts: No
Expand In Territory: Yes
Space Needs: 2,500 SF; FS, SC

SUPPORT & TRAINING PROVIDED:
Financial Assistance Provided: Yes(I)
Site Selection Assistance: Yes
Lease Negotiation Assistance: Yes
Co-Operative Advertising: Yes
Franchisee Assoc./Member: No
Size Of Corporate Staff: 30
On-Going Support: A,B,C,D,E,F,G,H,I
Training: 80 Hours at Corporate Training Center; 40 Hours On-Site.

SPECIFIC EXPANSION PLANS:
US: All United States
Canada: All Canada
Overseas: All Countries

<< >>

WOMEN'S 17-MINUTE WORKOUT

4790 Douglas Cir., NW
Canton, OH 44718-3632
Tel: (888) 832-1717 (330) 305-1717
Fax: (330) 497-6453
E-Mail: wo17minute@aol.com
www.womens17minuteworkout.com
Mr. Jeff Stone, Jr., Fran. Dev.

A totally unique women-only fitness club franchise opportunity. Backed by 25 years of experience, our proprietary system teaches women the truth about women's fitness and offers the fitness-minded entrepreneur the opportunity to own a very lucrative results-oriented business. Our members' results are incredible...and that spells success for everyone involved.

BACKGROUND: IFA MEMBER
Established: 1996; 1st Franchised: 1998
Franchised Units: 9
Company-Owned Units 5
Total Units: 14
Dist.: US-6; CAN-0; O'seas-0
North America: 1 State
Density: 6 in OH
Projected New Units (12 Months): 12
Qualifications: 3, 3, 4, 2, 2, 5
Registered: FL,IL,IN,MD,MI,MN,NY,RI, VA,WI,DC

FINANCIAL/TERMS:
Cash Investment: $45K
Total Investment: $158-197K

Minimum Net Worth:	$200K
Fees: Franchise -	$22.5K
Royalty - 6%/1.85K/Mo.;	Ad. - 1%
Earnings Claim Statement:	No
Term of Contract (Years):	5/5
Avg. # Of Employees:	4 FT, 4 PT
Passive Ownership:	Discouraged
Encourage Conversions:	Yes
Area Develop. Agreements:	Yes/5
Sub-Franchising Contracts:	No
Expand In Territory:	Yes

Space Needs: 1,800 SF; SC

SUPPORT & TRAINING PROVIDED:

Financial Assistance Provided:	No
Site Selection Assistance:	Yes
Lease Negotiation Assistance:	Yes
Co-Operative Advertising:	N/A
Franchisee Assoc./Member:	No
Size Of Corporate Staff:	10
On-Going Support:	A,B,C,D,E,F,G,H,I

Training: 3-4 Weeks Canton, OH.

SPECIFIC EXPANSION PLANS:

US:	All United States
Canada:	No
Overseas:	No

<< >>

SUPPLEMENTAL LISTING OF FRANCHISORS

A. T. C. HEALTHCARE SERVICES, 1983 Marcus Ave., # 200, Lake Success, NY 11042 ; (800) 444-4633 (516) 358-1000; (516) 358-3678

BALLY TOTAL FITNESS CENTER, 8700 Bryn Mawr Ave., 2nd Fl., Chicago, IL 60631 ; (800) 410-2582 (773) 380-3000; (773) 380-7679

BEAUX VISAGES EUROPEAN SKIN CARE CENTERS, 270 Mount Hope Dr., Albany, NY 12202-1058 ; (518) 465-1420; (518) 465-0364

BODY SHOP, THE, P.O. Box 1409, Wake Forest, NC 27588-1409 ; (919) 554-4900; (919) 554-4361

CARDINAL HEALTH, 700 Cardinal Pl., Dublin, OH 43107 ; (614) 757-7769; (314) 872-5500

COMFORT KEEPERS, 6450 Poe Ave., # 551, Dayton, OH 45414 ; (800) 387-2415 (937) 264-1933; (937) 264-3103

CONTEMPO WOMEN'S WORKOUT WORLD, 16015 Harlem Ave., Tinley Park, IL 60477 ; (708) 429-7766; (708) 429-9741

CONTOURS EXPRESS, 979 S. Main St., Nicholasville, KY 40356 ; (877) 227-2282 (859) 885-6441; (425) 920-0534

COPA CA TANA TANNING SALONS, 222 N. Sepulveda Blvd., # 2000, El Segundo, CA 90245 ; (877) 584-2399 (310) 364-5220; (310) 364-1611

CURVES FOR WOMEN, 400 Schroeder Dr., Waco, TX 76710-6948 ; (800) 848-1096 (254) 399-9285; (254) 399-9731

DISCOUNT SPORT NUTRITION, 1525 N. Stemmons Frwy., # 200, Carrollton, TX 75006 ; (877) 9sport3 (972) 245-1798; (972) 245-5306

DOCTORS & NURSES WEIGHT CONTROL CENTER, 1386B Shoreline Dr., Gulf Breeze, FL 32561 ; (800) 367-6391 (850) 934-8006; (850) 934-0340

FABUTAN SUN TAN STUDIOS, 5925 3rd St. SE, Calgary, AB T2H 1K3 CANADA; (800) 565-3658 (403) 640-2100; (403) 640-2116

FITNESS CENTERS OF AMERICA, 221 Bonita Ave., # 712, Piedmont, CA 94611 ; (510) 839-5471; (510) 547-3245

HEALTH CLUBS OF AMERICA, 2400 E. Commercial Blvd., # 808, Ft. Lauderdale, FL 33305 ; (305) 492-1201

INCHES A WEIGH, P.O. Box 59346, Birmingham, AL 35209 ; (800) 241-8663 (205) 879-8614; (205) 879-2106

IRLY BIRD, 7846 128th St., P.O. Box 9010, Surrey, BC V3T 4X7 CANADA; (604) 596-1551; (604) 597-3693

JENEAL STUDIOS, 3798 Westchase, Houston, TX 77042 ; (800) 7JE-NEAL (713) 781-2263; (713) 789-8585

LADY SLENDER, 10924 Vance Jackson Rd., # 401, San Antonio, TX 78230 ; (888) 227-8187 (210) 877-1500; (210) 877-1505

MEDIHEALTH SOLUTIONS, 4700 Westown Pkwy., # 300, West Des Moines, IA 50266-6718 ; (888) 595-9244 (515) 224-8388; (515) 224-8415

MITEX MATTRESS HYGIENICS, Box 10, Site 15, RR # 3, Olds, AB T4H 1P4 CANADA; (403) 556-1332; (403) 556-1336

NU-BEST DIAGNOSTIC LABS, 4159 Corporate Ct., Palm Harbor, FL 34683 (800) 839-6757 (727) 942-8324; (727) 943-7198

OUR WEIGH, 3637 Park Ave., # 201, Memphis, TN 38111-5614 ; (901) 458-7546

PALM BEACH TAN, 2387 Midway Rd., Carrollton, TX 75006-2521 ; (888) 725-6826 (972) 931-6595; (972) 931-6594

PASSPORT HEALTH, 845 E. Fort Ave., Baltimore, MD 21230 ; (888) 499-7277 (410) 727-0556; (410) 727-0696

PHYSICIANS WEIGHT LOSS CENTRES (CANADA), 395 Springside Dr., Akron, OH 44333 ; (800) 205-7887 (330) 666-7952; (330) 666-2197

PLANET BEACH, 3910 General De Gaulle, New Orleans, LA 70114-8210 ; (888) 290-8266 (504) 361-5550; (504) 361-5540

ROSEGLEN WEIGHT LOSS & WELLNESS OF CANADA, 1106 Union Ave., Laconia, NH 03246-2127 ; (866) 808-3505 (603) 524-4903; (603) 524-4591

SOLAR PLANET TANNING SALONS, 856 Folsom St., San Francisco, CA 94107 (800) 886-8486 (415) 908-6869; (415) 908-6860

STATE BEAUTY SUPPLY, 10405-B E. 55th Pl., Tulsa, OK 74146 ; (918) 627-8000; (918) 627-8660

SUNBANQUE ISLAND TANNING, 2533A Yonge St., Toronto, ON M4P 2H9 CANADA; (416) 488-5838; (416) 488-3712

SUNCHAIN TANNING CENTERS, 8102 E. McDowell, # 2C, Scottsdale, AZ 85257 ; (480) 421-9630; (480) 994-5162

SUPERIOR SENIOR CARE, P.O. Box 505, Hot Springs, AR 71902-0505 ; (800) 951-9792 (501) 783-1206; (501) 623-7853

VOLPE NAILS, P.O. Box 19979, Sarasota, FL 34276-2979 ; (800) 848-6573 (941) 925-7410; (941) 925-7213

WEIGHT WATCHERS INTERNATIONAL, 175 Crossways Park W., Woodbury, NY 11797-2016 ; (516) 390-1400; (516) 390-1510

Laundry & Dry Cleaning

Chapter

21

Laundry & Dry Cleaning Industry Profile

Total # Franchisors in Industry Group	23
Total # Franchised Units in Industry Group	2,374
Total # Company-Owned Units in Industry Group	36
Total # Operating Units in Industry Group	2,410
Average # Franchised Units/Franchisor	103.2
Average # Company-Owned Units/Franchisor	1.6
Average # Total Units/Franchisor	104.8
Ratio of Total # Franchised Units/Total # Company-Owned Units	65.9:1
Industry Survey Participants	11
Representing % of Industry	47.8%
Average Franchise Fee*:	$19.2K
Average Total Investment*:	$224.3K
Average On-Going Royalty Fee*:	6.6%

*If a range was provided, the mid-point of the range was used. See detailed profiles for actual ranges.

Five Largest Participants in Survey

Company	# Franchised Units	# Co-Owned Units	# Total Units	Franchise Fee	On-Going Royalty	Total Investment
1. Martinizing Dry Cleaning	763	0	763	30K	4%	210-300K
2. Pressed 4 Time	125	0	125	12.5K	6%	15.2-22.3K
3. Wedding Gown Specialists	119	1	120	N/A	20%	2.5K+
4. Eagle Cleaners	95	1	96	15K	5%/$195	200-250K
5. Nu-Look One-Hour Cleaners	50	3	53	20K	2%	125-200K+

All of the data provided are proprietary and should not be quoted without acknowledging *Bond's Franchise Guide.*

1-800-DRYCLEAN

3948 Ranchero Dr.
Ann Arbor, MI 48108-2775
Tel: (866) 822-6115 (734) 822-6800
Fax: (734) 822-6888
E-Mail: opportunity@1800dryclean.com
Web Site: www.1800dryclean.com
Mr. Marc A. Kiekenapp, VP Development

Without being a drycleaner, you can be a leader in this $10 billion market. The consumer wants convenience - the industry is not providing it. 1-800-DRYCLEAN delivers the solution! Big business does not necessarily mean big investment. For under $25,000, your 1-800-DRYCLEAN pick up and delivery service can be well on its way to becoming a fleet operation.

BACKGROUND: IFA MEMBER
Established: 2000; 1st Franchised: 2000
Franchised Units: 10
Company-Owned Units 0
Total Units: 10
Dist.: US-18; CAN-0; O'seas-0
North America: 9 States
Density: 5 in FL, 2 in MI, 2 in AL
Projected New Units (12 Months): 25
Qualifications: 3, 3, 1, 3, 4, 5
Registered: CA,FL,IL,IN,MD,MI,MN,NY, OR,RI,VA,WA,WI,DC

FINANCIAL/TERMS:
Cash Investment: $20K
Total Investment: $16.8-27.2K
Minimum Net Worth: $100K
Fees: Franchise - $6.9K
Royalty - 7%; Ad. - 0%
Earnings Claim Statement: No
Term of Contract (Years): 10/10
Avg. # Of Employees: 5 FT
Passive Ownership: Discouraged
Encourage Conversions: Yes
Area Develop. Agreements: No
Sub-Franchising Contracts: No
Expand In Territory: Yes
Space Needs: 200 SF; HB

SUPPORT & TRAINING PROVIDED:
Financial Assistance Provided: Yes(I)
Site Selection Assistance: Yes
Lease Negotiation Assistance: No
Co-Operative Advertising: No
Franchisee Assoc./Member: NR
Size Of Corporate Staff: 17
On-Going Support: C,D,E,G,h,I
Training: 5 Days Home Office; 4 Days Franchise Location; 6 Months Field Right-Start Program.

SPECIFIC EXPANSION PLANS:
US: All United States
Canada: All Canada
Overseas: All Countries

<< >>

AMERICA'S WASH-N-STOR

201 Barton Springs Rd.
Austin, TX 78704
Tel: (512) 457-1337
Fax: (512) 457-1335
E-Mail: gary@wash-n-stor.com
Web Site: www.wash-n-stor.com
Mr. Garyt Stillwell, President

A combination business of coin laundry, self-storage units and self-service car wash, all in one location.

BACKGROUND:
Established: 1998; 1st Franchised: 1998
Franchised Units: 1
Company-Owned Units 2
Total Units: 3
Dist.: US-1; CAN-0; O'seas-0
North America: 1 State
Density: 1 in NM
Projected New Units (12 Months): 11
Qualifications: 3, 2, 2, 1, 4, 4
Registered: NR

FINANCIAL/TERMS:
Cash Investment: $60-130K
Total Investment: $630-775K
Minimum Net Worth: $150K
Fees: Franchise - $12.5K
Royalty - 7.5%/600 Min.;
Ad. - 1.5%/$150
Earnings Claim Statement: No
Term of Contract (Years): 10/10
Avg. # Of Employees: 1 FT, 2 PT
Passive Ownership: Allowed
Encourage Conversions: No
Area Develop. Agreements: Yes/2
Sub-Franchising Contracts: No
Expand In Territory: Yes
Space Needs: 23,400 SF; FS

SUPPORT & TRAINING PROVIDED:
Financial Assistance Provided: Yes
Site Selection Assistance: Yes
Lease Negotiation Assistance: N/A
Co-Operative Advertising: N/A
Franchisee Assoc./Member: No
Size Of Corporate Staff: 2
On-Going Support: a,b,C,D,E,G,h,I
Training: 2 Days Austin, TX; 2 Days On-Site New Mexico; 2-7 Days on Opening of Facility.

SPECIFIC EXPANSION PLANS:
US: All United States
Canada: No
Overseas: No

<< >>

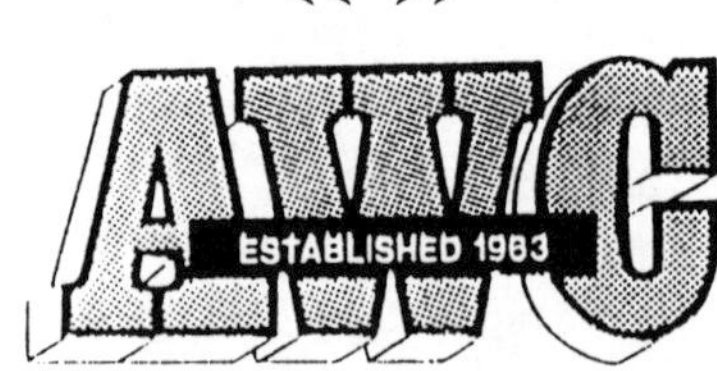

AWC COMMERCIAL WINDOW COVERINGS

825 W. Williamson
Fullerton, CA 92832
Tel: (800) 252-2280 (714) 879-3880
Fax: (714) 879-8419
Web Site: www.ibos.com/pub/ibos/awc
Mr. Leland B. Daniels, President

Mobile non-toxic drapery dry cleaning services provided on location for commercial customers; as well as sales, installation & repairs of all types of window coverings at competitive prices through centralized buying. Nationwide accounts will be serviced by the franchisees as they are established. Utilizing the customer base, references and reputation of the franchisor, developed over the past 37 years makes this an exceptional opportunity with endless possibilities and immediate credibility.

BACKGROUND:
Established: 1963; 1st Franchised: 1992
Franchised Units: 6
Company-Owned Units 4
Total Units: 10
Dist.: US-14; CAN-0; O'seas-0
North America: 5 States
Density: 6 in CA, 1 in NJ, 1 in DC
Projected New Units (12 Months): 3
Qualifications: 3, 4, 3, 3, 4, 4
Registered: CA,DC,MD

FINANCIAL/TERMS:
Cash Investment: $25-50K
Total Investment: $112.5-181.4K
Minimum Net Worth: $N/A
Fees: Franchise - $25K
Royalty - 5-12.5%; Ad. - 2.5%
Earnings Claim Statement: No
Term of Contract (Years): 10/10
Avg. # Of Employees:
1 FT, PT As Needed
Passive Ownership: Not Allowed

Encourage Conversions: Yes
Area Develop. Agreements: Yes
Sub-Franchising Contracts: No
Expand In Territory: Yes
Space Needs: N/A SF; HB

SUPPORT & TRAINING PROVIDED:
Financial Assistance Provided: Yes(I)
Site Selection Assistance: N/A
Lease Negotiation Assistance: Yes
Co-Operative Advertising: Yes
Franchisee Assoc./Member: No
Size Of Corporate Staff: 8
On-Going Support: A,B,C,D,F,h,I
Training: 2 Weeks at Plant and On-Site; On-Going.

SPECIFIC EXPANSION PLANS:
US: All United States
Canada: All Canada
Overseas: All Countries

<< >>

CHAMPION CLEANERS

2305 Hickory Valley Rd., #1A
Chattanooga, TN 37421-6797
Tel: (800) 357-0797 (423) 296-1150
Fax: (423) 296-1170
E-Mail: roldham@championcleaners.com
Web Site: www.championcleaners.com
Mr. Ray Oldham, President

CHAMPION CLEANERS provides an up-scale, state-of-the-art drycleaning and laundry facility that places its emphasis on quality and service. The package includes extensive training and comprehensive manuals covering every aspect of the business. Additional assistance is provided in areas of demographic studies, site selection, lease negotiation, construction, marketing and advertising.

BACKGROUND: IFA MEMBER
Established: 1994; 1st Franchised: 1995
Franchised Units: 27
Company-Owned Units 0
Total Units: 27
Dist.: US-10; CAN-0; O'seas-4
North America: 3 States
Density: 7 in TN, 2 in CO, 1 in MA
Projected New Units (12 Months): 12
Qualifications: 4, 4, 1, 4, 4, 4
Registered: FL

FINANCIAL/TERMS:
Cash Investment: $100K
Total Investment: $374-396K
Minimum Net Worth: $500K
Fees: Franchise - $25K
Royalty - 2%; Ad. - NR
Earnings Claim Statement: No
Term of Contract (Years): 10/5
Avg. # Of Employees: 12 FT, 2 PT
Passive Ownership: Discouraged
Encourage Conversions: No
Area Develop. Agreements: Yes/5
Sub-Franchising Contracts: Yes
Expand In Territory: Yes
Space Needs: 3,200 SF; FS, SC

SUPPORT & TRAINING PROVIDED:
Financial Assistance Provided: No
Site Selection Assistance: Yes
Lease Negotiation Assistance: Yes
Co-Operative Advertising: Yes
Franchisee Assoc./Member: Yes/Yes
Size Of Corporate Staff: 6
On-Going Support: C,D,E,G,H,I
Training: 2 Weeks Corporate Training Facility; 2 Weeks Franchisee's New Facility.

SPECIFIC EXPANSION PLANS:
US: Southeast
Canada: No
Overseas: No

<< >>

CLEAN 'N' PRESS AMERICA

500 Airport Blvd., # 100
Burlingame, CA 94010
Tel: (800) 237-1711 (650) 344-2377
Fax: (650) 344-2545
Mr. Alan Block, President

Dry cleaning and laundry service utilizing a central plant with satellite stores and pick-up and delivery service, providing quality for less. We provide you with a complete and highly-efficient system, including marketing programs, ranging from a single van to a multiple plant/store combination. You are given full training and support through an extensive hands-on training program with detailed manuals.

BACKGROUND:
Established: 1991; 1st Franchised: 1991
Franchised Units: 37
Company-Owned Units 0
Total Units: 37
Dist.: US-40; CAN-0; O'seas-0
North America: 3 States
Density: 40 in MN
Projected New Units (12 Months): 20
Qualifications: 4, 4, 1, 3, 3, 5
Registered: CA,MN

FINANCIAL/TERMS:
Cash Investment: $150K
Total Investment: $20-400K
Minimum Net Worth: $365K
Fees: Franchise - $9.5-40K
Royalty - 5%; Ad. - Varies
Earnings Claim Statement: No
Term of Contract (Years): 10/10
Avg. # Of Employees: Varies
Passive Ownership: Discouraged
Encourage Conversions: Yes
Area Develop. Agreements: Yes/Varies
Sub-Franchising Contracts: Yes
Expand In Territory: Yes
Space Needs: 850-3,500 SF; HB, SF, SC

SUPPORT & TRAINING PROVIDED:
Financial Assistance Provided: Yes(I)
Site Selection Assistance: Yes
Lease Negotiation Assistance: Yes
Co-Operative Advertising: N/A
Franchisee Assoc./Member: No
Size Of Corporate Staff: 6
On-Going Support: C,D,E,F,I
Training: 1-3 Weeks Phoenix, AZ or Other Location.

SPECIFIC EXPANSION PLANS:
US: All United States
Canada: All Canada
Overseas: Asia, Europe, North and South America

EAGLE CLEANERS

1750 University Dr., # 111
Coral Springs, FL 33071-8903
Tel: (800) 275-9751 (954) 346-9501
Fax: (954) 346-9505
E-Mail: G2eagle@aol.com
Mr. Gerard J. Teeven, Executive Vice President

Franchisor of state-of-the-art dry-cleaning stores, offering turn-key plants and drop stores, complete training, site evaluation and a marketing strategy that separates us from the rest of the dry cleaning industry.

BACKGROUND: IFA MEMBER
Established: 1991; 1st Franchised: 1993
Franchised Units: 95
Company-Owned Units 1
Total Units: 96
Dist.: US-92; CAN-0; O'seas-0
North America: 16 States
Density: CT, NY, FL
Projected New Units (12 Months): 40
Qualifications: 4, 5, 1, 4, 5, 4
Registered: FL,IL,MI,NY

FINANCIAL/TERMS:
Cash Investment: $75-110K
Total Investment: $200-250K

Minimum Net Worth: $250K
Fees: Franchise - $15K
Royalty - 5%/$195; Ad. - 3%
Earnings Claim Statement: No
Term of Contract (Years): 10/10
Avg. # Of Employees: 3 FT, 1 PT
Passive Ownership: Discouraged
Encourage Conversions: No
Area Develop. Agreements: Yes/10
Sub-Franchising Contracts: Yes
Expand In Territory: Yes
Space Needs: 1,800-2,200 SF; FS, SC

SUPPORT & TRAINING PROVIDED:
Financial Assistance Provided: Yes(I)
Site Selection Assistance: Yes
Lease Negotiation Assistance: Yes
Co-Operative Advertising: N/A
Franchisee Assoc./Member: No
Size Of Corporate Staff: 16
On-Going Support: A,C,D,E,F,G,H,I
Training: 3 Weeks Coral Springs, FL; 1 Week Opening; 90-120 Post-Opening.

SPECIFIC EXPANSION PLANS:
US: East, Midwest
Canada: No
Overseas:
Mexico, South America, Latin America

<< >>

HARVEY WASHBANGERS

106 29th Ave. N., P.O. Box 50582
Nashville, TN 37205
Tel: (615) 985-0029
Fax: (615) 985-0029
E-Mail: harvey@harveywashbangers.com
Web Site: www.harveywashbangers.com
Mr. David Harvey, President

HARVEY WASHBANGERS franchises combine laundry, restaurant and bar facilities all under one roof. It's without a doubt the most fun one can have doing the dirty laundry.

BACKGROUND:
Established: 1986; 1st Franchised: 1996
Franchised Units: 5
Company-Owned Units 1
Total Units: 6
Dist.: US-5; CAN-0; O'seas-0
North America: 3 States
Density: 2 in TN, 1 in CA, 1 in TX
Projected New Units (12 Months): 4
Qualifications: 3, 5, 2, 3, 2, 5
Registered: CA,FL

FINANCIAL/TERMS:
Cash Investment: $75K
Total Investment: $250-425K
Minimum Net Worth: $250K
Fees: Franchise - $20K
Royalty - 5%; Ad. - 0%
Earnings Claim Statement: No
Term of Contract (Years): 10/10
Avg. # Of Employees: 4 FT, 6 PT
Passive Ownership: Discouraged
Encourage Conversions: No
Area Develop. Agreements: No
Sub-Franchising Contracts: No
Expand In Territory: Yes
Space Needs: 4,500 SF; FS, SC

SUPPORT & TRAINING PROVIDED:
Financial Assistance Provided: Yes(I)
Site Selection Assistance: Yes
Lease Negotiation Assistance: Yes
Co-Operative Advertising: Yes
Franchisee Assoc./Member: No
Size Of Corporate Staff: 2
On-Going Support: C,D,E,F,G,h,i
Training: 2 Weeks Home Office; 1 Week Your Store.

SPECIFIC EXPANSION PLANS:
US: All United States
Canada: No
Overseas: No

<< >>

MARTINIZING DRY CLEANING

2005 Ross Ave.
Cincinnati, OH 45212-2009
Tel: (800) 827-0345 (513) 351-6211
Fax: (513) 731-0818
E-Mail: cleanup@martinizing.com
Web Site: www.martinizing.com
Mr. Jerald E. Laesser, Vice President

New franchisees receive the full benefit of MARTINIZING DRY CLEANING's 50 plus years of experience in site selection, training and marketing. MARTINIZING focuses totally on assisting its franchisees before, during and after opening. MARTINIZING is the most recognized name in dry-cleaning. We're rated # 1 in our industry by Entrepreneur Magazine.

BACKGROUND: IFA MEMBER
Established: 1949; 1st Franchised: 1949
Franchised Units: 763
Company-Owned Units 0
Total Units: 763
Dist.: US-522; CAN-36; O'seas-205
North America: 41 States, 6 Provinces
Density: 10 in MI, 82 in CA, 40 in TX
Projected New Units (12 Months): 25
Qualifications: 5, 4, 1, 3, 1, 5
Registered: All States

FINANCIAL/TERMS:
Cash Investment: $80K
Total Investment: $210-300K
Minimum Net Worth: $180K
Fees: Franchise - $30K
Royalty - 4%; Ad. - 0.5%
Earnings Claim Statement: No
Term of Contract (Years): 20
Avg. # Of Employees: 2 FT, 4 PT
Passive Ownership: Discouraged
Encourage Conversions: Yes
Area Develop. Agreements: Yes/3-20
Sub-Franchising Contracts: Yes
Expand In Territory: Yes
Space Needs: 1,500-2,000 SF; FS, SC

SUPPORT & TRAINING PROVIDED:
Financial Assistance Provided: Yes(I)
Site Selection Assistance: Yes
Lease Negotiation Assistance: Yes
Co-Operative Advertising: Yes
Franchisee Assoc./Member: Yes/Yes
Size Of Corporate Staff: 16
On-Going Support: C,D,E,G,H,I
Training: 1 Week Classroom; 2 Weeks In-Store.

SPECIFIC EXPANSION PLANS:
US: All United States
Canada: All Except AB
Overseas: Europe, Far and Middle East

<< >>

NU-LOOK 1-HR. CLEANERS

15 NE Second Ave.
Deerfield Beach, FL 33441-3503
Tel: (800) 413-7881 (954) 426-1111
Fax: (954) 570-6248
E-Mail: marketing@nu-look.com
Web Site: www.nu-look.com
Mr. Karl N. Dickey, President/CEO

Retail dry cleaner.

BACKGROUND:
Established: 1967; 1st Franchised: 1967
Franchised Units: 50
Company-Owned Units 3
Total Units: 53
Dist.: US-41; CAN-0; O'seas-12
North America: 4 States
Density: 24 in FL, 12 in MD, 10 in VA
Projected New Units (12 Months): 25
Qualifications: 2, 4, 2, 2, 3, 4
Registered: FL,MD,VA

FINANCIAL/TERMS:
Cash Investment: $45-75K
Total Investment: $125-200K+
Minimum Net Worth: $150K
Fees: Franchise - $20K
Royalty - 2%; Ad. - 3%
Earnings Claim Statement: No
Term of Contract (Years): 20/10
Avg. # Of Employees: 2 FT, 2 PT
Passive Ownership: Discouraged
Encourage Conversions: Yes
Area Develop. Agreements: Yes
Sub-Franchising Contracts: Yes
Expand In Territory: Yes
Space Needs: 1,200-1,400 SF; FS, SC

SUPPORT & TRAINING PROVIDED:
Financial Assistance Provided: Yes(I)
Site Selection Assistance: Yes
Lease Negotiation Assistance: Yes
Co-Operative Advertising: Yes
Franchisee Assoc./Member: No
Size Of Corporate Staff: 4
On-Going Support: C,D,E,G,H
Training: 4 Weeks Deerfield Beach, FL.

SPECIFIC EXPANSION PLANS:
US: All United States
Canada: All Canada
Overseas: All Countries

≺≺ ≻≻

PRESSED 4 TIME

124 Boston Post Rd.
Sudbury, MA 01776
Tel: (800) 423-8711 (978) 443-9200
Fax: (978) 443-0709
E-Mail: randy@pressed4time.com
Web Site: www.pressed4time.com
Mr. Randy Erb, Dir. Franchise Development

The nation's first and foremost dry-cleaning/shoe repair, pick-up and delivery franchise. Coast to coast, more than 50,000 customers smile when they see our franchisees. Dry-cleaning and shoe repair are performed by local merchants. Experience in the 7 billion-dollar dry-cleaning industry is not needed. If you like people and can work on your own, then this leading home-based, mobile franchise is probably for you!

BACKGROUND: IFA MEMBER
Established: 1987; 1st Franchised: 1990
Franchised Units: 125
Company-Owned Units 0
Total Units: 125
Dist.: US-107; CAN-4; O'seas-22
North America: 31 States, 2 Provinces
Density: 13 in PA, 7 in OH, 7 in MA
Projected New Units (12 Months): 36
Qualifications: 2, 1, 1, 3, 3, 3
Registered: CA,FL,IL,IN,MD,MI,MN,NY,OR,RI,VA,WA,WI

FINANCIAL/TERMS:
Cash Investment: $15.2-22.3K
Total Investment: $15.2-22.3K
Minimum Net Worth: $N/A
Fees: Franchise - $12.5K
Royalty - 6%; Ad. - None
Earnings Claim Statement: No
Term of Contract (Years): 10/10
Avg. # Of Employees: 1 FT
Passive Ownership: Not Allowed
Encourage Conversions: Yes
Area Develop. Agreements: No
Sub-Franchising Contracts: No
Expand In Territory: Yes
Space Needs: N/A SF; HB

SUPPORT & TRAINING PROVIDED:
Financial Assistance Provided: No
Site Selection Assistance: Yes
Lease Negotiation Assistance: N/A
Co-Operative Advertising: N/A
Franchisee Assoc./Member: No
Size Of Corporate Staff: 5
On-Going Support: a,b,C,D,E,G,H,I
Training: 2 Days Corporate at Sudbury, MA; 2 Days at Franchise; 1 Day at Franchise.

SPECIFIC EXPANSION PLANS:
US: All United States
Canada: All Canada
Overseas: No

≺≺ ≻≻

WEDDING GOWN SPECIALISTS/ RESTORATION

1270 Cedars Rd.
Lawrenceville, GA 30045
Tel: (800) 543-8987 (770) 998-3111
Fax: (770) 682-8736
Mr. Garah (Gary) I. Webster, Founder

Chemically restores discolored/stained wedding and christening gowns to true color without damage to fabric or dye. We also treat museum items, old quilts, etc.

BACKGROUND:
Established: 1987; 1st Franchised: 1987
Franchised Units: 119
Company-Owned Units 1
Total Units: 120
Dist.: US-100; CAN-10; O'seas-10
North America: 35 States, 4 Provinces
Density: 7 in OH, 5 in CA, 5 in NC
Projected New Units (12 Months): 15
Qualifications: 3, 3, 3, 3, 3, 3
Registered: NR

FINANCIAL/TERMS:
Cash Investment: $2.5K+
Total Investment: $2.5K+
Minimum Net Worth: $N/A
Fees: Franchise - $N/A
Royalty - 20% Fee; Ad. - 0%
Earnings Claim Statement: No
Term of Contract (Years): 1-Ind./1
Avg. # Of Employees: 1 FT, 1 PT
Passive Ownership: Discouraged
Encourage Conversions: No
Area Develop. Agreements: Yes/1-Indef.
Sub-Franchising Contracts: No
Expand In Territory: Yes
Space Needs: 500-1,000 SF; FS, SF, SC, RM, HB

SUPPORT & TRAINING PROVIDED:
Financial Assistance Provided: No
Site Selection Assistance: No
Lease Negotiation Assistance: No
Co-Operative Advertising: Yes
Franchisee Assoc./Member: Yes/Yes
Size Of Corporate Staff: 3
On-Going Support: b,c,d,G,h,I
Training: Not Required.

SPECIFIC EXPANSION PLANS:
US: All United States
Canada: All Canada
Overseas: All Free Nations

≺≺ ≻≻

SUPPLEMENTAL LISTING OF FRANCHISORS

APPARELMASTER USA, 104 Harrison Ave., Harrison, OH 45030 ; (877) 543-1678 (513) 202-1600; (513) 202-1660

COMET ONE-HOUR CLEANERS, 406 W. Division St., Arlington, TX 76011 ; (817) 461-3555; (817) 861-4779

DRY CLEANING STATION, 8301 Golden Valley Rd., # 230, Minneapolis, MN 55427 ; (800) 655-8134 (763) 541-0832; (763) 542-2246

DRYCLEAN - U. S. A., 290 NE 68th St., Miami, FL 33138-5520 ; (800) 746-4583 (305) 754-9966; (305) 754-8010

HANGERS CLEANERS, 7516 Precision Dr., Raleigh, NC 27613 ; (919) 313-2102; (919) 313-2103

Lawn & Garden

Chapter 22

Lawn & Garden Industry Profile

Total # Franchisors in Industry Group	23
Total # Franchised Units in Industry Group	1,385
Total # Company-Owned Units in Industry Group	416
Total # Operating Units in Industry Group	1,801
Average # Franchised Units/Franchisor	60.2
Average # Company-Owned Units/Franchisor	18.0
Average # Total Units/Franchisor	78.2
Ratio of Total # Franchised Units/Total # Company-Owned Units	3.3:1
Industry Survey Participants	11
Representing % of Industry	47.8%
Average Franchise Fee*:	$34.0K
Average Total Investment*:	$80.0K
Average On-Going Royalty Fee*:	6.9%

*If a range was provided, the mid-point of the range was used. See detailed profiles for actual ranges.

Five Largest Participants in Survey

Company	# Franchised Units	# Co-Owned Units	# Total Units	Franchise Fee	On-Going Royalty	Total Investment
1. Lawn Doctor	408	270	678	0K	10%	41K
2. Weed Man	161	0	161	20-34K	$8.8K/Vehicle	75K
3. Scotts Lawn Service	46	40	86	30-250K	6-10%	86-406K
4. U.S. Lawns	85	0	85	29K	3-4%	40-70K
5. Nitro-Green Professional Lawn and Tree Care	40	16	56	19.5K	7-8.5%	35-50K

All of the data provided are proprietary and should not be quoted without acknowledging *Bond's Franchise Guide.*

CLINTAR GROUNDSKEEPING SERVICES

70 Esna Park Dr., # 1
Markham, ON L3R 1E3 CANADA
Tel: (800) 361-3542 (905) 943-9530
Fax: (905) 943-9529
E-Mail: info@clintar.com
Web Site: www.clintar.com
Mr. Robert C. Wilton, President

Company provides a full-service, year-round grounds care service to Fortune 500 clients and government agencies. The average size business is $1,000,000. It provides landscape maintenance services, power sweeping, and snow and ice control services.

BACKGROUND:
Established: 1973; 1st Franchised: 1984
Franchised Units: 9
Company-Owned Units 1
Total Units: 10
Dist.: US-0; CAN-9; O'seas-0
North America: 1 Province
Density: 9 in ON
Projected New Units (12 Months): 2
Qualifications: 4, 5, 2, 3, 4, 5
Registered: NR

FINANCIAL/TERMS:
Cash Investment: $50-75K
Total Investment: $90-150K
Minimum Net Worth: $100K
Fees: Franchise - $30K
Royalty - 8%; Ad. - 0%
Earnings Claim Statement: No
Term of Contract (Years): 10/5
Avg. # Of Employees: 10 FT, 15 PT
Passive Ownership: Not Allowed
Encourage Conversions: Yes
Area Develop. Agreements: Yes
Sub-Franchising Contracts: No
Expand In Territory: Yes
Space Needs: 3,000 SF; FS, Multi-Unit Industrial

SUPPORT & TRAINING PROVIDED:
Financial Assistance Provided: Yes(I)
Site Selection Assistance: Yes
Lease Negotiation Assistance: Yes
Co-Operative Advertising: Yes
Franchisee Assoc./Member: Yes/Yes
Size Of Corporate Staff: 9
On-Going Support: a,B,C,D,E,F,H,I
Training: 2 Weeks in Toronto, ON.

SPECIFIC EXPANSION PLANS:
US: Northwest (Great Lakes Area)
Canada: All Canada
Overseas: No

<< >>

ENVIRO MASTERS LAWN CARE

P.O. Box 178
Caledon East, ON L0N 1E0 CANADA
Tel: (905) 584-9592
Fax: (905) 584-0402
Mr. Martin Fielding, President

Enjoy the Great Outdoors! and be part of a great new approach to lawn care. Organic and environmentally considerate. Home based. Excellent opportunity. Protected territories. Repeat business. Full training and marketing support. Business, turf management and in-field training.

BACKGROUND:
Established: 1987; 1st Franchised: 1991
Franchised Units: 17
Company-Owned Units 2
Total Units: 19
Dist.: US-0; CAN-19; O'seas-0
North America: NR
Density: NR
Projected New Units (12 Months): 6
Qualifications: 3, 2, 1, 2, 3, 3
Registered: NR

FINANCIAL/TERMS:
Cash Investment: $30-40K
Total Investment: $30-40K
Minimum Net Worth: $25K
Fees: Franchise - $15-25K
Royalty - 5%/2.5K; Ad. - 2%
Earnings Claim Statement: No
Term of Contract (Years): 10/10
Avg. # Of Employees: 1 FT, 1 PT
Passive Ownership: Discouraged
Encourage Conversions: Yes
Area Develop. Agreements: No
Sub-Franchising Contracts: Yes
Expand In Territory: No
Space Needs: NR SF; HB

SUPPORT & TRAINING PROVIDED:
Financial Assistance Provided: Yes(D)
Site Selection Assistance: Yes
Lease Negotiation Assistance: N/A
Co-Operative Advertising: Yes
Franchisee Assoc./Member: No
Size Of Corporate Staff: 4
On-Going Support: B,C,D,E,F,G,H,I
Training: 1-2 Weeks in Caledon East, ON.

SPECIFIC EXPANSION PLANS:
US: No
Canada: All Canada
Overseas: All Countries

<< >>

GREENLAND IRRIGATION

150 Ambleside Dr.
London, ON N6G 4R1 CANADA
Tel: (800) 661-0221 (519) 439-0220
Fax: (519) 433-9780
E-Mail: barrysmith@greenlandirrigation.com
Web Site: www.greenlandirrigation.com
Mr. Barry Smith, Vice President

Installation and service for lawn sprinklers' commercial and residential application. Complete training for TORO, Hunter, Rainbird and Nelson equipment. A niche market with tremendous opportunities.

BACKGROUND:
Established: 1986; 1st Franchised: 1995
Franchised Units: 12
Company-Owned Units 2
Total Units: 14
Dist.: US-0; CAN-14; O'seas-0
North America: 2 Provinces
Density: NR
Projected New Units (12 Months): 5
Qualifications: 4, 4, 2, 4, 4, 4
Registered: NR

FINANCIAL/TERMS:
Cash Investment: $25K
Total Investment: $25-50K
Minimum Net Worth: $100K
Fees: Franchise - $10K
Royalty - 10-3%; Ad. - 0%
Earnings Claim Statement: No
Term of Contract (Years): Lifetime
Avg. # Of Employees: 4 FT
Passive Ownership: Not Allowed
Encourage Conversions: No
Area Develop. Agreements: No
Sub-Franchising Contracts: No
Expand In Territory: Yes
Space Needs: N/A SF; HB

SUPPORT & TRAINING PROVIDED:
Financial Assistance Provided: Yes(I)
Site Selection Assistance: Yes
Lease Negotiation Assistance: N/A
Co-Operative Advertising: Yes
Franchisee Assoc./Member: No
Size Of Corporate Staff: 5
On-Going Support: A,B,C,D,E,G,H,I
Training: NR
SPECIFIC EXPANSION PLANS:
US: All United States
Canada: All Canada
Overseas: No

LAWN DOCTOR

142 State Rte. 34, P.O. Box 401
Holmdel, NJ 07733-2090
Tel: (800) 631-5660 (732) 946-0029
Fax: (732) 946-9089
E-Mail: franchiseinformation@lawndoctor.com
Web Site: www.lawndoctor.com
Mr. Edward L. Reid, National Franchise Sales Dir.

LAWN DOCTOR is an automated lawn care service. We use all natural and regular fertilization, plus control application, using our exclusive Turf Tamer equipment, manufactured and used only by LAWN DOCTOR, supplemented by a broad range of cultural care practices, utilizing integrated Pest Control Management to develop the health and beauty of turf and landscape areas with environmentally-balanced care.

BACKGROUND: IFA MEMBER
Established: 1967; 1st Franchised: 1967
Franchised Units: 408
Company-Owned Units 270
Total Units: 678
Dist.: US-350; CAN-0; O'seas-0
North America: 34 States
Density: 63 in NJ, 37 in NY, 35 in PA
Projected New Units (12 Months): 30
Qualifications: 3, 1, 1, 2, 1, 5
Registered: FL,IL,IN,MD,MI,MN,NY,RI,SD,VA,WI,DC
FINANCIAL/TERMS:
Cash Investment: $22K
Total Investment: $41K
Minimum Net Worth: $50K
Fees: Franchise - $0
Royalty - 10%; Ad. - 10%
Earnings Claim Statement: No
Term of Contract (Years): 20/5/5
Avg. # Of Employees: 2 PT
Passive Ownership: Discouraged
Encourage Conversions: Yes
Area Develop. Agreements: No
Sub-Franchising Contracts: No
Expand In Territory: Yes
Space Needs: N/A SF; HB
SUPPORT & TRAINING PROVIDED:
Financial Assistance Provided: Yes(D)
Site Selection Assistance: N/A
Lease Negotiation Assistance: No
Co-Operative Advertising: Yes
Franchisee Assoc./Member: Yes/Yes
Size Of Corporate Staff: 50
On-Going Support: B,C,D,G,H,I
Training: 2 Weeks NJ.
SPECIFIC EXPANSION PLANS:
US: All Except CA,WA,OR
Canada: No
Overseas: No

NATURALAWN OF AMERICA

1 E. Church St.
Frederick, MD 21701
Tel: (800) 989-5444 (301) 694-5440
Fax: (301) 846-0320
E-Mail: franchise@nl-amer.com
Web Site: www.nl-amer.com
Mr. Randy Loeb, VP Franchise Development

NATURALAWN of America is the only nationwide lawn care franchise offering an environmentally friendly lawn care service incorporating natural, organic-based fertilizers and biological controls. Our franchise owners provide residential and commercial customers with fertilization, weed control, insect control, disease control and lawn diagnosis services using safer and healthier products, eliminating the need for harsh chemicals and pesticides.

BACKGROUND:
Established: 1987; 1st Franchised: 1989
Franchised Units: 50
Company-Owned Units 4
Total Units: 54
Dist.: US-52; CAN-1; O'seas-0
North America: 25 States
Density: 6 in MD, 5 in PA, 5 in VA
Projected New Units (12 Months): 10-12
Qualifications: 4, 4, 1, 4, 3, 5
Registered: CA,FL,IL,IN,MD,MI,MN,NY,OR,VA,WA,WI
FINANCIAL/TERMS:
Cash Investment: $50K
Total Investment: $75-150K
Minimum Net Worth: $250K
Fees: Franchise - $29.5K
Royalty - Varies; Ad. - 0%
Earnings Claim Statement: Yes
Term of Contract (Years): 5/10
Avg. # Of Employees: 1-3 FT
Passive Ownership: Discouraged
Encourage Conversions: Yes
Area Develop. Agreements: No
Sub-Franchising Contracts: Yes
Expand In Territory: Yes
Space Needs: 1,200 SF; Warehouse
SUPPORT & TRAINING PROVIDED:
Financial Assistance Provided: Yes(I)
Site Selection Assistance: Yes
Lease Negotiation Assistance: Yes
Co-Operative Advertising: N/A
Franchisee Assoc./Member: No
Size Of Corporate Staff: 14
On-Going Support: A,B,C,D,E,F,G,h,I
Training: 1 Week Home Office; 1 Week Field Office; 1 Week OnSite.
SPECIFIC EXPANSION PLANS:
US: All United States
Canada: All Canada
Overseas: No

NITRO-GREEN PROFESSIONAL LAWN & TREE CARE

99 Weatherstone Dr., # 920
Woodstock, GA 30188
Tel: (888) 509-9500
Fax: (954) 340-7546
E-Mail: nitrogreen@mindspring.com
Web Site: www.nitrogreen.com
Mr. Randy Caldararo, Dir. Franchise Development

We award lawn and tree care franchises to qualified individuals who are willing to become an active partner with us. Our mission is to make the customer the focus of everything we do.

BACKGROUND:
Established: 1977; 1st Franchised: 1979
Franchised Units: 40
Company-Owned Units 16
Total Units: 56
Dist.: US-55; CAN-0; O'seas-0

North America: 14 States
Density: 8 in MT, 5 in ND, 5 in CA
Projected New Units (12 Months): 10
Qualifications: 5, 3, 2, 1, 4, 4
Registered: CA

FINANCIAL/TERMS:

Cash Investment: $35-40K
Total Investment: $35-50K
Minimum Net Worth: $50K
Fees: Franchise - $19.5K
Royalty - 7-8.5%; Ad. - N/A
Earnings Claim Statement: No
Term of Contract (Years): 20/10
Avg. # Of Employees: 1 FT, 1-2 PT
Passive Ownership: Allowed
Encourage Conversions: Yes
Area Develop. Agreements: No
Sub-Franchising Contracts: No
Expand In Territory: Yes
Space Needs: NR SF; FS, HB

SUPPORT & TRAINING PROVIDED:

Financial Assistance Provided: Yes(I)
Site Selection Assistance: Yes
Lease Negotiation Assistance: N/A
Co-Operative Advertising: Yes
Franchisee Assoc./Member: Yes/Yes
Size Of Corporate Staff: 8
On-Going Support: C,D,E,G,H,I
Training: Franchise and Company Locations.

SPECIFIC EXPANSION PLANS:

US: All United States
Canada: No
Overseas: No

<< >>

NUTRI-LAWN, ECOLOGY-FRIENDLY LAWN CARE

5397 Eglinton Ave. W., # 110
Toronto, ON M9C 5K6 CANADA
Tel: (800) 396-6096 (416) 620-7100
Fax: (416) 620-7771
E-Mail: nli@istar.ca
Web Site: www.nutri-lawn.com
Mr. Larry Maydonik, President

NUTRI-LAWN offers ecology-friendly lawn care to meet increasing consumer demand. We focus on fertilization and reduced control product usage through our spot treating and integrated pest management approach. We create large lawn care operations through our proven program and systems.

BACKGROUND: IFA MEMBER
Established: 1985; 1st Franchised: 1987
Franchised Units: 37
Company-Owned Units 0
Total Units: 37
Dist.: US-2; CAN-34; O'seas-1
North America: 2 States, 8 Provinces
Density: 20 in ON, 7 in BC
Projected New Units (12 Months): 6
Qualifications: 5, 4, 1, 3, 3, 5
Registered: VA

FINANCIAL/TERMS:

Cash Investment: $30-60K
Total Investment: $50-100K
Minimum Net Worth: $100K
Fees: Franchise - $25K
Royalty - 6%; Ad. - 1.5%
Earnings Claim Statement: No
Term of Contract (Years): 5/10
Avg. # Of Employees: 1 FT
Passive Ownership: Not Allowed
Encourage Conversions: Yes
Area Develop. Agreements: Yes
Sub-Franchising Contracts: No
Expand In Territory: Yes
Space Needs: 0 SF; SC

SUPPORT & TRAINING PROVIDED:

Financial Assistance Provided: No
Site Selection Assistance: Yes
Lease Negotiation Assistance: Yes
Co-Operative Advertising: Yes
Franchisee Assoc./Member: Yes/Yes
Size Of Corporate Staff: 4
On-Going Support: B,C,D,E,G,H
Training: 1 Week Toronto, ON.

SPECIFIC EXPANSION PLANS:

US: Northeast, Northwest
Canada: All Canada
Overseas: All Countries

<< >>

NUTRITE HYDRO AGRI CANADA

P.O. Box 1000
Brossard, PQ J4Z 3N2 CANADA
Tel: (800) 561-7449 (450) 462-2555
Fax: (450) 462-3634
E-Mail: Jacques.Cardinal@hydro.com
Mr. M. Jacques Cardinal, Dir. Franchising

Your venture - If you dream of starting your own business, or want to add new services to an existing business, you should think seriously about owning a NUTRITE LAWN CARE franchise. The bottom line is - A NUTRITE franchise is a wise investment. Join the NUTRITE group now!

BACKGROUND:
Established: 1967; 1st Franchised: 1984
Franchised Units: 43
Company-Owned Units 0
Total Units: 43
Dist.: US-0; CAN-44; O'seas-0
North America: 3 Provinces
Density: 37 in PQ, 5 in ON, 2 in NB
Projected New Units (12 Months): 3
Registered: CA

FINANCIAL/TERMS:

Cash Investment: $40K
Total Investment: $40K
Minimum Net Worth: $NR
Fees: Franchise - $10K
Royalty - $3.5K/Yr.; Ad. - 0%
Earnings Claim Statement: Yes
Term of Contract (Years): 5/5
Avg. # Of Employees: 2 FT
Passive Ownership: Allowed
Encourage Conversions: Yes
Area Develop. Agreements: No
Sub-Franchising Contracts: No
Expand In Territory: No
Space Needs: NR SF; NR

SUPPORT & TRAINING PROVIDED:

Financial Assistance Provided: No
Site Selection Assistance: Yes
Lease Negotiation Assistance: No
Co-Operative Advertising: No
Franchisee Assoc./Member: NR
Size Of Corporate Staff: 30
On-Going Support: A,B,C,D,F,G,h,i
Training: No Limit on Location.

SPECIFIC EXPANSION PLANS:

US: No
Canada: All Canada
Overseas: No

<< >>

SCOTTS LAWN SERVICE

14111 Scottslawn Rd.
Marysville, OH 43041
Tel: (800) 221-1760 (937) 644-7297
Fax: (937) 644-7422
E-Mail: jim_miller@scottslawnservice.com
Web Site: www.scottslawnservice.com
Mr. Jim Miller, Dir. Franchising

SCOTTS, the leading marketer of home lawn and garden products, has entered the lawn service business, the result ... SCOTTS LAWN SERVICE. As a franchise system, we offer very strong brand name awareness, powerful sales and marketing programs, extensive training and premium products.

BACKGROUND:
Established: 1998; 1st Franchised: 1998
Franchised Units: 46
Company-Owned Units 40
Total Units: 86
Dist.: US-86; CAN-0; O'seas-0
North America: NR
Density: 4 in OH, 3 in GA
Projected New Units (12 Months): 15
Qualifications: 4, 3, 3, 2, 2, 5
Registered: FL,IL,IN,MD,MI,MN,ND,OR,SD,VA,WA,WI

FINANCIAL/TERMS:
Cash Investment: $30-60K
Total Investment: $85.7-405.9K
Minimum Net Worth: $100-500K
Fees: Franchise - $30-250K
Royalty - 6-10%; Ad. - 0%
Earnings Claim Statement: Yes
Term of Contract (Years): 10/10
Avg. # Of Employees: 2+ FT
Passive Ownership: Discouraged
Encourage Conversions: Yes
Area Develop. Agreements: No
Sub-Franchising Contracts: No
Expand In Territory: Yes
Space Needs: 400 SF; FS, HB

SUPPORT & TRAINING PROVIDED:
Financial Assistance Provided: Yes(I)
Site Selection Assistance: N/A
Lease Negotiation Assistance: No
Co-Operative Advertising: N/A
Franchisee Assoc./Member: No
Size Of Corporate Staff: 20
On-Going Support: B,C,D,E,F,H,I
Training: 2 Weeks.

SPECIFIC EXPANSION PLANS:
US: All United States
Canada: Yes
Overseas: No

<< >>

U. S. LAWNS
4777 Old Winter Garden Rd.
Orlando, FL 33811
Tel: (800) 875-2967 (407) 522-1630
Fax: (407) 522-1669
E-Mail: info@uslawns.com
Web Site: www.uslawns.com
Mr. Paul C. Wolbert, Director of Development

Train and support franchisees in a commercial landscape market.

BACKGROUND: IFA MEMBER
Established: 1986; 1st Franchised: 1987
Franchised Units: 85
Company-Owned Units 0
Total Units: 85
Dist.: US-82; CAN-0; O'seas-0
North America: 14 States
Density: FL, MD, CA
Projected New Units (12 Months): 36
Qualifications: 2, 4, 3, 2, 3, 5
Registered: CA,FL,IL,MD,MI,VA,WI

FINANCIAL/TERMS:
Cash Investment: $10-40K
Total Investment: $40-70K
Minimum Net Worth: $50K
Fees: Franchise - $29K
Royalty - 3-4%; Ad. - 1%
Earnings Claim Statement: No
Term of Contract (Years): 5/5
Avg. # Of Employees: 8-10 FT
Passive Ownership: Discouraged
Encourage Conversions: Yes
Area Develop. Agreements: Yes
Sub-Franchising Contracts: No
Expand In Territory: Yes
Space Needs: NR SF; N/A

SUPPORT & TRAINING PROVIDED:
Financial Assistance Provided: Yes
Site Selection Assistance: Yes
Lease Negotiation Assistance: Yes
Co-Operative Advertising: Yes
Franchisee Assoc./Member: Yes/Yes
Size Of Corporate Staff: 18
On-Going Support: A,b,C,D,G,H,I
Training: 5 Days in FL; 5 Days at Your Location.

SPECIFIC EXPANSION PLANS:
US: PA,NJ,CT,MA,FL,CA,NC,SC
Canada: No
Overseas: No

<< >>

Weed Man

WEED MAN
50 Skagway Ave., # B
Toronto, ON M1M 3V1 CANADA
Tel: (888) 321-9333 (416) 269-5754
Fax: (416) 269-8233
E-Mail: turfholdings@aol.com
Web Site: www.weed-man.com
Ms. Jennifer Lemcke, VP Operations

Professional lawn care services.

BACKGROUND: IFA MEMBER
Established: 1970; 1st Franchised: 1976
Franchised Units: 161
Company-Owned Units 0
Total Units: 161
Dist.: US-40; CAN-120; O'seas-1
North America: 21 States,10 Provinces
Density: NR
Projected New Units (12 Months): 24
Qualifications: 3, 4, 1, 3, 3, 4
Registered: CA,CT,FL,IL,IN,KY,MD,MI,MN,ND,NE,NY,OR,RI,TX,WA,WI

FINANCIAL/TERMS:
Cash Investment: $25K
Total Investment: $75K
Minimum Net Worth: $50K
Fees: Franchise - $20-34K
Royalty - $8.8K/Vehcl.;
Ad. - 20% Royalty
Earnings Claim Statement: Yes
Term of Contract (Years): 10/10
Avg. # Of Employees: 5 FT
Passive Ownership: Discouraged
Encourage Conversions: Yes
Area Develop. Agreements: No
Sub-Franchising Contracts: Yes
Expand In Territory: Yes
Space Needs: NR SF; HB, SC

SUPPORT & TRAINING PROVIDED:
Financial Assistance Provided: No
Site Selection Assistance: Yes
Lease Negotiation Assistance: No
Co-Operative Advertising: Yes
Franchisee Assoc./Member: Yes
Size Of Corporate Staff: 9
On-Going Support: B,C,D,F,G,H
Training: 2 Weeks Scarborough, ON.

SPECIFIC EXPANSION PLANS:
US: All United States
Canada: All Canada
Overseas: Australia

<< >>

SUPPLEMENTAL LISTING OF FRANCHISORS

BOBBY LAWN CARE, P.O. Box 35062, London, ON N5W 5Z6 CANADA; (519) 455-5912; (519) 455-5915

GARDENER, THE, 300 John St., # 327, Thornhill, ON L3T 5W4 CANADA; (905) 889-1532; (800) 970-6947

JIM'S MOWING, 210 Lark Ln., Euless, TX 76039 ; (817) 684-0192;

LIQUI-GREEN LAWN & TREE CARE, 9601 N. Allen Rd., Peoria, IL 61615 ; (800) 747-5211 (309) 243-5815; (309) 243-5247

NATURE'S PRO, 382 S. Franklin St., Hempstead, NY 11550-6895 ; (800) 645-6464 (516) 538-6444; (516) 538-2042

SERVISTAR HOME & GARDEN SHOWPLACE, 8600 W. Bryn Mawr Ave., Chicago, IL 60631 ; (888) 474-9752 (773) 695-5379; (773) 695-7049

SPRING-GREEN LAWN CARE, 11909 Spaulding School Dr., Plainfield, IL 60544 (800) 435-4051 (815) 436-8777; (815) 436-9056

SUPER LAWNS, 15901 Derwood Rd., P.O. Box 5677, Rockville, MD 20855 ; (800) 44-LAWN1 (301) 948-8181; (301) 948-8461

TRUGREEN / CHEMLAWN, 855 Ridge Lake Blvd., Memphis, TN 38120 ; (800) 228-2814 (901) 681-2008; (901) 681-2010

TRUSERVE GROUNDSCARE, 70 Esna Park Dr., # 1, Markham, ON L3R 1E3 CANADA; (905) 943-9530; (905) 943-9529

Lodging

Chapter 23

Lodging Industry Profile

Total # Franchisors in Industry Group	74
Total # Franchised Units in Industry Group	28,676
Total # Company-Owned Units in Industry Group	3,581
Total # Operating Units in Industry Group	32,257
Average # Franchised Units/Franchisor	387.5
Average # Company-Owned Units/Franchisor	48.4
Average # Total Units/Franchisor	435.9
Ratio of Total # Franchised Units/Total # Company-Owned Units	8.0:1
Industry Survey Participants	21
Representing % of Industry	28.4 %
Average Franchise Fee*:	$31.7K
Average Total Investment*:	$3,621.0K
Average On-Going Royalty Fee*:	4.8%

*If a range was provided, the mid-point of the range was used. See detailed profiles for actual ranges.

Five Largest Participants in Survey

Company	# Franchised Units	# Co-Owned Units	# Total Units	Franchise Fee	On-Going Royalty	Total Investment
1. Cendant Corporation	6,588	0	6,588	Varies	Varies	205K-6.2MM
2. Choice Hotels International	4,371	0	4,371	25-50K	3.5-5.25%	4-6MM
3. Six Continent Hotels	2,751	510	3,261	$500/Room, 40K Min.	5%	Varies
4. Hampton Inn	1,136	27	1,163	45K	4% MGRR	4.9-8.7MM

AMERICINN INTERNATIONAL

250 Lake Dr. E.
Chanhassen, MN 55317-9364
Tel: (952) 294-5000
Fax: (952) 294-5001
E-Mail: franchise@americinn.com
Web Site: www.americinn.com
Mr. Jon D. Kennedy, SVP Mktg./Franchise Dev.

AMERICINN is an up-scale, limited-service, value-oriented chain. Currently, AMERICINN has over 190 franchises and continues to grow. Typically, the motels are located along major highways in cities with populations of between 10,000 and 300,000. AMERICINN has been successful with both travelers and vacationers because of their up-scale amenities and economy rates.

BACKGROUND:

Established: 1984; 1st Franchised: 1984
Franchised Units: 201
Company-Owned Units 6
Total Units: 207
Dist.: US-190; CAN-0; O'seas-0
North America: 20 States
Density: 72 in MN, 37 in WI, 22 in IA
Projected New Units (12 Months): 200
Qualifications: 5, 5, 4, 4, 4,
Registered: All States

FINANCIAL/TERMS:

Cash Investment: $25% Budget
Total Investment: $1.83MM
Minimum Net Worth: $1MM
Fees: Franchise - $35K
Royalty - 5%; Ad. - 2%
Earnings Claim Statement: No
Term of Contract (Years): 20
Avg. # Of Employees: 20 FT, 9 PT
Passive Ownership: Allowed
Encourage Conversions: N/A
Area Develop. Agreements: No
Sub-Franchising Contracts: No
Expand In Territory: Yes
Space Needs: 60,000 SF; FS

SUPPORT & TRAINING PROVIDED:

Financial Assistance Provided: Yes(I)
Site Selection Assistance: Yes
Lease Negotiation Assistance: Yes
Co-Operative Advertising: Yes
Franchisee Assoc./Member: Yes/Yes
Size Of Corporate Staff: 50
On-Going Support: a,b,C,D,E,G,H,I
Training: 3 Different Properties, 1 Week at Each.

SPECIFIC EXPANSION PLANS:

US: All United States
Canada: All Canada
Overseas: All Countries

<< >>

BAYMONT INNS & SUITES

250 E. Wisconsin Ave., # 1750
Milwaukee, WI 53202-4232
Tel: (414) 905-2000
Fax: (414) 905-2496
E-Mail: gilsimon@baymontinns.com
Web Site: www.baymontinns.com
Mr. Dick Kinney, Dir. Franchise Support Svcs.

BAYMONT INNS AND SUITES is positioned to appeal to both business and leisure travelers offering many amenities - frequent travelers' rewards, complimentary breakfast, voice mail, coffee makers and much more for $49.00 - 69.00.

BACKGROUND: IFA MEMBER

Established: 1935; 1st Franchised: 1986
Franchised Units: 79
Company-Owned Units 96
Total Units: 195
Dist.: US-172; CAN-0; O'seas-0
North America: 30 States
Density: 20 in MI, 18 in IL, 17 in WI
Projected New Units (12 Months): 40
Qualifications: 5, 5, 3, 2, 1, 3
Registered: All States

FINANCIAL/TERMS:

Cash Investment: $70%
Total Investment: $3.5MM+
Minimum Net Worth: $3MM
Fees: Franchise - $35K
Royalty - 5%; Ad. - 2%
Earnings Claim Statement: Yes
Term of Contract (Years): 20/10
Avg. # Of Employees: 4 FT, 12-18 PT
Passive Ownership: Allowed
Encourage Conversions: Yes
Area Develop. Agreements: Yes
Sub-Franchising Contracts: No
Expand In Territory: No
Space Needs: 2 Acres SF; FS

SUPPORT & TRAINING PROVIDED:

Financial Assistance Provided: Yes(I)
Site Selection Assistance: Yes
Lease Negotiation Assistance: No
Co-Operative Advertising: Yes
Franchisee Assoc./Member: Yes/Yes
Size Of Corporate Staff: 76
On-Going Support: C,D,E,G,H,I
Training: 1-2 Weeks Milwaukee, WI.

SPECIFIC EXPANSION PLANS:

US: All United States
Canada: All Canada
Overseas: No

<< >>

BEST INNS & SUITES

13 Corporate Sq., # 250
Atlanta, GA 30329
Tel: (800) TELL-US5 (404) 321-4045
Fax: (404) 321-4482
E-Mail: mikemuir@usfsi.com
Web Site: www.bestinn.com
Mr. Mike Muir, SVP Franchise Sales

BEST INNS & SUITES is a high-quality, mid-level, limited service hotel brand. With 145 hotels open, 31 under construction and another 26 signed agreements, BEST continues to expand around the country. BEST INNS & SUITES is primarily a conversion brand for existing hotel owners looking for a better way to do business. U. S. Franchise Systems, franchisor of the brand, is a recognized leader in the hotel industry, with 3 growing brands and a reputation for treating our franchisees fairly.

BACKGROUND: IFA MEMBER

Established: 1995; 1st Franchised: 1995
Franchised Units: 150
Company-Owned Units 0
Total Units: 150
Dist.: US-145; CAN-0; O'seas-0
North America: 35 States
Density: 17 in CA, 11 in IL, 9 in OR
Projected New Units (12 Months): 50
Qualifications: 3, 4, 4, 2, 2, 3
Registered: All States

FINANCIAL/TERMS:

Cash Investment: $190-330K
Total Investment: $190K-2.0MM
Minimum Net Worth: $N/A
Fees: Franchise - $35K
Royalty - 3-5%; Ad. - 2.5%
Earnings Claim Statement: Yes
Term of Contract (Years): 20/10
Avg. # Of Employees: 10-25 FT
Passive Ownership: Allowed
Encourage Conversions: Yes
Area Develop. Agreements: No

Sub-Franchising Contracts: No
Expand In Territory: Yes
Space Needs: NR SF; FS

SUPPORT & TRAINING PROVIDED:

Financial Assistance Provided: Yes(I)
Site Selection Assistance: No
Lease Negotiation Assistance: Yes
Co-Operative Advertising: Yes
Franchisee Assoc./Member: Yes/Yes
Size Of Corporate Staff: 135
On-Going Support: B,C,D,E,G,H,I
Training: 5 Days Atlanta, GA; 2-5 Days On-Site at Hotel.

SPECIFIC EXPANSION PLANS:

US: All United States
Canada: No
Overseas: No

<< >>

CANDLEWOOD SUITES/ CAMBRIDGE SUITES

8621 E. 21st St. N., # 200
Wichita, KS 67206
Tel: (316) 631-1361
Fax: (316) 631-1333
E-Mail: bgordon@candlewoodsuites.com
Web Site: www.candlewoodsuites.com
Mr. Chick Armstrong, VP Franchise Sales

CANDLEWOOD SUITES is a unique, high-quality, mid-priced hotel brand designed to deliver exceptional value to both owners and guests. CAMBRIDGE SUITES, established in 1998, is another tremendous opportunity to build or convert an existing hotel into the newest concept in lodging for the up-scale traveler.

BACKGROUND: IFA MEMBER

Established: 1995; 1st Franchised: 1996
Franchised Units: 23
Company-Owned Units 75
Total Units: 98
Dist.: US-98; CAN-0; O'seas-0
North America: 32 States
Density: 14 in TX, 8 in IL, 8 in CA
Projected New Units (12 Months): NR
Qualifications: 3, 3, 2, 2, 2, 3
Registered: All States Except HI

FINANCIAL/TERMS:

Cash Investment: $700K-2MM
Total Investment: $3-7MM
Minimum Net Worth: $N/A
Fees: Franchise - $400/Key/40K
Royalty - 4-5%RR; Ad. - 1.5%RR
Earnings Claim Statement: Yes
Term of Contract (Years): 20
Avg. # Of Employees: 6-13 FT
Passive Ownership: Allowed
Encourage Conversions: Yes
Area Develop. Agreements: No
Sub-Franchising Contracts: No
Expand In Territory: Yes
Space Needs: 56,628-108,90 SF; FS

SUPPORT & TRAINING PROVIDED:

Financial Assistance Provided: NR
Site Selection Assistance: No
Lease Negotiation Assistance: Yes
Co-Operative Advertising: No
Franchisee Assoc./Member: Yes/Yes
Size Of Corporate Staff: 100
On-Going Support: C,D,G,H,I
Training: Extensive Training Program.

SPECIFIC EXPANSION PLANS:

US: All United States
Canada: All Canada
Overseas: All Countries

<< >>

CENDANT CORPORATION

1 Sylvan Way
Parsippany, NJ 07054-3878
Tel: (800) 758-8999 (973) 428-9700
Fax: (973) 496-5915
Web Site: www.cendant.com
Ms. Nicole Johnson-Reece, Dir. Diversity/ Emerging Market

Franchisees looking for a hotel franchise to serve the growing business and leisure demand often turn to the Cendant portfolio of hotel brands. And for good reason. Cendant is the world's largest hotel franchisor with more than 6400 hotels, nearly 540,000 rooms and 5200 lodging franchisees. Cendant brands cover a wide cross-section of lodging markets, ranging from mid-priced, to economy to extended stay facilities, catering to both business and pleasure travelers.

BACKGROUND:

Established: 1990; 1st Franchised: 1990
Franchised Units: 6,588
Company-Owned Units 0
Total Units: 6,588
Dist.: US-6588; CAN-0; O'seas-0
North America: 50 States
Density: 478 in CA, 435 in TX, 423 FL
Projected New Units (12 Months): NR
Registered: NR

FINANCIAL/TERMS:

Cash Investment: $N/A
Total Investment: $205K-6.2MM
Minimum Net Worth: $N/A
Fees: Franchise - $Varies
Royalty - Varies; Ad. - Varies
Earnings Claim Statement: Yes
Term of Contract (Years): 15-20/N/A
Avg. # Of Employees: Varies
Passive Ownership: NR
Encourage Conversions: NR
Area Develop. Agreements: Yes-Int.
Sub-Franchising Contracts: NR
Expand In Territory: No
Space Needs: Varies SF; FS

SUPPORT & TRAINING PROVIDED:

Financial Assistance Provided: NR
Site Selection Assistance: No
Lease Negotiation Assistance: No
Co-Operative Advertising: Yes
Franchisee Assoc./Member: Yes
Size Of Corporate Staff: 724
On-Going Support: b,C,D,E,G,h,I
Training: Varies by Brand.

SPECIFIC EXPANSION PLANS:

US: All United States
Canada: NR
Overseas: NR

<< >>

CHOICE HOTELS CANADA

5090 Explorer Dr., # 500
Mississauga, ON L4W 4T9 CANADA
Tel: (905) 602-2222
Fax: (905) 624-7796
E-Mail: franchising@choicehotels.ca
Web Site: www.choicehotels.ca
Mr. Scott T. Duff, VP Franchise Development

Canada's largest hotel chain, with over 255 locations open and under development. We franchise 8 brands coast-to-coast: CLARION, QUALITY, COMFORT, COMFORT SUITES, SLEEP INN, RODEWAY INN, ECONO LODGE and MAINSTAY SUITES.

BACKGROUND:

Established: 1993; 1st Franchised: 1993
Franchised Units: 255
Company-Owned Units 0
Total Units: 255
Dist.: US-0; CAN-255; O'seas-0
North America: 10 Provinces

Density: 100 in ON, 40 in PQ,20 in AB
Projected New Units (12 Months): 35
Qualifications: 4, 5, 4, 3, 3, 4
Registered: AB

FINANCIAL/TERMS:
Cash Investment: $50% of Total
Total Investment: $2-10MM
Minimum Net Worth: $Varies
Fees: Franchise - $25-50K
Royalty - 3-5%; Ad. - 1.3%
Earnings Claim Statement: Yes
Term of Contract (Years): 20
Avg. # Of Employees: Varies
Passive Ownership: Allowed
Encourage Conversions: Yes
Area Develop. Agreements: No
Sub-Franchising Contracts: No
Expand In Territory: No
Space Needs: 60,000 SF; FS

SUPPORT & TRAINING PROVIDED:
Financial Assistance Provided: No
Site Selection Assistance: No
Lease Negotiation Assistance: N/A
Co-Operative Advertising: Yes
Franchisee Assoc./Member: Yes/Yes
Size Of Corporate Staff: 40
On-Going Support: A,B,C,D,e,G,h
Training: 3 Days to 1 Week On-Site Opening; 1-2 Day Seminar On-Going On-Site.

SPECIFIC EXPANSION PLANS:
US: No
Canada: All Canada
Overseas: No

CHOICE HOTELS INTERNATIONAL

10750 Columbia Pk.
Silver Spring, MD 20901-4447
Tel: (800) 547-0007 (301) 592-5000
Fax: (301) 592-6205
E-Mail: franchise_info@choicehotels.com
Web Site: www.choicehotels.com
Mr. Tom Mirgan, SVP Administration

CHOICE HOTELS INTERNATIONAL is one of the largest hotel franchises in the world with more than 4,000 hotels, inns, all-suite hotels and resorts in 36 countries under the brand names CLARION, QUALITY, COMFORT, SLEEP INN, RODEWAY INN, ECONO LODGE and MAINSTAY SUITES.

BACKGROUND: IFA MEMBER
Established: 1980; 1st Franchised: 1981
Franchised Units: 4,371
Company-Owned Units 0
Total Units: 4,371
Dist.: US-3234; CAN-234; O'seas-903
North America: 50 States,10 Provinces
Density: 223 in TX, 222 in CA, 191 FL
Projected New Units (12 Months): 300
Qualifications: 4, 4, 4, 2, 1, 1
Registered: All States

FINANCIAL/TERMS:
Cash Investment: $10-35% Dev. $
Total Investment: $4-6MM
Minimum Net Worth: $Varies
Fees: Franchise - $25-50K
Royalty - 3.5-5.25%; Ad. - 1-3.5% Rev.
Earnings Claim Statement: Yes
Term of Contract (Years): 20/None
Avg. # Of Employees: Varies
Passive Ownership: Allowed
Encourage Conversions: Yes
Area Develop. Agreements: No
Sub-Franchising Contracts: No
Expand In Territory: No
Space Needs: 31,000-33,000 SF; FS

SUPPORT & TRAINING PROVIDED:
Financial Assistance Provided: Yes(B)
Site Selection Assistance: No
Lease Negotiation Assistance: N/A
Co-Operative Advertising: N/A
Franchisee Assoc./Member: Yes/Yes
Size Of Corporate Staff: 2,025
On-Going Support: C,D,E,G,h,I
Training: 1 Week in Silver Spring, MD.

SPECIFIC EXPANSION PLANS:
US: All United States
Canada: All Canada
Overseas: All Countries

A cozy stay at a comfortable price®

COUNTRY INNS & SUITES BY CARLSON

P.O. Box 59159, Carlson Pkwy.
Minneapolis, MN 55459-8203
Tel: (800) 456-4000 (763) 212-2525
Fax: (763) 212-1338
E-Mail: njohnson@countryinns.com
Web Site: www.countryinns.com
Ms. Nancy Johnson, SVP Development

COUNTRY INNS & SUITES locations feature traditional architecture and sophisticated residential interior design with hardwood flooring and decorative ceiling borders. Each hotel welcomes guests with traditional furnishings that blend rich woods and elegant patterned fabrics. The brand is known for its consistently high-quality accommodations and personal, warm hospitality.

BACKGROUND: IFA MEMBER
Established: 1987; 1st Franchised: 1987
Franchised Units: 296
Company-Owned Units 4
Total Units: 300
Dist.: US-270; CAN-14; O'seas-16
North America: 37 States, 7 Provinces
Density: 38 in MN, 23 in WI, 22 in GA
Projected New Units (12 Months): 45
Qualifications: 5, 5, 5, 3, 5, 5
Registered: All States

FINANCIAL/TERMS:
Cash Investment: $780K-1.45MM
Total Investment: $3.1-5.4MM
Minimum Net Worth: $1MM
Fees: Franchise - $40K
Royalty - 4.5%; Ad. - 3%
Earnings Claim Statement: Yes
Term of Contract (Years): 15/0
Avg. # Of Employees: 10 FT, 6 PT
Passive Ownership: Allowed
Encourage Conversions: Yes
Area Develop. Agreements: No
Sub-Franchising Contracts: No
Expand In Territory: No
Space Needs: 65,340 SF; FS

SUPPORT & TRAINING PROVIDED:
Financial Assistance Provided: Yes(I)
Site Selection Assistance: No
Lease Negotiation Assistance: No
Co-Operative Advertising: Yes
Franchisee Assoc./Member: Yes/Yes
Size Of Corporate Staff: 41
On-Going Support: B,C,D,E,G,H
Training: 1 Week Minneapolis, MN (Brand Orientation); 3 Days Opening On-Site; 3 Days New Franchisee.

SPECIFIC EXPANSION PLANS:
US: All United States
Canada: All Canada
Overseas: Europe, Asia, South and Central America

<< >>

HAMPTON INN/HAMPTON INN & SUITES

9336 Civic Center Dr.
Beverly Hills, CA 90210
Tel: (800) 286-0645 (310) 278-4321

Fax: (310) 205-7655
E-Mail: bill_fortier@hilton.com
Web Site: www.hamptonfranchise.com
Mr. Bill Fortier, SVP Franchise Development

Hilton Hotels Corporation is recognized internationally as a preeminent hospitality company. The company develops, owns, manages or franchises more than 2,000 hotels, resorts and vacation ownership properties. Its portfolio includes many of the world's best known and most highly regarded hotel brands, including Hilton Conrad, Doubletree, Embassy Suites Hotels, HAMPTON INN, HAMPTON INN & SUITES, Harrison Conference Ctrs., Hilton Garden Inn, Hilton Grand Vacations Co. and Homewood Suites by Hilton.

BACKGROUND: IFA MEMBER
Established: 1983; 1st Franchised: 1983
Franchised Units: 1,136
Company-Owned Units <u>27</u>
Total Units: 1,163
Dist.: US-1142; CAN-11; O'seas-10
North America: 11 States
Density: 97 in FL, 80 in NC, 72 in GA
Projected New Units (12 Months): NR
Qualifications: 4, 5, 5, 2, 1, 3
Registered: All States

FINANCIAL/TERMS:
Cash Investment: $1.2MM-3.9MM
Total Investment: $4.9-8.7MM
Minimum Net Worth: $2MM
Fees: Franchise - $45K
Royalty - 4% MGRR; Ad. - 4% MGRR
Earnings Claim Statement: Yes
Term of Contract (Years): 20/N/A
Avg. # Of Employees: 4 FT, 14 PT
Passive Ownership: Allowed
Encourage Conversions: Yes
Area Develop. Agreements: No
Sub-Franchising Contracts: No
Expand In Territory: Yes
Space Needs: 1.5-3 Acres SF; FS

SUPPORT & TRAINING PROVIDED:
Financial Assistance Provided: No
Site Selection Assistance: Yes
Lease Negotiation Assistance: No
Co-Operative Advertising: Yes
Franchisee Assoc./Member: No
Size Of Corporate Staff: 200+
On-Going Support: A,b,C,D,E,G,H,I
Training: 3 Days of New Owner Orientation; 10 Days of GM Training.

SPECIFIC EXPANSION PLANS:
US: All United States
Canada: All Canada
Overseas: Mexico & Latin America

<< >>

HAWTHORN SUITES®

HAWTHORN SUITES HOTELS INTERNATIONAL

13 Corporate Sq., # 250
Atlanta, GA 30329
Tel: (888) 777-7511 (404) 321-4045
Fax: (404) 321-4482
E-Mail: franchise.info@usfsi.com
Web Site: www.hawthorn.com
Mr. Tim Muir, SVP Franchise Dales/Dev.

HAWTHORN SUITES is one of the fastest-growing suite-oriented hotel brands in the US. With 140 hotels open, 23 under construction and another 115 executed agreements in place, HAWTHORN continues to expand in major and tertiary markets. The Hyatt reservations systems provides reservations referrals for HAWTHORN when a Hyatt is unavailable in the same market. Proven track record of successful development, strong operating performance and sustainable growth in mid- to upper-level market.

BACKGROUND: IFA MEMBER
Established: 1995; 1st Franchised: 1995
Franchised Units: 140
Company-Owned Units <u>0</u>
Total Units: 140
Dist.: US-139; CAN-0; O'seas-1
North America: 40 States
Density: 13 in TX, 11 in OR, 10 in IL
Projected New Units (12 Months): 25
Qualifications: 4, 4, 4, 2, 2, 3
Registered: All States

FINANCIAL/TERMS:
Cash Investment: $500K-2.0MM
Total Investment: $3.1-6.9MM
Minimum Net Worth: $N/A
Fees: Franchise - $40K
Royalty - 5%; Ad. - 2.5%
Earnings Claim Statement: Yes
Term of Contract (Years): 20/10
Avg. # Of Employees: 20-100FT
Passive Ownership: Allowed
Encourage Conversions: Yes
Area Develop. Agreements: No
Sub-Franchising Contracts: No
Expand In Territory: Yes
Space Needs: NR SF; FS

SUPPORT & TRAINING PROVIDED:
Financial Assistance Provided: Yes(I)
Site Selection Assistance: No
Lease Negotiation Assistance: Yes
Co-Operative Advertising: Yes
Franchisee Assoc./Member: Yes/Yes
Size Of Corporate Staff: 135
On-Going Support: B,C,D,E,G,H,I
Training: 5 Days Training in Atlanta, GA; 5 Days Sales Training in Atlanta, GA.

SPECIFIC EXPANSION PLANS:
US: All United States
Canada: All Canada
Overseas: Europe, South America, Latin America.

HOSPITALITY INTERNATIONAL

1726 Montreal Cir.
Tucker, GA 30084
Tel: (800) 892-8405 (770) 270-1180
Fax: (770) 270-1077
Web Site: www.reservahost.com
Ms. Chhaya Patel, Franchise Development Coord.

Hotel franchisor of MASTER HOSTS INNS AND RESORTS, RED CARPET INN, SCOTTISH INNS, PASSPORT INN, DOWNTOWNER INNS, with over 252 franchised properties. HOSPITALITY INTERNATIONAL is proud of the fact that approximately 75% of its current franchisees are minorities. The company is actively pursuing the addition of new minority-owned franchises in all of the U.S.

BACKGROUND:
Established: 1982; 1st Franchised: 1982
Franchised Units: 252
Company-Owned Units <u>0</u>
Total Units: 252
Dist.: US-252; CAN-0; O'seas-0
North America: 32 States
Density: 30 in FL, 39 in GA, 18 in TN

Projected New Units (12 Months): 25
Qualifications: 3, 5, 4, 3, 2, 5
Registered: All States Except HI,WA

FINANCIAL/TERMS:

Cash Investment: $70-200K
Total Investment: $1.0-5.0MM
Minimum Net Worth: $Varies
Fees: Franchise - $2.5-5K
Royalty - 3-4%; Ad. - 2%
Earnings Claim Statement: No
Term of Contract (Years): 5
Avg. # Of Employees: 6 FT, 3 PT
Passive Ownership: Allowed
Encourage Conversions: Yes
Area Develop. Agreements: No
Sub-Franchising Contracts: No
Expand In Territory: N/A
Space Needs: 288/Guest SF; N/A

SUPPORT & TRAINING PROVIDED:

Financial Assistance Provided: Yes(I)
Site Selection Assistance: Yes
Lease Negotiation Assistance: Yes
Co-Operative Advertising: Yes
Franchisee Assoc./Member: Yes/Yes
Size Of Corporate Staff: 36
On-Going Support: B,C,D,E,G,H,I
Training: 2 Days in Tucker, GA.

SPECIFIC EXPANSION PLANS:

US: All United States
Canada: All Canada
Overseas: Mexico, Asia, South America

<< >>

KAMPGROUNDS OF AMERICA / KOA

P.O. Box 30558
Billings, MT 59114
Tel: (800) 548-7239 (406) 248-7444
Fax: (406) 254-7440
E-Mail: licensing@koa.net
Web Site: www.koakampgrounds.com
Mr. Arthur Peterson, CEO

KAMPGROUNDS OF AMERICA is North America's largest franchise system of open-to-the public campgrounds; no membership fees or annual dues are required. All KOA campgrounds offer RV and tent sites; 90% also offer Kamping Kabins. Nearly 2 million copies of the KOA directory are printed and distributed to campers. KOA campgrounds are located in 45 of the contiguous United States, 8 Canadian Provinces, Mexico and Japan.

BACKGROUND: IFA MEMBER
Established: 1961; 1st Franchised: 1962
Franchised Units: 496
Company-Owned Units 12
Total Units: 508
Dist.: US-463; CAN-34; O'seas-11
North America: 45 States, 8 Provinces
Density: 30 in CA, 30 in FL, 29 in CO
Projected New Units (12 Months): 8
Qualifications: 5, 3, 2, 3, 4, 4
Registered: All States

FINANCIAL/TERMS:

Cash Investment: $100-500K
Total Investment: $200K-4MM
Minimum Net Worth: $200K
Fees: Franchise - $25K
Royalty - 8%; Ad. - 2%
Earnings Claim Statement: Yes
Term of Contract (Years): 10/10
Avg. # Of Employees: 5 PT (Varies)
Passive Ownership: Discouraged
Encourage Conversions: Yes
Area Develop. Agreements: No
Sub-Franchising Contracts: No
Expand In Territory: Yes
Space Needs: 5+ acres SF; NR

SUPPORT & TRAINING PROVIDED:

Financial Assistance Provided: No
Site Selection Assistance: Yes
Lease Negotiation Assistance: Yes
Co-Operative Advertising: Yes
Franchisee Assoc./Member: Yes/Yes
Size Of Corporate Staff: 65
On-Going Support: A,B,C,D,E,F,G,h,I
Training: 2 Days at Customer Location; 3 Days at Billings, MT; 5 Days at Billings, MT.

SPECIFIC EXPANSION PLANS:

US: All United States
Canada: All Canada
Overseas: Europe, Central America, Mexico

<< >>

MICROTEL INNS & SUITES

13 Corporate Sq., # 250
Atlanta, GA 30329-1906
Tel: (888) 771-7171 (404) 321-4045
Fax: (404) 235-7460
E-Mail: franchise.info@usfsi.com
Web Site: www.microtelinn.com
Mr. Tim Muir, SVP Franchise Sales/Dev.

MICROTEL INNS & SUITES is one of the fastest-growing, all-new construction budget hotel franchise brands in the US. With nearly 215 hotels open, 37 under construction and another 226 signed agreements in place, MICROTEL is positioned for continued growth. MICROTEL offers a proven track record of successful development, strong operating performance and sustainable growth in the budget market. If you are looking to build a budget hotel, you need to look into MICROTEL.

BACKGROUND: IFA MEMBER
Established: 1995; 1st Franchised: 1995
Franchised Units: 255
Company-Owned Units 0
Total Units: 255
Dist.: US-252; CAN-0; O'seas-3
North America: 46 States
Density: 15 in TX, 12 in NC, 11 in TN
Projected New Units (12 Months): 35
Qualifications: 3, 4, 4, 2, 2, 3
Registered: All States

FINANCIAL/TERMS:

Cash Investment: $400-600K
Total Investment: $2.5-3.4MM
Minimum Net Worth: $N/A
Fees: Franchise - $35K
Royalty - 4-6%; Ad. - 2-3%
Earnings Claim Statement: Yes
Term of Contract (Years): 20/10
Avg. # Of Employees: 10-25 FT
Passive Ownership: Allowed
Encourage Conversions: No
Area Develop. Agreements: No
Sub-Franchising Contracts: No
Expand In Territory: Yes
Space Needs: NR SF; FS

SUPPORT & TRAINING PROVIDED:

Financial Assistance Provided: Yes(I)
Site Selection Assistance: No
Lease Negotiation Assistance: Yes
Co-Operative Advertising: Yes
Franchisee Assoc./Member: Yes/Yes
Size Of Corporate Staff: 135
On-Going Support: B,C,D,E,G,H,I
Training: 5 Days Training in Atlanta, GA.

SPECIFIC EXPANSION PLANS:

US: All United States
Canada: All Canada
Overseas: Europe, South America

<< >>

MOTEL 6
14651 Dallas Pkwy., # 500
Dallas, TX 75254
Tel: (888) 668-3503 (972) 702-6951
Fax: (972) 702-3610
E-Mail: arcinfo@airmail.net
Web Site: www.motel6.com
Mr. Dean Savas, SVP of Franchising

MOTEL 6 has a quality product, proven operational results, easy to operate. Many open markets are available. MOTEL 6 is a well established brand. Part of ACCOR ECONOMY LODGING organization. Largest owner/operator of economy lodging in the U.S.

BACKGROUND: IFA MEMBER
Established: 1962; 1st Franchised: 1996
Franchised Units: 127
Company-Owned Units 688
Total Units: 815
Dist.: US-811; CAN-4; O'seas-0
North America: 48 States
Density: 164 in CA, 103 in TX, 44 AZ
Projected New Units (12 Months): 29
Qualifications: 4, 4, 1, 1, 1, 3
Registered: All States

FINANCIAL/TERMS:
Cash Investment: $100-500K
Total Investment: $1.8-2.2MM
Minimum Net Worth: $1.5MM
Fees: Franchise - $25K
Royalty - 4%; Ad. - 3.5%
Earnings Claim Statement: Yes
Term of Contract (Years): 10-15/10
Avg. # Of Employees: 2-4 FT, 4-10 PT
Passive Ownership: Allowed
Encourage Conversions: Yes
Area Develop. Agreements: Yes/2-5
Sub-Franchising Contracts: No
Expand In Territory: No
Space Needs: 15,000 SF; FS

SUPPORT & TRAINING PROVIDED:
Financial Assistance Provided: Yes(I)
Site Selection Assistance: N/A
Lease Negotiation Assistance: No
Co-Operative Advertising: Yes
Franchisee Assoc./Member: Yes/Yes
Size Of Corporate Staff: 537
On-Going Support: A,B,C,D,E,G,h,I
Training: 1.5 Weeks Dallas, TX for Owners and Managers.

SPECIFIC EXPANSION PLANS:
US: All United States
Canada: All Canada
Overseas: No

RAMADA FRANCHISE CANADA
36 Toronto St., # 750
Toronto, ON M5C 2C5 CANADA
Tel: (800) 249-4656 (416) 361-1010
Fax: (416) 361-9577
E-Mail: wadamson@afmcorp.com
Web Site: www.ramada.ca
Mr. Warren B. Adamson, President

Multi-tiered hotel franchise organization, with representation across Canada. 41 PLAZA INN and limited properties comprising good rooms nationwide. Franchise offers marketing, training, advertising, loyalty programs and site selection.

BACKGROUND: IFA MEMBER
Established: 1991; 1st Franchised: 1992
Franchised Units: 63
Company-Owned Units 0
Total Units: 63
Dist.: US-0; CAN-41; O'seas-0
North America: 8 Provinces
Density: 20 in ON, 12 in BC, 4 in PQ
Projected New Units (12 Months): 8-10
Qualifications: 5, 4, 1, 5, 1, 5
Registered: AB

FINANCIAL/TERMS:
Cash Investment: $1-7MM
Total Investment: $2-20MM
Minimum Net Worth: $Varies
Fees: Franchise - $35K
Royalty - 3%; Ad. - 4%
Earnings Claim Statement: No
Term of Contract (Years): 5/5/5/5
Avg. # Of Employees: 0.4/Room; 80FT, 20PT
Passive Ownership: Allowed
Encourage Conversions: Yes
Area Develop. Agreements: Yes/5
Sub-Franchising Contracts: No
Expand In Territory: Yes
Space Needs: NR SF; FS

SUPPORT & TRAINING PROVIDED:
Financial Assistance Provided: N/A
Site Selection Assistance: Yes
Lease Negotiation Assistance: Yes
Co-Operative Advertising: Yes
Franchisee Assoc./Member: Yes/Yes
Size Of Corporate Staff: 15
On-Going Support: A,B,C,D,E,G,H,I
Training: 3-5 Days On-Site.

SPECIFIC EXPANSION PLANS:
US: No
Canada: All Canada
Overseas: No

<< >>

RED ROOF INNS
14651 Dallas Pkwy., # 500
Dallas, TX 75254
Tel: (888) 668-3503 (972) 702-6951
Fax: (972) 702-3610
E-Mail: arcinfo@airmail.net
Web Site: www.redroof.com
Mr. Dean Savas, SVP of Franchising

RED ROOF has quality product, proven operational results and is easy to operate. Many open markets are available. RED ROOF is a well established brand. Part of ACCOR ECONOMY LODGING's organization. Largest owner/operator of economy lodging in the US.

BACKGROUND: IFA MEMBER
Established: 1972; 1st Franchised: 1996
Franchised Units: 101
Company-Owned Units 259
Total Units: 360
Dist.: US-360; CAN-0; O'seas-0
North America: 39 States
Density: 37 in OH, 25 in TX, 22 in GA
Projected New Units (12 Months): 17
Qualifications: 4, 4, 1, 1, 1, 3
Registered: All States

FINANCIAL/TERMS:
Cash Investment: $100-500K
Total Investment: $2.6-3.4MM
Minimum Net Worth: $1.5MM
Fees: Franchise - $30K
Royalty - 4.5-5%; Ad. - 4%
Earnings Claim Statement: Yes
Term of Contract (Years): 20/10
Avg. # Of Employees: 2-4 FT, 4-10 PT
Passive Ownership: Allowed
Encourage Conversions: Yes

Area Develop. Agreements: No
Sub-Franchising Contracts: No
Expand In Territory: No
Space Needs: 15,000+ SF; FS
SUPPORT & TRAINING PROVIDED:
Financial Assistance Provided: Yes(I)
Site Selection Assistance: N/A
Lease Negotiation Assistance: No
Co-Operative Advertising: Yes
Franchisee Assoc./Member: Yes/Yes
Size Of Corporate Staff: 537
On-Going Support: A,B,C,D,E,G,h,I
Training: 2.5 Weeks Columbus, OH.
SPECIFIC EXPANSION PLANS:
US: All United States
Canada: All Canada
Overseas: No

<< >>

Top 50

SIX CONTINENTS HOTELS
3 Ravinia Dr., # 2900
Atlanta, GA 30346-2118
Tel: (770) 604-2107
Fax: (770) 604-8442
E-Mail: brown.kessler@6c.com
Web Site: www.sixcontinenthotels.com
Mr. Brown Kessler, VP Franchise Sales/ Dev.

SIX CONTINENTS HOTELS is the world's global hotel company. Operates or franchises more than 3,260 hotels and 514,000 guest rooms in more than 100 countries. Franchisor of INTER-CONTINENTAL HOTELS, CROWNE PLAZA HOTELS, HOLIDAY INN, HOLIDAY INN EXPRESS AND STAYBRIDGE SUITES HOTELS.

BACKGROUND: IFA MEMBER
Established: 1952; 1st Franchised: 1952
Franchised Units: 2,751
Company-Owned Units 510
Total Units: 3,261
Dist.: US-; CAN-; O'seas-
North America: 50 States
Density: 186 in CA,183 in TX, 167 FL
Projected New Units (12 Months): 100+
Qualifications: 5, 4, 4
Registered: All States and AB
FINANCIAL/TERMS:
Cash Investment: $1-20MM
Total Investment: $Varies
Minimum Net Worth: $Varies
Fees: Franchise - $500/Rm,40Kmin
Royalty - 5%; Ad. - 2.5-3%
Earnings Claim Statement: Yes
Term of Contract (Years): 10/10
Avg. # Of Employees: Varies
Passive Ownership: Allowed
Encourage Conversions: Yes
Area Develop. Agreements: No
Sub-Franchising Contracts: No
Expand In Territory: Yes
Space Needs: NR SF; FS
SUPPORT & TRAINING PROVIDED:
Financial Assistance Provided: Yes(I)
Site Selection Assistance: Yes
Lease Negotiation Assistance: No
Co-Operative Advertising: Yes
Franchisee Assoc./Member: Yes
Size Of Corporate Staff: 1,000
On-Going Support: C,D,E,H,I
Training: 4 - 5 Days Atlanta, GA. 4 - 5 Days Regional.
SPECIFIC EXPANSION PLANS:
US: All United States
Canada: All Canada
Overseas: All Countries

<< >>

STUDIO 6
14651 Dallas Pkwy., # 500
Dallas, TX 75254
Tel: (888) 668-3503 (972) 702-6951
Fax: (972) 702-3610
E-Mail: arcinfo@airmail.net
Web Site: www.motel6.com
Mr. Dean Savas, SVP of Franchising

STUDIO 6 is part of the ACCOR ECONOMY LODGING organization. Largest owner/operator of economy lodging in the US. Designed for travelers staying 5 nights or longer. STUDIO 6 has furnished studios and fully-equipped kitchens, including refrigerators and microwaves, at affordable rates.

BACKGROUND: IFA MEMBER
Established: 1962; 1st Franchised: 1999
Franchised Units: 2
Company-Owned Units 35
Total Units: 37
Dist.: US-33; CAN-4; O'seas-0
North America: 11 States
Density: 17 in TX, 4 in GA
Projected New Units (12 Months): 2
Qualifications: 4, 4, 1, 1, 1, 3
Registered: All States
FINANCIAL/TERMS:
Cash Investment: $100-500K
Total Investment: $2.7-3.4MM
Minimum Net Worth: $1.5MM
Fees: Franchise - $25K
Royalty - 5%; Ad. - 2%
Earnings Claim Statement: No
Term of Contract (Years): 10-15/10
Avg. # Of Employees: 2-4 FT, 4-10 PT
Passive Ownership: Allowed
Encourage Conversions: Yes
Area Develop. Agreements: No
Sub-Franchising Contracts: No
Expand In Territory: No
Space Needs: 15,000 SF; FS
SUPPORT & TRAINING PROVIDED:
Financial Assistance Provided: Yes(I)
Site Selection Assistance: N/A
Lease Negotiation Assistance: No
Co-Operative Advertising: No
Franchisee Assoc./Member: No/No
Size Of Corporate Staff: 537
On-Going Support: A,B,C,D,E,G,h,I
Training: 2 Weeks in Dallas, TX for Owners and Managers.
SPECIFIC EXPANSION PLANS:
US: All United States
Canada: All Canada
Overseas: No

<< >>

U. S. FRANCHISE SYSTEMS
13 Corporate Sq., # 250
Atlanta, GA 30329
Tel: (404) 321-4045
Fax: (404) 321-4482
E-Mail: tim.muir@usfsi.com
Web Site: www.usfsi.com
Mr. Michael Leven, President/CEO

Hotel franchisor of MICROTEL INNS & SUITES, BEST INNS & SUITES and HAWTHORN SUITES brands. MICROTEL -- all new construction, budget. BEST INNS -- middle level limited service. HAWTHORN -- upscale, suite-oriented brand. USFS is known as the "fair franchisor" with the most 2-sided agreement, lower than average fee structure, and no-hidden fees. Brands range from low-capital requirements (MICROTEL) to high (HAWTHORN).

BACKGROUND:
Established: 1995; 1st Franchised: 1995
Franchised Units: 517
Company-Owned Units 0
Total Units: 517
Dist.: US-430; CAN-3; O'seas-78
North America: 49 States
Density: NR
Projected New Units (12 Months): 60
Qualifications: 4, 4, 4, 3, 3, 4
Registered: All States

FINANCIAL/TERMS:
Cash Investment: $300K-2MM
Total Investment: $1.2-7MM
Minimum Net Worth: $N/A
Fees: Franchise - $35-40K
Royalty - 5-6%; Ad. - 2.5%
Earnings Claim Statement: Yes
Term of Contract (Years): 20/10
Avg. # Of Employees: 10-25 FT
Passive Ownership: Allowed
Encourage Conversions: Yes
Area Develop. Agreements: No
Sub-Franchising Contracts: No
Expand In Territory: Yes
Space Needs: 45,000 SF; FS, Raw land for development

SUPPORT & TRAINING PROVIDED:
Financial Assistance Provided: Yes(I)
Site Selection Assistance: No
Lease Negotiation Assistance: Yes
Co-Operative Advertising: No
Franchisee Assoc./Member: Yes
Size Of Corporate Staff: 150
On-Going Support: B,C,D,E,G,H,I
Training: 3-4 Days Atlanta, GA; On-Site as Needed.

SPECIFIC EXPANSION PLANS:
US: All United States
Canada: All Canada
Overseas: All Countries

<< >>

WOODFIELD SUITES

250 E. Wisconsin Ave., # 1750
Milwaukee, WI 53202
Tel: (414) 905-1376
Fax: (414) 905-2496
Web Site: www.budgetelinns.com
Mr. Daniel Daniele, SVP Development

WOODFIELD SUITES is positioned to appeal to both business and longer term business travelers offering many amenities - complimentary executive continental breakfast, complimentary hospitality and Jacuzzi suites and fully-equipped kitchens available in all suites, including a microwave, oven, refrigerator, coffeemaker. Suites also include an ironing board, hair dryer and voice mail.

BACKGROUND: IFA MEMBER
Established: 1988; 1st Franchised: 1998
Franchised Units: 0
Company-Owned Units 8
Total Units: 8
Dist.: US-8; CAN-0; O'seas-0
North America: 5 States
Density: 3 in WI, 1 in IL, 1 in TX
Projected New Units (12 Months): 0
Qualifications: 5, 5, 3, 2, 1, 3
Registered: All States

FINANCIAL/TERMS:
Cash Investment: $70%
Total Investment: $8.6-9.8MM
Minimum Net Worth: $8-9MM
Fees: Franchise - $30K
Royalty - 4.5%; Ad. - 1%
Earnings Claim Statement: No
Term of Contract (Years): 20/0
Avg. # Of Employees: 9 FT, 18-23 PT
Passive Ownership: Allowed
Encourage Conversions: Yes
Area Develop. Agreements: No
Sub-Franchising Contracts: No
Expand In Territory: Yes
Space Needs: 130,680 (3ac) SF; FS

SUPPORT & TRAINING PROVIDED:
Financial Assistance Provided: No
Site Selection Assistance: Yes
Lease Negotiation Assistance: No
Co-Operative Advertising: Yes
Franchisee Assoc./Member: No
Size Of Corporate Staff: 4
On-Going Support: C,d,e,h,I
Training: 1 Week in Milwaukee, WI.

SPECIFIC EXPANSION PLANS:
US: All United States
Canada: No
Overseas: No

<< >>

YOGI BEAR JELLYSTONE PARK CAMP-RESORTS

50 W. TechnaCentre Dr., # G
Milford, OH 45150-9798
Tel: (800) 626-3720 (513) 831-2100
Fax: (513) 576-8670
Web Site: www.campjellystone.com
Mr. Robert E. Schutter, Jr., President/COO

A unique recreation camp-resort for the entire family. YOGI and friends offer daily activities with a full amenity package, clean restrooms and YOGI souvenirs. Each camp-resort is independently owned and operated and maintains system standards.

BACKGROUND:
Established: 1969; 1st Franchised: 1969
Franchised Units: 68
Company-Owned Units 0
Total Units: 68
Dist.: US-66; CAN-5; O'seas-0
North America: 25 States, 2 Provinces
Density: 8 in IN, 7 in MI, 7 in WI
Projected New Units (12 Months): 4
Registered: CA,FL,IL,IN,MD,MI,MN, NY,VA,WI

FINANCIAL/TERMS:
Cash Investment: $30K
Total Investment: $30K
Minimum Net Worth: $NR
Fees: Franchise - $20-30K
Royalty - 6%; Ad. - 1%
Earnings Claim Statement: NR
Term of Contract (Years): 5-20/5-10
Avg. # Of Employees: 3 FT, 25 PT
Passive Ownership: Discouraged
Encourage Conversions: Yes
Area Develop. Agreements: No
Sub-Franchising Contracts: No
Expand In Territory: No
Space Needs: NR SF; NR

SUPPORT & TRAINING PROVIDED:
Financial Assistance Provided: Yes(D)
Site Selection Assistance: Yes
Lease Negotiation Assistance: Yes
Co-Operative Advertising: Yes
Franchisee Assoc./Member: NR
Size Of Corporate Staff: 6
On-Going Support: B,C,D,E,G,H,I
Training: 2-3 Days On-Site; 3-4 Days Headquarters; 1-3 Days/Year On-Site.

SPECIFIC EXPANSION PLANS:
US: All United States
Canada: All Canada
Overseas: No

<< >>

SUPPLEMENTAL LISTING OF FRANCHISORS

AMERISUITES, 700 Rte. 46 E., Fairfield, NJ 07007 ; (888) 778-3111 (973) 882-1010; (973) 882-1991

BUDGETEL INNS, 250 E. Wisconsin Ave., # 1750, Milwaukee, WI 53202 ; (414) 905-1376; (414) 905-2496

CASTLETON, 3400 Encrete Ln., Dayton, OH 45439 ; (800) 554-8265 (937) 294-8265; (937) 534-0426

CLUB HOTELS BY DOUBLETREE, 755 Crossover Ln., Memphis, TN 38117 ; (901) 374-5000; (901) 374-5008

CLUBHOUSE INNS OF AMERICA, 1950 Stemmons Fwy., # 6001, Dallas, TX 75207 ; (214) 863-1000; (214) 863-1665

COURTYARD BY MARRIOTT, 1 Marriott Dr., Dept. 55/514.01, Washington, DC 20058 ; (301) 380-7658; (301) 380-6699

DAYS INNS OF AMERICA, 1 Sylvan Way, Parsippany, NJ 07054-3878 ; (800) 952-3297 (973) 428-9700; (973) 496-7658

DOUBLETREE HOTEL SYSTEMS, 9336 Civic Center Dr., Beverly Hills, CA 90210 ; (800) 286-0645 (310) 378-4321; (310) 205-7655

DOWNTOWNER INNS, 1726 Montreal Cir., Tucker, GA 30084 ; (800) 892-8405 (770) 270-1180; (770) 270-1077

EMBASSY SUITES HOTELS, 9336 Civic Center Dr., Beverly Hills, CA 90210 ; (800) 286-0645 (310) 278-4321; (310) 205-7655

FAIRFIELD INN BY MARRIOTT, 1 Marriott Dr., Dept. 55/514.01, Washington, DC 20058 ; (301) 380-7658; (301) 380-6699

FAMILY INNS OF AMERICA, P.O. Box 10, Pigeon Forge, TN 37868 ; (615) 453-1766; (615) 453-0220

HILTON GARDEN INN, 9336 Civic Center Dr., Beverly Hills, CA 90210 ; (800) 286-0645 (310) 205-7655

HILTON INNS, 9336 Civic Center Dr., Beverly Hills, CA 90210 ; (800) 286-0645 (310) 278-4321; (310)205-7655

HOLIDAY INN WORLDWIDE, 3 Ravinia Dr., #2900, Atlanta, GA 30346-2149 ; (770) 604-5600; (770) 604-2107

HOMEGATE FRANCHISING, 700 Rte. 46 E., P.O. Box 2700, Fairfield, NJ 07007 (888) 778 3111 (973) 882-1010; (973) 882-1991

HOWARD JOHNSON HOTELS (CANADA), 36 Toronto St., # 750, Toronto, ON M5C 2C5 CANADA; (800) 249-4656 (416) 361-1010; (416) 361-9577

HOWARD JOHNSON INTERNATIONAL, 1 Sylvan Way, Parsippany, NJ 07054-3878 ; (800) 932-4656 (973) 496-9700; (973) 496-6057

INN SUITES HOTELS, 1615 E. Northern Ave., # 102, Phoenix, AZ 85020-3932 (800) 842-4242 (602) 944-1500; (602) 678-0281

ITT SHERATON CANADA, 45 Church St., Stoney Creek, ON L8E 2X7 CANADA; (905) 664-3337; (905) 664-1113

KNIGHTS FRANCHISE SYSTEM, 1 Sylvan Way, Parsippany, NJ 07054-3878 (800) 932-3300 (973) 496-1591; (973) 496-1359

MAINSTAY SUITES, 10750 Columbia Pk., Silver Spring, MD 20901 ; (800) 547-0007 (301) 592-5000; (301) 592-6205

MARRIOTT INTERNATIONAL, 1 Marriott Dr., Dept. 514.01, Washington, DC 20058 ; (800) 638-8108 (301) 380-9000; (301) 380-8957

NATIONAL 9 INNS, SUITES, MOTELS, 2285 S. Main St., Salt Lake City, UT 84115 (801) 466-9826; (801) 466-9856

PRIME HOSPITALITY CORP., 700 Rte. 46 E., P.O. Box 2700, Fairfield, NJ 07007-2700 ; (973) 882-1010; (973) 882-1991

PROMUS HOTELS, 755 Crossover Ln., Memphis, TN 38117 ; (901) 374-5103; (901) 374-5050

RAMADA INNS, 339 Jefferson Rd., P.O. Box 278, Parsippany, NJ 07054-3878 ; (800) 758-8999 (973) 428-9700; (973) 496-5915

RED LION HOTELS & INNS, 9336 Civic Center Dr., Beverly Hills, CA 90210 ; (310) 278-4321; (310) 205-7655

REGENT INTERNATIONAL HOTELS, P.O. Box 59159, Carlson Pwky., Minneapolis, MN 55459-8254 ; (612) 212-1458; (612) 212-3350

RESIDENCE INN BY MARRIOTT, 1 Marriott Dr., Dept. 514.01, Washington, DC 20058 ; (301) 380-9000; (301) 380-8957

SHONEY'S INNS, 130 Maple Dr. N., Hendersonville, TN 37075 ; (800) 222-2222 (615) 264-8000; (615) 264-3497

SPRINGHILL SUITES BY MARRIOT, 1 Marriott Dr., Dept. 55/514.01, Washington, DC 20058-0001 ; (301) 380-7658; (301) 380-6699

STARWOOD HOTELS & RESORTS WORLDWIDE, 100 Galleria Pkwy., # 1350, Atlanta, GA 30102 ; (770) 857-2000; (770) 857-2040

SUPER 8 MOTELS, 1 Sylvan Way, Parsippany, NJ 07054-3878 ; (800) 889-8847 (973) 496-5581; (973) 497-5351

TRAVELODGE / THRIFTLODGE, 1 Sylvan Way, Parsippany, NJ 07054-3878 ; (973) 428-9700; (973) 496-2284

VILLAGER LODGE, 1 Sylvan Way, Parsippany, NJ 07054-3878 ; (800) 694-6428 (973) 496-8429; (973) 496-2055

WELLESLEY INNS, 700 Rte. 46 E., P.O. Box 2700, Fairfield, NJ 07007 ; (888) 778 3111 (973) 882-1010; (973) 882-1991

WINGATE INNS, 1 Sylvan Way, Parsippany, NJ 07054-0278 ; (800) 567-4283 (973) 428-9700; (973) 496-1354

WOODFIN SUITE HOTELS, 12730 High Bluff Dr., # 250, San Diego, CA 92130 ; (619) 794-2338; (619) 794-2348

Maid Services & Home Cleaning

Chapter

24

Lodging Industry Profile

Total # Franchisors in Industry Group	24
Total # Franchised Units in Industry Group	3,526
Total # Company-Owned Units in Industry Group	170
Total # Operating Units in Industry Group	3,696
Average # Franchised Units/Franchisor	146.9
Average # Company-Owned Units/Franchisor	7.1
Average # Total Units/Franchisor	154.0
Ratio of Total # Franchised Units/Total # Company-Owned Units	20.7:1
Industry Survey Participants	14
Representing % of Industry	58.3%
Average Franchise Fee*:	$13.1K
Average Total Investment*:	$49.3K
Average On-Going Royalty Fee*:	5.4%

*If a range was provided, the mid-point of the range was used. See detailed profiles for actual ranges.

Five Largest Participants in Survey

Company	# Franchised Units	# Co-Owned Units	# Total Units	Franchise Fee	On-Going Royalty	Total Investment
1. Merry Maids	1,294	122	1,416	16-24K	5-7%	32.5-49.5K
2. Molly Maid	570	0	570	6.9K	7-3%	36-65K
3. Maids, The	437	9	446	17.5K	3.3-7%	56-245K
4. Maid Brigade Services	299	6	305	18.5K	3-7%	43.5K+
5. Maid To Perfection	243	0	243	10K	5-7%	35-44K

All of the data provided are proprietary and should not be quoted without acknowledging *Bond's Franchise Guide.*

CLASSY MAIDS

P.O. Box 8552
Madison, WI 53708-8552
Tel: (800) 347-5406 (608) 345-5689
Fax: (608) 839-8807
E-Mail: williamolday@charter.net
Mr. William D. Olday, Vice President

Residential cleaning program with customized one-on-one training and support. Wide variety of services available to offer clients. Large margins for operating. Franchisee is the boss of their business.

BACKGROUND:
Established: 1984; 1st Franchised: 1985
Franchised Units: 8
Company-Owned Units 0
Total Units: 8
Dist.: US-3; CAN-0; O'seas-0
North America: 4 States
Density: 2 in WI, 2 in TN
Projected New Units (12 Months): 2
Qualifications: 3, 3, 1, 1, 4, 4
Registered: None

FINANCIAL/TERMS:
Cash Investment: $5-10K
Total Investment: $7-12K
Minimum Net Worth: $5K
Fees: Franchise - $5.9K
Royalty - 6% or flat fee; Ad. - 0%
Earnings Claim Statement: No
Term of Contract (Years): 10/10,5/5
Avg. # Of Employees: 1 FT, 5-8 PT
Passive Ownership: Discouraged
Encourage Conversions: Yes
Area Develop. Agreements: Yes/5
Sub-Franchising Contracts: No
Expand In Territory: Yes
Space Needs: NR SF; HB

SUPPORT & TRAINING PROVIDED:
Financial Assistance Provided: Yes(D)
Site Selection Assistance: N/A
Lease Negotiation Assistance: N/A
Co-Operative Advertising: No
Franchisee Assoc./Member: No
Size Of Corporate Staff: 2
On-Going Support: b,c,d,G,h,I
Training: 5 Days Madison, WI or 5 Days at Franchisee Location.

SPECIFIC EXPANSION PLANS:
US: All United States
Canada: No
Overseas: No

<< >>

CLEANING AUTHORITY, THE

9017 Red Branch Rd., # G
Columbia, MD 21045
Tel: (800) 783-6243 (410) 740-1900
Fax: (410) 740-1906
E-Mail: tim@thecleaningauthority.com
Web Site: www.thecleaningauthority.com
Mr. Tim Evankovich, President

THE CLEANING AUTHORITY offers franchisees new and innovative methods in developing a successful maid service. Our unique, high-response marketing, coupled with our state-of-the-art proprietary software system, sets us far above the competition in supporting the franchisee. Join us to make your future more successful. Member Platinum 200.

BACKGROUND: IFA MEMBER
Established: 1978; 1st Franchised: 1996
Franchised Units: 42
Company-Owned Units 1
Total Units: 43
Dist.: US-41; CAN-0; O'seas-0
North America: 18 States
Density: 6 in MD, 5 in FL, 4 in TX
Projected New Units (12 Months): 12
Qualifications: 2, 3, 1, 1, 2, 5
Registered: CA,FL,MD,MI,VA

FINANCIAL/TERMS:
Cash Investment: $15-25K
Total Investment: $50-70K
Minimum Net Worth: $50K
Fees: Franchise - $18-28K
Royalty - 4-6%; Ad. - 2%
Earnings Claim Statement: Yes
Term of Contract (Years): 10/5
Avg. # Of Employees: Varies
Passive Ownership: Not Allowed
Encourage Conversions: Yes
Area Develop. Agreements: No
Sub-Franchising Contracts: No
Expand In Territory: Yes
Space Needs: 800-1,200 SF; Industrial

SUPPORT & TRAINING PROVIDED:
Financial Assistance Provided: Yes(I)
Site Selection Assistance: Yes
Lease Negotiation Assistance: No
Co-Operative Advertising: Yes
Franchisee Assoc./Member: Yes/Yes
Size Of Corporate Staff: 12
On-Going Support: b,C,D,G,H,I
Training: 2 Weeks Corporate Office in Columbia, MD.

SPECIFIC EXPANSION PLANS:
US: All United States
Canada: All Canada
Overseas: No

COTTAGECARE

6323 W. 110th St.
Overland Park, KS 66211
Tel: (800) 718-8200 (913) 469-8778
Fax: (913) 469-0822
E-Mail: franchiseinfo@cottagecare.com
Web Site: www.cottagecare.com
Mr. Thomas P. Schrader, President

Big business approach to housecleaning. We do the marketing and sign up new customers for you! You retain customers and manage the business, not clean houses. "Jumbo" exclusive territories are 4 times larger than industry standards, leading to 'Jumbo' sales.

BACKGROUND:
Established: 1988; 1st Franchised: 1989
Franchised Units: 53
Company-Owned Units 2
Total Units: 55
Dist.: US-48; CAN-7; O'seas-0
North America: 20 States, 3 Provinces
Density: 4 in MO, 5 in AB
Projected New Units (12 Months): 15
Qualifications: 4, 4, 2, 2, 1, 5
Registered: All States

FINANCIAL/TERMS:
Cash Investment: $39K
Total Investment: $39K
Minimum Net Worth: $N/A
Fees: Franchise - $4K
Royalty - 5.5%; Ad. - As needed
Earnings Claim Statement: Yes
Term of Contract (Years): 10/10
Avg. # Of Employees: 1 FT, 16 PT
Passive Ownership: Discouraged
Encourage Conversions: No
Area Develop. Agreements: Yes
Sub-Franchising Contracts: Yes
Expand In Territory: Yes
Space Needs: 400 SF; FS, SF, SC

SUPPORT & TRAINING PROVIDED:
Financial Assistance Provided: Yes(I)
Site Selection Assistance: Yes
Lease Negotiation Assistance: Yes
Co-Operative Advertising: Yes
Franchisee Assoc./Member: No
Size Of Corporate Staff: 14
On-Going Support: C,D,G,H
Training: 2 Weeks Overland Park, KS Headquarters.

SPECIFIC EXPANSION PLANS:
US: All United States
Canada: All Canada
Overseas: No

<< >>

DIAMOND HOME CLEANING SERVICES

4887 E. La Palma Ave., # 708
Anaheim, CA 92807
Tel: (800) 393-6243 (714) 701-9771
Fax: (714) 693-8106
E-Mail: mtgi@diamondhomecleaning.com
Web Site: www.diamondhomecleaning.com
Mr. Tom Devlin, President

3 franchise concepts - 1 franchise fee when you join the DIAMOND HOME CLEANING SERVICES franchise system. After completion of our extensive training program, you will be an expert in maid services, carpet cleaning and window cleaning services. Benefits include explosive 20% annual customer growth demand; home-based business; no weekends (have a life!); low investment of $25-60K, including start-up/working capital; and prime territories available.

BACKGROUND:
Established: 1993; 1st Franchised: 1997
Franchised Units: 26
Company-Owned Units 8
Total Units: 24
Dist.: US-34; CAN-0; O'seas-0
North America: 2 States
Density: 13 in CA
Projected New Units (12 Months): 12
Qualifications: 5, 3, 1, 3, 3, 5
Registered: CA

FINANCIAL/TERMS:
Cash Investment: $25K
Total Investment: $25-61K
Minimum Net Worth: $100K
Fees: Franchise - $5K
Royalty - 4-6%; Ad. - 0%
Earnings Claim Statement: No
Term of Contract (Years): 10/5
Avg. # Of Employees: 3 FT, 24 PT
Passive Ownership: Discouraged
Encourage Conversions: Yes
Area Develop. Agreements: No
Sub-Franchising Contracts: No
Expand In Territory: Yes
Space Needs: 500 SF; HB

SUPPORT & TRAINING PROVIDED:
Financial Assistance Provided: Yes(I)
Site Selection Assistance: Yes
Lease Negotiation Assistance: Yes
Co-Operative Advertising: No
Franchisee Assoc./Member: No
Size Of Corporate Staff: 6
On-Going Support: B,C,D,E,F,G,H,I
Training: 1 Week Anaheim, CA.

SPECIFIC EXPANSION PLANS:
US: Southwest
Canada: No
Overseas: No

<< >>

HOME CLEANING CENTERS OF AMERICA

10851 Mastin Blvd., # 130
Overland Park, KS 66210
Tel: (800) 767-1118 (913) 327-5227
Fax: (913) 327-5272
E-Mail: mcalhoon@aol.com
Web Site: www.homecleaningcenters.com
Mr. Mike Calhoon, President

Very large franchise zones. Quality Quality Quality. Owners do not clean houses. Every corporate policy is made by the franchise owners. Each and every owner is hand picked - having money is not enough. Corporate 'Mission Statement' is to have the largest grossing, highest-quality offices in the industry.

BACKGROUND: IFA MEMBER
Established: 1981; 1st Franchised: 1984
Franchised Units: 25
Company-Owned Units 0
Total Units: 25
Dist.: US-25; CAN-0; O'seas-0
North America: 9 States
Density: 7 in MO, 4 in KS, 4 in CO
Projected New Units (12 Months): 3
Qualifications: 3, 3, 1, 3, 5, 5
Registered: CA,IL,IN,MI,MN,NY,OR

FINANCIAL/TERMS:
Cash Investment: $20-30K
Total Investment: $30-50K
Minimum Net Worth: $N/A
Fees: Franchise - $9.5K
Royalty - 4.5-5%; Ad. - 0%
Earnings Claim Statement: Yes
Term of Contract (Years): 10/10
Avg. # Of Employees: 12 FT
Passive Ownership: Discouraged
Encourage Conversions: No
Area Develop. Agreements: No
Sub-Franchising Contracts: No
Expand In Territory: Yes
Space Needs: 500 SF; Non-Retail

SUPPORT & TRAINING PROVIDED:
Financial Assistance Provided: No
Site Selection Assistance: Yes
Lease Negotiation Assistance: Yes
Co-Operative Advertising: No
Franchisee Assoc./Member: Yes/Yes
Size Of Corporate Staff: 2
On-Going Support: b,C,D,E,F,G,H,I
Training: 5 Days Denver, CO or 5 days at St. Louis, MO.

SPECIFIC EXPANSION PLANS:
US: All United States
Canada: No
Overseas: No

<< >>

MAID BRIGADE SERVICES

Four Concourse Pkwy., # 200
Atlanta, GA 30328
Tel: (800) 722-6243 (770) 551-9630
Fax: (770) 391-9092
E-Mail: chay@maidbrigade.com
Web Site: www.maidbrigade.com
Ms. Cathy Hay, VP Franchise Development

MAID BRIGADE offers the best opportunity in the industry with our 3 new Large, Major and Regional Market Franchises. Our exclusive territory sizes range from 20,000 to 150,000 qualified households. We provide unparalleled support, business development and the latest technology in the industry. Our focus is to build strong businesses. Master franchises available outside the USA.

BACKGROUND: IFA MEMBER
Established: 1979; 1st Franchised: 1984
Franchised Units: 299
Company-Owned Units 6
Total Units: 305
Dist.: US-233; CAN-70; O'seas-2
North America: 31 States, 7 Provinces
Density: 43 in VA, 20 in TX, 18 in WA
Projected New Units (12 Months): 25
Qualifications: 4, 3, 2, 3, 2, 5
Registered: CA,FL,HI,IL,MD,MI,MN,NY,OR,VA,WA,WI,DC

FINANCIAL/TERMS:
Cash Investment: $43.5K+
Total Investment: $43.5K+

Minimum Net Worth:	$100K
Fees: Franchise -	$18.5K
Royalty - 3-7%;	Ad. - 2%
Earnings Claim Statement:	No
Term of Contract (Years):	10/10
Avg. # Of Employees:	15 FT
Passive Ownership:	Allowed
Encourage Conversions:	Yes
Area Develop. Agreements:	Yes/5
Sub-Franchising Contracts:	Yes
Expand In Territory:	Yes

Space Needs: 500-1,000 SF; HB, SF, SC

SUPPORT & TRAINING PROVIDED:

Financial Assistance Provided:	Yes(I)
Site Selection Assistance:	Yes
Lease Negotiation Assistance:	Yes
Co-Operative Advertising:	Yes
Franchisee Assoc./Member:	Yes/Yes
Size Of Corporate Staff:	13
On-Going Support:	A,B,C,D,E,F,G,H,I

Training: 5 Days in Atlanta, GA; 10 Days On-Site Week of Opening; Training Videos/Manuals.

SPECIFIC EXPANSION PLANS:

US:	All United States
Canada:	All Canada
Overseas:	All Countries

<< >>

MAID TO PERFECTION

1101 Opal Ct.
Hagerstown, MD 21740
Tel: (800) 648-6243 (301) 790-7900
Fax: (301) 790-3949
E-Mail: maidsvc@aol.com
Web Site: www.maidtoperfectioncorp.com
Mr. Michael Katzenberger, President/CEO

MAID TO PERFECTION ® is the only major cleaning franchise that provides access to every residential and commercial service dollar, within an exclusive territory. Ranked #1 for franchisee support/satisfaction in Success, April, 1999; cited as one of only 15 Great, Low-Investment franchises by Black Enterprise, September, 1999.

BACKGROUND: IFA MEMBER

Established: 1980; 1st Franchised: 1990

Franchised Units:	243
Company-Owned Units	0
Total Units:	243
Dist.:	US-220; CAN-23; O'seas-0
North America:	22 States, 2 Provinces
Density:	50 in MD, 33 in PA, 20 in CA
Projected New Units (12 Months):	50
Qualifications:	5, 5, 2, 4, 4, 5

Registered: CA,FL,IL,IN,MD,MI,MN,NY, ND,OR,RI,VA,WA,WI,DC

FINANCIAL/TERMS:

Cash Investment:	$36-44K
Total Investment:	$36-44K
Minimum Net Worth:	$80K
Fees: Franchise -	$10K
Royalty - 5-7%;	Ad. - 0%
Earnings Claim Statement:	No
Term of Contract (Years):	10/10
Avg. # Of Employees:	15 FT, 5 PT
Passive Ownership:	Discouraged
Encourage Conversions:	Yes
Area Develop. Agreements:	Yes/5
Sub-Franchising Contracts:	No
Expand In Territory:	Yes

Space Needs: 400-800 SF; FS, HB, Non-Retail

SUPPORT & TRAINING PROVIDED:

Financial Assistance Provided:	Yes(B)
Site Selection Assistance:	Yes
Lease Negotiation Assistance:	Yes
Co-Operative Advertising:	No
Franchisee Assoc./Member:	Yes/Yes
Size Of Corporate Staff:	17
On-Going Support:	C,D,E,G,H,I

Training: 1 Week at Corporate Headquarters; 1 Week On-Site.

SPECIFIC EXPANSION PLANS:

US:	All United States
Canada:	All Canada
Overseas:	All Countries

<< >>

MAIDPRO

180 Canal St.
Boston, MA 02114
Tel: (888) 624-3776 (617) 742-8787
Fax: (617) 720-0700
E-Mail: info@maidpro.com
Web Site: www.maidpro.com
Mr. Richard Sparacio, Dir. Franchise Development

MaidPro®

MAIDPRO is setting the trend in the home and office cleaning industry. MAIDPRO has a contemporary approach to this high-growth service. With unmatched graphic design and marketing, a completely paperless office and the ability for clients to request service on the Internet, MAIDPRO's franchisees have become successful in running a larger business.

BACKGROUND:

Established: 1991; 1st Franchised: 1997

Franchised Units:	22
Company-Owned Units	2
Total Units:	24
Dist.:	US-24; CAN-0; O'seas-0
North America:	13 States
Density:	8 in MA, 3 in FL, 2 in NH
Projected New Units (12 Months):	15
Qualifications:	3, 3, 1, 2, 4, 5

Registered: All States

FINANCIAL/TERMS:

Cash Investment:	$10-15K
Total Investment:	$28-50K
Minimum Net Worth:	$N/A
Fees: Franchise -	$7.9K
Royalty - 3-6%;	Ad. - N/A
Earnings Claim Statement:	No
Term of Contract (Years):	10/5
Avg. # Of Employees:	15 FT, 3 PT
Passive Ownership:	Not Allowed
Encourage Conversions:	Yes
Area Develop. Agreements:	No
Sub-Franchising Contracts:	No
Expand In Territory:	Yes

Space Needs: 500-1,500 SF; SF, OB

SUPPORT & TRAINING PROVIDED:

Financial Assistance Provided:	Yes(I)
Site Selection Assistance:	Yes
Lease Negotiation Assistance:	Yes
Co-Operative Advertising:	Yes
Franchisee Assoc./Member:	No
Size Of Corporate Staff:	5
On-Going Support:	C,d,E,G,h,I

Training: 2 Weeks in Boston, MA.

SPECIFIC EXPANSION PLANS:

US:	All United States
Canada:	No
Overseas:	No

<< >>

MAIDS, THE

4820 Dodge St.
Omaha, NE 68132-3111
Tel: (800) 843-6243 (402) 558-5555
Fax: (402) 558-4112
E-Mail: franchising@themaids.com
Web Site: www.maids.com
Mr. Michael Fagen, EVP Sales

AMERICA'S MAID SERVICE - THE MAIDS is the premier residential cleaning franchise. Our cleaning system is the most thorough in the industry and sets us ahead of all competition. We offer low investment, comprehensive training and on-going support that set the industry standard. Call THE MAIDS today and discover why we are AMERICA'S MAID SERVICE.

BACKGROUND: IFA MEMBER
Established: 1979; 1st Franchised: 1980
Franchised Units: 437
Company-Owned Units 9
Total Units: 446
Dist.: US-415; CAN-13; O'seas-0
North America: 40 States, 5 Provinces
Density: 34 in CA, 23 in NY, 20 in IL
Projected New Units (12 Months): 40
Qualifications: 4, 4, 1, 3, 1, 4
Registered: All States

FINANCIAL/TERMS:
Cash Investment: $14-61K
Total Investment: $56-245K
Minimum Net Worth: $180-350K
Fees: Franchise - $17.5K
Royalty - 3.3-7%; Ad. - 1%
Earnings Claim Statement: Yes
Term of Contract (Years): 20/20
Avg. # Of Employees: 1-2 FT, 8-12 PT
Passive Ownership: Discouraged
Encourage Conversions: Yes
Area Develop. Agreements: No
Sub-Franchising Contracts: Yes
Expand In Territory: Yes
Space Needs: 200 SF; FS, SC, SF

SUPPORT & TRAINING PROVIDED:
Financial Assistance Provided: Yes(I)
Site Selection Assistance: Yes
Lease Negotiation Assistance: No
Co-Operative Advertising: Yes
Franchisee Assoc./Member: Yes/Yes
Size Of Corporate Staff: 35
On-Going Support: A,B,C,D,G,H,I
Training: 8 Days Each in Both Managerial and Technical Training at Headquarters; 90 Days On-Site.

SPECIFIC EXPANSION PLANS:
US: All United States
Canada: All Canada
Overseas: All Countries

<< >>

Top 50

MERRY MAIDS

860 Ridge Lake Blvd.
Memphis, TN 38120
Tel: (800) 798-8000 (901) 537-8100
Fax: (901) 537-8140
E-Mail: franchisesales@mmhomeoffice.com
Web Site: www.merrymaids.com
Mr. Rob Sanders, Franchise Sales Mgr.

MERRY MAIDS is the largest and most recognized company in the home cleaning industry. The company's commitment to training and on-going support is unmatched. MERRY MAIDS is highly-ranked as the hottest and fastest-growing franchise opportunity according to leading national publications. We offer low investment, cross-selling promotions with our partner companies, research and development and commitment to quality.

BACKGROUND: IFA MEMBER
Established: 1979; 1st Franchised: 1980
Franchised Units: 1,294
Company-Owned Units 122
Total Units: 1,416
Dist.: US-862; CAN-63; O'seas-484
North America: 49 States, 7 Provinces
Density: 114 in CA, 45 in TX, 45 IL
Projected New Units (12 Months): 40
Qualifications: 5, 3, 1, 3, 4, 5
Registered: All States

FINANCIAL/TERMS:
Cash Investment: $16.5-22.5K
Total Investment: $32.5-49.5K
Minimum Net Worth: $Varies
Fees: Franchise - $16-24K
Royalty - 5-7%; Ad. - 0.25-1%
Earnings Claim Statement: No
Term of Contract (Years): 5/5
Avg. # Of Employees: 2 FT, 12 PT
Passive Ownership: Discouraged
Encourage Conversions: Yes
Area Develop. Agreements: No
Sub-Franchising Contracts: No
Expand In Territory: Yes
Space Needs: 800 SF; FS

SUPPORT & TRAINING PROVIDED:
Financial Assistance Provided: Yes(D)
Site Selection Assistance: No
Lease Negotiation Assistance: No
Co-Operative Advertising: N/A
Franchisee Assoc./Member: No
Size Of Corporate Staff: 60
On-Going Support: C,D,G,H,I
Training: 8 Days Headquarters, Memphis, TN.

SPECIFIC EXPANSION PLANS:
US: All United States
Canada: All Canada
Overseas: All Countries

<< >>

MERRY MAIDS OF CANADA

6540 Tomken Rd.
Mississauga, ON L5T 2E9 CANADA
Tel: (800) 263-5928 (905) 670-0000
Fax: (905) 670-0077
E-Mail: thould@svm.com
Web Site: www.servicemaster.com
Ms. Terry Hould, Franchise Director

Largest company in the residential cleaning industry. The company's commitment to training and on-going support is unmatched. Highly ranked as the hottest and fastest-growing franchise opportunity according to leading national publications.

BACKGROUND:
Established: 1991; 1st Franchised: 1991
Franchised Units: 54
Company-Owned Units 0
Total Units: 54
Dist.: US-800; CAN-54; O'seas-1300
North America: 9 Provinces
Density: 25 in ON, 7 in BC
Projected New Units (12 Months): 8
Qualifications: 2, 3, 1, 2, 3, 4
Registered: AB

FINANCIAL/TERMS:
Cash Investment: $17.5-24.5K
Total Investment: $40-50K
Minimum Net Worth: $50K
Fees: Franchise - $17.5-24.5K
Royalty - 5-7%; Ad. - 0%
Earnings Claim Statement: No
Term of Contract (Years): 5/5
Avg. # Of Employees: 2 FT, 2 PT
Passive Ownership: Discouraged
Encourage Conversions: Yes
Area Develop. Agreements: No
Sub-Franchising Contracts: No
Expand In Territory: Yes
Space Needs: 300-500 SF; Warehouse

SUPPORT & TRAINING PROVIDED:
Financial Assistance Provided: Yes
Site Selection Assistance: No
Lease Negotiation Assistance: No
Co-Operative Advertising: No
Franchisee Assoc./Member: Yes/CFA
Size Of Corporate Staff: 50
On-Going Support: B,C,D,G,h,I
Training: 8 Days Memphis, TN.

SPECIFIC EXPANSION PLANS:
US: N/A
Canada: All Canada
Overseas: N/A

<< >>

MOLLY MAID

3948 Ranchero Dr.
Ann Arbor, MI 48108-2775
Tel: (800) 665-5962 (734) 822-6800
Fax: (734) 822-6888
E-Mail: info@mollymaid.com
Web Site: www.mollymaid.com
Mr. Marc A. Kiekenapp, Dir. Franchise Development

MOLLY MAID is # 1 in the industry in residential cleaning and home care service. Ranked in INC 500, Entrepreneur's Top 100, Platinum 200, Entrepreneur 509 and Business Start-Ups As Top 200 Hottest Franchises. MOLLY MAID's technology won The Windows Worldwide Open in 1995 sponsored by Bill Gates.

BACKGROUND: IFA MEMBER
Established: 1979; 1st Franchised: 1979
Franchised Units: 570
Company-Owned Units 0
Total Units: 570
Dist.: US-280; CAN-167; O'seas-100
North America: 36 States, 3 Provinces
Density: 146 in ON, 52 in CA, 22 MI
Projected New Units (12 Months): 40
Qualifications: 3, 3, 1, 3, 4, 5
Registered: CA,FL,IL,IN,MD,MI,MN,NY,OR,RI,VA,WA,WI,DC

FINANCIAL/TERMS:
Cash Investment: $15-25K
Total Investment: $36-65K
Minimum Net Worth: $150K
Fees: Franchise - $6.9K
Royalty - 7-3%; Ad. - $75/Qtr.
Earnings Claim Statement: Yes
Term of Contract (Years): 10/10
Avg. # Of Employees: 12 FT
Passive Ownership: Discouraged
Encourage Conversions: Yes
Area Develop. Agreements: No
Sub-Franchising Contracts: No
Expand In Territory: Yes
Space Needs: 400 SF; Other

SUPPORT & TRAINING PROVIDED:
Financial Assistance Provided: Yes(I)
Site Selection Assistance: Yes
Lease Negotiation Assistance: No
Co-Operative Advertising: Yes
Franchisee Assoc./Member: Yes/Yes
Size Of Corporate Staff: 33
On-Going Support: C,D,F,G,h,I
Training: 5 Days in Home Office; 6 Months in Right Start Program; 2 Days at Franchise Location.

SPECIFIC EXPANSION PLANS:
US: All United States
Canada: All Canada
Overseas: Japan, United Kingdom

<< >>

SERVICEMASTER RESIDENTIAL/ COMMERCIAL (CANADA)

6540 Tomken Rd.
Mississauga, ON L5T 2E9 CANADA
Tel: (800) 263-5928 (905) 670-0000
Fax: (905) 670-0077
Web Site: www.svm.com
Mr. David Messenger, VP Franchise Market Dev.

One of Canada's oldest and best-respected franchise opportunities. SERVICEMASTER provides clean-up and reconstruction services after fire and floods, janitorial services, commercial carpet cleaning and residential carpet and upholstery cleaning services.

BACKGROUND:
Established: 1947; 1st Franchised: 1947
Franchised Units: 160
Company-Owned Units 0
Total Units: 160
Dist.: US-0; CAN-160; O'seas-0
North America: 10 Provinces
Density: 80 in ON, 19 in BC, 11 in AB
Projected New Units (12 Months): 9
Qualifications: 3, 3, 1, 2, 3, 4
Registered: AB

FINANCIAL/TERMS:
Cash Investment: $11.5-28.5K
Total Investment: $20-49K
Minimum Net Worth: $145K
Fees: Franchise - $11.5-28.5K
Royalty - 4-9%; Ad. - 1%
Earnings Claim Statement: No
Term of Contract (Years): 5/5
Avg. # Of Employees: Varies
Passive Ownership: Not Allowed
Encourage Conversions: Yes
Area Develop. Agreements: No
Sub-Franchising Contracts: No
Expand In Territory: Yes
Space Needs: NR SF; N/A

SUPPORT & TRAINING PROVIDED:
Financial Assistance Provided: Yes(D)
Site Selection Assistance: N/A
Lease Negotiation Assistance: N/A
Co-Operative Advertising: Yes
Franchisee Assoc./Member: Yes
Size Of Corporate Staff: 100
On-Going Support: B,C,D,G,h,I
Training: 2 Weeks Memphis, TN.

SPECIFIC EXPANSION PLANS:
US: All United States
Canada: All Canada
Overseas: No

<< >>

SUPPLEMENTAL LISTING OF FRANCHISORS

CLASSY MAIDS, P.O. Box 8552, Madison, WI 53708-8552 ; (800) 347-5406 (608) 345-5689; (608) 839-8807

HOME CLEANING CENTERS OF AMERICA, 10851 Mastin Blvd., # 130, Overland Park, KS 66210 ; (800) 767-1118 (913) 327-5227; (913) 327-5272

MAIDS TO ORDER, 919 E. Cherry St., Canal Fulton, OH 44614 ; (800) 701-6243 (330) 854-9382

MERRY MAIDS OF CANADA, 6540 Tomken Rd., Mississauga, ON L5T 2E9 CANADA; (800) 263-5928 (905) 670-0000; (905) 670-0077

MINI MAID, 2727 Canton Rd., # 550, Marietta, GA 30066 ; (800) 627-6464 (770) 794-9938; (770) 794-1877

OTHER WOMAN MAID FRANCHISE, THE, 9136 NE Glisan St., Portland, OR 97220 ; (800) 846-6052 (503) 252-4336; (503) 252-9259

SWISHER MAIDS, 6849 Fairview Rd., Charlotte, NC 28210-3363 ; (800) 444-4138 (704) 364-7707; (704) 365-8941

WORKENDERS, 4400 N. Federal Hwy., # 210, Boca Raton, FL 33431 ; (888) 249-0074 (561) 477-5352; (561) 477-5321

Maintenance/Cleaning/Sanitation

Chapter 25

Maintenance/Cleaning/Sanitation Industry Profile

Total # Franchisors in Industry Group	129
Total # Franchised Units in Industry Group	37,044
Total # Company-Owned Units in Industry Group	604
Total # Operating Units in Industry Group	37,648
Average # Franchised Units/Franchisor	287.2
Average # Company-Owned Units/Franchisor	4.7
Average # Total Units/Franchisor	291.9
Ratio of Total # Franchised Units/Total # Company-Owned Units	61.3:1
Industry Survey Participants	66
Representing % of Industry	51.2%
Average Franchise Fee*:	$19.3K
Average Total Investment*:	$63.5K
Average On-Going Royalty Fee*:	9.9%

*If a range was provided, the mid-point of the range was used. See detailed profiles for actual ranges.

Five Largest Participants in Survey

Company	# Franchised Units	# Co-Owned Units	# Total Units	Franchise Fee	On-Going Royalty	Total Investment
1. Jani-King International	7,700	35	7,735	8-33K	10%	2.9-40K
2. Coverall North America	5,941	0	5,941	6-32.2K	5%	6.2-35.9K
3. Servicemaster Clean	4,460	0	4,460	14.5-26.5K	4-10%	21.9-72.1K
4. Chem-Dry Carpet and Upholstery Cleaning	3,903	0	3,903	19.9K	$198/ Month	6.9-27.6K
5. Cleannet USA	2,146	7	2,153	2-25.5K	3%	2.9-35.7K

All of the data provided are proprietary and should not be quoted without acknowledging *Bond's Franchise Guide.*

1-800-GOT-JUNK?

201-2182 W. 12th Ave.
Vancouver, BC V6K 2N4 CANADA
Tel: (877) 408-5865 (604) 731-5782
Fax: (801) 751-0634
E-Mail: wmillet@1800gotjunk.com
Web Site: www.1800gotjunk.com
Mr. Wayne Millet, VP Development

1-800-GOT-JUNK? has revolutionized customer service in junk removal for over 10 years. By setting the mark for service standards and professionalism, an industry that once operated without set rates, price lists or receipts, now has top service standards. You will have the expert advice and support that is key to success. Our intensive training program will get you on track; our on-going support and continuing education will keep you there. Centralized call center allows you to focus on your business.

BACKGROUND: IFA MEMBER
Established: 1989; 1st Franchised: 1999
Franchised Units: 22
Company-Owned Units 1
Total Units: 23
Dist.: US-11; CAN-10; O'seas-0
North America: 7 States, 3 Provinces
Density: 5 in CA, 5 in ON, 2 inWA
Projected New Units (12 Months): 36
Qualifications: 5, 5, 1, 2, 4, 5
Registered: All States

FINANCIAL/TERMS:
Cash Investment: $45-70K
Total Investment: $45-70K
Minimum Net Worth: $50K
Fees: Franchise - $28K
Royalty - 8%; Ad. - 1%
Earnings Claim Statement: No
Term of Contract (Years): 5/15
Avg. # Of Employees: 6 FT, 4 PT
Passive Ownership: Discourged
Encourage Conversions: No
Area Develop. Agreements: No
Sub-Franchising Contracts: No
Expand In Territory: Yes
Space Needs: 350 SF; OB

SUPPORT & TRAINING PROVIDED:
Financial Assistance Provided: Yes(I)
Site Selection Assistance: N/A
Lease Negotiation Assistance: N/A
Co-Operative Advertising: Yes
Franchisee Assoc./Member: Yes/Yes
Size Of Corporate Staff: 18
On-Going Support: a,B,C,D,G,H,I
Training: 5-10 Days Vancouver, BC; 3-5 Days in Assigned Territory.

SPECIFIC EXPANSION PLANS:
US: All United States
Canada: No
Overseas: No

<< >>

AEROWEST & WESTAIR DEODORIZING SERVICES

3882 Del Amo Blvd., # 602
Torrance, CA 90503
Tel: (888) 663-6726 (310) 793-4242
Fax: (310) 793-4250
E-Mail: westsaninc@aol.com
Web Site: www.westsanitation.com
Mr. Chris Ratay, Franchise Manager

WEST provides unique odor counteractant dispensers and fluids at cost to franchisees for their service work in the 'high end' market, including hospitals, offices, government and municipal buildings, etc. Administrative support is performed by WEST on behalf of the franchisee, including billings and collections (gross franchise income is advanced at time of billing), allowing franchisees to concentrate on sales and service.

BACKGROUND: IFA MEMBER
Established: 1983; 1st Franchised: 1983
Franchised Units: 46
Company-Owned Units 29
Total Units: 75
Dist.: US-75; CAN-0; O'seas-0
North America: 30 States
Density: 13 in CA, 9 in NY, 7 in IL
Projected New Units (12 Months): 8
Qualifications: 2, 3, 3, 2, 2, 4
Registered: CA,KY,MD,IL,NY,WA,MI

FINANCIAL/TERMS:
Cash Investment: $3-10K
Total Investment: $3-40K
Minimum Net Worth: $10K
Fees: Franchise - $2K
Royalty - 35%; Ad. - 0%
Earnings Claim Statement: Yes
Term of Contract (Years): 5/1
Avg. # Of Employees: 1 FT
Passive Ownership: Discouraged
Encourage Conversions: N/A
Area Develop. Agreements: N/A
Sub-Franchising Contracts: No
Expand In Territory: Yes
Space Needs: N/A SF; HB

SUPPORT & TRAINING PROVIDED:
Financial Assistance Provided: Yes(D)
Site Selection Assistance: N/A
Lease Negotiation Assistance: N/A
Co-Operative Advertising: N/A
Franchisee Assoc./Member: No
Size Of Corporate Staff: 12
On-Going Support: A,B,C,D,G,H,I
Training: 1-2 Weeks Local, Near Franchisee's Home.

SPECIFIC EXPANSION PLANS:
US: All United States
Canada: No
Overseas: Europe, Asia

<< >>

AIRE-MASTER OF AMERICA

1821 N. Highway CC, P.O. Box 2310
Nixa, MO 65714
Tel: (800) 525-0957 (417) 725-2691
Fax: (417) 725-5737
E-Mail: fran1@airemaster.com
Web Site: www.airemaster.com
Mr. Jim M. Roudenis, Franchise Director

AIRE-MASTER is a unique system of odor control and restroom fixture cleaning. Unlike the majority of 'air-fresheners' on the market, AIRE-MASTER deodorizers and deodorant products actually eliminate odors by oxidation. You don't need prior experience in the odor control/sanitary supply industry to qualify for an AIRE-MASTER franchise. Customer base is built by making sales calls and providing good customer service. Complete training. Entrepreneur Magazine ranked Aire-Master #1 in the restroom hygiene.

BACKGROUND:
Established: 1958; 1st Franchised: 1976
Franchised Units: 57
Company-Owned Units 5

Total Units: 62
Dist.: US-60; CAN-2; O'seas-0
North America: 37 States, 2 Provinces
Density: 5 in MO, 5 in CA, 3 in NJ
Projected New Units (12 Months): 14
Qualifications: 5, 5, 5, 5, 5, 5
Registered: CA,IL,MD,NY

FINANCIAL/TERMS:
Cash Investment: $30K
Total Investment: $30-80K
Minimum Net Worth: $NR
Fees: Franchise - $22K
Royalty - 5%; Ad. - 0%
Earnings Claim Statement: No
Term of Contract (Years): 20/3
Avg. # Of Employees: 2-3 FT
Passive Ownership: Discouraged
Encourage Conversions: Yes
Area Develop. Agreements: No
Sub-Franchising Contracts: No
Expand In Territory: N/A
Space Needs: N/A SF; HB

SUPPORT & TRAINING PROVIDED:
Financial Assistance Provided: Yes(D)
Site Selection Assistance: N/A
Lease Negotiation Assistance: Yes
Co-Operative Advertising: Yes
Franchisee Assoc./Member: Yes/Yes
Size Of Corporate Staff: 70
On-Going Support: a,B,C,D,E,G,h,I
Training: 5 Days Headquarters, Nixa, MO; 5 Days Franchisee's Location.

SPECIFIC EXPANSION PLANS:
US: All United States
Canada: All Canada
Overseas: No

<< >>

Top 50

AMERICAN LEAK DETECTION
888 Research Dr., # 100, P.O. Box 1701
Palm Springs, CA 92263
Tel: (800) 755-6697 (760) 320-9991
Fax: (760) 320-1288
E-Mail: sbangs@leakbusters.com
Web Site: www.leakbusters.com
Ms. Sheila T. Bangs, Dir. Franchise Sales/ Marketing

Electronic detection of water, drain, waste, sewer and gas leaks under concrete slabs of homes, commercial buildings, pools, spas, fountains, etc. with equipment commissioned/ manufactured by company.

BACKGROUND: IFA MEMBER
Established: 1974; 1st Franchised: 1985
Franchised Units: 309
Company-Owned Units 1
Total Units: 310
Dist.: US-227; CAN-8; O'seas-75
North America: 38 States, 3 Provinces
Density: 63 in CA, 34 in FL, 17 in TX
Projected New Units (12 Months): 6
Qualifications: 3, 3, 2, 2, 2, 3
Registered: CA,FL,HI,IL,IN,MD,MI,MN, NY,OR,RI,VA,WA,WI,DC,AB

FINANCIAL/TERMS:
Cash Investment: $58-120K
Total Investment: $85-150K
Minimum Net Worth: $Varies
Fees: Franchise - $55K+
Royalty - 6-10%; Ad. - N/A
Earnings Claim Statement: No
Term of Contract (Years): 10/10
Avg. # Of Employees: 1-4 FT, 2 PT
Passive Ownership: Discouraged
Encourage Conversions: N/A
Area Develop. Agreements: No
Sub-Franchising Contracts: No
Expand In Territory: Yes
Space Needs: NR SF; NR

SUPPORT & TRAINING PROVIDED:
Financial Assistance Provided: Yes(D)
Site Selection Assistance: N/A
Lease Negotiation Assistance: N/A
Co-Operative Advertising: Yes
Franchisee Assoc./Member: Yes/Yes
Size Of Corporate Staff: 37
On-Going Support: a,B,C,D,f,G,H,I
Training: 6-10 Weeks Palm Springs, CA.

SPECIFIC EXPANSION PLANS:
US: Northeast, Midwest
Canada: MB, SK, AB
Overseas: Western Europe, Far East, South America

<< >>

AMERICARE RESTROOM HYGIENE & SUPPLY
225 Laura Dr., # A
Addison, IL 60101
Tel: (800) 745-6191 (630) 458-1990
Fax: (630) 458-1994
Mr. Richard F. Gac, President

Aroma enhancement plus infection control systems for retail, commercial and industrial manufacturing, specializing in full line of high profit products and services for germ killing, restroom supplies and maintenance.

BACKGROUND:
Established: 1990; 1st Franchised: 1993
Franchised Units: 21
Company-Owned Units 20
Total Units: 41
Dist.: US-41; CAN-0; O'seas-0
North America: 3 States
Density: 36 in IL, 3 in IN, 2 in WI
Projected New Units (12 Months): 4
Qualifications: 3, 2, 1, 2, 3, 5
Registered: IL,WI

FINANCIAL/TERMS:
Cash Investment: $5K
Total Investment: $9.5-95K
Minimum Net Worth: $100K
Fees: Franchise - $9.5K
Royalty - 15%; Ad. - NR
Earnings Claim Statement: No
Term of Contract (Years): 10/10
Avg. # Of Employees: 1 FT, 2 PT
Passive Ownership: Not Allowed
Encourage Conversions: N/A
Area Develop. Agreements: Yes
Sub-Franchising Contracts: Yes
Expand In Territory: Yes
Space Needs: N/A SF; HB

SUPPORT & TRAINING PROVIDED:
Financial Assistance Provided: Yes
Site Selection Assistance: N/A
Lease Negotiation Assistance: N/A
Co-Operative Advertising: Yes
Franchisee Assoc./Member: No
Size Of Corporate Staff: 10
On-Going Support: A,B,C,D,E,F,G,H,I
Training: 2 Weeks in Addison, IL.

SPECIFIC EXPANSION PLANS:
US: IL, IN, MI, WI
Canada: No
Overseas: No

<< >>

ANAGO CLEANING SYSTEMS
1515 University, # 203
Coral Springs, FL 33071
Tel: (800) 213-5857 (954) 745-0193
Fax: (954) 656-1014
E-Mail: david@goanago.com
Web Site: www.goanago.com
Ms. Mary Barker, VP Franchise Development

We are the Digital generation of cleaning franchises. We provide you with customers!!! Plus invoicing and collection services. We give you unparalleled training, progressive business development and equipment and supplies at the best pricing available. Business insurance is available, as well as financing for all of our programs. Master franchises available for select territories.

BACKGROUND:
Established: 2000; 1st Franchised: 2001
Franchised Units: 180
Company-Owned Units 0
Total Units: 180
Dist.: US-180; CAN-0; O'seas-0
North America: 5 States
Density: 120 in FL, 30 in OH, 20 IL
Projected New Units (12 Months): 200
Qualifications: 3, 3, 2, 2, 3, 5
Registered: CA,FL,IL,MI,VA

FINANCIAL/TERMS:
Cash Investment: $1-25K
Total Investment: $4-30K
Minimum Net Worth: $2K
Fees: Franchise - $8.3K
Royalty - 10%; Ad. - 0%
Earnings Claim Statement: No
Term of Contract (Years): 10/10
Avg. # Of Employees: 1 FT, 3-5 PT
Passive Ownership: Allowed
Encourage Conversions: Yes
Area Develop. Agreements: Yes/10
Sub-Franchising Contracts: Yes
Expand In Territory: Yes
Space Needs: N/A SF; N/A

SUPPORT & TRAINING PROVIDED:
Financial Assistance Provided: Yes(D)
Site Selection Assistance: Yes
Lease Negotiation Assistance: Yes
Co-Operative Advertising: Yes
Franchisee Assoc./Member: No
Size Of Corporate Staff: 12
On-Going Support: A,B,C,D,E,F,G,H,I
Training: Approximately 75 Hours Local Regional Office.

SPECIFIC EXPANSION PLANS:
US: All United States
Canada: All Canada
Overseas: All Countries

<< >>

BIOLOGIX
1561 Fairview Ave.
St. Louis, MO 63132-1324
Tel: (800) 747-1885 (314) 423-1945
Fax: (314) 423-4394
Mr. James C. Jones, VP/Director

BIOLOGIX provides guaranteed environmental waste elimination services to clients in the food service and hospitality industry. This is a ground floor opportunity to purchase exclusive rights to a territory in the Biotechnology/Environmental service field. Business-to-business sales, renewable income and a positive environmental impact make BIOLOGIX a tremendous opportunity.

BACKGROUND: IFA MEMBER
Established: 1989; 1st Franchised: 1995
Franchised Units: 22
Company-Owned Units 2
Total Units: 24
Dist.: US-2; CAN-0; O'seas-0
North America: 12 States
Density: 4 in MO, 3 in OH, 2 in TX
Projected New Units (12 Months): 22
Qualifications: 4, 4, 3, 4, 4, 5
Registered: IL,IN,MD,MI,RI,VA,WI

FINANCIAL/TERMS:
Cash Investment: $23.9-43.6K
Total Investment: $NR
Minimum Net Worth: $30K
Fees: Franchise - $12.5K
Royalty - 4%; Ad. - N/A
Earnings Claim Statement: No
Term of Contract (Years): 5/5
Avg. # Of Employees: 2 FT, 2 PT
Passive Ownership: Discouraged
Encourage Conversions: N/A
Area Develop. Agreements: No
Sub-Franchising Contracts: No
Expand In Territory: Yes
Space Needs: NR SF; HB

SUPPORT & TRAINING PROVIDED:
Financial Assistance Provided: No
Site Selection Assistance: N/A
Lease Negotiation Assistance: N/A
Co-Operative Advertising: N/A
Franchisee Assoc./Member: No
Size Of Corporate Staff: 30
On-Going Support: A,B,C,D,F,G,H,I
Training: 1 Week St. Louis, MO.

SPECIFIC EXPANSION PLANS:
US: All United States
Canada: No
Overseas: NR

<< >>

BONUS
BUILDING CARE ®

BONUS BUILDING CARE
P.O. Box 300
Indianola, OK 74442
Tel: (800) 931-1102 (918) 823-4990
Fax: (918) 823-4994
E-Mail: bonusinc@aol.com
Web Site: www.bonusbuildingcare.com
Ms. Arleen Cavanaugh, President

Commercial cleaning. Turn-key operation, with customers, training, operations assistance, equipment, business insurance and clerical support. Best cleaning franchise on the market today because of lower fees, personalized support, less restrictions and quicker start-up. We're not the biggest, but we are the best. Master franchises available. IFA Member.

BACKGROUND: IFA MEMBER
Established: 1996; 1st Franchised: 1996
Franchised Units: 211
Company-Owned Units 3
Total Units: 214
Dist.: US-214; CAN-0; O'seas-0
North America: 5 States
Density: TN, MO, TX
Projected New Units (12 Months): 100
Qualifications: 1, 1, 2, 2, 3, 3
Registered: IL, IN

FINANCIAL/TERMS:
Cash Investment: $Varies
Total Investment: $Varies
Minimum Net Worth: $N/A
Fees: Franchise - $6.5K
Royalty - 10%; Ad. - 0%
Earnings Claim Statement: No
Term of Contract (Years): 20/20
Avg. # Of Employees: Varies
Passive Ownership: Discouraged
Encourage Conversions: Yes
Area Develop. Agreements: No
Sub-Franchising Contracts: Yes
Expand In Territory: No
Space Needs: N/A SF; BH

SUPPORT & TRAINING PROVIDED:
Financial Assistance Provided: Yes(D)
Site Selection Assistance: N/A
Lease Negotiation Assistance: N/A
Co-Operative Advertising: N/A
Franchisee Assoc./Member: Yes/No

Size Of Corporate Staff: 6
On-Going Support: B,C,D,I
Training: Minimum 20 Hours On-Site; Minimum 10 Hours Classroom; as Needed Self-Study.

SPECIFIC EXPANSION PLANS:
US: All United States
Canada: All Canada
Overseas: All Countries

<< >>

BRITE SITE

4616 W. Fullerton Ave.
Chicago, IL 60639-1816
Tel: (800) 352-7483 (773) 772-7300
Fax: (773) 772-7631
Mr. Andreas R. Vassilos, President

BRITE SITE specializes in cleaning retail stores. We offer a proven system of operations, backed by over 25 years of experience. Our existing client base includes regional and national chain stores. Exclusive territories available. No experience necessary.

BACKGROUND:
Established: 1971; 1st Franchised: 1993
Franchised Units: 7
Company-Owned Units 1
Total Units: 8
Dist.: US-7; CAN-0; O'seas-0
North America: 3 States
Density: 6 in IL, 1 in IN, 1 in WI
Projected New Units (12 Months): 5
Qualifications: 2, 3, 3, 1, 1, 5
Registered: IL,IN

FINANCIAL/TERMS:
Cash Investment: $5-50K
Total Investment: $8-100K
Minimum Net Worth: $15K
Fees: Franchise - $5-15K+
Royalty - 10%; Ad. - 0-2%
Earnings Claim Statement: No
Term of Contract (Years): 10/10
Avg. # Of Employees: NR
Passive Ownership: Discouraged
Encourage Conversions: Yes
Area Develop. Agreements: Yes/10
Sub-Franchising Contracts: Yes
Expand In Territory: Yes
Space Needs: NR SF; SF, HB, Industrial Park

SUPPORT & TRAINING PROVIDED:
Financial Assistance Provided: Yes(B)
Site Selection Assistance: N/A
Lease Negotiation Assistance: Yes
Co-Operative Advertising: Yes
Franchisee Assoc./Member: Yes/Yes
Size Of Corporate Staff: 6
On-Going Support: A,B,C,D,E,G,H,I
Training: 3-14 Days Home Office and Field.

SPECIFIC EXPANSION PLANS:
US: Midwest
Canada: No
Overseas: No

<< >>

BUILDING SERVICES OF AMERICA

11900 W. 87th St., # 135
Lenexa, KS 66215
Tel: (913) 599-6200
Fax: (913) 599-4441
E-Mail: howard@buildingservicesofamerica.com
Web Site: www.buildingservicesofamerica.com
Mr. Howard Capps, President

Franchised commercial cleaning.

BACKGROUND:
Established: 1992; 1st Franchised: 1991
Franchised Units: 35
Company-Owned Units 1
Total Units: 36
Dist.: US-36; CAN-0; O'seas-0
North America: 2 States
Density: 15 in KS, 21 in MO
Projected New Units (12 Months): 6
Qualifications: 2, 2, 1, 2, 2, 2
Registered: NR

FINANCIAL/TERMS:
Cash Investment: $1.5-15K
Total Investment: $7.5-20K
Minimum Net Worth: $0K
Fees: Franchise - $1.5-15K
Royalty - 8%; Ad. - 0%
Earnings Claim Statement: No
Term of Contract (Years): 10/10
Avg. # Of Employees: Varies
Passive Ownership: Not Allowed
Encourage Conversions: N/A
Area Develop. Agreements: No
Sub-Franchising Contracts: No
Expand In Territory: Yes
Space Needs: NR SF; N/A

SUPPORT & TRAINING PROVIDED:
Financial Assistance Provided: Yes(D)
Site Selection Assistance: No
Lease Negotiation Assistance: No
Co-Operative Advertising: No
Franchisee Assoc./Member: Yes/Yes
Size Of Corporate Staff: 7
On-Going Support: A,C,D,G,H
Training: 1-2 Weeks at Corporate Office.

SPECIFIC EXPANSION PLANS:
US: All United States
Canada: No
Overseas: No

<< >>

CHEM-DRY CANADA

8472 Harvard Pl.
Chilliwack, BC V2P 7Z5 CANADA
Tel: (888) CHEM-DRY (604) 795-9918
Fax: (604) 795-7071
E-Mail: chemdry@chemdry.ca
Web Site: www.chemdry.ca
Ms. Trudy V. Miller, Franchise Marketing/Licensing

The world's largest carpet & upholstery franchise rated 'The Best of the Best' by Entrepreneur magazine for 12 consecutive years. Our unique patented, non-toxic, heated carbonating cleaner allows most carpets to dry in one hour. State-of-the-art equipment, 22 years experience, on-going research, in-field training, technical support, a monthly newsletter and annual conventions makes a CHEM-DRY franchise a good business.

BACKGROUND:
Established: 1977; 1st Franchised: 1978
Franchised Units: 135
Company-Owned Units 0
Total Units: 135
Dist.: US-0; CAN-135; O'seas-0
North America: 10 Provinces
Density: 48 in ON, 28 in BC, 18 in AB
Projected New Units (12 Months): 20
Qualifications: 3, 1, 1, 1, 1, 1
Registered: AB

FINANCIAL/TERMS:
Cash Investment: $17-25K
Total Investment: $37.9K
Minimum Net Worth: $40K
Fees: Franchise - $11K
Royalty - $310/Mo.; Ad. - $0
Earnings Claim Statement: No
Term of Contract (Years): 5/5
Avg. # Of Employees: 1-5 FT, 2-4 PT
Passive Ownership: Discouraged
Encourage Conversions: N/A
Area Develop. Agreements: No
Sub-Franchising Contracts: No
Expand In Territory: Yes
Space Needs: 500 SF; HB

SUPPORT & TRAINING PROVIDED:
Financial Assistance Provided: Yes(D)

Site Selection Assistance: N/A
Lease Negotiation Assistance: No
Co-Operative Advertising: No
Franchisee Assoc./Member: Yes/Yes
Size Of Corporate Staff: 14
On-Going Support: B,C,D,G,H,I
Training: 1 Week Head Office.

SPECIFIC EXPANSION PLANS:
US: N/A
Canada: All Canada
Overseas: No

<< >>

Top 50

CHEM-DRY CARPET & UPHOLSTERY CLEANING

1530 N. 1000 West
Logan, UT 84321-1900
Tel: (800) 841-6583 (435) 755-0099
Fax: (435) 755-0021
E-Mail: charlie@chemdry.com
Web Site: www.chemdry.com
Mr. Karwin R. Weaver, Franchise Sales Rep.

We have over 20 years of experience, state-of-the-art, patented equipment, on-going research and development and technical support. CHEM-DRY lets you offer a unique, patented, hot carbonating carpet and upholstery cleaning service that is second-to-none! Entrepreneur Magazine has rated us #1 in our field for the past 10 years.

BACKGROUND: IFA MEMBER
Established: 1977; 1st Franchised: 1978
Franchised Units: 3,903
Company-Owned Units 0
Total Units: 3,903
Dist.: US-2505; CAN-124; O'seas-1330
North America: 50 States, 11Provinces
Density: 433 in CA, 177 in TX, 151 FL
Projected New Units (12 Months): 225-250
Qualifications: 2, 3, 1, 1, 3, 5
Registered: All States

FINANCIAL/TERMS:
Cash Investment: $7K Down Pay.
Total Investment: $6.9-27.6K
Minimum Net Worth: $N/A
Fees: Franchise - $19.9K
Royalty - $198/Mo.; Ad. - 0%
Earnings Claim Statement: No
Term of Contract (Years): 5/5
Avg. # Of Employees: 3 FT
Passive Ownership: Allowed
Encourage Conversions: N/A
Area Develop. Agreements: No
Sub-Franchising Contracts: No
Expand In Territory: No
Space Needs: N/A SF; N/A

SUPPORT & TRAINING PROVIDED:
Financial Assistance Provided: Yes(D)
Site Selection Assistance: N/A
Lease Negotiation Assistance: N/A
Co-Operative Advertising: Yes
Franchisee Assoc./Member: Yes/No
Size Of Corporate Staff: 60
On-Going Support: B,C,D,G,H,I
Training: 5 Days Logan, UT; 8 Hour Home Study with Video.

SPECIFIC EXPANSION PLANS:
US: All United States
Canada: All Canada
Overseas: Most Countries

<< >>

CHEMSTATION INTERNATIONAL

3400 Encrete Ln.
Dayton, OH 45439
Tel: (800) 554-8265 (937) 294-8265
Fax: (937) 294-5360
E-Mail: franchise@chemstation.com
Web Site: www.chemstation.com
Mr. Steven Cox, Dir. Franchise Sales

CHEMSTATION is an affiliation of manufacturing centers which offer their customers the unique service of custom manufactured cleaning chemicals delivered in bulk to refillable containers that eliminate the waste and inefficiencies of drums.

BACKGROUND: IFA MEMBER
Established: 1983; 1st Franchised: 1984
Franchised Units: 44
Company-Owned Units 3
Total Units: 47
Dist.: US-42; CAN-0; O'seas-0
North America: 27 States
Density: 5 in OH, 3 in MI, 3 in IN
Projected New Units (12 Months): 2
Qualifications: 5, 4, 3, 2, 1, 5
Registered: NR

FINANCIAL/TERMS:
Cash Investment: $150-300K
Total Investment: $500-700K
Minimum Net Worth: $NR
Fees: Franchise - $45K
Royalty - 4%; Ad. - 2%
Earnings Claim Statement: No
Term of Contract (Years): 10/5
Avg. # Of Employees: 6 FT
Passive Ownership: Discouraged
Encourage Conversions: N/A
Area Develop. Agreements: No
Sub-Franchising Contracts: No
Expand In Territory: Yes
Space Needs: 6,000 SF; Commercial/Industrial

SUPPORT & TRAINING PROVIDED:
Financial Assistance Provided: No
Site Selection Assistance: Yes
Lease Negotiation Assistance: Yes
Co-Operative Advertising: Yes
Franchisee Assoc./Member: Yes
Size Of Corporate Staff: 35
On-Going Support: A,B,C,D,E,F,G,H,I
Training: 1 Week Dayton, OH and On-Going.

SPECIFIC EXPANSION PLANS:
US: West, NY, Northeast
Canada: All Canada
Overseas: All Countries

<< >>

CLEANNET USA

9861 Broken Land Pkwy., # 208
Columbia, MD 21046
Tel: (800) 735-8838 (301) 621-8839
Fax: (410) 720-5307
Web Site: www.cleannetusa.com
Mr. Dennis M. Urner, Executive VP

Full-service, turn-key commercial office cleaning franchise, offering guaranteed customer accounts, training equipment, supplies, local office support, quality control backup, billing/invoicing and guaranteed payment for services provided. Company also sells master licenses for markets with metropolitan populations of 500,000 and up.

BACKGROUND:
Established: 1987; 1st Franchised: 1988
Franchised Units: 2,146
Company-Owned Units 7
Total Units: 2,153
Dist.: US-1725; CAN-0; O'seas-0
North America: 13 States
Density: 366 in MD, 308 in NJ, 195 PA
Projected New Units (12 Months): 400
Qualifications: 4, 3, 2, 1, 3, 4
Registered: CA,FL,IL,MD,MI,VA

FINANCIAL/TERMS:
Cash Investment: $0-25K

Total Investment: $2.9-35.7K
Minimum Net Worth: $0-100K
Fees: Franchise - $2-25.5K
Royalty - 3%; Ad. - 0%
Earnings Claim Statement: No
Term of Contract (Years): 20/20
Avg. # Of Employees: 2 FT, 10 PT
Passive Ownership: Discouraged
Encourage Conversions: N/A
Area Develop. Agreements: Yes/20
Sub-Franchising Contracts: Yes
Expand In Territory: Yes
Space Needs: 2,000 SF; Multi-Tenant

SUPPORT & TRAINING PROVIDED:
Financial Assistance Provided: Yes(D)
Site Selection Assistance: Yes
Lease Negotiation Assistance: Yes
Co-Operative Advertising: No
Franchisee Assoc./Member: No
Size Of Corporate Staff: 75
On-Going Support: A,B,C,D,E,G,H,I
Training: 8 Days to 2 Weeks Company Offices; 4 Days to 3 Weeks Job Site or Master Offices.

SPECIFIC EXPANSION PLANS:
US: All United States
Canada: All Canada
Overseas: South Africa, Korea, Southeast Asia, Europe, Australia, U.K.

<< >>

Experience You Can Trust.

COIT SERVICES

897 Hinckley Rd.
Burlingame, CA 94010-1502
Tel: (800) 243-8797 (650) 697-5471
Fax: (650) 697-6117
E-Mail: nick@coit.com
Web Site: www.coit.com
Mr. Nick Granato, Chief Operating Officer

Granting large, exclusive territories, COIT SERVICES provides a proven opportunity in the carpet, upholstery, drapery, area rug air-duct cleaning and hard surface renewal business. COIT franchisees enjoy use of a universal 800# (1-800-FOR-COIT), along with successful marketing and business development that have been developed in 50 years of operational experience.

BACKGROUND: IFA MEMBER
Established: 1950; 1st Franchised: 1963
Franchised Units: 60
Company-Owned Units 10
Total Units: 70
Dist.: US-66; CAN-3; O'seas-1
North America: 26 States, 2 Provinces
Density: 16 in CA, 4 in WA, 4 in OH
Projected New Units (12 Months): 51
Qualifications: 3, 5, 4, 3, 1, 5
Registered: All States

FINANCIAL/TERMS:
Cash Investment: $40-60K
Total Investment: $100K
Minimum Net Worth: $No Minimum
Fees: Franchise - $25K
Royalty - 2-6%; Ad. - 0%
Earnings Claim Statement: Yes
Term of Contract (Years): 10/10
Avg. # Of Employees: 2 FT, 1 PT
Passive Ownership: Discouraged
Encourage Conversions: Yes
Area Develop. Agreements: No
Sub-Franchising Contracts: No
Expand In Territory: Yes
Space Needs: 1,000 SF; Industrial

SUPPORT & TRAINING PROVIDED:
Financial Assistance Provided: Yes(D)
Site Selection Assistance: Yes
Lease Negotiation Assistance: Yes
Co-Operative Advertising: Yes
Franchisee Assoc./Member: Yes/Yes
Size Of Corporate Staff: 19
On-Going Support: A,a,B,C,D,E,G,H,I
Training: 7 Days Corporate Headquarters; 1-2 Weeks in Field.

SPECIFIC EXPANSION PLANS:
US: Northeast, Southeast,Midwest
Canada: All Canada
Overseas: All Countries

<< >>

COUSTIC-GLO INTERNATIONAL

7115 Ohms Ln. # 7111
Minneapolis, MN 55439
Tel: (800) 333-8523 (952) 835-1338
Fax: (952) 835-1395
E-Mail: cgiinc@aol.com
Web Site: www.coustic-glo.com
Mr. Scott L. Smith, Dir. Fran. Marketing

Building restoration products which enable you to clean and restore all types of ceiling and wall areas. Very specialized market which is growing as buildings age and the indoor environmental concerns continue to grow nationwide.

BACKGROUND: IFA MEMBER
Established: 1975; 1st Franchised: 1984
Franchised Units: 150
Company-Owned Units 1
Total Units: 151
Dist.: US-210; CAN-26; O'seas-26
North America: NR
Density: 12 in GA, 6 in FL, 5 in TX
Projected New Units (12 Months): 50
Qualifications: 4, 4, 3, 3, 3, 3
Registered: All States

FINANCIAL/TERMS:
Cash Investment: $12-25K
Total Investment: $12-25K
Minimum Net Worth: $20K
Fees: Franchise - $12K
Royalty - 5%; Ad. - 1%
Earnings Claim Statement: Yes
Term of Contract (Years): 10/5
Avg. # Of Employees: 1 FT
Passive Ownership: Allowed
Encourage Conversions: N/A
Area Develop. Agreements: Yes/10
Sub-Franchising Contracts: Yes
Expand In Territory: Yes
Space Needs: N/A SF; N/A

SUPPORT & TRAINING PROVIDED:
Financial Assistance Provided: Yes(I)
Site Selection Assistance: N/A
Lease Negotiation Assistance: N/A
Co-Operative Advertising: Yes
Franchisee Assoc./Member: Yes/Yes
Size Of Corporate Staff: 20
On-Going Support: B,C,D,G,H,I
Training: 2 Weeks On-Location.

SPECIFIC EXPANSION PLANS:
US: All United States
Canada: All Canada
Overseas: All Countries

<< >>

COVERALL NORTH AMERICA

500 W. Cypress Creek Rd., # 580
Ft. Lauderdale, FL 33309
Tel: (800) 537-3371 (954) 351-1110
Fax: (954) 492-5044
E-Mail: info@coverall.com
Web Site: www.coverall.com
Mr. Jack Caughey, VP Franchise Development

Comprehensive janitorial franchise which includes state-of-the-art training, franchise development, equipment and supplies, billing and collection services, as well as customer assistance services. Additional training, bulk volume-buying power, insurance and benefit packages also available. Master franchises also available. Master insurance plans offered.

BACKGROUND: IFA MEMBER
Established: 1985; 1st Franchised: 1985
Franchised Units: 5,941
Company-Owned Units 0
Total Units: 5,941
Dist.: US-5676; CAN-88; O'seas-177
North America: 32 States, 2 Provinces
Density: 807 in CA, 714 in FL, 445 OH
Projected New Units (12 Months): 1,782
Qualifications: 3, 3, 2, 2, 3, 5
Registered: All States Except SD

FINANCIAL/TERMS:
Cash Investment: $1.5-25.5K
Total Investment: $6.2-35.9K
Minimum Net Worth: $1.5K
Fees: Franchise - $6-32.2K
Royalty - 5%; Ad. - 2%
Earnings Claim Statement: No
Term of Contract (Years): 20/20
Avg. # Of Employees: 1-2 FT, 2-3 PT
Passive Ownership: Allowed
Encourage Conversions: Yes
Area Develop. Agreements: Yes/20
Sub-Franchising Contracts: Yes
Expand In Territory: Yes
Space Needs: N/A SF; N/A

SUPPORT & TRAINING PROVIDED:
Financial Assistance Provided: Yes(D)
Site Selection Assistance: Yes
Lease Negotiation Assistance: No
Co-Operative Advertising: Yes
Franchisee Assoc./Member: No/No
Size Of Corporate Staff: 60
On-Going Support: A,B,C,D,G,H,I
Training: Approximately 40 Hours at Local Regional Office; Training Varies with Type of Franchise.

SPECIFIC EXPANSION PLANS:
US: All United States
Canada: All Canada
Overseas: All Countries

<< >>

DUCTBUSTERS

29160 US Hwy. 19 N.
Clearwater, FL 33761-2400
Tel: (800) 786-3828 (727) 787-7087
Fax: (727) 442-3380
E-Mail: billh@ductbusters.com
Web Site: www.ductbusters.com
Mr. Thomas J. Yacobellis, President/CEO

DUCTBUSTERS is the largest franchisor of duct-cleaning businesses selling exclusively to air conditioning contractors. You receive a protected territory, full use of the nationally registered name and logo, the Busterlink computer software, training for production-sales-and management, 14-volume training and reference manuals, equipment recommendations and continual on-going support.

BACKGROUND:
Established: 1989; 1st Franchised: 1992
Franchised Units: 29
Company-Owned Units 1
Total Units: 30
Dist.: US-25; CAN-0; O'seas-3
North America: 8 States
Density: 17 in FL, 3 in LA, 2 in TX
Projected New Units (12 Months): 16
Qualifications: 3, 4, 5, 2, 3, 5
Registered: CA,FL,IL,MD

FINANCIAL/TERMS:
Cash Investment: $7.5K
Total Investment: $2.5-50K
Minimum Net Worth: $N/A
Fees: Franchise - $7.5-24K
Royalty - 7%; Ad. - 0%
Earnings Claim Statement: No
Term of Contract (Years): 10/5
Avg. # Of Employees: 6 FT
Passive Ownership: Discouraged
Encourage Conversions: Yes
Area Develop. Agreements: NR
Sub-Franchising Contracts: NR
Expand In Territory: Yes
Space Needs: NR SF; N/A

SUPPORT & TRAINING PROVIDED:
Financial Assistance Provided: Yes(B)
Site Selection Assistance: N/A
Lease Negotiation Assistance: N/A
Co-Operative Advertising: N/A
Franchisee Assoc./Member: No
Size Of Corporate Staff: 6
On-Going Support: A,B,C,D,F,H,I
Training: 5 Days Clearwater, FL; 2 Days Franchisee's Facilities.

SPECIFIC EXPANSION PLANS:
US: All United States
Canada: All Canada
Overseas: All Countries

<< >>

DURACLEAN INTERNATIONAL

220 Campus Dr.
Arlington Heights, IL 60004-1485
Tel: (800) 251-7070 (847) 704-7100
Fax: (847) 704-7101
E-Mail: info@duraclean.com
Web Site: www.duraclean.com
Mr. Tom Mallory, Marketing. Development Mgr.

DURACLEAN offers distinct services, markets and revenue center packages to fit your needs for independence and growth. Carpet cleaning, ceiling and wall cleaning, upholstery and drapery cleaning, fire/smoke/water restoration, janitorial, pressure washing, hard surface floor care, duct cleaning and ultrasonic cleaning are all services that we offer. We are the most diversified cleaning franchise in the world.

BACKGROUND: IFA MEMBER
Established: 1930; 1st Franchised: 1945
Franchised Units: 516
Company-Owned Units 2
Total Units: 518
Dist.: US-267; CAN-22; O'seas-59
North America: 50 States
Density: 38 in FL, 34 in IL, 30 in CA
Projected New Units (12 Months): 30
Qualifications: 4, 4, 3, 3, 3, 3
Registered: All States

FINANCIAL/TERMS:
Cash Investment: $25K
Total Investment: $54-70K
Minimum Net Worth: $N/A
Fees: Franchise - $10K
Royalty - 6-8%; Ad. - 0%
Earnings Claim Statement: No
Term of Contract (Years): 5/5
Avg. # Of Employees: 2 FT, 1 PT
Passive Ownership: Discouraged
Encourage Conversions: Yes
Area Develop. Agreements: No
Sub-Franchising Contracts: No
Expand In Territory: Yes
Space Needs: N/A SF; HB

SUPPORT & TRAINING PROVIDED:
Financial Assistance Provided: Yes(D)
Site Selection Assistance: N/A
Lease Negotiation Assistance: N/A
Co-Operative Advertising: No
Franchisee Assoc./Member: Yes/No
Size Of Corporate Staff: 25
On-Going Support: C,D,G,H,I
Training: 6 Days Success Institute, Corp. Office; 2 Days On-Site Cleaning; Home Study Program.

SPECIFIC EXPANSION PLANS:
US: All United States
Canada: All Canada
Overseas: All Countries

<< >>

E. P. I. C. SYSTEMS

402 E. Maryland
Evansville, IN 47711
Tel: (800) 230-3742 (812) 428-7750
Fax: (812) 428-4162
E-Mail: epic_sys@hotmail.com
Mr. Jeffrey R. Schaperjohn, President

Complete janitorial service franchising master units for $25,000 per million population, single units for $6,500. We can assist with financing with good credit.

BACKGROUND:
Established: 1993; 1st Franchised: 1994
Franchised Units: 7
Company-Owned Units 0
Total Units: 7
Dist.: US-7; CAN-0; O'seas-0
North America: 2 States
Density: 4 in KY, 3 in IN
Projected New Units (12 Months): 6
Qualifications: 5, 3, 4, 3, 5, 4
Registered: FL,IN,MI

FINANCIAL/TERMS:
Cash Investment: $6.5-28.5K
Total Investment: $6.5-60K
Minimum Net Worth: $10.2-28.5K
Fees: Franchise - $6.5K
Royalty - 4-10%; Ad. - N/A
Earnings Claim Statement: No
Term of Contract (Years): 10/10
Avg. # Of Employees: 1 FT, 5 PT
Passive Ownership: Discouraged
Encourage Conversions: Yes
Area Develop. Agreements: Yes/10
Sub-Franchising Contracts: Yes
Expand In Territory: Yes
Space Needs: 250-1,000 SF; HB, OB

SUPPORT & TRAINING PROVIDED:
Financial Assistance Provided: Yes(D)
Site Selection Assistance: Yes
Lease Negotiation Assistance: No
Co-Operative Advertising: No
Franchisee Assoc./Member: No
Size Of Corporate Staff: 4
On-Going Support: c,D,I
Training: 2 Weeks at Headquarters.

SPECIFIC EXPANSION PLANS:
US: Midwest, Southeast
Canada: No
Overseas: No

<< >>

ENERGY WISE

215 Dutton Ave.
Sebastopol, CA 95472
Tel: (800) 553-6800 (707) 824-8775
Fax: (707) 824-6967
E-Mail: franchise@energywiseinc.com
Web Site: www.energywiseinc.com
Mr. Michael D. Gross, President

ENERGY WISE provides a yearly preventive maintenance program of the major appliances in the home, which save our customers money, while providing them with peace of mind. In addition, we offer a line of products and services which increase energy efficiency, improve air and water quality and provide for easier home maintenance - an excellent home-based business.

BACKGROUND: IFA MEMBER
Established: 1990; 1st Franchised: 1996
Franchised Units: 6
Company-Owned Units 1
Total Units: 7
Dist.: US-3; CAN-0; O'seas-0
North America: 1 State
Density: 3 in CA
Projected New Units (12 Months): 3
Qualifications: 4, 3, 3, 3, 4, 5
Registered: CA,VA

FINANCIAL/TERMS:
Cash Investment: $28-49.5K
Total Investment: $28-49.5K
Minimum Net Worth: $50K
Fees: Franchise - $12.5K
Royalty - 5%; Ad. - 0%
Earnings Claim Statement: No
Term of Contract (Years): 10/5
Avg. # Of Employees: 1 FT
Passive Ownership: Discouraged
Encourage Conversions: No
Area Develop. Agreements: No
Sub-Franchising Contracts: No
Expand In Territory: Yes
Space Needs: NR SF; HB

SUPPORT & TRAINING PROVIDED:
Financial Assistance Provided: No
Site Selection Assistance: N/A
Lease Negotiation Assistance: N/A
Co-Operative Advertising: No
Franchisee Assoc./Member: No
Size Of Corporate Staff: NR
On-Going Support: C,F,G,H,I
Training: 1 Week Sonoma County, CA.

SPECIFIC EXPANSION PLANS:
US: All United States
Canada: No
Overseas: No

<< >>

Top 50

ENVIRONMENTAL BIOTECH

1701 Biotech Way
Sarasota, FL 34243
Tel: (800) 314-6263 (941) 358-9112
Fax: (941) 359-9744
E-Mail: info@environmentalbiotech.com
Web Site: www.environmentalbiotech.com
Mr. Rick Bisio, VP Global Development

A sales to solutions service company. Utilizing the latest proprietary biotechnologies, we provide maintenance services to eliminate waste build-up in drain lines. Our target is the commercial and industrial food-service market, as well as hospitals and other producers of grease, oil, sugar, starch, and gelatin waste.

BACKGROUND: IFA MEMBER
Established: 1991; 1st Franchised: 1991
Franchised Units: 54
Company-Owned Units 5
Total Units: 59
Dist.: US-49; CAN-1; O'seas-9
North America: 3 States, 1 Province
Density: 3 in FL, 1 in TX, 1 in PA
Projected New Units (12 Months): 20
Qualifications: 4, 5, 2, 2, 4, 4
Registered: CA,DC,FL,HI,IL,IN,MD,MI, MN,NY,VA,WA

FINANCIAL/TERMS:
Cash Investment: $45-100K
Total Investment: $100K
Minimum Net Worth: $200K
Fees: Franchise - $35K
Royalty - 5%; Ad. - 1%
Earnings Claim Statement: Yes
Term of Contract (Years): 5/5/5
Avg. # Of Employees: 2 FT, 1 PT
Passive Ownership: Allowed
Encourage Conversions: No
Area Develop. Agreements: No
Sub-Franchising Contracts: No
Expand In Territory: No
Space Needs: 1,000 SF; Office

SUPPORT & TRAINING PROVIDED:
Financial Assistance Provided: Yes(D)
Site Selection Assistance: N/A
Lease Negotiation Assistance: Yes
Co-Operative Advertising: No
Franchisee Assoc./Member: Yes/Yes
Size Of Corporate Staff: 30
On-Going Support: b,C,D,F,G,h,I

Training: 2 Weeks at Headquarters; 3+ Weeks in Field.

SPECIFIC EXPANSION PLANS:

US: All United States
Canada: All Canada
Overseas: Most Developed Countries

<< >>

FABRIZONE CLEANING SYSTEMS

3135 Universal Dr., # 6
Mississauga, ON L4X 2E2 CANADA
Tel: (888) 781-1123 (416) 201-1010
Fax: (905) 602-7821
E-Mail: headoffice@fabrizone.com
Web Site: www.fabrizone.com
Mr. David S. Collier, President

FABRI-ZONE offers a full-service affiliate concept to start with a turn-key system with an environmentally-sensitive cleaning program, a patented dry cleaning and purification carpet cleaning process. Steam finishing process cleans upholstery and draperies. 14 profit centers mean high returns for affiliates. Recommended by carpet manufacturers.

BACKGROUND:

Established: 1981; 1st Franchised: 1984
Franchised Units: 39
Company-Owned Units 1
Total Units: 40
Dist.: US-7; CAN-30; O'seas-3
North America: NR
Density: NR
Projected New Units (12 Months): 8
Qualifications: 3, 4, 1, 4, 4, 4
Registered: NR

FINANCIAL/TERMS:

Cash Investment: $6K
Total Investment: $14K
Minimum Net Worth: $NR
Fees: Franchise - $Varies
Royalty - $150/mo.; Ad. - 0%
Earnings Claim Statement: NR
Term of Contract (Years): 3/3
Avg. # Of Employees: 2 FT, 4 PT
Passive Ownership: Not Allowed
Encourage Conversions: Yes
Area Develop. Agreements: Yes
Sub-Franchising Contracts: NR
Expand In Territory: NR
Space Needs: N/A SF; Home Based

SUPPORT & TRAINING PROVIDED:

Financial Assistance Provided: Yes
Site Selection Assistance: N/A
Lease Negotiation Assistance: N/A
Co-Operative Advertising: N/A
Franchisee Assoc./Member: No
Size Of Corporate Staff: 20
On-Going Support: B,C,d,e,G,H,I
Training: 8 Days Toronto, ON.

SPECIFIC EXPANSION PLANS:

US: All of United States
Canada: All Canada
Overseas: All Countries

<< >>

FIBRECLEAN SUPPLIES

1 - 3611 27 St. N.E.
Calgary, AB T1Y 5E4 CANADA
Tel: (403) 291-2870
Fax: (403) 291-3786
E-Mail: kbrown@fibreclean.com
Web Site: www.fibreclean.com
Ms. Kathy Brown, Franchise Operations Mgr.

FIBRECLEAN SUPPLIES distributes specialty wholesale supplies to the rapidly-expanding cleaning industry. We are the leading soft fibre supplier in Canada, with product lines that are recognizable throughout the industry. FIBRECLEAN offers franchisees existing sales to start with, exclusive territories, comprehensive training, customized software, in-house marketing department, centralized purchasing, certified instructors, product R & D, national and local mailers and much more.

BACKGROUND:

Established: 1977; 1st Franchised: 1996
Franchised Units: 4
Company-Owned Units 4
Total Units: 8
Dist.: US-0; CAN-8; O'seas-0
North America: 5 Provinces
Density: 3 in BC, 2 in AB, 1 in ON
Projected New Units (12 Months): 3
Qualifications: 5, 5, 2, 2, 2, 5
Registered: AB

FINANCIAL/TERMS:

Cash Investment: $75-125K
Total Investment: $100-200K
Minimum Net Worth: $100K
Fees: Franchise - $Varies
Royalty - 5%; Ad. - 1.25%
Earnings Claim Statement: No
Term of Contract (Years): 5/5
Avg. # Of Employees: 3 FT
Passive Ownership: Discouraged
Encourage Conversions: Yes
Area Develop. Agreements: Yes/Varies
Sub-Franchising Contracts: Yes
Expand In Territory: yes
Space Needs: 2,500 SF; Industrial Storefront

SUPPORT & TRAINING PROVIDED:

Financial Assistance Provided: No
Site Selection Assistance: Yes
Lease Negotiation Assistance: Yes
Co-Operative Advertising: Yes
Franchisee Assoc./Member: No
Size Of Corporate Staff: 31
On-Going Support: B,C,D,E,F,h
Training: 2 Weeks Calgary, AB; 1 Week On-Site.

SPECIFIC EXPANSION PLANS:

US: No
Canada: MB,PQ, Maritime
Overseas: No

<< >>

FISH WINDOW CLEANING SERVICES

148 #G Chesterfield Industrial Blvd.
Chesterfield, MO 63005
Tel: (877) 707-3474 (636) 530-7334
Fax: (636) 530-7856
E-Mail: campaign117@fishwindowcleaning.com
Web Site: www.fishwindowcleaning.com
Mr. Tim Church, Dir. Franchise Development

FISH WINDOW CLEANING provides 23 years of experience that gives the franchisee the keys to successfully manage his/her own business. FWC specializes in year-round residential and commercial window cleaning for structures 1 to 3 stories. FWC provides a service everyone appreciates with a catchy name everyone remembers. Large territories are awarded to allow the franchise owner to develop a thriving business and not just buy a job.

BACKGROUND: IFA MEMBER

Established: 1978; 1st Franchised: 1998
Franchised Units: 40
Company-Owned Units 2
Total Units: 42
Dist.: US-25; CAN-0; O'seas-0

North America: 12 States
Density: 7 in IN, 6 in OH, 5 in CO
Projected New Units (12 Months): 30
Qualifications: 4, 4, 1, 2, 3, 5
Registered: CA,FL,HI,IL,IN,MI,MN,NY, OR,RI,SD,VA,WA,WI,AB

FINANCIAL/TERMS:
Cash Investment: $25-100K
Total Investment: $27.83-119.85K
Minimum Net Worth: $70-500K
Fees: Franchise - $18.5-69.5K
Royalty - 6-8%; Ad. - 0%
Earnings Claim Statement: No
Term of Contract (Years): 10/5
Avg. # Of Employees: 5 FT
Passive Ownership: Discouraged
Encourage Conversions: Yes
Area Develop. Agreements: No
Sub-Franchising Contracts: No
Expand In Territory: Yes
Space Needs: 120 SF; Other

SUPPORT & TRAINING PROVIDED:
Financial Assistance Provided: Yes(D)
Site Selection Assistance: No
Lease Negotiation Assistance: No
Co-Operative Advertising: Yes
Franchisee Assoc./Member: Yes
Size Of Corporate Staff: 5
On-Going Support: A,B,C,D,G,H,I
Training: 2 Weeks, Chesterfield, MO; 2 Weeks, Franchisee's City.

SPECIFIC EXPANSION PLANS:
US: All United States
Canada: All Canada
Overseas: No

<< >>

HANDYMAN MATTERS
1251 S. Huron St., # C
Denver, CO 80228
Tel: (866) 808-8401
Fax: (720) 570-5017
E-Mail: andy@handymanmatters.com
Web Site: www.handymanmatters.com
Mr. Andy Bell, President/CEO

HANDYMAN MATTERS is an industry leader in the growing handyman repair and improvement category for residential and commercial properties. HANDYMAN MATTERS provides the convenience of one-call-does-it-all and is experiencing extremely high client satisfaction. We operate strictly as a time-plus-material service, choosing to employ our handymen for control, and offering our clients one handyman to perform carpentry, plumbing, electrical, drywall, masonry, roofing, and other tasks.

BACKGROUND: IFA MEMBER
Established: 1998; 1st Franchised: 2000
Franchised Units: 10
Company-Owned Units 3
Total Units: 13
Dist.: US-13; CAN-0; O'seas-0
North America: 4 States
Density: 6 in CO, 3 in CA, 2 in TX
Projected New Units (12 Months): 12
Qualifications: 3, 4, 4, 3, 3, 5
Registered: CA,IN,MI

FINANCIAL/TERMS:
Cash Investment: $50K
Total Investment: $50-75K
Minimum Net Worth: $150K
Fees: Franchise - $25K
Royalty - 6%; Ad. - 2%
Earnings Claim Statement: Yes
Term of Contract (Years): 10/5
Avg. # Of Employees: 12 FT
Passive Ownership: Allowed
Encourage Conversions: No
Area Develop. Agreements: Yes/10
Sub-Franchising Contracts: No
Expand In Territory: Yes
Space Needs: 600-1,000 SF; FS, HB

SUPPORT & TRAINING PROVIDED:
Financial Assistance Provided: Yes(I)
Site Selection Assistance: Yes
Lease Negotiation Assistance: Yes
Co-Operative Advertising: Yes
Franchisee Assoc./Member: No
Size Of Corporate Staff: 18
On-Going Support: a,C,D,E,G,h,I
Training: 1-2 Weeks in Denver, CO.

SPECIFIC EXPANSION PLANS:
US: All United States
Canada: All Canada
Overseas: Ireland

<< >>

HEAVEN'S BEST CARPET/ UPHOLST. CLEANING
247 N. 1st E., P.O. Box 607
Rexburg, ID 83440
Tel: (800) 359-2095 (208) 359-1106
Fax: (208) 359-1236
E-Mail: moinc@ida.net
Web Site: www.heavensbest.com
Mr. Dan Child

Unique low moisture cleaning process. There is no better franchise opportunity than this. Our franchisees are happy, our customers are happy. Our franchise is very affordable. Call for our free video.

BACKGROUND:
Established: 1983; 1st Franchised: 1983
Franchised Units: 530
Company-Owned Units 0
Total Units: 530
Dist.: US-491; CAN-4; O'seas-9
North America: 28 States
Density: 48 in CA, 46 in ID, 25 in CO
Projected New Units (12 Months): 100
Registered: CA,IL,IN,MN,OR,WA

FINANCIAL/TERMS:
Cash Investment: $7.5-20K
Total Investment: $16-40K
Minimum Net Worth: $10K
Fees: Franchise - $2.9K
Royalty - $80/Mo.; Ad. - NR
Earnings Claim Statement: No
Term of Contract (Years): 5/5
Avg. # Of Employees: 1 FT
Passive Ownership: Allowed
Encourage Conversions: Yes
Area Develop. Agreements: No
Sub-Franchising Contracts: Yes
Expand In Territory: Yes
Space Needs: N/A SF; N/A

SUPPORT & TRAINING PROVIDED:
Financial Assistance Provided: Yes
Site Selection Assistance: N/A
Lease Negotiation Assistance: N/A
Co-Operative Advertising: Yes
Franchisee Assoc./Member: Yes/Yes
Size Of Corporate Staff: 7
On-Going Support: A,B,F,G,H,I
Training: 4 Days Rexburg, ID.

SPECIFIC EXPANSION PLANS:
US: All United States
Canada: All Canada
Overseas: All Countries

<< >>

HYDRO PHYSICS PIPE INSPECTION
1855 W. Union Ave., # N
Englewood, CO 80110
Tel: (800) 781-3164 (303) 781-2474
Fax: (303) 781-0477
E-Mail: hydrophys@aol.com
Web Site: www.hydrophysics.com
Mr. Thomas J. Suiter, President

HYDRO PHYSICS specializes in the video inspection of underground pipes.

By seeing exactly what and where the problems are located, we can save our customers thousands of dollars in unnecessary repair costs. We are the only franchise specializing in this type of work.

BACKGROUND:
Established: 1991; 1st Franchised: 1998
Franchised Units: 9
Company-Owned Units 1
Total Units: 10
Dist.: US-10; CAN-0; O'seas-0
North America: 4 States
Density: 1 in CO, 1 in ID, 1 in MO
Projected New Units (12 Months): 15
Qualifications: 4, 3, 2, 2, 2, 5
Registered: CA,VA

FINANCIAL/TERMS:
Cash Investment: $25-80K
Total Investment: $68-125K
Minimum Net Worth: $250K
Fees: Franchise - $19.5K
Royalty - 7.5%; Ad. - 2%
Earnings Claim Statement: No
Term of Contract (Years): 10/10
Avg. # Of Employees: 1 FT
Passive Ownership: Not Allowed
Encourage Conversions: N/A
Area Develop. Agreements: Yes/10
Sub-Franchising Contracts: No
Expand In Territory: Yes
Space Needs: NR SF; N/A

SUPPORT & TRAINING PROVIDED:
Financial Assistance Provided: Yes(I)
Site Selection Assistance: N/A
Lease Negotiation Assistance: N/A
Co-Operative Advertising: N/A
Franchisee Assoc./Member: No
Size Of Corporate Staff: 2
On-Going Support: B,C,D,e,F,G,H,I
Training: 2 Weeks in Englewood, CO.

SPECIFIC EXPANSION PLANS:
US: All United States
Canada: No
Overseas: No

<< >>

JANI-KING INTERNATIONAL

16885 Dallas Pkwy.
Addison, TX 75001
Tel: (800) 526-4546 (972) 991-0900
Fax: (972) 991-5723
E-Mail: info@janiking.com
Web Site: www.janiking.com
Mr. Jerry L. Crawford, President

JANI-KING INTERNATIONAL is the world's largest commercial cleaning franchisor, with locations in 11 countries and nearly 100 regions in the U. S. and abroad. Our franchise opportunity includes initial customer contracts, training, continuous local support , administrative and accounting assistance, an equipment leasing program and national advertising. If you are searching for a flexible business opportunity, look no further.

BACKGROUND: IFA MEMBER
Established: 1969; 1st Franchised: 1974
Franchised Units: 7,700
Company-Owned Units 35
Total Units: 7,735
Dist.: US-4724; CAN-351; O'seas-528
North America: 39 States, 7 Provinces
Density: 880 in TX, 737 in CA, 307 FL
Projected New Units (12 Months): 1,500
Qualifications: 2, 2, 1, 2, 2, 3
Registered: CA,FL,HI,IL,IN,MI,MN,NY, OR,SD,VA,WA,WI,DC

FINANCIAL/TERMS:
Cash Investment: $2.9-33K
Total Investment: $2.9-40K
Minimum Net Worth: $2.9-33K
Fees: Franchise - $8-33K
Royalty - 10%; Ad. - 0%
Earnings Claim Statement: Yes
Term of Contract (Years): 20/20
Avg. # Of Employees: NR
Passive Ownership: Allowed
Encourage Conversions: N/A
Area Develop. Agreements: Yes/20
Sub-Franchising Contracts: Yes
Expand In Territory: Yes
Space Needs: NR SF; HB

SUPPORT & TRAINING PROVIDED:
Financial Assistance Provided: Yes(D)
Site Selection Assistance: N/A
Lease Negotiation Assistance: N/A
Co-Operative Advertising: N/A
Franchisee Assoc./Member: Yes/Yes
Size Of Corporate Staff: 65
On-Going Support: A,B,C,D,G,H,I
Training: 2 Weeks Local Regional Office.

SPECIFIC EXPANSION PLANS:
US: All United States
Canada: All Canada
Overseas: All Countries

<< >>

JAN-PRO CLEANING SYSTEMS

383 Strand Industrial Dr.
Little River, SC 29566
Tel: (800) 668-1001 (843) 399-9895
Fax: (843) 399-9890
E-Mail: janpro1@aol.com
Web Site: www.jan-pro.com
Ms. Carol McLennan, Vice President

JAN-PRO has built a solid reputation as a quality franchise organization within the commercial cleaning industry. We have been highly ranked in magazines such as Entrepreneur, Income Opportunities, Home Business and Business Start-Up. JAN-PRO franchise owners are in business for themselves, but not by themselves.

BACKGROUND:
Established: 1991; 1st Franchised: 1992
Franchised Units: 810
Company-Owned Units 0
Total Units: 810
Dist.: US-0; CAN-0; O'seas-0
North America: 16 States
Density: 75 in NJ, 55 in GA, 45 in IL
Projected New Units (12 Months): NR
Registered: NR

FINANCIAL/TERMS:
Cash Investment: $1-35K
Total Investment: $2.8-44K
Minimum Net Worth: $3K
Fees: Franchise - $1-35K
Royalty - 8%; Ad. - 0%
Earnings Claim Statement: No
Term of Contract (Years): 10/20
Avg. # Of Employees: 2 FT, 2 PT
Passive Ownership: Allowed
Encourage Conversions: NR
Area Develop. Agreements: No
Sub-Franchising Contracts: Yes
Expand In Territory: Yes
Space Needs: NR SF; HB

SUPPORT & TRAINING PROVIDED:
Financial Assistance Provided: NR
Site Selection Assistance: N/A
Lease Negotiation Assistance: N/A
Co-Operative Advertising: N/A
Franchisee Assoc./Member: No
Size Of Corporate Staff: NR
On-Going Support: A,B,C,D,G,H
Training: 5 On-Site Training Sessions.

SPECIFIC EXPANSION PLANS:
US: All United States
Canada: NR
Overseas: NR

<< >>

JANTIZE AMERICA

15449 Middlebelt
Livonia, MI 48154
Tel: (800) 968-9182 (734) 421-4733
Fax: (734) 421-4936
E-Mail: asi500@aol.com
Mr. Jerry Grabowski, President

You can own your own business for less than the cost of a new car! A JANTIZE commercial office cleaning franchise has it all - computerized procedures, audio/visual training, on-going assistance and more!

BACKGROUND:

Established: 1985; 1st Franchised: 1988
Franchised Units: 11
Company-Owned Units 0
Total Units: 11
Dist.: US-14; CAN-0; O'seas-0
North America: 2 States
Density: 13 in MI, 1 in NV
Projected New Units (12 Months): 5
Qualifications: 4, 4, 3, 2, 2, 5
Registered: MI

FINANCIAL/TERMS:

Cash Investment: $9-11.5K
Total Investment: $20K
Minimum Net Worth: $NR
Fees: Franchise - $3.5-16K
Royalty - 9%; Ad. - 0%
Earnings Claim Statement: No
Term of Contract (Years): 10/10
Avg. # Of Employees: 3-20 PT
Passive Ownership: Discouraged
Encourage Conversions: Yes
Area Develop. Agreements: No
Sub-Franchising Contracts: Yes
Expand In Territory: No
Space Needs: NR SF; NR

SUPPORT & TRAINING PROVIDED:

Financial Assistance Provided: Yes(D)
Site Selection Assistance: Yes
Lease Negotiation Assistance: No
Co-Operative Advertising: No
Franchisee Assoc./Member: NR
Size Of Corporate Staff: 8
On-Going Support: a,D,E,G,H,I
Training: 3-6 Days Headquarters; 3 Days Franchisee Location.

SPECIFIC EXPANSION PLANS:

US: All United States
Canada: All Canada
Overseas: No

KWIK DRY INTERNATIONAL

25665 Caton Farm Rd.
Plainfield, IL 60544
Tel: (815) 436-0333
Fax: (815) 436-7519
E-Mail: kwikdryint@hotmail.com
Web Site: www.kwikdry.com
Mr. Jim Boyd, Operations Manager

You would control your time and income, be new, yet run a business with 30 years of experience, using the dry extraction method of cleaning both carpets and furniture. KWIK DRY is very user-friendly (easy on the operator), utilizing an all natural cleaner. We put great emphasis on marketing (getting the jobs). Ideal as a second income business. Choice locations available.

BACKGROUND:

Established: 1967; 1st Franchised: 1995
Franchised Units: 16
Company-Owned Units 0
Total Units: 16
Dist.: US-12; CAN-0; O'seas-0
North America: 5 States
Density: 6 in IL, 3 in MO
Projected New Units (12 Months): 20
Qualifications: 1, 1, 1, 1, 4, 5
Registered: IL

FINANCIAL/TERMS:

Cash Investment: $5.7K
Total Investment: $11.7K
Minimum Net Worth: $10K
Fees: Franchise - $6K
Royalty - $175/Mo.; Ad. - 0%
Earnings Claim Statement: No
Term of Contract (Years): 5/5
Avg. # Of Employees: 1 FT
Passive Ownership: Allowed
Encourage Conversions: N/A
Area Develop. Agreements: No
Sub-Franchising Contracts: No
Expand In Territory: Yes
Space Needs: NR SF; HB

SUPPORT & TRAINING PROVIDED:

Financial Assistance Provided: Yes(D)
Site Selection Assistance: N/A
Lease Negotiation Assistance: N/A
Co-Operative Advertising: N/A
Franchisee Assoc./Member: No
Size Of Corporate Staff: NR
On-Going Support: B,G,h
Training: 5 Days Plainsfield, IL.

SPECIFIC EXPANSION PLANS:

US: All United States
Canada: No
Overseas: No

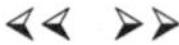

LANGENWALTER CARPET DYEING

1111 S. Richfield Rd.
Placentia, CA 92870-6790
Tel: (800) 422-4370 (714) 528-7610
Fax: (714) 528-7620
E-Mail: langdy@aol.com
Web Site: www.home.Navisoft.com/langenwalter
Mr. John Langenwalter, VP Fran. Dev.

We offer complete carpet color correction. The franchisees are carpet color correction experts. They can take care of problems such as sunfading, pet stains, bleach spots, chemical stains, etc. Complete color changes are also done to save the customer 85% of carpet replacement costs.

BACKGROUND:

Established: 1975; 1st Franchised: 1981
Franchised Units: 170
Company-Owned Units 3
Total Units: 173
Dist.: US-152; CAN-19; O'seas-2
North America: 25 States, 3 Provinces
Density: 75 in CA, 10 in BC, 9 in MA
Projected New Units (12 Months): 50
Qualifications: 3, 2, 1, 1, 2, 4
Registered: CA,FL,IN,MD,MI,MN,NY,OR,RI,VA,WA,WI,AB

FINANCIAL/TERMS:

Cash Investment: $30K
Total Investment: $30K
Minimum Net Worth: $30K
Fees: Franchise - $18K
Royalty - $110/Mo.; Ad. - 0%
Earnings Claim Statement: No
Term of Contract (Years): 3/3
Avg. # Of Employees: 1 PT
Passive Ownership: Not Allowed
Encourage Conversions: No
Area Develop. Agreements: No
Sub-Franchising Contracts: No
Expand In Territory: Yes
Space Needs: NR SF; HB

SUPPORT & TRAINING PROVIDED:

Financial Assistance Provided: No
Site Selection Assistance: N/A
Lease Negotiation Assistance: N/A
Co-Operative Advertising: Yes
Franchisee Assoc./Member: No
Size Of Corporate Staff: 10
On-Going Support: G,h,I
Training: 5 Days Placentia, CA.

SPECIFIC EXPANSION PLANS:

US: All United States
Canada: All Canada
Overseas: All Countries

<< >>

LASER CHEM ADVANCED CARPET & UPHOLSTERY DRY-CLEAN.

7022 S. 400 W.
Midvale, UT 84047

Tel: (888) 569-9533 (801) 569-9500
Fax: (801) 569-8400
Mr. Michael Jenkins

The LASER CHEM ADVANCED CARPET CLEANING cleans deep down, dries in minutes and leaves no residue. Customers are amazed! We also train you on the 6 methods of cleaning all types of upholstery. We provide on-going support.

BACKGROUND:
Established: 1993; 1st Franchised: 1994

Franchised Units:	36
Company-Owned Units	1
Total Units:	37
Dist.:	US-10; CAN-0; O'seas-0
North America:	8 States
Density:	2 in CA, 2 in OH, 1 in NJ
Projected New Units (12 Months):	10
Qualifications:	2, 1, 1, 1, 1, 1

Registered: NR

FINANCIAL/TERMS:

Cash Investment:	$6K+
Total Investment:	$6K+
Minimum Net Worth:	$5K
Fees: Franchise -	$10K
Royalty - $135/Mo.;	Ad. - 0%
Earnings Claim Statement:	No
Term of Contract (Years):	5/5
Avg. # Of Employees:	1 FT, 1 PT
Passive Ownership:	Allowed
Encourage Conversions:	Yes
Area Develop. Agreements:	No
Sub-Franchising Contracts:	No
Expand In Territory:	Yes

Space Needs: NR SF; N/A

SUPPORT & TRAINING PROVIDED:

Financial Assistance Provided:	Yes(D)
Site Selection Assistance:	N/A
Lease Negotiation Assistance:	N/A
Co-Operative Advertising:	N/A
Franchisee Assoc./Member:	No
Size Of Corporate Staff:	5
On-Going Support:	B,F,G,h,I

Training: 3-4 Days Midvale, UT.

SPECIFIC EXPANSION PLANS:

US:	All United States
Canada:	No
Overseas:	No

<< >>

LASER CHEM WHITE GLOVE COMMERCIAL CLEANING

7022 S. 400 W.
Midvale, UT 84047
Tel: (888) 569-9533 (801) 569-9500
Fax: (801) 569-8400
E-Mail: customercare@laserchem.com
Web Site: www.laserchem.com
Mr. Michael Jenkins, President

We are the only franchisor that we know of to offer full janitorial cleaning support and training, along with complete and detailed training on the famous LASER CHEM Advanced Carpet and Upholstery Cleaning Systems. We operate a very profit-oriented residential carpet cleaning business during the day while managing commercial buildings at night. We help you every step of the way.

BACKGROUND:
Established: 1993; 1st Franchised: 1994

Franchised Units:	35
Company-Owned Units	1
Total Units:	36
Dist.:	US-10; CAN-0; O'seas-0
North America:	1 State
Density:	10 in UT
Projected New Units (12 Months):	12
Qualifications:	2, 1, 1, 1, 1, 1

Registered: NR

FINANCIAL/TERMS:

Cash Investment:	$1.3K
Total Investment:	$8-19.2K
Minimum Net Worth:	$79.5K
Fees: Franchise -	$6.8K
Royalty - 7%;	Ad. - 0%
Earnings Claim Statement:	No
Term of Contract (Years):	10/10
Avg. # Of Employees:	1 FT, 2 PT
Passive Ownership:	Allowed
Encourage Conversions:	Yes
Area Develop. Agreements:	No
Sub-Franchising Contracts:	No
Expand In Territory:	Yes

Space Needs: NR SF; N/A

SUPPORT & TRAINING PROVIDED:

Financial Assistance Provided:	Yes(D)
Site Selection Assistance:	N/A
Lease Negotiation Assistance:	N/A
Co-Operative Advertising:	N/A
Franchisee Assoc./Member:	No
Size Of Corporate Staff:	5
On-Going Support:	a,B,C,D,F,G,h,I

Training: 34 Hours at Midvale, UT.

SPECIFIC EXPANSION PLANS:

US:	All United States
Canada:	No
Overseas:	No

<< >>

MAINTAIN CLEANING SYSTEMS

P.O. Box 867
Milford, OH 45150
Tel: (800) 861-4168 (513) 576-6622
Fax: (800) 867-0056
Mr. Allen Atkinson, President

Operate your own commercial cleaning service with outstanding local support. We will train and support you every step of the way.

BACKGROUND:
Established: 1993; 1st Franchised: 1993

Franchised Units:	49
Company-Owned Units	0
Total Units:	49
Dist.:	US-49; CAN-0; O'seas-0
North America:	2 States
Density:	40 in OH, 9 in KY
Projected New Units (12 Months):	40
Qualifications:	3, 3, 3, 3, 5, 5

Registered: NR

FINANCIAL/TERMS:

Cash Investment:	$1-5K
Total Investment:	$8.5-25K
Minimum Net Worth:	$N/A
Fees: Franchise -	$7K
Royalty - 5%;	Ad. - N/A
Earnings Claim Statement:	No
Term of Contract (Years):	5/2
Avg. # Of Employees:	1 PT
Passive Ownership:	Not Allowed
Encourage Conversions:	Yes
Area Develop. Agreements:	No
Sub-Franchising Contracts:	No
Expand In Territory:	N/A

Space Needs: NR SF; N/A

SUPPORT & TRAINING PROVIDED:

Financial Assistance Provided:	Yes(B)
Site Selection Assistance:	N/A
Lease Negotiation Assistance:	N/A
Co-Operative Advertising:	N/A
Franchisee Assoc./Member:	No
Size Of Corporate Staff:	10
On-Going Support:	A,C,D,E,H,I

Training: 2 Days Cincinnati, OH.

SPECIFIC EXPANSION PLANS:

US:	Midwest Only
Canada:	No
Overseas:	No

<< >>

MASTER CARE

555 6th St., # 327
New Westminster, BC V3L 4Y4
CANADA
Tel: (800) 889-2799 (604) 525-8221

Fax: (604) 526-2235
E-Mail: gerhard@mastercare.com
Web Site: www.mastercare.com
Mr. Gerhard Hoffman, President

Commercial janitorial services.

BACKGROUND:
Established: 1960; 1st Franchised: 1987
Franchised Units: 211
Company-Owned Units 1
Total Units: 212
Dist.: US-0; CAN-212; O'seas-0
North America: 1 Province
Density: 108 in BC
Projected New Units (12 Months): 30
Qualifications: 3, 3, 1, 1, 2, 3
Registered: NR

FINANCIAL/TERMS:
Cash Investment: $2-75K
Total Investment: $5-200K
Minimum Net Worth: $25K
Fees: Franchise - $4.5-125K
Royalty - 5-15%; Ad. - 1%
Earnings Claim Statement: No
Term of Contract (Years): 5/5
Avg. # Of Employees: 2 FT
Passive Ownership: Discouraged
Encourage Conversions: Yes
Area Develop. Agreements: Yes/10
Sub-Franchising Contracts: Yes
Expand In Territory: Yes
Space Needs: NR SF; N/A

SUPPORT & TRAINING PROVIDED:
Financial Assistance Provided: Yes(D)
Site Selection Assistance: Yes
Lease Negotiation Assistance: N/A
Co-Operative Advertising: Yes
Franchisee Assoc./Member: Yes/Yes
Size Of Corporate Staff: 4
On-Going Support: A,B,C,D,E,G,h,I
Training: 1-6 Weeks at Head Office.

SPECIFIC EXPANSION PLANS:
US: Master Franchises Only
Canada: Master Franchise
Overseas: No

<< >>

MAXCARE PROFESSIONAL CLEANING SYSTEMS

210 Town Park Dr.
Kennesaw, GA 30144
Tel: (800) 707-4332 (678) 355-4005
Fax: (678) 355-4977
E-Mail: kkaplan@maximgp.com
Web Site: www.maxcarecleaning.com
Mr. Ken Kaplan

All surfaces floor maintenance featuring state-of-the-art equipment, such as 'dust free' wood refinishing, and interior powerwashing of tile surfaces with no overspray. Many pre-established relationships with insurance companies, retailers, home improvement centers and real estate companies.

BACKGROUND:
Established: 1997; 1st Franchised: 1997
Franchised Units: 85
Company-Owned Units 0
Total Units: 85
Dist.: US-28; CAN-0; O'seas-0
North America: 34 States
Density: 11 in FL, 8 in TX, 6 in IL
Projected New Units (12 Months): 100
Qualifications: 3, 3, 3, 2, 3, 3
Registered: All States

FINANCIAL/TERMS:
Cash Investment: $NR
Total Investment: $12.5-50K
Minimum Net Worth: $50K
Fees: Franchise - $8.7K
Royalty - 6%; Ad. - 2%
Earnings Claim Statement: No
Term of Contract (Years): 10/10
Avg. # Of Employees: 3 FT
Passive Ownership: Allowed
Encourage Conversions: N/A
Area Develop. Agreements: No
Sub-Franchising Contracts: No
Expand In Territory: Yes
Space Needs: NR SF; HB

SUPPORT & TRAINING PROVIDED:
Financial Assistance Provided: Yes(D)
Site Selection Assistance: N/A
Lease Negotiation Assistance: N/A
Co-Operative Advertising: N/A
Franchisee Assoc./Member: No
Size Of Corporate Staff: 12
On-Going Support: B,C,D,E,G,H,I
Training: 10-16 Days Atlanta, GA.

SPECIFIC EXPANSION PLANS:
US: All United States
Canada: All Canada
Overseas: No

<< >>

MILLICARE COMMERCIAL CARPET CARE

201 Lukken Industrial Dr., W.
LaGrange, GA 30240-5913
Tel: (888) 88M-CARE (706) 880-5741
Fax: (706) 880-3279
E-Mail: nancy_heflin@millicare.com
Web Site: www.millicare.com
Ms. Caroil Brewton, Dir. Marketing

Buy into experience and professionalism. MILLICARE ENVIRONMENTAL SERVICES is currently seeking to select people to become franchisees in select cities in North America. The MILLICARE system includes a variety of services provided to commercial facility managers including carpet maintenance, carpet recycling, panel and upholstery cleaning and entryway systems. Franchisees receive world-class training, sales and marketing programs from a strong, experienced global franchisor.

BACKGROUND: IFA MEMBER
Established: 1984; 1st Franchised: 1996
Franchised Units: 74
Company-Owned Units 0
Total Units: 74
Dist.: US-71; CAN-7; O'seas-2
North America: NR
Density: NR
Projected New Units (12 Months): 15-20
Qualifications: 5, 4, 3, 3, 4, 5
Registered: CA,FL,HI,IL,IN,MD,MI,MN, NY,OR,RI,VA,WA,WI,DC,AB

FINANCIAL/TERMS:
Cash Investment: $30-50K
Total Investment: $70-170K
Minimum Net Worth: $100K
Fees: Franchise - $20K
Royalty - 6%; Ad. - 2%
Earnings Claim Statement: No
Term of Contract (Years): 5/5
Avg. # Of Employees: 1-20 FT
Passive Ownership: Allowed
Encourage Conversions: No
Area Develop. Agreements: Poss.
Sub-Franchising Contracts: No
Expand In Territory: Possible
Space Needs: 2,000 SF; Warehouse

SUPPORT & TRAINING PROVIDED:
Financial Assistance Provided: Yes(I)
Site Selection Assistance: No
Lease Negotiation Assistance: N/A
Co-Operative Advertising: Yes
Franchisee Assoc./Member: Yes
Size Of Corporate Staff: 6
On-Going Support: C,D,E,G,H,I
Training: 3 Days La Grange, GA; 3 Days Model Franchise Location, DE; 2 Days Franchisee's Location.

SPECIFIC EXPANSION PLANS:
US: All Major 2ndary Metro Areas
Canada: Toronto,Montreal
Overseas: Mexico

<< >>

Modernistic

MODERNISTIC CARPET & UPHOLSTERY CLEANING CO.

1460 Rankin St.
Troy, MI 48083
Tel: (800) 609-1000 (248) 589-1700
Fax: (248) 589-2660
E-Mail: vic@kfdc.com
Web Site: www.kfdc.com
Mr. Vic Koppang, President/CEO

We are a full-service carpet and upholstery cleaning company, established in 1972 and the largest of its kind in Michigan. We rank in the top 5 nationally among all independent companies, we grant larger territories and we are looking for qualified people to represent our brand name in major U.S. markets.

BACKGROUND: IFA MEMBER
Established: 1972; 1st Franchised: 1999
Franchised Units: 4
Company-Owned Units 0
Total Units: 4
Dist.: US-4; CAN-0; O'seas-0
North America: 1 State
Density: 4 in MI
Projected New Units (12 Months): 8-15
Qualifications: 3, 4, 2, 3, 3, 4
Registered: FL,IL,IN,MI,OR,WI

FINANCIAL/TERMS:
Cash Investment: $50K
Total Investment: $50-100K
Minimum Net Worth: $50K
Fees: Franchise - $12-40K
Royalty - 6%; Ad. - 14%
Earnings Claim Statement: No
Term of Contract (Years): Life
Avg. # Of Employees: 2 FT
Passive Ownership: Discouraged
Encourage Conversions: Yes
Area Develop. Agreements: Yes
Sub-Franchising Contracts: Yes
Expand In Territory: Yes
Space Needs: N/A SF; SF

SUPPORT & TRAINING PROVIDED:
Financial Assistance Provided: Yes(I)
Site Selection Assistance: Yes
Lease Negotiation Assistance: Yes
Co-Operative Advertising: Yes
Franchisee Assoc./Member: Yes/Yes
Size Of Corporate Staff: 70
On-Going Support: B,C,D,E,G,h,I
Training: 2 Weeks in Troy, MI; 1 Week On-Site.

SPECIFIC EXPANSION PLANS:
US: 43 States Where Registered
Canada: No
Overseas: No

<< >>

Top 50

MR. ROOTER CORP.

1020 N. University Parks Dr.
Waco, TX 76707
Tel: (800) 298-6855 (254) 745-2439
Fax: (800) 209-7621
E-Mail: mhawkins@dwyergroup.com
Web Site: www.mrrooter.com
Mr. Mike Hawkins, VP Franchising

Full-service plumbing and sewer/drain cleaning. Franchise specializing in conversion of existing trades people to our method of doing business.

BACKGROUND: IFA MEMBER
Established: 1968; 1st Franchised: 1972
Franchised Units: 263
Company-Owned Units 0
Total Units: 263
Dist.: US-181; CAN-17; O'seas-65
North America: 41 States, 4 Provinces
Density: 35 in CA, 18 in ON, 17 in TX
Projected New Units (12 Months): 40
Qualifications: 3, 3, 5, 2, 3, 4
Registered: All States

FINANCIAL/TERMS:
Cash Investment: $NR
Total Investment: $NR
Minimum Net Worth: $Varies
Fees: Franchise - $22.5K
Royalty - 3-6%; Ad. - 2%
Earnings Claim Statement: No
Term of Contract (Years): 10/5
Avg. # Of Employees: Depends on Sales
Passive Ownership: Not Allowed
Encourage Conversions: Yes
Area Develop. Agreements: Yes/10
Sub-Franchising Contracts: Yes
Expand In Territory: Yes
Space Needs: NR SF; N/A

SUPPORT & TRAINING PROVIDED:
Financial Assistance Provided: Yes(I)
Site Selection Assistance: N/A
Lease Negotiation Assistance: N/A
Co-Operative Advertising: No
Franchisee Assoc./Member: No
Size Of Corporate Staff: 13
On-Going Support: C,D,E,F,G,H,I
Training: 1 Week Waco, TX.

SPECIFIC EXPANSION PLANS:
US: Uncovered Areas
Canada: All Canada
Overseas: All Countries

<< >>

NATIONAL MAINTENANCE CONTRACTORS

1801 130th Ave. NE
Bellevue, WA 98005
Tel: (800) 347-7844 (425) 881-0500
Fax: (425) 883-4785
E-Mail: lyle.graddon@natmainco
Web Site: www.natmainco
Mr. Lyle R. Graddon, President

NATIONAL MAINTENANCE CONTRACTORS is a janitorial business.

BACKGROUND:
Established: 1975; 1st Franchised: 1975
Franchised Units: 409
Company-Owned Units 0
Total Units: 409
Dist.: US-409; CAN-0; O'seas-0
North America: 2 States
Density: 275 in WA, 139 in OR
Projected New Units (12 Months): 25
Qualifications: 5, 2, 5, 1, 1, 5
Registered: OR,WA

FINANCIAL/TERMS:
Cash Investment: $1-20K
Total Investment: $2-22K
Minimum Net Worth: $N/A
Fees: Franchise - $1-20K
Royalty - 6%; Ad. - 0%
Earnings Claim Statement: No
Term of Contract (Years): 5/5
Avg. # Of Employees: 1-4 FT
Passive Ownership: Discouraged
Encourage Conversions: Yes
Area Develop. Agreements: No
Sub-Franchising Contracts: No
Expand In Territory: Yes
Space Needs: N/A SF; NR

SUPPORT & TRAINING PROVIDED:
Financial Assistance Provided: Yes(D)
Site Selection Assistance: N/A
Lease Negotiation Assistance: N/A
Co-Operative Advertising: N/A
Franchisee Assoc./Member: No
Size Of Corporate Staff: 32

On-Going Support: A,C,D,G,H,I
Training: 5 Days Headquarters.
SPECIFIC EXPANSION PLANS:
US: WA, OR Only
Canada: No
Overseas: No

<< >>

NATURZONE PEST CONTROL

1899 Porter Lake Dr., #103
Sarasota, FL 34240
Tel: (877) 3-NOPEST (941) 378-3334
Fax: (941) 378-8584
E-Mail: travis@naturzone.com
Web Site: www.naturzone.com
Mr. Travis Wellbrock, President

Natural, non-allergenic pest control + lawn care/fertilization. Serves both commercial units and residential homes.

BACKGROUND:
Established: 1988; 1st Franchised: 1999
Franchised Units: 5
Company-Owned Units 1
Total Units: 6
Dist.: US-4; CAN-0; O'seas-0
North America: 2 States
Density: 3 in FL, 1 in KY
Projected New Units (12 Months): 10
Qualifications: 3, 3, 2, 1, 3, 4
Registered: FL
FINANCIAL/TERMS:
Cash Investment: $5K
Total Investment: $25K
Minimum Net Worth: $50K
Fees: Franchise - $15K
Royalty - 5%; Ad. - N/A
Earnings Claim Statement: No
Term of Contract (Years): On-Going
Avg. # Of Employees: 3 FT
Passive Ownership: Discouraged
Encourage Conversions: Yes
Area Develop. Agreements: Yes
Sub-Franchising Contracts: No
Expand In Territory: Yes
Space Needs: NR SF; FS, HB, SC
SUPPORT & TRAINING PROVIDED:
Financial Assistance Provided: Yes(I)
Site Selection Assistance: No
Lease Negotiation Assistance: No
Co-Operative Advertising: Yes
Franchisee Assoc./Member: No
Size Of Corporate Staff: 10
On-Going Support: C,D,h
Training: 2-3 Weeks in Sarasota, FL.
SPECIFIC EXPANSION PLANS:
US: All United States
Canada: All Canada
Overseas: All Countries

<< >>

OMEX INTERNATIONAL

3905 Hartzdale Dr., # 506
Camp Hill, PA 17078
Tel: (800) 827-6639 (717) 737-7311
Fax: (717) 737-9271
E-Mail: kabato@omexcorp.com
Web Site: www.omexcorp.com
Mr. Gerald Boarman, II, President

OMEX provides commercial contract cleaning services to first class office facilities including Fortune 500 companies, large office buildings, banks and medical clinics. Seeking prospects with good management, sales or business backgrounds determined to succeed and willing to follow our system. Low investment! Low royalties! Major territories! Free franchise renewal!

BACKGROUND:
Established: 1979; 1st Franchised: 1994
Franchised Units: 12
Company-Owned Units 1
Total Units: 13
Dist.: US-12; CAN-0; O'seas-0
North America: 9 States
Density: 4 in PA
Projected New Units (12 Months): NR
Registered: NR
FINANCIAL/TERMS:
Cash Investment: $40K
Total Investment: $40.4-70.6K
Minimum Net Worth: $150K
Fees: Franchise - $15-25K
Royalty - 4%; Ad. - N/A
Earnings Claim Statement: No
Term of Contract (Years): 10/10
Avg. # Of Employees: Varies
Passive Ownership: Discouraged
Encourage Conversions: NR
Area Develop. Agreements: No
Sub-Franchising Contracts: No
Expand In Territory: Yes
Space Needs: 800-1200 SF; Prime Location Not Required
SUPPORT & TRAINING PROVIDED:
Financial Assistance Provided: NR
Site Selection Assistance: No
Lease Negotiation Assistance: Yes
Co-Operative Advertising: Yes
Franchisee Assoc./Member: No
Size Of Corporate Staff: 7
On-Going Support: A,B,C,D,E,G,H,h, I
Training: 1 Week, Corporate Headquarters; 1 Week, Franchisee's Territory.
SPECIFIC EXPANSION PLANS:
US: All United States
Canada: NR
Overseas: NR

<< >>

O.P.E.N.
CLEANING
SYSTEMS

OPENWORKS

2777 E. Camelback Rd., # 350
Phoenix, AZ 85016-4347
Tel: (800) 777-6736 (602) 224-0440
Fax: (602) 468-3788
E-Mail: info@OpenWorksWeb.com
Web Site: www.OpenWorksWeb.com
Ms. Stacey Deakins, Marketing Coord.

OPENWORKS has been granting commercial cleaning franchises since 1983. Our program is centered around on-going training and support in addition to guaranteed initial customers. All franchises include a customer base, equipment and advanced business training. We also offer Master Franchises on an exclusive basis for certain metropolitan areas. Contact us today for more information.

BACKGROUND: IFA MEMBER
Established: 1983; 1st Franchised: 1983
Franchised Units: 387
Company-Owned Units 3
Total Units: 390
Dist.: US-390; CAN-0; O'seas-0
North America: 3 States
Density: 188 in AZ, 126 in WA, 76 CA
Projected New Units (12 Months): 100
Qualifications: 3, 3, 1, 2, 4, 4
Registered: CA,WA
FINANCIAL/TERMS:
Cash Investment: $5-150K
Total Investment: $14-150K
Minimum Net Worth: $10-500K
Fees: Franchise - $5-150K
Royalty - 10%; Ad. - 1%
Earnings Claim Statement: No
Term of Contract (Years): 10/10
Avg. # Of Employees: 3+ FT

Passive Ownership: Discouraged
Encourage Conversions: Yes
Area Develop. Agreements: Yes/20
Sub-Franchising Contracts: Yes
Expand In Territory: Yes
Space Needs: 3,000(master) SF; Master

SUPPORT & TRAINING PROVIDED:

Financial Assistance Provided: Yes(D)
Site Selection Assistance: No
Lease Negotiation Assistance: Yes
Co-Operative Advertising: N/A
Franchisee Assoc./Member: No
Size Of Corporate Staff: 25
On-Going Support: A,B,C,D,E,G,H,I
Training: 2 Wks. Regional Office (Janitorial); 4 Wks. Regional Off. & 3 Wks. Master's Off. (Master).

SPECIFIC EXPANSION PLANS:

US: All United States
Canada: All Canada
Overseas: All Countries

<< >>

PROFESSIONAL CARPET SYSTEMS

4211 Atlantic Ave.
Raleigh, NC 27604
Tel: (800) 925-5055 (919) 875-8871
Fax: (919) 875-9855
E-Mail: fthompson@procarpetsys.com
Web Site: www.procarpetsys.com
Mr. Fritz D. Thompson, President

PROFESSIONAL CARPET SYSTEMS is the leader in "on-site" carpet re-dyeing, servicing thousands of apartment complexes, hotels and motels worldwide. Services also include carpet cleaning, rejuvenation, repair, water and flood damage restoration and "guaranteed odor control." A total carpet care concept serving commercial and residential customers.

BACKGROUND:

Established: 1978; 1st Franchised: 1979
Franchised Units: 70
Company-Owned Units 0
Total Units: 70
Dist.: US-114; CAN-8; O'seas-14
North America: 43 States, 6 Provinces
Density: 24 in CA, 12 in FL, 9 in NC
Projected New Units (12 Months): 15
Registered: All States

FINANCIAL/TERMS:

Cash Investment: $10K+
Total Investment: $19.7K+
Minimum Net Worth: $NR
Fees: Franchise - $14.7K
Royalty - 6%; Ad. - 0%
Earnings Claim Statement: No
Term of Contract (Years): 10/10
Avg. # Of Employees: 1 FT With Truck
Passive Ownership: Discouraged
Encourage Conversions: No
Area Develop. Agreements: No
Sub-Franchising Contracts: No
Expand In Territory: Yes
Space Needs: NR SF; HB

SUPPORT & TRAINING PROVIDED:

Financial Assistance Provided: No
Site Selection Assistance: Yes
Lease Negotiation Assistance: N/A
Co-Operative Advertising: N/A
Franchisee Assoc./Member: NR
Size Of Corporate Staff: 8
On-Going Support: A,B,C,D,F,G,H,I
Training: 2 Weeks Headquarters.

SPECIFIC EXPANSION PLANS:

US: All United States
Canada: All Canada
Overseas: All Countries

<< >>

"professional polish"
A Total Franchise System

PROFESSIONAL POLISH

5450 East Loop 820 South
Fort Worth, TX 76119
Tel: (800) 255-0488 (817) 572-7353
Fax: (817) 561-6193
E-Mail: carren@professionalpolish.com
Web Site: www.professionalpolish.com
Ms. Carren Cavanaugh, Owner

Janitorial, lawn and building repair. Alto distributor. We make our franchisor make money.

BACKGROUND:

Established: 1981; 1st Franchised: 1986
Franchised Units: 34
Company-Owned Units 2
Total Units: 36
Dist.: US-36; CAN-0; O'seas-0
North America: 2 States
Density: 1 in TX, 1 in NC
Projected New Units (12 Months): 4
Qualifications: 5, 5, 5, 5, 5, 5
Registered: FL

FINANCIAL/TERMS:

Cash Investment: $7.5K
Total Investment: $20K
Minimum Net Worth: $25K
Fees: Franchise - $4.5K
Royalty - 15%; Ad. - 0%
Earnings Claim Statement: No
Term of Contract (Years): 20/20
Avg. # Of Employees: 2 FT, 1 PT
Passive Ownership: Discouraged
Encourage Conversions: N/A
Area Develop. Agreements: No
Sub-Franchising Contracts: No
Expand In Territory: Yes
Space Needs: N/A SF; N/A

SUPPORT & TRAINING PROVIDED:

Financial Assistance Provided: NR
Site Selection Assistance: N/A
Lease Negotiation Assistance: N/A
Co-Operative Advertising: Yes
Franchisee Assoc./Member: No
Size Of Corporate Staff: 6
On-Going Support: A,B,C,D,F,G,H,I
Training: 2 Weeks On-Site; 1 Week Fort Worth, TX; 1 Week Followup On-Site.

SPECIFIC EXPANSION PLANS:

US: Southwest, Southeast
Canada: No
Overseas: No

<< >>

PROPERTY DAMAGE APPRAISERS

6100 Southwest Blvd., # 200
Fort Worth, TX 76109-3964
Tel: (800) 749-7324 (817) 731-5555
Fax: (817) 731-5550
Web Site: www.pdahomeoffice.com
Mr. Rick Cutler, Dir. Training/Development

The industry's largest, franchised appraisal company, with national marketing support, a computerized office management system, training and on-going management assistance. No initial franchise fee is required - only a royalty on completed business. Automobile damage appraising experience a pre-requisite.

BACKGROUND:

Established: 1963; 1st Franchised: 1963
Franchised Units: 259
Company-Owned Units 0
Total Units: 259
Dist.: US-263; CAN-0; O'seas-0
North America: 47 States
Density: 25 in TX, 21 in CA, 15 in FL
Projected New Units (12 Months): 20
Qualifications: 3, 3, 5, 3, , 5
Registered: All States

FINANCIAL/TERMS:

Cash Investment: $9.2-23K
Total Investment: $9.2-23K

Minimum Net Worth: $NR
Fees: Franchise - $0
Royalty - 15%; Ad. - 0%
Earnings Claim Statement: No
Term of Contract (Years): 3/5
Avg. # Of Employees: 2 FT
Passive Ownership: Not Allowed
Encourage Conversions: Yes
Area Develop. Agreements: No
Sub-Franchising Contracts: No
Expand In Territory: Yes
Space Needs: NR SF; N/A

SUPPORT & TRAINING PROVIDED:
Financial Assistance Provided: No
Site Selection Assistance: Yes
Lease Negotiation Assistance: N/A
Co-Operative Advertising: Yes
Franchisee Assoc./Member: No
Size Of Corporate Staff: 36
On-Going Support: A,C,D,G,H,I
Training: 1 Week Corporate Headquarters; 4 Days On-Site.

SPECIFIC EXPANSION PLANS:
US: All United States
Canada: No
Overseas: No

PUROFIRST/PUROCLEAN

5350 NW 35th Ave.
Ft. Lauderdale, FL 33309
Tel: (800) 247-9047 (954) 777-2431
Fax: (954) 931-1915
E-Mail: rodwyer@purofirst.com
Web Site: www.puroclean.com
Mr. Rory O'Dwyer, Vice President

Franchisees provide specialty, high-profit, casualty restoration work. Franchisees work both directly with insurance companies and the property owners. Franchisees work for most national insurance companies. Fast start-up means quicker profits.

BACKGROUND:
Established: 1985; 1st Franchised: 1991
Franchised Units: 74
Company-Owned Units 0
Total Units: 74
Dist.: US-74; CAN-0; O'seas-0
North America: 25 States
Density: 13 in CA, 10 in PA, 6 in NJ
Projected New Units (12 Months): 18
Qualifications: 3, 1, 1, 3, 1, 3
Registered: CA,FL,IL,IN,MI,NY,OR,VA, WA,WI

FINANCIAL/TERMS:
Cash Investment: $10K
Total Investment: $66.2-107.7K
Minimum Net Worth: $NR
Fees: Franchise - $25K
Royalty - 10-8%; Ad. - 0%
Earnings Claim Statement: Yes
Term of Contract (Years): 10/10
Avg. # Of Employees: 2 FT, 2 PT
Passive Ownership: Discouraged
Encourage Conversions: No
Area Develop. Agreements: No
Sub-Franchising Contracts: No
Expand In Territory: No
Space Needs: Varies SF; FS, SF,HB

SUPPORT & TRAINING PROVIDED:
Financial Assistance Provided: Yes(D)
Site Selection Assistance: No
Lease Negotiation Assistance: No
Co-Operative Advertising: No
Franchisee Assoc./Member: Yes/Yes
Size Of Corporate Staff: 13
On-Going Support: C,G,H,I
Training: 10 Days Ft. Lauderdale, FL; 5 Days Franchise Location.

SPECIFIC EXPANSION PLANS:
US: All US, Esp. CA, PA, FL
Canada: No
Overseas: No

<< >>

RACS INTERNATIONAL

8515 Cedar Place Dr., # 108
Indianapolis, 462 46269
Tel: (317) 259-7227
Fax: (317) 259-7410
Web Site: www.racsclean.com
Mr. Mark O'Brien,

RACS INTERNATIONAL is a name known for quality, integrity and outstanding service, with over 20 years of commercial cleaning experience. Currently, it is among the top 20 franchises in terms of low investment start-up costs. RACS has developed a highly-trained network of commercial cleaning franchises with excellent ratings.

BACKGROUND:
Established: 1989; 1st Franchised: 1991
Franchised Units: 10
Company-Owned Units 0
Total Units: 10
Dist.: US-42; CAN-0; O'seas-0
North America: 2 States
Density: 23 in FL, 11 in IN
Projected New Units (12 Months): 25
Registered: FL,IN

FINANCIAL/TERMS:
Cash Investment: $1.5-28K
Total Investment: $4.4-43.1K
Minimum Net Worth: $N/A
Fees: Franchise - $3-31.5K
Royalty - 5%; Ad. - 1%
Earnings Claim Statement: No
Term of Contract (Years): 20/20
Avg. # Of Employees: 5 FT
Passive Ownership: Not Allowed
Encourage Conversions: Yes
Area Develop. Agreements: Yes/10
Sub-Franchising Contracts: Yes
Expand In Territory: Yes
Space Needs: 1,500 SF; HB, Other

SUPPORT & TRAINING PROVIDED:
Financial Assistance Provided: Yes(D)
Site Selection Assistance: Yes
Lease Negotiation Assistance: Yes
Co-Operative Advertising: Yes
Franchisee Assoc./Member: No
Size Of Corporate Staff: 11
On-Going Support: A,b,C,D,G,I
Training: 18 Hours RACS Office; 12 Hours On-the-Job.

SPECIFIC EXPANSION PLANS:
US: All United States
Canada: No
Overseas: No

<< >>

RAINBOW INTERNATIONAL CARPET CARE & RESTORATION

P.O. Box 3146
Waco, TX 76707
Tel: (800) 280-9963 (254) 745-2439
Fax: (800) 209-7621
E-Mail: mhawkins@dwyergroup.com
Web Site: www.rainbowintl.com
Mr. Mike Hawkins, VP Franchising

Nationally acclaimed carpet care and restoration franchisor, with 16 years of experienced, positioned to help franchisees tap into the expanding insurance restoration industry, only one of the more than ten profit centers from which franchisees can gain competitive advantage. Success of our franchisees is attributed to our proven niche marketing methods, comprehensive 12-hour technical support and consumer awareness of RAINBOW. Featured in Entrepreneur's Top 100.

BACKGROUND: IFA MEMBER
Established: 1980; 1st Franchised: 1981
Franchised Units: 438
Company-Owned Units 0
Total Units: 438
Dist.: US-283; CAN-15; O'seas-130
North America: 42 States, 6 Provinces
Density: 50 in TX, 20 in CA, 15 in FL
Projected New Units (12 Months): 24
Qualifications: 3, 2, 1, 2, 3, 5
Registered: All States

FINANCIAL/TERMS:
Cash Investment: $15-20K
Total Investment: $47-77K
Minimum Net Worth: $30K
Fees: Franchise - $15.9K
Royalty - 7%; Ad. - 2%
Earnings Claim Statement: No
Term of Contract (Years): 10/5
Avg. # Of Employees: 2 FT, 1 PT
Passive Ownership: Discouraged
Encourage Conversions: No
Area Develop. Agreements: No
Sub-Franchising Contracts: No
Expand In Territory: Yes
Space Needs: NR SF; HB

SUPPORT & TRAINING PROVIDED:
Financial Assistance Provided: Yes(D)
Site Selection Assistance: N/A
Lease Negotiation Assistance: No
Co-Operative Advertising: No
Franchisee Assoc./Member: No
Size Of Corporate Staff: 14
On-Going Support: A,b,C,D,G,H,I
Training: 2 Weeks at Corporate Headquarters.

SPECIFIC EXPANSION PLANS:
US: All United States
Canada: All Canada
Overseas: Japan, Middle East, Europe, Latin America

<< >>

ROTO-ROOTER
300 Ashworth Rd.
West Des Moines, IA 50265
Tel: (800) 575-7737 (515) 223-1343
Fax: (515) 223-6109
E-Mail: pbarkman@rrsc.com
Web Site: www.rotorooter.com
Mr. Michael Higgins, Dir. Franchise Development

World's largest plumbing repair and sewer and drain cleaning company, providing service to residential, commercial and municipal customers.

BACKGROUND: IFA MEMBER
Established: 1935; 1st Franchised: 1935
Franchised Units: 500
Company-Owned Units 100
Total Units: 600
Dist.: US-598; CAN-23; O'seas-0
North America: 50 States, 5 Provinces
Density: 44 in CA, 28 in TX, 24 in FL
Projected New Units (12 Months): 2
Qualifications: 3, 4, 5, 2, 2, 2
Registered: All States and AB

FINANCIAL/TERMS:
Cash Investment: $15-75K
Total Investment: $25-99K
Minimum Net Worth: $N/A
Fees: Franchise - $10K
Royalty - Varies; Ad. - Varies
Earnings Claim Statement: No
Term of Contract (Years): 10/10
Avg. # Of Employees: NR
Passive Ownership: Discouraged
Encourage Conversions: Yes
Area Develop. Agreements: No
Sub-Franchising Contracts: No
Expand In Territory: Yes
Space Needs: NR SF; N/A

SUPPORT & TRAINING PROVIDED:
Financial Assistance Provided: Yes(I)
Site Selection Assistance: N/A
Lease Negotiation Assistance: N/A
Co-Operative Advertising: Yes
Franchisee Assoc./Member: Yes/No
Size Of Corporate Staff: 25
On-Going Support: B,G,h,I
Training: N/A.

SPECIFIC EXPANSION PLANS:
US: No
Canada: No
Overseas: All Countries

<< >>

ROTO-STATIC INTERNATIONAL
90 Delta Park Blvd., Bldg. A
Brampton, ON L6T 5E7 CANADA
Tel: (905) 458-7002
Fax: (905) 458-8650
E-Mail: success@rotostatic.com
Web Site: www.rotostatic.com
Mr. Greg Inkster, Vice President

Profit from offering 6 services, including a unique system of carpet cleaning, , using Static Attraction principle, water damage restoration and odor removal services. Complete training in head office. On-going support systems. A company with a proven past.

BACKGROUND:
Established: 1977; 1st Franchised: 1977
Franchised Units: 141
Company-Owned Units 0
Total Units: 141
Dist.: US-0; CAN-141; O'seas-0
North America: 9 Provinces
Density: ON, PQ, BC
Projected New Units (12 Months): 10
Registered: AB

FINANCIAL/TERMS:
Cash Investment: $5-20K
Total Investment: $45-60K
Minimum Net Worth: $NR
Fees: Franchise - $15K
Royalty - 5%; Ad. - 2%
Earnings Claim Statement: No
Term of Contract (Years): 10/10
Avg. # Of Employees: 1-2 FT
Passive Ownership: Not Allowed
Encourage Conversions: NR
Area Develop. Agreements: Yes
Sub-Franchising Contracts: Yes
Expand In Territory: No
Space Needs: NR SF; NR

SUPPORT & TRAINING PROVIDED:
Financial Assistance Provided: Yes(I)
Site Selection Assistance: N/A
Lease Negotiation Assistance: N/A
Co-Operative Advertising: N/A
Franchisee Assoc./Member: Yes
Size Of Corporate Staff: 7
On-Going Support: C,D,E,F,G,H,I

Training: 4 Days Toronto, ON.
SPECIFIC EXPANSION PLANS:
US: All United States
Canada: All Canada
Overseas: U.K., Germany, France, Australia, Japan, Mexico, Spain

<< >>

SANIBRITE

9040 Leslie St., # 218
Richmond Hill, ON L4B 3M4 CANADA
Tel: (416) 410-7264
Fax: (416) 410-7264
E-Mail: sanibrit@idirect.com
Web Site: www.sanibrite.on.ca
Mr. Hossein Companieh, President

SANIBRITE is a unique company that is embarking on one of the most dynamic and totally new ideas in Canada. We have combined the success rate of franchising with a profitable and growing field of commercial cleaning. As a weary investor, SANIBRITE will provide you with the best business investment available for your money. It is a business that will be immune to economic problems, such as depreciation, recession and inflation.

BACKGROUND:
Established: 1987; 1st Franchised: 1989
Franchised Units: 45
Company-Owned Units 1
Total Units: 46
Dist.: US-1; CAN-44; O'seas-1
North America: 2 States
Density: 44 in ON, 1 in PQ
Projected New Units (12 Months): 5
Qualifications: 4, 3, 4, 3, 3, 4
Registered: NR
FINANCIAL/TERMS:
Cash Investment: $2-20K
Total Investment: $2-20K
Minimum Net Worth: $NR
Fees: Franchise - $0.95-15K
Royalty - 9.5%; Ad. - 4%
Earnings Claim Statement: Yes
Term of Contract (Years): 10/5/5
Avg. # Of Employees: 2 FT, 1 PT
Passive Ownership: Not Allowed
Encourage Conversions: Yes
Area Develop. Agreements: Yes/10/5
Sub-Franchising Contracts: Yes
Expand In Territory: No
Space Needs: 700-1,000 SF; Varies
SUPPORT & TRAINING PROVIDED:
Financial Assistance Provided: Yes(D)
Site Selection Assistance: Yes
Lease Negotiation Assistance: Yes
Co-Operative Advertising: Yes
Franchisee Assoc./Member: Yes
Size Of Corporate Staff: 5
On-Going Support: A,B,C,D,E,G,H,I
Training: 3 Hours Head Office; 5 Days On-Site.
SPECIFIC EXPANSION PLANS:
US: All United States
Canada: All Canada
Overseas: All Countries

<< >>

SEALMASTER

P.O. Box 2218
Sandusky, OH 44870
Tel: (800) 395-7325 (419) 626-4375
Fax: (419) 626-5477
E-Mail: info@sealmaster.net
Web Site: www.sealmaster.net
Mr. Roger Auker, Franchise Development Dir.

SEALMASTER is now offering manufacturing/sales opportunities in the billion dollar pavement products industry. This is a business-to-business franchise, offering pavement sealers, crack fillers, asphalt repair products, tennis court/running track coatings, traffic striping paints, tools, equipment and more. Turnkey operations available with on-going training and support.

BACKGROUND: IFA MEMBER
Established: 1969; 1st Franchised: 1993
Franchised Units: 23
Company-Owned Units 2
Total Units: 25
Dist.: US-18; CAN-0; O'seas-0
North America: 17 States
Density: NR
Projected New Units (12 Months): 6
Qualifications: 5, 3, 2, 2, 3, 4
Registered: CA,FL,HI,IL,IN,MD,MI,MN, NY,OR,RI,VA,WA,WI,DC
FINANCIAL/TERMS:
Cash Investment: $175K
Total Investment: $223.3-426K
Minimum Net Worth: $300-500K
Fees: Franchise - $35K
Royalty - 5%; Ad. - 1.5%
Earnings Claim Statement: No
Term of Contract (Years): 10/5/5/5
Avg. # Of Employees: 3 FT, 3 PT
Passive Ownership: Discouraged
Encourage Conversions: Yes
Area Develop. Agreements: NR
Sub-Franchising Contracts: NR
Expand In Territory: NR
Space Needs: 7,000-10,000 SF; FS
SUPPORT & TRAINING PROVIDED:
Financial Assistance Provided: NR
Site Selection Assistance: Yes
Lease Negotiation Assistance: NR
Co-Operative Advertising: Yes
Franchisee Assoc./Member: No
Size Of Corporate Staff: 27
On-Going Support: A,B,C,D,E,G,I
Training: 2 Weeks Corporate Headquarters, OH.
SPECIFIC EXPANSION PLANS:
US: All United States
Canada: All Canada
Overseas: All Countries

<< >>

SERVICEMASTER CLEAN

860 Ridge Lake Blvd.
Memphis, TN 38120-9792
Tel: (800) 230-2360 (901) 684-7500
Fax: (901) 684-7580
E-Mail: mporada@smclean.com
Web Site: www.ownafranchise.com
Mr. David Messenger, Vice President

SERVICEMASTER CLEAN provides heavy-duty cleaning services to both residential and commercial customers. Services include carpet, upholstery, window, drapery, disaster restoration and janitorial cleaning that is recognized around the world. With over 50 years experience, SERVICEMASTER offers state-of-the-art equipment, research and development, continuous training, cross-selling promotions with our partner companies and a strong franchise relations base.

BACKGROUND: IFA MEMBER
Established: 1947; 1st Franchised: 1952
Franchised Units: 4,488
Company-Owned Units 0
Total Units: 4,488
Dist.: US-2,914; CAN-176; O'seas-1,398
North America: 50 States, 9 Provinces
Density: 214 in IL, 156 in CA, 145 OH
Projected New Units (12 Months): 130
Qualifications: 5, 3, 2, 2, 3, 5
Registered: All States and AB

FINANCIAL/TERMS:

Cash Investment: $10-20K
Total Investment: $20.3-84.5K
Minimum Net Worth: $100K
Fees: Franchise - $15.9-28.5K
Royalty - 4-10%; Ad. - 0.5-1%
Earnings Claim Statement: No
Term of Contract (Years): 5/5
Avg. # Of Employees: 3 FT, 2 PT
Passive Ownership: Discouraged
Encourage Conversions: Yes
Area Develop. Agreements: No
Sub-Franchising Contracts: Yes
Expand In Territory: Yes
Space Needs: N/A SF; N/A

SUPPORT & TRAINING PROVIDED:

Financial Assistance Provided: Yes(D)
Site Selection Assistance: No
Lease Negotiation Assistance: No
Co-Operative Advertising: Yes
Franchisee Assoc./Member: Yes/Yes
Size Of Corporate Staff: 200
On-Going Support: A,B,C,D,F,G,H,I
Training: 2 Weeks Memphis, TN; 1 Week on Location.

SPECIFIC EXPANSION PLANS:

US: All United States
Canada: All Canada
Overseas: All Countries

SERVPRO

575 Airport Blvd.
Gallatin, TN 37066
Tel: (800) 826-9586 (615) 451-0600
Fax: (615) 451-4861
E-Mail: franchise@servpronet.com
Web Site: www.servpro.com
Mr. Kevin Brown, Dir. Fran. Expansion

A completely diversified cleaning and restoration business, with multiple income opportunities. The insurance restoration market (fire, smoke and water damages) is our main focus. We also specialize in commercial and residential cleaning. SERVPRO teaches effective management, marketing and technical skills. We are seeking qualified individuals with the desire to own their own business and become part of the SERVPRO team. If you want to be the best, join the best team. Call 1-800-826-9586.

BACKGROUND:

Established: 1967; 1st Franchised: 1969
Franchised Units: 1,069
Company-Owned Units 0
Total Units: 1,069
Dist.: US-1031; CAN-0; O'seas-0
North America: 49 States
Density: 105 in CA, 78 in FL, 50 OH
Projected New Units (12 Months): 80
Qualifications: 3, 4, 1, 3, 4, 4
Registered: All States

FINANCIAL/TERMS:

Cash Investment: $30-50K
Total Investment: $59-95K
Minimum Net Worth: $50K
Fees: Franchise - $45K
Royalty - 8-10%; Ad. - Up to 3%
Earnings Claim Statement: No
Term of Contract (Years): 5/5
Avg. # Of Employees: 4 FT, Varied PT
Passive Ownership: Discouraged
Encourage Conversions: Yes
Area Develop. Agreements: No
Sub-Franchising Contracts: No
Expand In Territory: No
Space Needs: NR SF; N/A

SUPPORT & TRAINING PROVIDED:

Financial Assistance Provided: Yes(D)
Site Selection Assistance: N/A
Lease Negotiation Assistance: No
Co-Operative Advertising: No
Franchisee Assoc./Member: No
Size Of Corporate Staff: 85
On-Going Support: B,C,D,E,G,H
Training: 2 Weeks Gallatin, TN; 1 Week Franchisee's Business Location.

SPECIFIC EXPANSION PLANS:

US: All United States
Canada: No
Overseas: No

SPARKLE WASH

26851 Richmond Rd.
Bedford Heights, OH 44146
Tel: (800) 321-0770 (216) 464-4212
Fax: (216) 464-8869
E-Mail: pfunku@en.com
Web Site: www.sparklewash.com
Mr. Michael A. Klavora, President

SPARKLE WASH provides mobile power-cleaning and restoration, providing broad market opportunities to our franchisees for the commercial, industrial, residential and fleet markets. SPARKLE WASH franchisees can also provide special services, including wood restoration, all using our environmentally-friendly products.

BACKGROUND: IFA MEMBER

Established: 1965; 1st Franchised: 1967
Franchised Units: 173
Company-Owned Units 1
Total Units: 174
Dist.: US-93; CAN-0; O'seas-79
North America: 32 States
Density: 13 in OH, 13 in PA, 8 in NY
Projected New Units (12 Months): 10
Qualifications: 3, 3, 1, 2, 4, 5
Registered: All States

FINANCIAL/TERMS:

Cash Investment: $19.3-21.3K
Total Investment: $50K
Minimum Net Worth: $60K
Fees: Franchise - $15K
Royalty - 3-5%; Ad. - 0%
Earnings Claim Statement: Yes
Term of Contract (Years): Continual
Avg. # Of Employees: 2 FT, 2 PT
Passive Ownership: Allowed
Encourage Conversions: Yes
Area Develop. Agreements: No
Sub-Franchising Contracts: No
Expand In Territory: Yes
Space Needs: NR SF; N/A

SUPPORT & TRAINING PROVIDED:

Financial Assistance Provided: Yes(B)
Site Selection Assistance: N/A
Lease Negotiation Assistance: N/A
Co-Operative Advertising: No
Franchisee Assoc./Member: Yes/Yes
Size Of Corporate Staff: 15
On-Going Support: B,C,D,G,H,I
Training: 1 Week Headquarters; 3 Days Franchisee Location; 3 Days National/Regional Meetings.

SPECIFIC EXPANSION PLANS:

US: All United States
Canada: All Canada
Overseas: All Countries

STEAMATIC

303 Arthur St.
Fort Worth, TX 76107
Tel: (800) 527-1295 (817) 332-1575
Fax: (817) 332-5349
E-Mail: bsims@steamatic.com
Web Site: www.steamatic.com
Mr. Bill Sims, VP Franchise Development

The total cleaning and restoration franchise, serving the residential, commercial and industrial markets. Greatest emphasis is on combating many of the problems associated with indoor air pollution, such as cleaning/sanitation of the HVAC system, air ducts and coils, carpet cleaning, etc. Emphasis also on water/storm damage cleaning and restoration of residential/commercial buildings. Plus, general residential and commercial cleaning.

BACKGROUND: IFA MEMBER
Established: 1946; 1st Franchised: 1968
Franchised Units: 360
Company-Owned Units 9
Total Units: 369
Dist.: US-193; CAN-72; O'seas-21
North America: 50 States,10 Provinces
Density: 19 in TX, 15 in FL, 8 in IL
Projected New Units (12 Months): 40
Registered: All States

FINANCIAL/TERMS:
Cash Investment: $35-100K
Total Investment: $25-75K
Minimum Net Worth: $NR
Fees: Franchise - $5-18K
Royalty - 5-8%; Ad. - 0%
Earnings Claim Statement: No
Term of Contract (Years): 10/5
Avg. # Of Employees: 5-40 FT, 3-10 PT
Passive Ownership: Discouraged
Encourage Conversions: Yes
Area Develop. Agreements: No
Sub-Franchising Contracts: No
Expand In Territory: No
Space Needs: NR SF; Warehouse

SUPPORT & TRAINING PROVIDED:
Financial Assistance Provided: Yes(D)
Site Selection Assistance: N/A
Lease Negotiation Assistance: N/A
Co-Operative Advertising: N/A
Franchisee Assoc./Member: Yes/Yes
Size Of Corporate Staff: 32
On-Going Support: A,B,C,D,E,F,G,H,I
Training: 2 Weeks Ft. Worth, TX.

SPECIFIC EXPANSION PLANS:
US: All United States
Canada: All Canada
Overseas: All Countries

<< >>

SWISHER HYGIENE

6849 Fairview Rd.
Charlotte, NC 28210
Tel: (800) 444-4138 (704) 364-7707
Fax: (704) 364-1202
E-Mail: bmullan@swisheronline.com
Web Site: www.swisheronline.com
Mr. Bruce Mullan, VP Sales

SWISHER HYGIENE is the world's largest commercial restroom hygiene franchise. This unique niche franchise offers limited competition with high profit returns. Complete training and an extensive support program are provided. Franchisees provide a weekly service that is a combination of a sanitary cleaning and product supply.

BACKGROUND:
Established: 1981; 1st Franchised: 1990
Franchised Units: 128
Company-Owned Units 1
Total Units: 129
Dist.: US-98; CAN-8; O'seas-6
North America: 40 States, 4 Provinces
Density: 12 in CA, 8 in FL, 6 in MI
Projected New Units (12 Months): 20
Qualifications: 4, 4, 4, 3, 4, 3
Registered: All States

FINANCIAL/TERMS:
Cash Investment: $50-100K
Total Investment: $50-100K
Minimum Net Worth: $N/A
Fees: Franchise - $15-85K
Royalty - 6%; Ad. - 2%
Earnings Claim Statement: No
Term of Contract (Years): 5/5
Avg. # Of Employees: 5 FT
Passive Ownership: Discouraged
Encourage Conversions: N/A
Area Develop. Agreements: No
Sub-Franchising Contracts: No
Expand In Territory: Yes
Space Needs: 900-1,200 SF; HB, SC

SUPPORT & TRAINING PROVIDED:
Financial Assistance Provided: Yes(D)
Site Selection Assistance: No
Lease Negotiation Assistance: No
Co-Operative Advertising: No
Franchisee Assoc./Member: No
Size Of Corporate Staff: 55
On-Going Support: A,B,C,D,G,H,I
Training: 1 Week Charlotte, NC.

SPECIFIC EXPANSION PLANS:
US: All United States
Canada: All Canada
Overseas: All Countries

<< >>

TOWER CLEANING SYSTEMS

P.O. Box 2468
Southeastern, PA 19399
Tel: (800) 355-4000 (610) 278-9000
Fax: (610) 275-7662
E-Mail: towerclean@aol.com
Web Site: www.toweronline.com
Mr. Chuck Lomagro, Vice President

TOWER CLEANING was rated in the top 100 franchises by "Entrepreneur"; "Inc. Magazine" says we are one of the country's fastest-growing franchises of 1997. We feature a tested, proven program with your initial clients already obtained; full start-up package, complete step-by-step and on-going training; professional administrative support (customer relations, accounting, invoicing, on-going marketing).

BACKGROUND:
Established: 1988; 1st Franchised: 1990
Franchised Units: 615
Company-Owned Units 0
Total Units: 615
Dist.: US-1270; CAN-0; O'seas-0
North America: 19 States
Density: 480 in PA, 235 in NJ, 225 WA
Projected New Units (12 Months): 500
Qualifications: 3, 3, 3, 2, 1, 5
Registered: All States

FINANCIAL/TERMS:
Cash Investment: $1.5-25K
Total Investment: $3.4-34K
Minimum Net Worth: $10K
Fees: Franchise - $4-33.6K
Royalty - 3%; Ad. - 0%
Earnings Claim Statement: No
Term of Contract (Years): 10/10
Avg. # Of Employees: 1-5 FT
Passive Ownership: Allowed
Encourage Conversions: Yes
Area Develop. Agreements: Yes/10
Sub-Franchising Contracts: No
Expand In Territory: Yes
Space Needs: N/A SF; NR

SUPPORT & TRAINING PROVIDED:
Financial Assistance Provided: Yes(D)
Site Selection Assistance: N/A
Lease Negotiation Assistance: N/A
Co-Operative Advertising: N/A
Franchisee Assoc./Member: No
Size Of Corporate Staff: 50+
On-Going Support: A,B,C,D,G,H,I
Training: 1 Week Local Office; 2-3 Days On-Site.

SPECIFIC EXPANSION PLANS:
US: All United States
Canada: All Canada
Overseas: No

<< >>

TRULY NOLEN PEST CONTROL

3636 E. Speedway
Tucson, AZ 85716-4018
Tel: (800) 458-3664 (520) 327-3447
Fax: (520) 322-4010
E-Mail: franchisesupport@truly.com

Web Site: www.trulynolen.com
Mr. Chuck Nygren, VP Franchising

Pest, lawn, termite, inspection based upon a unique and memorably established business system.

BACKGROUND: IFA MEMBER
Established: 1938; 1st Franchised: 1996
Franchised Units: 9
Company-Owned Units 79
Total Units: 88
Dist.: US-91; CAN-0; O'seas-0
North America: 13 States
Density: 42 in FL, 19 in AZ, 8 in CA
Projected New Units (12 Months): 4
Qualifications: 2, 2, 2, 2, 2, 5
Registered: CA, FL, MI, NY

FINANCIAL/TERMS:
Cash Investment: $5-100K
Total Investment: $1.5-200K
Minimum Net Worth: $25K
Fees: Franchise - $45K
Royalty - 7%; Ad. - 0%
Earnings Claim Statement: No
Term of Contract (Years): 5
Avg. # Of Employees: 10 FT, 1 PT
Passive Ownership: Discouraged
Encourage Conversions: Yes
Area Develop. Agreements: No
Sub-Franchising Contracts: No
Expand In Territory: Yes
Space Needs: NR SF; N/A

SUPPORT & TRAINING PROVIDED:
Financial Assistance Provided: No
Site Selection Assistance: No
Lease Negotiation Assistance: No
Co-Operative Advertising: No
Franchisee Assoc./Member: No
Size Of Corporate Staff: 25
On-Going Support: C,c,D,d,h,I
Training: 1 Week in Pompano Beach, FL; On-Site as Determined.

SPECIFIC EXPANSION PLANS:
US: All United States
Canada: All Canada
Overseas: No

<< >>

UNICLEAN SYSTEMS

1010 W. Cleans Rd., #200
North Vancouver, BC V7R 4S9 CANADA
Tel: (604) 986-4750
Fax: (604) 987-6838
Mr. Jack B. Karpowicz, President

Commercial office cleaning on a long-term contract basis.

BACKGROUND:
Established: 1976; 1st Franchised: 1981
Franchised Units: 398
Company-Owned Units 1
Total Units: 399
Dist.: US-48; CAN-347; O'seas-0
North America: 12 States, 5 Provinces
Density: 167 in BC, 89 in ON, 35 PQ
Projected New Units (12 Months): 20
Qualifications: 2, 3, 2, 2, 4, 5
Registered: CL,IL,OR,WA

FINANCIAL/TERMS:
Cash Investment: $5.5-16.5K
Total Investment: $5.5-16.5K
Minimum Net Worth: $N/A
Fees: Franchise - $1.5K
Royalty - 15%; Ad. - 0-5%
Earnings Claim Statement: No
Term of Contract (Years): 3/3
Avg. # Of Employees: N/A
Passive Ownership: Discouraged
Encourage Conversions: No
Area Develop. Agreements: Yes/10
Sub-Franchising Contracts: Yes
Expand In Territory: Yes
Space Needs: N/A SF; HB

SUPPORT & TRAINING PROVIDED:
Financial Assistance Provided: Yes(I)
Site Selection Assistance: N/A
Lease Negotiation Assistance: No
Co-Operative Advertising: Yes
Franchisee Assoc./Member: No
Size Of Corporate Staff: 8
On-Going Support: A,b,c,D,G,H
Training: 1-2 Weeks Home Office, North Vancouver, BC.

SPECIFIC EXPANSION PLANS:
US: All United States
Canada: All Except AB
Overseas: No

<< >>

VANGUARD CLEANING SYSTEMS

3 Twin Dolphin Dr., # 295
Redwood City, CA 94065
Tel: (800) 564-6422 (650) 594-1500
Fax: (650) 591-1545
E-Mail: rlee@vanguardcleaning.com
Web Site: www.vanguardcleaning.com
Mr. Raymond C. Lee, President

VANGUARD CLEANING SYSTEMS has been successfully franchising in the commercial cleaning industry since 1984. VANGUARD is currently seeking unit and master franchisees in the United States. A VANGUARD Master has 2 key responsibilities: recruiting individual unit franchisees and securing commercial cleaning accounts for them.

BACKGROUND: IFA MEMBER
Established: 1984; 1st Franchised: 1984
Franchised Units: 211
Company-Owned Units 3
Total Units: 214
Dist.: US-214; CAN-0; O'seas-0
North America: 1 State
Density: 211 in CA
Projected New Units (12 Months): 80
Qualifications: 3, 5, 1, 3, 4, 5
Registered: CA,FL

FINANCIAL/TERMS:
Cash Investment: $37.5K(Master)
Total Investment: $100-220K (M)
Minimum Net Worth: $100K (Master)
Fees: Franchise - $75K (Master)
Royalty - 4% (Master); Ad. - NR
Earnings Claim Statement: No
Term of Contract (Years): 20/20
Avg. # Of Employees: 5 FT, 2 PT
Passive Ownership: Discouraged
Encourage Conversions: Yes
Area Develop. Agreements: No
Sub-Franchising Contracts: Yes
Expand In Territory: Yes
Space Needs: N/A SF; N/A

SUPPORT & TRAINING PROVIDED:
Financial Assistance Provided: Yes(D)
Site Selection Assistance: N/A
Lease Negotiation Assistance: N/A
Co-Operative Advertising: N/A
Franchisee Assoc./Member: No
Size Of Corporate Staff: 14
On-Going Support: A,b,C,D,G,I
Training: 3 Weeks+ Redwood City, CA.

SPECIFIC EXPANSION PLANS:
US: All United States
Canada: All Canada
Overseas: All Countries

<< >>

WINDOW BUTLER

6355 E. Kemper Rd., # 250
Cincinnati, OH 45241
Tel: (800) 808-6470 (513) 489-4000
Fax: (513) 469-2226

E-Mail: wbutler@one.net
Web Site: www.windowbutler.com
Mr. Steve Cohen,

Home services are in demand! A WINDOW BUTLER franchise provides busy homeowners with window cleaning and all the maintenance services they need. It is a business built around managing people, not doing the work yourself. Our complete package was developed by the founders of 2 highly successful service-related franchises with over 500 units collectively.

BACKGROUND: IFA MEMBER
Established: 1997; 1st Franchised: 1997
Franchised Units: 15
Company-Owned Units 0
Total Units: 15
Dist.: US-15; CAN-0; O'seas-0
North America: 10 States
Density: 2 in CA, 3 in TN, 2 in KS
Projected New Units (12 Months): 12
Qualifications: 3, 4, 1, 2, 3, 5
Registered: CA,FL,IL,IN,MD,MI,NY,OR,VA,DC

FINANCIAL/TERMS:
Cash Investment: $10-20K
Total Investment: $19.2-40.1K
Minimum Net Worth: $10K
Fees: Franchise - $9.9-23.9K
Royalty - 6%; Ad. - 3%
Earnings Claim Statement: No
Term of Contract (Years): 10/10
Avg. # Of Employees: 3 FT
Passive Ownership: Not Allowed
Encourage Conversions: Yes
Area Develop. Agreements: Yes/10
Sub-Franchising Contracts: No
Expand In Territory: N/A
Space Needs: N/A SF; HB

SUPPORT & TRAINING PROVIDED:
Financial Assistance Provided: Yes(D)
Site Selection Assistance: No
Lease Negotiation Assistance: No
Co-Operative Advertising: No
Franchisee Assoc./Member: No
Size Of Corporate Staff: 3
On-Going Support: A,B,C,D,F,G,H,I
Training: 5 Days Cincinnati, OH.

SPECIFIC EXPANSION PLANS:
US: All United States
Canada: No
Overseas: No

<< >>

WINDOW GENIE
350 Gest St.
Cincinnati, OH 45203
Tel: (800) 700-0022 (513) 241-8443
Fax: (513) 412-7760
E-Mail: squegeepro@aol.com
Web Site: www.windowgenie.com
Mr. Richard Nonelle, President

Residential window cleaning and pressure washing business.

BACKGROUND:
Established: 1994; 1st Franchised: 1998
Franchised Units: 30
Company-Owned Units 0
Total Units: 30
Dist.: US-21; CAN-0; O'seas-0
North America: 10 States
Density: 6 in OH, 2 in KY, 2 in PA
Projected New Units (12 Months): 19
Qualifications: 4, 4, 1, 3, 3, 5
Registered: CA,FL,IN,MI

FINANCIAL/TERMS:
Cash Investment: $10-15K
Total Investment: $28-42K
Minimum Net Worth: $Varies
Fees: Franchise - $19.5K
Royalty - 6%; Ad. - 1%
Earnings Claim Statement: No
Term of Contract (Years): 10/5
Avg. # Of Employees: 2 FT, 2 PT
Passive Ownership: Discouraged
Encourage Conversions: Yes
Area Develop. Agreements: No
Sub-Franchising Contracts: No
Expand In Territory: Yes
Space Needs: N/A SF; N/A

SUPPORT & TRAINING PROVIDED:
Financial Assistance Provided: No
Site Selection Assistance: N/A
Lease Negotiation Assistance: N/A
Co-Operative Advertising: N/A
Franchisee Assoc./Member: No
Size Of Corporate Staff: 3
On-Going Support: B,C,D,E,F,G,H,I
Training: 5 Days Corporate, Cincinnati, OH; 5 Days On-Site.

SPECIFIC EXPANSION PLANS:
US: All United States
Canada: All Canada
Overseas: No

<< >>

SUPPLEMENTAL LISTING OF FRANCHISORS

ARODAL, 6171 Conin Dr., Mississauga, ON L4V 1N8 CANADA; (905) 678-6888; (905) 678-6967

BEE-CLEAN, 4505 101st, Edmonton, AB T6E 5C6 CANADA; (780) 462-0069; (780) 436-9528

BUILDING STARS, 2300 Westport Plaza Dr., # 204, St. Louis, MO 63146 ; (314) 878-8861; (314) 878-0545

CAPITAL CARPET CLEANING & DYE, 22410 Woodward, Ferndale, MI 48220 ; (248) 542-3636; (248) 542-4566

CLEANING CONSULTANT SERVICES, 3693 E. Marginal Way S., P.O. Box 1273, Seattle, WA 98111 ; (206) 682-9748; (206) 622-6876

CLEANING IDEAS, P.O. Box 7269, San Antonio, TX 78207 ; (210) 227-9161; (210) 227-0002

DRIRITE, 4000 Dow Rd., # 10, Melbourne, FL 32934-9276 ; (800) 462-5845 (407) 422-6688

EARTH-CLEAN.COM, 7649 Old Georgetown Rd., # 200A, Bethesda, MD 20814 ; (800) 571-5422 (301) 654-4986; (301) 654-4476

ELECTROLUX, 5956 Sherry Ln., # 1500, Dallas, TX 75225-6531 ; (214) 378-4040; (214) 378-4053

ENVIROBATE, 3301 E. 26th St., Minneapolis, MN 55406 ; (800) 926-1776 (612) 729-1080; (612) 729-1021

FIBRENEW INTERNATIONAL LTD., Box 33, Site 16, Rural Rt. 8, Calgary, AB T2J 2T9 CANADA; (800) 345-2951 (403) 278-7818; (403) 278-1434

GOOD LOOKIN' CARPET CLEANING, 40 Burnbank St., Ottawa, ON K2G OH4 CANADA; (613) 831-2604; (613) 831-3784

GUMBUSTERS INTERNATIONAL, 5203 Leesburg Pk., # 907, Falls Church, VA 22041 ; (877) 486-2878 (703) 575-3440; (703) 575-3456

INTERNATIONAL MASTER CARE JANITORIAL, 555 6th St., # 327, New Westminster, BC V3L 5H1 CANADA; (800) 889-2799 (604) 525-8221; (604) 526-2235

JANI-KING (CANADA), 23 Cornwallis St., Kentville, NS B4N 2E2 CANADA; (800) 565-1873 (902) 678-3200; (902) 678-3500

JDI CLEANING SYSTEMS, 3390 South Service Rd., Burlington, ON L7N 3J5 CANADA; (800) 567-5091 (905) 634-5228; (905) 634-8790

MASTER CARE, 555 6th St., # 327, New Westminster, BC V3L 4Y4 CANADA; (800) 889-2799 (604) 525-8221; (604) 526-2235

NATIONAL MAINTENANCE CONTRACTORS, 1801 130th Ave. NE, Bellevue, WA 98005 ; (800) 347-7844 (425) 881-0500; (425) 883-4785

ONE SOURCE FRANCHISE SYSTEM, 1600 Parkwood Cir., # 400, Atlanta, GA 30339-2119; (770) 436-9900; (770) 799-0247

P.E.S.T. MACHINE TEAM, THE, 3616 Lake Rd., Ponca City, OK 74604-5100 (800) 654-4541 (580) 762-6614; (580) 765-4613

PAUL W. DAVIS SYSTEMS, 1 Independent Dr., # 2300, Jacksonville, FL 32202 (800) 722-1818 (904) 737-2779; (904) 730-4204

REMODELING CONTRACTORS & CLEANING, 13845 W. 107th St., Lenexa, KS 66215 ; (800) 289-1389 (913) 327-8700; (913) 327-8701

ROOTER MAN, 268 Rangeway Rd., North Billerica, MA 01862 ; (800) 698-2244 (978) 667-1144; (978) 663-3976

S/M FRANCHISE SERVICES GROUP, 860 Ridge Lake Blvd., Memphis, TN 38120 ; (901) 537-8160; (901) 537-8161

SCRUBWAY, 1880 Markley St., 2nd Fl., Morristown, PA 19401 ; (800) 355-3000 (610) 278-9000; (610) 275-7360

SERV U-1ST, 2706 NE Sandy Blvd., Portland, OR 97219 ; (503) 244-7628; (503) 234-3989

SERVICE ONE, 5104 N. Orange Blossom Tr., # 114, Orlando, FL 32810 ; (800) 522-7111 (407) 293-7645; (407) 299-4306

SERVICEMASTER OF CANADA, 6540 Tomken Rd., Mississauga, ON L5T 2E9 CANADA; (905) 670-0000; (905) 670-0077

SERVICE-TECH CORPORATION, 7589 First Pl., Cleveland, OH 44146-6711 (800) 992-9302 (440) 735-1505; (440) 735-1433

STANLEY STEEMER CARPET CLEANER, 5500 Stanley Steemer Pkwy., Dublin, OH 43016 ; (800) 848-7496 (614) 764-2007; (614) 764-1506

STEAM BROTHERS PROFESSIONAL CLEANING & RESTORATION, 933 1/2 Basin Ave., Bismarck, ND 58504 ; (800) 767-5064 (701) 222-1263; (701) 222-1372

SYSTEMS PAVING, 1600 Dove St., # 250, Newport Beach, CA 92660-2432 (800) 801-7283 (949) 263-8300; (949) 263-0452

TRI-COLOR CARPET DYEING AND CLEANING, 603 W. Main St., Glasgow, KY 42141 ; (800) 452-9065 (502) 651-7879; (502) 651-6048

VALUE LINE MAINTENANCE SYSTEMS, P.O. Box 6450, Great Falls, MT 59406 ; (800) 824-4838 (406) 761-4471; (406) 761-4486

WINCO WINDOW CLEANING & MAINTENANCE, Colonial Ter., # 27, Knoxville, IA 50138 ; (641) 828-77944

WINDOW GENIE, 350 Gest St., Cincinnati, OH 45203 ; (800) 700-0022 (513) 241-8443; (513) 412-7760

For a full explanation of the data provided in the Franchisor Profiles, please refer to **Chapter 2, "How to Use the Data."**

Medical/Optical/Dental Products & Services

Chapter

26

Medical/Optical/Dental Products & Services Industry Profile

Total # Franchisors in Industry Group	18
Total # Franchised Units in Industry Group	1,832
Total # Company-Owned Units in Industry Group	353
Total # Operating Units in Industry Group	2,185
Average # Franchised Units/Franchisor	101.8
Average # Company-Owned Units/Franchisor	19.6
Average # Total Units/Franchisor	121.4
Ratio of Total # Franchised Units/Total # Company-Owned Units	5.2:1
Industry Survey Participants	4
Representing % of Industry	22.2%
Average Franchise Fee*:	$27.4K
Average Total Investment*:	$214.7K
Average On-Going Royalty Fee*:	5.0%

*If a range was provided, the mid-point of the range was used. See detailed profiles for actual ranges.

Company	# Franchised Units	# Co-Owned Units	# Total Units	Franchise Fee	On-Going Royalty	Total Investment
1. Miracle-Ear	930	185	1,115	28-60K	$46.50/Unit	100-200K
2. Amigo Mobility Center	42	5	47	20K	2-5%	65-89K
3. Hemorrhoid Clinic, The	32	1	33	25K	6%	140-225K
4. Women's Health Boutique	19	3	22	20.8K	4-7%	215-235K

AMIGO MOBILITY CENTER

6693 Dixie Hwy.
Bridgeport, MI 48722-0402
Tel: (800) 821-2710 (517) 777-6370
Fax: (517) 777-6537
Web Site: www.concentric.net/nmchihq
Mr. David Crispin, Chief Executive Officer

An AMIGO MOBILITY CENTER is a sales and service outlet, specializing in mobility products for mobility-impaired individuals or anyone with difficulty walking. Our Centers sell and service a variety of items, including battery-powered scooters, wheelchairs and conversion vans to the home health care market.

BACKGROUND:
Established: 1968; 1st Franchised: 1984
Franchised Units: 42
Company-Owned Units 5
Total Units: 47
Dist.: US-47; CAN-0; O'seas-0
North America: 16 States
Density: 9 in MI, 5 in FL, 5 in OH
Projected New Units (12 Months): 10
Qualifications: 4, 2, 2, 2, 3, 5
Registered: FL,IL,IN,MI,NY,MN

FINANCIAL/TERMS:
Cash Investment: $40-50K
Total Investment: $65-89K
Minimum Net Worth: $NR
Fees: Franchise - $20K
Royalty - 2-5%; Ad. - 1%
Earnings Claim Statement: Yes
Term of Contract (Years): 10/5
Avg. # Of Employees: 2 FT, 2 PT
Passive Ownership: Discouraged
Encourage Conversions: Yes
Area Develop. Agreements: Yes
Sub-Franchising Contracts: No
Expand In Territory: Yes
Space Needs: 1,600 SF; Upper-Scale Industrial Park

SUPPORT & TRAINING PROVIDED:
Financial Assistance Provided: Yes(I)
Site Selection Assistance: Yes
Lease Negotiation Assistance: Yes
Co-Operative Advertising: Yes
Franchisee Assoc./Member: Yes
Size Of Corporate Staff: 9
On-Going Support: A,B,C,D,E,F,G,H,I
Training: 14 Days Corporate Headquarters; 14-18 Days Franchise Center.

SPECIFIC EXPANSION PLANS:
US: Midwest, SW, NE and Sunbelt
Canada: No
Overseas: All Countries

<< >>

HEMORRHOID CLINIC, THE

P.O. Box 12488
Oakland, CA 94604
Tel: (510) 839-5471
Fax: (510) 547-3245
Dr. Roberto Y. Annings, President

Highly efficient and automated out-patient clinics for hemorrhoid and related rectal procedures. Proprietary laser techniques developed by Dr. Anning insure painless, 20-minute procedure and minimal recuperative discomfort. Lucrative business that takes advantage of the fact that 1 in 8 adults requires rectal surgery. 12 week training at headquarters clinic. All procedures on video. Excellent opportunity to work with the best!

BACKGROUND:
Established: 1987; 1st Franchised: 1988
Franchised Units: 32
Company-Owned Units 1
Total Units: 33
Dist.: US-27; CAN-3; O'seas-3
North America: 10 States, 2 Provinces
Density: 5 in OH, 2 in KY, 2 in MS
Projected New Units (12 Months): 2
Registered: NR

FINANCIAL/TERMS:
Cash Investment: $80-125K
Total Investment: $140-225K
Minimum Net Worth: $NR
Fees: Franchise - $25K
Royalty - 6%; Ad. - 1%
Earnings Claim Statement: Yes
Term of Contract (Years): 10/10
Avg. # Of Employees: 3 FT, 4 PT
Passive Ownership: Not Allowed
Encourage Conversions: Yes
Area Develop. Agreements: Yes/10
Sub-Franchising Contracts: Yes
Expand In Territory: Yes
Space Needs: 1,500-2,000 SF; FS, SF

SUPPORT & TRAINING PROVIDED:
Financial Assistance Provided: Yes(I)
Site Selection Assistance: Yes
Lease Negotiation Assistance: Yes
Co-Operative Advertising: Yes
Franchisee Assoc./Member: NR
Size Of Corporate Staff: 12
On-Going Support: C,D,E,G,H,I
Training: 12 Weeks Anning Clinic; 3 Weeks On-Site; On-Going Video Training Procedures.

SPECIFIC EXPANSION PLANS:
US: All United States
Canada: ON Only
Overseas: No

<< >>

MIRACLE-EAR

5000 Cheshire Ln. N.
Plymouth, MN 55446
Tel: (800) 234-7714 (612) 520-9500
Fax: (763) 268-4254
E-Mail: jdarland@miracle-ear.com
Web Site: www.miracle-ear.com
Mr. Jim Darland

Manufacturer and world's largest retailer of hearing systems, with 1,287 offices nationally. MIRACLE-EAR also has master franchisors in 20 foreign countries.

BACKGROUND:
Established: 1948; 1st Franchised: 1983
Franchised Units: 930
Company-Owned Units 185
Total Units: 1,115
Dist.: US-1267; CAN-0; O'seas-20
North America: 50 States
Density: 96 in CA, 39 in TX, 74 in FL
Projected New Units (12 Months): 125
Qualifications: 4, 4, 2, 3, 4, 4
Registered: All States

FINANCIAL/TERMS:
Cash Investment: $50-150K
Total Investment: $100-200K
Minimum Net Worth: $100K
Fees: Franchise - $28-60K
Royalty - $46.50/Unit;Ad. - $26/Inquiry
Earnings Claim Statement: No
Term of Contract (Years): 5/5
Avg. # Of Employees: 2 FT, 1 PT
Passive Ownership: Not Allowed
Encourage Conversions: N/A
Area Develop. Agreements: Yes/1-1.5
Sub-Franchising Contracts: No
Expand In Territory: Yes
Space Needs: 750 SF; FS, SF, SC, RM

SUPPORT & TRAINING PROVIDED:
Financial Assistance Provided: N/A
Site Selection Assistance: N/A
Lease Negotiation Assistance: No
Co-Operative Advertising: Yes
Franchisee Assoc./Member: No
Size Of Corporate Staff: 3
On-Going Support: A,C,D,E,G,h,I
Training: 2 Weeks Corporate Headquarters; 10 Weeks On-Site.

SPECIFIC EXPANSION PLANS:
US: West, Midwest
Canada: No
Overseas: All Countries

<< >>

WOMEN'S HEALTH BOUTIQUE
12715 Telge Rd.
Cypress, TX 77429
Tel: (888) 280-2053 (281) 256-4100
Fax: (281) 256-4178
E-Mail: w-h-bsales@w-h-b.com
Web Site: www.w-h-b.com
Mr. Bob Dolan, VP Franchise Sales

One-stop shopping for women with special needs in a tasteful environment, attended by knowledgeable, highly trained, compassionate saleswomen. Real products and services for post breast surgery, pre- and post-natal, post-mastectomy, compression therapy, hair loss, incontinence, skin care, wigs and turbans and personal care.

BACKGROUND: IFA MEMBER
Established: 1988; 1st Franchised: 1993
Franchised Units: 19
Company-Owned Units 3
Total Units: 22
Dist.: US-18; CAN-0; O'seas-0
North America: 10 States
Density: 5 in TX, 3 in MI, 2 in GA
Projected New Units (12 Months): 12
Qualifications: 4, 4, 3, 2, 5, 5
Registered: All Except HI,ND,SD

FINANCIAL/TERMS:
Cash Investment: $55K
Total Investment: $214.7-234.7K
Minimum Net Worth: $200K
Fees: Franchise - $20.8K
Royalty - 4-7%; Ad. - 0%
Earnings Claim Statement: No
Term of Contract (Years): 10/10
Avg. # Of Employees: 2-3 FT
Passive Ownership: Not Allowed
Encourage Conversions: N/A
Area Develop. Agreements: No
Sub-Franchising Contracts: No
Expand In Territory: Yes
Space Needs: 1,500 SF; SC, Medical Center

SUPPORT & TRAINING PROVIDED:
Financial Assistance Provided: Yes(I)
Site Selection Assistance: Yes
Lease Negotiation Assistance: Yes
Co-Operative Advertising: No
Franchisee Assoc./Member: Yes/Yes
Size Of Corporate Staff: NR
On-Going Support: C,D,E,G,H,I
Training: Approximately 5 Weeks.

SPECIFIC EXPANSION PLANS:
US: All United States
Canada: No
Overseas: No

<< >>

SUPPLEMENTAL LISTING OF FRANCHISORS

AMERICAN PHYSICAL REHABILITATION NETWORK, 4747 Holland Sylvania Rd., 2nd Fl., Sylvania, OH 43560 ; (800) 331-3058 (419) 824-3434; (419) 824-3435

COHEN'S FASHION OPTICAL, 1500 Hempstead Turnpike, East Meadow, NY 11554-1558 ; (516) 599-5500; (516) 465-6930

DENTIST'S CHOICE, THE, 34700 Pacific Coast Hwy., # 200, Capistrano Beach, CA 92677 ; (800) 757-1333 (949) 443-2070; (949) 443-2074

DIVERSIFIED DENTAL SERVICES, P.O. Box 36003, Saint Petersburg, FL 33736 ; (800) 374-6273 (727) 367-6801; (727) 367-9751

OPTION CARE, 100 Corporate North, # 212, Bannockburn, IL 60015 ; (800) 879-6137 (847) 615-1690; (847) 615-0326

OPTOMETRIC EYE CARE CENTER, P.O. Box 7185, Rocky Mount, NC 27804 (800) 334-3937 (252) 937-6650; (252) 937-6358

STERLING OPTICAL, 1500 Hempstead Turnpike, East Meadow, NY 11554 ; (800) 332-6302 (516) 390-2100; (516) 390-2110

TEXAS STATE OPTICAL, 4925 W. Cardinal Dr., Beaumont, TX 77705 ; (409) 842-4113; (409) 842-3522

TOTAL MEDICAL COMPLIANCE, 99 NW Miami Gardens Dr., # 206, North Miami Beach, FL 33169 ; (800) 840-6742 (305) 690-9890; (305) 690-9992

Packaging & Mailing

Chapter 27

Packaging & Mailing Industry Profile

Total # Franchisors in Industry Group	20
Total # Franchised Units in Industry Group	9,099
Total # Company-Owned Units in Industry Group	49
Total # Operating Units in Industry Group	9,148
Average # Franchised Units/Franchisor	455.0
Average # Company-Owned Units/Franchisor	2.4
Average # Total Units/Franchisor	457.4
Ratio of Total # Franchised Units/Total # Company-Owned Units	185.7:1
Industry Survey Participants	14
Representing % of Industry	70.0%
Average Franchise Fee*:	$25.3K
Average Total Investment*:	$93.0K
Average On-Going Royalty Fee*:	5.7%

*If a range was provided, the mid-point of the range was used. See detailed profiles for actual ranges.

Five Largest Participants in Survey

Company	# Franchised Units	# Co-Owned Units	# Total Units	Franchise Fee	On-Going Royalty	Total Investment
1. Mail Boxes Etc.	4,535	0	4,535	29.9K	5%	141-217K
2. Postnet Postal & Business Centers	712	0	712	26.9K	4%	91-122K
3. Packaging and Shipping Specialists	571	6	577	27.5K	0%	79.9-128K
4. Pak Mail	400	1	400	28K	5% Sliding	70-115K
5. Unishippers Association	306	1	307	10-50K	16.5%	10-100K

All of the data provided are proprietary and should not be quoted without acknowledging *Bond's Franchise Guide.*

AIM MAIL CENTERS

15550-D Rockfield Blvd.
Irvine, CA 92618
Tel: (800) 669-4246 (949) 837-4151
Fax: (949) 837-4537
E-Mail: mherrera@aimmailcenters.com
Web Site: www.aimmailcenters.com
Mr. Michael R. Herrera, VP Franchise Development

AIM MAIL CENTERS take care of all business service needs. AIM's services include renting mailboxes, buying stamps, sending faxes, notary, making copies and passport photos. AIM is also an authorized UPS and FedEx Shipping Outlet. It's like having a post office, office supply store, gift shop, and copy shop all rolled into one.

BACKGROUND: IFA MEMBER
Established: 1985; 1st Franchised: 1989
Franchised Units: 64
Company-Owned Units 0
Total Units: 64
Dist.: US-64; CAN-0; O'seas-0
North America: 7 States
Density: 46 in CA, 2 in WA, 4 in NV
Projected New Units (12 Months): 36
Qualifications: 4, 1, 1, 3, 4, 5
Registered: All States

FINANCIAL/TERMS:
Cash Investment: $30-35K
Total Investment: $95-105K
Minimum Net Worth: $125K
Fees: Franchise - $23.9K
Royalty - 5%; Ad. - 2%
Earnings Claim Statement: Yes
Term of Contract (Years): 15
Avg. # Of Employees: 1 FT, 2 PT
Passive Ownership: Discouraged
Encourage Conversions: Yes
Area Develop. Agreements: No
Sub-Franchising Contracts: No
Expand In Territory: Yes
Space Needs: 1,000 SF; SF, SC, Anchored Center

SUPPORT & TRAINING PROVIDED:
Financial Assistance Provided: Yes(I)
Site Selection Assistance: Yes
Lease Negotiation Assistance: Yes
Co-Operative Advertising: Yes
Franchisee Assoc./Member: Yes
Size Of Corporate Staff: 10
On-Going Support: C,D,E,G,H,I
Training: 2 Weeks Corporate Headquarters; 3 Days in Store.

SPECIFIC EXPANSION PLANS:
US: All United States
Canada: All Except AB
Overseas: All Countries

<< >>

CRATERS & FREIGHTERS

7000 E. 47th Ave., # 100
Denver, CO 80216
Tel: (800) 949-9931 (303) 399-8190
Fax: (303) 399-9964
E-Mail: Franchise@cratersandfreighters.com
Web Site: www.cratersandfreighters.com
Mr. Bob Molnar, Dir. Franchise Development

As specialty freight handlers, CRATERS & FREIGHTERS is the best-niched concept in the industry. We're the exclusive source for reliable, affordable specialty shipping services for pieces that are too big for UPS and too small for movers. We provide high-demand packing, crating and shipping with iron-clad insurance to an up-scale clientele. Serve your large territory from low overhead warehouse space.

BACKGROUND: IFA MEMBER
Established: 1990; 1st Franchised: 1991
Franchised Units: 60
Company-Owned Units 0
Total Units: 60
Dist.: US-60; CAN-0; O'seas-0
North America: 30 States
Density: 6 in CA, 6 in FL, 5 in TX
Projected New Units (12 Months): 14
Qualifications: 5, 4, 2, 1, 3, 5
Registered: CA,FL,MD,MI

FINANCIAL/TERMS:
Cash Investment: $NR
Total Investment: $88-127K
Minimum Net Worth: $150K
Fees: Franchise - $27K
Royalty - 5%; Ad. - 1%
Earnings Claim Statement: No
Term of Contract (Years): 15/15
Avg. # Of Employees: 3 FT
Passive Ownership: Discouraged
Encourage Conversions: N/A
Area Develop. Agreements: No
Sub-Franchising Contracts: No
Expand In Territory: Yes
Space Needs: 2000-2500 SF; Warehouse

SUPPORT & TRAINING PROVIDED:
Financial Assistance Provided: Yes(I)
Site Selection Assistance: Yes
Lease Negotiation Assistance: Yes
Co-Operative Advertising: Yes
Franchisee Assoc./Member: Yes
Size Of Corporate Staff: 12
On-Going Support: A,B,C,D,E,G,h,I
Training: 7 Days Home Office in Denver, CO.

SPECIFIC EXPANSION PLANS:
US: All United States
Canada: All Canada
Overseas: All Countries

<< >>

HANDLE WITH CARE PACKAGING STORE

5675 DTC Blvd., # 280
Greenwood Village, CO 80111
Tel: (866) 738-6820 (720) 529-0932
Fax: (303) 741-6653
E-Mail: dft@gonavis.com
Web Site: www.navisfranchiseinfo.com
Ms. Dee. F. Thomsen, Franchise Development Dir.

HANDLE WITH CARE PACKAGING STORES specialize in packaging and shipping fragile, large, awkward and valuable items--what we call FLAV. Unlike the saturated mail and parcel industry, the market for FLAV logistics is uncrowded and growing. We provide exceptional training and support, lead generation for local and national accounts, proprietary insurance and discounts with major freight carriers.

BACKGROUND: IFA MEMBER
Established: 1980; 1st Franchised: 1984
Franchised Units: 170
Company-Owned Units 0
Total Units: 170
Dist.: US-160; CAN-1; O'seas-9
North America: 38 States +
Density: 38 in CA, 15 in VA, 12 in FL
Projected New Units (12 Months): 30-40
Qualifications: 4, 4, 2, 3, 1, 4
Registered: All States

FINANCIAL/TERMS:
Cash Investment: $40-50K
Total Investment: $61.5-100.5K
Minimum Net Worth: $NR
Fees: Franchise - $24.5K
Royalty - 5%; Ad. - 3%
Earnings Claim Statement: No
Term of Contract (Years): 10/10
Avg. # Of Employees: 3-4 FT
Passive Ownership: Not Allowed
Encourage Conversions: Yes
Area Develop. Agreements: No
Sub-Franchising Contracts: No
Expand In Territory: Yes

Space Needs: 1,500-2,500 SF; SF, SC, Mini Warehouse

SUPPORT & TRAINING PROVIDED:

Financial Assistance Provided:	Yes(D)
Site Selection Assistance:	No
Lease Negotiation Assistance:	No
Co-Operative Advertising:	Yes
Franchisee Assoc./Member:	No
Size Of Corporate Staff:	21
On-Going Support:	C,D,E,G,h,I

Training: 3 Weeks Denver, CO; 3 Days Franchisee's Site.

SPECIFIC EXPANSION PLANS:

US:	All North America
Canada:	All Canada
Overseas:	No

<< >>

MAIL BOXES ETC.
MAKING BUSINESS EASIER® WORLDWIDE.

MAIL BOXES ETC.

6060 Cornerstone Ct. W.
San Diego, CA 92121-3795
Tel: (877) MBE-SALE
Fax: (858) 546-7492
E-Mail: fransale@mbe.com
Web Site: www.mbe.com
Mr. John Dring, Dir. Domestic Fran. Sales

Mail Boxes Etc., a UPS company, is the world's largest franchisor of retail postal and business services. Headquartered in San Diego, MBE boasts more than 4400 independently-owned locations around the world. The global leader in its industry, MBE provides convenient and value-added business services to general consumers, corporate "road warriors," and the small-office/home (SOHO) market.

BACKGROUND: IFA MEMBER

Established: 1980;	1st Franchised: 1980
Franchised Units:	4,535
Company-Owned Units	0
Total Units:	4,535
Dist.:	US-3527; CAN-264; O'seas-744
North America:	50 States,10 Provinces
Density:	501 in CA, 293 in FL, 190 TX
Projected New Units (12 Months):	200
Qualifications:	5, 4, 3, 3, 3, 5
Registered: All States	

FINANCIAL/TERMS:

Cash Investment:	$50K
Total Investment:	$141-217K
Minimum Net Worth:	$150K
Fees: Franchise -	$29.9K
Royalty - 5%;	Ad. - 3.5%
Earnings Claim Statement:	No
Term of Contract (Years):	10/10
Avg. # Of Employees:	2 FT, 2+ PT
Passive Ownership:	Allowed
Encourage Conversions:	Yes
Area Develop. Agreements:	Yes/10
Sub-Franchising Contracts:	No
Expand In Territory:	Yes

Space Needs: NR SF; FS, SF, SC, RM, Non-Tradit.

SUPPORT & TRAINING PROVIDED:

Financial Assistance Provided:	Yes
Site Selection Assistance:	Yes
Lease Negotiation Assistance:	Yes
Co-Operative Advertising:	Yes
Franchisee Assoc./Member:	Yes/Yes
Size Of Corporate Staff:	300
On-Going Support:	B,C,D,E,G,H,I

Training: 2 Weeks San Diego, CA; 2 Weeks In-Center.

SPECIFIC EXPANSION PLANS:

US:	All United States
Canada:	All Canada
Overseas:	All Countries

<< >>

MAIL BOXES ETC. (CANADA)

505 Iroquois Shore Rd., # 4
Oakville, ON L6H 2R3 CANADA
Tel: (800) 661-MBEC (905) 338-9754
Fax: (905) 338-7491
E-Mail: dwarren@ca.mbe.com
Web Site: www.mbe.com
Mr. Ralph Askar, EVP/COO

Business and communication services.

BACKGROUND:

Established: 1990;	1st Franchised: 1990
Franchised Units:	255
Company-Owned Units	2
Total Units:	257
Dist.:	US-0; CAN-216; O'seas-0
North America:	9 Provinces
Density:	NR
Projected New Units (12 Months):	50
Qualifications:	5, 4, 3, 3, 3, 4
Registered: NR	

FINANCIAL/TERMS:

Cash Investment:	$60K
Total Investment:	$110-135K
Minimum Net Worth:	$125K
Fees: Franchise -	$29.9K
Royalty - 6%;	Ad. - 2%
Earnings Claim Statement:	No
Term of Contract (Years):	10/10
Avg. # Of Employees:	2 FT, 1 PT
Passive Ownership:	Discouraged
Encourage Conversions:	Yes
Area Develop. Agreements:	Yes/10
Sub-Franchising Contracts:	No
Expand In Territory:	Yes

Space Needs: 1,200 SF; FS, SF, SC

SUPPORT & TRAINING PROVIDED:

Financial Assistance Provided:	Yes
Site Selection Assistance:	Yes
Lease Negotiation Assistance:	Yes
Co-Operative Advertising:	Yes
Franchisee Assoc./Member:	Yes/No
Size Of Corporate Staff:	20
On-Going Support:	a,B,C,D,e,G,h

Training: 2 Weeks at Corporate Office; 1.5 Weeks in Center.

SPECIFIC EXPANSION PLANS:

US:	All United States
Canada:	All Canada
Overseas:	U.K. and Ireland

<< >>

NAVIS PACK & SHIP CENTER

5675 DTC Blvd., # 280
Greenwood Village, CO 80111
Tel: (866) 738-6820 (720) 529-0932
Fax: (303) 741-6653
E-Mail: dft@gonavis.com
Web Site: www.navisfranchiseinfo.com
Franchise Development Dept.

Looking at franchising? Look no further than Navis Pack & Ship Centers. We specialize in packaging and shipping fragile, large, awkward and valuable items--what we call FLAV. Unlike the saturated mail and parcel industry, the market for FLAV logistics is uncrowded and growing. We provide exceptional training and support, lead generation for local and national accounts, proprietary insurance and discounts with major freight carriers. Come help us build our brand.

BACKGROUND: IFA MEMBER

Established: 2000;	1st Franchised: 2001
Franchised Units:	12
Company-Owned Units	0
Total Units:	12
Dist.:	US-10; CAN-2; O'seas-0

North America: 8 States +
Density: 3 in CO, 2 in FL, 1 in OR
Projected New Units (12 Months): NR
Registered: NR

FINANCIAL/TERMS:

Cash Investment: $30-50K
Total Investment: $100.5K
Minimum Net Worth: $NR
Fees: Franchise - $24.5K
Royalty - 5%; Ad. - 3%
Earnings Claim Statement: No
Term of Contract (Years): 10/10
Avg. # Of Employees: 4 FT
Passive Ownership: Allowed
Encourage Conversions: NR
Area Develop. Agreements: N/A
Sub-Franchising Contracts: N/A
Expand In Territory: Yes
Space Needs: 1,500-2,500 SF; SF, SC, Mini Warehouse

SUPPORT & TRAINING PROVIDED:

Financial Assistance Provided: Yes(I)
Site Selection Assistance: No
Lease Negotiation Assistance: Yes
Co-Operative Advertising: Yes
Franchisee Assoc./Member: Yes
Size Of Corporate Staff: 21
On-Going Support: A,B,C,D,e,f,G,H,I
Training: 3 Weeks Denver, CO; 3 Days Franchisee's Site.

SPECIFIC EXPANSION PLANS:

US: All United States
Canada: All Canada
Overseas: NR

PACK MART

13529 U. S. Hwy., # 1
Sebastian, FL 32958
Tel: (800) 234-7411 (561) 234-0208
Fax: (561) 589-0680
Mr. Bob Calistri, VP Marketing

Pack and shipping center. Mini centers from $4,775 and full store operations from $60,175.

BACKGROUND:

Established: 1993; 1st Franchised: 1995
Franchised Units: 3
Company-Owned Units 3
Total Units: 6
Dist.: US-4; CAN-0; O'seas-0
North America: 1 State
Density: 4 in FL
Projected New Units (12 Months): 8
Qualifications: 4, 4, 3, 3, 3, 3
Registered: FL

FINANCIAL/TERMS:

Cash Investment: $5-30K
Total Investment: $5-75K
Minimum Net Worth: $100K
Fees: Franchise - $1.5-15K
Royalty - 5%; Ad. - 1%
Earnings Claim Statement: No
Term of Contract (Years): 5/5
Avg. # Of Employees: 1 FT, 1 PT
Passive Ownership: Discouraged
Encourage Conversions: Yes
Area Develop. Agreements: Yes/5
Sub-Franchising Contracts: Yes
Expand In Territory: Yes
Space Needs: 100-1,000 SF; FS, SF, SC, RM

SUPPORT & TRAINING PROVIDED:

Financial Assistance Provided: Yes
Site Selection Assistance: Yes
Lease Negotiation Assistance: Yes
Co-Operative Advertising: Yes
Franchisee Assoc./Member: No
Size Of Corporate Staff: NR
On-Going Support: C,d,E,f,h,I
Training: 3 Weeks Sebastian, FL.

SPECIFIC EXPANSION PLANS:

US: Southwest, Southeast
Canada: No
Overseas: No

PACKAGING AND SHIPPING SPECIALISTS

5211 85th St., # 104
Lubbock, TX 79424
Tel: (800) 877-8884 (806) 794-9996
Fax: (806) 794-9997
E-Mail: mike@packship.com
Web Site: www.packship.com
Mr. Mike Gallagher, President

We are the only company that does not charge royalties and one of the most affordable and knowledgeable companies in this industry. A complete copy center and mail center with an array of related retail items for the consumer.

BACKGROUND:

Established: 1981; 1st Franchised: 1985
Franchised Units: 571
Company-Owned Units 6
Total Units: 577
Dist.: US-562; CAN-5; O'seas-10
North America: 37 States,10 Provinces
Density: 55 in TX
Projected New Units (12 Months): 40
Qualifications: 3, 2, 1, 2, 2, 2
Registered: All States

FINANCIAL/TERMS:

Cash Investment: $20-45K
Total Investment: $79.9-128K
Minimum Net Worth: $100K
Fees: Franchise - $27.5K
Royalty - 0%; Ad. - 0%
Earnings Claim Statement: No
Term of Contract (Years): 10/10
Avg. # Of Employees: 2 FT, 2 PT
Passive Ownership: Allowed
Encourage Conversions: Yes
Area Develop. Agreements: Yes/20
Sub-Franchising Contracts: Yes
Expand In Territory: Yes
Space Needs: 1,500 SF; SF, SC

SUPPORT & TRAINING PROVIDED:

Financial Assistance Provided: Yes(I)
Site Selection Assistance: Yes
Lease Negotiation Assistance: Yes
Co-Operative Advertising: No
Franchisee Assoc./Member: No
Size Of Corporate Staff: 18
On-Going Support: C,D,E,f,G,h,I
Training: 10-14 Days in Ann Arbor, MI; 10-14 Days in Dallas, TX.

SPECIFIC EXPANSION PLANS:

US: All United States
Canada: All Canada
Overseas: All Countries

PAK MAIL

7173 S. Havana St., # 600
Englewood, CO 80112
Tel: (800) 833-2821 (303) 957-1000
Fax: (800) 336-7363
E-Mail: sales@pakmail.com
Web Site: www.pakmail.com
Ms. Tonya Sarina, VP Sales/Marketing

PAK MAIL is a convenient center for packaging, shipping and business support services, offering both residential and commercial customers air, ground, and ocean carriers, custom packaging and crating, private mailbox rental, mail services, packaging and moving supplies, copy and fax service and internet access and related services. We ship anything, anywhere.

BACKGROUND: IFA MEMBER
Established: 1983; 1st Franchised: 1984
Franchised Units: 400
Company-Owned Units 0
Total Units: 400
Dist.: US-370; CAN-8; O'seas-22
North America: 42 States
Density: 91 in FL, 41 in GA, 22 in CA
Projected New Units (12 Months): 50
Qualifications: 3, 2, 2, 2, 2, 5
Registered: All States and AB

FINANCIAL/TERMS:
Cash Investment: $30-108K
Total Investment: $70-115K
Minimum Net Worth: $100K
Fees: Franchise - $28K
Royalty - 5% Sliding; Ad. - 2%
Earnings Claim Statement: Yes
Term of Contract (Years): 10/10
Avg. # Of Employees: 1 FT, 1 PT
Passive Ownership: Discouraged
Encourage Conversions: Yes
Area Develop. Agreements: Yes/5
Sub-Franchising Contracts: No
Expand In Territory: Yes
Space Needs: 1,200 SF; SC

SUPPORT & TRAINING PROVIDED:
Financial Assistance Provided: Yes(I)
Site Selection Assistance: Yes
Lease Negotiation Assistance: Yes
Co-Operative Advertising: Yes
Franchisee Assoc./Member: Yes/Yes
Size Of Corporate Staff: 22
On-Going Support: B,C,D,E,F,G,H,I
Training: 10 Days in Englewood, CO; 3 Days in Existing Center; 3 Days In New Center at Opening.

SPECIFIC EXPANSION PLANS:
US: All United States
Canada: All Canada
Overseas: All Countries

<< >>

PARCEL PLUS
12715 Telge Rd.
Cypress, TX 77429-2289
Tel: (888) 280-2053
Fax: (281) 256-4178
E-Mail: ppsales@iced.net
Web Site: www.parcelplus.com
Mr. Bob Dolan, VP Franchise Sales

Our five-year commitment to integrate logistics with the internet has created http://www.netship.com. Visit our site and you will quickly see that we are far more than a retail pack-and-ship chain.

BACKGROUND: IFA MEMBER
Established: 1986; 1st Franchised: 1988
Franchised Units: 106
Company-Owned Units 0
Total Units: 106
Dist.: US-129; CAN-0; O'seas-0
North America: 30 States
Density: 31 in VA, 29 in MD, 19 in TX
Projected New Units (12 Months): 15
Qualifications: 5, 5, 2, 4, , 5
Registered: FL,IL,IN,MD,MI,MN,VA,DC

FINANCIAL/TERMS:
Cash Investment: $80-100K
Total Investment: $45-80K
Minimum Net Worth: $150K
Fees: Franchise - $22.5K
Royalty - 4%; Ad. - 1%
Earnings Claim Statement: Yes
Term of Contract (Years): 10/10
Avg. # Of Employees: 2 FT, 2 PT
Passive Ownership: Discouraged
Encourage Conversions: Yes
Area Develop. Agreements: No
Sub-Franchising Contracts: No
Expand In Territory: Yes
Space Needs: 1,000-1,200 SF; SC

SUPPORT & TRAINING PROVIDED:
Financial Assistance Provided: Yes(I)
Site Selection Assistance: Yes
Lease Negotiation Assistance: Yes
Co-Operative Advertising: No
Franchisee Assoc./Member: Yes/Yes
Size Of Corporate Staff: 10
On-Going Support: A,B,C,D,E,F,G,H,I
Training: 1 Week Orientation at National Support Center; 2 Weeks Cargo Training; 2 Weeks at Stores.

SPECIFIC EXPANSION PLANS:
US: All United States
Canada: No
Overseas: No

<< >>

POSTAL ANNEX+
7580 Metropolitan Dr., # 200
San Diego, CA 92108
Tel: (800) 456-1525 (619) 563-4800
Fax: (619) 563-9850
Web Site: www.postalannex.com
Mr. Mike Watorski, Dir. Franchise Development

Retail business service center, providing: packaging, shipping, copying, postal, mail box rental, printing fax, notary, office supplies and more.

BACKGROUND: IFA MEMBER
Established: 1985; 1st Franchised: 1986
Franchised Units: 230
Company-Owned Units 0
Total Units: 230
Dist.: US-229; CAN-0; O'seas-1
North America: 27 States
Density: 130 in CA, 20 in OR, 17 MI
Projected New Units (12 Months): 36
Qualifications: 5, 3, 1, 1, 3, 3
Registered: CA,FL,IL,MD,MI,NY,OR,WA,WI,DC

FINANCIAL/TERMS:
Cash Investment: $35K
Total Investment: $111.9-169.7K
Minimum Net Worth: $200K
Fees: Franchise - $29.95K
Royalty - 5%; Ad. - 2%
Earnings Claim Statement: Yes
Term of Contract (Years): 15/15
Avg. # Of Employees: 1 FT, 2 PT
Passive Ownership: Allowed
Encourage Conversions: Yes
Area Develop. Agreements: Yes/10
Sub-Franchising Contracts: No
Expand In Territory: Yes
Space Needs: 1,200 SF; Supermarket Anchored

SUPPORT & TRAINING PROVIDED:
Financial Assistance Provided: Yes(I)
Site Selection Assistance: Yes
Lease Negotiation Assistance: Yes
Co-Operative Advertising: Yes
Franchisee Assoc./Member: Yes/Yes
Size Of Corporate Staff: 21
On-Going Support: c,d,E,G,H,I
Training: 2 Weeks San Diego, CA; 1 Week On-Site.

SPECIFIC EXPANSION PLANS:
US: All United States
Canada: All Canada
Overseas: All Countries

<< >>

POSTAL CONNECTIONS OF AMERICA
287 S. Robertson Blvd.
Beverly Hills, CA 90211
Tel: (800) 767-8257 (310) 360-1215
Fax: (310) 360-6765

E-Mail: info@postalconnections.com
Web Site: www.postalconnections.com
Mr. Stanley Grant, VP Franchise Development

POSTAL CONNECTIONS OF AMERICA franchises are specialty postal and copy service centers offering a variety of services, including packing, shipping, mailbox rentals, fax, moneygrams and notary services. Our newer outlets also include state-of-the-art technology features, such as computer work stations with high speed Internet access, e-mail address, video conferencing and meeting rooms, truly making our locations "virtual offices."

BACKGROUND:
Established: 1985; 1st Franchised: 1995
Franchised Units: 35
Company-Owned Units 7
Total Units: 42
Dist.: US-42; CAN-0; O'seas-0
North America: 13 States
Density: 13 in CA, 7 in AZ, 4 in OR
Projected New Units (12 Months): 36
Qualifications: 4, 1, 1, 3, 1, 4
Registered: All States

FINANCIAL/TERMS:
Cash Investment: $25-35K
Total Investment: $80-120K
Minimum Net Worth: $100K
Fees: Franchise - $18.9K
Royalty - 4%; Ad. - 2%
Earnings Claim Statement: No
Term of Contract (Years): 10/10
Avg. # Of Employees: 1 FT, 2 PT
Passive Ownership: Discouraged
Encourage Conversions: Yes
Area Develop. Agreements: Yes/10
Sub-Franchising Contracts: No
Expand In Territory: Yes
Space Needs: 1,200 SF; SF, SC

SUPPORT & TRAINING PROVIDED:
Financial Assistance Provided: Yes(I)
Site Selection Assistance: Yes
Lease Negotiation Assistance: Yes
Co-Operative Advertising: No
Franchisee Assoc./Member: No
Size Of Corporate Staff: 8
On-Going Support: B,C,d,e,h,I
Training: 7 Days Home Office, Beverly Hills, CA; 3 Days, New Location.

SPECIFIC EXPANSION PLANS:
US: All United States
Canada: All Canada
Overseas: Asia, Europe, South America

<< >>

Top 50

POSTNET POSTAL & BUSINESS CENTERS

181 N. Arroyo Grande Blvd., # 100 A
Henderson, NV 89014-1630
Tel: (800) 841-7171 (702) 792-7100
Fax: (702) 792-7115
E-Mail: info@postnet.net
Web Site: www.postnet.net
Mr. Brian Spindel, Executive VP

Become a POSTNET Pro! POSTNET's franchise opportunity offers a proven method of marketing products and services, which consumers need on a daily basis. The opportunity to get in on the ground floor of a rapidly expanding business is a rarity -- POSTNET's domestic and international franchisees have the opportunity to tap into the world market, offering personal and business services including UPS and FedEx Shipping, B/W and color copy services, private mail boxes, fax, printing and much more.

BACKGROUND: IFA MEMBER
Established: 1985; 1st Franchised: 1993
Franchised Units: 712
Company-Owned Units 0
Total Units: 712
Dist.: US-392; CAN-61; O'seas-314
North America: 39 States, 2 Provinces
Density: 17 in CA, 14 in IL, 11 in FL
Projected New Units (12 Months): 60
Qualifications: 4, 3, 2, 3, 4, 5
Registered: All States and AB

FINANCIAL/TERMS:
Cash Investment: $35-50K
Total Investment: $91-122K
Minimum Net Worth: $150K
Fees: Franchise - $26.9K
Royalty - 4%; Ad. - 1%
Earnings Claim Statement: No
Term of Contract (Years): 10/10
Avg. # Of Employees: 2 FT, 1 PT
Passive Ownership: Not Allowed
Encourage Conversions: Yes
Area Develop. Agreements: Yes/10
Sub-Franchising Contracts: No
Expand In Territory: Yes
Space Needs: 1,200 SF; SC

SUPPORT & TRAINING PROVIDED:
Financial Assistance Provided: Yes(I)
Site Selection Assistance: Yes
Lease Negotiation Assistance: Yes
Co-Operative Advertising: No
Franchisee Assoc./Member: Yes
Size Of Corporate Staff: 30
On-Going Support: C,D,E,G,H,I
Training: 1 Week Henderson, NV; 1 Week at Store Opening; 2-3 Days Follow-Up.

SPECIFIC EXPANSION PLANS:
US: All United States
Canada: All Canada
Overseas: All Countries

<< >>

UNISHIPPERS ASSOCIATION

746 E. Winchester St., # 200
Salt Lake City, UT 84107
Tel: (800) 999-8721 (801) 487-0600
Fax: (801) 487-0623
E-Mail: christine.kocherhans@unishippers.com
Web Site: www.unishippers.com
Ms. Christine Kocherhans, Coordinator, Franchise Sales

UNISHIPPERS, the largest reseller of transportation services in the United States, is looking for goal-oriented Master Franchisees as it expands into the global market. UNISHIPPERS combines the shipping volumes of thousands of businesses to obtain discounts and benefits from major overnight express and other transportation service carriers. These discounts and benefits, usually available only to large corporations, are then passed on to our customers, primarily small- to medium-sized businesses.

BACKGROUND: IFA MEMBER
Established: 1987; 1st Franchised: 1987
Franchised Units: 306
Company-Owned Units 1
Total Units: 307
Dist.: US-306; CAN-0; O'seas-1
North America: 48 States
Density: 27 in CA, 20 in NY, 20 in TX
Projected New Units (12 Months): 4
Qualifications: 4, 5, 1, 1, 5, 5
Registered: CA,FL,HI,IN,MD,MI,MN,NY,ND,OR,RI,SD,VA,WA,WI,DC

FINANCIAL/TERMS:
Cash Investment: $10-50K
Total Investment: $10-100K
Minimum Net Worth: $N/A
Fees: Franchise - $10-50K
Royalty - 16.5%; Ad. - 1% Gross
Earnings Claim Statement: Yes

Term of Contract (Years): 5/5
Avg. # Of Employees: 1 FT
Passive Ownership: Allowed
Encourage Conversions: N/A
Area Develop. Agreements: No
Sub-Franchising Contracts: Yes
Expand In Territory: No
Space Needs: NR SF; N/A

SUPPORT & TRAINING PROVIDED:
Financial Assistance Provided: Yes
Site Selection Assistance: N/A
Lease Negotiation Assistance: No
Co-Operative Advertising: N/A
Franchisee Assoc./Member: No
Size Of Corporate Staff: 35
On-Going Support: C,D,G,h,I
Training: 1 Week Salt Lake City, UT; 2 Days at Franchisee's Location.

SPECIFIC EXPANSION PLANS:
US: No
Canada: All Canada
Overseas: Western Europe, Pacific Rim

<< >>

SUPPLEMENTAL LISTING OF FRANCHISORS

CGI WORLDWIDE EXPRESS SERVICES, 7111-7115 Ohms Ln., Minneapolis, MN 55439-2142 ; (800) 758-7447 (612) 835-1338; (612) 835-1395

EXPRESS ONE, 7910 S. 3500 E., Salt Lake City, UT 84121 ; (800) 399-3971 (801) 944-1661; (801) 944-4448

PACKY THE SHIPPER/PACK 'N SHIP/PNS, 6115 Washington Ave., 2nd Fl., Racine, WI 53408 ; (800) 547-2259 (414) 504-2490; (414) 504-2499

PILOT AIR FREIGHT CORPORATION, 314 N. Middletown Rd., Lima, PA 19037 ; (800) 447-4568 (610) 891-8100; (610) 891-9341

QUIK-PAC & SHIP, P.O. Box 130, Morrisville, SC 27560 ; (800) 538-8521 (888) 724-2249

WORLDWIDE EXPRESS, P.O. Box 132518, Dallas, TX 75313 ; (800) 758-7447 (214) 720-2400; (214) 720-2446

Printing & Graphics

Chapter 28

Printing & Graphics Industry Profile

Total # Franchisors in Industry Group	26
Total # Franchised Units in Industry Group	5,200
Total # Company-Owned Units in Industry Group	40
Total # Operating Units in Industry Group	5,240
Average # Franchised Units/Franchisor	200.0
Average # Company-Owned Units/Franchisor	1.5
Average # Total Units/Franchisor	201.5
Ratio of Total # Franchised Units/Total # Company-Owned Units	130.0:1
Industry Survey Participants	15
Representing % of Industry	57.7%
Average Franchise Fee*:	$25.7K
Average Total Investment*:	$271.3K
Average On-Going Royalty Fee*:	5.6%

*If a range was provided, the mid-point of the range was used. See detailed profiles for actual ranges.

Five Largest Participants in Survey

Company	# Franchised Units	# Co-Owned Units	# Total Units	Franchise Fee	On-Going Royalty	Total Investment
1. Minuteman Press International	900	0	900	44.5K	6%	100-120K
2. Kwik-Kopy Printing	756	0	756	25K	4-8%	296-358 K
3. Sir Speedy	660	1	661	20K	4-6%	316-391K
4. Allegra Network LLC	548	0	548	19.5K	3-6%	273-441K
5. Proforma	525	0	525	19.5K	9%	22-27K

All of the data provided are proprietary and should not be quoted without acknowledging *Bond's Franchise Guide.*

ALLEGRA PRINT & IMAGING
AMERICAN SPEEDY PRINTING
INSTY-PRINTS
QUICK PRINT
SPEEDY PRINTING
ZIPPY PRINT

ALLEGRA NETWORK LLC

1800 W. Maple Rd.
Troy, MI 48084-7104
Tel: (800) 726-9050 (248) 614-3700
Fax: (248) 614-3719
E-Mail: mmenna@allegranetwork.com
Web Site: www.allegranetwork.com
Ms. Meredith Menna, Development Coord.

Our owners operate full-service communications centers, marketing a range of products including high-speed duplicating, color copying, desktop publishing, 2-4 color printing and digital capabilities. Our franchisees set themselves apart through exceptional personalized customer service. Printers plan order entry software.

BACKGROUND: IFA MEMBER
Established: 1976; 1st Franchised: 1977
Franchised Units: 548
Company-Owned Units 0
Total Units: 548
Dist.: US-500; CAN-37; O'seas-11
North America: 41 States, 3 Provinces
Density: 67 in MI, 38 in MN, 37 in IL
Projected New Units (12 Months): 0
Qualifications: 5, 2, 1, 2, 2, 2
Registered: All States

FINANCIAL/TERMS:
Cash Investment: $25-100K
Total Investment: $273-441K
Minimum Net Worth: $N/A
Fees: Franchise - $19.5K
Royalty - 3-6%; Ad. - 1-2%
Earnings Claim Statement: No
Term of Contract (Years): 20/20
Avg. # Of Employees: 3 FT, 1 PT
Passive Ownership: Not Allowed
Encourage Conversions: Yes
Area Develop. Agreements: No
Sub-Franchising Contracts: Yes
Expand In Territory: Yes
Space Needs: 1,500 SF; FS, SF, SC

SUPPORT & TRAINING PROVIDED:
Financial Assistance Provided: Yes
Site Selection Assistance: Yes
Lease Negotiation Assistance: Yes
Co-Operative Advertising: Yes
Franchisee Assoc./Member: Yes/Yes
Size Of Corporate Staff: 57
On-Going Support: C,D,E,F,G,h,I
Training: 2 Weeks at Home Office; 1 Week On-Site; On-Going

SPECIFIC EXPANSION PLANS:
US: All United States
Canada: All Canada
Overseas: No

<< >>

alphagraphics®
DESIGN ■ COPY ■ PRINT

Top 50

ALPHAGRAPHICS PRINTSHOPS OF THE FUTURE

268 S. State St., # 300
Salt Lake City, UT 84111
Tel: (800) 955-6246 (801) 595-7270
Fax: (801) 595-7273
E-Mail: mwitte@alphagraphics.com
Web Site: www.alphagraphics.com
Mr. Keith M. Gerson, VP Global Development

ALPHAGRAPHICS PRINTSHOPS OF THE FUTURE are the leading providers of print-related and digital publishing services for business worldwide. Our mission is to enable our customers to easily and effectively communicate in any publishing medium - anywhere in the world, any time. Our franchisees enjoy an average $949,477 in annual sales, the industry's highest. Services include design, high-speed duplication, single and multi-color printing, digital publishing, binding, CD-ROM and Web site services.

BACKGROUND: IFA MEMBER
Established: 1970; 1st Franchised: 1980
Franchised Units: 326
Company-Owned Units 1
Total Units: 327
Dist.: US-261; CAN-2; O'seas-81
North America: 42 States, 1 Province
Density: 33 in AZ, 29 in TX, 25 in IL
Projected New Units (12 Months): 40
Qualifications: 5, 5, 1, 4, 3, 5
Registered: CA,FL,IL,IN,MD,MI,MN,NY,OR,RI,VA,WA,WI

FINANCIAL/TERMS:
Cash Investment: $100-150K
Total Investment: $256.4-447.9K
Minimum Net Worth: $350K
Fees: Franchise - $25.9K
Royalty - 1.5-8%; Ad. - 2.5%
Earnings Claim Statement: Yes
Term of Contract (Years): 20/20
Avg. # Of Employees: 5 FT
Passive Ownership: Not Allowed
Encourage Conversions: Yes
Area Develop. Agreements: Yes/N/A
Sub-Franchising Contracts: No
Expand In Territory: Yes
Space Needs: 2,000-2,400 SF; FS, SC

SUPPORT & TRAINING PROVIDED:
Financial Assistance Provided: Yes(I)
Site Selection Assistance: Yes
Lease Negotiation Assistance: No
Co-Operative Advertising: Yes
Franchisee Assoc./Member: Yes
Size Of Corporate Staff: 99
On-Going Support: B,C,D,E,G,h,I
Training: 4 Weeks Tucson Service Center; 1 Week Field Location.

SPECIFIC EXPANSION PLANS:
US: All United States
Canada: All Canada
Overseas: All Countries

<< >>

AMERICAN WHOLESALE THERMOGRAPHERS / AWT

12715 Telge Rd.
Cypress, TX 77429-0777
Tel: (888) 280-2053 (281) 256-4100
Fax: (281) 256-4178
E-Mail: bdolan@inotes.iced.net
Web Site: www.iced.net
Mr. Bob Dolan, VP Franchise Sales

Wholesale printing, providing next-day raised-letter printed materials to retail printers, copy centers and business service centers. Products include quality business cards, stationery, announcements and invitations.

BACKGROUND: IFA MEMBER
Established: 1980; 1st Franchised: 1981
Franchised Units: 24
Company-Owned Units 0
Total Units: 24
Dist.: US-16; CAN-4; O'seas-0
North America: 14 States, 2 Provinces
Density: 3 in ON, 2 in OK, 2 in CA
Projected New Units (12 Months): 2
Qualifications: 5, 4, 1, 2, 1, 5
Registered: FL,IL,IN,MI,NY,VA,WI

FINANCIAL/TERMS:
Cash Investment: $90K
Total Investment: $340-352K
Minimum Net Worth: $250K
Fees: Franchise - $30K
Royalty - 5%; Ad. - NR

Earnings Claim Statement: Yes
Term of Contract (Years): 25/25
Avg. # Of Employees: 9 FT, 4 PT
Passive Ownership: Not Allowed
Encourage Conversions: No
Area Develop. Agreements: No
Sub-Franchising Contracts: No
Expand In Territory: Yes
Space Needs: 2,500-3,000 SF; Business Park, Warehouse

SUPPORT & TRAINING PROVIDED:

Financial Assistance Provided: Yes(B)
Site Selection Assistance: Yes
Lease Negotiation Assistance: Yes
Co-Operative Advertising: Yes
Franchisee Assoc./Member: Yes/Yes
Size Of Corporate Staff: NR
On-Going Support: B,C,D,E,G,h,I
Training: 2 Weeks Headquarters; 2 Weeks Operating Store; 2 Weeks On-Site.

SPECIFIC EXPANSION PLANS:

US: All United States
Canada: All Canada
Overseas: No

BCT

3000 NE 30th Pl., 5th Fl.
Ft. Lauderdale, FL 33306
Tel: (800) 627-9998 (954) 563-1224
Fax: (954) 565-0742
E-Mail: peter.posk@bctonline.com
Web Site: www.bctintl.com
Mr. Peter Posk, VP Marketing

Join the 24-year old industry-leading wholesale, manufacturing franchise with the competitive advantage. We are recession-resistant, high-volume, quick-turn around, wholesale only manufacturers, specializing in next-day delivery of thermographed and offset-printed products and rubber stamps to retail printers, mailing centers, office supply stores and other retailers. Comprehensive training, excellent support and nationally praised.

BACKGROUND: IFA MEMBER

Established: 1975; 1st Franchised: 1977
Franchised Units: 87
Company-Owned Units 0
Total Units: 87
Dist.: US-86; CAN-7; O'seas-1
North America: 38 States, 5 Provinces
Density: 16 in CA, 7 in FL, 5 in NY
Projected New Units (12 Months): 2
Qualifications: 4, 4, 3, 3, 3, 5
Registered: All States

FINANCIAL/TERMS:

Cash Investment: $115-151K
Total Investment: $354-441K
Minimum Net Worth: $250K
Fees: Franchise - $35K
Royalty - 6%; Ad. - N/A
Earnings Claim Statement: No
Term of Contract (Years): 25/10
Avg. # Of Employees: 10 FT, 6 PT
Passive Ownership: Not Allowed
Encourage Conversions: Yes
Area Develop. Agreements: No
Sub-Franchising Contracts: No
Expand In Territory: No
Space Needs: 4,000+ SF; FS, SC, Commercial Park

SUPPORT & TRAINING PROVIDED:

Financial Assistance Provided: Yes(I)
Site Selection Assistance: Yes
Lease Negotiation Assistance: Yes
Co-Operative Advertising: No
Franchisee Assoc./Member: Yes
Size Of Corporate Staff: 32
On-Going Support: a,B,C,d,E,G,h,I
Training: 2 Weeks Ft. Lauderdale, FL; 1 Week Pre-Opening at New-Site; 2 Weeks after and On-Going.

SPECIFIC EXPANSION PLANS:

US: NJ, NE
Canada: No
Overseas: No

COPY CLUB

12715 Telge Rd.
Cypress, TX 77429-0777
Tel: (888) 280-2053 (281) 256-4100
Fax: (281) 256-4178
E-Mail: bdolan@inotes.iced.net
Web Site: www.iced.net
Mr. Bob Dolan, VP Franchise Sales

High-visibility, high-traffic digital imaging and copying and business/communications center, open 24 hours a day. Dynamic retail environment. Also offering self-service copying and computer rental.

BACKGROUND: IFA MEMBER

Established: 1992; 1st Franchised: 1994
Franchised Units: 24
Company-Owned Units 0
Total Units: 24
Dist.: US-14; CAN-0; O'seas-0
North America: 4 States
Density: TX, CA, GA
Projected New Units (12 Months): 5
Qualifications: 5, 5, 3, 1, 1, 4
Registered: CA,FL,IL,NY,VA,WA

FINANCIAL/TERMS:

Cash Investment: $95K
Total Investment: $361.6-495.4K
Minimum Net Worth: $500K
Fees: Franchise - $30K
Royalty - 7%; Ad. - 0%
Earnings Claim Statement: Yes
Term of Contract (Years): 25/25
Avg. # Of Employees: 8 FT, 5 PT
Passive Ownership: Allowed
Encourage Conversions: No
Area Develop. Agreements: Yes/10
Sub-Franchising Contracts: Yes
Expand In Territory: Yes
Space Needs: 4,000 SF; FS

SUPPORT & TRAINING PROVIDED:

Financial Assistance Provided: Yes(I)
Site Selection Assistance: Yes
Lease Negotiation Assistance: Yes
Co-Operative Advertising: No
Franchisee Assoc./Member: Yes/Yes
Size Of Corporate Staff: NR
On-Going Support: C,D,E,G,h,I
Training: 3 Weeks in Classroom; 2 Weeks On-Site.

SPECIFIC EXPANSION PLANS:

US: All United States
Canada: No
Overseas: No

FRANKLIN'S SYSTEMS

12715 Telge Rd.
Cypress, TX 77429
Tel: (888) 280-2053 (281) 256-4100
Fax: (281) 256-4178
E-Mail: bdolan@inotes.iced.net
Web Site: www.iced.net
Mr. Bob Dolan, VP Franchise Sales

Part of the ICED family of franchises, now in our 30th year, with over 1,000 franchises in 21 countries. We maintain a position of leadership in our traditional printing and digital publishing, including Webpage design and maintenance, as well as legendary outside sales consultant training. Your corporate management skills are transferable in our business-to-business environment.

BACKGROUND: IFA MEMBER

Established: 1971; 1st Franchised: 1977
Franchised Units: 66
Company-Owned Units 0
Total Units: 66

Dist.: US-66; CAN-0; O'seas-0
North America: 14 States
Density: 22 in GA, 11 in FL, 7 in TN
Projected New Units (12 Months): 5
Registered: FL,VA

FINANCIAL/TERMS:

Cash Investment: $84K
Total Investment: $296.4-359.8K
Minimum Net Worth: $250K
Fees: Franchise - $25K
Royalty - 4-8%; Ad. - 0%
Earnings Claim Statement: No
Term of Contract (Years): 25/25
Avg. # Of Employees: 3-7 FT, 1 PT
Passive Ownership: Not Allowed
Encourage Conversions: No
Area Develop. Agreements: No
Sub-Franchising Contracts: No
Expand In Territory: Yes
Space Needs: 1,500-2,000 SF; SC, SF, Business Park

SUPPORT & TRAINING PROVIDED:

Financial Assistance Provided: Yes(I)
Site Selection Assistance: Yes
Lease Negotiation Assistance: Yes
Co-Operative Advertising: No
Franchisee Assoc./Member: Yes/Yes
Size Of Corporate Staff: NR
On-Going Support: B,C,D,E,G,h,I
Training: 5 Weeks Training (Lodging and Airfare Included.)

SPECIFIC EXPANSION PLANS:

US: All United States
Canada: No
Overseas: No

INK WELL, THE

12715 Telge Rd.
Cypress, TX 77429
Tel: (888) 280-2053 (281) 256-4100
Fax: (281) 256-4178
E-Mail: bdolan@inotes.iced.net
Web Site: www.iced.net
Mr. Bob Dolan, VP Franchise Sales

THE INK WELL printing centers are positioned to provide high-quality, full-service printing and copying, typesetting and design services to the business community.

BACKGROUND: IFA MEMBER
Established: 1972; 1st Franchised: 1981
Franchised Units: 39
Company-Owned Units 0
Total Units: 39
Dist.: US-40; CAN-0; O'seas-0
North America: 8 States
Density: 24 in OH, 5 in IL, 3 in FL
Projected New Units (12 Months): 4
Qualifications: 5, 4, 1, 2, 1, 5
Registered: FL

FINANCIAL/TERMS:

Cash Investment: $84K
Total Investment: $296.4-357.8K
Minimum Net Worth: $250K
Fees: Franchise - $25K
Royalty - 4-6%; Ad. - 2%
Earnings Claim Statement: No
Term of Contract (Years): 25/25
Avg. # Of Employees: 4-6 FT, 1 PT
Passive Ownership: Not Allowed
Encourage Conversions: No
Area Develop. Agreements: No
Sub-Franchising Contracts: No
Expand In Territory: Yes
Space Needs: 1,500-2,000 SF; SC, SC, Business Park

SUPPORT & TRAINING PROVIDED:

Financial Assistance Provided: Yes(D)
Site Selection Assistance: Yes
Lease Negotiation Assistance: Yes
Co-Operative Advertising: Yes
Franchisee Assoc./Member: Yes/Yes
Size Of Corporate Staff: NR
On-Going Support: B,C,D,E,G,h,I
Training: 5 Weeks Headquarters; 1 Week in Field; 8 Days On-Site.

SPECIFIC EXPANSION PLANS:

US: All United States
Canada: No
Overseas: No

KWIK-KOPY PRINTING

1 Entrepreneur Way
Cypress, TX 77429
Tel: (888) 280-2053 (281) 256-4100
Fax: (281) 256-4178
E-Mail: kksales@kwikkopy.combdolan@inotes.ic
Web Site: www.iced.net
Mr. Bob Dolan, VP Franchise Sales

Part of the ICED family of franchises, now in our 30th year, with over 1,000 franchises in 21 countries. As a member of the ICED family of franchises, we maintain a position of leadership with our traditional printing and digital publishing, including Website design and maintenance, as well as legendary outside sales consultant training. Your corporate management skills are transferable in our business-to-business environment.

BACKGROUND: IFA MEMBER
Established: 1967; 1st Franchised: 1967
Franchised Units: 756
Company-Owned Units 0
Total Units: 756
Dist.: US-365; CAN-76; O'seas-332
North America: 39 States, 6 Provinces
Density: 147 in TX, 32 in IL, 27 CA
Projected New Units (12 Months): 8
Registered: All Except SD,ND,HI

FINANCIAL/TERMS:

Cash Investment: $84K
Total Investment: $296.4-357.8K
Minimum Net Worth: $250K
Fees: Franchise - $25K
Royalty - 4-8%; Ad. - 0%
Earnings Claim Statement: Yes
Term of Contract (Years): 25/25
Avg. # Of Employees: 3-7 FT, 1 PT
Passive Ownership: Not Allowed
Encourage Conversions: No
Area Develop. Agreements: No
Sub-Franchising Contracts: No
Expand In Territory: Yes
Space Needs: 1,500-2,000 SF; SC, SF, Business Park

SUPPORT & TRAINING PROVIDED:

Financial Assistance Provided: Yes(D)
Site Selection Assistance: Yes
Lease Negotiation Assistance: Yes
Co-Operative Advertising: No
Franchisee Assoc./Member: Yes/Yes
Size Of Corporate Staff: NR
On-Going Support: B,C,D,E,G,h,I
Training: 5 Weeks for 2 People, Lodging Included; $1,500 Allowance for Meals/Airfare; Other Credits.

SPECIFIC EXPANSION PLANS:

US: All United States
Canada: All Canada
Overseas: All Countries

KWIK-KOPY PRINTING CANADA

1550 16th Ave.
Richmond Hill, ON L4B 3K9 CANADA
Tel: (800) 387-9725 (416) 798-7007
Fax: (905) 780-0575
E-Mail: kkpcc@kwikkopy.ca
Web Site: www.kwikkopy.ca
Mr. C. John Woodburn, Dir. Franchising

Full-service print franchise, on-site printing, copying and digital printing/copying. Canada's largest and most successful print franchise. Strong support and training programs -- no industry experience necessary -- over 1,000 outlets worldwide.

BACKGROUND:
Established: 1979; 1st Franchised: 1979
Franchised Units: 73
Company-Owned Units 5
Total Units: 78
Dist.: US-0; CAN-78; O'seas-0
North America: 9 Provinces
Density: 55 in ON, 5 in AB, 5 in BC
Projected New Units (12 Months): 6
Qualifications: 3, 4, 1, 3, 4, 5
Registered: All States and AB

FINANCIAL/TERMS:
Cash Investment: $80K
Total Investment: $175-200K
Minimum Net Worth: $200K
Fees: Franchise - $29.5K
Royalty - 7%; Ad. - 3%
Earnings Claim Statement: No
Term of Contract (Years): 10/10
Avg. # Of Employees: 2 FT
Passive Ownership: Not Allowed
Encourage Conversions: Yes
Area Develop. Agreements: Yes/10
Sub-Franchising Contracts: No
Expand In Territory: Yes
Space Needs: 800-1,500 SF; FS, Office Tower, Ind. Park

SUPPORT & TRAINING PROVIDED:
Financial Assistance Provided: Yes(I)
Site Selection Assistance: Yes
Lease Negotiation Assistance: Yes
Co-Operative Advertising: Yes
Franchisee Assoc./Member: Yes/No
Size Of Corporate Staff: 15
On-Going Support: C,D,E,G,h,I
Training: 3 Weeks Houston, TX; 1 Week Toronto, ON; 1 Week On-Site.

SPECIFIC EXPANSION PLANS:
US: N/A
Canada: All Canada
Overseas: Middle East, India, Asian Pacific Rim, Africa

<< >>

LAZERQUICK
29900 SW Kinsman
Wilsonville, OR 97070
Tel: (800) 477-2679 (503) 682-0185
Fax: (503) 682-7816
E-Mail: mybiz@lazerquick.com
Web Site: www.lazerquick.com
Mr. Rick Hinthorne

LAZERQUICK centers are complete, one-stop printing and copying centers. All centers feature state-of-the-art electronic publishing, digital graphics and imaging services that support our range of quality, fast-service offset printing, high-speed copying and related bindery and finishing services. The LAZERQUICK franchise is based on value and performance. Affiliates benefit from our unique and innovative programs.

BACKGROUND: IFA MEMBER
Established: 1968; 1st Franchised: 1990
Franchised Units: 24
Company-Owned Units 21
Total Units: 45
Dist.: US-47; CAN-0; O'seas-0
North America: 7 States
Density: 29 in OR, 13 in WA, 1 in CA
Projected New Units (12 Months): 6
Qualifications: 4, 3, 2, 3, 3, 5
Registered: CA,FL,IL,IN,MD,MI,MN,NY, OR,VA,WA,WI

FINANCIAL/TERMS:
Cash Investment: $51.8-82.5K
Total Investment: $172.5-275K
Minimum Net Worth: $N/A
Fees: Franchise - $25K
Royalty - 3-5%/$500; Ad. - 1.5%/$250
Earnings Claim Statement: Yes
Term of Contract (Years): 7/7/7
Avg. # Of Employees: 2 FT, 2 PT
Passive Ownership: Not Allowed
Encourage Conversions: Yes
Area Develop. Agreements: Yes/Varies
Sub-Franchising Contracts: No
Expand In Territory: No
Space Needs: 1,400-1,800 SF; SC

SUPPORT & TRAINING PROVIDED:
Financial Assistance Provided: Yes(I)
Site Selection Assistance: Yes
Lease Negotiation Assistance: Yes
Co-Operative Advertising: N/A
Franchisee Assoc./Member: No
Size Of Corporate Staff: 32
On-Going Support: C,D,E,G,I
Training: 5-7 Weeks at Corporate Headquarters.

SPECIFIC EXPANSION PLANS:
US: All United States
Canada: All Exc. AB,PQ
Overseas: No

<< >>

MINUTEMAN PRESS INTERNATIONAL
1640 New Hwy.
Farmingdale, NY 11735
Tel: (800) 645-3006 (631) 249-1370
Fax: (631) 249-5618
E-Mail: mpihq@aol.com
Web Site: www.minuteman-press.com
Mr. Robert Titus, President

Full-service printing and graphic centers, specializing in multi-color commercial printing at instant print prices. A one-stop printing and graphics business.

BACKGROUND: IFA MEMBER
Established: 1975; 1st Franchised: 1975
Franchised Units: 900
Company-Owned Units 0
Total Units: 900
Dist.: US-770; CAN-70; O'seas-50
North America: 46 States, 5 Provinces
Density: 75 in CA, 66 in NY, 58 in TX
Projected New Units (12 Months): 50
Qualifications: 1, 1, 1, 1, 2, 5
Registered: All States and AB

FINANCIAL/TERMS:
Cash Investment: $35-60K
Total Investment: $100-120K
Minimum Net Worth: $NR
Fees: Franchise - $44.5K
Royalty - 6%; Ad. - 0%
Earnings Claim Statement: Yes
Term of Contract (Years): 35/10
Avg. # Of Employees: 3 FT to Start
Passive Ownership: Discouraged
Encourage Conversions: Yes
Area Develop. Agreements: No
Sub-Franchising Contracts: No
Expand In Territory: Yes
Space Needs: 1,200 SF; FS, SF, SC

SUPPORT & TRAINING PROVIDED:
Financial Assistance Provided: Yes(I)
Site Selection Assistance: Yes
Lease Negotiation Assistance: Yes
Co-Operative Advertising: No
Franchisee Assoc./Member: No
Size Of Corporate Staff: 160
On-Going Support: b,C,D,E,F,G,H,I
Training: 3 Weeks New York; On-Site As Needed.

SPECIFIC EXPANSION PLANS:
US: All United States
Canada: All Canada
Overseas: U.K., South Africa, Australia

<< >>

PIP PRINTING
26722 Plaza Dr., # 200
Mission Viejo, CA 92691-6390
Tel: (800) 292-4747 (949) 282-3800
Fax: (949) 282-3899
E-Mail: fransales@pipprinting.com
Web Site: www.pip.com
Ms. Karen Brock, Mgr. Franchise Development

PIP PRINTING locations provide a full range of business communications from initial concept to finished printed product. PIP's service menu includes affordable, short-run full and multi-color printing, high-volume copying, desktop publication, layout, design and finishing on an array of products including newsletters, brochures, stationery and forms.

BACKGROUND: IFA MEMBER
Established: 1965; 1st Franchised: 1968
Franchised Units: 501
Company-Owned Units 0
Total Units: 501
Dist.: US-469; CAN-0; O'seas-16
North America: 38 States
Density: 104 in CA, 32 in NY,30 in FL
Projected New Units (12 Months): 5
Qualifications: 5, 4, 2, 2, 3, 5
Registered: All States Except ND

FINANCIAL/TERMS:
Cash Investment: $5-40K
Total Investment: $21-172K
Minimum Net Worth: $200-300K
Fees: Franchise - $5-22K
Royalty - 6%; Ad. - 2%
Earnings Claim Statement: Yes
Term of Contract (Years): 10/10
Avg. # Of Employees: 5 FT
Passive Ownership: Not Allowed
Encourage Conversions: Yes
Area Develop. Agreements: No
Sub-Franchising Contracts: No
Expand In Territory: Yes
Space Needs: 2,000 SF; FS, SF, SC, HB

SUPPORT & TRAINING PROVIDED:
Financial Assistance Provided: Yes(I)
Site Selection Assistance: Yes
Lease Negotiation Assistance: Yes
Co-Operative Advertising: Yes
Franchisee Assoc./Member: Yes/Yes
Size Of Corporate Staff: 40
On-Going Support: A,B,C,D,E,G,H,I
Training: 2 1/2 Weeks at Corporate Headquarters; 3 Days at Store Location After 30, 60, and 90 Days.

SPECIFIC EXPANSION PLANS:
US: All U.S., Especially CA
Canada: No
Overseas: No

<< >>

PROFORMA

8800 E. Pleasant Valley Rd.
Cleveland, OH 44131
Tel: (800) 825-1525 (216) 520-8400
Fax: (216) 520-8444
E-Mail: franchopp@proforma.com
Web Site: www.proforma.com
Ms. Theresa Huszka, Franchise Development

Home-based franchise. Franchise owners market and distribute printing and promotional products to other businesses. Major player in a $150 billion industry! Low overhead. Full marketing and administrative support. $9,500 initial investment. Expanding rapidly throughout North America.

BACKGROUND: IFA MEMBER
Established: 1978; 1st Franchised: 1985
Franchised Units: 525
Company-Owned Units 0
Total Units: 525
Dist.: US-260; CAN-20; O'seas-0
North America: 42 States, 2 Provinces
Density: 18 in CA, 10 in OH, 10 in NY
Projected New Units (12 Months): 75
Qualifications: 3, 5, 1, 3, 1, 5
Registered: All States

FINANCIAL/TERMS:
Cash Investment: $5-10K
Total Investment: $22-27K
Minimum Net Worth: $100K
Fees: Franchise - $19.5K
Royalty - 9%; Ad. - 1%
Earnings Claim Statement: No
Term of Contract (Years): 10/10
Avg. # Of Employees: 1 FT
Passive Ownership: Not Allowed
Encourage Conversions: Yes
Area Develop. Agreements: No
Sub-Franchising Contracts: No
Expand In Territory: N/A
Space Needs: NR SF; HB

SUPPORT & TRAINING PROVIDED:
Financial Assistance Provided: Yes(D)
Site Selection Assistance: N/A
Lease Negotiation Assistance: N/A
Co-Operative Advertising: Yes
Franchisee Assoc./Member: NR
Size Of Corporate Staff: 140
On-Going Support: A,C,D,F,G,H,I
Training: 1 Week Headquarters; 2 Days Regional 2 Days National; 2 Days Field Visit.

SPECIFIC EXPANSION PLANS:
US: All United States
Canada: All Canada
Overseas: No

<< >>

SIGNAL GRAPHICS PRINTING

6789 S. Yosemite St., # 100
Englewood, CO 80112
Tel: (800) 852-6336 (303) 779-6789
Fax: (303) 779-8445
E-Mail: sampacorp@ aol.com
Web Site: www.signalgraphics.com
Mr. Mike Latham, Dir. Fran. Dev.

A full range of services places SIGNAL GRAPHICS PRINTING ahead of the competition. Our franchising program will enable the owner having no previous printing experience to market quick printing, copying, desktop publishing, digital services, typesetting and high-quality commercial printing to a wide range of customers in the business community. Just the right size system to offer prime locations and personalized support.

BACKGROUND: IFA MEMBER
Established: 1974; 1st Franchised: 1982
Franchised Units: 50
Company-Owned Units 2
Total Units: 52
Dist.: US-46; CAN-0; O'seas-3
North America: 18 States
Density: 18 in CO, 3 in CA, 5 in TX
Projected New Units (12 Months): 10
Registered: All States Except ND,SD

FINANCIAL/TERMS:
Cash Investment: $60K Minimum
Total Investment: $190-230K
Minimum Net Worth: $NR
Fees: Franchise - $18K
Royalty - 0-5%; Ad. - $100/Mo.
Earnings Claim Statement: Yes
Term of Contract (Years): 25/25
Avg. # Of Employees: 4 FT, 1 PT
Passive Ownership: Discouraged
Encourage Conversions: Yes
Area Develop. Agreements: No
Sub-Franchising Contracts: No
Expand In Territory: Yes
Space Needs: 1,500 SF; SC

SUPPORT & TRAINING PROVIDED:
Financial Assistance Provided: Yes(I)
Site Selection Assistance: Yes
Lease Negotiation Assistance: Yes
Co-Operative Advertising: Yes
Franchisee Assoc./Member: Yes/Yes
Size Of Corporate Staff: NR
On-Going Support: B,C,d,E,G,H,I
Training: 3 Weeks Headquarters; 2 Weeks On-Site.

SPECIFIC EXPANSION PLANS:
US: All United States

Canada: All Canada
Overseas: All Countries

<< >>

SIR SPEEDY
26722 Plaza Dr.
Mission Viejo, CA 92691-6390
Tel: (800) 854-3321 (949) 348-5000
Fax: (949) 348-5068
E-Mail: ahuston@sirspeedy.com
Web Site: www.sirspeedy.com
Ms. Anne Huston, Sales Coordinator

A Monday through Friday business-to-business service, it provides copying, printing, digital communication and graphic design for a diverse range of corporate clients. It's global digital link facilitates instantaneous communication and transfer of material between all centers in the group.

BACKGROUND: IFA MEMBER
Established: 1968; 1st Franchised: 1968
Franchised Units: 660
Company-Owned Units 1
Total Units: 661
Dist.: US-752; CAN-5; O'seas-125
North America: 47 States, 1 Province
Density: 86 in CA, 72 in FL, 41 in IL
Projected New Units (12 Months): 40
Qualifications: 5, 4, 1, 3, 3, 5
Registered: All States

FINANCIAL/TERMS:
Cash Investment: $100-150K
Total Investment: $316-391K
Minimum Net Worth: $300K
Fees: Franchise - $20K
Royalty - 4-6%; Ad. - 1-2%
Earnings Claim Statement: Yes
Term of Contract (Years): 20/10
Avg. # Of Employees: 5+ FT
Passive Ownership: Discouraged
Encourage Conversions: Yes
Area Develop. Agreements: No
Sub-Franchising Contracts: No
Expand In Territory: Yes
Space Needs: 2,000-12,000 SF; FS, SC

SUPPORT & TRAINING PROVIDED:
Financial Assistance Provided: Yes(I)
Site Selection Assistance: Yes
Lease Negotiation Assistance: Yes
Co-Operative Advertising: No
Franchisee Assoc./Member: No
Size Of Corporate Staff: 50
On-Going Support: B,C,D,E,F,G,H,I
Training: 3 Weeks in Mission Viejo, CA; 6 Weeks at Franchisee's Site.

SPECIFIC EXPANSION PLANS:
US: All United States
Canada: ON
Overseas: Most Countries

<< >>

SUPPLEMENTAL LISTING OF FRANCHISORS

FRANKLIN'S PRINTING, DIGITAL IMAGING AND COPYING, 12715 Telge Rd., Cypress, TX 77410-0777 ; (888) 280 2053 (281) 256-4100; (281) 245-4178

INSTY-PRINTS, 8091 Wallace Rd., Eden Prairie, MN 55344 ; (800) 779-1000 (612) 975-6200; (612) 975-6262

POSTAL PRINTING & COMMUNICATIONS, 250 Auburn Ave., # 304, Atlanta, GA 30303 ; (800) 691-0636 (404) 659-5644; (404) 659-5646

PRINT THREE, 160 Nashdene Rd., Chatham, ON M1V 4CA CANADA; (800) 335-5918 (416) 754-8700; (416) 754-8441

SCREEN PRINTING USA, 534 W. Shawnee Ave., Plymouth, PA 18651-2009

SURE GRAPHICS, 101, 12465-82 Ave., Surrey, BC V3W 3E8 CANADA; (604) 594-8334; (604) 594-8320

Publications

Chapter 29

Publications Industry Profile

Total # Franchisors in Industry Group	27
Total # Franchised Units in Industry Group	1,077
Total # Company-Owned Units in Industry Group	61
Total # Operating Units in Industry Group	1,138
Average # Franchised Units/Franchisor	39.9
Average # Company-Owned Units/Franchisor	2.3
Average # Total Units/Franchisor	42.2
Ratio of Total # Franchised Units/Total # Company-Owned Units	17.7:1
Industry Survey Participants	6
Representing % of Industry	22.2%
Average Franchise Fee*:	$12.0K
Average Total Investment*:	$21.4K
Average On-Going Royalty Fee*:	8.1%

*If a range was provided, the mid-point of the range was used. See detailed profiles for actual ranges.

Five Largest Participants in Survey

Company	# Franchised Units	# Co-Owned Units	# Total Units	Franchise Fee	On-Going Royalty	Total Investment
1. Coffee News	276	3	279	2K	$20-75/Wk.	2.5K
2. Bingo Bugle Newspaper	71	0	71	1.5-10K	10%	1.5-10K
3. RSVP Publications	70	0	70	30K	7%	35-70K+
4. Perfect Wedding Guide, The	53	2	55	25-35K	6%	35-50K
5. Finderbinders/Sourcebook	18	1	19	1K	5-10%	10-15K

All of the data provided are proprietary and should not be quoted without acknowledging *Bond's Franchise Guide.*

BINGO BUGLE NEWSPAPER

P.O. Box 527
Vashon Island, WA 98070-0527
Tel: (800) 327-6437 (206) 463-5656
Fax: (206) 463-5630
E-Mail: tara@bingobugle.com
Web Site: www.bingobugle.com
Ms. Tara Snowden, Vice President

THE BINGO BUGLE is North America's largest network of newspapers devoted to bingo & gaming. Circulation over 1 million copies monthly. Listed in Entrepreneur's Annual Franchise 500 as one of the lowest cost franchise opportunities. Franchise fees range from $1,500 to $7,000. Complete training and support. Modest investment. Call 1-800-327-6437 for details.

BACKGROUND: IFA MEMBER
Established: 1981; 1st Franchised: 1983
Franchised Units: 71
Company-Owned Units 0
Total Units: 71
Dist.: US-66; CAN-5; O'seas-0
North America: 30 States, 2 Provinces
Density: 12 in CA, 6 in NY, 5 in FL
Projected New Units (12 Months): 6
Qualifications: 2, 4, 4, 2, 2, 1
Registered: IL,FL,SD,VA

FINANCIAL/TERMS:
Cash Investment: $1.5-6K
Total Investment: $1.5-10K
Minimum Net Worth: $NR
Fees: Franchise - $1.5-10K
Royalty - 10%; Ad. - 0%
Earnings Claim Statement: No
Term of Contract (Years): 5/5
Avg. # Of Employees: 0
Passive Ownership: Allowed
Encourage Conversions: No
Area Develop. Agreements: No
Sub-Franchising Contracts: No
Expand In Territory: No
Space Needs: N/A SF; N/A

SUPPORT & TRAINING PROVIDED:
Financial Assistance Provided: No
Site Selection Assistance: N/A
Lease Negotiation Assistance: No
Co-Operative Advertising: No
Franchisee Assoc./Member: Yes/Yes
Size Of Corporate Staff: 2
On-Going Support: NR
Training: 2.5 Days Seattle, WA.

SPECIFIC EXPANSION PLANS:
US: Northeast, Central US, NC
Canada: All Canada
Overseas: No

<< >>

COFFEE NEWS

P.O. Box 8444
Bangor, ME 04402-8444
Tel: (207) 941-0860
Fax: (207) 941-0860
E-Mail: bill@coffeednewsusa.com
Web Site: www.coffeenewsusa.com
Mr. William A. Buckley, President

COFFEE NEWS is an international, fun-filled weekly publication produced and delivered free of charge by local franchisors to restaurants, coffee shops and the hospitality industry. Each issue contains short stories, trivia, horoscopes, interesting facts and jokes, plus a local event section edited by the franchisee. Income is derived from the sale of ads to small businesses in each community.

BACKGROUND:
Established: 1994; 1st Franchised: 1996
Franchised Units: 276
Company-Owned Units 3
Total Units: 279
Dist.: US-109; CAN-135; O'seas-35
North America: NR
Density: 31 in BC, 28 in ME, 23 in ON
Projected New Units (12 Months): 100
Qualifications: 1, 5, 5, 3, 3, 3
Registered: CA,FL,HI,MN,NY,OR,SD, WI,AB

FINANCIAL/TERMS:
Cash Investment: $2.5K
Total Investment: $2.5K
Minimum Net Worth: $None
Fees: Franchise - $2K
Royalty - $20-75/Wk.; Ad. - 0%
Earnings Claim Statement: No
Term of Contract (Years): 4/4
Avg. # Of Employees: 1 FT, 1 PT
Passive Ownership: Discouraged
Encourage Conversions: N/A
Area Develop. Agreements: No
Sub-Franchising Contracts: No
Expand In Territory: Yes
Space Needs: N/A SF; N/A

SUPPORT & TRAINING PROVIDED:
Financial Assistance Provided: No
Site Selection Assistance: Yes
Lease Negotiation Assistance: No
Co-Operative Advertising: No
Franchisee Assoc./Member: No
Size Of Corporate Staff: 5
On-Going Support: G
Training: Quarterly Sales Meetings in ME.

SPECIFIC EXPANSION PLANS:
US: All United States
Canada: All Canada
Overseas: All Countries

<< >>

FINDERBINDER / SOURCEBOOK DIRECTORIES

8546 Chevy Chase Dr.
La Mesa, CA 91941-5325
Tel: (800) 255-2575 (619) 463-5050
Fax: (619) 463-5097
Web Site: www.marketing-tactics.com
Mr. Gary Beals, President

The FINDERBINDER News Media Directory and the SOURCEBOOK Directory of Clubs and Associations are locally-produced reference books created by existing communications firms, such as an advertising agency or public relations consultants. It is an added profit center that builds public awareness for the local company.

BACKGROUND:
Established: 1974; 1st Franchised: 1978
Franchised Units: 18
Company-Owned Units 1
Total Units: 19
Dist.: US-22; CAN-0; O'seas-0
North America: 15 States
Density: 4 in CA
Projected New Units (12 Months): 3
Registered: CA

FINANCIAL/TERMS:
Cash Investment: $NR
Total Investment: $10-15K
Minimum Net Worth: $30K
Fees: Franchise - $1K
Royalty - 5-10%; Ad. - N/A
Earnings Claim Statement: No
Term of Contract (Years): Open
Avg. # Of Employees: 2 FT, 1 PT
Passive Ownership: Discouraged
Encourage Conversions: No
Area Develop. Agreements: No
Sub-Franchising Contracts: No
Expand In Territory: Yes
Space Needs: N/A SF; N/A

SUPPORT & TRAINING PROVIDED:
Financial Assistance Provided: No
Site Selection Assistance: N/A
Lease Negotiation Assistance: N/A
Co-Operative Advertising: Yes
Franchisee Assoc./Member: No
Size Of Corporate Staff: 3
On-Going Support: C,D,E,G,H,I

Training: 1 Day in San Diego.
SPECIFIC EXPANSION PLANS:
US: All United States
Canada: All Canada
Overseas: U.K., Australia, New Zealand

<< >>

HOMESTEADER

P.O. Box 2824
Framingham, MA 01703
Tel: (800) 941-9907 (508) 820-4311
Fax: (508) 820-0280
Web Site: www.thehomesteader.com
Mr. Allen Nitschelm, President

THE HOMESTEADER is a publication direct-mailed to new homeowners, one of the best target markets for businesses to reach. This is a low-cost, home-based opportunity with great income potential for anyone with a sales, publishing or business background.

BACKGROUND:
Established: 1990; 1st Franchised: 1993
Franchised Units: 13
Company-Owned Units 3
Total Units: 16
Dist.: US-17; CAN-0; O'seas-0
North America: 4 States
Density: 11 in MA, 4 in CT, 1 in NY
Projected New Units (12 Months): 6-10
Qualifications: 3, 3, 4, 2, 4, 2
Registered: CA,FL,NY,VA
FINANCIAL/TERMS:
Cash Investment: $3.3-22K
Total Investment: $3.3-22K
Minimum Net Worth: $10K
Fees: Franchise - $3.4K
Royalty - 10%; Ad. - 0-2%
Earnings Claim Statement: Yes
Term of Contract (Years): 10/10
Avg. # Of Employees: 1 FT
Passive Ownership: Allowed
Encourage Conversions: N/A
Area Develop. Agreements: No
Sub-Franchising Contracts: No
Expand In Territory: No
Space Needs: NR SF; HB
SUPPORT & TRAINING PROVIDED:
Financial Assistance Provided: Yes(I)
Site Selection Assistance: N/A
Lease Negotiation Assistance: N/A
Co-Operative Advertising: N/A
Franchisee Assoc./Member: No
Size Of Corporate Staff: 4
On-Going Support: d,H
Training: 2-3 Days Framingham, MA.
SPECIFIC EXPANSION PLANS:
US: All United States
Canada: All Canada
Overseas: No

<< >>

PERFECT WEDDING GUIDE, THE

1206 N C.R. 427
Longwood, FL 32750
Tel: (888) 222-7433 (407) 331-6212
Fax: (407) 331-5004
E-Mail: patrick@perfectweddingguide.com
Web Site: www.perfectweddingguide.com
Mr. Patrick J. McGroder, President

THE PERFECT WEDDING GUIDE is a comprehensive buyers' guide to wedding and honeymoon products and services. As the owner of a PERFECT WEDDING GUIDE, you will publish a magazine that thousands of people will read every day. With the guidance of the nation's premier wedding magazine publisher, you will own and manage your own business!

BACKGROUND: IFA MEMBER
Established: 1991; 1st Franchised: 1998
Franchised Units: 53
Company-Owned Units 2
Total Units: 55
Dist.: US-54; CAN-1; O'seas-0
North America: 22 States
Density: 4 in FL, 2 in TX
Projected New Units (12 Months): 24
Qualifications: 4, 3, 3, 3, 5, 5
Registered: FL
FINANCIAL/TERMS:
Cash Investment: $30-50K
Total Investment: $35-50K
Minimum Net Worth: $50K
Fees: Franchise - $25-35K
Royalty - 6%; Ad. - 1%
Earnings Claim Statement: No
Term of Contract (Years): 10/10
Avg. # Of Employees: 2 FT
Passive Ownership: Discouraged
Encourage Conversions: NR
Area Develop. Agreements: No
Sub-Franchising Contracts: No
Expand In Territory: Yes
Space Needs: N/A SF; HB
SUPPORT & TRAINING PROVIDED:
Financial Assistance Provided: Yes(D)
Site Selection Assistance: N/A
Lease Negotiation Assistance: N/A
Co-Operative Advertising: No
Franchisee Assoc./Member: No
Size Of Corporate Staff: 7
On-Going Support: a,b,C,d,G,h,I
Training: 5 Days Longwood, FL; 5 Days Franchise Territory.
SPECIFIC EXPANSION PLANS:
US: All United States
Canada: All Canada
Overseas: No

<< >>

RSVP PUBLICATIONS

1156 NE Cleveland St.
Clearwater, FL 33755
Tel: (800) 360-7787 (727) 442-4000
Fax: (727) 441-1315
E-Mail: dave@rsvppublications.com
Web Site: www.rsvppublications.com
Mr. Dave Tropf, President

RSVP PUBLICATIONS, "direct mail to the upscale," is ideal for sales or marketing pros. RSVP regularly reaches 7 million of the most affluent homes in the U.S. With over 9,000 satisfied clients, we know what works and how to produce it to markets across the U.S. We offer extensive training that makes a new franchise buyer successful

BACKGROUND:
Established: 1985; 1st Franchised: 1986
Franchised Units: 70
Company-Owned Units 0
Total Units: 70
Dist.: US-70; CAN-0; O'seas-0
North America: 30 States
Density: 16 in CA, 5 in FL, 5 in OH
Projected New Units (12 Months): 10
Qualifications: 2, 2, 5, 3, 3, 4
Registered: CA,FL,HI,IL,IN,MI,MN,NY, OR,RI,VA,WA,WI,DC
FINANCIAL/TERMS:
Cash Investment: $30-60K

Total Investment:	$35-70K+
Minimum Net Worth:	$35K
Fees: Franchise -	$30K
Royalty - 7%;	Ad. - 0%
Earnings Claim Statement:	No
Term of Contract (Years):	10/10
Avg. # Of Employees:	2 FT, 1 PT
Passive Ownership:	Discouraged
Encourage Conversions:	N/A
Area Develop. Agreements:	No
Sub-Franchising Contracts:	No
Expand In Territory:	Yes
Space Needs: N/A SF; HB	

SUPPORT & TRAINING PROVIDED:

Financial Assistance Provided:	Yes(D)
Site Selection Assistance:	N/A
Lease Negotiation Assistance:	N/A
Co-Operative Advertising:	N/A
Franchisee Assoc./Member:	No
Size Of Corporate Staff:	N/R
On-Going Support:	B,D,H,I
Training: 2 Weeks in Tampa, FL.	

SPECIFIC EXPANSION PLANS:

US:	MW, NE
Canada:	All Canada
Overseas:	No

SUPPLEMENTAL LISTING OF FRANCHISORS

4 SEASONS PUBLISHING INC., # 9, 3151 Lakeshore Rd., # 112, Kelowna, BC V1W 2S9 CANADA; (877) 868-0729 (250) 868-0728; (250) 868-0730

ABOUT MAGAZINES, 576 Sigman Rd., # 200, Conyers, GA 30013 ; (877) 607-4768 (770) 761-3331; (770) 761-9889

DISCOVERY MAP INTERNATIONAL, 1909 Skyline Way, # 101, Anacortes, WA 98221-2992; (360) 588-0144; (360) 588-8344

FIESTA CARTOON MAPS, 942 N. Orlando, Mesa, AZ 85205 ; (800) 541-4963 (480) 396-8226; (480) 981-3570

GIRL'S LIFE, 4517 Hartford Rd., Baltimore, MD 21214-3122 ; (410) 254-9200; (410) 254-0991

HOME GUIDE MAGAZINE, 1600 Capital Cir., SW, Tallahassee, FL 32310; (800) 726-6683 (850) 574-2111; (850) 574-2525

HOMES & LAND MAGAZINE, P.O. Box 5018, Tallahassee, FL 32314 ; (800) 726-6683 (850) 574-2111; (850) 574-2525

K & O PUBLISHING, 5744 NE 61st St., P.O. Box 51189, Seattle, WA 98115-1189; (800) 447-1958 (206) 527-4958; (206) 527-9756

MUSCLEMAG INTERNATIONAL, 5775 McLaughlin Rd., Mississauga, ON L5R 3P7 CANADA; (905) 507-3545; (905) 507-3064

PENNYSAVER, 80 Eighth Ave., New York, NY 10011; (212) 243-6800; (212) 243-7457

PICKET FENCE PREVIEW, 1 Kennedy Dr., # 5, South Burlington, VT 05403 (800) 201-0338 (802) 660-3167; (802) 863-8965

TELEVISION + ENTERTAINMENT PUBLICATIONS, Liberty Square, Danvers, MA 01923; (888) 977-4666 (781) 777-9225; (781) 595-9237

TOWN PLANNER, 16600 Sprague Rd., # 440, Cleveland, OH 44130 ; (800) 383-1253 (440) 243-1229; (440) 243-1299

Real Estate Inspection Services

Chapter 30

Real Estate Inspection Services Industry Profile

Total # Franchisors in Industry Group	21
Total # Franchised Units in Industry Group	2,237
Total # Company-Owned Units in Industry Group	362
Total # Operating Units in Industry Group	2,599
Average # Franchised Units/Franchisor	106.5
Average # Company-Owned Units/Franchisor	17.2
Average # Total Units/Franchisor	123.7
Ratio of Total # Franchised Units/Total # Company-Owned Units	6.2:1
Industry Survey Participants	11
Representing % of Industry	52.4%
Average Franchise Fee*:	$20.4K
Average Total Investment*:	$29.3K
Average On-Going Royalty Fee*:	7.1%

*If a range was provided, the mid-point of the range was used. See detailed profiles for actual ranges.

Five Largest Participants in Survey

Company	# Franchised Units	# Co-Owned Units	# Total Units	Franchise Fee	On-Going Royalty	Total Investment
1. Terminix Termite & Pest Control	225	312	537	25-50K	7%	25-50K
2. Housemaster Home Inspection	382	0	382	8.5-24K	7.5%	14.3-47.5K
3. Amerispec Home Inspection	369	2	371	14.9-24.9K	7%	18.9-59.5K
4. Hometeam Inspection Service	333	0	333	13.9-23.9K	7%/$200	20.9-42.9K
5. Pillar to Post	323	0	323	11.9-29.9K	6%	17.5-45K

All of the data provided are proprietary and should not be quoted without acknowledging *Bond's Franchise Guide.*

AMERISPEC HOME INSPECTION SERVICE

860 Ridge Lake Blvd.
Memphis, TN 38120-9421
Tel: (800) 426-2270 (901) 820-8500
Fax: (901) 820-8520
E-Mail: sales@amerispec.net
Web Site: www.amerispecfranchise.com
Mr. Jim Sullivan, VP Sales/Operations

AMERISPEC delivers productivity enhancing tools to our owners like AMERISPEC HOME INSPECTOR (R), proprietary home inspection software loaded on an affordable hand-held computer. A private intranet permits two-way communication with and among our owners. Consider our extensive training, the acclaimed and recognized 'AMERISPEC report,' our ongoing educational support and the package is complete.

BACKGROUND: IFA MEMBER
Established: 1987; 1st Franchised: 1988
Franchised Units: 369
Company-Owned Units 2
Total Units: 371
Dist.: US-293; CAN-76; O'seas-0
North America: 48 States, 8 Provinces
Density: 23 in CA, 15 in FL, 11 in IL
Projected New Units (12 Months): 40
Qualifications: 3, 3, 3, 3, 1, 5
Registered: All States

FINANCIAL/TERMS:
Cash Investment: $10-15K
Total Investment: $18.9-59.5K
Minimum Net Worth: $25K
Fees: Franchise - $14.9-24.9K
Royalty - 7%; Ad. - 3%
Earnings Claim Statement: No
Term of Contract (Years): 5/5
Avg. # Of Employees: 1 FT, 2 PT
Passive Ownership: Allowed
Encourage Conversions: Yes
Area Develop. Agreements: No
Sub-Franchising Contracts: No
Expand In Territory: Yes
Space Needs: N/A SF; HB

SUPPORT & TRAINING PROVIDED:
Financial Assistance Provided: Yes(D)
Site Selection Assistance: N/A
Lease Negotiation Assistance: N/A
Co-Operative Advertising: N/A
Franchisee Assoc./Member: No
Size Of Corporate Staff: 30
On-Going Support: C,D,E,G,h,I
Training: 2 Weeks Memphis, TN.

SPECIFIC EXPANSION PLANS:
US: All United States
Canada: All Canada
Overseas: No

<< >>

AMERISPEC OF CANADA

6540 Tomken Rd.
Mississauga, ON L5T 2E9 CANADA
Tel: (800) 263-5928 (905) 670-0000
Fax: (905) 670-0077
Web Site: www.svm.com
Mr. David Messenger, VP Franchise Market Devel.

North America's largest provider of home inspection and related services in an exploding industry. Superior marketing, training, computer applications and support make this low capital, home-based franchise an exceptional opportunity.

BACKGROUND:
Established: 1988; 1st Franchised: 1988
Franchised Units: 53
Company-Owned Units 0
Total Units: 53
Dist.: US-0; CAN-50; O'seas-0
North America: 8 Provinces
Density: ON, PQ
Projected New Units (12 Months): 12
Qualifications: 2, 2, 2, 2, 3, 4
Registered: AB

FINANCIAL/TERMS:
Cash Investment: $14.9-24.9K
Total Investment: $20-35K
Minimum Net Worth: $50K
Fees: Franchise - $14.9-24.9K
Royalty - 7%; Ad. - 3%
Earnings Claim Statement: No
Term of Contract (Years): 5/5
Avg. # Of Employees: 1 FT, 2 PT
Passive Ownership: Not Allowed
Encourage Conversions: Yes
Area Develop. Agreements: No
Sub-Franchising Contracts: No
Expand In Territory: No
Space Needs: NR SF; N/A

SUPPORT & TRAINING PROVIDED:
Financial Assistance Provided: Yes(D)
Site Selection Assistance: N/A
Lease Negotiation Assistance: N/A
Co-Operative Advertising: Yes
Franchisee Assoc./Member: Yes/Yes
Size Of Corporate Staff: 100
On-Going Support: B,C,D,G,h,I
Training: 2 Weeks Memphis, TN.

SPECIFIC EXPANSION PLANS:
US: No
Canada: All Canada
Overseas: No

<< >>

BRICKKICKER, THE

849 N. Ellsworth
Naperville, IL 60563
Tel: (800) 821-1820 (630) 420-9900
Fax: (630) 420-2270
E-Mail: jallen@brickkicker.com
Web Site: www.brickkicker.com
Mr. Jay Allen, Dir. Marketing Services

Home and building inspections. Operating our own business since 1989 gives us a unique insight into the entrepreneurial aspects required to be an impact player in the industry. We've packaged our experience into a dynamic, aggressive program, including a heavy emphasis on 'live,' on-the-job training. Every BRICKKICKER benefits from the roll up our sleeves attitude in which we operate.

BACKGROUND:
Established: 1989; 1st Franchised: 1995
Franchised Units: 113
Company-Owned Units 1
Total Units: 114
Dist.: US-79; CAN-0; O'seas-0
North America: 7 States
Density: 16 in MI, 8 in WI, 7 in IN
Projected New Units (12 Months): 45
Qualifications: 3, 4, 2, 3, 3, 4
Registered: All States

FINANCIAL/TERMS:
Cash Investment: $9.4-24.9K
Total Investment: $19.4-39.9K
Minimum Net Worth: $10K
Fees: Franchise - $6.9-12.9K
Royalty - 6%; Ad. - 2%
Earnings Claim Statement: No
Term of Contract (Years): 7/20
Avg. # Of Employees: 1 FT
Passive Ownership: Discouraged
Encourage Conversions: Yes
Area Develop. Agreements: No
Sub-Franchising Contracts: No
Expand In Territory: Yes
Space Needs: NR SF; NR

SUPPORT & TRAINING PROVIDED:
Financial Assistance Provided: Yes(D)
Site Selection Assistance: N/A

Lease Negotiation Assistance: N/A
Co-Operative Advertising: N/A
Franchisee Assoc./Member: Yes/Yes
Size Of Corporate Staff: 7
On-Going Support: B,C,D,E,G,H,I
Training: 10 Days, Naperville, IL; 3 Days On-Site.

SPECIFIC EXPANSION PLANS:
US: All United States
Canada: All Canada
Overseas: No

<< >>

CRITERIUM ENGINEERS

22 Monument Sq., # 600
Portland, ME 04101
Tel: (800) 242-1969 (207) 828-1969
Fax: (207) 775-4405
Web Site: www.criterium-engineers.com
Mr. Peter E. Hollander, Dir. Marketing/ Development

CRITERIUM ENGINEERS is a consulting franchise available to licensed professional engineers. Company specializes in building inspection and evaluation services for buyers, investors, corporations, attorneys, insurance companies, lenders and government. Services include pre-purchase inspections, insurance investigations, due diligence, maintenance planning, expert testimony, reserve studies, environmental assessments, design and construction review.

BACKGROUND:
Established: 1957; 1st Franchised: 1958
Franchised Units: 66
Company-Owned Units 0
Total Units: 66
Dist.: US-66; CAN-0; O'seas-0
North America: 37 States
Density: 4 in CA, 2 in FL, 2 in NJ
Projected New Units (12 Months): 6
Registered: CA,FL,IN, IL, NY,OR

FINANCIAL/TERMS:
Cash Investment: $6K
Total Investment: $25K
Minimum Net Worth: $NR
Fees: Franchise - $21.5K
Royalty - 6%; Ad. - 1%
Earnings Claim Statement: No
Term of Contract (Years): 15/5
Avg. # Of Employees: 2 FT, 2 PT
Passive Ownership: Not Allowed
Encourage Conversions: N/A
Area Develop. Agreements: No
Sub-Franchising Contracts: No
Expand In Territory: Yes
Space Needs: 300 SF; NR

SUPPORT & TRAINING PROVIDED:
Financial Assistance Provided: Yes
Site Selection Assistance: N/A
Lease Negotiation Assistance: No
Co-Operative Advertising: N/A
Franchisee Assoc./Member: NR
Size Of Corporate Staff: 10
On-Going Support: B,C,D,G,H,I
Training: 1 Week Headquarters.

SPECIFIC EXPANSION PLANS:
US: All Legally Permitted
Canada: All Canada
Overseas: All Countries

<< >>

CRITTER CONTROL.

CRITTER CONTROL

9435 E. Cherry Bend Rd.
Traverse City, MI 49684
Tel: (800) 451-6544 (231) 947-2400
Fax: (231) 947-9440
E-Mail: crittercontrol@coslink.net
Web Site: www.crittercontrol.com
Mr. Sean Carruth, Staff Biologist

Urban Wildlife Management Specialists. Nation's leading animal control firm. Humane animal removal, prevention and repairs of animal damage.

BACKGROUND:
Established: 1983; 1st Franchised: 1988
Franchised Units: 78
Company-Owned Units 23
Total Units: 101
Dist.: US-99; CAN-2; O'seas-0
North America: NR
Density: 10 in MI, 9 in FL, 6 in OH
Projected New Units (12 Months): 10
Qualifications: 2, 3, 3, 3, 3, 4
Registered: CA,IN,MD,MI,NY,VA,WI

FINANCIAL/TERMS:
Cash Investment: $3-5K
Total Investment: $5-25K
Minimum Net Worth: $N/A
Fees: Franchise - $15-24K
Royalty - 6-16%; Ad. - 1-2%
Earnings Claim Statement: No
Term of Contract (Years): 10/10
Avg. # Of Employees: 2 FT, 1 PT
Passive Ownership: Discouraged
Encourage Conversions: N/A
Area Develop. Agreements: No
Sub-Franchising Contracts: No
Expand In Territory: Yes
Space Needs: NR SF; HB

SUPPORT & TRAINING PROVIDED:
Financial Assistance Provided: No
Site Selection Assistance: Yes
Lease Negotiation Assistance: N/A
Co-Operative Advertising: Yes
Franchisee Assoc./Member: Yes/Yes
Size Of Corporate Staff: 8
On-Going Support: C,D,G,H,I
Training: 1 Week Columbus, OH.

SPECIFIC EXPANSION PLANS:
US: All United States
Canada: All Canada
Overseas: No

<< >>

HOMETEAM INSPECTION SERVICE, THE

6355 E. Kemper Rd., # 250
Cincinnati, OH 45241
Tel: (800) 598-5297 (513) 469-2100
Fax: (513) 469-2226
E-Mail: hometeam@one.net
Web Site: www.homteam.com
Mr. Greg Haskett, VP Operations

Ranked #1 fastest-growing home inspection franchise in North America. Unique and field-proven marketing system that produces leads and appointments. Exclusive, protected territory. Extensive and continuous training. Sales hotline to build your business. Financing provided.

BACKGROUND: IFA MEMBER
Established: 1992; 1st Franchised: 1992
Franchised Units: 323
Company-Owned Units 0
Total Units: 323
Dist.: US-292; CAN-5; O'seas-0
North America: 48 States, 2 Provinces
Density: 29 in FL, 20 in OH, 16 in MI
Projected New Units (12 Months): 29
Qualifications: 2, 3, 2, 3, 3, 5
Registered: CA,FL,IL,IN,MD,MI,MN,NY, ND,OR,RI,SD,VA,WA,WI,DC

FINANCIAL/TERMS:
Cash Investment: $6.5-15.7K
Total Investment: $17.5-45K
Minimum Net Worth: $N/A
Fees: Franchise - $11.9-29.9K
Royalty - 6%; Ad. - 3%
Earnings Claim Statement: No
Term of Contract (Years): 10/10/10
Avg. # Of Employees: 1 FT
Passive Ownership: Discouraged

Encourage Conversions: N/A
Area Develop. Agreements: No
Sub-Franchising Contracts: No
Expand In Territory: Yes
Space Needs: N/A SF; N/A

SUPPORT & TRAINING PROVIDED:
Financial Assistance Provided: Yes(D)
Site Selection Assistance: N/A
Lease Negotiation Assistance: N/A
Co-Operative Advertising: Yes
Franchisee Assoc./Member: Yes/Yes
Size Of Corporate Staff: 20
On-Going Support: A,B,C,D,G,H,I
Training: 2 Weeks Corporate Headquarters, Cincinnati, OH.

SPECIFIC EXPANSION PLANS:
US: All United States
Canada: All Canada
Overseas: No

<< >>

Top 50

HOUSEMASTER HOME INSPECTIONS

421 W. Union Ave.
Bound Brook, NJ 08805
Tel: (800) 526-3939 (732) 469-6565
Fax: (732) 469-7405
E-Mail: jgranito@housemaster.com
Web Site: www.housemaster.com
Mr. John J. Granito, Dir. Franchise Sales

HOUSEMASTER is the oldest and most experienced home inspection franchise. HOUSEMASTER is the recognized authority on home inspections and has been featured as such on CNN, CNBC, Our Home Show and many more! You will be impressed with the level of expertise and the unsurpassed level of support that HOUSEMASTER franchise owners enjoy.

BACKGROUND: IFA MEMBER
Established: 1979; 1st Franchised: 1979
Franchised Units: 382
Company-Owned Units 0
Total Units: 382
Dist.: US-349; CAN-33; O'seas-0
North America: 48 States,10 Provinces
Density: 23 in NJ, 20 in NY, 18 in FL
Projected New Units (12 Months): 72
Qualifications: 4, 3, 2, 2, 5, 5
Registered: All States

FINANCIAL/TERMS:
Cash Investment: $12-35K
Total Investment: $14.3-47.5K
Minimum Net Worth: $75K
Fees: Franchise - $8.5-24K
Royalty - 7.5%; Ad. - 2.5%
Earnings Claim Statement: No
Term of Contract (Years): 5/5
Avg. # Of Employees: Varies
Passive Ownership: Allowed
Encourage Conversions: N/A
Area Develop. Agreements: No
Sub-Franchising Contracts: No
Expand In Territory: Yes
Space Needs: N/A SF; HB

SUPPORT & TRAINING PROVIDED:
Financial Assistance Provided: Yes(D)
Site Selection Assistance: N/A
Lease Negotiation Assistance: N/A
Co-Operative Advertising: N/A
Franchisee Assoc./Member: Yes/Yes
Size Of Corporate Staff: 22
On-Going Support: D,G,H,I
Training: 2-3 Weeks Bound Brook, NJ.

SPECIFIC EXPANSION PLANS:
US: All United States
Canada: All Canada
Overseas: Most Countries

<< >>

NATIONAL PROPERTY INSPECTIONS

11620 Arbor St., # 100
Omaha, NE 68144-2935
Tel: (800) 333-9807 (402) 333-9807
Fax: (800) 933-2508
E-Mail: info@npiweb.com
Web Site: www.npiweb.com
Ms. Julie Erickson, Dir. Franchise Sales

Nationally-acclaimed residential and commercial property inspection franchise. Low start-up costs. Exclusive territories. Expansion encouraged. Award-winning national referral program. Intensive, interactive, 2-week training course. Ongoing marketing management and technical support. Fee includes state-of-the-art computer package and everything needed for first year of business

BACKGROUND:
Established: 1987; 1st Franchised: 1987
Franchised Units: 139
Company-Owned Units 0
Total Units: 139
Dist.: US-85; CAN-1; O'seas-0
North America: 37 States, 1 Province
Density: 7 in IL, 5 in WI, 5 in NY
Projected New Units (12 Months): 24
Qualifications: 3, 3, 4, 3, 4, 4
Registered: All States and AB

FINANCIAL/TERMS:
Cash Investment: $5-8K
Total Investment: $17.8-25.8K
Minimum Net Worth: $NR
Fees: Franchise - $17.8-25.8K
Royalty - 8%; Ad. - 0%
Earnings Claim Statement: No
Term of Contract (Years): 5/5
Avg. # Of Employees: 1 FT
Passive Ownership: Discouraged
Encourage Conversions: Yes
Area Develop. Agreements: Yes
Sub-Franchising Contracts: No
Expand In Territory: Yes
Space Needs: NR SF; N/A

SUPPORT & TRAINING PROVIDED:
Financial Assistance Provided: Yes(D)
Site Selection Assistance: N/A
Lease Negotiation Assistance: N/A
Co-Operative Advertising: N/A
Franchisee Assoc./Member: No
Size Of Corporate Staff: 18
On-Going Support: D,G,H,I
Training: 2 Weeks Omaha, NE in NPI Corporate Office.

SPECIFIC EXPANSION PLANS:
US: All United States
Canada: All Canada
Overseas: No

<< >>

PILLAR TO POST

13902 N. Dale Mabry Hwy., # 300
Tampa, FL 33618
Tel: (877) 963-3129 (813) 962-4461
Fax: (813) 963-5301
E-Mail: frandev@pillartopost.com
Web Site: www.pillartopost.com
Mr. Allen Castleman, Dir. Franchising

PILLAR TO POST is the #1 home inspection franchise in the U.S. PTP offers a proven system of home inspection with training and support that has no equal. Successful and imaginative marketing programs. Materials, technical support and operational advice are provided. Husband and wife teams do very well.

BACKGROUND: IFA MEMBER
Established: 1994; 1st Franchised: 1994
Franchised Units: 333
Company-Owned Units 0
Total Units: 333
Dist.: US-177; CAN-90; O'seas-0
North America: 40 States, 8 Provinces
Density: 15 in OH, 12 in NY, 11 in FL
Projected New Units (12 Months): 90
Qualifications: 3, 3, 3, 3, 3, 3
Registered: All States

FINANCIAL/TERMS:
Cash Investment: $13.9-23.9K
Total Investment: $20.9-42.9K
Minimum Net Worth: $50K
Fees: Franchise - $13.9-23.9K
Royalty - 7%/$200; Ad. - 2%/$100
Earnings Claim Statement: No
Term of Contract (Years): 5/5
Avg. # Of Employees: 1 FT, 1 PT
Passive Ownership: Not Allowed
Encourage Conversions: N/A
Area Develop. Agreements: N/A
Sub-Franchising Contracts: No
Expand In Territory: No
Space Needs: N/A SF; N/A

SUPPORT & TRAINING PROVIDED:
Financial Assistance Provided: Yes
Site Selection Assistance: N/A
Lease Negotiation Assistance: N/A
Co-Operative Advertising: N/A
Franchisee Assoc./Member: No
Size Of Corporate Staff: 15
On-Going Support: b,C,D,F,G,h,I
Training: 2 Weeks Corporate Head Office.

SPECIFIC EXPANSION PLANS:
US: All United States
Canada: All Canada
Overseas: Europe

<< >>

PROFESSIONAL HOUSE DOCTORS

1406 E. 14th St.
Des Moines, IA 50316-2406
Tel: (800) 288-7437 (515) 265-6667
Fax: (515) 278-2070
Web Site: www.prohousedr.com
Mr. Dane J. Shearer, President

Environmental and building science specialists providing home and building inspections, radon testing and mitigation, plus over 20 other specialized services.

BACKGROUND:
Established: 1982; 1st Franchised: 1991
Franchised Units: 3
Company-Owned Units 1
Total Units: 4
Dist.: US-3; CAN-0; O'seas-0
North America: 1 State
Density: 3 in IA
Projected New Units (12 Months): 2
Qualifications: 3, 3, 2, 2, 4, 5
Registered: NR

FINANCIAL/TERMS:
Cash Investment: $20K
Total Investment: $20K
Minimum Net Worth: $100K
Fees: Franchise - $15K
Royalty - 6%; Ad. - 2%
Earnings Claim Statement: No
Term of Contract (Years): 5/5
Avg. # Of Employees: 1 FT, 1 PT
Passive Ownership: N/A
Encourage Conversions: N/A
Area Develop. Agreements: No
Sub-Franchising Contracts: No
Expand In Territory: Yes
Space Needs: Minimal SF; HB

SUPPORT & TRAINING PROVIDED:
Financial Assistance Provided: Yes(B)
Site Selection Assistance: Yes
Lease Negotiation Assistance: N/A
Co-Operative Advertising: Yes
Franchisee Assoc./Member: Yes/Yes
Size Of Corporate Staff: NR
On-Going Support: A,B,C,D,E,F,G,H,I
Training: 2 Weeks at Corporate Office.

SPECIFIC EXPANSION PLANS:
US: All United States
Canada: No
Overseas: No

<< >>

TERMINIX TERMITE & PEST CONTROL

855 Ridge Lake Blvd.
Memphis, TN 38120
Tel: (800) 654-7848 (901) 766-1351
Fax: (901) 766-1208
E-Mail: terminix@terminix.com
Web Site: www.terminix.com
Mr. John Geelan, Dir. Fran. Recruit.

Termite and pest control company.

BACKGROUND: IFA MEMBER
Established: 1927; 1st Franchised: 1927
Franchised Units: 225
Company-Owned Units 312
Total Units: 537
Dist.: US-524; CAN-0; O'seas-61
North America: 45 States
Density: 58 in CA, 49 in TX, 47 in FL
Projected New Units (12 Months): 5
Qualifications: 4, 5, 5, 3, , 5
Registered: CA,IL,IN,MD,MI,MN,NY,ND, OR,RI,SD,VA,WA,WI

FINANCIAL/TERMS:
Cash Investment: $7.1-25.55K
Total Investment: $25-50K
Minimum Net Worth: $Varies
Fees: Franchise - $25-50K
Royalty - 7%; Ad. - 2%
Earnings Claim Statement: No
Term of Contract (Years): 5-7/5
Avg. # Of Employees: Varies on Size
Passive Ownership: Discouraged
Encourage Conversions: Yes
Area Develop. Agreements: NR
Sub-Franchising Contracts: No
Expand In Territory: Yes
Space Needs: N/A SF; NR

SUPPORT & TRAINING PROVIDED:
Financial Assistance Provided: Yes
Site Selection Assistance: N/A
Lease Negotiation Assistance: N/A
Co-Operative Advertising: Yes
Franchisee Assoc./Member: Yes/No
Size Of Corporate Staff: 7215
On-Going Support: B,C,D,G,h,I
Training: 5-6 Days in Memphis, TN (Initial); 6 Weeks On-Location Training.

SPECIFIC EXPANSION PLANS:
US: All United States
Canada: All Canada
Overseas: Central America, China, Japan

WORLD INSPECTION NETWORK

6500 6th Ave. NW
Seattle, WA 98117-5099
Tel: (800) 967-8127 (206) 728-8100
Fax: (206) 441-3655
E-Mail: joinwin@wini.com
Web Site: www.wini.com
Mr. Tom Raymond, VP Franchise Development

The home inspection business is the highest growth business in real estate services today and we have the highest professional standards of any home inspection company in the industry. Our strategic partnership philosophy with our franchisees makes us different. We work together to build a strong market presence for our brand, WORLD INSPECTION NETWORK. Ask to see our strategic market growth plan for your area.

BACKGROUND: IFA MEMBER
Established: 1993; 1st Franchised: 1994
Franchised Units: 120
Company-Owned Units 0
Total Units: 120
Dist.: US-120; CAN-0; O'seas-0
North America: 26 States
Density: 21 in WA, 20 in CA, 9 in OR
Projected New Units (12 Months): 25
Qualifications: 5, 5, 2, 2, 5, 5
Registered: CA,FL,IL,IN,MI,MN,NY,OR, VA,WA,WI

FINANCIAL/TERMS:
Cash Investment: $10K
Total Investment: $33.1-47.8K
Minimum Net Worth: $N/A
Fees: Franchise - $23.9K
Royalty - 7; Ad. - 3%
Earnings Claim Statement: Yes
Term of Contract (Years): 5/5
Avg. # Of Employees: 1 FT
Passive Ownership: Discouraged
Encourage Conversions: Yes
Area Develop. Agreements: No
Sub-Franchising Contracts: No
Expand In Territory: Yes
Space Needs: N/A SF; HB

SUPPORT & TRAINING PROVIDED:
Financial Assistance Provided: Yes(D)
Site Selection Assistance: N/A
Lease Negotiation Assistance: N/A
Co-Operative Advertising: Yes
Franchisee Assoc./Member: Yes/Yes
Size Of Corporate Staff: 10
On-Going Support: B,C,D,G,H,I
Training: 2 Weeks Training Facility, Seattle, WA.

SPECIFIC EXPANSION PLANS:
US: All United States and Canada
Canada: All Canada
Overseas: No

≺≺ ≻≻

SUPPLEMENTAL LISTING OF FRANCHISORS

ALLSTATE HOME INSPECTION/ TESTING, 2097 N. Randolph Rd., Randolph Center, VT 05061 ; (800) 245-9932 (802) 728-4015; (802) 728-5534

AMBIC BUILDING INSPECTION CONSULTANTS, 1200 Rte. 130, Robbinsville, NJ 08691 ; (800) 88-AMBIC (609) 448-3900; (609) 426-1236

AMERICAN LEAD CONSULTANTS, 200 S. Broad St., 6th Fl., Philadelphia, PA 19102 ; (800) 441-5323 (215) 732-9449; (215) 732-9559

CAN-AM HOME INSPECTION SERVICES, 964 Thermal Dr., # 110, Coquilam, BC V3J 6S1 CANADA; (800) 828-3883 (604) 522-6833; (604) 469-6508

ENVIROFREE INSPECTIONS, 4763 S. Old U.S. 23, # A, Brighton, MI 48114-8685 ; (800) 220-0013 (810) 220-2767; (810) 220-2772

GRASSROOTS - HOME INSPECTION SPECIALISTS, 214 Martindale Rd., St. Catharines, ON L2R 6P9 CANADA; (800) 774-2538 (905) 687-1925; (905) 685-8125

INSPECT-IT 1ST PROPERTY INSPECTION, 3420 E. Shea Blvd., # 115, Phoenix, AZ 85028 ; (800) 510-9100 (602) 971-9400; (602) 992-3127

PESTMASTER FRANCHISE NETWORK, 137 E. South St., Bishop, CA 93514 ; (800) 525-8866 (760) 873-8100; (760) 873-3268

Real Estate Services

Chapter 31

Real Estate Services Industry Profile

Total # Franchisors in Industry Group	57
Total # Franchised Units in Industry Group	18,465
Total # Company-Owned Units in Industry Group	471
Total # Operating Units in Industry Group	18,936
Average # Franchised Units/Franchisor	323.9
Average # Company-Owned Units/Franchisor	8.3
Average # Total Units/Franchisor	332.2
Ratio of Total # Franchised Units/Total # Company-Owned Units	39.2:1
Industry Survey Participants	21
Representing % of Industry	36.8%
Average Franchise Fee*:	$13.6K
Average Total Investment*:	$99.1K
Average On-Going Royalty Fee*:	5.8%

*If a range was provided, the mid-point of the range was used. See detailed profiles for actual ranges.

Four Largest Participants in Survey

Company	# Franchised Units	# Co-Owned Units	# Total Units	Franchise Fee	On-Going Royalty	Total Investment
1. RE/MAX International	4,184	19	4,203	10-25K	Varies	20-150K
2. Century 21 Real Estate	4,196	0	4,196	0-25K	$500/6%	10.9-521K
3. Coldwell Banker Residential	2,449	0	2,449	0-20.5K	6%	151-477K
4. ERA Franchise Systems	1,027	0	1,027	0-20K	$540/6%	42.7-206K

All of the data provided are proprietary and should not be quoted without acknowledging *Bond's Franchise Guide.*

APARTMENT SELECTOR

P.O. Box 8355
Dallas, TX 75205-0060
Tel: (800) 324-3733 (214) 361-4420
Fax: (214) 361-8677
E-Mail: aptsel@aptselector.com
Web Site: www.aptselector.com
Mr. Kendall A. Laughlin, President

APARTMENT SELECTOR is the nation's oldest and largest FREE apartment and home rental service. Our fee is paid by apartment owners. Extensive training systems for agents and management. Referral network called Official Relocation Network.

BACKGROUND:

Established: 1959; 1st Franchised: 1983
Franchised Units: 24
Company-Owned Units 0
Total Units: 24
Dist.: US-21; CAN-0; O'seas-0
North America: 6 States
Density: 8 in TX
Projected New Units (12 Months): 2
Qualifications: 3, 3, 4, 3, 1, 1
Registered: All States

FINANCIAL/TERMS:

Cash Investment: $3K+
Total Investment: $NR
Minimum Net Worth: $N/A
Fees: Franchise - $2.5-10K
Royalty - 5%; Ad. - 1%
Earnings Claim Statement: No
Term of Contract (Years): 3/3
Avg. # Of Employees: 3 FT, 3 PT
Passive Ownership: Discouraged
Encourage Conversions: Yes
Area Develop. Agreements: No
Sub-Franchising Contracts: No
Expand In Territory: No
Space Needs: 250 SF; SC

SUPPORT & TRAINING PROVIDED:

Financial Assistance Provided: No
Site Selection Assistance: Yes
Lease Negotiation Assistance: No
Co-Operative Advertising: No
Franchisee Assoc./Member: No
Size Of Corporate Staff: 3
On-Going Support: c,d,E,g,h,I
Training: 1 Week Dallas, TX.

SPECIFIC EXPANSION PLANS:

US: Southeast, West
Canada: No
Overseas: No

<< >>

ASSIST-2-SELL

1610 Meadow Wood Ln.
Reno, NV 89502
Tel: (800) 528-7816 (775) 688-6060
Fax: (775) 688-6069
E-Mail: info@assist2sell.com
Web Site: www.assist2sell.com
Mr. Lyle Martin, Vice President

America's 'full service with sav' discount real estate franchise. Real estate license required. The future of real estate will focus around a 'menu of services' concept. Lower commissions will be the norm. Don't be left behind: catch our vision and step into the future.

BACKGROUND:

Established: 1987; 1st Franchised: 1993
Franchised Units: 138
Company-Owned Units 1
Total Units: 139
Dist.: US-125; CAN-0; O'seas-0
North America: 33 States
Density: 17 in CO, 14 in CA, 9 in MA
Projected New Units (12 Months): 35
Qualifications: 2, 4, 5, 2, 3, 4
Registered: CA,FL,IL,IN,MD,MN,NY,ND, OR,RI,SD,VA,WA,WI

FINANCIAL/TERMS:

Cash Investment: $0K
Total Investment: $25.5-52K
Minimum Net Worth: $N/A
Fees: Franchise - $10K
Royalty - 5%; Ad. - 0%
Earnings Claim Statement: No
Term of Contract (Years): 7/7
Avg. # Of Employees: 3 FT
Passive Ownership: Discouraged
Encourage Conversions: Yes
Area Develop. Agreements: No
Sub-Franchising Contracts: No
Expand In Territory: Yes
Space Needs: 150 SF; OB

SUPPORT & TRAINING PROVIDED:

Financial Assistance Provided: No
Site Selection Assistance: Yes
Lease Negotiation Assistance: Yes
Co-Operative Advertising: No
Franchisee Assoc./Member: No
Size Of Corporate Staff: 6
On-Going Support: d,G,H,I
Training: 4 Days in Reno, NV.

SPECIFIC EXPANSION PLANS:

US: All United States
Canada: All Canada
Overseas: All Countries

<< >>

BETTER HOMES REALTY

1777 Botelho Dr., # 390
Walnut Creek, CA 94596-8181
Tel: (800) 642-4428 (925) 937-9001
Fax: (925) 988-2770
E-Mail: flo@bhrcorp.com
Web Site: www.bhr.com
Ms. Florence Stevens, Vice President

Established identity, legal hot line support, no institutional advertising fee, franchise cap each calendar year, excellent corporate support, free DRE renewal, corporate advertising, hands-on regional support.

BACKGROUND:

Established: 1964; 1st Franchised: 1969
Franchised Units: 42
Company-Owned Units 0
Total Units: 42
Dist.: US-40; CAN-0; O'seas-0
North America: 1 State
Density: 39 in CA
Projected New Units (12 Months): 10
Qualifications: 3, 3, 3, 2, 1, 1
Registered: CA

FINANCIAL/TERMS:

Cash Investment: $10-60K
Total Investment: $N/A
Minimum Net Worth: $N/A
Fees: Franchise - $9.95K
Royalty - 6% w/Cap/4.5%; Ad. - 0%
Earnings Claim Statement: Yes
Term of Contract (Years): 5/5
Avg. # Of Employees: N/A
Passive Ownership: Allowed
Encourage Conversions: Yes
Area Develop. Agreements: NR
Sub-Franchising Contracts: Yes
Expand In Territory: Yes
Space Needs: N/A SF; N/A

SUPPORT & TRAINING PROVIDED:

Financial Assistance Provided: Yes(I)
Site Selection Assistance: N/A
Lease Negotiation Assistance: N/A
Co-Operative Advertising: Yes
Franchisee Assoc./Member: No
Size Of Corporate Staff: 7
On-Going Support: b,C,D,G,H,I
Training: Varies. 0.5-1 Day.

SPECIFIC EXPANSION PLANS:

US: West
Canada: No
Overseas: No

<< >>

BUYER'S AGENT, THE

1255 A Lynnfield Rd., # 273
Memphis, TN 38119
Tel: (800) 766-8728 (901) 767-1077
Fax: (901) 767-3577
E-Mail: rebuyragt@aol.com
Web Site: www.forbuyers.com
Mr. Joe Schmitter, Dir. Fran. Dev.

The nation's oldest and largest real estate franchise in the business of exclusive buyer representation.

BACKGROUND:

Established: 1988;	1st Franchised: 1988
Franchised Units:	62
Company-Owned Units	0
Total Units:	62
Dist.:	US-70; CAN-0; O'seas-0
North America:	28 States
Density:	8 in FL, 8 in CA, 5 in TN
Projected New Units (12 Months):	50
Qualifications:	3, 3, 2, 3, 3, 3
Registered:	CA,FL,HI,IN,MD,MI,MN,NY,OR,RI,VA,WA,WI

FINANCIAL/TERMS:

Cash Investment:	$20-30K
Total Investment:	$25-50K
Minimum Net Worth:	$50K
Fees: Franchise -	$14.9K
Royalty - 5%;	Ad. - 1%
Earnings Claim Statement:	No
Term of Contract (Years):	5/5
Avg. # Of Employees:	5-15 FT
Passive Ownership:	Discouraged
Encourage Conversions:	Yes
Area Develop. Agreements:	Consider
Sub-Franchising Contracts:	No
Expand In Territory:	Yes
Space Needs:	2,000 SF; FS, SF, SC

SUPPORT & TRAINING PROVIDED:

Financial Assistance Provided:	Yes(I)
Site Selection Assistance:	Yes
Lease Negotiation Assistance:	Yes
Co-Operative Advertising:	Yes
Franchisee Assoc./Member:	No
Size Of Corporate Staff:	12
On-Going Support:	A,B,C,D,E,G,H,I
Training:	5 Days Memphis, TN.

SPECIFIC EXPANSION PLANS:

US:	All United States
Canada:	All Canada
Overseas:	No

<< >>

CASTLES UNLIMITED

837 Beacon St.
Newton Centre, MA 02459
Tel: (888) 887-0777 (617) 964-3300
Fax: (617) 244-5847
E-Mail: franchise@castlesunltd.com
Web Site: www.castlesunltd.com
Mr. James D. Lowenstern, President

CASTLES UNLIMITED is the originator of the 100% Plus Commission Marketing Program which accelerates real estate broker production and competitiveness. The company also encourages brokers in Massachusetts to call to investigate special alliances.

BACKGROUND:

Established: 1985;	1st Franchised: 1990
Franchised Units:	2
Company-Owned Units	1
Total Units:	3
Dist.:	US-5; CAN-0; O'seas-0
North America:	1 State
Density:	5 in MA
Projected New Units (12 Months):	10
Qualifications:	2, 2, 5, 3, 3, 4
Registered:	NR

FINANCIAL/TERMS:

Cash Investment:	$10-25K
Total Investment:	$15-30K
Minimum Net Worth:	$100K
Fees: Franchise -	$11K
Royalty - 4.5%;	Ad. - 1%
Earnings Claim Statement:	No
Term of Contract (Years):	10/10
Avg. # Of Employees:	10 FT, 5 PT
Passive Ownership:	Discouraged
Encourage Conversions:	Yes
Area Develop. Agreements:	Yes
Sub-Franchising Contracts:	Yes
Expand In Territory:	Yes
Space Needs:	1,500 SF; SF

SUPPORT & TRAINING PROVIDED:

Financial Assistance Provided:	Yes(D)
Site Selection Assistance:	Yes
Lease Negotiation Assistance:	Yes
Co-Operative Advertising:	Yes
Franchisee Assoc./Member:	Yes
Size Of Corporate Staff:	2
On-Going Support:	b,C,d,e,f,G,H,I
Training:	2 Days at Newton, MA.

SPECIFIC EXPANSION PLANS:

US:	New England
Canada:	All Canada
Overseas:	All Countries

<< >>

CENTURY 21 REAL ESTATE

1 Campus Dr.
Parsippany, NJ 07054
Tel: (877) 221-5737
Fax: (973) 496-5806
E-Mail: c21info@aol.com
Web Site: www.century21.com
Mr. David Hardy, SVP Franchise Development

The franchise offered is for the operation of a real estate brokerage office, including services such as the listing and sale of properties, property management and other services generally provided by a licensed real estate broker.

BACKGROUND: IFA MEMBER

Established: 1972;	1st Franchised: 1972
Franchised Units:	4,196
Company-Owned Units	0
Total Units:	4,196
Dist.:	US-3931; CAN-265; O'seas-1442
North America:	All States & Provinces
Density:	486 in CA, 328 in FL, 263 TX
Projected New Units (12 Months):	417
Qualifications:	4, 4, 5, 4, 4, 4
Registered:	All States

FINANCIAL/TERMS:

Cash Investment:	$0-25K
Total Investment:	$10.9-521.2K
Minimum Net Worth:	$25K
Fees: Franchise -	$0-25K
Royalty - 6%/$500;	Ad. - 2%/$289
Earnings Claim Statement:	No
Term of Contract (Years):	10/5-10
Avg. # Of Employees:	Varies
Passive Ownership:	Not Allowed
Encourage Conversions:	Yes
Area Develop. Agreements:	No
Sub-Franchising Contracts:	No
Expand In Territory:	Yes
Space Needs:	1,000 SF; FS, SF, SC

SUPPORT & TRAINING PROVIDED:

Financial Assistance Provided:	No
Site Selection Assistance:	No
Lease Negotiation Assistance:	No
Co-Operative Advertising:	Yes
Franchisee Assoc./Member:	Yes/Yes
Size Of Corporate Staff:	176
On-Going Support:	A,C,D,E,G,H,I
Training:	5 Days in Parsippany, NJ; 3-7 Sessions on Telephone; 1 Day On-Site.

SPECIFIC EXPANSION PLANS:

US:	All United States
Canada:	All Canada
Overseas:	All Countries

<< >>

COLDWELL BANKER AFFILIATES (CANADA)

1 Richmond St. W., # 701
Toronto, ON M5H 3W4 CANADA
Tel: (800) 268-9599 (416) 947-9229
Fax: (416) 777-4604
Web Site: www.coldwellbanker.ca
Mr. Gacy Hockey, SVP Business Development

The most complete full-service real estate franchise in Canada. Offering unsurpassed revenue generating capabilities, leading-edge technology and outstanding support services consistent with our trademark of 'ultimate service.'

BACKGROUND:
Established: 1989; 1st Franchised: 1989
Franchised Units: 230
Company-Owned Units 0
Total Units: 230
Dist.: US-0; CAN-230; O'seas-0
North America: 9 Provinces
Density: 136 in ON, 36 in BC, 25 AB
Projected New Units (12 Months): 30
Qualifications: 4, 4, 5, 2, 4, 4
Registered: AB

FINANCIAL/TERMS:
Cash Investment: $10-100K
Total Investment: $10-200K
Minimum Net Worth: $Varies
Fees: Franchise - $7.5-18K
Royalty - 6%; Ad. - $40/Person
Earnings Claim Statement: No
Term of Contract (Years): 5-10/5-10
Avg. # Of Employees: 3 FT, 1 PT
Passive Ownership: Discouraged
Encourage Conversions: Yes
Area Develop. Agreements: No
Sub-Franchising Contracts: No
Expand In Territory: Yes
Space Needs: Varies SF; All Possible

SUPPORT & TRAINING PROVIDED:
Financial Assistance Provided: No
Site Selection Assistance: Yes
Lease Negotiation Assistance: No
Co-Operative Advertising: Yes
Franchisee Assoc./Member: No
Size Of Corporate Staff: 26
On-Going Support: A,C,d,E,G,H,I
Training: Varies.

SPECIFIC EXPANSION PLANS:
US: No
Canada: All Canada
Overseas: No

<< >>

COLDWELL BANKER COMMERCIAL AFFILIATES

1 Campus Dr.
Parsippany, NJ 07054
Tel: (800) 222-2162 (973) 496-5705
Fax: (973) 496-0199
E-Mail: commercial@coldwellbanker.com
www.coldwellbankercommercial.com
Mr. Arnie Kernus, SVP, SVP Franchise Development

The franchise is for a commercial real estate brokerage office, offering real estate brokerage and leasing services from a specified location under the registered name Coldwell Banker Commercial.

BACKGROUND:
Established: 1906; 1st Franchised: 1996
Franchised Units: 51
Company-Owned Units 23
Total Units: 74
Dist.: US-51; CAN-0; O'seas-0
North America: 25 States
Density: 16 in CA
Projected New Units (12 Months): 25
Registered: NR

FINANCIAL/TERMS:
Cash Investment: $37.15-108.9K
Total Investment: $37.15-108.9K
Minimum Net Worth: $50-100K
Fees: Franchise - $0-27.5K
Royalty - 6%; Ad. - 1%/$283
Earnings Claim Statement: No
Term of Contract (Years): 10/10
Avg. # Of Employees: 6 FT
Passive Ownership: Not Allowed
Encourage Conversions: Yes
Area Develop. Agreements: No
Sub-Franchising Contracts: No
Expand In Territory: Yes
Space Needs: 1,000 SF; FS,SF,SC,PROFBLDG

SUPPORT & TRAINING PROVIDED:
Financial Assistance Provided: NR
Site Selection Assistance: No
Lease Negotiation Assistance: No
Co-Operative Advertising: Yes
Franchisee Assoc./Member: No
Size Of Corporate Staff: 15
On-Going Support: A,C,D,E,G,H,I
Training: 1-2 Days On-Site.

SPECIFIC EXPANSION PLANS:
US: All United States
Canada: All Canada
Overseas: All Countries

<< >>

COLDWELL BANKER REAL ESTATE

1 Campus Dr.
Parsippany, NJ 07054
Tel: (973) 428-8600
Fax: (973) 496-7217
Web Site: www.coldwellbanker.com
Mr. David Hardy, SVP Franchise Development

The franchise is a real estate brokerage office offering defined real estate brokerage services from a specified location under the registered name Coldwell Banker.

BACKGROUND: IFA MEMBER
Established: 1902; 1st Franchised: 1982
Franchised Units: 2,449
Company-Owned Units 0
Total Units: 2,449
Dist.: US-2225; CAN-224; O'seas-0
North America: 50 States,11 Provinces
Density: 238 in CA, 155 in TX, 142 NY
Projected New Units (12 Months): 225
Qualifications: 4, 4, 5, 3, 2, 4
Registered: All States

FINANCIAL/TERMS:
Cash Investment: $23.5-65.6K
Total Investment: $150.6-477.3K
Minimum Net Worth: $25K
Fees: Franchise - $0-20.5K
Royalty - 6%; Ad. - 2.5%/$245
Earnings Claim Statement: No
Term of Contract (Years): 10/10
Avg. # Of Employees: NR
Passive Ownership: Not Allowed
Encourage Conversions: Yes
Area Develop. Agreements: No
Sub-Franchising Contracts: No
Expand In Territory: Yes
Space Needs: 1,000 SF; FS, SF, SC

SUPPORT & TRAINING PROVIDED:
Financial Assistance Provided: Yes(D)
Site Selection Assistance: No
Lease Negotiation Assistance: No
Co-Operative Advertising: Yes
Franchisee Assoc./Member: Yes
Size Of Corporate Staff: 136
On-Going Support: C,d,G,h,I
Training: 4 Days in Parsippany, NJ

SPECIFIC EXPANSION PLANS:
US: All United States
Canada: All Canada
Overseas: All Countries

<< >>

ELLIOTT & COMPANY APPRAISERS

7 Oak Branch Dr., # C
Greensboro, NC 27407
Tel: (800) 854-5889 (336) 854-3075
Fax: (336) 854-7734
E-Mail: elliottco@elliottco.com
Web Site: www.elliottco.com
Mr. Charlie W. Elliott, Jr., President

The franchisor provides a comprehensive package of services designed to assist the franchisee in marketing residential and commercial appraisals and managing the appraisal office.

BACKGROUND:
Established: 1985; 1st Franchised: 1994
Franchised Units: 8
Company-Owned Units 3
Total Units: 11
Dist.: US-10; CAN-0; O'seas-0
North America: 2 States
Density: 7 in NC, 3 in SC
Projected New Units (12 Months): 4
Qualifications: 3, , 5, , , 4
Registered: FL,VA

FINANCIAL/TERMS:
Cash Investment: $5.1-17.1K
Total Investment: $5.1-17.1K
Minimum Net Worth: $N/A
Fees: Franchise - $7.5K
Royalty - 8%/$200 Min.;
Ad. - 2%/$50 Min.
Earnings Claim Statement: No
Term of Contract (Years): 5/5
Avg. # Of Employees: 1 FT
Passive Ownership: Allowed
Encourage Conversions: No
Area Develop. Agreements: No
Sub-Franchising Contracts: No
Expand In Territory: Yes
Space Needs: N/A SF; Commercial Office

SUPPORT & TRAINING PROVIDED:
Financial Assistance Provided: Yes(D)
Site Selection Assistance: Yes
Lease Negotiation Assistance: Yes
Co-Operative Advertising: Yes
Franchisee Assoc./Member: No
Size Of Corporate Staff: 3
On-Going Support: C,D,E,h,I
Training: 2 Days Greensboro, NC.

SPECIFIC EXPANSION PLANS:
US: All United States
Canada: No
Overseas: No

<< >>

ERA FRANCHISE SYSTEMS

1 Campus Dr.
Parsippany, NJ 07054
Tel: (800) 869-1260 (973) 428-9700
Fax: (973) 496-0255
Web Site: www.era.com
Mr. David Hardy, SVP Franchise Development

The franchisee or "Member" will operate a real estate office offering listing and marketing of real property for sale and related services.

BACKGROUND: IFA MEMBER
Established: 1972; 1st Franchised: 1972
Franchised Units: 1,027
Company-Owned Units 0
Total Units: 1,027
Dist.: US-1027; CAN-0; O'seas-
North America: 50 States
Density: 137 in FL, 69 in CA, 59 NJ
Projected New Units (12 Months): NR
Registered: NR

FINANCIAL/TERMS:
Cash Investment: $0-20K
Total Investment: $42.7-205.9K
Minimum Net Worth: $25K
Fees: Franchise - $0-20K
Royalty - 6%/$540; Ad. - 2%/$207
Earnings Claim Statement: No
Term of Contract (Years): 10/7
Avg. # Of Employees: Varies
Passive Ownership: Not Allowed
Encourage Conversions: NR
Area Develop. Agreements: No
Sub-Franchising Contracts: No
Expand In Territory: Yes
Space Needs: 1,000 SF; FS, SF, SC

SUPPORT & TRAINING PROVIDED:
Financial Assistance Provided: NR
Site Selection Assistance: No
Lease Negotiation Assistance: No
Co-Operative Advertising: Yes
Franchisee Assoc./Member: Yes/Yes
Size Of Corporate Staff: 84
On-Going Support: A,C,D,E,G,H,I
Training: 1 Week in Parsippany, NJ; 2-3 days On-Site

SPECIFIC EXPANSION PLANS:
US: All United States
Canada: All Canada
Overseas: Central and South America

<< >>

GROUP TRANS-ACTION BROKERAGE SERVICES

550 Sherbrooke St. W., # 775, W. Tower
Montreal, PQ H3A 1B9 CANADA
Tel: (514) 288-6777
Fax: (514) 288-7543
Mr. Jean-Louis Bernard, General Manager

Group of independent real estate brokers everywhere in Quebec. Complete real estate services.

BACKGROUND:
Established: 1979; 1st Franchised: 1982
Franchised Units: 64
Company-Owned Units 0
Total Units: 64
Dist.: US-0; CAN-64; O'seas-0
North America: 1 Province
Density: 55 in PQ
Projected New Units (12 Months): 6
Registered: AB

FINANCIAL/TERMS:
Cash Investment: $10K
Total Investment: $10-50K
Minimum Net Worth: $NR
Fees: Franchise - $6-17K
Royalty - Flat; Ad. - Flat
Earnings Claim Statement: No
Term of Contract (Years): 5/1
Avg. # Of Employees: 10 FT
Passive Ownership: Not Allowed
Encourage Conversions: N/A
Area Develop. Agreements: Yes
Sub-Franchising Contracts: No
Expand In Territory: Yes
Space Needs: 1,000 SF; FS, SF

SUPPORT & TRAINING PROVIDED:
Financial Assistance Provided: Yes(I)
Site Selection Assistance: Yes
Lease Negotiation Assistance: Yes
Co-Operative Advertising: Yes
Franchisee Assoc./Member: NR
Size Of Corporate Staff: 4
On-Going Support: a,b,c,D,E,f,G,H,i
Training: 1 Week Headquarters.

SPECIFIC EXPANSION PLANS:
US: No
Canada: All Canada
Overseas: No

<< >>

HELP-U-SELL

6800 Jericho Tpk., # 208E
Syosset, NY 11791
Tel: (800) 366-1177 (516) 364-9650
Fax: (516) 364-8757
E-Mail: husann@aol.com

Web Site: www.helpusell.com
Ms. Ann Reynolds, VP Franchise Sales

HELP-U-SELL is the largest and oldest consumer-focused real estate company in North America. Consumers can receive comprehensive professional assistance in marketing and selling their home while saving thousands of dollars. Proven marketing system generate continuous buyer and seller leads.

BACKGROUND:
Established: 1976; 1st Franchised: 1976
Franchised Units: 246
Company-Owned Units 0
Total Units: 246
Dist.: US-145; CAN-2; O'seas-0
North America: 29 States, 1 Province
Density: 45 in CA, 19 in FL, 6 in MD
Projected New Units (12 Months): 50
Qualifications: 4, 4, 5, 3, 3, 4
Registered: CA,FL,HI,IN,MD,MI,OR,RI, SD,WA,WI,DC,AB

FINANCIAL/TERMS:
Cash Investment: $4.5K
Total Investment: $15-45K
Minimum Net Worth: $N/A
Fees: Franchise - $4.5K
Royalty - 3-5.5%; Ad. - 1%
Earnings Claim Statement: No
Term of Contract (Years): 5/5
Avg. # Of Employees: 4-10 FT
Passive Ownership: Discouraged
Encourage Conversions: Yes
Area Develop. Agreements: No
Sub-Franchising Contracts: Yes
Expand In Territory: No
Space Needs: 1,000 SF; FS, SF, SC, RM, Exec. Suite

SUPPORT & TRAINING PROVIDED:
Financial Assistance Provided: No
Site Selection Assistance: Yes
Lease Negotiation Assistance: No
Co-Operative Advertising: No
Franchisee Assoc./Member: No
Size Of Corporate Staff: NR
On-Going Support: c,D,e,G,h,I
Training: 4 Days San Bernadino, CA Headquarters.

SPECIFIC EXPANSION PLANS:
US: All United States
Canada: All Canada
Overseas: Asia

<< >>

HOMEOWNERS CONCEPT
611 N. Mayfair Rd.
Wauwatosa, WI 53226
Tel: (800) 800-9890 (414) 258-7778
Fax: (414) 258-8276
Mr. Peter M. Skanavis, President

HOMEOWNERS CONCEPT offers a unique flat fee real estate program of consulting/sales. Extremely efficient, high-volume, very profitable operation on the cutting edge of providing "value" to the consumer. Large, exclusive territory.

BACKGROUND:
Established: 1982; 1st Franchised: 1984
Franchised Units: 34
Company-Owned Units 0
Total Units: 34
Dist.: US-38; CAN-1; O'seas-0
North America: 8 States, 1 Province
Density: 7 in WI, 6 in OH, 4 in TX
Projected New Units (12 Months): 15
Qualifications: 2, 4, 3, 2, 4, 5
Registered: IL,WI,NY,FL,WA

FINANCIAL/TERMS:
Cash Investment: $16-20K
Total Investment: $16-20K
Minimum Net Worth: $50K
Fees: Franchise - $4.5K
Royalty - 3%; Ad. - NR
Earnings Claim Statement: No
Term of Contract (Years): 10/10
Avg. # Of Employees: 5 FT
Passive Ownership: Not Allowed
Encourage Conversions: Yes
Area Develop. Agreements: No
Sub-Franchising Contracts: No
Expand In Territory: Yes
Space Needs: 700 SF; OB

SUPPORT & TRAINING PROVIDED:
Financial Assistance Provided: No
Site Selection Assistance: Yes
Lease Negotiation Assistance: No
Co-Operative Advertising: No
Franchisee Assoc./Member: No
Size Of Corporate Staff: 2
On-Going Support: d,G,H,I
Training: 1 Week Milwaukee, WI.

SPECIFIC EXPANSION PLANS:
US: All United States
Canada: All Canada
Overseas: No

<< >>

HOMEVESTORS OF AMERICA
11910 Greenville Ave., # 300
Dallas, TX 75243-3596
Tel: (888) 701-3888 (972) 761-0046
Fax: (972) 761-9022
E-Mail: hvmarketing@homevestors.com
Web Site: www.homevestors.com
Mr. Mark McKeller, Franchise Development

HOMEVESTORS franchise owners are real estate investors that specialize in buying and selling single-family houses. The franchise provides a system to by houses wholesale; financing to purchase houses; training and other services.

BACKGROUND: IFA MEMBER
Established: 1989; 1st Franchised: 1996
Franchised Units: 60
Company-Owned Units 0
Total Units: 60
Dist.: US-33; CAN-0; O'seas-0
North America: 6 States
Density: 13 in TX, 3 in FL, 3 in MO
Projected New Units (12 Months): 15
Qualifications: 4, 4, 3, 2, 4, 5
Registered: NR

FINANCIAL/TERMS:
Cash Investment: $75-125K
Total Investment: $151-180K
Minimum Net Worth: $100K
Fees: Franchise - $25-35K
Royalty - $775/Transaction;
Ad. - $125/Trans.
Earnings Claim Statement: No
Term of Contract (Years): 5/5
Avg. # Of Employees: 3 FT, 1 PT
Passive Ownership: Discouraged
Encourage Conversions: Yes
Area Develop. Agreements: No
Sub-Franchising Contracts: No
Expand In Territory: No
Space Needs: 500 SF; SF

SUPPORT & TRAINING PROVIDED:
Financial Assistance Provided: No
Site Selection Assistance: Yes
Lease Negotiation Assistance: No
Co-Operative Advertising: No
Franchisee Assoc./Member: No
Size Of Corporate Staff: 14
On-Going Support: A,C,D,E,G,H
Training: 5 Days in Dallas, TX; 2 Days at Franchise Location.

SPECIFIC EXPANSION PLANS:
US: Southwest, Southeast
Canada: No
Overseas: No

NATIONAL TENANT NETWORK
525 SW First, # 105, P.O. Box 1664
Lake Oswego, OR 97034
Tel: (800) 228-0989 (503) 635-1118
Fax: (503) 638-2450
E-Mail: ntn@ntnnet.com

Web Site: www.ntnnet.com
Mr. Edward F. Byczynski, President

NATIONAL TENANT NETWORK (NTN) is a network providing tenant screening services to the real estate industry. Through the NTN centralized data system of nationally networked servers, subscribers have instant access to the data maintained exclusively by NTN in 21 states. Automated, 24-hour a day, 7 days a week access through phone, fax, PC and modem and over the Internet. On-line service provides tenant performance data, retail credit reports, analysis, scoring, etc. On-line reports in 15-seconds.

BACKGROUND:
Established: 1980; 1st Franchised: 1987
Franchised Units: 25
Company-Owned Units 2
Total Units: 27
Dist.: US-25; CAN-0; O'seas-0
North America: 21 States
Density: 4 in TX, 2 in CA, 2 in NJ
Projected New Units (12 Months): 4
Qualifications: 2, 3, 2, 4, 4, 3
Registered: CA,FL,IL,IN,OR,VA,WA,AB

FINANCIAL/TERMS:
Cash Investment: $40-65K
Total Investment: $80-100K
Minimum Net Worth: $N/A
Fees: Franchise - $25K
Royalty - 10%; Ad. - 2%
Earnings Claim Statement: No
Term of Contract (Years): 10/10
Avg. # Of Employees: 2 FT, 1 PT
Passive Ownership: Discouraged
Encourage Conversions: N/A
Area Develop. Agreements: Yes/10
Sub-Franchising Contracts: No
Expand In Territory: Yes
Space Needs: 300-500 SF; FS

SUPPORT & TRAINING PROVIDED:
Financial Assistance Provided: Yes(D)
Site Selection Assistance: No
Lease Negotiation Assistance: No
Co-Operative Advertising: Yes
Franchisee Assoc./Member: No
Size Of Corporate Staff: 10
On-Going Support: a,B,C,D,E,G,H,I
Training: 2 Weeks Franchisee Location.

SPECIFIC EXPANSION PLANS:
US: All United States
Canada: All Canada
Overseas: No

<< >>

PROPERTY INVESTMENT GROUP SERVICES

312 12th St., NW
Canton, OH 44703
Tel: (800) 949-7447 (330) 456-8911
Fax: (330) 453-5420
Web Site: www.propertyinvestmentgroupo.com
Mr. Steve Vandegrift, Franchise Director

Urban redevelopment program. Specializing in the purchase, renovation and sales of distressed properties. Full corporate office training and support. Limited partnership template and supporting documents also provided -- designed to raise capital for home purchases and renovations. Since 1992, more than 350 homes have been purchased, renovated, and sold in the Canton, OH market, earning the praise of community leaders.

BACKGROUND:
Established: 1992; 1st Franchised: 1998
Franchised Units: 1
Company-Owned Units 1
Total Units: 2
Dist.: US-1; CAN-0; O'seas-0
North America: 1 State
Density: 1 in OH
Projected New Units (12 Months): 12
Qualifications: 4, 4, 3, 2, 3, 5
Registered: NR

FINANCIAL/TERMS:
Cash Investment: $65-215K
Total Investment: $100-250K
Minimum Net Worth: $250K
Fees: Franchise - $35K
Royalty - $1.3K/Sale; Ad. - 1.5%
Earnings Claim Statement: No
Term of Contract (Years): 5/5
Avg. # Of Employees: 1-2 FT
Passive Ownership: Discouraged
Encourage Conversions: N/A
Area Develop. Agreements: No
Sub-Franchising Contracts: No
Expand In Territory: No
Space Needs: N/A SF; NR

SUPPORT & TRAINING PROVIDED:
Financial Assistance Provided: Yes(I)
Site Selection Assistance: No
Lease Negotiation Assistance: Yes
Co-Operative Advertising: N/A
Franchisee Assoc./Member: No
Size Of Corporate Staff: 7
On-Going Support: C,D,G,h,I
Training: 5 Days at Corporate Office; 5 Days at Franchise Territory.

SPECIFIC EXPANSION PLANS:
US: All United States
Canada: No
Overseas: No

<< >>

RE/MAX INTERNATIONAL

P.O. Box 3907
Englewood, CO 80155-3907
Tel: (800) 525-7452 (303) 770-5531
Fax: (303) 796-3599
E-Mail: vtracey@remax.net
Web Site: www.remax.com
Mr. Vinnie Tracey, VP Marketing

The RE/MAX real estate franchise network, now in its 30th year of consecutive growth, is a global system of more than 4,200 independently-owned and operated offices in 39 countries, engaging 71,000 members. RE/MAX sales associates lead the industry in professional designations, experience and production while providing real estate services in residential, commercial, referral, relocation and asset management. For more information visit www.remax.com.

BACKGROUND: IFA MEMBER
Established: 1973; 1st Franchised: 1975
Franchised Units: 4,184
Company-Owned Units 19
Total Units: 4,203
Dist.: US-2946; CAN-544; O'seas-713
North America: 50 States,12 Provinces
Density: 309 in CA, 178 in TX, 159 IL
Projected New Units (12 Months): 500
Qualifications: 3, 4, 5, 1, 4, 4
Registered: All States

FINANCIAL/TERMS:
Cash Investment: $20-200K
Total Investment: $20-150K
Minimum Net Worth: $Varies
Fees: Franchise - $10-25K
Royalty - Varies; Ad. - Varies
Earnings Claim Statement: No
Term of Contract (Years): 5/5
Avg. # Of Employees: 2-4 FT, 1 PT
Passive Ownership: Discouraged
Encourage Conversions: Yes
Area Develop. Agreements: No
Sub-Franchising Contracts: Yes
Expand In Territory: Varies
Space Needs: Varies SF; FS, SF, SC, RM

SUPPORT & TRAINING PROVIDED:
Financial Assistance Provided: Yes(D)
Site Selection Assistance: Yes
Lease Negotiation Assistance: Yes
Co-Operative Advertising: N/A
Franchisee Assoc./Member: No
Size Of Corporate Staff: 250
On-Going Support: C,D,G,h,I
Training: 40+ Hours at Headquarters in Englewood, CO.

SPECIFIC EXPANSION PLANS:
US: All United States
Canada: All Canada
Overseas: All Free World Countries. Already in 39 countries. Yet to open in Japan.

<< >>

REALTY EXECUTIVES INTERNATIONAL

4427 N. 36th St., # 100
Phoenix, AZ 85018
Tel: (800) 252-3366 (602) 957-0747
Fax: (602) 224-5542
E-Mail: billpowers@realtyexecutives.com
Web Site: www.realtyexecutives.com
Mr. William A. Powers, COO

The originators of the 100% Commission Concept. Awarding franchises to use the REALTY EXECUTIVES' name.

BACKGROUND:
Established: 1965; 1st Franchised: 1987
Franchised Units: 514
Company-Owned Units 0
Total Units: 514
Dist.: US-564; CAN-35; O'seas-25
North America: 45 States, 5 Provinces
Density: NR
Projected New Units (12 Months): 150
Qualifications: 4, 5, 5, 2, 3, 4
Registered: NR

FINANCIAL/TERMS:
Cash Investment: $25K
Total Investment: $25-82.5K
Minimum Net Worth: $30-50K
Fees: Franchise - $15K
Royalty - $35-50/agent/mo;
Ad. - $5-10/Agent
Earnings Claim Statement: No
Term of Contract (Years): 5/5
Avg. # Of Employees: 1 FT
Passive Ownership: Allowed
Encourage Conversions: Yes
Area Develop. Agreements: Yes/5
Sub-Franchising Contracts: Yes
Expand In Territory: Yes
Space Needs: NR SF; N/A

SUPPORT & TRAINING PROVIDED:
Financial Assistance Provided: No
Site Selection Assistance: No
Lease Negotiation Assistance: No
Co-Operative Advertising: Yes
Franchisee Assoc./Member: No
Size Of Corporate Staff: 12
On-Going Support: G,h,I
Training: 4 Days at Company Headquarters in Phoenix.

SPECIFIC EXPANSION PLANS:
US: All United States
Canada: All Canada
Overseas: All Countries

<< >>

REMERICA REAL ESTATE

40500 Ann Arbor Rd., # 102
Plymouth, MI 48170
Tel: (800) REM-ERICA (734) 459-4500
Fax: (734) 459-1566
E-Mail: jim.preston@remerica.com
Web Site: www.remerica.com
Mr. James A. Courtney

A cutting-edge residential real estate franchising organization. We offer broker, agent (experience and new), training, secretarial training, assist in recruiting, your own dynamic and interactive Website, intranet, technical support, TV and print advertising. See www.remerica.com and REMERICA FINANCIAL AND TITLE GROUP.

BACKGROUND:
Established: 1988; 1st Franchised: 1990
Franchised Units: 32
Company-Owned Units 0
Total Units: 32
Dist.: US-32; CAN-0; O'seas-0
North America: 1 State
Density: 34 in MI
Projected New Units (12 Months): 10
Qualifications: 5, 4, 5, 4, 2, 5
Registered: NR

FINANCIAL/TERMS:
Cash Investment: $15-70K
Total Investment: $20-100K
Minimum Net Worth: $25-100K
Fees: Franchise - $10K
Royalty - 6%; Ad. - 2%
Earnings Claim Statement: No
Term of Contract (Years): 5/5
Avg. # Of Employees: NR
Passive Ownership: Discouraged
Encourage Conversions: Yes
Area Develop. Agreements: No
Sub-Franchising Contracts: No
Expand In Territory: Yes
Space Needs: NR SF; FS, SF, SC, RM

SUPPORT & TRAINING PROVIDED:
Financial Assistance Provided: Yes(I)
Site Selection Assistance: Yes
Lease Negotiation Assistance: Yes
Co-Operative Advertising: Yes
Franchisee Assoc./Member: No
Size Of Corporate Staff: 12
On-Going Support: A,B,C,D,E,F,G,H,I
Training: 20+ Hours Plymouth, MI.

SPECIFIC EXPANSION PLANS:
US: All United States
Canada: All Canada
Overseas: No

<< >>

TUCKER ASSOCIATES

9279 N. Meridian St.
Indianapolis, IN 46260
Tel: (800) 659-0432 (317) 571-2200
Fax: (317) 571-2204
Web Site: www.talktotucker.com
Mr. Mark Bush, Senior Vice President

Real estate franchisor for the State of Indiana, offering marketing, recruiting, training and relocation leads for franchisees. Number one company in Indiana and recently named # 10 brand name of independently-owned companies.

BACKGROUND:

Established: 1918; 1st Franchised: 1989

Franchised Units:	23
Company-Owned Units	14
Total Units:	37
Dist.:	US-37; CAN-0; O'seas-0
North America:	1 State
Density:	33 in IN
Projected New Units (12 Months):	3-4
Qualifications:	5, 5, 5, 3, 4, 5

Registered: IL,IN

FINANCIAL/TERMS:

Cash Investment:	$100-200K
Total Investment:	$125-250K
Minimum Net Worth:	$25K
Fees: Franchise -	$0
Royalty - 6%;	Ad. - 0%
Earnings Claim Statement:	No
Term of Contract (Years):	6/5
Avg. # Of Employees:	1-2 FT, 3 PT
Passive Ownership:	Discouraged
Encourage Conversions:	Yes
Area Develop. Agreements:	No
Sub-Franchising Contracts:	No
Expand In Territory:	Yes

Space Needs: 1,500 SF; FS, SF, SC

SUPPORT & TRAINING PROVIDED:

Financial Assistance Provided:	Yes
Site Selection Assistance:	Yes
Lease Negotiation Assistance:	Yes
Co-Operative Advertising:	N/A
Franchisee Assoc./Member:	No
Size Of Corporate Staff:	3
On-Going Support:	a,B,C,D,E,G,h

Training: 2 Weeks Indianapolis, IN.

SPECIFIC EXPANSION PLANS:

US:	IN, Surrounding States
Canada:	No
Overseas:	No

≺≺ ≻≻

SUPPLEMENTAL LISTING OF FRANCHISORS

AMERICA'S CHOICE, 636 N. French, # 10, Amherst, NY 14228 ; (800) 831-2493 (716) 691-0596; (716) 691-0650

APARTMENT SEARCH INTERNATIONAL, 7200 France Ave. S., # 237, Edina, MN 55435-4309 ; (800) 989-3764 (612) 830-0509

BETTER LIFESTYLES REAL ESTATE, P.O. Box 540912, Linden Hill, NY 11354 ; (917) 776-4325

BUYER'S RESOURCE INTERNATIONAL, 393 Hanover Center Blvd., Etna, NH 03750 ; (800) 359-4092 (603) 643-9300; (603) 643-0404

CENTURY 21 REAL ESTATE CANADA, 700-1199 W. Pender St., Vancouver, BC V6E 2R1 CANADA; (604) 606-2100; (604) 606-2125

COMMISSION EXPRESS, 8306 Professional Hill Dr., Fairfax, VA 22031 (888) 560-5501 (703) 560-5500; (703) 560-5502

EWM, INC., 4760 Rte. 9, S., Howell, NJ 07731 ; (800) 396-4621 (732) 364-5900; (732) 905-8606

FAIR REALTY EXECUTIVES COMPANY, 320 N. Lake St., Aurora, IL 60506 ; (800) 553-3247 (630) 897-7600; (630) 897-7750

GMAC REAL ESTATE SERVICES, 477 Martinsville Rd., P.O. Box 880, Liberty Corner, NJ 07938-0880 ; (800) 274-7653 (908) 542-5500; (908) 604-4962

HER REAL ESTATE, 4656 Executive Dr., Columbus, OH 43220 ; (800) 848-7400 (614) 459-7400; (614) 442-2880

INTERNATIONAL REALTY PLUS, 1912 E. Andy Devine Ave., Kingman, AZ 86401 ; (888) 825-0811 (520) 753-4964; (520) 753-5492

KELLER WILLIAMS REALTORS, 3701 Bee Cave Rd., # 200, Austin, TX 78746 ; (512) 327-3070; (512) 328-1433

NATIONAL APARTMENT SERVICES, 7941 L-3 Angus Center, Springfield, VA 22153 ; (888) 356-3535 ; (703) 455-3475

NATIONAL REAL ESTATE SERVICE, 4100 Newport Pl., # 730, Newport Beach, CA 92660 ; (800) 654-7653 (949) 660-1919; (949) 660-1910

PRUDENTIAL REAL ESTATE AFFILIATES, 3333 Michelson Dr., # 1000, Irvine, CA 92612 ; (800) 477-7732 (949) 794-7900; (949) 794-7031

QPOINT HOME MORTGAGE NETWORK, 10900 NE 4th St., # 1800, Bellevue, WA 98004-5873 ; (800) 709-4965 (425) 462-6562; (425) 462-4691

REAL ESTATE ONE, 521 Randolph, Traverse City, MI 49684 ; (616) 946-4040; (616) 946-4339

REALTEC, 4230 L.B.J. Fwy., # 570, Dallas, TX 75244 ; (800) 732-5832 (972) 458-9388; (972) 458-8558

REALTY WORLD, 4100 Newport Place, # 720, Newport Beach, CA 92660 ; (800) 685-4984 (949) 251-0745; (949) 251-1066

RED CARPET KEIM, 189 E. Big Beaver, # 209, Troy, MI 48083 ; (800) 992-9119 (248) 680-7300; (248) 680-3014

SEARS TERMITE & PEST CONTROL, 6359 Edgewater Dr., Orlando, FL 32810 ; (800) 528-7287 ; (407) 523-9888

SHOWHOMES OF AMERICA, 3010 LBJ Fwy., # 555, Dallas, TX 75234 ; (972) 243-1900; (972) 243-3909

STATE WIDE REAL ESTATE SERVICES, P.O. Box 297, Escanaba, MI 49829 ; (800) 682-9123 (906) 786-8392; (906) 786-1388

WEICHERT REAL ESTATE AFFILIATES, 225 Littleton Rd., Morris Plains, NJ 07950 ; (973) 359-8395; (073) 292-1428

WHY USA REAL ESTATE, P.O. Box 497, 2110 US Hwy. 12 West, Menomonie, WI 54751-0497 ; (888) 990-7355 (715) 235-9546; (715) 235-9738

Recreation & Entertainment

Chapter 32

Recreation & Entertainment Industry Profile

Total # Franchisors in Industry Group	41
Total # Franchised Units in Industry Group	2,547
Total # Company-Owned Units in Industry Group	151
Total # Operating Units in Industry Group	2,698
Average # Franchised Units/Franchisor	62.1
Average # Company-Owned Units/Franchisor	3.7
Average # Total Units/Franchisor	65.8
Ratio of Total # Franchised Units/Total # Company-Owned Units	16.9:1
Industry Survey Participants	12
Representing % of Industry	29.3%
Average Franchise Fee*:	$20.6K
Average Total Investment*:	$371.9K
Average On-Going Royalty Fee*:	8.5%

*If a range was provided, the mid-point of the range was used. See detailed profiles for actual ranges.

Five Largest Participants in Survey

Company	# Franchised Units	# Co-Owned Units	# Total Units	Franchise Fee	On-Going Royalty	Total Investment
1. World Gym International	278	0	278	13K	$6.5K/Yr.	275K-1MM
2. American Poolplayers Association	245	0	245	Varies	20%	10.6-13K
3. Putt-Putt Golf Courses of America	200	1	201	5-30K	5%	100K-5MM
4. Complete Music	152	1	153	15.5K	8%	15.5-35K
5. Fred Astaire Dance Studios	108	0	108	15-35K	7-8%	138.5-357K

All of the data provided are proprietary and should not be quoted without acknowledging *Bond's Franchise Guide.*

AMERICAN DARTERS ASSOCIATION

1000 Lake St. Louis Blvd., # 310
Lake St. Louis, MO 63367
Tel: (888) 327-8752 (636) 625-8621
Fax: (636) 625-2975
E-Mail: adadarts@inlink.com
Web Site: www.adadarters.com
Mr. Glenn Remick, President

ADA franchisees offer recreational dart leagues using the Neutralizer, a copyrighted handicap system that neutralizes play. The league currently consists of 15,000 members who compete in year-round weekly play. Franchisees receive customized software, complete training, technical updates, support and networking opportunities at the national convention.

BACKGROUND:

Established: 1990; 1st Franchised: 1991
Franchised Units: 75
Company-Owned Units 0
Total Units: 75
Dist.: US-75; CAN-0; O'seas-0
North America: 26 States
Density: TX, IL, MO
Projected New Units (12 Months): 12
Qualifications: 3, 3, 3, 3, 3, 2
Registered: All States Except OR,AB

FINANCIAL/TERMS:

Cash Investment: $1-2.3K
Total Investment: $1.5-2.8K
Minimum Net Worth: $Varies
Fees: Franchise - $By Population
Royalty - 20%; Ad. - N/A
Earnings Claim Statement: No
Term of Contract (Years): 1.5/5
Avg. # Of Employees: Varies
Passive Ownership: Not Allowed
Encourage Conversions: N/A
Area Develop. Agreements: No
Sub-Franchising Contracts: No
Expand In Territory: Yes
Space Needs: N/A SF; N/A

SUPPORT & TRAINING PROVIDED:

Financial Assistance Provided: No
Site Selection Assistance: Yes
Lease Negotiation Assistance: N/A
Co-Operative Advertising: No
Franchisee Assoc./Member: No
Size Of Corporate Staff: 2
On-Going Support: A,B,C,D,F,G,H,I
Training: 3 Days Lake Saint Louis, MO.

SPECIFIC EXPANSION PLANS:

US: All United States
Canada: No
Overseas: No

<< >>

AMERICAN MOBILE SOUND

600 Ward Dr., # A-1
Santa Barbara, CA 93111
Tel: (800) 788-9007 (805) 681-8132
Fax: (805) 681-8134
Mr. Tad Clark, Fran. Dev. Coordinator

Each franchisee receives a comprehensive, step-by-step, customer-oriented training program enabling him or her to provide the highest-quality, most consistent, affordable disc jockey service, utilizing state-of-the art, high-quality sound and with professionally-trained DJ's for any event, as well as a complete music library with updates - 'Imagine...a career you can truly enjoy.'

BACKGROUND:

Established: 1991; 1st Franchised: 1994
Franchised Units: 31
Company-Owned Units 0
Total Units: 31
Dist.: US-28; CAN-0; O'seas-0
North America: 12 States
Density: 9 in CA, 5 in CO, 3 in TX
Projected New Units (12 Months): 12
Qualifications: 2, 2, 1, 1, 3, 5
Registered: CA

FINANCIAL/TERMS:

Cash Investment: $10-87K
Total Investment: $10-87K
Minimum Net Worth: $10K
Fees: Franchise - $6-15K
Royalty - 7%/$150; Ad. - 0%
Earnings Claim Statement: No
Term of Contract (Years): 10/10
Avg. # Of Employees: 5 PT
Passive Ownership: Allowed
Encourage Conversions: N/A
Area Develop. Agreements: No
Sub-Franchising Contracts: No
Expand In Territory: Yes
Space Needs: 250 SF; HB, OB

SUPPORT & TRAINING PROVIDED:

Financial Assistance Provided: Yes
Site Selection Assistance: Yes
Lease Negotiation Assistance: Yes
Co-Operative Advertising: N/A
Franchisee Assoc./Member: Yes/Yes
Size Of Corporate Staff: 2
On-Going Support: b,C,D,d,E,G,H,I
Training: 9 Days Santa Barbara, CA.

SPECIFIC EXPANSION PLANS:

US: All United States
Canada: No
Overseas: No

<< >>

AMERICAN POOLPLAYERS ASSOCIATION

1000 Lake St. Louis Blvd., # 325
Lake St. Louis, MO 63367-1340
Tel: (800) 372-2536 (636) 625-8611
Fax: (636) 625-2975
E-Mail: apa@poolplayers.com
Web Site: www.poolplayers.com
Mr. Kevin Hinkebein, Franchise Development Mgr.

APA franchisees operate recreational pool leagues utilizing "The Equalizer", a unique handicap system that equalizes play. The League, previously known as the Bud Light Pool League or the Camel pool League and now known nationally as the "APA Pool League", currently consists of over 200,000 members who compete in year-round weekly play. Franchisees receive customized software, technical updates, complete training, marketing support and networking opportunities at the annual convention.

BACKGROUND: IFA MEMBER

Established: 1980; 1st Franchised: 1982
Franchised Units: 245
Company-Owned Units 0
Total Units: 245
Dist.: US-228; CAN-17; O'seas-0
North America: 47 States, 6 Provinces
Density: 14 in IL, 13 in ON, 16 in FL
Projected New Units (12 Months): 20
Qualifications: 3, 3, 2, 2, 1, 5
Registered: All States

FINANCIAL/TERMS:

Cash Investment: $10.6-13K
Total Investment: $10.6-13K
Minimum Net Worth: $N/A
Fees: Franchise - $Varies
Royalty - 20%; Ad. - N/A
Earnings Claim Statement: No
Term of Contract (Years): 2/5/10
Avg. # Of Employees: Varies
Passive Ownership: Not Allowed
Encourage Conversions: N/A

Area Develop. Agreements: No
Sub-Franchising Contracts: No
Expand In Territory: N/A
Space Needs: N/A SF; HB

SUPPORT & TRAINING PROVIDED:

Financial Assistance Provided: Yes(D)
Site Selection Assistance: Yes
Lease Negotiation Assistance: N/A
Co-Operative Advertising: Yes
Franchisee Assoc./Member: Yes/No
Size Of Corporate Staff: 40+
On-Going Support: A,D,G,H
Training: 6 Days APA Home Office.

SPECIFIC EXPANSION PLANS:

US: All United States
Canada: All Canada
Overseas: No

CERAMICS TO GO

2340 Plaza Del Amo, #105
Torrance, CA 90501
Tel: (888) 316-TOGO (310) 533-0311
Fax: (310) 533-5955
E-Mail: ceramicstogo@aol.com
Web Site: www.ceramicstogo.com
Ms. Judy McConnell, President

Fun to own - fun to operate - retail ceramic do-it-yourself studio. Customers can paint it there (at no hourly charge) or take the project "to go." Complete kits with bisque, paints, etc. Paint kiln-fired ceramics anywhere.

BACKGROUND:

Established: 2001; 1st Franchised: 2001
Franchised Units: 0
Company-Owned Units 2
Total Units: 2
Dist.: US-2; CAN-0; O'seas-0
North America: 1 State
Density: 2 in CA
Projected New Units (12 Months): NR
Registered: NR

FINANCIAL/TERMS:

Cash Investment: $73.5-98.5K
Total Investment: $73.5-98.5K
Minimum Net Worth: $N/A
Fees: Franchise - $30K
Royalty - 5%; Ad. - 3%
Earnings Claim Statement: No
Term of Contract (Years): 10/10
Avg. # Of Employees: 4 PT
Passive Ownership: Discouraged
Encourage Conversions: NR
Area Develop. Agreements: No
Sub-Franchising Contracts: No
Expand In Territory: No
Space Needs: NR SF; SF, SC

SUPPORT & TRAINING PROVIDED:

Financial Assistance Provided: NR
Site Selection Assistance: Yes
Lease Negotiation Assistance: Yes
Co-Operative Advertising: No
Franchisee Assoc./Member: No
Size Of Corporate Staff: NR
On-Going Support: a,B,C,d,E,f,h,I
Training: 3 Days, Torrance, CA; 3 Days, Your Shop Location.

SPECIFIC EXPANSION PLANS:

US: All United States
Canada: NR
Overseas: NR

<< >>

COMPLETE MUSIC

7877 L St.
Omaha, NE 68127
Tel: (800) 843-3866 (402) 339-0001
Fax: (402) 339-1285
E-Mail: comucorp@aol.com
Web Site: www.cmusic.com
Mr. Kem Matthews, Franchise Director

COMPLETE MUSIC is the leader in disc jockey entertainment, providing dance music for over 1 million people each year. The uniqueness of this business allows owners, who need not be entertainers, to use their skills in management to hire and book their own musically-trained DJ's for all types of special events.

BACKGROUND:

Established: 1972; 1st Franchised: 1982
Franchised Units: 152
Company-Owned Units 1
Total Units: 153
Dist.: US-140; CAN-4; O'seas-0
North America: 31 States, 1 Province
Density: 21 in TX, 11 in NE, 8 in CO
Projected New Units (12 Months): 6-12
Qualifications: 3, 4, 1, 4, 4, 3
Registered: CA,FL,IL,IN,MD,MI,MN,OR, SD,WA,WI

FINANCIAL/TERMS:

Cash Investment: $9.5-24.5K
Total Investment: $15.5-35K
Minimum Net Worth: $N/A
Fees: Franchise - $15.5K
Royalty - 8%; Ad. - 4%
Earnings Claim Statement: Yes
Term of Contract (Years): Lifetime
Avg. # Of Employees: 2 FT, 5-40 PT
Passive Ownership: Discouraged
Encourage Conversions: Yes
Area Develop. Agreements: No
Sub-Franchising Contracts: No
Expand In Territory: Yes
Space Needs: N/A SF; HB

SUPPORT & TRAINING PROVIDED:

Financial Assistance Provided: Yes(D)
Site Selection Assistance: Yes
Lease Negotiation Assistance: Yes
Co-Operative Advertising: Yes
Franchisee Assoc./Member: Yes/Yes
Size Of Corporate Staff: 5
On-Going Support: B,c,D,E,F,G,h,i
Training: 9 Days Omaha, NE; 4 Days On-Site.

SPECIFIC EXPANSION PLANS:

US: All United States
Canada: All Canada
Overseas: No

DUFFERIN GAME ROOM STORE

3770 Nashua Dr.
Mississauga, ON L4V 1M6 CANADA
Tel: (800) 268-2597 (905) 677-7665
Fax: (800) 387-3157
Ms. Sarah Stone, Contract Manager

Canada's premier retailer of family games, specializing in high-quality DUFFERIN billiard equipment and 3,000 other games to enjoy quality time with family and friends.

BACKGROUND:

Established: 1986; 1st Franchised: 1987
Franchised Units: 18
Company-Owned Units 26
Total Units: 44
Dist.: US-0; CAN-44; O'seas-0
North America: 7 Provinces
Density: 20 in ON, 9 in AB, 6 in BC
Projected New Units (12 Months): 2-3
Qualifications: 5, 4, 3, 3, 3, 5
Registered: AB

FINANCIAL/TERMS:

Cash Investment: $143K
Total Investment: $357K

Minimum Net Worth: $TBA
Fees: Franchise - $28.6K
Royalty - 5%; Ad. - 2%
Earnings Claim Statement: No
Term of Contract (Years): 10/5
Avg. # Of Employees: 3 FT, 6 PT
Passive Ownership: Not Allowed
Encourage Conversions: No
Area Develop. Agreements: No
Sub-Franchising Contracts: No
Expand In Territory: No
Space Needs: 3,000-3,500 SF; FS, SC, RM

SUPPORT & TRAINING PROVIDED:

Financial Assistance Provided: No
Site Selection Assistance: Yes
Lease Negotiation Assistance: Yes
Co-Operative Advertising: Yes
Franchisee Assoc./Member: Yes/Yes
Size Of Corporate Staff: 300
On-Going Support: C,D,E,F,G,h,I
Training: Head Office.

SPECIFIC EXPANSION PLANS:

US: No
Canada: No
Overseas: No

<< >>

FRED ASTAIRE DANCE STUDIOS

7900 Glades Rd., # 630
Boca Raton, FL 33431
Tel: (800) 278-2473 (561) 218-3237
Fax: (561) 218-3299
E-Mail: dancefads@aol.com
Web Site: www.fredastaire.com
Ms. Linda Milo, Franchise Manager

FRED ASTAIRE DANCE STUDIOS (FADS) provides its franchised community with a 50+ year tradition that gives the individual franchisee worldwide name recognition identified with dance excellence unsurpassed in its industry. The original teaching methods of the great Fred Astaire are still in place today at the company that proudly bears his name. FADS provides its franchisees with extensive business and dance training, and ensures that its franchises operate under the strictest code of ethics.

BACKGROUND: IFA MEMBER

Established: 1947; 1st Franchised: 1950
Franchised Units: 108
Company-Owned Units 0
Total Units: 108
Dist.: US-110; CAN-6; O'seas-0
North America: 28 States, 1 Province
Density: 16 in FL, 13 in NY, 12 in OH
Projected New Units (12 Months): 8-10
Qualifications: 5, 4, 3, 2, 2, 5
Registered: CA,FL,MD,MN,NY,OR,RI, VA,WI

FINANCIAL/TERMS:

Cash Investment: $125K
Total Investment: $138.5-357K
Minimum Net Worth: $150K
Fees: Franchise - $15-35K
Royalty - 7-8%; Ad. - 0.2%/$25Min
Earnings Claim Statement: No
Term of Contract (Years): 5/5
Avg. # Of Employees: 10 FT
Passive Ownership: Discouraged
Encourage Conversions: Yes
Area Develop. Agreements: No
Sub-Franchising Contracts: Yes
Expand In Territory: Yes
Space Needs: 2,500 Min. SF; FS, SC

SUPPORT & TRAINING PROVIDED:

Financial Assistance Provided: Yes(I)
Site Selection Assistance: Yes
Lease Negotiation Assistance: Yes
Co-Operative Advertising: Yes
Franchisee Assoc./Member: No
Size Of Corporate Staff: 9
On-Going Support: A,b,c,d,E,f,G,h,I
Training: 8 Hours Dance or Management (Franchisee's Site) or 16 Hours Management (Existing Site).

SPECIFIC EXPANSION PLANS:

US: All United States
Canada: All Canada
Overseas: Under Trade Name Megadance International

<< >>

GRAND GATHERINGS

240 W. Tampa Avenue
Venice, FL 34285
Tel: (866) 484-7263 (941) 484-1312
Fax: (941) 484-5531
E-Mail: grandgatherings@aol.com
Web Site: www.aboutgrandgatherings.com
Ms. Marianne Bedard, President

GRAND GATHERINGS provides an event-planning service that is based on the concept of 'No Fee' to the client. This instantly translates into a high volume of clients from the start-up phase. Our marketing expertise and proven systems will give you a competitive advantage in gaining clients who are planning social celebrations, family gatherings, weddings and business functions. Easy to learn and fun to operate.

BACKGROUND:

Established: 1993; 1st Franchised: 2000
Franchised Units: 1
Company-Owned Units 1
Total Units: 2
Dist.: US-2; CAN-0; O'seas-0
North America: 1 State
Density: 2 in FL
Projected New Units (12 Months): 10
Qualifications: 4, 5, 3, 3, 4, 5
Registered: NR

FINANCIAL/TERMS:

Cash Investment: $32-40.5K
Total Investment: $32-40.5
Minimum Net Worth: $50K
Fees: Franchise - $23.5K
Royalty - 1.5%; Ad. - 0%
Earnings Claim Statement: Yes
Term of Contract (Years): 5/5
Avg. # Of Employees: 1 FT, 1 PT
Passive Ownership: Discouraged
Encourage Conversions: No
Area Develop. Agreements: No
Sub-Franchising Contracts: No
Expand In Territory: Yes
Space Needs: 800 SF; Office

SUPPORT & TRAINING PROVIDED:

Financial Assistance Provided: No
Site Selection Assistance: Yes
Lease Negotiation Assistance: No
Co-Operative Advertising: No
Franchisee Assoc./Member: No
Size Of Corporate Staff: 3
On-Going Support: b,c,d,G,H,I
Training: 3 Days in Venice, Florida.

SPECIFIC EXPANSION PLANS:

US: All United States
Canada: No
Overseas: No

PUTT-PUTT GOLF COURSES OF AMERICA

P.O. Box 35237
Fayetteville, NC 28303-0237
Tel: (910) 485-7131
Fax: (910) 485-1122
Web Site: www.putt-putt.com

Mr. Scott Anderson, National Franchise Dir.

PUTT-PUTT GOLF is now in its 44th year of operation. It is the oldest and largest operator/franchisor of miniature golf and family entertainment centers in the world. PUTT-PUTT GOLF operates in 28 states and in 8 foreign countries and specializes in the development of PUTT-PUTT GOLF, gamerooms, batting cages, bumpercars, go-carts, laser tag and total play.

BACKGROUND:

Established: 1954; 1st Franchised: 1955
Franchised Units: 200
Company-Owned Units 1
Total Units: 201
Dist.: US-186; CAN-1; O'seas-21
North America: 28 States, 1 Province
Density: 28 in TX, 25 in NC, 21 in OH
Projected New Units (12 Months): 12
Qualifications: 4, 5, 2, 3, 3, 4
Registered: All States and AB

FINANCIAL/TERMS:

Cash Investment: $30K-1MM
Total Investment: $100K-5MM
Minimum Net Worth: $100K
Fees: Franchise - $5-30K
Royalty - 5%; Ad. - 2%
Earnings Claim Statement: No
Term of Contract (Years): 40
Avg. # Of Employees: NR
Passive Ownership: Allowed
Encourage Conversions: N/A
Area Develop. Agreements: No
Sub-Franchising Contracts: No
Expand In Territory: No
Space Needs: 3-7 acres SF; N/A

SUPPORT & TRAINING PROVIDED:

Financial Assistance Provided: Yes(I)
Site Selection Assistance: Yes
Lease Negotiation Assistance: Yes
Co-Operative Advertising: No
Franchisee Assoc./Member: No
Size Of Corporate Staff: 24
On-Going Support: C,D,G,H,I
Training: 1 Week in Fayetteville, NC; 3-7 Days at Franchisee's Location.

SPECIFIC EXPANSION PLANS:

US: All United States
Canada: All Canada
Overseas: South America

<< >>

THEMED MINIATURE GOLF COURSES

P.O. Box 2435
Myrtle Beach, SC 29578-2435
Tel: (843) 249-2118
Fax: (843) 249-2118
E-Mail: chgrove@sccoast.net
Mr. Charles H. Grove, President

Themed, contoured adventure-type miniature golf courses with lakes, streambeds and waterfalls. Lush landscaping and the very finest designed, unique, playable holes that invite repeat participation. We also design and build complete family entertainment centers.

BACKGROUND:

Established: 1977; 1st Franchised: 1985
Franchised Units: 12
Company-Owned Units 4
Total Units: 16
Dist.: US-16; CAN-0; O'seas-0
North America: 10 States
Density: SC, FL, TX
Projected New Units (12 Months): 5
Qualifications: 5, 4, 2, 2, 3, 4
Registered: NR

FINANCIAL/TERMS:

Cash Investment: $62.5K-100K
Total Investment: $250-400K
Minimum Net Worth: $N/A
Fees: Franchise - $N/A
Royalty - N/A; Ad. - N/A
Earnings Claim Statement: No
Term of Contract (Years): Unlimited
Avg. # Of Employees: 2 FT, 2 PT
Passive Ownership: Allowed
Encourage Conversions: N/A
Area Develop. Agreements: No
Sub-Franchising Contracts: No
Expand In Territory: Yes
Space Needs: 30,000 SF; FS

SUPPORT & TRAINING PROVIDED:

Financial Assistance Provided: N/A
Site Selection Assistance: Yes
Lease Negotiation Assistance: Yes
Co-Operative Advertising: No
Franchisee Assoc./Member: Yes/Yes
Size Of Corporate Staff: 5
On-Going Support: B,C,D
Training: NR

SPECIFIC EXPANSION PLANS:

US: All United States
Canada: All Canada
Overseas: No

<< >>

WOODY'S WOOD SHOPS

1814 Franklin St., # 820
Oakland, CA 94612
Tel: (510) 839-5462
Fax: (510) 839-2104
Dr. Christo Y. Bruisers, President

WOODY'S WOOD SHOPS offer instruction and use of virtually all shop tools in a fully-outfitted wood shop. After detailed instruction and testing, members have full use of shop and related facilities. Open 15 hours/day, 7 days/week. Also sell small tools and all power equipment at cost plus 5%. Members pay front-end fees plus dues.

BACKGROUND:

Established: 1978; 1st Franchised: 1980
Franchised Units: 28
Company-Owned Units 14
Total Units: 42
Dist.: US-33; CAN-6; O'seas-0
North America: 7 States, 2 Provinces
Density: 16 in CA, 8 in OR, 3 in WA
Projected New Units (12 Months): 4
Registered: NR

FINANCIAL/TERMS:

Cash Investment: $72K
Total Investment: $85-185K
Minimum Net Worth: $NR
Fees: Franchise - $22K
Royalty - 6%; Ad. - 2%
Earnings Claim Statement: Yes
Term of Contract (Years): 15/15
Avg. # Of Employees: 1 FT, 4 PT
Passive Ownership: Discouraged
Encourage Conversions: Yes
Area Develop. Agreements: Yes/15
Sub-Franchising Contracts: Yes
Expand In Territory: No
Space Needs: 2,800-3,400 SF; FS, Warehouse

SUPPORT & TRAINING PROVIDED:

Financial Assistance Provided: Yes(D)
Site Selection Assistance: Yes
Lease Negotiation Assistance: Yes
Co-Operative Advertising: Yes
Franchisee Assoc./Member: NR
Size Of Corporate Staff: 21
On-Going Support: A,C,D,g,H,i
Training: 3 Weeks Headquarters; 2 Weeks On-Site; On-Going.

SPECIFIC EXPANSION PLANS:

US: All United States
Canada: ON Only
Overseas: No

<< >>

WORLD GYM INTERNATIONAL

3223 Washington Blvd.
Marina Del Rey, CA 90292
Tel: (800) 544-7441 (310) 827-7705
Fax: (310) 827-6355
E-Mail: info@worldgym.com
Web Site: www.worldgym.com
Mr. Mike Uretz, President/CEO

Service oriented fitness centers featuring circuit training, cardiovascular equipment, free weights and personal training.

BACKGROUND:

Established: 1977; 1st Franchised: 1985
Franchised Units: 278
Company-Owned Units 0
Total Units: 278
Dist.: US-262; CAN-3; O'seas-13
North America: 34 States
Density: 30 in FL, 24 in CA, 21 in NY
Projected New Units (12 Months): 45
Registered: CA,FL,HI,IL,IN,MD,MI,MN, NY,ND,RI,SD,VA,WA

FINANCIAL/TERMS:

Cash Investment: $275K-1MM
Total Investment: $275K-1MM
Minimum Net Worth: $300K-1MM
Fees: Franchise - $13K
Royalty - $6.5K/Yr.; Ad. - 0%
Earnings Claim Statement: No
Term of Contract (Years): 5/5
Avg. # Of Employees: 8-15 FT, 5 PT
Passive Ownership: Allowed
Encourage Conversions: Yes
Area Develop. Agreements: Yes/6
Sub-Franchising Contracts: No
Expand In Territory: Yes
Space Needs: 9500 SF; FS,SF,SC,RM

SUPPORT & TRAINING PROVIDED:

Financial Assistance Provided: No
Site Selection Assistance: N/A
Lease Negotiation Assistance: Yes
Co-Operative Advertising: No
Franchisee Assoc./Member: No
Size Of Corporate Staff: 3
On-Going Support: c,d,G,H,I
Training: 1-3 Day Seminars and Universities Throughout the Year, All US.

SPECIFIC EXPANSION PLANS:

US: All United States
Canada: All Canada
Overseas: All Countries

<< >>

SUPPLEMENTAL LISTING OF FRANCHISORS

ADVANTAGE GOLF TOURNAMENT SERVICE, 3790 Realty Rd., Addison, TX 75001 ; (800) 659-2815 (972) 243-6209; (972) 243-4252

AMACADE CENTERS, P.O. Box 24, Fayetteville, AR 72702 ; (501) 443-6791; (501) 443-4024

ATEC GRAND SLAM U. S. A., 10931 Crabapple Rd. # 103A, Roswell, GA 30075 ; (800) 775-2607 ; (707) 552-3503

BODY BALANCE FOR PERFORMANCE, 280 East Magnolia Blvd., Burbank, CA 91502 ; (800) 473-6211 ; (818) 957-9343

FAMILY SPORTS CONCEPTS, 505 E. Jackson St., # 308, Tampa, FL 33602-4989 (813) 226-2333; (813) 226-0030

FAMILY TREE DIGITAL VIDEO, 2966 Wildwood Dr., El Cajon, CA 92019 ; (800) 832-6459 (619) 444-2190; (619) 444-9432

GOLD'S GYM, 358 Hampton Dr., Venice, CA 90291-2624 ; (800) 457-5375 (310) 392-3005; (310) 392-4680

HOOP MOUNTAIN, 130 Centre St., # 7, Danvers, MA 01923 ; (800) 819-8445 ; (978) 774-8628

PARMASTERS GOLF TRAINING CENTERS, 9600 Cameron St., # 314, Burnaby, BC V3J 7N3 CANADA; (800) 663-2331 (604) 663-2331; (800) 416-6325

PUMP RADIO NETWORK, 2820 Jefferson Ave., Midland, MI 48640 ; (877) 682-5537 (517) 837-2460; (517) 837-3597

RIGHT ONE, THE, 160 Old Derby St., # 339, Hingham, MA 02043 ; (800) 348-3283 (781) 749-5700; (781) 749-2390

TABLE FOR EIGHT, 60 Thackeray Rd., Wellesley, MA 02481 ; (888) 8-TABLE8 (781) 239-3370; (781) 431-0106

TOGETHER DATING SERVICE, 5026 Dorsey Hall, # 205, Ellicott City, MD 21024 ; (877) 730-8866 (410) 730-8866; (410) 992-6910

VILLARI'S SELF DEFENSE CENTERS, 101 Cedar Grove Ln., # 105, Somerset, NJ 08873 ; (732) 563-0707; (732) 563-0325

Chapter 33
Rental Services

Rental Services Industry Profile

Total # Franchisors in Industry Group	10
Total # Franchised Units in Industry Group	2,442
Total # Company-Owned Units in Industry Group	533
Total # Operating Units in Industry Group	2,975
Average # Franchised Units/Franchisor	244.2
Average # Company-Owned Units/Franchisor	53.3
Average # Total Units/Franchisor	297.5
Ratio of Total # Franchised Units/Total # Company-Owned Units	4.6:1
Industry Survey Participants	8
Representing % of Industry	80.0%
Average Franchise Fee*:	$16.4K
Average Total Investment*:	$208.8K
Average On-Going Royalty Fee*:	5.3%

*If a range was provided, the mid-point of the range was used. See detailed profiles for actual ranges.

Five Largest Participants in Survey

Company	# Franchised Units	# Co-Owned Units	# Total Units	Franchise Fee	On-Going Royalty	Total Investment
1. Grand Rental Station/Taylor	1,250	0	1,250	1.5K	1.3%	225-250K
2. Aaron's Sales & Lease Ownership	203	357	560	35K	5%	263-502K
3. Nation-Wide General Rental	376	1	377	0K	0%	80-178K
4. Colortyme	326	0	326	25K	4%	293-517K
5. Gingiss Formal Wear	170	85	255	15K	8%	99-243K

All of the data provided are proprietary and should not be quoted without acknowledging *Bond's Franchise Guide.*

AARON'S SALES & LEASE OWNERSHIP

309 E. Paces Ferry Rd., N. E.
Atlanta, GA 30305-2367
Tel: (800) 551-6015 (404) 237-4016
Fax: (404) 240-6540
E-Mail: kim.vanwagner@aaronsfranchise.com
Web Site: www.aaronsfranchise.com
Mr. Kim VanWagner, Dir. Franchise Development

AARON'S SALES & LEASE OWNERSHIP is one of the fastest-growing rental purchase companies in the U.S., specializing in furniture, electronics and appliances. AARON'S SALES & LEASE OWNERSHIP offers franchisees the expertise, advantages and support of a well-established company, plus the opportunity to realize a significant financial return in a booming market segment.

BACKGROUND: IFA MEMBER
Established: 1955; 1st Franchised: 1992
Franchised Units: 203
Company-Owned Units 357
Total Units: 560
Dist.: US-560; CAN-0; O'seas-0
North America: 46 States
Density: TX, FL, GA
Projected New Units (12 Months): 40
Qualifications: 5, 5, 1, 4, 5, 5
Registered: CA,FL,HI,IL,IN,MI,NY,ND,OR,RI,SD,VA,WA,WI

FINANCIAL/TERMS:
Cash Investment: $200K
Total Investment: $263-502.4K
Minimum Net Worth: $350K
Fees: Franchise - $35K
Royalty - 5%; Ad. - 2.5%
Earnings Claim Statement: Yes
Term of Contract (Years): 10/10
Avg. # Of Employees: 6 FT
Passive Ownership: Allowed
Encourage Conversions: N/A
Area Develop. Agreements: Yes/Varies
Sub-Franchising Contracts: No
Expand In Territory: Yes
Space Needs: 8,000 SF; SC

SUPPORT & TRAINING PROVIDED:
Financial Assistance Provided: Yes(I)
Site Selection Assistance: Yes
Lease Negotiation Assistance: Yes
Co-Operative Advertising: Yes
Franchisee Assoc./Member: Yes
Size Of Corporate Staff: 3,500
On-Going Support: A,B,C,D,E,F,H,I
Training: 3 Weeks Corporate Headquarters; 2 Weeks Minimum On-Site; On-Going Varies.

SPECIFIC EXPANSION PLANS:
US: All United States
Canada: All Canada
Overseas: Yes

<< >>

BABY'S AWAY

14023 E. Hampden Pl.
Aurora, CO 80014
Tel: (800) 984-9030 (303) 596-8864
Fax: (303) 750-6668
E-Mail: jwierzba@babysaway.com
Web Site: www.babyaway.com
Mr. John Wierzba, President

Rental, delivery and pick-up of baby/child equipment to traveling families.

BACKGROUND:
Established: 1990; 1st Franchised: 1994
Franchised Units: 18
Company-Owned Units 12
Total Units: 30
Dist.: US-23; CAN-7; O'seas-0
North America: 10 States, 4 Provinces
Density: 4 in CO, 3 in CA, 3 in SC
Projected New Units (12 Months): 4
Qualifications: 3, 4, 3, 3, 3, 5
Registered: CA,IL

FINANCIAL/TERMS:
Cash Investment: $16-25K
Total Investment: $16-25K
Minimum Net Worth: $N/A
Fees: Franchise - $8K
Royalty - 7%; Ad. - 3%
Earnings Claim Statement: No
Term of Contract (Years): 10/5/5
Avg. # Of Employees: 1 FT
Passive Ownership: Allowed
Encourage Conversions: Yes
Area Develop. Agreements: Yes
Sub-Franchising Contracts: No
Expand In Territory: Yes
Space Needs: NR SF; HB

SUPPORT & TRAINING PROVIDED:
Financial Assistance Provided: Yes(D)
Site Selection Assistance: Yes
Lease Negotiation Assistance: No
Co-Operative Advertising: No
Franchisee Assoc./Member: No
Size Of Corporate Staff: 3
On-Going Support: b,C,D,F,G,I
Training: 3 Days in Corporate Headquarters in Denver, CO; 3 Days at Franchisee's Residence.

SPECIFIC EXPANSION PLANS:
US: All United States
Canada: No
Overseas: No

<< >>

COLORTYME

5700 Tennyson Pkwy., # 180
Plano, TX 75024
Tel: (800) 411-8963 (972) 608-5376
Fax: (972) 403-4923
E-Mail: pat@colortyme.com
Web Site: www.colortyme.com
Mr. Pat Sumner, Dir. Franchise Development

The nation's largest rental-purchase franchise company, specializing in electronics, furniture, appliances and computers. We help our customers find what's right for them and give our franchisees the support needed to be successful, at the best profit margins in the industry.

BACKGROUND: IFA MEMBER
Established: 1979; 1st Franchised: 1981
Franchised Units: 326
Company-Owned Units 0
Total Units: 326
Dist.: US-326; CAN-0; O'seas-0
North America: 41 States
Density: 57 in TX, 18 in KS, 1 in IN
Projected New Units (12 Months): 30
Qualifications: 4, 4, 4, 3, 3, 4
Registered: CA,FL,HI,IL,IN,MD,MI,NY,ND,OR,RI,SD,VA,WA,WI,DC

FINANCIAL/TERMS:
Cash Investment: $120-160K
Total Investment: $293-517K
Minimum Net Worth: $300K
Fees: Franchise - $25K
Royalty - 4%; Ad. - $250/Mo.
Earnings Claim Statement: Yes
Term of Contract (Years): 5-10/5-10
Avg. # Of Employees: 6 FT
Passive Ownership: Allowed
Encourage Conversions: Yes
Area Develop. Agreements: Yes/5

Sub-Franchising Contracts: No
Expand In Territory: Yes
Space Needs: 3,500 SF; FS, SF, SC, RM

SUPPORT & TRAINING PROVIDED:

Financial Assistance Provided: Yes(I)
Site Selection Assistance: Yes
Lease Negotiation Assistance: Yes
Co-Operative Advertising: Yes
Franchisee Assoc./Member: Yes/No
Size Of Corporate Staff: 21
On-Going Support: B,C,D,E,F,G,H
Training: 4 Weeks Varied Training.

SPECIFIC EXPANSION PLANS:

US: All United States
Canada: No
Overseas: No

<< >>

GENT'S FORMAL WEAR

404 E. Wright St.
Pensacola, FL 32501
Tel: (850) 434-3272
Fax: (850) 439-2177
E-Mail: gentsformalwear@aol.com
Web Site: www.gentsformalwear.com
Mr. Richard Crenshaw, President

Men's formal wear, rental and sales.

BACKGROUND:

Established: 1980; 1st Franchised: 1991
Franchised Units: 2
Company-Owned Units 1
Total Units: 3
Dist.: US-3; CAN-0; O'seas-0
North America: 2 States
Density: 2 in FL, 1 in MS
Projected New Units (12 Months): 2
Qualifications: 5, 4, 3, 3, 3, 4
Registered: FL

FINANCIAL/TERMS:

Cash Investment: $50K
Total Investment: $50-75K
Minimum Net Worth: $100K
Fees: Franchise - $10K
Royalty - 6%; Ad. - 0%
Earnings Claim Statement: Yes
Term of Contract (Years): 5/5
Avg. # Of Employees: 2 FT, 1 PT
Passive Ownership: Discouraged
Encourage Conversions: Yes
Area Develop. Agreements: No
Sub-Franchising Contracts: Yes
Expand In Territory: Yes
Space Needs: 1,000 SF; FS, SC

SUPPORT & TRAINING PROVIDED:

Financial Assistance Provided: No
Site Selection Assistance: Yes
Lease Negotiation Assistance: Yes
Co-Operative Advertising: No
Franchisee Assoc./Member: Yes/Yes
Size Of Corporate Staff: 2
On-Going Support: A,B,C,d,E,F,h
Training: 2 Weeks Home Office.

SPECIFIC EXPANSION PLANS:

US: Southeast
Canada: No
Overseas: No

<< >>

Top 50

GINGISS FORMALWEAR

2101 Executive Dr.
Addison, IL 60101-1482
Tel: (800) 621-7125 (630) 620-9050
Fax: (630) 620-8840
E-Mail: gingiss@gingiss.com
Web Site: www.gingiss.com
Mr. Tom C. Ryan, VP Franchise Development

GINGISS FORMALWEAR specializes in the rental and sale of men's and boys' tuxedos and related accessories. GINGISS is the leader in the formalwear wedding industry that does not go out of style, and is the only national formalwear chain that can coordinate groomsmen from coast to coast. GINGISS manufactures its own proprietary lines of formalwear, including exclusive designers such as Oleg Cassini.

BACKGROUND: IFA MEMBER

Established: 1936; 1st Franchised: 1968
Franchised Units: 170
Company-Owned Units 85
Total Units: 255
Dist.: US-255; CAN-0; O'seas-0
North America: 33 States
Density: 41 in TX, 38 in IL, 30 in CA
Projected New Units (12 Months): 15
Qualifications: 3, 3, 3, 3, 3, 3
Registered: CA,FL,IL,IN,MD,MI,MN,NY,OR,RI,VA,WA,WI,DC

FINANCIAL/TERMS:

Cash Investment: $59-107K
Total Investment: $98.7-242.7K
Minimum Net Worth: $NR
Fees: Franchise - $15K
Royalty - 8%; Ad. - 2%
Earnings Claim Statement: Yes
Term of Contract (Years): 10/10
Avg. # Of Employees: 2 FT, 4 PT
Passive Ownership: Discouraged
Encourage Conversions: Yes
Area Develop. Agreements: Yes
Sub-Franchising Contracts: No
Expand In Territory: Yes
Space Needs: 1,100-1,200 SF; FS, SF, SC, RM

SUPPORT & TRAINING PROVIDED:

Financial Assistance Provided: Yes(I)
Site Selection Assistance: Yes
Lease Negotiation Assistance: Yes
Co-Operative Advertising: Yes
Franchisee Assoc./Member: Yes/Yes
Size Of Corporate Staff: 50
On-Going Support: B,C,D,E,F,G,H
Training: 1 Week Corporate Headquarters; 1 Week Company Operated Store; On-Going on Location.

SPECIFIC EXPANSION PLANS:

US: All US, Except West Coast
Canada: All Canada
Overseas: No

<< >>

GRAND RENTAL STATION/ TAYLOR RENTAL

203 Jandus Rd.
Cary, IL 60013-2861
Tel: (800) 833-3004 (773) 695-5310
Fax: (847) 516-9921
E-Mail: hadler@truserv.com
Web Site: www.grandrental.com
Mr. Woody Adler, Dir. National Sales

Complete equipment rental operation, specializing in light contractor, home owner and party/special occasion rentals. We provide a complete support program including market/site evaluation, store design, inventory customization, hands-on-training and on-going field and technical support.

BACKGROUND: IFA MEMBER

Established: 1910; 1st Franchised: 1985
Franchised Units: 1,250
Company-Owned Units 0
Total Units: 1,250
Dist.: US-1272; CAN-0; O'seas-0
North America: 42 States
Density: MA, PA, NY
Projected New Units (12 Months): 60
Qualifications: 4, 4, 1, 1, 2, 4
Registered: All States

FINANCIAL/TERMS:
Cash Investment: $75-150K
Total Investment: $225-250K
Minimum Net Worth: $100K
Fees: Franchise - $1.5K
Royalty - 1.3%; Ad. - $30/Mo.
Earnings Claim Statement: No
Term of Contract (Years): 10/10
Avg. # Of Employees: 3 FT, 3 PT
Passive Ownership: Discouraged
Encourage Conversions: Yes
Area Develop. Agreements: No
Sub-Franchising Contracts: No
Expand In Territory: Yes
Space Needs: 5,000 SF; FS, SC
SUPPORT & TRAINING PROVIDED:
Financial Assistance Provided: No
Site Selection Assistance: Yes
Lease Negotiation Assistance: Yes
Co-Operative Advertising: Yes
Franchisee Assoc./Member: Yes/Yes
Size Of Corporate Staff: 16
On-Going Support: B,C,D,E,F,G,H,I
Training: 1 Week in Gary, IL.
SPECIFIC EXPANSION PLANS:
US: All United States
Canada: All Canada
Overseas: All Countries

<< >>

JOE RENT ALL/LOUE TOUT

28 Vanier St.
Chateauguay, PQ J6J 3W8 CANADA
Tel: (800) 361-2070 (450) 692-6268
Fax: (450) 692-2848
E-Mail: mrjoe@videotron.ca
Web Site: www.joelouetoutrentall.ca
Mr. J. Maurice Bissonnette, President

Equipment rental in 4 different options: tools, recreational vehicles, special events, motorcycles. Full operating support, including school. Buying group with central billing. Specific insurance plans. Own computer program.

BACKGROUND:
Established: 1979; 1st Franchised: 1982
Franchised Units: 80
Company-Owned Units 0
Total Units: 80
Dist.: US-0; CAN-80; O'seas-0
North America: 4 States
Density: 63 in PQ, 12 in ON
Projected New Units (12 Months): 8
Qualifications: 4, 4, 3, 4, 2, 4
Registered: NR
FINANCIAL/TERMS:
Cash Investment: $25-65K
Total Investment: $75-500K
Minimum Net Worth: $50K
Fees: Franchise - $20K
Royalty - 4%; Ad. - 3%
Earnings Claim Statement: Yes
Term of Contract (Years): 5/5
Avg. # Of Employees: 2-6 FT
Passive Ownership: Discouraged
Encourage Conversions: Yes
Area Develop. Agreements: No
Sub-Franchising Contracts: No
Expand In Territory: Yes
Space Needs: 2,500 SF; FS, SF
SUPPORT & TRAINING PROVIDED:
Financial Assistance Provided: Yes(I)
Site Selection Assistance: No
Lease Negotiation Assistance: Yes
Co-Operative Advertising: Yes
Franchisee Assoc./Member: Yes/Yes
Size Of Corporate Staff: 5
On-Going Support: A,B,C,D,E,F,G,H,I
Training: 1 Week Office; 2 Weeks to 1 Month at Franchisee's Location.
SPECIFIC EXPANSION PLANS:
US: As Master Franchisor
Canada: All Canada
Overseas: Yes, As Master Franchisor

<< >>

NATION-WIDE GENERAL RENTAL CENTERS

5510 Hwy. 9 N.
Alpharetta, GA 30004
Tel: (800) 227-1643 (770) 664-7765
Fax: (770) 664-0052
E-Mail: office@nation-widerental.com
Web Site: www.nation-widerental.com
Mr. Ike Goodvin, President

Tool and equipment rental business (since 1976) for homeowners, party and contractors. A complete turn-key package with proven equipment. No franchise fee or royalties. A complete training program with a buy-back agreement. This may be your business opportunity - act now! See our Website.

BACKGROUND:
Established: 1976; 1st Franchised: 1976
Franchised Units: 376
Company-Owned Units 1
Total Units: 377
Dist.: US-375; CAN-0; O'seas-2
North America: 29 States
Density: NR
Projected New Units (12 Months): 18
Qualifications: 2, 1, 1, 2, 1, 5
Registered: NR
FINANCIAL/TERMS:
Cash Investment: $40-50K
Total Investment: $80-178K
Minimum Net Worth: $40-50K
Fees: Franchise - $0
Royalty - 0%; Ad. - 0%
Earnings Claim Statement: Yes
Term of Contract (Years): 3/1
Avg. # Of Employees: 1 PT
Passive Ownership: Discouraged
Encourage Conversions: No
Area Develop. Agreements: No
Sub-Franchising Contracts: No
Expand In Territory: Yes
Space Needs: 2,500 SF; FS, SF, SC
SUPPORT & TRAINING PROVIDED:
Financial Assistance Provided: Yes
Site Selection Assistance: Yes
Lease Negotiation Assistance: Yes
Co-Operative Advertising: No
Franchisee Assoc./Member: Yes/Yes
Size Of Corporate Staff: NR
On-Going Support: B,C,D,E,F,I
Training: 7 Days Atlanta, GA.
SPECIFIC EXPANSION PLANS:
US: All United States
Canada: All Canada
Overseas: No

<< >>

SUPPLEMENTAL LISTING OF FRANCHISORS

AL'S FORMAL WEAR, P.O. Box 379, Bedford, TX 76095 ; (800) 879-1777 (817) 355-4444; (817) 355-4455

PRESIDENT TUXEDO, 32185 Hollingsworth, Warren, MI 48092 ; (800) 837-TUXS (810) 264-0600; (810) 264-7119

Retail: Art, Art Supplies & Framing

Chapter

34

Retail: Art, Art Supplies & Framing Industry Profile

Total # Franchisors in Industry Group	11
Total # Franchised Units in Industry Group	684
Total # Company-Owned Units in Industry Group	31
Total # Operating Units in Industry Group	715
Average # Franchised Units/Franchisor	62.2
Average # Company-Owned Units/Franchisor	2.8
Average # Total Units/Franchisor	65.0
Ratio of Total # Franchised Units/Total # Company-Owned Units	22.1:1
Industry Survey Participants	7
Representing % of Industry	63.6%
Average Franchise Fee*:	$28.2K
Average Total Investment*:	$127.6K
Average On-Going Royalty Fee*:	5.5%

*If a range was provided, the mid-point of the range was used. See detailed profiles for actual ranges.

Five Largest Participants in Survey

Company	# Franchised Units	# Co-Owned Units	# Total Units	Franchise Fee	On-Going Royalty	Total Investment
1. Fastframe USA	204	7	211	25K	7.5%	93.5-131K
2. Deck the Walls	169	4	173	25K	6%	160-280K
3. Great Frame Up, The	119	0	119	25K	6%	108-156K
4. Color Me Mine	58	1	59	20K	5%	125-165K
5. Framing and Art Centre	53	0	53	25K	6%	110-160K

BUDGET FRAMER

4313 E. Tradewinds Ave.
Ft. Lauderdale, FL 33308
Tel: (954) 491-0129
Fax: (954) 491-0129
E-Mail: thadden@aol.com
Web Site: www.budgetframerinc.com
Ms. Terrie L. Hadden, CEO

Complete turnkey operation with low costs and low royalty. Training is located in your store, which means no traveling to the franchisor. Franchisees conduct reasonable business hours, usually in a strip center setting. They will receive continual support from the BUDGET FRAMER with site selection and lease negotiation.

BACKGROUND:
Established: 1986; 1st Franchised: 1992
Franchised Units: 18
Company-Owned Units 1
Total Units: 19
Dist.: US-26; CAN-0; O'seas-0
North America: 6 States
Density: NR
Projected New Units (12 Months): 5
Qualifications: 4, 3, 1, 5, 4, 5
Registered: FL

FINANCIAL/TERMS:
Cash Investment: $35K min.
Total Investment: $95K
Minimum Net Worth: $300K
Fees: Franchise - $30K
Royalty - 4%; Ad. - 0%
Earnings Claim Statement: No
Term of Contract (Years): 5/5
Avg. # Of Employees: 2 FT, 1 PT
Passive Ownership: Discouraged
Encourage Conversions: NR
Area Develop. Agreements: No
Sub-Franchising Contracts: No
Expand In Territory: Yes
Space Needs: 1,000-1,200 SF; SC

SUPPORT & TRAINING PROVIDED:
Financial Assistance Provided: Yes(D)
Site Selection Assistance: Yes
Lease Negotiation Assistance: Yes
Co-Operative Advertising: No
Franchisee Assoc./Member: No
Size Of Corporate Staff: 1
On-Going Support: G
Training: 5-7 Days in Your Franchise Store.

SPECIFIC EXPANSION PLANS:
US: Eastern Seaboard
Canada: No
Overseas: No

<< >>

Top 50

COLOR ME MINE

14721 Califa St.
Van Nuys, CA 91411-3107
Tel: (888) 265-6764 (818) 989-8401
Fax: (818) 780-1442
E-Mail: maria@colormemine.com
Web Site: www.colormemine.com
Mr. Mike Mooslin, Chief Executive Officer

COLOR ME MINE is the world's leader in contemporary ceramics and crafts studios. Our comprehensive training and support system includes glazing, firing and design techniques, construction marketing, accounting services and manufacturing plants to ensure consistency and supply.

BACKGROUND: IFA MEMBER
Established: 1992; 1st Franchised: 1996
Franchised Units: 58
Company-Owned Units 1
Total Units: 59
Dist.: US-49; CAN-10; O'seas-59
North America: 13 States
Density: 22 in CA, 5 in PA, 4 in NJ
Projected New Units (12 Months): 25
Qualifications: 4, 3, 2, 3, 5, 5
Registered: CA,FL,HI,IL,IN,MD,MI,MN, NY,OR,VA,WA,WI,DC,AB

FINANCIAL/TERMS:
Cash Investment: $50K
Total Investment: $125-165K
Minimum Net Worth: $150K
Fees: Franchise - $20K
Royalty - 5%; Ad. - 1%
Earnings Claim Statement: Yes
Term of Contract (Years): 5/5
Avg. # Of Employees: 2 FT, 4 PT
Passive Ownership: Discouraged
Encourage Conversions: Yes
Area Develop. Agreements: No
Sub-Franchising Contracts: No
Expand In Territory: Yes
Space Needs: 1,300-2,000 SF; SF, SC, RM, Entertainment Cent

SUPPORT & TRAINING PROVIDED:
Financial Assistance Provided: No
Site Selection Assistance: Yes
Lease Negotiation Assistance: Yes
Co-Operative Advertising: No
Franchisee Assoc./Member: Yes
Size Of Corporate Staff: 15
On-Going Support: A,B,C,D,E,F,G,H,I
Training: 2 Weeks at Home Office in Van Nuys, CA; 5-7 Days at Franchised Location.

SPECIFIC EXPANSION PLANS:
US: All United States
Canada: All Canada
Overseas: All Countries

<< >>

DECK THE WALLS

Top 50

DECK THE WALLS

100 Glenborough Dr., # 1400
Houston, TX 77067-3600
Tel: (800) 543-3325 (281) 775-5267
Fax: (281) 775-5250
E-Mail: franinfo@fcibiz.com
Web Site: www.dtwfraninfo.com
Ms. Ann Nance, Franchise Development Mgr.

DECK THE WALLS is the nation's largest specialty retailer of art, custom framing and wall décor. Each store carries a large selection of limited and open edition prints, custom frame molding and mats. Easy to learn and operate; exceptional training & support; national buying power and proven marketing programs. Stores located in high-traffic regional malls and shopping centers. Rewarding business in a growing industry.

BACKGROUND: IFA MEMBER
Established: 1979; 1st Franchised: 1981
Franchised Units: 169
Company-Owned Units 4
Total Units: 173
Dist.: US-173; CAN-0; O'seas-0
North America: 38 States
Density: 26 in TX, 15 in PA, 12 in FL
Projected New Units (12 Months): 15
Qualifications: 5, 3, 3, 3, 4, 5
Registered: CA,FL,IL,IN,MD,MI,MN,NY, ND,OR,RI,SD,VA,WA,WI

FINANCIAL/TERMS:
Cash Investment: $80K
Total Investment: $160-280K
Minimum Net Worth: $250K
Fees: Franchise - $25K

Royalty - 6%; Ad. - 2%
Earnings Claim Statement: No
Term of Contract (Years): 10/10
Avg. # Of Employees: 2 FT, 3 PT
Passive Ownership: Allowed
Encourage Conversions: Yes
Area Develop. Agreements: No
Sub-Franchising Contracts: No
Expand In Territory: Yes
Space Needs: 1,500-2,000 SF; RM, SC

SUPPORT & TRAINING PROVIDED:
Financial Assistance Provided: Yes(I)
Site Selection Assistance: Yes
Lease Negotiation Assistance: Yes
Co-Operative Advertising: Yes
Franchisee Assoc./Member: Yes/Yes
Size Of Corporate Staff: 48
On-Going Support: B,C,D,E,F,G,H,I
Training: 2 Weeks Houston, TX.

SPECIFIC EXPANSION PLANS:
US: All United States
Canada: All Canada
Overseas: All Countries

<< >>

FASTFRAME USA
1200 Lawrence Dr., # 300
Newbury Park, CA 91320-1234
Tel: (888) TO-FRAME (805) 498-4463
Fax: (805) 498-8983
E-Mail: brenda@fastframe.com
Web Site: www.fastframe.com
Ms. Brenda Hales, Franchise Development

Over the past 14 years, FASTFRAME USA has captured its share of the market with its 200+ franchises within the US, along with affiliates in Brazil, Japan and Australia. FASTFRAME has emerged as a leader in the custom picture framing industry. FASTFRAME has built it foundation and reputation by providing high-quality craftsmanship, in a variety of products, at competitive prices, with immediate turn-around capabilities while guaranteeing customer satisfaction.

BACKGROUND: IFA MEMBER
Established: 1986; 1st Franchised: 1987
Franchised Units: 204
Company-Owned Units 7
Total Units: 211
Dist.: US-203; CAN-0; O'seas-9
North America: 24 States
Density: 94 in CA, 18 in IL, 11 in GA
Projected New Units (12 Months): 30
Qualifications: 5, 4, 1, 1, 1, 5
Registered: CA,HI,IL,IN,MN,NY,VA

FINANCIAL/TERMS:
Cash Investment: $30K
Total Investment: $93.5-131K
Minimum Net Worth: $93.5K
Fees: Franchise - $25K
Royalty - 7.5%; Ad. - 3%
Earnings Claim Statement: No
Term of Contract (Years): 10/10
Avg. # Of Employees: 1 FT, 2 PT
Passive Ownership: Not Allowed
Encourage Conversions: Yes
Area Develop. Agreements: Yes/8
Sub-Franchising Contracts: Yes
Expand In Territory: Yes
Space Needs: 1,200-1,400 SF; FS, SF, SC

SUPPORT & TRAINING PROVIDED:
Financial Assistance Provided: Yes(I)
Site Selection Assistance: Yes
Lease Negotiation Assistance: Yes
Co-Operative Advertising: Yes
Franchisee Assoc./Member: Yes/Yes
Size Of Corporate Staff: 16
On-Going Support: A,b,C,D,E,F,G,H,I
Training: 2 Weeks at Corporate Headquarters; 1 Week at Franchisee Location.

SPECIFIC EXPANSION PLANS:
US: All United States
Canada: No
Overseas: All Countries

<< >>

Top 50

FRAMING & ART CENTRE
1800 Appleby Line
Burlington, ON L7L 6A1 CANADA
Tel: (905) 332-6116
Fax: (905) 335-5377
E-Mail: framing@worldchat.com
Mr. Paul Misener, Franchise Development

FRAMING & ART CENTRE is Canada's only national art & custom framing store, specializing in a hands-on, artistic environment. Each store offers a large selection of design samples, prints and posters with custom framing in a creative atmosphere. Easy to learn and operate, exceptional training and support, national buying power and proven marketing programs. Air Miles offered.

BACKGROUND: IFA MEMBER
Established: 1974; 1st Franchised: 1977
Franchised Units: 53
Company-Owned Units 0
Total Units: 53
Dist.: US-0; CAN-53; O'seas-0
North America: 5 Provinces
Density: 29 in ON, 12 in BC, 6 in AB
Projected New Units (12 Months): 5
Qualifications: 4, 3, 3, 3, 3, 5
Registered: AB

FINANCIAL/TERMS:
Cash Investment: $30K
Total Investment: $110-160K
Minimum Net Worth: $150K
Fees: Franchise - $25K
Royalty - 6%; Ad. - 1%
Earnings Claim Statement: No
Term of Contract (Years): 10/5
Avg. # Of Employees: 2 FT, 2 PT
Passive Ownership: Discouraged
Encourage Conversions: Yes
Area Develop. Agreements: Yes
Sub-Franchising Contracts: No
Expand In Territory: Yes
Space Needs: 1,000-1,200 SF; SF, SC

SUPPORT & TRAINING PROVIDED:
Financial Assistance Provided: Yes(I)
Site Selection Assistance: Yes
Lease Negotiation Assistance: Yes
Co-Operative Advertising: Yes
Franchisee Assoc./Member: No
Size Of Corporate Staff: 4
On-Going Support: A,B,C,D,E,F,G,H,I
Training: 10 Days Burlington, ON.

SPECIFIC EXPANSION PLANS:
US: No
Canada: All Canada
Overseas: No

<< >>

The Great Frame Up®
Where Picture Framing is an Art™

GREAT FRAME UP, THE
100 Glenborough Dr., # 1450
Houston, TX 77067-3600
Tel: (800) 443-3325 (281) 775-5200
Fax: (281) 872-1646
E-Mail: franinfo@fcibiz.com
Web Site: www.tgfufraninfo.com
Ms. Ann Nance, Fran. Development Dir.

THE GREAT FRAME UP is part of the world's largest retail franchisor of affordable, high-quality custom framing. Specializing in custom framing in a hands-on, artistic environment featuring wide selections of custom frame moldings & mat styles, a proprietary framing system, superior design center & more. Easy to learn & operate; exceptional training & support; national buying power & proven marketing programs. Growth industry.

BACKGROUND: IFA MEMBER
Established: 1971; 1st Franchised: 1975
Franchised Units: 119
Company-Owned Units 0
Total Units: 119
Dist.: US-119; CAN-0; O'seas-0
North America: 26 States
Density: 25 in IL, 16 in GA, 15 in CA
Projected New Units (12 Months): 12
Qualifications: 5, 3, 3, 3, 4, 5
Registered: All States

FINANCIAL/TERMS:
Cash Investment: $50K
Total Investment: $108-156K
Minimum Net Worth: $200K
Fees: Franchise - $25K
Royalty - 6%; Ad. - 2%
Earnings Claim Statement: No
Term of Contract (Years): 10/10
Avg. # Of Employees: 3 FT, 2 PT
Passive Ownership: Allowed
Encourage Conversions: Yes
Area Develop. Agreements: No
Sub-Franchising Contracts: No
Expand In Territory: Yes
Space Needs: 1,500-2,000 SF; SC

SUPPORT & TRAINING PROVIDED:
Financial Assistance Provided: Yes(I)
Site Selection Assistance: Yes
Lease Negotiation Assistance: Yes
Co-Operative Advertising: Yes
Franchisee Assoc./Member: Yes/Yes
Size Of Corporate Staff: 38
On-Going Support: B,C,D,E,F,G,H,I
Training: 2 Weeks Houston, TX.

SPECIFIC EXPANSION PLANS:
US: All United States
Canada: No
Overseas: No

<< >>

MARAD FINE ART

65 High Ridge Rd., # 409
Stamford, CT 06905
Tel: (203) 322-7666
Fax: (203) 322-7666
E-Mail: maradart@aol.com
Web Site: www.maradfineart.com
Mr. Dick Fierstein, President

MARAD FINE ART offers qualified individuals with a flair for sales and an appreciation of art the chance to operate their own commercial art business from their home or office. MARAD's product line contains over 15,000 of the world's best-loved art reproductions in quality, custom frames at the same low price for each piece. Comprehensive sales training, exclusive territories and a turn-key ordering/fulfillment system allow for easy start-up and operational efficiency - little overhead/no inventory.

BACKGROUND:
Established: 1938; 1st Franchised: 2002
Franchised Units: 0
Company-Owned Units 1
Total Units: 1
Dist.: US-1; CAN-0; O'seas-0
North America: 1 State
Density: 1 in CT
Projected New Units (12 Months): 4
Qualifications: 3, 4, 2, 2, 3, 4
Registered: FL

FINANCIAL/TERMS:
Cash Investment: $NR
Total Investment: $39-69K
Minimum Net Worth: $NR
Fees: Franchise - $35-60K
Royalty - 4%; Ad. - 2%
Earnings Claim Statement: Yes
Term of Contract (Years): 10/5
Avg. # Of Employees: 1 FT
Passive Ownership: Not Allowed
Encourage Conversions: N/A
Area Develop. Agreements: No
Sub-Franchising Contracts: No
Expand In Territory: Yes
Space Needs: N/A SF; HB

SUPPORT & TRAINING PROVIDED:
Financial Assistance Provided: Yes(I)
Site Selection Assistance: N/A
Lease Negotiation Assistance: N/A
Co-Operative Advertising: No
Franchisee Assoc./Member: No
Size Of Corporate Staff: 1
On-Going Support: C,D,G
Training: 1 Day Stamford CT; 1 Day Hauppage, NY.

SPECIFIC EXPANSION PLANS:
US: All United States
Canada: No
Overseas: No

<< >>

SUPPLEMENTAL LISTING OF FRANCHISORS

FRAME & SAVE, 27 Spiral Dr., Florence, KY 41042 ; (800) 543-5464 (606) 647-4400; (606) 647-4405

KENNEDY STUDIOS, 140 Tremont St., Boston, MA 02111 ; (800) 448-0027 (617) 542-0868; (617) 695-0957

Retail: Athletic Wear/Sporting Goods

Chapter 35

Retail: Athletic Wear/Sporting Goods Industry Profile

Total # Franchisors in Industry Group	17
Total # Franchised Units in Industry Group	1,753
Total # Company-Owned Units in Industry Group	243
Total # Operating Units in Industry Group	1,996
Average # Franchised Units/Franchisor	103.1
Average # Company-Owned Units/Franchisor	14.3
Average # Total Units/Franchisor	117.4
Ratio of Total # Franchised Units/Total # Company-Owned Units	7.2:1
Industry Survey Participants	13
Representing % of Industry	76.5%
Average Franchise Fee*:	$31.4K
Average Total Investment*:	$256.0K
Average On-Going Royalty Fee*:	11.3%

*If a range was provided, the mid-point of the range was used. See detailed profiles for actual ranges.

Five Largest Participants in Survey

Company	# Franchised Units	# Co-Owned Units	# Total Units	Franchise Fee	On-Going Royalty	Total Investment
1. Athlete's Foot, The	521	185	706	35K	5%	200-650K
2. Play It Again Sports	557	1	558	25K	5%	170-205K
3. Pro Golf of America	148	1	149	49.5K	2.5%	400-600K
4. Golf USA	96	4	100	34-44K	2%	196-350K
5. International Golf	64	6	70	42K	2%	250-300K

All of the data provided are proprietary and should not be quoted without acknowledging *Bond's Franchise Guide.*

A. J. BARNES BICYCLE EMPORIUM

1401 Johnson Ferry Rd., # 148
Marietta, GA 30062
Tel: (770) 977-7426
Fax: (770) 977-7237
E-Mail: ajb@ajbarnes.com
Web Site: www.ajbarnes.com
Mr. Rob Richey, Dir. Franchise Sales

A. J. BARNES BICYCLE EMPORIUM is a full-service bicycle retail franchise chain with a fun, old-fashioned theme. Featuring major brands and an innovative open-kitchen-style service area so customers can actually watch their bicycle being serviced. A. J. BARNES is the premium-quality bicycle retail franchise, offering top-flite business operations training and on-going support from a highly-experienced management team with years of franchise operation.

BACKGROUND:
Established: 1989; 1st Franchised: 1992
Franchised Units: 34
Company-Owned Units 0
Total Units: 34
Dist.: US-34; CAN-0; O'seas-0
North America: 3 States
Density: 11 in FL, 2 in GA, 1 in TN
Projected New Units (12 Months): 20
Qualifications: 3, 3, 1, 1, 1, 5
Registered: FL

FINANCIAL/TERMS:
Cash Investment: $40K
Total Investment: $100-115K
Minimum Net Worth: $100K
Fees: Franchise - $25K
Royalty - 6%; Ad. - 0%
Earnings Claim Statement: No
Term of Contract (Years): 10/10
Avg. # Of Employees: 2 FT, 1 PT
Passive Ownership: Allowed
Encourage Conversions: No
Area Develop. Agreements: Yes/10
Sub-Franchising Contracts: No
Expand In Territory: Yes
Space Needs: 2,000 SF; SC

SUPPORT & TRAINING PROVIDED:
Financial Assistance Provided: Yes(I)
Site Selection Assistance: Yes
Lease Negotiation Assistance: Yes
Co-Operative Advertising: Yes
Franchisee Assoc./Member: Yes/Yes
Size Of Corporate Staff: 5
On-Going Support: A,C,D,E,F,G,H,I
Training: 14 Days Total at West Palm Beach, FL; 3 Days on Location.

SPECIFIC EXPANSION PLANS:
US: All United States
Canada: No
Overseas: Western Europe

<< >>

ATHLETE'S FOOT, THE

1950 Vaughn Rd.
Kennesaw, GA 30144
Tel: (800) 524-6444 (770) 514-4523
Fax: (770) 514-4843
E-Mail: pfranetovich@theathletesfoot.com
Web Site: www.theathletesfoot.com
Mr. Peter Franetovich, Director Franchise Sales

THE ATHLETE'S FOOT, with more than 700 stores in 45 countries, is the leading international franchisor of name-brand athletic footwear. As a franchisee, you will benefit from headquarters' support, including training, advertising, product selection, special vendor discount programs, continual footwear research at our exclusive-wear test center and much more.

BACKGROUND: IFA MEMBER
Established: 1971; 1st Franchised: 1972
Franchised Units: 521
Company-Owned Units 185
Total Units: 706
Dist.: US-371; CAN-2; O'seas-333
North America: 47 States, 1 Province
Density: NR
Projected New Units (12 Months): 120
Qualifications: 4, 5, 3, 3, 2, 5
Registered: All States

FINANCIAL/TERMS:
Cash Investment: $75-125K
Total Investment: $200-650K
Minimum Net Worth: $400K
Fees: Franchise - $35K
Royalty - 5%; Ad. - 0.6%
Earnings Claim Statement: No
Term of Contract (Years): 10/5
Avg. # Of Employees: 2 FT, 6 PT
Passive Ownership: Discouraged
Encourage Conversions: Yes
Area Develop. Agreements: Yes/10
Sub-Franchising Contracts: Yes
Expand In Territory: Yes
Space Needs: 1,200 SF; FS, SF, SC, RM

SUPPORT & TRAINING PROVIDED:
Financial Assistance Provided: Yes(I)
Site Selection Assistance: Yes
Lease Negotiation Assistance: Yes
Co-Operative Advertising: No
Franchisee Assoc./Member: Yes/Yes
Size Of Corporate Staff: 180
On-Going Support: B,C,D,E,f,G,H,I
Training: 1 Wek at Headquarters in Atlanta; 1 Wk. Prior to and during Opening on Location; On-Going.

SPECIFIC EXPANSION PLANS:
US: All United States
Canada: All Canada
Overseas: All Countries

EMPOWERED WOMEN'S GOLF SHOPS

5344 Belt Line Rd.
Dallas, TX 75240-2216
Tel: (800) 533-7309 (972) 253-8807
Fax: (972) 233-9079
E-Mail: empowrdgolf@earthlink.net
Web Site: www.empoweredgolf.com
Mr. Barry Dixon, VP Operations

Golf retailer for women only.

BACKGROUND:
Established: 1993; 1st Franchised: 1997
Franchised Units: 7
Company-Owned Units 1
Total Units: 8
Dist.: US-6; CAN-0; O'seas-0
North America: 5 States
Density: 2 in TX, 1 in AR, 1 in NV
Projected New Units (12 Months): 4
Qualifications: 5, 5, 1, 3, 3, 5
Registered: CA,FL

FINANCIAL/TERMS:
Cash Investment: $100-200K
Total Investment: $350-450K
Minimum Net Worth: $500K
Fees: Franchise - $25K
Royalty - 3%; Ad. - 1%
Earnings Claim Statement: No
Term of Contract (Years): 5/10
Avg. # Of Employees: 2 FT, 1 PT
Passive Ownership: Allowed
Encourage Conversions: N/A
Area Develop. Agreements: Yes/10
Sub-Franchising Contracts: No
Expand In Territory: Yes
Space Needs: 2,800 SF; SC

SUPPORT & TRAINING PROVIDED:
Financial Assistance Provided: N/A
Site Selection Assistance: Yes
Lease Negotiation Assistance: Yes
Co-Operative Advertising: Yes
Franchisee Assoc./Member: Yes
Size Of Corporate Staff: 3
On-Going Support: C,D,e,F,g
Training: 2 Weeks in Dallas, TX.
SPECIFIC EXPANSION PLANS:
US: All United States
Canada: No
Overseas: No

<< >>

FIELD OF DREAMS
5017 Hiatas Rd.
Sunrise, FL 33351
Tel: (800) 749-7529 (954) 749-8544
Fax: (954) 742-7044
Ms. Dawna Dunn Olarte

FIELD OF DREAMS, the ultimate sports and celebrity gift store.

BACKGROUND:
Established: 1990; 1st Franchised: 1991
Franchised Units: 38
Company-Owned Units 0
Total Units: 38
Dist.: US-23; CAN-1; O'seas-1
North America: 18 States
Density: 3 in GA, 3 in CA, 2 in TX
Projected New Units (12 Months): 10
Qualifications: 5, 4, 5, 4, 5, 5
Registered: CA,FL,MI,OR
FINANCIAL/TERMS:
Cash Investment: $60-245K
Total Investment: $160-225K
Minimum Net Worth: $150K
Fees: Franchise - $32.5K
Royalty - 6%; Ad. - 3%
Earnings Claim Statement: No
Term of Contract (Years): Lease
Avg. # Of Employees: 1 FT, 2 PT
Passive Ownership: Discouraged
Encourage Conversions: N/A
Area Develop. Agreements: Yes
Sub-Franchising Contracts: No
Expand In Territory: Yes
Space Needs: 900-1,400 SF; RM
SUPPORT & TRAINING PROVIDED:
Financial Assistance Provided: Yes(I)
Site Selection Assistance: Yes
Lease Negotiation Assistance: Yes
Co-Operative Advertising: Yes
Franchisee Assoc./Member: No
Size Of Corporate Staff: 9
On-Going Support: C,D,E,h,I
Training: 10 Days Orlando, FL.
SPECIFIC EXPANSION PLANS:
US: All United States
Canada: All Canada
Overseas: All Countries

<< >>

GOLF ETC. OF AMERICA
2201 Commercial Ln.
Granbury, TX 76048
Tel: (800) 806-8633 (817) 279-7888
Fax: (817) 279-9882
E-Mail: sales@golfetc.com
Web Site: www.golfetc.com
Mr. Don Willingham, Dir. Franchise Development

Total turn-key golf pro shop franchise. Retail center for golf equipment, accessories, gift items and furniture. Service center built inside for precision custom fitting and repair of golf clubs. Exciting and fun sports and entertainment industry.

BACKGROUND:
Established: 1992; 1st Franchised: 1996
Franchised Units: 57
Company-Owned Units 1
Total Units: 58
Dist.: US-30; CAN-0; O'seas-0
North America: 28 States
Density: 15 in TX, 10 in FL, 5 in LA
Projected New Units (12 Months): 24
Registered: NR
FINANCIAL/TERMS:
Cash Investment: $50-60K
Total Investment: $200K+
Minimum Net Worth: $130-145K
Fees: Franchise - $NR
Royalty - Call; Ad. - N/A
Earnings Claim Statement: No
Term of Contract (Years): NR
Avg. # Of Employees: 1 FT, 2 PT
Passive Ownership: Allowed
Encourage Conversions: NR
Area Develop. Agreements: NR
Sub-Franchising Contracts: No
Expand In Territory: NR
Space Needs: 3,000 SF; SF, SC, RM
SUPPORT & TRAINING PROVIDED:
Financial Assistance Provided: NR
Site Selection Assistance: Yes
Lease Negotiation Assistance: Yes
Co-Operative Advertising: No
Franchisee Assoc./Member: No
Size Of Corporate Staff: 11
On-Going Support: b,D,E,G,H,I
Training: 1 Week Granbury, TX.
SPECIFIC EXPANSION PLANS:
US: All United States
Canada: NR
Overseas: NR

<< >>

GOLF USA
3705 W. Memorial Rd., # 801
Oklahoma City, OK 73134
Tel: (800) 488-1107 (405) 751-0015
Fax: (405) 755-0065
E-Mail: franchise@gusahq.com
Web Site: www.golfusa.com
Mr. Rick Benson, VP Franchising

Discount golf retail stores, complete with name-brand, pro-line equipment, apparel and accessories. Indoor driving range/ swing analyzer.

BACKGROUND: IFA MEMBER
Established: 1986; 1st Franchised: 1989
Franchised Units: 96
Company-Owned Units 4
Total Units: 100
Dist.: US-81; CAN-5; O'seas-14
North America: 33 States, 3 Provinces
Density: 7 in TX, 7 in NC, 5 in KS
Projected New Units (12 Months): 12
Qualifications: 4, 5, 2, 2, 2, 3
Registered: CA,FL,HI,IL,IN,MD,MI,MN, NY,OR,RI,SD,VA,WA,WI
FINANCIAL/TERMS:
Cash Investment: $50-100K
Total Investment: $196-350K
Minimum Net Worth: $100K
Fees: Franchise - $34-44K
Royalty - 2%; Ad. - 1%
Earnings Claim Statement: No
Term of Contract (Years): 20/20

Avg. # Of Employees: 2 FT, 1 PT
Passive Ownership: Discouraged
Encourage Conversions: Yes
Area Develop. Agreements: Yes/4
Sub-Franchising Contracts: Yes
Expand In Territory: Yes
Space Needs: 2,500-4,500 SF; FS, SF, SC

SUPPORT & TRAINING PROVIDED:
Financial Assistance Provided: No
Site Selection Assistance: Yes
Lease Negotiation Assistance: Yes
Co-Operative Advertising: Yes
Franchisee Assoc./Member: Yes
Size Of Corporate Staff: 15
On-Going Support: A,B,C,D,E,F,G,H,I
Training: 2 Weeks Oklahoma City, OK; 5 Days at New Location.

SPECIFIC EXPANSION PLANS:
US: All United States
Canada: All Canada
Overseas: All Countries

INTERNATIONAL GOLF

9101 N. Thornydale Rd.
Tucson, AZ 85742
Tel: (800) 204-2600 (520) 744-1840
Fax: (520) 744-2076
Ms. Sheila J. White, Franchise Director

Off-course retail golf store, with complete selection of golf and golf-related merchandise, possibly complementing tennis or ski merchandise.

BACKGROUND:
Established: 1976; 1st Franchised: 1981
Franchised Units: 64
Company-Owned Units 6
Total Units: 70
Dist.: US-70; CAN-0; O'seas-0
North America: 17 States
Density: 12 in MI, 6 in OK, 6 in CA
Projected New Units (12 Months): 5
Qualifications: 4, 4, 3, 3, , 4
Registered: All States

FINANCIAL/TERMS:
Cash Investment: $125-150K
Total Investment: $250-300K
Minimum Net Worth: $NR
Fees: Franchise - $42K
Royalty - 2%; Ad. - 0%
Earnings Claim Statement: Yes
Term of Contract (Years): 15/15
Avg. # Of Employees: 2-3 FT, 2-3 PT
Passive Ownership: Discouraged
Encourage Conversions: Yes
Area Develop. Agreements: No
Sub-Franchising Contracts: No
Expand In Territory: Yes
Space Needs: 3,500 SF; FS, SF, SC

SUPPORT & TRAINING PROVIDED:
Financial Assistance Provided: Yes(I)
Site Selection Assistance: Yes
Lease Negotiation Assistance: Yes
Co-Operative Advertising: Yes
Franchisee Assoc./Member: No
Size Of Corporate Staff: 15
On-Going Support: A,B,C,D,E,F,G,h,I
Training: 10-14 Days Oklahoma City, OK; 7 Days On-Site.

SPECIFIC EXPANSION PLANS:
US: All United States
Canada: All Canada
Overseas: All Countries

<< >>

PLAY IT AGAIN SPORTS

4200 Dahlberg Dr., # 100
Minneapolis, MN 55422
Tel: (800) 592-8047 (763) 520-8480
Fax: (763) 520-85011
Web Site: www.playitagainsports.com
Mr. Jim Wellman, Franchise Development

Our retail stores blend the sale of used and new, name-brand sports equipment along with promoting trade-in discounts. This sales mix creates ultra-high value for the customer while providing significantly higher gross profit margins than traditional retailers.

BACKGROUND: IFA MEMBER
Established: 1983; 1st Franchised: 1988
Franchised Units: 557
Company-Owned Units 1
Total Units: 558
Dist.: US-623; CAN-69; O'seas-1
North America: 50 States,10 Provinces
Density: 67 in CA, 38 in ON, 34 in MI
Projected New Units (12 Months): 35
Qualifications: 5, 3, 2, 1, 1, 5
Registered: All States

FINANCIAL/TERMS:
Cash Investment: $60-70K
Total Investment: $170-205K
Minimum Net Worth: $225K
Fees: Franchise - $25K
Royalty - 5%; Ad. - 5%
Earnings Claim Statement: Yes
Term of Contract (Years): 10/10
Avg. # Of Employees: 3 FT, 2 PT
Passive Ownership: Discouraged
Encourage Conversions: Yes
Area Develop. Agreements: No
Sub-Franchising Contracts: No
Expand In Territory: Yes
Space Needs: 2,500-3,000 SF; FS, SC

SUPPORT & TRAINING PROVIDED:
Financial Assistance Provided: Yes(I)
Site Selection Assistance: Yes
Lease Negotiation Assistance: Yes
Co-Operative Advertising: Yes
Franchisee Assoc./Member: NR
Size Of Corporate Staff: 283
On-Going Support: B,C,D,E,F,G,H,I
Training: 2 1/2 Days Minneapolis, MN; 2 1/2 Days Minneapolis, M; 5 Days Minneapolis, MN.

SPECIFIC EXPANSION PLANS:
US: All United States
Canada: All Canada
Overseas: No

<< >>

PRO GOLF OF AMERICA

32751 Middlebelt Rd.
Farmington Hills, MI 48334-1726
Tel: (800) 521-6388 (248) 737-0553
Fax: (248) 737-9077
E-Mail: drose@progolfamerica.com
Web Site: www.progolf-discount.com
Mr. Don Rose, VP Operations

PRO GOLF offers the best opportunity to make money among the golf franchise stores available today. We have the best training, the largest selection of private label and exclusive products to sell and the best name - PRO GOLF. Come visit PRO GOLF and learn how a successful retail golf store should operate.

BACKGROUND: IFA MEMBER
Established: 1962; 1st Franchised: 1974
Franchised Units: 148
Company-Owned Units 1
Total Units: 149

Dist.: US-122; CAN-22; O'seas-4
North America: 30 States, 4 Provinces
Density: 13 in MI, 12 in CA, 9 in FL
Projected New Units (12 Months): 20
Qualifications: 5, 4, 3, 4, , 5
Registered: All States

FINANCIAL/TERMS:

Cash Investment: $200-350K
Total Investment: $400-600K
Minimum Net Worth: $450K
Fees: Franchise - $49.5K
Royalty - 2.5%; Ad. - 0%
Earnings Claim Statement: No
Term of Contract (Years): 15/10
Avg. # Of Employees: 4 FT, 3 PT
Passive Ownership: Discouraged
Encourage Conversions: Yes
Area Develop. Agreements: Yes/Negot.
Sub-Franchising Contracts: No
Expand In Territory: Yes
Space Needs: 4,000-6,000 SF; FS, SC

SUPPORT & TRAINING PROVIDED:

Financial Assistance Provided: Yes(I)
Site Selection Assistance: Yes
Lease Negotiation Assistance: Yes
Co-Operative Advertising: Yes
Franchisee Assoc./Member: No
Size Of Corporate Staff: 15
On-Going Support: B,C,D,E,F,G,H,I
Training: 8-12 Days at the Corporate Office in MI; 4-6 Days at Your Location.

SPECIFIC EXPANSION PLANS:

US: All United States
Canada: All Canada
Overseas: All That Have Golfers

SOCCER POST INTERNATIONAL

111 Melrose Dr.
New Rochelle, NY 10804
Tel: (914) 235-9161
Fax: (914) 636-8434
E-Mail: soccerpost@msn.com
Web Site: www.soccerpost.com
Mr. Jerome L. Kellert, President/CEO

A soccer specialty retail business, featuring top-of-the-line, cutting-edge soccer equipment from Adidas, Nike, Reebok, Xara, etc. Owner of store will become the center of soccer activity in the communities they serve. Must be soccer savvy!

BACKGROUND:

Established: 1978; 1st Franchised: 1991
Franchised Units: 25
Company-Owned Units 7
Total Units: 32
Dist.: US-32; CAN-0; O'seas-0
North America: NR
Density: 8 in PA 7 in NJ, 2 in IL
Projected New Units (12 Months): 12
Qualifications: 5, 3, 1, 3, 4, 5
Registered: CA,FL,IL,IN,MD.MI,NY, RI,WA

FINANCIAL/TERMS:

Cash Investment: $190-250K
Total Investment: $190-250K
Minimum Net Worth: $300K
Fees: Franchise - $19.5K
Royalty - 3-5%; Ad. - 1.5-3%
Earnings Claim Statement: Yes
Term of Contract (Years): 5/5
Avg. # Of Employees: 1 FT, 2-4 PT
Passive Ownership: Allowed
Encourage Conversions: Yes
Area Develop. Agreements: Yes/10
Sub-Franchising Contracts: Yes
Expand In Territory: Yes
Space Needs: 3,200 SF; SC

SUPPORT & TRAINING PROVIDED:

Financial Assistance Provided: Yes
Site Selection Assistance: Yes
Lease Negotiation Assistance: Yes
Co-Operative Advertising: Yes
Franchisee Assoc./Member: No
Size Of Corporate Staff: 9
On-Going Support: C,D,E,F,G,h,I
Training: 2 Weeks Plus Store, Voorhees, NJ.

SPECIFIC EXPANSION PLANS:

US: All United States
Canada: No
Overseas: No

<< >>

SPORT SHOE, THE

1770 Corporate Dr., # 500
Norcross, GA 30093
Tel: (800) 944-7463 (770) 279-7494
Fax: (770) 279-7180
E-Mail: franchise@thesportshoe.com
Web Site: www.thesportshoe.com
Mrs. Jan Judd, Dir. Franchising

For over 25 years, THE SPORT SHOE has been one of America's premier athletic shoe stores and sports-related activewear. THE SPORT SHOE offers continuing professional support, including site selection, lease negotiation, in-store operation and product knowledge, marketing and merchandising assistance, in-store set up and grand opening assistance.

BACKGROUND: IFA MEMBER

Established: 1974; 1st Franchised: 1989
Franchised Units: 7
Company-Owned Units 25
Total Units: 32
Dist.: US-32; CAN-0; O'seas-0
North America: 4 States
Density: 4 in GA, 1 in NC, 1 in AL
Projected New Units (12 Months): 6
Qualifications: 5, 5, 4, 4, 4, 4
Registered: FL,IN,MI

FINANCIAL/TERMS:

Cash Investment: $150K
Total Investment: $300K+
Minimum Net Worth: $300K
Fees: Franchise - $25K
Royalty - 4%; Ad. - N/A
Earnings Claim Statement: No
Term of Contract (Years): 10/5/5
Avg. # Of Employees: 2-4 FT, 6-8 PT
Passive Ownership: Allowed
Encourage Conversions: Yes
Area Develop. Agreements: Yes
Sub-Franchising Contracts: No
Expand In Territory: Yes
Space Needs: 3,000 SF; FS, SC

SUPPORT & TRAINING PROVIDED:

Financial Assistance Provided: No
Site Selection Assistance: Yes
Lease Negotiation Assistance: Yes
Co-Operative Advertising: Yes
Franchisee Assoc./Member: No
Size Of Corporate Staff: 60
On-Going Support: C,D,E,H,I
Training: 6-8 Weeks Corporate Office and Store.

SPECIFIC EXPANSION PLANS:

US: All United States
Canada: No
Overseas: No

<< >>

STROKES GOLF INTERNATIONAL

3223 Crow Canyon Rd., # 240
San Ramon, CA 94583
Tel: (888) 847-9792 (925) 355-1152
Fax: (925) 355-1153
E-Mail: doug@strokesgolf.com
Web Site: www.strokesgolf.com
Mr. Douglas T. Perkins, VP Franchise Licensing

Retail pro golf store with golf accessories and branded golf clothing line. An emphasis on selling PGA certified lessons and custom fitted quality golf clubs the average golfer can afford. Strokes has a lifetime guarantee for its clubs and uses a video capture swing-analysis system with the lessons.

BACKGROUND:
Established: 2000; 1st Franchised: 2000
Franchised Units: 10
Company-Owned Units 0
Total Units: 10
Dist.: US-7; CAN-0; O'seas-0
North America: 2 States
Density: 2 in CA
Projected New Units (12 Months): NR
Registered: NR

FINANCIAL/TERMS:
Cash Investment: $35-40K
Total Investment: $72-122K
Minimum Net Worth: $N/A
Fees: Franchise - $37.5K
Royalty - $90/week; Ad. - NR
Earnings Claim Statement: No
Term of Contract (Years): 10/5
Avg. # Of Employees: 1 FT
Passive Ownership: Allowed
Encourage Conversions: NR
Area Develop. Agreements: No
Sub-Franchising Contracts: No
Expand In Territory: Yes
Space Needs: 1200-1500 SF; SC

SUPPORT & TRAINING PROVIDED:
Financial Assistance Provided: NR
Site Selection Assistance: Yes
Lease Negotiation Assistance: Yes
Co-Operative Advertising: Yes
Franchisee Assoc./Member: Yes/No
Size Of Corporate Staff: 10
On-Going Support: A,B,C,D,E,F,G,H,I
Training: 5 Days in San Ramon, CA.

SPECIFIC EXPANSION PLANS:
US: All United States
Canada: NR
Overseas: NR

<< >>

WORLD CLASS ATHLETE
1814 Franklin St., # 820
Oakland, CA 94612
Tel: (510) 839-5462
Fax: (510) 839-2104
Mr. Jeffe Y. Merkin, President

WORLD CLASS ATHLETE offers a unique, specialty sporting goods concept. Product mix concentrates on athletic footwear, running, tennis and swimwear. Emphasis on race sponsorship, training programs and custom fitting. All major lines of footwear, accessories, warm-up suits and bags. Custom re-soling at Company-owned distribution centers. Founded by world class athlete Jeff Bond.

BACKGROUND:
Established: 1976; 1st Franchised: 1977
Franchised Units: 33
Company-Owned Units 4
Total Units: 37
Dist.: US-79; CAN-9; O'seas-4
North America: 15 States, 2 Provinces
Density: 25 in CA, 8 in WA, 7 in KY
Projected New Units (12 Months): 14
Qualifications: 3, 5, 4, 2, 3, 5
Registered: CA,FL,HI,IL,MN,MI,NY,OR, WA,WI,AB

FINANCIAL/TERMS:
Cash Investment: $90K
Total Investment: $150K
Minimum Net Worth: $250K
Fees: Franchise - $22K
Royalty - 6%; Ad. - 2%
Earnings Claim Statement: Yes
Term of Contract (Years): 15/15
Avg. # Of Employees: 2 FT, 4 PT
Passive Ownership: Not Allowed
Encourage Conversions: Yes
Area Develop. Agreements: Yes/15
Sub-Franchising Contracts: Yes
Expand In Territory: No
Space Needs: 1,800-2,200 SF; FS, SC, RM

SUPPORT & TRAINING PROVIDED:
Financial Assistance Provided: Yes(D)
Site Selection Assistance: Yes
Lease Negotiation Assistance: Yes
Co-Operative Advertising: Yes
Franchisee Assoc./Member: No
Size Of Corporate Staff: 12
On-Going Support: a,B,C,D,E,f,G,G,I
Training: 3 Weeks Headquarters; 2 Weeks On-Site; On-Going.

SPECIFIC EXPANSION PLANS:
US: All United States
Canada: All Canada
Overseas: Europe, U.K., Australia, New Zealand

SUPPLEMENTAL LISTING OF FRANCHISORS

FAN-A-MANIA SPORTS AND ENTERTAINMENT, 1393 W. 9000 St., # 250, West Jordan, UT 94088 ; (801) 253-7798; (801) 253-0931

GOLF AUGUSTA PRO SHOPS, 217 Bobby Jones Expwy., Augusta, GA 30907 (800) GOLF-051 (706) 863-9905; (706) 863-9909

OTTAWA ALGONQUIN TRAVEL, 657 Bronson Ave., Ottawa, ON K1S 4E7 CANADA; (800) 668-1743 (613) 233-7713; (613) 233-7805

SPORTS TRADERS, 508 Discovery St., Victoria, BC V8T 1G8 CANADA; (800) 792-3111 (250) 383-6443; (250) 383-2853

Retail: Clothing/Shoes/Accessories

Chapter **36**

Retail: Clothing/Shoes/Accessories Industry Profile

Total # Franchisors in Industry Group	6
Total # Franchised Units in Industry Group	105
Total # Company-Owned Units in Industry Group	113
Total # Operating Units in Industry Group	218
Average # Franchised Units/Franchisor	17.5
Average # Company-Owned Units/Franchisor	18.8
Average # Total Units/Franchisor	36.3
Ratio of Total # Franchised Units/Total # Company-Owned Units	0.9:1
Industry Survey Participants	3
Representing % of Industry	50.0%
Average Franchise Fee*:	$21.7K
Average Total Investment*:	$104.5K
Average On-Going Royalty Fee*:	5.7%

*If a range was provided, the mid-point of the range was used. See detailed profiles for actual ranges.

Three Largest Participants in Survey

Company	# Franchised Units	# Co-Owned Units	# Total Units	Franchise Fee	On-Going Royalty	Total Investment
1. Panda Shoes	41	5	46	25K	4%	80-125K
2. Mainstream Fashions	4	15	19	15K	8%	31.5-40.3K
3. Educational Outfitters	2	1	3	25K	5%	175K

All of the data provided are proprietary and should not be quoted without acknowledging *Bond's Franchise Guide.*

EDUCATIONAL OUTFITTERS

8002 E. Brainerd Rd.
Chattanooga, TN 37421
Tel: (877) 814-1222 (423) 894-1222
Fax: (423) 894-9222
E-Mail: info@eschoolclothes.com
Web Site: www.eschoolclothes.com
Mr. Brian Elrod, President

A new franchise that sells school uniforms and school dress-code apparel to parents of students who attend private, parochial, Christian and public schools. A booming market, low competition, vendor relationships with preferred pricing and credit terms, great potential returns, exclusive territories and extensive training

BACKGROUND:
Established: 1998; 1st Franchised: 2000
Franchised Units: 2
Company-Owned Units 1
Total Units: 3
Dist.: US-21; CAN-0; O'seas-0
North America: NR
Density: NR
Projected New Units (12 Months): 5
Qualifications: 3, 3, 1, 2, 3, 3
Registered: FL
FINANCIAL/TERMS:
Cash Investment: $75K
Total Investment: $175K
Minimum Net Worth: $300K
Fees: Franchise - $25K
Royalty - 5%; Ad. - 3%
Earnings Claim Statement: No
Term of Contract (Years): 10/5
Avg. # Of Employees: 3 PT
Passive Ownership: Not Allowed
Encourage Conversions: No
Area Develop. Agreements: No
Sub-Franchising Contracts: No
Expand In Territory: Yes
Space Needs: 2,000 SF; SF, SC
SUPPORT & TRAINING PROVIDED:
Financial Assistance Provided: No
Site Selection Assistance: Yes
Lease Negotiation Assistance: Yes
Co-Operative Advertising: Yes
Franchisee Assoc./Member: No
Size Of Corporate Staff: 2
On-Going Support: C,D,E,f,G,H,I
Training: 6 Days in Chattanooga, TN; 6 Days On-Site.
SPECIFIC EXPANSION PLANS:
US: SE and SW
Canada: No
Overseas: No

<< >>

MAINSTREAM FASHIONS

13877 Elkhart Rd.
Apple Valley, MN 55124
Tel: (612) 423-6254
Fax: (612) 322-3013
E-Mail: FashLady@aol.com
Web Site: www.mainstreamfashions.com
Mr. Nick DeNicola, VP Franchise Development

MAINSTREAM FASHIONS is a home-based business which markets contemporary women's and children's clothing through home and office shows. We're looking for entrepreneur-minded individuals with some business experience and a passion for fashion. Must be motivated to succeed in a fun, flexible and rewarding business environment.

BACKGROUND: IFA MEMBER
Established: 1991; 1st Franchised: 1998
Franchised Units: 4
Company-Owned Units 15
Total Units: 19
Dist.: US-19; CAN-0; O'seas-0
North America: 4 States
Density: 15 in MN, 2 in IA, 1 in WI
Projected New Units (12 Months): NR
Registered: NR
FINANCIAL/TERMS:
Cash Investment: $31.5-40.3K
Total Investment: $31.5-40.3K
Minimum Net Worth: $40K
Fees: Franchise - $15K
Royalty - 8%; Ad. - 0-2%
Earnings Claim Statement: Yes
Term of Contract (Years): 10/10
Avg. # Of Employees: 1 FT
Passive Ownership: Discouraged
Encourage Conversions: NR
Area Develop. Agreements: No
Sub-Franchising Contracts: No
Expand In Territory: Yes
Space Needs: N/A SF; HB
SUPPORT & TRAINING PROVIDED:
Financial Assistance Provided: NR
Site Selection Assistance: N/A
Lease Negotiation Assistance: N/A
Co-Operative Advertising: N/A
Franchisee Assoc./Member: No
Size Of Corporate Staff: 3
On-Going Support: B,C,D,E,G,H
Training: Approximately 3 Days Apple Valley, MN; 2-3 Days in Territory.
SPECIFIC EXPANSION PLANS:
US: Most States
Canada: NR
Overseas: NR

<< >>

PANDA SHOES

305 Marc Aurele Fortin Blvd.
Laval, PQ H7L 2A3 CANADA
Tel: (450) 622-4833
Fax: (450) 622-2939
E-Mail: info@pandashoes.com
Web Site: www.pandashoes.com
Ms. Linda Goulet, President

Children's shoe specialist - locations in major malls across Canada - 62 stores. Complete training program, including selling, merchandising, administration, etc. National advertising. Best selection of footwear for kids.

BACKGROUND:
Established: 1972; 1st Franchised: 1974
Franchised Units: 41
Company-Owned Units 5
Total Units: 46
Dist.: US-0; CAN-62; O'seas-0
North America: 6 Provinces
Density: 38 in PQ, 12 in ON, 9 in BC
Projected New Units (12 Months): 2
Registered: NR
FINANCIAL/TERMS:
Cash Investment: $60K
Total Investment: $80-125K
Minimum Net Worth: $NR
Fees: Franchise - $25K
Royalty - 4%; Ad. - 0.5%
Earnings Claim Statement: No
Term of Contract (Years): 5/Lease
Avg. # Of Employees: 3 FT, 2 PT
Passive Ownership: Discouraged
Encourage Conversions: Yes
Area Develop. Agreements: No
Sub-Franchising Contracts: No
Expand In Territory: Yes
Space Needs: 800 SF; RM
SUPPORT & TRAINING PROVIDED:
Financial Assistance Provided: No
Site Selection Assistance: Yes
Lease Negotiation Assistance: Yes
Co-Operative Advertising: Yes
Franchisee Assoc./Member: NR

Size Of Corporate Staff: 8
On-Going Support: B,C,D,E,F,G,H
Training: 2 Weeks Toronto, ON; 2 Weeks On-Site (at Opening).

SPECIFIC EXPANSION PLANS:
US: No
Canada: All Except AB
Overseas: No

<< >>

SUPPLEMENTAL LISTING OF FRANCHISORS

HAPPYDAYS HANDBAG & LUGGAGE COMPANY, 1441 Craigflower Rd., #409, Victoria, BC V9A 2Y9 CANADA; (250) 595-8934; (250) 595-8935

MARK'S WORK WEARHOUSE, 1035 64th Ave. SE, # 30, Calgary, AB T2H 2J7 CANADA; (800) 663-6275 (403) 255-9220; (403) 255-6005

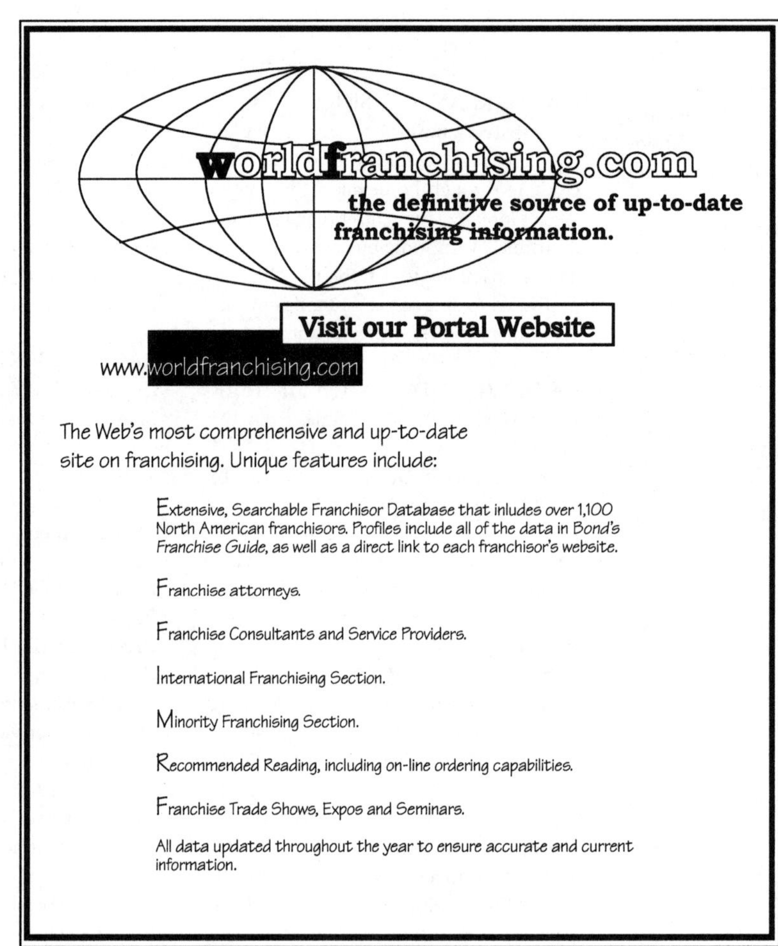

Retail: Convenience Stores/Supermarkets/Drugs

Chapter

37

Retail: Convenience Stores/Supermarkets/Drugs Industry Profile

Total # Franchisors in Industry Group	28
Total # Franchised Units in Industry Group	29,583
Total # Company-Owned Units in Industry Group	6,451
Total # Operating Units in Industry Group	36,034
Average # Franchised Units/Franchisor	1,056.5
Average # Company-Owned Units/Franchisor	230.4
Average # Total Units/Franchisor	1,286.9
Ratio of Total # Franchised Units/Total # Company-Owned Units	4.6:1
Industry Survey Participants	11
Representing % of Industry	39.3%
Average Franchise Fee*:	$22.7K
Average Total Investment*:	$353.2K
Average On-Going Royalty Fee*:	4.3%

*If a range was provided, the mid-point of the range was used. See detailed profiles for actual ranges.

Five Largest Participants in Survey

Company	# Franchised Units	# Co-Owned Units	# Total Units	Franchise Fee	On-Going Royalty	Total Investment
1. 7-Eleven, Inc.	18,504	2,638	21,142	61K	N/A	Varies
2. Circle K	3,800	2,400	6,200	15K	4%	400K-1.5MM
3. Medicine Shoppe, The	1,298	15	1,313	10-18K	2-5.5%	100K+
4. Health Mart	600	0	600	50K	0%	150-300K
5. White Hen Pantry	295	0	295	25K	8%+	Flexible

All of the data provided are proprietary and should not be quoted without acknowledging *Bond's Franchise Guide.*

Top 50

7-ELEVEN, INC.

2711 N. Haskell Ave., P.O. Box 711
Dallas, TX 75204
Tel: (800) 255-0711 (214) 828-7764
Fax: (214) 841-6776
E-Mail: jwebbj01@7-11.com
Web Site: www.7-eleven.com
Ms. Joanne Webb-Joyce, National Franchise Mgr.

7-ELEVEN stores were born from the simple concept of giving people 'what they want, when and where they want it.' This idea gave rise to the entire convenience store industry. While this formula still works today, customers' needs are changing at an accelerating pace. We are meeting this challenge with an infrastructure of daily distribution of fresh perishables, regional production of fresh foods and pastries and an information system that greatly improves ordering and merchandising decisions.

BACKGROUND: IFA MEMBER
Established: 1927; 1st Franchised: 1964
Franchised Units: 19,992
Company-Owned Units 2,656
Total Units: 22,648
Dist.: US-5771; CAN-499; O'seas-16378
North America: 36 States, 5 Provinces
Density: 1,183 in CA, 613 VA, 547 FL
Projected New Units (12 Months): 150
Qualifications: 4, 4, 3, 3, 5, 5
Registered: CA,IL,IN,MD,MI,NY,OR,RI, VA,WA, WI

FINANCIAL/TERMS:
Cash Investment: $81K
Total Investment: $118
Minimum Net Worth: $12.5K
Fees: Franchise - $64K
Royalty - N/A; Ad. - N/A
Earnings Claim Statement: No
Term of Contract (Years): 10
Avg. # Of Employees: 4 FT, 4 PT
Passive Ownership: Not Allowed
Encourage Conversions: N/A
Area Develop. Agreements: No
Sub-Franchising Contracts: No
Expand In Territory: No
Space Needs: 2,400 SF; FS, SC

SUPPORT & TRAINING PROVIDED:
Financial Assistance Provided: Yes(D)
Site Selection Assistance: N/A
Lease Negotiation Assistance: N/A
Co-Operative Advertising: No
Franchisee Assoc./Member: Yes/No
Size Of Corporate Staff: 1,000
On-Going Support: A,B,C,D,E,F,G,H,I
Training: 6 Weeks at Various Training Stores throughout US.

SPECIFIC EXPANSION PLANS:
US: NW,SW,MW,NE, Great Lakes
Canada: No
Overseas: No

<< >>

ARROW PRESCRIPTION CENTER

312 Farmington Ave.
Farmington, CT 06062
Tel: (800) 203-2776 (860) 676-1222
Fax: (860) 676-1499
E-Mail: info@arrowrx.com
Web Site: www.arrowrx.com
Mr. Ron Kaufman, VP Business Dev.

ARROW CORPORATION is one of the nation's largest franchisors of retail pharmacies, offering opportunities in traditional and alternative settings. At the core of ARROW'S philosophy is the delivery of pharmacy services directly to the patient by the pharmacist.

BACKGROUND: IFA MEMBER
Established: 1989; 1st Franchised: 1990
Franchised Units: 48
Company-Owned Units 22
Total Units: 70
Dist.: US-59; CAN-0; O'seas-0
North America: 6 States
Density: 42 in CT, 5 in MI, 5 in MA
Projected New Units (12 Months): 16
Qualifications: 4, 4, 5, 5, 4, 4
Registered: NR

FINANCIAL/TERMS:
Cash Investment: $20% of Total
Total Investment: $Varies
Minimum Net Worth: $100K
Fees: Franchise - $15K
Royalty - 6%; Ad. - Varies
Earnings Claim Statement: No
Term of Contract (Years): 20/10
Avg. # Of Employees: 2 FT, 1-6 PT
Passive Ownership: Discouraged
Encourage Conversions: Yes
Area Develop. Agreements: Yes/5
Sub-Franchising Contracts: No
Expand In Territory: No
Space Needs: 1,500 SF; FS, SC

SUPPORT & TRAINING PROVIDED:
Financial Assistance Provided: Yes(B)
Site Selection Assistance: Yes
Lease Negotiation Assistance: No
Co-Operative Advertising: Yes
Franchisee Assoc./Member: Yes
Size Of Corporate Staff: 30
On-Going Support: A,C,D,E,F,G,H,I
Training: 1-2 Weeks Corporate Training Center.

SPECIFIC EXPANSION PLANS:
US: All United States
Canada: No
Overseas: No

<< >>

Top 50

CIRCLE K

1500 N. Priest Dr.
Tempe, AZ 85281
Tel: (800) 813-7677 (602) 728-8000
Fax: (602) 728-5248
E-Mail: mrials@ppco.com
Web Site: www.circlek.com
Mr. Mike Rials, Franchise Development

Unlike any other convenience store and petroleum company, we offer you a CIRCLE K license opportunity that helps to build a business with leading brands in both the convenience store and petroleum industries (CIRCLE K/ 76). Licensing leading brands in these industries provides you with the ability to offer your customers a one-of-a-kind convenience experience. We also offer superior business systems, extensive training and effective promotional tools. This unique combination is the CIRCLE K advantage.

BACKGROUND: IFA MEMBER
Established: 1951; 1st Franchised: 1995
Franchised Units: 3,800
Company-Owned Units 2,400

Total Units: 6,200
Dist.: US-2700; CAN-0; O'seas-3500
North America: 37 States
Density: 550 in AZ, 400 in FL, 200 CA
Projected New Units (12 Months): 50
Qualifications: 5, 4, 5, 3, 3, 5
Registered: CA,FL,HI,MD,OR,VA,WA

FINANCIAL/TERMS:
Cash Investment: $300-450K
Total Investment: $400K-1.5MM
Minimum Net Worth: $500K
Fees: Franchise - $15K
Royalty - 4%; Ad. - 2%
Earnings Claim Statement: Yes
Term of Contract (Years): 10/5/5
Avg. # Of Employees: 8 FT, 4 PT
Passive Ownership: Discouraged
Encourage Conversions: Yes
Area Develop. Agreements: Yes/10
Sub-Franchising Contracts: No
Expand In Territory: Yes
Space Needs: 3,000 SF; FS

SUPPORT & TRAINING PROVIDED:
Financial Assistance Provided: Yes(I)
Site Selection Assistance: Yes
Lease Negotiation Assistance: No
Co-Operative Advertising: N/A
Franchisee Assoc./Member: No
Size Of Corporate Staff: 1,200
On-Going Support: B,C,D,E,F,G,H,I
Training: 4 Weeks in Phoenix, AZ.

SPECIFIC EXPANSION PLANS:
US: WA, OR, CA, HI
Canada: No
Overseas: Asia, South America, Europe

EXPRESS MART CONVENIENT STORE

6567 Kinne Rd.
Dewitt, NY 13214
Tel: (315) 446-0125
Fax: (315) 446-1355
Ms. Robbin Jeran, Mgr. Franchise Admin.

Convenience-store franchise with petroleum emphasis, currently offering development territories and master franchise agreements for U.S. and foreign countries.

BACKGROUND: IFA MEMBER
Established: 1975; 1st Franchised: 1990
Franchised Units: 21
Company-Owned Units 47
Total Units: 68
Dist.: US-67; CAN-0; O'seas-0
North America: 4 States
Density: 56 in NY, 8 in MA, 2 in CT
Projected New Units (12 Months): 3
Qualifications: 4, 3, 3, 3, 4, 4
Registered: CT,NY

FINANCIAL/TERMS:
Cash Investment: $40-60K
Total Investment: $136-460K
Minimum Net Worth: $Varies
Fees: Franchise - $15K
Royalty - 4%; Ad. - 1%
Earnings Claim Statement: No
Term of Contract (Years): 5/5/5/5
Avg. # Of Employees: 6 FT, 4 PT
Passive Ownership: Allowed
Encourage Conversions: Yes
Area Develop. Agreements: No
Sub-Franchising Contracts: Yes
Expand In Territory: Yes
Space Needs: 800-5,000 SF; FS

SUPPORT & TRAINING PROVIDED:
Financial Assistance Provided: Yes
Site Selection Assistance: Yes
Lease Negotiation Assistance: Yes
Co-Operative Advertising: Yes
Franchisee Assoc./Member: Yes
Size Of Corporate Staff: 300
On-Going Support: B,C,D,E,F
Training: 1 Week Corporate Headquarters; 1 Week Store Training.

SPECIFIC EXPANSION PLANS:
US: All United States
Canada: All Canada
Overseas: No

HEALTH MART

1 Post St.
San Francisco, CA 94104
Tel: (800) 369-5467 (415) 983-8300
Fax: (415) 983-9353
Mr. Jerry Josephson, Dir. Franchise Services

The largest full-line pharmacy franchise for independent store owners.

BACKGROUND:
Established: 1981; 1st Franchised: 1983
Franchised Units: 600
Company-Owned Units 0
Total Units: 600
Dist.: US-600; CAN-0; O'seas-0
North America: 34 States
Density: 83 in IL, 64 in MO, 59 in LA
Projected New Units (12 Months): 100
Qualifications: 3, 4, 5, 5, 1, 3
Registered: All States

FINANCIAL/TERMS:
Cash Investment: $5-15K
Total Investment: $150-300K
Minimum Net Worth: $NR
Fees: Franchise - $50K
Royalty - 0%; Ad. - $150/Mo.
Earnings Claim Statement: Yes
Term of Contract (Years): 5/5
Avg. # Of Employees: 2 FT, 1 PT
Passive Ownership: Allowed
Encourage Conversions: Yes
Area Develop. Agreements: No
Sub-Franchising Contracts: No
Expand In Territory: Yes
Space Needs: 500+ SF; FS, SF, SC, RM

SUPPORT & TRAINING PROVIDED:
Financial Assistance Provided: N/A
Site Selection Assistance: No
Lease Negotiation Assistance: No
Co-Operative Advertising: Yes
Franchisee Assoc./Member: No
Size Of Corporate Staff: 5
On-Going Support: b,C,D,e,G,h,I
Training: 1-3 Days On-Site.

SPECIFIC EXPANSION PLANS:
US: All United States
Canada: No
Overseas: No

JACKPOT CONVENIENCE STORES

P.O. Box 24447
Seattle, WA 98124
Tel: (800) 772-5765 (206) 286-6436
Fax: (206) 283-8036
Mr. Steven C. Gray, Franchise Manager

JACKPOT offers a franchise that includes a system of retail grocery services. JACKPOT licenses to franchisees its business system, know-how and its licensed trade name and service marks. JACKPOT provides training, continuing support, administration and marketing and promotion services.

BACKGROUND:
Established: 1981; 1st Franchised: 1990
Franchised Units: 109
Company-Owned Units 10
Total Units: 119
Dist.: US-114; CAN-0; O'seas-0
North America: NR
Density: NR
Projected New Units (12 Months): NR
Qualifications: 5, 4, 5, 1, 3, 4
Registered: CA,OR,WA

FINANCIAL/TERMS:
Cash Investment: $40-75K

Total Investment: $75-250K
Minimum Net Worth: $60K
Fees: Franchise - $5K
Royalty - 0.5%; Ad. - 1%
Earnings Claim Statement: No
Term of Contract (Years): 3/3
Avg. # Of Employees:
No Recommendation
Passive Ownership: Not Allowed
Encourage Conversions: N/A
Area Develop. Agreements: No
Sub-Franchising Contracts: No
Expand In Territory: No
Space Needs: NR SF; N/A

SUPPORT & TRAINING PROVIDED:
Financial Assistance Provided: No
Site Selection Assistance: N/A
Lease Negotiation Assistance: N/A
Co-Operative Advertising: N/A
Franchisee Assoc./Member: Yes/Yes
Size Of Corporate Staff: NR
On-Going Support: A,C,D,E,F,G,h,I
Training: 4 Weeks Seattle, WA.

SPECIFIC EXPANSION PLANS:
US: WA, OR, CA, NV, ID
Canada: No
Overseas: No

<< >>

We'll always make time for you.

Top 50

MEDICAP PHARMACY
4350 Westown Pkwy., # 400
West Des Moines, IA 50266-6718
Tel: (800) 445-2244 (515) 224-8400
Fax: (515) 224-8415
E-Mail: cjames@medihealthsolutions.com
Web Site: www.medihealthsolutions.com
Mr. Calvin C. James, VP Franchise Development

MEDICAP PHARMACY - convenient, low-cost, professional pharmacies. The stores operate in an average of 1,500 square feet. We average 90% RX and the remaining 10% over-the-counter products, including MEDICAP-brand private label. We specialize in starting new stores and converting existing full-line drug stores and independent pharmacies to the MEDICAP concept. We teach independent pharmacists how to survive in today's marketplace.

BACKGROUND: IFA MEMBER
Established: 1971; 1st Franchised: 1974
Franchised Units: 173
Company-Owned Units <u>18</u>
Total Units: 191
Dist.: US-197; CAN-0; O'seas-0
North America: 38 States
Density: 50 in IA, 11 in SC, 10 in IL
Projected New Units (12 Months): 25
Qualifications: 3, 1, 4, 5, 3, 5
Registered: CA,FL,IL,IN,MD,MN,ND, OR,SD,WA,WI

FINANCIAL/TERMS:
Cash Investment: $10K-45K
Total Investment: $20-324.7K
Minimum Net Worth: $NR
Fees: Franchise - $8.5-15K
Royalty - 2-4%; Ad. - 1%
Earnings Claim Statement: Yes
Term of Contract (Years): 20/20
Avg. # Of Employees: 2 FT
Passive Ownership: Allowed
Encourage Conversions: Yes
Area Develop. Agreements: No
Sub-Franchising Contracts: No
Expand In Territory: Yes
Space Needs: 1,500 SF; FS, SF, SC

SUPPORT & TRAINING PROVIDED:
Financial Assistance Provided: Yes(I)
Site Selection Assistance: Yes
Lease Negotiation Assistance: Yes
Co-Operative Advertising: N/A
Franchisee Assoc./Member: NR
Size Of Corporate Staff: 52
On-Going Support: B,C,D,E,F,G,H,I
Training: 5 Days Headquarters; 3 Days On-Site; 3 Days Computer.

SPECIFIC EXPANSION PLANS:
US: All United States
Canada: All Canada
Overseas: All Countries

<< >>

MEDICINE SHOPPE, THE
1100 N. Lindbergh Blvd.
St. Louis, MO 63132-2992
Tel: (800) 325-1397 (314) 993-6000
Fax: (314) 872-5500
E-Mail: clane@medicineshoppe.com
Web Site: www.medicineshoppe.com
Ms. Con T. Lane, National Dir. of Sales

Medicine Shoppe International is the largest and fastest growing chain of franchised pharmacies in the world. MSI offers its owners numerous ways to enter pharmacy ownership, i.e. acquisition of existing pharmacies, new store development, supermarkets clinic locations. Diversify your portfolio and participate in the graying of America.

BACKGROUND: IFA MEMBER
Established: 1970; 1st Franchised: 1970
Franchised Units: 1,298
Company-Owned Units <u>15</u>
Total Units: 1,313
Dist.: US-1133; CAN-0; O'seas-180
North America: 47 States
Density: 121 in PA, 111 in FL, 71 CA
Projected New Units (12 Months): 65
Qualifications: 3, 3, 4, 5, 2, 4
Registered: All States

FINANCIAL/TERMS:
Cash Investment: $10-18K
Total Investment: $100K+
Minimum Net Worth: $50K
Fees: Franchise - $10-18K
Royalty - 2-5.5%; Ad. - $200/month
Earnings Claim Statement: Yes
Term of Contract (Years): 10/15
Avg. # Of Employees: 2 FT, 1 PT
Passive Ownership: Allowed
Encourage Conversions: Yes
Area Develop. Agreements: Yes
Sub-Franchising Contracts: No
Expand In Territory: Yes
Space Needs: 1,200 SF; FS, SF, SC

SUPPORT & TRAINING PROVIDED:
Financial Assistance Provided: Yes(D)
Site Selection Assistance: Yes
Lease Negotiation Assistance: Yes
Co-Operative Advertising: Yes
Franchisee Assoc./Member: No
Size Of Corporate Staff: 240
On-Going Support: A,B,C,D,E,F,G,H,I
Training: 6 Days St. Louis, MO.

SPECIFIC EXPANSION PLANS:
US: All United States
Canada: Master License
Overseas: All Countries

<< >>

OPEN PANTRY FOOD MARTS
10505 Corporate Dr., # 101
Pleasant Prairie, WI 53158-1605
Tel: (800) 242-1018 (262) 632-3161
Fax: (262) 632-1463
E-Mail: RABuhler@clmail.com
Web Site: www.openpantry.com
Mr. John Schonert, VP Fran. Operations

Convenience store operations.

BACKGROUND:
Established: 1966; 1st Franchised: 1966

Franchised Units: 38
Company-Owned Units 16
Total Units: 54
Dist.: US-54; CAN-0; O'seas-0
North America: 2 States
Density: 53 in WI, 1 in IL
Projected New Units (12 Months): 6
Qualifications: 5, 5, 5, 4, 4, 5
Registered: WI

FINANCIAL/TERMS:
Cash Investment: $15-30K
Total Investment: $NR
Minimum Net Worth: $75K
Fees: Franchise - $10K
Royalty - NR; Ad. - NR
Earnings Claim Statement: No
Term of Contract (Years): NR
Avg. # Of Employees: 3 FT, 3 PT
Passive Ownership: Not Allowed
Encourage Conversions: No
Area Develop. Agreements: No
Sub-Franchising Contracts: No
Expand In Territory: NR
Space Needs: NR SF; FS, SF, SC

SUPPORT & TRAINING PROVIDED:
Financial Assistance Provided: Yes(I)
Site Selection Assistance: No
Lease Negotiation Assistance: N/A
Co-Operative Advertising: Yes
Franchisee Assoc./Member: No
Size Of Corporate Staff: 18
On-Going Support: C,D,E,G,H,I
Training: NR

SPECIFIC EXPANSION PLANS:
US: NR
Canada: No
Overseas: NR

<< >>

UNCLESAM'S CONVENIENT STORE

P.O. Box 870
Elsa, TX 78543-0870
Tel: (888) 786-7373 (956) 262-7273
Fax: (956) 262-7290
E-Mail: uscs12@aol.com
Web Site: www.unclesamscstore.com
Mr. Jackie L. Thomas, Executive VP

A turn-key convenience store franchise program available in 31 states. Affiliated with major fuel and merchandise suppliers. Attractive financing available to qualified candidates. Training, site evaluation, store design, operations manual, software package, advertising, promotions, security systems, deli, car wash and many more benefits.

BACKGROUND:
Established: 1970; 1st Franchised: 1997
Franchised Units: 1
Company-Owned Units 52
Total Units: 53
Dist.: US-52; CAN-0; O'seas-0
North America: 1 State
Density: 52 in TX
Projected New Units (12 Months): 10
Qualifications: 4, 5, 3, 4, 3, 5
Registered: FL,OR

FINANCIAL/TERMS:
Cash Investment: $100K+
Total Investment: $800K+
Minimum Net Worth: $300K
Fees: Franchise - $25K
Royalty - 5%; Ad. - 1%
Earnings Claim Statement: No
Term of Contract (Years): 5/5/5/5/5
Avg. # Of Employees: 6 FT, 2 PT
Passive Ownership: Discouraged
Encourage Conversions: Yes
Area Develop. Agreements: Yes/5
Sub-Franchising Contracts: No
Expand In Territory: Yes
Space Needs: 2,500+ SF; FS

SUPPORT & TRAINING PROVIDED:
Financial Assistance Provided: Yes(I)
Site Selection Assistance: Yes
Lease Negotiation Assistance: Yes
Co-Operative Advertising: Yes
Franchisee Assoc./Member: Yes/No
Size Of Corporate Staff: 6
On-Going Support: a,B,C,d,E,F,I
Training: 4 Weeks at Corporate Headquarters.

SPECIFIC EXPANSION PLANS:
US: South, SW, SE, East, West
Canada: No
Overseas: No

<< >>

WHITE HEN PANTRY

3003 Butterfield Rd.
Oak Brook, IL 60523
Tel: (800) 726-8791 (630) 366-3000
Fax: (630) 366-3447
Web Site: www.whitehen.com
Ms. Gail M. Bosch, Franchising Manager

WHITE HEN PANTRY is a neighborhood convenience store, specializing in fresh-brewed coffee, full-service deli, custom-made sandwiches and salads, fresh produce and a bakery.

BACKGROUND: IFA MEMBER
Established: 1965; 1st Franchised: 1965
Franchised Units: 295
Company-Owned Units 0
Total Units: 295
Dist.: US-295; CAN-0; O'seas-0
North America: 4 States
Density: 233 in IL, 56 in MA, 6 in IN
Projected New Units (12 Months): 10
Qualifications: 2, 4, 3, 2, 3, 5
Registered: IL,IN

FINANCIAL/TERMS:
Cash Investment: $56.8K+
Total Investment: $Flexible
Minimum Net Worth: $N/A
Fees: Franchise - $25K
Royalty - 8%+; Ad. - Included
Earnings Claim Statement: Yes
Term of Contract (Years): 10/10
Avg. # Of Employees: 2 FT, 12 PT
Passive Ownership: Not Allowed
Encourage Conversions: N/A
Area Develop. Agreements: No
Sub-Franchising Contracts: No
Expand In Territory: No
Space Needs: 2,500 SF; SC

SUPPORT & TRAINING PROVIDED:
Financial Assistance Provided: Yes(D)
Site Selection Assistance: N/A
Lease Negotiation Assistance: N/A
Co-Operative Advertising: N/A
Franchisee Assoc./Member: Yes
Size Of Corporate Staff: 260
On-Going Support: A,C,D,E,F,G,H,I
Training: 1 Week Corporate Office; 2 Weeks On-Site.

SPECIFIC EXPANSION PLANS:
US: IL, IN, MA, NH Only
Canada: No
Overseas: No

<< >>

SUPPLEMENTAL LISTING OF FRANCHISORS

AM/PM MINI-MARKET, 4 Centerpointe Dr., La Palma, CA 90623-1066 ; (800) 322-2726 (714) 670-5393; (714) 670-5439

COGO'S, 2589 Boyce Plaza Rd., Pittsburgh, PA 15241-3981 ; (800) 472-1481 (412) 257-1550; (412) 257-9174

CONVENIENT FOOD MART, 467 North State St., Painesville, OH 44077

(800) 860-4844 (440) 639-6515; (440) 639-6526

DAIRY MART CONVENIENCE STORES INTERNATIONAL, 300 Executive Pkwy. W., Hudson, OH 44236 ; (330) 342-6758; (330) 342-6752

DRUG EMPORIUM, 155 Hidden Ravines Dr., Powell, OH 43065 ; (740) 548-7080; (740) 548-6541

GIANT EAGLE, 101 Kappa Dr., Pittsburgh, PA 15238 ; (412) 963-2560; (412) 963-0374

GIANT TIGER STORES, 2480 Walkley Rd., Ottawa, ON K1G 6A9 CANADA; (613) 521-8222; (613) 521-4474

IGA CANADA, 304 The East Mall, # 700, Etobicoke, ON M9B 6E2 CANADA; (416) 232-2880; (416) 234-7013

J. J. PEPPER'S FOOD STORE, 121 E. Grand Ave., Northlake, IL 60164 ; (708) 409-0001; (708) 409-0003

JOHNNY QUIK FOOD STORES, 5816 E. Shields Ave., Fresno, CA 93727 ; (559) 291-7136; (559) 291-1656

PIGGLY WIGGLY, P.O. Box 1719, Memphis, TN 38101 ; (800) 800-8215 (901) 395-8215; (901) 395-8475

QUICKWAY, 44 Grand St., Sidney, NY 13838 ; (800) 934-9480 (607) 561-2700; (607) 563-1460

QUIK STOP MARKETS, 4567 Enterprise St., Fremont, CA 94538 ; (510) 657-1544

SAV-MOR DRUG STORES, 43155 W. Nine Mile Rd., Novi, MI 48376 ; (248) 348-1570; (248) 348-4316

SHOPPERS DRUG MART, 225 Yorkland Blvd., Willowdale, ON M2J 4Y7 CANADA; (416) 490-2648; (416) 490-2700

SUGAR CREEK CONVENIENCE STORES & FUEL, 760 Brooks Ave., Rochester, NY 14619 ; (716) 436-2691; (716) 328-7374

TEDESCHI FOOD SHOPS, 14 Howard St., Rockland, MA 02370 ; (800) 833-3724 (781) 878-8210; (781) 878-0476

For a full explanation of the data provided in the Franchisor Profiles, please refer to **Chapter 2, "How to Use the Data."**

Retail: Home Furnishings

Chapter

38

Retail: Home Furnishings Industry Profile

Total # Franchisors in Industry Group	44
Total # Franchised Units in Industry Group	2,743
Total # Company-Owned Units in Industry Group	128
Total # Operating Units in Industry Group	2,871
Average # Franchised Units/Franchisor	62.3
Average # Company-Owned Units/Franchisor	2.9
Average # Total Units/Franchisor	65.2
Ratio of Total # Franchised Units/Total # Company-Owned Units	21.4:1
Industry Survey Participants	17
Representing % of Industry	38.6%
Average Franchise Fee*:	$21.1K
Average Total Investment*:	$163.5
Average On-Going Royalty Fee*:	4.1%

*If a range was provided, the mid-point of the range was used. See detailed profiles for actual ranges.

Five Largest Participants in Survey

Company	# Franchised Units	# Co-Owned Units	# Total Units	Franchise Fee	On-Going Royalty	Total Investment
1. Decorating Den Interiors	465	1	466	23.9K	7% Sliding	12-60K
2. Budget Blinds	240	0	240	25K	4-5%	30-45K
3. Floor Coverings International	187	0	187	16K	$325/Mo/5%	31.1-41.3K
4. GCO Carpet Outlet	125	7	132	25K	3-5%	260-522K
5. Norwalk-The Furniture Idea	73	12	85	50K	1.5%	350-400K

All of the data provided are proprietary and should not be quoted without acknowledging *Bond's Franchise Guide.*

A SHADE BETTER

3615 Superior Ave., Bldg. # 42
Cleveland, OH 44114
Tel: (800) 722-8676 (216) 391-5267
Fax: (216) 391-8118
E-Mail: info@ashadebetter.com
Web Site: www.ashadebetter.com
Mr. James P. Prexta, President

Distinctive retail stores selling beautiful lamp shades, lamps and accessories. Franchisees will also have the opportunity to develop and service the wholesale market in their exclusive territory.

BACKGROUND:

Established: 1988; 1st Franchised: 1993
Franchised Units: 10
Company-Owned Units 7
Total Units: 17
Dist.: US-18; CAN-0; O'seas-0
North America: 7 States
Density: 5 in OH, 3 in IL, 2 in TX
Projected New Units (12 Months): 12
Qualifications: 4, 4, 2, 2, 3, 5
Registered: CA,FL,IL,IN,MD,MI,WI

FINANCIAL/TERMS:

Cash Investment: $75-100K
Total Investment: $114-156K
Minimum Net Worth: $300K
Fees: Franchise - $35K
Royalty - 6%; Ad. - 1%
Earnings Claim Statement: No
Term of Contract (Years): 5/5/5/5
Avg. # Of Employees: 2 FT, 2 PT
Passive Ownership: Discouraged
Encourage Conversions: Yes
Area Develop. Agreements: Yes/Varies
Sub-Franchising Contracts: No
Expand In Territory: Yes
Space Needs: 1,800 SF; SC

SUPPORT & TRAINING PROVIDED:

Financial Assistance Provided: No
Site Selection Assistance: Yes
Lease Negotiation Assistance: Yes
Co-Operative Advertising: No
Franchisee Assoc./Member: No
Size Of Corporate Staff: 6
On-Going Support: B,C,D,E,h,I
Training: 6 Days Cleveland, OH or Phoenix, AZ; 6 Days On-Site.

SPECIFIC EXPANSION PLANS:

US: Midwest, Southwest
Canada: No
Overseas: No

<< >>

BIG BOB'S NEW & USED CARPET SHOPS

9320 W. 75th Street
Shawnee Mission, KS 66204
Tel: (877) 644-2627 (913) 789-7773
Fax: (913) 789-7126
E-Mail: BBB97INC@aol.com
Web Site: www.bigbobscarpet.com
Mr. David Elyachar, President

To provide an affordable opportunity to franchise, drawing from the unique used, second, promotionals, and private lines of flowing and in turn providing an excellent margin and excellent prices to the franchisee and the customer. BIG BOB'S uses unique and proven advertising. There will be full training and counsel when needed.

BACKGROUND:

Established: 1983; 1st Franchised: 1993
Franchised Units: 33
Company-Owned Units 3
Total Units: 36
Dist.: US-36; CAN-0; O'seas-0
North America: 19 States
Density: 6 in OH, 5 in TX, 4 in FL
Projected New Units (12 Months): 7
Qualifications: 2, 3, 3, 2, 4, 4
Registered: CA,FL,IL,IN,MD,MI,MN, NY,VA,WA

FINANCIAL/TERMS:

Cash Investment: $60-140K
Total Investment: $60-140K
Minimum Net Worth: $Not Required
Fees: Franchise - $7.5K
Royalty - 1-5%; Ad. - N/A
Earnings Claim Statement: No
Term of Contract (Years): 5/5
Avg. # Of Employees: 3-5 FT
Passive Ownership: Discouraged
Encourage Conversions: Yes
Area Develop. Agreements: No
Sub-Franchising Contracts: No
Expand In Territory: Yes
Space Needs: 7,000-12,000 SF; FS, SF

SUPPORT & TRAINING PROVIDED:

Financial Assistance Provided: Yes(I)
Site Selection Assistance: Yes
Lease Negotiation Assistance: No
Co-Operative Advertising: No
Franchisee Assoc./Member: No
Size Of Corporate Staff: 4
On-Going Support: B,C,D,E,F,G,H,I
Training: 1 Week in Kansas City, KS; Other Optional Areas.

SPECIFIC EXPANSION PLANS:

US: All United States
Canada: No
Overseas: No

<< >>

BUDGET BLINDS

733 W. Taft Ave.
Orange, CA 92865
Tel: (800) 420-5374 (714) 637-2100
Fax: (714) 637-1400
E-Mail: franchise@budgetblinds.com
Web Site: www.budgetblinds.com
Mr. Shelby Wilson, Sales Manager

BUDGET BLINDS trains individuals to own and operate a home-based business that sells and installs window coverings, via a well-equipped mobile showroom. What makes our franchise unique is that we actually teach people how to run a business, versus teaching people how to do a job. By business we mean hiring, monitoring and maintaining employees, working from cash flow, profit loss and balance statements, We teach what business owners need to know, not what job operators want to know.

BACKGROUND: IFA MEMBER

Established: 1992; 1st Franchised: 1994
Franchised Units: 240
Company-Owned Units 0
Total Units: 240
Dist.: US-240; CAN-0; O'seas-0
North America: 36 States
Density: 60 in CA, 15 in GA, 14 in AZ
Projected New Units (12 Months): 350
Qualifications: 2, 4, 1, 2, 3, 5
Registered: All States

FINANCIAL/TERMS:

Cash Investment: $50K
Total Investment: $30-45K
Minimum Net Worth: $30K
Fees: Franchise - $25K
Royalty - 4-5%; Ad. - $150
Earnings Claim Statement: Yes
Term of Contract (Years): 5/5
Avg. # Of Employees: 1-5 FT
Passive Ownership: Discouraged
Encourage Conversions: Yes
Area Develop. Agreements: No
Sub-Franchising Contracts: No
Expand In Territory: Yes
Space Needs: NR SF; HB

SUPPORT & TRAINING PROVIDED:
Financial Assistance Provided: Yes(I)
Site Selection Assistance: N/A
Lease Negotiation Assistance: N/A
Co-Operative Advertising: Yes
Franchisee Assoc./Member: No/No
Size Of Corporate Staff: 25
On-Going Support: A,B,C,D,G,H
Training: 10 Days Orange, CA.
SPECIFIC EXPANSION PLANS:
US: All United States
Canada: All Canada
Overseas: No

<< >>

CARPET NETWORK
109 Gaither Dr., # 302
Mount Laurel, NJ 08054-1704
Tel: (800) 248-1067 (856) 273-9393
Fax: (856) 273-0160
E-Mail: info@carpetnetwork.com
Web Site: www.carpetnetwork.com
Mr. Leonard Rankin, President/CEO

'The Traveling Floor and Window Store.' A mobile business offering carpet, area rugs, laminate, wood, vinyl flooring and window treatments in the convenience of the consumer's home or business. Over 4,000 selections from leading manufacturers, serving today's 'time starved' consumer. Large exclusive territories, marketing strategy - training - 24-hour support and much more.

BACKGROUND: IFA MEMBER
Established: 1991; 1st Franchised: 1992
Franchised Units: 46
Company-Owned Units 1
Total Units: 47
Dist.: US-47; CAN-0; O'seas-0
North America: 18 States
Density: 8 in PA, 4 in NY, 3 in NJ
Projected New Units (12 Months): 24
Qualifications: 3, 3, 1, 3, 3, 5
Registered: FL,IN,MN,NY
FINANCIAL/TERMS:
Cash Investment: $13K
Total Investment: $13K
Minimum Net Worth: $13K
Fees: Franchise - $9.9K
Royalty - 2-7%; Ad. - $165/Mo.
Earnings Claim Statement: No
Term of Contract (Years): 15/15
Avg. # Of Employees: 1 FT, 1 PT
Passive Ownership: Discouraged
Encourage Conversions: N/A
Area Develop. Agreements: Yes
Sub-Franchising Contracts: No
Expand In Territory: Yes
Space Needs: N/A SF; HB
SUPPORT & TRAINING PROVIDED:
Financial Assistance Provided: Yes(D)
Site Selection Assistance: N/A
Lease Negotiation Assistance: N/A
Co-Operative Advertising: N/A
Franchisee Assoc./Member: Yes/Yes
Size Of Corporate Staff: 5
On-Going Support: C,D,G,h,I
Training: 6 Days at Corporate Office, Mt. Laurel, NJ.
SPECIFIC EXPANSION PLANS:
US: All United States
Canada: No
Overseas: No

<< >>

DECORATING DEN INTERIORS
19100 Montgomery Village Ave., # 200
Montgomery Village, MD 20886-3701
Tel: (800) 332-3367 (301) 272-1500
Fax: (301) 272-1520
E-Mail: decden@decoratingden.com
Web Site: www.decoratingden.com
Ms. Victoria Jenkins, VP Franchise Marketing

Established in 1969, DECORATING DEN INTERIORS is the oldest international, shop-at-home interior decorating franchise in the world. Our company-trained interior decorators bring thousands of samples including window coverings, wallcoverings, floor coverings, furniture and accessories to their customers' homes in our uniquely equipped COLORVAN ©. Special business features include: home-based, marketing systems, business systems, training, support and complete sampling.

BACKGROUND: IFA MEMBER
Established: 1969; 1st Franchised: 1970
Franchised Units: 465
Company-Owned Units 1
Total Units: 466
Dist.: US-401; CAN-50; O'seas-15
North America: NR
Density: 33 in FL, 28 in NC, 27 in TX
Projected New Units (12 Months): 50
Qualifications: 5, 5, 3, 3, 5, 5
Registered: All States
FINANCIAL/TERMS:
Cash Investment: $12-40K
Total Investment: $12-60K
Minimum Net Worth: $50K
Fees: Franchise - $23.9K
Royalty - 7% (Sliding);
Ad. - 4%/$100 Min
Earnings Claim Statement: Yes
Term of Contract (Years): 10/10
Avg. # Of Employees: 1 FT
Passive Ownership: Not Allowed
Encourage Conversions: Yes
Area Develop. Agreements: Yes/10
Sub-Franchising Contracts: Yes
Expand In Territory: No
Space Needs: N/A SF; HB
SUPPORT & TRAINING PROVIDED:
Financial Assistance Provided: Yes(D)
Site Selection Assistance: N/A
Lease Negotiation Assistance: N/A
Co-Operative Advertising: Yes
Franchisee Assoc./Member: Yes/Yes
Size Of Corporate Staff: 40
On-Going Support: C,D,E,G,H,I
Training: 10.5 Days in Montgomery Village, MD.
SPECIFIC EXPANSION PLANS:
US: All United States
Canada: All Canada
Overseas: No

<< >>

DECOR-AT-YOUR-DOOR INTERNATIONAL
23 Heather Green Ct.
Ocoee, FL 34761
Tel: (800) 936-3326 (407) 877-3033
Fax: (407) 877-8088
E-Mail: info@decor-at-your-door.com
Web Site: www.decor-at-your-door.com
Ms. Lori Marshall, President/CEO

Assist business and home owners in choosing and purchasing window treatments and floor coverings. We offer quality service, the top brands and the most reasonable franchise fees in the industry. Check the competition and compare DECOR-AT-YOUR-DOOR is listed among the Top 50 New Franchises by Entrepreneur Magazine.

BACKGROUND:
Established: 1995; 1st Franchised: 2000

Franchised Units: 11
Company-Owned Units 1
Total Units: 12
Dist.: US-12; CAN-0; O'seas-0
North America: 12 States
Density: NR
Projected New Units (12 Months): 5
Qualifications: 1, 3, 3, 2, 2, 5
Registered: FL

FINANCIAL/TERMS:
Cash Investment: $9-15K
Total Investment: $9-15K
Minimum Net Worth: $NR
Fees: Franchise - $7K
Royalty - 1%/$100; Ad. - 1%
Earnings Claim Statement: No
Term of Contract (Years): 10/10
Avg. # Of Employees: 1 FT, 1 PT
Passive Ownership: Discouraged
Encourage Conversions: N/A
Area Develop. Agreements: No
Sub-Franchising Contracts: No
Expand In Territory: Yes
Space Needs: NR SF; HB

SUPPORT & TRAINING PROVIDED:
Financial Assistance Provided: No
Site Selection Assistance: N/A
Lease Negotiation Assistance: No
Co-Operative Advertising: Yes
Franchisee Assoc./Member: No
Size Of Corporate Staff: 1
On-Going Support: b,E,G,h
Training: 1 Week or 5 Days in Orlando, FL.

SPECIFIC EXPANSION PLANS:
US: All United States, Target SE
Canada: No
Overseas: No

<< >>

FLOOR COVERINGS INTERNATIONAL

5182 Old Dixie Hwy., # B
Forest Park, GA 30297
Tel: (800) 955-4324 (404) 361-5047
Fax: (404) 366-4606
E-Mail: lmcbride@carpetvan.com
Web Site: www.floorcoveringsintl.com
Ms. Karen Childers

FLOOR COVERINGS INTERNATIONAL is the 'Flooring Store at your Door.' FCI is the first and leading mobile 'shop at home' flooring store. Customers can select from over 3,000 styles and colors of flooring right in their own home! All the right ingredients are there to simplify a buying decision. We offer all the brand names you and your customers will be familiar with. We carry all types of flooring, as well as window blinds.

BACKGROUND:
Established: 1988; 1st Franchised: 1989
Franchised Units: 187
Company-Owned Units 0
Total Units: 187
Dist.: US-150; CAN-16; O'seas-60
North America: 43 States, 5 Provinces
Density: 15 in PA, 11 in OH, 9 in IL
Projected New Units (12 Months): 45
Qualifications: 5, 5, 4, 3, 4, 4
Registered: All States

FINANCIAL/TERMS:
Cash Investment: $25-35K
Total Investment: $31.1-41.3K
Minimum Net Worth: $50K
Fees: Franchise - $16K
Royalty - 5%/$325/Mo.;
Ad. - 2%/$130/Mo.
Earnings Claim Statement: No
Term of Contract (Years): 10/10
Avg. # Of Employees: 1 FT, 1PT
Passive Ownership: Discouraged
Encourage Conversions: Yes
Area Develop. Agreements: Yes/10
Sub-Franchising Contracts: No
Expand In Territory: Yes
Space Needs: NR SF; Mobile Van

SUPPORT & TRAINING PROVIDED:
Financial Assistance Provided: Yes(D)
Site Selection Assistance: Yes
Lease Negotiation Assistance: N/A
Co-Operative Advertising: Yes
Franchisee Assoc./Member: Yes
Size Of Corporate Staff: 15
On-Going Support: A,B,C,D,E,G,H,I
Training: 2 Weeks Home Study; 2 Weeks Atlanta, GA.

SPECIFIC EXPANSION PLANS:
US: All United States
Canada: All Canada
Overseas: U.K.

<< >>

FLOOR TO CEILING

2999 W. Country Rd. 42, # 145
Burnsville, MN 55306
Tel: (952) 890-8979
Fax: (952) 890-3818
E-Mail: mscherer@floortoceiling.com
Web Site: www.floortoceiling.com
Mr. Mike Scherer, Franchise Sales Dir.

FLOOR TO CEILING offers a comprehensive retail franchise opportunity in the fast-growing home decorating market. FTC franchisees benefit from national buying power in floorcovering, kitchen and bath and decorative products from the nation's leading manufacturers. Our service is complete with software, advertising, rebates, insurance, consumer financing, HR and much more!

BACKGROUND:
Established: 1990; 1st Franchised: 1996
Franchised Units: 51
Company-Owned Units 1
Total Units: 52
Dist.: US-63; CAN-0; O'seas-0
North America: 9 States
Density: 23 in MN, 14 in WI, 6 in IL
Projected New Units (12 Months): 15-20
Qualifications: 5, 4, 5, 3, 4, 5
Registered: IL,IN,MN,ND,SD,WA,WI

FINANCIAL/TERMS:
Cash Investment: $Varies
Total Investment: $Varies
Minimum Net Worth: $Varies
Fees: Franchise - $3-6K
Royalty - $350+/Mo.; Ad. - 0%
Earnings Claim Statement: Yes
Term of Contract (Years): 5/5-10
Avg. # Of Employees: 4 FT, 2 PT
Passive Ownership: Allowed
Encourage Conversions: Yes
Area Develop. Agreements: Yes/Varies
Sub-Franchising Contracts: NR
Expand In Territory: Yes
Space Needs: 8,000-14,000 SF; FS, SF, SC

SUPPORT & TRAINING PROVIDED:
Financial Assistance Provided: N/A
Site Selection Assistance: No
Lease Negotiation Assistance: No
Co-Operative Advertising: Yes
Franchisee Assoc./Member: Yes/Yes
Size Of Corporate Staff: 10
On-Going Support: A,C,D,E,G,H
Training: Variable Amount of Time at Home Office.

SPECIFIC EXPANSION PLANS:
US: All United States
Canada: No
Overseas: No

<< >>

GCO CARPET OUTLET

210 Town Park Dr., NW
Kennesaw, GA 30144-5514
Tel: (800) 279-8345 (678) 355-4362
Fax: (678) 355-4981
E-Mail: mbennett@gcocarpet.com
Web Site: www.gcocarpet.com
Mr. Randy G. Burgan, Dir. Fran. Dev.

A new idea in floorcovering stores. GCO CARPET OUTLET stores sell premium, in-stock flooring at everyday low prices to the price-conscious consumer. This cash-and-carry outlet concept eliminates traditional problems faced by flooring retailers: installation subcontracting, receivables, measuring and delivery and special ordering of merchandise. GCO offers support in all stages of franchise. Over 60% of growth is from existing GCO franchisees.

BACKGROUND:
Established: 1988; 1st Franchised: 1989
Franchised Units: 125
Company-Owned Units 7
Total Units: 132
Dist.: US-108; CAN-0; O'seas-0
North America: 26 States
Density: 19 in FL, 9 in MN, 8 in WI
Projected New Units (12 Months): 40
Qualifications: 5, 4, 3, 3, 3, 4
Registered: All States Except DC

FINANCIAL/TERMS:
Cash Investment: $100K
Total Investment: $260-522K
Minimum Net Worth: $400K
Fees: Franchise - $25K
Royalty - 3-5%; Ad. - $500/Mo.
Earnings Claim Statement: Yes
Term of Contract (Years): 10/5/5
Avg. # Of Employees: 4 FT, 1 PT
Passive Ownership: Discouraged
Encourage Conversions: Yes
Area Develop. Agreements: No
Sub-Franchising Contracts: No
Expand In Territory: Yes
Space Needs: 10,000 SF; FS, SF, SC

SUPPORT & TRAINING PROVIDED:
Financial Assistance Provided: Yes
Site Selection Assistance: Yes
Lease Negotiation Assistance: Yes
Co-Operative Advertising: Yes
Franchisee Assoc./Member: Yes/No
Size Of Corporate Staff: 33
On-Going Support: A,B,C,D,E,f,G,H,I
Training: 2 Weeks at Montgomery, AL.

SPECIFIC EXPANSION PLANS:
US: All United States
Canada: No
Overseas: No

<< >>

LIVING LIGHTING

4699 Keele St., # 1
Downsview, ON M3J 2N8 CANADA
Tel: (416) 661-9916
Fax: (416) 661-9706
Ms. Janine De Freitas

Full line of retail lighting, home lighting and home decorating centers.

BACKGROUND:
Established: 1968; 1st Franchised: 1970
Franchised Units: 22
Company-Owned Units 0
Total Units: 22
Dist.: US-0; CAN-28; O'seas-0
North America: 2 Provinces
Density: 27 in ON, 1 in BC
Projected New Units (12 Months): NR
Registered: AB

FINANCIAL/TERMS:
Cash Investment: $80K
Total Investment: $200-225K
Minimum Net Worth: $NR
Fees: Franchise - $30K
Royalty - 4%; Ad. - 1%
Earnings Claim Statement: Yes
Term of Contract (Years): NR
Avg. # Of Employees: NR
Passive Ownership: NR
Encourage Conversions: NR
Area Develop. Agreements: NR
Sub-Franchising Contracts: NR
Expand In Territory: NR
Space Needs: NR SF; NR

SUPPORT & TRAINING PROVIDED:
Financial Assistance Provided: No
Site Selection Assistance: Yes
Lease Negotiation Assistance: Yes
Co-Operative Advertising: Yes
Franchisee Assoc./Member: Yes/Yes
Size Of Corporate Staff: 18
On-Going Support: NR
Training: NR

SPECIFIC EXPANSION PLANS:
US: NR
Canada: All Canada
Overseas: No

<< >>

MORE SPACE PLACE, THE

12555 Enterprise Blvd., # 101
Largo, FL 33773
Tel: (888) 731-3051 (727) 539-1611
Fax: (727) 524-6382
E-Mail: clarkwilliams@ij.net
Web Site: www.morsspaceplace.com
Mr. Clark Williams, COO

Quality storage and space utilization systems. A collection of unique furniture, Murphy Beds, Pocket Office Desk System, custom closets and more. TMSP is poised to help consumers and business save one of today's most precious commodities: SPACE.

BACKGROUND: IFA MEMBER
Established: 1989; 1st Franchised: 1993
Franchised Units: 22
Company-Owned Units 1
Total Units: 23
Dist.: US-23; CAN-0; O'seas-0
North America: 2 States
Density: 20 in FL, 3 in MI
Projected New Units (12 Months): 6
Qualifications: 4, 4, 1, 3, 2, 5
Registered: FL,MI

FINANCIAL/TERMS:
Cash Investment: $85-153.8K
Total Investment: $85-153.8K
Minimum Net Worth: $250K
Fees: Franchise - $22.5K
Royalty - 4.5%/$500/W;
Ad. - 2.5%/$250/M
Earnings Claim Statement: No
Term of Contract (Years): 10/10
Avg. # Of Employees: 3 FT, 1 PT
Passive Ownership: Allowed
Encourage Conversions: Yes
Area Develop. Agreements: Yes/10
Sub-Franchising Contracts: No
Expand In Territory: Yes
Space Needs: 2,500 SF; FS, SF, SC

SUPPORT & TRAINING PROVIDED:
Financial Assistance Provided: No
Site Selection Assistance: Yes
Lease Negotiation Assistance: Yes
Co-Operative Advertising: Yes
Franchisee Assoc./Member: No
Size Of Corporate Staff: 30
On-Going Support: B,C,D,E,F,H
Training: 1 Week Headquarters Largo, FL; 4 Days On-Site.

SPECIFIC EXPANSION PLANS:
US: All United States
Canada: No
Overseas: No

<< >>

MOUNTAIN COMFORT FURNISHINGS

P.O. Box 767
Frisco, CO 80443
Tel: (888) 686-2638 (970) 668-3661
Fax: (970) 668-5329
E-Mail: mtncmft@colorado.net
Web Site: www.mountaincomfort.net
Mr. Bill Jarski, President

Franchises for the establishment and operation of a specialty furniture store which sells distinctive mountain life-style furnishings and specialty décor items. Group buying and marketing benefits. Low yearly license fee.

BACKGROUND:
Established: 1984; 1st Franchised: 1991
Franchised Units: 3
Company-Owned Units 2
Total Units: 5
Dist.: US-5; CAN-0; O'seas-0
North America: 2 States
Density: 3 in CO, 1 in OR, 1 in CA
Projected New Units (12 Months): 6
Qualifications: 4, 4, 2, 3, 3, 4
Registered: None

FINANCIAL/TERMS:
Cash Investment: $Varies
Total Investment: $190-410.8K
Minimum Net Worth: $150K
Fees: Franchise - $22.5K
Royalty - $10K/Yr.; Ad. - 0.5%/Mo.
Earnings Claim Statement: No
Term of Contract (Years): 5/5
Avg. # Of Employees: 3 FT, 2 PT
Passive Ownership: Discouraged
Encourage Conversions: Yes
Area Develop. Agreements: No
Sub-Franchising Contracts: No
Expand In Territory: Yes
Space Needs: 3,000-8,000 SF; FS, SC

SUPPORT & TRAINING PROVIDED:
Financial Assistance Provided: Yes(I)
Site Selection Assistance: Yes
Lease Negotiation Assistance: Yes
Co-Operative Advertising: Yes
Franchisee Assoc./Member: Yes/Yes
Size Of Corporate Staff: 4
On-Going Support: b,C,D,E,F,G,H,I
Training: 2+ Weeks Frisco or Vail, CO; 6+ Days at Franchise Location.

SPECIFIC EXPANSION PLANS:
US: Rocky Mtn. States and NE
Canada: No
Overseas: No

<< >>

NAKED FURNITURE

1157 Lackawanna Trail, P.O. Box F
Clarks Summit, PA 18411
Tel: (800) 352-2522 (570) 587-7800
Fax: (570) 586-8587
E-Mail: nkdfurn@epix.net
Web Site: www.nakedfurniture.com
Mr. Bruce C. MacGowan, President

NAKED FURNITURE is the nation's largest retailer of custom-finished and ready-to-finish solid wood home furnishings. We offer a wide range of innovative and affordable choices. We serve our markets with attractive, professionally-run stores and a diverse selection of quality furniture and accessories that allow our store owners to maintain their leadership position in the rapidly-growing specialty furniture market.

BACKGROUND:
Established: 1972; 1st Franchised: 1979
Franchised Units: 26
Company-Owned Units 2
Total Units: 28
Dist.: US-37; CAN-0; O'seas-0
North America: 12 States
Density: 9 in MI, 8 in IL, 5 in PA
Projected New Units (12 Months): 6
Qualifications: 4, 3, 1, 1, 3, 5
Registered: CA,FL,IL,IN,MD,MI,MN,ND, NY,RI,VA,WA,WI

FINANCIAL/TERMS:
Cash Investment: $72-123K
Total Investment: $143-245K
Minimum Net Worth: $NR
Fees: Franchise - $19.5K
Royalty - 4%; Ad. - 1%
Earnings Claim Statement: No
Term of Contract (Years): 10/10
Avg. # Of Employees: 3 FT, 2 PT
Passive Ownership: Allowed
Encourage Conversions: Yes
Area Develop. Agreements: Yes
Sub-Franchising Contracts: No
Expand In Territory: Yes
Space Needs: 6,500+ SF; FS, SF, SC, RM

SUPPORT & TRAINING PROVIDED:
Financial Assistance Provided: Yes
Site Selection Assistance: Yes
Lease Negotiation Assistance: Yes
Co-Operative Advertising: No
Franchisee Assoc./Member: Yes/Yes
Size Of Corporate Staff: 19
On-Going Support: a,B,C,D,E,F,G,h,I
Training: 1 Week Headquarters; 1 Week On-Site.

SPECIFIC EXPANSION PLANS:
US: All United States
Canada: No
Overseas: No

<< >>

NORWALK - THE FURNITURE IDEA

100 Furniture Pkwy.
Norwalk, OH 44857-9587
Tel: (800) NORWALK (800) 837-2565
Fax: (419) 744-3212
E-Mail: mike_turbeville@norwalk-furniture
Web Site: www.norwalkfurnitureidea.com
Mr. Mike Turbeville, Retail Development

Living room specialty stores offering consumers 1000 fabrics and leathers available in 500 styles with delivery in just 35 days.

BACKGROUND: IFA MEMBER
Established: 1902; 1st Franchised: 1987
Franchised Units: 73
Company-Owned Units 12
Total Units: 85
Dist.: US-79; CAN-8; O'seas-0
North America: 29 States, 3 Provinces
Density: 14 in FL, 5 in TX, 5 in CA
Projected New Units (12 Months): 6
Qualifications: 4, 3, 3, 2, 3, 4
Registered: All States

FINANCIAL/TERMS:
Cash Investment: $75-175K
Total Investment: $350-400K
Minimum Net Worth: $250K
Fees: Franchise - $50K
Royalty - 1.5%; Ad. - 0%
Earnings Claim Statement: No
Term of Contract (Years): 20/5
Avg. # Of Employees: 12 FT
Passive Ownership: Discouraged
Encourage Conversions: Yes
Area Develop. Agreements: Yes/1
Sub-Franchising Contracts: No

Expand In Territory: Yes
Space Needs: 4,000 SF; FS, SC

SUPPORT & TRAINING PROVIDED:

Financial Assistance Provided: Yes(I)
Site Selection Assistance: Yes
Lease Negotiation Assistance: Yes
Co-Operative Advertising: Yes
Franchisee Assoc./Member: Yes/Yes
Size Of Corporate Staff: 10
On-Going Support: a,b,C,D,E,F,h,I
Training: 2 Weeks, Cleveland; 1 Week Co-owned Store, 2 Weeks, Franchisee's Store.

SPECIFIC EXPANSION PLANS:

US: All United States
Canada: All Canada
Overseas: All Countries

<< >>

SLUMBERLAND INTERNATIONAL

3060 Centerville Rd.
Little Canada, MN 55117
Tel: (651) 482-7500
Fax: (651) 490-0479
Web Site: www.slumberland-furniture.com
Mr. Keith Freeburg, Executive Director Franchising

SLUMBERLAND is a home furnishings specialty retailer, featuring name-brand mattresses, sleep sofas, reclining chairs, sofas and chairs, daybeds and related bedroom furniture. SLUMBERLAND is a market-driven retailer that outpaces national averages in sales/SF and gross margins.

BACKGROUND: IFA MEMBER

Established: 1967; 1st Franchised: 1978
Franchised Units: 39
Company-Owned Units 22
Total Units: 61
Dist.: US-67; CAN-0; O'seas-0
North America: 7 States
Density: 33 in MN, 12 in IA, 8 in SD
Projected New Units (12 Months): 8
Registered: IL,MN,ND,SD,WI

FINANCIAL/TERMS:

Cash Investment: $NR
Total Investment: $100-400K
Minimum Net Worth: $NR
Fees: Franchise - $12.5K
Royalty - 3%; Ad. - 2%
Earnings Claim Statement: No
Term of Contract (Years): 10/10
Avg. # Of Employees: 4 FT, 2 PT
Passive Ownership: Discouraged
Encourage Conversions: Yes
Area Develop. Agreements: No
Sub-Franchising Contracts: No
Expand In Territory: Yes
Space Needs: 15,000 SF; FS, SC

SUPPORT & TRAINING PROVIDED:

Financial Assistance Provided: No
Site Selection Assistance: No
Lease Negotiation Assistance: Yes
Co-Operative Advertising: N/A
Franchisee Assoc./Member: NR
Size Of Corporate Staff: NR
On-Going Support: B,c,d,G,H,i
Training: 3 Days Headquarters; 2 Weeks On-Site.

SPECIFIC EXPANSION PLANS:

US: Central Midwest
Canada: No
Overseas: No

<< >>

Top 50

VERLO MATTRESS FACTORY STORES

W3130 Hwy 59, P.O. Box 298
Whitewater, WI 53190
Tel: (800) 229-8957 (262) 473-8957
Fax: (262) 473-4623
E-Mail: franchise@verlo.com
Web Site: www.verlofranchise.com
Mr. James M. Young, VP Franchising

VERLO MATTRESS FACTORY STORES (R) is the nation's largest CRAFTSMAN DIRECT (R) retailer. Each franchise assembles hand-crafted mattresses to the customer's specifications.

BACKGROUND: IFA MEMBER

Established: 1958; 1st Franchised: 1981
Franchised Units: 59
Company-Owned Units 7
Total Units: 66
Dist.: US-66; CAN-0; O'seas-0
North America: 10 States
Density: 23 in WI, 22 in IL, 4 in FL
Projected New Units (12 Months): 14
Qualifications: 4, 3, 2, 3, 4, 5
Registered: All States Except CA and HI

FINANCIAL/TERMS:

Cash Investment: $40-100K
Total Investment: $178-500K
Minimum Net Worth: $300K
Fees: Franchise - $30K
Royalty - 5%; Ad. - $300/Mo.
Earnings Claim Statement: Yes
Term of Contract (Years): 5/5
Avg. # Of Employees: 5 FT
Passive Ownership: Allowed
Encourage Conversions: Yes
Area Develop. Agreements: Yes/Varies
Sub-Franchising Contracts: No
Expand In Territory: Yes
Space Needs: 3,000-10,000 SF; FS, SF

SUPPORT & TRAINING PROVIDED:

Financial Assistance Provided: No
Site Selection Assistance: Yes
Lease Negotiation Assistance: Yes
Co-Operative Advertising: No
Franchisee Assoc./Member: Yes/Yes
Size Of Corporate Staff: 13
On-Going Support: B,C,D,E,G,H,i
Training: 5-10 Days Corporate Office; 5-7 Days On-Site; On-Going.

SPECIFIC EXPANSION PLANS:

US: All United States
Canada: No
Overseas: No

<< >>

WINDOW WORKS

5821 Cedar Lake Rd.
Minneapolis, MN 55344-3516
Tel: (800) 326-2659 (952) 943-4353
Fax: (952) 943-9050
E-Mail: info@windowworks.net
Web Site: www.windowworks.net
Mr. Thomas Bodin, President

WINDOW WORKS showroom retails custom window treatments and accessories all within a 1,000 to 1,500 SF facility. Designers offer in-home consultation service, selling top-quality drapery, shutters, blinds and bedding. Exclusive Windcom software tracks day-to-day business and generates 27 reports from marketing to sales tax.

BACKGROUND:

Established: 1978; 1st Franchised: 1979
Franchised Units: 6

Company-Owned Units	0
Total Units:	6
Dist.:	US-6; CAN-0; O'seas-0
North America:	6 States
Density:	1 in MI, 1 in CO
Projected New Units (12 Months):	3-4
Qualifications:	3, 2, 1, 2, 3, 4

Registered: IL,IN,MD,MI,MN,VA,WA

FINANCIAL/TERMS:

Cash Investment:	$NR
Total Investment:	$60-90K
Minimum Net Worth:	$NR
Fees: Franchise -	$17.5K
Royalty - 4%;	Ad. - 1%
Earnings Claim Statement:	No
Term of Contract (Years):	15/15
Avg. # Of Employees:	2 FT, 1 PT
Passive Ownership:	Discouraged
Encourage Conversions:	No
Area Develop. Agreements:	No
Sub-Franchising Contracts:	No
Expand In Territory:	No

Space Needs: 1,000-1,500 SF; SC

SUPPORT & TRAINING PROVIDED:

Financial Assistance Provided:	No
Site Selection Assistance:	Yes
Lease Negotiation Assistance:	Yes
Co-Operative Advertising:	Yes
Franchisee Assoc./Member:	No
Size Of Corporate Staff:	4
On-Going Support:	C,D,E,G,H,I

Training: 1-2 Weeks Corporate Window Works - MN; Store Site, as Needed.

SPECIFIC EXPANSION PLANS:

US:	Most Areas; Not CA or NY
Canada:	No
Overseas:	No

<< >>

SUPPLEMENTAL LISTING OF FRANCHISORS

ABBEY CARPET COMPANY, 3471 Bonita Bay Blvd., Bonita Springs, FL 34134 ; (800) USE-ABBEY (941) 948-0900; (941) 948-0999

CARPET MASTER, 179 Christopher St., New York, NY 10014 ; (800) 596-7847 (516) 798-7000; (516) 795-3545

CARPETERIA, 25322 Rye Canyon Rd., Valencia, CA 91355-1151 ; (800) 356-6763 (805) 295-1000; (805) 257-4958

CARPETMAX, 210 Town Park Dr., Kennesaw, GA 30144 ; (800) 331-1744 (678) 355-4000; (678) 355-4995

CARPETS PLUS, 210 Town Park Dr., Kennesaw, GA 30144 ; (678) 355-4000; (678) 355-4995

CLASSY CLOSETS ETC., 1235 S. Akimel Ln., # 5063, Chandler, AZ 85226-5170; (800) 992-2448 (602) 967-2200; (602) 438-2304

DECOR & YOU, 900 Main St. S., Bldg. # 2, Southbury, CT 06488 ; (800) 477-3326 (203) 264-3500; (203) 264-3516

DESIGNS OF THE INTERIOR (DOTI), 1226 W. Northwest Hwy., Palatine, IL 60067 ; (888) 382-7488 (847) 776-7477; (847) 776-7459

EXPRESSIONS CUSTOM FURNITURE, 902 Napoleon Ave., New Orleans, LA 70115 ; (800) 323-1160 (504) 812-0720; (504) 887-8874

EXPRESSIONS IN FABRICS, 401 11th St., NW, Hickory, NC 28601 ; ; (704) 328-2176

FURNITURE REP'S WAREHOUSE, 294 Carlton Dr., Carol Stream, IL 60188 ; (630) 588-9270; (630) 588-1754

LIFESTYLE MOBILE CARPET SHOWROOM, P.O. Box 3876, Dalton, GA 30721 ; (800) 346-4531 (706) 278-7919; (706) 278-7711

NATIONWIDE FLOOR & WINDOW COVERINGS, 111 E. Kilbourn Ave., # 2400, Milwaukee, WI 53202-6611 ; (800) 366-8088 (414) 765-9900; (414) 765-1300

PANHANDLER, THE, 4699 Keele St., # 1, Downsview, ON M3J 2N8 CANADA; (416) 661-9916; (416) 661-9706

SEARS CARPET & UPHOLSTERY CARE, 8101 N. High St., # 260, Columbus, OH 43235-1406 ; (800) 586-1603 (614) 318-3003; (614) 847-4055

SPRING CREST DRAPERY CENTERS, 4375 Prado Rd., # 104, Corona, CA 91720 (800) 552-5523 (909) 340-2293; (909) 340-2078

TODAY'S WINDOW FASHIONS, 3121 Mt. Pinos Way, Box 549, Frazier Park, CA 93225 ; (888) 649-1600 (805) 245-2443; (805) 245-1909

Retail: Home Improvement & Hardware

Chapter

39

Retail: Home Improvement & Hardware Industry Profile

Retail: Home Improvement & Hardware Industry Profile

Total # Franchisors in Industry Group	16
Total # Franchised Units in Industry Group	10,785
Total # Company-Owned Units in Industry Group	308
Total # Operating Units in Industry Group	11,093
Average # Franchised Units/Franchisor	674.0
Average # Company-Owned Units/Franchisor	19.3
Average # Total Units/Franchisor	693.3
Ratio of Total # Franchised Units/Total # Company-Owned Units	35.0:1
Industry Survey Participants	6
Representing % of Industry	37.5%
Average Franchise Fee*:	$30.2K
Average Total Investment*:	$303.5K
Average On-Going Royalty Fee*:	4.7%

*If a range was provided, the mid-point of the range was used. See detailed profiles for actual ranges.

Five Largest Participants in Survey

Company	# Franchised Units	# Co-Owned Units	# Total Units	Franchise Fee	On-Going Royalty	Total Investment
1. Snap-On Tools	4,562	99	4,661	5K	$50/Mo.	156-248K
2. Matco Tools	1,374	28	1,404	0K	0%	54-147K
3. Stained Glass Overlay	285	0	285	45K	5%	80K
3. Color Your World	44	130	174	35-80K	7%	180-300K
5. United States Seamless	87	11	98	8.5K	$2.5/Mach.	49.5-147K

All of the data provided are proprietary and should not be quoted without acknowledging *Bond's Franchise Guide.*

ACE HARDWARE

2200 Kensington Ct.
Oak Brook, IL 60523-2100
Tel: (800) 4-ACE-HDW (630) 472-4041
Fax: (630) 571-0977
E-Mail: bjabl@acehardware.com
Web Site: www.acehardware.com
Mr. Bill Jablonowski, Fran. Program Mgr.

ACE HARDWARE is a Fortune 500 company of over 5,100 retailers selling hardware and related home improvement products. ACE is now offering franchise opportunities in selected markets nationwide. Come grow in this new endeavor with the backing of a company possessing 75 years of success, along with outstanding purchasing power, brand recognition and retail practices.

BACKGROUND:
Established: 1924; 1st Franchised: 1999
Franchised Units: 0
Company-Owned Units 13
Total Units: 13
Dist.: US-13; CAN-0; O'seas-0
North America: 3 States
Density: NR
Projected New Units (12 Months): 10
Qualifications: 5, 4, 3, 3, 3, 5
Registered: All States

FINANCIAL/TERMS:
Cash Investment: $150-250K
Total Investment: $1.0-1.2MM
Minimum Net Worth: $1MM
Fees: Franchise - $35K
Royalty - 2%; Ad. - 1.3%/$6.5K
Earnings Claim Statement: No
Term of Contract (Years): 20/5
Avg. # Of Employees: 3 FT, 10-12 PT
Passive Ownership: Not Allowed
Encourage Conversions: Yes
Area Develop. Agreements: No
Sub-Franchising Contracts: No
Expand In Territory: Yes
Space Needs: 10,000-15,000 SF; FS, SC

SUPPORT & TRAINING PROVIDED:
Financial Assistance Provided: Yes(I)
Site Selection Assistance: Yes
Lease Negotiation Assistance: Yes
Co-Operative Advertising: Yes
Franchisee Assoc./Member: Not Yet
Size Of Corporate Staff: 5,000
On-Going Support: A,B,C,D,e,F,G
Training: 6 Weeks Oak Brook, IL.

SPECIFIC EXPANSION PLANS:
US: Selected Markets in US.
Canada: No
Overseas: No

<< >>

COLOR YOUR WORLD

2600 Steeles Ave. W.
Concord, ON L4K 3C8 CANADA
Tel: (800) 387-7311 (905) 738-7477
Fax: (905) 738-9723
Mr. Bob Crookston, Franchise Sales Mgr.

Canada's largest paint and wallpaper retailer, selling to the do-it-yourself and trade markets.

BACKGROUND:
Established: 1912; 1st Franchised: 1977
Franchised Units: 44
Company-Owned Units 130
Total Units: 174
Dist.: US-0; CAN-276; O'seas-0
North America: 10 Provinces
Density: ON, BC, AB
Projected New Units (12 Months): NR
Qualifications: 5, 5, 2, 3, 4, 5
Registered: AB

FINANCIAL/TERMS:
Cash Investment: $90-150K
Total Investment: $180-300K
Minimum Net Worth: $N/A
Fees: Franchise - $35-80K
Royalty - 7%; Ad. - 4%
Earnings Claim Statement: No
Term of Contract (Years): 10/5
Avg. # Of Employees: 4 FT, 3 PT
Passive Ownership: Discouraged
Encourage Conversions: N/A
Area Develop. Agreements: No
Sub-Franchising Contracts: No
Expand In Territory: No
Space Needs: 3,000 SF; FS

SUPPORT & TRAINING PROVIDED:
Financial Assistance Provided: N/A
Site Selection Assistance: N/A
Lease Negotiation Assistance: N/A
Co-Operative Advertising: N/A
Franchisee Assoc./Member: Yes/No
Size Of Corporate Staff: NR
On-Going Support: A,B,C,D,F,G,h,I
Training: 8 Weeks at Various Locations.

SPECIFIC EXPANSION PLANS:
US: No
Canada: All Canada
Overseas: No

<< >>

MAC TOOLS

4635 Hilton Corp. Dr.
Columbus, OH 43232
Tel: (800) 622-8665 (330) 929-4949
Fax: (330) 926-5320
E-Mail: angie.mccartney@mactools.com
Web Site: www.mactools.com
Ms. Angie McCartney, Franchise Sales Admin.

Mobile distributors of "World Class" MATCO TOOLS, diagnostic computers and service equipment to professional automotive technicians at their place of employment.

BACKGROUND: IFA MEMBER
Established: 1978; 1st Franchised: 1993
Franchised Units: 1,374
Company-Owned Units 28
Total Units: 1,404
Dist.: US-1360; CAN-0; O'seas-0
North America: 50 States
Density: NR
Projected New Units (12 Months): 290
Qualifications: 3, 2, 2, 1, 2, 5
Registered: All States

FINANCIAL/TERMS:
Cash Investment: $15.5-26K
Total Investment: $54-147K
Minimum Net Worth: $15K
Fees: Franchise - $0
Royalty - 0%; Ad. - 0%
Earnings Claim Statement: No
Term of Contract (Years): 10/10
Avg. # Of Employees: 1 FT
Passive Ownership: Allowed
Encourage Conversions: Yes
Area Develop. Agreements: No
Sub-Franchising Contracts: No
Expand In Territory: Yes
Space Needs: N/A SF; N/A

SUPPORT & TRAINING PROVIDED:
Financial Assistance Provided: Yes(D)
Site Selection Assistance: N/A
Lease Negotiation Assistance: N/A
Co-Operative Advertising: N/A
Franchisee Assoc./Member: Yes/Yes
Size Of Corporate Staff: 180
On-Going Support: A,B,C,D,E,F,G,H,I
Training: 6 Day Classroom Stow, OH; 3 Weeks On-Site.

SPECIFIC EXPANSION PLANS:
US: All United States
Canada: No
Overseas: No

<< >>

SNAP-ON TOOLS

2801 80th St.
Kenosha, WI 53141-1410
Tel: (800) 786-6600 (262) 656-6516

Fax: (262) 656-5088
E-Mail: franchise@snapon.com
Web Site: www.snapon.com
Mr. M. Raymond Moore, Dir. Franchise Operations

Snap-on

The premier solutions provider to the vehicle service industry. Premium quality products, delivered and sold with premium service. We are proud of our heritage and are boldly addressing the future needs of our customers with improved efficiency, creating products and services from hand tools to data and management systems. Contact us today for discussion.

BACKGROUND: IFA MEMBER
Established: 1920; 1st Franchised: 1991
Franchised Units: 4,562
Company-Owned Units 99
Total Units: 4,661
Dist.: US-3374; CAN-355; O'seas-833
North America: All States & Provinces
Density: 360 in CA, 241 in TX, 190 PA
Projected New Units (12 Months): 682
Qualifications: 3, 4, 2, 2, 5, 5
Registered: All States

FINANCIAL/TERMS:
Cash Investment: $Low Cost
Total Investment: $156-248K
Minimum Net Worth: $NR
Fees: Franchise - $5K
Royalty - $50/Mo.; Ad. - 0%
Earnings Claim Statement: Yes
Term of Contract (Years): 10/5
Avg. # Of Employees: 1 FT
Passive Ownership: Not Allowed
Encourage Conversions: Yes
Area Develop. Agreements: No
Sub-Franchising Contracts: No
Expand In Territory: Yes
Space Needs: NR SF; N/A

SUPPORT & TRAINING PROVIDED:
Financial Assistance Provided: Yes(D)
Site Selection Assistance: N/A
Lease Negotiation Assistance: N/A
Co-Operative Advertising: N/A
Franchisee Assoc./Member: No
Size Of Corporate Staff: NR
On-Going Support: A,B,C,D,E,F,G,h,I
Training: 1 Week at Branch or Regional Office; 1 Week at Branch; 3 Weeks On-the-Job.

SPECIFIC EXPANSION PLANS:
US: All United States
Canada: All Canada
Overseas: Japan, UK, Germany, Australia, New Zealand, S. Africa

<< >>

STAINED GLASS OVERLAY
1827 North Case St.
Orange, CA 92865
Tel: (800) 944-4746 (714) 974-6124
Fax: (714) 974-6529
E-Mail: info@stainedglassoverlay.com
Web Site: www.stainedglassoverlay.com
Ms. Cathy Cooper, Franchise Services

We are the leading decorative glass franchisor in the world. Combine our patented technology and proven format into a great business. Design works of SGO, for homes, business and religious institutions. We don't require that you have an artistic or glass industry background. We provide training in all required skills.

BACKGROUND: IFA MEMBER
Established: 1981; 1st Franchised: 1982
Franchised Units: 285
Company-Owned Units 0
Total Units: 285
Dist.: US-141; CAN-14; O'seas-130
North America: 39 States, 6 Provinces
Density: 26 in CA, 7 in IL, 6 in FL
Projected New Units (12 Months): 25
Qualifications: 4, 4, 3, 2, 2, 5
Registered: All States Exc. ND and HI, plus AB

FINANCIAL/TERMS:
Cash Investment: $80K
Total Investment: $80K
Minimum Net Worth: $200K
Fees: Franchise - $45K
Royalty - 5%; Ad. - 2%
Earnings Claim Statement: No
Term of Contract (Years): 5/5
Avg. # Of Employees: 3 FT
Passive Ownership: Discouraged
Encourage Conversions: Yes
Area Develop. Agreements: No
Sub-Franchising Contracts: No
Expand In Territory: Yes
Space Needs: 1,100 SF; SC

SUPPORT & TRAINING PROVIDED:
Financial Assistance Provided: Yes(I)
Site Selection Assistance: Yes
Lease Negotiation Assistance: No
Co-Operative Advertising: No
Franchisee Assoc./Member: Yes/Yes
Size Of Corporate Staff: 17
On-Going Support: B,C,d,e,F,G,h,I
Training: 2 x 1 Week Sessions at Headquarters in Orange, CA.

SPECIFIC EXPANSION PLANS:
US: All United States
Canada: All Can. Exc. PQ
Overseas: Western Europe

UNITED STATES SEAMLESS
2001 1st Ave. N.
Fargo, ND 58102-2426
Tel: (800) 615-9318 (701) 241-8888
Fax: (701) 241-9999
E-Mail: info@usseamless.com
Web Site: www.usseamless.com
Mr. David E. Hedman, National Sales Mgr.

UNITED STATES SEAMLESS, ranked the #1 seamless siding franchise in America by Entrepreneur Magazine, is offering protected franchise territories for the sale and installation of seamless steel siding, gutters and vinyl replacement windows. The franchise offers 14 solid PVC colors, 12 of which have matching accessories. We also offer 7 colors in the exclusive Mountain Cedar two-tone steel siding coil.

BACKGROUND:
Established: 1991; 1st Franchised: 1992
Franchised Units: 87
Company-Owned Units 11
Total Units: 98
Dist.: US-98; CAN-0; O'seas-0
North America: 14 States
Density: 32 in MN, 10 in IA, 9 in ND
Projected New Units (12 Months): 11
Qualifications: 5, 5, 4, 3, 4, 5
Registered: IL,IN,MI,MN,ND,OR,SD, WA,WI

FINANCIAL/TERMS:
Cash Investment: $20-40K
Total Investment: $49.5-147K
Minimum Net Worth: $40K
Fees: Franchise - $8.5K
Royalty - $2.5K/Mach.;
Ad. - $200-500/Mo
Earnings Claim Statement: No

Term of Contract (Years):	15/15
Avg. # Of Employees:	3 FT
Passive Ownership:	Not Allowed
Encourage Conversions:	No
Area Develop. Agreements:	No
Sub-Franchising Contracts:	No
Expand In Territory:	Yes

Space Needs: 2,000 SF; HB, Office/ Warehouse

SUPPORT & TRAINING PROVIDED:

Financial Assistance Provided:	Yes(D)
Site Selection Assistance:	Yes
Lease Negotiation Assistance:	No
Co-Operative Advertising:	No
Franchisee Assoc./Member:	No
Size Of Corporate Staff:	10
On-Going Support:	B,C,d,G,H,I

Training: 1 Week Fargo, ND.

SPECIFIC EXPANSION PLANS:

US:	All United States
Canada:	No
Overseas:	No

<< >>

SUPPLEMENTAL LISTING OF FRANCHISORS

AMERICAN HERITAGE SHUTTERS, 6655 Poplar Ave., # 204, Germantown, TN 38138-0643 ; (901) 751-1000; (901) 755-8666

AUSTIN HARDWOODS, 2119 Goodrich, Austin, TX 78704 ; (512) 442-4001; (512) 441-6444

DO IT BEST CORP., Nelson Rd., P.O. Box 868, Fort Wayne, IN 46801 ; (888) 364-8237 (219) 748-5300; (219) 748-5478

FEATHER RIVER WOOD & GLASS, 2345 Forest Ave., Chico, CA 95928-7641 (800) 395-3667 (530) 895-0762; (530) 895-9207

FLOORING AMERICA, 210 Town Park Dr., NW, Kennesaw, GA 30144-5514 ; (678) 355-4000; (678) 355-4995

FLOORTASTIC, 1638 S. Research Loop Rd., # 160, Tuscon, AZ 85710 ; (800) 332-7397 (520) 722-9718; (520) 296-4393

NITE TIME DÉCOR, P.O. Box 5183, Lubbock, TX 79404 ; (800) 687-9551 (806) 722-1225; (806) 722-9627

SERVICE WORLD, 3820 Premier Ave., Memphis, TN 38188 ; (901) 368-3361; (901) 368-1144

SNAP-ON TOOLS (CANADA), 2325 Skymark Ave., Mississauga, ON L4W 5A9 CANADA; (800) 665-8665 (905) 624-0066; (905) 238-9658

Retail: Pet Products & Services

Chapter 40

Retail: Pet Products & Services Industry Profile

Total # Franchisors in Industry Group	29
Total # Franchised Units in Industry Group	1,403
Total # Company-Owned Units in Industry Group	239
Total # Operating Units in Industry Group	1,642
Average # Franchised Units/Franchisor	48.4
Average # Company-Owned Units/Franchisor	8.2
Average # Total Units/Franchisor	56.6
Ratio of Total # Franchised Units/Total # Company-Owned Units	5.9:1
Industry Survey Participants	10
Representing % of Industry	34.5%
Average Franchise Fee*:	$17.6K
Average Total Investment*:	$149.3K
Average On-Going Royalty Fee*:	5.4%

*If a range was provided, the mid-point of the range was used. See detailed profiles for actual ranges.

Five Largest Participants in Survey

Company	# Franchised Units	# Co-Owned Units	# Total Units	Franchise Fee	On-Going Royalty	Total Investment
1. Pet Valu International	273	120	393	20K	N/A	85.4-208K
2. Petland	148	1	149	25K	4.5%	180-500K
3. Aussie Pet Mobile	129	1	130	17.5-27.5K	8%	45-165K
4. Pet Pantry International, The	35	0	35	20K	0%	65K
5. Pet Nanny of America	18	0	18	4.8K	5% Min./$25K/Wk.	5.3-6.8K

All of the data provided are proprietary and should not be quoted without acknowledging *Bond's Franchise Guide.*

ANIMAL ADVENTURE PETS

5453 S. 76th St.
Greendale, WI 53129
Tel: (800) 289-5665
Fax: (414) 423-7351
E-Mail: mike@AnimalAdventurePets.com
Web Site: www.petstorefranchise.com
Mr. Mike Edwards, President

Retail pet & supply store designed to make the most of pet enjoyment by customers and employees. Each unit has a distinctive store design that sets it apart from typical pet shops and discount pet food stores. The store has playful live animals, cheerful sounds of song birds, talking parrots and other small animals. The tropical environment & sales people keep customers coming back.

BACKGROUND:
Established: 1999; 1st Franchised: 1999
Franchised Units: 3
Company-Owned Units 3
Total Units: 6
Dist.: US-6; CAN-0; O'seas-0
North America: 1 State
Density: 6 in WI
Projected New Units (12 Months): 2
Qualifications: 3, 3, 2, 4, 3, 5
Registered: IL,WI,MI

FINANCIAL/TERMS:
Cash Investment: $80K
Total Investment: $248-345K
Minimum Net Worth: $200K
Fees: Franchise - $25K
Royalty - 4%; Ad. - 5%
Earnings Claim Statement: Yes
Term of Contract (Years): 10/3-5
Avg. # Of Employees: 6 FT, 7PT
Passive Ownership: Discouraged
Encourage Conversions: Yes
Area Develop. Agreements: No
Sub-Franchising Contracts: No
Expand In Territory: No
Space Needs: 7,500 SF; FS, SF, SC

SUPPORT & TRAINING PROVIDED:
Financial Assistance Provided: No
Site Selection Assistance: Yes
Lease Negotiation Assistance: Yes
Co-Operative Advertising: No
Franchisee Assoc./Member: No
Size Of Corporate Staff: 2
On-Going Support: C,d,E,F,G,H
Training: 15 Days in Milwaukee, WI; 5 Days at Store Location during Opening.

SPECIFIC EXPANSION PLANS:
US: Midwest
Canada: No
Overseas: No

<< >>

AUSSIE PET MOBILE

34189 Pacific Coast Hwy., # 203
Dana Point, CA 92629-2814
Tel: (949) 234-0680
Fax: (949) 234-0688
E-Mail: dlouy@aussiepetmobile.com
Web Site: www.aussiepetmobile.com
Mr. David Louy, VP Franchise Sales

AUSSIE PET MOBILE is an internationally proven franchise system of mobile pet grooming with new U.S. headquarters in Orange County, CA. We pride ourselves on our innovative trailer design, heated hydrobath and a 15-step grooming maintenance process. No experience is required. The AUSSIE PET MOBILE franchise package includes a comprehensive training course. Franchisees enjoy a protected territory with regional and national advertising support. Area development programs for absentee executives/investors.

BACKGROUND: IFA MEMBER
Established: 1996; 1st Franchised: 1997
Franchised Units: 156
Company-Owned Units 1
Total Units: 157
Dist.: US-105; CAN-0; O'seas-52
North America: 12 States
Density: CA, CO, TX
Projected New Units (12 Months): NR
Qualifications: 2, 1, 1, 3, 3, 5
Registered: CA,FL,IL,IN,MD,MI,MN,NY, OR,RI,VA,WA,WI

FINANCIAL/TERMS:
Cash Investment: $52.5K
Total Investment: $135-165K
Minimum Net Worth: $250K
Fees: Franchise - $17.5-27.5K
Royalty - 8%; Ad. - 4%
Earnings Claim Statement: No
Term of Contract (Years): 10/10+10
Avg. # Of Employees: 1-3 FT
Passive Ownership: Allowed
Encourage Conversions: No
Area Develop. Agreements: Yes/10
Sub-Franchising Contracts: No
Expand In Territory: Yes
Space Needs: NR SF; N/A

SUPPORT & TRAINING PROVIDED:
Financial Assistance Provided: Yes(I)
Site Selection Assistance: N/A
Lease Negotiation Assistance: N/A
Co-Operative Advertising: Yes
Franchisee Assoc./Member: Yes/Yes
Size Of Corporate Staff: 9
On-Going Support: A,B,C,D,E,F,G,H,I
Training: 5 Days for Employees; 1 Day for Area Developers.

SPECIFIC EXPANSION PLANS:
US: All United States
Canada: All Canada
Overseas: All Countries

<< >>

PET HABITAT

6921 Heather St.
Vancouver, BC V6P 3P5 CANADA
Tel: (604) 266-2721
Fax: (604) 266-5880
Mr. Ernest Ang, President

Up-scale retail pet center.

BACKGROUND:
Established: 1979; 1st Franchised: 1991
Franchised Units: 8
Company-Owned Units 2
Total Units: 10
Dist.: US-0; CAN-10; O'seas-5
North America: 1 Province
Density: 10 in BC
Projected New Units (12 Months): 3
Qualifications: 3, 3, 2, 3, 4, 4
Registered: None

FINANCIAL/TERMS:
Cash Investment: $50K+
Total Investment: $150-500K
Minimum Net Worth: $100K
Fees: Franchise - $10K+
Royalty - 5%; Ad. - 2%

Earnings Claim Statement: Yes
Term of Contract (Years): 5/5
Avg. # Of Employees: 3 FT, 3 PT
Passive Ownership: Discouraged
Encourage Conversions: Yes
Area Develop. Agreements: No
Sub-Franchising Contracts: Yes
Expand In Territory: Yes
Space Needs: 1,500+ SF; RM

SUPPORT & TRAINING PROVIDED:
Financial Assistance Provided: Yes(I)
Site Selection Assistance: Yes
Lease Negotiation Assistance: Yes
Co-Operative Advertising: Yes
Franchisee Assoc./Member: No
Size Of Corporate Staff: 6
On-Going Support: a,b,C,D,e,F,H
Training: 1 Week Head Office; 2 Weeks Corporate Store.

SPECIFIC EXPANSION PLANS:
US: No
Canada: BC
Overseas: Asia, South America

<< >>

PET NANNY OF AMERICA
310 N. Clippert St., # 5
Lansing, MI 48912
Tel: (517) 336-8622
Fax: (517) 336-8624
E-Mail: petnanny@arc.net
Web Site: www.petnanny.com
Ms. Rebecca Ann Brevitz, President

PET NANNY, the professional pet-sitting business system, was developed in 1983 specifically for full-time, serious operators in the fascinating pet care world. Our program gives specialists the quality competitive edge necessary to dominate in any market. In training, all areas of operation are covered including pet development and training, marketing, advertising, newsletters and contracts.

BACKGROUND:
Established: 1987; 1st Franchised: 1988
Franchised Units: 18
Company-Owned Units 0
Total Units: 18
Dist.: US-17; CAN-0; O'seas-0
North America: NR
Density: 3 in MI, 1 in FL, 1 in AZ
Projected New Units (12 Months): 6
Qualifications: 1, 3, 3, 3, 5, 5
Registered: FL,MI,OR

FINANCIAL/TERMS:
Cash Investment: $2.9-6.8K
Total Investment: $5.3-6.8K
Minimum Net Worth: $50K
Fees: Franchise - $4.8K
Royalty - 5%/Min. $25/wk; Ad. - 2%
Earnings Claim Statement: No
Term of Contract (Years): 5/5
Avg. # Of Employees: 1 FT, 6 PT
Passive Ownership: Discouraged
Encourage Conversions: Yes
Area Develop. Agreements: No
Sub-Franchising Contracts: No
Expand In Territory: Yes
Space Needs: N/A SF; HB

SUPPORT & TRAINING PROVIDED:
Financial Assistance Provided: Yes(D)
Site Selection Assistance: N/A
Lease Negotiation Assistance: N/A
Co-Operative Advertising: Yes
Franchisee Assoc./Member: No
Size Of Corporate Staff: 5
On-Going Support: a,B,c,D,G,h
Training: 3-5 Days in Lansing, MI.

SPECIFIC EXPANSION PLANS:
US: Most States
Canada: ON
Overseas: U.K.

PET PANTRY INTERNATIONAL, THE
1657 Highway 395, # 202
Minden, NV 89423
Tel: (800) 381-7387 (775) 783-9722
Fax: (775) 783-9513
E-Mail: wadew@thepetpantry.com
Web Site: www.thepetpantry.com
Mr. Wade Webster, VP Business Dev.

THE PET PANTRY can offer you a spectacular growth opportunity because the forecast calls for it to continue reigning cats and dogs! No royalties; protected marketing areas; little competition; advertising and marketing support; comprehensive, ongoing educational and training programs; on-going business development support. Our free home delivery of super-premium dog and cat food is a profitable way to build your future. Call 1-800-381-7387.

BACKGROUND:
Established: 1995; 1st Franchised: 1995
Franchised Units: 35
Company-Owned Units 0
Total Units: 35
Dist.: US-39; CAN-0; O'seas-0
North America: 22 States
Density: 8 in CA, 4 in WA, 2 in PA
Projected New Units (12 Months): 50
Qualifications: 4, 3, 1, 2, 1, 5
Registered: All States

FINANCIAL/TERMS:
Cash Investment: $20K
Total Investment: $65K
Minimum Net Worth: $100K
Fees: Franchise - $20K
Royalty - 0%; Ad. - 0%
Earnings Claim Statement: No
Term of Contract (Years): 7/7
Avg. # Of Employees: 1 FT
Passive Ownership: Allowed
Encourage Conversions: No
Area Develop. Agreements: No
Sub-Franchising Contracts: No
Expand In Territory: Yes
Space Needs: 600 SF; HB

SUPPORT & TRAINING PROVIDED:
Financial Assistance Provided: No
Site Selection Assistance: Yes
Lease Negotiation Assistance: No
Co-Operative Advertising: Yes
Franchisee Assoc./Member: No
Size Of Corporate Staff: 13
On-Going Support: B,C,D,F,g,H,I
Training: 5 Days in Minden, NV at Corporate Office.

SPECIFIC EXPANSION PLANS:
US: All United States
Canada: All Canada
Overseas: All as Master Franchisor

<< >>

PET VALU INTERNATIONAL
2 Devon Sq., # 200, 744 W. Lancaster
Wayne, PA 19087
Tel: (888) 564-6784 (610) 225-0800
Fax: (610) 225-0822
E-Mail: petvalu@aol.com
Web Site: www.petvalu.com
Mr. David J. Wheat, VP Franchise Development

Discount retailer of pet foods and supplies. 'Your Neighborhood Store With Superstore Prices.'

BACKGROUND:
Established: 1976; 1st Franchised: 1987
Franchised Units: 273
Company-Owned Units 120

Total Units: 393
Dist.: US-95; CAN-328; O'seas-0
North America: 5 States, 2 Provinces
Density: 227 in ON, 30 in PA,26 in NJ
Projected New Units (12 Months): TBD
Qualifications: 4, 3, 2, 3, 4, 5
Registered: MD,NY,VA

FINANCIAL/TERMS:

Cash Investment: $15-95K
Total Investment: $85.4-207.9K
Minimum Net Worth: $40-160K
Fees: Franchise - $20K
Royalty - N/A; Ad. - N/A
Earnings Claim Statement: No
Term of Contract (Years): 10/5/5
Avg. # Of Employees: 2 FT, 2 PT
Passive Ownership: Not Allowed
Encourage Conversions: No
Area Develop. Agreements: No
Sub-Franchising Contracts: No
Expand In Territory: No
Space Needs: 2,000-3,000 SF; SC

SUPPORT & TRAINING PROVIDED:

Financial Assistance Provided: Yes(B)
Site Selection Assistance: N/A
Lease Negotiation Assistance: Yes
Co-Operative Advertising: Yes
Franchisee Assoc./Member: Yes
Size Of Corporate Staff: 59
On-Going Support: A,C,E,F,I
Training: 1 Day at Head Office, Wayne, PA; 3 Weeks at Head Office and Operating Store.

SPECIFIC EXPANSION PLANS:

US: Northeast
Canada: MB, ON
Overseas: No

PETLAND

250 Riverside St., P.O. Box 1606
Chillicothe, OH 45601-5606
Tel: (800) 221-5935 (740) 775-2464
Fax: (740) 775-2575
E-Mail: jwhitman@petland.com
Web Site: www.petland.com
Mr. Jim Whitman, Director Fran. Dev.

PETLAND is a full-service, pet retail store that features live animals, including tropical fish, marine fish, small mammals, reptiles, amphibians, tropical, domestically-bred birds, puppies and kittens. The PETLAND concept also features over 4,000 merchandise items to support the pets sold to or already in the homes of its customers. Over 1,500 merchandise items are PETLAND brands, sold exclusively through PETLAND retail stores.

BACKGROUND:

Established: 1967; 1st Franchised: 1972
Franchised Units: 148
Company-Owned Units 1
Total Units: 149
Dist.: US-93; CAN-46; O'seas-6
North America: 32 States, 5 Provinces
Density: 19 in OH, 14 in FL, 11 in IL
Projected New Units (12 Months): 18
Qualifications: 3, 5, 1, 3, 4, 5
Registered: AB

FINANCIAL/TERMS:

Cash Investment: $60-120K
Total Investment: $180-500K
Minimum Net Worth: $250K
Fees: Franchise - $25K
Royalty - 4.5%; Ad. - N/A
Earnings Claim Statement: No
Term of Contract (Years): 20/20
Avg. # Of Employees: 5 FT, 7 PT
Passive Ownership: Discouraged
Encourage Conversions: Yes
Area Develop. Agreements: No
Sub-Franchising Contracts: No
Expand In Territory: Yes
Space Needs: 5,000 SF; FS, SC, RM

SUPPORT & TRAINING PROVIDED:

Financial Assistance Provided: Yes(I)
Site Selection Assistance: Yes
Lease Negotiation Assistance: Yes
Co-Operative Advertising: Yes
Franchisee Assoc./Member: No
Size Of Corporate Staff: 38
On-Going Support: B,C,D,E,F,G,H,I
Training: 1.5 Weeks Training Store, Chillicothe, OH; 1 Week Classroom; 2 Weeks New Store Location.

SPECIFIC EXPANSION PLANS:

US: All United States
Canada: All Canada
Overseas: Western Europe, Australia, South America

<< >>

PETS ARE INN

5100 Edina Blvd., # 206
Minneapolis, MN 55439
Tel: (800) 248-PETS (952) 944-8298
Fax: (952) 829-3828
E-Mail: jplatt@petsareinn.com
Web Site: www.petsareinn.com
Mr. Jim Platt, President

When a family goes on vacation, they prefer to have their pet cared for in a loving - caring - home environment. We are looking for individuals that recognize the need for PETS ARE INN in their area. An individual that has a proven track record as a professional in other areas but has made a conscious decision to change career paths - to be involved in business and in the community. Our unique niche in the hospitality/travel industry provides our customers and their pets with worry free services.

BACKGROUND:

Established: 1982; 1st Franchised: 1992
Franchised Units: 18
Company-Owned Units 0
Total Units: 18
Dist.: US-17; CAN-0; O'seas-0
North America: NR
Density: 6 in MN, 3 in TX, 2 in WA
Projected New Units (12 Months): 4
Qualifications: 5, 4, 3, 5, 5, 4
Registered: CA,HI,IL,IN,MD,MI,MN,WA

FINANCIAL/TERMS:

Cash Investment: $20K
Total Investment: $35-65K
Minimum Net Worth: $NR
Fees: Franchise - $15K
Royalty - 5-10%; Ad. - 1%
Earnings Claim Statement: Yes
Term of Contract (Years): 10/10
Avg. # Of Employees: 2 FT, 4 PT
Passive Ownership: Not Allowed
Encourage Conversions: N/A
Area Develop. Agreements: No
Sub-Franchising Contracts: No
Expand In Territory: No
Space Needs: NR SF; HB

SUPPORT & TRAINING PROVIDED:

Financial Assistance Provided: No
Site Selection Assistance: Yes
Lease Negotiation Assistance: Yes
Co-Operative Advertising: Yes
Franchisee Assoc./Member: No
Size Of Corporate Staff: 5
On-Going Support: A,B,C,D,E,G,H,I
Training: 5 Days in Minneapolis, MN.

SPECIFIC EXPANSION PLANS:

US: Central Time Zone
Canada: No
Overseas: No

<< >>

RUFFIN'S PET CENTRES

109 Industrial Dr.
Dunnville, ON N1A 2X5 CANADA

Tel: (905) 774-7079
Fax: (905) 774-1096
Mr. Mark Reynolds, President

RUFFIN'S PET CENTER is a unique combination of a traditional pet store and a discount, pet-food outlet. The union of these two types of stores increases the strength of both. The high traffic of a pet store increases the on-going pet food sales. This strong concept, combined with great office support, equals a successful franchise.

BACKGROUND:

Established: 1981; 1st Franchised: 1986

Franchised Units:	14
Company-Owned Units	0
Total Units:	14
Dist.:	US-0; CAN-14; O'seas-0
North America:	1 Province
Density:	14 in ON
Projected New Units (12 Months):	3
Qualifications:	4, 2, 1, 1, 2, 4

Registered: NR

FINANCIAL/TERMS:

Cash Investment:	$NR
Total Investment:	$65-85K
Minimum Net Worth:	$Varies
Fees: Franchise -	$20K
Royalty - 4%;	Ad. - 1%
Earnings Claim Statement:	No
Term of Contract (Years):	5/5
Avg. # Of Employees:	1 FT, 3 PT
Passive Ownership:	Not Allowed
Encourage Conversions:	Yes
Area Develop. Agreements:	No
Sub-Franchising Contracts:	No
Expand In Territory:	No

Space Needs: 1,500 SF; SC, RM

SUPPORT & TRAINING PROVIDED:

Financial Assistance Provided:	No
Site Selection Assistance:	Yes
Lease Negotiation Assistance:	Yes
Co-Operative Advertising:	Yes
Franchisee Assoc./Member:	No
Size Of Corporate Staff:	3
On-Going Support:	B,C,D,E,f,G,H

Training: 1 Week Operating Store Close to Franchise; 1-2 Weeks Head Office; 1-2 Weeks On-Site.

SPECIFIC EXPANSION PLANS:

US:	No
Canada:	ON
Overseas:	No

STEIN-WAY DOG TRAINING

1 Sarah Wells Trail
Goshen, NY 10924
Tel: (888) 636-7171 (845) 294-6880
Fax: (845) 294-8613
E-Mail: franchise@stein-way.com
Web Site: www.stein-way.com
Ms. Linda Stein, President/CEO

STEIN-WAY DOG TRAINING offers franchises to people who would love to spend their work week training dogs and the people that love them. Our unique system teaches dogs Manners, Obedience and Housebreaking in One 3-hour session. We include a guarantee that has worked for over 20 years for more than 6,000 dogs. You'll be selling others a wonderful and valuable service to a growing market sector - busy pet owners.

BACKGROUND:

Established: 1980; 1st Franchised: 2002

Franchised Units:	0
Company-Owned Units	0
Total Units:	0
Dist.:	US-0; CAN-0; O'seas-0
North America:	N/A
Density:	N/A
Projected New Units (12 Months):	3-6
Qualifications:	2, 4, 1, 4, 4, 5

Registered: NR

FINANCIAL/TERMS:

Cash Investment:	$21.5-47.5K
Total Investment:	$21.5-47.5K
Minimum Net Worth:	$N/A
Fees: Franchise -	$12.5-15K
Royalty - 500-700/Mo.;	Ad. - 3%
Earnings Claim Statement:	No
Term of Contract (Years):	10/10
Avg. # Of Employees:	None
Passive Ownership:	Not Allowed
Encourage Conversions:	No
Area Develop. Agreements:	Yes
Sub-Franchising Contracts:	No
Expand In Territory:	Yes

Space Needs: NR SF; FS, SF

SUPPORT & TRAINING PROVIDED:

Financial Assistance Provided:	No
Site Selection Assistance:	Yes
Lease Negotiation Assistance:	No
Co-Operative Advertising:	Yes
Franchisee Assoc./Member:	No
Size Of Corporate Staff:	NR
On-Going Support:	C,D,e,G,h,I

Training: 2 Weeks Goshen, NY.

SPECIFIC EXPANSION PLANS:

US:	NE, Mid-Atlantic, SE
Canada:	No
Overseas:	No

<< >>

SUPPLEMENTAL LISTING OF FRANCHISORS

BARK BUSTERS, 3881 E. Mallard, Highlands Ranch, CO 80126 ; (877) 280-7100 (303) 471-4935; (303) 471-4935

BONE APPETIT BAKERY, THE, 925 L St., Lincoln, NE 68508 ; (888) 81-BONES (402) 434-5888; (402) 434-5624

CANINE COUNSELORS, 1660 Southern Blvd. A, West Palm Beach, FL 33406 ; (800) 456-DOGS (561) 640-3970; (561) 640-3973

CRITTER CARE OF AMERICA, 1519 Kirkwood Ave., Nashville, TN 37221 (800) 256-3014 (615) 850-2273; (615) 463-8527

PET CITY, 1325 S. Cherokee St., Denver, CO 80223 ; (800) 526-7387 (303) 744-6131; (303) 777-5762

PET GUARD USA, 33 Pheasant Ln., Hamden, CT 06518 ; (866) DOG-FENCE (203) 288-7964

PET SUPPLIES PLUS, 37720 Amrhein, Livonia, MI 48150 ; (734) 464-2700; (734) 464-7500

PET VALU INTERNATIONAL (CANADA), 7300 Warden Ave., # 400, Markham, ON L3R 9Z6 CANADA; (888) 564-6784 (905) 946-1200; (905) 946-0659

PETPEOPLE, 722 Genevieve St., # E, Solana Beach, CA 92075 ; (800) 655-6595 (619) 481-3335; (619) 481-3337

PET-TENDERS, P.O. Box 23622, San Diego, CA 92193 ; (800) 738-8363 (619) 298-3033

Retail: Photographic Products & Services

Retail: Photographic Products & Services Industry Profile

Total # Franchisors in Industry Group	19
Total # Franchised Units in Industry Group	942
Total # Company-Owned Units in Industry Group	173
Total # Operating Units in Industry Group	1,115
Average # Franchised Units/Franchisor	49.6
Average # Company-Owned Units/Franchisor	9.1
Average # Total Units/Franchisor	58.7
Ratio of Total # Franchised Units/Total # Company-Owned Units	5.4:1
Industry Survey Participants	6
Representing % of Industry	31.6%
Average Franchise Fee*:	$20.2K
Average Total Investment*:	$132.2K
Average On-Going Royalty Fee*:	6.0%

*If a range was provided, the mid-point of the range was used. See detailed profiles for actual ranges.

Five Largest Participants in Survey

Company	# Franchised Units	# Co-Owned Units	# Total Units	Franchise Fee	On-Going Royalty	Total Investment
1. Motophoto (SM)	315	50	365	15K	6%	310K
2. Glamour Shots	152	2	154	15K	0%	150K
3. Sports Section, The	150	1	151	11-31K	0%	15-45K
4. One Hour Motophoto and Portrait (Canada)	53	3	56	35K	6%	225-250K
5. I.N.V.U. Portraits	51	0	51	12K	6%	28-66K

GLAMOUR SHOTS

1300 Metropolitan Ave.
Oklahoma City, OK 73108
Tel: (800) 336-4550 (405) 947-8747
Fax: (405) 951-7343
E-Mail: reesa@glamourshots.com
Web Site: www.glamourshots.com
Ms. Reesa Hembree, Franchise Sales Coord.

GLAMOUR SHOTS is more than you ever pictured. We are the industry leader in high-fashion photography. We provide pre-opening assistance, comprehensive training, operational training and systems and regional field consultants, as well as solid, on-going support. Come join the leader!

BACKGROUND: IFA MEMBER
Established: 1988; 1st Franchised: 1992
Franchised Units: 152
Company-Owned Units 2
Total Units: 154
Dist.: US-144; CAN-5; O'seas-9
North America: 42 States, 1 Province
Density: 25 in TX, 21 in FL, 14 in CA
Projected New Units (12 Months): 25
Qualifications: 5, 1, 1, 2, 2, 5
Registered: CA,FL,HI,IL,IN,MD,MI,MN,NY,OR,RI,SD,VA,WA,WI,DC

FINANCIAL/TERMS:
Cash Investment: $15K
Total Investment: $150K
Minimum Net Worth: $200K
Fees: Franchise - $15K
Royalty - 0%; Ad. - $357/Mo.
Earnings Claim Statement: No
Term of Contract (Years): 10/10
Avg. # Of Employees: NR
Passive Ownership: Not Allowed
Encourage Conversions: Yes
Area Develop. Agreements: Yes
Sub-Franchising Contracts: No
Expand In Territory: Yes
Space Needs: 800-1,200 SF; RM

SUPPORT & TRAINING PROVIDED:
Financial Assistance Provided: Yes(I)
Site Selection Assistance: Yes
Lease Negotiation Assistance: Yes
Co-Operative Advertising: Yes
Franchisee Assoc./Member: Yes
Size Of Corporate Staff: NR
On-Going Support: A,B,C,D,E,G,H
Training: 1 Week at National Training Center; 4 Wks. at Training Store; As Needed at Your Location.

SPECIFIC EXPANSION PLANS:
US: All United States
Canada: All Canada
Overseas: All Countries

<< >>

Top 50

I.N.V.U. PORTRAITS

563 W. 500 S., # 250
Bountiful, UT 84020
Tel: (801) 292-4688
Fax: (801) 299-1625
E-Mail: randy@invuportraits.com
Web Site: www.invuportraits.com
Mr. Randy S. Olson

I.N.V.U. PORTRAITS combine heartwarming, one-of-a-kind photography with the up-scale creative touch of hand coloring and sepia toning. The resulting combination is a cherished piece. If you've ever considered owning your own home-based business and are able to put your creative talents and energies into an exciting and rewarding industry, we want to speak with you.

BACKGROUND:
Established: 1995; 1st Franchised: 1996
Franchised Units: 51
Company-Owned Units 0
Total Units: 51
Dist.: US-51; CAN-0; O'seas-0
North America: 30 States
Density: 4 in CA, 4 in FL, 3 in VA
Projected New Units (12 Months): 60
Qualifications: 5, 4, 2, 1, 4, 5
Registered: CA,FL,IL,IN,MD,MI,MN,NY,OR,RI,VA,WA,WI,DC

FINANCIAL/TERMS:
Cash Investment: $28-66K
Total Investment: $28-66K
Minimum Net Worth: $50K
Fees: Franchise - $12K
Royalty - 6%; Ad. - 2%
Earnings Claim Statement: No
Term of Contract (Years): 10/5
Avg. # Of Employees: 4 FT
Passive Ownership: Not Allowed
Encourage Conversions: No
Area Develop. Agreements: No
Sub-Franchising Contracts: No
Expand In Territory: Yes
Space Needs: N/A SF; HB

SUPPORT & TRAINING PROVIDED:
Financial Assistance Provided: No
Site Selection Assistance: N/A
Lease Negotiation Assistance: N/A
Co-Operative Advertising: N/A
Franchisee Assoc./Member: No
Size Of Corporate Staff: 45
On-Going Support: b,C,D,G,h
Training: 5 Days Salt Lake City, UT.

SPECIFIC EXPANSION PLANS:
US: All United States
Canada: All Canada
Overseas: No

<< >>

MOTOPHOTO

Top 50

MOTOPHOTO (SM)

4444 Lake Center Dr.
Dayton, OH 45426-0096
Tel: (800) 733-6686 (937) 854-6686
Fax: (937) 854-0140
E-Mail: franchise@motophoto.com
Web Site: www.motophoto.com
Mr. Paul Pieschel, SVP Franchise Development

MOTOPHOTO is an up-scale specialty retailer in the $14 billion and still-growing photo processing and portrait industries. MOTOPHOTO stores feature on-site processing, portrait studios, select merchandise and digital applications. This is a happy, clean and up-scale business, operating with a small, professional staff and requiring a modest inventory investment with strong profit potential. Ranked #4 in Income Opportunities' Platinum 2000 and # 15 in Success Franchise Gold 100.

BACKGROUND: IFA MEMBER
Established: 1981; 1st Franchised: 1982
Franchised Units: 315
Company-Owned Units 50
Total Units: 365
Dist.: US-335; CAN-38; O'seas-47
North America: 27 States, 1 Province
Density: 50 in NJ, 44 in ON, 27 in IL
Projected New Units (12 Months): 20
Qualifications: 5, 4, 1, 4, 3, 5
Registered: CA,FL,HI,IL,IN,MD,MI,NY,RI,VA,WI,DC

FINANCIAL/TERMS:
Cash Investment: $60K
Total Investment: $310K
Minimum Net Worth: $150K

Fees: Franchise - $15K
Royalty - 6%; Ad. - 0.5%
Earnings Claim Statement: Yes
Term of Contract (Years): 10/10
Avg. # Of Employees: 3 FT, 3 PT
Passive Ownership: Allowed
Encourage Conversions: Yes
Area Develop. Agreements: Yes/5/5/5/5
Sub-Franchising Contracts: No
Expand In Territory: Yes
Space Needs: 1,200-1,400 SF; FS, SF, SC, RM

SUPPORT & TRAINING PROVIDED:
Financial Assistance Provided: Yes(D)
Site Selection Assistance: Yes
Lease Negotiation Assistance: Yes
Co-Operative Advertising: Yes
Franchisee Assoc./Member: No
Size Of Corporate Staff: 70
On-Going Support: B,C,D,E,G,H,I
Training: 3 Weeks Dayton, OH; 3 Weeks Local Market.

SPECIFIC EXPANSION PLANS:
US: All United States
Canada: ON, W Provinces
Overseas: All Countries

<< >>

ONE HOUR MOTOPHOTO & PORTRAIT STUDIO (CANADA)

1315 Lawrence Ave. E., # 509
Don Mills, ON M3A 3R3 CANADA
Tel: (416) 443-1900
Fax: (416) 443-1653
E-Mail: franchise@motophoto.com
Web Site: www.motophoto.com
Mr. John Blatchly, Fran. Dev.

Own a franchise that's fun to run! MOTOPHOTO is an up-scale, specialty retail concept, featuring one hour processing, photo-related merchandise and a portrait studio. We're dedicated to enhancing our customers' enjoyment of their imaging experiences better than any other provider.

BACKGROUND:
Established: 1986; 1st Franchised: 1987
Franchised Units: 53
Company-Owned Units 3
Total Units: 56
Dist.: US-0; CAN-56; O'seas-26
North America: 1 Province
Density: 56 in ON
Projected New Units (12 Months): 6-8
Qualifications: 5, 5, 1, 4, 4, 5
Registered: NR

FINANCIAL/TERMS:
Cash Investment: $85-90K
Total Investment: $225-250K
Minimum Net Worth: $250K
Fees: Franchise - $35K
Royalty - 6%; Ad. - 6%
Earnings Claim Statement: Yes
Term of Contract (Years): 10/2-5
Avg. # Of Employees: 3 FT, 2 PT
Passive Ownership: Not Allowed
Encourage Conversions: Yes
Area Develop. Agreements: No
Sub-Franchising Contracts: No
Expand In Territory: Yes
Space Needs: 1,000-1,200 SF; SF, SC, RM

SUPPORT & TRAINING PROVIDED:
Financial Assistance Provided: Yes(I)
Site Selection Assistance: Yes
Lease Negotiation Assistance: Yes
Co-Operative Advertising: Yes
Franchisee Assoc./Member: Yes/Yes
Size Of Corporate Staff: 10
On-Going Support: A,B,C,D,E,F,G,H
Training: 3 Weeks Corporate Training.

SPECIFIC EXPANSION PLANS:
US: N/A
Canada: ON, BC
Overseas: No

<< >>

SPORTS SECTION, THE

3871 Lakefield Dr., # 100
Suwanee, GA 30024
Tel: (800) 321-9127 (770) 622-4900
Fax: (770) 622-4949
E-Mail: jan@office.sports-section.com
Web Site: www.sports-section.com
Mr. Jan Rhodes, Dir. Fran. Dev.

'The Best in Youth & Sports Memories.' THE SPORTS SECTION franchisees earn income from 3 profit centers: youth and sports photo keepsakes, uniforms and trophies/awards. Complete training is provided. No experience in photography required. Exclusive, protected territories. No royalties. Operate from home or office, full or part-time. Finance plan available.

BACKGROUND: IFA MEMBER
Established: 1983; 1st Franchised: 1984
Franchised Units: 150
Company-Owned Units 1
Total Units: 151
Dist.: US-143; CAN-3; O'seas-0
North America: 43 States
Density: 12 in GA, 10 in FL, 9 in CA
Projected New Units (12 Months): 25
Qualifications: 5, 4, 1, 3, 3, 4
Registered: All States

FINANCIAL/TERMS:
Cash Investment: $10.9-30.9K
Total Investment: $15-45K
Minimum Net Worth: $N/A
Fees: Franchise - $10.9-30.9K
Royalty - 0%; Ad. - 0%
Earnings Claim Statement: Yes
Term of Contract (Years): 10/10
Avg. # Of Employees: 2 FT, 2 PT
Passive Ownership: Discouraged
Encourage Conversions: Yes
Area Develop. Agreements: Yes (Int'l.)
Sub-Franchising Contracts: Yes
Expand In Territory: Yes
Space Needs: N/A SF; HB, OB

SUPPORT & TRAINING PROVIDED:
Financial Assistance Provided: No
Site Selection Assistance: N/A
Lease Negotiation Assistance: N/A
Co-Operative Advertising: N/A
Franchisee Assoc./Member: Yes/Yes
Size Of Corporate Staff: 35
On-Going Support: A,b,C,D,G,H,h,I
Training: 2-3 Days in Franchisee's Territory; On-Going Training.

SPECIFIC EXPANSION PLANS:
US: All United States
Canada: All Canada
Overseas: Master Franchises Only

<< >>

VISUAL IMAGE, THE

100 E. Brockman Way
Sparta, TN 38583
Tel: (800) 344-0323 (931) 836-2800
Fax: (931) 836-6279
E-Mail: info@thevisualimageinc.com
Web Site: www.thevisualimageinc.com
Mr. Donald Holman, Vice President

VISUAL IMAGE combines the advantages of high mark-up photography with the low overhead of home-based business. Because we do all our photography on location, you save the high cost of retailspace and the confinement of retail hours! We go to preschools and pet shops and take portraits for busy, working parents. Because we do studio-quality portraiture, preschools love our work and invite us back season after season. Creative, fulfilling work, financial and physical rewards.

BACKGROUND:

Established: 1984;	1st Franchised: 1994
Franchised Units:	17
Company-Owned Units	3
Total Units:	20
Dist.:	US-20; CAN-0; O'seas-0
North America:	12 States
Density:	4 in FL, 4 in TN, 2 in NC
Projected New Units (12 Months):	3
Qualifications:	3, 4, 1, 1, 3, 5
Registered: FL,MI	

FINANCIAL/TERMS:

Cash Investment:	$30-40K
Total Investment:	$35-40K
Minimum Net Worth:	$50K
Fees: Franchise -	$23.5K
Royalty - 0%;	Ad. - 0%
Earnings Claim Statement:	Yes
Term of Contract (Years):	3/5
Avg. # Of Employees:	1 FT, 1 PT
Passive Ownership:	Discouraged
Encourage Conversions:	N/A
Area Develop. Agreements:	No
Sub-Franchising Contracts:	No
Expand In Territory:	Yes
Space Needs: N/A SF; HB	

SUPPORT & TRAINING PROVIDED:

Financial Assistance Provided:	Yes(I)
Site Selection Assistance:	N/A
Lease Negotiation Assistance:	N/A
Co-Operative Advertising:	Yes
Franchisee Assoc./Member:	Yes
Size Of Corporate Staff:	3
On-Going Support:	B,C,D,G,h,I

Training: 1 Week Home Base; 1 Week Training Center; I Week Training Center/Your Location.

SPECIFIC EXPANSION PLANS:

US:	All United States
Canada:	No
Overseas:	No

SUPPLEMENTAL LISTING OF FRANCHISORS

BRUSHSTROKES - WORKS OF ART, 4338 Glendale-Milford Rd., Cincinnati, OH 45242-3706 ; (888) 292-7992 ; (513) 563-2691

IMAGE ARTS, ETC., 8340 Camino Santa Fe, # E, San Diego, CA 92121-2665 ; (800) 865-4333 (858) 578-7200; (858) 453-4218

JAPAN CAMERA CENTRE 1 HOUR PHOTO, 205 Riviera Dr., # 1, Markham, ON L3R 5J8 CANADA; (800) 268-7740 (416) 445-1481; (416) 445-0519

LIL' ANGELS PHOTOGRAPHY, 6080 Quince Rd., Memphis, TN 38119 ; (800) 766-5052 (901) 682-4470; (901) 682-2018

MASTER PHOTOGRAPHY, P.O. Box 2239, Aspen, CO 81612 ; (800) 482-2505 (970) 927-2505; (970) 927-2522

ZAIO.COM, 93 Center Pointe Dr., St. Charles, MO 63304 ; (877) 233-9563 (636) 447-4429; (636) 498-0293

Retail: Specialty

Chapter 42

Retail: Specialty Industry Profile

Total # Franchisors in Industry Group	112
Total # Franchised Units in Industry Group	8,175
Total # Company-Owned Units in Industry Group	2,494
Total # Operating Units in Industry Group	10,669
Average # Franchised Units/Franchisor	73.0
Average # Company-Owned Units/Franchisor	22.3
Average # Total Units/Franchisor	95.3
Ratio of Total # Franchised Units/Total # Company-Owned Units	3.3:1
Industry Survey Participants	46
Representing % of Industry	41.1%
Average Franchise Fee*:	$25.1K
Average Total Investment*:	$193.6K
Average On-Going Royalty Fee*:	5.3%

*If a range was provided, the mid-point of the range was used. See detailed profiles for actual ranges.

Five Largest Participants in Survey

Company	# Franchised Units	# Co-Owned Units	# Total Units	Franchise Fee	On-Going Royalty	Total Investment
1. General Nutrition Centers	2,842	1,718	4,560	35K	6%	132.7-182K
2. Party Land	400	0	400	35K	5%	249-329K
3. Christmas Décor	340	0	340	9.5-16K	2-4.5%	15.9-31.9K
4. Book Rack, The	283	1	284	6K	$75/Month	18K+
5. Wild Birds Unlimited	281	0	281	18K	4	80-140K

All of the data provided are proprietary and should not be quoted without acknowledging *Bond's Franchise Guide.*

ASHLEY AVERY'S COLLECTABLES

100 Glenborough Dr., # 1450
Houston, TX 77067
Tel: (800) 543-3325 (281) 775-5290
Fax: (281) 775-5250
E-Mail: franinfo@fcibit.com
Web Site: www.ashleyaverys.com
Ms. Ann Nance, Franchise Development Mgr.

ASHLEY AVERY'S COLLECTABLES is America's largest chain of gifts & collectables, featuring exclusive pieces from world-renowned names such as Swarovski, Armani, Ilardo, Hummel and many more. Each store features an elegant, gallery-like atmosphere with fascinating works of all kinds. Located in up-scale regional malls. Easy to learn & operate; exceptional training and support; national buying power & proven marketing programs.

BACKGROUND: IFA MEMBER
Established: 1981; 1st Franchised: 1981
Franchised Units: 40
Company-Owned Units 1
Total Units: 41
Dist.: US-41; CAN-0; O'seas-0
North America: 13 States
Density: 17 in TX, 5 in FL, 2 in GA
Projected New Units (12 Months): 10
Qualifications: 5, 3, 3, 3, 4, 5
Registered: CA,FL,IL,IN,MD,MI,MN,NY, ND,RI,SD,VA,WA,WI

FINANCIAL/TERMS:
Cash Investment: $150K
Total Investment: $272-403K
Minimum Net Worth: $400K
Fees: Franchise - $30K
Royalty - 6%; Ad. - 2%
Earnings Claim Statement: No
Term of Contract (Years): 10
Avg. # Of Employees: 2 FT, 2 PT
Passive Ownership: Allowed
Encourage Conversions: Yes
Area Develop. Agreements: No
Sub-Franchising Contracts: No
Expand In Territory: Yes
Space Needs: 900-1,200 SF; RM, Kiosk (200sf)

SUPPORT & TRAINING PROVIDED:
Financial Assistance Provided: Yes(I)
Site Selection Assistance: Yes
Lease Negotiation Assistance: Yes
Co-Operative Advertising: Yes
Franchisee Assoc./Member: Yes/Yes
Size Of Corporate Staff: 7
On-Going Support: A,B,C,D,E,F,G,H,I
Training: 7 Days Houston, TX.

SPECIFIC EXPANSION PLANS:
US: All United States
Canada: No
Overseas: No

<< >>

BOOK RACK, THE

2715 E. Commercial Blvd.
Ft. Lauderdale, FL 33308
Tel: (954) 984-1918
Fax:
Mr. Fred M. Darnell, President

New and used paperback books.

BACKGROUND:
Established: 1963; 1st Franchised: 1966
Franchised Units: 283
Company-Owned Units 1
Total Units: 284
Dist.: US-283; CAN-1; O'seas-0
North America: NR
Density: TX, FL, TN
Projected New Units (12 Months): 19
Qualifications: 3, 3, 5, 3, 1, 2
Registered: All States Except ND,SD

FINANCIAL/TERMS:
Cash Investment: $16-34K
Total Investment: $18K+
Minimum Net Worth: $16K
Fees: Franchise - $6K
Royalty - $75/Mo.; Ad. - 0%
Earnings Claim Statement: No
Term of Contract (Years): Lifetime
Avg. # Of Employees: 1 FT, 1 PT
Passive Ownership: Allowed
Encourage Conversions: Yes
Area Develop. Agreements: No
Sub-Franchising Contracts: No
Expand In Territory: Yes
Space Needs: 1,200-6,000 SF; SC

SUPPORT & TRAINING PROVIDED:
Financial Assistance Provided: No
Site Selection Assistance: Yes
Lease Negotiation Assistance: Yes
Co-Operative Advertising: No
Franchisee Assoc./Member: No
Size Of Corporate Staff: 8
On-Going Support: C,D,E,F,G,H
Training: 7-10 Days Ft. Lauderdale, FL.

SPECIFIC EXPANSION PLANS:
US: All United States
Canada: All Canada
Overseas: No

<< >>

BUTTERFIELDS, ETC.

1040 Wm. Hilton Pkwy., Circle Bldg.
Hilton Head Island, SC 29928
Tel: (843) 842-6000
Fax: (843) 842-6999
Mr. Jim Lunceford, President

Retail gourmet kitchen store, located in up-scale malls. Our merchandise mix includes high-quality cookware, largest assortment of kitchen gadgets, cookbooks, decorative ceramics, linens, cutlery and fresh-roasted coffee beans.

BACKGROUND:
Established: 1979; 1st Franchised: 1986
Franchised Units: 19
Company-Owned Units 0
Total Units: 19
Dist.: US-26; CAN-0; O'seas-0
North America: NR
Density: NR
Projected New Units (12 Months): NR
Registered: NR

FINANCIAL/TERMS:
Cash Investment: $50K
Total Investment: $150-225K
Minimum Net Worth: $250K
Fees: Franchise - $20K
Royalty - 4-5%; Ad. - NR
Earnings Claim Statement: No
Term of Contract (Years): 10
Avg. # Of Employees: NR
Passive Ownership: Not Allowed
Encourage Conversions: Yes
Area Develop. Agreements: NR
Sub-Franchising Contracts: NR
Expand In Territory: NR
Space Needs: NR SF; NR

SUPPORT & TRAINING PROVIDED:
Financial Assistance Provided: Yes(I)
Site Selection Assistance: Yes
Lease Negotiation Assistance: Yes
Co-Operative Advertising: No
Franchisee Assoc./Member: No
Size Of Corporate Staff: NR
On-Going Support: NR
Training: 2 Weeks.

SPECIFIC EXPANSION PLANS:
US: NR
Canada: No
Overseas: No

<< >>

CANDLEMAN CORPORATION

1021 Industrial Park Rd.
Brainerd, MN 56401
Tel: (800) 328-3453 (218) 829-0592

Fax: (218) 825-2449
E-Mail: info@candleman.com
Web Site: www.candleman.com
Ms. Sara Wise, Vice President

Candleman is a focused franchise system is a leader in upscale retailing of unique candles and accessories. With an experienced professional management team to assist franchisees, Candleman provides an extremely comprehensive support program for its franchisees involving every aspect of setting up and operating a store. The successful franchisee is a partner couple who enjoys people, has a flair for home décor and would like working collectively with fellow franchisees.

BACKGROUND: IFA MEMBER
Established: 1991; 1st Franchised: 1992
Franchised Units: 62
Company-Owned Units 1
Total Units: 63
Dist.: US-58; CAN-5; O'seas-0
North America: 24 States, 3 Provinces
Density: 6 in PA, 5 in MN, 4 in WA
Projected New Units (12 Months): 10
Qualifications: 4, 4, 2, 2, 4, 5
Registered: All States
FINANCIAL/TERMS:
Cash Investment: $70K
Total Investment: $150-350K
Minimum Net Worth: $200K
Fees: Franchise - $25K
Royalty - 6%; Ad. - $100/Mo.
Earnings Claim Statement: No
Term of Contract (Years): 10/10
Avg. # Of Employees: 1 FT, 4-5 PT
Passive Ownership: Not Allowed
Encourage Conversions: No
Area Develop. Agreements: No
Sub-Franchising Contracts: No
Expand In Territory: No
Space Needs: 800-1,200 SF; RM
SUPPORT & TRAINING PROVIDED:
Financial Assistance Provided: Yes(I)
Site Selection Assistance: Yes
Lease Negotiation Assistance: Yes
Co-Operative Advertising: No
Franchisee Assoc./Member: Yes/Yes
Size Of Corporate Staff: 13
On-Going Support: C,D,E,F,G,H,I
Training: 7 Days in Headquarters; 3 Days On-Site.
SPECIFIC EXPANSION PLANS:
US: All United States
Canada: All Canada
Overseas: Europe, Middle East, Australia, South America

CHRISTMAS DECOR

P.O. Box 5946
Lubbock, TX 79413
Tel: (800) 687-9551 (806) 772-1225
Fax: (806) 722-9627
E-Mail: info@christmasdecor.net
Web Site: www.christmasdecor.net
Mr. Jim Ketchum, Chief Executive Officer

Holiday and event decorating services provided to homes and businesses. Fun, high-margin business that offers annual income by working only 4-6 months of the year. Also, an excellent add-on business for landscape, pool and spa, electrical and other seasonal service contractors. Landscape lighting franchise available also to create year round business.

BACKGROUND: IFA MEMBER
Established: 1986; 1st Franchised: 1996
Franchised Units: 340
Company-Owned Units 0
Total Units: 340
Dist.: US-160; CAN-5; O'seas-0
North America: 44 States, 2 Provinces
Density: 23 in TX, 14 in OH, 13 in MI
Projected New Units (12 Months): 100
Qualifications: 2, 4, 2, 3, 3, 4
Registered: All States and AB
FINANCIAL/TERMS:
Cash Investment: $6.6-9.5K
Total Investment: $15.9-31.9K
Minimum Net Worth: $N/A
Fees: Franchise - $9.5-15.9K
Royalty - 2-4.5%; Ad. - $180/Yr.
Earnings Claim Statement: No
Term of Contract (Years): 5/5
Avg. # Of Employees: 2-4 FT, 3-20 PT
Passive Ownership: Discouraged
Encourage Conversions: N/A
Area Develop. Agreements: No
Sub-Franchising Contracts: No
Expand In Territory: No
Space Needs: Varies SF; HB, Many Add-On Businesses
SUPPORT & TRAINING PROVIDED:
Financial Assistance Provided: Yes(D)
Site Selection Assistance: Yes
Lease Negotiation Assistance: No
Co-Operative Advertising: No
Franchisee Assoc./Member: Yes/Yes
Size Of Corporate Staff: 18
On-Going Support: A,B,D,G,h,I
Training: 3 Days Major Cities in US; 2 Days of Continuing Education in Major Cities.
SPECIFIC EXPANSION PLANS:
US: All United States
Canada: All Canada
Overseas: All Christian Countries

COMPUTER MOMS INTERNATIONAL

537 Woodward St., # D
Austin, TX 78704
Tel: (888) HIRE-MOMS (512) 477-6667
Fax: (512) 305-0132
E-Mail: franchisee@computermoms.com
Web Site: www.computermoms.com
Mr. Russell Harrell, Chief Executive Officer

Home-based business providing one-on-one computer training and support at the client's home or office on their computer with their applications. Prospective franchisees should have an intermediate level of Windows literacy and proficiency in common PC applications. Master franchises available now.

BACKGROUND: IFA MEMBER
Established: 1994; 1st Franchised: 1998
Franchised Units: 63
Company-Owned Units 1
Total Units: 64
Dist.: US-55; CAN-0; O'seas-0
North America: 2 States
Density: 54 in TX, 1 in OK
Projected New Units (12 Months): 36-72
Qualifications: 2, 3, 4, 2, 4, 4
Registered: NR
FINANCIAL/TERMS:
Cash Investment: $8.76-95.25K
Total Investment: $9.75-100K
Minimum Net Worth: $N/A
Fees: Franchise - $9.75K
Royalty - 14%; Ad. - 3%/$25/Wk.
Earnings Claim Statement: No
Term of Contract (Years): 7/7
Avg. # Of Employees: 1 FT, 0-10 PT
Passive Ownership: Not Allowed
Encourage Conversions: Yes
Area Develop. Agreements: Yes/5

Sub-Franchising Contracts: Yes
Expand In Territory: Yes
Space Needs: NR SF; N/A

SUPPORT & TRAINING PROVIDED:
Financial Assistance Provided: Yes(D)
Site Selection Assistance: N/A
Lease Negotiation Assistance: N/A
Co-Operative Advertising: N/A
Franchisee Assoc./Member: No
Size Of Corporate Staff: 8
On-Going Support: A,B,C,d,H,I
Training: 2 1-Week Sessions in Austin, TX.

SPECIFIC EXPANSION PLANS:
US: All United States
Canada: No
Overseas: No

<< >>

COMPUTER RENAISSANCE

124 S. Florida Ave., # 202
Lakeland, FL 33801
Tel: (888) 266-7736 (604) 730-5553
Fax: (604) 738-4080
E-Mail: rlancit@compren.com
Web Site: www.compren.com
Mr. Rob Lancit, VP Franchise Development

COMPUTER RENAISSANCE, a full-service retail store specializing in quality used, refurbished and new computer hardware, software and related accessories. Our stores also provide custom-built computers, system upgrades and superior technical service. With constant upgrades to computers in both the hardware and software fields, you can ensure your spot in a highly innovative industry by becoming part of a continuing market demand.

BACKGROUND: IFA MEMBER
Established: 1988; 1st Franchised: 1993
Franchised Units: 120
Company-Owned Units 4
Total Units: 124
Dist.: US-114; CAN-10; O'seas-0
North America: 34 States, 6 Provinces
Density: 8 in MN, 6 in IL, 6 in TX
Projected New Units (12 Months): 15
Qualifications: 4, 5, 2, 3, 4, 5
Registered: MI, OR, WI

FINANCIAL/TERMS:
Cash Investment: $75-100K
Total Investment: $70-280K
Minimum Net Worth: $100K
Fees: Franchise - $25K
Royalty - 5%; Ad. - 2%
Earnings Claim Statement: No
Term of Contract (Years): 5/5
Avg. # Of Employees: 4 FT, 2 PT
Passive Ownership: Discouraged
Encourage Conversions: Yes
Area Develop. Agreements: No
Sub-Franchising Contracts: No
Expand In Territory: Yes
Space Needs: 2,000 SF; SF, SC

SUPPORT & TRAINING PROVIDED:
Financial Assistance Provided: Yes(I)
Site Selection Assistance: Yes
Lease Negotiation Assistance: Yes
Co-Operative Advertising: No
Franchisee Assoc./Member: Yes/Yes
Size Of Corporate Staff: 20
On-Going Support: B,C,D,E,F,G,h,I
Training: 2 Weeks in Florida.

SPECIFIC EXPANSION PLANS:
US: All United States
Canada: All Canada
Overseas: All Countries

<< >>

CONNOISSEUR, THE

201 Torrance Blvd.
Redondo Beach, CA 90277
Tel: (310) 374-9768
Fax: (310) 372-9097
E-Mail: info@giftsofwine.com
Web Site: www.giftsofwine.com
Mr. Sandy French, President

Personalized gifts of fine wines, champagnes, gourmet, crystal and special occasion items.

BACKGROUND:
Established: 1975; 1st Franchised: 1989
Franchised Units: 7
Company-Owned Units 1
Total Units: 8
Dist.: US-7; CAN-0; O'seas-0
North America: 5 States
Density: 2 in CO, 2 in CA, 1 in IL
Projected New Units (12 Months): 25
Registered: All States

FINANCIAL/TERMS:
Cash Investment: $175K
Total Investment: $175K
Minimum Net Worth: $NR
Fees: Franchise - $29.5K
Royalty - 6%; Ad. - 1%
Earnings Claim Statement: No
Term of Contract (Years): 10/10
Avg. # Of Employees: 1 FT, 2 PT
Passive Ownership: Discouraged
Encourage Conversions: No
Area Develop. Agreements: Yes/10/10
Sub-Franchising Contracts: Yes
Expand In Territory: Yes
Space Needs: 2,000 SF; FS, SC, RM

SUPPORT & TRAINING PROVIDED:
Financial Assistance Provided: No
Site Selection Assistance: Yes
Lease Negotiation Assistance: Yes
Co-Operative Advertising: No
Franchisee Assoc./Member: NR
Size Of Corporate Staff: 4
On-Going Support: A,B,C,D,E,F,H
Training: 1 Week Headquarters.

SPECIFIC EXPANSION PLANS:
US: All United States
Canada: No
Overseas: No

<< >>

Country Clutter
Gifts, Collectibles & Home Decor
Top 50

COUNTRY CLUTTER

3333 Vaca Valley Pkwy., # 900
Vacaville, CA 95688
Tel: (800) 425-8883 (707) 451-6890
Fax: (707) 451-0410
E-Mail: franchiseinfo@countryclutter.com
Web Site: www.countryclutter.com
Mr. Terry Odneal, VP Franchise Development

A charming country store for gifts, collectibles and home decor. A unique business that offers old fashioned quality, selection and customer service. A complete franchise program professionally designed, computerized and planned to sell a perfected blend of country merchandise made by primarily American manufacturers and crafters. Rich arrangements and displays of textures, colors and aromas make shopping at COUNTRY CLUTTER a true sensory delight.

BACKGROUND:
Established: 1991; 1st Franchised: 1992
Franchised Units: 56

Company-Owned Units 3
Total Units: 59
Dist.: US-54; CAN-0; O'seas-0
North America: 23 States
Density: 16 in CA, 4 in GA, 5 in TX
Projected New Units (12 Months): 15
Qualifications: 5, 3, 3, 3, 4, 5
Registered: CA,FL,HI,IL,IN,MD,MI,NY, OR,RI,VA,WA, WI, DC

FINANCIAL/TERMS:

Cash Investment: $70-85K
Total Investment: $155-307K
Minimum Net Worth: $250K
Fees: Franchise - $25K
Royalty - 5.5%; Ad. - 1%
Earnings Claim Statement: Yes
Term of Contract (Years): 5/5
Avg. # Of Employees: 2 FT, 5 PT
Passive Ownership: Discouraged
Encourage Conversions: Yes
Area Develop. Agreements: Yes/Open
Sub-Franchising Contracts: No
Expand In Territory: No
Space Needs: 1,800-2,400 SF; RM, Factory Outlets

SUPPORT & TRAINING PROVIDED:

Financial Assistance Provided: No
Site Selection Assistance: Yes
Lease Negotiation Assistance: Yes
Co-Operative Advertising: No
Franchisee Assoc./Member: Yes/Yes
Size Of Corporate Staff: 19
On-Going Support: C,D,E,F,G,h,I
Training: 3-5 Days Headquarters; 3-5 Days On-Site; 40 Hours Home Training with Computer.

SPECIFIC EXPANSION PLANS:

US: All United States
Canada: No
Overseas: No

<< >>

CROWN TROPHY

9 Skyline Dr.
Hawthorne, NY 10532-1402
Tel: (800) 583-8228 (914) 347-7700
Fax: (914) 347-0211
E-Mail: scott@crowntrophy.com
Web Site: www.crownfranchise.com
Mr. Scott Kelly, Executive Vice President

The only franchise of its kind in America, CROWN TROPHY is the largest supplier and fastest growing retailer of trophies and awards in the country. Crown offers a full-service facility utilizing state-of-the-art equipment along with the most innovative product line in the industry. CROWN TROPHY is truly a one of a kind, unique franchise opportunity.

BACKGROUND: IFA MEMBER

Established: 1978; 1st Franchised: 1987
Franchised Units: 101
Company-Owned Units 1
Total Units: 102
Dist.: US-94; CAN-0; O'seas-0
North America: 35 States
Density: 13 in NY, 6 in NJ, 6 in PA
Projected New Units (12 Months): 12
Qualifications: 2, 2, 1, 3, 5, 5
Registered: CA,FL,IL,IN,MD,MI,MN,ND, NY,OR,SD,WI

FINANCIAL/TERMS:

Cash Investment: $90K
Total Investment: $135-145K
Minimum Net Worth: $100K
Fees: Franchise - $32K
Royalty - 5%; Ad. - None
Earnings Claim Statement: No
Term of Contract (Years): 10/5/5
Avg. # Of Employees: 1 FT, 2 PT
Passive Ownership: Discouraged
Encourage Conversions: Yes
Area Develop. Agreements: No
Sub-Franchising Contracts: No
Expand In Territory: Yes
Space Needs: 1,500-1,600 SF; SF, SC

SUPPORT & TRAINING PROVIDED:

Financial Assistance Provided: Yes(I)
Site Selection Assistance: Yes
Lease Negotiation Assistance: Yes
Co-Operative Advertising: No
Franchisee Assoc./Member: No
Size Of Corporate Staff: 10
On-Going Support: C,D,E,F,H,I
Training: 10 Days Corporate Office; 5 Days On-Site.

SPECIFIC EXPANSION PLANS:

US: All United States
Canada: No
Overseas: No

<< >>

EARFUL OF BOOKS

907 W. 5th St., # 203
Austin, TX 78703
Tel: (888) EAR-FULS (512) 343-2620
Fax: (512) 343-2751
E-Mail: contactus@earful.com
Web Site: www.earfulcom
Mr. Jim Grant, VP Franchise Development

Rental and sale of audio books in cassette and CD format.

BACKGROUND:

Established: 1991; 1st Franchised: 1998
Franchised Units: 17
Company-Owned Units 7
Total Units: 26
Dist.: US-13; CAN-0; O'seas-0
North America: 5 States
Density: 7 in TX, 3 in NC
Projected New Units (12 Months): 20
Qualifications: 5, 4, 3, 4, 5, 5
Registered: CA,IL,MD,NY,VA,WA,WI,DC

FINANCIAL/TERMS:

Cash Investment: $100K
Total Investment: $225-275K
Minimum Net Worth: $250K
Fees: Franchise - $25K
Royalty - 4%; Ad. - 1%
Earnings Claim Statement: No
Term of Contract (Years): 10/5
Avg. # Of Employees: 2 FT, 4 PT
Passive Ownership: Allowed
Encourage Conversions: Yes
Area Develop. Agreements: Yes
Sub-Franchising Contracts: No
Expand In Territory: Yes
Space Needs: 2,000-2,500 SF; SC

SUPPORT & TRAINING PROVIDED:

Financial Assistance Provided: No
Site Selection Assistance: Yes
Lease Negotiation Assistance: Yes
Co-Operative Advertising: Yes
Franchisee Assoc./Member: Yes/Yes
Size Of Corporate Staff: 10
On-Going Support: D,E,F,I
Training: 1 Week at Home Office; 1 Week On-Site.

SPECIFIC EXPANSION PLANS:

US: All United States
Canada: Yes, Considered
Overseas: No

<< >>

ECOSMARTE PLANET FRIENDLY

730 West 78th St.
Richfield, MN 55423
Tel: (800) 466-7946 (612) 866-1200
Fax: (612) 866-0152
E-Mail: ecosmarte@visi.com
Web Site: www.ecosmarte.com
Mr. Joe Cantin, North American Sales Mgr.

Environmental technology retail store, specializing in non-chlorine, non-brine water systems for home, business pool and spa. Oxygen and natural products.

BACKGROUND:

Established: 1994;	1st Franchised: 1996
Franchised Units:	5
Company-Owned Units	2
Total Units:	7
Dist.:	US-7; CAN-0; O'seas-0
North America:	6 States
Density:	3 in MN, 1 in AZ, 1 in TX
Projected New Units (12 Months):	6
Qualifications:	3, 3, 1, 4, 3, 4
Registered: NR	

FINANCIAL/TERMS:

Cash Investment:	$75-245K
Total Investment:	$100-245K
Minimum Net Worth:	$250K
Fees: Franchise -	$15-30K
Royalty - 0%;	Ad. - 0%
Earnings Claim Statement:	No
Term of Contract (Years):	5/5
Avg. # Of Employees:	2 FT, 4 PT
Passive Ownership:	Discouraged
Encourage Conversions:	No
Area Develop. Agreements:	Yes/5
Sub-Franchising Contracts:	No
Expand In Territory:	Yes
Space Needs: 1,500 SF; SF, SC, HB	

SUPPORT & TRAINING PROVIDED:

Financial Assistance Provided:	Yes(I)
Site Selection Assistance:	Yes
Lease Negotiation Assistance:	Yes
Co-Operative Advertising:	Yes
Franchisee Assoc./Member:	No
Size Of Corporate Staff:	20
On-Going Support:	B,C,D,e,h,I
Training: 10 Days at Phoenix, AZ; 7 Days Minneapolis, MN.	

SPECIFIC EXPANSION PLANS:

US:	Southwest, Northeast
Canada:	All Canada
Overseas:	All Countries

<< >>

ELEPHANT WALK

318 N. Carson St., # 214
Carson City, NV 89701
Tel: (800) 654-5156 (775) 882-1963
Fax: (800) 654-5161
Mr. John (Jack) D. Pomeroy, President

CAPTURE THE BEAUTY! You'll love owning an ELEPHANT WALK Gift Gallery. Unique, handcrafted, nature-themed gifts--sculptures, jewelry, home decorative products and more. Developed and refined in Hawaii... Now rapidly reaching malls across the nation.

BACKGROUND:

Established: 1983;	1st Franchised: 1996
Franchised Units:	0
Company-Owned Units	10
Total Units:	10
Dist.:	US-9; CAN-0; O'seas-0
North America:	2 States
Density:	8 in HI, 1 in NV
Projected New Units (12 Months):	4
Qualifications:	3, 3, 2, 3, 4, 5
Registered: HI	

FINANCIAL/TERMS:

Cash Investment:	$75-100K
Total Investment:	$145-195K
Minimum Net Worth:	$250K
Fees: Franchise -	$25K
Royalty - 6%;	Ad. - 1%
Earnings Claim Statement:	No
Term of Contract (Years):	5/5/5/5
Avg. # Of Employees:	1 FT, 4 PT
Passive Ownership:	Discouraged
Encourage Conversions:	Yes
Area Develop. Agreements:	No
Sub-Franchising Contracts:	No
Expand In Territory:	Yes
Space Needs: 1,000 SF; SF, RM, Airport, Resort Area	

SUPPORT & TRAINING PROVIDED:

Financial Assistance Provided:	N/A
Site Selection Assistance:	Yes
Lease Negotiation Assistance:	Yes
Co-Operative Advertising:	No
Franchisee Assoc./Member:	No
Size Of Corporate Staff:	6
On-Going Support:	C,D,E,F,G,H,I
Training: 10 Days Honolulu, HI (I.E.L. University).	

SPECIFIC EXPANSION PLANS:

US:	All United States
Canada:	No
Overseas:	No

<< >>

EXPETEC TECHNOLOGY SERVICES

12 2nd Ave. SW
Aberdeen, SD 57401
Tel: (888) 297-2292 (605) 225-4122
Fax: (605) 225-5176
E-Mail: jenniferR@cdfs.com
Web Site: www.expetec.biz
Ms. Jennifer Roberts, VP Sales & Strategic Alliances

EXPETEC locations provide mobile, on-site or in-shop computer and printer repair, sales, service and upgrades. A multiple profit center in one franchise, with unlimited market potential, including communications, phone systems and retail point-of-sale systems.

BACKGROUND: IFA MEMBER

Established: 1992;	1st Franchised: 1996
Franchised Units:	150
Company-Owned Units	0
Total Units:	150
Dist.:	US-150; CAN-0; O'seas-0
North America:	28 States
Density:	19 in FL, 8 in TX, 5 in SD
Projected New Units (12 Months):	50
Registered: NR	

FINANCIAL/TERMS:

Cash Investment:	$30K
Total Investment:	$53.8-80K
Minimum Net Worth:	$100K
Fees: Franchise -	$27K
Royalty - 5%;	Ad. - 2%
Earnings Claim Statement:	No
Term of Contract (Years):	10
Avg. # Of Employees:	2 FT
Passive Ownership:	Discouraged
Encourage Conversions:	NR
Area Develop. Agreements:	Yes/10
Sub-Franchising Contracts:	Yes
Expand In Territory:	Yes
Space Needs: 300-700 SF; FS, SF, SC	

SUPPORT & TRAINING PROVIDED:

Financial Assistance Provided:	NR
Site Selection Assistance:	Yes
Lease Negotiation Assistance:	Yes
Co-Operative Advertising:	No
Franchisee Assoc./Member:	Yes/Yes
Size Of Corporate Staff:	13
On-Going Support:	B,C,D,E,F,G,H,I
Training: 3 Weeks in Aberdeen, SD.	

SPECIFIC EXPANSION PLANS:

US:	All United States
Canada:	No
Overseas:	No

<< >>

FAST-FIX JEWELRY REPAIRS

1300 NW 17th Ave., # 170
Delray Beach, FL 33445
Tel: (800) 359-0407 (561) 330-6060

Fax: (561) 330-6062
E-Mail: franchise@fastfix.com
Web Site: www.fastfix.com
Mr. Mark Goldstein, VP Franchise Development

FAST-FIX JEWELRY REPAIRS ® is a proven business with an 18-year track record in the multi-billion dollar jewelry and watch repair industry. FAST-FIX stores operate only in major regional malls, which guarantee high visibility and traffic. Most repairs can be completed within an hour while customers watch or enjoy shopping. FAST-FIX JEWELRY REPAIRS ® has more than 115 franchise locations nationwide. The chain's innovative and complete training program is conducted at the site of each new store.

BACKGROUND: IFA MEMBER
Established: 1984; 1st Franchised: 1987
Franchised Units: 116
Company-Owned Units 0
Total Units: 116
Dist.: US-116; CAN-0; O'seas-0
North America: 23 States + PR
Density: 19 in FL, 19 in CA, 16 in TX
Projected New Units (12 Months): 25
Qualifications: 3, 5, 1, 1, 1, 4
Registered: CA,DC, FL,IL,MD,MI,MN, NY,OR,RI,VA,WA,WI

FINANCIAL/TERMS:
Cash Investment: $40-60K
Total Investment: $113-200K
Minimum Net Worth: $N/A
Fees: Franchise - $30K
Royalty - 5%; Ad. - 0%
Earnings Claim Statement: No
Term of Contract (Years): 10/10
Avg. # Of Employees: 3 FT, 1 PT
Passive Ownership: Discouraged
Encourage Conversions: NR
Area Develop. Agreements: Yes/10
Sub-Franchising Contracts: No
Expand In Territory: Yes
Space Needs: 150-850 SF; RM

SUPPORT & TRAINING PROVIDED:
Financial Assistance Provided: Yes(I)
Site Selection Assistance: Yes
Lease Negotiation Assistance: Yes
Co-Operative Advertising: N/A
Franchisee Assoc./Member: Yes/Yes
Size Of Corporate Staff: 9
On-Going Support: B,C,D,E,G,H,I
Training: 8 Days at National Training Center in Dallas and On-Site Training.

SPECIFIC EXPANSION PLANS:
US: All United States
Canada: All Canada
Overseas: Yes

<< >>

FOLIAGE DESIGN SYSTEMS
4496 35th St.
Orlando, FL 32811-6504
Tel: (800) 933-7351 (407) 245-7776
Fax: (407) 245-7533
E-Mail: info@foliagedesign.com
Web Site: www.foliagedesign.com
Mr. John S. Hagood, Chairman

FOLIAGE DESIGN SYSTEMS is one of the largest interior plant maintenance companies in the U. S., according to Interiorscape Magazine. FOLIAGE DESIGN franchisees learn the business from the ground up in an intensive training program followed by training sessions in the field. Franchisees are taught design, sales and maintenance of interior foliage plants.

BACKGROUND:
Established: 1971; 1st Franchised: 1980
Franchised Units: 36
Company-Owned Units 4
Total Units: 40
Dist.: US-40; CAN-0; O'seas-0
North America: 14 States
Density: 19 in FL, 4 in SC, 3 in MS
Projected New Units (12 Months): 3
Registered: FL

FINANCIAL/TERMS:
Cash Investment: $15-50K
Total Investment: $35-150K
Minimum Net Worth: $NR
Fees: Franchise - $20-100K
Royalty - 6%; Ad. - 0%
Earnings Claim Statement: No
Term of Contract (Years): 20/5
Avg. # Of Employees: 4 FT, 2 PT
Passive Ownership: Discouraged
Encourage Conversions: No
Area Develop. Agreements: No
Sub-Franchising Contracts: Yes
Expand In Territory: Yes
Space Needs: 200 SF; Greenhouse, Warehouse

SUPPORT & TRAINING PROVIDED:
Financial Assistance Provided: No
Site Selection Assistance: Yes
Lease Negotiation Assistance: No
Co-Operative Advertising: No
Franchisee Assoc./Member: NR
Size Of Corporate Staff: 8
On-Going Support: a,B,C,D,F,G,H,I
Training: 2 Weeks Headquarters; 3-5 Days in Field.

SPECIFIC EXPANSION PLANS:
US: All United States
Canada: All Canada
Overseas: Europe, Asia, Mexico, South America

<< >>

FOOT SOLUTIONS
1730 Cumberland Point Dr., # 5
Marietta, GA 30067
Tel: (866) 338-2597 (770) 955-0099
Fax: (770) 951-2666
E-Mail: fscorp@footsolutions.com
Web Site: www.footsolutions.com
Mr. Raymond J. Margiano, President

FOOT SOLUTIONS offers foot care services, including computer foot scanning, custom insoles and a line of specialty shoes and foot care products.

BACKGROUND:
Established: 2000; 1st Franchised: 2000
Franchised Units: 28
Company-Owned Units 0
Total Units: 28
Dist.: US-26; CAN-2; O'seas-0
North America: 13 States
Density: 2 in NC, 2 in OH, 2 in OR
Projected New Units (12 Months): 40
Qualifications: 4, 4, 3, 3, 3, 4
Registered: CA,FL,IL,IN,MD,MI,MN, NY,VA,WA

FINANCIAL/TERMS:
Cash Investment: $35-75K
Total Investment: $150-200K
Minimum Net Worth: $250K
Fees: Franchise - $25K
Royalty - 5%; Ad. - 2%
Earnings Claim Statement: No
Term of Contract (Years): 20/10/10
Avg. # Of Employees: 2 FT, 1 PT
Passive Ownership: Discouraged
Encourage Conversions: No

Area Develop. Agreements: No
Sub-Franchising Contracts: No
Expand In Territory: Yes
Space Needs: 1,000-1,500 SF; SF, SC

SUPPORT & TRAINING PROVIDED:
Financial Assistance Provided: Yes
Site Selection Assistance: Yes
Lease Negotiation Assistance: Yes
Co-Operative Advertising: Yes
Franchisee Assoc./Member: No
Size Of Corporate Staff: 22
On-Going Support: B,C,D,E,H,I
Training: 2 Weeks Atlanta, GA and On-Site.

SPECIFIC EXPANSION PLANS:
US: All United States
Canada: All Canada
Overseas: Limited

<< >>

FOR THE BRIDE TO BE

P.O. Box 4437
Cordova, TN 33088-4437
Tel: (866) 843-7378 (901) 753-9867
Fax: (901) 624-6810
E-Mail: john@forthebridetobe.com
Web Site: www.forthebridetobe.com
Mr. John A. Ferrante, CEO-Franchise Div.

A FOR THE BRIDE TO BE franchise is a retail boutique that specializes in the sale of accessories, gifts, invitations and specialty items for the wedding consumer. As a FOR THE BRIDE TO BE franchisee, you have the freedom and challenge of owning your own business, with the added support of proven business and sales methods, products and the guidance of experienced franchisor-business owners.

BACKGROUND:
Established: 1994; 1st Franchised: 2001
Franchised Units: 0
Company-Owned Units 1
Total Units: 1
Dist.: US-1; CAN-0; O'seas-0
North America: 1 State
Density: 1 in TN
Projected New Units (12 Months): 5
Qualifications: 2, 4, 4, 3, 4, 5
Registered: FL,MI

FINANCIAL/TERMS:
Cash Investment: $10-25K
Total Investment: $150-270K
Minimum Net Worth: $N/A
Fees: Franchise - $25K
Royalty - 5%; Ad. - 1%
Earnings Claim Statement: No
Term of Contract (Years): 10/10
Avg. # Of Employees: 1 FT, 1 PT
Passive Ownership: Allowed
Encourage Conversions: Yes
Area Develop. Agreements: No
Sub-Franchising Contracts: No
Expand In Territory: No
Space Needs: 2,000 SF; SC

SUPPORT & TRAINING PROVIDED:
Financial Assistance Provided: Yes(I)
Site Selection Assistance: Yes
Lease Negotiation Assistance: Yes
Co-Operative Advertising: Yes
Franchisee Assoc./Member: No
Size Of Corporate Staff: 3
On-Going Support: C,D,E,F,G,I
Training: 2 Weeks in Memphis, TN.

SPECIFIC EXPANSION PLANS:
US: TN, KY, OK, MI, FL, AL
Canada: No
Overseas: No

<< >>

GNC LiveWell.

Top 50

GENERAL NUTRITION CENTERS

300 Sixth Ave.
Pittsburgh, PA 15222-2514
Tel: (800) 766-7099 (412) 288-2043
Fax: (412) 288-2033
E-Mail: livewell@gncfranchising.com
Web Site: www.gncfranchising.com
Mr. Bruce Pollack, Dir. Franchising

GNC is the leading national specialty retailer of vitamins, minerals, herbs and sports nutrition supplements and is uniquely positioned to capitalize on the accelerating self-care trend. As the leading provider of products and information for personal health enhancement, the company holds the largest specialty-retail share of the nutritional supplement market. GNC was ranked America's #1 retail franchise in 1998/1999 by Entrepreneur International.

BACKGROUND: IFA MEMBER
Established: 1935; 1st Franchised: 1988
Franchised Units: 2,842
Company-Owned Units 1,718
Total Units: 4,560
Dist.: US-4188; CAN-134; O'seas-266
North America: 50 States, 1 Province
Density: 408 in CA,340 in FL,293 TX
Projected New Units (12 Months): NR
Qualifications: 5, 5, 1, 1, 1, 4
Registered: All States

FINANCIAL/TERMS:
Cash Investment: $60K
Total Investment: $132.7-182K
Minimum Net Worth: $100K
Fees: Franchise - $35K
Royalty - 6%; Ad. - 3%
Earnings Claim Statement: Yes
Term of Contract (Years): 10/5
Avg. # Of Employees: 1 FT, 3-5 PT
Passive Ownership: Not Allowed
Encourage Conversions: Yes
Area Develop. Agreements: Yes/Varies
Sub-Franchising Contracts: No
Expand In Territory: Yes
Space Needs: 1,402 (avg.) SF; SC, RM

SUPPORT & TRAINING PROVIDED:
Financial Assistance Provided: Yes(D)
Site Selection Assistance: Yes
Lease Negotiation Assistance: Yes
Co-Operative Advertising: Yes
Franchisee Assoc./Member: Yes/Yes
Size Of Corporate Staff: 700+
On-Going Support: A,B,C,D,E,F,G,H,I
Training: 1 Wk. On-Site in Local Corporate Store; 1 Wk. in Pittsburgh, PA; 1 Wk. Opening Assistance.

SPECIFIC EXPANSION PLANS:
US: All United States
Canada: PQ Only
Overseas: Middle East, Japan, Malaysia, New Zealand, Africa.

<< >>

GROWER DIRECT FRESH CUT FLOWERS

4220 - 98 St., # 301
Edmonton, AB T6E 6A1 CANADA
Tel: (800) 567-7258 (780) 436-7774
Fax: (780) 436-3336
Mr. John Paton, Franchise Coordinator

As the largest floral chain retailer, our independently operated franchise locations sell the world's highest-quality fresh cut roses and other flowers in a unique 'boutique-style' setting. Product is sourced directly from the finest producers known and transported weekly to our stores via GROWER DIRECT's distribution system. Rapid product sales translate into 50-60 inventory turns annually and help make the enjoyment of FRESH CUT FLOWERS an affordable and everyday event for our customers.

BACKGROUND:
Established: 1991; 1st Franchised: 1991
Franchised Units: 121
Company-Owned Units 1
Total Units: 122
Dist.: US-0; CAN-122; O'seas-0
North America: 10 Provinces
Density: 38 in AB, 22 in ON, 15 in BC
Projected New Units (12 Months): 12
Qualifications: 4, 4, 2, 2, 4, 4
Registered: AB

FINANCIAL/TERMS:
Cash Investment: $40K
Total Investment: $35-40K
Minimum Net Worth: $50K
Fees: Franchise - $25K
Royalty - $240/Wk.; Ad. - $15/Wk.
Earnings Claim Statement: No
Term of Contract (Years): 10/10
Avg. # Of Employees: 1 FT, 2 PT
Passive Ownership: Discouraged
Encourage Conversions: Yes
Area Develop. Agreements: No
Sub-Franchising Contracts: Yes
Expand In Territory: Yes
Space Needs: 400-1,000 SF; SC

SUPPORT & TRAINING PROVIDED:
Financial Assistance Provided: No
Site Selection Assistance: Yes
Lease Negotiation Assistance: Yes
Co-Operative Advertising: Yes
Franchisee Assoc./Member: Yes/Yes
Size Of Corporate Staff: 14
On-Going Support: b,C,D,E,G,H,I
Training: 5 Days in Store; 5 Days in Classroom; 5 Days Industry Tours.

SPECIFIC EXPANSION PLANS:
US: No
Canada: All Canada
Overseas: No

<< >>

HEALTHY BACK

P.O. Box 1296
Newington, VA 22122-1296
Tel: (703) 339-1300
Fax: (703) 339-0671
Web Site: www.healthyback.com
Mr. Howard J. Margolis, Franchise Manager

The Healthy Back is a retail store which specializes in selling ergonomically designed products such as office chairs, recliners, beds, pillows, supports, massagers, desks, foot rests, books, videos and other products which help prevent and relieve back/neck and improve a person's daily comfort.

BACKGROUND:
Established: 1993; 1st Franchised: 1999
Franchised Units: 12
Company-Owned Units 10
Total Units: 22
Dist.: US-22; CAN-0; O'seas-0
North America: 19 States
Density: 4 in CO, 1 in Each of rest
Projected New Units (12 Months): 6
Qualifications: 5, 4, 3, 4, 2, 5
Registered: NR

FINANCIAL/TERMS:
Cash Investment: $100K
Total Investment: $167.1-279.9K
Minimum Net Worth: $650K
Fees: Franchise - $25K
Royalty - 5%; Ad. - 1.5%
Earnings Claim Statement: No
Term of Contract (Years): 5/5
Avg. # Of Employees: 2 PT
Passive Ownership: Not Allowed
Encourage Conversions: N/A
Area Develop. Agreements: No
Sub-Franchising Contracts: No
Expand In Territory: No
Space Needs: 2,500 SF; SC

SUPPORT & TRAINING PROVIDED:
Financial Assistance Provided: Yes(I)
Site Selection Assistance: Yes
Lease Negotiation Assistance: Yes
Co-Operative Advertising: No
Franchisee Assoc./Member: Yes/Yes
Size Of Corporate Staff: 16
On-Going Support: C,D,E,F,G,h,I
Training: 9 Days in Washington, DC Area.

SPECIFIC EXPANSION PLANS:
US: All United States
Canada: No
Overseas: No

<< >>

HOBBYTOWN USA

6301 S. 58th St.
Lincoln, NE 68516
Tel: (800) 858-7370 (402) 434-5050
Fax: (402) 434-5055
E-Mail: dfo@hobbytown.com
Web Site: www.hobbytown.com
Ms. Nichole Ernst, Dir. Franchise Opportunities

HOBBYTOWN USA stores are full-line hobby stores, featuring hobby trains, models, radio-controlled vehicles, games, collectible cards, diecast toys, gifts, accessories and much more! The HOBBYTOWN USA system provides store owners with a comprehensive package of systems and services to be competitive in the hobby and entertainment industries.

BACKGROUND: IFA MEMBER
Established: 1969; 1st Franchised: 1986
Franchised Units: 122
Company-Owned Units 1
Total Units: 123
Dist.: US-129; CAN-0; O'seas-0
North America: 36 States
Density: 7 in AZ, 7 in TX, 6 in CA
Projected New Units (12 Months): 30
Qualifications: 4, 3, 2, 2, 2, 5
Registered: All States

FINANCIAL/TERMS:
Cash Investment: $50-90K
Total Investment: $120-250K
Minimum Net Worth: $120K
Fees: Franchise - $19.5K
Royalty - 2.5%; Ad. - N/A
Earnings Claim Statement: No
Term of Contract (Years): 10/10
Avg. # Of Employees: 1-2 FT, 2-3 PT
Passive Ownership: Discouraged
Encourage Conversions: Yes
Area Develop. Agreements: No
Sub-Franchising Contracts: No
Expand In Territory: Yes
Space Needs: 2,500 SF; SC, RM

SUPPORT & TRAINING PROVIDED:
Financial Assistance Provided: Yes(I)
Site Selection Assistance: Yes
Lease Negotiation Assistance: Yes
Co-Operative Advertising: Yes
Franchisee Assoc./Member: Yes
Size Of Corporate Staff: 27
On-Going Support: A,C,D,E,F,G,H,I
Training: 1 Week Home Office; 2 Weeks On-Site.

SPECIFIC EXPANSION PLANS:
US: All United States
Canada: No
Overseas: No

<< >>

JUST-A-BUCK

301 N. Main St., #5
New City, NY 10956

Tel: (800) 332-2229 (845) 638-4111
Fax: (845) 638-3878
E-Mail: rs@spyral.net
Web Site: www.just-a-buck.com
Mr. Ronald Sommers, Dir. Franchise Development

Merchandise that would sometimes cost as much as ten times more at any other store makes JUST-A-BUCK fun to shop and fun to run. America's only franchised dollar store. Each location is neat and clean. It takes hard work but the concept is simple and it's made even easier with on-going support, training and help with everything from marketing to merchandising. IFA Member. Entrepreneur Top 500.

BACKGROUND: IFA MEMBER
Established: 1988; 1st Franchised: 1992
Franchised Units: 35
Company-Owned Units 11
Total Units: 46
Dist.: US-46; CAN-0; O'seas-0
North America: 7 States
Density: 19 in NY, 10 in NJ, 4 in CT
Projected New Units (12 Months): 15
Qualifications: 4, 3, 2, 2, 2, 4
Registered: FL,MD,MI,NY,VA,DC

FINANCIAL/TERMS:
Cash Investment: $40-60K
Total Investment: $126.7-265.9K
Minimum Net Worth: $150K
Fees: Franchise - $25K
Royalty - 4%; Ad. - 2%
Earnings Claim Statement: No
Term of Contract (Years): 10/20
Avg. # Of Employees: 7 FT, 10 PT
Passive Ownership: Not Allowed
Encourage Conversions: Yes
Area Develop. Agreements: No
Sub-Franchising Contracts: No
Expand In Territory: Yes
Space Needs: 3,500 SF; SC, RM

SUPPORT & TRAINING PROVIDED:
Financial Assistance Provided: Yes(I)
Site Selection Assistance: Yes
Lease Negotiation Assistance: Yes
Co-Operative Advertising: No
Franchisee Assoc./Member: No
Size Of Corporate Staff: 18
On-Going Support: A,B,C,D,E,F,G,H,I
Training: 10 Days NY State; 10 Days On-Site.

SPECIFIC EXPANSION PLANS:
US: All United States
Canada: No
Overseas: No

<< >>

LATEX CITY

1814 Franklin St., # 820
Oakland, CA 94612
Tel: (510) 839-5462
Fax: (510) 839-2104
Mr. BruceY. Mowat, President

Unique ground-floor specialty retailing opportunity in booming latex novelty aid business. Complete line of proprietary products. Turn-key package includes lease negotiation, fully-stocked inventory, in-store merchandising/display. On-going support. LATEX CITY is ideal for aggressive couples. This is not smut - but a highly profitable, high-margin, fully legal business.

BACKGROUND:
Established: 1972; 1st Franchised: 1986
Franchised Units: 26
Company-Owned Units 4
Total Units: 30
Dist.: US-25; CAN-2; O'seas-3
North America: 17 States, 1 Province
Density: 3 in CA, 3 in NY, 2 in OR
Projected New Units (12 Months): 10
Registered: NR

FINANCIAL/TERMS:
Cash Investment: $65K
Total Investment: $85-235K
Minimum Net Worth: $NR
Fees: Franchise - $15K
Royalty - 6%; Ad. - 2%
Earnings Claim Statement: Yes
Term of Contract (Years): 10/10
Avg. # Of Employees: 2 FT
Passive Ownership: Discouraged
Encourage Conversions: Yes
Area Develop. Agreements: Yes/5
Sub-Franchising Contracts: No
Expand In Territory: No
Space Needs: 1,000-1,400 SF; FS, SF, SC, RM

SUPPORT & TRAINING PROVIDED:
Financial Assistance Provided: Yes(D)
Site Selection Assistance: Yes
Lease Negotiation Assistance: Yes
Co-Operative Advertising: Yes
Franchisee Assoc./Member: NR
Size Of Corporate Staff: 6
On-Going Support: A,B,C,D,G,H
Training: 3 Weeks Headquarters; 1 Week Plant; 2 Weeks On-Site.

SPECIFIC EXPANSION PLANS:
US: All United States
Canada: Major Cities
Overseas: No

<< >>

LEMSTONE BOOKS

311 S. County Farm Rd., # E
Wheaton, IL 60187
Tel: (630) 682-1400
Fax: (630) 682-1828
E-Mail: phild@lemstone.com
Web Site: www.lemstone.com
Mr. Phil Darr, VP Sales/Admin.

Since 1982, LEMSTONE has been helping Christians own, operate and succeed in Christian retailing. Our franchise concept provides a 'road map for success' for Christian retailers who possess a heart for people and an entrepreneurial spirit. We currently have over 75 stores in 27 states. LEMSTONE stores are located in premier regional malls within growing markets. Our stores enjoy maximum market exposure every day as thousands of customers shop.

BACKGROUND: IFA MEMBER
Established: 1981; 1st Franchised: 1982
Franchised Units: 63
Company-Owned Units 2
Total Units: 65
Dist.: US-77; CAN-0; O'seas-0
North America: 27 States
Density: 8 in TN, 8 in OH, 7 in IL
Projected New Units (12 Months): 12
Qualifications: 5, 2, 1, 2, 2, 4
Registered: CA,FL,IL,IN,MD,MI,MN,NY, OR,WA,WI

FINANCIAL/TERMS:
Cash Investment: $60K
Total Investment: $150-240K
Minimum Net Worth: $350K
Fees: Franchise - $30K
Royalty - 4%; Ad. - 1%
Earnings Claim Statement: NR
Term of Contract (Years): 10/10
Avg. # Of Employees: 1 FT, 4 PT
Passive Ownership: Discouraged
Encourage Conversions: No
Area Develop. Agreements: No
Sub-Franchising Contracts: No
Expand In Territory: Yes
Space Needs: 1,300-2,000 SF; RM

SUPPORT & TRAINING PROVIDED:
Financial Assistance Provided: No
Site Selection Assistance: Yes
Lease Negotiation Assistance: Yes
Co-Operative Advertising: Yes
Franchisee Assoc./Member: Yes/Yes
Size Of Corporate Staff: 14
On-Going Support: A,B,C,D,E,F,G,H

Training: 8 Days Headquarters; 5 Days On-Site.
SPECIFIC EXPANSION PLANS:
US: All United States
Canada: No
Overseas: No

<< >>

LITTLE PROFESSOR BOOK CENTERS

405 Little Lake Dr., # C
Ann Arbor, MI 48103
Tel: (800) 899-6232 (734) 994-1212
Fax: (734) 994-9009
E-Mail: lpbchome@aol.com
Web Site: www.littleprofessor.com
Mr. John Glazer, President

Full-line, full-service, community-oriented general bookstore.

BACKGROUND:
Established: 1964; 1st Franchised: 1969
Franchised Units: 65
Company-Owned Units 0
Total Units: 65
Dist.: US-80; CAN-0; O'seas-0
North America: 29 States
Density: 12 in OH, 8 in WI, 8 in MI
Projected New Units (12 Months): 10
Qualifications: 5, 4, 2, 3, 3, 5
Registered: CA,FL,IL,IN,MI,MN,NY,RI, VA,WI
FINANCIAL/TERMS:
Cash Investment: $100-500K
Total Investment: $300K-1.5MM
Minimum Net Worth: $250K
Fees: Franchise - $37K
Royalty - 3%; Ad. - 0.5%
Earnings Claim Statement: Yes
Term of Contract (Years): 10/10
Avg. # Of Employees: 2 FT, 6 PT
Passive Ownership: Discouraged
Encourage Conversions: Yes
Area Develop. Agreements: No
Sub-Franchising Contracts: No
Expand In Territory: Yes
Space Needs: 3,000-15,000 SF; FS, SF, SC
SUPPORT & TRAINING PROVIDED:
Financial Assistance Provided: Yes(I)
Site Selection Assistance: Yes
Lease Negotiation Assistance: Yes
Co-Operative Advertising: Yes
Franchisee Assoc./Member: Yes/Yes
Size Of Corporate Staff: 10
On-Going Support: A,b,C,d,E,F,G,H,h,I
Training: 1 Week Ann Arbor, MI (Home Office), 1-2 Weeks On-Site, LPBC Coventions Once a Year
SPECIFIC EXPANSION PLANS:
US: Midwest
Canada: No
Overseas: No

<< >>

LOVE BOUTIQUE, THE

17551 - 108 Ave. NW
Edmonton, AB T5T 3M6 CANADA
Tel: (888) 296-2588 (780) 486-0433
Fax: (780) 486-5114
E-Mail: virginiaf@telfordinvestments.com
Web Site: www.theloveboutique.com
Ms. Virginia Falkenberg, Franchise Mgr.

Adult store franchise system, specializing in lingerie, oils, games, magazines, books, videos, toys and other products. Up-to-date selection ensures sales with better than average margin. Franchisor is Canada's complete distributor of lingerie and adult product.

BACKGROUND:
Established: 1982; 1st Franchised: 1999
Franchised Units: 2
Company-Owned Units 19
Total Units: 21
Dist.: US-0; CAN-21; O'seas-0
North America: 1 Province
Density: 21 in Alberta
Projected New Units (12 Months): 3
Qualifications: 5, 3, 1, 1, 1, 5
Registered: AB
FINANCIAL/TERMS:
Cash Investment: $128-193K
Total Investment: $128-193K
Minimum Net Worth: $NR
Fees: Franchise - $30K
Royalty - 5%; Ad. - 2%
Earnings Claim Statement: No
Term of Contract (Years): 5/5
Avg. # Of Employees: 1 FT, 2-3 PT
Passive Ownership: Not Allowed
Encourage Conversions: N/A
Area Develop. Agreements: No
Sub-Franchising Contracts: No
Expand In Territory: No
Space Needs: 1,200-1,600 SF; FS, SF, SC, RM
SUPPORT & TRAINING PROVIDED:
Financial Assistance Provided: N/A
Site Selection Assistance: Yes
Lease Negotiation Assistance: N/A
Co-Operative Advertising: Yes
Franchisee Assoc./Member: No
Size Of Corporate Staff: 18
On-Going Support: A,B,C,D,E,F
Training: 1 Week Corporate Store Location.
SPECIFIC EXPANSION PLANS:
US: All United States
Canada: All Canada
Overseas: No

<< >>

MACBIRDIE GOLF GIFTS

7399 Bush Lake Rd.
Edina, MN 55439
Tel: (800) 343-1033 (952) 830-1033
Fax: (952) 830-1055
E-Mail: info@macbirdie.com
Web Site: www.macbirdie.com
Mr. Marcel Kole, President/CEO

MACBIRDIE GOLF GIFTS is a national retailer/franchisor of an exciting mix of unique golf products & gifts. Its product line serves consumers looking for unique golf gifts, home décor, & other decorative products, novelty items, and corporate tournaments & events

BACKGROUND:
Established: 1989; 1st Franchised: 1994
Franchised Units: 3
Company-Owned Units 2
Total Units: 5
Dist.: US-5; CAN-0; O'seas-0
North America: 4 States
Density: 2 in MN, 1 in TX
Projected New Units (12 Months): 3-4
Qualifications: 5, 4, 4, 3, 3, 3
Registered: All States Except, OR, RI, AB
FINANCIAL/TERMS:
Cash Investment: $30-60K
Total Investment: $120-180K
Minimum Net Worth: $250K
Fees: Franchise - $15K
Royalty - 5%; Ad. - 1-3%

Earnings Claim Statement: No
Term of Contract (Years): 7/5
Avg. # Of Employees: 1 FT, 2-3 PT
Passive Ownership: Discouraged
Encourage Conversions: No
Area Develop. Agreements: Yes/5
Sub-Franchising Contracts: No
Expand In Territory: Yes
Space Needs: 1,200 SF; RM

SUPPORT & TRAINING PROVIDED:

Financial Assistance Provided: N/A
Site Selection Assistance: Yes
Lease Negotiation Assistance: Yes
Co-Operative Advertising: N/A
Franchisee Assoc./Member: No
Size Of Corporate Staff: 4
On-Going Support: A,B,C,D,E,G,h,I
Training: 1 Week in Edina, MN.

SPECIFIC EXPANSION PLANS:

US: All United States
Canada: No
Overseas: No

<< >>

Top 50

MERKINSTOCK

P.O. Box 12488
Oakland, CA 94604
Tel: (510) 839-5462
Fax: (510) 839-2104
Dr. David Y. Brown, President

World's largest selection of merkins - both natural and synthetic. Over 35 models, 15 color selections. Custom fitting in discrete environment. Also custom dyeing. Guaranteed satisfaction. 15 stores in Far East and Europe prove that concept is ripe for aggressive expansion into the U. S. market. Looking for entrepreneurs with the desire to succeed.

BACKGROUND:

Established: 1992; 1st Franchised: 1995
Franchised Units: 21
Company-Owned Units 6
Total Units: 27
Dist.: US-3; CAN-2; O'seas-15
North America: 2 States, 1 Province
Density: 2 in CA, 1 in NV
Projected New Units (12 Months): 10
Qualifications: 3, 5, 4, 2, 3, 5
Registered: CA

FINANCIAL/TERMS:

Cash Investment: $90K
Total Investment: $150K
Minimum Net Worth: $250K
Fees: Franchise - $20K
Royalty - 6%; Ad. - 2%
Earnings Claim Statement: Yes
Term of Contract (Years): 15/15
Avg. # Of Employees: 2 FT
Passive Ownership: Not Allowed
Encourage Conversions: Yes
Area Develop. Agreements: Yes/15
Sub-Franchising Contracts: Yes
Expand In Territory: No
Space Needs: 1,200 SF; FS, SC, RM

SUPPORT & TRAINING PROVIDED:

Financial Assistance Provided: Yes(D)
Site Selection Assistance: Yes
Lease Negotiation Assistance: Yes
Co-Operative Advertising: Yes
Franchisee Assoc./Member: No
Size Of Corporate Staff: 4
On-Going Support: a,B,C,D,E,f,G,G,I
Training: 3 Weeks Headquarters; 2 Weeks On-Site; On-Going.

SPECIFIC EXPANSION PLANS:

US: All United States
Canada: All Canada
Overseas: All Countries

<< >>

Top 50

MUSIC-GO-ROUND

4200 Dahlberg Dr., # 100
Minneapolis, MN 55422-4836
Tel: (800) 645-7298 (763) 520-8485
Fax: (763) 520-8501
E-Mail: ljensen@winmark.com
Web Site: www.musicgoround.com
Ms. Lynn Jensen, Franchise Development

MUSIC GO ROUND is a franchised, retail music store that buys, sells, trades and consigns used and new musical instruments, gear and equipment. Our success formula is based on buying and selling used products, aggressive marketing, retail site selection and support of franchises.

BACKGROUND: IFA MEMBER

Established: 1986; 1st Franchised: 1994
Franchised Units: 67
Company-Owned Units 8
Total Units: 75
Dist.: US-80; CAN-0; O'seas-0
North America: 30 States
Density: 12 in MN, 9 in IL, 4 in WI
Projected New Units (12 Months): 30
Qualifications: 3, 3, 4, 3, 4, 5
Registered: All States

FINANCIAL/TERMS:

Cash Investment: $45-60K
Total Investment: $186.4-254.9K
Minimum Net Worth: $200K Appx.
Fees: Franchise - $20K
Royalty - 3%; Ad. - $500/Yr.
Earnings Claim Statement: Yes
Term of Contract (Years): 10/10
Avg. # Of Employees: 2 FT, 2 PT
Passive Ownership: Discouraged
Encourage Conversions: Yes
Area Develop. Agreements: Yes/3
Sub-Franchising Contracts: No
Expand In Territory: Yes
Space Needs: 2,500 SF; SC

SUPPORT & TRAINING PROVIDED:

Financial Assistance Provided: Yes(I)
Site Selection Assistance: Yes
Lease Negotiation Assistance: Yes
Co-Operative Advertising: Yes
Franchisee Assoc./Member: No
Size Of Corporate Staff: 175
On-Going Support: A,C,D,E,F,G,h,I
Training: 11 Days at Home Office.

SPECIFIC EXPANSION PLANS:

US: All United States
Canada: All Canada
Overseas: No

<< >>

NATURE OF THINGS STORE, THE

10700 W. Venture Dr.
Franklin, WI 53132
Tel: (800) 283-2921 (414) 529-2192
Fax: (414) 529-2253
Web Site: www.natureofthingsstore.com
Mr. Tony Aiello, Franchise Director

Join the aniMALL kingdom and travel beyond the ordinary. THE NATURE OF THINGS STORE is a retail chain, specializing in the sale of science and nature-related gift and education items, with an emphasis on endangered species. Become a member of this fast- growing franchise.

BACKGROUND:

Established: 1989; 1st Franchised: 1991
Franchised Units: 11

Company-Owned Units 0
Total Units: 11
Dist.: US-8; CAN-0; O'seas-0
North America: 5 States
Density: 4 in WI, 2 in MO, 1 in CO
Projected New Units (12 Months): 2-3
Qualifications: 4, 3, 2, 3, 4, 4
Registered: FL,IL,IN,MI,MN,NY,SD,WI

FINANCIAL/TERMS:

Cash Investment: $50-100K
Total Investment: $168-288K
Minimum Net Worth: $200-250K
Fees: Franchise - $25K
Royalty - 5%; Ad. - 1%
Earnings Claim Statement: No
Term of Contract (Years): 10/10
Avg. # Of Employees: 1 FT, 4 PT
Passive Ownership: Discouraged
Encourage Conversions: N/A
Area Develop. Agreements: No
Sub-Franchising Contracts: No
Expand In Territory: Yes
Space Needs: 1,500-1,800 SF; RM

SUPPORT & TRAINING PROVIDED:

Financial Assistance Provided: Yes(I)
Site Selection Assistance: Yes
Lease Negotiation Assistance: Yes
Co-Operative Advertising: Yes
Franchisee Assoc./Member: No
Size Of Corporate Staff: 4
On-Going Support: A,C,D,E,G,H,I
Training: 1 Week Corporate Office and Corporate Stores.

SPECIFIC EXPANSION PLANS:

US: All United States
Canada: No
Overseas: No

<< >>

PAPER WAREHOUSE/ PARTY UNIVERSE

7630 Excelsior Blvd.
Minneapolis, MN 55426-4504
Tel: (800) 229-1792 (952) 936-1000
Fax: (952) 936-9800
E-Mail: mike.anderson@paperwarehouse.com
Web Site: www.paperwarehouse.com
Mr. Mike Anderson, VP Franchising

PAPER WAREHOUSE specializes in party supplies and paper goods. They operate under the names PAPER WAREHOUSE, PARTY UNIVERSE and www.paperwarehouse.com. PAPER WAREHOUSE stores offer an extensive assortment of special occasion, seasonal and everyday party and entertainment supplies, gift wrap, greeting cards and catering supplies at everyday low prices.

BACKGROUND: IFA MEMBER

Established: 1983; 1st Franchised: 1987
Franchised Units: 55
Company-Owned Units 87
Total Units: 142
Dist.: US-141; CAN-1; O'seas-0
North America: 24 States
Density: 29 in MN, 14 in CO, 14 in OK
Projected New Units (12 Months): 15
Qualifications: 5, 3, 3, 3, 3, 3
Registered: All States Except Hawaii

FINANCIAL/TERMS:

Cash Investment: $75-100K
Total Investment: $184-445K
Minimum Net Worth: $450K+
Fees: Franchise - $35K
Royalty - 5%; Ad. - 0%
Earnings Claim Statement: No
Term of Contract (Years): 10/10
Avg. # Of Employees: 5-6 FT
Passive Ownership: Allowed
Encourage Conversions: Yes
Area Develop. Agreements: Yes/10
Sub-Franchising Contracts: No
Expand In Territory: N/A
Space Needs: 7,200 SF; SC

SUPPORT & TRAINING PROVIDED:

Financial Assistance Provided: Yes(I)
Site Selection Assistance: Yes
Lease Negotiation Assistance: Yes
Co-Operative Advertising: No
Franchisee Assoc./Member: Yes/IFA
Size Of Corporate Staff: 65
On-Going Support: A,C,D,E,G,I
Training: 1 Week in Minneapolis, MN.

SPECIFIC EXPANSION PLANS:

US: All United States
Canada: All Canada
Overseas: No

PAPYRUS

500 Chadbourne Rd., P.O. Box 6030
Fairfield, CA 94533
Tel: (800) 872-7978 (707) 428-0200
Fax: (707) 428-0641
E-Mail: kathyl@papyrus-sfp.com
Web Site: www.papyrusonline.com
Ms. Kathleen A. Low, Dir. Franchise Development

A unique concept, featuring fine greeting cards, stationery, designer gift wrap and associated products in fine paper. Merchandise mix emphasizes superior design, style and quality.

BACKGROUND:

Established: 1973; 1st Franchised: 1988
Franchised Units: 73
Company-Owned Units 59
Total Units: 132
Dist.: US-130; CAN-0; O'seas-0
North America: 29 States
Density: NR
Projected New Units (12 Months): 30
Qualifications: 5, 5, 3, 5, 1, 5
Registered: All Except ND,SD

FINANCIAL/TERMS:

Cash Investment: $75-100K
Total Investment: $205-417K
Minimum Net Worth: $400K
Fees: Franchise - $29.5K
Royalty - 6%; Ad. - 1%
Earnings Claim Statement: Yes
Term of Contract (Years): 10/5/5
Avg. # Of Employees: 1-2 FT, 4 PT
Passive Ownership: Discouraged
Encourage Conversions: Yes
Area Develop. Agreements: Yes/Varies
Sub-Franchising Contracts: No
Expand In Territory: Yes
Space Needs: 1,000 SF; SF, RM

SUPPORT & TRAINING PROVIDED:

Financial Assistance Provided: Yes(I)
Site Selection Assistance: Yes
Lease Negotiation Assistance: Yes
Co-Operative Advertising: Yes
Franchisee Assoc./Member: Yes/Yes
Size Of Corporate Staff: 30
On-Going Support: A,B,C,D,E,F,G,H,I
Training: 9 Days Corporate Headquarters.

SPECIFIC EXPANSION PLANS:

US: All United States
Canada: All Canada
Overseas: No

PARTY LAND

5215 Militia Hill Rd.
Plymouth Meeting, PA 19462-1216
Tel: (800) 778-9563 (610) 941-6200
Fax: (610) 941-6301
E-Mail: jbarry@partyland.com
Web Site: www.partyland.com
Mr. John L. Barry, VP Franchise Sales

World's largest international retail party supply franchise, specializing in service, selection and savings. The official party store for the 'new millennium.'

BACKGROUND:
Established: 1986; 1st Franchised: 1988
Franchised Units: 400
Company-Owned Units 0
Total Units: 400
Dist.: US-362; CAN-4; O'seas-38
North America: 23 States, 3 Provinces
Density: 20 in PA, 8 in TX, 3 in CO
Projected New Units (12 Months): 20
Qualifications: 5, 4, 2, 1, 5, 5
Registered: All States and AB

FINANCIAL/TERMS:
Cash Investment: $80K
Total Investment: $249-329K
Minimum Net Worth: $250K
Fees: Franchise - $35K
Royalty - 5%; Ad. - 4%
Earnings Claim Statement: No
Term of Contract (Years): 20/10
Avg. # Of Employees: 2 FT, 6 PT
Passive Ownership: Allowed
Encourage Conversions: Yes
Area Develop. Agreements: Yes/5
Sub-Franchising Contracts: Yes
Expand In Territory: No
Space Needs: NR SF; FS, SF, SC

SUPPORT & TRAINING PROVIDED:
Financial Assistance Provided: Yes(I)
Site Selection Assistance: Yes
Lease Negotiation Assistance: Yes
Co-Operative Advertising: Yes
Franchisee Assoc./Member: Yes/Yes
Size Of Corporate Staff: 30+
On-Going Support: A,B,C,D,E,F,G,H,I
Training: 1 Week Party Land University.

SPECIFIC EXPANSION PLANS:
US: All United States
Canada: All Canada
Overseas: All Countries

PINCH-A-PENNY

P.O. Box 6025
Clearwater, FL 33758
Tel: (727) 531-8913
Fax: (727) 536-8066
Mr. John C. Thomas, President

PINCH-A-PENNY is the nation's largest franchise retailer of swimming pool, spa and patio supplies.

BACKGROUND:
Established: 1974; 1st Franchised: 1976
Franchised Units: 138
Company-Owned Units 2
Total Units: 140
Dist.: US-140; CAN-0; O'seas-0
North America: 3 States
Density: 137 in FL, 1 in GA, 2 in AL
Projected New Units (12 Months): 10
Registered: FL

FINANCIAL/TERMS:
Cash Investment: $NR
Total Investment: $75-594K
Minimum Net Worth: $NR
Fees: Franchise - $15-50K
Royalty - 6%; Ad. - 4%
Earnings Claim Statement: No
Term of Contract (Years): 5/20
Avg. # Of Employees: NR
Passive Ownership: Discouraged
Encourage Conversions: No
Area Develop. Agreements: No
Sub-Franchising Contracts: No
Expand In Territory: Yes
Space Needs: 1,000-3,500 SF; SC

SUPPORT & TRAINING PROVIDED:
Financial Assistance Provided: No
Site Selection Assistance: Yes
Lease Negotiation Assistance: Yes
Co-Operative Advertising: N/A
Franchisee Assoc./Member: NR
Size Of Corporate Staff: NR
On-Going Support: A,B,C,D,E,H,I
Training: 4 Weeks Headquarters.

SPECIFIC EXPANSION PLANS:
US: All United States
Canada: No
Overseas: No

RAFTERS

4699 Keele St., # 1
Downsview, ON M3J 2N8 CANADA
Tel: (416) 661-9916
Fax: (416) 661-9706
Ms. Janine De Freitas

Full-line gift store with distinct kitchen department.

BACKGROUND:
Established: 1978; 1st Franchised: 1980
Franchised Units: 13
Company-Owned Units 0
Total Units: 13
Dist.: US-0; CAN-16; O'seas-0
North America: 3 Provinces
Density: 8 in AB, 7 in ON, 1 in BC
Projected New Units (12 Months): NR
Registered: AB

FINANCIAL/TERMS:
Cash Investment: $40K
Total Investment: $110K
Minimum Net Worth: $NR
Fees: Franchise - $25K
Royalty - 6%; Ad. - 1%
Earnings Claim Statement: Yes
Term of Contract (Years): NR
Avg. # Of Employees: NR
Passive Ownership: NR
Encourage Conversions: NR
Area Develop. Agreements: NR
Sub-Franchising Contracts: NR
Expand In Territory: NR
Space Needs: NR SF; NR

SUPPORT & TRAINING PROVIDED:
Financial Assistance Provided: No
Site Selection Assistance: NR
Lease Negotiation Assistance: Yes
Co-Operative Advertising: Yes
Franchisee Assoc./Member: Yes/Yes
Size Of Corporate Staff: 18
On-Going Support: D,E,G
Training: NR

SPECIFIC EXPANSION PLANS:
US: NR
Canada: All Canada
Overseas: No

RELAX THE BACK

10350 Heritage Park Dr., # 202
Santa Fe Springs, CA 90670
Tel: (800) 290-2225 (562) 941-1913
Fax: (562) 946-4396
E-Mail: davidl@relaxtheback.com
Web Site: www.relaxtheback.com
Mr. David Lamb, Sr. VP Franchising

North America's largest specialty retailer of ergonomic and back care products. We are in the comfort business, many of our products are designed to relieve or eliminate back and neck pain.

BACKGROUND: IFA MEMBER
Established: 1983; 1st Franchised: 1989
Franchised Units: 71
Company-Owned Units 15
Total Units: 86
Dist.: US-84; CAN-2; O'seas-0
North America: 34 States, 1 Province
Density: 20 in CA, 6 in FL, 6 in TX

Projected New Units (12 Months): 15
Qualifications: 4, 4, 3, 3, 2, 5
Registered: All States

FINANCIAL/TERMS:

Cash Investment: $100K
Total Investment: $180-300K
Minimum Net Worth: $300K
Fees: Franchise - $25K
Royalty - 4%; Ad. - 1%
Earnings Claim Statement: No
Term of Contract (Years): 10/10
Avg. # Of Employees: 3 FT, 1 PT
Passive Ownership: Discouraged
Encourage Conversions: N/A
Area Develop. Agreements: Yes/Varies
Sub-Franchising Contracts: No
Expand In Territory: No
Space Needs: 2,600 SF; FS, SF, SC, RM

SUPPORT & TRAINING PROVIDED:

Financial Assistance Provided: Yes(I)
Site Selection Assistance: Yes
Lease Negotiation Assistance: Yes
Co-Operative Advertising: Yes
Franchisee Assoc./Member: Yes/Yes
Size Of Corporate Staff: 25
On-Going Support: B,C,D,E,G,H,I
Training: 8 Days Corp HQ; 1 Week On-Site.

SPECIFIC EXPANSION PLANS:

US: All United States
Canada: All Canada
Overseas: No

<< >>

RESCUECOM CORPORATION

2560 Burnet Ave.
Syracuse, NY 13206
Tel: (800) 737-2837 (315) 433-0002
Fax: (315) 433-5228
E-Mail: franchise@rescuecom.com
Web Site: www.rescuecom.com
Mr. David A. Milman, President

For the best computer technical talent, RESCUECOM offers the freedom of business ownership without the requirements (and headaches) of the mundane day to day business functions.

BACKGROUND:

Established: 1997; 1st Franchised: 1999
Franchised Units: 6
Company-Owned Units 5
Total Units: 11
Dist.: US-5; CAN-0; O'seas-0
North America: 3 States
Density: 3 in NY, 1 in IL, 1 in CA
Projected New Units (12 Months): 3
Qualifications: 3, 3, 5, 4, 4, 4
Registered: CA,FL,IL,IN,MI,NY,AB

FINANCIAL/TERMS:

Cash Investment: $1.5-15K
Total Investment: $29.4-53.2K
Minimum Net Worth: $25K
Fees: Franchise - $15K
Royalty - 18%; Ad. - 2%
Earnings Claim Statement: Yes
Term of Contract (Years): 10/5
Avg. # Of Employees: 1-3 FT
Passive Ownership: Not Allowed
Encourage Conversions: Yes
Area Develop. Agreements: No
Sub-Franchising Contracts: No
Expand In Territory: NR
Space Needs: N/A SF; HB

SUPPORT & TRAINING PROVIDED:

Financial Assistance Provided: Yes
Site Selection Assistance: Yes
Lease Negotiation Assistance: Yes
Co-Operative Advertising: Yes
Franchisee Assoc./Member: No
Size Of Corporate Staff: 20
On-Going Support: A,B,C,D,E,F,H,I
Training: 10 Days in Syracuse, NY.

SPECIFIC EXPANSION PLANS:

US: All United States
Canada: All Canada
Overseas: Europe

<< >>

RIDER'S HOBBY SHOPS

4627 Platt Rd.
Ann Arbor, MI 48108-9726
Tel: (888) 530-9780
Fax: (517) 796-2679
Web Site: www.riders.com
Mr. Brent Martin, Dir. Business Development

RIDER'S HOBBY SHOPS sell FUN! When families walk into a RIDER'S HOBBY SHOP, childhood dreams come alive and imaginations run wild. The family-oriented recreational products displayed throughout the store offer something fun and exciting for just about everyone. RIDER'S HOBBY SHOPS sell radio controlled cars, boats, airplanes, helicopters, electric trains, models of all types, games, telescopes, specialty tools, kites, rockets, doll houses, slotcars, educational toys for kids and much more.

BACKGROUND:

Established: 1946; 1st Franchised: 1996
Franchised Units: 4
Company-Owned Units 6
Total Units: 10
Dist.: US-13; CAN-0; O'seas-0
North America: 3 States
Density: 11 in MI, 1 in TX, 1 in VA
Projected New Units (12 Months): 15-20
Qualifications: 4, 4, 3, 2, 4, 5
Registered: IL,IN,MI

FINANCIAL/TERMS:

Cash Investment: $80-120K
Total Investment: $200-300K
Minimum Net Worth: $300K
Fees: Franchise - $17.5K
Royalty - 3.5%; Ad. - 1%
Earnings Claim Statement: Yes
Term of Contract (Years): 10/5
Avg. # Of Employees: 3-4 FT, 6-10 PT
Passive Ownership: Discouraged
Encourage Conversions: Yes
Area Develop. Agreements: No
Sub-Franchising Contracts: No
Expand In Territory: No
Space Needs: 3,000-5,000 SF; SC

SUPPORT & TRAINING PROVIDED:

Financial Assistance Provided: No
Site Selection Assistance: Yes
Lease Negotiation Assistance: Yes
Co-Operative Advertising: Yes
Franchisee Assoc./Member: No
Size Of Corporate Staff: 8
On-Going Support: A,B,C,D,E,F,G,H,I
Training: 5 Days Corporate Headquarters; 14 Days Franchisee's Retail Location.

SPECIFIC EXPANSION PLANS:

US: Focus on Midwest
Canada: No
Overseas: Master Franchisee in the U.K.

SHEFIELD GOURMET GROUP OF COMPANIES

2265 W. Railway St., Box 490
Abbotsford, BC V2S 5Z5 CANADA
Tel: (604) 859-1014
Fax: (604) 859-1711
E-Mail: shefield@uniserve.com
Web Site: www.shefieldgourmet.com
Mr. T. Hartford, Franchise Director

Retail outlet, featuring tobaccos and related products, but also offering other merchandise, including beverages, confectionery, reading material, giftware and lottery that caters to everyday needs and impulse buying.

BACKGROUND:

Established: 1976; 1st Franchised: 1976

Franchised Units: 111
Company-Owned Units 2
Total Units: 113
Dist.: US-0; CAN-113; O'seas-0
North America: 7 Provinces
Density: 39 in BC, 32 in ON, 23 in AB
Projected New Units (12 Months): 5
Registered: AB

FINANCIAL/TERMS:

Cash Investment: $40-100K
Total Investment: $180K
Minimum Net Worth: $NR
Fees: Franchise - $10-25K
Royalty - 2-8%; Ad. - NR
Earnings Claim Statement: NR
Term of Contract (Years): 5/5
Avg. # Of Employees: 1 FT, 1 PT
Passive Ownership: Discouraged
Encourage Conversions: Yes
Area Develop. Agreements: No
Sub-Franchising Contracts: No
Expand In Territory: Yes
Space Needs: 250-1,500 SF; RM, SC

SUPPORT & TRAINING PROVIDED:

Financial Assistance Provided: No
Site Selection Assistance: Yes
Lease Negotiation Assistance: Yes
Co-Operative Advertising: Yes
Franchisee Assoc./Member: NR
Size Of Corporate Staff: 8
On-Going Support: C,D,E,G,I
Training: 1 Week On-Site.

SPECIFIC EXPANSION PLANS:

US: No
Canada: All Canada
Overseas: No

<< >>

Top 50

TALKING BOOK WORLD

25900 Greenfield Rd., # 255
Oak Park, MI 48237
Tel: (800) 403-2933 (248) 968-4080
Fax: (707) 897-7996
E-Mail: franchise@talkingbooks.com
Web Site: www.talkingbookworld.com
Mr. Richard Simtob, Dir. Franchise Sales

TALKING BOOK WORLD is the world's largest audio book retail store. TALKING BOOK WORLD has the largest selection of audiobooks for rent, with NO DUE DATES.

BACKGROUND:

Established: 1993; 1st Franchised: 1995
Franchised Units: 22
Company-Owned Units 23
Total Units: 45
Dist.: US-43; CAN-2; O'seas-0
North America: 9 States, 1 Province
Density: 16 in MI, 15 in CA, 1 in FL
Projected New Units (12 Months): 10
Qualifications: 3, 3, 3, 4, 5, 5
Registered: CA,FL,IL,IN,MD,MI,NY,VA

FINANCIAL/TERMS:

Cash Investment: $20-225K
Total Investment: $150-225K
Minimum Net Worth: $100K
Fees: Franchise - $25K
Royalty - 5%; Ad. - 2%
Earnings Claim Statement: No
Term of Contract (Years): 15/15
Avg. # Of Employees: 1 FT, 2 PT
Passive Ownership: Discouraged
Encourage Conversions: Yes
Area Develop. Agreements: Yes/3
Sub-Franchising Contracts: No
Expand In Territory: Yes
Space Needs: 1,800 SF; FS, SF, SC

SUPPORT & TRAINING PROVIDED:

Financial Assistance Provided: Yes(I)
Site Selection Assistance: Yes
Lease Negotiation Assistance: Yes
Co-Operative Advertising: Yes
Franchisee Assoc./Member: Yes/Yes
Size Of Corporate Staff: 8
On-Going Support: C,D,E,F,G,H,I
Training: 2 Weeks Michigan/California; 1 Week On Site; Unlimited Any Corporate Store.

SPECIFIC EXPANSION PLANS:

US: All United States
Canada: All Canada
Overseas: No

<< >>

Top 50

TINDER BOX INTERNATIONAL

3 Bala Plaza East, # 102
Bala Cynwyd, PA 19004-2449
Tel: (800) 846-3372 (610) 668-4220
Fax: (610) 668-4266
E-Mail: tbiltd@ix.netcom.com
Web Site: www.tinderbox.com
Mr. Neal Baratt, Franchise Development

The world's largest and oldest chain of premium cigar, tobacco, smoking accessory and gift stores, with 70 years' experience as the undisputed industry leader.

BACKGROUND: IFA MEMBER

Established: 1928; 1st Franchised: 1965
Franchised Units: 128
Company-Owned Units 3
Total Units: 131
Dist.: US-116; CAN-1; O'seas-0
North America: 50 States
Density: 17 in CA, 9 in IL, 9 in OH
Projected New Units (12 Months): 25
Qualifications: 5, 3, 1, 2, 4, 5
Registered: All Except ND,SD

FINANCIAL/TERMS:

Cash Investment: $75-100K
Total Investment: $175-250K
Minimum Net Worth: $250-300K
Fees: Franchise - $30K
Royalty - 4-5%; Ad. - 3%
Earnings Claim Statement: Yes
Term of Contract (Years): 10/5
Avg. # Of Employees: 1-2 FT, 2-3 PT
Passive Ownership: Allowed
Encourage Conversions: Yes
Area Develop. Agreements: Yes/5
Sub-Franchising Contracts: No
Expand In Territory: Yes
Space Needs: 800-1,500 SF; FS, SF, SC, RM

SUPPORT & TRAINING PROVIDED:

Financial Assistance Provided: Yes
Site Selection Assistance: Yes
Lease Negotiation Assistance: Yes
Co-Operative Advertising: Yes
Franchisee Assoc./Member: No
Size Of Corporate Staff: 10
On-Going Support: a,C,D,E,F,G,H,I
Training: 5 Days Home Office; 3-5 Days at Franchisee's Store; Follow-Up Store Visit within 30 Days.

SPECIFIC EXPANSION PLANS:

US: All United States
Canada: All Canada
Overseas: All Countries

<< >>

WICKS 'N' STICKS

333 N. Sam Houston Pkwy. E, # 610
Houston, TX 77060-2484
Tel: (888) 55-WICKS (281) 618-4011

Fax: (281) 618-4000
Web Site: www.wicksnstick.com
Mr. Mark L. Jameson, Executive Vice President

Wicks'n'Sticks™

Nation's largest and most respected franchised retailer of quality candles, fragrancing and related home decorative products. Franchisees are offered outstanding name recognition, comprehensive training and extensive start up and on-going support. Rated a top franchise by both Success Gold 200 and Income Opportunities Platinum 2000.

BACKGROUND: IFA MEMBER
Established: 1968; 1st Franchised: 1968
Franchised Units: 148
Company-Owned Units 7
Total Units: 155
Dist.: US-155; CAN-0; O'seas-0
North America: 37 States
Density: 14 in TX, 14 in CA, 13 in FL
Projected New Units (12 Months): 17
Qualifications: 5, 3, 3, 3, 3, 5
Registered: CA,IL,IN,MD,MI,MN,NY,ND,OR,RI,SD,VA,WA,WI

FINANCIAL/TERMS:
Cash Investment: $65K
Total Investment: $198.5-330.72K
Minimum Net Worth: $70K Liquid
Fees: Franchise - $35K
Royalty - 2.5% (in 2002); Ad. - None
Earnings Claim Statement: No
Term of Contract (Years): 5+
Avg. # Of Employees: 1 FT, 6 PT
Passive Ownership: N/A
Encourage Conversions: N/A
Area Develop. Agreements: No
Sub-Franchising Contracts: No
Expand In Territory: Yes
Space Needs: 1000-1700 SF; RM

SUPPORT & TRAINING PROVIDED:
Financial Assistance Provided: No
Site Selection Assistance: Yes
Lease Negotiation Assistance: Yes
Co-Operative Advertising: Yes
Franchisee Assoc./Member: Yes
Size Of Corporate Staff: 21
On-Going Support: A,C,D,E,F,G,H,I
Training: 8 Days Corporate Office, Houston, TX.

SPECIFIC EXPANSION PLANS:
US: All United States
Canada: No
Overseas: No

<< >>

WILD BIRD CENTER

7370 MacArthur Blvd.
Glen Echo, MD 20812-1200
Tel: (800) 945-3247 (301) 229-9585
Fax: (301) 320-6154
E-Mail: georgep@wildbirdcenter.com
Web Site: www.wildbirdcenter.com
Mr. George H. Petrides, President

A WBCA franchise is more than a store; it is a valued community resource. The story of THE WILD BIRD CENTERS OF AMERICA, Inc. is one of enthusiasm about wild birds and a professional approach to the birding market. The customer enjoys friendly, personal service in a peaceful environment with the feel of a relaxing backyard. The owner provides this service with the help of highly-efficient systems and support.

BACKGROUND: IFA MEMBER
Established: 1985; 1st Franchised: 1988
Franchised Units: 99
Company-Owned Units 1
Total Units: 100
Dist.: US-98; CAN-2; O'seas-0
North America: 33 States, 1 Province
Density: 9 in MD, 8 in PA, 6 in CO
Projected New Units (12 Months): 20
Qualifications: 5, 4, 2, 4, 2, 5
Registered: All Except HI

FINANCIAL/TERMS:
Cash Investment: $35-50K
Total Investment: $75-131K
Minimum Net Worth: $150K
Fees: Franchise - $19.5K
Royalty - 3-4.5%; Ad. - 0%
Earnings Claim Statement: No
Term of Contract (Years): 5/5x5
Avg. # Of Employees: 1 FT, 2 PT
Passive Ownership: Discouraged
Encourage Conversions: No
Area Develop. Agreements: No
Sub-Franchising Contracts: No
Expand In Territory: Yes
Space Needs: 1,500-2,400 SF; SC

SUPPORT & TRAINING PROVIDED:
Financial Assistance Provided: Yes(I)
Site Selection Assistance: Yes
Lease Negotiation Assistance: Yes
Co-Operative Advertising: Yes
Franchisee Assoc./Member: Yes/Yes
Size Of Corporate Staff: 15
On-Going Support: C,d,E,F,G,h
Training: 10 Days Home Office.

SPECIFIC EXPANSION PLANS:
US: All United States
Canada: All Canada
Overseas: No

<< >>

WILD BIRD MARKETPLACE

4317 Elm Tree Rd.
Bloomfield, NY 14469
Tel: (888) 926-2473 (716) 229-5897
Fax: (716) 229-5448
E-Mail: jfg@wildbirdmarketplace.com
Web Site: www.wildbirdmarketplace.org
Mr. John F. Gardner, President

WILD BIRD MARKETPLACE is committed to providing an outstanding franchise opportunity - one that provides personal satisfaction, community recognition and profitability based on personal motivation, qualification and commitment.

BACKGROUND:
Established: 1988; 1st Franchised: 1990
Franchised Units: 15
Company-Owned Units 0
Total Units: 15
Dist.: US-15; CAN-0; O'seas-0
North America: 10 States
Density: 4 in PA, 2 in NC, 2 in WY
Projected New Units (12 Months): 4
Qualifications: 4, 3, 2, 1, 3, 4
Registered: FL,IL,IN,MD,MI,NY,RI,SD,WI,AB

FINANCIAL/TERMS:
Cash Investment: $30-50K
Total Investment: $90-150K
Minimum Net Worth: $150K
Fees: Franchise - $20K
Royalty - 4%; Ad. - 0%
Earnings Claim Statement: No
Term of Contract (Years): 10/10
Avg. # Of Employees: 1 FT, 2 PT
Passive Ownership: Discouraged
Encourage Conversions: Yes
Area Develop. Agreements: Yes
Sub-Franchising Contracts: Yes
Expand In Territory: Yes

Space Needs: 2,000 SF; FS, SF, SC

SUPPORT & TRAINING PROVIDED:

Financial Assistance Provided:	Yes(I)
Site Selection Assistance:	Yes
Lease Negotiation Assistance:	Yes
Co-Operative Advertising:	N/A
Franchisee Assoc./Member:	No
Size Of Corporate Staff:	3
On-Going Support:	C,D,E,F,G,H,I

Training: 5 Days Corporate Headquarters; 5 Days at Store.

SPECIFIC EXPANSION PLANS:

US:	NE, SE, Midwest
Canada:	No
Overseas:	No

<< >>

WILD BIRDS UNLIMITED

11711 N. College Ave., # 146
Carmel, IN 46032-5601
Tel: (888) 302-2473 (317) 571-7100
Fax: (317) 571-7110
E-Mail: pickettp@wbu.com
Web Site: www.wbu.com
Mr. Paul E. Pickett, Dir. Franchise Development

WILD BIRDS UNLIMITED is North America's original and largest group of retail stores catering to the backyard birdfeeding and nature enthusiast. We currently have over 280 stores in the U. S. and Canada. Stores provide birdseed, feeders, houses, optics and nature-related gifts. Additionally, stores provide extensive educational programs regarding backyard birdfeeding. Franchisees are provided an all-inclusive support system.

BACKGROUND: IFA MEMBER

Established: 1981; 1st Franchised: 1983

Franchised Units:	281
Company-Owned Units	0
Total Units:	281
Dist.:	US-267; CAN-16; O'seas-0
North America:	42 States, 3 Provinces
Density:	19 in MI, 18 in TX, 13 in IL
Projected New Units (12 Months):	35
Qualifications:	5, 5, 1, 3, 2, 5

Registered: CA,FL,IL,IN,MD,MI,MN,NY, OR,RI,VA,WA,WI,DC

FINANCIAL/TERMS:

Cash Investment:	$32-45K
Total Investment:	$80-140K
Minimum Net Worth:	$150K
Fees: Franchise -	$18K
Royalty - 4%;	Ad. - NR
Earnings Claim Statement:	Yes
Term of Contract (Years):	10/5
Avg. # Of Employees:	2 FT, 4 PT
Passive Ownership:	Not Allowed
Encourage Conversions:	N/A
Area Develop. Agreements:	No
Sub-Franchising Contracts:	No
Expand In Territory:	Yes

Space Needs: 1,400-1,800 SF; FS, SC

SUPPORT & TRAINING PROVIDED:

Financial Assistance Provided:	Yes(I)
Site Selection Assistance:	Yes
Lease Negotiation Assistance:	Yes
Co-Operative Advertising:	No
Franchisee Assoc./Member:	Yes/Yes
Size Of Corporate Staff:	40
On-Going Support:	C,D,E,F,G,H,I

Training: 6 Days in Indianapolis, IN; 1 Day at Store Site.

SPECIFIC EXPANSION PLANS:

US:	All United States
Canada:	All Canada
Overseas:	No

<< >>

SUPPLEMENTAL LISTING OF FRANCHISORS

ABINGTON'S COLLECTIBLES, 4699 Keele St., # 1, Downsview, ON M3J 2N8 CANADA; (416) 661-9916; (416) 661-9706

BABIES 'N' BELLS, 4489 Mira Vista Dr., Frisco, TX 75034-7519 ; (888) 418-2229 (972) 335-3535; (469) 384-0138

BACCHUS WINE MADE SIMPLE, 1000 Manhattan Ave., Manhattan Beach, CA 90266 ; (310) 372-2021; (310) 372-5541

BETTER BACK STORE, THE, P.O. Box 1296, Newington, VA 22122 ; (800) 501-2225 (703) 339-1300; (703) 339-0671

BIRDERS NATURE STORE, 4699 Keele St., # 1, Downsview, ON M3J 2N8 CANADA; (416) 661-9916; (416) 661-9706

CAR PHONE STORE, THE, 2608 Berlin Turnpike, Newington, CT 06109 ; (860) 571-7600; (860) 257-1818

CASH CONVERTERS CANADA, 185 The West Mall, Toronto, ON M9C 5L5 CANADA; (888) 677-2274 (416) 695-2321; (416) 695-9051

CLEANING SUPPLIER, 6544 S. State St., Murray, UT 84107 ; (801) 270-8300; (801) 270-8500

CONROY'S/1-800-FLOWERS, 1600 Stewart Ave., Westbury, NY 11590 ; (800) 557-4770 (516) 237-6000; (516) 237-6097

CRAFTERS MARKETPLACE, 2624 Dunwin Dr., # 3, Mississauga, ON L5J 4B6 CANADA; (800) 292-2585 ; (972) 478-2404

D' VINE WINE, 514 Camden Cir., Mississauga, ON L4Z 2P2 CANADA; (888) 464-9463 (905) 501-8520; (905) 712-3871

FLICKERS, 1101 N.E. 40th Ct, # 5, Ft. Lauderdale, FL 33334-3093 ; (877) 563-9744 (954) 563-9744; (954) 563-9755

FLOWERAMA OF AMERICA, 3165 W. Airline Hwy., Waterloo, IA 50703 ; (800) 728-6004 (319) 291-6004; (319) 291-8676

FOREMOST LIQUOR STORES, 4001 W. Devon, Chicago, IL 60646 ; (773) 545-3111; (312) 545-3330

GREAT CANADIAN DOLLAR STORE, 302-31 Bastion Sq., Victoria, BC V8W 1J1 CANADA; (877) 388-0123 (250) 388-0123; (250) 388-9763

HALOWEEN EXPRESS, 1860 Georgetown Rd., Owenton, KY 40359 ; (828) 277-8188; (828) 277-8159

HAMMETT'S LEARNING WORLD, P.O. Box 859057, Braintree, MA 02185-9057 ; (800) 955-2200 (781) 848-1000; (781) 848-3970

HANNOUSH JEWELERS, 134 Capital Dr., West Springfield, MA 01089-1331 (888) 325-3935 (413) 846-4640; (413) 788-7588

HAT ZONE, THE, 1036 A NE Jib Court, Lakewood Bus. Pk., Lee's Summit, MO 64064 ; (800) 440-6894 (816) 795-8702; (816) 795-9159

INACOM COMPUTER CENTERS, 10810 Farnam Dr., Omaha, NE 68154 (800) 843-2762 (402) 758-3900; (402) 330-9608

LASERNETWORKS, 785 Pacific Rd., # 1, Oakville, ON L6L 6M3 CANADA; (800) 461-4879 (905) 847-5990; (905) 847-5991

MGM LIQUOR STORES, 1124 Larpenteur Ave. W., St. Paul, MN 55113-6317 ; (651) 487-1006; (651) 487-9401

NATURE'S 10, 12200 E. Briarwood Ave., # 250, Englewood, CO 80112-6702

OFFICE 1 SUPERSTORE INTERNATIONAL, P.O. Box 5093, East Hampton, NY 11937 ; (516) 537-4290; (516) 537-4293

PARTY CITY, 400 Commons Way, Rockaway, NJ 07866 ; (800) 883-2100 (973) 983-0888; (973) 983-1333

PARTY FAIR, Pond Rd. Shopping Center, Freehold, NJ 07728 ; (732) 780-1110; (732) 780-5174

PCHUT.COM, 1205 Hwy. 20, Mountain Home, ID 83647-3962 ; (208) 580-2574; (208) 363-9201

PINCH-A-PENNY, P.O. Box 6025, Clearwater, FL 33758 ; (727) 531-8913; (727) 536-8066

PLATO'S CLOSET, 4200 Dahlberg Dr., # 100, Minneapolis, MN 55422 ; (800) 839-3921 (763) 520-8630; (763) 520-8501

POT POURRI, 216 Migneron, Ville Saint-Lauren, QC H4T 1Y7 CANADA; (514) 341-4000; (514) 341-4241

RECYCLED PAPER GREETINGS, 3636 N. Broadway, Chicago, IL 60613 (800) 777-3331 (312) 348-6410; (312) 296-6291

RETOOL, 4200 Dalhberg Dr., Minneapolis, MN 55422 ; (800) 645-7297 (763) 520-8485; (612) 520-8501

SHAVER CENTER/CENTRE DU RASOIR, 3151 rue Joseph Dubreuil, Lachine, PQ H8T 3HT CANADA; (514) 636-4512; (514) 636-8356

SHEFFIELD&SONSTOBACCONISTS, P.O. Box 490, Abbotsford, AB U2S S2S CANADA; (604) 859-1014; (604) 859-1711

SHE'S FLOWERS, 100 N. Glendora Ave., # 106, Glendora, CA 91741 ; (800) 777-2582 (626) FLO-RIST; (626) 335-2039

SOFTUB, 21100 Superior St., Chatsworth, CA 91311 ; (800) 266-7882 (818) 407-4646; (818) 407-4658

SOX APPEAL, 7167 Shady Oak Rd., Eden Prairie, MN 55344 ; (800) 899-8478 (612) 943-1011; (612) 934-9050

SUCCESSORIES, 2520 Diehl Rd., Aurora, IL 60504 ; (800) 621-1423 (630) 820-7200; (630) 820-3856

TFM, 10333 - 174 St., Edmonton, AB T5S 1H1 CANADA; (780) 483-3217; (780) 486-7528

TRUE FRIENDS, 318 N. Carson St., # 214, Carson City, NV 89701 ; (800) 654-5156 (702) 882-1963; (800) 654-5161

T-SHIRTS PLUS, P.O. Box 9423, College Station, TX 77842 ; (800) 880-0721 (254) 776-8872; (254) 776-6838

WOODCRAFT FRANCHISING, 1177 Rosemar Rd., Parkersburg, WV 26105 ; (304) 422-5412; (304) 485-1938

YARD CARDS, 3990 State St., Abilene, TX 79603; (915) 672-9444; (915) 672-9444

ZLAND.COM, 240 Briggs Rd., Costa Mesa, CA 92626-4511 ; (877) 682-0922 (714) 436-2500

Retail: Video/Audio/Electronics

Chapter

43

Retail: Video/Audio/Electronics Industry Profile

Total # Franchisors in Industry Group	19
Total # Franchised Units in Industry Group	4,160
Total # Company-Owned Units in Industry Group	8,452
Total # Operating Units in Industry Group	12,612
Average # Franchised Units/Franchisor	218.9
Average # Company-Owned Units/Franchisor	444.8
Average # Total Units/Franchisor	663.7
Ratio of Total # Franchised Units/Total # Company-Owned Units	0.5:1
Industry Survey Participants	4
Representing % of Industry	21.1%
Average Franchise Fee*:	$20.0K
Average Total Investment*:	$95.3K
Average On-Going Royalty Fee*:	4.0%

*If a range was provided, the mid-point of the range was used. See detailed profiles for actual ranges.

Four Largest Participants in Survey

Company	# Franchised Units	# Co-Owned Units	# Total Units	Franchise Fee	On-Going Royalty	Total Investment
1. Radio Shack Select	2,154	5,033	7,187	25K	0%	60K
2. CD Warehouse	240	64	304	20K	5/4%	132-169K
3. Microplay Interactive	100	1	101	15K	3.4% Avg.	115-200K
4. Video Data Services	80	0	80	20K	$750/Year	20-23K

All of the data provided are proprietary and should not be quoted without acknowledging *Bond's Franchise Guide.*

CD WAREHOUSE

900 N. Broadway
Oklahoma City, OK 73102
Tel: (800) 641-9394 (405) 236-8742
Fax: (405) 232-3710
E-Mail: franchise.development@cdwarehouse.com
Web Site: www.cdwarehouse.com
Mrs. Whitney L. Gebard, Mgr. Fran. Dev.

CD WAREHOUSE is a rapidly-growing franchise, specializing in the sale of pre-owned CDs and DVDs. Our stores also buy and trade used CD's, sell Top 100 new CDs, and sell other music-related items. Our proprietary software makes it easy to buy and sell pre-owned CDs, even without prior music knowledge.

BACKGROUND: IFA MEMBER
Established: 1992; 1st Franchised: 1992
Franchised Units: 216
Company-Owned Units 64
Total Units: 280
Dist.: US-263; CAN-7; O'seas-10
North America: 36 States, 3 Provinces
Density: 51 in TX, 21 in FL, 17 in CA
Projected New Units (12 Months): 15
Qualifications: 5, 3, 1, 2, 4, 4
Registered: CA,FL,IL,IN,MD,MI,NY,OR,RI,VA,WI

FINANCIAL/TERMS:
Cash Investment: $40-60K
Total Investment: $122-162K
Minimum Net Worth: $150K
Fees: Franchise - $20K
Royalty - 5%/4%; Ad. - 1.75%
Earnings Claim Statement: No
Term of Contract (Years): 10/10
Avg. # Of Employees: 2-3 FT, 3-4 PT
Passive Ownership: Discouraged
Encourage Conversions: N/A
Area Develop. Agreements: Yes
Sub-Franchising Contracts: No
Expand In Territory: Yes
Space Needs: 1,500-2,000 SF; FS, SC

SUPPORT & TRAINING PROVIDED:
Financial Assistance Provided: Yes(I)
Site Selection Assistance: Yes
Lease Negotiation Assistance: Yes
Co-Operative Advertising: Yes
Franchisee Assoc./Member: Yes/No
Size Of Corporate Staff: 25
On-Going Support: C,D,E,G,H,I
Training: 5-6 Days at Oklahoma City, OK Training Center.

SPECIFIC EXPANSION PLANS:
US: All United States
Canada: All Canada
Overseas: All Countries

<< >>

MICROPLAY INTERACTIVE

706 Giddings Ave., # 1-C
Annapolis, MD 21401 CANADA
Tel: (877) 221-6685 (410) 990-1115
Fax: (410) 990-1118
E-Mail: mcopeland@microplay.com
Web Site: www.microplay.com
Mr. Mason Copeland, Franchise Director

MICROPLAY stores take video game specialty retailing to a whole new level. We buy, sell, rent and accessorize all popular games and systems, including Nintendo, Sony, Sega and PC CD-ROM. Our well-stocked stores offer variety, expertise and great value. In short, 'We sell fun!' We welcome you to discover why MICROPLAY is ranked #1 in video games.

BACKGROUND: IFA MEMBER
Established: 1985; 1st Franchised: 1993
Franchised Units: 100
Company-Owned Units 1
Total Units: 101
Dist.: US-13; CAN-84; O'seas-4
North America: 7 States, 9 Provinces
Density: 47 in ON, 8 in PQ, 8 in BC
Projected New Units (12 Months): 25
Qualifications: 3, 3, 4, 3, 2, 5
Registered: NR

FINANCIAL/TERMS:
Cash Investment: $40-80K
Total Investment: $115-200K
Minimum Net Worth: $300K
Fees: Franchise - $15K
Royalty - 3.4% Avg.; Ad. - 1%
Earnings Claim Statement: No
Term of Contract (Years): 10/10
Avg. # Of Employees: 2 FT, 1 PT
Passive Ownership: Discouraged
Encourage Conversions: Yes
Area Develop. Agreements: Yes/10
Sub-Franchising Contracts: Yes
Expand In Territory: No
Space Needs: 1,400 SF; SC

SUPPORT & TRAINING PROVIDED:
Financial Assistance Provided: Yes(I)
Site Selection Assistance: Yes
Lease Negotiation Assistance: Yes
Co-Operative Advertising: Yes
Franchisee Assoc./Member: Yes/Yes
Size Of Corporate Staff: 14
On-Going Support: A,B,C,D,E,F,G,H,I
Training: 2 Days Concord, ON; 3 Days Training Store, Toronto, ON; 3 Days Pre-Opening/Grand Opening.

SPECIFIC EXPANSION PLANS:
US: NY,NJ,DE,CT,PA,OH, Midwest
Canada: All Canada
Overseas: England

<< >>

RADIO SHACK SELECT

300 W. 3rd St., # 1600
Fort Worth, TX 76102
Tel: (800) 826-3905 (817) 415-3499
Fax: (817) 415-8651
E-Mail: paul.crump@radioshack.com
Web Site: www.radioshack.com
Mr. Paul Crump, Fran. Dir./New Stores

RADIO SHACK is a consumer electronics retailer.

BACKGROUND: IFA MEMBER
Established: 1921; 1st Franchised: 1969
Franchised Units: 2,154
Company-Owned Units 5,033
Total Units: 7,187
Dist.: US-7091; CAN-0; O'seas-54
North America: 48 States
Density: CA, NY, IL
Projected New Units (12 Months): 150
Qualifications: 5, 5, 5, 1, 1, 4
Registered: CA,FL,IL,IN,MD,MI,MN,NY,ND,OR,SD,VA,WA,WI,DC

FINANCIAL/TERMS:
Cash Investment: $20% Down
Total Investment: $60K
Minimum Net Worth: $N/A
Fees: Franchise - $25K
Royalty - 0%; Ad. - 0%
Earnings Claim Statement: No
Term of Contract (Years): 10/Annual
Avg. # Of Employees: NR
Passive Ownership: Discouraged
Encourage Conversions: No
Area Develop. Agreements: No
Sub-Franchising Contracts: No
Expand In Territory: Yes
Space Needs: 500 SF; FS, SF, SC, RM

SUPPORT & TRAINING PROVIDED:
Financial Assistance Provided: Yes(D)
Site Selection Assistance: No
Lease Negotiation Assistance: No
Co-Operative Advertising: Yes
Franchisee Assoc./Member: Yes/Yes
Size Of Corporate Staff: 150
On-Going Support: A,B,C,D,E,F,G,H,I
Training: 5 Days On-Site.
SPECIFIC EXPANSION PLANS:
US: All States Except Hawaii
Canada: No
Overseas: No

<< >>

VIDEO DATA SERVICES

2200 Dunbarton Dr., # D
Chesapeake, VA 23325
Tel: (800) 836-9461
Fax: (757) 424-8693
E-Mail: corporate@videomasteronline.com
Web Site: www.vdsvideo.com
Mr. Rory Graham

VIDEO DATA SERVICES provide a unique, video-photography service to businesses and consumers. The complete package includes all equipment, training, marketing and field assistance. It can be started part-time and is ideal as a family or retirement business. VIDEO DATA SERVICES is the largest video-taping service in North America. We also provide film-to-tape transfers and editing services.

BACKGROUND:
Established: 1981; 1st Franchised: 1984
Franchised Units: 80
Company-Owned Units 0
Total Units: 80
Dist.: US-230; CAN-6; O'seas-0
North America: NR
Density: 24 in CA, 12 to VA, 8 in NY
Projected New Units (12 Months): 30
Qualifications: 5, 3, 1, 3, 3, 2
Registered: CA,IL,NY,VA,MI,WA
FINANCIAL/TERMS:
Cash Investment: $10-20K
Total Investment: $20-23K
Minimum Net Worth: $75K
Fees: Franchise - $20K
Royalty - $750/Yr.; Ad. - 0%
Earnings Claim Statement: No
Term of Contract (Years): 10/10
Avg. # Of Employees: 1 FT, 1 PT
Passive Ownership: Not Allowed
Encourage Conversions: N/A
Area Develop. Agreements: No
Sub-Franchising Contracts: No
Expand In Territory: No
Space Needs: 200 SF; HB
SUPPORT & TRAINING PROVIDED:
Financial Assistance Provided: Yes(I)
Site Selection Assistance: N/A
Lease Negotiation Assistance: N/A
Co-Operative Advertising: N/A
Franchisee Assoc./Member: Yes/No
Size Of Corporate Staff: 4
On-Going Support: B,G,H,I
Training: 3 Days San Diego, CA; 3 Days Rochester, NY.
SPECIFIC EXPANSION PLANS:
US: All United States
Canada: All Canada
Overseas: No

<< >>

SUPPLEMENTAL LISTING OF FRANCHISORS

@WIRELESS, 50 Methodist Hill Dr., # 1500, Rochester, NY 14623 ; (800) 613-2355 (716) 359-3390; (716) 359-3253

BANG & OLUFSEN RETAILING CONCEPT, 1200 Business Center Dr., # 100, Mount Prospect, IL 60056 ; (877) 507-1234 (847) 299-9380; (847) 699-1475

BLOCKBUSTER INTERNATIONAL, 1201 Elm St., # 2100, Dallas, TX 75270 (888) 309-2234 (214) 854-3488; (214) 854-3788

COMPUTER TROUBLE SHOOTERS, 3904 N. Druid Hills Rd., # 323, Decatur, GA 30033 ; (877) 704-1702 (770) 454-6382; (770) 454-6766

DISC GO ROUND, 900 N. Broadway, Oklahoma City, OK 73102 ; (800) 476-9249 (405) 236-8742; (405) 949-2566

IT'S ABOUT GAMES, 4200 Dahlberg Dr., Minneapolis, MN 55422 ; (800) 824-6360 (612) 520-8500; (612) 520-8501

MR. MOVIES, 7625 Parklawn, # 200, Edina, MN 55435 ; (800) 562-7667 (612) 835-3321; (612) 835-1144

RADIO SHACK (CANADA), 1 Tandy Center, 16th Fl., Fort Worth, TX 76102 ; (705) 728-6242; (705) 728-2012

VIDEO UPDATE, 3100 World Trade Center, 30 E. 7th St., St. Paul, MN 55101-4913 ; (651) 222-0006; (612) 312-2666

VIRTUAL PCS, 1546 Dartford, Maumee, OH 43537-1374 ; (888) 990-8324 (419) 866-2005; (419) 866-2500

Retail: Miscellaneous

Chapter 44

Retail: Miscellaneous Industry Profile

Total # Franchisors in Industry Group	13
Total # Franchised Units in Industry Group	1,311
Total # Company-Owned Units in Industry Group	150
Total # Operating Units in Industry Group	1,461
Average # Franchised Units/Franchisor	100.8
Average # Company-Owned Units/Franchisor	11.5
Average # Total Units/Franchisor	112.3
Ratio of Total # Franchised Units/Total # Company-Owned Units	8.7:1
Industry Survey Participants	5
Representing % of Industry	38.5%
Average Franchise Fee*:	$24.2K
Average Total Investment*:	$139.8K
Average On-Going Royalty Fee*:	4.3%

*If a range was provided, the mid-point of the range was used. See detailed profiles for actual ranges.

Five Largest Participants in Survey

Company	# Franchised Units	# Co-Owned Units	# Total Units	Franchise Fee	On-Going Royalty	Total Investment
1. Heel Quik!	680	0	680	2.5-17.5K	4%	8.9-154K
2. A Buck Or Two Stores	255	34	289	50K	6%	160K
3. Dollar Discount Stores of America	148	0	148	18K	3%	199K
4. Grand & Toy	25	48	73	15K	Varies	100K
5. Terri's Consign & Design	8	8	16	28K	4%	100-200K

All of the data provided are proprietary and should not be quoted without acknowledging *Bond's Franchise Guide.*

A BUCK OR TWO STORES

8200 Jane St.
Concord, ON L4K 5A7 CANADA
Tel: (800) 890-8633 (905) 738-3180
Fax: (905) 738-3176
franchise_opportuni@denninghouse.com
Web Site: www.buckortwo.com
Mr. Dennis Klein, President/CEO

We're approaching 200 fun, exciting A BUCK OR TWO locations across Canada, well defined by simplicity, offering first-quality merchandise, presented in a visually appealing format, departmentalized, at prices of $2 or less. Sales and profit are maximized with a great selection of core and seasonal merchandise, as well as aggressively-priced special opportunity buys, where volume purchasing power allows franchisees to continually benefit.

BACKGROUND: IFA MEMBER
Established: 1987; 1st Franchised: 1989
Franchised Units: 255
Company-Owned Units 34
Total Units: 289
Dist.: US-0; CAN-190; O'seas-0
North America: 9 Provinces
Density: 80 in ON, 19 in BC, 17 in NS
Projected New Units (12 Months): 25
Qualifications: 4, 5, 4, 4, 3, 5
Registered: AB

FINANCIAL/TERMS:
Cash Investment: $50-70K
Total Investment: $160K
Minimum Net Worth: $200K
Fees: Franchise - $50K
Royalty - 6%; Ad. - 1%
Earnings Claim Statement: No
Term of Contract (Years): 5/5
Avg. # Of Employees: Varies
Passive Ownership: Discouraged
Encourage Conversions: N/A
Area Develop. Agreements: No
Sub-Franchising Contracts: No
Expand In Territory: Yes
Space Needs: 2,500-4,000 SF; RM

SUPPORT & TRAINING PROVIDED:
Financial Assistance Provided: Yes(D)
Site Selection Assistance: N/A
Lease Negotiation Assistance: N/A
Co-Operative Advertising: Yes
Franchisee Assoc./Member: Yes/Yes
Size Of Corporate Staff: 100
On-Going Support: a,C,D,E,G,h
Training: 1 Week Hamilton, ON; 2 Weeks Site Location.

SPECIFIC EXPANSION PLANS:
US: No
Canada: All Canada
Overseas: Mexico, South America, Europe, Australia

<< >>

DOLLAR DISCOUNT STORES OF AMERICA

1362 Naamans Creek Rd.
Boothwyn, PA 19061
Tel: (800) 227-5314 (610) 497-1991
Fax: (610) 485-6439
E-Mail: info@dollardiscount.com
Web Site: www.dollardiscount.com
Mr. Mitchel Insel, Franchise Director

Dollar stores.

BACKGROUND: IFA MEMBER
Established: 1982; 1st Franchised: 1987
Franchised Units: 148
Company-Owned Units 0
Total Units: 148
Dist.: US-148; CAN-0; O'seas-0
North America: NR
Density: PA, NJ, FL
Projected New Units (12 Months): 40
Qualifications: 3, 2, 2, 3, 3, 5
Registered: All States Except HI

FINANCIAL/TERMS:
Cash Investment: $20-30K
Total Investment: $199K
Minimum Net Worth: $100K
Fees: Franchise - $18K
Royalty - 3%; Ad. - 1%
Earnings Claim Statement: No
Term of Contract (Years): 10/15
Avg. # Of Employees: 1-2 FT, 5-6 PT
Passive Ownership: Discouraged
Encourage Conversions: N/A
Area Develop. Agreements: No
Sub-Franchising Contracts: No
Expand In Territory: No
Space Needs: 2,000-4,000 SF; FS, SF, SC, RM

SUPPORT & TRAINING PROVIDED:
Financial Assistance Provided: Yes(I)
Site Selection Assistance: Yes
Lease Negotiation Assistance: Yes
Co-Operative Advertising: No
Franchisee Assoc./Member: Yes/Yes
Size Of Corporate Staff: 19
On-Going Support: A,B,C,D,E,F,G,H,I
Training: 5 Days in Boothwyn, PA.

SPECIFIC EXPANSION PLANS:
US: All United States
Canada: No
Overseas: No

<< >>

GATEWAY NEWSTANDS

9554 Yonge St., # 400
Richmond Hill, ON L4C 9M5 CANADA
Tel: (800) 942-5351 (905) 737-7755
Fax: (905) 737-7757
E-Mail: info@gatewaynewstands.com
Web Site: www.gatewaynewstands.com
Mr. Michael Aychental, Chief Executive Officer

Newsstand, candy, lotto and limited food. Service locations in high-rise office towers, shopping centers and transit locations throughout the United States.

BACKGROUND:
Established: 1983; 1st Franchised: 1983
Franchised Units: 319
Company-Owned Units 0
Total Units: 319
Dist.: US-66; CAN-222; O'seas-1
North America: NR
Density: 193 in ON, 19 in IL, 16 NY
Projected New Units (12 Months): 50
Qualifications: 5, 3, 2, 1, 2, 3
Registered: NR

FINANCIAL/TERMS:
Cash Investment: $40-150K
Total Investment: $50-200K
Minimum Net Worth: $NR
Fees: Franchise - $Varies
Royalty - 3%; Ad. - 0%
Earnings Claim Statement: No
Term of Contract (Years): 5-10/5
Avg. # Of Employees: 1 FT, 2 PT
Passive Ownership: Not Allowed
Encourage Conversions: No
Area Develop. Agreements: No
Sub-Franchising Contracts: Yes
Expand In Territory: Yes
Space Needs: 100-1,000 SF; SF, RM, Transit Location

SUPPORT & TRAINING PROVIDED:
Financial Assistance Provided: Yes
Site Selection Assistance: Yes
Lease Negotiation Assistance: Yes
Co-Operative Advertising: Yes
Franchisee Assoc./Member: No
Size Of Corporate Staff: 11

On-Going Support: C,D,E,F,I
Training: 2 Days to 2 Weeks in Store.
SPECIFIC EXPANSION PLANS:
US: All United States
Canada: All Canada
Overseas: U.K.

<< >>

GRAND & TOY

33 Green Belt Dr.
Don Mills, ON M1W 1G6 CANADA
Tel: (416) 391-8581
Fax: (416) 441-6084
Web Site: www.grandtoy.com
Ms. Anne MacPhee, Dir. Franchising

GRAND & TOY sells stationary, general office services, office machines and equipment, office furniture, office electronic products, drafting and art supplies, office business books, manuals and journals, school supplies, office bulk beverages, computer hardware and software, cellular phones, pagers, gift items, social stationary, cards and other office supplies and furniture.

BACKGROUND:
Established: 1982; 1st Franchised: 1993
Franchised Units: 25
Company-Owned Units 48
Total Units: 73
Dist.: US-0; CAN-73; O'seas-0
North America: 1 Province
Density: 73 in ON
Projected New Units (12 Months): 4
Qualifications: 4, 4, 5, 2, 3, 5
Registered: N/A
FINANCIAL/TERMS:
Cash Investment: $50-80K
Total Investment: $100K
Minimum Net Worth: $150K
Fees: Franchise - $15K
Royalty - Varies; Ad. - Incl. Roy.
Earnings Claim Statement: Yes
Term of Contract (Years): 3
Avg. # Of Employees: 5 FT, 10 PT
Passive Ownership: Not Allowed
Encourage Conversions: N/A
Area Develop. Agreements: No
Sub-Franchising Contracts: No
Expand In Territory: Yes
Space Needs: 3,400 SF; RM, OB
SUPPORT & TRAINING PROVIDED:
Financial Assistance Provided: Yes(I)
Site Selection Assistance: N/A
Lease Negotiation Assistance: No
Co-Operative Advertising: Yes
Franchisee Assoc./Member: Yes
Size Of Corporate Staff: 2,500
On-Going Support: B,C,D,E,F,H
Training: 2 Weeks in Head Office; 4 Weeks in Store.
SPECIFIC EXPANSION PLANS:
US: No
Canada: ON
Overseas: Most Countries

<< >>

HEEL QUIK!®

Top 50

HEEL QUIK!

1730 Cumberland Point Dr., # 5
Marietta, GA 30067
Tel: (800) 255-8145 (770) 951-9440
Fax: (770) 933-8268
E-Mail: hqcorp@bellsouth.net
Web Site: www.heelquik.net
Mr. Raymond J. Margiano, Pres./CEO

HEEL/SEW QUIK! Shoe repair and personal services (clothing alterations, monogramming, keymaking and sale of related retail items.

BACKGROUND:
Established: 1984; 1st Franchised: 1985
Franchised Units: 680
Company-Owned Units 0
Total Units: 680
Dist.: US-100; CAN-0; O'seas-580
North America: 20 States
Density: 15 in GA, 10 in FL, 3 in TX
Projected New Units (12 Months): 5
Qualifications: 3, 2, 1, 2, 2, 3
Registered: FL,MI
FINANCIAL/TERMS:
Cash Investment: $5-100K
Total Investment: $8.9-153.5K
Minimum Net Worth: $45K
Fees: Franchise - $2.5-17.5K
Royalty - 4%; Ad. - 2%
Earnings Claim Statement: No
Term of Contract (Years): 20/10
Avg. # Of Employees: 2 FT, 1 PT
Passive Ownership: Discouraged
Encourage Conversions: Yes
Area Develop. Agreements: Yes/10/10
Sub-Franchising Contracts: No
Expand In Territory: Yes
Space Needs: 65-1,200 SF; FS,SF,SC,RM,HB,Inside Business
SUPPORT & TRAINING PROVIDED:
Financial Assistance Provided: Yes(I)
Site Selection Assistance: Yes
Lease Negotiation Assistance: Yes
Co-Operative Advertising: Yes
Franchisee Assoc./Member: Yes/Yes
Size Of Corporate Staff: 9
On-Going Support: b,C,D,E,F,G,H,I
Training: 2 Weeks Atlanta, GA; 3 Days On-Site
SPECIFIC EXPANSION PLANS:
US: All United States
Canada: All Canada
Overseas: All Countries

<< >>

TERRI'S CONSIGN & DESIGN FURNISHINGS

1375 W. Drivers Way
Tempe, AZ 85284
Tel: (800) 455-0400 (480) 969-1121
Fax: (480) 969-5052
E-Mail: marcusc@terris-cdf.com
Web Site: www.eterris.com
Mr. Marcus Curtis, President

Nation's leader in consignment home furnishings. We deal in furnishings acquired from model homes, estates, factory liquidations, skilled craftsmen and fine homes. Quality brand-name furnishings, accessories, office furnishings, art and antiques. Business has high sales volume with high margin and no initial cost inventory. Ground floor opportunities still available.

BACKGROUND:
Established: 1979; 1st Franchised: 1993
Franchised Units: 8
Company-Owned Units 8
Total Units: 16
Dist.: US-13; CAN-0; O'seas-0
North America: 5 States
Density: 7 in AZ, 2 in NV, 2 in CA
Projected New Units (12 Months): 4
Qualifications: 4, 4, 3, 3, 3, 5
Registered: CA,OR,WA
FINANCIAL/TERMS:
Cash Investment: $75-175K
Total Investment: $100-200K
Minimum Net Worth: $250K+
Fees: Franchise - $28K
Royalty - 4%; Ad. - 1%
Earnings Claim Statement: Yes
Term of Contract (Years): 10/5/5
Avg. # Of Employees: 10 FT, 3 PT
Passive Ownership: Not Allowed
Encourage Conversions: Yes
Area Develop. Agreements: Yes/10

Sub-Franchising Contracts: No
Expand In Territory: Yes
Space Needs: 20,000 SF; FS, SC, Warehouse

SUPPORT & TRAINING PROVIDED:

Financial Assistance Provided: Yes(I)
Site Selection Assistance: Yes
Lease Negotiation Assistance: Yes
Co-Operative Advertising: No
Franchisee Assoc./Member: No
Size Of Corporate Staff: 7
On-Going Support: C,D,E,G,H,I
Training: 1 Week Mesa, AZ; 5 Days Store Location upon Opening.

SPECIFIC EXPANSION PLANS:

US: All United States
Canada: No
Overseas: No

SUPPLEMENTAL LISTING OF FRANCHISORS

CASH CONVERTERS, 1450 E. American Ln., # 1350, Schaumburg, IL 60173-6083 ; (888) 910-2274 (847) 330-1122; (847) 330-1660

HAKKY INSTANT SHOE REPAIR, 1739 Sands Pl., # F, Marietta, GA 30067 ; (770) 956-8651; (770) 951-0355

MIGHTY DOLLAR, 528 Hood Rd., Markham, ON L3R 3K9 CANADA; (905) 513-8191; (905) 513-6387

MONEYSWORTH & BEST QUALITY SHOE REPAIR, 501 Downtree Dairy Rd., # 5, Vaughan, ON L4L 8H8 CANADA; (800) 363-SHOE (416) 674-6148; (416) 674-8945

STREET CORNER NEWS, 2945 SW Wanamaker Dr., Topeka, KS 66614 ; (800) 789-NEWS (785) 272-8529; (785) 272-2384

Security & Safety Systems

Chapter 45

Security & Safety Systems Industry Profile

Total # Franchisors in Industry Group	16
Total # Franchised Units in Industry Group	757
Total # Company-Owned Units in Industry Group	112
Total # Operating Units in Industry Group	869
Average # Franchised Units/Franchisor	47.3
Average # Company-Owned Units/Franchisor	7.0
Average # Total Units/Franchisor	54.3
Ratio of Total # Franchised Units/Total # Company-Owned Units	6.8:1
Industry Survey Participants	4
Representing % of Industry	25.0%
Average Franchise Fee*:	$26.1K
Average Total Investment*:	$217.1K
Average On-Going Royalty Fee*:	6.8%

*If a range was provided, the mid-point of the range was used. See detailed profiles for actual ranges.

Four Largest Participants in Survey

Company	# Franchised Units	# Co-Owned Units	# Total Units	Franchise Fee	On-Going Royalty	Total Investment
1. Sonitrol	178	34	212	20-50K	2.5%	250-600K
2. Fire Defense Centers	19	44	63	20.5K	10%	42-45K
3. Proshred Security	34	1	35	35K	8%	350K
4. Roll-A-Way	26	5	31	7.9-21.7K	0%	35-65K

All of the data provided are proprietary and should not be quoted without acknowledging *Bond's Franchise Guide.*

FIRE DEFENSE CENTERS
6110-20 Powers Ave., # 144
Jacksonville, FL 32217
Tel: (800) 554-3028 (904) 731-1833
Fax:
Ms. I. A. La Russo, President

Dealing with national accounts on servicing of fire extinguishers, automatic restaurant hood systems, municipal supplies and first aid kits. Warranty on equipment sold to business and guaranteed fire code compliance to business. Provide consultation for businesses to comply with city and state governments.

BACKGROUND:
Established: 1973; 1st Franchised: 1986
Franchised Units: 19
Company-Owned Units 44
Total Units: 63
Dist.: US-63; CAN-0; O'seas-0
North America: 15 States
Density: 20 in FL
Projected New Units (12 Months): 3
Qualifications: 5, 2, 1, 2, 1, 5
Registered: All States

FINANCIAL/TERMS:
Cash Investment: $40-45K
Total Investment: $42-45K
Minimum Net Worth: $NR
Fees: Franchise - $20.5K
Royalty - 10%; Ad. - 1%
Earnings Claim Statement: No
Term of Contract (Years): 10/10
Avg. # Of Employees: 2-20 FT
Passive Ownership: Allowed
Encourage Conversions: No
Area Develop. Agreements: No
Sub-Franchising Contracts: No
Expand In Territory: Yes
Space Needs: 1,500 SF; Warehouse

SUPPORT & TRAINING PROVIDED:
Financial Assistance Provided: Yes
Site Selection Assistance: Yes
Lease Negotiation Assistance: Yes
Co-Operative Advertising: Yes
Franchisee Assoc./Member: Yes/Yes
Size Of Corporate Staff: 18
On-Going Support: A,B,C,D,E,F,G,H,I
Training: 2 Weeks Headquarters.

SPECIFIC EXPANSION PLANS:
US: All United States
Canada: No
Overseas: No

<< >>

PROSHRED SECURITY
2200 Lakeshore Blvd. W., # 104
Toronto, ON M8V 1A4 CANADA
Tel: (800) 461-9760 (416) 251-4272
Fax: (416) 251-7121
E-Mail: proshred@proshred.com
Web Site: www.proshred.com
Mr. Sean O'Dea, President

PROSHRED SECURITY is a franchise for business people. Our license owners provide at-your-door document shredding services to area businesses. Customers include all levels of business and government. Operating in the U. S., Canada and Europe, PROSHRED is the largest in North America. Company management has a long, successful history in franchising.

BACKGROUND:
Established: 1985; 1st Franchised: 1990
Franchised Units: 34
Company-Owned Units 1
Total Units: 35
Dist.: US-4; CAN-31; O'seas-0
North America: 3 States, 10 Provinces
Density: NR
Projected New Units (12 Months): 4
Registered: CA,FL,MD,MI,OR,DC

FINANCIAL/TERMS:
Cash Investment: $200K
Total Investment: $350K
Minimum Net Worth: $NR
Fees: Franchise - $35K
Royalty - 8%; Ad. - 0%
Earnings Claim Statement: No
Term of Contract (Years): 5/5/5/5
Avg. # Of Employees: 5 FT, 2 PT
Passive Ownership: Not Allowed
Encourage Conversions: Yes
Area Develop. Agreements: Yes/10
Sub-Franchising Contracts: No
Expand In Territory: Yes
Space Needs: NR SF; N/A

SUPPORT & TRAINING PROVIDED:
Financial Assistance Provided: Yes(I)
Site Selection Assistance: N/A
Lease Negotiation Assistance: N/A
Co-Operative Advertising: N/A
Franchisee Assoc./Member: No
Size Of Corporate Staff: 11
On-Going Support: A,C,D,E,G,H,I
Training: 9 Days Toronto, ON; 5 Days Local.

SPECIFIC EXPANSION PLANS:
US: All United States
Canada: All Canada
Overseas: Europe, Australia, Asia

<< >>

ROLL-A-WAY
10601 Oak St., N.E.
St. Petersburg, FL 33716
Tel: (888) 765-5292 (727) 576-6044
Fax: (727) 579-9410
Web Site: www.roll-a-way.com
Mr. Bill Salin, VP Franchise Development

ROLL-A-WAY manufactures rolling-security and storm shutters for residential and commercial applications. We are the largest and oldest manufacturer in the U. S. The franchise consists of training in sales, marketing and installation of the shutter system. The franchisee purchases directly from the manufacturer, and the business is very profitable and gaining in popularity every day. The shutters are excellent for saving money on utilities.

BACKGROUND:
Established: 1955; 1st Franchised: 1994
Franchised Units: 26
Company-Owned Units 5
Total Units: 31
Dist.: US-50; CAN-0; O'seas-0
North America: 17 States
Density: 3 in CA, 3 in NC, 3 in TX
Projected New Units (12 Months): 10
Qualifications: 4, 4, 3, 3, 2, 4
Registered: CA,FL,MD,NY,RI,VA,WA, WI

FINANCIAL/TERMS:
Cash Investment: $15.8-40K
Total Investment: $35-65K
Minimum Net Worth: $250K
Fees: Franchise - $7.9-21.7K
Royalty - 0%; Ad. - 0%
Earnings Claim Statement: No
Term of Contract (Years): 10/5/5
Avg. # Of Employees: 2 FT, 2 PT
Passive Ownership: Discouraged
Encourage Conversions: N/A
Area Develop. Agreements: No
Sub-Franchising Contracts: No
Expand In Territory: Yes
Space Needs: NR SF; N/A

SUPPORT & TRAINING PROVIDED:
Financial Assistance Provided: No

Site Selection Assistance: N/A
Lease Negotiation Assistance: No
Co-Operative Advertising: No
Franchisee Assoc./Member: No
Size Of Corporate Staff: 30
On-Going Support: B,C,D,F,h
Training: 2 Weeks Corporate Office, St. Petersburg, FL.

SPECIFIC EXPANSION PLANS:

US: All United States
Canada: All Canada
Overseas: All Countries

<< >>

SONITROL

211 North Union, # 350
Alexandria, VA 22314
Tel: (800) 328-5607 (703) 684-6606
Fax: (703) 684-6612
E-Mail: bmeares@sonitrol.com
Web Site: www.sonitrol.com
Mr. William Meares, Chief Operating Officer

SONITROL offers a broad line of security systems to commercial and residential subscribers. A majority of SONITROL products are sold to businesses which have typically been in operations for over a year. The signature system is based on a sound activated audio. This process allows for verification of alarms and has resulted in the apprehension of over 135,000 criminals.

BACKGROUND: IFA MEMBER
Established: 1964; 1st Franchised: 1965
Franchised Units: 178
Company-Owned Units 34
Total Units: 212
Dist.: US-177; CAN-1; O'seas-2
North America: 41 States
Density: 24 in CA, 14 in FL, 11 in NY
Projected New Units (12 Months): 3
Qualifications: 4, 5, 3, 2, 5, 4
Registered: FL,IL,VA

FINANCIAL/TERMS:

Cash Investment: $100-200K
Total Investment: $250-600K
Minimum Net Worth: $250K
Fees: Franchise - $20-50K
Royalty - 2.5%; Ad. - N/A
Earnings Claim Statement: No
Term of Contract (Years): 10/10
Avg. # Of Employees: Varies
Passive Ownership: Not Allowed
Encourage Conversions: N/A
Area Develop. Agreements: No
Sub-Franchising Contracts: No
Expand In Territory: No
Space Needs: NR SF; N/A

SUPPORT & TRAINING PROVIDED:

Financial Assistance Provided: N/A
Site Selection Assistance: N/A
Lease Negotiation Assistance: No
Co-Operative Advertising: No
Franchisee Assoc./Member: Yes/Yes
Size Of Corporate Staff: 11
On-Going Support: C,d,E,G,h,I
Training: Business Training On-Site; 1 Wk. Technical Training in Orlando; 1 Wk. Sales Tr. in Dallas.

SPECIFIC EXPANSION PLANS:

US: All United States
Canada: No
Overseas: No

<< >>

SUPPLEMENTAL LISTING OF FRANCHISORS

FIREMASTER, 520 Broadway, # 650, Santa Monica, CA 90401 ; (800) 944-3473 (310) 451-8888; (310) 395-7048

IDENT-A-KID SERVICES OF AMERICA, 2810 Scherer Dr., # 100, St. Petersburg, FL 33716 ; (800) 890-1000 (727) 577-4646; (727) 576-8528

MACE SECURITY CENTERS, 662 S. Fulton St., Denver, CO 80231 ; (800) 836-8220 (303) 363-7968; (303) 367-9962

PAYSTATION, 5155 Spectrum Way, # 17, Mississauga, ON L4W 5A1 CANADA; (800) 268-1440 (905) 625-8500; (905) 625-6254

PROSHRED SECURITY, 2200 Lakeshore Blvd. W., # 104, Toronto, ON M8V 1A4 CANADA; (800) 461-9760 (416) 251-4272; (416) 251-7121

SAFE NOT SORRY, 421 W. Union Ave., Bound Brook, NJ 08805 ; (888) 469-3900; (732) 469-0096

SECURITY WORLD INTERNATIONAL, 3403 NW 55th St., Bldg. # 10, Ft. Lauderdale, FL 33309 ; (800) 669-7328 (954) 846-2400; (954) 846-9686

VOCAM USA, 855 E. Golf Rd., # 2145, Arlington Heights, IL 60005-5222 ; (888) 38-VOCAM (847) 734-3000; (847) 734-7159

Signs

Chapter 46

Signs Industry Profile

Total # Franchisors in Industry Group	17
Total # Franchised Units in Industry Group	2,007
Total # Company-Owned Units in Industry Group	7
Total # Operating Units in Industry Group	2,014
Average # Franchised Units/Franchisor	118.1
Average # Company-Owned Units/Franchisor	0.4
Average # Total Units/Franchisor	118.5
Ratio of Total # Franchised Units/Total # Company-Owned Units	286.7:1
Industry Survey Participants	8
Representing % of Industry	47.1%
Average Franchise Fee*:	$23.7K
Average Total Investment*:	$114.8K
Average On-Going Royalty Fee*:	5.9%

*If a range was provided, the mid-point of the range was used. See detailed profiles for actual ranges.

Five Largest Participants in Survey

Company	# Franchised Units	# Co-Owned Units	# Total Units	Franchise Fee	On-Going Royalty	Total Investment
1. Sign-A-Rama	612	0	612	37.5K	6%	102-108K
2. Fastsigns	438	0	438	20K	6%	142-219K
3. Signs Now	263	0	263	25K	5%	150-250K
4. Signs By Tomorrow	112	1	113	24.5K	3-6%	97-179K
5. American Sign Shops	42	1	43	20K	6%	66-92K

All of the data provided are proprietary and should not be quoted without acknowledging *Bond's Franchise Guide.*

AMERICAN SIGN SHOPS

3803-B Computer Dr., # 200
Raleigh, NC 27609
Tel: (800) 966-2700 (919) 787-1557
Fax: (919) 787-3830
E-Mail: info@amerisign.com
Web Site: www.amerisign.com
Mr. Andrew Akers, Vice President

Latest technology in computer-generated signs. Full color digital graphics production and we provide full training and on-going support. Local assistance. Franchise highly rated by Success and Entrepreneur Magazines. Operated in a clean, retail environment, hours 9 to 5. We choose highly-motivated franchisees who want to succeed as entrepreneurs. Franchise Advisory Council and Mentor Program instituted by company. You can't find better franchise support!

BACKGROUND: IFA MEMBER
Established: 1984; 1st Franchised: 1987
Franchised Units: 42
Company-Owned Units 1
Total Units: 43
Dist.: US-43; CAN-0; O'seas-0
North America: 11 States
Density: 15 in NC, 13 in MI, 4 in OH
Projected New Units (12 Months): 10
Qualifications: 5, 4, 1, 3, 3, 5
Registered: IL,MI,VA,WI

FINANCIAL/TERMS:
Cash Investment: $30-40K
Total Investment: $66-92K
Minimum Net Worth: $150K
Fees: Franchise - $20K
Royalty - 6%; Ad. - 0%
Earnings Claim Statement: No
Term of Contract (Years): 20/20
Avg. # Of Employees: 2 FT, 2 PT
Passive Ownership: Discouraged
Encourage Conversions: No
Area Develop. Agreements: No
Sub-Franchising Contracts: No
Expand In Territory: Yes
Space Needs: 1,600 SF; FS, SF, SC

SUPPORT & TRAINING PROVIDED:
Financial Assistance Provided: Yes(I)
Site Selection Assistance: Yes
Lease Negotiation Assistance: Yes
Co-Operative Advertising: No
Franchisee Assoc./Member: Yes/No
Size Of Corporate Staff: 6
On-Going Support: C,D,E,G,h,I
Training: 8 Hours Home Study; 2 Weeks Headquarters; 1 Week Franchisee Location.

SPECIFIC EXPANSION PLANS:
US: East of Rocky Mountains
Canada: No
Overseas: No

<< >>

BEYOND SIGNS

36 Apple Creek Blvd.
Markham, ON L3R 4Y4 CANADA
Tel: (800) 265-7446 (905) 415-9809
Fax: (905) 415-1583
Mr. Glenn Kerekes, President

VINYLGRAPHICS is a Canadian franchisor of custom sign centres that offer interior/exterior signage, window lettering, vehicle and boat decoration, magnetic signs and more, to today's business community. The lettering for the signs is generated utilizing state-of-the-art technology and proven vinyl films.

BACKGROUND:
Established: 1983; 1st Franchised: 1990
Franchised Units: 14
Company-Owned Units 0
Total Units: 14
Dist.: US-0; CAN-14; O'seas-0
North America: 1 Province
Density: 14 in ON
Projected New Units (12 Months): 6
Registered: NR

FINANCIAL/TERMS:
Cash Investment: $35K
Total Investment: $90K
Minimum Net Worth: $NR
Fees: Franchise - $25K
Royalty - 8%; Ad. - 0%
Earnings Claim Statement: No
Term of Contract (Years): 10/5
Avg. # Of Employees: 3 FT
Passive Ownership: Not Allowed
Encourage Conversions: Yes
Area Develop. Agreements: Yes/15
Sub-Franchising Contracts: Yes
Expand In Territory: Yes
Space Needs: 1,500 SF; SC

SUPPORT & TRAINING PROVIDED:
Financial Assistance Provided: Yes
Site Selection Assistance: Yes
Lease Negotiation Assistance: Yes
Co-Operative Advertising: Yes
Franchisee Assoc./Member: Yes/Yes
Size Of Corporate Staff: 8
On-Going Support: B,C,D,e,G,H,I
Training: 5 Weeks Toronto, ON.

SPECIFIC EXPANSION PLANS:
US: All United States
Canada: All Canada
Overseas: All Countries

<< >>

FASTSIGNS.

Top 50

FASTSIGNS

2550 Midway Rd., # 150
Carrollton, TX 75006-2357
Tel: (800) 827-7446 (972) 447-0777
Fax: (972) 248-8201
E-Mail: bill.mcpherson@fastsigns.com
Web Site: www.fastsigns.com
Mr. Bill McPherson, VP Franchise Sales

FASTSIGNS sign centers produce complete computer-generated signs and graphics for the business community. FASTSIGNS is the acknowledged leader of the quick sign industry. Rated #7 in Success Magazine's 1999 Franchisee Satisfaction Survey. Quality systems include comprehensive 3 week training, on-going support, unique marketing materials and National Accounts program. Site selection assistance and the latest industry equipment.

BACKGROUND: IFA MEMBER
Established: 1985; 1st Franchised: 1986
Franchised Units: 438
Company-Owned Units 0
Total Units: 438
Dist.: US-370; CAN-9; O'seas-59
North America: 41 States, 2 Provinces
Density: 47 in TX, 34 in CA, 20 in IL
Projected New Units (12 Months): 20
Qualifications: 5, 4, 1, 1, 3, 5
Registered: All States and AB

FINANCIAL/TERMS:
Cash Investment: $50-75K
Total Investment: $148-219K
Minimum Net Worth: $200K
Fees: Franchise - $20K
Royalty - 6%; Ad. - 2%
Earnings Claim Statement: Yes
Term of Contract (Years): 20/10
Avg. # Of Employees: 6 FT
Passive Ownership: Not Allowed
Encourage Conversions: Yes
Area Develop. Agreements: Yes
Sub-Franchising Contracts: Int
Expand In Territory: Yes
Space Needs: 1,400 SF; SC

SUPPORT & TRAINING PROVIDED:
Financial Assistance Provided: Yes(I)
Site Selection Assistance: Yes

Lease Negotiation Assistance: Yes
Co-Operative Advertising: Yes
Franchisee Assoc./Member: Yes
Size Of Corporate Staff: 75
On-Going Support: C,D,E,G,H,I
Training: 3 Weeks in Dallas, TX.

SPECIFIC EXPANSION PLANS:
US: All United States
Canada: All Canada
Overseas: France, Germany, Italy, Spain, UK, New Zealand, Australia, Colombia, Mexico, Brazil

<< >>

SIGN-A-RAMA

1801 Australian Ave., S.
West Palm Beach, FL 33409
Tel: (800) 776-8105 (561) 640-5570
Fax: (561) 640-5580
E-Mail: kwheeler@signarama.com
Web Site: www.signarama.com
Mr. Kevin Wheeler, Dir. Minority Development

World's largest full-service sign franchise. Over 550 locations in 20 countries. Ranked #1 in industry. No experience needed. Full training, local back-up and support. Financing available.

BACKGROUND: IFA MEMBER
Established: 1986; 1st Franchised: 1987
Franchised Units: 612
Company-Owned Units 0
Total Units: 612
Dist.: US-612; CAN-0; O'seas-612
North America: 44 States
Density: 44 in CA, 28 in FL, 23 in NJ
Projected New Units (12 Months): 100
Qualifications: 5, 4, 1, 1, 4, 5
Registered: All States and AB

FINANCIAL/TERMS:
Cash Investment: $40-50K
Total Investment: $102-108K
Minimum Net Worth: $60K
Fees: Franchise - $37.5K
Royalty - 6%; Ad. - 0%
Earnings Claim Statement: No
Term of Contract (Years): 35/35
Avg. # Of Employees: 3 FT
Passive Ownership: Discouraged
Encourage Conversions: Yes
Area Develop. Agreements: No Domestic
Sub-Franchising Contracts: Yes
Expand In Territory: Yes
Space Needs: 1,200 SF; SC

SUPPORT & TRAINING PROVIDED:
Financial Assistance Provided: Yes(I)
Site Selection Assistance: Yes
Lease Negotiation Assistance: Yes
Co-Operative Advertising: Yes
Franchisee Assoc./Member: Yes/Yes
Size Of Corporate Staff: 85
On-Going Support: A,B,C,D,E,F,G,H,I
Training: 2 Weeks West Palm Beach, FL; 2 Weeks On-Site; 1 Week Mentor.

SPECIFIC EXPANSION PLANS:
US: All United States
Canada: All Canada
Overseas: All Countries

<< >>

SIGNS BY TOMORROW

6460 Dobbin Rd.
Columbia, MD 21045
Tel: (800) 765-7446 (410) 992-7192
Fax: (410) 992-7675
E-Mail: fransales@signsbytomorrow.com
Web Site: www.signsbytomorrow.com
Mr. Robert G. Nunn, III, Dir. Franchise Development

Computer-generated, one day, vinyl sign shop. Business-to-business, high growth, high gross margins, service-oriented, multiples possible. Most extensive training and support system. Aggressive R & D program. High rate of franchisee success and satisfaction. No tech experience necessary.

BACKGROUND: IFA MEMBER
Established: 1986; 1st Franchised: 1987
Franchised Units: 112
Company-Owned Units 1
Total Units: 113
Dist.: US-113; CAN-0; O'seas-0
North America: 30 States
Density: 15 in PA, 15 in MD, 8 in NJ
Projected New Units (12 Months): 20
Qualifications: 4, 5, 1, 4, 5, 5
Registered: All States

FINANCIAL/TERMS:
Cash Investment: $40-50K
Total Investment: $97-179K
Minimum Net Worth: $140K
Fees: Franchise - $24.5K
Royalty - 3-6%; Ad. - 1%
Earnings Claim Statement: Yes
Term of Contract (Years): 20/20
Avg. # Of Employees: 3 FT, 2 PT
Passive Ownership: Not Allowed
Encourage Conversions: No
Area Develop. Agreements: Yes/Negot.
Sub-Franchising Contracts: No
Expand In Territory: No
Space Needs: 1,800 SF; SC

SUPPORT & TRAINING PROVIDED:
Financial Assistance Provided: Yes(I)
Site Selection Assistance: Yes
Lease Negotiation Assistance: Yes
Co-Operative Advertising: Yes
Franchisee Assoc./Member: Yes/Yes
Size Of Corporate Staff: 18
On-Going Support: B,C,D,E,F,G,H,I
Training: 2 Weeks Headquarters; 2 Weeks in Store.

SPECIFIC EXPANSION PLANS:
US: All United States
Canada: No
Overseas: No

SIGNS FIRST

813 Ridge Lake Blvd., # 390
Memphis, TN 38120
Tel: (800) 852-2163 (901) 682-2264
Fax: (901) 682-2475
E-Mail: signsfirst1@earthlink.net
Web Site: www.signsfirst.net
Ms. Peggy Cahoon, Office Manager

SIGNS FIRST is the only franchise with over 25 years sign industry experience. We specialize in computer-generated, one-day temporary and permanent signs for retail, professional and commercial businesses on a cash and carry basis. Franchisee support is unparalleled with comprehensive training, on-going technological support and marketing assistance.

BACKGROUND:
Established: 1966; 1st Franchised: 1989
Franchised Units: 33
Company-Owned Units 0
Total Units: 33
Dist.: US-42; CAN-0; O'seas-0
North America: 17 States
Density: 13 in TN, 12 in MS, 3 in CO
Projected New Units (12 Months): 5
Qualifications: 3, 4, 3, 1, 3, 5

Registered: FL

FINANCIAL/TERMS:

Cash Investment:	$20K
Total Investment:	$20-65K
Minimum Net Worth:	$250K
Fees: Franchise -	$10-15K
Royalty - 6%;	Ad. - 0%
Earnings Claim Statement:	No
Term of Contract (Years):	10/10
Avg. # Of Employees:	2 FT
Passive Ownership:	Discouraged
Encourage Conversions:	Yes
Area Develop. Agreements:	Yes/10
Sub-Franchising Contracts:	No
Expand In Territory:	Yes

Space Needs: 1,500 SF; FS, SF, SC, RM

SUPPORT & TRAINING PROVIDED:

Financial Assistance Provided:	N/A
Site Selection Assistance:	Yes
Lease Negotiation Assistance:	Yes
Co-Operative Advertising:	No
Franchisee Assoc./Member:	No
Size Of Corporate Staff:	6
On-Going Support:	B,C,D,E,F,G,I

Training: 2 Weeks Memphis, TN; 1 Week + Follow-Up Visit in Store.

SPECIFIC EXPANSION PLANS:

US:	All United States
Canada:	No
Overseas:	No

<< >>

SIGNS NOW

4900 Manatee Ave. W.
Bradenton, FL 34209-3859
Tel: (800) 356-3373 (941) 747-7747
Fax: (941) 750-8604
E-Mail: franchiseinfo@signsnow.com
Web Site: www.signsnow.com
Mr. Dennis Staub, Dir. Fran. Dev.

SIGNS NOW is the professional graphics solution. We are the "one stop shop" for all graphics and signage needs! We offer an international system of sign centers, with new century image with unparalleled support in training, marketing, site selection and operating systems.

BACKGROUND: IFA MEMBER

Established: 1986; 1st Franchised: 1986

Franchised Units:	263
Company-Owned Units	0
Total Units:	263
Dist.:	US-228; CAN-20; O'seas-14
North America:	41 States
Density:	29 in FL, 23 in IL, 15 in NC
Projected New Units (12 Months):	50
Qualifications:	5, 5, 2, 3, 2, 5

Registered: All States

FINANCIAL/TERMS:

Cash Investment:	$55-75K
Total Investment:	$150-250K
Minimum Net Worth:	$150K
Fees: Franchise -	$25K
Royalty - 5%;	Ad. - 2%
Earnings Claim Statement:	Yes
Term of Contract (Years):	20/20
Avg. # Of Employees:	3 FT
Passive Ownership:	Not Allowed
Encourage Conversions:	Yes
Area Develop. Agreements:	No
Sub-Franchising Contracts:	No
Expand In Territory:	Yes

Space Needs: 1800 minimum SF; SF, SC

SUPPORT & TRAINING PROVIDED:

Financial Assistance Provided:	Yes(I)
Site Selection Assistance:	Yes
Lease Negotiation Assistance:	Yes
Co-Operative Advertising:	N/A
Franchisee Assoc./Member:	No
Size Of Corporate Staff:	38
On-Going Support:	B,C,D,E,G,H,I

Training: 3 Weeks, Bradenton, FL; 1 Week, Regional Ctr.; 1 Week, Actual Ctr.

SPECIFIC EXPANSION PLANS:

US:	All United States
Canada:	All Canada
Overseas:	All Countries

<< >>

SIGNS ON SITE

5350 Corporate Grove Blvd. SE
Grand Rapids, MI 49512
Tel: (888) 715-7446 (616) 656-9770
Fax: (616) 656-9775
E-Mail: mail@signs-on-site.com
Web Site: www.signs-on-site.com
Mr. Jeffrey R. Lewis, President/CEO

SIGNS ON SITE is different from all other 'sign' franchises. There is no need to manufacture. You can start from your home, and the initial investment is low. You go to the client and provide periodic signage solutions to corporations, hospitals and institutions.

BACKGROUND:

Established: 1997; 1st Franchised: 1998

Franchised Units:	6
Company-Owned Units	0
Total Units:	6
Dist.:	US-6; CAN-0; O'seas-0
North America:	5 States
Density:	NR
Projected New Units (12 Months):	7
Qualifications:	2, 4, 2, 4, 3, 5

Registered: CA,FL,IL,IN,MD,MI,MN,MO, NY,OR,PA,RI,TX,VA,WA,WI,DC

FINANCIAL/TERMS:

Cash Investment:	$30-60K
Total Investment:	$60-100K
Minimum Net Worth:	$N/A
Fees: Franchise -	$25K
Royalty - 6%;	Ad. - 1%
Earnings Claim Statement:	No
Term of Contract (Years):	7/7
Avg. # Of Employees:	2 FT, 1 PT
Passive Ownership:	Discouraged
Encourage Conversions:	Yes
Area Develop. Agreements:	Yes/7
Sub-Franchising Contracts:	No
Expand In Territory:	No

Space Needs: 1,000-1,200 SF; HB

SUPPORT & TRAINING PROVIDED:

Financial Assistance Provided:	Yes(D)
Site Selection Assistance:	Yes
Lease Negotiation Assistance:	Yes
Co-Operative Advertising:	Yes
Franchisee Assoc./Member:	No
Size Of Corporate Staff:	7
On-Going Support:	C,D,E,G,H,I

Training: 2 Weeks Grand Rapids, MI.

SPECIFIC EXPANSION PLANS:

US:	All United States
Canada:	All Canada
Overseas:	No

<< >>

SUPPLEMENTAL LISTING OF FRANCHISORS

ASI SIGN SYSTEMS, 3890 W. Northwest Hwy., # 102, Dallas, TX 75220 ; (800) 274-7732 (214) 352-9140; (214) 352-9741

SIGN EXPRESS, 4900 Manatee Ave. W., Bradenton, FL 34209 ; (800) 525-7446 (941) 747-7747; (941) 747-5074

SIGNS & MORE IN 24, 1739 St. Mary's Ave., Parkersburg, WV 26101 ; (800) 358-2358 (800) 424-7446; (304) 422-7449

SIGNS PLUS USA, 2750 Harbor Blvd., Costa Mesa, CA 92626 ; (714) 444-4545

Travel

Chapter 47

Travel Industry Profile

Total # Franchisors in Industry Group	22
Total # Franchised Units in Industry Group	5,199
Total # Company-Owned Units in Industry Group	577
Total # Operating Units in Industry Group	5,776
Average # Franchised Units/Franchisor	236.3
Average # Company-Owned Units/Franchisor	26.2
Average # Total Units/Franchisor	262.5
Ratio of Total # Franchised Units/Total # Company-Owned Units	9.0:1
Industry Survey Participants	6
Representing % of Industry	27.3%
Average Franchise Fee*:	$20.0K
Average Total Investment*:	$52.2K
Average On-Going Royalty Fee*:	2.3%

*If a range was provided, the mid-point of the range was used. See detailed profiles for actual ranges.

Five Largest Participants in Survey

Company	# Franchised Units	# Co-Owned Units	# Total Units	Franchise Fee	On-Going Royalty	Total Investment
1. Carlson Wagonlit Travel	1,302	419	1,721	Included	Varies	6.6-156K
2. Uniglobe Travel	1,100	0	1,100	2-25K	$275-550/Mo.	21-104K
3. Travel Network	507	1	508	5-30K	$350-750/Mo.	10-100K
4. Cruise One	430	0	430	9.8K	3%	10-22K
5. Caribbean Cruise Lines/Golfahoy.com	26	1	27	31K	$750/Mo.	49.6-63.75K

CARIBBEAN CRUISE LINES/ GOLFAHOY.COM

1430 Webber Ctr., 5555 Calgary Trail S.
Edmonton, AB T6H 5P9 CANADA
Tel: (877) 415-5442 (780) 415-5442
Fax: (780) 468-4665
E-Mail: aw@golfahoy.com
Web Site: www.golfahoy.com
Mr. Anthony Webber, Chairman/CEO

Own your dream golf business franchise! Unique opportunity in the fastest growing segment of the $3.7 trillion world travel industry. Golf cruises! Comprehensive training and support. What do we do differently? We focus on the golf experience, the cruiseliner becomes fabulous transportation from one exotic golf course to the next. Home-based office opportunity for golfers accustomed to six-figure income.

BACKGROUND:
Established: 1988; 1st Franchised: 1999
Franchised Units: 26
Company-Owned Units 1
Total Units: 27
Dist.: US-19; CAN-7; O'seas-1
North America: 9 States, 3 Provinces
Density: 2 in FL, 2 in NJ, 2 in ON
Projected New Units (12 Months): 20
Qualifications: 3, 4, 1, 4, 3, 5
Registered: CA, FL, IL, WI, DC, AB

FINANCIAL/TERMS:
Cash Investment: $49.6-63.75K
Total Investment: $49.6-63.75K
Minimum Net Worth: $49.6-63.75K
Fees: Franchise - $31K
Royalty - 750/mo.; Ad. - 0%
Earnings Claim Statement: No
Term of Contract (Years): 10/10
Avg. # Of Employees: 1 FT
Passive Ownership: Not Allowed
Encourage Conversions: N/A
Area Develop. Agreements: Yes/10
Sub-Franchising Contracts: Yes
Expand In Territory: Yes
Space Needs: N/A SF; HB

SUPPORT & TRAINING PROVIDED:
Financial Assistance Provided: Yes(D)
Site Selection Assistance: N/A
Lease Negotiation Assistance: N/A
Co-Operative Advertising: Yes
Franchisee Assoc./Member: Yes/No
Size Of Corporate Staff: 5
On-Going Support: A,b,G,h,I
Training: 7 Days on Caribbean Golf Cruise; 4 Days in Training/Golf Resort.

SPECIFIC EXPANSION PLANS:
US: All United States
Canada: All Canada
Overseas: W. Europe, Asia, S. Africa, Australia, New Zealand, Asia

<< >>

CARLSON WAGONLIT TRAVEL

Carlson Parkway, P.O. Box 59159
Minneapolis, MN 55441
Tel: (800) 678-8241 (612) 212-1611
Fax: (612) 212-2302
E-Mail: jrisner@carslon.com
Web Site: www.carlsontravel.com
Mr. John Risner, Dir. Fran. Dev.

Start-up and conversion travel agencies available. Preferred supplier program; national and local marketing and advertising newsletters; brochures; assistance with commercial business development; regional meetings; participation in CARLSON Selling Systems; Associate consulting service; hotel programs; 24-hour service center; centralized support department; international rate desk; and professional development programs. Leading technology to maximize efficiency.

BACKGROUND: IFA MEMBER
Established: 1900; 1st Franchised: 1984
Franchised Units: 1,302
Company-Owned Units 419
Total Units: 1,721
Dist.: US-1404; CAN-0; O'seas-400
North America: 49 States
Density: 160 in CA, 80 in MN, 55 TX
Projected New Units (12 Months): 100
Qualifications: 3, 4, 5, 4, 3, 4
Registered: All States Except MN,,NY,DC

FINANCIAL/TERMS:
Cash Investment: $4-34.5K
Total Investment: $6.6-156.2K
Minimum Net Worth: $N/A
Fees: Franchise - $Included
Royalty - Varies; Ad. - Varies
Earnings Claim Statement: No
Term of Contract (Years): 3-10/3-10
Avg. # Of Employees: Varies
Passive Ownership: Discouraged
Encourage Conversions: Yes
Area Develop. Agreements: No
Sub-Franchising Contracts: No
Expand In Territory: Yes
Space Needs: NR SF; FS, SF, SC, RM, Other

SUPPORT & TRAINING PROVIDED:
Financial Assistance Provided: No
Site Selection Assistance: Yes
Lease Negotiation Assistance: Yes
Co-Operative Advertising: Yes
Franchisee Assoc./Member: Yes/Yes
Size Of Corporate Staff: 80
On-Going Support: d,E,g,h,i
Training: 2 Weeks in Minneapolis/On-Site for Start-Ups; 2 Days in Minneapolis for Conversions.

SPECIFIC EXPANSION PLANS:
US: All United States
Canada: No
Overseas: No

<< >>

CRUISEONE

1415 NW 62nd St., # 205
Ft. Lauderdale, FL 33309-1955
Tel: (800) 892-3928 (954) 958-3701
Fax: (954) 958-3697
E-Mail: franchise@cruiseone.com
Web Site: www.cruiseone.com
Mr. Lee Mitchell

CRUISEONE is a nationwide, home-based cruise-only franchise company representing all major cruise lines. Franchisees are professionally trained in a 7-day extensive program. How to close the sale and service the client, on-board ship inspections, sales and marketing techniques and customized software use are just the beginning. National Account Status offers consumers cruises for the lowest possible price and pays highest commissions in the industry. 1997 sales exceeded $80 million. Low start-up costs.

BACKGROUND: IFA MEMBER
Established: 1992; 1st Franchised: 1993
Franchised Units: 430
Company-Owned Units 0
Total Units: 430
Dist.: US-430; CAN-0; O'seas-0
North America: 45 States
Density: 40 in FL, 39 in CA, 33 in TX
Projected New Units (12 Months): 120
Qualifications: 3, 4, 2, 3, 5, 4
Registered: All States

FINANCIAL/TERMS:
Cash Investment: $10-22K

Total Investment: $10-22K
Minimum Net Worth: $N/A
Fees: Franchise - $9.8K
Royalty - 3%; Ad. - 0%
Earnings Claim Statement: No
Term of Contract (Years): 5
Avg. # Of Employees: 1 FT
Passive Ownership: Not Allowed
Encourage Conversions: N/A
Area Develop. Agreements: No
Sub-Franchising Contracts: No
Expand In Territory: Yes
Space Needs: N/A SF; HB

SUPPORT & TRAINING PROVIDED:

Financial Assistance Provided: Yes(D)
Site Selection Assistance: N/A
Lease Negotiation Assistance: N/A
Co-Operative Advertising: Yes
Franchisee Assoc./Member: No
Size Of Corporate Staff: 42
On-Going Support: A,B,C,D,F,g,h,I
Training: 7 Days Ft. Lauderdale, FL.

SPECIFIC EXPANSION PLANS:

US: All United States
Canada: No
Overseas: No

<< >>

ENCHANTED HONEYMOONS

2927 S. 108th St.
Omaha, NE 68144
Tel: (800) 253-2863 (402) 390-9291
Fax: (402) 393-8096
Web Site: www.enchantedhoneymoons.com
Mr. Kem Matthews, President

ENCHANTED HONEYMOONS services the most exciting aspect of the travel industry: honeymoon and leisure travel. Join the fascinating world of travel without years of schooling. Part time or full time startup.

BACKGROUND:

Established: 1995; 1st Franchised: 1998
Franchised Units: 6
Company-Owned Units 1
Total Units: 7
Dist.: US-4; CAN-0; O'seas-0
North America: 3 States
Density: 2 in NE, 1 in KS, 1 in MN
Projected New Units (12 Months): 10
Qualifications: 3, 3, 1, 3, 2, 1
Registered: MN

FINANCIAL/TERMS:

Cash Investment: $25.5-37.5K
Total Investment: $25.5-37.5K
Minimum Net Worth: $NR
Fees: Franchise - $21.5K
Royalty - 0.5%; Ad. - 2% or N/A
Earnings Claim Statement: Yes
Term of Contract (Years): 10/10
Avg. # Of Employees:
1 FT (in beginning)
Passive Ownership: Discouraged
Encourage Conversions: Yes
Area Develop. Agreements: No
Sub-Franchising Contracts: No
Expand In Territory: Yes
Space Needs: 600-1,200 SF; SF, SC, RM

SUPPORT & TRAINING PROVIDED:

Financial Assistance Provided: Yes(D)
Site Selection Assistance: Yes
Lease Negotiation Assistance: Yes
Co-Operative Advertising: Yes
Franchisee Assoc./Member: No
Size Of Corporate Staff: 4
On-Going Support: B,C,D,E,G,H
Training: 5 Days Corporate Office in Omaha, NE; 2 Days On-Site.

SPECIFIC EXPANSION PLANS:

US: All United States
Canada: No
Overseas: No

<< >>

TRAVEL NETWORK

560 Sylvan Ave.
Englewood Cliffs, NJ 07632
Tel: (800) 669-9000 (201) 567-8500
Fax: (201) 567-4405
E-Mail: info@travnet.com
Web Site: www.travnet.com
Ms. Stephanie Abrams, Executive VP

Join the exciting travel industry with the leading travel franchisor as the owner of a TRAVEL NETWORK full-service travel agency catering to the business and leisure traveler. A TRAVEL NETWORK VACATION CENTRAL agency focuses solely on the lucrative leisure travel markets, or, as the owner of a full-service agency, catering to the business traveler as well as the leisure traveler. Our program includes complete start-up assistance, site selection and more.

BACKGROUND:

Established: 1982; 1st Franchised: 1983
Franchised Units: 507
Company-Owned Units 1
Total Units: 508
Dist.: US-454; CAN-3; O'seas-51
North America: 35 States, 1 Province
Density: 65 in NY, 32 in NJ, 26 in CA
Projected New Units (12 Months): 50
Qualifications: 5, 4, 2, 4, 3, 5
Registered: CA,FL,IL,IN,MD,MI,MN,NY,OR,RI,VA,WA,WI,DC

FINANCIAL/TERMS:

Cash Investment: $5-50K
Total Investment: $10-100K
Minimum Net Worth: $150K
Fees: Franchise - $5-30K
Royalty - $350-750/Mo; Ad. - $200/Mo.
Earnings Claim Statement: No
Term of Contract (Years): 15/15
Avg. # Of Employees: 2 FT, 1 PT
Passive Ownership: Discouraged
Encourage Conversions: Yes
Area Develop. Agreements: Yes/20
Sub-Franchising Contracts: Yes
Expand In Territory: Yes
Space Needs: 800-1,000 SF; FS, SF, SC, RM, HB

SUPPORT & TRAINING PROVIDED:

Financial Assistance Provided: Yes
Site Selection Assistance: Yes
Lease Negotiation Assistance: Yes
Co-Operative Advertising: Yes
Franchisee Assoc./Member: Yes
Size Of Corporate Staff: 25
On-Going Support: A,B,C,D,E,F,G,H,I
Training: 1 Week in NJ; 1 Week in Orlando, FL; 1 Week in Houston, TX; 1 Week On-Site at Store.

SPECIFIC EXPANSION PLANS:

US: All United States
Canada: All Canada
Overseas: All Countries

<< >>

UNIGLOBE TRAVEL

1199 W. Pender St., # 900
Vancouver, BC V6E 2R1 CANADA
Tel: (800) 863-1606 (604) 718-2600
Fax: (949) 623-9008
E-Mail: franchise@uniglobe.com
Web Site: www.uniglobefranchise.com
Mr. John Henry, SVP Global Franchise Dev.

Entrepreneur has consistently awarded UNIGLOBE TRAVEL the #1 company in travel-agency franchising. All UNIGLOBE travel agency franchisees benefit from programs and systems designed to handle the needs of both the corporate and leisure client. UNIGLOBE franchisees benefit from money-saving automation agreements and top-notch incentive commission programs with major airline, hotel, car rental, tour and cruise-line companies.

BACKGROUND: IFA MEMBER
Established: 1979; 1st Franchised: 1980
Franchised Units: 1,100
Company-Owned Units 0
Total Units: 1,100
Dist.: US-756; CAN-200; O'seas-100
North America: 50 States, 9 Provinces
Density: 109 in CA,45 in IL,41 in OH
Projected New Units (12 Months): 100
Qualifications: 5, 4, 1, 3, 4, 5
Registered: All States

FINANCIAL/TERMS:
Cash Investment: $2-25K
Total Investment: $21-104K
Minimum Net Worth: $60K
Fees: Franchise - $2-25K
Royalty - $275-550; Ad. - $550
Earnings Claim Statement: No
Term of Contract (Years): 10/5
Avg. # Of Employees: 3 FT, 1 PT
Passive Ownership: Discouraged
Encourage Conversions: Yes
Area Develop. Agreements: Yes/5
Sub-Franchising Contracts: Yes
Expand In Territory: Yes
Space Needs: 1,200 SF; FS, SF, SC, RM, HB

SUPPORT & TRAINING PROVIDED:
Financial Assistance Provided: Yes
Site Selection Assistance: Yes
Lease Negotiation Assistance: Yes
Co-Operative Advertising: Yes
Franchisee Assoc./Member: Yes/No
Size Of Corporate Staff: 100
On-Going Support: B,C,D,e,G,h,I
Training: 3 -5 Days in Irvine, CA.

SPECIFIC EXPANSION PLANS:
US: All United States
Canada: All Canada
Overseas: All Countries

<< >>

SUPPLEMENTAL LISTING OF FRANCHISORS

ADMIRAL OF THE FLEET CRUISE CENTERS, 3430 Pacific Ave. SE, # A-5, Olympia, WA 98501 ; (800) 877-7447 (360) 438-1191; (360) 438-2618

ALGONQUIN TRAVEL, 657 Bronson Ave., Ottawa, ON K1S 4E7 CANADA; (800) 668-1743 (613) 233-7713; (613) 233-7805

BTI AMERICA'S PARTNER GROUP, 400 Skokie Blvd., # 675, Northbrook, IL 60062 ; (800) 775-7702 (847) 753-6700; (847) 753-6730

BYEBYENOW.COM, 1100 Park Blvd., S, # 1800, Pompano Beach, FL 33064-2232; (800) 626-2469 (954) 979-6647; (954) 935-0178

CRUISE HOLIDAYS INTERNATIONAL, P.O. Box 59159, Minnetonka, MN 55459-8207 ; (800) 866-7245 (763) 212-1168; (763) 212-1242

CRUISE PLANNERS, 3300 University Dr., # 602, Coral Springs, FL 33065 ; (888) 582-2150 (954) 344-8060; (954) 344-4479

CRUISE VACATIONS, 2025 W. Broadway, Vancouver, BC V6J 1Z6 CANADA; (800) 665-1882 (604) 731-5546; (604) 736-6513

CRUISESHIPCENTERS, 344 River Oaks Blvd. W., Oakville, ON L6H 5E8 CANADA; (905) 257-3505; (905) 257-6560

EMPRESS TRAVEL, 465 Smith St., Farmingdale, NY 11735 ; (800) 284-0022 (613) 420-9200; (613) 420-0511

EXA INTERNATIONAL, 440 S. Federal Hwy., #104, Deerfield Beach, FL 33441 ; (305) 670-3833; (305) 670-4904

GALAXSEA CRUISES & TOURS, 13150 Coit Rd., # 125, Dallas, TX 75240 ; (800) 820-4710 (972) 671-7245; (972) 671-1151

KIRBY TOURS, 18977 West Ten Mile Rd., # 103, Southfield, MI 48075-2616 ; (248) 423-6400; (248) 443-0600

TPI TRAVEL SERVICES, 10012 Dale Mabry Hwy., # 102, Tampa, FL 33618-4425 ; (888) TPI-DEAL (813) 269-4960; (813) 281-4969

VACATIONBOUND SYSTEMS, 1315 Autrim Dr., Roseville, CA 95747 ; (916) 783-8473; (916) 783-8473

Chapter 48

Miscellaneous

Miscellaneous Industry Profile

Total # Franchisors in Industry Group	111
Total # Franchised Units in Industry Group	14,189
Total # Company-Owned Units in Industry Group	1,116
Total # Operating Units in Industry Group	15,305
Average # Franchised Units/Franchisor	127.8
Average # Company-Owned Units/Franchisor	10.1
Average # Total Units/Franchisor	137.9
Ratio of Total # Franchised Units/Total # Company-Owned Units	12.7:1
Industry Survey Participants	23
Representing % of Industry	20.7%
Average Franchise Fee*:	$37.4K
Average Total Investment*:	$152.3K
Average On-Going Royalty Fee*:	7.8%

*If a range was provided, the mid-point of the range was used. See detailed profiles for actual ranges.

Five Largest Participants in Survey

Company	# Franchised Units	# Co-Owned Units	# Total Units	Franchise Fee	On-Going Royalty	Total Investment
1. Culligan	704	53	757	5K	5%	103-225K
2. Ecowater Systems	725	0	725	0K	None	250K
3. House Doctors Handyman Service	225	0	225	12-30K	6%	19-46K
4. Benvinco	194	1	195	39.9K	$12/Audit	40K
5. Color Your Carpet	192	1	193	15K	3%	739-49K

All of the data provided are proprietary and should not be quoted without acknowledging *Bond's Franchise Guide.*

A ALL ANIMAL CONTROL

P.O. Box 33087-8087
Northglenn, CO 80233
Tel: (888) WILDPESTS (303) 452-2113
Fax: (303) 452-7572
E-Mail: info@aallanimalcontrol.com
Web Site: www.aallanimalcontrol.com
Mr. Mark E. Dotson, Chief Executive Officer

A ALL ANIMAL CONTROL specializes in resolving wild life conflicts in residential & commercial structures. We offer humane & environmentally conscious solutions to wildlife problems. Not only are we capable of removing & relocating wildlife, we can also follow through by de-odorizing, repairing damage and preventing potential future problems.

BACKGROUND:
Established: 1995; 1st Franchised: 2000
Franchised Units: 0
Company-Owned Units 1
Total Units: 1
Dist.: US-1; CAN-0; O'seas-0
North America: 1 State
Density: 1 in Colorado
Projected New Units (12 Months): 5
Qualifications: 3, 3, 4, 2, 3, 4
Registered: NR

FINANCIAL/TERMS:
Cash Investment: $10-20K
Total Investment: $30-35K
Minimum Net Worth: $25K
Fees: Franchise - $7.5-15.5K
Royalty - 5%; Ad. - 1%
Earnings Claim Statement: No
Term of Contract (Years): 10/10
Avg. # Of Employees: 1 FT
Passive Ownership: Not Allowed
Encourage Conversions: Yes
Area Develop. Agreements: Yes/10
Sub-Franchising Contracts: No
Expand In Territory: Yes
Space Needs: N/A SF; HB

SUPPORT & TRAINING PROVIDED:
Financial Assistance Provided: N/A
Site Selection Assistance: N/A
Lease Negotiation Assistance: N/A
Co-Operative Advertising: No
Franchisee Assoc./Member: No
Size Of Corporate Staff: 2
On-Going Support: C,D,E,F,G,H,I
Training: 2 Weeks in Denver, CO.

SPECIFIC EXPANSION PLANS:
US: All United States
Canada: No
Overseas: No

<< >>

AIR BROOK LIMOUSINE

P.O. Box 123
Rochelle Park, NJ 07662
Tel: (201) 368-3974
Fax: (201) 368-2247
Web Site: www.aribrook.com
Mr. Jim Bziekonski, Franchise Director

Limousine Service / Ground Transportation.

BACKGROUND:
Established: 1969; 1st Franchised: 1971
Franchised Units: 73
Company-Owned Units 0
Total Units: 73
Dist.: US-73; CAN-0; O'seas-0
North America: 1 State
Density: 73 in NJ
Projected New Units (12 Months): 10
Qualifications: 2, 2, 2, 2, 3, 4
Registered: NR

FINANCIAL/TERMS:
Cash Investment: $5.5-11K
Total Investment: $10.5-20K
Minimum Net Worth: $N/A
Fees: Franchise - $7.5-12.5K
Royalty - 40%; Ad. - 0%
Earnings Claim Statement: No
Term of Contract (Years): 10/2
Avg. # Of Employees: 2 FT
Passive Ownership: Allowed
Encourage Conversions: N/A
Area Develop. Agreements: No
Sub-Franchising Contracts: No
Expand In Territory: Yes
Space Needs: N/A SF; N/A

SUPPORT & TRAINING PROVIDED:
Financial Assistance Provided: Yes(D)
Site Selection Assistance: N/A
Lease Negotiation Assistance: N/A
Co-Operative Advertising: N/A
Franchisee Assoc./Member: No
Size Of Corporate Staff: 57
On-Going Support: A,B,C,D,G,H,I
Training: 3 Days Rochelle Park, NJ.

SPECIFIC EXPANSION PLANS:
US: NJ Only
Canada: No
Overseas: No

<< >>

APARTMENT MOVERS ETC.

3168 Winners Cir.
Charleston, SC 29414
Tel: (800) 847-2861 (843) 767-0073
Fax: (843) 573-0350
E-Mail: apartmentmovers@mindspring.com
Web Site: www.apartmentmoversetc.com
Ms.Brenda Bucceri, Operation/Sales Mgr.

Residential and Commercial Moving Company. Offering customers a guaranteed lowest move price. Customized software price quotes by phone, any size move. Unique logo reaches market niche. Comprehensive operations manual, proven success methods, high profit margins, training. Excellent profitable business opportunity.

BACKGROUND:
Established: 1995; 1st Franchised: 1998
Franchised Units: 5
Company-Owned Units 0
Total Units: 5
Dist.: US-5; CAN-0; O'seas-0
North America: 5 States
Density: 4 in SC, 1 in KY
Projected New Units (12 Months): 6
Qualifications: 2, 1, 1, 1, 1, 1
Registered: FL, IL, IN, MI

FINANCIAL/TERMS:
Cash Investment: $30K
Total Investment: $60-150K
Minimum Net Worth: $100K
Fees: Franchise - $19.5K
Royalty - 5%; Ad. - 1%
Earnings Claim Statement: No
Term of Contract (Years): 10/10
Avg. # Of Employees: 4 FT, 3 PT
Passive Ownership: Allowed
Encourage Conversions: Yes
Area Develop. Agreements: Yes/10
Sub-Franchising Contracts: Yes
Expand In Territory: Yes
Space Needs: Minimal SF; Parking for Trucks

SUPPORT & TRAINING PROVIDED:
Financial Assistance Provided: Yes(I)
Site Selection Assistance: Yes
Lease Negotiation Assistance: Yes
Co-Operative Advertising: Yes
Franchisee Assoc./Member: No
Size Of Corporate Staff: 4
On-Going Support: A,C,D,E,F,G,H,I
Training: 10 Days On-Site.

SPECIFIC EXPANSION PLANS:
US: Eastern and Central
Canada: No
Overseas: No

<< >>

ATLANTIC MOWER PARTS & SUPPLIES

13421 S.W. 14th Pl.
Ft. Lauderdale, FL 33325
Tel: (954) 474-4942
Fax: (954) 475-0414
Mr. Robert J. Bettelli, President

Lawn mower replacement after-market. Parts for national brands (Snapper, Toro, MTD, Murray, etc.).

BACKGROUND:
Established: 1978; 1st Franchised: 1988
Franchised Units: 12
Company-Owned Units 1
Total Units: 13
Dist.: US-15; CAN-0; O'seas-0
North America: 1 State
Density: 15 in FL
Projected New Units (12 Months): 5
Qualifications: 2, 3, 3, 4, 1, 5
Registered: FL

FINANCIAL/TERMS:
Cash Investment: $~45K
Total Investment: $45K
Minimum Net Worth: $NR
Fees: Franchise - $15.9K
Royalty - 5%; Ad. - 0.5%
Earnings Claim Statement: No
Term of Contract (Years): 10/10
Avg. # Of Employees: 1 FT
Passive Ownership: Allowed
Encourage Conversions: Yes
Area Develop. Agreements: Yes/1
Sub-Franchising Contracts: Yes
Expand In Territory: Yes
Space Needs: 250 SF; Warehouse

SUPPORT & TRAINING PROVIDED:
Financial Assistance Provided: No
Site Selection Assistance: Yes
Lease Negotiation Assistance: Yes
Co-Operative Advertising: No
Franchisee Assoc./Member: NR
Size Of Corporate Staff: 3
On-Going Support: B,C,D,E
Training: 5 Days Headquarters; 5 Days On-Site.

SPECIFIC EXPANSION PLANS:
US: All United States
Canada: No
Overseas: No

BEVINCO

250 Consumers Rd., # 1103
Toronto, ON M2J 4V6 CANADA
Tel: (888) 238-4626 (416) 490-6266
Fax: (416) 490-6899
E-Mail: info@bevinco.com
Web Site: www.bevinco.com
Mr. Barry Driedger, President

Liquor inventory auditing and control service for bars and restaurants. Utilizing our computerized weighing system, franchisees will identify and resolve the shrinkage problems associated with the bar business. On-going weekly accounts make for an excellent executive income.

BACKGROUND:
Established: 1987; 1st Franchised: 1990
Franchised Units: 194
Company-Owned Units 1
Total Units: 195
Dist.: US-139; CAN-36; O'seas-20
North America: 40 States, 7 Provinces
Density: 9 in CA, 8 in OH, 6 in TX
Projected New Units (12 Months): 50
Qualifications: 3, 4, 4, 3, 3, 3
Registered: All States

FINANCIAL/TERMS:
Cash Investment: $40K
Total Investment: $40K
Minimum Net Worth: $40K
Fees: Franchise - $39.9K
Royalty - $12/Audit; Ad. - $2/Audit
Earnings Claim Statement: No
Term of Contract (Years): 5/5
Avg. # Of Employees: 1-3 FT, 1-3 PT
Passive Ownership: Not Allowed
Encourage Conversions: N/A
Area Develop. Agreements: Yes/5
Sub-Franchising Contracts: No
Expand In Territory: N/A
Space Needs: NR SF; N/A

SUPPORT & TRAINING PROVIDED:
Financial Assistance Provided: Yes(I)
Site Selection Assistance: N/A
Lease Negotiation Assistance: N/A
Co-Operative Advertising: N/A
Franchisee Assoc./Member: Yes/Yes
Size Of Corporate Staff: 4
On-Going Support: A,b,D,G,H,I
Training: 10 Days at Head Office in Toronto; 5 Days Franchisee's Location.

SPECIFIC EXPANSION PLANS:
US: All United States
Canada: All Canada
Overseas: All Countries

<< >>

COLOR YOUR CARPET

2465 Ridgecrest Ave.
Orange Park, FL 32065
Tel: (800) 321-6567 (904) 272-6567
Fax: (904) 272-6750
E-Mail: angel@franchise411.com
Web Site: www.franchise411.com/dyetech
Ms. Connie D'Imperio, President

No competition! The ONLY on-site, 100% carpet dyeing and color restoration service in the world. Advanced technology provides cost-effective, convenient alternative to costly carpet replacement. Design dyeing, spot dyeing and color matching taught by experts. Large protected territory expansion program.

BACKGROUND:
Established: 1979; 1st Franchised: 1990
Franchised Units: 192
Company-Owned Units 1
Total Units: 193
Dist.: US-112; CAN-48; O'seas-32
North America: 14 States, 4 Provinces
Density: 18 in FL, 12 in AB
Projected New Units (12 Months): 24
Qualifications: 3, 4, 1, 4, 5, 5
Registered: FL,HI,IL,MD,MI,MN,OR, VA,WA,DC

FINANCIAL/TERMS:
Cash Investment: $25-35K
Total Investment: $39-49K
Minimum Net Worth: $150K
Fees: Franchise - $15K
Royalty - 3%; Ad. - 0%
Earnings Claim Statement: Yes
Term of Contract (Years): 5/5
Avg. # Of Employees: 1 FT, 1 PT
Passive Ownership: Allowed
Encourage Conversions: No
Area Develop. Agreements: Yes/10
Sub-Franchising Contracts: Yes
Expand In Territory: Yes
Space Needs: N/A SF; HB

SUPPORT & TRAINING PROVIDED:
Financial Assistance Provided: No
Site Selection Assistance: N/A
Lease Negotiation Assistance: N/A
Co-Operative Advertising: N/A
Franchisee Assoc./Member: Yes/Yes
Size Of Corporate Staff: 6
On-Going Support: A,B,C,D,E,F,G,H,I
Training: 2 Weeks Home Study; 1 Week Orange Park, FL; 1 Week On-the-Job Existing Franchisee's Site.

SPECIFIC EXPANSION PLANS:
US: All United States
Canada: All Canada
Overseas: Primarily South America, Europe, Asia, Middle East

<< >>

COMPUTER BUILDERS WAREHOUSE

1993 Tobsal Ct.
Warren, MI 48091
Tel: (888) 668-0900 (810) 756-2600
Fax: (810) 756-8715
E-Mail: gthomas@cbwnet.com
Web Site: www.computerfranchise.com
Mr. Eugene J. Thomas, President

Exciting and unique franchise opportunity. Our franchisees take advantage of our state of the art manufacturing and warehouse facility. The testing center provides customers with reliable built to order computer products, while in-store service labs provide complete computer service, parts and components. A turnkey operation is provided.

BACKGROUND:
Established: 1990; 1st Franchised: 1999
Franchised Units: 4
Company-Owned Units 1
Total Units: 5
Dist.: US-5; CAN-0; O'seas-0
North America: 1 State
Density: 5 in MI
Projected New Units (12 Months): 15
Qualifications: 5, 3, 2, 3, 3, 5
Registered: CA,FL,HI,IL,IN,MD,MI,MN,NY,ND,OR,RI,SD,VA,WA,WI,DC

FINANCIAL/TERMS:
Cash Investment: $100K
Total Investment: $300-350K
Minimum Net Worth: $200K
Fees: Franchise - $35K
Royalty - 1.5%; Ad. - 2%
Earnings Claim Statement: No
Term of Contract (Years): 10/5
Avg. # Of Employees: 7 FT, 2 PT
Passive Ownership: Not Allowed
Encourage Conversions: Yes
Area Develop. Agreements: No
Sub-Franchising Contracts: No
Expand In Territory: No
Space Needs: 3,500 SF; FS,SF,SC

SUPPORT & TRAINING PROVIDED:
Financial Assistance Provided: Yes(I)
Site Selection Assistance: Yes
Lease Negotiation Assistance: Yes
Co-Operative Advertising: Yes
Franchisee Assoc./Member: No
Size Of Corporate Staff: 75
On-Going Support: B,C,D,E,F,G,H
Training: 3 Weeks at Company Headquarters; 2-4 Weeks On-Site.

SPECIFIC EXPANSION PLANS:
US: All United States
Canada: No
Overseas: No

<< >>

CULLIGAN

One Culligan Pkwy.
Northbrook, IL 60062-6209
Tel: (800) CULLIGAN (847) 205-5823
Fax: (847) 205-6050
E-Mail: kwood@culligan.com
Web Site: www.culligan.com
Mr. Kenneth E. Wood, Dir. Market Development

CULLIGAN is looking for franchisees to start a business selling 5 gallon bottles of water for delivery to homes and offices. CULLIGAN is a manufacturer of water conditioners, filters and drinking water devices.

BACKGROUND: IFA MEMBER
Established: 1936; 1st Franchised: 1939
Franchised Units: 704
Company-Owned Units 53
Total Units: 757
Dist.: US-801; CAN-48; O'seas-0
North America: 50 States
Density: 40 in MN, 40 in IA, 35 in WI
Projected New Units (12 Months): 8
Qualifications: 5, 5, 2, 3, 4, 4
Registered: All States

FINANCIAL/TERMS:
Cash Investment: $103-225K
Total Investment: $103-225K
Minimum Net Worth: $250K
Fees: Franchise - $5K
Royalty - 5%; Ad. - 0%
Earnings Claim Statement: No
Term of Contract (Years): 10/10
Avg. # Of Employees: 6 FT
Passive Ownership: Discouraged
Encourage Conversions: Yes
Area Develop. Agreements: No
Sub-Franchising Contracts: No
Expand In Territory: No
Space Needs: 2,500 SF; SF

SUPPORT & TRAINING PROVIDED:
Financial Assistance Provided: No
Site Selection Assistance: No
Lease Negotiation Assistance: No
Co-Operative Advertising: No
Franchisee Assoc./Member: No
Size Of Corporate Staff: 20
On-Going Support: C,D,G,H,I
Training: 1 Week Chicago, IL.

SPECIFIC EXPANSION PLANS:
US: SE, Pacific NW, Northeast
Canada: All Canada
Overseas: Mexico, South America

<< >>

DISCOUNT IMAGING

P.O. Box 699
West Monroe, LA 71294-0699
Tel: (800) 987-8258 (318) 324-8258
Fax: (318) 324-1211
E-Mail: bradh@discountimaging.com
Web Site: www.difcorp.com
Mr. Brad Hargrove, National Sales Mgr.

Single source providers of printer, fax and copier supplies and service to businesses of all types. Program features proprietary product line, purchasing power and other support services.

BACKGROUND: IFA MEMBER
Established: 1995; 1st Franchised: 1998
Franchised Units: 6
Company-Owned Units 1
Total Units: 7
Dist.: US-13; CAN-0; O'seas-0
North America: 5 States
Density: 2 in AR, 1 in FL, 1 in AL
Projected New Units (12 Months): 2
Qualifications: 4, 3, 2, 1, 4, 5
Registered: FL,TX

FINANCIAL/TERMS:
Cash Investment: $25-40K
Total Investment: $56-62K
Minimum Net Worth: $75K
Fees: Franchise - $25K
Royalty - 3-6%; Ad. - 0%
Earnings Claim Statement: No
Term of Contract (Years): 10/5
Avg. # Of Employees: 4 FT, 1 PT
Passive Ownership: Discouraged
Encourage Conversions: No
Area Develop. Agreements: No
Sub-Franchising Contracts: No
Expand In Territory: Yes
Space Needs: NR SF; HB

SUPPORT & TRAINING PROVIDED:
Financial Assistance Provided: Yes(I)
Site Selection Assistance: Yes
Lease Negotiation Assistance: No
Co-Operative Advertising: No
Franchisee Assoc./Member: No
Size Of Corporate Staff: 6
On-Going Support: C,d,E,F,G,h,I
Training: 2 Weeks Corporate; 4 Weeks On-Site.

SPECIFIC EXPANSION PLANS:
US: South, Southeast
Canada: All Canada
Overseas: No

<< >>

ECOWATER SYSTEMS

P.O. Box 64420
St. Paul, MN 55164
Tel: (800) 942-5415 (651) 731-7438
Fax: (651) 739-4547
E-Mail: johnsonj@ecowater.com
Web Site: www.ecowater.com
Mr. Jerry Johnson, Mgr. Franchise Development

Manufacturer & distributor of water treatment products for residential, commercial and industrial uses. Established in 1925, EcoWater has been providing high quality computerized water treatment and products worldwide. As the world's largest manufacturer of residential water systems, you build your business, in protected territories, servicing your customers and controlling your future.

BACKGROUND:
Established: 1925; 1st Franchised: 1927
Franchised Units: 725
Company-Owned Units 0
Total Units: 725
Dist.: US-600; CAN-50; O'seas-75
North America: 50 States, 5 Provinces
Density: NR
Projected New Units (12 Months): 20
Qualifications: 5, 4, 1, 2, 4, 5
Registered: All States
FINANCIAL/TERMS:
Cash Investment: $125K
Total Investment: $250K
Minimum Net Worth: $200K
Fees: Franchise - $0
Royalty - None; Ad. - Varies
Earnings Claim Statement: No
Term of Contract (Years): 2-10/2-10
Avg. # Of Employees: 4 FT, 2 PT
Passive Ownership: Discouraged
Encourage Conversions: Yes
Area Develop. Agreements: Yes/1
Sub-Franchising Contracts: Yes
Expand In Territory: Yes
Space Needs: 2,500 SF; FS, SF, SC
SUPPORT & TRAINING PROVIDED:
Financial Assistance Provided: Yes(D)
Site Selection Assistance: Yes
Lease Negotiation Assistance: No
Co-Operative Advertising: Yes
Franchisee Assoc./Member: No
Size Of Corporate Staff: 500
On-Going Support: B,C,D,E,G,H,I
Training: 3-5 Days On-Site; 5 Days at Corporate Office.
SPECIFIC EXPANSION PLANS:
US: All United States
Canada: All Canada
Overseas: Yes - Contact Company

<< >>

ENGLISH BUTLER CANADA

39 King St.
St. John, NB E2L 4W3 CANADA
Tel: (416) 966-9802
Fax: (416) 966-9803
E-Mail: nassad@accessv.com
Web Site: www.englishbutler.com
Mr. Nicholas Assad, Franchise Director

Elegant, traditional gifts and home decorating accessories. Merchandise ranges from printer to pictures, afghans to table linens and collectibles to seasonal giftware.

BACKGROUND:
Established: 1984; 1st Franchised: 1994
Franchised Units: 18
Company-Owned Units 3
Total Units: 21
Dist.: US-0; CAN-20; O'seas-0
North America: 3 Provinces
Density: 15 in ON, 3 in NB, 2 in NS
Projected New Units (12 Months): 6-8
Qualifications: 4, 4, 3, 3, 4, 5
Registered: NR
FINANCIAL/TERMS:
Cash Investment: $75K
Total Investment: $250K
Minimum Net Worth: $100K
Fees: Franchise - $25K
Royalty - 6%; Ad. - 0.5%
Earnings Claim Statement: No
Term of Contract (Years): 10/5
Avg. # Of Employees: 2 FT, 3-5 PT
Passive Ownership: Discouraged
Encourage Conversions: No
Area Develop. Agreements: No
Sub-Franchising Contracts: No
Expand In Territory: Yes
Space Needs: 2,000 SF; RM
SUPPORT & TRAINING PROVIDED:
Financial Assistance Provided: Yes(I)
Site Selection Assistance: Yes
Lease Negotiation Assistance: Yes
Co-Operative Advertising: Yes
Franchisee Assoc./Member: Yes/Yes
Size Of Corporate Staff: 7
On-Going Support: B,D,E,F,h
Training: 3 Weeks Corporate Stores.
SPECIFIC EXPANSION PLANS:
US: No
Canada: ON, PQ, AB
Overseas: No

<< >>

FILTERFRESH

378 University Ave.
Westwood, MA 02090
Tel: (800) 332-6771 (781) 461-8734
Fax: (781) 461-8732
Web Site: www.filterfresh.com
Mr. Roger Cohen, President

High-tech office coffee service, using a patented single-cup coffeemaker. FILTERFRESH brews coffee by-the-cup from fresh-ground coffee in seconds. Choice exclusive territories are available as a franchise or joint-venture with corporate. The FILTERFRESH franchise provides access to patented equipment, detailed training in sales and service, on-going support and supply services.

BACKGROUND:
Established: 1986; 1st Franchised: 1987
Franchised Units: 60
Company-Owned Units 10
Total Units: 70
Dist.: US-49; CAN-0; O'seas-1
North America: 25 States
Density: 8 in NY, 6 in NJ, 3 in CA
Projected New Units (12 Months): 4
Qualifications: 4, 5, 2, 3, 4, 4
Registered: CA,FL,IL,IN,MD,MI,MN,NY, OR,RI,VA,WA
FINANCIAL/TERMS:
Cash Investment: $150-500K
Total Investment: $50-500K
Minimum Net Worth: $500K
Fees: Franchise - $24.5K
Royalty - 5%; Ad. - 2%
Earnings Claim Statement: No
Term of Contract (Years): 10/10
Avg. # Of Employees: 4 FT, 2 PT
Passive Ownership: Not Allowed
Encourage Conversions: N/A
Area Develop. Agreements: No
Sub-Franchising Contracts: No
Expand In Territory: Yes
Space Needs: 1,500 SF; Warehouse
SUPPORT & TRAINING PROVIDED:
Financial Assistance Provided: Yes(I)
Site Selection Assistance: Yes

Lease Negotiation Assistance: No
Co-Operative Advertising: Yes
Franchisee Assoc./Member: Yes/No
Size Of Corporate Staff: 30
On-Going Support: A,B,C,D,E,F,G,H,I
Training: 1 Week Montreal, PQ; 2 Weeks On-Site; 1 Week Westwood, MA.

SPECIFIC EXPANSION PLANS:
US: All United States
Canada: No
Overseas: All Countries

<< >>

GUARDIAN, THE CHILD SUPPORT PEOPLE

14121 NW Fwy., # B
Houston, TX 77040
Tel: (888) 829-3335 (713) 462-1139
Fax: (713) 462-8177
E-Mail: info@911guardian.com
Web Site: www.911guardian.com
Ms. Suzanne Hill, Dir. Franchise Training

We assist custodial parents in collecting their unpaid child support. We offer a contingency fee-based service, so the custodial parent does not have any out-of-pocket, up-front expenses or fees to pay.

BACKGROUND:
Established: 1999; 1st Franchised: 2000
Franchised Units: 6
Company-Owned Units 1
Total Units: 7
Dist.: US-7; CAN-0; O'seas-0
North America: 3 States
Density: 3 in TX, 3 in FL
Projected New Units (12 Months): 10
Qualifications: 3, 4, 1, 3, 3, 5
Registered: FL

FINANCIAL/TERMS:
Cash Investment: $35K+
Total Investment: $62-96K
Minimum Net Worth: $150K
Fees: Franchise - $35K
Royalty - Varies; Ad. - Varies
Earnings Claim Statement: No
Term of Contract (Years): 5/5
Avg. # Of Employees: 2 FT
Passive Ownership: Not Allowed
Encourage Conversions: N/A
Area Develop. Agreements: No
Sub-Franchising Contracts: No
Expand In Territory: Yes
Space Needs: 700 SF; SF, SC

SUPPORT & TRAINING PROVIDED:
Financial Assistance Provided: No
Site Selection Assistance: Yes
Lease Negotiation Assistance: Yes
Co-Operative Advertising: Yes
Franchisee Assoc./Member: No
Size Of Corporate Staff: 17
On-Going Support: A,B,C,D,E,G,h,I
Training: 3 Weeks Corporate Site; 1 Week/Quarter Franchisee Location.

SPECIFIC EXPANSION PLANS:
US: South and Southeast
Canada: No
Overseas: No

<< >>

HOUSE DOCTORS HANDYMAN SERVICE

6355 E. Kemper Rd., # 250
Cincinnati, OH 45241
Tel: (800) 319-3359 (513) 469-2443
Fax: (513) 469-2226
E-Mail: housedr@one.net
Web Site: www.housedoctors.com
Mr. Steve Cohen, President

There's big money in house calls. Millions of dollars are being spent every day on those odd jobs around the house that people don't have the time or skill to do. You don't need a screwdriver or hammer to own this franchise. Financing and training provided.

BACKGROUND: IFA MEMBER
Established: 1994; 1st Franchised: 1995
Franchised Units: 225
Company-Owned Units 0
Total Units: 225
Dist.: US-224; CAN-0; O'seas-1
North America: 42 States
Density: 10 in OH, 9 in IN, 9 in IL
Projected New Units (12 Months): 30
Qualifications: 2, 3, 2, 2, 4, 5
Registered: CA,FL,IL,IN,MD,MI,MN,NY, ND,OR,RI,VA,WA,WI

FINANCIAL/TERMS:
Cash Investment: $12-23K
Total Investment: $19-46K
Minimum Net Worth: $10K
Fees: Franchise - $12-30K
Royalty - 6%; Ad. - 3%
Earnings Claim Statement: No
Term of Contract (Years): 10/10/10
Avg. # Of Employees: 3 FT, 2 PT
Passive Ownership: Discouraged
Encourage Conversions: Yes
Area Develop. Agreements: Yes/10
Sub-Franchising Contracts: No
Expand In Territory: No
Space Needs: N/A SF; N/A

SUPPORT & TRAINING PROVIDED:
Financial Assistance Provided: Yes(D)
Site Selection Assistance: N/A
Lease Negotiation Assistance: N/A
Co-Operative Advertising: N/A
Franchisee Assoc./Member: No
Size Of Corporate Staff: 12
On-Going Support: A,B,C,D,E,G,H,I
Training: 1 Week Cincinnati, OH.

SPECIFIC EXPANSION PLANS:
US: All United States
Canada: All Canada
Overseas: All Countries

MAGIS FUND RAISING SPECIALISTS

845 Heathermoor Ln.
Perrysburg, OH 43551-2933
Tel: (419) 874-4459
Fax: (419) 874-4459
Dr. Richard W. Waring, President

Conducts annual giving, endowment, capital campaigns, feasibility studies, fund raising audits, personnel searches, corporate solicitations, etc. Presents seminars, designs brochures, presentations, etc. for churches, schools, hospitals, etc. 30 years of fund raising experience. Contract with small- to medium-sized charities who cannot afford full-time development directors. The first fund raising franchise with a guarantee in the U. S. and Canada. $180 million raised.

BACKGROUND:
Established: 1991; 1st Franchised: 1991
Franchised Units: 8
Company-Owned Units 2
Total Units: 10
Dist.: US-6; CAN-3; O'seas-0
North America: 2 States, 1 Province
Density: 3 in MI, 3 in OH, 3 in ON
Projected New Units (12 Months): 6
Qualifications: 5, 5, 4, 4, 4, 5

Registered: All Except AB

FINANCIAL/TERMS:

Cash Investment: $17K
Total Investment: $28.5K
Minimum Net Worth: $100K
Fees: Franchise - $7.5K
Royalty - 8%; Ad. - 2%
Earnings Claim Statement: No
Term of Contract (Years): 5/5
Avg. # Of Employees: 2 FT, 4 PT
Passive Ownership: Not Allowed
Encourage Conversions: Yes
Area Develop. Agreements: Yes
Sub-Franchising Contracts: Yes
Expand In Territory: Yes
Space Needs: 500 SF; HB

SUPPORT & TRAINING PROVIDED:

Financial Assistance Provided: Yes(I)
Site Selection Assistance: N/A
Lease Negotiation Assistance: N/A
Co-Operative Advertising: Yes
Franchisee Assoc./Member: No
Size Of Corporate Staff: 2
On-Going Support: a,B,c,d,E,G,h
Training: 1 Week Home Study; 1 Week Support Service Center; 1 Week On-Site.

SPECIFIC EXPANSION PLANS:

US: All United States
Canada: All Canada
Overseas: All Countries

Metal Supermarkets (Canada) Ltd.
The Convenience Stores of the Metal Industry

Top 50

METAL SUPERMARKETS INTERNATIONAL

170 Wilkinson Rd., # 17/18
Brampton, ON L6T 4Z5 CANADA
Tel: (888) 807-8755 (905) 459-0466
Fax: (905) 459-3690
E-Mail: miller-joe@compuserve.com
Web Site: www.metalsupermarkets.com
Mr. Joe H. Miller, President Franchise Division

METAL SUPERMARKETS is a highly specialized supplier of small quantities of virtually all types and forms of metal. Customers are maintenance departments of all types of industries. As 'convenience stores of the metal industry,' we have no minimum order We offer fast delivery, custom cutting and can source rare metals.

BACKGROUND: IFA MEMBER

Established: 1985; 1st Franchised: 1987
Franchised Units: 57
Company-Owned Units 23
Total Units: 80
Dist.: US-38; CAN-32; O'seas-10
North America: 23 States, 8 Provinces
Density: 13 in ON, 5 in FL, 3 in PA
Projected New Units (12 Months): 18
Qualifications: 5, 3, 3, 3, 3, 5
Registered: All States

FINANCIAL/TERMS:

Cash Investment: $100K
Total Investment: $200-225K
Minimum Net Worth: $200K
Fees: Franchise - $38K
Royalty - 6%; Ad. - 0%
Earnings Claim Statement: No
Term of Contract (Years): 10/10
Avg. # Of Employees: 3 FT, 1 PT
Passive Ownership: Discouraged
Encourage Conversions: Yes
Area Develop. Agreements: Yes/10
Sub-Franchising Contracts: No
Expand In Territory: Yes
Space Needs: 3500 SF; Industrial Park

SUPPORT & TRAINING PROVIDED:

Financial Assistance Provided: No
Site Selection Assistance: Yes
Lease Negotiation Assistance: Yes
Co-Operative Advertising: No
Franchisee Assoc./Member: Yes/Yes
Size Of Corporate Staff: 15
On-Going Support: C,D,E,F,G,h,I
Training: 1 Week in Toronto, ON; 2 Weeks Corporate Store; 2 Weeks Own Store.

SPECIFIC EXPANSION PLANS:

US: All United States
Canada: PQ
Overseas: Europe

<< >>

OPTIONS TALENT

7001 Lake Ellenor Dr., # 200
Orlando, FL 32809-5792
Tel: (888) 771-5043 (407) 240-1656
Fax: (407) 240-4177
E-Mail: tbears@optionstalent.com
Web Site: www.optionstalent.com
Ms. Terri Bears, Senior Vice President

eModel.com is the largest scouting company in the world. We expose our models through digital comp cards on our website to thousands of agencies, models and clients.

BACKGROUND: IFA MEMBER

Established: 1996; 1st Franchised: 1999
Franchised Units: 92
Company-Owned Units 6
Total Units: 98
Dist.: US-98; CAN-0; O'seas-0
North America: 23 States
Density: 9 in CA, 8 in FL, 6 in TX
Projected New Units (12 Months): 37
Qualifications: 3, 4, 2, 3, 3, 3
Registered: All States

FINANCIAL/TERMS:

Cash Investment: $35-50K
Total Investment: $30K
Minimum Net Worth: $50K
Fees: Franchise - $20K
Royalty - 0; Ad. - $1,500/Mo.
Earnings Claim Statement: Yes
Term of Contract (Years): 3/3
Avg. # Of Employees: 2 FT, 1 PT
Passive Ownership: Discouraged
Encourage Conversions: NR
Area Develop. Agreements: No
Sub-Franchising Contracts: No
Expand In Territory: No
Space Needs: 2,000 SF; FS

SUPPORT & TRAINING PROVIDED:

Financial Assistance Provided: NR
Site Selection Assistance: Yes
Lease Negotiation Assistance: No
Co-Operative Advertising: Yes
Franchisee Assoc./Member: IFA
Size Of Corporate Staff: 230
On-Going Support: A,C,D
Training: 3 Weeks in Orlando, FL.

SPECIFIC EXPANSION PLANS:

US: All United States
Canada: All Canada
Overseas: Africa, S. America

<< >>

PURIFIED WATER TO GO

5160 S. Valley View Blvd., # 110
Las Vegas, NV 89118-1778
Tel: (800) 976-9283 (702) 895-9350
Fax: (702) 895-9306
E-Mail: lventresca@watertogo.com
Web Site: www.watertogo.com
Mr. Lou Ventresca

PURIFIED WATER TO GO, recently featured on NBC nightly news, is a full-service or express retail outlet, selling purified water by the gallon, purified ice and related products. As the leader in water store franchises, PURIFIED WATER TO GO answers today's need for superior quality drinking water. Water is purified on store premises, and customers are drawn to the appeal of our sparkling clean, blue and white interior design.

BACKGROUND:
Established: 1991; 1st Franchised: 1995
Franchised Units: 51
Company-Owned Units 0
Total Units: 51
Dist.: US-33; CAN-0; O'seas-0
North America: 12 States
Density: 12 in WA, 5 in NV, 5 in NM
Projected New Units (12 Months): 15
Qualifications: 4, 2, 1, 3, 4, 5
Registered: All States

FINANCIAL/TERMS:
Cash Investment: $25-50K
Total Investment: $75-145K
Minimum Net Worth: $150K
Fees: Franchise - $23-29K
Royalty - 4-6%; Ad. - $150-200/Mo
Earnings Claim Statement: No
Term of Contract (Years): 10/10
Avg. # Of Employees: 1 FT, 1 PT
Passive Ownership: Discouraged
Encourage Conversions: N/A
Area Develop. Agreements: Yes/10
Sub-Franchising Contracts: No
Expand In Territory: Yes
Space Needs: 500-1,000 SF; SF, SC

SUPPORT & TRAINING PROVIDED:
Financial Assistance Provided: Yes(I)
Site Selection Assistance: Yes
Lease Negotiation Assistance: Yes
Co-Operative Advertising: Yes
Franchisee Assoc./Member: Yes
Size Of Corporate Staff: 9
On-Going Support: B,C,D,E,F,G,H,I
Training: 5 Days Corporate Office in Las Vegas, NV.

SPECIFIC EXPANSION PLANS:
US: All United States
Canada: All Canada
Overseas: All Countries

RESETTLERS, THE

5811 Kennett Pk.
Centreville, DE 19807
Tel: (302) 658-9110
Fax: (302) 658-5809
E-Mail: resettlers@att.net
Web Site: www.resettlers.com
Mr. Len Adams, Dir. Fran. Dev.

THE RESETTLERS is a customized and caring moving service for seniors, which includes professional packing, unpacking and complete resettlement of the new home. A pioneer in the moving service concept, the company guides clients through every state of the moving process and assists with move preparation and organization through their Rent-A-Daughter program. Antiques, collectibles, furniture and household items no longer needed in the new residence are sold through our retail outlets.

BACKGROUND: IFA MEMBER
Established: 1985; 1st Franchised: 1997
Franchised Units: 1
Company-Owned Units 1
Total Units: 2
Dist.: US-3; CAN-0; O'seas-0
North America: 2 States
Density: 2 in DE, 1 in WI
Projected New Units (12 Months): 2-3
Qualifications: 5, 5, 3, 3, 2, 5
Registered: NR

FINANCIAL/TERMS:
Cash Investment: $40-75K
Total Investment: $Varies
Minimum Net Worth: $NR
Fees: Franchise - $20K
Royalty - 5%; Ad. - 2%
Earnings Claim Statement: Yes
Term of Contract (Years): 10/10
Avg. # Of Employees: 10-15 PT
Passive Ownership: Not Allowed
Encourage Conversions: N/A
Area Develop. Agreements: Yes
Sub-Franchising Contracts: No
Expand In Territory: Yes
Space Needs: 2.500 SF; SF, FS

SUPPORT & TRAINING PROVIDED:
Financial Assistance Provided: No
Site Selection Assistance: Yes
Lease Negotiation Assistance: Yes
Co-Operative Advertising: Yes
Franchisee Assoc./Member: No
Size Of Corporate Staff: 6
On-Going Support: C,D,E,F,G,I
Training: 2 Weeks in Wilmington, DE; 1 Week On-Site.

SPECIFIC EXPANSION PLANS:
US: All United States
Canada: No
Overseas: No

SHRED-IT

601 Central Park Dr.
Sanford, FL 32771
Tel: (407) 445-8066
E-Mail: info@shredit.com
Web Site: www.shredit.com
Mr. Jeff Kish, Dir. Franchise Operations

Business service, offering mobile paper shredding and recycling, serving Fortune 1,000 companies, hospitals, medical facilities, banks, financial institutions, investment and professional firms and the government.

BACKGROUND:
Established: 1988; 1st Franchised: 1992
Franchised Units: 52
Company-Owned Units 19
Total Units: 71
Dist.: US-55; CAN-10; O'seas-6
North America: 27 States, 7 Provinces
Density: 6 in CA, 5 in FL, 3 in OH
Projected New Units (12 Months): 23
Qualifications: 5, 5, 1, 3, 4, 5
Registered: CA,FL,IL,IN,MD,MI,NY,WA, WI,DC,AB

FINANCIAL/TERMS:
Cash Investment: $70-140K
Total Investment: $350-450K
Minimum Net Worth: $350K
Fees: Franchise - $55K
Royalty - 5%; Ad. - 1.5%
Earnings Claim Statement: No
Term of Contract (Years): 10/10/10
Avg. # Of Employees: 6 FT
Passive Ownership: Not Allowed
Encourage Conversions: N/A
Area Develop. Agreements: Yes/10/10
Sub-Franchising Contracts: No
Expand In Territory: Yes
Space Needs: 1,500 SF; Industrial Flex Space

SUPPORT & TRAINING PROVIDED:
Financial Assistance Provided: Yes(I)
Site Selection Assistance: Yes
Lease Negotiation Assistance: Yes
Co-Operative Advertising: N/A
Franchisee Assoc./Member: Yes/Yes
Size Of Corporate Staff: 40
On-Going Support: B,C,D,E,G,H,I
Training: 2 Weeks in Oakville, ON.

SPECIFIC EXPANSION PLANS:
US: All United States

Canada: SK, PQ
Overseas: All Countries

<< >>

TWO MEN AND A TRUCK

2152 Commons Pkwy.
Okemos, MI 48864
Tel: (800) 345-1070 (517) 482-6683
Fax: (800) 278-6114
E-Mail: ronl@twomen.com
Web Site: www.twomen.com
Mr. Ron Lovejoy, Franchise Sales Coord.

TWO MEN AND A TRUCK franchises provide local residential and commercial moving services, boxes and packing services and supplies. Our Stick Men University and First Gear Training program provide the most comprehensive initial and on-going training in the industry. We are the 7th largest moving company in the nation! The 'Company That's On The Move."

BACKGROUND: IFA MEMBER
Established: 1985; 1st Franchised: 1989
Franchised Units: 105
Company-Owned Units 0
Total Units: 105
Dist.: US-95; CAN-0; O'seas-0
North America: 22 States
Density: 21 in MI, 8 in FL, 7 in TX
Projected New Units (12 Months): 24
Qualifications: 3, 4, 1, 3, 5, 5
Registered: CA,FL,IL,IN,MI,MN,NY,OR, RI,WA,WI

FINANCIAL/TERMS:
Cash Investment: $65K+
Total Investment: $75K+
Minimum Net Worth: $80K
Fees: Franchise - $28K
Royalty - 6%; Ad. - 1%
Earnings Claim Statement: No
Term of Contract (Years): 5/5
Avg. # Of Employees: 2 FT, 6 PT
Passive Ownership: Discouraged
Encourage Conversions: Yes
Area Develop. Agreements: No
Sub-Franchising Contracts: No
Expand In Territory: Yes
Space Needs: 500+ SF; Varies Dramatically

SUPPORT & TRAINING PROVIDED:
Financial Assistance Provided: No
Site Selection Assistance: Yes
Lease Negotiation Assistance: No
Co-Operative Advertising: No
Franchisee Assoc./Member: Yes/Yes
Size Of Corporate Staff: 28
On-Going Support: A,C,D,G,H,I
Training: 5 Days Lansing, MI at Stick Men University.

SPECIFIC EXPANSION PLANS:
US: All United States
Canada: No
Overseas: No

<< >>

UCC TOTALHOME

8450 Broadway
Merrillville, IN 46410
Tel: (800) 827-6400 (219) 736-1100
Fax: (219) 755-6208
E-Mail: dbowen@ucctotalhome.com
Web Site: www.ucctotalhome.com
Ms. Debbie Bowen, Dir. Franchise Development

UCC TOTALHOME offers consumers the unparalleled opportunity to buy merchandise at manufacturer's invoice cost. Our hundreds of thousands of members purchase directly from more than 800 manufacturers. No mark-up, no middleman, no kidding. UCC TOTALHOME franchise owners enroll members through our time-tested marketing system and service these members with the support of more than 150 specialists at the UCC Corporate Support Center.

BACKGROUND: IFA MEMBER
Established: 1971; 1st Franchised: 1972
Franchised Units: 71
Company-Owned Units 13
Total Units: 84
Dist.: US-77; CAN-15; O'seas-0
North America: 21 States, 4 Provinces
Density: 10 in MI, 8 in NY, 7 in OH
Projected New Units (12 Months): 8
Qualifications: 4, 4, 1, 3, 1, 5
Registered: All States

FINANCIAL/TERMS:
Cash Investment: $88-237K
Total Investment: $88-237K
Minimum Net Worth: $100K
Fees: Franchise - $35-55K
Royalty - 22%; Ad. - N/A
Earnings Claim Statement: No
Term of Contract (Years): 12/12
Avg. # Of Employees: 12 FT, 2 PT
Passive Ownership: Discouraged
Encourage Conversions: N/A
Area Develop. Agreements: No
Sub-Franchising Contracts: No
Expand In Territory: No
Space Needs: 4,000-6,000 SF; Business Park

SUPPORT & TRAINING PROVIDED:
Financial Assistance Provided: Yes(B)
Site Selection Assistance: Yes
Lease Negotiation Assistance: No
Co-Operative Advertising: N/A
Franchisee Assoc./Member: No
Size Of Corporate Staff: 150
On-Going Support: A,B,C,D,E,G,H,h
Training: 3 Weeks Merrillville, IN; 5 Weeks in an Operating Franchise.

SPECIFIC EXPANSION PLANS:
US: All United States
Canada: All Canada
Overseas: No

<< >>

UNITED STATES BASKETBALL LEAGUE

46 Quirk Rd.
Milford, CT 06460
Tel: (800) THE USBL (203) 877-9508
Fax: (203) 878-8109
E-Mail: usbl96@aol.com
Web Site: www.usbl.com
Mr. Daniel Meisenheimer, III, President

The USBL is the first and only sports league structured as a franchisor and the only publicly-traded sports league (OTCBB: USBL). The USBL is 16 years old with 10 teams and 132 USBL players have made the NBA. Visit the USBL Website at www.usbl.com.

BACKGROUND:
Established: 1985; 1st Franchised: 1990
Franchised Units: 10
Company-Owned Units 0
Total Units: 10
Dist.: US-10; CAN-0; O'seas-0
North America: 4 States
Density: 2 in NY, 2 in FL, 2 in NJ
Projected New Units (12 Months): 6
Qualifications: 4, 4, 3, 3, 3, 4
Registered: FL,NY,DC

FINANCIAL/TERMS:
Cash Investment: $500K
Total Investment: $500-750K
Minimum Net Worth: $1MM

Fees: Franchise - $300K
Royalty - 5%/$20K; Ad. - 1%/$3K
Earnings Claim Statement: No
Term of Contract (Years): 10/10
Avg. # Of Employees: 4 FT, 15 PT
Passive Ownership: Not Allowed
Encourage Conversions: N/A
Area Develop. Agreements: Yes/10
Sub-Franchising Contracts: Yes
Expand In Territory: Yes
Space Needs: N/A SF; FS

SUPPORT & TRAINING PROVIDED:

Financial Assistance Provided: Yes(D)
Site Selection Assistance: Yes
Lease Negotiation Assistance: Yes
Co-Operative Advertising: Yes
Franchisee Assoc./Member: Yes/Yes
Size Of Corporate Staff: 8
On-Going Support: A,b,C,d,e,f,G,h,I
Training: 2 Weeks CT or PA.

SPECIFIC EXPANSION PLANS:

US: All U.S., East of Miss.
Canada: All Canada
Overseas: Europe, Far East

<< >>

SUPPLEMENTAL LISTING OF FRANCHISORS

A QUIK SERVICES, 1730 Cumberland Point Dr., # 5, Marietta, GA 30067 ; (800) 255-8145 (770) 951-9440; (770) 933-8268

AIT FREIGHT SYSTEMS, P.O. Box 66730, Chicago, IL 60666 ; (800) 669-4248 (630) 766-8300; (630) 766-0305

ARMOLOY CORPORATION, THE, 114 Simonda Ave., DeKalb, IL 60115 ; (815) 758-6657; (815) 758-0268

ARMOR SHIELD, Box 2, 1 School Road, Flanouth, KY 45249 (BAD) ; (800) 543-1838 (513) 684-0040; (513) 684-0079

BLADERUNNER MOBILE SHARPENING SYSTEM, 6431 Orr Rd., Charlotte, NC 28213 ; (800) 742-7754 (704) 597-8266; (704) 598-7111

BUTTON KING, 925 Howard St., San Francisco, CA 94103-4108 ; (415) 543-2256; (415) 495-8617

CAREY INTERNATIONAL, 4530 Wisconsin Ave., NW, Washington, DC 20016 ; (202) 895-1200; (202) 895-1209

CASE HANDYMAN SERVICES, 4701 Sangamore Rd., # P-40, Bethesda, MD 20816 ; (800) 426-9434 (301) 229-4600; (301) 229-2089

CLEANWAY INDUSTRIES, 16 Library Ave., Westhampton Beach, NY 11978 (800) 332-6996 (516) 288-6300; (516) 288-6483

DIAL A ROSE, 12216 U. S. Hwy. # 1, West Palm Beach, FL 33418 ; (800) 378-ROSE (561) 622-1843; (561) 622-1843

DIAL ONE, 1551 S. Fanklin Rd., Indianapolis, IN 46239 ; (800) 342-5111 (317) 375-2168; (317) 375-2178

DISCOUNT IMAGING, P.O. Box 699, West Monroe, LA 71294-0699 ; (800) 987-8258 (318) 324-8258; (318) 324-1211

EMBROIDME, 1601 Belvedere Rd., 501 S., West Palm Beach, FL 33406-1541 (800) 727-6720 (561) 640-7367; (561) 640-6062

FRANCHISE DEVELOPMENT CENTER, 4360 Chamlee Dunwoody Rd., # 410, Atlanta, GA 30341-1049 ; (770) 455-4300; (770) 455-4422

GLASS MAGNUM, 17815 Shawnee Tr., Tualatin, OR 97062 ; (800) 642-1141 (503) 641-6926; (503) 612-9441

HISTORICAL RESEARCH CENTER, THE, 632 S. Military Trl., Deerfield Beach, FL 33442 ; (800) 940-7991 (954) 421-8713; (954) 360-9005

INDEPENDENT LIGHTING FRANCHISE, 873 Seahawk Cir., Virginia Beach, VA 23452 ; (800) 637-5483 (804) 468-5448; (804) 468-1514

INTERQUEST DETECTION CANINES, 21900 Tomball Pkwy., Houston, TX 77070-1526 ; (800) 481-7768 (281) 320-1231; (281) 320-2512

INTERSTATE ALL BATTERY CENTERS, 1700 Dixon St., Des Moines, IA 50316 ; (800) 203-6549 ; (800) 246-1024

K & N MOBILE DISTRIBUTION SYSTEMS, 4909 Rondo Dr., Fort Worth, TX 76106 ; (800) 433-2170 (817) 626-2885; (817) 624-3721

LEROS POINT TO POINT, 17 Grammercy Pl., Thornwood, NY 10594 (800) 82-LEROS (914) 747-2300; (914) 747-2917

MINI-TANKERS USA, 4739 University Way, NE. # 1620, Seattle, WA 98105 ; (877) 218-3003 (905) 607-7129; (888) 682-2213

NAUT-A-CARE FRANCHISING, 2507 W. Pacific Coast Hwy., # 204, Newport Beach, CA 92663-4722 ; (887) 582-5823 (949) 631-2660; (949) 631-2502

NELSON'S DIRECT CASKET OUTLET, 210 W. Maple, Independence, MO 64051 ; (816) 252-0979; (816) 252-1216

OPTIONS TALENT, 7001 Lake Ellenor Dr., # 200, Orlando, FL 32809-5792 ; (407) 240-1656; (407) 240-4177

PIRTEK USA, 501 Haverty Ct., Rockledge, FL 32955 ; (888) 774-7835 (321) 504-4422; (321) 504-4433

PROTOCOL, INC., 1370 Mendota Heights Rd., Mendota Heights, MN 55120 ; (800) 247-8363 (651) 454-0518; (651) 454-9542

PURE WATER, INC., 3725 Touzalin Ave., Lincoln, NE 68501 ; (800) 875-5915 (402) 467-9300; (402) 467-9393

RAINSOFT WATER TREATMENT SYSTEMS, 2080 E. Lunt Ave., Elk Grove, IL 60007 ; (800) 724-6763 (847) 437-9400; (847) 437-1594

SUBURBAN CYLINDER EXPRESS, 240 Rte. 10 W., P.O. Box 206, Whippany, NJ 07981-0206 ; (800) 526-0620 (973) 503-9871; (973) 515-5996

WATERCARE CORPORATION, 125 E. Alberta Dr., P.O. Box 1717, Manitowoc, WI 54221 ; (920) 682-6823; (920) 682-7673

WE THE PEOPLE, 1501 State St., Santa Barbara, CA 93101 ; (805) 962-4100; (805) 962-9602

WORLD CLASS PARKING, 525 Plymouth Rd., # 319, Plymouth Meeting, PA 19462 ; (888) 680-7275 (610) 828-1908; (610) 834-2937

FRANCHISOR QUESTIONNAIRE
www.worldfranchising.com and 2002 BOND'S FRANCHISE GUIDE

1. Franchise Trade Name: ______________________________

2. Address: ______________________________
   City ______________________ State/Province________ Zip/Postal Code ______________
   Telephone: (800) ______________________ or ( ) ______________________
   Fax Number: ( ) ______________ ; E-Mail Address: ______________________
   Internet: www.______________________ (Note: To ensure accuracy, please attach business card/letterhead)

3. Contact: ______________________ Position: ______________________

4. President/CEO ______________________ (**Note:** This data will not be published.)

5. Description of Business: (Use the full space available to set yourself apart from other franchising opportunities, i.e. sell your system to the potential franchisee.)

____

____

____

____

____

6. Company was founded in 19 _____. First year as franchisor was 19 _____.

7. Actual number of Franchised Units __________ Units

8. Actual number of Company-Owned Units __________ Units
   Total Operating Units __________ Units

9. Of Total Operating Units listed in # 8 above, _______ were in the U.S.
   _______ were in Canada.
   _______ were Overseas.

10. Of the Total Operating Units listed in # 8 above, A) in how many States/Provinces did you have operating units and B) what 3 States/Provinces had the largest number of operating units?

A) Franchisor Has Operating Units in	B) Top 3 States/Provinces	# Units in Each of B)
__________ U. S. States	1. __________________	____________
__________ Canadian Provinces	2. __________________	____________
__________ Foreign Countries	3. __________________	____________

11. How many **New Units** do you plan to open in the next 12 months? ________ Units

12. Do you provide potential franchisees with an **Earnings Claim Statement**? ❑ Yes ❑ No

13. What is the **minimum net worth** required of the franchisee? $ ______________

14. Even though the cash investment may vary substantially by individual unit, what is the range of **equity capital** (up-front cash) required? $ ______________

15. What is the range of **total investment** required? $______________

16. How much is the **initial franchise fee** for a new franchisee? $______________

17. How much is the **on-going royalty fee**? ________ % or ____________

18. How much is the **on-going advertising fee**? ________ % or ____________

19. The following States/Province require a separate registration (or disclosure, indicated by an *) document. In which are you **currently registered to franchise**?

❑ All Below or	❑ IN	❑ ND	❑ WA
❑ CA	❑ MD	❑ OR*	❑ WI
❑ FL*	❑ MI*	❑ RI	❑ DC
❑ HI	❑ MN	❑ SD	
❑ IL	❑ NY	❑ VA	❑Alberta

20. What is the **term of the original franchise agreement**? ________ Years

21. What is the **term of the renewal period**? ________ Years

22. Do you have **Area Development Agreements**? ❑ Yes ❑ No; If Yes, for what period? _____ Years

23. Do you have **Sub-Franchisor Contracts** covering specified territories? ❑ Yes ❑ No

24. Can the franchisee establish **additional outlets** within his area? ❑ Yes ❑ No

25. Is **passive ownership** of the initial unit ❑ Allowed ❑ Allowed, But Discouraged ❑ Not Allowed

26. Do you **encourage conversions**? ❑ Yes ❑ No ❑ Not Applicable

27. Is **financial assistance** available? ❑ Yes ❑ No ❑ N.A.; If Yes, ❑ Direct or ❑ Indirect

28. Do you assist the franchisee in **site selection**? ❑ Yes ❑ No ❑ Not Applicable

29. What **square footage and types of sites** do most of your franchise units require? ________ SF
❑ Free-Standing Building ❑ Storefront ❑ Strip Center ❑ Regional Mall
❑ Home-Based ❑ Other ________ ❑ Not Applicable

30. Do you assist the franchisee in **lease negotiations**? ❑ Yes ❑ No ❑ Not Applicable

31. Do you participate in **co-operative advertising**? ❑ Yes ❑ No ❑ Not Applicable

32. Including the owner/operator, **how many employees** are recommended to properly staff the average franchised unit? ________ Full-Time ________ Part-Time

33. How many full-time, paid personnel are currently on your **corporate staff**? ________

34. In qualifying a potential franchisee, please rank the following criteria from Unimportant to Very Important:

	Unimportant				Very Important
Financial Net Worth	1	2	3	4	5
General Business Experience	1	2	3	4	5
Specific Industry Experience	1	2	3	4	5
Formal Education	1	2	3	4	5
Psychological Profile	1	2	3	4	5
Personal Interview(s)	1	2	3	4	5

35. What are the location and duration of any **initial training sessions** included in the franchise fee?

	Location	Duration
A.	__________	__________
B.	__________	__________
C.	__________	__________

36. Which of the following **on-going services** do you provide to the franchisee?

Service	Included in Fees	At Additional Cost	N.A.
Central Data Processing	A. ❑	a. ❑	❑
Central Purchasing	B. ❑	b. ❑	❑
Field Operations Evaluation	C. ❑	c. ❑	❑
Field Training	D ❑	d. ❑	❑
Initial Store Opening	E. ❑	e. ❑	❑
Inventory Control	F. ❑	f. ❑	❑
Franchisee Newsletter	G. ❑	g. ❑	❑
Regional Or National Meetings	H. ❑	h. ❑	❑
800 Telephone Hotline	I. ❑	i. ❑	❑

37. Does your system have a **franchisee association**? ❑ Yes ❑ No;
If Yes, are you a member? ❑ Yes ❑ No

38. In which specific regions of the U.S. are you actively seeking new franchisees? For example: All U.S., or NW & SW, or NJ Only. ____________________

39. Are you actively seeking franchisees in Canada? ❑ Yes ❑ No
If Yes, in which Provinces? ❑ All or ____________________

40. Are you actively seeking franchisees Overseas? ❑ Yes ❑ No
If Yes, in which Countries? ____________________

41. Stock symbol and exchange if Company is publicly traded. __________ Symbol; ______ Exchange

Name of Respondent: ____________________ Telephone No: (   ) __________

Thank you very much for your time and prompt attention. Please return to:

Source Book Publications
1814 Franklin Street, Suite 820
Oakland, CA 94612
(510) 839-5471 ❖ FAX (510) 839-2104

Alphabetical Listing of Franchisors

* Indicates Full Franchisor Profile

#

A

B

C

D

E

F

G

H

I

J

K

L

M

N

O

P

Q

R

S

T

U

V

W

X

Y

Z

* Indicates Full Franchisor Profile

DEFINITIVE FRANCHISOR DATABASE AVAILABLE FOR RENT

SAMPLE FRANCHISOR PROFILE

Name of Franchise:	**BLIMPIE SUBS AND SALADS**
Address:	1775 The Exchange, # 800
City/State/Zip/Postal Code:	Atlanta, GA 30339
Country:	U. S. A.
800 Telephone #:	(800) 447-6256
Local Telephone #:	(770) 984-2707
Alternate Telephone #:	
Fax #:	(770) 980-9176
E-Mail:	chuckt@blimpie.com
Internet Address:	www.blimpie.com
# Franchised Units:	1,955
# Company-Owned Units:	1
# Total Units:	1,956
Company Contact:	Mr. Chuck Taylor
Contact Title/Position:	National Business Development
Contact Salutation:	Mr. Taylor
President:	Mr. Jeffrey Endervelt
President Title:	President
President Salutation:	Mr. Endervelt
Industry Category (of 45):	16 / Rental Services
IFA Member:	International Franchise Association
CFA Member:	

KEY FEATURES

• Number of Active North American Franchisors	~ 2,500
% US	~85%
% Canadian	~15%
• Data Fields (See Above)	24
• Industry Categories	45
• % With Toll-Free Telephone Numbers	67%
• % With Fax Numbers	97%
• % With Name of Preferred Contact	99%
• % With Name of President	97%
• % With Number of Total Operating Units	95%
• Guaranteed Accuracy - $.50 Rebate/Returned Bad Address	
• Converted to Any Popular Database or Contact Management Program	
• Initial Front-End Cost	$700
• Quarterly Up-Dates	$75
• Mailing Labels Only - One-Time Use	$400

For More Information, Please Contact

Source Book Publications

1814 Franklin Street, Suite 820, Oakland, California 94612

(800) 841-0873 ❖ (510) 839-5471 ❖ FAX (510) 839-2104